Water for food Water for life

WITHDRAWN

UTSA LIBRARIES

A Comprehensive Assessment of Water Management in Agriculture

First published by Earthscan in the UK and USA in 2007

Copyright © 2007
International Water Management Institute

All rights reserved

ISBN: 978-1-84407-396-2 paperback
ISBN: 978-1-84407-397-9 hardback

Creative direction and editing by Communications Development Incorporated,
Washington, D.C.
Typesetting by Elaine Wilson of Communications Development Incorporated.
Design by Peter Grundy of Peter Grundy Art & Design, London, UK

Most of the illustrations opening the chapters are winning submissions from an art competition soliciting illustrations of the main messages of the Comprehensive Assessment of
Water Management in Agriculture.

For a full list of publications please contact:
Earthscan
8–12 Camden High Street
London, NW1 0JH, UK
Tel: +44 (0)20 7387 8558
Fax: +44 (0)20 7387 8998
Email: earthinfo@earthscan.co.uk
Web: www.earthscan.co.uk

22883 Quicksilver Drive, Sterling, VA 20166-2012, USA

Published with the International Water Management Institute

A catalogue record for this book is available from the British Library

Library of Congress Cataloging-in-Publication Data has been applied for

This volume should be cited as:
Comprehensive Assessment of Water Management in Agriculture. 2007. *Water for Food,
Water for Life: A Comprehensive Assessment of Water Management in Agriculture.* London:
Earthscan, and Colombo: International Water Management Institute.

To purchase the full report, *Water for Food, Water for Life: A Comprehensive Assessment
of Water Management in Agriculture* (Earthscan, 2007), visit www.earthscan.co.uk.

Water
for food
Water
for life

A Comprehensive Assessment of Water Management in Agriculture

Edited by David Molden

for Comprehensive
assessment
of water management in agriculture

IWMI
**International
Water Management
Institute**

EARTHSCAN

Library
University of Texas
at San Antonio

"The world water crisis has caught us unawares, with a series of local hydrological pinch-points rapidly escalating into a global pandemic of empty rivers, dry boreholes, and wrecked wetlands as profound as, and often linked to, climate change. The water crisis has badly needed its equivalent of the reports of the Intergovernmental Panel on Climate Change. And for the two-thirds of the world's water that is used for agriculture, the Comprehensive Assessment provides just that. Timely, forensic, and unflinching in its analysis, forward thinking and strategic in its search for practical solutions, this is a landmark."

Fred Pearce
Author of *When The Rivers Run Dry* and frequent contributor to *NewScientist*

"This assessment is critical. Not only because it concerns a critical life resource like water. But because it involves an assessment that is comprehensive, analytical, and timely. The issue must become the world's obsession: growing and eating food that is water-prudent. I would encourage, indeed urge, you to use this rich and rigorous assessment to make changes in policy and practice."

Sunita Narain, Stockholm Water Prize Winner 2005
Director, Centre for Science and Environment

"A wake-up call to policymakers, bringing attention, understanding, and ultimately hope to the crucial need for better agricultural water management in all its forms to feed future generations and sustain thriving rural communities and ecosystems."

Peter Lee
President, International Commission on Irrigation and Drainage

"This is perhaps the most extraordinary recipe book ever produced: Take one world already being exhausted by 6 billion people. Find the ingredients to feed another 2 billion people. Add demand for more food, more animal feed, and more fuel. Use only the same amount of water the planet has had since creation. And don't forget to restore the environment that sustains us. Stir very carefully."

Margaret Catley-Carlson
Chair, Global Water Partnership

"Is there enough water to meet the world's food needs without decimating freshwater ecosystems? The Comprehensive Assessment says 'Yes'—but only by getting more nutritional value per drop and by adopting strategies that integrate the goals of food security, poverty reduction, and ecological health. This timely assessment provides valuable guidance for policymakers, planners, and practitioners the world over. Yes, there is enough water. But is there enough willpower?"

Sandra Postel
Author of *Pillar of Sand: Can the Irrigation Miracle Last?*
Coauthor of *Rivers for Life: Managing Water for People and Nature*

Table of contents

Foreword

In 1998–2000 I had the privilege of working on "World Water Vision," a public policy exercise in which more than 15,000 people participated in developing visions on water issues affecting their country, region, or sector, firmly rooted in the ideas of integrated water resources management. The process culminated in the 2nd World Water Forum and Ministerial Conference in The Hague, the largest gathering to that date of people concerned with water. What struck me then, particularly at the forum, was how the water for food and agriculture and the water and nature groups were working completely at cross-purposes. It was not so much that they disagreed—they were not even in the same room, let alone talking to each other! Their conclusions, however well integrated and thought-out within their own sectors, were completely at loggerheads.

The water and nature groups took their cues from the well accepted environmental sustainability goals. They concluded that large abstractions of water, particularly for agriculture—much of it presumed to be used wastefully—had already caused major environmental damage. They accepted the need to provide more water for growing cities and industry but wanted to stop or reverse the degradation of environmental quality. Their conclusion was that agriculture would clearly have to relinquish some water and that it could do so by increasing irrigation efficiency.

The water for agricultural groups took their cues from the well-accepted hunger and poverty reduction goals. They concluded that to feed a growing, wealthier world population and reduce hunger, increased diversions of water to agriculture would be unavoidable, even if all possible efforts were made to increase irrigation efficiency.

What this shows is that the amount of water abstracted from nature for agriculture is a critical variable. It is critical in all scenarios that try to assess global scarcity or the severity of the world water crisis. And in 2000 there was no agreement on how much this ought to be.

When I applied to become Director General of the International Water Management Institute (IWMI), I proposed that the institute play a major role in answering the question: How much water does irrigated agriculture really need? Now, seven years later, I feel privileged to write the foreword for the final report of the Comprehensive Assessment of

Water Management in Agriculture. In many ways this report is the definitive answer to that crucial question. The report answers many other critical questions as well. Involvement in the assessment quickly spread beyond the scientists of IWMI to almost all other centers of the Consultative Group on International Agricultural Research (CGIAR) and beyond that to many outside the CGIAR as well.

The Comprehensive Assessment started as a research program to span some of the key knowledge gaps related to water, food, and the environment. David Molden and his colleagues in the Comprehensive Assessment Steering Committee gradually transformed the program into a true assessment of the state of water management in agriculture over the last 50 years and projections for another 50 years into the future.

Fortunately, a lot has changed in seven years. Many useful bridges have been built between the agriculturalists and the environmentalists involved in water. Agriculture and wetlands is now discussed among the ecologists in the Ramsar Convention, while biodiversity in agroecosystems is on the agenda for agriculturalists. Dialogue has improved on many fronts. The Comprehensive Assessment on Water Management in Agriculture complements the Millennium Ecosystem Assessment. Where the Millennium Ecosystem Assessment focused on the environment, with inputs from agriculture, the Comprehensive Assessment focuses on agriculture, with strong inputs from an environmental perspective. The Comprehensive Assessment will also provide a major input into the new International Assessment of Agriculture Science and Technology for Development.

So what does this assessment conclude? Is there enough water? Or are we running out? The Comprehensive Assessment's answer is that we are running out of water to satisfy all demands in many locations—the closed and closing river basins—and that this will worsen if current policies continue. That is the bad news. But the assessment also identifies key opportunities to alleviate or prevent such water crises. One of the most surprising conclusions, presented with authority, is the optimistic view on rainfed agriculture. The assessment concludes that a key opportunity to address poverty and improve water productivity lies in Africa's savannahs. While many may be skeptical that major progress can be made in such a difficult environment, where real success has eluded us despite decades of trying, the evidence shows that this is indeed possible. In Brazil, the savannahs have been developed successfully, and crop and water productivity have both increased dramatically.

The Comprehensive Assessment puts forward key recommendations for improving water management in agriculture to address the world water crisis, backed by the authority of more than 700 scientists and careful analysis. I am confident that the Comprehensive Assessment—with proper adaptation to regional, national, and basin realities—will be a crucial guide for water policy in agriculture. It already has been important for sharing knowledge among researchers and research organizations and for setting research agendas. I hope—and expect—that the investments made by so many in this assessment will be a stepping stone out of poverty for millions of poor rural people who struggle with water scarcity today.

Frank Rijsberman
Director General
International Water Management Institute

Preface

The Comprehensive Assessment of Water Management in Agriculture is a critical evaluation of the benefits, costs, and impacts of the past 50 years of water development, the water management challenges communities face today, and the solutions people have developed around the world. It is a multi-institute process aimed at assessing the current state of knowledge and stimulating ideas on how to manage water resources to meet the growing needs for agricultural products, to help reduce poverty and food insecurity, and to contribute to environmental sustainability. The findings will enable better investment and management decisions in water and agriculture in the near future by considering their impact over the next 50 years.

The assessment was produced by a broad partnership of practitioners, researchers, and policymakers using an assessment process that engaged networks of partners to produce and synthesize knowledge and elaborate innovative methods and responses. An assessment, as distinct from a review, is undertaken for decisionmakers rather than scientists, is driven by a specific problem rather than more general scientific curiosity, requires a clear judgment as well as objective analysis, and deals with a range of uncertainty without being exhaustive.

The target audience of this assessment are the people who make the investment and management decisions in water management for agriculture—agricultural producers, water managers, investors, policymakers, and civil society. In addition, the assessment should inform the general public about these important issues, so that we can all help to make better decisions through our political processes.

The scope of this assessment is water management in agriculture, including fisheries and livestock, and the full spectrum of crop production from soil tillage through supplemental irrigation and water harvesting to full irrigation in a sustainable environment context. The assessment was originally framed by 10 questions, later expanded as interest grew (see box), and includes the overarching question: how can water in agriculture be developed and managed to help end poverty and hunger, ensure environmentally sustainable practices, and find the right balance between food and environmental security?

The Comprehensive Assessment places water management in agriculture in a social, ecological, and political context and assesses the dominant drivers of change. It explicitly addresses multiple use, feedbacks, and dynamic interactions between water for production systems, livelihood support, and the environment. It analyzes past and current water development efforts from the perspective of costs, benefits, and impacts, considering society (economic and rural development, increased food security, agricultural development, health, and poverty) and the environment (conservation and degradation of ecosystems and agriculture).

The Comprehensive Assessment covers major ground identified as important but not given thorough coverage in related assessments. The Millennium Ecosystem Assessment identified agriculture as a key driver of ecosystem change and at a global scale addressed the reasons for this and the responses available (MEA 2005). The World Water Assessment Programme considers all aspects of water and touches on water for agriculture in its report, but does not go into detailed analysis (UN–Water 2006). The ongoing International Assessment of Agricultural Science and Technology for Development (IAASTD) lists water as a key issue and draws on the results of the Comprehensive Assessment.

The Comprehensive Assessment used a participatory, open assessment process (Watson and Gitay 2004) that

- Provided a critical and objective evaluation of information for guiding decisions on a complex public issue.
- Engaged stakeholders early in the process and in building consensus or debating contentious issues.

Initial framing questions of the Comprehensive Assessment

These 10 questions were defined in 2001 by the Steering Committee of the Comprehensive Assessment:

1. What are the options and their consequences for improving water productivity in agriculture?
2. What have been the benefits, costs, and impacts of irrigated agricultural development, and what conditions those impacts?
3. What are the consequences of land and water degradation on water productivity and on the multiple users of water in catchments?
4. What are the extent and significance of use of low-quality water in agriculture (saline and wastewater), and what are the options for its use?
5. What are the options for better management of rainwater to support rural livelihoods, food production, and land rehabilitation in water-scarce areas?
6. What are the options and consequences for using groundwater?
7. How can water be managed to sustain and enhance capture fisheries and aquaculture systems?
8. What are the options for integrated water resources management in basins and catchments?
9. What policy and institutional frameworks are appropriate under various conditions for managing water to meet the goals of food and environmental security?
10. How much water will be needed for agriculture, given the need to meet food security and environmental sustainability goals?

- Provided technically accurate, evidence-based analysis, summation, and synthesis that reduced complexity but added value to existing information.
- Was conducted by a large and diverse team of experts (scientists, practitioners, policymakers) to incorporate relevant geographic and disciplinary representation.
- Summarized its findings with simple and understandable messages for the target audience through clear answers to their questions, taking into account the multidisciplinary and multistakeholder involvement.
- Included external reviews with demonstrated response to the reviews to further strengthen objectivity, representation, and wide ownership.

To realize an informed, consultative, and inclusive assessment, scientists, policymakers, practitioners, and stakeholders were invited to participate. Through dialogue, debate, and other exchange, pertinent questions were identified and discussed. Background assessment research was conducted in a separate phase and is documented in a book series and reports (see www.iwmi.cgiar.org/assessment). Through collaboration with more than 700 individuals, numerous organizations, and networks, background material was developed and chapters were developed, reviewed, and improved.

Each chapter's writing team consisted of one to three coordinating lead authors, generally two to four lead authors, and five to ten contributing authors as well as a network of some 50 expert consultants. Each chapter went through two rounds of reviews with about 10 reviewers per round. A review editor verified that each review comment was addressed. The extensive review process represented another effort to engage civil society groups, researchers, and policymakers, among others. Cross-cutting issues of the Comprehensive Assessment were health, gender, and climate change. Groups of experts from these fields provided invaluable information and feedback to all of the chapters and commented on drafts of the texts. The process provided a mechanism for knowledge sharing, but also stimulated new thinking about water and food. The results thus provide not only an assessment of existing knowledge and experiences, but also new understanding of water management in agriculture.

The advantages of such an approach are numerous. It provides science-backed and policy-relevant findings, disseminates results throughout the process, and maintains high-quality science through the guidance of coordinating lead authors and the review process. Such an inclusive and collaborative procedure not only ensures greater scientific rigor, but also underscores authority and contributes to widespread ownership. The hope is that these efforts will result in significant changes in thinking and action on water management.

The Consultative Group on International Agricultural Research (CGIAR), the Secretariat of the Convention on Biological Diversity, the Food and Agriculture Organization of the United Nations, and the Ramsar Convention on Wetlands are co-sponsors of the assessment. While they have not formally endorsed the findings of the assessment, they have contributed to them and have expressed an interest in the results. Their role was to:

- Shape the assessment process by recommending key issues for assessment.
- Participate in developing the assessment.
- Transmit the results of the assessment to their constituents.

The Comprehensive Assessment (www.iwmi.cgiar.org/assessment) is organized through the CGIAR's Systemwide Initiative on Water Management (SWIM), which is convened by the International Water Management Institute, which initiated the process and provided a secretariat to facilitate the work. Involving food and environment communities together has been an important step in finding sustainable agricultural solutions.

Each chapter opens with artwork illustrating a main message of the assessment. Most of these illustrations are winning submissions from an art competition sponsored by the Comprehensive Assessment to communicate its key messages to a wide audience in innovative ways.

References

International Assessment of Agricultural Science and Technology for Development website. [www. agassessment.org].

MEA (Millennium Ecosystem Assessment). 2005. *Ecosystems and Human Well-being: Synthesis.* Washington, D.C.: Island Press.

UN–Water (United Nations World Water Assessment Programme). 2006. *United Nations World Water Development Report: Water, a Shared Responsibility.* Paris.

Watson, R.T., and H. Gitson. 2004. "Mobilization, Diffusion, and Use of Scientific Expertise." Report commissioned by the Institute for Sustainable Development and International Relations. Paris. [www.iddri.org/iddri/telecharge/gie/wp/iddri_IEG-expertise.pdf].

Team for the preparation of the Comprehensive Assessment of Water Management in Agriculture and its summary report

Overall coordinator: David Molden

Chapter coordinating lead authors: Deborah Bossio, Bas Bouman, Gina E. Castillo, Patrick Dugan, Malin Falkenmark, Jean-Marc Faurès, C. Max Finlayson, Charlotte de Fraiture, Line J. Gordon, Douglas J. Merrey, David Molden, François Molle, Regassa E. Namara, Theib Y. Oweis, Don Peden, Manzoor Qadir, Johan Rockström, Tushaar Shah, and Dennis Wichelns

Chapter lead authors: Akiça Bahri, Randolph Barker, Christophe Béné, Malcolm C.M. Beveridge, Prem S. Bindraban, Randall E. Brummett, Jacob Burke, David Coates, William Critchley, Pay Drechsel, Karen Frenken, Kim Geheb, Munir A. Hanjra, Nuhu Hatibu, Phil Hirsch, Elizabeth Humphreys, Maliha H. Hussein, Eiman Karar, Eric Kemp-Benedict, Jacob. W. Kijne, Bancy Mati, Peter McCornick, Ruth Meinzen-Dick, Paramjit Singh Minhas, A.K. Misra, Peter P. Mollinga, Joke Muylwijk, Liqa Raschid-Sally, Helle Munk Ravnborg, Claudia Sadoff, Lisa Schipper, Laurence Smith, Pasquale Steduto, Veliyil Vasu Sugunan, Mark Svendsen, Girma Tadesse, To Phuc Tuong, Hugh Turral, Domitille Vallée, Godert van Lynden, Karen Villholth, Suhas Wani, Robin L. Welcomme, and Philippus Wester

Review editors: Sawfat Abdel-Dayem, Paul Appasamy, Fatma Attia, Jean Boroto, David Coates, Rebecca D'Cruz, John Gowing, Richard Harwood, Jan Lundqvist, David Seckler, Mahendra Shah, Miguel Solanes, Linden Vincent, and Robert Wasson

Statistical advisors: Charlotte de Fraiture and Karen Frenken

Summary report writing team: David Molden, Lisa Schipper, Charlotte de Fraiture, Jean-Marc Faurès, and Domitille Vallée

Editors: Bruce Ross-Larson, principal editor, working with his colleagues Meta de Coquereaumont and Christopher Trott of Communications Development Incorporated in Washington, D.C.

Sponsors of the Comprehensive Assessment (who helped shape the assessment, provided key input, and will transmit the results to their constituents):

Consultative Group on International Agricultural Research
Convention on Biological Diversity
Food and Agriculture Organization of the United Nations
Ramsar Convention on Wetlands

Steering Committee: David Molden, Chair (International Water Management Institute); Bas Bouman (International Rice Research Institute); Gina E. Castillo (Oxfam Novib); Patrick Dugan (WorldFish Center); Jean-Marc Faurès (Food and Agriculture Organization of the United Nations); Eiman Karar (Water Research Commission of South Africa); Theib Y. Oweis (International Center for Agricultural Research in the Dry Areas); Johan Rockström (Stockholm Environment Institute); and Suhas Wani (International Crops Research Institute for the Semi-Arid Tropics)

Comprehensive Assessment Secretariat: David Molden (Coordinator), Sithara Atapattu, Naoya Fujimoto, Sepali Goonaratne, Mala Ranawake, Lisa Schipper, and Domitille Vallée

Core support for the assessment process leading to the production of this book was provided by: the governments of the Netherlands, Sweden (through the Swedish Water House), and Switzerland; the World Bank in support of Systemwide Programs; the Consultative Group on International Agricultural Research (CGIAR) Challenge Program on Water and Food; and donors to the International Water Management Institute. Project-specific support was provided by the governments of Austria, Japan, and Taiwan; EU support to the Institutional and Social Innovations in Irrigation Mediterranean Management Project; the Food and Agriculture Organization of the United Nations; the Organization of Petroleum Exporting Countries Fund; the Rockefeller Foundation; Oxfam Novib; and the CGIAR Gender and Diversity Program. In addition, the many individuals and organizations involved in the assessment supplied countless hours of in-kind contributions.

Agricultural water use—meeting the challenge of food security, poverty reduction, and environmental sustainability

Artist: Surendra Pradhan, Nepal

Summary for decisionmakers

Will there be enough water to grow enough food? Yes, if...

Question: Is there enough land, water, and human capacity to produce food for a growing population over the next 50 years—or will we "run out" of water?

The Comprehensive Assessment's answer: It is possible to produce the food—but it is probable that today's food production and environmental trends, if continued, will lead to crises in many parts of the world. Only if we act to improve water use in agriculture will we meet the acute freshwater challenges facing humankind over the coming 50 years.

Why is the situation different now?

Fifty years ago the world had fewer than half as many people as it has today. They were not as wealthy. They consumed fewer calories, ate less meat, and thus required less water to produce their food. The pressure they inflicted on the environment was lower. They took from our rivers a third of the water that we take now.

Today the competition for scarce water resources in many places is intense. Many river basins do not have enough water to meet all the demands or even enough for their rivers to reach the sea. Further appropriation of water for human use is not possible because limits have been reached and in many cases breached. Basins are effectively "closed," with no possibility of using more water. The lack of water is thus a constraint to producing food for hundreds of millions of people. Agriculture is central in meeting this challenge because the production of food and other agricultural products takes 70% of the freshwater withdrawals from rivers and groundwater.

Greater competition raises questions: Who will get the water, and how will allocations be decided? Conflict will grow between pastoralists and herders, between farms and cities, between those upstream and those downstream.

Not all contenders are human. Water used for agriculture is simply not available for wetlands, streams, deltas, and plants and animals. And as aquatic and terrestrial ecosystems are damaged, ecosystems change. Ecosystem services are threatened by the way we grow food. The climate is changing, affecting every facet of societies, ecosystems, and economies.

' Only if we act to improve water use in agriculture will we meet the acute freshwater challenges facing humankind over the coming 50 years

The trendlines shout out that we are not doing the right things. Inequity in the benefits of water use will grow between haves and have-nots to the detriment of food production. The pollution and depletion of rivers and groundwater will continue. Enough food grown at the aggregate global level does not mean enough food for everyone.

The Comprehensive Assessment of Water Management in Agriculture pulls together five years of work by more than 700 scientists and practitioners from around the world. Their strong and urgent message: problems will intensify unless they are addressed—and now.

Where is there hope? Increasing the productivity of land and water

The hope lies in closing the gap in agricultural productivity in many parts of the world—often today no greater than that on the fields of the Roman Empire—and in realizing the unexplored potential that lies in better water management along with nonmiraculous changes in policy and production techniques. The world has enough freshwater to produce food for all its people over the next half century. But world leaders must take action now—before the opportunities to do so are lost.

Some good news: 75% of the additional food we need over the next decades could be met by bringing the production levels of the world's low-yield farmers up to 80% of what high-yield farmers get from comparable land. Better water management plays a key role in bridging that gap.

More good news: the greatest potential increases in yields are in rainfed areas, where many of the world's poorest rural people live and where managing water is the key to such increases. Only if leaders decide to do so will better water and land management in these areas reduce poverty and increase productivity.

Even more good news: while there will probably be some need to expand the amount of land we irrigate to feed 8–9 billion people, and while we will have to deal with the associated adverse environmental consequences, with determined and focused change there is real scope to improve production on many existing irrigated lands. Doing so would lessen the need for more water in these areas and for even greater expansion of irrigated land. In South Asia—where more than half the crop area is irrigated and productivity is low—with determined policy change and robust institutions almost all additional food demand could be met by improving water productivity in already irrigated crop areas. In rural Sub-Saharan Africa comprehensive water management policies and sound institutions would spur economic growth for the benefit of all. And despite the bad news about groundwater depletion, there is still potential in many areas for highly productive pro-poor groundwater use, for example, the lower Gangetic plains and parts of Sub-Saharan Africa.

What changes are needed?

Such gains, although far from impossible, require big changes in the policy agenda for water management. That agenda must be grounded in the reality that ensuring food security and protecting ecosystems are vital to human survival and must be achieved in harmony. Water systems must be built for many purposes and managed to provide a wide range of ecosystem services. And there are opportunities—in rainfed, irrigated, livestock, and fisheries systems—for preserving, even restoring, healthy ecosystems.

Different strategies are required for different situations. Sub-Saharan Africa requires investments in infrastructure, considering the range of options available. Where infrastructure is already heavily developed, as in much of Asia, a focus on improving productivity, reallocating supplies, and rehabilitating ecosystems is required. In all cases, supporting institutions, adapted to changing needs, are essential.

There are also different pathways out of poverty. In some settings low-cost technologies can be viewed as a stepping stone—they are simple and can be rapidly implemented, reaping quick gains in food security and income for many people. And with favorable institutional and market conditions, other options will arise, such as larger scale irrigation or other income-generating and employment opportunities. But the first step is important.

> Thinking differently about water is essential for achieving our triple goal of ensuring food security, reducing poverty, and conserving ecosystems.

What policy actions are needed?

Start with eight:

- *Policy action 1. Change the way we think about water and agriculture.* Thinking differently about water is essential for achieving our triple goal of ensuring food security, reducing poverty, and conserving ecosystems. Instead of a narrow focus on rivers and groundwater, view rain as the ultimate source of water that can be managed. Instead of blueprint designs, craft institutions while recognizing the politically contentious nature of the reform process. And instead of isolating agriculture as a production system, view it as an integrated multiple-use system and as an agroecosystem, providing services and interacting with other ecosytsems.

- *Policy action 2. Fight poverty by improving access to agricultural water and its use.* Target livelihood gains of smallholder farmers by securing water access through water rights and investments in water storage and delivery infrastructure where needed, improving value obtained by water use through pro-poor technologies, and investing in roads and markets. Multiple-use systems—operated for domestic use, crop production, aquaculture, agroforestry, and livestock—can improve water productivity and reduce poverty.

- *Policy action 3. Manage agriculture to enhance ecosystem services.* Good agricultural practice can enhance other ecosystem services. In agroecosystems there is scope to promote services beyond the production of food, fiber, and animal protein. Agricultural production does not have to be at the expense of other services that water provides in rivers and wetlands. But because of increased water and land use, and intensification, some ecosystem change is unavoidable, and difficult choices are necessary.

- *Policy action 4. Increase the productivity of water.* Gaining more yield and value from less water can reduce future demand for water, limiting environmental degradation and easing competition for water. A 35% increase in water productivity could reduce additional crop water consumption from 80% to 20%. More food can be produced per unit of water in all types of farming systems, with livestock systems deserving attention. But this optimism should be met with caution because in areas of high productivity only small gains are possible. Larger potential exists in getting more value per unit of water, especially through integrated systems and higher value production systems and through reductions in social and environmental costs. With careful targeting, the poor can benefit from water productivity gains in crop, fishery, livestock, and mixed systems.

- *Policy action 5. Upgrade rainfed systems—a little water can go a long way.* Rainfed agriculture is upgraded by improving soil moisture conservation and, where feasible, providing supplemental irrigation. These techniques hold underexploited potential for quickly lifting the greatest number of people out of poverty and for increasing water productivity, especially in Sub-Saharan Africa and parts of Asia. Mixed crop and livestock systems hold good potential, with the increased demand for livestock products and the scope for improving the productivity of these systems.

- *Policy action 6. Adapt yesterday's irrigation to tomorrow's needs.* The era of rapid expansion of irrigated agriculture is over. A major new task is adapting yesterday's irrigation systems to tomorrow's needs. Modernization, a mix of technological and managerial upgrading to improve responsiveness to stakeholder needs, will enable more productive and sustainable irrigation. As part of the package irrigation needs to be better integrated with agricultural production systems to support higher value agriculture and to integrate livestock, fisheries, and forest management.

- *Policy action 7. Reform the reform process—targeting state institutions.* Following a realistic process to suit local needs, a major policy shift is required for water management investments important to irrigated and rainfed agriculture. A wider policy and investment arena needs to be opened by breaking down the divides between rainfed and irrigated agriculture and by better linking fishery and livestock practices to water management. Reform cannot follow a blueprint. It takes time. It is specific to the local institutional and political context. And it requires negotiation and coalition building. Civil society and the private sector are important actors. But the state is often the critical driver, though state water institutions are often the most in need of reform.

- *Policy action 8. Deal with tradeoffs and make difficult choices.* Because people do not adapt quickly to changing environments, bold steps are needed to engage with stakeholders. Informed multistakeholder negotiations are essential to make decisions about the use and allocation of water. Reconciling competing demands on water requires transparent sharing of information. Other users—fishers, smallholders without official title, and those dependent on ecosystem services—must develop a strong collective voice.

> A wider policy and investment arena needs to be opened by breaking down the divides between rainfed and irrigated agriculture and by better linking fishery and livestock practices to water management

4

Divergent views—divergent understanding

Views diverge sharply on the competing choices for water for food and for ecosystems. Some emphasize developing more water through large infrastructure to relieve scarcity, fuel economic growth, protect vulnerable people, and relieve pressure on the environment. Projects to transfer water from water-abundant to water-scarce basins follow this approach. At the other end of the spectrum are calls for a halt to agricultural and hydraulic infrastructure expansion—and for practices that restore ecosystems.

> A major reason for the diverging views on competing choices for water for food and water for ecosystems is divergent understanding of some basic premises

A major reason for the diverging views is divergent understanding of some basic premises. How much water is used in agriculture? How much irrigation is there? What is the contribution of groundwater? And what is the present use and future potential of rainfed agriculture? Different people place different values on water use. There is also a lack of knowledge and awareness of past impacts and the current situation of water use. By bringing together a diverse group of people with different perspectives, this assessment has made strides in finding common ground.

How much water is used for agriculture?

To produce enough food to satisfy a person's daily dietary needs takes about 3,000 liters of water converted from liquid to vapor—about 1 liter per calorie. Only about 2–5 liters of water are required for drinking. In the future more people will require more water for food, fiber, industrial crops, livestock, and fish. But the amount of water per person can be reduced by changing what people consume and how they use water to produce food.

Imagine a canal 10 meters deep, 100 meters wide, and 7.1 million kilometers long—long enough to encircle the globe 180 times. That is the amount of water it takes each year to produce food for today's 6.5 billion people. Add 2–3 billion people and accommodate their changing diets from cereals to more meat and vegetables and that could add another 5 million kilometers to the channel of water needed to feed the world's people.

About 80% of agricultural evapotranspiration—when crops turn water into vapor (box 1)—comes directly from rain, and about 20% from irrigation (map 1). Arid areas like the Middle East, Central Asia, and the western United States tend to rely on irrigation. There has also been large-scale irrigation development in South and East Asia, less in Latin America, and very little in Sub-Saharan Africa.

Withdrawals of water by agriculture (70%), industry (20%), and municipalities (10%)

Consider how we use water from rivers, lakes, and groundwater—blue water. Total global freshwater withdrawals are estimated at 3,800 cubic kilometers, with 2,700 cubic kilometers (or 70%) for irrigation, with huge variations across and within countries. Industrial and domestic use is growing relative to that for agriculture. And water for energy generation—hydropower and thermo cooling—is growing rapidly. Not all water withdrawn is "lost." Much is available for reuse in river basins, but often its quality is degraded.

Water, the blood of the biosphere, connects ecosystems across the landscape. When agricultural activities change the quality, quantity, and timing of water flows,

box **1** | **Water use in rainfed and irrigated agriculture**

The illustration shows how water is used globally and the services each use provides. The main source of water is rain falling on the earth's land surfaces (110,000 cubic kilometers). The arrows express the magnitude of water use, as a percentage of total rainfall, and the services provided. So, for example, 56% of green water is evapotranspired by various landscape uses that support bioenergy, forest products, livestock grazing lands, and biodiversity, and 4.5% is evapotranspired by rainfed agriculture supporting crops and livestock. Globally, about 39% of rain (43,500 cubic kilometers) contributes to blue water sources, important for supporting biodiversity, fisheries, and aquatic ecosystems. Blue water withdrawals are about 9% of total blue water sources (3,800 cubic kilometers), with 70% of withdrawals going to irrigation (2,700 cubic kilometers). Total evapotranspiration by irrigated agriculture is about 2,200 cubic kilometers (2% of rain), of which 650 cubic kilometers are directly from rain (green water) and the remainder from irrigation water (blue water). Cities and industries withdraw 1,200 cubic kilometers but return more than 90% to blue water, often with degraded quality. The remainder flows to the sea, where it supports coastal ecosystems. The variation across basins is huge. In some cases people withdraw and deplete so much water that little remains to flow to the sea.

Global water use

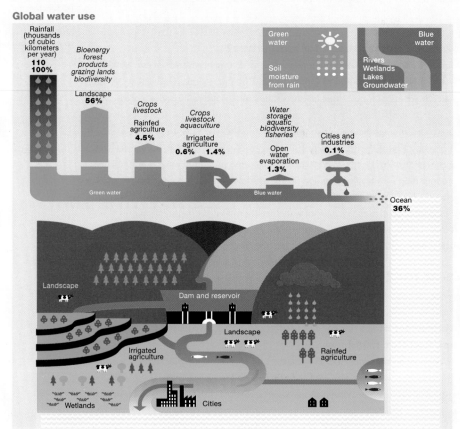

Source: Calculations for the Comprehensive Assessment of Water Management in Agriculture based on data from T. Oki and S. Kanae, 2006, "Global Hydrological Cycles and World Water Resources," *Science* 313 (5790): 1068–72; UNESCO–UN World Water Assessment Programme, 2006, *Water: A Shared Responsiblity,* The United Nations World Water Development Report 2, New York, UNESCO and Berghahn Books.

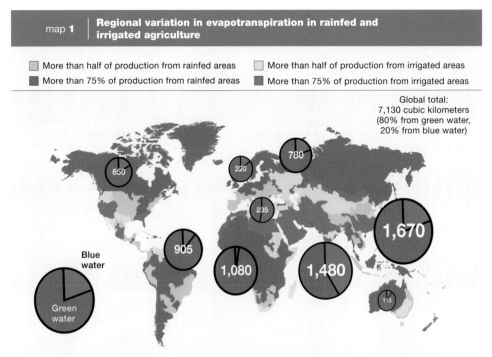

| map 1 | **Regional variation in evapotranspiration in rainfed and irrigated agriculture** |

More than half of production from rainfed areas   More than half of production from irrigated areas

More than 75% of production from rainfed areas   More than 75% of production from irrigated areas

Global total:
7,130 cubic kilometers
(80% from green water,
20% from blue water)

650

220

780

235

Blue water

905

1,670

Green water

1,080

1,480

110

Note: Production refers to gross value of production. The pie charts show total crop water evapotranspiration in cubic kilometers by region.

Source: International Water Management Institute analysis done for the Comprehensive Assessment for Water Management in Agriculture using the Watersim model; chapter 2.

this can change connected systems' capacity to produce ecosystem services other than food. Some changes to ecosystems are unavoidable simply because of the amount of water needed to produce food. But much ecosystem change is avoidable, if water is managed well.

Water for food—water for life

The last 50 years have seen remarkable developments in water resources and in agriculture. Massive developments in hydraulic infrastructure have put water at the service of people. While the world population grew from 2.5 billion in 1950 to 6.5 billion today, the irrigated area doubled and water withdrawals tripled.

Agricultural productivity grew thanks to new crop varieties and fertilizers, fueled by additional irrigation water. World food production outstripped population growth. Global food prices declined markedly (figure 1). And the greater use of water for irrigated agriculture benefited farmers and poor people—propelling economies, improving livelihoods, and fighting hunger.

But much unfinished business remains. In 2003, 850 million people in the world were food insecure, 60% of them living in South Asia and Sub-Saharan Africa, and 70%

figure **1** | **Irrigation expanding, food prices falling**

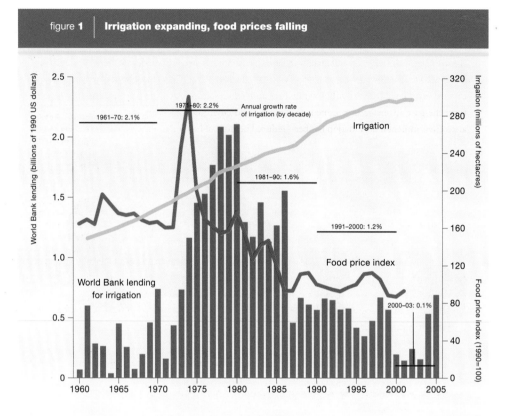

Source: Based on World Bank and Food and Agriculture Organization data; chapter 9.

of the poor live in rural areas. In Sub-Saharan Africa the number of food-insecure people rose from 125 million in 1980 to 200 million in 2000.

The last 50 years have also witnessed unprecedented changes in ecosystems, with many negative consequences. The Millennium Ecosystem Assessment pointed out that growth in agriculture has been responsible for much of this change. Agricultural practices have contributed primarily to the loss of regulating ecosystem services—such as pollination, biological pest control, flood retention capacity, and changes in microclimate regulation—and to the loss of biodiversity and habitats. Our message: better water management can mitigate many of the negative consequences.

Promising trends

■   Per capita consumption of food and total consumption of fruits, vegetables, and livestock products are steadily rising, leading to better nutrition for many and a decrease in the percentage of undernourished people. The average global per capita daily food supply increased from 2,400 kilocalories (kcal) in 1970 to 2,800 kcal in 2000, so enough food was produced globally to feed a growing population.

■ Land and water productivity are also rising steadily—with average grain yields rising from 1.4 metric tons per hectare to 2.7 metric tons over the past four decades.

■ New investments in irrigation and agricultural water management have the potential to spur economic growth within agriculture and other sectors. And using lessons from the past, investments can incur fewer social and environmental costs. In some areas environmental degradation has been reduced because of better natural resources management.

■ An increase in global trade in food products and in consequent flows of virtual water (the water embodied in food exports) offers prospects for better national food security and the possibility of relieving water stress.

Disturbing trends

■ The number of people malnourished remains about 850 million.

■ The average daily per capita food supply in South Asia (2,400 kcal) and Sub-Saharan Africa (2,200 kcal), while slowly rising, remains below the world average of 2,800 kcal in 2000 and far below the excessively high level in industrial countries (3,450 kcal). There are large losses of food between what is supplied and what is consumed by people—on the order of a third—an indirect waste of water.

■ Pollution is increasing, and rivers are drying up because of greater agricultural production and water consumption. Freshwater fisheries, important for the livelihoods of rural poor, have been damaged or are threatened. Land and water resources are being degraded through erosion, pollution, salinization, nutrient depletion, and the intrusion of seawater.

■ Pastoralists, many relying on livestock as their savings, are putting the world's grazing lands under great pressure.

■ In several river basins water is poorly managed, and allocations to users (including the environment) are overcommitted, so there is not enough water to meet all demands.

■ Groundwater levels are declining rapidly in densely populated areas of North Africa, North China, India, and Mexico because of overexploitation.

■ Water management institutions have been slow to build or change capacity and adapt to new issues and conditions.

Double-edged trends

■ Increasing water withdrawals and water depletion for irrigation in developing countries have been good for economic growth and poverty alleviation—but often bad for the environment.

■ Agricultural subsidies can be beneficial if applied judiciously as a management tool to support income generation by the rural poor and to protect the environment. If not so applied, they distort water and agricultural practices.

> Growth in agriculture has been responsible for much of the loss of biodiversity and habitats and of regulating ecosystem services. Better water management can mitigate many of the negative consequences.

- The growing demand of cities and industries for water offers possibilities for employment and income. But it also shifts water out of agriculture, puts extra strain on rural communities, and pollutes water.
- Consumption of fish and meat is rising, increasing the reliance on aquaculture and industrial livestock production, with benefits for income and well-being but with more pressure on water resources and the environment.

And emerging forces

A growing population is a major factor behind today's water scarcity, but the main reasons for water problems are lack of commitment and targeted investment, insufficient human capacity, ineffective institutions, and poor governance

- The climate is changing, affecting temperatures and precipitation patterns. Tropical areas with intense poverty, such as a large part of Sub-Saharan Africa, will be most adversely affected. Irrigators dependent on snow melt are even more vulnerable to changes in river flows.
- Globalization continues over the long run, providing new opportunities for commercial and high-value agriculture but presenting new challenges for rural development.
- Urbanization increases demand for water, generates more wastewater, and alters patterns of demand for agricultural products.
- Higher energy prices increase the costs of pumping water, applying fertilizers, and transporting products. Greater reliance on bioenergy will affect the production and prices of food crops and increase the amount of water used by agriculture.
- Perceptions and thinking about water are changing, with water professionals and policymakers realizing (again) the need to improve the use not only of blue water (in lakes, rivers, and aquifers) but also that of green water (soil moisture).
- More attention is being given to ecosystem and other integrated approaches and to understanding how forces outside water for agriculture influence both water and agriculture.

Water scarcity—water management

Without better water management in agriculture the Millennium Development Goals for poverty, hunger, and a sustainable environment cannot be met. Access to water is difficult for millions of poor women and men for reasons that go beyond the physical resource base. In some places water is abundant, but getting it to people is difficult because of lack of infrastructure and because of restricted access as a result of political and sociocultural issues. In other places, people's demands go beyond what the natural resource base can handle, and not everyone is assured access to water.

Water scarcity, defined in terms of access to water, is a critical constraint to agriculture in many areas of the world. A fifth of the world's people, more than 1.2 billion, live in areas of physical water scarcity, lacking enough water for everyone's demands. About 1.6 billion people live in water-scarce basins, where human capacity or financial resources are likely to be insufficient to develop adequate water resources (map 2). Behind today's water scarcity lie factors likely to multiply and gain in complexity over the coming years. A growing population is a major factor, but the main reasons for water problems lie elsewhere—lack of commitment to water and poverty, inadequate and inadequately targeted investment, insufficient human capacity, ineffective institutions, and poor governance.

Summary for
decisionmakers

| map **2** | **Areas of physical and economic water scarcity** |

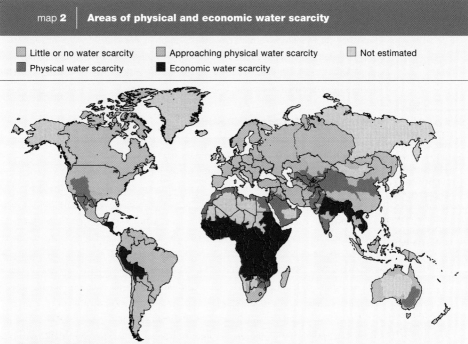

☐ Little or no water scarcity ☐ Approaching physical water scarcity ☐ Not estimated
■ Physical water scarcity ■ Economic water scarcity

Definitions and indicators
- *Little or no water scarcity.* Abundant water resources relative to use, with less than 25% of water from rivers withdrawn for human purposes.
- *Physical water scarcity (water resources development is approaching or has exceeded sustainable limits).* More than 75% of river flows are withdrawn for agriculture, industry, and domestic purposes (accounting for recycling of return flows). This definition—relating water availability to water demand—implies that dry areas are not necessarily water scarce.
- *Approaching physical water scarcity.* More than 60% of river flows are withdrawn. These basins will experience physical water scarcity in the near future.
- *Economic water scarcity (human, institutional, and financial capital limit access to water even though water in nature is available locally to meet human demands).* Water resources are abundant relative to water use, with less than 25% of water from rivers withdrawn for human purposes, but malnutrition exists.

Source: International Water Management Institute analysis done for the Comprehensive Assessment of Water Management in Agriculture using the Watersim model; chapter 2.

Economic scarcity

Economic scarcity is caused by a lack of investment in water or a lack of human capacity to satisfy the demand for water. Much of the scarcity is due to how institutions function, favoring one group over another and not hearing the voices of various groups, especially women.

Symptoms of economic water scarcity include scant infrastructure development, either small or large scale, so that people have trouble getting enough water for agriculture or drinking. And even where infrastructure exists, the distribution of water may be inequitable. Much of Sub-Saharan Africa is characterized by economic scarcity, so further water development could do much to reduce poverty.

Physical scarcity

Physical scarcity occurs when there is not enough water to meet all demands, including environmental flows. Arid regions are most often associated with physical water scarcity, but water scarcity also appears where water is apparently abundant, when water resources are overcommitted to various users due to overdevelopment of hydraulic infrastructure, most often for irrigation. In such cases there simply is not enough water to meet both human demands and environmental flow needs. Symptoms of physical water scarcity are severe environmental degradation, declining groundwater, and water allocations that favor some groups over others.

New challenges beyond scarcity

Energy affects water management now and will do so even more in the future. Energy prices are rising, pushing up the costs of pumping water, manufacturing fertilizers, and transporting products. This will have implications for access to water and irrigation. Increased hydropower will mean increased competition for water with agriculture.

Climate change policy is increasingly supporting greater reliance on bioenergy as an alternative to fossil fuel–based energy. But this is not consistently coupled with the water discussion. The Comprehensive Assessment estimates that with heavy reliance on bioenergy the amount of agricultural evapotranspiration in 2050 to support increased bioenergy use will be about what is depleted for all of agriculture today. Reliance on bioenergy will further intensify competition for water and land, so awareness of the "double-edged" nature of bioenergy needs to be raised.

Urbanization and the global market will dictate the choices of farmers around the world. Changes in the global market and the spread of globalization will determine the profitability of agriculture. Where suitable infrastructure and national policies are in place, a variety of shifting niche markets will emerge, creating opportunities for innovative entrepreneurial farmers. In some countries the contribution of farming to the national economy will shrink, with implications for smallholders and subsistence farmers who rely on extension, technology, and regional markets. The demographics of farming change with urbanization. Many women and older people will be left in rural areas to look after farms Yet agricultural development remains the single most promising engine of growth in the majority of Sub-Saharan countries. To ensure the sustainability of the agriculture sector in many of these countries, investments in technology and capacity building need to go hand in hand with policies that make farming profitable.

Climate change will affect all facets of society and the environment, directly and indirectly, with strong implications for water and agriculture now and in the future. The climate is changing at an alarming rate, causing temperature rise, shifting patterns of precipitation, and more extreme events. Agriculture in the subtropics—where most poor countries are situated—will be affected most. The future impacts of climate change need to be incorporated into project planning, with behavior, infrastructure, and investments all requiring adjusting to adapt to a changing set of climate parameters. Water storage and control investments will be important rural development strategies to respond to climate change. The impacts of policies and laws set up to reduce greenhouse gas emissions or adjust to a changing climate also need to be taken into account.

> Climate change will affect all facets of society and the environment, with strong implications for water and agriculture now and in the future

Future demand for food—and for water

As population grows, so will demand for food and water.

How much more food?

Food and feed crop demand will nearly double in the coming 50 years. The two main factors driving how much more food we will need are population growth and dietary change. With rising incomes and continuing urbanization, food habits change toward more nutritious and more varied diets—not only toward increasing consumption of staple cereals but also to a shift in consumption patterns among cereal crops and away from cereals toward livestock and fish products and high-value crops (figures 2 and 3).

Per capita food supply in Organisation for Economic Co-operation and Development (OECD) countries will level off well above 2,800 kcal, which is usually taken as

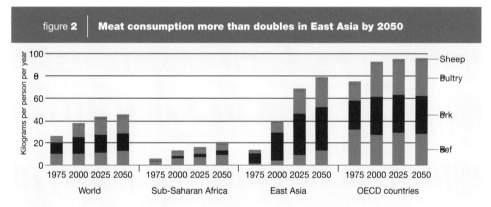

figure 2 | Meat consumption more than doubles in East Asia by 2050

Source: for 1975 and 2000, FAOSTAT statistical database; for 2025 and 2050, International Water Management Institute analysis done for the Comprehensive Assessment of Water Management in Agriculture using the Watersim model; chapter 3.

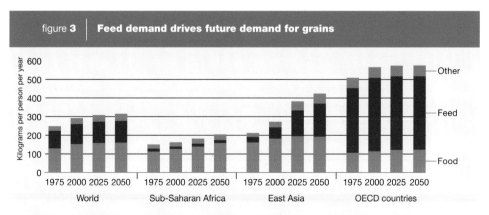

figure 3 | Feed demand drives future demand for grains

Source: for 1975 and 2000, FAOSTAT statistical database; for 2025 and 2050, International Water Management Institute analysis done for the Comprehensive Assessment of Water Management in Agriculture using the Watersim model; chapter 3.

a threshold for national food security. People in low- and middle-income countries will substantially increase their calorie intake, but a significant gap between poor and rich countries will likely remain in the coming decades.

Producing meat, milk, sugar, oils, and vegetables typically requires more water than producing cereals—and a different style of water management. Increasing livestock production requires even more grain for feed, leading to a 25% increase in grains. Thus, diets are a significant factor in determining water demands. While feed-based meat production may be water costly, grazing systems behave quite differently. From a water perspective grazing is probably the best option for large land areas, but better grazing and watering practices are needed.

'
Without further improvements in water productivity by 2050 the amount of water evaporated in crop production will almost double from today's amount

How much more water?

Without further improvements in water productivity or major shifts in production patterns, the amount of water consumed by evapotranspiration in agriculture will increase by 70%–90% by 2050. The total amount of water evaporated in crop production would amount to 12,000–13,500 cubic kilometers, almost doubling the 7,130 cubic kilometers of today. This corresponds to an average annual increase of 100–130 cubic kilometers, almost three times the volume of water supplied to Egypt through the High Aswan Dam every year.

On top of this is the amount of water needed to produce fiber and biomass for energy. Cotton demand is projected to grow by 1.5% annually, and demand for energy seems insatiable. By 2030 world energy demand will rise by 60%, two-thirds of the increase from developing countries, some from bioenergy.

Fortunately, water productivity in agriculture has steadily increased in the past decades, in large part due to increases in crop yields, and will continue to do so. The pace of this increase can vary substantially according to the type of policies and investments put in place, with substantial variation in impacts on the environment and the livelihoods of agricultural populations. Key options are explored below, using a set of scenarios (figure 4).

How can we meet food and fiber demand with our land and water resources?

The world's available land and water resources can satisfy future food demands in several ways.

- Investing to increase production in rainfed agriculture (rainfed scenario).
  - Increasing productivity in rainfed areas through enhanced management of soil moisture and supplemental irrigation where small water storage is feasible.
  - Improving soil fertility management, including the reversal of land degradation.
  - Expanding cropped areas.
- Investing in irrigation (irrigation scenario).
  - Increasing annual irrigation water supplies by innovations in system management, developing new surface water storage facilities, and increasing groundwater withdrawals and the use of wastewater.
  - Increasing water productivity in irrigated areas and value per unit of water by integrating multiple uses—including livestock, fisheries, and domestic use—in irrigated systems.
- Conducting agricultural trade within and between countries (trade scenario).

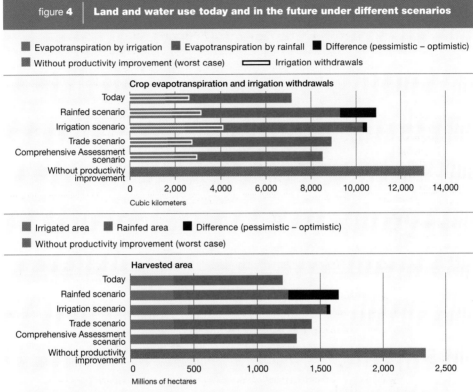

figure **4** | **Land and water use today and in the future under different scenarios**

■ Evapotranspiration by irrigation ■ Evapotranspiration by rainfall ■ Difference (pessimistic – optimistic)
■ Without productivity improvement (worst case) ▭ Irrigation withdrawals

Crop evapotranspiration and irrigation withdrawals

Today
Rainfed scenario
Irrigation scenario
Trade scenario
Comprehensive Assessment scenario
Without productivity improvement

0   2,000   4,000   6,000   8,000   10,000   12,000   14,000
Cubic kilometers

■ Irrigated area ■ Rainfed area ■ Difference (pessimistic – optimistic)
■ Without productivity improvement (worst case)

Harvested area

Today
Rainfed scenario
Irrigation scenario
Trade scenario
Comprehensive Assessment scenario
Without productivity improvement

0   500   1,000   1,500   2,000   2,500
Millions of hectares

Note: The figure shows projected amounts of water and land requirements under different scenarios. The Comprehensive Assessment scenario combines elements of the other approaches (see chapter 3 for details). The purple segments of the bars show the difference between optimistic and pessimistic assumptions for the two rainfed and two irrigated scenarios. The brown bar shows the worst cases scenario of no improvement in productivity.

Source: International Water Management Institute analysis done for the Comprehensive Assessment for Water Management in Agriculture using the Watersim model; chapter 3.

■ Reducing gross food demand by influencing diets, and reducing post-harvest losses, including industrial and household waste.

Each of these strategies will affect water use, the environment, and the poor—but in very different ways, depending on the local setting. The Comprehensive Assessment scenario combines elements of different approaches suited to each region.

Can upgrading rainfed agriculture meet future food demands?

Today, 55% of the gross value of our food is produced under rainfed conditions on nearly 72% of the world's harvested cropland. In the past, many countries focused their "water attention" and resources on irrigation development. The future food production that should come from rainfed or irrigated agriculture is the subject of intense debate, and the policy options have implications that go beyond national boundaries.

An important option is to upgrade rainfed agriculture through better water management practices. Better soil and land management practices can increase water productivity, adding a component of irrigation water through smaller scale interventions such as rainwater harvesting. Integrating livestock in a balanced way to increase the productivity of livestock water is important in rainfed areas.

At the global level the potential of rainfed agriculture is large enough to meet present and future food demand through increased productivity (see figure 4, rainfed scenario). An optimistic rainfed scenario assumes significant progress in upgrading rainfed systems while relying on minimal increases in irrigated production, by reaching 80% of the maximum obtainable yield. This leads to an average increase of yields from 2.7 metric tons per hectare in 2000 to 4.5 in 2050 (1% annual growth). With no expansion of irrigated area, the total cropped area would have to increase by only 7%, compared with 24% from 1961 to 2000, to keep pace with rising demand for agricultural commodities.

‘ At the global level the potential of rainfed agriculture is large enough to meet present and future food demand through increased productivity

But focusing only on rainfed areas carries considerable risks. If adoption rates of improved technologies are low and rainfed yield improvements do not materialize, the expansion in rainfed cropped area required to meet rising food demand would be around 53% by 2050 (figure 4). Globally, the land for this is available, but agriculture would then encroach on marginally suitable lands and add to environmental degradation, with more natural ecosystems converted to agriculture.

What can irrigated agriculture contribute?

Under optimistic assumptions about water productivity gains, three-quarters of the additional food demand can be met by improving water productivity on existing irrigated lands. In South Asia—where more than 50% of the cropped area is irrigated and productivity is low—additional food demand can be met by improving water productivity in irrigated agriculture rather than by expanding the area under production. But in parts of China and Egypt and in developed countries, yields and water productivity are already quite high, and the scope for further improvements is limited. In many rice-growing areas water savings during the wet season make little sense because they will not be easily available for other uses.

An alternative strategy is to continue expansion of irrigated land because it provides access to water to more people and can provide a more secure food future (see figure 4, irrigation scenario). Irrigation could contribute 55% of the total value of food supply by 2050. But that expansion would require 40% more withdrawals of water for agriculture, surely a threat to aquatic ecosystems and capture fisheries in many areas. In Sub-Saharan Africa there is very little irrigation, and expansion seems warranted. Doubling the irrigated area in Sub-Saharan Africa would increase irrigation's contribution to food supply from only 5% now to an optimistic 11% by 2050.

What is the potential of trade to release pressure on freshwater resources?

By importing agricultural commodities, a nation "saves" the amount of water it would have required to produce those commodities domestically. Egypt, a highly water-stressed country, imported 8 million metric tons of grain from the United States in 2000. To produce this amount of grain Egypt would have needed about 8.5 cubic kilometers of irrigation water (Egypt's annual supply from Lake Nasser is 55.6 cubic kilometers). Japan, a land-scarce country and the world's biggest grain importer, would require an additional 30 billion cubic meters of crop water consumption to grow the food it imports. Cereal trade has a moderating impact on the demand for irrigation water, because the major grain exporters—the United States, Canada, France, Australia, and Argentina—produce grain in highly productive rainfed conditions.

A strategic increase in international food trade could thus mitigate water scarcity and reduce environmental degradation (see figure 4, trade scenario). Instead of striving for food self-sufficiency, water-short countries would import food from water-abundant countries. But poor countries depend, to a large extent, on their national agriculture sector, and the purchasing power required to cover food needs from the world market is often low. Struggling with food security, these countries remain wary of depending on imports to satisfy basic food needs. A degree of food self-sufficiency is still an important policy goal. And despite emerging water problems, many countries view the development of water resources as a more secure option to achieving food supply goals and promoting income growth, particularly in poor rural communities. The implication is that under the present global and national geopolitical and economic situation, it is unlikely that food trade will solve water scarcity problems in the near term.

> But even in an optimistic investment scenario, by 2050 the cropped area will increase by 9% and water withdrawals for agriculture will increase by 13%

Influencing what happens next

With the increases in world food demand inevitable, agriculture will require more land and water. Part of the increase in food production can be achieved by improving crop yields and increasing crop water productivity, through appropriate investments in both irrigated and rainfed agriculture (table 1) as in the Comprehensive Assessment scenario. But even in an optimistic investment scenario (see figure 4, Comprehensive Assessment scenario), by 2050 the cropped area will increase by 9% and water withdrawals for agriculture will increase by 13%, taking resources away from other ecosystems. One challenge is to manage this additional water in a way that minimizes the adverse impacts on—and where possible enhances—ecosystem services and aquatic food production, while providing the necessary gains in food production and poverty alleviation. Doing so will require a water-food-environment policy agenda suited to each country and region.

table 1	Comprehensive Assessment scenario characteristics		
Region	**Scope for improved productivity in rainfed areas**	**Scope for improved productivity in irrigated areas**	**Scope for irrigated area expansion**
Sub-Saharan Africa	High	Some	High
Middle East and North Africa	Some	Some	Very limited
Central Asia and Eastern Europe	Some	Good	Some
South Asia	Good	High	Some
East Asia	Good	High	Some
Latin America	Good	Some	Some
OECD countries	Some	Some	Some

There is a need to invest in water. But the type of investment and how it is carried out make all the difference. The Comprehensive Assessment's view on investments is broad and considers a range of options (box 2). It includes investments in improving management, building effective institutions to meet changing demands, and increasing knowledge and human capacity. Despite good intentions it is difficult to make meaningful investments in crafting institutions and empowering people to make better choices about water. And it is often easier and politically more expedient to build large infrastructure without considering alternatives and the environmental and social costs. This must change.

A combination of investment, policy, and research approaches will clearly be needed, and each strategy will have risks and tradeoffs. Any strategy will require a concurrent policy shift. The global policy and economic environment will provide the overall framework for

box **2** | **The spectrum from rainfed to irrigated**

Managing water for agriculture includes a spectrum of options—from producing under fully irrigated to entirely rainfed conditions, to supporting livestock, forestry, and fisheries, and to interacting with important ecosystems. The continuum of water management practices starts with fields or grazing land entirely dependent on rainwater. On-farm conservation practices focus on storing water in the soil. Moving along the continuum, more surface water or groundwater is added to enhance crop production. This additional freshwater provides opportunities for multiple uses, including aquaculture and livestock within the production system.

Diverse options for agricultural water management along the spectrum

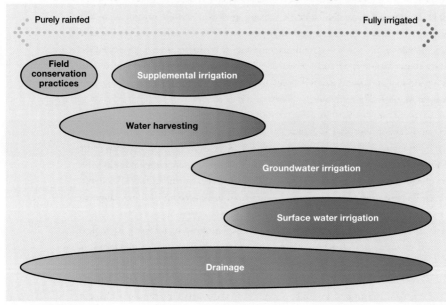

local agriculture, but local conditions will dictate the choices for future water investments in agriculture.

Change does not always require governments to spend huge sums of money. Many informed investment decisions can save money—a lot of money. And when the conditions are right, individuals will invest in water for their own welfare.

Policy action 1 Change the way we think about water and agriculture

Today's water management challenges—and tomorrow's—differ greatly from those of recent decades. More water will be needed for agriculture to reduce hunger and feed a growing population. But the impacts on poverty and ecosystems will depend on the type of investments. Thinking differently about water is a requirement if we want to achieve our triple goal of ensuring food security, reducing poverty, and conserving ecosystem integrity.

> Change does not always require governments to spend huge sums of money. Many informed investment decisions can save money

Like the challenges, the investments required today differ greatly from those in the last half century. They will have to increase human and institutional capacity and improve management and infrastructure, integrating the needs of diverse and changing demands on water resources (table 2). Investments will be more strategic, planned within the overall framework of agriculture and rural development.

It is time to abandon the obsolete divide between irrigated and rainfed agriculture. In the new policy approach rainfall will be acknowledged as the key freshwater resource, and all water resources, green and blue, will be explored for livelihood options at the appropriate scale for local communities. Also to be considered is the role of marginal-quality water in improving livelihoods. Rather than thinking of the water flowing out of cities as waste, it needs to be seen as a resource for many poor urban or periurban farmers. We need to consider agriculture as an ecosystem and to recognize the importance of preserving the natural resource base on which agricultural productivity rests. And we need to be cautious in using resources: overpumped aquifers and overdeveloped river basins are showing their limits, presenting a different set of problems.

But to support these changes, investments are required to build knowledge and to reform and develop institutions. Education, research, capacity building, and awareness raising are stepping stones toward better water management in agriculture. A new cadre of policymakers, managers, and extension providers is needed, with staff trained to understand and support producers in water management investments in farms and communities. But investments are not enough. They need to be accompanied by changes in governance and decisionmaking power.

Improving water management in agriculture requires learning by doing and a flexible, adaptive approach. Adaptive management is appropriate for variable resources in a context of continually fluctuating parameters. Adaptive management incorporates an understanding of the variability within systems, as well as long-term and slow-onset changes. It allows for management practices to be responsive to these variations, some of which can be rapid.

| table 2 | Evolution of thinking on water management in agriculture |

Past thinking	Current and future thinking
Focused attention, mainly on irrigation options and withdrawals from rivers and groundwater.	Considers options across a spectrum of water management in agriculture, including rainfed and irrigation, and integrating fisheries and livestock.
	Devotes more attention to managing rainwater, evapotranspiration, and reuse.
	Views land-use decisions as water-use decisions.
	Incorporates the interconnectedness of users through the hydrologic cycle.
Treated water for agriculture and for ecosystems as separate.	Treats agriculture as an ecosystem producing multiple services, interacting with ecosystem conservation.
Considered benefits and costs only of food production in a sectoral approach.	Adopts a broader livelihood agenda to increase assets of the poor, provide more voice in decisionmaking, raise incomes, and reduce risk and vulnerability.
Directed mainly at crop production.	Promotes the multiple functions and multiple goals of water in agriculture.
	Recognizes different roles based on gender, age, class, and caste.
Worked in a political vacuum, imposing single-factor ("magic bullet") reforms from the outside.	Structures context-specific approaches to negotiating and crafting effective institutions and policies, recognizing the contentious political nature of reforms.
Managed water in a command and control environment.	Makes irrigation services directed, flexible, reliable, and transparent.
Made investments to meet needs of poor people in the form of "interventions."	Places the means of getting out of poverty into the hands of poor people by focusing on water as a means to raise their own food.
	Increases participation in markets for higher incomes through diversification and local economic growth, creating more jobs both on and off the farm.
Expanded agricultural land to increase production.	Intensifies agriculture by increasing water and land productivity to limit additional water use and expansion onto new lands.
Saw the state as the responsible unit for resource development and management.	Makes decisions on water interventions more inclusive and transparent.
	Involves civil society organizations in decisionmaking.
Sidelined biodiversity as somebody else's problem and purely as a "conservation" issue.	Mainstreams biodiversity and ecosystem services to avoid their loss or mismanagement.
Viewed environmental use of water as "wasted" water.	Includes proper economic valuation of the environmental aspects of water use in tradeoffs and decisions for water use.

Policy action 2 Fight poverty by improving access to agricultural water and its use

Insecure access to reliable, safe, and affordable water keeps hundreds of millions of people from escaping poverty. Most of them rely directly on agriculture for their food and income. Unless bold action is taken, many more smallholder farmers, fishers, herders, and people dependent on wetlands will fall into poverty as rivers dry up, groundwater declines, and water rights are lost.

Broadly conceived, poverty reduction strategies will entail four elements:

- Empowering people to use water better, and targeting the right groups.
- Ensuring the right to secure access.
- Improving governance of water resources.
- Supporting the diversification of livelihoods.

Targeting smallholder farmers—particularly in largely rainfed areas, but also in ir- rigated areas—offers the best chance for reducing poverty quickly in developing countries. Smallholder farmers make up the majority of the world's rural poor. Often occupying mar- ginal land and depending mainly on rainfall for production, they are sensitive to droughts, floods, and shifts in markets and prices. In regions where agriculture constitutes a large proportion of the economy, water management in agriculture will remain a key element in strategies to reduce rural poverty. Smallholder farmers possess the greatest unexploited potential to directly influence land and water use management.

Focusing on livelihood gains by small-scale, individually managed water technologies holds great promise for poverty reduction in the semiarid and arid tropics. These include small pumps and innovative technologies such as low-cost drip irrigation, small affordable pumps, and small-scale water storage. These are affordable even for some of the poorest members of the community and can be implemented almost immediately, without the long delays of large projects. Private investments in pumps have improved the livelihoods and food security of millions of farmers and pastoralists in Africa and Asia. In the long run these can be viewed as a first step, followed by additional investments in infrastructure.

Clarifying water rights can ensure secure access to water for agriculture for poor women and men when carefully implemented. In certain circumstances collective wa- ter rights might be preferable to individual water rights. Redistributive policies can give the rural poor access to assets, markets, and services. Acknowledging customary laws and informal institutions can facilitate and encourage local management of water and other natural resources. The capacity of people to manage their water resources can be enhanced through specific training. Local management should be integrated with basin, regional, and national institutions—and based within the broader context of rural development.

Where there is equity in resource distribution, the poverty reducing impact of im- proved water management on agricultural productivity growth has been greater. Inequal- ity, particularly gender-based inequality, tempers the effectiveness of poverty reduction efforts. Women produce an estimated two-thirds of the food in most developing countries, yet they often have inadequate access to land, water, labor, capital, technologies, and other inputs and services. This situation is unjust and prevents women from realizing their full

Targeting smallholder farmers— particularly in largely rainfed areas, but also in irrigated areas—offers the best chance for reducing poverty quickly in developing countries

potential as human beings and citizens and compromises efforts to target water management for poverty reduction.

Small water management systems, built and operated by communities or individuals from groundwater, river water, and wastewater, are vital to many poor farmers but often are not officially recognized. Increased visibility of irrigation and water management of these informal systems will influence governments to provide policy and technical support and help to ensure poor farmers' continuing access.

Policymakers need to focus on both design and development of water resources infrastructure from a multiple-use system perspective. By doing so they can maximize the benefits per unit of water for poor women and men and ensure that institutional and legal frameworks guarantee the participation of rural people and marginal groups in all phases of policy development and decisionmaking for infrastructure investments. Multiple-use systems for domestic use, crop production, aquaculture, agroforestry, and livestock effectively improve water productivity and reduce poverty. The contributions to livelihoods, especially for poor households, of these multiple uses are substantial.

> **Multiple-use systems for domestic use, crop production, aquaculture, agroforestry, and livestock effectively improve water productivity and reduce poverty**

Agricultural water research should target poverty head on. It should look at low-cost technologies and practices adapted to accommodate gender and cultural differences. It should examine how to obtain more nutrition per drop—especially important for food security in areas without adequate market access. And it should examine how the capabilities of the poor can be enhanced to cope with floods, droughts, and other water-related hazards.

Fisheries should be better integrated in water resources management. They are an important source of livelihoods and nutrition. The value of freshwater fish production to human nutrition and incomes is far greater than gross national production figures suggest. The bulk of production is generated by small-scale activities, with exceedingly high levels of participation not only in catching and farming but also in the ancillary activities of processing and marketing.

Livestock, too, need to be better integrated in water resources management. In addition to enhancing income and food security, livestock play a big role in livelihood strategies for 70% of the world's rural poor, enabling families to survive crop failure, cope with income shocks, and meet unexpected or major family expenses by selling an animal.

Agricultural water management investments alone cannot eliminate poverty. Many poverty reduction gains come from better credit and insurance, better farm practices, stronger links to markets and support services, and improved health care. So water management approaches need to be better integrated into broader poverty reduction strategies.

Policy action 3 Manage agriculture to enhance ecosystem services

Land-use changes and water diversions for agriculture have been major drivers of the degradation and loss of ecosystems. Greater food production has come at the expense of biodiversity and ecosystem services—regulating, supporting, provisioning, and cultural—that are often important to poor people's livelihoods.

Why manage ecosystem services?

Ecosystem services of agricultural systems include flood mitigation, groundwater recharge, erosion control, and habitats for birds, fish, and other animals, in addition to food production. Many services (pollination, predation) are used as agricultural inputs.

Poor agricultural water management practices can damage ecosystems and their services in many ways. For example:

■ River and groundwater depletion and consequent degradation of downstream aquatic ecosystems, including wetlands, estuaries, and coastal ecosystems, with devastating effects on fisheries.

■ Drainage of wetlands and discharges of wastewater to surface water–dependent and groundwater-dependent ecosystems.

■ Pollution from overuse of nutrients and agrochemicals, with consequences both for terrestrial and aquatic ecosystems and for human health.

■ Poor land and water management leading to excessive erosion, causing siltation in rivers, wetlands, and coastal areas—in addition to poor soil conservation limiting green water utilization.

■ Loss of natural resource base, affecting people's livelihoods by changing coping strategies and making people more vulnerable to shocks.

> Many agricultural water management systems have evolved into diverse agroecosystems, rich in biodiversity and ecosystem services

How to manage for diverse agroecosystems

Even so, many agricultural water management systems have evolved into diverse agroecosystems, rich in biodiversity and ecosystem services far beyond food production. There are many examples where areas of paddy rice cultivation are semi-natural wetlands (figure 5).

Strategies for avoiding the adverse impacts:

■ *Improve agricultural practices to enhance a range of ecosystem services.* In agroecosystems there is scope to promote services beyond the production of food, fiber, and animal products. Agricultural production does not have to be at the expense of other services provided by water in wetlands and rivers.

■ *Align support for maintaining or improving ecosystem services by ensuring that the rural poor realize considerable benefits.* Otherwise, poverty alleviation and healthy ecosystems will seem in competition.

■ *Adapt to manage the water used by agroecosystems and to accommodate the uncertainty about ecosystem change.*

■ *Improve land and water management to incorporate a better understanding of the importance and role of biodiversity.* Biodiversity underpins ecosystem services, and its proper management is essential to maintaining and improving human well-being. Managing these relationships must be the responsibility of all who use water.

■ *Have managers manage for diversity and engineers engineer for diversity.* Diversity is good for economic and ecosystem prosperity, resilience, and sustainability. A way to maintain diversity is to manage agroecosystems to mimic as closely as possible their natural character and state—for example, by releasing environmental flows with a pattern close to the original. Simplifying parts of ecosystems to increase economic output for certain sectors or stakeholders (intense monocropping) is not necessarily

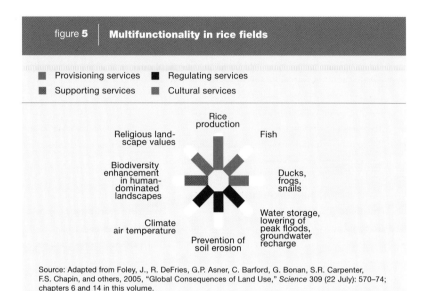

figure 5 | **Multifunctionality in rice fields**

■ Provisioning services ■ Regulating services
■ Supporting services ▓ Cultural services

Rice production

Religious land-scape values

Fish

Biodiversity enhancement in human-dominated landscapes

Ducks, frogs, snails

Climate air temperature

Water storage, lowering of peak floods, groundwater recharge

Prevention of soil erosion

Source: Adapted from Foley, J., R. DeFries, G.P. Asner, C. Barford, G. Bonan, S.R. Carpenter, F.S. Chapin, and others, 2005, "Global Consequences of Land Use," *Science* 309 (22 July): 570–74; chapters 6 and 14 in this volume.

bad and can be a productive use of ecosystems. But it must be conducted under a broader strategy that manages ecosystem services overall—and that promotes sustaining and rehabilitating ecosystem diversity.

■ *Raise awareness of the role and value of ecosystem services*—through education, information dissemination, and dialogues among stakeholders, sectors, and disciplines.

■ *Improve inventories, assessments, and monitoring*, especially of factors related to ecosystem resilience and thresholds that, once crossed, preclude a system from providing a range of services.

Policy action 4 Increase the productivity of water

Increasing water's productivity—gaining more yield and value from water—is an effective means of intensifying agricultural production and reducing environmental degradation. There are reasons to be optimistic. There is still ample scope for higher physical water productivity—getting more produce per unit of water—in low-yielding rainfed areas and in poorly performing irrigation systems, where poverty and food insecurity prevail. Good agricultural practices—managing soil fertility and reducing land degradation—are important for increasing crop per drop. Our assessment of livestock and fisheries reveals scope for improvements in these systems as well—important because of the growing demand for meat and fish.

Reasons for optimism—and caution

There are many well known crop per drop improvements. These include more reliable and precise distribution and application (such as drip) of irrigation water, supplemental and deficit irrigation, improved soil fertility, and soil conservation practices. In smallholder livestock systems, feeding animals crop residues can provide a severalfold increase in water productivity. Integrated approaches are more effective than single technologies.

But caution and care must be mixed with the optimism. Water productivity gains are often difficult to realize, and there are misperceptions about the scope for increasing physical water productivity. For example:

- Much of the potential gain in physical water productivity has already been met in high-productivity regions.
- Waste in irrigation is less than commonly perceived, especially because of reuse of water locally or downstream—farmers thirsty for water do not let it flow easily down the drain.
- Major gains and breakthroughs, as those in the past from breeding and biotechnology, are much less likely (box 3).
- A water productivity gain by one user may be a loss to another—upstream gain may be offset by a loss in fisheries, or the gain may put more agrochemicals into the environment.

There is greater reason to be optimistic about increasing economic water productivity—getting more value per unit of water. How? By switching to higher value agricultural uses. Or by reducing costs of production. Integrated approaches—agriculture-aquaculture systems, better integrating livestock in irrigated and rainfed systems, using irrigation water for household and small industries—all are important for increasing the value and jobs per drop. One example: better veterinary services can improve water productivity because healthier animals provide more benefits per unit of water.

Higher physical water productivity and economic water productivity reduce poverty in two ways. First, targeted interventions enable poor people or marginal producers to gain access to water or to use water more productively for nutrition and income generation. Second, the multiplier effects on food security, employment, and income can benefit the poor. But programs must ensure that the gains reach the poor, especially poor rural women, and are not captured by wealthier or more powerful users. Inclusive negotiations increase the chance that all voices will be heard.

> Increasing water's productivity is an effective means of intensifying agricultural production and reducing environmental degradation

With the right policy and institutional environment

Many known technologies and management practices promise considerable gains in water productivity. Achieving those gains requires a policy and institutional environment that

---

| box 3 | Can biotechnology improve water productivity? |

For the Comprehensive Assessment of Water Management in Agriculture we conclude that only moderate impacts on crop water productivity can be expected from genetic improvements to plants over the next 15–20 years. But these improvements will reduce the risk of crop failure. Gains from breeding non-traditional crops and fish can improve water productivity. They can be achieved through slow conventional breeding, but be sped up by using appropriate biotechnological tools, of which genetically modified organisms are only one means. Greater, easier, and less contentious gains are to be made through better management, because there is already such a wide gap between practice and biophysical potential.

aligns the incentives of various users at different scales—from field to basin to country—to encourage the uptake of new techniques and to deal with tradeoffs. It requires policies that:

- *Overcome risks.* Farmers face low prices for their output, uncertainties in markets, and uncertainties in water distribution and rain. Managing water reduces some of these risks. Better market access and information help. But some sort of insurance may also be needed.

> **Many known technologies and management practices promise considerable gains in water productivity. Achieving those gains requires a policy and institutional environment that aligns the incentives of various users at different scales**

- *Provide incentives for gains in water productivity.* The incentives of producers (more water for more produce and income) are often much different from those of broader society (less water for agriculture, more for cities and the environment). Rather than trying to charge farmers more for water use, the parts of society benefiting from re-allocations may need to compensate farmers for less water use in agriculture.

- *Adjust basin-level water allocation policies.* Changes in practices aimed at increasing water productivity result in changes in other parts of a river basin. Increasing agricultural pro-duction by using saved water or increasing water harvesting may leave less water for down-stream users—such as coastal fisheries. Before implementing change, there must be an un-derstanding of basin hydrology and an overall perspective on water allocation programs, so that there is a real increase in basin-level water productivity, not just local gains.

- *Target the poor with sustainable, water productivity-enhancing practices.* Wealthier and more powerful users tend to capture gains, especially in ill-devised development or relief programs. A long-term, carefully designed program—to integrate technologies, practices, and markets, to reduce risks, and to ensure profitability—is required for pro-poor gains.

- *Look for opportunities outside the water sector.* Many possibilities exist for addressing the vulnerability, risk, markets, and profitability of agricultural enterprise.

High priorities for water productivity improvement include:

- Areas where poverty is high and water productivity low, where the poor could benefit—much of Sub-Saharan Africa and parts of South Asia and Latin America (figures 6 and 7).

- Areas of physical water scarcity where there is intense competition for water—the Indus Basin and Yellow River—especially through gains in economic water productivity.

- Areas with little water resource development, such as Sub-Saharan Africa, where a little water can make a big difference.

- Areas of water-driven ecosystem degradation, such as falling groundwater tables and drying rivers.

Policy action 5 Upgrade rainfed systems— a little water can go a long way

About 70% of the world's poor people live in rural areas where livelihood options outside of agriculture are limited. Many rural poor rely mainly on rainfed farming for food, but variable rainfall, dry spells, and droughts make rainfed farming a risky business (map 3). Better management of rainwater, soil moisture, and supplemental irrigation is the key to helping the greatest number of poor people, for three main reasons:

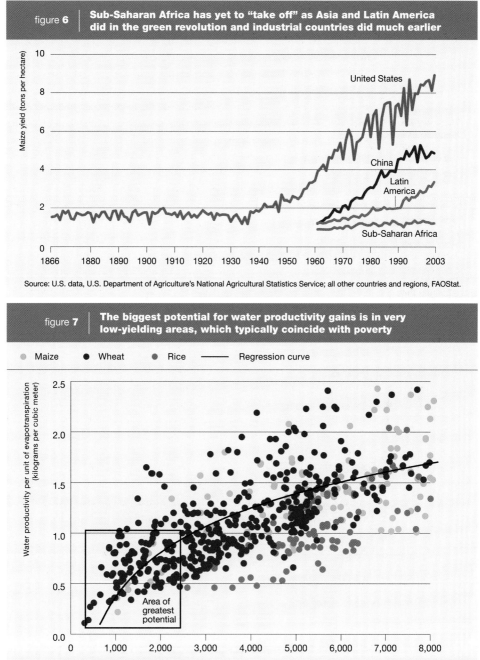

figure 6 | **Sub-Saharan Africa has yet to "take off" as Asia and Latin America did in the green revolution and industrial countries did much earlier**

Maize yield (tons per hectare)

United States

China

Latin America

Sub-Saharan Africa

1866 1880 1890 1900 1910 1920 1930 1940 1950 1960 1970 1980 1990 2003

Source: U.S. data, U.S. Department of Agriculture's National Agricultural Statistics Service; all other countries and regions, FAOStat.

figure 7 | **The biggest potential for water productivity gains is in very low-yielding areas, which typically coincide with poverty**

Maize   Wheat   Rice   —— Regression curve

Water productivity per unit of evapotranspiration (kilograms per cubic meter)

Area of greatest potential

Yield (kilograms per hectare)

Source: Adapted from Zwart, S.J., and W.G.M. Bastiaanssen, 2004, "Review of Measured Crop Water Productivity Values for Irrigated Wheat, Rice, Cotton and Maize," *Agricultural Water Management* 69 (2): 115–33; chapter 7.

- It cuts the yield losses from dry spells—which can claim one of every five harvests in Sub-Saharan Africa.
- It gives farmers the security they need to risk investing in other inputs such as fertilizers and high-yielding varieties. Farmers dare not risk the little they have buying inputs for a crop that may fail for lack of water.
- It allows farmers to grow higher value market crops, such as vegetables or fruits. These are more sensitive to water stress and require costlier inputs. Farmers can then move away from low-value staple foods and earn cash incomes.

Better management of rainwater and soil moisture is the key to helping the greatest number of poor people

Improving agricultural productivity in areas that depend on rainfall has the greatest potential to reduce poverty and hunger, especially for Sub-Saharan Africa and large parts of Asia. Current yields in many rainfed settings are low, and improving rainfed farming could double or quadruple yields. Such yields "gaps" are greatest for maize, sorghum, and millet in Sub-Saharan Africa. Closing those gaps promises huge social, economic, and environmental paybacks.

Slow uptake

While numerous studies document the benefits of upgrading rainfed agriculture by soil and water conservation practices, water harvesting, and supplemental irrigation, these tend to be isolated successes. Adoption rates have been low for four main reasons: the low profitability of agriculture, lack of markets, relatively high labor costs, and high risks. Past efforts have not changed national yields very much. Needed now is to improve farmers' access to markets,

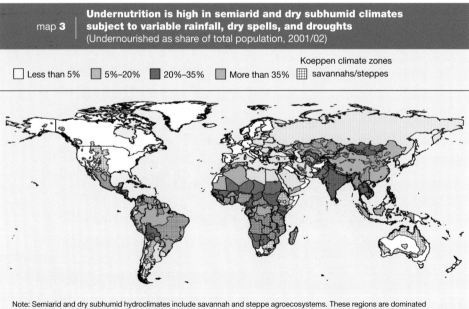

map 3 | **Undernutrition is high in semiarid and dry subhumid climates subject to variable rainfall, dry spells, and droughts**
(Undernourished as share of total population, 2001/02)

Koeppen climate zones

☐ Less than 5%   ■ 5%–20%   ■ 20%–35%   ■ More than 35%   ▦ savannahs/steppes

Note: Semiarid and dry subhumid hydroclimates include savannah and steppe agroecosystems. These regions are dominated by sedentary farming subject to the world's highest rainfall variability and occurrence of dry spells and droughts.
Source: UNStat database, 2005, United Nations Statistical Division, http://unstats.un.org/unsd/default.htm; chapter 8.

credits, and inputs (fertilizers). But the first step would be to target water—because without having water where and when it is needed, rural people risk crop failure and hunger.

Investments to reduce vulnerability to water-related risks and improve productivity in rainfed areas are compelling for equity and for the environment. Investment costs per hectare are lower in rainfed areas than in irrigated areas. The systems can be quickly implemented, yield fast and high marginal returns, and slash poverty. The technologies for upgrading rainfed agriculture already exist—and in some cases have been around for thousands of years. For example, conservation tillage, which disturbs the soil as little as possible to avoid soil moisture loss, is practiced on 45 million hectares, mostly in South and North America. In Rajasthan, India, the restoration of traditional water-harvesting structures that had fallen into disuse allowed farmers to gain a second cropping season, improve their productivity, and reduce groundwater pumping costs.

Realizing the potential of existing rainfed areas reduces the need for water withdrawals for new large-scale irrigation development, although improving rainfed production through water harvesting and supplemental irrigation also requires infrastructure, if smaller and more distributed.

Realizing this potential also requires measures of risk mitigation. Agricultural production in semiarid areas is highly vulnerable to variable climate and to future climate change. And too much reliance on rainfall may reduce farmers' ability to adapt to change. Water-harvesting techniques are useful to bridge short dry periods, but longer dry periods may lead to crop failure. Because of this risk, farmers are reluctant to invest in fertilizers, pesticides, and labor, creating a circular pattern of risk and poverty. Adding an irrigation component is often an important element of upgrading rainfed agricultre.

Nor is upgrading rainfed agriculture free of negative environmental consequences. Depending on the setting, harvesting rainwater increases the amount of water depleted by crops, leaving less for runoff to rivers and lakes or for groundwater recharge. Impacts on downstream resources need site-specific assessments.

> Investments to reduce vulnerability to water-related risks and improve productivity in rainfed areas are compelling for equity and for the environment

Accelerating progress

But with the right incentives and measures to mitigate risks for individual farmers, water management in rainfed agriculture holds large potential to increase food production and reduce poverty, while maintaining ecosystem services.

Key steps for tapping rainwater's potential to boost yields and incomes:

■ *Make more rainwater available to crops when it is most needed.* This can be done by capturing more rainfall, storing it for use when needed, adding irrigation to rainfed systems, using it more efficiently, and cutting the amount that evaporates unused. Water harvesting, supplemental irrigation, conservation tillage, and small-scale technologies (treadle pumps and simple drip-irrigation kits) are all proven options. For example, small investments providing 100 liters per square meter for supplemental irrigation during dry spells when crops are flowering or at the grain-filling stage could more than double agricultural and water productivity. This is much less than what is required for typical full-time irrigation.

■ *Build capacity.* Water planners and policymakers need to develop and apply rainwater management strategies, and extension services need the skills and commitment to get rainwater-exploitation techniques out to farmers and to work with them to adapt and innovate for their specific context. This has been a blind spot of river basin management

- *Expand water and agricultural policies and institutions.* Rainwater management in upper catchments and on farms should be included in management plans, and supporting water institutions are needed.

The challenge for irrigated agriculture in this century is to improve equity, reduce environmental damage, increase ecosystem services, and enhance water and land productivity in existing and new irrigated systems

Policy action 6 Adapt yesterday's irrigation to tomorrow's needs

In large parts of the developing world irrigation is still the backbone of rural economies (map 4). While irrigation will continue to be critical to meeting global food needs and to sustaining rural economies, the conditions that led to massive public investment in large-scale irrigation in the second half of the 20th century have changed greatly.

The era of rapid expansion of large-scale public irrigated agriculture is over: a major new task is adapting yesterday's irrigation systems to tomorrow's needs. More than anything, irrigation must respond to changing requirements, serving an increasingly productive agriculture. Reforming water management institutions is a priority—changing incentive structures and building capacities to meet new challenges.

Why invest in irrigation?

Investments in irrigation, though still needed, must become more strategic (box 4). Irrigation has to be seen in the context of other development investments, taking into consideration the big picture of costs and benefits, including social, cultural, economic, and environmental aspects. Also to be considered is the full spectrum of irrigation options—from large-scale systems providing water for all or most of a crop's needs to small-scale technologies supplying water to bridge dry spells in rainfed areas.

Improving the performance of existing systems and adding new irrigation can reduce poverty by increasing farmer incomes, providing employment for the landless, reducing staple food prices, and contributing to overall economic growth by inducing secondary benefits, such as boosting agroindustry.

What kind of investment and how much?

The challenge for irrigated agriculture in this century is to improve equity, reduce environmental damage, increase ecosystem services, and enhance water and land productivity in existing and new irrigated systems. Countries need to tailor irrigation investments to local circumstances—reflecting the stage of national development, integration into the world economy, degree of poverty and equity, availability of land and water, share of agriculture in the national economy, and comparative advantage in local, regional, and world markets.

In some areas there is scope for expanding irrigation, especially in Sub-Saharan Africa. In others the challenge is to get more from existing infrastructure—through technical upgrading and better management practices.

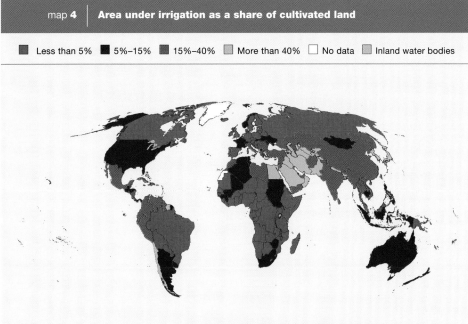

map 4 | **Area under irrigation as a share of cultivated land**

■ Less than 5%   ■ 5%–15%   ■ 15%–40%   ■ More than 40%   ☐ No data   ■ Inland water bodies

Source: Food and Agriculture Organization, 2006, FAOSTAT database, http://faostat.fao.org; chapter 9.

box 4 | **Four reasons to invest in irrigation**

1. To reduce poverty in rural areas. In countries and regions that rely on agriculture for a large part of their GDP (most of Sub-Saharan Africa), raising agricultural productivity is the most viable option for reducing poverty, and irrigation development can act as a springboard for economic development. Irrigation schemes can facilitate multiple uses of water that combine agriculture with livestock, fisheries, and other income-generating activities to enhance rural incomes and sustainability.

2. To keep up with global demand for agricultural products and adapt to changing food prefer-ences and societal demands. Feeding an additional 2–3 billion people by 2050 will require greater productivity on existing irrigated lands and some expansion of irrigation. Urbanization in many devel-oping countries shifts demand from staple crops to fruits, vegtables, and livestock products.

3. To adapt to urbanization, industrialization, and increasing allocations to the environment. In-creasing competition for water will require investments that enable farmers to grow more food with less water.

4. To respond to climate change. Climate variability and extremes may require large water storage facilities, further irrigation development, and changes in the operation of existing schemes.

While in places these reasons will justify investments in new irrigated infrastructure, the bulk of fu-ture investments will focus on preserving and modernizing existing irrigation systems to improve their performance and adapt them to their new function. This is particularly relevant to South Asia, where yields are low, inequity is substantial, and water logging and salinization are pervasive.

Productivity gains are possible across the full spectrum of existing irrigated agriculture, driven by the market and incentives that lead to profitable farm incomes. Large-scale surface irrigation systems need to incorporate better information and water control, have more of a service-oriented culture, and be more responsive to the needs of farmers, livestock keepers, fishers, and those who use water for small industry or domestic use.

Irrigation management must also increase the reliability of water supply. More finance will be required for well conceived improvements in water control and delivery, automation and measurement, and for better training and professional development of staff.

More investments in technical and managerial upgrading are required in countries with aging irrigation infrastructure. Investments in drainage are likely to continue at fairly modest levels. There will thus be considerable tension between financial needs and a government's willingness and ability to finance them.

> In some areas there is scope for expanding irrigation—in others the challenge is to get more from existing infrastructure

Manage groundwater sustainably

Thanks to a global groundwater boom, millions of farmers and pastoralists in Asia and Africa have improved their livelihoods and food security. Groundwater has contributed significantly to growth in irrigated areas since the 1970s, especially in South Asia and the North China Plains, regions with high concentrations of rural poverty. Overwhelming evidence from Asia suggests that groundwater irrigation promotes greater interpersonal, intergender, interclass, and spatial equity than does large surface irrigation.

But the boom has turned to bust. Runaway expansion in groundwater irrigation poses an environmental threat but remains a mainstay of smallholder agrarian livelihoods. The energy-groundwater nexus has created a curious political economy paradox: soaring energy prices may help save the aquifers but threaten groundwater-based livelihood systems. Improving the energy efficiency of groundwater irrigation may help save aquifers and livelihoods. In those areas current trends in groundwater use will not be sustained unless accompanied by far more intensive resource management.

But in other areas groundwater's potential could be further exploited. In areas with good aquifers and recharge and a high prevalence of poverty, such as the Gangetic plains, groundwater irrigation remains an important development strategy. How best to manage it? Participatory approaches to sustainable groundwater management will need to combine supply-side measures (artificial recharge, aquifer recovery, interbasin transfers) with demand-side measures (groundwater pricing, legal and regulatory control, water rights and withdrawal permits, water-saving crops and technologies).

Supply-side measures have proved easier to implement than demand-side measures—even in technologically advanced countries. But the only way to relax aquifer systems to an acceptable degree may be to reduce irrigated areas, improve farming practices, and switch to water-saving crops—difficult to implement, especially in developing countries.

Make the best use of marginal-quality water where it matters

Freshwater of marginal quality is an important source of water. Millions of small-scale farmers in urban and periurban areas of developing countries irrigate with wastewater from residential, commercial, and industrial sources, in many areas not treated before use. Millions of other farmers in deltaic areas and tailend sections of large-scale irrigation schemes irrigate with a blend of canal water, saline drainage water, and wastewater. Many of them cannot control the volume or quality of water they receive within a week, month, or season.

Wastewater reuse in agriculture is difficult to assess, but it is clearly important in several areas, largely in arid and wet environments. In Hanoi, Viet Nam, 80% of vegetables are irrigated with water mixed with wastewater, and in Kumasi, Ghana, recorded informal irrigation, much of it using wastewater, covers 11,900 hectares, about a third of the officially recorded irrigated area of the country. There are three main policy approaches for improving management of marginal-quality water: reduce the amount of marginal-quality water generated, minimize the risks when it is used in agriculture, and minimize the risks when handling food grown with such water.

Change the governance of irrigation

Needed, above all, is to change the governance of irrigation. With the general decline in construction of new systems and the shift of management responsibilities to users, the role of public irrigation agencies is rapidly changing. Activities in planning and designing systems, contracting for and supervising civil works, and delivering water to farms will be less important. New responsibilities will include resource allocation, bulk water delivery, basin-level management, sector regulation, and the achievement of global social and environmental goals such as the Millennium Development Goals.

Policy action 7 Reform the reform process—targeting state institutions

The state will retain its role as the main driver of reform, but it is also the institution most in need of reform. There are cases of "failing states" in addition to situations where structural adjustment has brought major transformations to the detriment of agriculture and water management. The state must take responsibility for ensuring greater equity in access to water resources and foster investments to reduce poverty. Protecting essential ecosystem services is also vital, especially to poor people's livelihoods.

The last 30 years of attempts at agricultural water reform have, with few exceptions, shown disappointing results. Despite repeated calls for decentralization, integration, reform, and better governance, implementation has not been entirely successful, and much remains to be done to achieve effective changes (box 5).

The approach to reform needs to be reconsidered. Instead of the linear, prescriptive models that have dominated thinking for the past several decades, the Comprehensive Assessment proposes a more nuanced and organic approach to institutional reform—one grounded in the local socioeconomic, political, and physical environment and cognizant of the dynamic nature of institutions (box 6).

Why have previous approaches so often failed?

Many reforms have not taken into account the history, culture, environment, and vested interests that shape the scope for institutional change. They have often been based

> Reforms have focused on formal irrigation or water management policies and organizations and have ignored the many other factors that affect water use in agriculture—policies in other sectors, user institutions, and broader social institutions

| box **5** | **Prescriptive models of reform often fail to deliver expected benefits** |

- *Irrigation management transfer.* To reduce government expenditure and improve irrigation performance, many countries have pursued a policy of transferring irrigation management from the state to user groups (water user associations or farmer organizations).

  This has demonstrated potential, but the results have been mixed.
- *River basin organizations.* Centralized basin organizations have been widely touted as the ideal organizational model for managing competition for water and for implementing integrated water resources management.

  Countries would do well to consider placing more emphasis on developing, managing, and maintaining collaborative relationships for basin governance—building on existing organizations, customary practices, and administrative structures.
- *Pricing irrigation water.* Pricing irrigation water has been promoted as the way to achieve water-use efficiency and to cover the costs of construction and operation and maintenance of infrastructure.

  Implementation has frequently foundered on political opposition, compounded by difficulties in measuring water deliveries and collecting fees from large numbers of small users. Applied as a blanket measure, pricing—at a level to be effective as a demand-management mechanism—risks aggravating water deprivation and poverty.
- *Tradable water rights.* The other aspect of pricing that has attracted attention is related to water markets. In countries where water rights exist and are separate from land rights, markets can, in theory, ensure efficient reallocation of water among sectors through trading.

  In practice, water trading has thus far only reallocated small volumes of the resource (less than 1% a year of permanent entitlements in Australia and the western United States). Based on experience thus far, water markets are unlikely to have a big impact on agricultural water use in Asia or Sub-Saharan Africa in the coming 20–30 years.

on "blueprint" solutions—solutions that follow a model that may have been successful elsewhere. Another reason reforms fall short is a focus on a single type of organization rather than the larger institutional context. Focusing on formal irrigation or water management policies and organizations, most reforms have ignored the many other factors that affect water use in agriculture—policies and government agencies in other sectors, informal user institutions, and the macroeconomic environment and broader social institutions.

Other common stumbling blocks include:
- *Inadequate support for reform at required levels.* Change requires support at the policy and decisionmaking level and at the implementation level.
- *Inadequate capacity building and incentives for change.* For individuals and organizations to change their way of doing things, they often need new skills and knowledge.
- *Repeated underestimation of the time, effort, and investment required to change.* Particularly for reforms tied to time-bound, donor-funded projects, there is a tendency to expect too much too quickly. The result: reforms are prematurely judged unsuccessful and are left incomplete or abandoned.

| box 6 | Seven imperatives for today's agricultural water management |

1. Get technical water bureaucracies to see water management not just as a technical issue but also as a social and political issue. This would require meeting the multiple water needs of poor women and men—for growing food, for drinking, for enabling hygiene and sanitation, and for generating income through a range of activities.

2. Support more integrated approaches to agricultural water management. Examples include managing water to enhance ecosystem services in addition to crop production, incorporating livestock and fisheries into water management, improving rainwater management and encouraging investments to upgrade rainfed production, and supporting systems and services that encompass multiple water uses, safe reuse of wastewater, and joint use of surface water and groundwater.

3. Create incentives for water users and government agency staff to improve the equity, efficiency, and sustainability of water use.

4. Improve the effectiveness of the state, particularly in its regulatory role, and find the right balance between action by the state and by other institutional actors.

5. Develop effective coordination and negotiation mechanisms among the state, civil society, and private organizations in water development and management and in related sectors.

6. Empower women and marginalized groups who have a stake but currently not a voice in water management. Specific support institutions are needed to progress toward the Millennium Development Goals.

7. Build coalitions among government, civil society, and private and community users—and harness market forces for successful reform.

Crafting reform strategies

Moving forward requires strategies for institutional and policy reform that take into account today's (and yesterday's) realities. First, reform is an inherently political process. Second, the state is the primary, but not the only, driver in reform. Third, the pluralism and social embeddedness of institutions affect water development, management, and use. Fourth, capacity building, information sharing, and public debate are essential. Fifth, implementation plans must be responsive to new knowledge and opportunities.

Policy action 8 Deal with tradeoffs and make difficult choices

Water management today requires making difficult choices and learning to deal with tradeoffs. In reality, win-win situations will be hard to find. But a consultative and inclusive process for reaching decisions can help ensure that tradeoffs do not have inequitable effects.

Reform and change are unpredictable. Even with the best science there will always be a high level of uncertainty about external drivers and about the impacts of decisions. One of the biggest drivers will be climate change, which will affect productivity and ecosystems and will require policies and laws in response to change. Water management institutions must take an adaptive management approach. They need the capacity to identify danger signs and the flexibility to change policy when better understanding emerges. Informed multistakeholder negotiations are required to deal with tradeoffs, and innovative means to apply decisions.

The big tradeoffs

- *Water storage for agriculture—water for the environment.* The Comprehensive Assessment points to the need for more storage of water including, as locally appropriate, that behind large and small dams, in groundwater, and by water harvesting—albeit at a slower rate. Storage will be a widespread response to changing rainfall in many regions as a result of climate change. But it will also take water away from environmental uses.

- *Reallocation—overallocation.* Providing access to water and safeguarding rights to water were identified as key poverty concerns. But in many "closed" basins resources are already overallocated, making allocation decisions particularly difficult. New allocations of water in closed basins will require renegotiating water allocation. Who will benefit the most from water gains? And how will losses be compensated?

- *Upstream—downstream.* Freshwater fisheries, environmental flows, and coastal areas are all affected by developments upstream in river basins, often without discussion. Part of the difficulty is that cause-effect relations are difficult to identify, so actions are taken without knowing the consequence. And poor fishers lack the voice or political clout to retain their water.

- *Equity—productivity.* Promoting productive and efficient agriculture tends to favor the wealthy, and promoting more equitable agriculture is not necessarily productive.

- *This generation—the next ones.* Some choices made now can be a benefit, or a cost, for future generations. With groundwater levels dropping in many areas, mining it further today may mean that someone tomorrow will not enjoy the same resource. But encouraging economic growth by using groundwater now could mean that people in the future can move more easily away from dependence on groundwater.

> The Comprehensive Assessment finds that more balanced outcomes are generally reached when there is a mix of political space allowed by the state and active organization of civil society to defend causes or population groups

Making difficult choices

The state's role in driving reform may be critical, but it cannot make changes alone. Alone, writing new laws or passing administrative orders achieves little. Good governance is rarely triggered by well intentioned policy documents or participatory rhetoric. The Comprehensive Assessment finds that more balanced outcomes are generally reached when there is a mix of political space allowed by the state and active organization of civil society to defend causes or population groups.

There is a need to identify incentives or mechanisms to compensate those who stand to lose in water allocation decisions. The concept of payment for environmental services has given ecosystems a voice in this.

Elements critical for negotiating tradeoffs:

- *Foster social action and public debate.* Public debate based on shared information creates more trust, legitimacy, and understanding of the reasons for change—increasing the likelihood of implementation. Such debate creates opportunities to include poor stakeholders—those with the most to gain (or lose), among them the too-often

unrecognized landless, fishers, pastoralists, and those dependent on wetland and forest ecosystem services.

■ *Develop better tools for assessing tradeoffs.* Such tools can help in deciding which ecosystem services in a particular area most benefit society. Existing tools include cost-
benefit analyses, valuation of nonmarket services, assessments of risk and vulnerability, and models for estimating the water flows required by wetlands.

■ *Share knowledge and information equitably.* More data need to be generated, turned
into reliable information, and shared widely with stakeholders to empower them
through better awareness and understanding—that is, through knowledge. New
skills and capacities in water management institutions are critical—at a time when
government capacities to attract and hold people with this expertise are weakening.

Part 1 | Setting the scene

Chapter 1 sets the scene, introduces the context of the assessment, and describes key concepts used throughout the assessment.

Agricultural water use supports life

Artists: Jhun Jhun Jha and Hira Karn, Nepal

1 | Setting the scene

Authors: David Molden, Jean-Marc Faurès, C. Max Finlayson, Habiba Gitay, Joke Muylwijk, Lisa Schipper, Domitille Vallée, and David Coates

We face unprecedented challenges of water management—how to use water sustainably to respond to the increasing demand for agricultural products in many areas and how to find practical solutions where water use has exceeded sustainable limits. We need both more solutions and innovative ways of looking for them. This assessment starts with the premise that there are ways to ensure economic and social development while satisfying the increasing needs for safer and more sustainable agricultural practices.

Modern agricultural practices, including major investments in high-yielding plant varieties and farming systems using high inputs of agrochemicals and water, have enabled growth in world food production to outpace population growth and caused global food prices to fall. Increased water use for agriculture has benefited farmers and poor people globally. But there remains much unfinished business and many complex challenges for the agriculture sector: providing rural people with resources and opportunities to live healthy and productive lives, producing more and better quality food using less water per unit of output, applying clean technologies that ensure environmental sustainability, and contributing productively to local and national economies.

And despite abundant food and lower food prices, the task of providing food security to all remains incomplete. At the beginning of the 21st century 850 million people in the world remain food insecure, 60% of them living in South Asia and Sub-Saharan Africa, and 70% of the poor live in rural areas. Many of these people live in regions where financial and institutional resources and ill-adapted policies constrain agricultural and human development. In households responsibility for food security falls mainly on women, who receive insufficient attention in policymaking related to this basic need.

Relatively neglected during the green revolution in agriculture has been the role of water for healthy ecosystems. There are too many examples of fragmented, desiccated, and polluted rivers; endangered aquatic species; accumulations of agricultural chemicals; and loss and degradation of natural ecosystems (MEA 2005). Rapidly growing urban areas burgeoning industries, and rising use of chemicals in agriculture have undermined the quality of many rivers, lakes, aquifers, and other ecosystems. Groundwater resources, an increasingly preferred source of agricultural and drinking water, are becoming polluted or are depleted to levels that make access difficult or uneconomical and unsustainable.

> Ensuring equitable access to water and its benefits now and for future generations is a major challenge as scarcity and competition increase

The aim of the Comprehensive Assessment of Water Management in Agriculture

The outlook for the coming decades is that agriculture will require more water to meet the demands of growing populations. Ensuring equitable access to water and its benefits now and for future generations is a major challenge as scarcity and competition increase. With growing concern for the environment, some difficult choices will have to be made. Further tradeoffs cannot be avoided and will be politically contested. Choices about water use and management in agriculture will determine to a large extent whether societies reach the interlinked multiple goals of economic and social development and environmental sustainability as articulated in the Millennium Development Goals (table 1.1).

How should water be managed for agriculture in the future? World Water Vision, culminating in The Hague in 2000, produced the *Vision for Water and Nature* (IUCN 2000) and "A Vision for Water for Food and Rural Development" (van Hofwegen and Svendsen 2000). These two "visions" contain widely diverging views on the need to develop additional water resources for agriculture, on how society should use water, and on the benefits and costs of such developments. A major reason for the divergence? The difference in understanding of some basic premises, such as how effectively water is used for

table **1.1**	Relationship of water management in agriculture to the Millennium Development Goals
Millennium Development Goal	**Role of water management in agriculture**
Goal 1 Eradicate extreme poverty and hunger	Increase agricultural production and productivity to keep up with rising demand and maintain affordable food prices for the poor; improve access to factors of production and markets for the rural poor.
Goal 3 Promote gender equality and empower women	Enhance equitable access to water and thus the ability to produce food.
Goal 4 Reduce child mortality	Contribute to better hygiene and diets, particularly through the appropriate use of marginal-quality water and the integration of multiple water-use approaches into new and existing agricultural water management systems, including domestic and productive functions.
Goal 5 Improve maternal health	
Goal 6 Combat HIV/AIDS, malaria, and other diseases.	
Goal 7 Ensure environmental sustainability	Integrate the principles of sustainable development into agricultural water development to reverse the loss of environmental resources.
Goal 8 Develop a global partnership for development	Involve the diverse range of practitioners, researchers, and decisionmakers in the preparation of water management actions.

poverty reduction, the extent of ecological impact, the contribution of groundwater, and the current use and future potential of rainfed agriculture. Both technical and institutional solutions are proposed, but uptake is difficult and potential impacts are under debate. Lacking is adequate knowledge of past impacts and a clear sense of the present situation of water use.

A major step toward creating more equitable and effective use of water in agriculture in developing countries is to take stock of how water is currently managed for agriculture and of the impacts of its use on food and environmental sustainability. To move forward we need to combine knowledge of what has worked and what has failed and who has benefited and who has not, with information on promising and less conventional approaches that may hold the key to future water management. And we need to identify the range of sources of potential increases in agricultural water productivity and the ways to realize them. The Comprehensive Assessment of Water Management in Agriculture was designed to come to grips with these issues on a practical level, provide a better understanding of approaches that are likely to succeed, and identify key gaps in knowledge.

> The Comprehensive Assessment was designed to come to grips with issues on a practical level, provide a better understanding of approaches that are likely to succeed, and identify key gaps in knowledge

Key concepts

Water management in agriculture requires an interdisciplinary and integrated approach. The issues span numerous fields of inquiry and dimensions of livelihoods. Key concepts that are used repeatedly throughout the assessment are explained below.

Agricultural water sources and flows

The Comprehensive Assessment starts with rain as the ultimate source of water. This is different from the conventional view of water for agriculture, which focuses on withdrawals of water from surface sources (rivers, lakes) and groundwater sources for irrigation. Rainfall is partitioned into runoff, which contributes to river flow, and water stored temporarily within soils, which is converted to liquid vapor through evaporation and transpiration. We use concepts of *blue water* and *green water* to describe this complex of sources and flows. Blue water is water in rivers, groundwater aquifers, reservoirs, and lakes and is the main water source for irrigated agriculture. Green water refers to the soil moisture generated from rainfall that infiltrates the soil and is available for uptake by plants. It constitutes the main water resource in rainfed agriculture. Agricultural water management systems rely on several sources, including rainfall, groundwater, water withdrawals from surface water, and water that is used and then recycled.

Agricultural water management

In agriculture, water is managed for the production of crops for food, fiber, fuel, and oils and for fisheries and livestock husbandry. In generating outputs, agricultural producers aim to meet their specific livelihood objectives. Water is only one input to production, and its relative importance and the way it is managed vary by agricultural system. The impacts of water uses for agriculture are far-reaching because water management draws heavily on natural and human resource bases.

The Comprehensive Assessment considers a range of agricultural water management systems. It assesses the increasing use of groundwater and marginal-quality water (saline, brackish, urban wastewater, irrigation drainage water) by smallholders for wealth generation. It also looks at the pressure imposed by the increasing use of water resources on livelihoods. It follows the flow of water from rain to the sea; how water is used and reused by cities, agriculture, and ecosystems; and how it is used and consumed by various uses and users.

There is a palette of water management options between purely rainfed and purely irrigated agriculture (figure 1.1). The Comprehensive Assessment considers farming systems that rely fully on rainfall, those that use supplemental irrigation in combination with rainfall, and those that rely fully on abstracting and transporting surface water or groundwater directly to the fields (irrigation).

These systems are categorized based on the relative reliance on green water sources (soil moisture) or blue water sources (groundwater, rivers, and lakes). Field conservation practices tend to conserve rain on the field, while both groundwater and surface water irrigation have critical blue water components. Toward the middle of the continuum—supplemental irrigation, water harvesting, and groundwater irrigation—is where some of the most interesting, but perhaps less explored solutions are found. These sources of water can be small or large scale, serving one or several people. Agricultural drainage (removal of water to create a favorable environment for agricultural production) is considered important for increasing productivity and sustainability for both rainfed and irrigated systems.

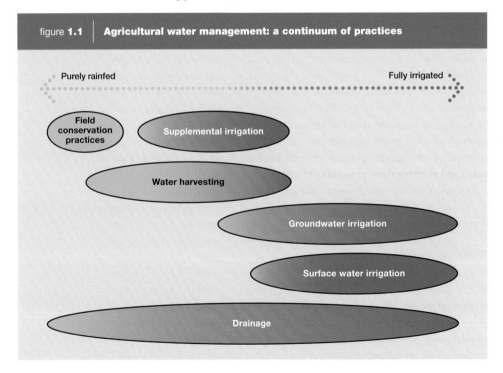

figure **1.1** | **Agricultural water management: a continuum of practices**

Many rural poor people depend on livestock raising for their livelihood. Domestic animals provide meat, milk, hides, blood, cash income, farm power, and manure for fuel and soil nutrients (see chapter 13 on livestock). Like other agricultural activities, livestock raising requires large quantities of water. When livestock systems are poorly managed, they can contribute to degradation and contamination of land and water resources. Similarly, fishing is an important source of food and income for many poor people (see chapter 12 on inland fisheries). Nearly all inland waters support fisheries in one form or another, and fish production is one of the most basic services provided by these ecosystems. Thus fisheries and livestock are included in the water management palette of options.

Important dimensions of agricultural water management are:

■ The scale and management of systems, and whether they are individually or communally managed.

■ The institutional environment, including land and water rights, and policies toward infrastructure development, water allocation, and environmental protection.

■ Payment for infrastructure, its operation and maintenance, and the water services provided, and whether these are from individual, private, community, or public funds.

> Important dimensions of agricultural water management are the scale and management of systems, the institutional environment, and payment for infrastructure and water services

Livelihoods

The concept of livelihoods encompasses the various ways of living that meet individual, household, and community needs. The livelihoods approach to development places people at the center of development strategies by assessing the strengths and vulnerabilities of poor people in terms of five types of capital: human, social, natural, physical, and financial.

Achieving sustainable livelihoods is a means of supporting human well-being through measures to enhance human health, education, and opportunity and to ensure a healthy environment and a decent standard of living. The sustainability component of the livelihood approach is achieved by helping people build resilience to external shocks and stresses, maintain the long-term productivity of natural resources, move away from dependence on unsustainable outside support, and avoid undermining the livelihood options of others. Effective responses to livelihood issues generally emerge from policies and approaches that address the needs of individual groups or subgroups rather than those that view the poor as a homogeneous group. Appropriate responses can be developed by listening to poor people and involving them in the policy processes (Chambers and Conway 1991) and by emphasizing governance issues that can support livelihood outcomes.

Power balance, gender, social settings, and diversity

Roles, rights, and responsibilities of women and men are socially defined, culturally based, and reflected in formal and informal power structures that influence how management decisions are taken and that may favor or deprive certain groups. Agriculture, water management, and all other activities related to it have an impact on social interactions and structures. Therefore any change in water management or in production systems will affect the relations between men and women of different classes and age groups. Understanding social dynamics in water management in agriculture requires looking at the diverse forms of social differentiation such as gender, poverty, class, caste, religion, and ethnicity and analyzing them within their context of diversity. All of these aspects are interlinked and are equally important when working with communities.

Thus, practitioners, extension workers, scientists, and policymakers will always directly or indirectly affect these social relations when trying to guide or change management or production dynamics. Water management interventions, by taking these impacts into account, can be designed to strengthen, break, or adapt existing gender patterns and dynamics within the specific social, cultural, economic, technical, and productive contexts.

> Water management interventions can be designed to strengthen, break, or adapt existing gender patterns and dynamics within the specific social, cultural, economic, technical, and productive contexts

Ecosystems and ecosystem services

An ecosystem is a functional unit consisting of all the living organisms (plants, animals, and microbes) in a given area and all the nonliving physical and chemical factors of their environment, linked together through nutrient cycling and energy flow. Ecosystems vary widely in size and type, but they always function as a unit. Ecosystem services are the benefits that people derive from ecosystems (see chapter 6 on ecosystems). The Millennium Ecosystem Assessment (MEA 2005) identifies four categories of sometimes overlapping services:

■ *Provisioning services.* The products obtained from ecosystems, including food, freshwater, fuel, and genetic resources.

■ *Regulating services.* The benefits derived from the regulation of ecosystem processes, including pollination, erosion control, storm protection, biological control, regulation of human diseases, climate and water regulation, and water purification and waste treatment.

■ *Cultural services.* The nonmaterial benefits obtained from ecosystems, including cultural diversity and heritage, aesthetic values, and recreation and tourism.

■ *Supporting services.* The services that are necessary for the production of all the other services, often with only indirect impact on people, including soil formation and retention, primary production, nutrient and water cycling, and provisioning of habitats.

Agricultural systems (agroecosystems) are ecosystems that are being modified by activities designed to favor agricultural production. The difference between an agroecosystem and other ecosystems is largely conceptual and based on a qualitative opinion about the degree of human intervention that favors agricultural production. The same does not necessarily hold for fisheries production, which tends to focus on wild catches, although in places fish stocking and habitat modifications have been used to increase catches and overall production. Aquaculture, the farming of fish and other animals, involves increased management of production through highly diverse extensive to intensive farming systems. Whether highly managed or not, many ecosystems contribute other valuable services that support food production, such as pollination, pest control, water storage, and soil formation.

Biodiversity. Biodiversity includes all ecosystems—managed or unmanaged—and the species and genetic resources that they support. Biodiversity is an encompassing concept that supports managed and unmanaged systems. Many managed systems have unique biodiversity associated with them. Such biodiversity is often maintained by human activities, in particular agriculture. Agriculture in turn depends on biodiversity, which supports ecosystem functions beyond the limits of the managed system itself.

Biodiversity is important for agriculture as a source of agricultural products, such as animal and plant genetic resources. It supports agriculture indirectly, such as by sustaining pollinators for agricultural crops, maintaining soil quality though soil biodiversity, and contributing to nutrient recycling and control of land erosion. It is important for sustaining water provision for agriculture (by maintaining the water cycle and condition of catchments). And it contributes to recycling and absorbing pollution caused by agriculture.

Agriculture also has a major impact on biodiversity, as it is the dominant human use of land, a major driver of biodiversity loss, and the major user of water. But it also relieves other stresses on the environment such as poverty and hunger. Consequently, agriculture plays a significant role in the improved management of biodiversity for the benefit of agriculture itself and also in providing substantial benefits beyond agriculture.

Agriculture has left a footprint on the environment that is reflected in changes in biodiversity. Reducing that footprint benefits other users of biodiversity and agriculture. Looking at how biodiversity responds to management therefore offers a tool to assist in planning for sustainable agriculture. Global agreements such as the Convention on Biological Diversity and the Ramsar Convention on Wetlands support the development process to conserve and sustainably use all forms of biodiversity, backed by commitments to significantly reduce the rate of biodiversity loss and an understanding that this is required to achieve human development targets (see www.biodiv.org).

> As water becomes more scarce, output per unit of water—water productivity—becomes more relevant than output per unit area as the measure of agricultural productivity

Water productivity

The amount of output per unit area—such as yield in tons per hectare—is the most common measure of agricultural productivity. But as water becomes more scarce, considering the output per unit of water—water productivity—becomes more relevant (see chapter 7 on water productivity). We consider physical water productivity as the mass of agricultural output from crops, fish, or livestock products per unit of water. Economic water productivity is the value of output per unit of water, reflecting gross returns plus livelihood and ecosystem values, benefits, and costs. The unit of water is important and is expressed as either water delivered to a use (from rainwater plus withdrawals from blue water sources) or depleted by a use (by evaporation, transpiration, pollution, or flows to a sink where it cannot be reused).

River basins—open, closed, and closing

River basins are the geographic area contained within the watershed limits of a system of streams and rivers converging toward the same terminus, generally the sea or sometimes an inland water body. Basins are an important unit of analysis in this assessment because water flows within a basin connect users and ecosystems. In many river basins use of water for human purposes through investments in water infrastructure for urban, industrial, and agricultural growth is approaching or exceeding limits, so that river discharges cannot meet downstream environmental needs (for example, environmental flows, flushing of salts or sediment) or allocation commitments during all or part of a year—a process of basin closure. Basins are "closed" when there is an overcommitment of water to human uses, and "closing" when the situation is approaching this condition.

The conceptual framework

The Comprehensive Assessment thus examines options for improving water management in a context of increasing tension between agriculture and ecosystems over conflicting requirements for water. Its aim is to reach the common goals embodied in the Millennium Development Goals: to use water and other resources to produce enough food for everyone and to do so in a way that is environmentally sustainable. The approach recognizes that water management lies within the sphere of agricultural systems and that that sphere is a part of the greater natural resource base that includes land, water, biodiversity, and people. The entire arrangement is embedded in a social and political context (figure 1.2).

The Comprehensive Assessment framework considers dynamic interactions between agricultural systems, people, management, and life support systems across time (50 years back and 50 years forward) and scales (from local to global levels). It relates drivers of change to agricultural water management and the evolution of agricultural systems and to their outcomes and impacts and goals. The framework provides a perspective on the interactions between these key components, but it is only a snapshot of the linkages; it cannot fully capture the importance of the social, cultural, political, and institutional dimensions of water management in agriculture and all their permutations in rural and local settings.

> The Comprehensive Assessment framework considers dynamic interactions between agricultural systems, people, management, and life support systems across time and scales

Drivers

The Comprehensive Assessment recognizes that water management in agriculture does not operate in isolation. A complex, interlinked set of drivers has affected the evolution of agricultural systems, their water management, and their capacity to produce and will continue to do so over the next 50 years. Furthermore, these drivers will themselves undergo change over the coming decades. The Comprehensive Assessment has identified eight drivers as especially important to agricultural water management: policies, institutions, and power; population and diets; availability and access to markets; water storage, delivery, and drainage infrastructure; urbanization; agricultural knowledge, science, and technology; global integration and trade; environmental change; and energy production and use.

In some cases there will also be direct and indirect feedback loops, so that changes in water management will affect the dimensions, direction, rate, and impact of the drivers, which in turn will affect water management. Some drivers can be influenced this way, but many others are manifested only over decades or centuries, and their magnitude and rate of change cannot be influenced in the short term. Further, many of these drivers are influenced much more strongly by other processes, such as global political developments.

Outcomes and impacts

Agricultural water management contributes to the production of agricultural outputs, which in turn contribute to livelihoods through food and nutrition, health, income, and employment. Clearly, to meet the Millennium Development Goals it is important to consider the consequence of investments and management decisions for the various dimensions of the outcomes.

| figure **1.2** | **A conceptual framework for the Comprehensive Assessment of Water Management in Agriculture** |

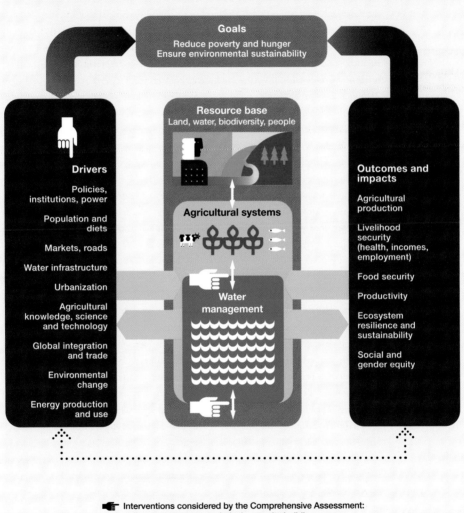

Interventions considered by the Comprehensive Assessment: policy, management, technical, capacity building

The types of outcomes and impacts that the Comprehensive Assessment considers include agricultural production, livelihood security (health, incomes, employment), food security, productivity, ecosystem resilience and sustainability, and social and gender equity.

Because agriculture manipulates the natural resource base, it affects ecosystems. Whether these outcomes are positive, negative, or mixed depends on what management choices are made. Some interventions could increase the amount of food within a country without improving food security for individuals. Many past interventions increased food production at the cost of environmental sustainability.

Different spatial and temporal scales

International, national, regional, and local levels have different stakeholders and actors, and intervention decisions are made at different levels, from those of individual farmers and their families and communities to those of international development banks. Interventions at one level can influence outcomes at others. Individuals and groups command different levels of power, wealth, influence, and ability to express their needs, concerns, and rights. Temporal and spatial connections across scales, both hydrologic and policy, require the engagement of multiple disciplines that can consider the dynamics within and across levels.

> Many past interventions increased food production at the cost of environmental sustainability

Various actors can change power and authority by working at different levels. They can alter access to resources and decisionmaking processes with respect to those resources. Scale choices can be a means of inclusion or exclusion of people from water management choices and benefits. Water management and agricultural development problems are often experienced and managed at a scale different from that corresponding to the jurisdiction of decisionmaking bodies. How water is managed on a farm or in an irrigation system can affect other users within a river basin. This can result in a mismatch between development, policies, and needs.

While strategies described as "local" can be associated with a clear objective, things get blurred as the scale gets larger. For example, increasing water supply locally through farm ponds, groundwater use, water harvesting, or small tanks may capture water that would have been used downstream. In certain circumstances such uses of water may be a more productive and sustainable alternative to larger reservoirs further downstream, so the picture is increasingly complex.

National interventions by governments and adjustments by local actors are also interrelated. For example, subsidies for adoption of microirrigation or soil conservation techniques are meant to foster local conservation by farmers, while farmers' use of groundwater will provoke national interventions or policy responses. Politics and social structures will have a direct bearing on the kinds of agricultural choices adopted by local actors and the kinds of water development actions at all levels.

At the global level sectoral and market linkages have spatial implications for basin agricultural production and water use. Relative or shifting factor prices, taxation or subsidies, migration, the World Trade Organization or other free trade agreements, and the evolution of world markets can have sweeping consequences.

Time also matters. Agricultural and water systems are the results of thousands of years of interventions and evolution. Some processes happen in a relatively short period—the application of water to crops—but others critical to sustainability may take years, such as the buildup of salinity or a drop in groundwater levels.

Interventions and response options

The Comprehensive Assessment considers the use and effectiveness of a range of interventions and options for responding to the need for sustainable water management in

agriculture for poverty reduction and environmental sustainability. It considers the most important entry points for attaining these goals through three processes:

■   Changing the way water is managed in agricultural systems (changes in technologies or management practices).

■   Managing the interaction with the natural resource base and other ecosystems (withdrawals of water from the resource base, return flows of altered quality to the resource base).

■   Influencing the relevant drivers through policies and institutional changes.

An effective strategy will involve a mix of interventions through all three entry points.

Interventions can be implemented through laws, regulations, incentives, structural investments, and enforcement schemes; partnerships and collaborations, including with civil society; information and knowledge sharing, including capacity building; and public, collective, and private actions. The choice of options will be greatly influenced by the temporal and physical scales, the uncertainty of outcomes, cultural contexts, gender and power relations, politics, and the implications for equity and tradeoffs. Institutions at different levels have different response options available to them, and special care is required to ensure policy coherence.

Decisionmaking processes are value laden and combine political and technical elements to varying degrees. Management choices may be based on synergies or tradeoffs between goals and outcomes that may be in competition and that change the type, magnitude, and relative mix of services provided by agriculture and ecosystems.

> The choice of options will be greatly influenced by the temporal and physical scales, the uncertainty of outcomes, cultural contexts, gender and power relations, politics, and the implications for equity and tradeoffs

Several pathways are possible, but which is just and sustainable? The use of scenarios

The future of agricultural water management is highly uncertain. First, there is insufficient information on the current state of agricultural systems and their driving forces, including the interconnectivity of different systems and the extent of adverse feedback from degraded ecosystems in the wider landscape. Second, even with exact information it is not possible to predict surprises and random events such as major disasters and the consequences of declining ecosystem resilience and increasing climate variability. Recurring floods and droughts have a major impact on agricultural water management, but there is relatively high uncertainty regarding the specifics of future climate change and resulting changes in the frequency of extreme events. Third, the future is unknown because it depends on decisions that have yet to be made. For example, will water or ecosystem services be priced? Will integrated water resources management be the guiding principle in future water decisions? How will declining ecosystem resilience affect agricultural systems?

Instead of trying to predict the most likely future, the Comprehensive Assessment uses a set of scenarios to explore possible futures based on different types of investment choices. Scenario analysis provides insights about how different drivers of change work by exploring the consequences of a range of investments.

The Comprehensive Assessment recognizes that solutions must address all of the issues of poverty, environment, and food security collectively. It also recognizes that trying to attain any one of these goals without simultaneously considering the other goals eventually leads to a worsening of the situation because the three are so closely linked. Thus, it is also necessary to identify and to try to minimize the negative effects that these components have on each other.

Uncertainty in the Comprehensive Assessment

Instead of trying to predict the most likely future, the Comprehensive Assessment uses a set of scenarios to explore possible futures based on different types of investment choices

Given the need for synthesis and judgments on the veracity and uncertainty of evidence, the uncertainty associated with the conclusions and outcomes of the assessment has to be clearly labeled. This can be done quantitatively or qualitatively. The Intergovernmental Panel on Climate Change (IPCC) assessments that deal with the global climate system and that are based on models of the coupled atmosphere-ocean systems use a quantitative scale with a probabilistic outcome (IPCC 2001). This assessment uses a qualitative scale based on the scheme for judging uncertainty developed for the IPCC (Moss and Schneider 2000) and subsequently used in the Millennium Ecosystem Assessment. The scale is based on the amount of evidence and the extent of agreement within the scientific and expert community on that evidence (figure 1.3) and is used throughout the report.

Structure of the assessment

Part 2 of the Comprehensive Assessment synthesis volume begins by examining *trends* in water management in agriculture that have shaped thinking and influenced past interventions and investments. The volume then looks ahead to the future and discusses *scenarios* for water management in the context of a number of key drivers of water management in the future (see figure 1.2). Part 3 looks at the major cross-cutting issues that we consider crucial to all water management decisions and activities: *poverty, policies and institutions, ecosystems*, and *water productivity*. In part 4 thematic chapters capture the essence of current knowledge on major components of water management: *rainfed agriculture, irrigation, groundwater, marginal-quality water, inland fisheries, livestock, rice, land*, and *river basins*.

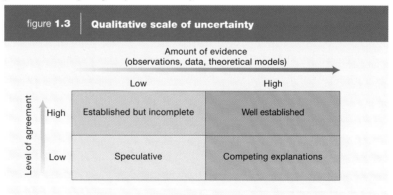

figure **1.3**   **Qualitative scale of uncertainty**

Source: Adapted from Moss and Schneider 2000.

References

Chambers, R., and G. Conway. 1991. *Sustainable Rural Livelihoods: Practical Concepts for the 21st Century*. IDS Discussion Paper 296. Institute of Development Studies, Brighton, UK.

IPCC (Intergovernmental Panel on Climate Change). 2001. *Climate Change 2001: Synthesis Report*. A Contribution of Working Groups I, II, and III to the Third Assessment Report of the Intergovernmental Panel on Climate Change. Cambridge, UK: Cambridge University Press.

IUCN (World Conservation Union). 2000. *Vision for Water and Nature: A World Strategy for Conservation and Sustainable Management of Water Resources in the 21st Century*. Gland, Switzerland.

MEA (Millennium Ecosystem Assessment). 2005. *Ecosystems and Human Well-being: Synthesis*. Washington, D.C.: Island Press.

Moss, R.H., and S.H. Schneider. 2000. "Uncertainties in the IPCC TAR: Recommendations to Lead Authors for More Consistent Assessment and Reporting." In R. Pachauri, T. Taniguchi, and K. Tanaka, eds., *Guidance Papers on the Cross-Cutting Issues of the Third Assessment Report of the IPCC*. Geneva: World Meteorological Organization.

Van Hofwegen, P., and M. Svendsen. 2000. "A Vision for Water for Food and Rural Development." Paper presented to the 2nd World Water Forum, 17–22 March, The Hague, Netherlands.

Part 2 | Trends and scenarios

These chapters consider key water, food, livelihood, and environment drivers, trends, and societal responses to show the trajectory of water use and management for agriculture, review the situation today, and explore options for the future.

Changing diets lead to changing water use in agriculture

Artist: Sineal Yap Fui Yee, Malaysia

2 | Trends in water and agricultural development

Lead authors: David Molden, Karen Frenken, Randolph Barker, Charlotte de Fraiture, Bancy Mati, Mark Svendsen, Claudia Sadoff, and C. Max Finlayson

Contributing authors: Sithara Attapatu, Mark Giordano, Arlene Inocencio, Mats Lannerstad, Nadia Manning, François Molle, Bert Smedema, and Domitille Vallée

Overview

To meet the objectives of increasing food production and alleviating poverty and hunger in an environmentally sustainable manner will require a renewed focus on agricultural water management and institutional innovations for managing water. In some areas of the world demand for water for various uses exceeds supply. But for much of the world there is a pending crisis of water supply not because of a shortage of water but because of mismanagement of water resources. This report defines water scarcity from the perspective of individual water users who lack secure access to safe and affordable water to consistently satisfy their needs for food production, drinking, washing, or livelihoods.

About 2.8 billion people, more than 40% of the world's population, live in river basins where water scarcity must be reckoned with [competing explanations]. About 1.6 billion people live in areas of economic water scarcity where human, institutional, and financial capital limit access to water even though water in nature is available locally to meet human demands. Symptoms of economic water scarcity include lack of or underdeveloped water infrastructure, whether small-scale (water harvesting structures) or large-scale (reservoirs, distribution networks); high vulnerability to short- and long-term drought; and difficult access to reliable supplies, especially for rural people. These conditions are prevalent in much of South Asia and Sub-Saharan Africa. Another 1.2 billion people live under conditions of physical water scarcity in river basins where water resources development has exceeded sustainable limits. In these cases symptoms include environmental degradation and competition for water. While it is possible with good management to treat the symptoms of water scarcity, it is also possible with bad management to create water problems in areas of no water scarcity.

Throughout the developing world income and nutrition levels are improving in aggregate, but poverty and malnutrition persist in many regions, including Asia, Sub-Saharan Africa, and parts of Latin America. There has been a steady increase in the per capita consumption of food, including fruits, vegetables, and animal products, leading to better nutrition for many and a decrease in famines. The average global per capita daily food supply increased from 2,400 kilocalories (kcal) in 1970 to 2,800 kcal in 2000, which means that enough food was produced globally to feed the growing population. Fish and meat consumption is rising, increasing reliance on aquaculture and industrial livestock production, with some positive well-being and income benefits, but greater pressure on water resources and the environment. However, pockets of food insecurity remain. The average daily per capita food supply in South Asia (2,400 kcal) and Sub-Saharan Africa (2,200 kcal), while slowly rising, was below the world average of 2,800 kcal in 2000.

While it is possible with good management to treat the symptoms of water scarcity, it is also possible with bad management to create water problems in areas of no water scarcity

Key trends and their drivers

During the second half of the 20th century the global food system was able to respond to the doubling of world population by more than doubling food production [well established]. From 1963 to 2000 food production grew more rapidly in developing countries than in developed countries, with growth in food production exceeding growth in population, except in Africa. However, there was wide variability in food production within and across regions. Intensification and yield growth have been the dominant factors, and irrigated agriculture has played a major role. Nearly all the growth in cereal production since 1970 has been from higher yields. Yield increases have come at different times in different regions of the world. In some areas yields have reached their upper limits and are showing signs of leveling off.

Globally, about 80% of agricultural water use (evapotranspiration) is directly from green water (rainfall stored in soil moisture), with the rest from blue water sources (water withdrawals from rivers, reservoirs, lakes, and aquifers) [well established]. There is considerable variation across regions. Irrigation is relatively important in Asia and North Africa, while rainfed agriculture dominates in Sub-Saharan Africa. Groundwater levels are declining in many areas where there is a high dependence on groundwater for agriculture and population demands are high. Demand for water for industrial and domestic uses is growing relative to demand for agriculture. As competition for water intensifies, agriculture can expect to receive a decreasing share of developed freshwater resources.

Despite dramatic increases in large-scale irrigation infrastructure over the past half century, the bulk of the world's agricultural production still comes from predominantly rainfed lands [well established]. Some 55% of the gross value of crop production is grown under rainfed agriculture on 72% of harvested land.[1] Many people dependent on rainfed agriculture are highly vulnerable to both short-term dry spells and long-term drought and thus are reluctant to invest in agricultural inputs that could increase yields. In developing countries growth in both productivity improvements and area expansion has been slower in rainfed agriculture than in irrigated agriculture. The potential exists for raising the productivity of many rainfed systems in Sub-Saharan Africa, but this potential has been exceptionally difficult to realize.

The world's harvested land increased by about 24% from 1961 to 2003 to 1.2 billion hectares (ha), 28% of it irrigated, while the area equipped for irrigation[2] nearly doubled, from 139 million ha to 277 million ha, funded initially by investments by international development banks, donor agencies, and national governments but later increasingly by small-scale private investments [established but incomplete]. Irrigation water was essential to achieve the gains from high-yielding fertilizer-responsive crop varieties. Approximately 70% of the world's irrigated land is in Asia, where it accounts for almost 35% of cultivated land. By contrast, there is very little irrigation in Sub-Saharan Africa. Globally, donor spending on agricultural water reached a peak of more than $1 billion a year in the late 1970s and early 1980s and then fell to less than half that level by the late 1980s. Benefit-cost ratios deteriorated with falling cereal prices and rising construction costs. Recognition of the poor performance of large-scale irrigation systems spread, and opposition mounted to the environmental degradation and social dislocation sometimes caused by large dams. Today, there appears to be consensus that the appropriate scale of infrastructure should be determined by the specific environmental, social, and economic conditions and goals, with the participation of all stakeholders.

> The potential exists for raising the productivity of many rainfed systems, but this potential has been exceptionally difficult to realize in many areas

Biological diversity is in rapid decline in all the world's major biomes [well established]. Loss of biodiversity is greatest among freshwater-dependent species—almost twice as fast as for marine or terrestrial species. The majority of biomes have been greatly modified, with 20%–50% of 14 global biomes transformed to croplands. For terrestrial ecosystems the most important direct driver of change in the past 50 years has been land cover change. Further land use changes causing habitat loss are associated primarily with the additional expansion of agriculture. For freshwater ecosystems the most important direct drivers of change include direct physical changes to freshwater habitat, such as draining wetlands and building dams, and modification of water regimes through water extraction and pollution. Many indirect drivers of change work through the impacts of land use arising from agriculture-related activities

The two major factors contributing to increased food demand, and thus to increased water use for food production, are population growth and changes in diets as living standards improve [well established]. Rising incomes lead not only to increasing consumption of staple cereals, but also to a shift in consumption patterns among cereal crops and away from cereals toward livestock products, fish, and high-value crops. A growing, wealthier population requires more food per person, and richer and more varied diets. The amount of water needed to produce food depends on diets and how the food is produced.

Rapid rural to urban migration in developing countries influences farming practices and water demand [established but incomplete]. In the 1960s two-thirds of the world's population lived in rural areas, and 60% of the economically active population worked in agriculture. Today, half of the people live in rural areas, and just a little more than 40% of the economically active population depend directly on agriculture. In absolute terms the rural population will start to decline in the next few years, and by 2050 two-thirds of the world's people will live in cities. In many poor countries in South Asia and Sub-Saharan Africa, however, the rural population will continue to grow until about 2030, and the number of people depending on agriculture will continue to rise. Cities are rapidly increasing their claim on water at the expense of rural uses such as farming. Urban centers represent a source of pollution that has impacts on downstream irrigation and aquatic ecosystems.

Farmers need to adjust to the agricultural transformation that occurs as economies develop, incomes rise, and urbanization spreads. Agriculture grows but not as fast as the nonagricultural sector, and food habits shift toward richer and more varied diets. Some farmers will shift from staples to higher value horticultural crops, livestock, and fisheries. Others will special ize in export crops. Farmers who continue to grow staple food crops will need to boost their productivity. The next step in agricultural transformation is access to value-added supply chains in the modern retail sector. In many parts of the developing world groups of professional farmers are emerging whose incomes come almost entirely from farming. Many more farm households are augmenting their incomes from nonfarm activities as labor has become more mobile. The way this transformation unfolds has implications for water investments to reduce poverty. In the early stages investments in water to increase productivity can be quite effective in reducing poverty. But as economies grow, this impact diminishes. Later, livelihood diversification becomes an important strategy. Ultimately, this could lead to an exit from agriculture, another means of escape from rural poverty *[competing explanations]*.

> Cities are rapidly increasing their claim on water at the expense of rural uses such as farming

Benefits and costs

Investments in water for agriculture have made a positive contribution to rural livelihoods, food security, and poverty reduction [established but incomplete]. The positive impact is felt through employment gains, affordable food prices, and more stable outputs. Through a multiplier effect investments in irrigation lead to a rise in crop yields and farm incomes that results in higher demand for goods and services in the nonfarm sector—multiplying the benefits of the original investment. A handful of studies indicate that the multiplier effect of investment in irrigation is in the range of 2.5 to 4. The additions to employment in the local nonfarm sector can be as high as twice that for the farm sector, with a major impact on poverty reduction.

Poorly conceived and implemented water management interventions have incurred high social and environmental costs [well established]. Social costs have included inequity in the allocation of benefits and loss of livelihood opportunities. Common property resources such as rivers and wetlands, important for poor fishers and resource gathers, have been appropriated for other uses, resulting in a loss of livelihood opportunities. Communities have been displaced, especially in areas behind dams, without adequate compensation. A large proportion of irrigation's negative environmental effects arise from the diversion of water away from natural aquatic ecosystems, such as rivers, lakes, oases, and other groundwater-dependent wetlands. Direct and indirect negative impacts have been well documented, including salinization, channel erosion, declines in biodiversity, introduction of invasive alien species, reduction of water quality, genetic isolation through habitat fragmentation, and reduced production of floodplain and other inland and coastal fisheries.

Changing responses over time to the water-food-environment challenge

Farmers, fishers, and pastoralists and their communities, often supported by community-based organizations, have responded to water scarcity with or without government support [established but incomplete]. The failure of large-scale public irrigation systems to provide water where and when farmers needed it spurred many to invest in individual pumps and other private irrigation systems. Where opportunities permit, farmers are benefiting from more flexible and reliable supplies or from small storage coupled with irrigation. However, local responses do not always meet the broader water-food-environment challenge because the primary focus is generally to enhance local food production and livelihoods. Particularly in semiarid areas unregulated exploitation of groundwater can lead to falling water tables or to rising water tables and increased salinity. The development of private facilities may further disadvantage poor farmers, who cannot afford the investment costs, and undermine farmer irrigation associations.

Responses at the national level generally express a broader view, but still reflect specific perspectives and priorities [competing explanations]. Often, institutional development did not keep pace with rapid infrastructure development, undermining the efficiency of investments and failing to adapt to changing economic, environmental, and social conditions. Many of today's water bureaucracies were set up to construct major water infrastructure facilities. This heavy focus on infrastructure sometimes led to institutions and practices that were well suited for construction, but less well suited for the adaptive management needed to operate long-lived, multipurpose water infrastructure. Today, despite repeated calls for integration, government responses tend to remain mostly sectoral. Management of water allocation between sectors remains fragmented and highly politicized in most countries. Even within agriculture irrigation receives the most attention while rainfed agriculture, fisheries, and livestock are rarely considered in discussions of water resources.

> Good practice in agriculture is increasingly sensitive to the role of ecosystems, and the environmental community has become increasingly aware of the importance of water, food, and livelihood issues

Although some people argue that water is essentially a local issue, global issues affect global water use, and thus global actions are necessary to resolve them [competing explanations]. Global issues of trade, energy, and subsidies have an impact on water use, but water is rarely a main topic of global discussions and agreements on these topics. The Second World Water Forum in 2000 was instrumental in mobilizing thinking around key global issues of the water crisis: water supply, agriculture, environment, and livelihoods. A divide in thinking was clearly illustrated by reports on water for food and rural development and reports on water and nature. With water again at the forefront of global issues, discussions are occurring in a more balanced context, with more consideration of the social and environmental tradeoffs that water management and development decisions entail.

In agricultural water new paradigms call for considering water management within a basin context and for including rainfed agriculture, fisheries, and livestock in water discussions. There is more attention to integration across sectors and to the appropriate roles of public and private sectors. Good practice in agriculture is also increasingly sensitive to the role of ecosystems, recognizing the importance of watershed protection, environmental flows, and sustainable management of aquatic ecosystems, springs, and aquifers. At the same time there has been an increasing awareness within the environmental community of the importance of water, food, and livelihoods issues.

The water situation today—is there a water crisis?

While the global quantity of freshwater is constant, the world population and therefore freshwater demand are growing. There is enough land, water, and human capacity in the world to produce sufficient food in aggregate for a growing population over the next

50 years, so in that sense water is not a constraint to global food production. So why is there talk of a water crisis?

There are many local crises that taken together could constitute a global water crisis. In some areas of the world demand for water for various uses exceeds supply. But for much of the world there is a pending crisis not because of a shortage of water but because of mismanagement of water resources. Avoiding this crisis will require institutional innovations that allow focusing simultaneously on the goals and tradeoffs in food security, poverty reduction, and environmental sustainability.

> For much of the world there is a pending crisis not because of a shortage of water but because of mismanagement of water resources

Water scarcity today

What is water scarcity? We define scarcity from the perspective of individual water users rather than the hydrology of an area. Individuals are water insecure when they lack secure access to safe and affordable water to consistently satisfy their needs for drinking, washing, food production, and livelihoods. An area is water scarce when a large number of people are water insecure (Rijsberman 2006).

Access to water is difficult for millions of people for reasons that go beyond the physical resource base. About 2.8 billion people live in areas facing water scarcity, and more than 1.2 billion of them—one fifth of the world's population—live in areas of physical water scarcity. Another 1.6 billion people live in basins that face economic water scarcity, where human capacity or financial resources are likely to be insufficient to develop adequate water resources even though adequate water in nature is available to meet human needs (map 2.1). Within these regions poor people suffer most from symptoms of scarcity. Lack of finance, lack of human capacity, poor management, and a lack of good governance all contribute to water scarcity.

Physical water scarcity. Physical water scarcity occurs when available water resources are insufficient to meet all demands, including minimum environmental flow requirements (see chapter 16 on river basins; photo 2.1). Arid regions are most often associated with physical water scarcity, but an alarming new trend is an artificially created physical water scarcity, even where water is apparently abundant. This is due to the overallocation and overdevelopment of water resources, leaving no scope for making water available to meet new demands except through interbasin transfers. There is not enough water to meet both human demands and environmental flow needs.

Symptoms of physical water scarcity include severe environmental degradation, such as river desiccation and pollution; declining groundwater tables; water allocation disputes; and failure to meet the needs of some groups. Some 1.2 billion people live in river basins where the physical scarcity of water is absolute (human water use has surpassed sustainable limits). And another 500 million people live in river basins that are fast approaching this situation. While physical scarcity introduces complex problems, investments in good management can mitigate many of them.

Economic water scarcity. Economic water scarcity occurs when investments needed to keep up with growing water demand are constrained by financial, human, or institutional

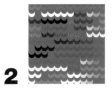

| map **2.1** | **Areas of physical and economic water scarcity** |

☐ Little or no water scarcity ☐ Approaching physical water scarcity ☐ Not estimated

■ Physical water scarcity ■ Economic water scarcity

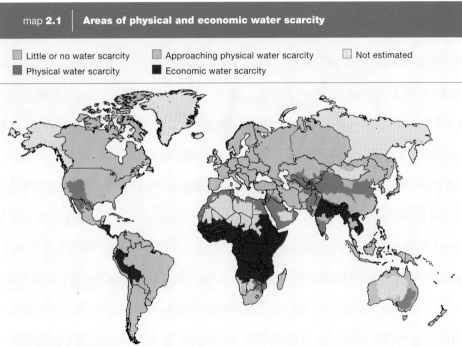

Definitions and indicators

- *Little or no water scarcity.* Abundant water resources relative to use, with less than 25% of water from rivers withdrawn for human purposes.
- *Physical water scarcity (water resources development is approaching or has exceeded sustainable limits).* More than 75% of river flows are withdrawn for agriculture, industry, and domestic purposes (accounting for recycling of return flows). This definition—relating water availability to water demand—implies that dry areas are not necessarily water scarce.
- *Approaching physical water scarcity.* More than 60% of river flows are withdrawn. These basins will experience physical water scarcity in the near future.
- *Economic water scarcity (human, institutional, and financial capital limit access to water even though water in nature is available locally to meet human demands).* Water resources are abundant relative to water use, with less than 25% of water from rivers withdrawn for human purposes, but malnutrition exists.

Source: International Water Management Institute analysis done for the Comprehensive Assessment of Water Management in Agriculture using the Watersim model.

capacity (photo 2.2). Much of the scarcity felt by people is due to the way institutions function—favoring one group over another, not listening to the voices of women and disadvantaged groups. Symptoms of economic water scarcity include inadequate infrastructure development, so that people have trouble getting enough water for agriculture and domestic purposes; high vulnerability to seasonal water fluctuations, including floods and long- and short-term drought; and inequitable distribution of water even though infrastructure exists. Much of Sub-Saharan Africa experiences economic water scarcity, and there are many pockets across the globe where water resources are inequitably distributed. Further water development could ease problems of poverty and inequality.

Poverty and undernourishment remain

Throughout the developing world income and nutrition levels are improving in aggregate. However, while food production has outpaced population growth globally and food

Photo by Karen Conniff

Photo 2.1 Physical water scarcity—water development is approaching or has exceeded sustainable limits

Photo by Mats Lannerstad

Photo 2.2 Economic water scarcity: water exists in nature, but access is difficult

prices have declined, poverty and malnutrition persist in many regions including Asia, Sub-Saharan Africa, and parts of Latin America. It is clear that the benefits of the gains made in agriculture have been unequally distributed.

The poverty statistics are bleak:

- More than 1 billion people lived below the $1 a day poverty line in 2001 (UNDP 2005).
- 1.5 billion people live on between $1 and $2 a day.
- The majority of people living in abject poverty are women and children (UN 2006a).
- 1.1 billion people had no access to clean water in 2004 (WHO and UNICEF 2006).
- 2.6 billion people had no access to improved sanitation in 2004 (WHO and UNICEF 2006).
- 850 million people are undernourished, 815 million of them in developing countries representing 17% of the population of these countries (FAO 2004).

Many poor people either do not produce sufficient food for their own consumption or do not earn enough to buy the food they need. The share of undernourished people in the developing world varies from about 10% in the Near East and North Africa and Latin America and the Caribbean regions to almost 33% in Sub-Saharan Africa (figure 2.1).

By optimistic projections the number of undernourished people in the world is expected to decline to 610 million by 2015 (Bruinsma 2003), still far greater than the 1996 World Food Summit target of 400 million (FAO 1997) and the Millennium Development

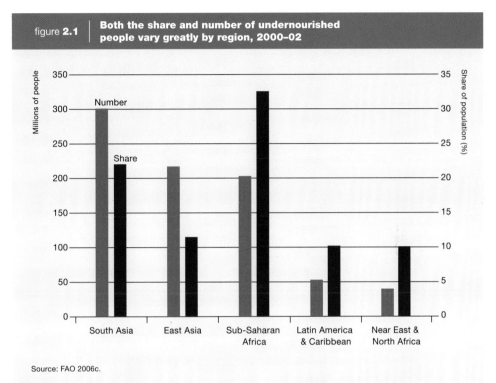

figure **2.1** | **Both the share and number of undernourished people vary greatly by region, 2000–02**

Source: FAO 2006c.

Goals target of halving, between 1990 and 2015, the proportion of people who suffer from hunger (UN 2006a).

The 850 million undernourished people (FAO 2004) depend on water for agriculture in different ways:

- Smallholder farmers (50%) depend on access to secure water supplies for food production, nutrition, income, and employment.
- The urban poor (20%) have benefited from the lower food prices made possible through productivity gains in agriculture. There is also a growing pattern of urban-rural family linkages, as part of the family, usually men, migrate to cities and support remaining family members back in the villages—often the elderly, women, and children.
- The rural landless (20%) could gain by employment and income brought about by agriculture.
- The remaining undernourished (10%) include pastoralists vulnerable to drought and climate change, fishers vulnerable to water pollution and river water depletion, and forest-dependents vulnerable to clearing of land for agriculture, road construction, and eventually deforestation.

Many more people are vulnerable to changes in water quantity, quality, and timing brought about by increased competition, climate change, floods, and droughts.

Agricultural development as a driver of ecosystem change and biodiversity loss

The Millennium Ecosystem Assessment (MEA 2005a,b) has reported that many eco-systems globally have been transformed as a consequence of human activities. A major driver in this change has been the doubling in world population, from 3 billion in 1959 to 6 billion in 1999. More land was converted to cropland in the 30 years after 1950 than in the 150 years between 1800 and 1950, with some 24% of the earth's land area now occupied by cultivated systems. Between 1960 and 2000 reservoir storage capacity quadrupled, changing the natural flow of rivers. Approximately 35% of mangrove forests have been lost

| figure **2.2** | **Threatened vertebrate species in 14 global biomes** |

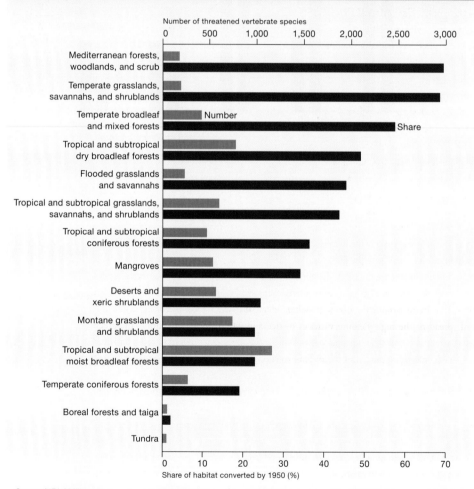

Number of threatened vertebrate species

Share of habitat converted by 1950 (%)

Source: MEA 2005b.

(based on countries with adequate data, which encompass about half the mangrove area), due mainly to transformation to agriculture or aquaculture. More than half of the 14 biomes (regional groupings of similar plants, animals, and climates on a global scale) assessed had experienced a 20%–50% conversion to human use, with temperate and Mediterranean forests and temperate grasslands the most affected (figure 2.2)

Key trends and their drivers: how did we get here?

What have been the key changes and ways of thinking, especially about agricultural development and the use of water, that have brought people to think about water as a scarce resource?

Agricultural productivity

During the second half of the 20th century the global food system was able to respond to the doubling of world population by more than doubling food production. Thus, food demand could be met if food supplies were evenly distributed. From 1963 to 2000 food production grew more rapidly in developing countries than in developed countries, with food production growth exceeding population growth, except in Africa (figure 2.3 and table 2.1). However, there was wide variability in food production within and across regions. And kilocalories per person per day, which in 2000 averaged 2,800 globally, ranged from 2,200 in Sub-Saharan Africa and 2,400 in South Asia to 2,850 in Latin America and 2,875 in East Asia, to a high of 3,450 in industrial countries (FAO 2006c).

This growth in crop production was achieved through a combination of expansion in arable land, increase in cropping intensities (multiple cropping or shorter fallow periods), and increases in yield. The increases in arable land were small, with much of the expansion onto marginal lands as urbanization spread onto good quality agricultural lands (Penning de Vries and others 2002). The amount of cropland per person is currently about 0.25 ha, compared with 0.45 ha in 1961. Intensification and yield growth have been the dominant factors in production growth, and irrigated agriculture has played a major role. Nearly all the growth in cereal grain production since 1970 has been from higher yields (see table 2.1). In developing countries growth accelerated in the 1970s with the introduction and spread of the high-yielding varieties of rice and wheat under irrigation—the green revolution.

Yield increases have come at different times in different regions of the world. For example, maize yields started rising before the 1940s in the United States, in the 1960s in China, in the 1970s and again in the 1990s in Latin America, but have not yet taken off in Africa (see figure 6 in summary; FAO 2006b). In some areas yields have reached their upper limits and are showing signs of leveling off.

Green and blue water use in agriculture

Agriculture uses water through evapotranspiration (transpiration by plants and evaporation from soils). A distinction can be made between the withdrawal of water from rivers, reservoirs, lakes, and aquifers (blue water) and the direct use of rainwater stored in the

> During the second half of the 20th century the global food system was able to respond to the doubling of world population by more than doubling food production

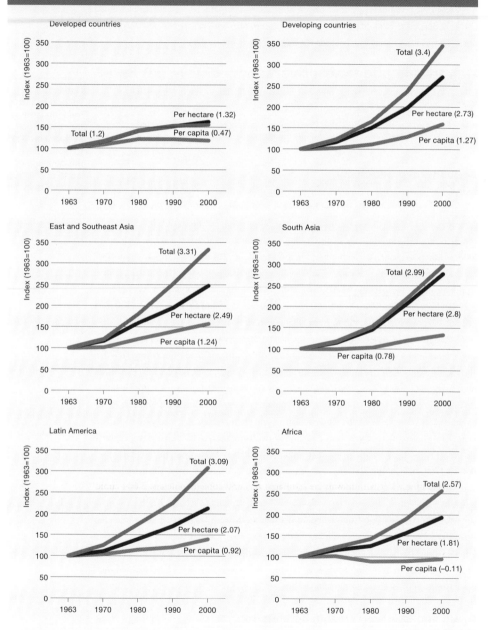

figure 2.3 **Growth in food production outpaced growth in population between 1963 and 2000 in all regions but Africa**

Note: Numbers in parentheses are average annual growth rates for 1963–2000.

Source: FAO 2006b; Hayami 2005.

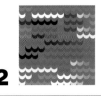

table **2.1**	Global cereal production, 1970–2005		
Year	Area (millions of hectares)	Yield (metric tons per hectare)	Production (millions of metric tons)
1970	676	1.77	1,192
1980	717	2.16	1,550
1990	708	2.75	1,952
2000	674	3.06	2,060
2005	686	3.27	2,240

Source: FAO 2006b; Falcon and Naylor 2005.

soil (green water). There is a range of options for using blue and green water for crop production. Pure rainfed agriculture uses only green water. Practices to upgrade rainfed agriculture supplement rainwater with blue water. Irrigation uses blue water in addition to green water to maintain adequate soil moisture levels, allowing crops to fulfill their yield potential. Blue water is the measured and managed freshwater resource that is also used to meet domestic, industrial, and hydropower demands and that sustains aquatic ecosystems in rivers and lakes (UN 2006b).

Globally, about 80% of agricultural evapotranspiration is directly from green water, with the rest from blue water sources (map 2.2). There is considerable variation between regions. Irrigation is relatively important in Asia and North Africa, while rainfed agriculture dominates in Sub-Saharan Africa.

The implications of green and blue water use are quite different (see chapter 6 on ecosystems). Increased evapotranspiration from blue water sources reduces stream flow and groundwater levels. Increased evapotranspiration from green water sources is usually due to expansion of agricultural land area, a terrestrial impact, but has less impact on blue water flows. Still, any change in land use can affect river flows. In South Africa recognition of the effects of "streamflow-reducing activities" has led to initiatives to control commercial forestry and to remove invasive tree species in order to reduce evapotranspiration and increase river flow (Hope 2006).

Global blue water withdrawals are estimated at 3,830 cubic kilometers, 2,664 cubic kilometers (70%) of which are for agriculture, including losses (table 2.2; FAO 2006a). The net evapotranspiration from irrigation is 1,570 cubic kilometers, while the remainder of the 7,130 cubic kilometers used is directly from rain. About 1,000 cubic kilometers (25%–30%) of the 3,830 cubic kilometers withdrawn originate from groundwater (see chapter 10 on groundwater), mostly for drinking water and irrigation. Groundwater levels are declining in areas of China, India, Mexico, Egypt, and other parts of North Africa, where dependence on groundwater for agriculture and population demands are high. Demand for water for industrial and municipal uses, including for energy generation, is growing relative to demand for agriculture (figure 2.4). As competition for water from these other sectors intensifies, agriculture can expect to receive a decreasing share of developed freshwater resources.

map **2.2** | **Food crop evapotranspiration from rain and irrigation**

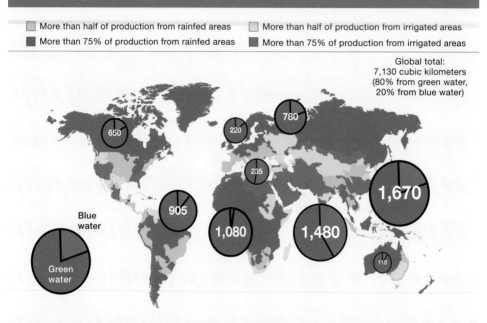

☐ More than half of production from rainfed areas   ☐ More than half of production from irrigated areas

■ More than 75% of production from rainfed areas   ■ More than 75% of production from irrigated areas

Global total:
7,130 cubic kilometers
(80% from green water,
20% from blue water)

Note: Production refers to gross value of production. The pie charts show total crop water evapotranspiration in cubic kilometers by region.

Source: International Water Management Institute analysis done for the Comprehensive Assessment for Water Management in Agriculture using the Watersim model.

table **2.2** | **Freshwater resources and withdrawal, 2000**
(cubic kilometers per year unless otherwise indicated)

Region	Renewable freshwater resources	Total freshwater withdrawal	Freshwater withdrawals						Withdrawal as share of renewable resources (%)
			Agriculture		Industry		Municipalities		
			Amount	Share (%)	Amount	Share (%)	Amount	Share (%)	
Africa	3,936	217	186	86	9	4	22	10	5.5
Asia	11,594	2,378	1,936	81	270	11	172	7	20.5
Latin America	13,477	252	178	71	26	10	47	19	1.9
Caribbean	93	13	9	68	1	9	3	23	14.4
North America	6,253	525	203	39	252	48	70	13	8.4
Oceania	1,703	26	19	72	3	10	5	18	1.5
Europe	6,603	418	132	32	223	53	63	15	6.3
World	43,659	3,830	2,664	70	785	20	381	10	8.8

Source: FAO 2006a.

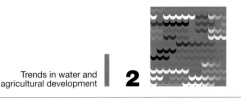

| figure **2.4** | **Sectoral competition is increasing for blue water withdrawals for human uses** |

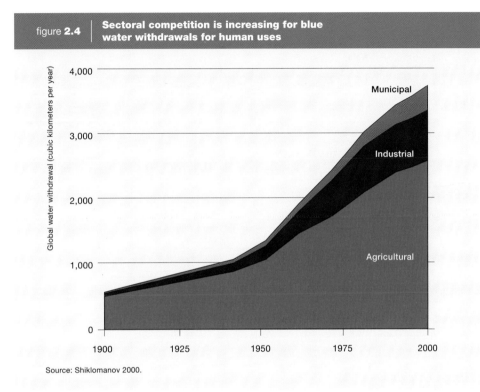

Source: Shiklomanov 2000.

Rainfed agriculture

Despite dramatic increases in large-scale irrigation infrastructure over the past half century the bulk of the world's agricultural production still comes from predominantly rainfed lands.[3] Some 55% of the gross value of crop production is grown under rainfed agriculture on 72% of harvested land (table 2.3; see also chapter 3 on scenarios). There are large regional differences in the percentage of rainfed cultivated land, from almost 95% in Sub-Saharan Africa and almost 90% in Latin America, to less than 70% in the Near East and North Africa and less than 60% in South Asia. In Southeast Asia the picture is more mixed.

Rainfed areas support both permanent crops such as rubber, tea, and coffee and annual crops such as wheat, maize, and rice. Some crops such as tubers, which are a staple crop of much of Sub-Saharan Africa, have been largely overlooked by the green revolution. In developing countries severe poverty is found in areas where the unpredictability of rainfall and flooding creates great uncertainty. Many people dependent on rainfed agriculture are highly vulnerable to both short-term (two to three weeks) dry spells and long-term (seasonal) drought and thus are reluctant to invest in agricultural inputs that could increase yields. This situation will become worse for many small farmers with climate change.

In developing countries growth in both productivity improvements and area expansion has been slower in rainfed agriculture than in irrigated agriculture (see below). Most irrigation has been installed on already cultivated rainfed land rather than on new land. In

table **2.3** | **Global water and land statistics**

Water (cubic kilometers)				Land (millions of hectares)		
Use	**Statistics**			**Use**	**Statistics**	
	Total precipitation over continents 110,000				Total terrestrial land	13,000
	Vapor flow back to the atmosphere 70,000	Runoff to the oceans 40,000				
	Evapotranspiration	Withdrawals				
Biomass consumed by grazing livestock	840			Grazing lands		3,430
Rainfed crops	4,910			Rainfed harvested lands		860
Irrigated crops	Irrigation 1,570 Rainfall 650		2,664	Irrigated cultivated lands	Harvested	340[a]
Municipal use	53		381			
Industrial use	88		785			
Reservoirs	208					

a. Of which 277 are equipped.

Source: For water withdrawal statistics and equipped irrigation area, FAO 2006a; for evapotranspiration, International Water Management Institute analysis using the Watersim model; for harvested irrigated crop area, chapter 3 on scenarios; for biomass consumed by grazing livestock, Stockholm Environment Institute calculations for the Comprehensive Assessment of Water Management in Agriculture; for municipal, industrial, and reservoir use, Shiklomanov 2000; for land statistics, FAO 2006b.

temperate regions with relatively reliable rainfall and good soils rainfed agriculture generates high yields, especially when supplemental irrigation practices are applied (see chapter 8 on rainfed agriculture). The potential exists for raising the productivity of many rainfed systems (in particular for maize, sorghum, and millet) in Sub-Saharan Africa, but this potential has been difficult to realize.

Irrigated agriculture

In the past half century there have been massive investments in large-scale public surface irrigation infrastructure as part of efforts to increase world staple food production and ensure food self-sufficiency. Irrigation water was essential to achieve the gains from high-yielding fertilizer-responsive crop varieties. These investments by international development banks, donor agencies, and national governments to develop and expand irrigation systems established the foundation of food security in much of the developing world. During this period more than half the agricultural budget in many countries, particularly in Asia, and more than half of World Bank agricultural lending was devoted to irrigation (Rosegrant and Svendsen 1993). At the same time irrigation demand dominated steadily increasing water withdrawals.

While the world's cultivated land increased by about 13% from 1961 to 2003 (from 1,368 million ha to 1,541 million ha), equipped irrigated area (photo 2.3) almost doubled, from 139 million ha to 277 million ha, an increase from 10% to 18% of cultivated area.

Harvested irrigated area, which includes double cropping, is estimated at 340 million ha (see table 2.3 and chapter 3 on scenarios). New incomplete evidence suggests that the harvested irrigated area might actually be higher because of a higher cropping intensity and unreported, often informal, groundwater or private irrigation (Thenkabail and others 2006). Approximately 70% of the world's irrigated land is in Asia (figure 2.5), where it accounts for 34% of cultivated land. China and India alone account for more than half of irrigated land in Asia. Over time Asia, with its high population densities, has come to rely increasingly on irrigated agriculture to boost agricultural productivity and thus to ensure domestic food security. More than two-thirds of the increase in cereal grain has come from irrigated land.

> While the world's cultivated land increased by about 13% from 1961 to 2003, equipped irrigated area almost doubled

By contrast, there is very little irrigation in Sub-Saharan Africa. Several large publicly funded irrigation schemes were commissioned in the 1960s and 1970s, mostly as settlement schemes funded through bilateral loans. Water application methods were largely surface irrigation, and little was done to improve water productivity. Decisionmaking was centralized, and profitability was low. Many of the schemes became unsustainable, and some closed. World Bank lending for irrigation and drainage fell sharply after 1985 (Donkor 2003).

During the 1990s most countries in East and Southern Africa emphasized implementation of poverty reduction strategies, which allocated inadequate budgets for agriculture, particularly water management. Meanwhile, as the costs of inputs escalated and inflation grew, the prices of farm produce plummeted. Even though lending for irrigation and drainage partially recovered in the late 1990s, lending for 2002–05 was still less than half the level for 1978–81, very low compared with lending in other regions. Also, investment in agricultural water in Sub-Saharan Africa has been only a small proportion of the total for the water sector—just 14% of African Development Bank lending to the water sector as a whole during 1968–2001, for example (Peacock, Ward, and Gambarelli forthcoming).

Photo by T.William Critchley

Photo 2.3 Large sprinkler system used in irrigated agriculture

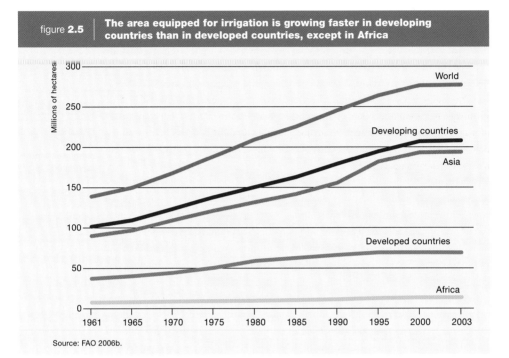

figure 2.5 The area equipped for irrigation is growing faster in developing countries than in developed countries, except in Africa

Millions of hectares

World

Developing countries

Asia

Developed countries

Africa

1961 1965 1970 1975 1980 1985 1990 1995 2000 2003

Source: FAO 2006b.

Globally, donor spending on irrigation reached a peak of more than $1 billion a year (in 1980 US dollars) in the late 1970s and early 1980s and then fell to less than half that level by the late 1980s (Rosegrant and Svendsen 1993). Four factors contributed to the decline in public investments in irrigation in the 1980s. First, there was a sharp drop in cereal prices in the 1980s. Second, there was growing recognition of the poor performance of irrigation systems.[4] Third, there was a rise in construction costs of irrigation infrastructure, although it is now decreasing (Inocencio and others forthcoming). Falling grain prices and rising construction costs reduced benefit-cost ratios, discouraging further investments. Fourth, there was growing opposition to large dams and to the environmental degradation and social dislocation they sometimes caused. Reflecting these environmental concerns, the World Commission on Dams, created in 1997, reviewed the experience with large dams and established a framework for decisionmaking regarding new large-scale dam projects (WCD 2000).

Recently, there has been renewed interest in investment in agricultural water management. The World Bank's new *Water Resources Sector Strategy*, for example, calls for a principled but pragmatic approach to balanced investment in both infrastructure and institutions and spells out a strategy for re-engaging in agricultural water management (World Bank 2004, 2006).

Two major investment trends exist today. One is the emergence of mega-projects such as the south-north diversion project in China and the interlinking rivers project in India, which intend to transfer water from water-abundant to water-scarce areas. The other is extensive individual and small-scale investments in irrigation and groundwater (photos 2.4 and 2.5).

Private and community-based irrigation systems in developing countries, particularly groundwater pumping (figure 2.6), have grown rapidly since the 1980s, propelled by the availability of cheap drilling technology, rural electrification, subsidized energy, and inexpensive small pumps that farmers can afford to purchase themselves. Pumping enabled small-scale irrigation to develop within rainfed systems and to supplement other sources of irrigation water. In India, with 26 million pump owners, irrigation from groundwater now exceeds irrigation from surface water systems. One consequence has been accelerating rates of groundwater decline.

Photo 2.4 One major investment trend is the emergence of mega-projects

Photo 2.5 Another is extensive individual investment in irrigation and groundwater

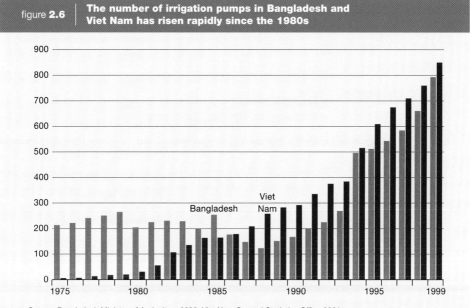

figure **2.6** | **The number of irrigation pumps in Bangladesh and Viet Nam has risen rapidly since the 1980s**

Source: Bangladesh Ministry of Agriculture 2000; Viet Nam General Statistics Office 2001.

A fairly polarized debate has arisen in some circles over the relative benefits of large- and small-scale infrastructure. In reality, the appropriate scale of infrastructure should be determined in the context of the specific environmental, social, and economic conditions and goals, with the participation of relevant stakeholders.

Drivers of biodiversity loss and ecosystem change

Biological diversity is in rapid decline in all the world's major biomes. While rates of loss differ between regions and biomes, loss of biodiversity is greatest among freshwater-dependent species—almost twice as fast as for marine and terrestrial species (figure 2.7). This has happened because biodiversity associated with inland waters is concentrated within limited areas, because many inland water-dependent species are especially vulnerable to changes in environmental conditions, and because freshwater is subject to rapidly escalating threats from land-based impacts as demands placed on water to meet growing populations and development pressures rises (MEA 2005a).

Many factors contribute to biodiversity change. The most important direct drivers of biodiversity loss are habitat change (land use change, physical modification of rivers, water withdrawal from rivers, damage to sea floors from trawling), climate change, invasive alien species, species overexploitation, and pollution. For most ecosystems the impacts are constant or growing.

- *Habitat transformation and fragmentation.* This includes the impact of land cover change, such as the conversion to agriculture and the release of nutrients into rivers, and of water withdrawals for irrigation.

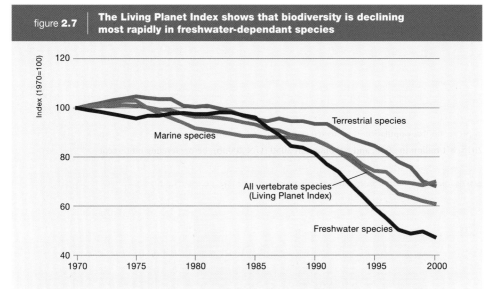

| figure **2.7** | **The Living Planet Index shows that biodiversity is declining most rapidly in freshwater-dependant species** |

Note: The index incorporates data on the abundance of 555 terrestrial species, 323 freshwater species, and 267 marine species around the world. While the index fell by some 40% between 1970 and 2000, the terrestrial index fell by about 30%, the freshwater index by about 50%, and the marine index by about 30%.

Source: MEA 2005b.

- *Modifications to water regimes.* Many rivers have been fragmented through the construction of dams and barrages. River-regulating structures have changed flow regimes (the quantity and timing of flow in rivers).
- *Spread of invasive alien species.* Increased trade and travel have contributed to the spread of invasive alien species (and disease organisms). The introduction of non-native invasive species is now a major cause of species decline in freshwater systems. While measures are increasingly being taken to control some of the pathways through which invasive species make inroads, many pathways remain inadequately regulated.
- *Nutrient loading.* Since 1950 anthropogenic increases in nitrogen, phosphorus, sulfur, and other nutrient-associated pollutants have emerged as one of the most important drivers of change in terrestrial, freshwater, and coastal ecosystems. Humans now produce more reactive (biologically available) nitrogen than all natural pathways combined.

The majority of biomes have been greatly modified, with 20%–50% of 14 global biomes transformed to croplands. For terrestrial ecosystems the most important direct driver of change in the past 50 years has been changes in land cover. Further land use changes causing habitat loss are associated primarily with the additional expansion of agriculture and secondarily with the expansion of cities and infrastructure.

For freshwater ecosystems the most important direct drivers of change in the past 50 years include direct physical changes to freshwater habitat, such as draining wetlands and building dams, and deliberate modification of water regimes through, for example, water extraction and pollution. All these factors are also influenced indirectly through the impacts of land use; for example, excessive erosion leads to sedimentation in rivers, estuaries, and lakes. Invasive species are also an important driver. Many of these drivers arise due to agriculture-related activities (including livestock, fisheries, and aquaculture).

People and diets

The two major factors contributing to increased food demand, and thus to increased water use for food production, are population growth and changes in diets as living standards improve. Global population is projected to grow from 6.1 billion in 2000 to 7.2 billion in 2015, 8.1 billion in 2030, and 8.9 billion in 2050 (UN 2003b), before leveling off (except in Sub-Saharan Africa). Rising incomes lead not only to increasing consumption of staple cereals, but also to a shift in consumption patterns among cereal crops and away from cereals toward livestock products, fish, and high-value crops.

The key variable used for measuring and evaluating the evolution of the world food situation is kilocalories per person per day (FAO 2006c). The world food supply increased from about 2,400 kcal per person per day in 1970 to 2,800 kcal per person per day in 2000.[5] However, large differences exist. In developed countries food supply increased from 3,050 kcal to 3,450 kcal per person per day over that period, while in Sub-Saharan Africa it increased from 2,100 kcal to about 2,200 kcal (figure 2.8).

The growth in per capita food consumption has been accompanied by significant changes in commodity composition. Cereals continue to be the most important source of

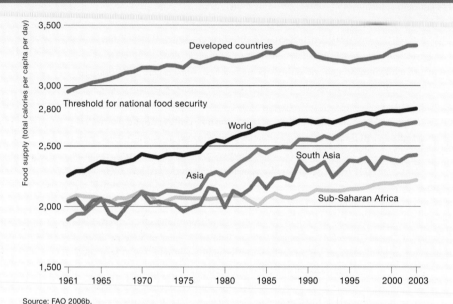

figure **2.8** | **There has been a steady increase in global nutritional status since the 1960s, but developing countries still lag behind**

Food supply (total calories per capita per day)

Developed countries

Threshold for national food security

World

South Asia

Asia

Sub-Saharan Africa

Source: FAO 2006b.

total food consumption in the world, but there are large regional differences in the com-modity composition of the diet (figure 2.9). In Sub-Saharan Africa roots and tubers are by far the most important component and are expected to remain so for some time. In all regions except Sub-Saharan Africa there has been a significant increase in the consumption of vegetable oils over the last three decades. Meat consumption increased in all regions except Sub-Saharan Africa. The industrial countries are by far the largest meat consumers, at 103 kilograms per person per year, a trend that is projected to continue for the next 50 years. The same pattern applies to dairy products.

A growing, wealthier population requires more food per person, and richer and more varied diets. The amount of water needed to produce food depends on diets and how the food is produced (see chapter 7 on water productivity). It is estimated that in 2000 crop production to feed 6.1 billion people used about 7,130 cubic kilometers of water through evapotranspiration (see chapter 3 on scenarios), excluding evaporation from grazing lands. About 1,570 cubic kilometers of the evapotranspiration was met using blue water from the 2,664 cubic kilometers withdrawn from rivers, lakes, and aquifers (see table 2.2). Crop evapotranspiration thus roughly corresponds to about 3,000 liters of water to feed one person per day, or 1 liter of water to produce 1 calo-rie. But this varies by water productivity and diet. A diet without meat requires an estimated 2,000 liters of water per day to produce, while a diet high in grainfed beef requires about 5,000 liters of water (Renault and Wallender 2000; see chapter 7 on water productivity).

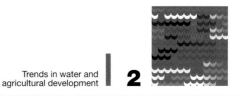

figure **2.9** | **Major diet components vary by region—and over time**

a. Includes Australia, Austria, Belgium, Canada, Denmark, Finland, France, Germany, Greece, Iceland, Ireland, Israel, Italy, Japan, Luxembourg, Malta, the Netherlands, New Zealand, Norway, Portugal, South Africa, Spain, Sweden, Switzerland, the United Kingdom, and the United States.

Source: FAO 2006c.

It is clear then that as more people add more animal products to their diets, more water will be required for agriculture. But that is not necessarily bad for water. Pasture-fed and free-roaming livestock do not use additional blue water, and in many places animals graze on land where no other form of agriculture can take place. Moreover, for many malnourished people livestock products are important for a balanced diet, while livestock rearing and fisheries are extremely important livelihood activities for many poor people.

The amount of water needed to produce food depends on diets and how the food is produced. Crop evapotranspiration roughly corresponds to about 3,000 liters of water to feed one person per day, or 1 liter to produce 1 calorie

Consumption and production of animal products are growing at about 2.5%–4% a year in developing countries, but at less than 0.5% a year in developed countries (see chapter 13 on livestock). But annual per capita meat consumption in developing countries is still lower than it was in developed countries 30 years ago and will remain so for the next 30 years. Most of the increased production will be met through mixed and industrial livestock systems, which depend on feed rather than grazing. More crops—and thus more water—will be needed for feed.

Freshwater fish consumption has been growing at a rate of 3.3% a year between 1970 and 2000 and 4.5% a year between 1990 and 2000. Fish, including shellfish and crustaceans, provide about 16% of animal protein consumed worldwide and are a valuable source of minerals and fatty acids. While fish harvests from marine capture have barely increased since the 1990s, annual freshwater fish production (from capture fisheries and aquaculture) doubled between 1990 and 2000.

Because both oceanic and freshwater capture fisheries have reached their limits of sustainability in many locations, the rising demand for fish will have to come from aquaculture. Aquaculture has been growing at a rate of 8% a year since 1980 and has increased its share in world fish supplies to 43% (FAO 2006d). Aquaculture in the coastal zone has been the method for meeting the increasing demand on fisheries and is also the fastest growing food sector in the world, with an output of 37.9 million metric tons in 2001 (Kura and others 2004). Aquaculture, like industrial livestock systems, requires freshwater to produce feed, and inland aquaculture has additional water requirements, adding to the competition for water resources.

Urbanization and migration

In the 1960s two-thirds of the world's population lived in rural areas (figure 2.10), and 60% of the economically active population worked in agriculture. Today, half of the people live in rural areas, and just a little more than 40% of the economically active population depend directly on agriculture. In absolute terms the rural population will start to decline in the next few years. By 2030 more than 60% of the world's people will live in cities. But, again, global averages mask considerable regional variation. In many poor countries in South Asia and Sub-Saharan Africa the rural population will continue to grow until about 2030, and the number of people depending on agriculture will continue to rise.

Rapid rural to urban migration in developing countries influences farming practices and water demand. Also, it is often the men who migrate to cities, leaving women, older people, and children behind in rural areas. As a consequence, in developing countries women's share in the economically active population in agriculture is growing, rising from

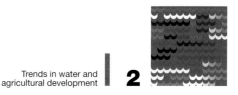

39% in 1961 to 44% in 2004, while in developed countries it is falling, dropping from 44% to 35% (FAO 2006b).

Cities are rapidly increasing their claim on water at the expense of rural uses such as farming. Furthermore, urban centers represent a source of pollution that has impacts on

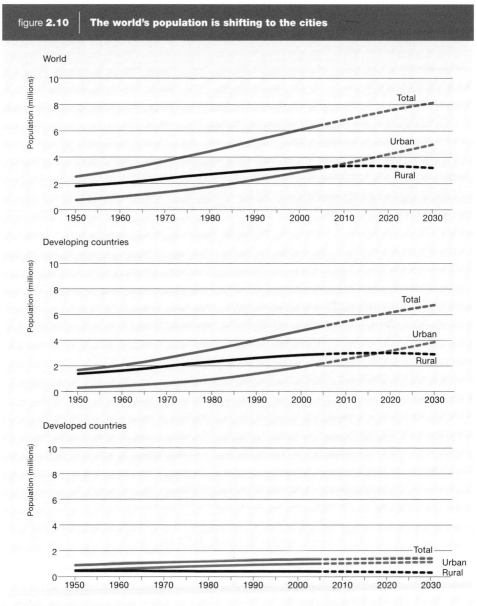

figure **2.10** | **The world's population is shifting to the cities**

Source: FAO 2006b.

downstream irrigation and aquatic ecosystems. City wastewater, often untreated, is an increasing source of irrigation water, especially in noncoastal cities. Wastewater use has its own unique set of health and environment considerations (see chapter 11 on marginal-quality water).

Agricultural transformations

Economic development typically begins with the development of agriculture. In the early stages of development agriculture provides labor and capital (often in the form of export earnings) to the industrial sector and in turn provides a market for industrial products. As the economy develops agriculture grows but not as fast as the nonagricultural sector. Agriculture's share of GDP declines. With rising incomes and urbanization, food habits change toward richer and more varied diets.

This agricultural transformation will take different forms in different countries or regions. To adapt to changes in consumer demand some farmers will shift from staples to higher value horticultural crops, livestock, and fisheries. Others will specialize in export crops. Farmers who continue to grow staple food crops will need to boost their productivity. Low-cost food grains will be important to poor people both because grains constitute a large share of their budgets and because the low wages made possible by cheap food make labor-intensive activities more profitable (Timmer 2005).

The next step in agricultural transformation is access to value-added supply chains in the modern retail sector, where the added value comes in the form of higher quality, timeliness, food safety, and labor standards in production (Timmer 2005). It is difficult to judge how fast this transition is occurring, but in many parts of the developing world groups of professional farmers are emerging whose incomes come almost entirely from farming. They are more innovative than conventional farmers, have larger farms, and have better access to resources such as credit and new marketing structures. Supermarkets play an increasingly important role as intermediaries in these value-added supply chains, ensuring quality, environmental standards, and market access.

A much larger number of farm households in developing countries are involved in transformation of a different sort, increasingly augmenting their incomes through nonfarm activities. Labor has become more mobile. The distinction between rural and urban is becoming blurred, as households move between both rural and urban worlds and earn a living in both agricultural and nonagricultural activities (Rigg 2005).

Management of water resources for agriculture will be shaped by this ongoing transition. For example, families with incomes essentially from nonfarm activities or those who invest in pumps to obtain water on demand will have less interest in assuming responsibilities for operation and maintenance of irrigation systems.

The way this transformation unfolds has implications for water investments to reduce poverty. In the early stages of the transformation investments in water to increase productivity can be quite effective in reducing poverty, especially through a multiplier effect. But as economies grow, this impact diminishes. Furthermore, other opportunities open up for the rural poor, including job opportunities in the cities. Later in the transformation livelihood diversification becomes an important strategy. It is hard to gain much wealth from agriculture alone unless farm sizes are large enough. Ultimately, this could lead to an exit

> The next step in agricultural transformation is access to value-added supply chains in the modern retail sector in the form of higher quality, timeliness, food safety, and labor standards in production

from agriculture, another escape from rural poverty. But throughout the transformation there will be pockets of rural poverty, where more targeted investments in water for food can make a difference in the nutrition, income, and health of the rural poor.

Benefits and costs, winners and losers

From a global perspective the economic benefits from investments in water for agriculture over the last 50 years have far exceeded the costs, but the gains could have been much more equitably distributed. Furthermore, the social and environmental costs have sometimes been severe, were often neglected in cost-benefit analyses, and could have been reduced with appropriate attention.

> From a global perspective the economic benefits from investments in water for agriculture over the last 50 years have far exceeded the costs, but the gains could have been much more equitably distributed

Gains in food security, economic growth, poverty reduction, and environmental sustainability

The major objectives of large-scale irrigation investments have been economic growth, food security, and poverty alleviation. Due largely to the expansion of irrigation and the adoption of green revolution technologies, global food grain prices have fallen dramatically. The growth dividend made possible by productivity gains has been shared between producers through higher incomes and consumers through lower prices. But consumers benefited much more than producers, particularly the poor who receive half or more of their calories from cereal grains.

Research shows that investments in water for agriculture have made a positive contribution to rural livelihoods, food security, and poverty reduction (Lipton, Litchfield, and Faurès 2003; Hasnip and others 2001; Hussain 2005). The positive impact is felt through employment gains, affordable food prices, and more stable outputs. Through a multiplier effect the investment in irrigation leads to a rise in crop yields and farm incomes that results in higher demand for goods and services in the nonfarm sector that multiplies the benefits of the original investment. A handful of studies on the multiplier effects of investment in irrigation indicate a range of 2.5 to 4 (Bhattarai, Barker, and Narayanamoorthy forthcoming). Mellor (2002) notes that the additions to employment in the local nonfarm sector can be as high as twice that for the farm sector, with a major impact on poverty reduction.

Water management practices have also contributed to environmental sustainability. Development of intensive irrigation has reduced the amount of land required for agriculture. Wetlands and agriculture have coexisted for 10,000 years, shaping many adaptations of biodiversity (Bambaradeniya and Amerasinghe 2004). Galraith, Amerasinghe, and Huber-Lee 2005 find that in recent years irrigation and water storage have created new habitats for water birds in Asia, leading to an increase in their population.

Social and environmental costs

Poorly conceived and implemented water management interventions have incurred high social and environmental costs. Social costs have included inequity in the allocation of benefits and loss of livelihood opportunities. Differential access to benefits has been common, especially between more and less powerful members of society: landed and landless, rich and poor, men and women, large and small landholders. Some projects have benefited upstream users at the expense of downstream users, who lose access to some or all good-quality water. Common-property resources such as rivers and wetlands, important for poor fishers and resource gathers, have been appropriated for other uses, resulting in a loss of livelihood opportunities (Gowing, Tuong, and Hoanh 2006). Communities have been displaced, especially in areas behind dams, without adequate compensation (WCD 2000).

A large proportion of irrigation's negative environmental effects arise from the diversion of water from natural aquatic ecosystems, such as rivers, lakes, oases, and other groundwater-dependent wetlands. Direct and indirect negative impacts have been well documented (for example, Richter and others 1997; Revenga and others 2000; WCD 2000; Bunn and Arthington 2002; MEA 2005a,b; see chapter 6 on ecosystems for details), including salinization, channel erosion, declines in biodiversity, introduction of invasive alien species, reduction of water quality, genetic isolation through habitat fragmentation, and reduced production of floodplain and other inland and coastal fisheries.

> A large proportion of irrigation's negative environmental effects arise from the diversion of water from natural aquatic ecosystems

Poor irrigation practices result in the buildup of salinity in the soil, though there is uncertainty about how much. Available but highly unreliable data suggest that some 20–30 million ha of irrigated land in the arid and semiarid zones are seriously affected by salinity—about 10% of all irrigated land and 20% of irrigated land in these susceptible regions. Current estimates are that about 0.25–0.5 million ha are lost from production every year as a result of salt buildup (FAO 2002), much less than the often quoted figure of 1–2 million ha. There has been a great slowdown in the growth in salinization as the development of new large-scale irrigation has slowed. Often, in new irrigation projects water tables rise rapidly, causing waterlogging and salinization, but eventually they drain or reach equilibrium. Much of the newer irrigation development comes from groundwater, which tends to drain lands.

Changing responses over time to the water-food-environment challenge

Meeting the water-food-environment challenge requires reducing poverty by producing food in an environmentally sustainable manner and by managing any negative consequences when tradeoffs must be made. Individuals, communities, governments, and the international community have all been responding to water problems, but in different ways over time.

Local responses by farmers and communities

Farmers, fishers, and pastoralists and their communities, often supported by community-based organizations, have responded to water scarcity with or without government support (Noble and others 2006). The failure of large-scale public irrigation systems to provide water where and when farmers needed it spurred many to invest in individual pumps and other private irrigation systems. This informal irrigation sector blossomed in many areas. Examples include water harvesting using age-old systems (such as the revival of *johads* in Rajastan, India; Shah and Raju 2002) or adapting systems to the local situation. Peri-urban irrigators use wastewater as a key source (Drechsel and others 2006; see also chapter 11 on marginal-quality water). Where opportunities permit, farmers are benefiting from more flexible and reliable supplies or from small storage coupled with micro, or localized, irrigation to shift from cereal grains to higher value crops.

However, local responses do not always meet the broader water-food-environment challenge because the primary focus is generally to enhance local food production and livelihoods. Farmers and communities, for example, do not bear all of the costs of their actions with regard to the environment or downstream impacts. Particularly in semiarid areas, unregulated exploitation of groundwater can lead to falling water tables (see chapter 10 on groundwater). Upstream development of water sources can decrease water availability downstream. Furthermore, the development of private facilities may further disadvantage poor farmers, who cannot afford the investment costs, and undermine farmer irrigation associations. Many have argued that uniting these local actions into larger programs or establishing regulatory policies could reduce the negative impacts.

> The focus on water infrastructure sometimes led to institutions and practices well suited for construction, but less well suited for the adaptive management needed to operate long-lived, multipurpose water infrastructure

National government responses

Responses at the national level generally express a broader view, but they still reflect specific perspectives and priorities. Governance in the water sector has often been the root cause of success or failure at the national level. Often, institutional development failed to keep pace with rapid infrastructure development, undermining the efficiency of investments and failing to adapt to changing economic, environmental, and social conditions. Many of today's water bureaucracies were set up to construct major water infrastructure facilities. This heavy focus on infrastructure sometimes led to institutions and practices that were well suited for construction, but less well suited for the adaptive management needed to operate long-lived, multipurpose water infrastructure (see chapters 9 on irrigation and 5 on policies and institutions).

In the 1990s investment in water infrastructure fell sharply as the focus shifted to water management. Efforts emphasized demand management, rationalized water allocation, institutions and capacity building, and market tools for promoting more efficient use and operations of existing water supplies.

A global consensus (discussed below) was emerging during this period on good practice in integrated water resources management, environmental water needs, and ecosystems approaches. It was increasingly being recognized that agricultural water management needs to be more integrated, looking at the full range of water resources, water uses, and management and supply development options. Important changes were gradually being made, such as the South African Water Law, which included the first designation of environmental allocations for water.

But despite repeated calls for integration, government responses remain mostly sectoral. Management of water allocation across sectors remains fragmented and highly politicized in most countries. Even within agriculture, irrigation receives the most attention while rainfed agriculture, fisheries, and livestock are rarely considered in discussions of water resources.

Global and regional responses

There is no global convention on water, unlike for desertification, wetlands, and biodiversity. Some argue that water is essentially a local issue, and thus there is no need for global action. But global issues affect global water use, and thus global actions are necessary to resolve them.

Consider recent events in Asian cereal grain production and trade. Food grain production in the Punjab region of India and Pakistan and the North China Plain, two of the breadbaskets of Asia, increased dramatically in the 1970s and 1980s. Today, however, the exploitation of water resources exceeds sustainable levels because more groundwater is being pumped for irrigation than is being recharged. A recent report notes that the threat to irrigation in the temperate regions of northern China could cause China to import a large share of its wheat needs, which would have a substantial impact on global production and trade (Lohmar and others 2003). In an effort to avert this outcome and to boost rural incomes, China instead introduced national cereal grain subsidies in 2004. This may result in extending the wheat-growing area further south in China into more humid climates, as occurred in eastern India and Bangladesh.

> National management of water allocation across sectors remains fragmented and highly politicized in most countries

The United Nations Conference on Environmental Development in Rio de Janeiro (Earth Summit) in 1992 was a milestone in the global call to action for better water management. A consensus emerged on global good practice in water management based on the Dublin Principles (ICWE 1992): freshwater is a finite and vulnerable resource, essential to sustain life, development, and the environment; water development and management should be based on a participatory approach, involving users, planners, and policymakers at all levels; women play a central part in the provision, management, and safeguarding of water; and water has an economic value in all its competing uses, and should be recognized as an economic good. There was also recognition of the urgency of the challenge, which many considered an impending water crisis, a crisis of water management as much as of water scarcity.

The Second World Water Forum in 2000 was instrumental in mobilizing thinking around key global issues of the water crisis: water supply, agriculture, environment, and livelihoods (HRH Prince of Orange and Rijsberman 2000). A divide in thinking was clearly illustrated by reports on water for food and rural development (van Hofwegen and Svendsen 2000) and reports on water and nature (IUCN 2000). Numerous programs, meetings, organizations, and activities were mobilized to address the issues that make up the global water crisis—the Global Water Partnership, UN–Water,[6] the World Water Council, World Water Week in Stockholm, the Consultative Group on International Agricultural Research Challenge Program on Water and Food, and this Comprehensive Assessment of Water Management in Agriculture.

With water again at the forefront of global issues, discussions are occurring in a more balanced context, with more consideration of the social and environmental tradeoffs that water management and development decisions entail (SIWI and IWMI 2004; World Bank 2004).

New paradigms call for considering agricultural water management within a basin context and for including rainfed agriculture, fisheries, and livestock in water discussions. There is more attention to integration across sectors and to the appropriate roles of public and private sectors. Good practice in agriculture is also increasingly more sensitive to the role of ecosystems, recognizing, for example, the importance of watershed protection, environmental flows, and sustainable management of aquatic ecosystems, springs, and aquifers.

At the same time there has been an increasing awareness within the environmental community of the importance of water, food, and livelihoods issues. This awareness builds on the Ramsar Convention on Wetlands' emphasis on the wise use of wetlands, which has long recognized that wetlands are being used for agriculture, but that this should be done in a sustainable manner. This dialogue about a balanced ecoagriculture to meet the needs of both societies and ecosystems can evolve still further, with wider all round benefits.

Reviewers

Chapter review editor: John Gowing.
Chapter reviewers: Gordana Beltram, Jeremy Berkoff, Jacob Burke, Joseph K. Chisenga, Victor A. Dukhovny, Jean-Marc Faurès, Francis Gichuki, M. Gopalakrishnan, Fitsum Hagos, Jippe Hoogeveen, Nancy Karanja, Jacob W. Kijne, Wulf Klohn, Gordano Kranjac-Berisavljevic, Jean Margat, Douglas J. Merrey, James Newman, Bart Schultz, David Seckler, Henri Tardieu, Jinxia Wang, and Philippus Wester.

Notes

1. Harvested area includes cropping intensity. Thus if two crops per year are grown on the same 100 hectares, the harvested area is 200 hectares.

2. Area equipped for irrigation refers to areas where irrigation infrastructure has been developed. Area actually irrigated may differ from area equipped for irrigation, and equipped area does not include cropping intensity.

3. The distinction between rainfed and irrigated agriculture is blurred, with rainfed areas receiving supplemental irrigation.

4. Improving irrigation management to overcome problems of poor irrigation performance was the motivation behind the establishment of the International Irrigation Management Institute, which later expanded its mandate and became the International Water Management Institute.

5. A dietary energy supply value of 2,800 kcal per person per day is usually taken as a threshold for national food security, considering dietary energy requirements (typically between 1,900 kcal and 2,500 kcal per person per day), inefficiencies in the food distribution chain, and inequalities in access to food through a national distribution function of dietary energy consumption.

6. UN–Water is the interagency mechanism established to follow up on the water-related decisions of the World Summit on Sustainable Development and the Millennium Development Goals concerning water.

References

Bambaradeniya, C.N.B., and F.P. Amerasinghe. 2004. "Biodiversity Associated with the Rice Field Agro-ecosystem in Asian Countries: A Brief Review." IWMI Working Paper 63. International Water Management Institute, Colombo.

Bangladesh, Ministry of Agriculture. 2000. "National Minor Irrigation Project." Dhaka.

Bhattarai, M., R. Barker, and A. Narayanamoorthy. Forthcoming. "Who Benefits from Irrigation Investments in India? Implications of Irrigation Multiplier Estimates for Cost Recovery and Irrigation Finance." *Irrigation and Drainage.*

Bruinsma, Jere. 2003. *World Agriculture: Towards 2015/2030. An FAO Perspective.* London: Earthscan.

Bunn, S.E., and A.H. Arthington. 2002. "Basic Principles and Ecological Consequences of Altered Flow Regimes for Aquatic Biodiversity." *Environmental Management* 30 (4): 492–507.

Donkor, S. 2003. "Development Challenges of Water Resource Management in Africa." *African Water Journal* 1: 1–19.

Drechsel, P., S. Graefe, M. Sonou, and O.O. Cofie. 2006. *Informal Irrigation in Urban West Africa: An Overview.* IWMI Research Report 102. Colombo: International Water Management Institute.

Falcon, W.P., and R.L. Naylor. 2005. "Rethinking Food Security for the Twenty-first Century." *American Journal of Agricultural Economics* 87 (5): 1113–27.

FAO (Food and Agriculture Organization). 1997. *Report of the World Food Summit, 13–17 November 1996.* Part I. Rome.

———. 2002. "Crops and Drops: Making the Best Use of Water for Irrigation." Rome.

———. 2004. *The State of Food Insecurity in the World 2004.* Rome.

———. 2006a. AQUASTAT database. Rome. [http://www.fao.org/ag/aquastat].

———. 2006b. FAOSTAT database. Rome. [http://faostat.external.fao.org].

————. 2006c. *World Agriculture: Towards 2030/2050. Prospects for Food, Nutrition, Agriculture and Major Commodity Groups.* Interim report. Global Perspective Studies Unit. Rome.

————2006d. *State of World Aquaculture 2006.* FAO Fisheries Technical Paper 500. Rome.

Galbraith, H., P. Amerasinghe, and A. Huber-Lee. 2005. "The Effects of Agricultural Irrigation on Wetland Ecosystems in Developing Countries: A Literature Review." CA Discussion Paper 1. Comprehensive Assessment Secretariat Colombo.

Gowing, J.W., T.P. Tuong, and C.T. Hoanh. 2006. "Land and Water Management in Coastal Zones: Dealing with Agriculture-Aquaculture-Fishery Conflicts." In *Environmental Livelihoods in Tropical Coastal Zones: Managing Agriculture-Fishery-Aquaculture Conflicts.* London: CABI Publishing.

Hasnip, N., S. Mandal, J. Morrison, P. Pradhan, and L. Smith L. 2001. "Contribution of Irrigation to Sustaining Rural Livelihoods." KAR Project R 7879, Literature Review. Report OD/TN 109. HR Wallingford and UK Department for International Development, Wallingford, UK.

Hayami, Y. 2005 "An Emerging Agrarian Problem in High-Performing Asian Economies." Presidential lecture at the 5th Conference of the Asian Society of Agricultural Economists, 29–31 August, Zahedan, Iran.

Hope, R.A. 2006. "Water, Workfare, and Poverty: The Impact of the Working for Water Programme on Rural Poverty Reduction." *Environment, Development, and Sustainability* 8 (1): 139–56.

HRH The Prince of Orange and F.R. Rijsberman. 2000. "Summary Report of the 2nd World Water Forum: From Vision to Action." *Water Policy* 2 (6): 387–95.

Hussain, I. 2005. *Pro-poor Intervention Strategies in Irrigated Agriculture in Asia—Poverty in Irrigated Agriculture: Issues, Lessons, Options and Guidelines.* Final Synthesis Report. Colombo: International Water Management Institute and Asian Development Bank.

ICWE (International Conference on Water and the Environment). 1992. *The Dublin Statement and Report of the Conference.* International Conference on Water and the Environment: Development Issues for the 21st Century, 26–31 January, Dublin.

Inocencio, A., D. Merrey, M. Tonosaki, A. Maruyama, I. de Jong, and M. Kikuchi. Forthcoming. "Costs and Performance of Irrigation Projects: A Comparison of sub-Saharan Africa and Other Developing Regions." IWMI Research Report. International Water Management Institute, Colombo.

IUCN (World Conservation Union). 2000. *Vision for Water and Nature: A World Strategy for Conservation and Sustainable Management of Water Resources in the 21st Century.* Gland, Switzerland.

Kura, Y., C. Revenga, E. Hoshino, and G. Mock. 2004. *Fishing for Answers.* Washington, D.C.: World Resources Institute.

Lipton, M., J. Litchfield, and J.M. Faurès. 2003. "The Effects of Irrigation on Poverty: A Framework for Analysis." *Water Policy* 5 (5–6): 413–27.

Lohmar, B., J.X. Wang, S. Rozelle, J.K. Huang, and D. Dawe. 2003. *China's Agricultural Water Policy Reforms: Increasing Investment, Resolving Conflicts, and Revising Incentives.* Information Bulletin 782. Washington, D.C.: U.S. Department of Agriculture, Economic Research Service, Market and Trade Economics Division.

MEA (Millennium Ecosystem Assessment). 2005a. *Ecosystem Services and Human Well-being: Wetlands and Water Synthesis.* Washington, D.C.: World Resources Institute.

————. 2005b. *Ecosystems and Human Well-being: Biodiversity Synthesis.* Washington, D.C.: World Resources Institute.

Mellor, J.W. 2002. "Irrigation Agriculture and Poverty Reduction: General Relationships and Specific Needs." In I. Hussain and E. Biltonen, eds., *Managing Water for the Poor.* Colombo: International Water Management Institute.

Noble, A.; D. Bossio, F.W.T. Penning De Vries, J. Pretty, and T.M. Thiyagarajan. 2006. *Intensifying Agricultural Sustainability: An Analysis of Impacts and Drivers in the Development of "Bright Spots."* Comprehensive Assessment of Water Management in Agriculture Research Report 13. Colombo: International Water Resources Management Institute.

Peacock, T., C. Ward, and G. Gambarelli. Forthcoming. *Investment in Agricultural Water for Poverty Reduction and Economic Growth in Sub-Saharan Africa. Synthesis Report.* Collaborative Programme of African Development Bank, Food and Agriculture Organization, International Fund for Agricultural Development, International Water Management Institute, and World Bank. Columbo.

Penning de Vries, F.W.T., H. Acquay, D. Molden, S.J. Scherr, C. Valentin, and O. Cofie. 2002. *Integrated Land and Water Management for Food and Environmental Security.* Research Report 1. International Water Management Institute, Colombo.

Renault, D., and W.W. Wallender. 2000. "Nutritional Water Productivity and Diets." *Agricultural Water Management* 45 (3): 275–96.

Revenga, C., J. Brunner, N. Henniger, K. Kassem, and R. Payner. 2000. *Pilot Analysis of Global Ecosystems, Freshwater Systems.* Washington, D.C.: World Resources Institute.

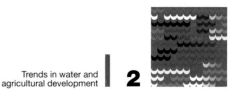

Richter, B.D., D.P. Braun, M.A. Mendelson, and L.L. Master. 1997. "Threats to Imperiled Freshwater Fauna." *Conservation Biology* 11 (5): 1081–93.

Rigg, J. 2005. "Land, Farming, Livelihoods, and Poverty: Rethinking the Links in the Rural South." *World Development* 34 (1): 180–202.

Rijsberman, F.R. 2006. "Water Scarcity: Fact or Fiction?" *Agricultural Water Management* 80 (1–3): 5–22.

Rosegrant, M.W., and M. Svendsen. 1993. "Asian Food Production in the 1990s: Irrigation Investment and Management Policy." *Food Policy* 18 (1): 13–32.

Shah, T., and K.V. Raju. 2002. "Rethinking Rehabilitation: Socio-ecology of Tanks and Water Harvesting in Rajasthan, North-West India." *Water Policy* 3 (6): 521–36.

Shiklomanov, I.A. 2000. "Appraisal and Assessment of World Water Resources." *Water International* 25 (1): 11–32.

SIWI (Stockholm International Water Institute) and IWMI (International Water Management Institute). 2004. *Water—More Nutrition Per Drop: Towards Sustainable Food Production and Consumption Patterns in a Rapidly Changing World.* Stockholm: Stockholm International Water Institute.

Thenkabail, P.S., C.M. Biradar, H. Turral, P. Noojipady, Y.J. Li, J. Vithanage, V. Dheeravath, M. Velpuri, M. Schull, X.L. Cai, and R. Dutta, R. 2006. *An Irrigated Area Map of the World (1999) Derived from Remote Sensing.*" Research Report 105. Colombo: International Water Management Institute.

Timmer, P. 2005. "Agriculture and Pro-Poor Growth: An Asian Perspective." Working Paper 63. Center for Global Development, Washington D.C.

UN (United Nations). 2003a. *Water for Food, Water for Life: The United Nations World Water Development Report 1.* Paris and New York: United Nations Educational, Scientific and Cultural Organization and Berghahn Books.

———. 2003b. *World Population Prospects: The 2002 Revision.* New York.

———. 2006a. Millennium Development Goals Indicators. The Official United Nations Site for the MDG Indicators. Accessed October 2006. [http://mdgs.un.org/].

———. 2006b. *Water—A Shared Responsibility: The United Nations World Water Development Report 2.* Paris and New York: United Nations Educational, Scientific and Cultural Organization and Berghahn Books.

UNDP (United Nations Development Programme). 2005. *Human Development Report 2005: International Cooperation at a Crossroads—Aid, Trade, and Security in an Unequal World.* New York,

Van Hofwegen, P., and M. Svendsen. 2000. "A Vision for Water for Food and Rural Development." Paper presented to the 2nd World Water Forum, 17–22 March, The Hague, Netherlands.

Viet Nam, General Statistics Office. 2001. *Statistical Data of Viet Nam Agriculture, Forestry, and Fishery, 1975-2000.* Hanoi: Statistical Publishing House, Department of Agriculture, Forestry, and Fishery.

WCD (World Commission on Dams). 2000. *Dams and Development: A New Framework for Decision-Making.* London: Earthscan.

WHO (World Health Organization) and UNICEF (United Nations Children's Fund). 2006. Joint Monitoring Programme for Water Supply and Sanitation database [www.wssinfo.org/].

World Bank. 2004. *Water Resources Sector Strategy: Strategic Directions for World Bank Engagement.* Washington, D.C.

———. 2006. *Reengaging in Agricultural Water Management: Challenges and Options.* Washington, D.C.

The path to success is not a single vector from the current status

Artist: Nathanael Kang, Malaysia

3

Looking ahead to 2050: scenarios of alternative investment approaches

Coordinating lead authors: Charlotte de Fraiture and Dennis Wichelns

Lead authors: Johan Rockström and Eric Kemp-Benedict

Contributing authors: Nishadi Eriyagama, Line J. Gordon, Munir A. Hanjra, Jippe Hoogeveen, Annette Huber-Lee, and Louise Karlberg

Overview

Food production requires enormous amounts of water and land. Yearly, some 7,130 cubic kilometers of water are consumed by crops to meet global food demand, the equivalent of 90 times the annual runoff of the Nile River, or more than 3,000 liters per person per day. Most of it (78%) comes directly from the rain, and 22% from irrigation. Already, 1.2 billion people live in river basins characterized by absolute physical water scarcity, while another 1.6 billion live in basins where economic constraints limit the pace of much-needed investments in water management. Today, food production requires about 2,500 square meters of cropland and 5,500 square meters of grazing land per person per year. Without proper investments water shortages, water quality deterioration, and land degradation are expected to intensify, particularly in resource-poor countries.

World food demand, and thus the consumption of agricultural water, will continue to increase during the coming decades, even though the rate of population growth is declining. With a growing population, rising incomes, and changes in diets, food demand may grow by 70%–90% by 2050. Without improvements in the efficiency of agricultural water use, crop water consumption would have to grow by the same order of magnitude.

Competition between water for food production and water for other sectors will intensify, but food production will remain the largest water user worldwide. Because of urbanization, demand for water in domestic and industrial sectors is expected to grow by a factor of 2.2 by 2050. With the increasing scarcity of water, reuse of urban wastewater will become more important in water-short areas. Crop production for energy generation also is increasing in several areas, with potentially substantial implications for land and water use in agriculture. While major tradeoffs will occur between all water using sectors, the tradeoffs will be particularly pronounced between agriculture and the environment, the two largest water-demanding sectors. Climate change will further increase pressures on water resources management.

Investments to improve productivity in rainfed areas are needed to increase food production, stimulate economic development, and protect the environment. Many rural poor people depend on rainfed agriculture. Assisting the poor often implies focusing on smallholders in rainfed areas. Investment costs per hectare to upgrade rainfed areas tend to be relatively low, particularly in Sub-Saharan Africa, where most rural poor people live in rainfed areas and more poor people may be lifted out of poverty by focusing investment on rainfed areas. An optimistic outlook on yield growth shows that rainfed agriculture could meet food demand in 2050. The potential is particularly high in low-yielding farming systems, which tend to be where poor people live. Realizing the yield growth potential of existing rainfed areas reduces the need for new large-scale irrigation development. But improving rainfed production through water harvesting and supplemental irrigation also requires infrastructure, though smaller and less centralized. In addition, impacts on downstream water resources are more disperse and difficult to assess. Harvesting rainwater increases the amount of water consumed by crops, leaving less water for runoff to rivers and lakes. Intensifying rainfed agriculture throughout a large region will affect surface water and groundwater resources. This negative impact on downstream water availability is partly offset by improvements in water productivity. Relying largely on rainfed agriculture is also risky and needs the right incentives and measures to mitigate risks to individual farmers to realize its full potential.

> There is greater scope for increasing food production by improving output per unit of water in existing irrigated areas than by expanding irrigated area

There is greater scope for increasing food production by improving output per unit of water in existing irrigated areas than by expanding irrigated area. In an optimistic yield growth scenario, in which 80% of the gap between actual and obtainable irrigated yields is bridged, more than half of additional food demand can be met by improving output per unit of water on existing irrigated lands. In South Asia, where more than 50% of the cropped area is irrigated and productivity is low, additional food demand can be met by improving output per unit of water in irrigated agriculture rather than by expanding area under production. Bridging 80% of the irrigated yield gap contributes 540 million metric tons of grains, or 75% of additional global demand by 2050. Expanding irrigated area by 35% contributes only 260 million metric tons of grain. Yield improvements increase required water diversions by 30%, but irrigated area expansion requires an increase of 55%. This would have serious impacts on water scarcity and the provision of environmental services. Further, the capital cost of improving water productivity is smaller than the cost of new construction for area expansion. The largest gains in value per unit of water likely will be achieved through diversification and by using water for many productive purposes, such as fisheries, livestock, home gardens, and other small enterprises.

Optimal investment strategies will require an appropriate mix of strategies, depending on the potential and constraints in different regions. With inevitable increases in world food demand agriculture will require more land and water resources. Part of the increase in food production can be achieved by improving crop yields and increasing output per unit of

Looking ahead to 2050:
scenarios of alternative
investment approaches | **3**

water, through appropriate investments in both irrigated and rainfed agriculture. However, even in an optimistic investment scenario, cropped area will increase by 9% and water withdrawals for agriculture will increase by 13% by 2050. One challenge is to manage this additional water in a way that minimizes adverse impacts on—and where possible enhances—environmental services, while providing the necessary gains in food production and poverty alleviation.

Drivers of agricultural water use

Competing claims on water resources will increase with rising demands from agriculture, households, and industry. Recent forecasts warn of impending global problems unless appropriate action is taken to improve water management and increase water use efficiency (Seckler and others 1998; Seckler and others 2000; Alcamo and others 1997; Rosegrant, Cai, and Cline 2002; Shiklomanov 2000; Vörösmarty and others 2004; Bruinsma 2003; SEI 2005; Falkenmark and Rockström 2004; Rosegrant and others 2006). About 1.2 billion people live in water-scarce river basins (closed basins), and another 500 million where the limit to water resources is fast approaching (closing basins; see chapters 2 on trends and 16 on basins). Another 1.6 billion people live in basins where economic constraints limit the pace of much-needed investments in water management.

With continuing population growth, rising incomes, and urbanization, food demand will roughly double in the next 50 years

Food supply and demand
With continuing population growth, rising incomes, and urbanization, food demand will roughly double in the next 50 years.

Changing diets. As incomes rise, food habits change in favor of more nutritious and more diversified diets. Rising incomes throughout much of Asia over the last three decades led not only to more consumption of staple cereals but also to a shift in consumption patterns among cereal crops and away from cereals toward livestock products and high-value crops. In middle-income countries (such as Thailand) per capita rice consumption stabilized or slightly declined while wheat consumption increased. Meat consumption more than tripled, while dairy demand more than doubled from 1967 to 1997. Consumption of high-value crops, such as fruit, sugar, and edible oils, also increased substantially (FAOSTAT 2006).

In the years ahead urbanization and income growth will continue to drive food demand toward higher per capita food intake and richer diets, particularly in low- and middle-income countries. The base scenario of the Comprehensive Assessment of Water Management in Agriculture estimates that more than 25% of the increase in grain demand will be due to changes in diets—mainly for the production of animal products—rather than to population growth. Such changes influence future agricultural water demand because livestock products, sugar, and oil typically require more water to produce than cereals and roots and tubers (see chapter 7 on water productivity).

While the changes in diets follow similar patterns (Rosegrant, Cai, and Cline 2002; Pingali 2004), regional and cultural differences are pronounced—and are expected to remain so in coming decades. Meat consumption will rise slower in India than in China, but

figure **3.1** | **The world will get richer, but large income gaps will remain**

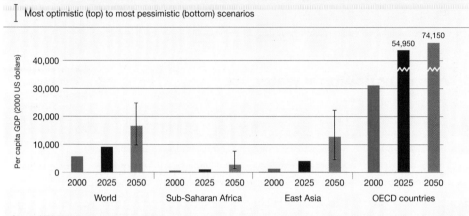

Most optimistic (top) to most pessimistic (bottom) scenarios

Source: MEA 2005; Alcamo and others 2005.

demand for dairy products will increase rapidly, with profound impacts on water resources (Singh and others 2004). In China per capita pork consumption is slightly higher than in the United States and increasing quickly, while per capita beef consumption is only 10% of that in the United States. Meat consumption in much of Sub-Saharan Africa is not directly related to income, because many pastoralists eat livestock products and bushmeat out of necessity.

Figures 3.1, 3.2, and 3.3 illustrate trends in income and per capita food consumption. Table 3.1 provides estimates of agricultural commodity demands used in this study, comparing them with projections published by others.

Income is a major driver of changes in diets. The income gap between rich and poor countries will decline, but remain large. In 2000 per capita GDP was estimated at $5,630 worldwide, $31,650 in Organisation for Economic Co-operation and Development (OECD) countries, $1,230 in East Asia, and $560 in Sub-Saharan Africa. According to projections by the Millennium Ecosystem Assessment, none of the developing regions will reach the OECD level by 2050. Projections exhibit great uncertainty. The I bars in figure 3.1 indicate the difference between the most optimistic and pessimistic among that assessment's scenarios. The colored bars depict the income projections we use in our scenario analysis (borrowed from the Millennium Ecosystem Assessment scenario TechnoGarden).

Global average meat consumption is estimated at 37 kilograms (kg) per capita per year in 2000, increasing to 48 kg in 2050 (see figure 3.2). Regional variation is large— meat consumption in Sub-Saharan Africa is about 12 kg per capita, less than one-sixth the meat consumption in OECD countries. With economic growth East Asia will move toward the same consumption level as OECD countries. Our estimates are comparable to those of other studies. The Millennium Ecosystem Assessment estimates global average annual meat demand by 2050 in the range of 41–70 kg per capita: 100–130 kg per capita for the OECD and 18–27 for Sub-Saharan Africa (Alcamo and others 2005). The Food

Looking ahead to 2050:
scenarios of alternative
investment approaches

3

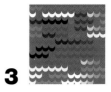

| figure **3.2** | **Meat consumption per person will roughly double in East Asia** |

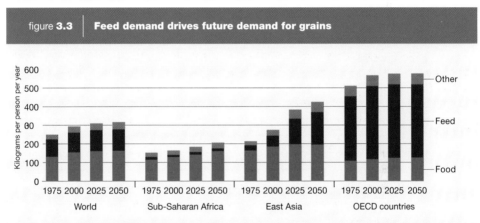

Source: For 1975 and 2000, FAOSTAT 2006; for 2025 and 2050, International Water Management Institute analysis done for the Comprehensive Assessment of Water Management in Agriculture using the Watersim model.

| figure **3.3** | **Feed demand drives future demand for grains** |

Source: For 1975 and 2000, FAOSTAT 2006; for 2025 and 2050, International Water Management Institute analysis done for the Comprehensive Assessment of Water Management in Agriculture using the Watersim model.

and Agriculture Organization's (FAO) interim report *Agriculture: Towards 2030/2050* provisionally estimates a global average of 52 kg per capita by 2050 (FAO 2006). Expected growth in per capita meat consumption in East Asia and the OECD will be much slower in the next 25 years than in the past 25 years (Alexandratos 1997, 2005). In OECD countries meat consumption will stabilize or decline, due partly to health considerations.

In high-income countries the growth rate in cereal consumption per capita declines over time, approaching zero by 2050 (see figure 3.3). In growing economies in East Asia (including China) cereal consumption continues to increase due to increasing feed grain demand, while per capita food consumption stabilizes. In Sub-Saharan Africa cereal food consumption continues to increase, but at a modest rate.

Increasing consumption of livestock products leads to higher feed grain demand, though the extent is subject to debate. Livestock are fed primarily by a combination of grass (grazing), crop residuals, and feedstuffs (primarily grains). Red meats require twice as much feed grain as white meats (Seckler and others 2000; Verdegem, Bosma, and Verreth 2006). In OECD countries, where cattle are raised largely on feed grains, cattle feeding accounts for two-thirds of the average per capita grain consumption. In Sub-Saharan Africa and India, where grazing is common and livestock are fed crop residuals and by-products, less than 10% of the grain supply is used for feed. Producing 1 kg of meat requires 2.3 kg of maize in the United States but only 0.1 kg in India (derived from FAOSTAT 2006).

An important question is how livestock will be fed in the future (Seckler and others 2000). Some argue that cattle will be raised largely on grass and crop residuals (as today) and that increases in feed demand will largely be offset by improving feed efficiency

table **3.1**	**Comparison of global demand projections**	
Variable	FAOSTAT 2006 Base year 2000	Comprehensive Assessment of Water Management in Agriculture 2025
Calories per capita (kilocalories per person per day)	2,790	3,100
Rice (millions of metric tons)	349	545
Wheat (millions of metric tons)	570	805
Maize (millions of metric tons)	610	870
Cereals for food (millions of metric tons)	940	1,230
Cereals for feed (millions of metric tons)	645	890
Cereals total[c] (millions of metric tons)	1,840	2,560
Roots and tubers (millions of metric tons)	685	625
Vegetables (millions of metric tons)	750	1,020
Oil crops (millions of metric tons)	370	585
Meat (millions of metric tons) demand[d]	220	360
Sugar[e] (millions of metric tons)	146	195
Aquaculture (millions of metric tons)	41	80
Milk and dairy (millions of metric tons)	476	720
Milk cows[g] (millions)	625	805
Beef cows[g] (millions)	300	405
Pigs[g] (millions)	1,150	1,500
Grazing land (millions of hectares)	3,450	4,660

a. Based on per capita gross food consumption including losses during processing and consumption. Most people actually consume fewer calories.
b. Production in millions of tons
c. Total cereals include cereals for food, feed, and other purposes
d. Beef, pork, poultry, and sheep.
e. Raw sugar equivalent.
f. Verdegem, Bosma, and Verreth 2006.

(continues on facing page)

Looking ahead to 2050:
scenarios of alternative
investment approaches

3

(Rosegrant, Cai, and Cline 2002) or by switching to other types of feed (Verdegem, Bosma, and Verreth 2006). Others claim that grain feeding will gain importance with decreasing opportunities to expand grazing land. In addition, with urbanization, livestock production will become more intensive and concentrated near cities (Keyzer and others 2005).

Figure 3.3 shows the potential impact on feed consumption, assuming that livestock feeding remains largely as it is today. Ways to improve livestock water productivity are described in chapter 13 on livestock.

General trends toward more diversified and meat-based diets are well documented (Pingali 2004; Alexandratos 1997, 2005), but considerable uncertainties remain regarding food and feed demand projections. Environmental concerns and emerging health

International Water Management Institute	International Food Policy Research Institute	Food and Agriculture Organization	Comprehensive Assessment of Water Management in Agriculture	Food and Agriculture Organization	Millennium Ecosystem Assessment
2025	2025	2030	2050	2050	2050
2,950		3,050	2,970[a]	3,130	2,970–3,600
	510	533	580	524[b]	
	770	851	890	908[b]	
	905		1,000		
1,175	1,240	1,406	1,480	1,445	
940	1,012	1,148	1,010		
2,435	2,606	2,838	2,980	3,012	2,864–3,229
	630	615	810	670	
			1,570		
			780		
	336	373	440	465	377–567
		216	250	240	
			122[f]		
		746	925	895	
		1,858[h]	1,070		
			510		
			1,790		
			5,220		

g. Assuming no changes in yield and extraction rates.

h. This is the total for milk and beef cows.

Source: For International Water Management Institute, Seckler and others 2000; for International Food Policy Research Institute, Rosegrant, Cai, and Cline 2002; for Food and Agriculture Organization 2030, FAO 2002, and for 2050, FAO 2006; for Millennium Ecosystem Assessment, MEA 2005; for grazing land, Stockholm Environment Institute projections done for the Comprehensive Assessment of Water Management in Agriculture.

problems related to obesity might generate new trends, particularly in high-income countries. Outbreaks of diseases such as mad cow disease and, more recently, avian flu might frighten consumers away from meat consumption. In addition, future feed grain requirements per kilogram of meat, milk, and eggs (see figure 3.3) and income projections that drive changes in diets are uncertain (see figure 3.1).

Changes in fish production. As fish stocks in oceans and fresh water bodies decline (Kura and others 2004; Worm and others 2006), the importance of aquaculture in meeting world fish demand will increase (see chapter 12 on inland fisheries). Between 1998 and 2003 global production from capture fisheries fluctuated between 87.7 and 95.5 million metric tons. In the same period aquaculture production increased steadily from 30.6 to 41 million metric tons (Verdegem, Bosma, and Verreth 2006). Projections of global fish production from aquaculture range from 15.6 kg per capita in 2030 to 22.5 kg per capita in 2030 (Ye 1999). The higher estimate corresponds to global aquaculture production of 186 million metric tons.

In many areas environmental flow regulations are needed to ensure adequate volumes and seasonal water patterns in rivers to maintain fisheries and other ecosystem services (Poff and others 1997; Arthington and others 2006). In water-scarce basins during the dry season aquacultural production and environmental requirements might compete with water diversions for irrigation. However, in some areas fish production is an integral part of an irrigated agricultural production system (Nguyen-Khoa and Smith 2004 and chapter 12 on inland fisheries).

And in some areas aquaculture is linked with capture fisheries. For example, production of high-value commodities such as shrimp and salmon can require up to 3 kg of fishmeal per kilogram of output (Naylor and others 1998, 2000). However, aquacultural production of shrimp and salmon accounts for a small portion of worldwide fish production. In aggregate, aquaculture is a net producer, generating 3–4 kg of food fish per kilogram of feed fish used in production (Tidwell and Allan 2001).

Assessments of the impacts of aquaculture on freshwater demand vary by an order of magnitude. Verdegem, Bosma, and Verreth (2006) estimate that aquaculture requires on average between 0.4 and 1.6 cubic meters of water per kilogram of fish produced from open water evaporation and seepage from ponds. Where fish are fed grains, this adds to the water requirements. Extensive aquaculture can require up to 45 cubic meters of water per kilogram of fish. Assuming production of 120 million metric tons of fish from aquaculture by 2050 and 1.6 cubic meters per kilogram (Verdegem, Bosma, and Verreth 2006), 190 cubic kilometers of water would be required, or about 8% of current irrigation withdrawals. This estimate does not account for seepage water that might recharge groundwater and be reused. Additional water for fish when aquaculture is combined with canals and reservoirs for irrigation is negligible at a global scale (see chapter 7 on water productivity). However, problems might arise locally if water is retained in an irrigation delivery system during peak demand. Integrating fisheries with irrigation is an important way to increase output and value per unit of water (see chapter 12 on inland fisheries).

> Assuming production of 120 million metric tons of fish from aquaculture by 2050 and 1.6 cubic meters of water per kilogram, 192 cubic kilometers of water would be required, or about 8% of current irrigation withdrawals

Looking ahead to 2050:
scenarios of alternative
investment approaches

3

Food, feed, and energy crops. Food production requires large amounts of water. On average, 1 kg of grain requires 1,600 liters of water, but estimates vary from 400 to more than 5,000 liters per kilogram of grain. The amount of water required to produce crops varies by crop and region, depending on climate, mode of cultivation (rainfed or irrigated, high-input or low-input agriculture), crop variety and length of growing season, and crop yields (see chapter 7 on water productivity). Following the water productivity framework in the livestock chapter, the water account for livestock includes water used to produce both feed crops and grass for grazing. By contrast, food wastes and crop residues are by-products, for which the water requirements have already been accounted. It is estimated that 7,130 cubic kilometers are consumed by crops globally, including both feed and food crops (table 3.2).

Nonfood crops such as cotton occupy 3% of the cropped area and 9% of irrigated area. The demand for cotton is expected to more than double by 2050. Crop production for energy also is increasing in several areas, with potentially substantial implications for land and water use in agriculture (Koplow 2006).

> Even with improvements in water productivity, agriculture will continue to consume a large portion of the world's developed water supply in 2050

Water for food production

Suppose improvements in land and water productivity or major shifts in production patterns do not take place. The amount of crop water consumption in 2050 would increase by 70%–90% depending on actual growth in population and income, and assumptions regarding the water requirements of livestock and fisheries. If that occurs, crop water consumption will reach 12,050–13,500 cubic kilometers, up from 7,130 cubic kilometers today. This estimated range includes crop water depletion for food and feed production, plus losses through evaporation from soil and open water. Evaporation from flooded rice paddies, irrigation canals, and reservoirs also is included, while evaporation from grasslands and aquaculture ponds is not. The estimate also excludes the impact of likely improvements in water productivity (see chapter 7 on water productivity). However, even with improvements in water productivity, agriculture will continue to consume a large portion of the world's developed water supply.

Only some of the water consumed by crops is diverted from surface and groundwater resources through irrigation—blue water. A large portion comes directly from rainfall that infiltrates the soil to generate soil moisture—green water (see chapters 1 on setting the scene and 8 on rainfed agriculture). Assessments of future water withdrawals for agriculture depend on assumptions regarding water sources. According to our estimates, 78% of the water consumed in agriculture is met from rain falling directly on land in both rainfed and irrigated areas.[1] The other 22% (1,570 cubic kilometers) is met by consumptive use of water withdrawn from rivers, lakes, and aquifers. To provide this 1,570 cubic kilometers, an estimated 2,630 cubic kilometers are withdrawn from surface water and groundwater resources. This means that 60% of the water withdrawn for agriculture is consumed (rendered unusable for further use) by crops and evaporation losses from soils and open water bodies, while 40% returns to surface water or groundwater.[2]

The ratio of consumption to withdrawals is commonly referred to as the consumptive or depleted fraction (Seckler and others 2000).[3] Consumptive fractions tend to be

table 3.2	Crop water consumption and water needed for grazing in 2000 (cubic kilometers unless otherwise indicated)				
	Crops				
Region	Total cereals[a]	Roots and tubers	Sugar	Vegetables and fruits	Soybeans
Sub-Saharan Africa	557	154	25	26	7
East Asia	960	99	67	172	68
South Asia	896	18	135	84	37
Central Asia & Eastern Europe	525	44	14	7	4
Latin America	336	29	163	35	176
Middle East & North Africa	166	4	6	32	1
OECD countries	640	12	24	15	134
World	4,089	363	434	370	427

Note: Water for aquaculture or inland fisheries is not included in these estimates.

a. Includes cereals used for feed.

b. Estimating the water transpired on grazing land is a fairly new exercise and relies on several uncertain factors—the feed energy supplied per kilogram of grass, feed energy requirements per animal, the mix of feeds for different kinds of livestock, and the water-use efficiency of grass production. The estimates for the composition of livestock feed from grazing are produced using the same assumptions as in chapter 13 on livestock of 5 kg of grass per tropical livestock unit per day and a water-use efficiency of 1.3 kg of dry matter per cubic meter of water, which corresponds to 750 liters per kilogram. This estimate is much lower than the amount of water evaporated from pastureland estimated

(continues on facing page)

low in water-abundant areas, where intensive water management is not cost effective, and higher in water-scarce areas, where plants use shallow groundwater and farmers reuse drainage water. In the Middle East and North Africa region we estimate a consumptive fraction of 77%, with peak values close to 100%. In water-abundant areas the consumptive fraction can be as low as 35%. Generally it is not feasible or desirable to achieve a consumptive fraction higher than 70% at the basin scale, due to substantial infrastructure and environmental costs (Molden, Sakthivaldivel, and Habib 2000 and chapter 16 on river basins).

Our estimate of 2,630 cubic kilometers withdrawn for agriculture in 2000 is consistent with estimates in other studies (box 3.1).

Ways to meet the demand for water for food. The estimated amount of additional water required to produce enough food in the future is large, given current trends in population, income, and diet. In addition, the increasing demand for nonagricultural water will intensify competition for limited resources. Without increases in productivity an additional 5,000 cubic kilometers of water will be required for crop production to meet future food demand, while the land area used for crops and livestock will increase by 50%–70% (Kemp-Benedict 2006b).

There are several ways to satisfy future food demands with the world's available land and water resources:

■   Expanding rainfed croplands.

Looking ahead to 2050:
scenarios of alternative
investment approaches

3

Crops			Livestock		
Other	Total	Share of water from rivers and aquifers (%)	Feed crops	Grazing[b]	Share of water for grazing (%)
312	1,071	6	68	218	76
325	1,661	22	277	96	26
335	1,505	41	16	27	63
193	772	20	277	61	18
169	895	12	190	240	56
30	225	61	59	13	18
181	990	17	426	185	30
1,547	7,130[c]	22	1,312	840	39

by Postel (1998): 5,800 cubic kilometers. Our estimates describe the amount of evaporation for grass actually consumed, rather than for the total area reported as "permanent pasture." Two factors explain the difference: in extensive grazing lands only a small portion of the grass biomass is consumed, and reported permanent pasture land tends to be overestimated, with part of the pasture land underused (Kemp-Benedict 2006b).

c. This estimate is comparable to other estimates, such as Rockström and others (1999), 6,800 cubic kilometers; Chapagain (2006), 6,390 cubic kilometers; and Postel (1998), 7,500 cubic kilometers.

Source: For crops, Watersim simulations, and for grazing, Stockholm Environment Institute computations, both done for the Comprehensive Assessment of Water Management in Agriculture.

■ Increasing water productivity and upgrading rainfed areas by enhancing management of rainwater and local runoff through in-situ and ex-situ water harvesting (adding small amounts of irrigation water where feasible).

■ Increasing annual irrigation water supplies by developing new surface water storage facilities and increasing groundwater withdrawals and use of wastewater.

■ Increasing water productivity in irrigated areas and the value per unit of water by integrating livestock and fisheries in irrigated systems.

■ Promoting agricultural trade from water-abundant and water-efficient producing areas to water-scarce areas.

■ Changing food demand patterns (influencing diets toward more water-efficient food mixes, such as less meat) and reducing waste (post-harvest losses).

Much effort has been devoted to agricultural water management in irrigated areas, while water management in rainfed areas has received less attention.[4] Yet there are notable opportunities to improve yields and water productivity in rainfed areas. The Comprehensive Assessment presents evidence on the opportunities to more than double yields for major rainfed crops in tropical developing countries through integrated soil, water, and crop management (see chapters 8 on rainfed agriculture and 15 on land).

Water productivity can be enhanced in rainfed areas by integrating in-situ management of rainfall (maximizing rainfall infiltration on farm fields), and soil fertility management with external management of local runoff (for supplemental irrigation). For example, farmers can use improved tillage methods (in-situ water harvesting),

box **3.1** | **Estimates of water withdrawals vary**

The concerns that water is a finite resource and that inappropriate uses of water can harm the environment are not new. Many researchers have estimated actual and future global water withdrawals and depletion for human purposes. Studies conducted in the 1960s and 1970s projected that by 2000 global water withdrawals would climb to 6,000–8,000 cubic kilometers of the 12,500 cubic kilometers of accessible resources, with dire consequences for the world's water resources (Gleick 1999). More recent assessments suggest that current annual global water withdrawals by all sectors are 3,100–3,700 cubic kilometers. Thus some of the earlier forecasts are two times the water demands actually observed (Gleick 1999), largely because water productivity improvements were not taken into account. The analysis in this chapter accounts for potential improvements in water productivity.

Estimates of water demands also vary because of differing definitions of *water use*. Some writers use the term to describe total withdrawals, while others refer to crop water depletion. In addition, data describing irrigation and basin efficiency are sparse, and estimates are subject to judgments about the amount of reuse of return flows (Seckler and others 2000; Molden, Sakthivaldivel, and Habib 2000). Furthermore, past projections have focused almost exclusively on withdrawals from rivers and groundwater, and consumptive use for irrigation, domestic, and industrial sectors. Recent estimates account more clearly for water consumption in rainfed agriculture (Rockström and others 1999; Falkenmark and Rockström 2004; Gordon and others 2005).

The following table presents some recent best estimates on water withdrawals for agriculture in 2025.

Projected increases in water withdrawals for irrigation, various sources
(cubic kilometers unless otherwise indicated)

Source	1995	2025	Increase (%) 1995–2025
Shiklomanov (2000)	2,488	3,097	24
Seckler and others (2000)	2,469	2,915	18
Faurès, Hoogeveen, and Bruinsma (2002)	2,128	2,420[a]	14

a. This estimate uses 2030 as the projection year and covers projects for developing countries only, constituting 75%–80% of global withdrawals.
Source: Molden and de Fraiture 2004.

fertilization methods, and higher yielding varieties to enhance yields and water productivity in rainfed agriculture (see chapters 8 on rainfed agriculture and 15 on land). Farmers can also implement soil and water conservation measures that reduce surface runoff and soil evaporation, while increasing the proportion of rainfall used effectively in crop production.

International trade is important in achieving national food security goals, with potentially interesting implications for global water resources. In 1995, without international trade in cereal crops, irrigation water consumption would have been higher by 11% (de Fraiture and others 2004; Oki and others 2003).

Post-harvest losses globally are estimated at 10%–35% of total production (WRI 1998). In the United States food waste in processing, retailing, and consumer use is

Looking ahead to 2050:
scenarios of alternative
investment approaches

3

about 27% of the food supply (WRI 1998). Preventing post-harvest losses in Africa—an estimated 10% of total production is lost on the farm[5]—might reduce crop water consumption by 95 cubic kilometers a year with current crop water productivity. Reducing pest and disease damage could improve water productivity substantially: 40% of potential output in Africa and Asia, and about 20% in the developed world, is lost to pests and pathogens (Somerville and Briscoe 2001). Much of the loss occurs after plants are fully grown, after most or all of the water required to produce a crop has been consumed. So, reducing losses to pests and pathogens will improve productivity per unit of evapotranspiration, generating a net water savings. But this will require chemicals that may reduce water quality.

Modifying diets, though difficult, can have large impacts on future food demands and water requirements (SIWI and IWMI 2004). Projections of global meat demand by 2050, as reported in the Millennium Ecosystem Assessment scenarios, vary from 41 to 70 kg per person per year depending on income, price, and public perceptions about health risks and environmental concerns (Alcamo and others 2005). The lower bound estimate (41 kg per person) might require 950 cubic kilometers (15%) less crop water consumption than the upper bound estimate (70 kg per person).

> Withdrawals for nonagricultural sectors are expected to more than double by 2050, increasing competition for water between sectors

Nonagricultural water use

More water to domestic and industrial purposes. The demand for water in industrial and domestic uses increases with urbanization. Withdrawals for nonagricultural sectors are expected to more than double by 2050, increasing competition for water between sectors (table 3.3). In most countries water for cities receives priority over water for agriculture—by law or by custom (Molle and Berkoff 2006). Greater competition for water will leave less for agriculture, particularly near large cities in water-short areas (such as the Middle East and North Africa, Central Asia, India, Pakistan, Mexico, and northern China). The estimates show also that while the proportion of water diverted for nonagricultural sectors increases, agriculture remains the largest water user among the productive sectors globally. While major tradeoffs will occur between all water-using sectors, they will be particularly pronounced between agriculture and the environment as the two largest water demanding sectors (Rijsberman and Molden 2001).

Only a small part of the water diverted for domestic and industrial purposes is consumed, with 75%–85% of water diverted to urban areas flowing back to rivers, lakes, and groundwater as return flow. In many urban areas, particularly in water-scarce developing countries, wastewater is used for high-value vegetable production, a livelihood activity for millions of city dwellers (Gupta and Gangopadhyay 2006; Hussain and others 2001, 2002; Raschid-Sally, Carr, and Buechler 2005; and chapter 11 on marginal-quality water).

The use of urban wastewater for irrigation will increase as water becomes more scarce in urbanizing areas. If by 2050 half the return flows from cities are reused, 200 cubic kilometers of wastewater might be used for irrigation. This would represent only 6%–8% of future agricultural withdrawals, but the economic values generated might be

table **3.3**	**Withdrawals by nonagricultural sector will increase by a factor of 2.2 by 2050** (cubic kilometers unless otherwise indicated)					

	Agriculture	Domestic		Manufacturing	
Region	**2000**	**2000**	**2050**	**2000**	**2050**
Sub-Saharan Africa	68	7	35	2	8
East Asia	518	48	185	21	159
South Asia	1,095	15	90	4	29
Central Asia & Eastern Europe	244	40	88	68	236
Latin America	175	31	78	12	42
Middle East & North Africa	173	14	51	3	10
OECD countries	233	121	152	135	131
World	2,630	278	681	245	617

Note: Seckler and others (2000) estimate domestic use at 265 cubic kilometers in 1995,with a 2.1% growth rate to 2025, and industrial use at 590 cubic kilometers, with a 1.6 % growth rate. Rosegrant, Cai, and Cline (2002) estimate growth in nonirrigation consumptive water use of 1.6% a year for 1995–2025 (withdrawals not reported). Shiklomanov (2000) estimates annual growth of 1.7% for 1995–2025 for domestic and industrial use.

(continues on facing page)

substantial. Much of the wastewater would be used to produce highly valued vegetables, helping sustain the livelihoods of millions of small farmers (Hussain and others 2001, 2002). While reuse of city wastewater for agriculture poses environmental and health risks, these can be minimized with proper management (see chapter 11 on marginal-quality water).

In many countries rising incomes are correlated with increasing demands for restoring and maintaining environmental services. The demand for environmental amenities adds pressure on scarce water resources. The environment has become a new competitor for water in some areas, as reflected in changing policies for water allocation and pricing (see chapter 6 on ecosystems). A first-cut estimate by Smakthin, Revenga, and Döll (2004) indicates that 20%–45% of long-term annual flows must be preserved to maintain essential ecosystem services.[6]

UNESCO (2006) suggests that 100 cubic kilometers need to be added to estimates of future water demands to account for current overexploitation of groundwater and 30 cubic kilometers must be added to account for the mining of fossil groundwater.

Exploring alternative strategies

The policies and investment strategies chosen to increase food production will affect water use, the environment, and rural and urban poverty. Feeding 3 billion more people by 2050 will require water development and management decisions that address tradeoffs between food and environmental security. Three broad investment strategies are to:

■   Improve productivity in rainfed settings.

Looking ahead to 2050:
scenarios of alternative
investment approaches

3

Thermo-cooling		Total nonagricultural				
			Share of total (%)		Share of total (%)	Annual increase (%)
2000	2050	2000	2000	2050	2050	2000–50
1	18	10	13	60	47	3.7
32	75	101	16	419	50	2.9
15	55	34	3	175	16	3.3
48	52	156	39	377	55	1.8
10	134	53	23	254	61	3.2
7	22	24	12	82	35	2.5
262	307	518	69	590	77	0.3
376	664	902	25	1,963	42	1.6

Source: Stockholm Environment Institute 2006 estimates done for the Comprehensive Assessment of Water Management in Agriculture.

- Increase production in irrigated areas.
- Expand international trade.

We examine these strategies and conclude with a plausible scenario that combines the best elements of the three: the Comprehensive Assessment scenario (table 3.4).

We use scenarios to illustrate the tradeoffs in these investment strategies. To explore the potential outcomes and impacts of each strategy, we highlight each alternative and contrast one with another. For example, we compare a scenario that emphasizes area expansion with a scenario that emphasizes productivity improvement. Actual improvements in agricultural water management will consist of more balanced combinations of measures rather than one set. The impacts of policy choices involve a complex web of feedback mechanisms. Our aim is not to describe the future in all of its complexities and manifestations in this analysis, but rather to illustrate tradeoffs by examining the potential implications of changes in a limited number of variables most amenable to policy changes. We present alternative policy choices and water management strategies, concluding with an optimistic scenario that builds on the regional relevance and opportunities of those strategies.

In constructing the scenarios, we use Watersim (de Fraiture forthcoming), a quantitative model consisting of two fully integrated modules: a food production and demand module based on a partial equilibrium framework, and a water supply and demand module based on a water balance and water accounting framework. Several relevant issues, such as impacts on the environment and poverty reduction, are difficult to model or quantify. Hence, we combine quantitative analysis with qualitative interpretations based on detailed analysis of the current situation in chapters 4–16.

table **3.4**

Overview of scenarios of irrigation, crop water use, crop yields, and water productivity in 2050

Variable	Base year 2000	Rainfed scenarios 2050	
		High yield	Low yield
Rationale		Emphasizes investments in rainfed areas: water harvesting and supplemental irrigation	Simulates the pessimistic case where upgrading rainfed agriculture is not successful
Irrigated area (millions of hectares)	340	340	340
Growth (%)		0	0
Rainfed area (millions of hectares)	860	920	1,320
Growth (%)		7	53
Irrigated cereal yield (metric tons per hectare)	3.70	5.02	4.94
Growth (%)		34	30
Rainfed cereal yield (metric tons per hectare)	2.46	4.24	2.96
Growth (%)		72	20
Water productivity, irrigated (kilograms per cubic meter)	0.68	0.84	0.83
Growth (%)		24	22
Water productivity, rainfed (kilograms per cubic meter)	0.49	0.66	0.54
Growth (%)		35	10
Cereals traded (millions of metric tons)	262	510	620
Share of consumption traded (%)	14	17	22
Crop water consumption, rainfall (cubic kilometers)	5,560	7,415	9,040
Growth (%)		33	63
Crop water consumption, irrigation (cubic kilometers)	1,570	1,870	1,870
Growth (%)		19	19
Withdrawals for irrigation (cubic kilometers)	2,630	3,155	3,160
Growth (%)		19	19
Share of value from irrigated area (%)	46	40	40
Investments costs (billions of US dollars)		40–250	30–210

Note: Scenarios were constructed using the Watersim model (de Fraiture forthcoming).   *(continues on facing page)*

Can upgrading rainfed agriculture meet future food demand?

Rainfed areas generate about 62% of global cereal production on 71% of the area harvested in cereals. More generally, rainfed areas generate an estimated 54% of the gross value of worldwide crop production on 72% of the harvested area (Watersim estimates for the Comprehensive Assessment). With rising concerns over the high cost of expanding large-scale irrigation and the environmental impacts of large dams, upgrading rainfed agriculture is gaining increased attention (see chapter 8 on rainfed agriculture and box 3.2).

There are several compelling reasons to invest in water management in rainfed agriculture. There is high potential to improve productivity, especially where yields are low. A majority of the rural poor are smallholders who depend on rainfed rather than irrigated agriculture, so assisting the poor often implies focusing on smallholders in rainfed areas.

Looking ahead to 2050:
scenarios of alternative
investment approaches

3

| Irrigation scenarios 2050 | | Trade scenario | Comprehensive Assessment of Water Management in Agriculture scenario |
Area expansion	Yield improvement	2050	2050
Emphasizes food self-sufficiency and stable food supply through expansion of irrigated areas	Emphasizes improving the performance of existing irrigated areas: increase in yield and water productivity	Simulates increased agricultural trade from water-abundant countries to water-scarce countries	Emphasizes optimal strategies that vary among regions: an optimistic, but plausible scenario
450	370	340	394
33	9	0	16
1,100	1,140	1,040	920
28	33	22	7
5.04	6.55	4.94	5.74
35	77	33	55
2.95	2.97	3.90	3.88
20	21	59	58
0.83	0.97	0.83	0.93
22	43	22	38
0.54	0.55	0.62	0.64
10	11	33	31
430	480	700	490
14	16	23	16
8,080	7,880	7,260	6,570
45	42	31	19
2,420	2,255	1,650	1,945
54	44	5	24
4,120	3,460	2,760	2,975
57	32	5	13
51	45	39	40
415	300	25–110	250–370

Realizing the potential of existing rainfed areas reduces the need for new large-scale irrigation development, which can generate adverse environmental impacts. And the cost of upgrading rainfed areas is generally lower than the cost of constructing irrigation schemes, particularly in Sub-Saharan Africa.

Nevertheless, the potential contribution of rainfed agriculture to world food production is the subject of debate, and forecasts of the relative roles of irrigated and rainfed agriculture vary considerably. Adoption rates of water-harvesting techniques are low, and extending successful local techniques over larger areas has proven difficult in the past. Relying on rainfed agriculture also involves considerable risk. Water-harvesting techniques are useful for bridging short dry spells, and investments in water management are thus a way to decrease risk in rainfed agriculture. But longer dry spells may lead to crop failure, and rainfed agriculture is generally more risky than fully irrigated agriculture.

| box **3.2** | **What is upgrading rainfed agriculture?** |

Upgrading rainfed agriculture through improved water management consists of:

- In-situ soil and water management and water harvesting techniques (conservation agriculture, bunds, terracing, contour cultivation, furrows, land leveling).
- Ex-situ water harvesting for supplemental irrigation (surface microdams, subsurface tanks, farm ponds).

These measures are implemented primarily by farmers, without external interventions or detailed engineering analysis. The measures are less technology intensive, more labor intensive and environmentally less disruptive than conventional large-scale irrigation.

Some of these measures might be considered as irrigation by some observers. However, we find it helpful to describe a continuum of partially irrigated areas between the extremes of areas completely dependent on rainfall and areas that are fully irrigated (Rockström 2003).

Source: Chapter 8 on rainfed agriculture.

| box **3.3** | **The GAEZ method and exploitable yield gaps** |

The Food and Agriculture Organization and the International Institute for Applied Systems Analysis have developed a method for assessing land suitability classes and maximum attainable yields under different input regimes using the Global Agro-Ecological Zones (GAEZ) concept (www.iiasa.ac.at/Research/LUC/GAEZ/index.htm).

The literature on yield gaps distinguishes two components: agroenvironmental and other non-transferable factors, and differences in crop management practices such as suboptimal use of inputs and other cultural practices. The portion of the gap due to the first component cannot be narrowed. The portion pertaining to the second component can be narrowed and is termed the "exploitable yield gap." Duwayri, Tran, and Nguyen (1999) suggest the theoretical maximum obtainable yields of wheat and rice might be as high as 20 metric tons per hectare. Yields of 17 metric tons per hectare have been achieved on experiment stations in subtropical climates and 10 metric tons per hectare in tropical climates. Wide yield differences are present even among countries with fairly similar agroecological environments. In such cases differences in the socioeconomic and policy environments play a major role (Bruinsma 2003, p. 297–303).

Rainfed scenarios: optimistic and pessimistic. To assess the potential of improving rainfed agriculture, we analyze two yield projections, low and high. We apply the Global Agro-Ecological Zones (GAEZ) methodology and use information describing exploitable yield gaps, the difference between actual and maximum attainable yields (box 3.3). The maximum attainable yield assumes high input levels and best suited varieties, depending on the quality of land. This approach provides realistic estimates based on known techniques, without assuming major breakthroughs (Fischer and others 2002; Bruinsma 2003).

The yield growth scenarios are formulated based on exploitable yield gaps (table 3.5). The high-yield scenario assumes—rather optimistically—that 80% of the gap will be bridged within the time horizon. This implies successful institutional reform, well functioning markets and credit systems, mechanization, improved use of fertilizers and

Looking ahead to 2050:
scenarios of alternative
investment approaches

3

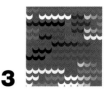

table **3.5**	**Yield scenarios for rainfed agriculture** (tons per hectare unless otherwise indicated)						
			Low-yield scenario		**High-yield scenario**		**Historical annual growth rate,[a] irrigated plus rainfed (%)**
Crop and region	**Actual yield 2000**	**Maximum potential yield**	**Simulated yield 2050**	**Annual growth rate (%) 2000–50**	**Simulated yield 2050**	**Annual growth rate (%) 2000–50**	
Wheat							
Sub-Saharan Africa	1.3	3.4	1.9	0.7	3.2	1.8	2.6
Middle East & North Africa	0.8	3.5	1.2	0.7	1.6	1.3	2.4
Central Asia & Eastern Europe	2.0	5.1	2.4	0.4	3.8	1.3	1.1
South Asia	1.6	2.7	1.7	0.2	2.5	1.0	2.8
East Asia	3.0	4.6	3.3	0.2	4.5	0.8	4.4
Latin America	2.2	3.9	2.6	0.3	3.7	1.0	1.4
OECD countries	3.4	5.6	3.8	n.a.	5.5	1.0	1.6
World	2.4	5.0	2.7	0.3	3.8	0.7	2.2
Rice							
Sub-Saharan Africa	1.0	4.0	1.5	0.8	3.2	2.4	0.4
Middle East & North Africa	n.a.	n.a.	n.a.	n.a.	n.a.	n.a.	1.4
Central Asia & Eastern Europe	n.a.	2.4	n.a.	n.a.	n.a.	n.a.	0.2
South Asia	1.6	3.5	2.1	0.6	3.3	1.5	1.7
East Asia	1.8	4.5	2.4	0.5	4.3	1.7	2.0
Latin America	1.4	4.5	2.1	0.8	3.8	2.0	2.0
OECD countries	n.a.	2.9	n.a.	n.a.	n.a.	n.a.	0.8
World	1.6	4.2	2.0	0.5	3.6	1.6	1.7
Maize							
Sub-Saharan Africa	1.4	6.6	2.1	0.7	4.1	2.1	0.8
Middle East & North Africa	0.9	4.3	1.3	0.6	1.7	1.2	3.0
Central Asia & Eastern Europe	3.2	3.8	3.3	0.1	3.5	0.2	1.9
South Asia	1.6	6.9	2.5	0.9	4.3	2.0	1.4
East Asia	3.6	5.5	3.9	0.2	5.0	0.7	3.2
Latin America	2.7	5.3	3.3	0.4	4.9	1.2	2.5
OECD countries	8.3	10.1	8.7	0.1	9.1	0.2	2.0
World	4.0	7.8	4.3	0.2	6.2	0.9	2.0

n.a. is not applicable because crop not grown under rainfed conditions.

a. Historical growth rates include the effects of conversion from rainfed to irrigated production, particularly in South and East Asia during the green revolution. Achieving these growth rates in purely rainfed systems will be difficult. Time series data disaggregated for irrigated and rainfed yields are not available.

Source: Actual yields in 2000 based on data underlying Bruinsma (2003); maximum attainable rainfed yields (high input) derived from GAEZ country-level data.

high-yielding varieties, and rapid adoption of water-harvesting techniques. The pessimistic yield scenario assumes that only 20% of the gap will be bridged, due to a slow rate of adoption of soil fertility and crop improvements, in-situ soil and water management, and external water-harvesting measures. Where yields are already high and the exploitable gap is small, as in OECD countries, projected growth rates are low. Where yields are low, as in Sub-Saharan Africa, potential improvements are large. In some cases productivity improves at a higher rate than historically observed.

The potential for growth is high in Sub-Saharan Africa, where yields are low and have been more or less stagnant during the past 40 years. Observed yields are less than one-third of the maximum attainable yields, suggesting considerable scope for improvement. In OECD countries, where yields have been increasing rapidly, the scope for further improvements is likely smaller (figure 3.4).

Improved water management in rainfed areas is essential. Bridging the yield gap in rainfed areas will happen only with the right mix of physical and institutional infrastructure. This requires effort and investment additional to business-as-usual scenarios developed by the International Water Management Institute (Seckler and others 2000) and the FAO study, *World Agriculture: Towards 2015/2030* (Bruinsma 2003).

figure **3.4** | **Past growth of maize yields and the potential for growth vary considerably by region**

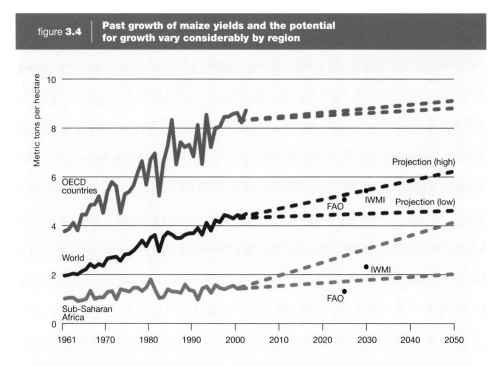

Note: Points marked FAO (Food and Agriculture Organization) are based on projections in Bruinsma (2003); those marked IWMI (International Water Management Institute) are based on projections in Seckler and others (2000).

Source: For 1960–2003, FAOSTAT 2006; for 2000–50, International Water Management Institute analysis done for the Comprehensive Assessment of Water Management in Agriculture using the Watersim model.

Looking ahead to 2050:
scenarios of alternative
investment approaches

3

Great potential—great uncertainties. The rainfed scenario that assumes zero growth in irrigated area shows that the potential of rainfed agriculture is sufficient to meet additional food requirements globally. Nearly all the additional food demand projected to 2050 can be met by increases in productivity. In an optimistic yield growth scenario in which cereal yields grow by 72%, the demand for agricultural commodities is met by increasing rainfed harvested area by only 7% (figure 3.5). The contribution of rainfed agriculture to the total gross value of food supply increases from 52% in 2000 to 60% in 2050. In the optimistic yield scenario Sub-Saharan Africa, Asia, and Latin America can be largely self-sufficient in producing major food crops. But East Asia must import maize to meet the large increase in feed demand. In addition, the Middle East and North Africa must import food because of lack of suitable lands for rainfed production. Global food trade increases from 14% to 17% of total production.

But the scenario analysis also demonstrates the risks inherent in a rainfed-based strategy. In the pessimistic scenario with a low rate of adoption of water harvesting

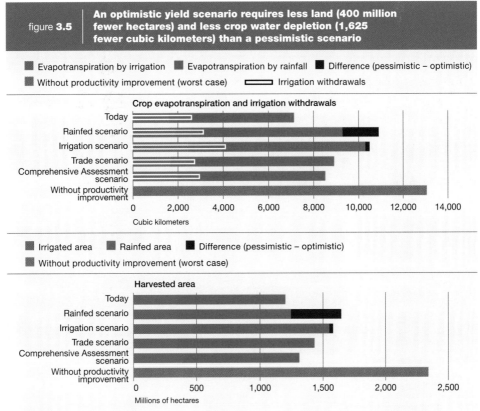

| figure **3.5** | An optimistic yield scenario requires less land (400 million fewer hectares) and less crop water depletion (1,625 fewer cubic kilometers) than a pessimistic scenario |

■ Evapotranspiration by irrigation ■ Evapotranspiration by rainfall ■ Difference (pessimistic – optimistic)
■ Without productivity improvement (worst case) ▭ Irrigation withdrawals

Crop evapotranspiration and irrigation withdrawals

Cubic kilometers

■ Irrigated area ■ Rainfed area ■ Difference (pessimistic – optimistic)
■ Without productivity improvement (worst case)

Harvested area

Millions of hectares

Note: The figure shows projected amounts of water and land requirements under different scenarios. The Comprehensive Assessment scenario combines elements of the other approaches. The purple segments of the bars show the difference between optimistic and pessimistic assumptions for the two rainfed and two irrigated scenarios. The brown bar shows the worst cases scenario of no improvement in productivity.

Source: International Water Management Institute analysis done for the Comprehensive Assessment for Water Management in Agriculture using the Watersim model.

and only modest improvements in rainfed yields, the area in rainfed production must increase by 53% to meet future food demands (an additional 400 million hectares as compared with the optimistic yield scenario; see figure 3.5). Globally, the land is available (table 3.6), but such a large expansion might have negative environmental consequences if production is extended to marginally suitable areas. Erosion and soil degradation might cause long-term declines in productivity. The large-scale conversion of forested and grazing areas to farmland also might have undesirable environmental consequences.

FAO estimates suggest ample scope to increase the area under crops except in South Asia and the Middle East and North Africa (see table 3.6). In Sub-Saharan Africa and Latin America only one-fifth of the potential land area is already in use. However, more than half of the land marked as potential is now under forests or protected areas (Alexandratos 2005). Furthermore, some of the land might be marginal in quality (Bruinsma 2003) or not suitable for cereal crops.

In the pessimistic yield scenario, countries without potential to expand rainfed areas—due either to lack of suitable land or to unreliable rainfall—must increase food imports. The Middle East and North Africa will import more than two-thirds of its agricultural needs. South and East Asia, due to land limitations, will become major importers of maize and other grains, importing 30%–50% of their domestic needs. Latin America, developed countries, and Central Asia and Eastern Europe, having the potential to expand land in agriculture, will increase their exports. Globally, food trade will increase from 14% of total agricultural production today to 22% in 2050. Large grain imports from East and South Asia will put upward pressure on food prices (the model results suggest an increase of 11%). There is a risk that poor countries may not be able to afford food imports, and household-level food insecurity and inequity might worsen.

Climate change, which is expected to increase the variability and intensity of weather events, exacerbates the risks of rainfed production, particularly in semiarid areas vulnerable to drought (Kurukulasuriya and others 2006). Floods may damage infrastructure (roads, bridges), with negative implications for marketing farm output.

table 3.6	Potential land suitable for agricultural expansion (millions of hectares unless otherwise indicated)	
Region	Area currently cropped[a] (irrigated plus rainfed)	Total area suitable for rainfed production
Sub-Saharan Africa	228	1,031
Middle East & North Africa	86	99
Central Asia & Eastern Europe	265	497
South Asia	207	220
East Asia	232	366
Latin America	203	1,066
Developed countries	387	874

a. Estimates of total cropped areas vary between 1.2 and 1.6 billion hectares depending on definitions of crop categories.
Source: Based on FAO (2002, p. 40).

Looking ahead to 2050:
scenarios of alternative
investment approaches

3

Both the optimistic and pessimistic rainfed scenarios lead to substantial increases in soil water consumption. Improved water management (including small amounts of supplemental irrigation) is a prerequisite for the yield improvements in the high-yield scenario. With higher yields water transpiration by crops must increase to produce enough biomass and economic yield. Part of the increased evapotranspiration might be offset by increasing water productivity, by improving the harvest index, by reducing losses from soil evaporation, or by increasing transpiration while reducing evaporation. When yields are low (below 50% of the potential), the scope to improve water productivity is high, but if yields are high, additional water is required to achieve even higher yields (figure 3.6). Thus the higher the initial yield, the lower the potential for water productivity gains.

In the optimistic rainfed yield scenario total evapotranspiration on cropland increases by 30%, from 7,130 to 9,280 cubic kilometers. While the global average of rainfed cereal yield improves by 72%, crop water productivity improves by 35%. In the pessimistic yield scenario global rainfed cereal yields improve by 20% and water productivity by 10%, while total crop water consumption increases by 54% to 10,980 cubic kilometers, an additional 3,850 cubic kilometers after the year 2000. Increases in soil water depletion of that order of magnitude will have impacts on river flows and groundwater recharge, with implications for downstream water users and those relying on groundwater resources. There might

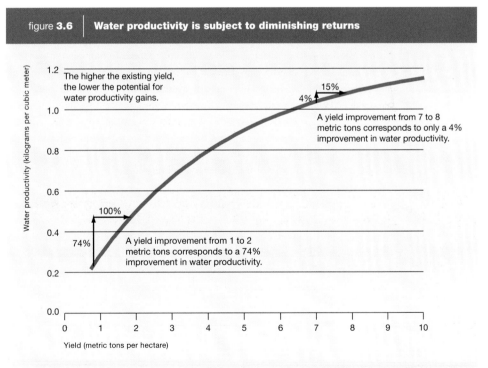

figure **3.6** | **Water productivity is subject to diminishing returns**

The higher the existing yield, the lower the potential for water productivity gains.

15%
4%

A yield improvement from 7 to 8 metric tons corresponds to only a 4% improvement in water productivity.

100%

74%

A yield improvement from 1 to 2 metric tons corresponds to a 74% improvement in water productivity.

Water productivity (kilograms per cubic meter)

Yield (metric tons per hectare)

Source: Based on the yield–water productivity relationship for rainfed cereals in Rockström (2003); see also chapter 7 on water productivity.

also be implications for atmospheric properties (Foley and others 2005, Gordon and Folke 2000; chapter 6 on ecosystems).

The estimated cost of improving rainfed agriculture varies substantially according to the situation. Assuming an investment cost range of $50–$250 per hectare and $2–$5 per 1,000 cubic meters of water (see chapter 8 on rainfed agriculture), the estimated capital cost of the low-yield scenario is between $30 billion and $210 billion and that of the high-yield scenario between $40 billion and $250 billion. While the impacts are described to 2050, the scenario assumes that investments are made in the next 20 years. Capital investments must come largely from public sources. Individual farmers complement these with private investments in enhanced farm inputs. Financing this scenario may prove difficult because donor investments tend to favor large infrastructure projects typically associated with large-scale irrigation rather than small, dispersed investments in rainfed agriculture.

> Upgraded rainfed agriculture can produce the food required in the future, but multiple conditions must be met for successful implementation, including substantial investments in water harvesting, agricultural research, supporting institutions, and rural infrastructure

Conclusion: upgrading rainfed agriculture offers good potential to meet future food demand. Upgraded rainfed agriculture can produce the food required in the future, but conditions must be met for successful implementation of a "rainfed strategy." The required productivity increases will not occur without substantial investments in water harvesting, agricultural research, supporting institutions, and rural infrastructure. In addition, crop yields will vary with economic incentives and crop prices, as farmers respond to those parameters when choosing key inputs. A high-yield scenario will evolve only if generating high yields is profitable for farmers. Resources are available to improve rainfed agriculture, but the institutional structure must encourage farm-level adoption of the recommended production practices. If incentives are missing or inappropriate, the environmental costs of achieving greater production could be substantial: 54% more crop water consumption and 38% more land (see figure 3.5). Such large increases in crop water consumption will likely have consequences for downstream ecosystems and water users. Moreover, a large expansion of agricultural land might reduce biodiversity and damage ecosystem services.

More irrigation?

Irrigated agriculture now provides 40% of the global cereal supply (60% of the cereals produced in developing countries). About 46% of the gross value of agricultural production (total production multiplied by world market prices in 2000) comes from irrigated areas, which make up 28% of the harvested area (Watersim estimates for the Comprehensive Assessment). Many expect that the contribution of irrigated agriculture to food production and rural development will increase in the coming decades (Seckler and others 2000; Bruinsma 2003).

After a decade of decline, international donors have shown renewed interest in irrigation investments, particularly in Sub-Saharan Africa, where irrigation development has remained well below its physical potential (see chapter 9 on irrigation). The Commission for Africa (2005) and the New Partnership for Africa's Development have described the need to invest in doubling the irrigated area in Sub-Saharan Africa to achieve the Millennium Development Goals.

Looking ahead to 2050:
scenarios of alternative
investment approaches

3

In India the groundwater boom, with millions of smallholders investing in private tubewells, continues despite environmental problems with groundwater overdraft and fossil groundwater mining (see chapter 10 on groundwater). Irrigation with wastewater is expanding in developing countries in areas near major cities (see chapter 11 on marginal-quality water). In India and Pakistan large investments are planned for rehabilitating and modernizing the Ganges and Indus River irrigation systems (Briscoe and others 2005).

The evidence suggests that despite environmental concerns about large-scale irrigation development (see chapter 6 on ecosystems), there remain good reasons to invest in irrigation development, improvement, and modernization. These include the potential for poverty alleviation, high potential to improve irrigation performance, maintenance of irrigation capacity, and concerns about climate change and its effects on rainfall variability (see chapter 9 on irrigation).

We examine scenarios that describe the implications of irrigated area expansion and the gains from enhancing the output per unit of water in irrigated areas.

Expanding irrigated areas. This scenario emphasizes food self-sufficiency and access to agricultural water for more people, particularly in Asia and Sub-Saharan Africa. Irrigated area increases by 0.6% per year from 340 million hectares (ha) in 2000 to 450 million ha in 2050,[7] simulating the expansion of the groundwater boom in South Asia, the intensification of irrigated areas in the Middle East and North Africa and in East Asia, and a doubling of irrigated area in Sub-Saharan Africa from 6.4 million ha to 12.8 million ha (table 3.7). Irrigated and rainfed yields increase at a modest pace—between 20% and 35% over 50 years.

With the expansion of irrigated area South and East Asia become largely self-sufficient in maize and other grains, while importing small amounts of wheat. East Asia continues exporting rice, but vegetable exports decline due to rapid increases in domestic demand. Sub-Saharan Africa becomes largely food self-sufficient, though it cannot

table **3.7**	Assumptions underlying the irrigated area expansion scenario					
	Area irrigated and harvested (millions of hectares)			Irrigated wheat yields (metric tons per hectare)		
Region	2000	2050	Cumulative growth (%) 2000–50	2000	2050	Cumulative growth (%) 2000–50
Sub-Saharan Africa	6.4	12.8	101	3.0	3.8	27
Middle East & North Africa	20.7	22.8	10	3.4	4.2	23
Central Asia & Eastern Europe	32.8	37.3	14	3.0	4.0	32
South Asia	104.3	135.2	30	2.8	4.0	44
East Asia	116.5	169.6	46	4.1	6.0	47
Latin America	16.5	23.4	42	4.8	6.3	31
OECD countries	45.4	49.8	10	4.4	4.9	10
World	341.3	454.4	33	3.4	4.7	38

maintain pace with the rapidly increasing domestic demand for maize. The rural economy in Sub-Saharan Africa is boosted as smallholders benefit from the opportunity to produce irrigated vegetables for the growing domestic market. As a result, Sub-Saharan Africa becomes largely self-sufficient in vegetables. Global trade in agricultural products remains at about the current level.

National food security and rural incomes are enhanced in this scenario, but pressure on water resources increases. Harvested area increases by 110 million ha, partly by increasing irrigation intensity (growing more crops per season) and partly by expanding the area by 76 million ha. Without improvements in application efficiency agricultural water diversions for irrigation increase from 2,630 cubic kilometers per year today to 4,100 cubic kilometers per year in 2050 (see figure 3.5). The increase is equivalent to 30 times the amount of water stored behind the Aswan Dams. With improvements in application efficiency global diversions might increase to only 3,650 cubic kilometers.

The cost of building, maintaining, and managing the required water infrastructure will be substantial, particularly in Sub-Saharan Africa, where irrigation costs are high and public funds are severely limited. At least $400 billion will be required to expand the harvested area by 110 million ha, a rough estimate based on incomplete data (table 3.8). Building the supporting infrastructure and creating the institutional capacity to manage newly built irrigation schemes, roads, and marketing facilities will add further to costs. Substantial investments will be required by public agencies, development banks, and other donor organizations.

Much of the irrigated area expansion in South Asia will involve groundwater development, which typically is privately funded. In Sub-Saharan Africa irrigation development will come largely from public investments. The average construction cost per hectare is higher in Sub-Saharan Africa than in South Asia, due partly to high transaction costs and partly to the high failure rate of irrigation projects. In a global sample of 314 publicly funded irrigation projects analyzed by Inocencio and others (2006), about half the projects in Sub-Saharan Africa were partial failures, the highest rate among regions in the sample. The authors argue that if only successful projects are considered, the investments costs in Sub-Saharan Africa are similar to those in other regions. An estimated $30–$40 billion are needed to double the area equipped with irrigation infrastructure, and additional funds are needed for complementary investments in roads, storage and processing facilities, communications, and institutions (Rosegrant and others 2005).

Physical water scarcity might increase while economic water scarcity declines. Already, 1.2 billion people (20% of the world's population) live in physically water-scarce basins. In the irrigated area expansion scenario this number increases to about 2.6 billion (28% of world population) in 2050 (map 3.1). Competition among sectors (agriculture, fisheries, cities, and industry) and transboundary water conflicts will likely intensify. In 36 of 128 basins minimum environmental flow requirements will not be satisfied, implying a potential increase in the adverse environmental impacts of agricultural water withdrawals on ecosystems and fisheries. Expanding irrigation infrastructure also increases the potential for aquaculture development, but we are unable to evaluate this tradeoff with data currently available.

> Under the irrigated area expansion scenario the number of people who live in physically water-scarce basins rises from 1.2 billion to 2.6 billion in 2050

Looking ahead to 2050:
scenarios of alternative
investment approaches

3

	table 3.8	**Capital investment cost of irrigated area expansion**				
Region	**Additional equipped area** (millions of hectares) **(1)**	**New irrigation costs** (US dollars per hectare) **(2)**	**Total area costs** (billions of US dollars) **(3 = 1 × 2)**	**Additional storage** (cubic kilometers) **(4)**	**Storage costs** (billions of US dollars) **(5)**	**Total costs** (billions of US dollars) **(6 = 3 + 5)**
Sub-Saharan Africa	6.2	5,600	35	89	10	45
Middle East & North Africa	3.1	6,000	19	71	8	26
Central Asia & Eastern Europe	4.5	3,500	16	61	7	22
South Asia	25.1	2,600	65	630	69	135
East Asia	30.4	2,900	88	459	50	139
Latin America	6.9	3,700	26	142	16	41
OECD countries	0.1	3,500	0.4	52	6	6
World	76.3	3,255	248	1,504	165	414

Note: Values may not sum to totals due to rounding.

Source: New irrigation cost estimates are from chapter 9 on irrigation; storage cost estimates are derived using the low estimate in Keller, Sakthivadivel, and Seckler (2000) of $0.11 per cubic meter.

map 3.1	**Irrigated area expansion leads to 2.6 billion people living in water-scarce basins by 2050**

 Water-scarce basins in 2000 and 2050    Water-scarce basins in 2050 but not in 2000

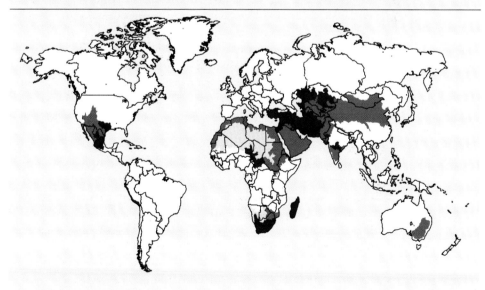

Source: International Water Management Institute analysis done for the Comprehensive Assessment of Water Management in Agriculture using the Watersim model.

Improving irrigation performance. Many irrigation schemes, particularly in South Asia, perform below potential (see chapter 9 on irrigation), and the scope for improving water productivity is high (Molden and de Fraiture 2004; Kijne, Barker, and Molden 2003). Here we explore the potential contribution to global food production of improving irrigation performance by formulating an irrigated yield growth scenario that assumes bridging 75%–80% of the exploitable yield gaps in coming decades (table 3.9). This simulates a rather optimistic—though not unrealistic—scenario of implementing institutional reforms (see chapter 5 on policies and institutions), resolving competition among headenders and tailenders, improving water allocation mechanisms (see chapter 16 on river basins), and motivating farmers and water managers to improve the productivity of land and water (Wang and others 2006; Luquet and others 2005). In addition to better water management, this entails higher soil fertility, better pest management, and improved seeds and other agronomic measures (see chapters 7 on water productivity and 15 on land).

This scenario shows the large potential for improving productivity in irrigated areas, particularly where yields are low.

■　South Asia can become self-sufficient in all grains, vegetables, and roots and tubers by improving irrigated yields and slightly expanding the harvested area (10% increase in irrigated area, 12% increase in rainfed area). India can meet all additional cereal demands by improving irrigated yields. The near doubling of yields depicted in this scenario is by no means easy but can be achieved with appropriate investments.

■　In East Asia, where yields are relatively high, the scope for improving productivity is smaller, yet the demand for agricultural commodities increases rapidly. Improving irrigation can meet 75% of the additional cereal requirements while the remainder is imported.

■　In the Middle East and North Africa, where opportunities to improve irrigation performance and expand irrigated area are limited, one-third of additional cereal requirements can be met by improving productivity, while the remainder is imported from OECD countries, Latin America, and Eastern Europe. Globally, agricultural commodity trade declines slightly.

■　In Sub-Saharan Africa, where more than 90% of production originates from rainfed areas, improving productivity on existing irrigated areas has only a small impact on food supply.

This scenario foresees a modest 9% expansion of irrigated area globally, while irrigation diversions increase by 32% (see figure 3.5). To achieve the improvements in irrigated yields depicted in this scenario, water supplies must be increased in existing irrigated areas. In India, for example, farmers install additional tubewells in command areas to supplement unreliable surface water supply (see chapter 10 on groundwater). In some areas yield improvements are achieved by augmenting water supplies in tailend areas, partly (but not entirely) at the expense of headend areas (see Hussain and others 2004 for a win-win case in Pakistan). Better timing of water deliveries also is helpful in improving crop yields. All of these measures lead to more water evaporated by crops, a precondition for increasing yields. As a result, water consumption and irrigation diversions increase substantially in this scenario.

Looking ahead to 2050:
scenarios of alternative
investment approaches

3

Part of the increase in water consumption is offset by improvements in water use efficiency[8] and water productivity. Improving efficiency implies that a larger portion of diverted water is used beneficially by crops, livestock, or other productive processes. This might be achieved, for example, by recycling drainage water or improving on-farm water management (Molden, Sakthivadivel, and Habib 2000; Seckler and others 2000). Improving water productivity implies that more output is obtained per unit of water consumed, perhaps by achieving a higher harvest index or reducing evaporation losses from soils. In the high-yield scenario the global consumptive fraction increases from 59% to 66%. Some authors suggest it is neither feasible nor desirable to increase this fraction further. Seckler and others (2000) explain that increases beyond the range of 70% often are associated with salinization and pollution problems, particularly if leaching requirements are ignored.

Investment costs in this scenario are about $300 billion (table 3.10).

Conclusion: both more irrigation and better irrigation are needed. Comparing both strategies in irrigation investments, the scenario analysis shows that the potential gains from enhancing productivity in irrigated areas are larger than the gains from area expansion. Improving irrigated cereal yields by 77% contributes 550 million metric tons of grains, or 50% of global additional demand by 2050. Expanding irrigated area by 33% contributes only 260 million metric tons of grains.

Arguably, the largest gains in water productivity in value per unit of water are achieved by diversification and by using water for many productive purposes—such as fisheries, livestock, home gardens, and other small enterprises (van Koppen, Moriarty, and Boelee 2006 and chapter 4 on poverty).[9] This may require changes in irrigation design to incorporate small dams, fisheries, and flood protection.

The analysis also demonstrates large regional differences. In South Asia there is substantial scope for improving productivity in irrigated areas while possibilities to expand areas are more limited or involve large infrastructure investments, such as the Linking of Rivers project in India. In East Asia there is some scope for area expansion, but most of the increase in production must come from productivity improvements. In Sub-Saharan Africa the scope for irrigated area expansion is sizable, but development costs are relatively high and historical success rates are relatively low. In water-scarce Middle East and North Africa area expansion is infeasible, and the scope for improving productivity is comparatively small. With rapid population growth, this region will depend increasingly on imports. In Latin America, OECD countries, Eastern Europe, and Central Asia there is potential to improve productivity in irrigated areas, but improving and expanding rainfed agriculture will be less expensive and might generate greater output gains.

Can trade offset water scarcity?

In the 1950s and 1960s agricultural policy in many developing countries favored import substitution, with food security equated with national food self-sufficiency. Farm lobbies were strong, and protecting agriculture was considered necessary for ensuring national food security. Subsidized water and irrigation infrastructure, marketing boards, tariffs, and input subsidies were viewed as necessary measures to promote food self-sufficiency

> The potential gains from enhancing productivity in irrigated areas are larger than the gains from area expansion. Improving irrigated cereal yields by 77% meets 50% of global additional demand by 2050, while expanding irrigated areas meets just 23%

table **3.9** | **Yield scenarios for irrigated agriculture**

Crop and region	Yield (metric tons per hectare)			Cumulative growth (%) 2000–50
	Actual 2000	Maximum potential[a]	Simulated 2050	
Wheat				
Sub-Saharan Africa	3.0	5.8	5.3	77
Middle East & North Africa	3.4	6.8	6.3	85
Central Asia & Eastern Europe	3.0	7.7	6.6	117
South Asia	2.8	4.5	4.5	61
East Asia	4.1	7.5	6.8	67
Latin America	4.8	6.3	5.9	23
OECD countries	4.4	7.9	7.7	72
World	3.4	7.1	5.7	70
Rice				
Sub-Saharan Africa	1.8	7.2	4.1	130
Middle East & North Africa	4.2	9.9	7.6	80
Central Asia & Eastern Europe	2.3	7.4	6.0	163
South Asia	2.6	8.2	6.3	138
East Asia	3.7	7.3	6.0	61
Latin America	3.4	6.7	6.1	81
OECD countries	4.6	8.4	7.6	64
World	3.4	7.4	6.1	83
Maize				
Sub-Saharan Africa	2.8	10.5	7.9	180
Middle East & North Africa	6.1	13.2	9.3	51
Central Asia & Eastern Europe	5.0	10.2	9.8	96
South Asia	2.6	10.8	7.3	176
East Asia	5.6	10.3	9.5	68
Latin America	4.9	10.9	9.1	87
OECD countries	9.9	11.3	10.8	10
World	6.1	10.9	9.6	57

a. Maximum attainable irrigated yields derived from GAEZ country-level data.

b. Historical growth rates from 1961–63 to 2001–03 of average yields, FAOSTAT (2006). Time series data disaggregated into rainfed and irrigated yields are not available.

(continues on facing page)

Looking ahead to 2050:
scenarios of alternative
investment approaches

3

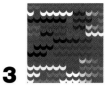

Annual growth rate (%)		Water productivity (kilograms per cubic meter of evapotranspiration)		
Simulated 2000–50	Historical, irrigated plus rainfed[b]	2000	Simulated 2050	Cumulative growth (%) 2000–50
1.1	2.6	0.37	0.53	45
1.2	4.4	0.43	0.60	37
1.6	2.8	0.44	0.71	61
1.0	1.1	0.46	0.63	36
1.0	1.4	0.63	0.88	40
0.4	2.4	0.69	0.74	8
1.1	1.6	0.70	0.96	37
1.1	2.2	0.54	0.74	38
2.2	0.4	0.18	0.31	72
1.2	2.0	0.37	0.48	30
2.0	1.7	0.26	0.46	78
1.8	0.2	0.27	0.50	86
1.0	2.0	0.54	0.78	46
1.2	1.4	0.40	0.61	52
1.0	0.8	0.53	0.72	36
1.2	1.7	0.46	0.75	65
2.1	0.8	0.36	0.70	96
0.8	3.2	0.77	0.95	23
1.4	1.4	0.81	1.16	43
2.1	1.9	0.30	0.55	83
1.0	2.5	0.84	1.14	36
1.3	3.0	0.44	0.63	42
0.2	2.0	1.33	1.40	5
0.9	2.0	0.87	1.13	31

Source: Derived from GAEZ country data, weighted averages over different land suitability classes. Based on data from Fischer and others (2002), provided by FAO.

table **3.10**	Capital investment cost of the improved irrigation performance scenario

Region	Rehabili-tated area (millions of hectares) (1)	Costs of rehabilitation (US dollars per hectare) (2)	Total costs of rehabilitated areas (billions of US dollars) (3 = 1 × 2)	Additional storage (cubic kilometers) (4)	Storage costs (billions of US dollars) (5)	Total costs (billions of US dollars) (6 = 3 + 5)
Sub-Saharan Africa	6	2,000	12	37	4	16
Middle East & North Africa	17	2,000	34	87	10	44
Central Asia & Eastern Europe	20	1,000	20	85	9	29
South Asia	81	900	73	322	35	108
East Asia	75	700	53	141	16	68
Latin America	18	1,300	23	78	9	32
OECD countries	5	1,000	5	16	2	7
World	222	990	220	766	84	304

Note: Values may not sum to totals because of rounding.

Source: Rehabilitation cost estimates are from chapter 9 on irrigation; storage cost estimates are derived using the low estimate in Keller, Sakthivadivel, and Seckler (2000) of $0.11 per cubic meter.

and minimize the risk of famines (Molden, Amarasinghe, and Hussain 2001; Kikuchi, Maruyama, and Hayami 2001; Barker and Molle 2004). The role of trade in domestic food supply was—and for most developing countries still is—modest.

Expanded international food trade can have significant impacts on national water demands. Allan (1998) coined the term "virtual water" to denote the water used to produce imported crops. By importing agricultural commodities, a country "saves" the amount of water it would have required to produce those commodities domestically. For example, Egypt, a highly water-stressed country, imported 8 million metric tons of grain from the United States in 2000. Producing that grain in Egypt would have required about 8.5 billion cubic meters of irrigation water—about one-sixth of Egypt's annual releases from Lake Nasser. Japan, a land-scarce country and the world's largest grain importer, would require an additional 30 billion cubic meters of irrigation water and rainfall to produce its food imports (de Fraiture and others 2004).

Globally, cereal trade has a moderating impact on the demand for irrigation water, as four of the five major grain exporters (United States, Canada, France, and Argentina) produce grain in highly productive rainfed conditions. Without cereal trade global demand for irrigation water in 1995 would have been 11% higher (de Fraiture and others 2004; Oki and others 2003).

Some authors have proposed increasing trade to mitigate water scarcity and reduce environmental degradation (Allan 2001; Hoekstra and Hung 2005; Chapagain 2006; Zimmer and Renault 2003). They suggest that instead of striving for food self-sufficiency, water-short countries should import food from water-abundant countries. Much of that analysis does not account for several key considerations that determine international trade

Looking ahead to 2050:
scenarios of alternative
investment approaches

3

patterns, such as domestic macroeconomic policies, socioeconomic goals, exchange rate policies, and political relationships. Nor does it consider the potential environmental impacts of increasing agricultural trade, such as extending agricultural areas and building new processing and packaging facilities in exporting countries. In addition, there may be substantial costs in shipping large volumes of food between countries and within importing countries. And with rising energy prices the per-unit costs of processing, storing, and shipping food will increase.

Trade scenario. In this scenario production occurs in North America, Europe, and Latin America, while in the rainfed scenarios Sub-Saharan Africa, South Asia, and East Asia increase their production to maintain a desired level of self-sufficiency in staple foods. Thus countries with abundant water resources and production capacities increase their agricultural production and export to water-short countries. North America, Latin America (mainly Brazil and Argentina), Northwestern Europe, and Eastern Europe (Russia and Ukraine) export to the Middle East and North Africa and to India, Pakistan, and China (map 3.2). Sub-Saharan Africa improves its rainfed agriculture but remains a minor importer. In the importing countries crop yields improve at a modest pace (25%) while irrigated and rainfed areas remain constant. China, India, and the Middle East and North Africa reduce their irrigated areas for cereals, shifting toward labor-intensive, higher valued

map **3.2** | **Virtual water embedded in agricultural trade**

■ Major virtual water exporter   □ Self-sufficient   □ Not estimated
■ Minor virtual water exporter   ■ Net virtual water importer

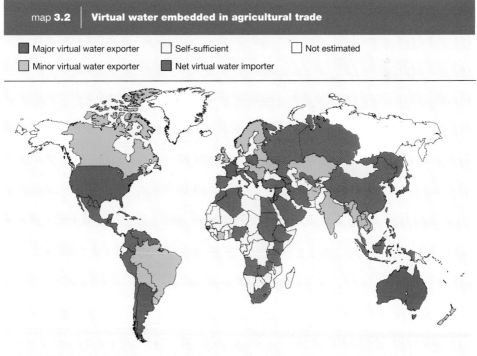

Source: De Fraiture and others 2004.

crops such as vegetables. Appropriate water pricing schemes and incentives such as credit and subsidies induce farmers to shift to crops with higher value output per unit of irrigation water. Water scarcity problems are lessened through better on-farm management and microirrigation in greenhouses. In exporting countries rainfed yields of staple crops—such as cereals, soybeans (oil crops), and roots and tubers—improve by 60% on average. Rainfed areas in exporting countries increase by 260 million ha, primarily in Latin America, where the scope for area expansion is still large.

Conclusion: high potential for water but many socioeconomic and political issues.
The scenario analysis reveals, in theory, that world food demands can be satisfied through international trade, without worsening water scarcity or requiring additional irrigation infrastructure (table 3.11). However, the analysis does not account for the political, social, and economic issues that countries consider when choosing trade strategies. It is not likely that a majority of water-short countries will greatly increase their food imports in the near term.

Food imports already are essential in countries where production is limited by water scarcity or other constraints, as in many countries of the Middle East and Sub-Saharan Africa. This is also true for some countries in Southeast Asia, like Japan and Malaysia, where the expanding industrial service sectors are creating severe labor resource constraints in agriculture. In some countries in Sub-Saharan Africa the costs of inland transportation motivate countries to feed coastal cities with imports rather than to rely on domestic production—at least in the near term, until rural infrastructure can be improved (Seckler and others 2000). Food trade (or aid) also buffers fluctuations in production due to climate variability. In other countries land, not water, is the binding constraint (Kumar and Singh 2005).

table **3.11**	**Demand and net trade flows of cereals under different scenarios**					

Region	Demand (millions of metric tons) 2000	Demand (millions of metric tons) 2050	Rainfed scenarios 2050 Low yield — Net trade flows (millions of metric tons)	Rainfed scenarios 2050 Low yield — Share of demand (%)	Rainfed scenarios 2050 High yield — Net trade flows (millions of metric tons)	Rainfed scenarios 2050 High yield — Share of demand (%)
Sub-Saharan Africa	98	213	−32	15	−14	7
Middle East & North Africa	99	208	−149	72	−141	68
Eastern Europe & Central Asia	234	295	151	51	56	19
South Asia	241	476	−88	19	−5	1
East Asia	505	807	−148	18	−57	7
Latin America	149	290	76	26	17	6
OECD countries	508	586	167	29	157	27

Note: Negative values indicate imports, and positive values indicate exports.

Source: International Water Management Institute analysis done for the Comprehensive Assessment of Water Management in Agriculture using the Watersim model.

(continues on facing page)

Looking ahead to 2050:
scenarios of alternative
investment approaches | **3**

Overall, most international food trade occurs for reasons not related to water resources. In 1995 less than one-quarter of global cereal trade was related to water scarcity
(de Fraiture and others 2004; Yang and others 2002). This might change as water becomes
more scarce and the prices of water-intensive crops increase. International trade provides
water-short countries an option for responding to increasing water scarcity. The importance of this option in the future will depend on many factors, including international
trade agreements, the costs of engaging in trade, and the nature of domestic economic
objectives and political considerations.

The cost of increasing international trade can be substantial for developing countries.
Food imports must be paid for with foreign exchange, earned by selling exports or obtained
through grants and loans. This fact is somewhat hidden by large amounts of donor assistance
in hard currency and historically heavily subsidized exports from Europe and the United
States (Seckler and others 2000). Many poor countries, particularly in Sub-Saharan Africa,
do not have sufficient exports to pay for imports. Oil-producing countries might face this
problem in future, if high prices accelerate their shift to an end-of-oil era (Margat 2006).
Further, poor countries relying on one or a few export products are vulnerable to fluctuations
in the terms of trade and therefore in purchasing power. Finally, trade requires substantial
amounts of energy for transporting goods, adding to the environmental costs of trade.

Poor countries struggling with issues of food security remain wary of depending on
imports to satisfy basic food needs. They view such a strategy as increasing their vulnerability to fluctuations in world prices and geopolitics. A certain degree of food self-sufficiency
is still an important policy goal, and despite emerging water problems, many countries
view the development of water resources as a more secure option for achieving food supply
goals and promoting income growth, particularly in poor rural communities. It is debatable

Irrigated scenarios 2050				Trade scenario 2050	
Area expansion		Yield improvement			
Net trade flows (millions of metric tons)	Share of demand (%)	Net trade flows (millions of metric tons)	Share of demand (%)	Net trade flows (millions of metric tons)	Share of demand (%)
−44	21	−22	10	−51	24
−131	63	−83	40	−156	75
49	17	3	1	181	61
−32	7	20	4	−119	25
−18	2	−34	4	−191	24
44	15	29	10	178	61
112	19	99	17	136	23

whether poor, water-scarce countries with limited investments in water infrastructure can afford to import large amounts of agricultural commodities. In addition, as recent discussions in the World Trade Organization illustrate, the economic and political interests associated with agricultural trade are substantial. Those interests might dominate water scarcity and environmental concerns in some countries (see Mehta and Madsen 2005). In sum, it is unlikely that food trade alone will solve problems of water scarcity in the near term.

International trade provides water-short countries an option for responding to increasing water scarcity. The importance of this option depends on many factors

Understanding tradeoffs

In the extreme case of no future productivity improvements, 13,050 cubic kilometers of crop water consumption and 2.4 billion ha of cropland would be required to produce the food and feed demanded in 2050. Though none of the scenarios depicts an increase of this magnitude, some scenarios involve more strain on available resources than others. In addition, some scenarios offer better prospects for poverty alleviation, environmental protection, and food security.

We examine linkages and tradeoffs involving terrestrial and aquatic ecosystems, poverty alleviation, and food security (figure 3.7). Our discussion is based on results presented above and discussion presented in other chapters.

Aquatic ecosystems

In all scenarios the demand for freshwater increases to meet future food demands. Water consumption increases substantially in irrigated and rainfed areas (figure 3.8).

Ecosystems provide a range of services such as food production, fisheries, flood protection, water filtration, and groundwater recharge (see chapter 6 on ecosystems). Many authors describe the adverse impacts of irrigation on ecosystem services other than food production (Pimentel and others 2004; Khan and others 2006; chapters 2 on trends and 6 on ecosystems). Extracting water from rivers and aquifers reduces the amount available to aquatic ecosystems and can affect groundwater tables. The infrastructure needed to divert water for irrigation (and other purposes) can alter hydrology, leading to river fragmentation, with negative consequences for aquatic habitats (see chapter 12 on inland fisheries). Reductions in ecosystem services often have severe consequences for poor people, who depend heavily on ecosystems for their livelihoods.

In the irrigated area expansion scenario withdrawals increase by 57%, with potentially large impacts on aquatic ecosystems and coastal zones. More dams and other water storage facilities are needed, which may alter the timing and variability of flows—important for sustaining ecosystem services (Poff and others 1997).

Innovative techniques and management methods are available for mitigating the effects, and the impacts of irrigation development on ecosystem services will vary. In some systems it has been possible to find synergies between fisheries and irrigation, especially in small and medium-scale irrigation schemes. For example, dams can provide fishing opportunities in reservoirs (Nguyen-Khoa and Smith 2004; Nguyen-Khoa and others 2005). Negative environmental impacts can also be limited by adhering to environmental flow regulations (see chapter 6 on ecosystems).

Looking ahead to 2050:
scenarios of alternative
investment approaches

3

| figure **3.7** | **Possible quantitative indicators to illustrate tradeoffs** |

Aquatic ecosystems
In all scenarios demand for freshwater increases to meet food demand. While some positive impacts can come from investment strategies that include a system perspective, adverse impacts on aquatic systems dominate, particularly in the irrigated area expansion scenario. The effects on aquatic systems of intensifying rainfed agriculture are less known.

Terrestrial ecosystems
Food production affects terrestrial ecosystems through changes in land cover (for example, conversion of forests and savannahs into agricultural land). In the optimistic rainfed yield scenario additional land requirements are lowest, but the rainfed strategy is risky. In a scenario where yields remain below expectations, land requirements are highest.

Poverty alleviation
The impact of different strategies on poverty alleviation is difficult to assess. Much depends on the type of irrigation intervention and how it is implemented. Expansion of smallholder irrigation techniques (both surface water and groundwater) has high potential for poverty alleviation. Improving rainfed agriculture has high potential but carries risks.

Food security
In semiarid areas expanding irrigated areas and improving yields in irrigated and rainfed agriculture offer good prospects for secure food supply. Reaching those whose productivity did not rise significantly and who experienced a net loss in food security because of falling commodity prices is the greatest challenge of coming decades.

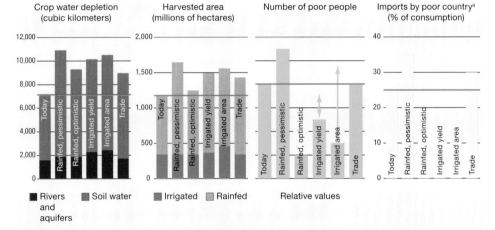

a. Poor countries are those with annual per capita incomes below $2,500. Imports include food aid. Note that the indicators here are used to illustrate tradeoffs rather than to quantitatively analyze the full range of issues.

Source: Results presented in the text and qualitative discussion presented in other chapters.

Examples of positive impacts of irrigation on ecosystem services include groundwater recharge, reduction of soil erosion through terracing, biodiversity in paddy fields and small tanks, and multiple use of irrigation water for domestic and productive purposes (Hussain and Hanjra 2003, 2004; Smith 2004). Studies show that about 80% of groundwater recharge occurs through canal systems in India and Pakistan (Ambast and others 2006; Ahmad, Bastiaanssen, and Feddes 2005). Groundwater recharge is not always positive, however, as it can lead to waterlogging in areas where deep percolation is restricted and drainage systems are inadequate (Scott and Shah 2004; Ambast, Tyagi, and Raul 2006).

Intensive irrigation has larger impacts on water volumes and quality than do low-input systems. Many of the improvements in water-use efficiency arise from greater use of external inputs, increased mechanization, and intensification of production. For example,

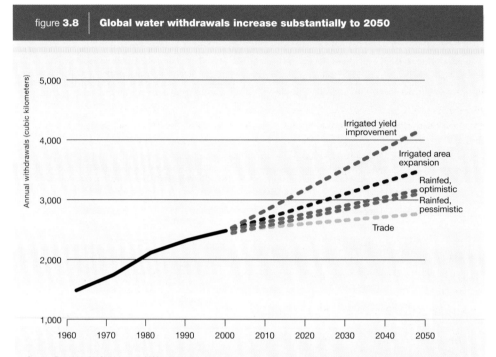

figure **3.8** | **Global water withdrawals increase substantially to 2050**

Annual withdrawals (cubic kilometers)

5,000

4,000 — Irrigated yield improvement

Irrigated area expansion

Rainfed, optimistic
3,000 — Rainfed, pessimistic

Trade

2,000

1,000

1960 1970 1980 1990 2000 2010 2020 2030 2040 2050

Source: For 1960–95, Shiklomanov 2000; 1995–2050, modeling results scenarios done for the Comprehensive Assessment of Water Management in Agriculture.

human activities have already doubled the amount of nitrogen sequestered globally, and tripled the phosphorous use (Vitousek and others 1997; Bennett, Carpenter, and Caraco 2001). This has led to eutrophication of lakes and coastal zones, damaging fisheries, reducing recreation values, and increasing the occurrence of toxic algae blooms. Pesticide levels in water can constitute a health threat.

The need for new irrigation investments can be reduced by improving agricultural production in rainfed areas. Because of negative impacts on aquatic systems associated with irrigation development, investments in rainfed agriculture seem compelling from an environmental perspective (see chapter 6 on ecosystems). However, there is ample evidence that land-use decisions alter hydrological flows, which can cause cascading effects to other systems. The impacts on subsurface and surface runoff can vary substantially. Proper land and water management is required to achieve the potential of rainfed agriculture. Intercepting rainwater increases the water consumed by crops, so less water is available for runoff and groundwater recharge. Improving rainfed production through supplemental irrigation requires infrastructure, though smaller and more distributed than in intensive irrigation. Impacts on downstream water resources are more dispersed and difficult to assess. Further intensification of rainfed agriculture is often associated with increased fertilizer and pesticide use, which can have adverse impacts on water quality.

Looking ahead to 2050:
scenarios of alternative
investment approaches

3

Terrestrial ecosystems

Food production affects terrestrial ecosystems when forests and savannahs are converted to agricultural land. The Millennium Ecosystem Assessment scenarios predict that land-use change will continue to put major pressure on ecosystem services (Alcamo and others 2005). In our scenarios land requirements increase a total of 6%–38% (0.1%–0.7% annual growth) between 2000 and 2050 (figure 3.9). This can have substantial impact on ecosystem services that depend on those habitats. The risks include biodiversity loss, loss of pollinator species, and increases in invasive species (Dudgeon 2000; Thrupp 2000; chapter 6 on ecosystems). Expansion of rainfed agriculture and the conversion of forests into cropland can alter biogeochemical cycles, including carbon sequestration capacity and hydrology (Foley and others 2005). It has been estimated that deforestation has reduced global evaporation by as much as irrigation has increased it (Gordon and others 2005). The changes in water vapor flows may have impacts on climate in some regions and locales (see chapter 6).

Investments in existing irrigated and rainfed areas will reduce the need to expand the area in agriculture, preventing further conversion of forests and natural lands. Improving crop yields will also reduce the need for additional land in agriculture. But if yield growth rates remain low, substantial additional land will be required to meet future demand,

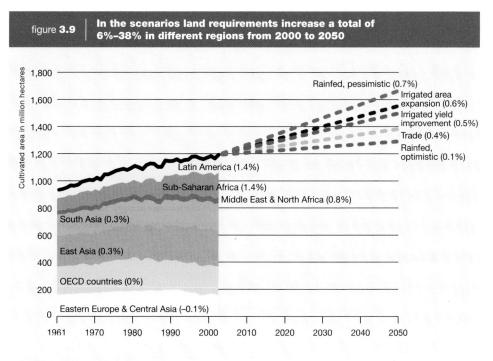

figure **3.9** | **In the scenarios land requirements increase a total of 6%–38% in different regions from 2000 to 2050**

Note: Numbers in parentheses are annual growth rates.

Source: For 1961–2002, FAOSTAT 2006; for 2000–2050, International Water Management Institute analysis done for the Comprehensive Assessment of Water Management in Agriculture using the Watersim model.

possibly leading to encroachment of marginal areas and terrestrial ecosystems. Rainfed agriculture, under conditions of poorly distributed rainfall or droughts, might lead to shifting cultivation, underinvestment in land conservation, and nonsustainable land use. Increased yields and intensification of rainfed and irrigated agriculture are often associated with monoculture and greater agrochemical use, which can lead to soil pollution, salinization, and waterlogging.

> Managing agricultural systems to generate more than one ecosystem service has been suggested as a method to reduce ecosystem service tradeoffs from agricultural expansion and intensification

Many agricultural investments generate benefits within and outside the agricultural sector (Pretty and others 2006; chapter 15 on land). For example, investments in land and water management often are helpful in reducing soil erosion. Investments that enhance the retention of soil organic matter reduce the rate at which carbon is released into the atmosphere. This impact, known also as carbon sequestration, is a globally important ecosystem service. In general, investments that generate ecological benefits can be viewed as helpful in offsetting some of the negative impacts of agricultural expansion and intensification (see chapter 6).

Food security

In semiarid areas, expanding irrigated area and improving irrigated yields offer better prospects for achieving secure food supplies than rainfed agriculture. Yields in irrigated areas are higher than in rainfed areas, and year-to-year fluctuations due to weather variability are smaller. With a secure water supply farmers are willing to invest in improved inputs to boost production further. Upgrading rainfed agriculture will offset these risks to a certain extent, but additional risk management strategies (such as cereal banks and crop insurance systems) may be necessary.

In many rainfed areas there is substantial scope for increasing yields, which can increase food security, particularly in poor countries with little ability to build and maintain irrigation infrastructure. But past efforts to improve rainfed agriculture have generated mixed results. In the pessimistic yield scenario, production declines and food prices rise. Countries with limited opportunities for expanding rainfed area increase imports, while facing higher food prices and larger trade deficits, which might adversely affect national food supply. Greater variability in annual weather patterns, due to climate change, might worsen this situation in rainfed areas. Brown and Lall (2006) find a statistically significant relationship between greater interannual rainfall variability and lower per capita GDP, particularly in poor countries. But there are ways to mitigate these risks (see chapter 8 on rainfed agriculture).

International trade provides opportunities to enhance national food security, but some developing countries lack sufficient foreign exchange and the political will required to sustain increased imports. International trade in food and other goods is driven more by politics and economics than by water management decisions.

Poverty alleviation

With increasing globalization, many poor farmers are affected by developments in international markets. Thus, productivity improvements alone might not be sufficient to ensure household food security if market prices decline when aggregate productivity increases. The challenge is to increase food production while not depressing prices below levels that

Looking ahead to 2050:
scenarios of alternative
investment approaches

3

enable farmers to earn sufficient revenue to achieve food security. Improving productivity at a pace that exceeds the rate of decline in market prices requires broader access to water (Evenson and Gollin 2003; chapter 4 on poverty). At the same time, the urban poor and the landless rural poor benefit from lower food prices. The landless rural poor also benefit from labor opportunities provided by large-scale irrigation development (chapter 4 on poverty).

Irrigation development creates the possibility for multiple uses of irrigation water, such as fish and livestock production and other income-generating activities that directly benefit the poor. Irrigation can also stabilize food prices, to the benefit of risk-averse poor farmers and poor urban consumers. Irrigation can also enhance human capital by attracting investments in such social services as education (Foster and Rosenzweig 2004).

The impact of irrigation development on poverty is strongly linked to the type of irrigation. In the past, particularly during the green revolution, large-scale irrigation development contributed to poverty alleviation directly and through multiplier effects (Bhattarai, Sakthivadivel, and Hussain 2002). However, with increasing financial and environmental concerns, the era of large-scale irrigation expansion seems over (see chapter 9 on irrigation).

Small-scale irrigation—such as treadle pumps and drip irrigation kits for home vegetable gardens—targeted directly to the poor can be a cost-effective alternative for reducing poverty (Polak 2005). But the successes observed with small-scale systems in South Asia might not be achievable in Sub-Saharan Africa, where aquifers are less suitable, population is less concentrated, and physical infrastructure and institutions are less developed (Goldman and Smith 1995; Mosley 2002). Livelihoods might be enhanced more effectively in Sub-Saharan Africa by improving rainfed agriculture, particularly where small investment costs per hectare enable improvements over a larger area than is possible with similar investments targeted to large-scale irrigation.

> Small-scale irrigation—such as treadle pumps and drip irrigation kits for home vegetable gardens—targeted directly to the poor can be a cost-effective alternative for reducing poverty

Comparing South Asia and Sub-Saharan Africa, homes to most of the world's poor

Optimal investment strategies will differ considerably by region. In the Middle East and North Africa water scarcity constrains further irrigation expansion, and the scope for improving rainfed agriculture is limited. In South Asia the lack of suitable land is becoming a constraint, and water resources are stressed in many basins. China has sufficient water in the south but not in the north. Land and water are sufficient in Latin America and most of Sub-Saharan Africa, but investment funds are limited, institutions are weak, and much of the infrastructure needed to support economic development is not yet in place.

In both Sub-Saharan Africa and South Asia the discussion of investments in water management is highly relevant and debated. The Commission for Africa (2005) and the New Partnership for Africa's Development propose doubling the area under irrigation to boost food production and enhance rural development. India is planning a multibillion-dollar Linking of Rivers project, and Pakistan plans to modernize its aging infrastructure in the Indus Basin. Proponents see investments in new irrigation and hydropower as needed to meet rapidly increasing demand for food and energy. Opponents of large-scale irrigation projects suggest improving rainfed areas where the poor will benefit the most. They claim it is cheaper—in financial, environmental, and social terms—to upgrade underperforming infrastructure, increase rainfed production, and import food. In both Sub-Saharan Africa and South Asia improvements in agricultural water management are needed to increase agricultural productivity and reduce the high rates of rural poverty (Hussain and Hanjra 2003, 2004).

> In an optimistic yield scenario for rainfed agriculture in Sub-Saharan Africa additional food demand can be met from the same harvested area without expansion. But low adoption rates of water harvesting techniques indicate that achieving success will be challenging

Sub-Saharan Africa: upgrade rainfed agriculture by adding irrigation and investing in transport and governance

Sub-Saharan Africa is largely self-sufficient in major staple crops such as cassava, sweet potatoes, other roots and tubers, maize, and coarse grains (millet, sorghum), but food production and its distribution are highly skewed. Except in rice and wheat, the roles of irrigation and trade in food supply are negligible, with 91% of the supply coming from rainfed agriculture and just under 4% imported from outside the region. Less than 4% of the harvested area is irrigated, and more than 60% of the irrigated area is in just three countries: South Africa, Sudan, and Madagascar (figure 3.10). Water-use approaches potential use in just a few river basins, such as the Limpopo, Orange, and South Madagascar. In most basins water scarcity is caused by inadequate water infrastructure, rather than lack of water resources. Of the potential irrigated area of 40 million ha, 7 million ha are developed (Frenken 2005).

Food demand in Sub-Saharan Africa will roughly triple in the coming 50 years. Increases in production likely will come from rainfed agriculture. Despite ample physical potential, irrigation will play a limited role in near-term food supply. Even if the area irrigated in Sub-Saharan Africa is doubled, as suggested by the Commission for Africa (2005), the impact of irrigation on staple food supply will remain small (7%–11% of total food production). The importance of international trade in providing Sub-Saharan Africa's food supply also might be limited in the short term because of a shortage of foreign exchange earnings in many countries. Food aid, which is vital to individual countries and groups in times of emergencies, contributes little to the overall food supply.

The investment cost of doubling the irrigated area is high (see table 3.10), and it is not clear that irrigated cereal production in Sub-Saharan Africa, plagued by high marketing and transportation costs, can compete with subsidized food imports from Europe and the United States. In addition, the institutional infrastructure and experience required for operation, maintenance, and management are lacking. Surface water irrigation schemes have had mixed results in Sub-Saharan Africa, and a groundwater revolution (as in South Asia) has not yet occurred in the region (Giordano 2006).

Without substantial improvements in the productivity of rainfed agriculture, food production will fall short of demand. Water harvesting and small-scale supplemental irrigation methods in rainfed areas—combined with increased input use—can boost productivity by a factor of two or three in Sub-Saharan Africa (Rockström and others 2004; Mati 2006; chapter 8 on rainfed agriculture).

In an optimistic yield scenario for rainfed agriculture additional food demand can be met from the same harvested area without expansion. But low adoption rates of

Looking ahead to 2050:
scenarios of alternative
investment approaches

3

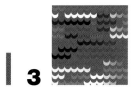

| figure **3.10** | **The proportion of harvested area that is irrigated is largest in South Asia and smallest in Sub-Saharan Africa** (millions of hectares, 2000) |

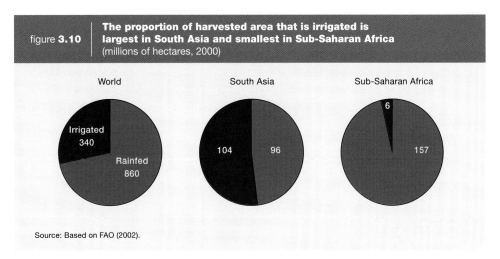

World   South Asia   Sub-Saharan Africa

Source: Based on FAO (2002).

water-harvesting techniques indicate that the extension of local successes throughout the region will be challenging. In a low-yield scenario for rainfed agriculture the cropped area expands by 70%. Where land suitable for agriculture is available, area expansion on such a scale will occur, at least to an extent, at the expense of natural lands and forests, increasing the likelihood of land degradation (Alexandratos 2005; chapter 15 on land).

Low profits and high risks discourage farmers from investing in land and water resources. Major limitations include the lack of domestic market infrastructure, barriers to international markets, and high marketing costs caused by poor roads (Rosegrant and others 2005, 2006). Other barriers include poor governance, institutional disincentives to profitable agriculture (taxes, corruption, lack of formal land titles), and high levels of risk discouraging farmers from investing in labor and other inputs (Hanjra, Ferede, and Gutta forthcoming).

South Asia: improving irrigation and rainfed performance

There is little scope for expanding the agricultural area in South Asia, where 94% of the suitable area already is cultivated (FAO 2002). In addition, more than half the harvested area is irrigated. South Asia has an established system of land and water rights, water institutions, trained manpower, and extensive experience in working with international donors to implement large-scale irrigation projects.

With current yields much lower than potential, output can be increased substantially by increasing productivity in the irrigated sector. In a high-productivity scenario all additional food demand can be met by improving land and water productivity in irrigated areas, without expanding irrigated areas.

The challenge in improving the performance of irrigated agriculture is more institutional than technical, but reforming irrigation bureaucracies is a daunting task (see chapter 5 on policies and institutions), and reducing the subsidies that distort the use of water and energy is politically difficult (Shah and others 2004). These institutional issues must be addressed to enhance the likelihood of achieving higher levels of land and water productivity.

The scope for improving rainfed agriculture in South Asia also is considerable. In a high-yield scenario all additional land and water for food can be met by improving land and water productivity. But if yields remain below expectation, due to low adoption of water-harvesting techniques or climate variability, imports will be needed. Supportive institutions and a supportive economic environment are vital to achieving the potential gains in this scenario.

For many years the Indian government has focused on achieving national food self-sufficiency in staple crops. More recently, as the imminent danger of famines has decreased and nonagricultural sectors have expanded, the national perspective on production and trade has changed. Food trade might become more important in the future, particularly as the relative contribution of nonfarm sectors to the Indian economy increases (Dasgupta and Singh 2005; Rigg 2005, 2006).

The Comprehensive Assessment scenario

Each of the scenarios described above has emphasized one strategy, such as improving rainfed agriculture through better rainwater management, improving yields and water productivity on existing irrigated areas, or expanding irrigated areas and trade. In reality, a combination of strategies will be implemented, building on regional strengths and limitations (table 3.12). Here we present an additional scenario, the Comprehensive Assessment's optimistic but plausible scenario emphasizing strategies that vary among regions.

In this scenario considerable investments are made in South Asia to improve irrigation performance and, to a smaller extent, improve water productivity in rainfed areas. Local fisheries and livestock are integrated as part of modernizing irrigation systems. The irrigated area expands by 18 million ha (18%). The area irrigated by groundwater is limited to avoid further aggravation of groundwater overdraft. New irrigation development is targeted mostly to small landholdings, with an emphasis on poverty reduction.

In Sub-Saharan Africa investments are targeted toward improving rainfed smallholder agriculture, again with an emphasis on poverty alleviation. The area under irrigation

> In a high-productivity scenario in South Asia all additional food demand can be met by improving land and water productivity in irrigated areas without expanding irrigated areas

table **3.12**	**Scope for productivity improvement and area expansion**		
Region	**Scope for improved productivity in rainfed areas**	**Scope for improved productivity in irrigated areas**	**Scope for expansion of irrigated area**
Sub-Saharan Africa	High	Some	High
Middle East & North Africa	Some	Some	Very limited
Central Asia & Eastern Europe	Some	Good	Some
South Asia	Good	High	Some
East Asia	Good	High	Some
Latin America	Good	Some	Some
OECD countries	Some	Some	Some

increases by 80%,[10] mainly through small-scale, informal irrigation, geared to producing high-value cash crops (sugar, cotton, fruits). Smallholders produce labor-intensive crops for local markets, such that Sub-Saharan Africa becomes largely self-sufficient in all food commodities including fruits and vegetables. To ensure economic feasibility and profitability for individual farmers, due attention is given to supporting physical and institutional infrastructure, such as favorable policies, credit, subsidies, education, and healthcare, capable government institutions, and water user associations. Investments in smallholder agriculture are seen as a necessary first step to promote rural growth and poverty alleviation. In the longer run, however, with more urbanization and diversification of economic activities, the number of people in farming decreases and farm sizes and incomes increase.

In the Middle East and North Africa water withdrawals for irrigation and groundwater overdrafts are reduced, and institutional reforms are implemented. Environmental flow regulations are strictly adhered to, even if the area under irrigation is reduced. The area under irrigated cereals is further reduced in favor of higher value crops (fruits and vegetables), which are exported to Europe. Cereal imports increase rapidly.

East Asia consolidates its position as a rice exporter, mainly by improving and intensifying existing irrigated production systems. The integration of fisheries in paddy production is promoted, and aquaculture production increases. China introduces environmental flow regulations to avoid overdrafts, and because of rapid economic growth and the associated demand for agricultural products, China becomes a major grain importer.

Eastern Europe and Central Asia and Latin America expand cultivated areas, primarily under rainfed conditions. Efforts are made to restore degraded river basins in Central Asia by imposing and enforcing stricter rules on environmental flows. Latin America increases its exports of sugar, soybeans, and biofuels. OECD countries emphasize restoring aquatic ecosystem services and reducing groundwater overdrafts. Agricultural exports decline in response to the reform of subsidies.

The global average rainfed cereal yield increases by 58%, while rainfed crop water productivity improves by 31% (table 3.13). Global irrigated yield increases by 55%, while crop water productivity improves by 38%. In monetary terms the output per unit of water increases more rapidly, as multiple uses of water are encouraged and fisheries and livestock production are integrated. Globally, harvested areas increase by 14%. Adverse impacts on terrestrial ecosystems are minimized by zoning regulations where rainfed area expands. Irrigated area increases by 16%, and much of the increase in harvested area comes from higher cropping intensity rather than from expansion of irrigated area.

Crop water consumption increases by 20%, while withdrawals by agriculture increase by 13% (345 cubic kilometers) to 2,975 cubic kilometers by 2050. Water use increases in response to higher food demands. Some of the increase is offset by improvements in crop water productivity and gains in water-use efficiency, although the latter is rather limited. Even in this optimistic scenario, withdrawals by agriculture increase. The challenge is to manage this water with minimal adverse impacts on ecosystem services, while providing the necessary gains in food production.

> Under the Comprehensive Assessment scenario crop water consumption increases by 20%, while withdrawals by agriculture increase by 13%. The challenge is to manage this increase in water use with minimal adverse impacts on environmental services

table **3.13**	| The Comprehensive Assessment scenario projections to 2050							
	Irrigated area		Rainfed area		Rainfed cereal yield		Irrigated cereal yield	
Region	Millions of hectares	Cumulative change (%)	Millions of hectares	Cumulative change (%)	Metric tons per hectare	Cumulative change (%)	Metric tons per hectare	Cumulative change (%)
Sub-Saharan Africa	11.3	80	174.2	10	2.34	98	4.37	99
Middle East & North Africa	21.5	5	16.1	−12	1.19	59	5.58	58
Central Asia & Eastern Europe	34.7	6	120.7	−5	3.00	47	6.06	78
South Asia	122.7	18	83.9	−12	2.54	91	4.84	89
East Asia	135.6	16	182.2	17	3.96	51	5.97	49
Latin America	19.5	18	147.9	46	3.90	58	6.77	68
OECD countries	47.3	4	179.0	4	6.35	33	8.03	22
World	394	16	920.0	10	3.88	58	5.74	55

Source: International Water Management Institute analysis done for the Comprehensive Assessment of Water Management in Agriculture using the Watersim model.

(continues on facing page)

Emerging issues

Water resources planning and management are increasingly affected by a range of emerging issues:

- *Energy.* Rising energy prices affect water use in agriculture in different ways. For example, biofuels production is a new competitor with food for water and land (box 3.4).
- *Climate change.* Climate change adds to the complexity of water resources planning and management. Uncertainty remains regarding how, when, and to what extent this will affect agricultural production and water demand and supply, and what adaptive management strategies may be required (box 3.5).
- *Globalization and trade policies.* Increasingly, decisions taken outside the water sector, such as those on domestic agricultural subsidies and international trade and politics, will influence the water-food-environment equation.
- *The changing role of state and local actors.* Many of the current concerns within the water sector (such as sustainability, efficiency in management, cost recovery, and water rights) will continue to be poorly addressed by top-down interventions mediated by the state and promoted by external development banks or agencies. Success in addressing these issues will reside in the adequate evolution of the roles of states, markets, communities, and civil society (see chapter 5 on policies and institutions).
- *Gender and the feminization of agriculture.* Women play a central role as producers of food, managers of natural resources, income earners, and caretakers of the household's food, water, and nutrition security. While the extent is debated, in many parts of the world women increasingly are involved in agriculture, as men

Looking ahead to 2050:
scenarios of alternative
investment approaches

3

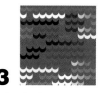

Rainfed water productivity		Irrigated water productivity		Crop water consumption		Irrigation water diversions		Trade	
Kilograms per cubic meter	Cumulative change (%)	Kilograms per cubic meter	Cumulative change (%)	Cubic kilometers	Cumulative change (%)	Cubic kilometers	Cumulative change (%)	Millions of metric tons	Share of consumption (%)
0.28	75	0.50	58	1,379	29	100	46	−25	12
0.25	47	0.82	41	272	7	228	8	−127	61
0.69	47	1.05	43	773	0	271	11	66	22
0.46	82	0.79	62	1,700	15	1,195	9	2	0
0.57	36	1.06	45	1,990	19	601	16	−97	12
0.63	50	0.91	52	1,361	52	196	12	18	6
1.30	25	1.42	18	1,021	4	238	2	151	26
0.64	31	0.93	38	8,515	20	2,975	13	490	15

box **3.4** | **Rising energy prices**

Crude oil prices have risen sharply in the past few years, and fluctuated around $60 a barrel in the first half of 2006. Higher energy prices affect agricultural water use in four ways:

- The demand for alternative energy sources, such as hydropower and bioenergy, increases, with potential impacts on water resource allocation.
- The cost of pumping groundwater increases.
- The viability of desalinization as a source of irrigation water declines (Younos 2005; Semiat 2000).
- Fertilizer prices and the unit costs of other oil-based inputs increase. Some farmers choose to expand irrigated area rather than improving yields, possibly leading to higher aggregate water demand.

Hydropower and bioenergy require substantial water, although hydropower production does not consume water. Multipurpose dams can produce energy, sustain irrigation and fisheries, enhance river regulation, and increase storage. However, dams often have adverse impacts on river ecosystems.

Bioenergy production is a consumptive use of water that might compete with food crop production for water and land resources (Berndes 2002). For example, one of the Millennium Ecosystem Assessment scenarios foresees that by 2050 one-quarter of the global energy supply will be met by energy from biomass (Alcamo and others 2005). Producing the necessary 8 billion tons of biomass requires 5,500 cubic kilometers of crop water consumption, roughly 75% of what is needed for the production of global food today (Kemp-Benedict 2006a, 2006c).

With rising energy prices the cost of groundwater pumping will increase. If India and other countries discontinue energy price subsidies, irrigation might become unaffordable for millions of smallholder farmers.

box **3.5** | **Changing climate and water resources**

The impacts of climate change on agricultural production and water resources are uncertain, with potentially great spatial variation. Semiarid and subtropical areas in Asia, Sub-Saharan Africa, Latin America, and the Middle East and North Africa will likely be affected the most through higher temperatures, greater rainfall variability, and greater frequency of extreme events (Bruinsma 2003; IPPC 2001; Dinar and others 1998; Kurukulasuriya and others 2006).

The Third Assessment report by the International Panel on Climate Change (IPCC 2001) foresees a temperature rise in the range of 2°–6° Celsius by 2100. Temperature increases in the Millennium Ecosystem Assessment scenarios are in the lower range of 1.5°–2.0° Celsius above pre-industrial revolution temperatures in 2050, and 2.0°–3.5° Celsius higher in 2100 (Alcamo and others 2005). Such temperature increases might lead to reductions in crop yields. But these losses might be offset by increases in yields because atmospheric carbon dioxide might act as a "fertilizer."

The combined effect of temperature rises and carbon dioxide enhancement varies among crops (Parry and others 1999; Alcamo and others 2005). Farmers might be able to adapt to temperature increases by changing planting dates, using different varieties, or switching to different crops (Droogers and Aerts 2005; Droogers 2004). Adaptations might generate substantial transaction costs (Pannell and others 2006).

While future regional temperatures are uncertain, still more uncertain are future precipitation patterns within regions. Most climate models agree on a global average precipitation increase in the 21st century, but they do not agree on the spatial patterns of changes in precipitation (Alcamo and others 2005), though some describe a trend of declining soil moisture (Dai, Qian, and Trenberth 2005).

Most climate change models indicate a strengthening of the summer monsoon. In Asia this might increase rainfall by 10%–20%. Even more important, it might generate a dramatic increase in interyear variability (WWF 2005). For paddy farmers this might imply less water scarcity but more damage from flooding and greater fluctuations in crop production. Some arid areas might become even drier, including the Middle East, parts of China, southern Europe, northeastern Brazil, and west of the Andes in Latin America. According to most climate models, the absolute amount of rainfall in Africa will decline as variability increases. In semiarid areas where rainfall already is unreliable, this might have severe impacts on crop production (Kurukulasuriya and others 2006) and the economy (Brown and Lall 2006). Irrigation might help smooth out variability, but is only useful if the total amount of rainfall remains sufficient to meet crop water demands.

Climate change might also affect agriculture if it causes substantial melting of glaciers that feed major rivers that are used for irrigation. Such melting could affect millions of hectares of irrigated land on the Indo-Gangetic plain. Millions of cubic meters of water are stored during the winter months in the form of ice and gradually released as melting water in spring. The warmer spring weather coincides with the start of the growing season. The disappearance of ice caps may change this flow, leading to greater summer runoff. Without additional storage to capture increased summer runoff, much water will flow unused to the ocean, leading to water scarcity in the drier months (Barnett, Adam, and Lettenmaier 2005; Wescoat 1991; Rees and Collins 2004; Dinar and others 1998).

migrate to cities and abroad in search of employment outside agriculture (see chapter 4 on poverty).

■ *Genetically modified crops.* The pros and cons and the potential role of genetically modified crops in improving water productivity and reducing poverty are subject to debate. Box 7.2 in chapter 7 on water productivity gives an overview of the issues.

Looking ahead to 2050:
scenarios of alternative
investment approaches   **3**

Summary statement

The path to success in enhancing agricultural production and ensuring food security is not a single, neatly formed vector from the current situation to a well defined target. Instead, the aggregate, global path will include many smaller paths representing the efforts of developing and industrialized countries seeking to ensure domestic food security and enhance public welfare. The smaller paths will become intertwined through international trade and the transfer of technology through the efforts of national and international research centers. We offer the Comprehensive Assessment scenario as one example of a strategy that might achieve the world's goals for food security, poverty reduction, and environmental sustainability.

Reviewers

Chapter review editor: Mahendra Shah.
Chapter reviewers: Angela Arthington, Habtamu Ayana, Gerold Bödeke, Deborah Bossio, Margaret Catley-Carlson, David Coates, Malin Falkenmark, Jean-Marc Faurès, Francis Gichuki, Jacob W. Kijne, Bruce Lankford, Jean Margat, Andrew McDonald, Douglas J. Merrey, James Newman, Sandra Postel, Manzoor Qadir, Claudia Sadoff, Chris Schwartz, David Seckler, Domitille Vallée, and Philippus Wester.

Notes

1. In rainfed areas 100% of crop water consumption is provided by precipitation. But in irrigated areas, too, part of the water is provided by rain falling in the command area. Irrigation professionals refer to this as "effective precipitation." This estimate is derived from International Water Management Institute analysis done for the Comprehensive Assessment of Water Management in Agriculture using the Watersim model; the FAO estimates 11%.

2. Our estimate of 2,630 cubic kilometers includes recycling within river basins. Seckler and others (1998, 2000) refer to this as "primary water." Summing all withdrawals from individual water users will lead to a higher estimate because of reuse of drainage flows by downstream users (Perry 1999; Molden, Sakthivaldivel, and Habib 2000). The interpretation of these numbers at such large scales is not always straightforward (Lankford 2006b). According to the FAO's estimate, 1,030 cubic kilometers of crop water evapotranspiration is provided by irrigation water, close to our estimate of 1,130 cubic kilometers.

3. Also refer to a recent web discussion among water experts on this topic (Winrock Water, www.winrockwater.org/forum.cfm).

4. Most literature related to rainfed agriculture describes soil conservation, fertility, pest management, and the like. Very little attention has been given to the need for rainwater management.

5. www.nepadst.org/platforms/foodloss.shtml.

6. The concept of minimum amounts of water has been superseded by the concept of the natural flow regime—flow quantities, temporal patterns, and overall flow variability (Arthington and others 2006). Smakthin, Revenga, and Döll (2004) is one of the few attempts at quantification.

7. This is similar to assumptions underlying the FAO's study *World Agriculture: Towards 2015/2030* (FAO 2002). Note that the expansion of irrigated harvested areas comes from expanding the area equipped and increasing the intensity of cropping (number of crops per year).

8. Efficiency of water use can be expressed by many indicators. In the Watersim model we use effective efficiency, defined as the amount of water beneficially used by plants or animals divided by total water consumption (Keller and Keller 1998), and depleted or consumptive fraction, defined as the ratio of water consumed to water withdrawn (Seckler and others 2000).

9. Frameworks for evaluating water productivity incorporating multiple uses of water exist (see chapters 12 on inland fisheries and 13 on livestock), but empirical observations and data are limited. Therefore, increases in water productivity by integrating fisheries and livestock could not be quantified in the scenario analysis.

10. This is comparable to the doubling envisaged by the Commission for Africa (2005), though its timeframe is shorter. Lankford (2006a) warns that doubling the irrigated area is not feasible without some large-scale irrigation. He recommends a slower rate of growth than foreseen by the Commission for Africa.

References

Ahmad, M.-U.-D., W. G. M. Bastiaanssen, and R.A. Feddes. 2005. "A New Technique to Estimate Net Groundwater Use Across Large Irrigated Areas by Combining Remote Sensing and Water Balance Approaches, Rechna Doab, Pakistan." *Hydrogeology Journal* 13 (5–6): 653–64.

Alcamo, J., P. Döll, F. Kaspar, and S. Siebert. 1997. *Global Change and Global Scenarios of Water Use and Availability: An Application of Water GAP 1.0.* Kassel, Germany: University of Kassel, Center for Environmental Systems Research.

Alcamo, J., D. van Vuuren, C. Ringler, W. Cramer, T. Masui, J. Alder, and K. Schulze. 2005. "Changes in Nature's Balance Sheet: Model-based Estimates of Future Worldwide Ecosystem Services." *Ecology and Society* 10 (2): 19.

Alexandratos, N. 1997. "China's Consumption of Cereals and the Capacity of the Rest of the World to Increase Exports." *Food Policy* 22 (3): 253–67.

———. 2005. "Countries with Rapid Population Growth and Resource Constraints: Issues of Food, Agriculture, and Development." *Population and Development Review* 31 (2): 237.

Allan, J.A. 1998. "Virtual Water: A Strategic Resource. Global Solutions to Regional Deficits." *Groundwater* 36 (4): 545–46.

———. 2001. Virtual Water—Economically Invisible and Politically Silent—A Way to Solve Strategic Water Problems. *International Water and Irrigation* 21 (4): 39–41.

Ambast, S.K., N.K. Tyagi, and S.K. Raul. 2006. "Management of Declining Groundwater in the Trans Indo-Gangetic Plain (India): Some Options." *Agricultural Water Management* 82 (3): 279–96.

Arthington, Angela H., Stuart E. Bunn, N. LeRoy Poff, and Robert J. Naiman. 2006. "The Challenge of Providing Environmental Flow Rules to Sustain River Ecosystems." *Ecological Applications* 16 (4): 1311–18.

Barker, R.; and F Molle. 2004. *Evolution of Irrigation in South and Southeast Asia.* Comprehensive Assessment Research Report 5. Colombo: International Water Management Institute.

Barnett., T.P, J.C. Adam, and D.P Lettenmaier. 2005 Potential Impacts of a Warming Climate on Water Availability in Snow-Dominated Regions. *Nature* 438 (17) 303–09.

Bennett, E.M., S.R. Carpenter, and N.F. Caraco. 2001. "Human Impact on Erodable Phosphorus and Eutrophication: A Global Perspective." *Bioscience* 51: 227–34.

Berndes, G. 2002. "Bioenergy and Water—The Implications of Large-scale Bioenergy Production for Water Use and Supply." *Global Environmental Change* 12 (2002) 253–71.

Bhattarai, M., R. Sakthivadivel, and I. Hussain. 2002. "Irrigation Impacts on Income Inequality and Poverty Alleviation: Policy Issues and Options for Improved Management of Irrigation Systems." Working Paper 39. International Water Management Institute, Colombo.

Briscoe, J., U. Qamar, M. Contijoch, P. Amir, and D. Blackmore. 2005. "Pakistan's Water Economy: Running Dry." World Bank, Washington, D.C., and Islamabad.

Brown, C., and U. Lall. 2006. "Water and Economic Development: The Role of Interannual Variability and a Framework for Resilience." Working paper. Columbia University, International Research Institute for Climate and Society, New York.

Bruinsma, J., ed. 2003. *World Agriculture: Towards 2015/2030. An FAO Perspective.* London: Food and Agriculture Organization and Earthscan.

Chapagain, A. 2006. "Globalization of Water. Opportunities and Threats of Virtual Water Trade." PhD thesis. UNESCO-IHE Delft, Water and Environmental Resources Management, Netherlands.

Commission for Africa. 2005. *Our Common Interest. Report of the Commission for Africa.* London: Penguin Books.

Dai, A., T. Qian, and K. E. Trenberth. 2005. "Has the Recent Global Warming Caused Increased Drying over Land?" Paper presented at the American Meteorological Society 16th Symposium on Global Change and Climate Variations, Symposium on Living with a Limited Water Supply, 9–13 January, San Diego, Calif.

Dasgupta, S., and A. Singh. 2005. "Will Services be the New Engine of Indian Economic Growth?" *Development and Change* 36 (6): 1035–57.

de Fraiture, C. Forthcoming. "Integrated Water and Food Analysis at the Global and Basin Level. An Application of WATERSIM." In E. Craswell, M. Bonell, D. Bossio, S. Demuth, and N. van de Giesen, eds., *Integrated Assessment of Water Resources and Global Change: A North-South Analysis.* New York: Springer.

de Fraiture, C., X. Cai, U. Amarasinghe, M. Rosegrant, and D. Molden. 2004. "Does Cereal Trade Save Water? The Impact of Virtual Water Trade on Global Water Use." Comprehensive Assessment of Water Management in Agriculture 4. International Water Management Institute, Colombo.

Dinar, A., R. Mendelsohn, R. Evenson, J. Parikh, A. Sanghi, K. Kumar, J. Mckinsey, and S. Lonergan. 1998. *Measuring the Impact of Climate Change on Indian Agriculture.* Technical Paper 402. Washington, D.C.: World Bank.

Looking ahead to 2050:
scenarios of alternative
investment approaches

3

Droogers, P. 2004. "Adaptation to Climate Change to Enhance Food Security and Preserve Environmental Quality: Example for Southern Sri Lanka." *Agricultural Water Management* 66 (1): 15–33.

Droogers, P., and J. Aerts. 2005. "Adaptation Strategies to Climate Change and Climate Variability: A Comparative Study between Seven Contrasting River Basins." *Physics and Chemistry of the Earth, Parts A/B/C* 30(6–7): 339–46.

Dudgeon, D. 2000. "Large-Scale Hydrological Changes in Tropical Asia: Prospects for Riverine Biodiversity." *BioScience* 50 (9): 793–806.

Duwayri, M., D.V. Tran, V.N. Nguyen. 1999. "Reflections on Yield Gaps in Rice Production." *International Rice Commission Newsletter* 48: 13–26.

Evenson, R.E., and D. Gollin. 2003. "Assessing the Impact of the Green Revolution 1960 to 2000." *Science* 300 (5620): 758–62.

Falkenmark, M., and J. Rockström. 2004. *Balancing Water for Humans and Nature: The New Approach in Ecohydrology.* London: Earthscan.

FAO (Food and Agriculture Organization). 2002. *World Agriculture: Towards 2015/2030. Summary Report.* Rome.

———. 2006. *World Agriculture: Towards 2030/2050. Interim Report.* Rome.

FAOSTAT. 2006. Statistical database. Accessed June 2006. [http://faostat.fao.org/].

Faurès, J-M., J. Hoogeveen, and J. Bruinsma. 2002. "The FAO Irrigated Area Forecast for 2030." Food and Agriculture Organization, Rome.

Fischer, G., H. van Velthuizen, M. Shah, and F.O. Nachtergaele. 2002. *Global Agro-ecological Assessment for Agriculture in the 21st Century: Methodology and Results.* CD-ROM. International Institute for Applied Systems Analysis and Food and Agriculture Organization: Laxenburg, Austria, and Rome.

Foley, J.A., R. DeFries, G. P. Asner, C. Barford, G. Bonan, S. R. Carpenter, F. S. Chapin, and others. 2005. "Global Consequences of Land Use." *Science* 309 (5734): 570–74.

Foster, A.D., and M.R. Rosenzweig. 2004. "Technological Change and the Distribution of Schooling: Evidence from Green-Revolution India." *Journal of Development Economics* 74 (1): 87–111.

Frenken, K., ed. 2005. *Irrigation in Africa in Figures. AQUASTAT Survey—2005.* Water Report 31. Rome: Food and Agriculture Organization.

Giordano, M. 2006. "Agricultural Groundwater Use and Rural Livelihoods in Sub-Saharan Africa: A First-Cut Assessment." *Hydrogeology Journal* 14 (3): 310–18.

Gleick, P.H. 1999. "Water Futures: A Review of Global Water Projections." In F.R. Rijsberman, ed., *World Water Scenarios: Analysis.* London: Earthscan.

Goldman, A., and J. Smith. 1995. "Agricultural Transformations in India and Northern Nigeria: Exploring the Nature of Green Revolutions." *World Development* 22 (12): 243–63.

Gordon, L., and C. Folke. 2000. "Ecohydrological Landscape Management for Human Well-being." *Water International* 25 (2): 178–84.

Gordon, L.J., W. Steffen, B.F. Jönsson, C. Folke, M. Falkenmark, and Å Johannessen. 2005. "Human Modification of Global Water Vapor Flows from the Land Surface." *Proceedings of the National Academy of Sciences of the United States* 102 (21): 7612–17.

Gupta, R., and S.G. Gangopadhyay. 2006. "Peri-urban Agriculture and Aquaculture." *Economic and Political Weekly* 41 (18): 1757–60.

Hanjra, M.A., T. Ferede, and D.G. Gutta. Forthcoming. "Pathways to Reduce Rural Poverty in Ethiopia: Investing in Irrigation Water, Education and Markets." *African Water Journal.*

Hoekstra, A.Y., and P.Q. Hung. 2005. "Globalisation of Water Resources: International Virtual Water Flows in Relation to Crop Trade." *Global Environmental Change* 15 (1): 45–56.

Hussain, I., and M.A. Hanjra. 2003. "Does Irrigation Water Matter for Rural Poverty Alleviation? Evidence from South and South-East Asia." *Water Policy* 5 (5): 429–42.

———. 2004. "Irrigation and Poverty Alleviation: Review of the Empirical Evidence." *Irrigation and Drainage* 53 (1): 1–15.

Hussain, I., M. Mudasser, M.A. Hanjra, U. Amrasinghe, and D. Molden. 2004. "Improving Wheat Productivity in Pakistan: Econometric Analysis using Panel Data from Chaj in the Upper Indus Basin." *Water International* 29 (2): 189–200.

Hussain, I., L. Raschid, M.A. Hanjra, F. Marikar, and W. van der Hoek. 2001. "A Framework for Analyzing Socioeconomic, Health and Environmental Impacts of Wastewater Use in Agriculture in Developing Countries." Working Paper 26. International Water Management Institute, Colombo.

———. 2002. "Wastewater Use in Agriculture: Review of Impacts and Methodological Issues in Valuing Impacts." Working Paper 37. International Water Management Institute, Colombo.

Inocencio, A., D. Merrey, M. Tonosaki, A. Maruyama, I. de Jong, and M. Kikuchi. 2006. "Costs and Performance of Irrigation Projects: A Comparison of Sub-Saharan Africa and Other Developing Regions." International Water Management Institute, Colombo.

IPCC (Intergovernmental Panel on Climate Change). 2001. *Third Assessment Report.* Cambridge, UK: Cambridge University Press.

Keller, A., and J. Keller. 1998. *Effective Efficiency: A Water Use Concept for Allocating Freshwater Resources.* Water Resources and Irrigation Division Discussion Paper 22. Arlington, Va.: Winrock International.

Keller, A., R. Sakthivadivel, and D. Seckler. 2000. *Water Scarcity and the Role of Storage in Development.* Research Report 39. Colombo: International Water Management Institute.

Kemp-Benedict, E. 2006a. "Energy Scenario Notes." Background technical report for the Comprehensive Assessment on Water Management in Agriculture for the International Water Management Institute. Stockholm Environmental Institute.

———. 2006b. "Land for Livestock Scenario Notes." Background technical report for the Comprehensive Assessment on Water Management in Agriculture for the International Water Management Institute. Stockholm Environmental Institute.

———. 2006c. "Water for Biomass in the Baseline CA Scenario." Background technical report for the Comprehensive Assessment on Water Management in Agriculture for the International Water Management Institute. Stockholm Environmental Institute.

Keyzer, M.A., M.D. Merbis, I.F.P.W. Pavel, and C.F.A. van Wesenbeeck. 2005. "Diet Shifts towards Meat and the Effects on Cereal Use: Can We Feed the Animals in 2030?" *Ecological Economics* 55 (2): 187–202.

Khan, S., R. Tariq, C. Yuanlai, and J. Blackwell. 2006. "Can Irrigation be Sustainable?" *Agricultural Water Management* 80 (1–3): 87–99.

Kijne, J., R. Barker, and D. Molden. 2003. *Water Productivity in Agriculture: Limits and Opportunities for Improvement.* Wallingford, UK: CABI Publishing.

Kikuchi, T., A. Maruyama, and Y. Hayami. 2001. "Investment Inducements to Public Infrastructure: Irrigation in the Philippines and Sri Lanka since Independence." International Rice Research Institute and International Water Management Institute, Manila and Colombo.

Koplow, D. 2006. *Biofuels—At What Cost? Government Support for Ethanol and Biodiesel in the United States.* Geneva: Institute for Sustainable Development, Global Subsidies Initiative.

Kumar, M.D., and O.P. Singh. 2005. "Virtual Water in Global Food and Water Policy Making: Is There a Need for Rethinking?" *Water Resources Management* 19 (6): 759–89.

Kura, Y., Carmen Revenga, Eriko Hoshino, and Greg Mock. 2004. *Fishing for Answers. Making Sense of the Global Fish Crisis.* World Resources Institute: Washington, D.C.

Kurukulasuriya, P., R. Mendelsohn, R. Hassan, J. Benhin, M. Diop, H.M. Eid, K.Y. Fosu, and others. 2006. "Will African Agriculture Survive Climate Change?" *World Bank Economic Review* 20 (3): 367–88.

Lankford, B.A. 2006a. "Exploring Policy Interventions for Agricultural Water Management in Africa." DEV/ODG Research Note. School of Development Studies, University of East Anglia, Norwich, UK.

———. 2006b. "Localising Irrigation Efficiency." *Irrigation and Drainage* 55 (4): 345–62.

Luquet, D., A. Vidal, M. Smith, and J. Dauzatd. 2005. "'More Crop per Drop': How to make it Acceptable for Farmers?" *Agricultural Water Management* 76 (2): 108–19.

Margat, J. 2006. "Diversity of Water Resources in Arid Areas and Consequences on Development." Paper presented at 1st International Conference on Water Ecosystems and Sustainable Development in Arid and Semiarid Zones, 9–15 October, Urumqi, China.

Mati, B. 2006. "Overview of Water and Soil Nutrient Management under Smallholder Rain-fed Agriculture in East Africa." Working Paper 105. International Water Management Institute, Colombo.

MEA (Millennium Ecosystem Assessment). 2005. *Millennium Ecosystem Assessment: Scenarios.* Washington D.C.: Island Press.

Mehta, L., and B.L.C. Madsen. 2005. "Is the WTO After Your Water? The General Agreement on Trade in Services (GATS) and Poor People's Right to Water." *Natural Resources Forum* 29 (2): 154–64.

Molden, D.J., and C. de Fraiture. 2004. *Investing in Water for Food, Ecosystems, and Livelihoods.* Comprehensive Assessment Blue Paper. Discussion draft. International Water Management Institute, Colombo

Molden, D.J., U. Amarasinghe, and I. Hussain. 2001. *Water for Rural Development.* Background paper on water for rural development prepared for the World Bank. Working Paper 32. Colombo: International Water Management Institute.

Molden, D.J., R. Sakthivadivel, and Z. Habib. 2000. *Basin-level Use and Productivity of Water: Examples from South Asia.* Research Report 49. Colombo: International Water Management Institute.

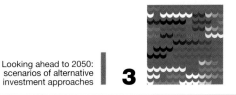

Molle, F., and J. Berkoff. 2006. "Cities versus Agriculture: Revisiting Intersectoral Water Transfers. Potential Gains and Conflicts." Comprehensive Assessment of Water Management in Agriculture 10. International Water Management Institute, Colombo.

Mosley, P. 2002. "The African Green Revolution as a Pro-poor Policy Instrument." *Journal of International Development* 14 (6): 695–724.

Naylor, R.L., R.J. Goldberg, H. Mooney, M.C. Beveridge, J. Clay, C. Folk, N. Kautsky, J. Lubchenco, J. Primavera, and M. Williams. 1998. "Nature's Subsidies to Shrimp and Salmon Farming." *Nature* 282 (5390): 883–84.

Naylor, R.L., R.J. Goldberg, J.H. Primavera, N. Kautsky, M.C. Beveridge, J. Clay, C. Folk, J. Lubchenco, H. Mooney, and M. Troell. 2000. "Effect of Aquaculture on World Fish Supplies." *Nature* 405 (6790): 1017–24.

Nguyen-Khoa, S., and L.E.D. Smith. 2004. "Irrigation and Fisheries: Irreconcilable Conflicts or Potential Synergies?" *Irrigation and Drainage* 53 (4): 415–27.

Nguyen-Khoa, S., C. Garaway, B. Chamsinhg, D. Siebert, and M. Randone. 2005. "Impacts of Irrigation on Fisheries in Rain-fed Rice-farming Landscapes." *Journal of Applied Ecology* 42 (5): 892–900.

Oki, T., M. Sato, A. Kawamura, M. Miyake, S. Kanae, and K. Musiake. 2003. "Virtual Water Trade to Japan and in the World." In A.Y. Hoekstra and P.Q. Hung, eds., *Proceedings of the International Expert Meeting on Virtual Water Trade.* Delft, Netherlands: IHE.

Pannell, D.J., G.R. Marshall, N. Barr, A. Curtis, F. Vanclay, and R. Wilkinson. 2006. "Understanding and Promoting Adoption of Conservation Technologies by rural landholders." *Australian Journal of Experimental Agriculture* 46 (11): 1407–24.

Parikh, J., and S. Gokarn. 1993. "Climate Change and India's Energy Policy Options: New Perspectives on Sectoral CO_2 Emissions and Incremental Costs." *Global Environmental Change* 3 (3): 276–91.

Parry, M., C. Rosenzweig, A. Iglesias, G. Fischer, and M. Livermore. 1999. "Climate Change and World Food Security: A New Assessment." *Global Environmental Change* 9 (S1): S51–S67.

Perry, C.J. 1999. "The IWMI Water Resources Paradigm—Definitions and Implications." *Agricultural Water Management* 40 (1): 45–50.

Pimentel, D., B. Berger, D. Filiberto, M. Newton, B. Wolfe, E. Karabinakis, S. Clark, E. Poon, E. Abbett, and S. Nandagopal. 2004. "Water Resources: Agricultural and Environmental Issues." *BioScience* 54 (10): 909–18.

Pingali, P. 2004. "Westernization of Asian Diets and the Transformation of Food Systems: Implications for Research and Policy." FAO-ESA Working Paper 04-17. Food and Agriculture Organization, Agricultural and Development Economics Division, Rome.

Poff, N.L., J.D. Allan, M.B. Bain, J.R. Karr, K.L. Prestegaard, B.D. Richter, R.E. Sparks, and J.C. Stromberg. 1997. "The Natural Flow Regime—A Paradigm for River Conservation and Restoration." *BioScience* 47 (11): 769–84.

Polak, P. 2005. "The Big Potential of Small Farms." *Scientific American* 293 (3): 62–69.

Postel. S.L. 1998. "Water for Food Production: Will There Be Enough in 2025?" *Bioscience* 48 (8): 629–37.

Pretty, J.N., A.D. Noble, D. Bossio, J. Dixon, R.E. Hine, F.W.T. Penning de Vries, and J.I.L. Morison. 2006. "Resource-conserving Agriculture Increases Yields in Developing Countries." *Environmental Science & Technology* 40 (4): 1114–19.

Raschid-Sally, L., R. Carr, and S. Buechler. 2005. "Managing Wastewater Agriculture to Improve Livelihoods and Environmental Quality in Poor Countries." *Irrigation and Drainage* 54 (S1): S11–S22.

Rees, G., and D. Collins. 2004. "An Assessment of the Potential Impacts of Deglaciation on the Water Resources of the Himalayas." HR Wallingford, UK.

Rigg, J. 2005. "Poverty and Livelihoods after Full-time Farming: A South-East Asian View." *Asia Pacific Viewpoint* 46 (2): 173–84.

———. 2006. "Land, Farming, Livelihoods, and Poverty: Rethinking the Links in the Rural South." *World Development* 34 (1): 180–202.

Rijsberman, F.R., and D.J. Molden. 2001. "Balancing Water Uses: Water for Food and Water for Nature." Thematic background paper for the International Conference on Freshwater, 3–7 December, Bonn, Germany.

Rockström, J. 2003. "Water for Food and Nature in Drought-prone Tropics: Vapour Shift in Rain-fed Agriculture." *Philosophical Transactions Royal Society B* 358 (1440): 1997–2009.

Rockström, J., L. Gordon, L. Falkenmark, M. Folke, and M. Engvall. 1999. "Linkages among Water Vapor Flows, Food Production and Terrestrial Services." *Conservation Ecology* 3 (2): 5.

Rockström, J., C. Folke, L. Gordon, N. Hatibu, G. Jewitt, F. Penning De Vries, F. Rwehumbiza, and E. Al. 2004. "A Watershed Approach to Upgrade Rainfed Agriculture in Water Scarce Regions through Water System Innovations: An Integrated Research Initiative on Water for Food and Rural Livelihoods in Balance with Ecosystem Functions." *Physics and Chemistry of the Earth, Parts A/B/C* 29 (15–18): 1109–18.

Rosegrant, M., X. Cai, and S. Cline. 2002. *World Water and Food to 2025. Dealing with Scarcity.* Washington, D.C.: International Food Policy Research Institute.

Rosegrant, M.W., S.A. Cline, W. Li, T.B. Sulser, and R.A. Valmonte-Santos. 2005. "Looking Ahead. Long Term Prospects for Africa's Agricultural Development and Food Security," 2020 Discussion paper 41. International Food Policy Research Institute, 2020 Vision for Food, Agriculture and the Environment, Washington, D.C.

Rosegrant, M.W., C. Ringler, T. Benson, X. Diao, D. Resnick, J. Thurlow, M. Torero, and D. Orden. 2006. *Agriculture and Achieving The Millennium Development Goals.* Washington, D.C.: World Bank, Agriculture and Rural Development Department.

Scott, C.A., and T. Shah. 2004. "Groundwater Overdraft Reduction through Agricultural Energy Policy: Insights from India and Mexico." *Water Resources Development* 20 (2): 149–64.

Seckler, D., D. Molden, U. Amarasinghe, and C. de Fraiture. 2000. *Water Issues for 2025: A Research Perspective.* Colombo: International Water Management Institute.

Seckler, D., U. Amarasinghe, D. Molden, R. de Silva, and R. Barker. 1998. *World Water and Demand and Supply, 1990 to 2025: Scenarios and Issues.* Research Report 19. Colombo: International Water Management Institute.

SEI (Stockholm Environment Institute). 2005. "Sustainable Pathways to Attain the Millennium Development Goals— Assessing the Role of Water, Energy and Sanitation." Document prepared for the UN World Summit, September 14, New York. Stockholm.

Semiat, R. 2000. "Desalination: Present and Future." *Water International* 25 (1): 54–65.

Shah, T., C. Scott, A. Kishore, and A. Sharma. 2004. *Energy-Irrigation Nexus in South Asia: Improving Groundwater Conservation and Power Sector Viability.* IWMI Research Report 70. Colombo: International Water Research Institute.

Shiklomanov, I. 2000. "Appraisal and Assessment of World Water Resources." *Water International* 25 (1): 11–32.

Singh, O.P., Amrita Sharma, Rahul Singh, and Tushaar Shah. 2004. "Virtual Water Trade in Dairy Economy. Irrigation Water Productivity in Gujarat." *Economic and Political Weekly* July 31: 3492–97.

SIWI (Stockholm International Water Institute) and IWMI (International Water Management Institute). 2004. *Water— More Nutrition Per Drop.* Stockholm.

Smakhtin, V., C. Revenga, and P. Döll. 2004. "A Pilot Global Assessment of Environmental Water Requirements and Scarcity." *Water International* 29 (3): 307–17.

Smith, L.E.D. 2004. "Assessment of the Contribution of Irrigation to Poverty Reduction and Sustainable Livelihoods." *Water Resources Development* 20 (2): 243–57.

Somerville, C., and J. Briscoe. 2001. "Genetic Engineering and Water." *Science* 292 (5525): 2217.

Thrupp, L.A. 2000. "Linking Agricultural Biodiversity and Food Security: The Valuable Role of Agrobiodiversity for Sustainable Agriculture." *International Affairs* 76 (2): 283–97.

Tidwell, J.H., and Geoff L. Allan. 2001. "Fish as Food: Aquaculture's Contribution." *EMBO Reports* 2 (11): 958–63.

UNESCO (United Nations Educational, Scientific and Cultural Organization). 2006. *Exploitation and Utilization of Groundwater Around the World.* CD-ROM. United Nations Educational, Scientific and Cultural Organization International Hydrological Programme and BRGM, Paris and Orléans, France.

Van Koppen, B., P. Moriarty, and E. Boelee. 2006. *Multiple-use Water Services to Advance the Millennium Development Goals.* Research Report 98. International Water Management Institute, Colombo.

Verdegem, M.C.J., R.H. Bosma, and J.A.J. Verreth. 2006. "Reducing Water Use for Animal Production through Aquaculture." *Water Resources Development* 22 (1): 101–13.

Vitousek, P.M., J.D. Aber, R.W. Howarth, G.E. Likens, P.A. Matson, D.W. Schindler, W.H. Schlesinger, and D.G. Tilman. 1997. "Human Alteration of the Global Nitrogen Cycle: Sources and Consequences." *Ecological Applications* 7 (3): 737–50.

Vörösmarty, C.J., D. Lettenmaier, C. Leveque, M. Meybeck, C. Pahl-Wostl, J. Alcamo, W. Cosgrove, and others. 2004. "Humans Transforming the Global Water System." *EOS, Transactions, American Geophysical Union* 85 (48): 509–14.

Wang, J., Z. Xu, J. Huang, and S. Rozelle. 2006. "Incentives to Managers or Participation of Farmers in China's Irrigation Systems: Which Matters Most for Water Savings, Farmer Income, and Poverty?" *Agricultural Economics* 34 (3): 315–30.

Wescoat, J.L., Jr. 1991. "Managing the Indus River basin in Light of Climate Change: Four Conceptual Approaches." *Global Environmental Change* 1 (5): 381–95.

World Bank. 2003. *World Development Report 2003.* World Bank and Oxford University Press: New York and Washington, D.C.

Worm, B., E. B. Barbier, N. Beaumont, J. E. Duffy, C. Folke, B.S. Halpern, J. B.C. Jackson, and others. 2006. "Impacts of Biodiversity Loss on Ocean Ecosystem Services." *Science* 314 (5800) 787 –90.

WRI (World Resources Institute) 1998. *World Resources 1998–99: Environmental Change and Human Health.* New York: Oxford University Press.

Looking ahead to 2050:
scenarios of alternative
investment approaches

3

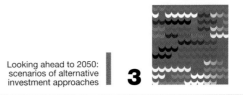

WWF. 2005. *An Overview of Glaciers, Glacier Retreat, and Subsequent Impacts in Nepal, India and China*. Kathmandu: WWF Nepal Program.

Yang, H., P. Reichert, K.A. Abbaspour, and A.J.B. Zehnder. 2002. "A Water Resources Threshold and its Implications for Food Security." *Environmental Science and Technology* 37 (14), 3048–54.

Ye, Yimin. 1999 *Historical Consumption and Future Demand for Fish and Fishery Products: Exploratory Calculations for the Years 2015/2030*. Fisheries Circular 946. Rome: Food and Agriculture Organization.

Younos, T. 2005. "The Economics of Desalination." *Journal of Contemporary Water Research and Education* 132: 39–54.

Zimmer, D., and D. Renault. 2003. "Virtual Water in Food Production and Global Trade: Review of Methodological Issues and Preliminary Results." In A.Y. Hoekstra and P.Q. Hung, eds., *Proceedings of the International Expert Meeting on Virtual Water Trade*. Delft, Netherlands: IHE.

Part 3 | Integrating issues

These chapters assess key concepts, trends, conditions, and response options for four cross-cutting issues: poverty, policies and institutions, ecosystems, and water productivity.

Water for farming to fight poverty

Artist: Thim Sophal, Cambodia

4 Reversing the flow: agricultural water management pathways for poverty reduction

Coordinating lead authors: Gina E. Castillo and Regassa E. Namara

Lead authors: Helle Munk Ravnborg, Munir A. Hanjra, Laurence Smith, and Maliha H. Hussein

Contributing authors: Christopher Béné, Simon Cook, Danielle Hirsch, Paul Polak, Domitille Vallée, and Barbara van Koppen

Overview

Access to water for productive and consumptive uses, poverty reduction, and sustainable livelihoods for rural people are all intimately linked [well established]. Apart from labor and land, water is one of the most important resources of poor people in rural areas. Improving access to water and productivity in its use can contribute to greater food security, nutrition, health status, income, and resilience in income and consumption patterns. In turn, this can contribute to other improvements in financial, human, physical, and social capital, simultaneously alleviating multiple dimensions of poverty. Indeed, the productivity of other assets often depends on water use, while sustainable patterns of water use can contribute to the conservation of all natural resources.

This chapter recognizes that poverty prevails in all farming systems and in all regions of the developing world, although with varying severity and intensity [well established]. For instance, in Sub-Saharan Africa, the absolute number of poor people is very high in rainfed systems. Although the underlying causes of poverty vary by farming system, difficult access to water and its growing scarcity stand as threats to future advances in poverty reduction in all such systems. Other water-dependent groups that are highly vulnerable to poverty include rural small-scale fishing and herding communities. For them, problems of access will worsen because of climate change and water-related disasters that can undermine their livelihood strategies.

Where there is equity in resource distribution, the impact of improved water management on agricultural productivity growth has been more poverty reducing [established but incomplete]. Inequality, particularly gender-based inequality, tempers the effectiveness of poverty reduction efforts. Women, who produce an estimated two-thirds of the food in most developing countries, are important stakeholders in poverty reduction in irrigated and rainfed systems. Yet they often have inadequate access to land, water, labor, capital, technologies, and other services. This situation is unjust and prevents women from realizing their full potential as human beings and citizens and compromises efforts to target water management for poverty reduction.

Water is an important livelihood asset, particularly for the rural poor who depend on agriculture [well established]. Better water management is a promising pathway to fight poverty, improve equity, and empower poor men and women. No blueprint strategies are presented here to reduce poverty and inequity. Strategies have to be context-specific and must begin with the recognition that water should be an integral part of realizing the right to a sustainable livelihood for poor men and women.

' **Better water management is a promising pathway to fight poverty, improve equity, and empower poor men and women**

Broadly conceived poverty reduction strategies will entail four elements:

- Ensuring the right to secure access to water for the poor (securing water and developing appropriate technologies and financing options).
- Empowering people to use water better (raising water productivity).
- Improving the governance of water resources.
- Supporting the diversification of livelihoods.

Based on a review of experiences, we propose broad areas of focus for investments in agricultural water resources development and management. These investments need to be informed by a thorough understanding of the constraints and aspirations of poor people themselves. Some of these proposed strategies are:

- Developing new water systems without repeating the mistakes of the last 50 years. For countries that have not yet developed their water resources, there are two basic approaches: large infrastructure development or a range of small-scale, low-cost technologies, including farmer-managed technologies, community irrigation systems, rainwater management, and informal irrigation. Both approaches are justified in different situations. Small-scale systems can target poverty head-on but may not be able to protect poor people's limited assets under conditions of greater climate variability. Investments in big infrastructure aim at general economic growth with the goal of reaching the poor both directly and through multiplier effects on production, consumption, and human capital.
- Increasing the productivity and equity of existing systems, including upgrading rainfed systems to improve crop and livestock productivity; diversifying into high-value, high water-productivity crops; and engaging in value-adding processing activities and other small businesses.
- Ensuring secure access to water for agriculture for poor women and men by clarifying water rights.
- Facilitating local management by acknowledging the importance of customary laws and informal institutions in the management of water and other natural resources.
- Providing policy and technical support to informal irrigation systems, which are vital to many poor farmers.

Reversing the flow:
agricultural water management
pathways for poverty reduction

4

- Designing and developing water resources infrastructure, applying a multiple-use systems perspective (including domestic use, livestock, fisheries, and aquaculture) to maximize benefits per unit of water for poor women and men.
- Supporting agricultural water research that targets poverty head-on, looks at low-cost and gender-suited technologies, and investigates policies most likely to reduce poverty and inequality.

While agricultural water management and development play an important part in poverty reduction, they cannot banish poverty alone [well established]. Also needed are complementary investments in education, health, rural infrastructure, capacity building, and supportive institutions, together with pro-poor, pro-gender research on low-cost and gender-suited technologies, crop research advances, and improved agronomic and water management practices and related dimensions of social exclusion, equity, and empowerment. This requires a complementarity of actors, including nongovernmental organizations (NGOs), research organizations, governments, the private sector, and donors. Holistic and integrated assessment of needs, possible interventions, and their interactions will be the key to achieving sustained improvements in water use for poverty reduction.

> Crop and livestock production, agroprocessing, fishing, eco-systems, and human health are all influenced by the quality and quantity of available water and in turn affect human well-being

Understanding water poverty

Water is essential for life and human well-being. Water is used in both productive and consumptive activities and contributes to rural and urban livelihoods in myriad ways. Adequate access to water is a prerequisite for realizing of the right to development.[1]

Lack of access to drinking water is an indicator of poverty, but the role of water in human well-being is far more complex. Crop and livestock production, agroprocessing, fishing, ecosystems, and human health are all influenced by the quality and quantity of available water (see chapters 6 on ecosystems, 12 on inland fisheries, and 13 on livestock) and in turn affect human well-being.

In many cases poor people lack access to enough water for both productive and consumptive uses simply because the resource is physically scarce (see chapter 2 on trends). Here, the issue is water availability. In other cases water resources development costs are prohibitive and water is economically scarce. In still others water is physically available but generates lower than potential economic gains and constricts human welfare. It has low water productivity (see chapter 7 on water productivity) because of poor management, or the gains are distributed inequitably in ways that disadvantage poor people (institutional water scarcity). Mismanagement of water resources can even contribute to poverty, as in the case of groundwater overdraft (see chapter 10 on groundwater). Changes in water allocation due to social preferences and political decisions may also create scarcity, as some groups get water while others are denied access. This can increase poverty and vulnerability.

It is highly likely that problems of water scarcity, mismanagement, and water-related disasters will intensify due to population increases, rising demand for water for agriculture and other uses, and greater climate variability. Pressure on coping structures will affect patterns of water ownership and accessibility. Increasing scarcity is likely to deepen current inequalities, to the detriment of the poor, particularly women and marginalized groups.

Human vulnerability will increase unless systems are able to adapt more rapidly to the ensuing shocks (Pannell and others 2006).

Water resource development can address poverty, improve well-being, and enhance people's freedoms and opportunities to accumulate assets to lead dignified lives. For many of today's rural poor, water security is vital for livelihood security. Essential accompanying factors include an enabling policy environment, supportive pro-poor institutions, appropriate cropping technologies, financial and technical support joined to local demand, and investments in institutions and training that enhance people's capacities and freedoms to participate in defining the development they want (see chapter 5 on policies and institutions).

The agricultural water rights and management agenda to fight poverty is clear. It entails ensuring the right to secure access to water for the poor, empowering people to use water more effectively, improving the governance of water resources and supporting services, and supporting the diversification of livelihoods.

Increasing overall water productivity for poor people remains the main pathway to reduce poverty, but how best to match the agricultural water management package (technology, institutions, policies) to the needs of the heterogeneous poor living in diverse agroecological settings remains unclear. Understanding how improvements in water management can reduce poverty and enabling the necessary changes are two of the most important policy and research challenges for the coming decades.

> Poverty and the availability of water are linked, but the prevalence and severity of poverty appear to depend more on the development of water resources than on the endowment

The profile of poverty and water

While the proportion of poor people may be falling, more than 1 billion people still live on less than $1 a day, and 2.8 billion live on less than $2 a day (OECD 2001). According to the UN Millennium Project (2005) the number of people living on less than a $1 a day dropped between 1990 and 2001, from 1.218 billion to 1.089 billion. But in some countries the absolute number of poor people is still rising. In Sub-Saharan Africa the number of poor people living on less than a $1 a day increased from 227 million in 1990 to 313 million in 2001 (UN Millennium Project 2005). Global poverty is highly regionalized, rural, and disproportionately female. Estimates of rural poverty range from 62% (CGIAR 2000) to 75% (IFAD 2001) of all poor people. South Asia and Sub-Saharan Africa are the core areas for absolute poverty, with 70% of the world's poor. South Asia has 44% of the people below $1 per day, but the depth of poverty is worse in Sub-Saharan Africa (map 4.1).

Poverty and the availability of water are linked. Not all poor regions lack adequate water resources, however, and other factors come into play. The water resources endowment of the most poverty-stricken regions compares reasonably well with that of better-off countries, and the prevalence and severity of poverty appear to depend more on the development of water resources than on the endowment. For instance, eastern India—part of South Asia's so-called poverty square—is endowed with enormous amounts of groundwater and surface water resources. But while western India forged ahead with the green revolution in 1960s and 1970s, eastern India lagged behind, due mainly to the slow pace of groundwater development (Shah 2001).

A third of the world's people experience water scarcity as a result of rising and competing demands for water from the rapid expansion of irrigation, growth in industry, power

Reversing the flow:
agricultural water management
pathways for poverty reduction

4

| map **4.1** | **Share of population below the poverty line** |

☐ 0%–15% ☐ 16%–25% ☐ 26%–35% ☐ 36%–45% ☐ 46%–55% ☐ More than 55%

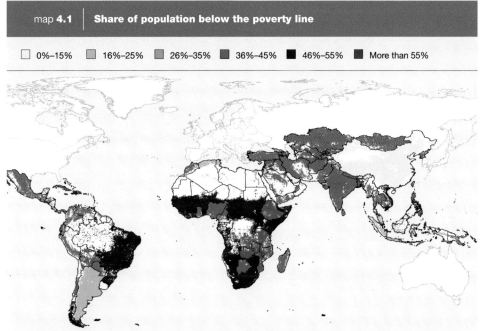

Note: The poverty line is roughly equivalent to a standard of living at $1 a day in purchasing power parity income, which adjusts for differences in price levels across countries.
Source: Thornton and others 2002.

generation, and demography or from the lack of investments in infrastructure or capacity (see chapters 2 on trends and 3 on scenarios). The available water supply and its productive capacity are further strained by climate change, land degradation, deterioration of water quality, and the need to maintain environmental flows and protect aquatic ecosystems (Murgai, Ali, and Byerlee 2001; Postel 1999; Janmaat 2004; Davidson 2000; World Bank 2003). The bulk of this "water-scarce" population resides in the semiarid regions of Asia and in Sub-Saharan Africa, where poverty is deep-rooted. The increasing competition for water tends to lead to growing inequity in its provision.

Mismanagement of water resources—as with extensive arsenic poisoning of groundwater in Bangladesh and fluoride contamination of well water in western India—produces health problems and affects livelihood opportunities (see chapter 10 on groundwater). The shifting allocation from rural to urban areas is common throughout the world and puts more pressure on water resources (Molle and Berkoff 2006). Future rapid shifts in rural-urban population ratios will intensify the scramble for water. In the high-altitude Andean watersheds rising competition for water is linked to increases in irrigated agriculture and urban populations. Water customarily used by peasants and indigenous peoples has been diverted for hydropower projects or for high-profit users who live outside the area (see chapter 16 on river basins). Finally, poor people are generally most vulnerable to these water-related issues because their limited access to assets means that they have low resilience to induced changes or shocks.

Farming systems, water, and livelihoods

Agriculture is the main source of livelihood for the world's rural poor and is pivotal to the economies of many developing countries. Women produce an estimated two-thirds of the food in most developing countries (UNDP 2006). Even with the diversification of rural livelihoods and with increasing urbanization, an estimated 50% or more of poor people will remain in rural areas by 2035, a significant number of whom will be smallholder producers (IFAD 2001). For poor farmers agriculture is a disadvantaged activity because of poor people's limited access to livelihood assets and their exclusion from formal decisionmaking and priority setting in agriculture. Water scarcity is one of the main factors that constrains their agricultural output, income, and profitability. The well-being that people derive from water therefore depends on the interaction between farming systems and livelihood systems.

Farming systems. Poverty prevails in all farming systems and in all regions of the developing world, with varying depth and severity. For instance, in Sub-Saharan Africa the incidence of poverty is lower in irrigated farming than in other farming systems, and the absolute number of poor is relatively small (Dixon and Gulliver 2001, p. 33). Poverty rates are generally lower in irrigated than in rainfed settings (figure 4.1). A study in the Mwea irrigation scheme in Kenya found that households outside the scheme are relatively

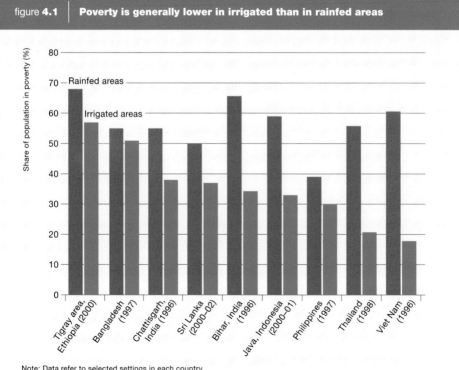

figure **4.1** | **Poverty is generally lower in irrigated than in rainfed areas**

Note: Data refer to selected settings in each country.
Source: Hanjra, Ferede, and Gutta forthcoming; Hussain and others 2006.

Reversing the flow:
agricultural water management
pathways for poverty reduction

4

income-poorer than their counterparts within the scheme. Households in the middle income quintile within the irrigation scheme are wealthier than households in the richest quintile outside the scheme (figure 4.2).

Although the underlying causes of poverty vary by farming system, growing scarcity and competition for water are a threat to future advances in poverty reduction. Indeed, most of the areas of persistent poverty can be described as "water scarce." However, many irrigated areas with large-scale systems, particularly in India and Pakistan, remain home to large numbers of poor people in both absolute and relative terms. This is due largely to inequity in access to land and water resources and the resulting low productivity, particularly in downstream areas.

Livelihood systems. The productivity of farming systems depends on the amount of capital assets available to farmers. The sustainable livelihoods framework is useful for portraying how various forms of capital shape rural livelihoods. It recognizes that in rural communities the capacity to resist poverty and to improve livelihoods often depends on the opportunities offered by natural resource–based production systems, conditioned by the wider economic, institutional, and political environment. Livelihoods analysis prompts assessment of the assets used for existence (both those owned and those obtained through formal or customary rights or exchange) and of how they are used in livelihood activities. Inequity in household access to assets is seen to affect the coping mechanisms of individuals within households and their ability to deal with crises and external risk factors

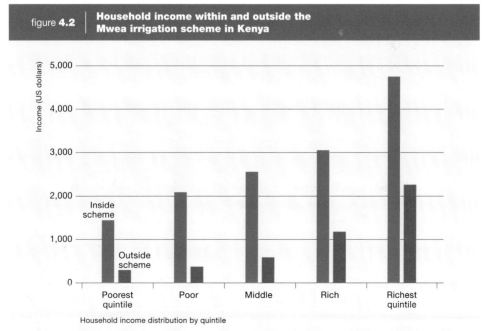

figure **4.2** | **Household income within and outside the Mwea irrigation scheme in Kenya**

Household income distribution by quintile

Source: Nguyo, Kaunga, and Bezuneh 2002.

(Bebbington 1999; IDS 1999). Men and women, because of their different access to assets, will have different capacities to withstand or escape poverty.

Along with land, water is generally the most important natural asset for poor people. Improving access to water and productivity in its use can contribute to other improvements in financial, human, physical, and social capital, simultaneously alleviating multiple dimensions of poverty. Productive but sustainable patterns of water use may also contribute to the conservation of water resources and other aspects of natural capital. Poverty and environmental degradation are closely linked (see chapter 6 on ecosystems). A degraded environment provides fewer development opportunities, less water security, greater health risks, and increased exposure to landslides, droughts, and soil erosion (PEP 2002). Hence, any assessment of how improvements in agricultural water management can affect poverty must consider impacts on these varied dimensions of poverty and their interactions. It must also consider whether changes are in absolute or relative terms and long lasting or transient and consider their distributional incidence in terms of gender and social groups.

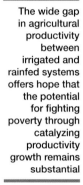

The wide gap in agricultural productivity between irrigated and rainfed systems offers hope that the potential for fighting poverty through catalyzing productivity growth remains substantial

Agricultural water management and its transmission pathways affecting poverty

This section looks at how the effects of investment in agricultural water management on poverty are transmitted through interrelated pathways (table 4.1). The poverty reduction impact can be direct or indirect, negative or positive, depending on the nature of these pathways (Hussain 2005). The net welfare effects of investments in agricultural water management depend individually and synergistically on investments in related agricultural science and technology, rural infrastructure, basic health and education, conducive policies and institutions, provision of public goods, quality of governance (such as the prevailing social power relations), gender roles, degree of participation of the poor in decisionmaking, and the natural resources endowment and climate (Dixon and Gulliver 2001).

Production and productivity. Improved agricultural water management boosts total farm output. Increased output may arise from improved yields, reduced crop loss, improved cropping intensity, and increased cultivated area. Reliable access to water enhances the use of complementary inputs such as high-yielding varieties and agrochemicals, which also increases output levels (Smith 2004; Bhattarai and Narayanamoorthy 2003; Hasnip and others 2001; Hussain and Hanjra 2003, 2004; Huang and others 2006). Food and Agriculture Organization (FAO 2003) data show that the major sources of growth in crop production for all developing countries during 1961–99 were yield increase (71%), area expansion (23%), and cropping intensity (6%). Empirical evidence for a sample of 40 countries shows that for each 1% improvement in crop productivity $1 a day poverty fell by about 1% and the human development index rose by 0.1% (Irz and others 2001). There seems to be a solid link between yield growth, poverty reduction, and human development.

The wide gap in agricultural productivity between irrigated and rainfed systems offers hope that the potential for fighting poverty through catalyzing productivity growth remains substantial (Hussain and others 2004). In some South and Southeast Asian countries

Reversing the flow:
agricultural water management
pathways for poverty reduction

4

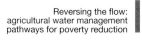

table **4.1**	**Agricultural water management and its transmission pathways for reducing or increasing poverty**		
Impact area	**Possible positive impacts**	**Possible negative impacts**	**Key target groups**
Production and productivity	Increased food production through yield improvement, area expansion, cropping intensity gains, and shift in cropping and production patterns	Higher production usually requires more water, leaving less water elsewhere (pasture land and watering points), affecting livestock and fish stock	Landowners
Employment	Increased demand for labor, higher wage earnings, reduced pressure on nonagricultural employment, less time accessing and collecting water, and more time for other productive and livelihood-enhancing activities	Loss of employment opportunities for nomadic herders, fishers, and those directly dependent on ecosystem services, and deterioration in labor relations	Landowners, landless laborers, poor urban dwellers
Consumption and food prices	Lower prices for staples and food	Downward pressure on producers' income	Rural and urban poor, landowners
Backward linkages and second-round effects	Increased use of production-intensifying inputs such as fertilizer, pesticides, improved seeds, and other agricultural services; shift to high-value crops and increased demand for crops of nonirrigated areas; increased employment in the agricultural services sector	May contribute to monoculture and to loss of local varieties and agrobiodiversity	Rural and urban poor, landowners
Nonfarm rural output and employment	Increased expenditure on nonfood products, increased demand for nonfood goods and services	Locally available wage employment may encourage child labor	Food processors, transporters, traders, construction firms, microentrepreneurs
Output and income stabilization	Reduced variance of output, employment, and income; increased spending on lifecycle events	Expensive credit, proclivity to spend on lifecycle events and indebtedness	Land owners, laborers and urban poor
Nutrition	More stable food supply, better balanced diet, with adequate intakes of micronutrients	Monocropping of cereals, may also lead to negative nutritional effects	Smallholders, urban poor
Multiple uses of agricultural water supply	Use irrigation water for drinking, sanitation, homestead gardens, trees, livestock, replenishment of aquifers, rural industry, artisanal fishing, aquaculture, and other purposes, which enhances value per drop of water	Possible use of polluted and unsafe water for drinking	Women, herders, poor farmers, fisher folk
Equity	Redistribution of public monies as broadly as possible among rural populations, and resettlement of poor people from overcrowded urban or marginal areas	Displacement of people and social disruptions, increased inequality between geographic areas, land consolidation in which poor people may lose rights to land and water	Rainfed farmers, women, urban poor
Environment and health	Intensification can ease pressure on natural resources by limiting expansion of land and water use; more income and better nutrition, leading to better health and well-being	When poorly managed can lead to land and water degradation (waterlogging and salinization), spread of waterborne diseases, pollution of surface and groundwater, propagation of aquatic weeds	Tailend irrigators, downstream water users, fisher folk

irrigated areas are more than twice as productive as nonirrigated areas, but productivity varies widely within and across systems (Hussain 2005). Variation depends on a range of factors, including policies, local conditions, system management, broader economic and political factors, and the agricultural water management regime. In India, for example, output per hectare is higher for groundwater irrigation than for both canal and tank irrigation systems (Lipton, Litchfield, and Faurès 2003). Productivity also varies widely in aquaculture and livestock systems.

Wood, You, and Zhang (2004), in their analysis of the spatial patterns of crop yields in Latin American and Caribbean countries, found that agricultural research and development in recent decades has been biased toward generating technologies for use in areas with better access to reliable water supplies or irrigated areas. Consider rice. About 90% of the estimated 275 new varieties released in Latin American countries over the past three decades were targeted to irrigated and rainfed wetlands. Average yields in irrigated regions rose from 2.8 metric tons per hectare in the mid 1960s to 4.4 metric tons per hectare in the mid-1990s, while average yields in rainfed regions have changed little over four decades (table 4.2).

table **4.2**	**Rice production in irrigated and rainfed areas in Latin American countries**				
Farming system	**Variety**	**1967**	**1981**	**1989**	**1995**
Irrigated					
Area	Modern	—	1,546.5	2,801.4	3,340.3
(thousands of hectares)	Traditional	1,573.1	924.4	446.8	462.4
Production	Modern	—	6,281.5	1,2490.7	1,5201.9
(thousands of metric tons)	Traditional	4,436.2	3,285.3	1,727.8	1,693.0
Yield	Modern	—	4.1	4.5	4.6
(metric tons per hectare)	Traditional	2.8	3.6	3.9	3.7
Rainfed					
Area	Modern	—	499.0	580.3	675.3
(thousands of hectares)	Traditional	4,258.1	5,285.9	3,847.1	2,373.2
Production	Modern	—	556.9	1,287.0	1,509.4
(thousands of metric tons)	Tradtional	5,945.2	5,607.3	4,323.4	2,680.8
Yield	Modern	—	1.1	2.2	2.2
(metric tons per hectare)	Traditional	1.4	1.1	1.1	1.1
Total					
Area (thousands of hectares)		5,831.2	8,255.9	7,675.7	6,851.2
Production (thousands of metric tons)		10,381.7	15,727.4	19,828.8	21,100.9
Yield (metric tons per hectare)		1.8	1.9	2.6	3.1

Note: Modern are semidwarf varieties.
Source: Wood, You, and Zhang 2004, p. 372.

Reversing the flow:
agricultural water management
pathways for poverty reduction

4

The Comprehensive Assessment finds that the rainfed areas of the semi-arid, arid, and subhumid tropics in developing countries have the greatest potential for productivity gains (see chapters 7 on water productivity and 8 on rainfed agriculture).

Employment. Investment in agricultural water management also affects poverty through its effects on employment by creating additional demand for labor (Damiani 2003; FAO 2000; van Imschoot 1992; Narayanamoorthy and Deshpande 2003; von Braun 1995). Water resources development and management projects require labor for construction and ongoing maintenance of canals, wells, and pumps (Hussain 2005), an important source of employment for the landless rural poor and rural households with excess labor. Increased farm output also stimulates demand for farm labor during the main cropping season and the dry cropping seasons made possible by improved water management, increasing both the number of workers required and the length of employment (Chambers 1988). For example, annual labor use per hectare in the Ganges-Kobadak irrigation system of Bangladesh is about 100 days more than that in nearby nonirrigated areas (Hussain 2005). The same holds for other settings (figure 4.3).

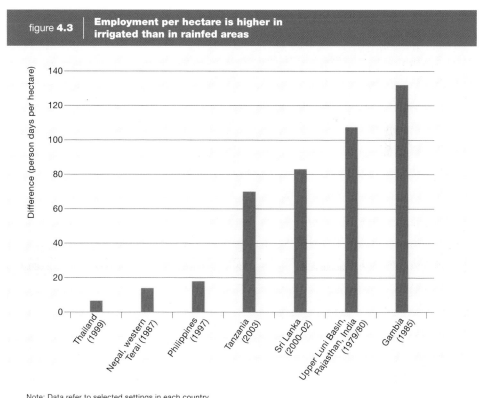

figure **4.3** | **Employment per hectare is higher in irrigated than in rainfed areas**

Note: Data refer to selected settings in each country.
Source: Hussain and Hanjra 2003, 2004 for Thailand, Philippines, Sri Lanka, and India; Thapa, Otsuka, and Barker 1992 for Nepal; Mwakalila 2006 for Tanzania; von Braun, Puetz, and Webb 1989 for Gambia.

The effects may extend to urban areas if water resources development and management projects reduce migration and so relieve the downward pressure on urban wages and the upward pressure on prices of housing and other urban infrastructure (Smith 2004). For landless laborers increased cropping intensity and cultivated area have the greatest impact on employment. In southern Palawan, in the Philippines, irrigation increased labor use on lowland farms, raising demand for local labor from 18 days per hectare in 1995 to 54 days per hectare in 2002 (Shively and Pagiola 2004).

The employment impact of irrigation may extend beyond command areas. For example, landless workers in the Terai in Nepal and Bihar State in India migrate long distances to take advantage of seasonal employment opportunities in intensively irrigated systems in the Indian states of Haryana and Punjab. Among upland households in southern Palawan 68% had at least one household member working on a lowland irrigated farm in 2002, and a substantial number of upland households consider wage employment on lowland farms as a viable alternative to upland cultivation (Shively 2006). However, irrigation benefits may approach a zero-sum game over the long run without structural change in the economy because areas with intensive irrigation development act as magnets that attract poverty from their surroundings (Shah and Singh 2004).

Consumption and food prices. Improved agricultural water management boosts food output and lowers staple food prices, making food available and affordable to the poor—nearly all consumers benefit (Datt and Ravallion 1998). Falling food prices put downward pressure on producers' income, but the losses are more than offset by gains in productivity, leaving all better off in irrigated areas. Those whose productivity does not rise, such as farmers in marginal rainfed areas, may suffer a loss of income. Reaching these poor households poses the largest challenge to poverty reduction efforts (Evenson and Gollin 2003). A major share of the consumption benefits that accrue to the poor do so indirectly through linkages and in the long run. Studies show that for every $1 in new farm income earned in Sub-Saharan Africa, at least one additional dollar could be realized from second-round effects. The estimates show that adding $1 of new farm income should boost total household income (including the original $1 stimulus) to $2.57 in Zambia, $2.48 in the Central Groundnut Basin of Senegal, $2.28 in Burkina Faso, and $1.96 in Niger. These estimates depend critically on the selections of a region's catchment area (local, regional, national) and the classification of commodities in terms of their tradability. Consumption linkages dominate; the share of growth linkages attributable to consumption linkages alone was 98% in Zambia, 93% in Burkina Faso, 79% in Niger, and 42% in Senegal (Delgado and others 1994, 1998).

Backward linkages and second-round effects. Access to agricultural water has second-round effects on poverty through output, employment, and prices. Access to reliable agricultural water encourages farmers and fishers to increase their use of inputs, fertilizers, pesticides, improved seeds, and other agricultural inputs and services (World Bank 2005). Modern inputs like fertilizers are highly complementary to water, and hence the demand for these inputs is influenced by the availability of water. Access to reliable water also enables farmers to switch from staples to higher value market-oriented products and to

> Improved agricultural water management boosts food output and lowers staple food prices, making food available and affordable to the poor

Reversing the flow:
agricultural water management
pathways for poverty reduction

4

practice more integrated approaches, including incorporation of livestock and fisheries. For such developments to play an even greater role in poverty reduction, farmers need to be able to manage market risks associated with price fluctuations. The switch in crops may also create or expand demand for crops of rainfed areas, leading to poverty reduction in these areas (Lipton and Longhurst 1989).

Nonfarm rural output and employment. As farm output and incomes rise and food prices fall, enriched farmers and workers will increase their expenditure on nonfood products, boosting demand and increasing employment opportunities in nonfarm income-generating activities. These may include transportation, construction, secondary processing of animal products, food preparation, and trading (World Bank 2005). However, such effects are likely to be less effective under certain conditions. One is when income and land distribution are highly skewed and the consumption patterns of the better-off are oriented to imports and capital-intensive goods and services rather than to the output of rural nonfarm suppliers. Another is when the poor face barriers to entry in nonfarm employment and microenterprises because of ethnicity or caste, gender, skill and education levels, access to information, mobility, transaction costs, and risks. A third is when diversification requires investment in specific assets for which the poor lack the necessary resources without access to well functioning credit and insurance markets (Reardon and others 2000).

Lower benefits to the poor through these pathways are plausible, since poor people are often badly positioned, locationally and otherwise, to benefit directly from nonfarm jobs. The literature points to a close association between nonfarm sector diversification and poverty reduction, but the causal links between the two are difficult to establish (Ellis 2000). Studies in Viet Nam (van de Walle and Cratty 2004) show that the determinants of participation in nonfarm markets and escape from poverty are not the same, though having irrigated land and education are common shared determinants.

> Reliable access to agricultural water not only raises crop output levels, but also usually reduces variance in output across seasons and years

Output and income stabilization. Access to agricultural water reduces poverty and vulnerability by lowering the variance of output, employment, and income. Two factors contribute to output fluctuations: rainfall variability and the relative prices of outputs. Food grain output is sensitive to variations in rainfall (Smith 2004; Lipton, Litchfield, and Faurès 2003). Reliable access to agricultural water not only raises crop output levels, but also usually reduces variance in output across seasons and years. For instance, the entropy index of rice yield dispersion in irrigated areas in Brazil fell from 5.3 in 1975 to 2.7 in 1995, while in rainfed areas it rose from 8.0 to 13.7. Moreover, the mean difference in yield between irrigated and rainfed areas also widened (Wood, You, and Zhang 2004). But stabilization of farm output cannot be achieved merely through a reliable system of agricultural water management. Reducing risk and increasing predictability for farmers requires improving the general environment for farming (Smith 2004).

Nutrition. Access to agricultural water may have positive impacts on nutritional outcomes through diversification of crops and greater stability and availability of food supplies (Lipton 2001) and domestic water, thus ensuring a better balanced diet with adequate intakes of micronutrients. A comparison of food security for households inside and outside the Mwea irrigation scheme in Kenya revealed that food insecurity was much lower inside the scheme (13% of households) than outside (33%; Nguyo, Kaunga and Bezuneh 2002). A study of rice irrigation projects in The Gambia (involving pump irrigation and drainage intervention) concluded that the projects increased real income by 13% (von Braun, Puetz, and Webb 1989). It found that a 10% increase in income leads to a 9.4% increase in food expenditure and a 4.8% increase in calorie consumption and that a 10% increase in calorie availability per capita leads to a 2.4% increase in the weight-for-age index, a robust indicator of nutritional status and poverty. The nutritional impact of the adoption of microirrigation technologies is particularly notable. Following the adoption of bucket kits, poor farm families in India and Nepal, especially female farmers, were able to improve their vegetable and fruit intake (Namara, Upadhyay, and Nagar 2005; Upadhyay, Samad, and Giordano 2004). Changes in agricultural water management may adversely affect the nutrition intake of the poor, however, when they lead to monocropping of cereals at the expense of pulses, oilseeds, and coarse grains. For instance, the rapid expansion in the area of boro rice and wheat facilitated by an expansion of irrigation infrastructure in Bangladesh was achieved partly through reduction in the area planted in pulses and oilseeds. These two crops are important sources of protein and micronutrients, particularly for the poor (Hossain, Naher, and Shahabuddin 2005).

Multiple uses of agricultural water supply. Poor rural households may use agricultural or domestic water in multiple ways. Agricultural water may be used for drinking, sanitation, homestead gardens, trees (outside formal irrigation system command areas), livestock, replenishment of aquifers, urban water supply, rural industries, artisanal fishing, and aquaculture. Examples of such multiple uses are abundant (Nguyen-Khoa, Smith, and Lorenzen 2005; Laamrani and others 2000; Moriarty, Butterworth, and van Koppen 2004; Jehangir, Mudasser, and Ali 2000) and are spreading rapidly (Alberts and van der Zee 2004). The benefits may be especially critical for women (for domestic and income-generating purposes) and for other vulnerable groups (who may depend on fishing or brick-making, for example). Thus when irrigation is seen as a low-value water use compared with alternatives, this range of uses and associated benefits may be neglected (Bhatia 1997; Meinzen-Dick 1997; Yoder 1983). Evidence from the Lower Mekong River, Lake Chad Basin, Amazon River, Lao PDR, and Sri Lanka shows how inland fisheries provide 10%–30% of incomes for farmers. A study in South Africa found that the income from productive uses of domestic water represents about 17% of average household income in villages with very limited domestic water provision compared with 31% in comparable villages with adequate domestic water provision (Perez de Mendiguren Castresana 2004).

Equity. Targeted investments in agricultural water management can be an effective way to reduce societal inequity when used to provide opportunities for the rural poor. For example, large public irrigation systems have been built to stimulate economic development in poor regions. Programs to support water harvesting and treadle pumps have

> Targeted investments in agricultural water management can be an effective way to reduce societal inequity when used to provide opportunities for the rural poor

Reversing the flow:
agricultural water management
pathways for poverty reduction

4

been introduced to reach the disadvantaged. But investments can increase inequity if the rich and powerful capture the benefits or if poor people are displaced (Cernea 2003). The equity impacts of agricultural water management projects vary with time, in both the nature and number of beneficiaries and the nature and extent of the benefits (Smith 2004). Tailend farmers, often the poorest, suffer a twin disadvantage—less water and more uncertainty (figure 4.4).

As agricultural water management spreads, inequality tends to fall. The full equity impacts can be assessed only after a significant time lag, and policies to facilitate adoption by the poorest may be merited (Kerr and Kolavalli 1999). Studies in China show that income from crops grown on irrigated land has the highest marginal effect on lowering inequality (Huang and others 2005). A 1% increase in income from crops grown on irrigated land for all households would decrease the Gini coefficient for total income inequality by 0.1%. Inequality is attenuated by the presence of irrigation (figure 4.5).

Factors that improve equity in agricultural water management include equitable land distribution, with secure ownership or tenancy rights; efficient input, credit, and product markets; access to information; and nondiscriminatory policies for smallholder producers and landless laborers (Hussain 2005; Smith 2004). These conditions are rarely met.

figure **4.4** | **Poverty is higher among tailend farmers**

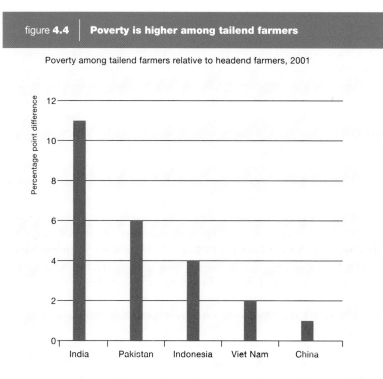

Poverty among tailend farmers relative to headend farmers, 2001

Note: Data refer to selected sites in each country.
Source: Hussain 2005.

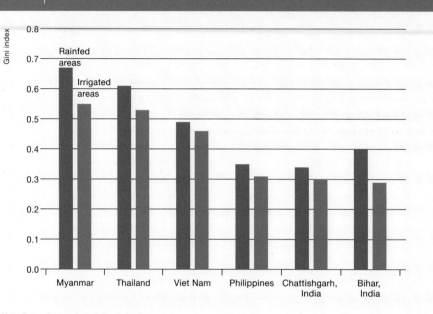

figure **4.5** | **Inequality is lower in irrigated than in rainfed areas**

Note: Data refer to selected sites in each country.
Source: Hussain and Hanjra 2003.

Absolute poverty for some may worsen if investments in agricultural water reinforce processes of land consolidation in which poor households lose rights to land and water or if investments are associated with displacement of labor by mechanization or herbicide use. Poor people may be displaced by the construction of reservoirs and canals, or their livelihoods may be adversely affected by upstream or downstream impacts (Hasnip and others 2001). Larger and relatively resource-rich water infrastructure users will benefit most, even if poor people usually still benefit in absolute terms.

Rising prosperity in irrigated areas has turned the spotlight on the plight of poor people in rainfed areas. Investment in agricultural water management will inevitably be better suited to some regions than to others, and hence geographic inequity may be unavoidable. Moreover, depression of output prices following the introduction of irrigation may reduce the income of poor rainfed farmers, when their productivity does not rise. Women typically have less access to productive resources such as land, water, credit, training, fertilizer, and marketing channels (Agarwal 1994). Women's traditional tasks such as livestock keeping, secondary processing of products, and weeding and transplanting increase with more reliable water, whereas plowing and land preparation, traditionally male tasks, may not. Thus training, credit, input delivery programs, and water delivery schedules that account for gender differentiation of labor, methods of production, and resource access within households can harness opportunities to reduce poverty by facilitating women's activities.

Reversing the flow:
agricultural water management
pathways for poverty reduction

4

Environment and health. Investments in agricultural water management have both negative and positive impacts on environment and health. Higher income due to better agricultural water management can enhance farmers' abilities to invest in land improvements that enhance sustainability (see chapter 15 on land; Morrison and Pearce 2000; Shively 1999). Investments in agricultural water management, by reducing pressure on surrounding marginal areas, can help to avoid deforestation, land degradation, and loss of biodiversity (Shively 2006; Shively and Pagiola 2004). The population absorption capacity of an irrigation-led strategy may be greater, and pressure on natural resources less severe, than for alternatives (Carruthers 1996). Agricultural water management improves health status through better nutrition, availability of drinking water, and increased spending to combat diseases like malaria.

The negative environmental impacts of water use in agriculture are extensively documented (see chapter 6 on ecosystems; Urama and Hodge 2004; Dougherty and Hall 1995; Goldsmith and Hildyard 1992; Petermann 1996). Most commonly cited are the upstream and downstream impacts of water diversions (Gichuki 2004), waterlogging and salinization within irrigation command areas (Khan and others 2006), and increased agrochemical usage and pollution and eutrophication of water bodies (Hendry and others 2006). Badly designed or managed irrigation can harm public health and human capital through the spread of waterborne diseases, usually with a greater effect on the poor (Ersado 2005). Negative social and environmental consequences often hurt the poor more than the nonpoor because the poor lack political power and the financial resources to avoid the potentially adverse impacts of irrigation, from physical displacements to health risks and land degradation (Hussain 2005).

A net welfare impact assessment of investments in agricultural water management that takes into consideration the total benefits (including the multiplier effects) and the total corresponding costs (including social, environmental, and health costs) has yet to be conducted (see chapter 9 on irrigation). What we can present here, however, are the direction and magnitude of the poverty impacts of potential agricultural water management interventions that are discussed throughout the book, differentiated by impact pathways (table 4.3).

The nature and magnitude of the poverty alleviation impacts of agricultural water management interventions change over time and with economic development (as illustrated in table 4.3). The marginal impact of agricultural water management on poverty reduction is strongest at the initial stage and then declines as economies grow. For example, the correlation coefficient between irrigation and poverty across 14 Indian states halved from 1973–74 (–0.63) to 1993–94 (–0.30) (Bhattarai and Narayanmoorthy 2003). Moreover, the relative significance of the poverty reduction pathways changes with time. The employment impact pathway is strong at the initial stage, whereas the effect of the productivity pathway is greater toward the later stage.

Using comprehensive datasets from 80 agroclimate subzones of India for 1984–85 and 1994–95, Saleth and others (2003) provide evidence for the declining impact of irrigation over time and for a change in the relative significance of its employment and productivity effects. The analysis shows that since the initial influences of irrigation were

> The marginal impact of agricultural water management on poverty reduction is strongest at the initial stage and then declines as economies grow

table **4.3**	Strength of poverty impacts of agricultural water management and related interventions by pathways			
Potential agricultural water management interventions	Production/ productivity	Employment	Consumption and price	Backward linkages and second-round output effects
1. New systems				
Large-scale public surface irrigation	High	Medium	High	High
Diffuse forms of irrigation: communal or private operated systems, groundwater, and so on	High	High	Medium	Medium
Fisheries and aquaculture	Medium	High	Low	Low
Multiple use systems: production plus, domestic plus	Low	Medium	Low	Low
Integrating livestock	Medium	Medium	Medium	Low
2. Maintaining ecosystem resilience	Low	Low	Low	Low
3. Improving existing systems				
Improving agricultural water productivity	Medium	Medium	Medium	High
Reversing land degradation	Medium	Low	Medium	Medium
Management of marginal-quality water resources	Low	Low	Low	Low
4. Rainwater management	Medium	Medium	Medium	Medium
5. Water policies and institutions	Medium	Low	Low	Low

a. Mixed positive and negative impacts.

(continues on facing page)

mostly in terms of expanded cultivation, intensive land use, and crop pattern changes, its poverty alleviation impact came largely through the employment pathway. But when the limits for these influences were reached, the poverty reduction contribution of irrigation through the employment pathway declined much faster than the increase in its contribution through the productivity pathway.

At a lower spatial scale an analysis of 256 districts in India shows that districts with above average stock of rural infrastructure have higher values of agricultural output than districts with below average levels of infrastructure, including irrigation, fertilizer, literacy, school, rural roads, and rural electrification (Narayanamoorthy and Hanjra 2006). The impact of infrastructure variables on the value of output turns out to be stronger when they are used as lagged variables in the regression analysis. In particular, the impact of irrigation infrastructure on the value of agricultural output appears to have increased over time.

Irrigation creates winners and losers. Often the gains are far larger than the losses. But who gains and who loses? Studies rarely capture the distributional impacts of irrigation across human and social scales. An exceptionally rare study by Gidwani (2002) shows that the effects of irrigation are ambiguous, both in shaping people's perceptions of well-being and in transforming the material landscape. It uses Sen's (1999) paradigm of "development as freedom" and disaggregates these impacts into a broad set of "functionings," or freedoms to achieve lives that the villagers value. It shows that both laborers (mostly members of the

Reversing the flow:
agricultural water management
pathways for poverty reduction

4

Nonfarm rural output and employment impacts	Income stabilization	Nutritional impacts	Multiple use	Socioeconomic effects	Environmental and health impacts
High	Medium	Medium	High	Mixed[a]	Mixed[a]
Medium	High	Medium	High	Mixed[a]	Mixed[a]
High	High	High	High	Medium	High
Low	Low	High	High	High	Medium
High	High	High	High	Medium	Mixed[a]
Medium	Low	Medium	High	Low	High
Medium	High	Medium	Low	Mixed[a]	Mixed[a]
Medium	High	Medium	Low	Low	High
Low	Medium	Mixed[a]	Low	Mixed[a]	Mixed[a]
Medium	High	Medium		High	Medium
Low	Medium	Low		High	Medium

lower castes) and employers (mostly members of the landowning and the trading castes) are better off as a result of canal irrigation. In particular, the well-being of laborers has improved or is generally rising on all counts, except their control over cultivable land. Laborers have experienced improvements in their employment conditions and social status or caste dominance, while employers' control over laborers has permanently diminished as has their caste dominance.

Generally, declining control over land by the laborers stems from expensive credit, lower mobility into nonfarm jobs, and a tendency to resort to land mortgages to raise money for marriages and other lifecycle events. Although irrigation seems to have created conditions for land transfers from weaker to richer population segments, it is far less clear that irrigation is the underlying cause of land mortgage transfers. The impact of irrigation intervention on the freedom of villagers is by no means unequivocal: there are often commonalities as well as divergences—laborers say that their employment and living conditions have improved, while employers complain about deterioration in labor relations; laborers are losing control over land, while employers are gaining control. There is nevertheless virtual unanimity among the residents of the irrigation project that despite various unanticipated negative effects, irrigation development has been a positive intervention: all have benefited, albeit disproportionately, depending on their initial entitlements.

The antipoverty impacts through agricultural water management pathways are conditioned by multiple socioeconomic and agroecological factors, shaping welfare and equity outcomes and impacts across spatial, temporal, and human scales. The main implications of this message are:

- In closed basins—where all water is already allocated and where the pathway for further poverty reduction through new investment initiatives is increasingly limited—improving the management of existing systems is the preferred strategy (see chapters 7 on water productivity and 16 on river basins). This is particularly the case for many countries in Asia, the Middle East, and North Africa.
- Where there is economic water scarcity—where exploitable water supplies are available in nature, but people have difficulty accessing them—investment in new agricultural water management (both small-scale irrigation to upgrade rainfed systems and larger scale irrigation) is recommended, but care must be taken to avoid the social and environmental ills of the past. Considerations for terrestrial and aquatic ecosystems; integration of fisheries, aquaculture, and livestock; and application of the multiple-use systems concepts (Van Koppen, Moriarty, and Boelee 2006) in the initial agricultural water management planning process would increase value per drop of water and ensure ecosystem resilience.

> In most food-producing areas of the world historical sources of growth in productivity are being rapidly exhausted and investments are urgently needed to buffer adverse effects and protect food and livelihood security.

Challenges and pressures

This section examines some of the challenges and pressures associated with improving agriculture and enhancing food production. The dramatic increase in world food production over the past half century has come from increased crop yields (see chapter 2 on trends). But in most food-producing areas of the world (Brazil, China, India, Iran, Pakistan, Western Europe) the historical sources of growth in productivity are being rapidly exhausted (Brown 2005; see chapter 7 on water productivity), and a significant share of irrigated land is now jeopardized by scarce river water, groundwater depletion, a fertility-sapping buildup of salts in the soil, or some combination of these factors (Postel 2003). Investments are urgently needed to buffer these adverse effects and protect food and livelihood security. In some areas land expansion is limited, and in closed basins water resources have been exhausted. In other areas, particularly in Sub-Saharan Africa, productive potential remains. In areas where the productive potential has been achieved, other opportunities, such as shifting to higher value produce, diversifying income sources, or even exiting from agriculture, must be sought.

Increasing the productivity of smallholder agriculture to reduce hunger and poverty

For smallholders to participate effectively in markets and to generate significant on-farm income, solving the water constraint is a necessary but insufficient condition. Raising productivity will require investments in transportation, communication, extension services, credit, capacity building, and education. New approaches to support information flows between farmers and markets are needed to encourage agricultural innovation.

Reversing the flow:
agricultural water management
pathways for poverty reduction | **4**

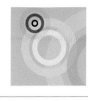

Government budgets do not prioritize these issues, as they are often externally financed and not sustainable in the long run. Partnerships between governments, private sector or NGO service providers, civil society organizations, and community-based groups are crucial to help farmers make the transition. A related challenge is to set up targeted safety nets for farmers who are unable to adjust quickly enough as the transformation of agriculture to market-oriented production accelerates over the coming decades. Safety nets that can provide credible insurance against catastrophic asset loss and facilitate rapid recovery will be crucial, given the expected impacts of climate change.

Strengthening water governance

Recognizing that the root cause of many water problems related to poverty is poor water governance, there has been a wide call for reform (see chapter 5 on policies and institutions). Common elements in such reform initiatives are decentralized decisionmaking, often involving institutionalization of user participation, assignment of private property or extensive use rights to water, and greater reliance on market mechanisms to ensure the most cost-effective allocation and management of scarce water resources.

Ensuring rural poor people's right to secure access to water represents a key challenge to water governance reform. Currently, access to water, particularly for agriculture, tends to be based on informal or customary rights associated with ownership of land containing water springs or flows or based on social norms or relations with owners of land or local water committee members. If such forms of access are not recognized and accommodated in reforms of water governance, the rural poor stand to lose their access to water for agriculture (Bauer 1997; Pradhan and others 1997). Women in particular confront severe problems in accessing water. Because access often depends on land ownership, gender inequalities and discrimination in access to land and in livelihood opportunities in general often reproduce gender inequalities in water.

A second challenge related to water governance is to ensure poor rural men and women a voice in decisionmaking on the development, allocation, and management of water resources. In many places the response to this challenge has been to create water user boards that aim to represent all relevant stakeholders. However, experience has been disappointing. Stakeholder participation in the formulation and renegotiation of water policy, legal, and regulatory frameworks has been limited. The ways social and economic relations shape access to and management of water and their effects on interactions among stakeholder representatives are rarely clearly recognized and addressed. In this situation and within limited and often unclear mandates, water user boards tend to reproduce existing power inequities among stakeholders and thus have come to legitimize rather than challenge and contest these relations (Ravnborg forthcoming; Webster, Merrey, and de Lange 2003).

Strengthening the voices of the poor in decisions affecting their well-being

A prerequisite for strengthening water governance is to increase awareness of "water poverty" as a core component of poverty and to ensure that the rights of the poor are properly addressed. Smallholder farmers, particularly women, have been unable to voice their

> Ensuring rural poor people's right to secure access to water represents a key challenge to water governance reform

economic interests in political forums (figure 4.6). The same is true for a large number of fishing and herding communities.

There are a large number of stakeholders in government agencies and the private sector with a keen interest in water allocation (including river flow management). As water becomes scarcer, the conflict over water allocation, rights, and entitlements at household, watershed, and basin levels is bound to intensify. One way to tackle this is to craft and support institutions and processes that have the ability to speak upward from the village level to higher levels, and to make the voices of the poor heard, as illustrated in box 4.1.

Having the right to voice opinions is not the same as having the power to set the agenda. Today, there are two mechanisms that allow for addressing water development in the context of poverty reduction: Poverty Reduction Strategy Papers (PRSPs) and integrated water resources management. However, achievements to date do not match their potential.

In the case of the PRSP processes prioritization of scarce financial resources often goes to more tangible sectors such as education and health and not to more contested sectors such as water resources, which often involve many stakeholders. As a result, water management actions are poorly represented in PRSPs (PEP 2002).

This challenge can be addressed through a three-pronged approach: first, recognize and protect the rights of the poor; second, prepare a transparent national water sector strategy with poor male and female farmers as a priority; and third, integrate the water strategy

> Smallholder farmers, particularly women, have been unable to voice their economic interests in political forums

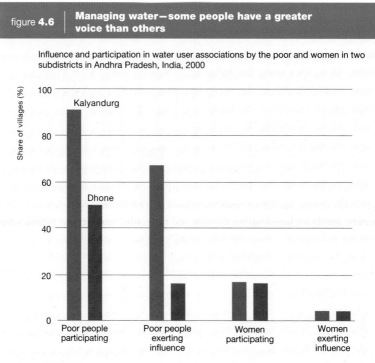

figure **4.6** | **Managing water—some people have a greater voice than others**

Influence and participation in water user associations by the poor and women in two subdistricts in Andhra Pradesh, India, 2000

Share of villages (%)

Kalyandurg

Dhone

Poor people participating | Poor people exerting influence | Women participating | Women exerting influence

Source: UNDP 2006.

Reversing the flow:
agricultural water management
pathways for poverty reduction

4

box **4.1**

Improving livelihoods through better water management and institution building

Cotahuasi is 2,600 meters above sea level in the Peruvian Andes. It is isolated and populated largely by indigenous people who suffer from poverty, illiteracy, and little access to basic social services. The area is recovering from years of terror and violence inflicted by the Shining Path guerrilla movement.

The NGO AEDES started working there in 1996 to implement the development program Local Agenda 21. Sustainable water management was identified as key to developing the area, which is in the Ocoña watershed. AEDES focused on improving incomes by capitalizing on people's knowledge of organic production and pest management. They revived and strengthened irrigator committees, improving irrigation techniques. Farmers' incomes have improved as AEDES located national and international markets for a niche crop, amaranth.

AEDES also began to facilitate roundtables, bringing together representatives of different government agencies, community groups, and the private sector to discuss a water management plan. In 2005 the watershed was declared a protected area, and plans call for development of ecotourism. AEDES has also developed a geographic information system–based database that facilitates development of a zoning plan and provides information to support local negotiation on the use of land and water. The database provides the roundtables with valuable input for their planning exercises and allows them to develop proposals that are acceptable to regional and even national decisionmakers. With the experience gained in Cotahuasi, AEDES is planning to scale up its activities to the other subbasins in the Ocoña watershed.

Source: Both ENDS and Gomukh 2005.

into national poverty reduction programs such as PRSPs (UNDP 2006). Over the past two years the World Bank (forthcoming) has assisted countries in Africa (Ethiopia, Tanzania), Latin America (Brazil, Honduras, Peru), Asia (China, India, Pakistan, the Philippines), and elsewhere (Azerbaijan, Iraq) to prepare such country water assistance strategies.

The ongoing debate on whether integrated water resources management contributes to poverty reduction or worsens poverty has not yet been resolved. Some argue that it can facilitate management of water resources and water services in ways that will help reduce poverty. Others strongly contest this claim (see chapters 5 on policy and institutions and 16 on river basins). In Africa, for example, the regulatory administrative water rights and registration systems introduced under the banner of the integrated water resources management agenda are biased against the poor and risk further eroding their limited water rights (Van Koppen and others 2004; Mumma 2005).

This water development agenda can fit the needs of the poor, unlike former interpretations of integrated water resources management as a blanket water agenda for everybody, including the poor. It offers an opportunity to reduce poverty by recognizing multiple-use systems approaches as appropriate in poor areas with backlogs in infrastructure development (GWP 2004). This recognition widens the interpretation of integrated water resources management in at least three aspects. It clearly includes water development. It acknowledges that water can be used for poverty alleviation and gender equity only if poor women and men get more and better access to water for both domestic and productive uses. And it recognizes that even if it becomes more expensive to develop water resources because the easier resources have already been developed, this should not stifle efforts to develop new water resources to provide for the basic domestic and productive water needs of all.

Improving gender equality and recognizing changes in demography and livelihoods

In many cases water resource policies have proven detrimental to women's water rights and to the sustainable management and use of water resources

In many cases water resource policies and programs have proven detrimental to women's land and water rights and, therefore, to their sustainable management and use (photo 4.1). Interventions such as irrigation habitually exacerbate rather than redress the existing imbalance between men and women's ownership rights, division of labor, and incomes (Ahlers 2000; Boelens and Zwarteveen 2002; Chancellor 2000). Where women constitute a significant proportion—if not the majority—of farm decisionmakers, as in large parts of Southern and Eastern Africa and elsewhere, strengthening women's land and water rights and gender-sensitive targeting of credit and input provision, training, and market linkages are central to increasing agricultural productivity (Quisumbing 1996; Van Koppen 2002). Efforts to increase water productivity, whether through new microirrigation technologies or community management of multifunctional irrigation structures, need to be well targeted to women farmers.

Water policies and agricultural water management activities also need to take into account the impact of the HIV/AIDS pandemic and its disproportionate effects on women and girls. In Sub-Saharan Africa, the epicenter of the HIV/AIDS pandemic, households with sick members need more water, while the loss of agricultural labor and the shift to low-input crops and activities that demand less labor all affect local water management.

Photo 4.1 Woman transporting water in gourds

Photo by Olufunke Cofie

Reversing the flow:
agricultural water management
pathways for poverty reduction

4

Improved agricultural water management and gender equality can create greater resilience among poor vulnerable households to withstand the poverty impacts of HIV/AIDS and other diseases. The financial burden of HIV/AIDS means that innovative cost-recovery measures are needed. Measures also need to take into account the loss of skilled people in the water sector (Ashton and Ramasar 2002). Inheritance rights to land and water need to be protected, especially where orphans and girls are ineligible to hold land or water rights and where water rights are customary rather than formal (Aliber and Walker 2006).

Ending terrestrial and aquatic ecosystem degradation

Ecosystems provide a range of benefits to humanity, including food, timber, fuel, fibers, climate regulation, erosion control, and regulation of water flows and quality (see chapter 6 on ecosystems). Unsustainable land and water management decreases the capacity of ecosystems to provide these services and hits the poor the hardest, as a large proportion of poor people depend on wetlands and other common property resources for their livelihoods—the land and water sources that have been among the most degraded. Further loss of these valuable ecosystems will result in less water security and increased poverty. The capacity of ecosystems to generate ecosystem services has diminished in response to management of water for agriculture and the extension of agriculture into marginal and fragile lands. While water may be a limiting factor for agriculture, more serious will be the degradation of ecosystems that provide and regulate water, which will lead to decreasing natural water supply and quality.

> Poverty reduction programs that are formulated without due regard to ecosystem resilience will not achieve sustainable poverty alleviation objectives

Aquatic ecosystems—and inland fisheries that rely on the sustainability of these ecosystems—are facing unprecedented threats, including physical encroachment and loss, pollution, and overharvesting of resources. By far the most important threat comes from the changes in land and water management, which can alter the hydrological dynamics that have driven the patterns of seasonal and interannual production in these ecosystems over millennia (see chapter 12 on inland fisheries). There are many examples of rivers in developing countries where water flow has already been altered significantly by dams and irrigation schemes and where the associated riverine floodplains and other wetlands have been degraded. Hence, poverty reduction programs that are formulated without due regard to ecosystem resilience will not achieve sustainable poverty alleviation objectives.

Reducing the vulnerability of poor people to climate shocks and other hazards

The last decade has seen a dramatic increase in the number and intensity of water-related disasters and other hazards. Globally, between 1991 and 2000 more than 665,000 people died in 2,557 natural disasters, 90% of them from water-related events such as floods, typhoons, and hurricanes (UN–Water 2005, p. 12). Most victims were in developing countries. Such disasters and the vulnerability they inflict can undermine any effort to break out of poverty and can even cast more people into poverty when the basis of their livelihoods is destroyed by a cataclysm.

Climate change has both short- and long-term effects. Short-term climate variability and its extremes influence the range and frequency of shocks that society absorbs or adjusts to, whereas longer term variability can lead to changes in the productive base of society, particularly in economies dependent on natural resources (Parry and others 1999).

The impacts of climate change penetrate all aspects of the environment, society, and economy so that other global trends influencing development reinforce the adverse effects of climate change to inflict greater harm on the poor. O'Brien and Leichenko (2000) note how exposure to climate change and globalization can produce a phenomenon they call "double exposure." Farmers who are already vulnerable to market fluctuations as a result of international trade will be double losers through losses in crops, livestock, or other agricultural assets from changes in weather patterns. These effects will be felt most acutely by poor farmers because they are less able to adapt to the changing context and respond to external shocks (Lambrou and Piana 2006). Analysis by Kurukulasuriya and others (2006) shows that climate change will hit agriculture hardest in Africa, a region already devastated by extreme poverty and episodes of famines. The post-disaster impact assessments in Sri Lanka show that the 2004 tsunami caused widespread destruction and contamination of coastal aquifers, destroyed open dug wells used for potable water supplies, increased groundwater salinity, and affected the long-term sustainability of the fragile agroecosystems, to the detriment mainly of poor coastal communities (Illangsekare and others 2006). The challenge is to define appropriate supportive institutional and policy frameworks that enable local adaptation and reduce risk and vulnerability at different scales (see Pannell and others 2006).

> An equitable pro-poor arrangement is to guarantee acceptable minimum quantities of water and land for all and to set rules for the few who want to claim any surplus

Reducing water poverty

The strategies for lifting most of the 800 million people who work on small farms out of poverty is necessarily multipronged. Broadly conceived it entails:

- Ensuring the right to secure access to water for the poor (securing water and developing appropriate technologies and financing options).
- Empowering people to use water better (raising water productivity).
- Improving governance of water resources.
- Supporting the diversification of livelihoods.

Such multifaceted strategies will require ensuring the right to secure access to water and a range of other complementary technologies, accompanied by dynamic policies and institutions that are responsive to the needs of the poor, as well as capacity building and support of pro-poor research. It is critical to create awareness among governments of the significance of water in the resource base and of the need to protect it not only as a strategy for sustainable economic development but as a critical measure for poverty reduction.

Ensuring the right to secure access to water for the poor

Securing water. Cremers, Ooijevaar, and Boelens (2005, p. 40) present security of access in terms of the possibility of materializing water use rights now and in the future and of avoiding or controlling the risks of unsustainable water management. To secure these rights it is important to consider the larger "bundle of rights" (water access and withdrawal rights, operational rights, decisionmaking rights) of which they are a part. Users can adopt strategies to secure rights. People often try to materialize their claims through rules, rights,

Reversing the flow:
agricultural water management
pathways for poverty reduction

4

and regulations that originate from different and sometimes divergent rights systems and that best represent their interests. But it is also essential that higher level institutions such as the national law and water administration provide policies and mechanisms that increase security of access for users and address entitlement gaps of the poor.

The rising demand for limited water resources makes sharing and prioritizing unavoidable and puts the poor at greater risk. Local norms generally guarantee that everyone has access to water for drinking. In many African countries local norms also tend to support equitable access to water for small-scale productive uses and livelihoods. Individuals who take large quantities of water and thus deprive others generally encounter community resistance (Derham, Hellum, and Sithole 2005). However, formal water legislation and priority setting under scarcity can often only weakly protect the poor. Local regulations and solutions in water management tend to be overlooked by official policies and intervention strategies. An equitable pro-poor arrangement, as practiced for example in parts of India and Sri Lanka, is to guarantee acceptable minimum quantities of water or land for all and to set rules for the few who want to claim any surplus (Van Koppen, Parthasarathy, and Safiliou 2002). Equity here refers to both the distribution of water access rights and to control over water management.

Investments or policies disrupting existing water access rules have an impact on livelihoods. For instance, informal irrigation systems, such as *dambos* in Southern Africa and *fadamas* in Nigeria, contribute to poverty reduction and food security. There are many instances in Africa where poor people have lost vital livelihood systems because government planning diverted water used in informal irrigation systems to formal water uses such as hydropower systems or medium- and large-scale irrigation systems.

An important way to increase the security of local water rights is to assign the rights to collectives rather than individuals (Boelens and Hoogendam 2002; Bruns and Meinzen-Dick 2000). Data from Chile, Ecuador, and Peru show that assigning water rights to individuals may create unstable situations, negatively affecting indigenous water rights and livelihoods (Bauer 1998; Brehm and Quiroz 1995). Communities can also compete for irrigation water, which often results in stretching the services beyond the planned capacity of the infrastructure (photo 4.2).

Although not recognized by formal legal frameworks in many places, rights to water are often claimed on the basis of land ownership. Owning land on which there is a spring, a stream, or an aquifer is a common mechanism for claiming a right to that water. Thus, where land distribution is skewed against the poor, water is also likely to be unevenly distributed. Adding to this, land with a water source tends to have a higher value than land without one, making land ownership–based rights to water even more inaccessible to the poor.

In the Nicaraguan hillsides approximately 60% of nonpoor households own land with a water source compared with about 15% of the poorest households (Ravnborg forthcoming). In Southwestern Tanzania, where land distribution within many communities was at least partially guided by social concerns to secure all households a right to land in the valley bottoms, almost 9 of 10 households have rights to traditionally irrigated (vinyungu) land, with no differences between nonpoor and the poorest households (Boesen and Ravnborg 1993).

> There are many instances in Africa where poor people have lost vital livelihood systems because government planning diverted water used in informal irrigation systems to formal water uses

Photo 4.2 Bringing water to the fields

Photo by David Molden

Access to water or water infrastructure may also be limited by access to financial resources, as is the case for most countries in Sub-Saharan Africa and South Asia (box 4.2). In South Asia's so-called poverty square, which comprises Bangladesh, eastern India, and Nepal's Terai, the gradual expansion of public and private tubewells during the 1960s and 1970s favored the elite, who had access to the necessary capital (Shah 2001; Shah and others 2000). Lack of access to capital may also limit the capacity of governments to provide the needed water infrastructure for the development of their citizens. Bilateral and multilateral investments in water infrastructure have diminished for many reasons; chief among them environmental pressure, poor performance, and lack of donor interest in agriculture (see chapter 2 on trends). Thus African countries are finding it increasingly difficult to secure funds to enable productive access to water resources for effective poverty reduction and food production.

Developing appropriate technologies and financing options. Small-scale localized water management systems are generally more suited to the needs of the poor. Examples of the successful development and marketing of such technologies are the treadle pump in Bangladesh during 1980s and the low-cost small-scale drip and sprinkler systems and water storage devices developed later.

- *Small-scale mechanized pumps.* In the 1980s the World Bank invested in a tubewell initiative in Bangladesh that made available subsidized diesel pump sets capable of irrigating 2–20 hectares. While these initiatives were successful in expanding irrigated acreage, they had a negative, or at best neutral, effect on poverty because they tilted access to irrigation toward larger, wealthier farmers. To facilitate the spread of the smaller technologies among small farmers and women, credit schemes were developed that allowed even women's groups to obtain loans and manage the pump sets for water sale (Van Koppen and Mahmud 1996).

box **4.2**	**Empowering rural women: creating local leaders**

Alivelamma, age 28 and belonging to a Scheduled caste, is a resident of Jettigundlapalli Village, Chittor District, Andra Pradesh, India. She lives with her husband, two daughters, and a son. The family had 1.4 hectares of land that they were unable to cultivate because of a lack of water. She and her husband worked as agricultural laborers. From their meager seasonal earnings, they had to meet all their expenses. Frequently, they had to go to moneylenders. Alivelamma took her daughter out of school because the cost was too high and the daughter needed to look after the youngest sibling.

In 2001 Alivelamma joined a rural microcredit group. The group's good performance helped them get a loan of 8,000 rupees (Rs). After a series of small loans, Alivelamma and two other members got a grant of Rs 60,000 for a bore well. With her share of water, she irrigates 0.6 hectare and grows tomatoes. She also sells water to nearby farmers. The increase in family income has given Alivelamma the confidence to take an additional loan to construct a new house. Her children are going to school, and the family eats better. Alivelamma buys what she needs and no longer must rely on her husband for money. She also travels outside her village to meet with government officials, whereas before she never dared to leave her village or to exercise her political rights.

Source: DHAN Foundation 2003.

Reversing the flow:
agricultural water management
pathways for poverty reduction

4

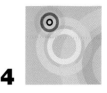

■ *Treadle pumps.* In the late 1980s International Development Enterprise implemented a program to stimulate the rural mass marketing of treadle pumps, promoting the emergence of 75 private sector manufacturers, several thousand village dealers and well drillers, and a variety of marketing and promotional activities (Heierli and Polak 2000). Over a 15-year period some 1.5 million treadle pumps were purchased and installed by small farmers at an unsubsidized fair market price, putting 300,000 hectares under irrigation at a total investment cost of $49.5 million. The cost of irrigating the same farmland with a conventional dam and canal system would have been at least $1.5 billion. This treadle pump investment is generating $150 million a year in continuing net income for poor smallholders (Polak 2005; Polak and Yoder 2006; Sauder 1992). The Food and Agriculture Organization and many other organizations are now involved in treadle pump programs in Asia and Sub-Saharan Africa (Kay and Brabben 2000). These small-scale technologies enable poor people to take a major step on the pathway out of poverty (figure 4.7).

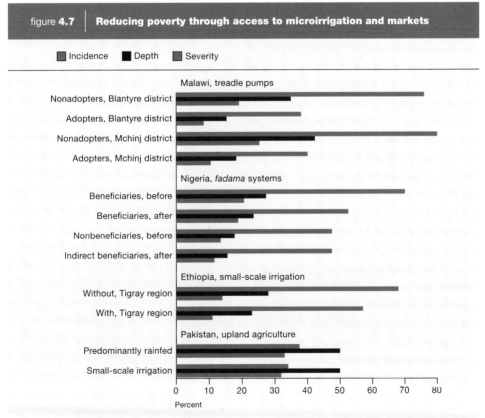

figure 4.7 | **Reducing poverty through access to microirrigation and markets**

Note: Data refer to selected sites in each country.
Source: Gichuki and Hanjra forthcoming.

- *Low-cost drip irrigation.* Low-cost drip systems have been made available to small-holder farmers through a private sector network of manufacturers, village dealers, and farmer-technicians who install a 1 acre drip system in two days for about $4. In addition to providing a reliable source of water, low-cost drip systems can improve crop quality, boost yield, and lower water use, leading to the cultivation of high-value marketable crops (Keller and others 2001).

- *Low-cost water storage.* In many semi-arid areas the bulk of annual rainfall occurs during a few monsoon months. Because irrigation water is either scarce or not available during dry months, when growing conditions are otherwise favorable and vegetable and fruit prices are at their highest, small-scale farmers are unable to compete in the market. Capturing and storing monsoon rainwater for future use are constrained by the high price of conventional water storage systems. Low-cost bagged water storage systems tailored to the needs of poor male and female farmers are particularly advantageous to poor farmers. Recent advances have lowered the costs of material, but the need for cheap on-farm water storage systems remains, particularly with the increasing variability in monsoon rainfall due to climate change (Polak and others 2004).

- *Informal irrigation systems.* Upland farming and hillside farming are most commonly equated with rainfed farming. Nevertheless, in many countries upland and hillside farmers have developed systems of informal irrigation ranging from drip irrigation constructed from water-filled plastic bottles placed to irrigate seedlings to more organizationally demanding systems of furrow irrigation in valley bottoms and along river beds to irrigate vegetables, green maize, and paddy. In most cases poor people are engaged in agricultural activities involving marginal-quality water (see chapter 11 on marginal-quality water). The use of marginal-quality water has mixed impacts on both irrigators and customers. While the use of such water can be economically attractive, the risks to the health of producers, consumers, and the environment need to be carefully managed through public policy interventions (Hussain and others 2001).

Such informal irrigation systems are rarely adequately reflected in official statistics or recognized by policymakers and agricultural support services such as research and extension (photos 4.3 and 4.4). In Ghana informal irrigation around cities in the center of the country covers an estimated 40,000 hectares compared with 5,478 hectares covered by the 22 formal

> Informal irrigation systems are rarely adequately reflected in official statistics or recognized by policymakers and agricultural support services such as research and extension

Photo 4.3

Photo 4.4

Photos by Olufunke Cofie

Many farmers use different sources of water with a variety of technologies, which are often not officially recognized

Reversing the flow:
agricultural water management
pathways for poverty reduction

4

schemes (Drechsel and others 2006). In mainland Tanzania an estimated 5% of cultivated land is irrigated, two-thirds of it under traditional irrigation initiated by farmers with no support by external agencies (FAO 2005). But even this statistic likely underestimates the importance of informal irrigation. A study of four hillside villages in Iringa District in Southwestern Tanzania found that 9 of 10 of rural households had land under informal irrigation (Boesen and Ravnborg 1993). In these villages informally irrigated land constitutes as much as 16% of cultivated land. In the Honduran and Nicaraguan hillsides 16%–39% of farming households have land on which there is a water source or that borders a stream. But these households lack access to the resources and technologies needed to make productive use of the water. In Miraflor and in the Condega District in the Nicaraguan hillsides only one-third of households with access to water have crops under some form of informal irrigation (Ravnborg 2002a, 2003).

Having the ability to water crops through such small-scale technologies and informal irrigation makes a tremendous difference to the livelihoods of farming households as it reduces the potentially negative impacts from dry spells during the rainy season and allows for the cultivation of water-demanding and often higher value crops such as vegetables (GWP 2003). Thus it reduces the vulnerability and increases the otherwise low returns associated with rainfed farming.

> A promising pathway to using water more effectively for poverty reduction and gender equity is an approach that takes poor women's and men's multiple water needs as the starting point

Empowering people to use water better

Using water better means improving the productivity of agricultural water in both irrigated and rainfed systems, through multiple-use water system, integrated water resources planning, and targeted research. This will entail understanding local contexts and constraints, developing appropriate training, and building capacity to empower users to use water to maximize benefits and reduce negative impacts on the environment.

Improving productivity and equity in existing large-scale irrigation systems. Productivity is low in many old established irrigation systems in Africa and Asia, and pockets of poverty persist. Findings on irrigation sites in India, Kyrgyzstan, and Nepal illustrate that inequitable water distribution coexists with a range of socioeconomic conditions (figure 4.8). The common elements found across the cases studies are weaknesses and power imbalances in relationships, inadequately developed knowledge and skills, and disadvantaged access for poor and female irrigators (Mott MacDonald 2006; Howarth and others forthcoming). From extensive case studies in Asia, interventions that might improve poverty reduction can be categorized into technical and institutional interventions (Hussain 2005). Technical interventions include promoting water saving and conservation measures, enhancing diversification of agricultural enterprise, introducing high-value crops, rehabilitating infrastructure, integrating management of surface water and groundwater, developing water control structures, and improving drainage management. But to be effective, these technical interventions must be complemented by institutional interventions, such as developing relationships and accountability between water users, user associations, and service providers; building the capacity of system officials and water user association members through targeted training; and improving headend and tailend equity in water distribution (Mott MacDonald 2006; Howarth and others forthcoming).

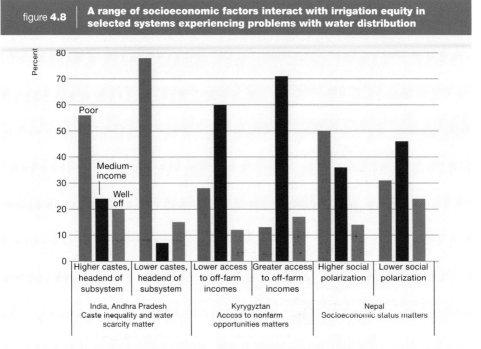

figure 4.8 | **A range of socioeconomic factors interact with irrigation equity in selected systems experiencing problems with water distribution**

Note: Well-being categories are based on local assessments by key informants and baseline survey.
Source: Mott MacDonald 2006.

Upgrading rainfed systems. Low-yielding rainfed systems in marginal areas hold the highest potential for productivity gains (see chapter 8 on rainfed agriculture). Because a large number of rural poor people depend on these systems for their livelihoods, upgrading these systems through soil water conservation, water harvesting, and supplemental irrigation can lift people out of poverty through productivity gains.

Recognizing multiple uses of water infrastructure. A promising pathway to using water more effectively for poverty reduction and gender equity is a multiple-use water services approach, which takes poor women's and men's multiple water needs as the starting point. This approach recognizes that when rural communities construct their own wells, village tanks, household storage, and other water infrastructure they typically do so for multiple uses: domestic purposes, sanitation, livestock, small-scale horticulture, cropping, fisheries and aquaculture, tree growing, beer making, and other small water-dependent businesses and ceremonial uses. For the poor, water is water whatever its designated purpose (photo 4.5). Communities also tap multiple conjunctive sources of water: rainfall, surface streams and lakes, wetlands, and groundwater. Multifunctionality, flexibility, and the tapping of conjunctive water sources enable poor people to accommodate for the range of water needs, seasonal variation, and the need to spread risks and cope with extreme events.

Reversing the flow:
agricultural water management
pathways for poverty reduction

4

Photo 4.5 Households often use water meant for drinking purposes for homestead irrigation

Multiple-use approaches are thought to be effective for poverty alleviation and gender equity for several reasons:

■ By taking poor women's and men's multiple water needs as a starting point, multiple-use approaches meet a broad range of basic water needs and alleviate more dimensions of multifaceted poverty: they reduce drudgery and improve health and food security and increase income from livestock, fish, crops, and small businesses.

■ Incremental capital costs are low compared with single-use approaches and represent good value for money in light of the considerably broader livelihood and scheme sustainability benefits derived.

■ Having a water user institution that includes all water users, instead of having parallel irrigation committees, domestic water committees, and traditional structures governing the same water resources could be more effective and sustainable.

■ Holistic water user associations are considerably more equitable if the multiple water needs of all are taken into consideration from the outset.

■ The opportunities of multiple-use approaches for widening livelihood benefits and enhancing scheme sustainability and equity at low incremental costs are generic and can be implemented on the ground according to locally specific conditions.

Integrating livestock and small-scale fisheries and aquaculture in the water resources planning process. Livestock rearing, fishing, and small-scale aquaculture activities represent a significant share of farm production in most farming systems of the developing world and are a major source of cash income for households with small landholdings (Turpie and others 1999; Maltsoglou and Rapsomanikis 2005; Thornton and others 2002). Promoting livestock production and integrating it into crop production systems are effective ways to target the rural poor; livestock income improves equity in favor of the poor more than crop incomes (Adams 1994). Similarly, integrated aquaculture-agriculture and inland artisanal fisheries and related activities such as small-scale fish processing and trading are usually operated by resource- and land-poor households (see chapter 12 on inland fisheries). In places where primarily women engage in livestock activities, targeting the livestock sector would also be a way of reaching rural women with income-generating activities.

Enhancing water productivity through targeted research. Pro-poor research on low-cost and gender-suited technologies, crop improvements, and better agronomic and water management practices can contribute significantly to poverty reduction. Crop research should focus on issues relevant to the circumstances of poor people in developing countries such as drought, rainfall failure, water logging, salinity, sodicity, pests and diseases, and soil nutrient deficiencies. The development of crop varieties tolerant of these biotic and abiotic stresses would improve the productivity of water (see chapter 7 on water productivity). There is also a great need for water research that locates water use as an embedded activity mediated through institutions, social relations, property rights, identity, and culture (Mosse 2003; Cleaver 2000; Mehta 2005). This can assist with more realistic proposals for how agricultural water management can reduce poverty and inequality.

> Pro-poor research on low-cost and gender-suited technologies, crop improvements, and better agronomic and water management practices can contribute significantly to poverty reduction

Improving governance of water resources

Improved governance of water resources can potentially contribute to poverty reduction by enabling secure rights to water and related services for the poor. Water rights of poor people are often informal and insecure, and they are not always sanctioned by social norms. The institutions charged with protecting the rights are frequently inaccessible or unresponsive to the poor. Water entitlements of poor people are often encroached on, physically or volumetrically. This section highlights how water governance agendas have made irrigation water more accessible to smallholders.

Multiple actors: linking local users to management and decisionmaking processes.

Developing sustainable water management and governance agendas requires the involvement of multiple actors (see chapter 5 on policies and institutions). NGOs can play a role in training and capacity building by mediating between stakeholders and empowering local populations to identify their problems in a systems context, to analyze causes and effects, to assess options, to arrive at well informed decisions, and even to assert their claims to unused land and water. NGOs working on water management have accumulated a wealth of experience on local strategies for poverty reduction through sustainable water management (Both ENDS and Gomukh 2005).

Supporting the diversification of livelihoods

Most poor farmers engage in several activities in addition to agriculture to increase their incomes, manage risks, and cope with uncertainty. Diversifying income sources and even exiting from agriculture are seen by many as viable strategies for escaping poverty (Dixon and Gulliver 2001) and indirectly reducing the pressure over local water resources when

Reversing the flow:
agricultural water management
pathways for poverty reduction

4

these are limited. In many countries income sources other than agriculture already constitute a substantial proportion of rural household income. In India more than a third of rural households derive their income from manufacturing and services. Poverty reduction efforts need to link these microrealities—expanding the asset base and the productivity of assets—with enabling macro-level policies. Investments in education and training programs and infrastructure are crucial. The private sector, governments, NGOs, research institutes, and aid agencies all have a role to play in this. The development of the rural nonfarm sector must be seen as a complement to and not a substitute for agriculturally led poverty reduction efforts.

Linking farmers to input and output markets. Agricultural water management and other production technologies and services are more effective when they enable smallholders to take advantage of market opportunities (Maltsoglou and Rapsomanikis 2005). Agricultural water management interventions are a strategic entry point for addressing a range of market constraints.

The income-generating potential of agricultural water management is directly related to the degree to which smallholders are integrated with input and output markets. Impacts are greatest when small farmers can access a range of complementary goods and services for the production and marketing of crops. Furthermore, when these goods and services are aligned along specific commodity value chains, a synergistic effect is created. Thus agricultural water management interventions are most effective where market linkages already exist or could be created.

The increasing concentration of global agribusiness supply chains means that small farmers must find ways to link up commercially with much larger players. Otherwise, they risk being squeezed out of the fastest growing domestic and export markets, which are increasingly controlled by supermarkets and agribusiness firms (Reardon and others 2003).Whether the smallholders are raising labor-intensive cash crops or livestock or fish, generating new income depends on removing constraints in access to markets where they sell their products (photo 4.6).

Supermarkets in both developed and developing countries are playing an increasingly dominant role in markets for fruits, vegetables, and other high-value crops that can be grown advantageously by many smallholders (Reardon and others 2003). To gain access to supermarket buyers, smallholders may need training to meet new quality standards. To meet market volume requirements, smallholders need stronger farmer organizations and mechanisms to aggregate their production. Bundling products and services for small-scale farmers in a vertically integrated fashion could be a key strategy in catalyzing the participation of growing numbers of poor rural producers in emerging high-value agricultural commodity markets.

Water markets can enhance poor people's access to water. As the price of the cheapest diesel pump in Bangladesh dropped over the years from $500 to $160, millions of smallholders increased their disposable income by installing treadle pumps and hundreds of thousands of smallholders in Bangladesh and eastern India started selling excess water to their neighbors. The water markets this created have expanded smallholder access to affordable irrigation water

> The income-generating potential of agricultural water management is directly related to the degree to which smallholders are integrated with input and output markets

Photo 4.6 Smallholder irrigated agricultural products are often perishable, requiring improvements in marketing systems

(Shah 2001). Twenty years ago villagers in Bangladesh reported that just 30% of small farmers in the village had access to affordable irrigation water. Two years ago that share had risen to between 70% and 100% (Nanes, Calavito, and Polak 2003). Thus, under certain circumstances, adaptive private agents' market responses can make up for failed public efforts.

Promoting crop diversification. Crop diversification is a key to the livelihood strategies of poor people, but smallholders face significant constraints to diversifying their enterprises. For instance, despite the high demand for fruits and vegetables poor farmers are not benefiting much from the production of economically more rewarding cash (export) crops, mainly because their subsistence orientation has kept them specializing in staple crops. For instance, in Kenya, Tanzania, and Uganda, where agricultural prices and trade have been liberalized, producers of export crops tend to be better off than producers of food crops (Peacock 2005). In Kenya 47% of subsistence farmers are below the poverty line, compared with 31% of cash-crop farmers. In Malawi the income of smallholder burley tobacco growers is more than double that of food crop growers in the poorest regions (Peacock 2005).

While real concerns have been raised about the impact of cash-crop production on nutrition, cash-crop producers are better off overall than subsistence or food crop producers. Thus, smallholder farmers should be supported to produce and market crops and other produce for which there is increasing demand and which therefore can generate an enhanced income. Strengthening farmer organizations, collection centers, and access to finance and knowledge will be crucial if poor farmers are to benefit. Efficient infrastructure networks will also be needed.

There are also emerging opportunities for improving economic water productivity and reducing poverty. These include rural-based production and processing, fresh fruits and vegetables, and bioenergy crops. Donors, governments, and the private sector should do more to foster innovation, including supporting value chain arrangements for niche products.

Reversing the flow:
agricultural water management
pathways for poverty reduction

4

The way forward

Clearly, increasing agricultural water productivity can play an important role in reducing poverty and vulnerability. A mix of small-scale technologies and water resources infrastructure designed from a multiple-use perspective can maximize benefits per unit of water for poor women and men. These efforts need to be combined with greater access to assets (land, water, working capital, human capital), markets, information, and services for poor people, particularly poor women. More priority needs to be given to equity and poverty reduction in water management projects and scaling up successful local innovations. Appropriate legal frameworks and functioning institutions that enable a wide ranging of stakeholders to share information and learn from successes and failures are critical for managing water in a way that ensures environmental sustainability and protects, promotes, and enhances poor people's rights, assets, and freedoms.

Reviewers

Chapter review editor: Jan Lundqvist.
Chapter reviewers: Rudolph Cleveringa, Mark Giordano, Nancy Johnson, Richard Palmer Jones, Stephane Jost, Eiman Karar, Douglas J. Merrey, François Molle, Anne Nicolaysen, Rosanno Quagliariello, Dina Safilou-Rothschild, Maria Saleth, Madar Samad, Kemi Seesink, and Marcel J. Silvius.

Notes

The title of this chapter is inspired by a quotation attributed to a farmer from the American West: "Water flows uphill towards money." We think that this is generally the unfortunate truth in too many countries today and want to see that water also flows to the poor.

1. This statement is made in full awareness of the contested nature of human rights declarations, of critiques of universalism and the rights based approach to development, and of the need to situate rights-based discourses in local contexts. However, water is fundamental, and many rights such as the right to life and food cannot be realized without the right to water. That human rights are necessary for combating poverty and ensuring sustainable development is reflected in the Millennium Declaration, the Copenhagen Declaration, the Vienna Declaration, and the work of the UN General Assembly. Advancing a right to water cannot be divorced from the important role that healthy ecosystems play in ensuring an adequate quantity and quality of freshwater for basic human needs, sustainable social and economic development, and poverty reduction.

References

Adams, R.H.J. 1994. "Non-farm Income and Inequality in Rural Pakistan: A Decomposition Analysis." *Journal of Development Studies* 31 (1): 110–33.

Adhiguru, P., and P. Ramasamy. 2003. "Agricultural-based Interventions for Sustainable Nutrition Security." Policy Paper 17. National Centre for Agricultural Economics and Policy Research, New Delhi.

Agarwal, B. 1994. *A Field of One's Own: Gender and Land Rights in South Asia*. Cambridge, UK: Cambridge University Press.

Ahlers, R. 2000. "Gender Issues in Irrigation." In C. Tortajada, ed., *Women and Water Management: The Latin American Experience*. New Delhi: Oxford University Press.

Alberts, J.H., and J.J. van der Zee. 2004. "A Multi-Sectoral Approach to Sustainable Rural Water Supply: The Role of the Rope Handpump in Nicaragua." In Patrick Moriarty, John Butterworth, and Barbara van Koppen, eds., *Beyond Domestic: Case Studies on Poverty and Productive Uses of Water at the Household Level*. IRC Technical Papers Series 41. Delft, Netherlands: International Water and Sanitation Centre, Natural Resources Institute, and International Water Management Institute.

Aliber, M., and C. Walker. 2006. "The Impact of HIV/AIDS on Land Rights: Perspectives from Kenya." *World Development* 34 (3): 704–27.

Ashton, P., and V. Ramasar. 2002. "Water and HIV/AIDS: Some Strategic Considerations in Southern Africa." In Anthony Turton and Roland Henwood, eds., *Hydropolitics in the Developing World: A Southern African Perspective*. Pretoria: African Water Issues Research Unit.

Bauer, C.J. 1997. "Bringing Water Markets Down to Earth: The Political Economy of Water Rights in Chile, 1976–1995." *World Development* 25 (5): 639–56.

———. 1998. *Against the Current: Privatization, Water Markets, and the State in Chile*. Norwell, Mass.: Kluwer Academic Publishers.

Bebbington, A. 1999. "Capitals and Capabilities: A Framework for Analysing Peasant Viability, Rural Livelihoods and Poverty." *World Development* 27 (12): 2021–44.

Bhatia, R. 1997. "Food Security Implications of Raising Irrigation Charges in Developing Countries." In M. Kay, T. Franks, and L.E.D. Smith, eds., *Water: Economics, Management and Demand*. London: E & FN Spon and Chapman & Hall.

Bhattarai, M., and A. Narayanamoorthy. 2003. "Impact of Irrigation on Rural Poverty in India: An Aggregate Panel-Data Analysis." *Water Policy* 5 (5–6): 443–58.

Boelens, R., and P. Hoogendam, eds. 2002. *Water Rights and Empowerment*. Assen, Netherlands: Van Gorcum.

Boelens, R., and M. Zwarteveen. 2002. "Gender Dimensions of Water Control in Andean Irrigation." In R. Boelens and P. Hoogendam, eds., *Water Rights and Empowerment*. Assen, Netherlands: Van Gorcum.

Boesen, J., and H.M. Ravnborg. 1993. "Peasant Production in Iringa District, Tanzania." CDR Project Paper 93.1. Centre for Development Research, Copenhagen.

Both ENDS and Gomukh. 2005. *River Basin Management: A Negotiated Approach*. Amsterdam.

Brehm, M.R., and J. Quiroz. 1995. *The Market for Water Rights in Chile: Major Issues*. World Bank Technical Paper 285. Washington, D.C.: World Bank.

Brown, L.R. 2005. *Outgrowing the Earth: The Food Security Challenge in an Age of Falling Water Tables and Rising Temperatures*. New York: W.W. Norton & Co.

Bruns, B.R., and R.S. Meinzen-Dick, eds. 2000. *Negotiating Water Rights*. New Delhi: Vistaar; and London: Intermediate Technology Press.

Carruthers, I. 1996. "Economics of Irrigation." In L. Pereira, R. Feddes, J. Gilley, and B. Lesaffre, eds., *Sustainability of Irrigated Agriculture*. Dordrecht, Netherlands: Kluwer Academic Publishers.

Cernea, M.M. 2003. "For a New Economics of Resettlement: A Sociological Critique of the Compensation Principle." *International Social Science Journal* 55 (175): 37–45.

CGIAR (Consultative Group on International Agricultural Research). 2000. "Charting CGIAR's Future: A New Vision for 2010." Paper prepared for the Mid-Term Meeting, 21–26 May, Dresden, Germany. Accessed August 15, 2005. [www.rimisp.cl/cg2010b/doc4.html#_ftn1].

Chambers, R. 1988. *Managing Canal Irrigation*. Cambridge, UK: Cambridge University Press.

Chancellor, F. 2000. "Sustainable Irrigation and the Gender Question in Southern Africa." In A. Pink, ed., *Sustainable Development International*. 3rd ed. London: ICG Publishing Ltd.

Cleaver, F. 2000. "Moral Ecological Rationality, Institutions and the Management of Common Property Resources." *Development and Change* 31 (2): 361–83.

Cremers, L., M. Ooijevaar, and R. Boelens. 2005. "Institutional Reform in the Andean Irrigation Sector: Enabling Policies for Strengthening Local Rights and Water Management." *Natural Resources Forum* 29 (1): 37–50.

Damiani, O. 2003. "Effects on Employment, Wages, and Labor Standards of Non-Traditional Export Crops in Northeast Brazil." *Latin American Research Review* 38 (1): 84–112.

Datt, G., and M. Ravallion. 1998. "Farm Productivity and Rural Poverty in India." *Journal of Development Studies* 34 (4): 62–85.

Davidson, A.P. 2000. "Soil Salinity, a Major Constraint to Irrigated Agriculture in the Punjab Region of Pakistan: Contributing Factors and Strategies for Amelioration." *American Journal of Alternative Agriculture* 15 (4): 154–59.

Delgado, C., P. Hazell, J. Hopkins, and V. Kelly. 1994. "Promoting Intersectoral Growth Linkages in Rural Africa through Agricultural Technology and Policy Reform." *American Journal of Agricultural Economics* 76 (5): 1166–71.

Delgado, C., J. Hopkins, V. Kelly, P. Hazell, A. Mckenna, P. Gruhn, B. Hojjati, J. Sil, and C. Courbois. 1998. *Agricultural Growth Linkages in Sub-Saharan Africa*. Research Report 107. International Food Policy Research Institute, Washington, D.C.

Derham, B., A. Hellum, and P. Sithole. 2005. "Intersections of Human Rights and Customs: A Livelihood Perspective on Water Laws." In B. van Koppen, J.A. Butterworth, and I. Juma, eds., *African Water Laws: Plural Legislative Frameworks for Rural Water Management in Africa*. Proceedings of a workshop held 26–28 January in Johannesburg, South Africa. Pretoria: International Water Management Institute.

DHAN (Development of Humane Action) Foundation. 2003. *Leadership Matters: Annual Report 2003*. Madurai, India.

Reversing the flow:
agricultural water management
pathways for poverty reduction

4

Dixon, J., and A. Gulliver. 2001. *Farming Systems and Poverty: Improving Farmers' Livelihoods in a Changing World.* Rome and Washington, D.C.: Food and Agriculture Organization and World Bank.

Dougherty, T.C., and A.W. Hall. 1995. *Environmental Impact Assessment of Irrigation and Drainage Projects.* Irrigation and Drainage Paper 53. Rome: Food and Agriculture Organization.

Drechsel, P., S. Graefe, M. Sonou, and O.O. Cofie. 2006. *Informal Irrigation in Urban West Africa: An Overview.* IWMI Research Report 102. Colombo: International Water Management Institute.

Ellis, F. 2000. "The Determinants of Rural Livelihood Diversification in Developing Countries." *Journal of Agricultural Economics* 51 (2): 289–302.

Ersado, L. 2005. "Small-Scale Irrigation Dams, Agricultural Production, and Health: Theory and Evidence from Ethiopia." Policy Research Working Paper 3494. World Bank, Washington, D.C.

Evenson, R.E., and D. Gollin. 2003. "Assessing the Impact of the Green Revolution 1960 to 2000." *Science* 300 (2 May): 758–62.

FAO (Food and Agriculture Organization). 2000. *Socio-economic Impact of Smallholder Irrigation Development in Zimbabwe: Case Studies of Ten Irrigation Schemes.* Sub-Regional Office for East and Southern Africa. Harare.

———. 2003. *World Agriculture: Towards 2015/2030. An FAO Perspective.* Rome: Food and Agriculture Organization and Earthscan.

———. 2005. AQUASTAT database. United Republic of Tanzania Country Profile. Accessed August 15. [www.fao.org/ag/agl/aglw/aquastat/countries/tanzania/index.stm].

Gichuki, F. 2004. "Managing the Externalities of Dry Season River Flow: A Case Study from the Ewaso Ngiro North River Basin, Kenya." *Water Resources Research* 40 (8).

Gichuki, F., and M.A. Hanjra. Forthcoming. "Agricultural Water Management Pathways to Breaking the Poverty Trap: Case Studies of Limpopo, Nile, Volta River Basins." *African Development Review.*

Gidwani, V. 2002. "The Unbearable Modernity of 'Development'? Canal Irrigation and Development Planning in Western India." *Progress in Planning* 58 (1): 1–80.

Goldsmith, E., and N. Hildyard. 1992. *The Social and Environmental Effects of Large Dams.* Volume III: A Review of the Literature. Bodmin, UK: Wadebridge Ecological Centre.

GWP (Global Water Partnership). 2003. "Poverty Reduction and IWRM." TEC Background Paper 8. Sweden.

———. 2004. *Catalyzing Change: A Handbook for Developing Integrated Water Resources Management (IWRM) and Water Efficiency Strategies.* Stockholm.

Hagos, F., and S. Holden. 2005. "Rural Household Poverty Dynamics in Northern Ethiopia 1997–2000: Analysis of Determinants of Poverty." Agricultural University of Norway, Department of Economics and Social Sciences, Aas, Norway.

Hanjra, M.A., T. Ferede, and D. Gutta. Forthcoming. "Pathways to Reduce Rural Poverty in Ethiopia: Investing in Irrigation Water, Education and Markets." *African Water Journal.*

Hasnip, N., S. Mandal, J. Morrison, P. Pradhan, and L.E.D. Smith. 2001. *Contribution of Irrigation to Sustaining Rural Livelihoods.* Wallingford, UK: HR Wallingford.

Heierli, Urs, with Paul Polak. 2000. *Poverty Alleviation as a Business.* Swiss Agency for Development and Cooperation, Berne.

Hendry, K., H. Sambrook, C. Underwood, R. Waterfall, and A. Williams. 2006. "Eutrophication of Tamar Lakes (1975–2003): A Case Study of Land-Use Impacts, Potential Solutions and Fundamental Issues for the Water Framework Directive." *Water and Environment Journal* 20 (3): 159–68.

Hossain, Mahabub, Firdousi Naher, and Quazi Shahabuddin. 2005. "Food Security and Nutrition in Bangladesh: Progress and Determinants." *Electronic Journal of Agricultural and Development Economics* 2 (2): 103–32.

Howarth, S.E., G. Nott, U.N. Parajuli, and N. Djailobayev. Forthcoming. "Irrigation, Governance and Water Access: Getting Better Results for the Poor." Paper prepared for the 4th Asian Regional Conference and 10th International Seminar on Participatory Irrigation Management, held by the Iranian National Committee on Irrigation and Drainage, the International Commission on Irrigation and Drainage, and the International Network on Participatory Irrigation Management, 2–5 May 2007, Tehran.

Huang, Q., David Dawe, Scott Rozelle, Jikun Huang, and Jinxia Wang. 2005. "Irrigation, Poverty and Inequality in Rural China." *Australian Journal of Agricultural and Resource Economics* 49 (2): 159–75.

Huang, Q., S. Rozelle, B. Lohmar, Jikun Huang, and Jinxia Wang. 2006. "Irrigation, Agricultural Performance and Poverty Reduction in China." *Food Policy* 31 (1): 30–52.

Hussain, I. 2005. *Pro-poor Intervention Strategies in Irrigation Agriculture in Asia: Poverty in Irrigated Agriculture—Issues, Lessons, Options and Guidelines.* Colombo: International Water Management Institute and Asian Development Bank.

Hussain, I., and M.A. Hanjra. 2003. "Does Irrigation Water Matter for Rural Poverty Alleviation? Evidence from South and South-East Asia." *Water Policy* 5 (5–6): 429–42.

———. 2004. "Irrigation and Poverty Alleviation: Review of the Empirical Evidence." *Irrigation and Drainage* 53 (1): 1–15.

Hussain, I., M. Mudasser, M.A. Hanjra, U. Amrasinghe, and D. Molden. 2004. "Improving Wheat Productivity in Pakistan: Econometric Analysis Using Panel Data from Chaj in the Upper Indus Basin." *Water International* 29 (2): 189–200.

Hussain, I., L. Raschid, M.A. Hanjra, F. Marikar, and W.V.D. Hoek. 2001. "A Framework for Analyzing Socioeconomic, Health and Environmental Impacts of Wastewater Use in Agriculture in Developing Countries." Working Paper 26. International Water Management Institute, Colombo.

Hussain, I., D. Wijerathna, S.S. Arif, Murtiningrum, A. Mawarni, and Suparmi. 2006. "Irrigation, Productivity and Poverty Linkages in Irrigation Systems in Java, Indonesia." *Water Resources Management* 20 (3): 313–36.

Hussain, M. 2004. "Impact of Small Scale Irrigation Schemes on Poverty Alleviation in Marginal Areas of Punjab, Pakistan." PhD Thesis. University of Agriculture, Agri-Economics, Faisalabad, Pakistan.

IDS (Institute for Development Studies). 1999. "Sustainable Livelihood Guidance Sheets." University of Sussex, Brighton, UK.

IFAD (International Fund for Agricultural Development). 2001. *Rural Poverty Report 2001: The Challenge of Ending Rural Poverty.* New York: Oxford University Press.

Illangasekare, T., S.W. Tyler, T.P. Clement, K.G. Villholth, A.P.G.R.L. Perera, J. Obeysekera, A. Gunatilaka, and others. 2006. "Impacts of the 2004 Tsunami on Groundwater Resources in Sri Lanka." *Water Resources Research* 42 (5): 1–9.

Irz, X., L. Lin, C. Thirtle, and S. Wiggins. 2001. "Agricultural Productivity Growth and Poverty Alleviation." *Development Policy Review* 19 (4): 449–66.

Janmaat, J. 2004. "Calculating the Cost of Irrigation Induced Soil Salinization in the Tungabhadra Project." *Agricultural Economics* 31 (1): 81–96.

Jehangir, W., M. Mudasser, and N. Ali. 2000. "Domestic Uses of Irrigation Water and its Impact on Human and Livestock Health in Pakistan." In *Proceedings of the US Committee on Irrigation and Drainage, Colorado, June 2000.* Boulder, Colo.: US Committee on Irrigation and Drainage.

Kay, M., and T. Brabben. 2000. *Treadle Pumps for Irrigation in Africa.* Knowledge Synthesis Report 1. International Programme for Technology and Research in Irrigation and Drainage, Rome.

Keller, J., D. Adhikari, M. Peterson, and S. Suryanwanshi. 2001. "Engineering Low-Cost Micro-Irrigation for Small Plots." International Development Enterprises, Lakewood, Colo.

Kerr, J., and S. Kolavalli. 1999. "Impact of Agricultural Research on Poverty Alleviation: Conceptual Framework with Illustrations from the Literature." EPTD Discussion Paper 56. International Food Policy Research Institute and Consultative Group on International Agriculture Research, Washington, D.C.

Khan, S., R. Tariq, C. Yuanlai, and J. Blackwell. 2006. "Can Irrigation be Sustainable?" *Agricultural Water Management* 80 (1–3): 87–99.

Kurukulasuriya, P., R. Mendelsohn, R. Hassan, J. Benhin, M. Diop, H.M. Eid, K.Y. Fosu, and others. 2006. "Will African Agriculture Survive Climate Change?" *World Bank Economic Review* 20 (3): 367–88.

Laamrani, H., K. Khallaayoune, M. Laghroubi, T. Abdelafid, E. Boelee, S.J. Watts, and B. Gryseels. 2000. "Domestic Use of Irrigation Water: The Metfia in Central Morocco." *Water International* 25 (3): 410–18.

Lambrou, Y., and G. Piana. 2006. *Gender: The Missing Component of the Response to Climate Change.* Rome: Food and Agriculture Organization, Sustainable Development Department, Gender and Population Division.

Lipton, M. 2001. "Challenges to Meet: Food and Nutrition Security in the New Millennium." *Proceedings of the Nutrition Society* 60 (2): 203–14.

Lipton, M., and R. Longhurst. 1989. *New Seeds and Poor People.* Baltimore, Md.: Johns Hopkins University Press.

Lipton, M., J. Litchfield, and Jean-Marc Faurès. 2003. "The Effects of Irrigation on Poverty: A Framework for Analysis." *Water Policy* 5 (5–6): 413–27.

Maltsoglou, I., and G. Rapsomanikis. 2005. "The Contribution of Livestock to Household Income in Viet Nam: A Household Typology Based Analyses." PPLPI Working Paper 21. Food and Agriculture Organization, Pro-Poor Livestock Policy Initiative, Rome.

Mangisoni, J.H. 2006. "Impact of Treadle Pump Irrigation Technology on Smallholder Poverty and Food Security in Malawi: A Case Study of Blantyre and Mchinji Districts." International Water Management Institute, Pretoria.

Mehta, L. 2005. *The Politics and Poetics of Water: Naturalising Scarcity in Western India.* New Delhi: Orient Longman.

Meinzen-Dick, R. 1997. "Valuing the Multiple Uses of Irrigation Water." In M. Kay, T. Franks, and L.E.D. Smith, eds., *Water: Economics, Management and Demand.* London: E & FN Spon and Chapman & Hall.

Molle, F., and J. Berkoff. 2006. "Cities Versus Agriculture: Revisiting Intersectoral Water Transfers, Potential Gains and Conflicts." Comprehensive Assessment Research Report 10. International Water Management Institute, Colombo.

Moriarty, Patrick, John Butterworth, and Barbara van Koppen, eds. 2004. *Beyond Domestic: Case Studies on Poverty and Productive Uses of Water at the Household Level.* IRC Technical Papers Series 41. Delft, Netherlands: International Water and Sanitation Centre, Natural Resources Institute, and International Water Management Institute.

Reversing the flow:
agricultural water management
pathways for poverty reduction | **4**

Morrison, J.A., and R. Pearce. 2000. "Interrelationships between Economic Policy and Agri-Environmental Indicators: An Investigative Framework with Examples from South Africa." *Ecological Economics* 34 (3): 363–77.

Mosse, David. 2003. *The Rule of Water: Statecraft, Ecology, and Collective Action in South India*. New Delhi: Oxford University Press.

Mott MacDonald. 2006. "Equity, Irrigation and Poverty: Guidelines for Sustainable Water Management: Final Report." Project R8338 for Department for International Development. Croydon, Surrey, UK.

Mumma, A. 2005. "Kenya's New Water Law: An Analysis of the Implications for the Rural Poor." In B. van Koppen, J.A. Butterworth, and I. Juma, eds., *African Water Laws: Plural Legislative Frameworks for Rural Water Management in Africa*. Proceedings of a workshop held 26–28 January in Johannesburg, South Africa,. Pretoria: International Water Management Institute.

Murgai, R., M. Ali, and D. Byerlee. 2001. "Productivity Growth and Sustainability in Post Green-Revolution Agriculture: The Case of Indian and Pakistani Punjabs." *World Bank Research Observer* 16 (2): 199–218.

Mwakalila, S. 2006. "Socio-economic Impacts of Irrigated Agriculture in Mbarali District of South-West Tanzania." *Physics and Chemistry of the Earth* 31 (15–16): 876–84.

Namara, R.E., B. Upadhyay, and R.K. Nagar. 2005. *Adoption and Impacts of Microirrigation Technologies: Empirical Results from Selected Localities of Maharashtra and Gujarat States of India*. Research Report 93. Colombo: International Water Management Institute.

Nanes, R., L. Calavito, and Paul Polak. 2003. "Report of Feasibility Mission for Smallholder Irrigation in Bangladesh." International Development Enterprises, Lakewood, Colo.

Narayanamoorthy, A., and R.S. Deshpande. 2003. "Irrigation Development and Agricultural Wages: An Analysis Across States." *Economic and Political Weekly* 38 (35): 3716–22.

Narayanamoorthy, A., and M.A. Hanjra. 2006. "Rural Infrastructure and Agricultural Output Linkages: A Study of 256 Indian Districts." *Indian Journal of Agricultural Economics* 61 (3): 444–59.

Nguyen-Khoa, S., L. Smith, and K. Lorenzen. 2005. *Impacts of Irrigation on Inland Fisheries: Appraisals in Laos and Sri Lanka*. Comprehensive Assessment Research Report 7. Imperial College London and International Water Management Institute, Colombo.

Nguyo, Wilson, Betty Kaunga, and Mesfin Bezuneh. 2002. *Alleviating Poverty and Food Insecurity: The Case of Mwea Irrigation Scheme in Kenya*. Madison, Wisc.: University of Wisconsin-Madison, BASIS Collaborative Research Support Program.

O'Brien, K.L., and R.M. Leichenko. 2000. "Double Exposure: Assessing the Impacts of Climate Change Within the Context of Economic Globalisation." *Global Environmental Change* 10 (3): 221–32.

OECD (Organization for Economic Co-operation and Development). 2001. "Rising to the Global Challenge: Partnership for Reducing World Poverty." Policy statement by the Development Assistance Committee High Level Meeting, 25–26 April, Paris.

Pandey, S. 1989. "Irrigation and Crop Yield Variability: A Review." In J.R. Anderson and P.B.R. Hazell, eds., *Variability in Grain Yield: Implications for Agricultural Research and Policy in Developing Countries*. Baltimore, Md.: John Hopkins University Press.

Pannell, D., G. Marshall, N. Barr, A. Curtis, F. Vanclay, and R. Wilkinson. 2006. "Understanding and Promoting Adoption of Conservation Practices by Rural Landholders." *Australian Journal of Experimental Agriculture* 46 (11): 1407–24.

Parry, M., C. Rosenzweig, A. Iglesias, G. Fischer, and M. Livermore. 1999. "Climate Change and World Food Security: A New Assessment." *Global Environmental Change* 9 (S1): S51–S67.

Peacock, T. 2005. "Agricultural Water Development for Poverty Reduction in Eastern and Southern Africa." Report submitted to the Collaborative Program on Investments in Agricultural Water Management in Sub-Saharan Africa. Draft. International Fund for Agricultural Development, Rome.

PEP (Poverty-Environment Partnership). 2002. *Linking Poverty Reduction and Water Management*. Stockholm and New York: Stockholm Environment Institute and United Nations Development Programme.

Perez de Mendiguren Castresana, J.C. 2004. "Productive Uses of Water at the Household Level: Evidence from Bushbuckridge, South Africa." In Patrick Moriarty, John Butterworth, and Barbara van Koppen, eds., *Beyond Domestic. Case Studies on Poverty and Productive Uses of Water at the Household Level*. IRC Technical Papers Series 41. Delft, Netherlands: International Water and Sanitation Centre, Natural Resources Institute, and International Water Management Institute.

Petermann, T. 1996. *Environmental Appraisals for Agricultural and Irrigated Land Development*. Zschortau, Germany: German Foundation for International Development (DSE) and Food and Agriculture Development Centre (ZEL).

Polak, P. 2005. "The Big Potential of Small Farms." *Scientific American* 293 (3): 84–91.

Polak, P., and R. Yoder. 2006. "Creating Wealth from Groundwater for Dollar-a-Day Farmers: Where the Silent Revolution and the Four Revolutions to End Rural Poverty Meet." *Hydrogeology Journal* 14 (3): 424–32.

Polak, P., J. Keller, R. Yoder, A. Sadangi, J.N. Ray, T. Pattanyak, S. Vaidya, N. Bembalkar, S. Chepe, D. Singh, and P. Bezbaruah. 2004. "A Low-Cost Storage System for Domestic and Irrigation Water for Small Farmers." International Development Enterprises, Lakewood, Colo.

Postel, S.L. 1999. *Pillar of Sand; Can the Irrigation Miracle Last?* New York: W.W. Norton.

———. 2003. "Securing Water for People, Crops, and Ecosystems: New Mindset and New Priorities." *Natural Resources Forum* 27 (2): 89–98.

Postel, S., P. Polak, F. Gonzales, and J. Keller. 2001. "Drip Irrigation for Small Farmers." *Water International* 26 (1): 3–13.

Pradhan, Rajendra, Franz von Bneda-Beckmann, Keebet von Benda-Beckmann, H.L.J. Spiertz, Shantam S. Khadka, and K. Azharul Haq, eds. 1997. *Water Rights, Conflict and Policy: Proceedings of Workshop held in Kathmandu, Nepal, January 22–24, 1996.* Colombo: International Irrigation Management Institute.

Quisumbing, Agnes. 1996. "Male-Female Differences in Agricultural Productivity: Methodological Issues and Empirical Evidence." *World Development* 24 (10): 1579–95.

Ravnborg, H.M. 2002a. "Perfiles de Pobreza para la Reserva Natural Miraflor-Moropotente, Municipio de Estelí, y el Municipio de Condega, Región I, Las Segovias, Nicaragua." CDR Working Paper 02.5. Centre for Development Research, Copenhagen.

———. 2002b. "Poverty and Soil Management—Evidence of Relationships from Three Honduran Watersheds." *Society and Natural Resources* 15 (6): 523–39.

———. 2003. "Poverty and Environmental Degradation in the Nicaraguan Hillsides." *World Development* 31 (11): 1933–46.

———. Forthcoming. "Water Management and the Poor. Issues and Scales of Action." Water International.

Reardon, T., C.P. Timmer, C.B. Barrett, and J. Berdegue. 2003. "The Rapid Rise of Supermarkets in Africa, Asia and Latin America." *American Journal of Agricultural Economics* 85 (5): 1140–46.

Reardon, T., J.E. Taylor, K. Stanoulis, P. Lanjouw, and A. Balisacan. 2000. "Effects of Nonfarm Employment on Rural Income Inequality in Developing Countries: An Investment Perspective." *Journal of Agricultural Economics* 51 (2): 266–88.

Saleth, R.M., R.E. Namara, and Madar Samad. 2003. "Dynamics of Irrigation Poverty Linkages in Rural India: Analytical Framework and Empirical Analysis." *Water Policy* 5 (5–6): 459–73.

Saleth, R.M., M. Samad, D. Molden, and I. Hussain. 2003. "Water, Poverty and Gender: An Overview of Issues and Policies." *Water Policy* 5 (5–6): 385–98.

Sauder, Allan. 1992. "International Development Enterprises Evaluation of Marketing Appropriate Technology Phase II." Canadian International Development Agency, Quebec.

Sen, A. 1999. *Development as Freedom.* New York: Oxford University Press.

Shah, T. 2001. *Wells and Welfare in the Ganga Basin: Public Policy and Private Initiative in Eastern Uttar Pradesh, India.* Research Report 54. Colombo: International Water Management Institute.

Shah, T., and O.P. Singh. 2004. "Irrigation Development and Rural Poverty in Gujarat, India: A Disaggregated Analysis." *Water International* 29 (2): 167–77.

Shah, Tushaar, M. Alam, Dinesh Kumar, R.K. Nagar, and Mahendra Singh. 2000. *Pedaling out of Poverty: Social Impact of a Manual Irrigation Technology in South Asia.* Research Report 45. Colombo: International Water Management Institute.

Shively, G.E. 1999. "Measuring the Environmental Impacts of Technical Progress in Low-income Agriculture: Empirical Evidence on Irrigation Development and Forest Pressure in Palawan, the Philippines." Paper presented at the Annual Meeting of the American Agricultural Economics Association, 8–11 August, Nashville, Tenn.

———. 2006. "Externalities and Labour Market Linkages in a Dynamic Two-Sector Model of Tropical Agriculture." *Environment and Development Economics* 11 (1): 59–75.

Shively, G.E., and S. Pagiola. 2004. "Agricultural Intensification, Local Labor Markets, and Deforestation in the Philippines." *Environment and Development Economics* 9 (2): 241–66.

Smith, L.E.D. 2004. "Assessment of the Contribution of Irrigation to Poverty Reduction and Sustainable Livelihoods." *Water Resources Development* 20 (2): 243–57.

Thapa, G., K. Otsuka, and R. Barker. 1992. "Effect of Modern Rice Varieties and Irrigation on Household Income Distribution in Nepalese Villages." *Agricultural Economics* 7 (3–4): 245–65.

Thirtle, C., I. Xavier, L. Lin, C. McKenzie-Hill, and S. Wiggins. 2001. *Relationship between Changes in Agricultural Productivity and the Incidence of Poverty in Developing Countries.* London: Department for International Development.

Thornton, P.K., R.L. Kruska, N. Henninger, P.M. Kristjanson, R.S. Reid, F. Atieno, A.N. Odero, and T. Ndegwa. 2002. *Mapping Poverty and Livestock in the Developing World.* Nairobi: International Livestock Research Institute.

Turpie, J., B. Smith, L. Emerton, and B. Barnes. 1999. *Economic Value of the Zambezi Basin Wetlands.* Cape Town: World Conservation Union Regional Office in Southern Africa.

UNDP (United Nations Development Programme). 2006. *Human Development Report 2006. Beyond Scarcity: Power, Poverty and the Global Water Crisis.* New York.

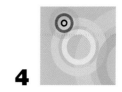

Reversing the flow:
agricultural water management
pathways for poverty reduction

4

UN Millennium Project. 2005. *Investing in Development: A Practical Plan to Achieve the Millennium Development Goals.* New York: Earthscan.

UN–Water. 2005. *Water for Life Decade 2005–2015.* Booklet. New York: United Nations.

Upadhyay, B., M. Samad, and M. Giordano. 2004. "Livelihoods and Gender Roles in Drip-irrigation Technology: A Case of Nepal." Working Paper 87. International Water Management Institute, Colombo.

Urama, K.C., and I. Hodge. 2004. "Irrigation Externalities and Agricultural Sustainability in South-Eastern Nigeria." *Journal of Agricultural Economics* 55 (3): 479–501.

Van De Walle, D., and D. Cratty. 2004. "Is the Emerging Non-Farm Market Economy the Route Out of Poverty in Vietnam?" *Economics of Transition* 12 (2): 237–74.

Van Imschoot, M. 1992. "Water as a Source of Employment." *International Labor Review* 131 (1): 125–37.

Van Koppen, Barbara. 2002. *A Gender Performance Indicator for Irrigation: Concepts, Tools, and Applications.* Research Report 59. Colombo: International Water Management Institute.

Van Koppen, Barbara, and Simeen Mahmud. 1996. *Women and Water Pumps in Bangladesh. The Impact of Participation in Irrigation Groups on Women's Status.* London: Intermediate Technology Publications.

Van Koppen, Barbara, Patrick Moriarty, and Eline Boelee. 2006. *Multiple-Use Water Services to Advance the Millennium Development Goals.* Research Report 98. Colombo: International Water Management Institute.

Van Koppen, Barbara, Regassa Namara, and Constantina Safilios-Rothschild. 2005. "Reducing Poverty through Investments in Agricultural Water Management." Working Paper 101. International Water Management Institute, Colombo.

Van Koppen, Barbara, R. Parthasarathy, and Constantina Safiliou. 2002. *Poverty Dimensions of Irrigation Management Transfer in Large-scale Canal Irrigation in Andra Pradesh and Gujarat, India.* Research Report 61. Colombo: International Water Management Institute.

Van Koppen, Barbara, Charles Sokile, Nuhu Hatibu, Bruce Lankford, Henry Mahoo, and Pius Yanda. 2004. "Formal Water Rights in Rural Tanzania: Deepening the Dichotomy?" IWMI Working Paper 71. International Water Management Institute, Colombo.

Von Braun, J., ed. 1995. *Employment for Poverty Reduction and Food Security.* Washington, D.C.: International Food Policy Research Institute.

Von Braun, J., D. Puetz, and P. Webb. 1989. *Irrigation Technology and the Commercialization of Rice in the Gambia: Effects on Income and Nutrition.* Research Report 75. Washington, D.C.: International Food Policy Research Institute.

Webster, P., D.J. Merrey, and M. de Lange. 2003. "Boundaries of Consent: Stakeholder Representation in River Basin Management in Mexico and South Africa." *World Development* 3 (5): 797–812.

Wood, Stanley, Liangzhi You, and Xiaobo Zhang. 2004. "Spatial Patterns of Crop Yields in Latin American and the Caribbean." *Cuadernos de Economia* 41 (124): 361–81.

World Bank. 2003. *World Development Report 2003: Sustainable Development in a Dynamic World—Transforming Institutions, Growth, and Quality of Life.* Washington, D.C.

———. 2005. *Shaping the Future of Water for Agriculture: A Sourcebook for Investment in Agricultural Water Management.* Washington, D.C.

———. Forthcoming. *Pakistan's Water Economy: Running Dry.* New York: Oxford University Press.

Yoder, R. 1983. *Non-agricultural Uses of Irrigation Systems: Past Experience and Implications for Planning and Design.* ODI Network Paper 7e. London: Overseas Development Institute.

Multiple-use systems

Artist: Titilope Shittu, Nigeria

5 | Policy and institutional reform: the art of the possible

Coordinating lead author: Douglas J. Merrey

Lead authors: Ruth Meinzen-Dick, Peter P. Mollinga, and Eiman Karar

Contributing authors: Walter Huppert, Judith Rees, Juana Vera, Kai Wegerich, and Pieter van der Zaag

Overview

Poverty, hunger, gender inequality, and environmental degradation continue to afflict developing countries not because of technical failings but because of political and institutional failings. Current policies and institutional arrangements are often ineffective, and the challenges are increasing. Institutional reform is critical, but many reforms have had mixed outcomes at best.

This chapter proposes a structured, context-specific approach to reforming, negotiating, and crafting effective institutions, organizations, and policies for water management in developing countries based on a careful assessment of experiences. This approach recognizes the inherently complex, political, and contentious nature of institutional transformation. It promotes careful analysis—of the current situation, available options, vested interests, potential costs and benefits, potential allies and opposition—as a basis for a strategic plan to guide reform. The plan should be a flexible guideline, responsive to experience and new opportunities. It recognizes that institutions, organizations, and policies are context specific.

While market forces and communities play critical roles in water management, the state will continue to have a central role because of its responsibility for providing public goods and for ensuring equity and sustainability. It is also responsible for maintaining a macroeconomic environment conducive to developing and using water resources effectively and equitably and for integrating the development and management of water resources into national programs in a way that optimizes the contribution of water to sustainable national growth. This includes, at a minimum, assessing the impacts of water policies, programs, and projects on national development, social well-being, and environmental quality. Policies, programs, and projects not complying with basic threshold requirements should be redesigned. The state is best placed to mobilize resources for large-scale water development and overall regulation. However, the state is not a monolithic entity, and with its often fragmented and even contradictory structures and processes, it is also a core component of the problem.

One challenge is to encourage technical water bureaucracies to see water management as a social and political as well as a technical issue and therefore to prioritize reducing poverty, increasing equity, and enhancing ecosystem services as their overarching goals. Another is to support more integrated approaches to agricultural water management, for example, incorporating livestock and fisheries, encouraging new lower cost technologies, and improving rainfed agricultural production. Meeting these challenges will be impossible in many developing countries without substantial changes in water management policies and institutions.

> One challenge is to encourage technical water bureaucracies to see water management as a social and political as well as a technical issue

The state should not be seen as the sole institution for delivering sound water management. Effective coordination and negotiation mechanisms are needed among the various state, civil society, and private sector organizations involved.

Political and institutional reforms are triggered by both internal and external pressures and opportunities, by pressures such as water scarcity, poverty, and food insecurity as well as by changes in global terms of trade and the requirements of development partners. The chapter reviews several major responses to these pressures. An early assumption that farmers were failing to respond to new irrigation opportunities ("blame the farmers") led to emphasizing training and on-farm infrastructure development. Next came attempts to transfer responsibilities to farmer organizations (irrigation management transfer). More recently, increasing interactions among water uses and users has led to the creation of river basin organizations, with mixed results. Market-inspired reforms including privatization and new water markets remain attractive to many donors, though not necessarily to developing countries. Radical changes in the balance of power in favor of water users and major restructuring of entrenched "hydro-bureaucracies" have not been on the agenda of any developing country. International development partners have not reflected sufficiently on the extent to which they have become part of the problem faced by developing countries rather than part of the solution.

A critical review of these experiences is organized around three themes:

■ The bias toward imposing blueprint solutions rather than critical evaluation of political and historical realities.

■ The need for changes in the larger institutional context, not simply in individual organizations or institutions.

■ The need to create an effective framework for relationships among actors and stakeholders.

Policies are produced and implemented in an institutional context. Therefore this chapter addresses both policies and institutions. The chapter argues against imposing solutions but for basing reforms and reform processes on basic principles such as the need for information sharing, transparency, accountability, equity, and empowerment of poor women and men.

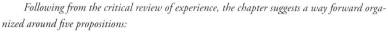

5

Following from the critical review of experience, the chapter suggests a way forward organized around five propositions:

1. Institutional reform processes are inherently political, making generalization and advocacy of single-dimensional solutions impractical. Needed instead are insightful analysis of what is possible, coalition building, and effective champions of change.

2. Reforms do not start from a blank slate, but are embedded in a sociotechnical context with a history, culture, environment, and vested interests that shape the scope for change. These well established conditions are in a state of flux that can create opportunities for negotiating reforms, but outcomes are inherently unpredictable.

3. The state will remain the main driver of reform for the foreseeable future but is also the institution most in need of reform. The state must take responsibility for ensuring greater equity in access to water resources and for using water development and management to reduce poverty. Protecting essential ecosystem services is also vital for many reasons, including their importance to poor people's livelihoods.

4. Knowledge and human capacity are critical to implementing successful integrated water resources management and to crafting institutions and policies for reducing poverty, promoting economic growth, and conserving essential ecosystem services. More reliable data are needed and must be shared widely with stakeholders to empower them through greater awareness and understanding. Further, new skills and capacities within water management institutions are critically important—at a time when various forces are weakening governments' capacities to attract and hold people with this expertise.

5. The state cannot make changes alone. Writing new laws and passing administrative orders achieve little by themselves. Investments of time and other resources in public debate based on shared, trusted information pay off by creating knowledge, legitimacy, and understanding of the reasons for change, and increase the likelihood of implementation. Knowledge sharing and debate create opportunities for including and empowering poor stakeholders—those with the most to gain (or lose). Coalitions of stakeholders and political reformers can lead a reform process that will strengthen both the state and civil society to play more effective roles in water management.

Research is urgently needed to support reform processes and reduce the uncertainty of reforms as sociopolitical processes. Paying more attention to ways to institutionalize social equity, poverty reduction, and ecosystem sustainability is critical. Negotiating reforms is the art of the possible, but informing that art with applied professional research will make successful outcomes more likely.

> The state will remain the main driver of reform for the foreseeable future but is also the institution most in need of reform

Reforming reform

How can agriculture and water management reform processes be made more effective for achieving food security, environmental sustainability, economic growth, social equity, and poverty reduction? The central message of the Comprehensive Assessment is that we need fundamental changes in how agricultural water is developed and managed. We need to internalize the agriculture-water-poverty-gender-environment nexus, to make real progress toward the Millennium Development Goals.

Institution refers to social arrangements that shape and regulate human behavior and have some degree of permanency and purpose transcending individual human lives and intentions. Examples are rotation schedules for water distribution, market mechanisms for obtaining crop credit, membership rules of water user associations, and property rights in water and infrastructure. Institutions are often referred to as the rules of the game in society (North 1990). Rules are interpreted and acted on differently by different people. Institutions, including rules, are dynamic and emerge, evolve, and disappear over time.

Organization refers to groups of people with shared goals and some formalized pattern of interaction, often defined in terms of roles such as president, water bailiff, or secretary. Examples are water user associations, government irrigation agencies, privatized water companies, water resources research organizations, farmer unions, consultancy firms, nongovernmental organizations, and regulatory bodies. There is enormous diversity in the form, scope, size, structure, permanency, and purpose of organizations. Bureaucracies are a particular type of organization characterized by role differentiation, hierarchical relationships, and formal, written, rules of procedure and accountability. This makes them very different from less formal local associations, but both are organizations.

A *policy* is "a set of interrelated decisions taken by a political actor or group concerning the selection of goals and the means of achieving them within a specified situation where these decisions should, in principle, be within the power of those actors to achieve" (Howlett and Ramesh 1995, p. 5, quoting Jenkins 1978). Any organization can have policies, but the focus here is on public policy.

How policy works is the focus of this chapter. A rationalist and linear perspective assumes that policymaking has sequential steps from problem formulation, to evaluation of alternatives, to implementation (policy as prescription; Mackintosh 1992). This perspective is associated with expert managerial approaches to intervention and with thinking in terms of models to be applied generally. Policymaking can also be seen as an inherently political activity, with different perceptions and interests contested at all stages (policy as process; Mackintosh 1992). Policy is a bargained outcome, the environment is conflictual, and the process is characterized by diversity and constraint. The intervention perspective emphasizes negotiation, participatory design and implementation, and situation specificity (Gordon, Lewis, and Young 1997). These different perspectives on policy directly translate into different understandings of reform, of transforming policy, institutions, organizations, and governance structures.

A second characteristic of policy processes is whether policymaking is more state centric or more society centric (Grindle 1999). In authoritarian systems policy processes tend to be highly state centric and confined to small circles of power, with negligible influence of civil society. In democratic societies policy processes are more society centric, with recognized opportunities for different interest groups to influence policymaking and implementation. However, a lot depends on the institutions through which civil society involvement takes place. Regardless of how policy is decided, it remains largely symbolic without effective institutions and organizational capacity to transform it into practical reality.

Governance is the way authority is organized and executed in society, and often includes the normative notion of the necessity of good governance. The Global Water Partnership defines water governance as "the range of political, social, economic, and administrative systems that are in place to develop and manage water resources, and the delivery of water services, at different level of society" (Rogers and Hall 2003, p. 7). *Governance* is therefore a broad term that includes institutions, organizations, and policies. The World Bank broadens the definition to include the process by which those in authority are selected, monitored, and replaced and the effectiveness of government in implementing sound policies (Jayal 1997).

That requires restructuring the institutions and organizations responsible for agricultural water management and policymaking, which in turn demands a transformation in reform strategies (see box 5.1 for definitions of *institution*, *organizations*, and *policy*). Reforming large formal organizations—governments, investment banks, donors, international nongovernmental organizations (NGOs)—is especially high priority though also most problematic. But local-level and informal institutions and organizations need to change as well. They are coming under increasing pressure as the large formal organizations and institutions have proven so ineffective in responding to new technologies and market conditions and dealing with inequities and social conflict at the local level.

The record in designing and promoting policy and institutional reforms is embarrassingly bad. The social engineering (box 5.2) panaceas of the past 30 years in agricultural water management and use have failed to achieve their objectives *[well established]*. Irrigation development has led to huge increases in food production and enabled large numbers of people to escape poverty, especially in Asia. But it has come at a very high cost financially (often through low returns to investments) and has exacerbated inequity, injustice, and environmental degradation and marginalized rainfed farmers, women, and other excluded people. Extreme poverty continues in many parts of Africa and Asia. If policy and institutional reforms had been more effective, irrigation investments would have yielded far higher benefits at much lower financial, social, and environmental costs.

The Comprehensive Assessment seeks to identify and promote innovative options and approaches to improve management of water resources for food and nature over the next 25 years. In most developing countries policies and institutional frameworks and capacities are inadequate to meet these challenges. Government organizations are often structured to address past challenges (for example, to construct irrigation schemes) and lack the personnel, culture, mandate, and financial resources to respond effectively to what is required of them today. Challenges are more complex. Rising demand for water is leading to scarcity and environmental threats. Climate change is threatening destabilizing impacts. Agricultural markets are globally linked. Expectations are also changing: water management organizations are expected to focus on new social goals such as poverty reduction, enhanced equity through targeting the poor, and environmental conservation.

The only way the Comprehensive Assessment can avoid becoming yet another failed panacea is by identifying practical and innovative approaches to enable institutions to formulate and implement new policies. This chapter contributes with a critical analysis

> Had policy and institutional reforms been more effective, irrigation investments would have yielded far higher benefits at much lower financial, social, and environmental costs

| box **5.2** | **What is "social engineering"?** |

The term *social engineering* is used here in a narrow sense to refer to linear models for changing societies or organizations, where blueprints are used to replicate a structure in a new context, that may have worked elsewhere. Application of this model to achieve social change—if x then y follows—is based on a misunderstanding of the complex, nondeterministic, and stochastic nature of social organizations. Social engineering as used here does not imply pessimism about the possibility of facilitating and guiding social change, but cautions against overly simple prescriptions.

of experience to date. It offers no magic potions or simple panaceas for investors. *Instead of more social engineering paradigms based on linear, mechanistic models of the sort that have hindered progress before (see box 5.2), we propose a structured, context-specific approach to negotiating and crafting effective institutions and realistic policies that recognize the inherently contentious and political nature of institutional transformation. This is the main message of the chapter.*

Since most of the literature deals with irrigation, the chapter has a clear bias in that direction.[1] That is not necessarily a problem, for at least two reasons. First, the lessons and principles apply more broadly: integrating management of water for crops, livestock, and fish; promoting water harvesting and microagricultural water management technologies (for example, treadle pumps, bucket and drip irrigation kits); targeting assistance to poor women and men; applying integrated basin management; establishing the conditions for producing more value per unit of water; and giving the environment as well as poor male and female stakeholders a voice in agricultural water policymaking—none of these objectives will be achieved unless we become far more effective at promoting policy and institutional reform. We can learn a lot from the experience of the irrigation sector.

> We propose a structured, context-specific approach to negotiating and crafting effective institutions and realistic policies that recognize the inherently contentious and political nature of institutional transformation

Second, in many countries governments remain heavily involved in irrigation development and management, so that improving irrigation performance through institutional and policy reform would make a large contribution to reducing poverty, promoting agricultural growth, and reducing environmental degradation (see chapter 9 on irrigation). However, there are important differences, depending on the source and use of water. For example, groundwater is a common pool resource (subtractable, high exclusion costs) subject to capture using private technologies and very difficult for government, markets, or community institutions to control or regulate access to (see chapter 10 on groundwater). This makes it more difficult to develop effective institutions to manage groundwater than surface water, which is more observable. Furthermore, fishing, livestock, small household gardens, and other agricultural water uses are often not taken into account in irrigation system management despite their critical importance to poor people's livelihoods.

Assessing institutional and policy challenges

This section discusses the leading role of the state in water development and management and the forces that have triggered reforms. It reviews some of the leading responses to these triggers: blaming and training farmers, organizing farmers, promoting river basin organizations, and experimenting with market-inspired reforms. None of these attempts has substantially improved water management at any scale.

The state will continue to lead institutional reform— but is itself in need of reform

The state has historically played a leading role in water development, both in supporting large-scale irrigation, hydropower, and flood control as well as in facilitating private and small-scale farmer-managed irrigation. The state was the central institution driving the boom in irrigation development in the second half of the 20th century. There are sound reasons for the state's central role, related to state authority, national welfare and development, and resource mobilization (see chapter 9 on irrigation). Vital natural resources are considered public goods to be regulated, managed, and used by the state for public welfare. Large-scale development of water resources requires substantial financial and human resources and a long-term perspective on returns to the investments. Since ancient times the state has been the only organization with the capacity to mobilize sufficient resources for investments requiring a long-term horizon with a large public good element.

Many countries adhere to some form of public trust doctrine, a principle dating back at least to Roman law, which maintains that control over water is an aspect of sovereignty (Ingram and Oggins 1992) and that the state holds navigable waters and other water resources as a common heritage for the benefit of the people. The state is accountable for allocating a scarce resource for which there is high demand, resulting in decisions that entail tradeoffs between resource sustainability and economic development. High levels of social inequity often require further state intervention to protect the silent vulnerable: the poor, the disenfranchised, the environment, and future generations. This is a tall order for any government and is proving to be a formidable challenge, especially in countries where the state is not effective. State-managed water systems have often performed poorly because of a lack of state capacity, poor incentives for agency staff and water users, and their inability to respond effectively to changes in demand, among other reasons.

> The challenges are to improve the effectiveness of the state itself and to find the right balance between state action and other institutional actors

While the state remains the main actor to initiate reforms, the challenges are to improve the effectiveness of the state itself and to find the right balance between state action and other institutional actors. States, like market and community institutions, are inherently imperfect. Each has serious limitations. The answer is to find the right balance and to achieve complementarity, no easy feat for policymakers.

Triggers that set off institutional and policy reforms

Governments everywhere are challenged by the need to provide food for their citizens, boost rural incomes, and reduce poverty while sustainably managing natural resources as well as water infrastructure. These challenges have to be managed in a rapidly changing world with competitive global markets, increasing competition for water, and an environment where agricultural welfare depends on much more than water availability. Policies and institutions that may have been effective 20 years ago cannot cope with these new pressures.

There are many sources of pressure for reforms in the irrigation sector. Governments, donors, and investors are concerned that returns on investments are too low, in part because crop yields, prices, and cropping intensity are below expectations. Poverty and socioeconomic inequity continue even in relatively "successful" irrigation schemes. The sustainability of both infrastructure and the environment raise serious questions. And increasing demand for water for other uses threatens the water supply for agriculture.

Many governments are implementing reforms triggered by a combination of internal and external pressures. Environmental, social, economic, and political dynamics; regime change; pressures from donors and development partners; and international macroeconomic trends such as globalization all play a role.

In South Africa the end of apartheid provided enormous political momentum for radical reforms to correct injustices in many domains, including the water sector. The internal political push for reform led to participatory processes to formulate a new water act and water policies (de Lange 2004), followed by the more complex and long-term process of implementing the reforms. In Chile tradable water rights were introduced as part of a strong domestic political commitment to a neoliberal, market-driven development paradigm. The military government that came to power in 1973 adopted radical free-market policies and gave a group of US-trained free-market economists unprecedented influence in rewriting Chilean laws to further their economic policy (Carrasco 1995). The results of those water reforms have been mixed (Bauer 1997, 2005). But post-1990 changes in Brazil, Chile, and South Africa (Peña and Solanes 2003) are examples of nationally driven consensus-based reforms that have had substantial impacts.

> Externally driven reforms are less likely to have a lasting impact unless they are also championed by strong domestic actors

Evidence from South America (Peña and Solanes 2003) and Asia (Molle 2005; Samad 2005) suggests that externally driven reforms are less likely to have a lasting impact unless they are also championed by strong domestic actors. Pakistan in the 1990s and Indonesia during the Suharto regime are cases in which irrigation reform was on the national agenda primarily because of pressure by international development funding agencies (van der Velde and Tirmizi 2004; Bruns 2004). There was little domestic momentum supporting reform. In both countries the irrigation bureaucracies neutralized whatever reform efforts were undertaken. In countries of geopolitical importance to the major donor countries, such as Egypt and Pakistan, international development agencies seem to have had little bargaining power to encourage or enforce reform (on reform in Egypt, see Merrey 1998).

Mexico and India are examples of combined internal and external triggers for reforms. In Mexico the seeming "big bang" irrigation reform of the early 1990s in fact had a long and complex history (Rap, Wester, and Pérez-Prado 2004). Changes in the relationship between the agencies responsible for agriculture and water resources and the evolution of their control over water resources, together with the role of international funding agencies in policy debates and in financing infrastructure development, culminated in far-reaching irrigation reform just at the time of a presidential election. Not only did the organization of irrigation management change, but the water bureaucracy regained its lost autonomy.

In India external influences on irrigation reform included both international funding agencies and participatory approaches to water management introduced by Ford Foundation–sponsored action research programs based on the Philippines irrigation reform models of the 1970s and 1980s. These experiments, combined with domestic debates on "underutilization" of irrigation systems, came to be known as "participatory irrigation management" reform. However, lacking strong political coalitions to support the reforms and their almost exclusive focus on local management, local successes were not scaled out and up. Andhra Pradesh attempted a big bang approach to irrigation reform in 1996–97 (based partly on the perceived quick and radical change in Mexico), enacting far-reaching statewide legislation, with strong political support. Vested interests in the water bureaucracy and at local levels limited its impact, however.

The Andhra Pradesh case shows that political will at the top may not suffice. Unless water users and government line agencies are strongly behind the reform, results will be limited because appropriation of the reform initiative by vested interests is relatively easy (Mollinga, Doraiswamy, and Engbersen 2004).

Failed responses to reform

What have been some of the main responses to these triggers of reform?

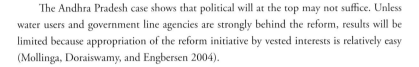

Blaming then training the farmers while ignoring the real problem. Triggered by the Asian food crises of the 1960s, governments made huge investments in new irrigation schemes, supported by bilateral donors and development banks (see chapter 9 on irrigation). By the mid-1970s, however, evidence was growing that while the green revolution had significantly reduced food shortages, the new publicly constructed and managed irrigation systems were performing far below expectations.

The initial response was to assume that the problems were largely on the farm, that farmers were mismanaging water and needed training to improve irrigation performance. In some cases farmers were perceived as illiterate, conservative, and too "traditional."[2] Throughout Asia the response was to develop programs that focused on educating farmers at the farm or turnout level on "proper" scientific irrigation and to impose "improved" infrastructure at this level. Examples include on-farm water management projects in Pakistan, the Command Area Development Authority in India, and similar large investment projects in Egypt, Indonesia, the Philippines, and elsewhere.

This blame-the-farmers analysis conveniently defined the problem as outside the domain of the managing water agencies and placed it squarely on the farmers' shoulders. The conditions to which farmers were responding, such as unreliable water services, were not acknowledged. The educate-the-farmers attitude persists today as a component of social engineering approaches to water sector reform.

Despite growing evidence that farmers were responding to unreliable and inequitable delivery at the main canal level (Wade and Chambers 1980)—which led the International Irrigation Management Institute in the late 1980s to focus its research at these higher levels (Merrey 1997)—the on-farm focus developed a momentum of its own that continued into the mid-1990s. Huge sums of money were spent with little visible impact on irrigation performance.

Organizing the farmers through irrigation management transfer, but ignoring the preconditions. An important dimension of the early attention to on-farm problems was attempts to organize farmers into water user associations. Observations showed farmer-managed irrigation systems to be functioning effectively, so the hope was that organizing farmers in government-managed schemes would show similar results. Water user associations, farmer training, and on-farm infrastructure development were expected to lead to better irrigation performance while also reducing government investment and operation and maintenance (O&M) costs. At this early stage, water user associations were perceived in narrow terms: they would take responsibility for rehabilitation, maintenance, and water

The initial response to the poor performance of irrigation systems was to assume that farmers were mismanaging water—conveniently defining the problem as outside the domain of the water agencies

distribution of irrigation systems at the tertiary level (the smallest canals from which a number of farmers take water directly). Before the 1990s few attempts had been made to give farmers a voice at higher levels of irrigation schemes (Gal Oya in Sri Lanka was an example; see Uphoff 1986, 1992). In a delayed response to pressures to "roll back the state," some governments made more serious attempts at irrigation management transfer during the 1990s, a movement that continues today and even has its own network (International Network for Participatory Irrigation Management, www.inpim.org).

Pilot projects to transfer management from the state to user groups on government-built schemes have rarely been scaled up effectively to cover larger areas. Many governments were reluctant, even when project documents promised to do so. Another reason was the failure to recognize the critical differences between government- and farmer-managed irrigation systems. Management transfer programs in countries as diverse as Australia, Colombia, Indonesia Mali, Mexico, New Zealand, Senegal, Sri Lanka, Turkey, and the United States have demonstrated some positive results from involving farmers and reducing government expenditures, but they have rarely shown improvements in output performance or quality of maintenance (Vermillion 1997; Vermillion and others 2000; Samad and Vermillion 1999; Vermillion and Garcés-Restrepo 1998). The few notable exceptions are middle-income developing countries such as Mexico and Turkey and high-income countries such as New Zealand and the United States. Research in the 1990s on irrigation management transfer processes and outcomes produced many case studies and some useful guidelines for implementation (for example, Vermillion and Sagardoy 1999). There is broad agreement on the necessary conditions, but very few cases where they have been met on a large scale (box 5.3).

> **Pilot projects to transfer management from the state to user groups on government-built schemes have rarely been scaled up effectively to cover larger areas**

Irrigation management transfer and similar decentralization schemes can also have unintended negative consequences, for example, by strengthening local strongmen (Klaphake 2005; Mollinga, Doraiswamy, and Engbersen 2004) or giving men unequal power over women (Meinzen-Dick and Zwarteveen 1998). Similarly, although some pilot projects have improved land productivity and helped poor farmers, most integrated watershed management projects have not delivered the expected benefits (Kerr 2002). Thus policies to devolve management to local collective action institutions have not been the solution to better performance of water systems.

Gulati, Meinzen-Dick, and Raju (2005) suggest that most user organizations failed in India because they focused on areas of concern to the government but not necessarily to the farmers. To be successful, they recommend that user organizations receive the authority to levy water fees, conduct maintenance, and represent farmers' interests to government agencies. Moreover, where user groups have stronger water rights, farmers' incentives to participate in O&M may also be stronger. Where farmers are involved in maintenance activities, the resources mobilized can be substantial—as much as several times the irrigation charges paid to the state. This demonstrates the potential—but the implication is that successful irrigation management transfer requires much greater policy and institutional changes *[well established]*. Even where the formal conditions seem to be in place, however, as in Andhra Pradesh, India, there is considerable evidence that the sticking point is the unwillingness of government organizations to delegate or share power with user organizations.

box **5.3**	**Conditions for successful irrigation management transfer**

The following conditions have been identified as necessary for successful irrigation management transfer:

- Firm, consistent long-term political commitment.
- Legal and political recognition of farmer organizations, including their right to raise revenue, enter into contracts, and apply sanctions.
- Clearly recognized and sustainable water rights and water service.
- Infrastructure that is compatible with the water service, water rights, and local management capacities (Perry 1995).
- Well specified management functions and assignment of authority.
- Effective accountability and incentives for management.
- Arrangements for viable and timely conflict resolution.
- Benefits that exceed costs and are proportional to farmer investments.
- Ability to mobilize adequate resources for irrigation.

The following conditions are important for sustainability following management transfer:

- Support services to farmer organizations as they evolve from single-purpose operation and maintenance to multipurpose commercial organizations.
- Periodic financial audit of the farmer organization.
- Higher level federations of local organizations for planning, allocating, and enforcing resource use at watershed or aquifer levels.

Source: Samad and Merrey (2005) and Merrey (1997), synthesizing from other sources.

This takes us back to the fundamental issue: while governments may be willing to transfer the hard work and expense of local water management to users, they are rarely willing to restructure their bureaucracies or to make the other legal and structural changes needed to achieve a new balance of political power favoring users (Mexico is a partial exception; see Rap, Wester, and Pérez-Prado 2004). Similarly, after a few papers in the 1980s (Wade 1982; Repetto 1986), the continuing problem of corruption—an institutional problem par excellence—has hardly been studied. Box 5.4 provides some recent insights into this issue.

Promoting river basin organizations—but one size rarely fits all. A more recent trend has been to promote river basin organizations to manage competition for water at the basin level. There is general agreement on the long-term benefits of effective integrated management of river basins, especially with increasing competition and environmental degradation. But attempts to impose particular models of river basin organizations in developing countries, especially models derived from the experiences of rich countries, are not likely to succeed because the objectives and institutional contexts differ so greatly (Shah, Makin, and Sakthivadivel 2005). Indeed, having a formal organization, even in highly developed basins, has been shown not to be a necessary condition (Svendsen 2005a).

Attempting to build organizations for managing river basins that represent the interests of all water users, including small farmers, is fraught with difficulties (Wester, Merrey,

Major sources of corruption in irrigation are lack of transparency leading to asymmetric information, and incompatible incentive structures between officials and farmers.

Preventing information asymmetry. In the Bolivian Andes, where traditional irrigation schemes apply the principle of rotating tasks (*cargos rotativos*), members of different age groups are responsible for different tasks in the operation and maintenance of the irrigation system (Huppert and Urban 1998). Over time, everyone becomes familiar with all the essential tasks needed to keep the system functional. This prevents any individual from gaining specialized knowledge not available to the others. It prevents the emergence of an asymmetrical information problem and thereby limits the risks of corruption and manipulation. Other means of limiting asymmetrical information include the use of comprehensive management information systems and co-ownership and team formation (for social control).

Improving incentives. In the Gascogne the French government is using a franchise system to prevent potential moral hazard risks in irrigation (Huppert and Hagen 1999). Compagnie d'Aménagement des Coteaux de Gascogne (CACG) was awarded a 10-year concession to provide operation and maintenance services to water users in irrigation systems. If CACG does not perform acceptably, another provider will be chosen for the next term. Creating a credible "threat" of competition between providers can act as an incentive not to deviate too far from the clients' interests when deciding on the allocation of scarce resources.

Other ways to improve incentives and bring the service providers' interests in line with those of clients include bonus payments and contractual provisions limiting the service provider's alternatives for action. Well functioning management information systems may also help. A guiding principle is to try to link service level and quality to the respective actor's payoffs (monetary and nonmonetary). Thus unifying decision rights over input resources with the right to collect payoffs in relation to the service benefit from those decisions may solve the problem. However, this must be coupled to the empowerment of farmer-clients to gain access to relevant information, especially where external influences (such as varying water availability) make it difficult to establish a fixed level of service. There are very few examples of such approaches being introduced and institutionalized in developing countries. Some years ago Svendsen and Huppert (2000) thought that the Andhra Pradesh, India, case was such an example, but more recent work (Mollinga, Doraiswamy, and Engbersen 2004) suggests that what they observed was not sustained.

Source: Huppert 2005.

and de Lange 2003; Wester, Shah, and Merrey 2005). The idea that a specific organization is necessary for integrated management of a basin may be based on the false belief that the physical reality of an integrated river basin system requires an organization coinciding with its boundaries. This not only ignores the fact that human social systems have entirely different (and often highly flexible) boundaries, but confuses organizations and institutions.

Governments are facing the complexities of managing increasing competition for water in river basins before they have found solutions to local and irrigation scheme–level problems. In many developing countries small-scale irrigation farmers are under threat from other sectoral demands for water considered of higher economic value. This threatens the livelihoods of millions of small farmers in economies with few alternative sources of employment (Svendsen 2005b). An externally imposed one-size-fits-all strategy for managing such complexity is unlikely to be effective. (Chapter 16 provides a more detailed analysis of river basin management issues.)

Experimenting with market-inspired reform has shown little promise so far. In electricity services, healthcare, and some other development sectors, disillusionment with state agencies has led to the promotion of markets and private sector participation. In the agricultural water sector this trend has been restrained by many sources of market failure, including the existence of monopolies and the potential for serious externalities. There have nonetheless been several types of reforms associated with some forms of privatization or market instruments.

> The idea that a specific organization is necessary for integrated management of a basin may be based on the false belief that the physical reality of an integrated river basin system requires an organization coinciding with its boundaries

Private sector involvement. Reforms associated with greater private sector involvement in the construction and management of water systems are often advocated in response to inefficiencies of public sector agencies, with the assumption that private companies will have lower labor costs or stronger incentives to provide better services. Private investment in construction is more common in the domestic water supply and sanitation sector than in large-scale irrigation, but the rapid expansion of private groundwater irrigation and pumping, particularly in South Asia, represents massive investments by individual farmers (see chapter 10 on groundwater; Shah and others 2000; Heierli and Polak 2000; Polak 2005). Privatization of O&M has been a component of many irrigation devolution programs, particularly where pumping or other equipment management requires specialized skills that farmers may lack. A private company may be hired to operate the pumps or heavy maintenance equipment, paid for by farmers or state budgets. The impact on service provision is affected by the arrangements for authorization, payment, and accountability (Huppert, Svendsen, and Vermillion 2001). Attempts to implement public-private partnerships for urban water and wastewater services in developing countries have had a high failure rate, mainly because of economic volatility or because effective monitoring and regulation systems are lacking (Braadbaart 2005).

Positive externalities may justify public investment in irrigation systems: the benefits are social (lower food costs to consumers, promotion of economic growth) and often slow in coming. Private investment can be encouraged for constructing complementary infrastructure, such as roads and electricity, and for providing individualized technologies, such as pumps and drip systems. In most developing countries interest rates are high and long-term credit is not available. It is unrealistic to expect that private investment can substitute for the traditional role of governments in investing in irrigation projects.

Nevertheless, there is an important role for the private sector in making low-cost agricultural water management technologies such as treadle pumps, small power pumps, and bucket and drip kits more widely available. Such technologies can be readily acquired and used by individual smallholder farmers, both men and women, and in many situations can substantially improve nutrition and incomes (see chapter 4 on poverty; Shah and others 2000; Mangisoni 2006; Namara, Upadhyay, and Nagar 2005; Merrey, Namara, and de Lange 2006). Restrictive policies in some Sub-Saharan African countries are retarding the wider use of these technologies, in marked contrast to South Asian countries.

Economic incentives for water allocation. Two major types of reform aim to create economic incentives for improved water management: water pricing and tradable water rights. With water-pricing policies, payment goes to the state or water agency, whereas with tradable water rights payment goes to the holder of the rights.

Water pricing may be used to create incentives for water conservation (which requires some form of volumetric pricing) or to raise resources for construction or O&M. However, such efforts have often foundered on political opposition as well as difficulties in measuring water deliveries and collecting fees (Dinar 2000; Molle and Berkoff forthcoming). Unreliable water delivery services are another reason farmers resist paying.

Generally, pricing policies for recovering the costs of infrastructure development and O&M, applied as a blanket measure, risk seriously aggravating water deprivation and poverty. A requirement to pay water fees may cause some poor farmers to give up farming. The potential to reduce poverty through subsidized new infrastructure development would be forfeited as well. Pushing poor people out of the agricultural water business is a perverse form of water conservation and demand management. A sliding-scale pricing strategy is one possible solution (Schreiner and van Koppen 2001). In many developing country situations, however, as in Sub-Saharan Africa and parts of India, formal irrigation systems may not be the most effective way to reduce poverty. Subsidized irrigation undermines the returns to already poor and marginal rainfed farmers and diverts scarce investment resources from where they may do the most good in terms of poverty reduction—improving rainfed agriculture. Critical to improving returns to rainfed agriculture is better agricultural water management, but this can often be achieved with lower cost interventions such as rainwater harvesting, conservation farming, and treadle pumps (see chapter 4 on poverty and chapter 8 on rainfed agriculture).

> The conditions necessary for market-based reforms to contribute to sustainable water management in agriculture are extremely rare in developing countries

Tradable water rights represent the greatest degree of privatization in water management, because they involve the private sector in water allocation as well as management. Individuals with water rights have the potential to gain from transferring their water to others through water markets, thereby offering positive as well as negative economic incentives for demand management. In addition to clearly defined water rights (including transfer rights), water markets require physical infrastructure that allows water to be transferred from one user to another, and institutional arrangements to protect against negative impacts on third parties when water is transferred (Easter, Rosegrant, and Dinar 1998 and Rosegrant and Binswanger 1994).

Market-inspired reforms have not lived up to their promise. Earlier enthusiasm for market-based water reforms was at best premature. The conditions necessary for market-based reforms to contribute to sustainable water management in agriculture are extremely rare in developing countries and uncommon even in rich countries. The Chile and Valencia (Spain) water market reforms have been held up as examples, but closer inspection raises many questions (Bauer 1997, 2005; Ingo 2004; Trawick 2005). As in all market and private property rights situations, questions of regulation (who sets the rules and what are the rules?) and capture of benefits (who wins and who loses in imperfect markets?) are central for assessing market-inspired reforms. A phased approach of vesting rights in existing users and currently excluded users and of clarifying regulatory mechanisms before developing detailed water market mechanisms may be more appropriate and politically more feasible than a rush to markets (see Bruns, Ringler, and Meinzen-Dick 2005).

Roads not traveled: empowering users and restructuring bureaucracies. Outside of some NGO-led watershed management projects, empowerment of water users (especially women and ethnic minorities) and radical bureaucratic restructuring are rarely discussed. Policies for irrigation management transfer sometimes do incrementally change the balance of power in favor of water users (for example, in Turkey), but they can also be neutralized or reversed (for example, in Andhra Pradesh, India; Indonesia; and the Philippines). Why there is so little to show after more than 30 years of attempted agricultural water management reforms is the topic of the next section.

Critical review of experiences: what are the lessons?

This section critically reviews approaches to institutional reform in the agricultural water management sector, highlighting three themes:

■ The dominance of social engineering paradigms and associated problems.

■ The benefits of a "problemshed" perspective rather than a watershed perspective.

■ The relevance and advantages of plurality in organizations, institutions, and water management objectives.

Figure 5.1 and box 5.5 summarize two conceptual and theoretical frameworks that heavily influenced this review.

> The tendency to think of institutions as things rather than as relationships and processes and to apply engineering metaphors and approaches rarely leads to effective institutional change

Need for context-specific, not social engineering solutions

Policies emphasizing public management, community-level collective action, and private sector roles follow different institutional approaches, but they share several tendencies.

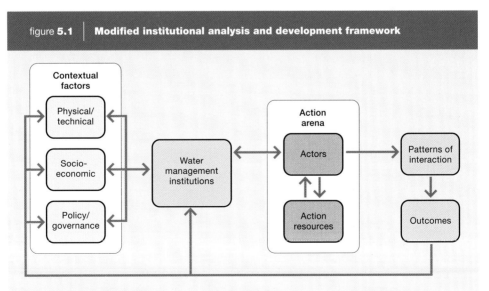

figure **5.1** | **Modified institutional analysis and development framework**

Source: Adapted from Ostrom (2005).

Tactics for reforming well entrenched policies and institutions are contingent, context specific, and nonlinear, and therefore the outcomes are uncertain. Nevertheless, the underlying principles of successful water resource management systems can be derived from theory and practical experience:
- Publicly available knowledge about resource availability over time and space.
- Policies establishing allocations, rights to the resources, priorities, cost recovery, and governance (who decides and how).
- Rules, laws, and regulations codifying how policies are to be implemented.
- Definition of roles and responsibilities (formal or informal organizations) for implementation of the rules.
- Infrastructure to deliver the services in terms of the rules and allocations.
- Incentives for people to participate and invest (relating especially to the profitability of water use in agriculture).
- Capacity to adapt to changing circumstances based on lessons (learning organization, adaptive capacity).

These principles are applicable in all locations and at all scales. Worldwide, there are many successful sustainable long-standing water resources management systems. These schemes are characterized not only by the basic elements of success but by a large degree of consistency and mutual synergy among the elements (Ostrom 1990, 1992). Water schemes that are not performing well are either missing one or more of the elements or have a mismatch among them.

Clearly the relationships among these elements are complex, and neither fixed nor absolute. They are interactive and dynamic with feedback loops. Change is based on new information. The dynamism is contentious but also a creative political process.

Intervening to change one element without paying attention to its consistency with the others is a recipe for failure—one that has been cooked repeatedly.

The nature of the water resource both sets limits on what kinds of policies or infrastructure are possible and provides opportunities to choose. Policies, rules, organizations, and infrastructure based on perceived water surplus will become increasingly counterproductive as water becomes scarcer or environmental concerns take center stage (Wester, Shah, and Merrey 2005). This is the fundamental problem facing large Asian irrigation bureaucracies: these organizations, the infrastructure they have constructed, and the policies and laws which they were implementing are now inappropriate as conditions have changed, yet the political process has failed to keep pace and introduce reforms needed to sustain and optimize the stream of benefits from these huge past investments.

Source: Adapted from Perry (1995, 2003a, 2003b).

One is an attempt at social engineering, the assumption that institutions can be shaped and reshaped like the physical landscape and that the role of institutional analysis is to chart some kind of blueprint for developing the "right" kinds of institutions (see box 5.2). Another is to compare the actual performance of one type of institution with the anticipated performance of an alternative type. This creates unrealistic expectations for the alternative type of institution. Moreover, repeated underestimation of the time, effort, and investment required to change institutions means that institutional reforms remain incomplete, especially if they are tied to a time-bound, donor-funded project. The result is that the expectations are not met, leading to yet another cycle of disappointment and experiments with another type of institution in search of a better "solution."[3]

The tendency to think of institutions as things rather than as relationships and processes and to apply engineering metaphors and approaches rarely leads to effective institutional change. Key aspects of institutions are that they persist over time and that change is path dependent—where an institution is going is shaped by where it has been (North 1990). These well established fundamentals are too often overlooked in the discussion of "models," "best practices," "toolboxes," and "blueprints," which often suggest that generalized sets of solutions are possible and undervalue the importance of context specificity and process. The disappointing outcomes of the numerous attempts to impose water user associations in such diverse contexts as South Asia, Sub-Saharan Africa, and the transition economies of Central Asia illustrate this error (box 5.6; Goldensohn 1994; Sivamohan 1986; Sivamohan and Scott 1994; Wade 1982; Shah and others 2002).

Instead of such social engineering approaches it is more useful to think of organic analogies, in which each institution is a product of its environment, rather than a replica of institutions elsewhere. Institutional change may be influenced, catalyzed, guided, or enabled, but not forced. Approaches need to be grounded in the local sociocultural, political, and physical environment. Changing long-standing social arrangements requires leadership and a structured long-term process. Reform tends to be slow and gradual, in an open-ended, nonlinear process with a high level of uncertainty. The processes are the outcome of human interaction, with scope for learning and adapting to new conditions.[4]

From watershed to "problemshed"

Until recently, water sector reform focused largely on irrigation. Irrigation policy reform has rarely been integrated with agricultural policy reform, often because the two are the responsibilities of different ministries. This disconnect continues and has not been well studied.

In the past decade the concept of integrated water resources management has come to dominate water reform discussions (GWP 2000; Merrey and others 2005), directing attention to the interconnections and interdependencies of different water uses and users. Irrigation needs to be understood in the context of multiple uses of water in both a river basin and a local context (see chapter 16 on river basins). Further, irrigation is increasingly seen as a threat to environmental sustainability (see chapter 6 on ecosystems), and questions have been raised about its impacts on poverty (see chapter 4 on poverty). At a time when irrigation institutions are still ineffective at managing water within irrigation schemes, they must now also defend the interests of irrigators against increasing competition for water, often from politically powerful entities (Vermillion and Merrey 1998; Wester, Shah, and Merrey 2005) and become more effective at addressing poverty, equity, and environmental issues. Thus water governance, management, and use must be considered comprehensively, within a problem analysis context that looks at "problemsheds"—the boundaries of a particular problem as defined by a network of issues—rather than as watersheds.

Water governance, management, and use cannot be treated independently. Both the causes of water problems and their solutions are embedded partly in processes and forces

| box **5.6** | **The state and water reform in Central Asian transition economies** |

Since the collapse of the Soviet Union there have been major changes in the agricultural sectors of the successor states. During the Soviet period the inputs for agricultural production were controlled and organized by the government in large-scale state and collective farms. After independence the successor states chose different privatization strategies. In Kazakhstan, Kyrgyzstan, and Tajikistan agricultural land was privatized and state control of crop production was abandoned. Turkmenistan and Uzbekistan continued tight governmental controls regulating supply and demand for agricultural inputs and products.

State and collective farm employees were specialized workers with only limited experience in all aspects of farm management. With privatization accountants, tractor drivers, teachers, and nurses became farmers. On state and collective farms large-scale farm inputs and outputs were centrally coordinated; with privatization this stopped and created a high degree of vulnerability.

Irrigation systems were designed for large-scale farms and mainly for a single crop. When these farms were divided into smaller units, water management became less efficient and created conflicts among farmers. Since privatization, small farmers have tended to shift from the cash crop cotton to food crops. Because of the old irrigation infrastructure, an appropriate irrigation service cannot be provided except by increasing the overall amount of water (Ul Hassan, Starkloff, and Nizamendik-hodjaeva 2004).

Some irrigation systems were built with a specific political rationale, when economic circumstances were different. Energy costs were low, and the Soviet government wanted to stabilize rural communities and secure borders. Pump stations were constructed to pump water to heights of 130 meters. With independence large-scale irrigation systems were often no longer financially feasible. According to a World Bank survey, in Tajikistan and Uzbekistan 11%–64% of irrigated land faces negative gross margins (if real energy costs are charged) affecting 250,000 people in Tajikistan and more than 1.1 million in Uzbekistan (Bucknall and others 2001).

Irrigation management transfer with full cost recovery is not feasible in certain regions of Central Asia because of high costs and low returns. It must be accompanied by complete redesign and reconstruction of irrigation systems rather than rehabilitation.

Source: Based on material provided by Kai Wegerich, contributing author.

in other domains. For example, farmers' water use behavior depends on household allocation decisions on labor, time, money, and other resources; the profitability of irrigated agriculture, fisheries, and livestock; the overall risk environment; and many other factors, and only partially, if at all, on increasing water-use efficiency. Intersectoral water allocation is to a large extent a product of broader political and economic considerations, such as the political clout of urban areas and industrial interests (see Molle and Berkoff 2005).

Failure to take this embeddedness into account has been a key factor limiting the success of previous reforms. Negotiating and crafting new types of organizational arrangements for managing irrigation, for example, are not possible without considering broader institutional arrangements and policies in the water, agricultural, and rural sectors as well as currency, trade, and overall macroeconomic policies. For example, the success of reforms of the Office du Niger in Mali lay in broader reforms to enhance the effectiveness of input and output markets as well as the restructuring of the management agency (box 5.7).

| box **5.7** | **A case of effective reform: Office du Niger, Mali** |

Office du Niger in Mali is a large-scale irrigation scheme created during the colonial period and expanded since then to cover about 70,000 hectares. Until about a decade ago it was seen as a hopeless case: low productivity, dissatisfied farmers, bankrupt. Today, the World Bank and others showcase Office du Niger as an example of what major policy, organizational, and institutional reforms can achieve. Between 1982 and 2002 rice yields increased by a factor of four, total production increased sixfold, incomes increased dramatically even as population exploded, women gained opportunities in farming and business, and new businesses were created. How did the government of Mali achieve this?

Aw and Diemer (2005) provide a detailed case study of the 20-year process of increasingly successful reforms. Until 1982 farmers had no voice; they were dissatisfied but poor and disorganized. However, various external and internal pressures forced the government to consider new options. Donors declined to finance further expansion until the scheme became financially sustainable. The government agreed to accept small reforms for obtaining assistance with physical improvements, including provision of credit to farmers and the first steps to organizing farmers as partners in scheme management. The support of a small group of Malian officials was crucial. Rice yields doubled, and power began to shift from agency staff to farmers as more government officials accepted the reforms. An alliance of the ruling party and donors introduced further reforms, leading to higher production and more control by farmers. After 1991 the one-party government was replaced by a democratic government committed to market reforms and further downsizing of the agency. Consultations among Office du Niger staff, farmers, ministries, and donors led to new legislation providing security of land tenure, full cost recovery, and joint management of the scheme by elected farmers' representatives and agency staff. A new balance of power was institutionalized through three-year, three-party (agency, government, farmers) performance contracts.

Aw and Diemer argue that some of the lessons learned in Mali are applicable to other countries. First, irrigation reforms are most successful when they are an integral part of a larger reform process. Second, government can begin with small politically feasible reforms that lead to benefits for farmers, creating a platform for building coalitions for further reform. Third, the key role played by powerful nonirrigation stakeholders, in Mali's case the ruling political parties and later the business community, enabled increasingly significant reforms. Fourth, there was a high degree of learning by doing, facilitated through the monitoring of results by farmers and others and sharing them widely. Finally, the reform process was long term, and the field staff committed to the welfare of farmers, with good access to decisionmakers, played a key role.

Source: Aw and Diemer 2005.

In practice, water governance, management, and use remain highly sector focused and demarcated. This is visible in the design of water organizations and in the disciplinary focus of water resources education. It is also characteristic of some multilateral investment banks and donors' internal structures, limiting their ability to foster reform in a broader national context (Molle 2005) and to foster innovative integrated water development at the local level through multiple-use water supply systems (see chapter 4 on poverty; Moriarty, Butterworth, and van Koppen 2004). Most observations in this chapter are as relevant to donors and multilateral banks as to developing countries, though less well studied at that level. A recent analysis has documented the serious institutional issues affecting the performance of multilateral banks and their relationships with client countries in Sub-Saharan Africa (Morardet and others 2005). The positive side of a single-purpose approach is that focused and concerted action is possible. This focus needs to be maintained but set in a broader, more comprehensive problem analysis context.

Three pluralities: multiple actors, institutions, and functions

Water governance, management, and use are characterized by three types of plurality—complex, overlapping, and sometimes competing networks of actors, rules, functions, and organizations.

- Multiple actors and organizations involved in water decisionmaking at different levels.
- Multiple rules and procedures applicable to a specific issue, as in legal pluralism.
- Multifunctionality of water resources systems and the range of values attached to these functions.

Clearly, such complexity and multiple pluralities require multiple reform strategies. However, policies for agricultural water management have tended to adopt "simplifications" (Scott 1998) to make rural societies more amenable to social engineering by states, to shape landscapes and people to their images of modernity. Standardized approaches and solutions are usually problematic. Our review is empirically oriented rather than theoretically or ideologically focused: the three pluralities exist and have to be dealt with more adequately in water sector reform than they have been so far to make progress on sustainable human development. Because of space limitations, we take for granted macro-level public economic and other policies and their impacts on water development but acknowledge their importance (Peña, Luraschi, and Valenzuela no date; Allan 1998; Allan, Thurton, and Nicol 2003).

Multiple actors in polycentric governance. There are many institutional and organizational models to choose from for water resources management: from direct public management to direct private management and from delegated management by an agency or utility to community self-management. But even if a system is formally under government management, farmers and private contractors still play an important role, and even in farmer-managed systems the state and markets are still critical.

Unfortunately, most water sector reform has been single-organization or single-institution focused. Most irrigation reforms have focused on one type of institution or organization: reform of water bureaucracies, irrigation management transfer to water user associations, development of water markets, or the introduction of river basin authorities. Almost invariably these reforms have ignored gender issues. This is like building on a single pillar. A more appropriate model is a tripod with several cross-supports (figure 5.2). Through mutual support the whole structure is stronger and more flexible than a single pillar.

What is critical is not finding a single "right" type of institution or organization but identifying the conditions under which each can play an effective role, understanding what can be done to strengthen them, and ensuring effective coordination and negotiation mechanisms among them. Huppert (1997) and Huppert and Urban (1998) provide a framework for examining the "exchange relationships" among organizations in irrigation

| figure **5.2** | **Tripod of water management** |

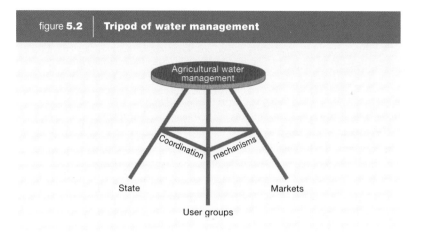

maintenance and service delivery, focusing on who authorizes the service, who provides it, and who pays for it, and the modes and mechanisms that govern the service relationship. Examining these relationships can reveal when the institutional arrangements create incentives for effective water management and when there are critical gaps that lead to poorly functioning systems.

Coordination and negotiation among organizations are particularly important when all stakeholders affected by water management are not represented in the organization entrusted to manage the water:

■ If responsibility for water management is transferred to an irrigators association, other water users in the local community will be affected but may not be included in official decisionmaking.[5]

■ Decentralization to locally elected government bodies may include additional (local) stakeholders in water resources decisionmaking, but not those living upstream or downstream who are affected by management of the resource.

■ A local government agency is often accountable to the central government, not locally. Sector divisions often limit their accountability to all stakeholders.

■ In most cases regulation is vested with the state as the representative of the people, but there may also be separate regulatory boards with representatives of at least some key stakeholder groups (farmers, fishers, environmental agencies, or groups) included. An example is the Project Management Committee in Sri Lankan irrigation systems (box 5.8). The definition and selection of who counts as a stakeholder are crucially important aspects of constituting inclusive planning and decisionmaking institutions.

Most reforms have focused on the organizations directly involved in irrigation or water management and not on the many other institutions that affect how water is managed in agriculture, from other sectors and other water uses to the overall economy, broader social and religious institutions, and other government agencies. Although some analysts and policymakers would like to streamline this complexity, for example, by collapsing it into a single river basin organization with a very broad mandate, organizational complexity persists. Applying integrated water resources management principles and achieving

box **5.8**	**Multiple water uses in Sri Lanka**

The Kirindi Oya system in southern Sri Lanka illustrates the complexities in meeting the needs of different types of users. Water is used for field crops, household gardens, livestock, fishing, and domestic use. Each use category does not represent a homogeneous interest group, but may be divided between the old irrigated area built hundreds of years ago, and the new area, with less reliable water. Each group may have its own association, and a government agency may be charged with responsibile for water use. The Project Management Committee, which decides on water release patterns, does not include cattle owners or fisher groups; and even domestic water supply and environment organizations are not formally represented. Garden irrigation, done mostly by women, is not a recognized water use and has neither a user organization nor a government agency to advocate for its water needs. Fishing and gardening add substantial value but are not formally recognized. Involving these other water users is essential for any plans to balance water use in a basin or locality.

Multiple water users in the Kirindi Oya system in Sri Lanka

Use	Users	Basis of claim	Supporting institutions
Field irrigation	Old area farmers	Customary use Recognized by government	Project Management Committee Farmer organizations
	New area farmers	Government allocation	Project Management Committee Farmer organizations
Garden irrigation	Mostly women	Well ownership Proximity	Well ownership Local norms
Livestock	Pastoralists	Historic use Not recognized by project	Cattle-owning farmer organization (not active in water issues) Divisional Secretary
	Farm households	Needed for livelihood	Local norms
Fishing	Mostly male farmers, part time	Use over time Membership in Fisher Cooperative Societies	Fisher Cooperative Societies (not in Project Management Committee)
Domestic	Old area households	Customary, necessary use Special allocations from reservoir	Project Management Committee reserves water for special water issues in dry season
	New area households	Reservoir allocations for water system Membership in standpipe committee Payment of fees	National Water Supply and Drainage Board (not in Project Management Committee), Standpipe committees Local norms
Environmental	Wildlife		Department of Wildlife Conservation (not in Project Management Committee)

Source: Adapted from Bakker and others (1999); see also Renwick (2001).

the Millennium Development Goals require cooperation among many actors and sectors beyond agriculture and water, but promoting interministerial and interdepartmental cooperation is difficult everywhere.

Ostrom, Schroeder, and Wynne (1993) argue that "polycentric governance" arrangements have advantages in allowing for experimentation in developing rules to fit a range of

conditions and to tap into local knowledge as well as technical expertise. Blomquist (1992) shows how a range of state and local government organizations as well as user organizations have evolved to manage groundwater in California. Working together to develop governance arrangements has been as important as the actual configuration of organizations. Another advantage of pluralistic organizational arrangements is redundancy: if one local organization becomes less effective its members may use other overlapping organizations to obtain services. Redundancy may also enhance the capacity of local populations to respond to external threats.

Institutional pluralism—both a strength and a constraint. Just as many organizations have overlapping mandates, there is often a plurality of institutions relevant to particular issues such as property rights arrangements for water and land (Boelens and Hoogendam 2002; Bruns and Meinzen-Dick 2000, 2005). In addition to state law, other sources of property rights for water include international treaties and law, development project regulations, religious law and practices, rules developed by user groups, and customary law (figure 5.3).

There are often inconsistencies among these categories, for example, between environmental legislation and other water acts or between different interpretations of customary law, and formal rules may differ from rules in use. Claims to water rights may be based on any of these, and each type of claim is only as strong as the institution that stands behind it. State law may be strong, but at the local level, especially in areas far from the

figure **5.3** | **Overlapping legal orders relating to water**

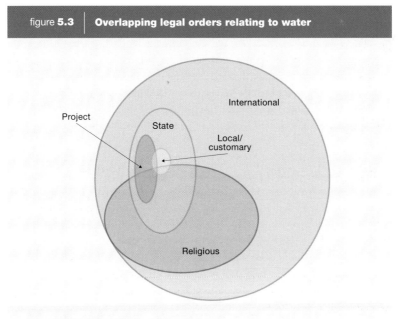

Source: Meinzen-Dick and Pradhan 2002.

capital city, state agencies may not have the capacity to monitor and enforce state definitions of water rights, and community norms may have greater influence. This can lead to confusion and conflict, but it is also an important mechanism for adapting water allocation to local conditions. Thus, water rights are more accurately understood as negotiated outcomes than as clearly following from written statutes.[6]

> Water rights are more accurately understood as negotiated outcomes than as clearly following from written statutes

A related, often problematic, area is ownership of hydraulic structures such as canals. There is a general understanding (even if no specific law) that the government owns the irrigation schemes it constructs. In most countries irrigation management transfer policies are notably vague on this issue: while farmers are expected to take responsibility for O&M, which can require substantial investment, they are not necessarily investing in "their" property. In farmer-built and -managed systems the property relationships are generally clear: ownership is shared with others in proportion to their investment or other criteria (Coward 1986a, 1986b). For long-term sustainability of infrastructure governments would do well to avoid creating government-owned property at the local level and offer instead to share costs with communities to encourage communities to create their own property.

As governments create new water laws for implementing integrated water resources management, the diversity and flexibility of local customary laws, principles, and practices may be replaced by uniform and rigid principles and requirements. Often, local practices are equitable and effective, and undermining them may be counterproductive. Sometimes, however, there may be serious equity issues, particularly biases against women in land and water rights that governments rightly may wish to address. However, national laws are not always be very effective in addressing such issues (for example, Trawick 2005; Vera forthcoming).

The plurality of organizations and institutions dealing with water management means that it is not realistic to plan sweeping reforms that impose new institutional and organizational arrangements supplanting all previous institutions and organizations. But within the limitations imposed by history, culture, and developmental pathways, there is also room to maneuver. Intentional reforms are possible, but there are so many factors at work that outcomes cannot be predicted, only anticipated with varying degrees of confidence.

Multifunctionality—added complexity and strength. Water sector reform strategies are increasingly expected to address concerns beyond water management issues, including reducing poverty and gender inequity, reversing environmental degradation, and giving voice to marginalized groups. In Asia irrigation investments contributed much to poverty reduction (Hussain 2005), but large-scale irrigation is at best a blunt instrument for achieving this purpose. Polak (2005) argues that while large-scale irrigation is a "prime mover" for achieving food security at the macro level, the greatest opportunity for improving the livelihoods of small farmers today is promoting low-cost, market-driven microagricultural water management technologies (see chapter 4 on poverty). In principle such an approach can be better targeted to women and is less likely to damage the environment than large-scale irrigation, but current capacities to implement such

targeted programs on a large scale are minimal (van Koppen, Safilios Rothschild, and Namara 2005).

Ecosystems provide many functions to societies, which are valued differently by different groups. To achieve sustainable outcomes, ecosystem functions and values need to be reflected in water policies, and mechanisms need to be in place to balance them (Abdeldayem and others 2005; see chapter 6 on ecosystems). In developed countries the environment has a strong political voice, but in developing countries attention to environmental conservation is often perceived as antipoor. It is important to find effective ways of linking ecosystem services directly to improving the livelihoods of the poor. This requires demonstrating strong evidence of a "win-win" approach and creating political coalitions to pursue them.

Another issue is how to give effective voice to poor and marginalized people—women, minorities, pastoralists, fishers. There are no easy solutions, but examining how explicit and implicit rules favor or exclude different groups is a good starting point (Vera forthcoming). Membership rules for local water user groups and higher level organizations such as project management committees or basin organizations may exclude certain categories of users—for example, fishers and female gardeners are excluded from irrigation project management committees in Sri Lanka (see box 5.8); women are excluded from water user associations in the Andes (Vera 2005); and the rural poor, including small-scale irrigators, are not represented in Mexico's river basin councils (Wester, Merrey, and de Lange 2003). Holding meetings in a language spoken mainly by the educated elite can exclude people from minority ethnic groups or those with less education, and the timing and location of meetings can make it difficult for women to participate.

Kerr (2002) found that in many watershed management projects in India, women and herders bore the highest costs of new practices, but downstream farmers received the greatest benefits. However, where nongovernmental organizations had been involved in working with marginalized groups on other activities, such as group credit, these groups developed more bargaining power. The move toward integrated water resources management should create space for involving herders, fishers, domestic water supply users, and others who depend on water resources for their livelihoods in decisionmaking, along with farmers, environmentalist, and state actors. Finding concrete ways to recognize the multiple claims on water resources use and to create situations in which the different functions of water, the different values attached to them, and the different outcomes its use produces for different groups can be negotiated more constructively is a major challenge of water sector reform.

To contribute to both poverty reduction and environmental sustainability, reforms should create a framework for development relationships among the key governance actors—government, nongovernmental organizations, civil society, and the private sector (see figure 5.2)—to identify the most effective resource uses and management modalities for empowering disadvantaged groups. Because incentives are lacking to engage poor people in the governance of water resources, the state needs to use its authority to enhance their voice and benefits. One way is to use water-related projects to generate income or employment. For example, South Africa's Working for Water Program to remove alien

> Water sector reform strategies are increasingly expected to address concerns beyond water management issues

plants from watersheds creates employment and trains local people in the skills required to manage small contracts—creating a new class of entrepreneurs (Görgens and van Wilgen 2004).

Recognizing all water users and developing institutional mechanisms to address their water needs is challenging. But it is critical for strengthening the agriculture-water-poverty-gender-environment nexus. It is often women and poor households that depend on other uses of water. Moreover, fishing, livestock, gardens, domestic, and environmental uses often have high value per unit of water, so including them can substantially increase the total value of agricultural water systems.

> **Recognizing all water users and developing institutional mechanisms to address their water needs is challenging— but it is critical**

The way forward

Successfully moving forward requires strategies for institutional and policy reform processes that take into account reform as an inherently political process; the social embeddedness of water institutions; the state as the driver of reform; capacity building, information sharing, and public debates; and implementation strategies.

Reform is a political process

Institutional transformation is inherently political and typically slow and difficult, with losers and winners and "outsiders" who also have their own interests. Some interests are more politically powerful than others, often distorting outcomes in favor of special interests. Policy actors and advisors need to make strategic assessments of how policies and institutions related to agriculture and water management can contribute to food security, environmental sustainability, economic growth, and poverty reduction—a process of transforming perceptions, interests, and objectives into strategies. This means taking into account political feasibility as well as desired outcomes.

Key questions to ask for each situation include:

- What will be the benefits of institutional and policy reform, and how will these benefits be distributed? What will be the costs, and who will bear them?
- What coalition of interest groups will push forward and implement the change? Around which issues can such efforts be organized most productively?
- How can these coalitions be supported?
- What can realistically be done to adapt the enabling and constraining conditions for this institutional transformation?
- How can knowledge producers and processors—academics, consultants, and reflective practitioners—play a more active role?

The answers to these questions depend on specific conditions. The tendency to impose generalized solutions has led only to failure. Factors affecting the answers include biophysical characteristics; social, cultural, and political context; and types of agricultural water infrastructure (canals, wells, small or large dams, rainfed). Analyzing each situation and drawing on experiences of other cases as a practical resource and on frameworks such as those illustrated in figure 5.1 and box 5.5 are necessary first steps for strategizing effective institutional transformation.

Water governance and institutions are embedded in a broader context

There is no blank slate starting point for institutional and organizational reforms: the entire process is embedded in a context with a history and culture that shape the scope for future change. Factors such as technology, water availability, cropping patterns, market development, social capital, government policies, and overall political factors shape institutions as well as how people manage water. Thus institutions that are effective in one environment cannot simply be transplanted to another environment and be expected to have the same effect.

Interventions to change water institutions and organizations must consider the consistency of the proposed reforms with hydrologic, social, economic, and political conditions (see box 5.5). For example, introducing water markets requires water rights that are clear and not tied to specific land parcels, laws and organizations capable of enforcing and facilitating transactions, and infrastructure with flexibility and measurement capacity. Transferring management of irrigation infrastructure to farmers is more likely to succeed where farmers' water rights are specified, there is legal support for farmer organizations, infrastructure is designed for decentralized management, and the property status of the infrastructure is clear. Policies emphasizing demand management and cost recovery require water delivery infrastructure and measurement capacity—neither of which is common in developing countries.

> Interventions to change water institutions and organizations must consider the consistency of the proposed reforms with hydrologic, social, economic, and political conditions

However, conditions are not static nor changed only by conscious reform. Conditions may change on their own and require institutional adjustments to catch up. A seasonal drought or increased water scarcity induced by climate change requires greater management intensity. HIV/AIDS and malaria may reduce the ability of farmers to do heavy maintenance or engage in time-critical management practices. Trade reform undermines the food-security rationale for massive public irrigation investments, while farmers with profitable niche opportunities may exert pressure for improved irrigation services or purchase their own equipment (see chapter 9 on irrigation). As river basins develop from being "open" to "closed," the types of policies and organizations required change dramatically (see chapter 16 on river basins).

There are several policy and institutional implications of this embeddedness of agricultural water management issues in a broader context:

- *Problemsheds: understanding issue-networks.* The single-sector perspective dominating agricultural water management needs to be replaced by an approach that starts with a concrete problem and then decides what is required and possible (defining the next step). It is more appropriate to look at "problemsheds"—the boundaries of a particular problem defined by the issue-network—than at watersheds.[7] Most social and political boundaries do not line up with hydrologic boundaries such as watersheds. In some cases it is better to build on existing administrative units than to force the development of new, hydrologically defined "watershed" organizations (Abdeldayem and others 2005; van der Zaag 2005; Moss 2003; Swallow, Johnson, and Meinzen-Dick 2001; see chapter 16 on river basins for further discussion).
- *Realistic expectations about feasible options.* More realistic expectations are needed about what can be achieved within given constraints and circumstances, and on the

basis of such assessments pragmatic and programmatic choices need to be made on where to allocate time and resources.

- *Out-of-the-sector policy entrepreneurship for better coordination.* More effective ways are needed to address the age-old problems of coordination, interaction, and collaboration among organizations. In addition to government agencies such coalitions should include various private and civil society interests for a truly integrated approach (Sabatier and others 2005). Water policymakers and implementers must also participate in decisionmaking outside the water sector to solve some water problems. Unfortunately, there are very few positive examples in the agricultural water sector of such integrated approaches.[8]

> In some cases it is better to build on existing administrative units than to force the development of new, hydrologically defined "watershed" organizations

- *Thoughtful practitioners.* Working in a constrained environment requires policy and administrative entrepreneurship, making creative and effective use of legal, administrative, and budget space in the system for developing creative responses. It requires people with the skills to assess situations, draw lessons from experience, and create effective strategies to move forward (Schön 1983; Forester 1999). For international donors, implementing agencies, and research institutions, which tend to be captured by prevailing donor paradigms, this will require self-reflection and revision of existing practices of planning, finance, and research prioritization.

Understanding how organizations and institutions are integral parts of a complex sociotechnical system with its own history, which changes as people respond to new opportunities and pressures, is essential for designing effective reform strategies—but the very complexity means that prediction is impossible and a social learning perspective is essential.

The state is the main driver of reform—but cannot succeed alone

Successful reforms of the water sector still require the state to play a leading role *[well established]*. There are a few examples of water sector reforms initiated by civil society movements in developing countries, such as a campaign to reduce pollution in the Bhavani Basin in India (Meinzen-Dick and others 2004), but these are rare and tend to be localized and partial. There are more examples of donor-led reforms, but these often do not last beyond the project period (if they are implemented at all). The private sector may create demand for institutional change (for example, the farm sector demand for better performing irrigation systems in Mexico after implementation of the North American Free Trade Agreement increased the opportunity cost of poorly performing systems), but this will not go far without state "ownership" of the reforms.

Accepting the state as the driver of reform poses its own dilemma. The state is often itself in need of reform. In most state institutions there are few incentives, for example, to overcome gender imbalances, the male-dominated engineering culture of water agencies, and elite capture of reforms. This is a political issue and requires leadership at the political level.

Although public agency roles in design, construction, and O&M are shrinking, there are new roles for the state in basin planning and management, water rights registration and monitoring, data collection and management, environmental monitoring and assessment, support of local management institutions, and accrediting of private service providers. Some of these new roles are essential but so new that there is a question whether

existing organizations can fulfill them effectively. The regulatory capacity of the state becomes more, not less, vital. The complexity of the task in transition economies is especially daunting, as illustrated in box 5.6.

Government resources will not be sufficient as the sole source of investment in water control; in many cases governments do not have the fiscal resources to provide adequate funding even for O&M. Other financing mechanisms are required, as discussed by Winpenny (2003). There is considerable interest in public-private partnerships, but these should not be limited to partnerships with multinational corporations. India has set up "Nigams" to tap into the domestic bond industry as a source of financing for large-scale systems; these have been successful in mobilizing finance and expediting construction but have not led to improved irrigation performance and cost recovery for sustainability (Gulati, Meinzen-Dick, and Raju 2005, chap. 5). Japan is using environmental service payments to supplement resources for irrigation O&M. But the greatest source of private financing is farmers themselves, who invest considerable amounts in irrigation infrastructure and O&M when it is in their interests to do so, for example, in tubewells under their own control. Penning de Vries, Sally, and Inocencio (2005) review the large potential for investment in agricultural water development by small farmers and businesspeople.

> An area critical to successful reform, but barely studied, is how governments allocate budgets and monitor outcomes of budget expenditures

An area critical to successful reform, but barely studied, is how governments allocate budgets and monitor outcomes of budget expenditures. Lack of transparency has led to calls for decentralized participatory budgeting. Budget allocations reflect government priorities, in turn often reflecting historical inertia and entrenched bureaucracies. If specific allocations target support for women, poverty reduction, and environmental services, for example, these are important steps, especially if accompanied by transparent monitoring. Gender-responsive budgeting provides a means to examine the priorities reflected in budgets at different levels and is being tried in many countries (Budlender 2000; Mukhopadhyay and others 2002). This concept could be applied to other priority areas as well (see Norton and Elston 2002; de Sousa Santos 1998; and www.odi.org.uk/pppg/cape for general discussion and examples). While such approaches are emerging in other sectors, they still need to be introduced in the water sector.

For such financing arrangements to lead to better performance, and not to uncoordinated development or poorly performing systems, transparency and appropriate coordination mechanisms are critical. First, this means sufficient accountability within government departments to ensure that public funds are well spent and to create incentives to deliver efficient services.[9] Second, it means appropriate regulation of private operators to ensure that they deliver agreed levels of services to all users equitably at agreed rates. Even when user groups are entrusted with water management, accountability is critical to ensure that all users (including women and marginalized groups) are served. The state capacity for regulation in many of these arenas is often weak. This remains a serious policy challenge. Third, it means developing mechanisms for effective coordination among government units.

The state will continue to be responsible for ensuring that poor people and environmental services receive the water that they need, even if they are unable to pay. This is essential for meeting basic needs and for conserving resources. In many cases basic needs are interpreted as the minimum requirements for domestic water use (for example, 20 liters a person per day). However, many customary systems, especially in Africa, recognize livelihood needs as part of the basic requirements (von Koppen and others forthcoming), as increasingly do some new national laws (South Africa) and some service providers (Moriarty, Butterworth, and van Koppen 2004). The state's primary responsibility to ensure that people have necessary services does not mean that the state must implement everything by itself. The gap between state capacities and the scale of the problem is too great. The state needs to work with the private sector and civil society to facilitate what each does best, while concentrating its scarce capacity where it has a comparative advantage.

> Information, knowledge, and the capacity to use it are critical to successful integrated water management and appropriate reforms—but their availability is often limited

Because the state is itself the focus of much of the required reform, while still being the critical driver of reforms, coalitions among the private sector and civil society are critically important for long-term success.

Knowledge and capacity for balanced policy processes

Information, knowledge, and the capacity to use it are critical to successful integrated water management and appropriate reforms. But the availability of reliable data transformed into credible information is often limited. In many cases the desired data do not exist (long time series of hydrological and meteorological data, density of measurement networks, gender-disaggregated household data, policy impact studies).

More often existing data are difficult to access. Hydrological data may become state secrets when interstate water conflicts emerge, or procedures for accessing data may be excessively cumbersome or expensive. The information may be unreliable if it is thought to support particular political agendas or if collection practices are not rigorous enough. Differential access to information, for example, by men or elites but not women or poor stakeholders, can make inequity worse (Vera 2005). To achieve sustainable agricultural water management, reliable information needs to be made available in the public domain and widely shared and debated, as a means to empower stakeholders by increasing their knowledge. As demand for water puts pressure on the supply, access to reliable information by all stakeholders becomes increasingly critical (Burton and Molden 2005).

Another critical area is the growing mismatch between the multidisciplinary technical capacity required for integrated water resources management and the narrow—and dwindling—capacities of most government water agencies. Budget reductions, unattractive salaries and career prospects compared with alternatives, and conservative university curricula are making it increasingly difficult for government agencies to attract and retain staff with the kinds of expertise required. There are a few bright spots. The most interesting may be two initiatives in Southern Africa that cooperate in capacity building and research (box 5.9).

As important as knowledge and capacity within government is public awareness of water issues and access to information. Transparency and accountability are critical for a democratic political process of institutional reform, whether it is government agencies, user groups, or private contractors that deliver water services. Sometimes, proposed reforms are thwarted by the deliberate dissemination of misinformation (Van der Velde and Tirmizi 2004). However, citizen committees and public hearings can contribute to

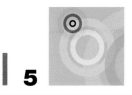

| box **5.9** | **Capacity building and research initiatives in Southern Africa** |

Waternet is a network for integrated water resources management capacity building with more than 50 member institutions in 12 countries in eastern and southern Africa. It is training a new generation of water professionals through a unique multidisciplinary, multi-institutional program. The Water Research Fund for Southern Africa (WARFSA) supports research by regional professionals. The two institutions, linked with the Southern Africa Development Community (SADC) and the Southern African chapter of the Global Water Partnership, sponsor an annual symposium to exchange and debate policy directions and new research findings.

Source: Swatuk 2005; van der Zaag 2005.

successful reform by creating greater accountability and trust (Moench, Caspari, and Dixit 1999; Sabatier and others 2005; Bruns, Ringler, and Meinzen-Dick 2005). Collaborative partnerships among the state, civil society, and the private sector may require investments in capacity for collaboration within partner organizations. However, the outcome of "participatory" processes is not pre-ordained: opposing parties may not converge on a common position, or one party may pressure others using superior power.

Balanced policy processes require capacity building of the groups and organizations in a disadvantaged position with regard to knowledge, notably small-scale water users and women. Sabatier's (1988) work on the advocacy coalition framework found that in reaching agreements on watershed management plans and practices in the western United States, there were alliances among government agencies, user groups, and environmental interest groups, among others. It is critical for successful outcomes of negotiations that each group has at least one trusted person who understands the information and models being used in multistakeholder dialogue and decisionmaking processes.

Most water management institutions focus on water quantity. But each user not only takes water out, but also returns something to the hydrological system. A looming challenge is regulation of water quality. Even small amounts of contaminants can make water unusable for others, and the contamination may persist. Many water control institutions do not have the capacity to monitor or regulate water quality, and agencies that do monitor quality are separate from agencies charged with agricultural water management. Greater investment in state capacity is needed, but the state cannot do it all. Informing the general public about water-quality issues is an important adjunct. Tools such as bio-monitoring can empower communities to check the quality of their water resources (Mthimkhulu and others forthcoming; Wepener and others 2005).

Even with the best management there will be conflicts over water. Some may be resolved locally through customary institutions, but the state has a responsibility to develop mechanisms to help users resolve conflicts. Technical information may help in some cases; in others cases arbitration and enforcement will be required. The large number of international river basins means that forums for negotiating sharing arrangements between countries are also needed, calling for strong negotiating skills within government agencies, user groups, and other stakeholders.

Implementing reform

Encouraging the emergence of a learning culture in organizations is critical to the success of reforms. In the long run organizations able to anticipate change and learn from experience are the most adaptive, and their reforms are the most sustainable. Where institutional change is needed, identifying a champion within senior political or agency levels will often help to create a vision of reform and to overcome obstacles, especially early in the process. It is also important to build coalitions around specific shared objectives, so that change becomes institutionalized. Such a structured context-specific approach precludes the usual practice of adopting single-factor panaceas to achieve a desired goal.

> It is remarkable how little research has been done to understand how to support agricultural water reform processes. With such a fundamental gap it is not surprising that so much uncertainty surrounds how to proceed with policy and institutional reform

The state is an essential driver of reforms, but it cannot make lasting changes alone. No matter how strong the state, customary law and institutions are not always amenable to being rewritten as statutory law. There is often a temptation to pass reforming legislation with little discussion, to minimize opposition (van der Velde and Tirmizi 2004). But reforms passed in this manner may never be implemented or may cause a public outcry when they become known. Public debate and policy formulation create broader legitimacy and understanding and increase the chances of implementation and sustainability. South Africa's debates over the reform of its water law created so much awareness among the public that there had to be follow-through (de Lange 2004), whereas other countries have reformed their water law (often in response to donor pressures, and with external models) with little fanfare and equally little impact.

Reducing uncertainty: research to support reform processes

Considering that the central importance of policies and institutional capacities to promote sustainable development has long been recognized, it is remarkable how little research has been done to understand how to support reform processes in the agricultural water sector. There are a few case studies, but most are too superficial or too partisan to contribute much. There are a few comparative analyses across countries and regions (a recent contribution is Dirksen and Huppert 2006), but almost no in-depth, long-term, or historical studies of processes and underlying drivers. Further, most research has focused more on what than on how. Many studies begin with an assumption of the desirability of a specific reform (management transfer, privatization, river basin organizations) without addressing the strategic process of implementation. With such a fundamental gap in the social science research it is not surprising that so much uncertainty surrounds how to proceed with policy and institutional reform.

Mollinga and Bolding (2004) propose a research program specific to irrigation reform, emphasizing the resilience of irrigation bureaucracies, the role of international development funding agencies, and the capture of irrigation reform implementation by elites. Studies should apply rigorous comparative analyses and contextualized case studies examining a representative range of successes, failures, and cases in between. A few of the topics needing urgent attention include:

- Studies of institutional reform as sociopolitical processes—what works, why, and under what conditions.
- Studies on incentives, positive and negative. There has been little work on rent seeking in the water sector since 1986 despite its continuing prominence, and there is almost no evidence on responses to water pricing in the agricultural sector. The role and politics of budget allocations in reform processes has been similarly neglected.
- Studies of the implementation and outcomes of integrated water resources management—a rhetorical buzzword, but little studied in practice.
- Comparative studies of the outcomes of various structural reforms, such as decentralization, alternative river basin management models, and alternative models for structuring ministries dealing with agricultural water.

A cross-cutting research topic of critical importance is how to promote greater attention to equity, including gender issues, poverty reduction, innovative ways of implementing integrated water supply systems at local levels, scale-up of new low-cost small-scale water technologies and improvements in the productivity of rainfed agriculture, and integration of ecosystem services and provision of other essential water services.

Clearly, much remains to be done. Because of the large number of contextual factors and overlapping institutions, institutional reforms are never going to be a certain process. There will be no textbook formulas for reforms, but further work in these areas can help to guide the process if supporting policy and institutional change processes are viewed as the art of the possible.

Reviewers

Chapter review editor: Miguel Solanes.
Chapter reviewers: Apichart Anukularmphai, Bryan Bruns, J.J. Burke, Belgin Cakmak, Frances Cleaver, Declan Conway, Rosa Garay-Flühmann, Mark Giordano, Line J. Gordon, Leon Hermans, Chu Thai Hoanh, Walter Huppert, Patricia Kabatabazi, Lyla Mehta, David Molden, François Molle, Esther Mwangi, Gladys Nott, Chris Perry, Claudia Ringler, V. Santhakumar, David Seckler, Ganesh Shivakothi, Amy Sullivan, Larry Swatuk, Paul Trawick, Olcay Unver, Philippus Wester, Dennis Wichelns, and James Winpenny.

Notes

1. Chapters 10 on groundwater and 16 on river basins, like this chapter, address largely policy and institutional issues; we have tried to avoid overlap. Chapter 9 on irrigation addresses quite different issues than those addressed here—there is therefore considerable complementarity.

2. For example, the US Agency for International Development's on-farm water management projects in Egypt and Pakistan documented farmers' alleged ignorance of rooting depths and irrigation requirements and inability to cooperate (Lowdermilk, Freeman, and Early 1978).

3. Benchmarking through systematic comparison can be useful under some circumstances, but it is important to compare likes with likes.

4. See Pahl-Wostl (2002) and Ebrahim (forthcoming) for examples and analysis of social learning in policymaking and adaptive management.

5. In South Africa in the transformation of irrigation boards whose members are white commercial farmers to inclusive water user associations, the problem became how to balance the interests of those who have large financial investments in irrigation with those making no such investment but needing water (Faysse 2004). In Andhra Pradesh, India, the law says that other water users can be observers or nonvoting members of irrigator-composed water user associations. This has not been implemented, and in irrigation tanks (small reservoirs) conflicts between fisheries and irrigation interests have emerged. In most Andean rural communities women are not allowed to be members of water user associations (Vera 2005).

6. Through which organizations competing property rights claims and interpretations are mediated is a separate question. State and customary law may have separate organizational frameworks for adjudication, but the same court organization may also have a mandate for addressing both. This is another example of the importance of distinguishing between institutions and organizations.

7. On the notion of "problemshed" and its use in water policy and discourse, see for instance, www.renpanteg.de/2005/proceedings/node172.html, http://cwrri.colostate.edu/pubs/newsletter/specinterest/parkcity.htm, www.ucowr.siu.edu/updates/pdf/V111_A1.pdf, http://frap.cdf.ca.gov/publications/cumim.pdf, www.ca9.uscourts.gov/ca9/newopinions.nsf/7DBD5DB043E626BF88256E5A00707D96/$file/0015967.pdf?openelement (all accessed October 31, 2005).

8. Positive examples include a small river basin in Namibia (Botes and others 2003; Manning and Seely 2005) and watershed management in the United States (Sabatier and others 2005); a less positive one is the Command Area Development Authority in India (Sivamohan 1986; Sivamohan and Scott 1994).

9. For more detail on such accountability mechanisms, see Small and Carruthers (1991) and Gulati, Meinzen-Dick, and Raju (2005).

References

Abdeldayem, S., J. Hoevenaars, P. P. Mollinga, W. Scheumann, R. Slootweg, and F. van Steenbergen. 2005. "Agricultural Drainage: Towards an Integrated Approach." *Irrigation and Drainage Systems* 19 (1): 71–87.

Allan, J. A., A. Turton, and A. Nicol. 2003. "Policy Options in Water-Stressed States: Emerging Lessons from the Middle East and Southern Africa." University of Pretoria, African Water Issues Research Unit, and Overseas Development Institute, Pretoria, and London.

Allan, T. 1998. "Moving Water to Satisfy Uneven Global Needs: 'Trading' Water as an Alternative to Engineering It." *ICID Journal* 47 (2): 1–8.

Aw, D., and G. Diemer. 2005. *Making a Large Irrigation Scheme Work: A Case Study from Mali.* Washington, D.C.: World Bank.

Bakker, M., R. Barker, R. S. Meinzen-Dick, and F. Konradsen, eds. 1999. "Multiple Uses of Water in Irrigated Areas: A Case Study from Sri Lanka." SWIM Report 8. International Water Management Institute, Colombo.

Bauer, C. J. 1997. "Bringing Water Markets Down to Earth: The Political Economy of Water Rights in Chile, 1976–1995." *World Development* 25 (5): 639–56.

———. 2005. *Siren Song: Chilean Water Law as a Model for International Reform.* Washington, D.C.: RFF Press.

Blomquist, W. 1992. *Dividing the Waters: Governing Groundwater in Southern California.* San Francisco, Calif.: ICS Press.

Boelens, R., and P. Hoogendam, eds. 2002. *Water Rights and Empowerment.* Assen, Netherlands: Van Gorcum.

Botes, A., J. Henderson, T. Nakale, K. Nantanga, K. Schachtschneider, and M. Seely. 2003. "Ephemeral Rivers and Their Development: Testing an Approach to Basin Management Committees on the Kuiseb River, Namibia." *Physics and Chemistry of the Earth* 28 (20–27): 853–58.

Braadbaart, O. 2005. "Privatizing Water and Wastewater in Developing Countries: Assessing the 1990s Experiments." *Water Policy* 7 (4): 329–44.

Bruns, B. 2004. "From Voice to Empowerment: Rerouting Irrigation Reform in Indonesia." In P. P. Mollinga and A. Bolding, eds., *The Politics of Irrigation Reform: Contested Policy Formulation and Implementation in Asia, Africa, and Latin America.* Hans, UK: Ashgate.

Bruns, B. R., and R. Meinzen-Dick. 2000. *Negotiating Water Rights.* London: Intermediate Technology Press.

———. 2005. "Framework for Water Rights: An Overview of Institutional Options." In B. R. Bruns, C. Ringler, and R. S. Meinzen-Dick, eds., *Water Rights Reform: Lessons for Institutional Design.* Washington, D.C.: International Food Policy Research Institute.

Bruns, B. R., C. Ringler, and R. S. Meinzen-Dick, eds. 2005. *Water Rights Reform: Lessons for Institutional Design.* Washington, D.C.: International Food Policy Research Institute.

Bucknall, J., I. Klytchnikova, J. Lampietti, M. Lundell, M. Scatasta, and M. Thurman. 2001. *Irrigation in Central Asia: Where to Rehabilitate and Why.* Washington, D.C.: World Bank.

Budlender, D. 2000. "The Political Economy of Women's Budgets in the South." *World Development* 28 (7): 1365–78.

Burton, M., and D. J. Molden. 2005. "Making Sound Decisions: Information Needs for Basin Water Management." In M. Svendsen, ed., *Irrigation and River Basin Management: Options for Governance and Institutions.* Wallingford, UK: CABI Publishing.

Carrasco, E. R. 1995. "Autocratic Transitions to Liberalism: A Comparison of Chilean and Russian Structural Adjustment." *Transnational Law and Contemporary Problems* 5 (99): 104–06. Quoted in Mentor, J. 2001. "Trading Water, Trading Places: Water Marketing in Chile and the Western United States." Presented at AWRA/ILWRI-University of Dundee

Specialty Conference, "Globalization and Water Resources Management: The Changing Value of Water," August 6–8, Dundee, UK. [Accessed November 21, 2005, at www.mentorlaw.com/tradingwater.pdf].

Coward, E. W., Jr. 1986a. "Direct or Indirect Alternatives for Irrigation Investment and the Creation of Property." In K. W. Easter, ed., *Irrigation Investment, Technology, and Management Strategies for Development.* Boulder, Colo., and London: Westview Press.

———. 1986b. "State and Locality in Asian Irrigation Development: The Property Factor." In K. C. Nobe and R. K. Sampath, eds., *Irrigation Management in Developing Countries: Current Issues and Approaches.* Boulder, Colo., and London: Westview Press.

De Lange, M. 2004. "Water Policy and Law Review Process in South Africa with a Focus on the Agricultural Sector." In P. P. Mollinga and A. Bolding, eds., *The Politics of Irrigation Reform: Contested Policy Formulation and Implementation in Asia, Africa, and Latin America.* Hans, UK: Ashgate.

De Sousa Santos, B. 1998. "Participatory Budgeting in Porto Alegro: Toward a Redistributive Democracy." *Politics and Society* 26 (4): 461–75.

Dinar, A., ed. 2000. *The Political Economy of Water Pricing Reforms.* New York: Oxford University Press.

Dirksen, W., and W. Huppert, eds. 2006. *Irrigation Sector Reform in Central and East European Countries.* Eschborn, Germany: Deutsche Gesellschaft für Technische Zusammenarbeit.

Easter, K. W., M. W. Rosegrant, and A. Dinar, eds. 1998. *Markets for Water: Potential and Performance.* Boston, Mass.: Kluwer Academic Publishers.

Ebrahim, A. Forthcoming. "Learning in Environmental Policy Making and Implementation." Draft. In K. Ahmed and E. Sanchez-Triana, eds., *Understanding Policy Strategic Environmental Assessment.* Washington, D.C.: World Bank.

Faysse, N. 2004. *An Assessment of Small-Scale Users' Inclusion in Large-Scale Water Users Associations of South Africa.* IWMI Research Report 84. Colombo: International Water Management Institute.

Forester, J. F. 1999. *The Deliberative Practitioner: Encouraging Participatory Planning Processes.* Boston, Mass.: MIT Press.

Goldensohn, M. 1994. "Participation and Empowerment: An Assessment of Water User Associations in Asia and Egypt." United States Agency for International Development, Irrigation Support Project for Asia and Near East, Washington, D.C.

Gordon, I., J. Lewis, and K. Young. 1997. "Perspectives on Policy Analysis." In M. Hill, ed., *The Policy Process: A Reader.* 2nd ed. London: Pearson-Prentice Hall.

Görgens, A. H. M., and B. W. van Wilgen. 2004. "Invasive Alien Plants and Water Resources in South Africa: Current Understanding, Predictive Ability and Research Challenges." *South African Journal of Science* 100 (1/2): 27–33.

Grindle, M. S. 1999. "In Quest of the Political: The Political Economy of Development Policy Making." CID Working Paper 17. Harvard University, Center for International Development, Cambridge, Mass.

Gulati, A., R. S. Meinzen-Dick, and K. V. Raju. 2005. *Institutional Reforms in Indian Irrigation.* New Delhi: Sage Publications.

GWP (Global Water Partnership). 2000. "Integrated Water Resources Management." GWP Technical Committee Background Paper 4. Stockholm.

Heierli, U., and P. Polak. 2000. "Poverty Alleviation as Business: The Market Creation Approach to Development." Swiss Agency for Development and Cooperation, Bern. Accessed May 30. [www.intercooperation.ch/sed/product/heierli/main.html].

Howlett, M., and M. Ramesh. 1995. *Studying Public Policy: Policy Cycles and Policy Subsystems.* Oxford, UK: Oxford University Press.

Huppert, W. 1997. "Irrigation Management Transfer: Changing Complex Delivery Systems for O&M Services." MAINTAIN Thematic Paper 7. Deutsche Gesellschaft für Technische Zusammenarbeit, Eschborn, Germany.

———. 2005. "Water Management in the 'Moral Hazard Trap': The Example of Irrigation." Paper presented at Stockholm Water Symposium, August 21, Stockholm.

Huppert, W., and C. Hagen. 1999. "Maintenance as a Service Provision in Irrigation—The Example of the 'Neste System' in Southern France." *Journal of Applied Irrigation Science* 37 (1): 63–88.

Huppert, W., and K. Urban. 1998. *Analysing Service Provision—Instruments for Development Cooperation Illustrated by Examples from Irrigation.* Frankfurt, Germany: Deutsche Gesellschaft für Technische Zusammenarbeit.

Huppert, W., M. Svendsen, and D. L. Vermillion. 2001. *Governing Maintenance Provision in Irrigation: A Guide to Institutionally Viable Maintenance Strategies.* Wiesbaden, Germany: Universum Verlagsanstalt.

Hussain, I. 2005. *Pro-Poor Intervention Strategies in Irrigated Agriculture in Asia: Poverty in Irrigated Agriculture—Issues, Lessons, Options, and Guidelines: Bangladesh, China, India, Pakistan, and Viet Nam.* Final synthesis report 1. Colombo: International Writer Management Institute.

Ingo, G. 2004. "El Derecho Local a los Recursos Hídricos y la Gestión Ambiental regional de Chile: estudios de caso." In F. Peña, ed., *Los Pueblos Indígenas y el Agua: desfíos de siglo XXI.* El Colegio de San Luis, Water Law and Indigenous

Rights (WALIR), Mexican Secretariat of the Environment (SEMARNAT), and Mexican Institute of Water Technology (IMTA), San Luis de Potosí, Mexico.

Ingram, H., and C. R. Oggins. 1992. "The Public Trust Doctrine and Community Values in Water." *Natural Resources Journal* 32 (3): 515–37.

Jayal, N. G. 1997. "The Governance Agenda. Making Democratic Development Dispensible. *Economic and Political Weekly* 32 (8): 407–12.

Jenkins, W. I. 1978. *Policy Analysis: A Political and Organizational Perspective.* London: Martin Robertson.

Kerr, J. M. 2002. *Watershed Development Projects in India: An Evaluation.* Research Report 127. Washington, D.C: International Food Policy Research Institute.

Klaphake, A. 2005. "Integrietes Flussgebietsmanagement in Brasilien?" [Integrated Basin Management in Brazil?] In S. Neubert, W. Scheumann, A. van Edig, and W. Huppert, eds., *Integrietes Wasserressourcen Management (IWRM): Ein Konzept in die Praxis überführen [Integrated Water Resource Management (IWRM): Putting a Concept into Practice].* Baden-Baden, Germany: Nomos-Verlag.

Lowdermilk, M. K., D. M. Freeman, and A. C. Early. 1978. *Farm Irrigation Constraints and Farmers' Responses: Comprehensive Field Survey in Pakistan.* Vols. 1–6. Fort Collins, Colo.: Colorado State University.

Mackintosh, M. 1992. "Introduction." In M. Wuyts, M. Mackintosh, and T. Hewitt, eds., *Development Policy and Public Action.* Oxford, UK: Oxford University Press.

Mangisoni, J. 2006. "Impact of Treadle Pump Irrigation Technology on Smallholder Poverty and Food Security in Malawi: A Case Study of Blantyre and Mchinji Districts." International Water Management Institute, Pretoria.

Manning, N., and M. Seely. 2005. "Forum for Integrated Resource Management (FIRM) in Ephemeral Basins: Putting Communities at the Centre of the Basin Management Process." *Physics and Chemistry of the Earth* 30 (11–16): 886–93.

Meinzen-Dick, R., and R. Pradhan. 2002. "Legal Pluralism and Dynamic Property Rights." CAPRi Working Paper 22. Consultative Group on International Agricultral Research, Washington, D.C.

Meinzen-Dick, R., and M. Zwarteveen. 1998. "Gendered Participation in Water Management: Issues and Illustrations from Water Users' Associations in South Asia." In D. Merrey and S. Baviskar, eds., *Gender Analysis and Reform of Irrigation Management: Concepts, Cases and Gaps in Knowledge.* Colombo: International Water Management Institute.

Meinzen-Dick, R. S., R. Pradhan, K. Palanisami, A. Dixit, and K. Athukorala. 2004. "Livelihood Consequences of Transferring Water out of Agriculture: Synthesis of Findings from South Asia." Ford Foundation, New Delhi.

Merrey, D. J. 1997. *Expanding the Frontiers of Irrigation Management Research: Results of Research and Development at the International Irrigation Management Institute 1984–1995.* Colombo: International Water Management Institute.

———. 1998. "Governance and Institutional Arrangements for Managing Water Resources in Egypt." In P. Mollinga, ed., *Water Control in Egypt's Canal Irrigation: A Discussion of Institutional Issues at Different Levels.* Wageningen, Netherlands: Wageningen Agricultural University and International Institute for Land Reclamation and Improvement.

Merrey, D. J., P. Drechsel, F. Penning de Vries, and H. Sally. 2005. "Integrating 'Livelihoods' into Integrated Water Resources Management: Taking the Integration Paradigm to Its Logical Next Step for Developing Countries." *Regional and Environmental Change* 5 (4): 197–204.

Merrey, D. J., R. Namara, and M. de Lange. 2006. "Agricultural Water Management Technologies for Small Scale Farmers in Southern Africa: An Inventory and Assessment of Experiences, Good Practices, and Costs." International Water Management Institute, Pretoria.

Moench, M., E. Caspari, and A. Dixit, eds. 1999. *Rethinking the Mosaic: Investigations into Local Eater Management.* Kathmandu: Nepal Water Conservation Foundation and the Institute for Social and Environmental Transition.

Molle, F. 2005. *Irrigation and Water Policies in the Mekong Region: Current Discourses and Practices.* IWMI Research Report 95. Colombo: International Water Management Institute.

Molle, F., and J. Berkoff. 2005. "Cities versus Agriculture: Revisiting Intersectoral Water Transfers, Potential Gains, and Conflicts." Comprehensive Assessment of Water Management in Agriculture Research Report 10. International Water Management Institute, Colombo.

———, eds. Forthcoming. *Irrigation Water Pricing Policy in Context: Exploring the Gap between Theory and Practice.* Wallingford, UK: CABI Publishing and International Water Management Institute.

Mollinga, P., and A. Bolding. 2004. "The Politics of Irrigation Reform: Research for Strategic Action." In P. Mollinga and A. Bolding, eds., *The Politics of Irrigation Reform: Contested Policy Formulation and Implementation in Asia, Africa, and Latin America.* Hans, UK: Ashgate.

Mollinga, P. P., R. Doraiswamy, and K. Engbersen. 2004. "Capture and Transformation: Participatory Irrigation Management in Andhra Pradesh, India." In P. Mollinga and A. Bolding, eds., *The Politics of Irrigation Reform: Contested Policy Formulation and Implementation in Asia, Africa, and Latin America.* Hans, UK: Ashgate.

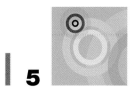

Morardet, S., D. J. Merrey, J. Seshoka, and H. Sally. 2005. "Improving Irrigation Project Planning and Implementation Processes in Sub-Saharan Africa: Diagnosis and Recommendations." IWMI Working Paper 99. International Water Management Institute, Colombo.

Moriarty, P., J. Butterworth, and B. van Koppen, eds. 2004. *Beyond Domestic: Case Studies on Poverty and Productive Uses of Water at the Household Level.* Delft, Netherlands: IRC International Water and Sanitation Centre.

Moss, T. 2003. "Solving Problems of 'Fit' at the Expense of Problems of 'Interplay'? The Spatial Reorganisation of Water Management following the EU Water Framework Directive." In H. Breit, A. Engels, T. Moss, and M. Troja, eds., *How Institutions Change: Perspectives on Social Learning in Global and Local Environmental Contexts.* Opladen, Germany: Leske + Budrich.

Mthimkhulu, S., H. Dallas, J. Dey, and Z. Hoko. Forthcoming. "Biological Assessment of the State of the Water Quality in the Mbuluzi River, Swaziland." *Physics and Chemistry of the Earth.*

Mukhopadhyay T., D. Elston, G. Hewitt, and D. Budlender. 2002. *Gender Budgets Make Cents: Understanding Gender Responsive Budgets.* London: Commonwealth Secretariat.

Namara, R., B. Upadhyay, and R. K. Nagar. 2005. *Adoption and Impacts of Microirrigation Technologies from Selected Localities of Maharashtra and Gujarat States of India.* IWMI Research Report 93. Colombo: International Water Management Institute.

North, D. 1990. *Institutions, Institutional Change, and Economic Performance.* Cambridge, UK: Cambridge University Press.

Norton, A., and D. Elston. 2002. "What Is behind the Budget? Politics, Rights, and Accountability in the Budget Process." Overseas Development Institute, London.

Ostrom, E. 1990. *Governing the Commons: The Evolution of Institutions for Collective Action.* New York: Cambridge University Press.

———. 1992. *Negotiating Institutions for Self-Governing Irrigation Systems.* San Francisco, Calif.: Institute for Contemporary Studies Press.

———. 2005. *Understanding Institutional Diversity.* Princeton, N.J.: Princeton University Press.

Ostrom, E., L. Schroeder, and S. G. Wynne. 1993. *Institutional Incentives and Sustainable Development: Infrastructure Policies in Perspective.* Boulder, Colo.: Westview Press.

Pahl-Wostl, C. 2002. "Towards Sustainability in the Water Sector—The Importance of Human Actors and Processes of Social Learning." *Aquatic Sciences* 64 (4): 394–411.

Peña, H., and M. Solanes. 2003. "Effective Water Governance in the Americas: A Key Issue." Paper presented at the Third World Water Forum, March 16–23, Kyoto, Japan.

Peña, H., M. Luraschi, and S. Valenzuela. n.d. "Water, Development, and Public Policies: Strategies for the Inclusion of Water in Sustainable Development." Draft Discussion Document for Global Water Partnership. Ministry of Public Works, Transport and Telecommunications, Santiago.

Penning de Vries, F. W. T., H. Sally, and A. Inocencio. 2005. "Opportunities for Private Sector Participation in Agricultural Water Development and Management." IWMI Working Paper 100. International Water Management Institute, Colombo.

Perry, C. J. 1995. "Determinants of Function and Dysfunction in Irrigation Performance and Implications for Performance Improvement." *International Journal of Water Resources Development* 11 (1): 25–38.

———. 2003a. "Non-State Actors and Water Resources Development—An Economic Perspective." *Non-State Actors and International Law* 3 (1): 99–110.

———. 2003b. "Successful Water Resources Management: A Solved Problem?" Keynote address at ICID.UK Research Day, April 3, Wallingford, UK.

Polak, P. 2005. "The Big Potential of Small Farms." *Scientific American,* 293 (3) 84–91.

Rap, E., P. Wester, and L. N. Pérez-Prado. 2004. "The Politics of Creating Commitment: Irrigation Reforms and the Reconstitution of the Hydraulic Bureaucracy in Mexico." In P. Mollinga and A. Bolding, eds., *The Politics of Irrigation Reform: Contested Policy Formulation and Implementation in Asia, Africa, and Latin America.* Hans, UK: Ashgate.

Renwick, M. 2001. *Valuing Water in Irrigated Agriculture and Reservoir Fisheries: A Multiple-Use Irrigation System in Sri Lanka.* IWMI Research Report 51. Colombo: International Water Management Institute.

Repetto, R. 1986. *Skimming the Water: Rent-Seeking and the Performance of Public Irrigation Systems.* Washington, D.C.: World Resources Institute.

Rogers, P., and A. Hall. 2003. "Effective Water Governance." GWP Technical Committee Background Paper 7. Global Water Partnership, Stockholm.

Rosegrant M. W., and H. Binswanger. 1994. "Markets in Tradable Water Rights: Potential for Efficiency Gains in Developing Country Water Resource Allocation." *World Development* 22 (11): 1–11.

Sabatier, P. 1988. "An Advocacy Coalition Model of Policy Change and the Role of Policy-Oriented Learning Therein." *Policy Sciences* 21: 129–68.

Sabatier, P., W. Focht, M. Lubell, Z. Trachtenberg, A. Vedlitz, and M. Matlock, eds. 2005. *Swimming Upstream: Collaborative Approaches to Watershed Management.* Boston, Mass.: MIT Press.

Samad, M. 2005. "Water Institutional Reforms in Sri Lanka." *Water Policy* 7 (1): 125–40.

Samad, M., and D. J. Merrey. 2005. "Water to Thirsty Fields: How Social Research Can Contribute." In M. Cernea and A. Kassam, eds., *Researching the Culture in Agriculture: Social Research for International Development.* Wallingford, UK: CABI Publishing.

Samad, M., and D. L. Vermillion. 1999. *Assessment of the Impact of Participatory Irrigation Management in Sri Lanka: Partial Reforms, Partial Benefits.* IWMI Research Report 34. Colombo: International Water Management Institute.

Schön, D. A. 1983. *The Reflective Practitioner: How Professionals Think in Action.* New York: Basic Books.

Schreiner, B., and B. van Koppen. 2001. "From Bucket to Basin: Poverty, Gender, and Integrated Water Management in South Africa." In C. L. Abernethy, ed., *Intersectoral Management of River Basins: Proceedings of an International Workshop on 'Integrated Water Management in Water Stressed River Basins in Developing Countries: Strategies for Poverty Alleviation and Agricultural Growth.'* Colombo: International Water Management Institute and German Foundation for International Development.

Scott, J. C. 1998. *Seeing Like a State: How Certain Schemes to Improve the Human Condition Have Failed.* Yale Agrarian Studies Series. New Haven, Conn., and London: Yale University Press.

Shah, T., M. Alam, D. Kumar, R. K. Nagar, and M. Singh. 2000. *Pedaling out of Poverty: Social Impacts of a Manual Irrigation Technology in South Asia.* IWMI Research Report 45. Colombo: International Water Management Institute.

Shah, T., I. Makin, and R. Sakthivadivel. 2005. "Limits to Leapfrogging: Issues in Transposing Successful River Basin Management Institutions in the Developing World." In M. Svendsen, ed., *Irrigation and River Basin Management: Options for Governance and Institutions.* Wallingford, UK: CABI Publishing.

Shah, T., B. van Koppen, D. Merrey, M. de Lange, and M. Samad. 2002. *Institutional Alternatives in African Smallholder Irrigation: Lessons from International Experience with Irrigation Management Transfer.* IWMI Research Report 60. Colombo: International Water Management Institute.

Sivamohan, M. V. K., ed. 1986. *Issues in Irrigated Agriculture and Command Area Development.* New Delhi: Ashish.

Sivamohan, M. V. K., and C. Scott. 1994. *India: Irrigation Management Partnerships.* Hyderabad, India: Booklinks Corporation.

Small, L. E., and I. Carruthers. 1991. *Farmer-Financed Irrigation: The Economics of Reform.* Cambridge, UK: Cambridge University Press.

Svendsen, M. 2005a. "Basin Management in a Mature Closed Basin: The Case of California's Central Valley." In M. Svendsen, ed., *Irrigation and River Basin Management: Options for Governance and Institutions.* Wallingford, UK: CABI Publishing.

———, ed. 2005b. *Irrigation and River Basin Management: Options for Governance and Institutions.* Wallingford, UK: CABI Publishing.

Svendsen, M., and W. Huppert. 2000. "Incentive Creation for Irrigation System Maintenance and Water Delivery: The Case of Recent Reforms in Andhra Pradesh." Deutsche Gesellschaft für Technische Zusammenarbeit, Eschborn, Germany.

Swallow, B. M., N. L. Johnson, and R. S. Meinzen-Dick. 2001. "Working with People for Watershed Management." *Water Policy* 3 (6): 449–56.

Swatuk, L. 2005. "Political Challenges to Implementing IWRM in Southern Africa." *Physics and Chemistry of the Earth* 30 (11–16): 872–80.

Trawick, P. 2005. "Going with the Flow: The State of Contemporary Studies of Water Management in Latin America." *Latin American Research Review* 40 (3): 443–56.

Ul Hassan, M., R. Starkloff, and N. Nizamedinkhodjaeva. 2004. *Inadequacies in the Water Reforms in the Kyrgyz Republic.* IWMI Research Report 81. Colombo: International Water Management Institute.

Uphoff, N. 1986. *Improving International Irrigation Management with Farmer Participation: Getting the Process Right.* Boulder, Colo.: Westview Press.

———. 1992. *Learning from Gal Oya: Possibilities for Participatory Development and Post-Newtonian Social Science.* Ithaca, N.Y.: Cornell University Press.

Van der Velde, E. J., and J. Tirmizi. 2004. "Irrigation Policy Reforms in Pakistan: Who's Getting the Process Right?" In P. Mollinga and A. Bolding, eds., *The Politics of Irrigation Reform: Contested Policy Formulation and Implementation in Asia, Africa, and Latin America.* Hans, UK: Ashgate.

Van der Zaag, P. 2005. "Integrated Water Resources Management: Relevant Concept or Irrelevant Buzzword? A Capacity Building and Research Agenda for Southern Africa." *Physics and Chemistry of the Earth* 30 (11–16): 867–71.

Van Koppen, B., C. Safilios Rothschild, and R. Namara. 2005. "Reducing Poverty through Investments in Agricultural Water Management: Poverty and Gender Issues and Synthesis of Sub-Saharan Africa Case Study Reports." IWMI Working Paper 101. International Water Management Institute, Colombo.

Van Koppen, B., J. Butterworth, I. Jum, and F. Maganga, eds. Forthcoming. *Community-based Water Law and Water Resource Management Reform in Developing Countries.* Wallingford, UK: CABI Publishing and International Water Management Instiute.

Vera, D. J. 2005. "Irrigation Management, the Participatory Approach, and Equity in an Andean Community." In V. Bennett, S. Dávila, and M. N. Rico, eds., *Opposing Currents: The Politics of Water and Gender in Latin America.* Pittsburgh, Pa.: University of Pittsburgh Press.

———. Forthcoming. "Derechos de Agua, Etnicidad y Sesgos de Género: Un Estudio comparativo de la Legislaciones Hídricas de tres país Andinos; Peru, Bolivia, y Ecuador." In R. Boelens, D. Gretches, and A. Guevera, eds., *Políticas Hídricas, Derechos Consuetudinarios e Identidades Locales.* Lima and Abya Ayala, Ecuador: Water Law and Indigenus Rights and Instituto de Estudios Peruanos.

Vermillion, D. L. 1997. *Impacts of Irrigation Management Transfer: A Review of the Evidence.* IWMI Research Report 11. Colombo: International Water Management Institute.

Vermillion, D. L., and C. Garcés-Restrepo. 1998. *Impacts of Colombia's Current Irrigation Management Transfer Program.* IWMI Research Report 25. Colombo: International Water Management Institute.

Vermillion, D .L., and D. J. Merrey. 1998. "What the Twenty-First Century Will Demand of Water Management Institutions." *Journal of Applied Irrigation Science* 33 (2): 145–64.

Vermillion, D. L., and J. A. Sagardoy. 1999. "Transfer of Irrigation Management Services, Guidelines." FAO Irrigation and Drainage Paper 58. Food and Agriculture Organization, Rome.

Vermillion, D. L., M. Samad, S. Pusposutardjo, S. S. Arif, and S. Rochdyanto. 2000. *An Assessment of Small-Scale Irrigation Management Turnover Program in Indonesia.* IWMI Research Report 38. Colombo: International Water Management Institute.

Wade, R. 1982. "The System of Administrative and Political Corruption: Canal Irrigation in South India." *Journal of Development Studies* 18 (3): 287–328.

Wade, R., and R. Chambers. 1980. "Managing the Main System: Canal Irrigation's 'Blind Spot.'" *Economic and Political Weekly* 15 (39): A107–A112.

Wepener, V., J. H. J. van Vuren, F. P. Chatiza, L. Slabert, and B. Masola. 2005. "Active Biomonitoring in Freshwater Environments: Early Warning Signals from Biomarkers in Assessing Biological Effects of Diffuse Sources of Pollutants." *Physics and Chemistry of the Earth* 30 (11–16): 751–61.

Wester, P., D. J. Merrey, and M. de Lange. 2003. "Boundaries of Consent: Stakeholder Representation in River Basin Management in Mexico and South Africa." *World Development* 31 (5): 797–812.

Wester, P., T. Shah, and D. J. Merrey. 2005. "Providing Irrigation Services in Water Scarce Basins: Representation and Support." In M. Svendsen, ed., *Irrigation and River Basin Management: Options for Governance and Management.* Wallingford, UK: CABI Publishing.

Winpenny, J. 2003. *Financing Water for All.* Report of the World Panel on Financing Water Infrastructure, chaired by Michel Camdessus. Kyoto: World Water Council, 3rd World Water Forum, and Global Water Partnership.

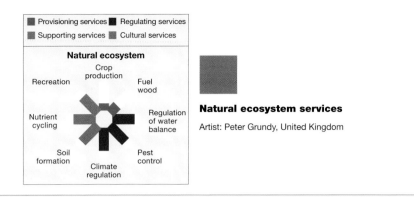

Provisioning services ■ Regulating services
Supporting services ■ Cultural services

Natural ecosystem

Recreation

Crop production

Fuel wood

Nutrient cycling

Regulation of water balance

Soil formation

Pest control

Climate regulation

Natural ecosystem services

Artist: Peter Grundy, United Kingdom

6

Agriculture, water, and ecosystems: avoiding the costs of going too far

Coordinating lead authors: Malin Falkenmark, C. Max Finlayson, and Line J. Gordon

Contributing authors: Elena M. Bennett, Tabeth Matiza Chiuta, David Coates, Nilanjan Ghosh, M. Gopalakrishnan, Rudolf S. de Groot, Gunnar Jacks, Eloise Kendy, Lekan Oyebande, Michael Moore, Garry D. Peterson, Jorge Mora Portuguez, Kemi Seesink, Rebecca Tharme, and Robert Wasson

Overview

Agricultural systems depend fundamentally on ecological processes and on the services provided by many ecosystems. These ecological processes and services are crucial for supporting and enhancing human well-being. Ecosystems support agriculture, produce fiber and fuel, regulate freshwater, purify wastewater and detoxify wastes, regulate climate, provide protection from storms, mitigate erosion, and offer cultural benefits, including significant aesthetic, educational, and spiritual benefits.

Agricultural management during the last century has caused widescale changes in land cover, watercourses, and aquifers, contributing to ecosystem degradation and undermining the processes that support ecosystems and the provision of a wide range of ecosystem services. Many agroecosystems have been managed as though they were disconnected from the wider landscape, with scant regard for maintaining the ecological components and processes that underpinned their sustainability. Irrigation, drainage, extensive clearing of vegetation, and addition of agrochemicals (fertilizers and pesticides) have often altered the quantity and quality of water in the agricultural landscape. The resultant modifications of water flows and water quality have had major ecological, economic, and social consequences, including effects on human health *[well established]*. Among them are the loss of provisioning services such as fisheries, loss of regulating services such as storm protection and nutrient retention, and loss of cultural services such as biodiversity and recreational values. Adverse ecological change, including land degradation through pollution, erosion, and salinization, and the loss of pollinators and animals that prey on pest species, can have negative feedback effects on food and fiber production *[well established]*. In extreme cases human health can also suffer, for example, through insect-borne disease or through changes in diet and nutrition. All too often the consequences of modifying agroecosystems have not been fully considered nor adequately monitored.

It has been increasingly recognized that agricultural management has caused some ecosystems to pass ecological thresholds (tipping points), leading to a regime change in the ecosystem and loss of ecosystem services. Ecosystem rehabilitation is likely to be costly, if possible at all. Some changes can be nearly irreversible (for example, the establishment of anoxic areas in marine water bodies). These changes can occur suddenly, although they often represent the cumulative outcome of a slow decline in biodiversity and reduced ecological resilience (the ability to undergo change and retain the same function, structure, identity, and feedbacks).

The poor people in rural areas who use a variety of ecosystem services directly for their livelihoods are likely to be the most vulnerable to changes in ecosystems. Therefore, failure to tackle the loss and degradation of ecosystems, such as that caused by the development and management of agriculture-related water resources, will ultimately undermine progress toward achieving the Millennium Development Goals of reducing poverty, combating hunger, and increasing environmental sustainability.

An integrated approach is needed for managing land and water resources and ecosystems that acknowledges the multifunctionality of agroecosystems in supporting food production and ecosystem resilience. That requires a better understanding of how agroecosystems generate multiple ecosystem services and of the value of maintaining biodiversity, habitat heterogeneity, and landscape connectivity in agricultural landscapes. Social issues, such as the importance of the role of gender in management decisions, also require more emphasis. Attention should be directed toward minimizing the loss of ecosystem resilience and building awareness of the importance of cumulative changes and of extreme events for generating ecosystem change. It is also necessary to meet the water requirements for sustaining ecosystem health and biodiversity in rivers and other aquatic ecosystems (marshes, lakes, estuaries) and to demonstrate the benefits of these services to society as a whole.

It has been estimated that by 2050 food demand will roughly double. As populations and incomes increase, demand for water allocations for agriculture will rise. Simplified, there are three main ways in which this increased water requirement can be met: through increased water use on current agricultural lands, through expansion of agricultural lands, and through increased water productivity. While all are plausible and a mix of solutions is likely, each has vastly different implications for nonagricultural ecosystems and the services they generate.

With the current high levels of land conversion and river regulation globally, greater consideration should be given to improving management of water demand within existing agricultural systems, rather than seeking further expansion of agriculture. Dependent on local conditions, technologies and management practices need to be substantially improved, and ecologically sound techniques implemented more widely to reduce the impacts from agriculture, whether extensive or intensive. Further intensification will require careful management to prevent further degradation and loss of ecosystem services through increased external effects and downstream water pollution. With the basis of many essential ecosystem services already seriously undermined, there is an urgent need not only to

> An integrated approach is needed for managing land, water, and ecosystems that acknowledges the multifunctionality of agroecosystems in supporting food production and ecosystem resilience

Agriculture, water, and
ecosystems: avoiding the
costs of going too far

6

minimize future impacts, but also to reverse loss and degradation through rehabilitation and, in some cases, full restoration.

An integrated approach to land, water, and ecosystems at basin or catchment scale is urgently needed to increase multiple benefits and to mitigate detrimental impacts among ecosystem services. This involves assessing the costs and benefits as well as all known risks to society as a whole and to individual stakeholders. Societally accepted tradeoffs are unlikely without wide stakeholder discussion of consequences, distribution of costs and benefits, and possible compensation. It is also important that the results feed into processes of social learning about ecosystem behavior and management. A few tools are available to assist in striking tradeoffs (including economic valuation and desktop procedures for establishing environmental flows), but more efficient and less sectorally specific tools are needed. Most of the tools were developed to enable better decisionmaking on well known problems and benefits. Needed are tools to address the lesser known problems and benefits and to prepare for surprises.

Decisions on tradeoffs under uncertain conditions should be based on a set of alternative scientifically informed arguments, with an understanding of the uncertainties that exist when dealing with ecological forecasting. To minimize the sometimes very high future costs of unexpected social and ecological impacts, it will be necessary to conceptualize uncertainty in decisionmaking. Adaptive management and scenario planning that improve assessment, monitoring, and learning are two components of this conceptualization.

Ongoing attention is required to communicate ecological messages across disciplinary and sectoral boundaries and to relevant policy and decisionmaking levels. The challenge is to produce simple messages about the multiple benefits of an ecosystem and about how ecosystems generate services—without oversimplifying the complexity of ecosystems.

In view of the huge scale of future demands on agriculture to feed humanity and eradicate hunger, and the past undermining of the ecological functions on which agriculture depends, it is essential that we change the way we have been doing business. To do this, we need to:

- Address social and environmental inequities and failures in governance and policy as well as on-ground management.
- Rehabilitate degraded ecosystems and, where possible, restore lost ecosystems.
- Develop institutional and economic measures to prevent further loss and to encourage further changes in the way we do business.
- Increase transparency in decisionmaking about agriculture-related water management and increase the exchange of knowledge about the consequences of these decisions. In the past many changes in ecosystem services have been unintended consequences of decisions taken for other purposes, often because the tradeoffs implicit in the decisionmaking were not transparent or were not known *[well established]*.

> There is a need not only to minimize future ecosystem impacts, but also to reverse loss and degradation through rehabilitation and, in some cases, full restoration

Water and agriculture—a challenge for ecosystem management

Changes in agriculture over the last century have led to substantial increases in food security through higher and more stable food production. However, the way that water has been managed in agriculture has caused widescale changes in land cover and watercourses, contributed to ecosystem degradation, and undermined the processes that support ecosystems and the provision of a wide range of ecosystem services essential for human well-being.

The Millennium Ecosystem Assessment, an international assessment by more than 1,300 scientists of the state of the world's ecosystems and their capacity to support human well-being, identified agricultural expansion and management as major drivers of ecosystem loss and degradation and the consequent decline in many ecosystem services and human well-being (www.maweb.org). Analyses illustrated that by 2000 almost a quarter of the global land cover had been converted for cultivation (map 6.1), with cropland covering more than 50% of the land area in many river basins in Europe and India and more than 30% in the Americas, Europe, and Asia. The Millennium Ecosystem Assessment also showed that the development of water infrastructure and the regulation of rivers for many purposes, including agricultural production, often resulted in the fragmentation of rivers (map 6.2) and the impoundment of large amounts of water (figure 6.1; Revenga and others 2000; Vörösmarty, Lévêque, and Revenga 2005).

Many scientists argue that as a society we are becoming more vulnerable to environmental change (Steffen and others 2004; Holling 1986), reducing our natural capital and degrading options for our current and future well-being (Jansson and others 1994; Arrow and others 1995; MEA 2005c). Natural and human-induced disasters, such as droughts and famine, are also likely to increase the pressure on vulnerable people, such as the rural poor, who depend most directly on their surrounding ecosystems (Silvius, Oneka, and Verhagen 2000; WRI and others 2005; Zwarts and others 2006).

Furthermore, as populations and incomes grow, it has been estimated that food demand will roughly double by 2050 and shift toward more varied and water-demanding diets, increasing water requirements for food production (see chapter 3 on scenarios).

map **6.1** | **Extent of cultivated systems in 2000**

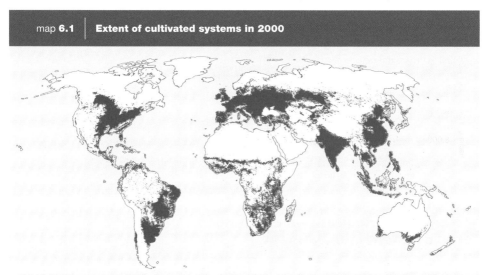

Note: Cultivated systems are defined as areas where at least 30% of the landscape is in croplands, shifting cultivation, confined livestock production, or freshwater aquaculture.
Source: MEA 2005c.

Agriculture, water, and
ecosystems: avoiding the
costs of going too far

6

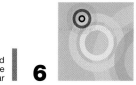

map **6.2** | **River channel fragmentation and flow regulation of global rivers**

■ Unfragmented   ■ Moderately fragmented   ■ Highly fragmented   □ No data   ■ Unassessed

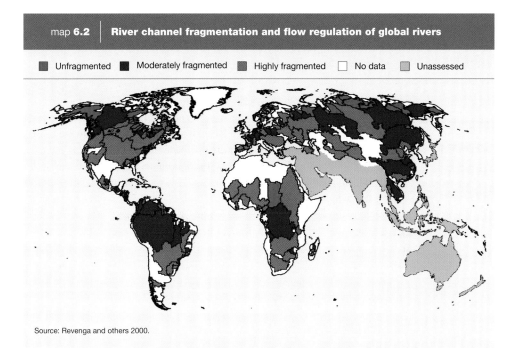

Source: Revenga and others 2000.

figure **6.1** | **Development of water infrastructure and regulation of rivers resulted in the impoundment of large amounts of water**

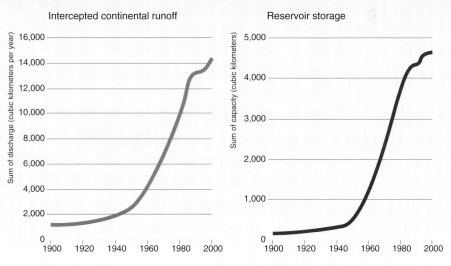

Note: The time series data are taken from a subset of large reservoirs (0.5 cubic kilometers maximum storage each), geographically referenced to global river networks and discharge.

Source: Millennium Ecosystem Assessment.

Simplified, there are three main ways to meet this water requirement: increasing water use on current agricultural lands through intensification of production (see chapters 8 on rainfed agriculture and 9 on irrigation), expanding agricultural lands, and increasing water productivity (see chapters 7 on water productivity and 15 on land).

These options have vastly different implications for ecosystems and the services they generate. Increased water use on agricultural lands through irrigation will reduce the availability of blue water resources (surface water and groundwater), especially for downstream aquatic systems, and can contribute to waterscape alterations, for example, through the introduction of dams for irrigation. Increased green water flows (soil moisture generated from rainfall that infiltrates the soil) through higher consumptive water use in rainfed agriculture (as a result of increased crop productivity) will also reduce the availability of water downstream, although the extent to which this could occur varies *[established but incomplete]*. Expanding agricultural land can alter the water flow in the landscape, with impacts on terrestrial and aquatic ecosystems. Finally, while increased water productivity is intended to produce more food without using more water, it can lead to deterioration in water quality through increased use of agrochemicals.

> Humanity is facing an enormous challenge in managing water to secure adequate food production without undermining the life support systems on which society depends

Humanity is facing an enormous challenge in managing water to secure adequate food production without undermining the life support systems on which society depends—and in some instances while simultaneously rehabilitating or restoring those systems. Research on ecosystems has generally been separate from research on water in agriculture, leading to a segregated view of humans and food security on one side and nature conservation on the other. In this chapter we challenge this view by describing recent understanding of how all ecosystems support human well-being, including ensuring food security and redressing social inequities.

We focus on the links between ecosystems and management of water in agriculture. Water functions as the "bloodstream of the biosphere" (Falkenmark 2003). It is vital for the generation of many ecosystem services in both terrestrial and aquatic ecosystems and provides a link between ecosystems, including agroecosystems. As for agricultural production, we consider the importance of both blue and green water (see chapter 1 on setting the scene) for ecosystems, both those characterized by the presence of blue water, such as marshes, rivers, and lakes, and terrestrial ecosystems that depend on and modify green water.

We first assess the ecosystem effects of past water-related management in agriculture, highlighting some of the often unintentional tradeoffs between water for food production and water for other ecosystem services. We then outline response options for improving water management. We emphasize the need to intentionally deal with the unavoidable and often surprising tradeoffs that arise when making decisions to increase food production, noting that these are often embedded within complex social situations where different stakeholders have highly diverse interests, skills, and influence (see, for example, chapters 5 on policies and institutions, 15 on land, and 17 on river basins).

Agriculture and ecosystems

While agricultural production is driven by human management (soil tillage, irrigation, nutrient additions), it is still influenced by the same ecological processes that shape and drive nonagricultural ecosystems, particularly those that support biomass production and others

Agriculture, water, and
ecosystems: avoiding the
costs of going too far

6

such as nitrogen uptake from the atmosphere and pollination of crops. Agricultural systems are thus viewed as ecosystems that are modified, at times highly, by activities designed to ensure or increase food production (box 6.1). These ecosystems are often referred to as agroecosystems; the difference between an agroecosystem and other ecosystems is considered to be largely conceptual, related to the extent of human intervention or management.

Disruption of the processes that maintain the structure and functioning of an ecosystem, such as water flow, energy transfer, and growth and production, can have dire consequences, including soil erosion and loss of soil structure and fertility. Severe disruption can result in the degradation or loss of the agroecosystem itself or other linked ecosystems and the ecosystem services that it supplies (see chapter 15 on land). The degradation of the Aral Sea is a dramatic example of human intervention having gone too far (box 6.2).

---

box 6.1 | Agriculture makes landscape modifications unavoidable

There are many land and water manipulations that can increase the productivity of agricultural land in order to meet increasing demands for more food. All have consequences for ecosystems. The key message is that agriculture makes landscape modification unavoidable, although smarter application of technology and more emphasis on ecosystemwide sustainability could reduce adverse impacts. These land and water manipulations include:

- *Shifting the distribution of plants and animals.* Most apparent are the clearing of native vegetation and its replacement with seasonally or annually sown crops, and the replacement of wild animals with domestic livestock.
- *Coping with climate variability to secure water for crops.* As water is a key material for photosynthesis, crop productivity depends intimately on securing water to ensure growth. Three different time scales need to be taken into account when considering water security: seasonal shortfalls in water availability that can be met by irrigation so that the growing season is extended and extra crops can be added; dry spells during the wet season that can be met by specific watering that can be secured, even in small-scale farming, if based on locally harvested rain; and recurrent drought that has traditionally been met by saving grain from good years to rely on during dry years.
- *Maintaining soil fertility.* The conventional way to secure enough air in the root zone is by drainage and ditching through plowing to ensure that rain water can infiltrate. However, this also leads to erosion and the removal of fertile soil by strong winds and heavy rain. These side effects can be limited by focusing on soil conservation actions, such as minimum tillage practices.
- *Coping with crop nutrient needs.* The nutrient supply of agricultural soils is often replenished through the application of manure or chemical fertilizers. Ideally, the amount added should balance the amount consumed by the crop, to limit the water-soluble surplus in the ground that may be carried to rivers and lakes.
- *Maintaining landscape-scale interactions.* When natural ecosystems are converted to agricultural systems, some ecological processes (such as species mobility and subsurface water flows) that connect parts of the landscape can be interrupted. This can have implications for agricultural systems as it can affect pest cycles, pollination, nutrient cycling, and water logging and salinization. Managing landscapes across larger scales thus becomes important; an increasing number of studies illustrate how to design landscapes to increase the productivity of agriculture while also generating other ecosystem services (Lansing 1991; Cumming and Spiesman 2006; Anderies 2005; McNeely and Scherr 2003).

It is thus important to adapt agricultural management (including crop types) to the ecological conditions. Growing crops unsuited to the climate conditions, for example, could have harmful consequences. When agricultural techniques that had been developed in the temperate climate of Europe were introduced in late 18th century Australia, the result was vast areas of salinized lands (Folke and others 2002). Trying to grow lucrative oil palms on saline soils in the Indus Delta and Pakistan and the acid sulphate soils of Southeast Asia is another example of a severe mismatch between agricultural activity and ecological conditions. In the 1970s it was argued that there was a climate bias—"water blindness"—that led to efforts to transfer inappropriate agricultural technology from developed to developing countries (Falkenmark 1979).

Human well-being and ecosystem services

The Millennium Ecosystem Assessment (MEA 2005c) showed that the well-being of human society was intimately linked to the capacity of ecosystems to provide ecosystem services and that securing multiple ecosystem services depended on healthy ecosystems.

box **6.2**	**The Aral Sea—an ecological catastrophe**

The Aral Sea is probably the most prominent example of how unsustainable water management for agriculture has led to a large-scale and possibly irreversible ecological and human disaster. Reduced water flow in the rivers supplying the sea has resulted in outcomes that have impaired human livelihoods and health, affected the local climate, and reduced biodiversity. Since 1960 the volume of water in the Aral Sea Basin has been reduced by 75%, due mainly to reduced inflows as a consequence of irrigation of close to 7 million hectares of land (UNESCO 2000; Postel 1999). This has led to the loss of 20 of 24 fish species and collapse of the fishing industry; the fish catch fell from 44,000 tons annually in the 1950s to zero, with the loss of 60,000 jobs (Postel 1996). Species diversity and wildlife habitat have also declined, particularly in the wetlands associated with the sea (Postel 1999). The water diversions together with polluted runoff from agricultural land have had serious human health effects, including an increase in pulmonary diseases as winds whipped up dust and toxins from the exposed sea bed (WMO 1997).

Wind storms pick up some 100 million tons of dust containing a mix of toxic chemicals and salt from the dry sea bed and dump them on the surrounding farmland, harming and killing crops as well as people (Postel 1996). The low flows into the sea have concentrated salts and toxic chemicals, making water supplies hazardous to drink (Postel 1996). In the Amu Darya River Basin chemicals such as dichlorodiphenyl-trichloroethane (DDT), lindane, and dioxin have been carried by agricultural runoff and spread through the aquatic ecosystems and into the human food chain. Secondary salinization is also occurring (Williams 2002).

Attempts to rehabilitate the Northern Sea are under way through the Syr Darya and Northern Aral Sea Project (www.worldbank.org.kz); initial results are seen as positive (Pala 2006). A dam has been constructed between the two parts of the sea to allow the accumulation of water and to help rehabilitate parts of the delta. While the project aims to reestablish and sustain fishery and agricultural activities and to reduce the harmful effects on the drinking water, the extent of past changes makes restoration highly unlikely. The ecological and social changes in the Aral Sea ecosystem are considered largely irreversible.

Agriculture, water, and
ecosystems: avoiding the
costs of going too far

6

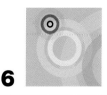

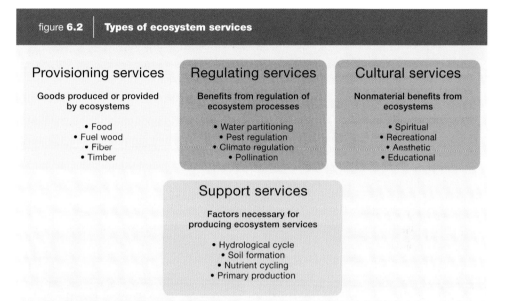

figure **6.2** | **Types of ecosystem services**

Provisioning services

**Goods produced or provided
by ecosystems**

- Food
- Fuel wood
- Fiber
- Timber

Regulating services

**Benefits from regulation of
ecosystem processes**

- Water partitioning
- Pest regulation
- Climate regulation
- Pollination

Cultural services

**Nonmaterial benefits from
ecosystems**

- Spiritual
- Recreational
- Aesthetic
- Educational

Support services

**Factors necessary for
producing ecosystem services**

- Hydrological cycle
- Soil formation
- Nutrient cycling
- Primary production

Source: Adapted from MEA 2003.

Whether an ecosystem is managed primarily for food production, water regulation, or for other services (figure 6.2), it is possible to secure these for the long term only if basic ecosystem functioning is maintained. In many agroecosystems considerable effort goes into ensuring crop production, but often at the expense of other important services, such as fisheries (Kura and others 2004), freshwater supply (Vörösmarty, Lévêque, and Revenga 2005), and regulation of floods (Daily and others 1997; Bravo de Guenni 2005).

Biodiversity—variability and diversity within and among species, habitats, and ecosystem services—is important for supporting ecosystem services and has value in its own right. Further, biodiversity can act as an insurance mechanism by increasing ecosystem resilience (box 6.3). Some species that do not seem to have an important role in ecosystems under stable conditions may be crucial in the recovery of an ecosystem after a disturbance. Similarly, if one species is lost, another with similar characteristics may be able to replace it. While the concept of biodiversity comprises ecosystems, species, and genetic components, most of the discussion in this chapter focuses on the functional role of ecosystems and species (or taxa) in terms of the ecosystem services that they provide.

There is increasing evidence that ecosystems play an important role in poverty reduction (Silvius, Onela, and Verhagen 2000; WRI and others 2005). Many rural poor people rely on a variety of sources of income and subsistence activities that are based on ecosystems and are thus most directly vulnerable to the loss of ecosystem services *[established]*. These sources of income, often generated by women and children, include small-scale farming and livestock rearing, fishing, hunting, and collecting firewood and other ecosystem products that may be sold for cash or used directly by households. Floodplain wetlands, for example, support many human activities, including fisheries, cropping, and gardening (photos 6.1–6.3).

box **6.3** | **Biodiversity and ecosystem resilience**

The decline of biodiversity globally, most severely manifested in freshwater systems (MEA 2005b), has renewed interest in ecosystem conservation and management and in the links between bio-diversity and ecosystem functioning (Holling and others 1995; Tilman and others 1997), including the role in human well-being (MEA 2005c) and the links to poverty (Adams and others 2004; WRI and others 2005). Many people highlight the ethical argument for conserving biodiversity for its own intrinsic value, and projects aimed at conserving endangered species (establishment of protected areas, changed land-use practices) have been common investment strategies, with different social outcomes (Adams and others 2004).

Research in recent decades has illustrated the importance of species diversity for ecosystem functioning (see photos of wetland biodiversity). The general theory is that a more diverse system contributes to more stable productivity by providing a means of coping with variation.

Pelicans

Dragonfly

Crocodile

Elephants

However, it has recently been argued that it is not the richness of species that contributes to eco-system functioning, but rather the existence of functional groups (predators, pollinators, herbivores, decomposers) with different and sometimes overlapping functions in relation to ecosystem process-es (Holling and others 1995). To understand the role of diversity for ecosystem functioning, it is necessary to analyze the identities, densities, biomasses, and interactions of populations of species in the ecosystem, as well as their temporal and spatial variations (Kremen 2005). Diversity of organ-isms within and between functional groups can be critical for maintaining resistance to change.

Species that may seem redundant during some stages of ecosystem development may be criti-cal for ecosystem reorganization after disturbance (Folke and others 2004). Response diversity (the differential responses of species to disturbance) helps to stabilize ecosystem services in the face of shocks (Elmqvist and others 2003).

Agriculture, water, and
ecosystems: avoiding the
costs of going too far

6

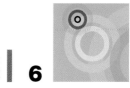

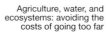

Photo 6.1

Photo 6.2

Photo 6.3

Photos by C. Max Finlayson

Fisheries, cropping, and gardening are among the many human activities supported by floodplain wetlands.

The Millennium Ecosystem Assessment concluded that a failure to tackle the decline in ecosystem services will seriously erode efforts to reduce rural poverty and social inequity and eradicate hunger; this is a critical issue in many regions, particularly in Sub-Saharan Africa (WRI and others 2005). It is also true that continued and increasing poverty can intensify pressure on ecosystems as many of the rural poor and other vulnerable people are left with no options but to overexploit the remaining natural resource base. The result is often a vicious cycle in which environmental degradation and increased poverty are mutually reinforcing forces (Silvius and others 2003). The Millennium Ecosystem Assessment (MEA 2005c) concluded that interventions that led to the loss and degradation of wetlands and water resources would ultimately undermine progress toward achieving the Millennium Development Goals of reducing poverty and hunger and ensuring environmental sustainability.

Consequences and ecosystem impacts

Modifications of the landscape to increase global food production have resulted in increased provisioning services, but also in adverse ecological changes in many ecosystems, with concomitant loss and degradation of services (MEA 2005c). Water management has caused changes in the physical and chemical characteristics of inland and coastal aquatic ecosystems and in the quality and quantity of water, as well as direct and indirect biological changes (Finlayson and D'Cruz 2005; Agardy and Alder 2005; Vörösmarty, Lévêque, and Revenga 2005). It has also caused changes in terrestrial ecosystems through the expansion of agricultural lands and changes in water balances (Foley and others 2005).

These changes have had negative feedback on the food and fiber production activities of agroecosystems, for example through reductions in pollinators (Kremen, Williams, and Thorp 2002) and degradation of land (see chapter 15 on land) *[established but incomplete]*. Adverse changes have varied in intensity, and some are seemingly irreversible, or at least difficult or expensive to reverse, such as the extensive dead zones in the Gulf of Mexico and the Baltic Sea (Dybas 2005). The catastrophic collapse of coastal fisheries as a consequence of environmental change is another example (see chapter 12 on inland fisheries). This chapter focuses on the consequences for ecosystems of green and blue water management in agriculture while acknowledging that many other human activities also play a role. Synergistic and cumulative effects can make it extremely difficult to attribute change to a single cause (box 6.4).

box **6.4**

**Cumulative changes—new challenges for
water management in agriculture**

New challenges are emerging for water managers in agriculture as a consequence of the cumulative and sometimes synergistic effects of multiple drivers, including climate change and invasive species.

Global climate change is expected to directly and indirectly alter and degrade many ecosystems (Gitay and others 2002). For example, it will exacerbate problems associated with already expanding demand for water where it leads to decreased precipitation, while in limited cases, where precipitation increases, it could lessen pressure on available water. There are also major expected consequences for wetland ecosystems and species, although the extent of change is not well established (Gitay and others 2002; van Dam and others 2002; Finlayson and others forthcoming).

There is growing recognition of the important role that invasive species can play in degradation of ecosystems and ecosystem services (MEA 2005c). Invasive species, spread through water regulation for transport and water transfer and through trade, have altered the character of many aquatic ecosystems (see photo). Once established, invasive plants can block channels and irrigation canals and decrease connectivity within and between rivers and wetlands, replace valuable species, and damage infrastructure (Finlayson and D'Cruz 2005).

Invasive species from forest plantations are also threatening water supply for downstream users, as shown in South Africa where cities such as Cape Town and Port Elisabeth depend on runoff from the natural low biomass vegetation in the catchment (Le Maitre and others 1996). Invasive species in riparian areas are a problem for water resources in several other parts of the world. The annual losses due to the invasive woody species tamarisk in the semiarid western United States reach $280–$450 a hectare, with restoration costs of approximately $7,400 a hectare (Zavaleta 2000).

Photo by C. Max Finlayson

Water hyacinth, a rapidly growing, free-floating invasive plant, has degraded many ecosystems

Aquatic ecosystems

Water-related agricultural modifications have had major ecological, economic, and social consequences, including effects on human health, through changes in the key ecological components and processes of rivers, lakes, floodplains, and groundwater-fed wetlands *[well established]*. These changes include alterations to the quantity, timing, and natural variability of flow regimes; alterations to the waterscape through the drainage of wetlands and the construction of irrigation storages; and increased concentrations of nutrients, trace elements, sediments, and agrochemicals.

Aquatic ecosystems provide a wide array of ecosystem services *[well established]*. Their nature and value are not consistent, however, and our understanding of how ecosystem processes support many of these services is inadequate (Finlayson and D'Cruz 2005; Baron and others 2002; Postel and Carpenter 1997). In several areas around the world changes have contributed to a loss of provisioning services such as fisheries, regulating services such as storm protection and nutrient retention, and cultural services such as recreational and aesthetic uses. In some cases ecosystems have passed thresholds

Agriculture, water, and
ecosystems: avoiding the
costs of going too far

6

or gone through regime shifts leading to a collapse of ecosystem services, making the costs of restoration (if possible at all) very high. These losses have adverse effects on livelihoods and economic production *[well established]*. There is ongoing debate whether the positive outcomes in terms of increased upstream production of food outweigh the negative consequences for people dependent on downstream ecosystem services. While most cost-benefit studies show that the costs of the losses have been higher than the gains, other scientists argue that these studies have many weaknesses (Balmford and others 2002).

Although agriculture, especially water management in agriculture, is a major driver behind the loss of downstream ecosystem services *[well established]*, there are competing explanations for the manner and importance of individual processes and events and the ultimate role of agriculture as a triggering force for degradation is in many situations unknown. Dams, overfishing, urban water withdrawals, and natural and anthropogenic climate variation can contribute to cumulative and synergistic effects, reduced resilience, and increased degradation of downstream ecosystems (photo 6.4). Uncertainty is often high when it comes to the exact location or timing of the response of downstream ecosystems to upstream water alterations. This does not mean that we can ignore the role of agriculture. But we need to address the problems as complex and interacting, and to consider a systems perspective for analyzing multiple drivers of change.

> Long-term trend analysis of 145 major world rivers indicates that discharge has declined in one-fifth of cases

The next two sections offer examples of how water-related management in agriculture has changed the capacity of downstream ecosystems to generate ecosystem services and a brief discussion of the consequences of some of these changes.

Water quantity and waterscape alterations. Increased cultivation in recent decades has resulted in increased diversion of freshwater, with some 70% of water now being used for agriculture and reaching as high as 85%–90% in parts of Africa, Asia, and the Middle

Photo by C. Max Finlayson

Photo 6.4 Dams provide many benefits for people, but also affect ecosystems by changing the hydrology and fragmenting rivers

East (Shiklomanov and Rodda 2003) *[well established]*. Regulation of the world's rivers has altered water regimes, with substantial declines in discharges to the ocean (Meybeck and Ragu 1997). Long-term trend analysis (more than 25 years) of 145 major world rivers indicates that discharge has declined in one-fifth of cases (Walling and Fang 2003). Worldwide, large artificial impoundments hold vast quantities of water and cause significant distortion of flow regimes (Vörösmarty and others 2003), often with harmful effects on human health (box 6.5).

Water diversion and the construction of hydraulic infrastructure (reservoirs, physical barriers) have altered downstream ecosystems through changes in the quantity and pattern of water flows and the seasonal inflows of freshwater (see global summaries in Vörösmarty, Lévêque, and Revenga 2005 and Finlayson and D'Cruz 2005). Negative effects include the loss of local livelihood options, fragmentation and destruction of aquatic habitats, changes in the composition of aquatic communities, loss of species, and health problems resulting from stagnant water. Less flooding means less sedimentation and deposition of nutrients on floodplains and reduced flows and nutrient deposition in parts of the coastal zone (Finlayson and D'Cruz 2005).

| box **6.5** | **Water management and human health** |

Many water-related diseases have been successfully controlled through water management (for example, malaria in some places), but others have been exacerbated by the degradation of inland waters through water pollution and changes in flow regimes (the spread of schistosomiasis). Where diseases have spread, the adverse effects on human health are due to a complex mix of environmental and social causes. The Millennium Ecosystem Assessment reported many instances where water management practices contributed to a decline in well-being and health (MEA 2005a; Finlayson and D'Cruz 2005). This includes diseases caused by the ingestion of water contaminated by human or animal feces; diseases caused by contact with contaminated water, such as scabies, trachoma, and typhus; diseases passed on by intermediate hosts such as aquatic snails or insects that breed in aquatic ecosystems, such as dracunculiasis and schistosomiasis, as well as dengue fever, filariasis, malaria, onchocerciasis, trypanosomiasis, and yellow fever; and diseases that occur when there is insufficient clean water for basic hygiene.

In addition to disease from inland waters, waterborne pollutants have a major effect on human health, often through their accumulation in the food chain. Many countries now experience problems with elevated levels of nitrates in groundwater from the large-scale use of organic and inorganic fertilizers. Excess nitrate in drinking water has been linked to methemoglobin anemia in infants.

There is increasing evidence from wildlife studies that humans are at risk from a number of chemicals that mimic or block the natural functioning of hormones, interfering with natural bodily processes, including normal sexual development. Chemicals such as DDT, dioxins, and those in many pesticides are endocrine disruptors, which may interfere with human hormone functions, undermining disease resistance and reproductive health.

The draining and burning of forested peat swamps in Southeast Asia have had devastating health effects (see box 6.6 later in this chapter) that extend across many countries and that may be long-lasting. The investigation of environment-related health effects linked with the ongoing degradation of the forested peat swamps is a major issue for health services in the region.

Agriculture, water, and
ecosystems: avoiding the
costs of going too far

6

Interbasin transfers of water, particularly large transfers between major river systems as are being planned in India, for example, are expected to be particularly harmful to downstream ecosystems (Gupta and Deshpande 2004; Alam and Kabir 2004) and to exacerbate pressures from hydrological regulation (Snaddon, Davies, and Wishart 1999). Where these are being considered, scientific and transparent assessments of the benefits and problems are strongly encouraged. Junk (2002) has highlighted the similar adverse consequences on water regimes expected from the construction of industrial waterways (hidrovias) through large wetlands, such as the Pantanal of Maso Grosso, Brazil. The nature of expected changes depends on the amount and timing of water being transferred and so needs to be assessed case by case.

Shrinking lakes. There are many instances where consumptive water use and water diversions have contributed to severe degradation of downstream ecosystem services. The degradation of the Aral Sea in Central Asia represents one of the most extreme cases (see box 6.2).

The desiccation of Lake Chad in West Africa is another example. It shrank from 25,000 square kilometers in surface area to one-twentieth that size over a 35-year period. However, there are competing explanations for this reduction. Natural rainfall variability is an important driver. The lake is very shallow, and at various times in its history it has assumed different states, with changes triggered by climate variability (Lemoalle 2003). It is unclear what role human-induced change has played, but different drivers include the withdrawal of irrigation water, land-use changes reducing precipitation through changes in albedo (the energy that is reflected by the earth and that varies with land surface characteristics), and reduced moisture recycling (Coe and Foley 2001).

Lake Chapala, the world's largest shallow lake, situated in the Lerma-Chapala Basin in central Mexico, is another example of consumptive water use upstream affecting the size of a lake. During 1979–2001 water volume in the lake dropped substantially to about 20% of capacity due to excessive water extraction for agricultural and municipal needs. Average annual rainfall from 1993 to 2003 was only 5% below the historical average and efforts were made to reduce water use in irrigation, but still the amount of surface and groundwater used in the basin exceeded supply by 9% on average (Wester, Scott, and Burton 2005). Above average rains in 2003 and 2004 increased the water volume to about 6,000 million cubic meters. There is still intense competition over water allocation, and environmental water requirements have yet to be determined, leaving the future of the lake and the allocation of water for urban and agricultural purposes under threat.

The high variability in lake volume in both Lake Chad and Lake Chapala means that the people depending on ecosystem services from these basins need to have a high adaptive capacity to cope with the rapidly changing circumstances, whether induced by people or nature.

Shrinking rivers. Consumptive use and interbasin transfers have transformed several of the world's largest rivers into highly stabilized and, in some cases, seasonally non-discharging, channels (Meybeck and Ragu 1997; Snaddon, Davies, and Wishart 1999; Cohen 2002). Streamflow depletion is a widespread phenomenon in tropical and subtropical regions in rivers with large-scale irrigation, including the Pangani (IUCN 2003),

> Worldwide, large artificial impoundments hold vast quantities of water and cause significant distortion of flow regimes, often with harmful effects on human health

Yellow (He, Cheng, and Luo 2005), Aral Sea tributaries, Chao Phraya, Ganges, Incomati, Indus, Murray-Darling, Nile, and Rio Grande (Falkenmark and Lannerstad 2005). Smakhtin, Revenga, and Döll (2004) suggest that the streamflow required for aquatic ecosystem health (environmental flow) has already been overappropriated in many rivers.

In the United States the construction of dams and water diversions for irrigation and other purposes in the Colorado Basin, together with large-scale interbasin transfers, has greatly reduced the flow of the river to the delta. A considerable portion of the delta has been transformed into mudflats, saltflats, and exposed sand. With the loss of the delta habitats, wetlands now exist mainly in areas where agricultural drainage has occurred (Postel 1996). The Ganges is among the major rivers of South Asia that no longer discharge year round to the sea. As a result there is a rapid upstream advance of a saline front, with consequent changes in mangrove communities, fish habitat, cropping, and human livelihoods (Postel 1996; Mirza 1998; Rahman and others 2000). On the Zambezi River in Southern Africa damming for electricity and agriculture has reduced flows to the coast and led to a decline in shrimp production that could have been worth as much as $10 million a year (Gammelsrod 1992).

> **The regulation of rivers has brought many benefits, but the adverse impacts have often failed to receive adequate and transparent consideration**

The regulation of rivers has brought many benefits to people, but the adverse impacts, especially those related to reduced downstream flows, have often failed to receive adequate and transparent consideration (WCD 2000; Revenga and others 2000; MEA 2005b).

Drainage of wetlands. Water regulation and drainage for agricultural development are the main causes of wetland habitat loss and degradation (Revenga and others 2000; Finlayson and D'Cruz 2005) and consequent loss of ecosystem services. By 1985 drainage and conversion of wetlands, mainly for agriculture, had affected an estimated 56%–65% of inland and coastal marshes in Europe and North America and 27% in Asia (OECD 1996). Drainage of wetlands often reduces important regulating ecosystem services, with such outcomes as increased vulnerability to storms and flooding and further eutrophication of lakes and coastal waters.

Harder to demonstrate is the cumulative effect of the loss of smaller sites, both individual sites and networks of sites, such as those used by migratory waterbirds (Davidson and Stroud forthcoming). The adverse effects are often assumed, but the evidence is incomplete. Still, there are many lessons, such as those from the drainage and subsequent burning of forested peat swamps in Southeast Asia (box 6.6), a case that has had dramatic health effects on many people across the region (see box 6.5). The loss of small wetlands (referred to as potholes) on the prairies of Canada and the United States through drainage and infilling has led to the loss of habitat for large numbers of migratory waterbirds (North American Waterfowl Management Plan 2004). The loss of forested riparian wetlands adjacent to the Mississippi River in the United States was seen as an important factor contributing to the severity and damage of the 1993 flood in the Mississippi Basin (Daily and others 1997).

Wetlands are often thought to act as "sponges" that soak up water during wet periods and release it during dry periods. While there are numerous examples of wetlands, notably floodplains, where this does occur, there is increasing evidence that such generalizations are not applicable for all hydrological contexts or wetland types (Bullock and Acreman

Agriculture, water, and
ecosystems: avoiding the
costs of going too far

6

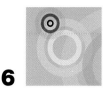

box **6.6**	**The widespread impacts of draining and burning in Southeast Asian peatlands**

Large parts of the tropical peat swamp forests in Southeast Asia have been seriously degraded, largely due to logging for timber and pulp (Wösten and others 2006; Page and others 2002). The process has been accelerated over the last two decades by the conversion of forests to agriculture, particularly oil palm plantations. Drainage and forest clearing threaten the stability of large tracts of forests in Indonesia and Malaysia and make them susceptible to fire.

Attempts to clear and drain the forests and establish agriculture have high rates of failure. Under the Mega Rice Project in Kalimantan, Indonesia, large areas of forest were cleared and some 4,600 kilometers of drainage canals were constructed in an attempt to grow rice on a grand scale using emigrant workers from the heavily populated neighboring island of Java. The cleared land was unsuited to rice production, and the scheme was abandoned. In 1997 land clearing and subsequent uncontrolled fires severely burned about 5 million hectares of forest and agricultural land in Kalimantan, releasing an estimated 0.8–2.6 billion tons of carbon dioxide into the atmosphere (Glover and Jessup 1999; Page and others 2002; Wooster and Strub 2002). The fires created a major atmospheric haze, with severe impacts on the health of 70 million people in six countries. In addition, there have been economic effects on timber and agricultural activities, with the fires compounding the loss of peatlands through clearing and failed attempts to cultivate large areas for rice.

Rehabilitation of some degraded areas is under way, but it is a slow and difficult process trying to reestablish the hydrology and vegetation (Wösten and others 2006). At a regional level the Association of Southeast Asian Nations (ASEAN) has taken an active interest in the problem through the ASEAN Peatland Management Initiative, facilitating the sharing of expertise and resources among the affected countries to prevent peatland fires and manage peatlands wisely. The regional initiatives are linked with national action plans. Monitoring mechanisms are in place, and a policy of zero burning for further land clearing has also been established, in particular for oil palm plantations.

Despite these steps, the problem of peatland degradation continues. The expansion of oil palm plantations is a major driver. The peat swamps are still being cleared and burned, undermining efforts to conserve and use the peatlands of Southeast Asia wisely and threatening the health of people locally and regionally.

2003). Indeed, there are instances where the opposite occurs: where wetlands reduce low flows, increase floods, or act as a barrier to groundwater recharge. Given the wide range of wetlands, from entirely groundwater-fed springs and mountain bogs to large inland river floodplains, such variation should not be surprising.

Changes in water quality. Many factors contribute to changes in water quality. This section looks at nutrient loads, agrochemicals, and siltation.

Nutrient loading. The use of fertilizers has brought major benefits to agriculture, but has also led to widespread contamination of surface water and groundwater through runoff. Over the past four decades excessive nutrient loading has emerged as one of the most important direct drivers of ecosystem change in inland and coastal wetlands, with the flux of reactive nitrogen to the oceans having increased by nearly 80% from 1860 to 1990 (MEA 2005c). Phosphorus applications have also increased, rising threefold since 1960, with a steady increase until 1990 followed by a leveling off at approximately the application rates of the 1980s (Bennett, Carpenter, and Caraco 2001). These changes are mirrored by phosphorus accumulation in soils, with high levels of phosphorus runoff. In developed countries annual storage peaked around 1975 and is now at about the same annual rate as in 1961. In developing countries, however, storage went from negative values in 1961 to about 5 teragrams per year in 1996.

Excessive nutrient loading can cause algal blooms, decreased drinking water quality, eutrophication of freshwater ecosystems and coastal zones, and hypoxia in coastal waters. In Lake Chivero, Zimbabwe, agricultural runoff is seen as responsible for algal blooms, infestations of water hyacinth, and fish declines as a result of high levels of ammonia and low oxygen levels (UNEP 2002). In Australia extensive algal blooms in coastal inlets and estuaries, inland lakes, and rivers have been attributed to increased nutrient runoff from agricultural fields (Lukatelich and McComb 1986; Falconer 2001). Diffuse runoff of nutrients from agricultural land is held to be largely responsible for increased eutrophication of coastal waters in the United States as well as for the periodic development, often varying from year to year, of anoxic conditions in coastal water in many parts of the world, such as the Baltic and Adriatic Seas and the Gulf of Mexico (Hall 2002).

> Nutrient management can be undermined by the loss of wetlands that assimilate nutrients and some pollutants

Nutrient management can be undermined by the loss of wetlands that assimilate nutrients (nitrogen, phosphorous, organic material) and some pollutants. Extensive evidence shows that up to 80% of the global incident nitrogen loading can be retained within wetlands (Green and others 2004; Galloway and others 2004). However, the ability of such ecosystems to cleanse nutrient-enriched water varies and is not unlimited (Alexander, Smith, and Schwarz 2000; Wollheim and others 2001). Verhoeven and others (2006) point out that many wetlands in agricultural catchments receive excessively high loadings of nutrients, with detrimental effects on biodiversity. Wetlands and lakes risk switching from a state in which they retain nutrients to one in which they release nutrients or emit

---

box 6.7 | **Regime shifts from excessive nutrient loads**

There are reported cases of regime shifts occurring in lakes because of increased nutrient loading, resulting in the loss of ecosystem services such as fisheries and tourism (Folke and others 2004). Some temperate lakes have experienced shifts between a turbid water and a clear water state, with the shift often attributed to an increase in phosphorous loading (Carpenter and others 2001). Some tropical lakes have shifted from a dominance of free-floating plants to submerged plants, with nutrient enrichment seemingly reducing the resilience of the submerged plants, possibly through shading and changes in underwater light (Scheffer and others 2001). Other wetlands and coastal habitats have also experienced similar shifts. In the United States nutrient enrichment caused a shift in emergent vegetation in the Everglades and a shift from clear water to murky water with algal blooms in Florida Bay (Gunderson 2001).

Other evidence comes from lakes subject to infilling and nutrient enrichment. In Lake Hornborga in Sweden emergent macrophytic vegetation proliferated after initial infilling of the lake margins and increased runoff of nutrients. The situation was reversed only after massive mechanical intervention and investment (Hertzman and Larsson 1999). In Australia agricultural runoff has resulted in shifts in vegetation dominance as a consequence of nutrient enrichment, increased inundation and salinization (Davis and others 2003; Strehlow and others 2005).

Agriculture, water, and
ecosystems: avoiding the
costs of going too far

6

the greenhouse gas nitrous oxide. Regime shifts are often rapid, but they have likely followed a slower and difficult to detect change in ecosystem resilience. It is generally difficult to monitor changes in resilience before a system hits the threshold and changes from one state to another (box 6.7; Carpenter, Westley, and Turner 2005).

Agrochemical contamination. Pollution and contamination from agricultural chemicals have been well documented since the publication of the seminal book *Silent Spring* (Carson 1962). Bioaccumulation as a consequence of the wide use of agrochemicals has had dire outcomes for many species that reside in or feed predominantly in wetlands or lakes that have accumulated residues from pesticides *[well established]*. The decline in the breeding success of raptors was a turning point in developing awareness about the dangers of using pesticides (Carson 1962).

An increasing amount of analytical and ecotoxicological data has become available for aquatic communities, and more recent research has also focused on risk assessments and the development of diagnostic tests that can guide management decisions about the use of such chemicals (van den Brink and others 2003). Taylor, Baird, and Soares (2002) have highlighted the high levels of pesticide use and low levels of environmental risk assessment in developing countries. They have promoted an integrated approach to evaluating environmental risks from pesticides that incorporates stakeholder consultation, chemical risk assessment, and ecotoxicological testing for ecological effects, also taking into account the potential effects on human health.

Vörösmarty, Lévêque, and Revenga (2005) report that water contamination by pesticides has increased rapidly since the 1970s despite increased regulation of the use of xenobiotic substances, especially in developed countries. However, bans on the use of these chemicals have generally been imposed only two to three decades after their first commercial use, as with DDT and atrazine. Many of these substances are highly persistent in the environment, but because of the generally poor monitoring of their long-term effects the global and long-term implications of their use cannot be fully assessed. Policy responses to contamination may lag far behind the event, as shown in the well documented case of agricultural pesticide bioaccumulation of DDT in the Zambezi Basin (Berg, Kilbus, and Kautsky 1992).

Siltation of rivers. In many parts of the world extensive sheet wash and gully erosion due to land management practices have devastated large areas, reduced the productivity of wide tracts of land, led to rapid siltation of reservoirs and threatened their longevity, and increased sediment loads in many rivers (see chapter 15 on land). On a regional scale some reservoirs in Southern Africa are at risk of losing more than a quarter of their storage capacity within 20–25 years (Magadza 1995). While many Australian and Southern African waters are naturally silty, many have experienced increased silt loads as a result of agricultural practices (Davies and Day 1998). Zimbabwe's more than 8,000 small to medium-size dams, for example, are threatened by sedimentation from soil erosion, while the Save River, an international river shared with Mozambique, has been reduced from a perennial to a seasonal river system due in large part to increased siltation as a result of soil erosion.

Globally, rivers discharge nearly 38,000 cubic kilometers of freshwater to the oceans and carry roughly 70% of the sediment input, though rivers draining only 10% of the

Water contamination by pesticides has increased rapidly since the 1970s despite increased regulation, especially in developed countries

land area contribute 60% of the total sediment discharge (Milliman 1991). The high sediment loads carried by Asian rivers are a consequence of land-use practices, particularly land-clearing practices for agriculture that lead to erosion, a situation likely to continue as a consequence of the expansion of agriculture in Africa, Asia, and Latin America (Hall 2002). A notable outcome of the supply of sediment and associated nutrients to the oceans is the increased frequency and intensity of anoxic conditions in recent years (Hall 2002).

There are also situations where river regulation has caused a decline in silt transport to downstream habitats, with reduced siltation along floodplains and in deltas and other downstream ecosystems. This has occurred in the Mesopotamian Marshes, where large-scale drainage is a bigger problem than silt-related changes in the downstream ecosystems (box 6.8).

Terrestrial ecosystems

Hydrological changes that occur as a result of agricultural expansion, particularly into forests, are seldom thought of in terms of water management in agriculture, although such changes are of at least the same magnitude as those resulting from irrigation (Gordon and others 2005). This is an area in need of further research, especially as biofuels and tree

---

box **6.8** | **Desiccation of the Mesopotamian wetlands**

The Mesopotamian wetlands, one of the cradles of civilization and a biodiversity center of global importance, used to cover more than 15,000 square kilometers in the lower Euphrates and Tigris Basins. Agricultural development and other drainage activities over the past 30 years have reduced them to 14% of their original size, and vast areas have been turned into bare land and salt crusts (Richardson and others 2005). The ecological implications have been severe, with drastic land degradation and impacts on wildlife, including bird migration and the extinction of endemic species, and on the ecology of the downstream Shatt el Arab and coastal fisheries in the Persian Gulf. The local population of half a million Marsh Arabs have become environmental refugees.

The causes of this severe ecological degradation are complex. Some of the causes were intentional, the results of drainage efforts to reclaim marshland, deal with soil salinization, improve agricultural productivity, and strengthen military security in southern Iraq in the 1980s and 1990s. Other causes were unintentional and included both the large-scale consumptive water use in irrigation systems and the return of saline drainage, agricultural and industrial chemical pollution, and the loss of flood flow, with its load of silt and nutrients, linked to recent large-scale streamflow regulation in upstream Turkey.

With the extent of existing regulation and degradation, the proposed rehabilitation of 30% of the Central Marshes upstream of the confluence of the Euphrates and Tigris could generate its own adverse impacts on aquatic ecosystems further downstream. The additional evaporation from just 1,000 square kilometers of restored open-water surfaces would consume an average flow of 67 cubic meters per second, or 25% of the original (pre-regulation) dry season flow, and reduce downstream streamflow even further. Without an increase in the amount of water available, simply returning the water to upstream areas may not be enough to restore the marshes and could further reduce the flow of water to downstream areas.

Source: Partow 2001; Italy, Ministry for the Environment and Territory, and Free Iraq Foundation 2004.

Agriculture, water, and
ecosystems: avoiding the
costs of going too far

6

plantations for carbon sequestration are new driving forces in the agricultural sector with potentially major, but largely unassessed, consequences for water use (Jackson and others 2005; Berndes 2002). Forest clearing for agriculture has hydrological consequences [*well established*], but site-specific responses will vary. Deforestation can lead to land degradation through salinization, soil loss, and waterlogging (for discussion on irrigation-induced salinity, see chapter 15 on land).

There is increasing speculation about how altered green water flows affect local, regional, and global climate. Most of the evidence comes from tropical semiarid to humid climates, with little from temperate regions. This section reviews the evidence of water-related changes in terrestrial ecosystems as a response to agriculture.

Changes in the water table. Water can build up in the soil profile if the rate of input, through irrigation, for example, exceeds the rate of throughput (for example, crop water consumption). This can cause water logging and salinization, which are extensively described for irrigated agriculture (Postel 1999). Continuous irrigation can result in soil salinization. Tanzania has an estimated 1.7–2.9 million hectares of saline soils and 300,000–700,000 hectares of sodic soils (FAO and UNESCO 2003), some of it now abandoned. Salt-affected soils in irrigation schemes are often related to poor soil and water management in addition to the unsuitability of many soils for irrigation (see chapters 9 on irrigation and 15 on land).

Clearing woody vegetation for pastures and crops can also lead to dryland salinization. Tree-covered landscape can provide an important regulating service by consuming rainfall by high evapotranspiration, limiting groundwater recharge, and keeping the groundwater low enough to prevent salt from being carried upward through the soil. Australia has had major problems with soil salinization since native woody vegetation was cleared in the 1930s for pastures and agricultural expansion (Farrington and Salama 1996). Consumptive water use has declined, the water table has risen, and salt has moved into the surface soils so that large tracts of land have become less suitable—and even unusable—for agriculture (Anderies and others 2001; Briggs and Taws 2003). Green water flows at a continental scale have been reduced by 10% (Gordon, Dunlop, and Foran 2003).

Decreased infiltration of water into the soil, often as a result of poor management of crop and grazing land, is another problem that can cause changes in the water table with effects on terrestrial systems, including a reduction in the capacity to produce biomass (Falkenmark and Rockström 1993). This is a well-known problem in many rainfed farming systems (see chapters 8 on rainfed agriculture and 15 on land). Desiccation of the soil in this manner is one of the factors behind what is often referred to as "desertification" or land degradation in the tropics.

Changes in runoff from vegetation change. The effects of alterations to vegetation (especially forests) on blue and green water flows are well studied at a local and regional scale. Catchment-scale experiments have shown that forested catchments in general have a higher green water flow and a lower blue water flow than grass or crop-dominated catchments with the same hydrology and climate. However, the effects of deforestation depend on the intensity and manner of forest clearance and on the character of the old and new land

> Decreased infiltration of water into the soil, often a result of poor management of crop and grazing land, can cause desiccation of the soil

cover and its management (McCulloch and Robinson 1993; Bosch and Hewlett 1982; Bruijnzeel 1990).

General work on the influence of vegetation, climate, and land cover on the water balance of a system has shown that there are vegetation-specific changes (L'vovich 1979; Calder 2005). Management of plant production that redirects blue water to green water can reduce the amount of water to downstream systems (Falkenmark 1999). For example, replacing crop or grasslands with forest plantations can decrease runoff and streamflow (Jewitt 2002). The South African Water Act classifies forest plantations as a "streamflow reduction activity," and forestry companies have to pay for their water use since less of the precipitation reaches the river.

Moisture recycling. Clearing land for agriculture and increasing use of irrigation have modified green water flows globally, reducing them by 3,000 cubic kilometers through forest clearing and increasing them by 1,000–2,600 cubic kilometers in irrigated areas (Döll and Siebert 2002; Gordon and others 2005). The ability of changes in land cover to influence climate through changes in green water flow has been increasingly recognized. It has been suggested that large-scale deforestation can reduce moisture recycling, affect precipitation (Savenije 1995, 1996; Trenberth 1999), and alter regional climate, with indications of global impacts (Kabat and others 2004; Nemani and others 1996; Marland and others 2003; Savenije 1995).

Pielke and others (1998) conclude that the evidence is convincing that land cover changes can significantly influence weather and climate and are as important as other human-induced changes for the Earth's climate. However, the models employed do not deal explicitly with green water flows, but rather with the compounded effects of changes in albedo, surface wind, leaf area index, and other indicators. Nevertheless, regional studies in West Africa (Savenije 1996; Zheng and Eltahir 1998), the United States (Baron and others 1998; Pielke and others 1999), and East Asia (Fu 2003) have illustrated that changes in land cover affect green water flows, with impacts on local and regional climates. Likewise, biome-specific models of land cover conversions from rainforest to grasslands have shown a decrease in vapor flows and precipitation as well as effects on circulation patterns (Salati and Nobre 1991) and savannahs (Hoffman and Jackson 2000). There are also indications that increased vapor flows through irrigation can alter local and regional climates (Pielke and others 1997; Chase and others 1999). The conversion of steppe to irrigated croplands in Colorado resulted in a 120% increase in vapor flows (Baron and others 1998), contributing to higher precipitation, lower temperatures, and an increase in thunderstorm activity (Pielke and others 1997).

Whether these changes can trigger rapid regime shifts (box 6.9), which in many cases may be irreversible, and changes to which farmers need to adapt is still speculative. In the Amazon the clearing of land has reduced moisture recycling, resulting in prolonged dry seasons and increased burning, and may have triggered an irreversible regime shift from rainforest vegetation to savannah (Oyama and Nobre 2003). There is also increasing concern about changes in the African and Asian monsoons, including weakening of the East Asian summer monsoon low-pressure system and an increase in irregular northerly flows (Fu 2003). Likewise, modeled vegetation changes for agricultural expansion in West Africa have shown potentially dramatic impacts on rainfall in the African monsoon circulation (Zheng and Eltathir 1998).

> There are indications that increased vapor flows through irrigation can alter local and regional climates

Agriculture, water, and
ecosystems: avoiding the
costs of going too far

6

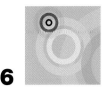

box **6.9**

Resilience and the increased risk of rapid regime shifts in ecosystems

Ecosystems change and evolve, with disturbance now seen as an inherent component of ecosystem processes *[well established]*. The speed of change in many ecosystems has, however, increased rapidly, and there is now concern that large-scale changes will increase the vulnerability of some ecosystems to water-related agricultural activities. Ecosystems are complex adaptive systems (Levin 1999), with nonlinear dynamics and thresholds between different "stable states." Nonlinear changes are sometimes abrupt and large, and they may be difficult, expensive, or impossible to reverse. The increased likelihood of nonlinear changes stems from drivers of ecosystem change that adversely affect the resilience of an ecosystem, its capacity to absorb disturbance, undergo change, and still retain essentially the same function, structure, identity, and feedbacks (Gunderson and Holling 2002; Carpenter and others 2001) and provide components for renewal and reorganization (Gunderson and Holling 2002).

Variability and flexibility are needed to maintain ecosystem resilience. Attempts to stabilize systems in some perceived optimal state, whether for conservation or production, have often reduced long-term resilience, making the system more vulnerable to change (Holling and Meffe 1996). While today's agricultural systems are able to better deal with local and small-scale variability, the simplifications of landscapes and reduction of other ecosystem services have decreased the capacity of agricultural systems and other ecosystems to cope with larger scale and more complex dynamics through reduced ecosystem resilience locally and across scales (Gunderson and Holling 2002).

Little is yet known about how to estimate resilience and detect thresholds before regime shifts occur (Fernandez and others 2002). Better mechanisms to monitor regime shifts include the identification and monitoring of slowly changing variables (Carpenter and Turner 2000) and measurable "surrogates of resilience" (Bennett, Cumming, and Peterson 2005; Cumming and others 2005).

Societal responses and opportunities

The negative effects of past agricultural management on ecosystem services and the need to produce more food for growing populations provide an unparalleled challenge. Meeting this challenge requires large-scale investments to improve agricultural management practices, increase the availability of techniques to minimize adverse ecological impacts, enhance our understanding of ecosystem-agriculture interactions, and reduce poverty and social inequities, including issues of gender, health, and education that affect ecosystem management decisions.

In presenting possible responses for meeting this challenge, we emphasize several ecological outcomes that we consider to be critical in this effort: maintenance or rehabilitation of the ecological connectivity, heterogeneity, and resilience in the landscape, which in turn implies maintenance or rehabilitation of the biodiversity that characterizes the landscape. We focus on integration and awareness of the negative consequences of choices in terms of the tradeoffs between food production and other ecosystem services. We do not propose specific responses for specific ecosystems or locations, although we aim to help national and local decisionmaking with a framework for addressing some of these issues. Many of the responses outlined are dependent on effective governance measures and policies that support sustainable development with a balance of ecological and social outcomes, issues covered in detail in chapters 5 on policies and institutions and 16 on river basins.

Improving agricultural technology and management practices

The Millennium Ecosystem Assessment (MEA 2005c) supports the view that intensification of agricultural systems will create fewer tradeoffs with ecosystem services than will expansion. Intensification will require improvements in agricultural productivity, especially in water productivity (see chapter 7 on water productivity) in water-scarce environments. However, because intensification can bring its own ecological problems, for example, through pollution or the introduction of invasive species, command and control approaches to management should be avoided (Holling and Meffe 1996). The potential problems of intensification could be lessened or avoided through the adoption of a systems approach to agriculture and integrated approaches to landscape management (see below).

Many of the chapters in this volume address agricultural techniques and improved management practices. Chapters 14 on rice and 15 on land highlight the need to consider techniques and practices that may not increase the production of one or a few specific crops but that support the provision of multiple benefits. Unless responses that restrict the potential adverse impacts of intensification are applied, intensification will not be any more environmentally and socially benign than many past agricultural practices.

> The potential problems of intensification could be lessened through the adoption of a systems approach to agriculture and integrated approaches to landscape management

Applying integrated approaches to water, agriculture, and other ecosystems

Integrated policy and management approaches are increasingly seen as crucial in facilitating decisionmaking and making tradeoffs between food and other ecosystem services. Integrated approaches have taken many forms, including integrated river basin management,

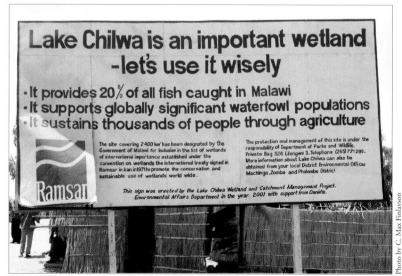

Photo 6.5 This use of wetlands in Malawi attempts to integrate multiple benefits and costs

Photo by C. Max Finlayson

Agriculture, water, and
ecosystems: avoiding the
costs of going too far

6

integrated land and water management, ecosystem approaches, integrated coastal zone management, and integrated natural resources management. Their general aim is often the same. They actively seek to address integration of all the benefits and costs associated with land-use and water decisions, including effects on ecosystem services, food production, and social equity, in a transparent manner; to involve key stakeholders and cross-institutional levels; and to cross relevant biophysical scales, addressing interconnectedness across subbasin, river basin, and landscape scales (photo 6.5).

While integrated approaches for environmental management are seen as an important effort and have long been promoted, there are few successful examples. The governance systems required to support the appropriate institutional and managerial arrangements, particularly for the allocation of resources and planning authority concomitant with responsibility at a local level, seem difficult to achieve (see, for example, chapter 16 on river basins). One complaint is that most of these approaches are based on a technocratic view of decisionmaking, whereas real life is far messier, with power struggles, lack of trust between and within stakeholder groups, and complex and evolutionary behavior of ecosystems that make it difficult to assess total benefits and impacts. Folke and others (2005) see a need for more emphasis on building, managing, and maintaining collaborative social relationships for river basin governance, which is in line with current thinking about ecosystem management.

> While integrated approaches for environmental management have long been promoted, there are few successful examples

Where river basin organizations have succeeded, that has often been because of their ability to deliver on the common aims of jurisdictions (such as coordinated water management to supply irrigation). The situation is more complex when dealing with international transboundary rivers, such as the Nile and the Mekong. An alternative to river basin processes may be to explore more regional guidance for common policies, as is being developed in Southern Africa (box 6.10).

The complexity of the social policy and institutional links that govern ecosystem management and influence necessary tradeoffs is shown for wetlands in figure 6.3. Differences in local contexts may affect the manner in which relationships between individuals

| box **6.10** | **National and regional policy initiatives on water and ecosystems** |

The South African National Water Act of 1998 protects the water requirements for ecosystems and supports them through an ongoing scientific effort. This is in line with the principles contained in the Southern African Development Commission (SADC) regional water policy of May 2004, which recognizes the environment as a legitimate user of water and calls on SADC members to adopt all necessary strategies and actions to sustain the environment. At the national level water reforms in South Africa and Zimbabwe have successfully mainstreamed environmental water requirements in water resources policy and legislation. Namibia is similarly considering policy that stresses sectoral coordination, integrated planning and management, and resource management aimed at coping with ecological and associated environmental risks.

Mexico's 1992 Law of National Waters is another example of national water reforms that consider ecosystem needs. It empowers the federal government to declare as disaster areas watersheds or hydrological regions that represent or may represent irreversible risks to an ecosystem.

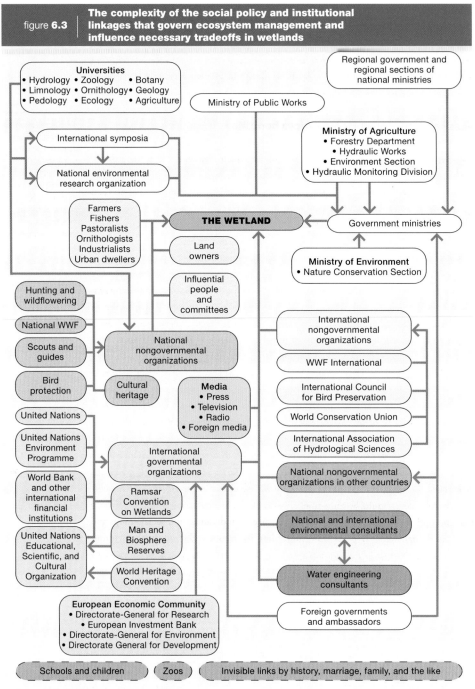

figure **6.3** The complexity of the social policy and institutional linkages that govern ecosystem management and influence necessary tradeoffs in wetlands

Universities
- Hydrology • Zoology • Botany
- Limnology • Ornithology • Geology
- Pedology • Ecology • Agriculture

Regional government and regional sections of national ministries

International symposia

National environmental research organization

Ministry of Public Works

Ministry of Agriculture
- Forestry Department
- Hydraulic Works
- Environment Section
- Hydraulic Monitoring Division

Farmers
Fishers
Pastoralists
Ornithologists
Industrialists
Urban dwellers

THE WETLAND

Government ministries

Land owners

Influential people and committees

Ministry of Environment
- Nature Conservation Section

Hunting and wildflowering

National WWF

Scouts and guides

National nongovernmental organizations

Bird protection

Cultural heritage

International nongovernmental organizations

WWF International

United Nations

Media
- Press
- Television
- Radio
- Foreign media

International Council for Bird Preservation

United Nations Environment Programme

International governmental organizations

World Conservation Union

International Association of Hydrological Sciences

World Bank and other international financial institutions

Ramsar Convention on Wetlands

National nongovernmental organizations in other countries

United Nations Educational, Scientific, and Cultural Organization

Man and Biosphere Reserves

National and international environmental consultants

World Heritage Convention

Water engineering consultants

European Economic Community
- Directorate-General for Research
- European Investment Bank
- Directorate-General for Environment
- Directorate General for Development

Foreign governments and ambassadors

Schools and children   Zoos   Invisible links by history, marriage, family, and the like

Source: Hollis 1994.

Agriculture, water, and
ecosystems: avoiding the
costs of going too far

6

and institutions are built and maintained. High levels of knowledge and human capacity are considered critical to crafting the institutions and policies required for successful integrated water management (see chapter 5 on policies and institutions). This chapter emphasizes the need to raise awareness of the role of ecosystem services in societal well-being in both multifunctional agricultural systems and across landscapes and on the importance of maintaining the ecological and social processes that support these.

Assessing and nurturing multiple benefits

Improving awareness and understanding. Integrated approaches help to deal with the competing interests in water resources They make it possible to share the multiple benefits and costs that are generated across a river basin and that are improved or degraded through agricultural interventions in the landscape.

Assessment of the multiple ecosystem services and the processes that support them is a key component of these approaches. Historically, decisions concerning ecosystem management have tended to favor either conversion of ecosystems or management for a single ecosystem service, such as water supply or food production, often without consideration of the effects on such groups as the rural poor, women, and children (MEA 2005c). Many ecosystem services do not have a price on the market and are often neglected in policymaking and decisionmaking. As we better understand the benefits provided by the entire array of ecosystem services, we also realize that some of the best response options will involve managing landscapes, including agriculture, for a broader array of services. That will entail taking greater account of social issues, such as gender-based roles and poverty, when making decisions about agriculture and water management (WRI and others 2005).

The Millennium Ecosystem Assessment has provided a major advance in understanding the links between the provision of ecosystem services and human well-being (www.maweb.org). Increased awareness is still needed on several different levels. The scientific knowledge of how ecosystem services contribute to human well-being within and between different sectors of society, and the role of water in sustaining these services, need to be improved. Dissemination of information on these issues and dialogue with stakeholders should be enhanced. Civil society organizations can help to ensure that appropriate consideration is given to the voices of individuals and social groups and to nonutilitarian values in decisionmaking. Minority groups and disadvantaged groups, such as indigenous people and women, in particular, need to be heard. Women play a critical and increasing role in agriculture in many parts of the developing world (Elder and Schmidt 2004).

Urbanization provides new challenges. For the first time in human history more people live in cities than in the rural areas. It has been estimated that the urban areas in the Baltic Sea region in northern Europe need an area of functioning ecosystems some 500 times the size of the cities themselves to generate the ecosystem services they depend on (Folke and others 1997). The green water needs for ecosystem services that support these cities are roughly 54 times larger than the blue water needs of households and industry (Jansson and others 1999). However, people who live in cities often become mentally

Historically, decisions concerning ecosystem management have tended to favor conversion of ecosystems or management for a single ecosystem service, such as food production disconnected from the ecological and hydrological processes that sustain their well-being. In this perspective farmers are the stewards of the landscape in which cities lie. This provides a new challenge for water and ecosystem management.

One of the main gaps in our scientific understanding of ecosystems and ecosystem services is where the thresholds lie and how far a system can be changed before it loses too many essential functions and totally changes its behavior (Gunderson and Holling 2002). Without this knowledge the early warning indicators required to provide advance warning of anticipated adverse change or of when a threshold is being approached cannot be developed.

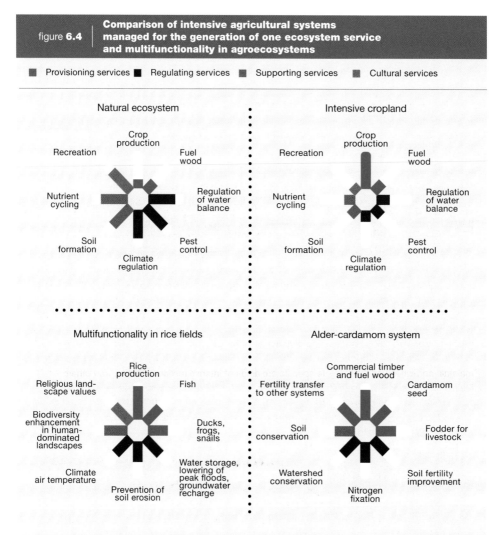

figure **6.4** | **Comparison of intensive agricultural systems managed for the generation of one ecosystem service and multifunctionality in agroecosystems**

■ Provisioning services ■ Regulating services ■ Supporting services ■ Cultural services

Natural ecosystem

Recreation — Crop production — Fuel wood

Nutrient cycling — Regulation of water balance

Soil formation — Pest control

Climate regulation

Intensive cropland

Recreation — Crop production — Fuel wood

Nutrient cycling — Regulation of water balance

Soil formation — Pest control

Climate regulation

Multifunctionality in rice fields

Religious landscape values — Rice production — Fish

Biodiversity enhancement in human-dominated landscapes — Ducks, frogs, snails

Climate air temperature — Water storage, lowering of peak floods, groundwater recharge

Prevention of soil erosion

Alder-cardamom system

Fertility transfer to other systems — Commercial timber and fuel wood — Cardamom seed

Soil conservation — Fodder for livestock

Watershed conservation — Soil fertility improvement

Nitrogen fixation

Source: Adapted from Foley and others 2005; chapters 14 and 15 in this volume.

Agriculture, water, and
ecosystems: avoiding the
costs of going too far

6

Managing agriculture for multiple outputs. Increasing attention to ecosystem services provides an opportunity to emphasize multifunctionality within agroecosystems and the connectivity between and within agroecosystems and other ecosystems. It is often assumed that agricultural systems are managed only for optimal (or maximum) production of one ecosystem service, food, or fiber (figure 6.4). But agricultural systems can generate other ecosystem services, and we need to improve our capacity to assess, quantify, and value these as well. Encouraging multiple benefits from these systems can generate synergies that result in the wider distribution of benefits across more people and sectors. Ecosystem-based approaches to water management need not constrain agricultural development but can be points of convergence for social equity, poverty reduction, resource conservation, and international concerns for global food security, biodiversity conservation, and carbon sequestration (see chapter 15 on land). Ecosystem-based approaches aim to maintain and where possible enhance diversity and to build the ecological resilience of the agricultural landscape as well as of ecosystems altered by agriculture (box 6.11).

The concept of multifunctional agriculture is not new; it has long been practiced in many forms and combinations. Integrated pest management is one way to manage a whole landscape in order to sustain an ecosystem service (pest control) that enhances agricultural production. This type of regional management requires integrated approaches based on an ecological understanding of fragmentation and landscape heterogeneity (Cumming and Spiesman 2006). Hydrological understanding is also important. Studies have shown that it is possible to control insect outbreaks by timing irrigation events (Lansing 1991) and that

| box **6.11** | **Some basic principles for maintaining ecosystem resilience** |

The resilience perspective shifts from policies that aspire to control change in systems assumed to be stable to policies to manage the capacity of social-ecological systems to cope with, adapt to, and shape change (Berkes, Colding, and Folke 2003). Managing for resilience enhances the likelihood of sustaining development in changing environments where the future is unpredictable.

Variability, disturbance, and change are important components of an ecosystem. For example, when variability in river flows is altered, marked changes in ecosystem functions can be expected (Richter and others 2003). Wetting and drying of soils can be important for the resilience of ecosystem functions, such as pest control and nutrient retention in wetlands. Exactly what level of variability to maintain and when variability is site specific are areas of intense research (Richter and others 2003). Maintaining diversity has been shown to be important for building ecosystem resilience, in particular for maintaining functional and response diversity (Elmqvist and others 2003; MEA 2005c). Responses should therefore seek to maintain and enhance diversity in ecosystems and across broader land-scapes while maintaining food production.

The driving variables behind the functioning of ecosystems tend to have slower dynamics than those that support the ecosystem services generated from that system (Carpenter and Turner 2000). Therefore, the monitoring of long-term ecosystem performance should cover the productivity of the ecosystem and the crucial variables that enable production. This is particularly evident when monitoring the productivity of croplands. Harvested yields are an important measure, but they may not tell the full story. Long-term productivity likely depends on slower variables, such as the accumulation and decomposition of soil organic matter.

planting trees in particular parts of the landscape can reduce vulnerability to waterlogging and salinization in other parts of the landscape (Andreis 2005).

Other chapters in this volume propose multifunctional agriculture as a response to the environmental degradation resulting from more narrowly based agricultural practices. For example, chapter 14 on rice illustrates the different ecosystem services generated in rice fields. Chapter 8 on rainfed agriculture illustrates how modifications to the water balance and erosion control can increase crop production. And chapter 9 on irrigation emphasizes multifunctionality in large-scale public irrigation systems that are dependent on surface water. Chapter 15 on land also presents a comprehensive overview of multifunctional agriculture and landscapes, including resource-conserving agriculture and emphasizes the synergies that arise between multiple users of ecosystem services when agriculture is treated as an integral part of the broader landscape. These chapters also illustrate the close links between environmental change and well-being and highlight the different roles and responsibilities of women and men in agriculture, the economy, and the household, and their different effects on the environment, issues requiring further study.

> Given past failures to secure the wider range of ecosystem services, we highlight the need for tools that can be used in striking tradeoffs between water for different ecosystem services

Assessing tradeoffs and tools for dealing with them

Scientists are increasingly questioning the wisdom of seeking economic development, including further development of agriculture and fisheries, at the expense of wider environmental and social consequences (International Council for Science 2002; SIWI and others 2005; Foley and others 2005; Kura and others 2004). Arrow and others (1995) have shown convincingly that economic development without due consideration of the ecological consequences may not provide the economic means to overcome environmental concerns in the future, particularly if the ecological resilience of the wider environment is undermined. The consequences of losing ecological resilience, especially when it results in irreversible change, have not been fully considered alongside the expected benefits (MEA 2005c).

It is anticipated that the management of water for agroecosystems alone will be subject to competition from wider environmental requirements (Lemly, Kingsford, and Thompson 2000; Molden and de Fraiture 2004) and may require further tradeoffs and the adoption of wider and more inclusive mechanisms. For example, the public sector is starting to buy back irrigation water from farmers to sustain or rehabilitate ecosystems or ecosystem services, sometimes even paying farmers not to irrigate. Governments may be able to buy the rights to water (whether the rights had previously been given away or obtained through the market), or nongovernmental organizations may be able to lease the water during dry years to support valued aquatic ecosystems. Water for the environment can thus be seen as a new driving force to which agriculture needs to adapt.

Ecosystem management is increasingly undertaken through collaborative planning and consultation processes, following past failures to transparently consider tradeoffs and wider societal interests (Carbonell, Nathai-Gyan, and Finlayson 2001). The Millennium Ecosystem Assessment (MEA 2005b,c) emphasizes the importance of overcoming sectoral divides and encompassing wider stakeholder participation in planning and development. Some of the people most vulnerable to ecosystem change depend directly on ecosystem

Agriculture, water, and
ecosystems: avoiding the
costs of going too far

6

services for their livelihoods, and they have often lacked a voice in making decisions about these services (Carbonell, Nathai-Gyan, and Finlayson 2001). Many local people who depend on ecosystems have had to develop management practices to deal with disturbances and change in a way that builds socioecological resilience (Berkes and Folke 1998). They can contribute their understanding of fundamental ecosystem processes (Olsson, Folke, and Hahn 2004). For the social mechanisms of dealing with the conflicts that occur when making tradeoffs see chapter 5 on policies and institutions and chapter 16 on river basins.

New tools are emerging for dealing with tradeoffs, including some that provide economic incentives and support the formulation of policies and regulations. Given past failures to secure the wider range of ecosystem services, we highlight the need for developing and adopting tools that can be used in striking tradeoffs between water for different ecosystem services. Such tools include economic valuation and cost-benefit analysis of ecosystem services, assessment of environmental flows, risk and vulnerability assessments, strategic and environmental impact assessments, and probability-based modeling.

Successful employment of such tools requires an adequate information base and improved predictive capacity about how ecosystems respond to change, and articulation of what is unknown or uncertain (Carpenter and others 2001). While the use of such tools has been increasingly promoted through international forums, conventions, and treaties, lack of awareness and capacity still seems to impede their use. We focus here on two tools that have considerable potential to assist in making tradeoffs: economic valuation of ecosystem services and allocation of environmental flows.

> A wide range of methods are available for valuing ecosystems beyond the use of direct market prices

Ecosystem valuation. Economic valuation is a powerful tool for addressing the tradeoffs between food production and other ecosystem services when making decisions about water management in agriculture. Its broad aim is to quantify the benefits (both market and nonmarket) that people obtain from ecosystem services to enable decisionmakers and the

---

box 6.12 | The total economic value of ecosystems

Total economic value involves assessing the value of four categories of ecosystem services:
- *Direct use values* are derived from ecosystem services that are used directly by people and include the value of consumptive uses, such as the harvesting of food products, timber, medicinal products, and the hunting of animals, as well as the value of nonconsumptive uses, such as the enjoyment of recreational and cultural amenities, water sports, and spiritual and social services.
- *Indirect use values* are derived from ecosystem services that provide benefits outside the ecosystem itself, for example, the water filtration function of wetlands, the storm protection function of mangrove forests and delta islands, and carbon sequestration by forests.
- *Option values* are derived from preserving the option to use services in the future rather than now, either by oneself (option value) or by heirs or others (bequest value).
- *Nonuse* (or existence) *values* refer to the value people may place on knowing that a resource exists even if they never use that resource directly.

Source: MEA 2005b.

public to evaluate the economic costs and benefits of any proposed change in an ecosystem and to facilitate comparison with other aspects of the economy. Economic valuation is just one way of assessing tradeoffs. It is especially useful in the context of economic arguments favoring actions leading to ecosystem degradation that fail to take full account of the economic costs. Ecosystem valuation assists in the efficient allocation of resources, enhances the scope for market creation, and can reduce the magnitude of market failures.

Total economic value (box 6.12) has become a widely used framework for identifying and quantifying ecosystem services (Balmford and others 2002; MEA 2005c). It considers the full range of ecosystem characteristics together—resource stocks or assets, flows of environmental services, and attributes of the ecosystem as a whole. It covers direct and indirect values and option and nonuse values.

---

box 6.13 | Commonly used valuation tools

A wide array of methods can be used for economic valuation of ecosystems. Some of the most common are:

- *Replacement costs*. Even where ecosystem services have no market value themselves, they often have alternatives or substitutes that can be bought and sold. These replacement costs can be used as a proxy for ecosystem resources, although they usually represent only partial estimates or are underestimates.
- *Effects on production*. Other economic processes often rely on ecosystem resources as inputs or on the essential life support provided by these services. Where they have a market, it is possible to look at the contribution of the services to the output or income of these wider production and consumption opportunities in order to assess their value.
- *Damage costs avoided*. The reduction or loss of ecosystem services frequently incurs costs in terms of damage to or reduction of other economic activities. The damage costs that are avoided can be taken to represent the economic losses forgone by conserving ecosystems.
- *Mitigative or avertive expenditures*. It is almost always necessary to take action to mitigate or avert the negative effects of the loss of ecosystem services so as to avoid economic damage. These costs can be used as indicators of the value of conserving ecosystems in terms of expenditures avoided.
- *Hedonic pricing*. Hedonic methods look at the differentials in property prices and wages between locations and isolate the proportion of this difference that can be ascribed to the existence or quality of ecosystem services.
- *Travel costs*. Many ecosystems typically hold a high value as a recreational resource or destination. Although in many cases no charge is made to view or enjoy less human-dominated ecosystems, people must still spend time and money to reach them. This expenditure—on transport, food, equipment, accommodations, time, and so on—can be calculated, and a demand function can be constructed relating visitation rates to expenditures made. These travel costs reflect the value that people place on the leisure, recreational, or tourism aspects of specified ecosystems.
- *Contingent valuation*. Even where ecosystem services have no market price and no close replacements or substitutes, they frequently have a high value to people. Contingent valuation techniques infer the value that people place on these services by asking about willingness to pay for them (or willingness to accept compensation for their loss) under the hypothetical scenario that they would be available for purchase.

Agriculture, water, and
ecosystems: avoiding the
costs of going too far

6

A wide range of methods are available for valuing ecosystems beyond the use of direct market prices. These include approaches that elicit preferences directly (such as contingent valuation methods) and those that use indirect methods to infer preferences from actions to purchase related services (for example, through production functions, dose-response relationships, travel costs, replacement costs, and mitigative expenditures). These methods are summarized in box 6.13.

While economic tools may prove useful in striking tradeoffs, they are unlikely to be useful in all circumstances. The more sophisticated the method, the less useful it is likely to be in situations where data are not available or where political issues hold sway. Economic tools can assist in understanding only the economic tradeoffs, not the political tradeoffs or the role of complex social relationships such as the role of gender and culture.

In the last two decades the notion of paying for ecosystem services has begun to emerge (WWF 2006). Such projects typically involve local land and water managers (including farmers) and use financial initiatives to encourage management changes that increase ecosystem services. The idea behind the initiatives is that beneficiaries of the service should compensate those who "provide" the environmental services by conserving natural ecosystems. Some of the better known projects concern watershed restoration (decreased erosion, decreased nutrient runoff).

> Tools have been developed to assist in making decisions for allocating water for both economic and environmental purposes

Environmental water flows. Environmental flows refer to the quantity, seasonality, and quality of water considered to be sufficient for protecting the structure and function of an ecosystem and its dependent species and services, taking into account temporal differences in water requirements and spatial variability. The allocation of an environmental flow is defined by the long-term availability of water, including the extent of natural and anthropogenic temporal and spatial variability and identified ecosystem responses (Dyson, Bergkamp, and Scanlon 2003). Environmental flows are often established through environmental, social, and economic assessments (King, Tharme, and Sabet 2000; Dyson, Bergkamp, and Scanlon 2003). Determining how much water can be allocated to consumptive human uses without the loss of ecosystem services is becoming a more common component of efforts to maintain and rehabilitate rivers and wetlands, including estuaries and other coastal ecosystems.

To date, most developing countries with significant irrigation have paid relatively little attention to safeguarding flows for the environment (Tharme 2003), but this situation is expected to change rapidly in the coming decades. Water legislation in South Africa and the Mekong Agreement are examples of the recognition of environmental water requirements in developing countries. More explicit bulk allocation of water to the environment may provide a major challenge to irrigators to manage with smaller and less dependable allocations for cropping. While the assessment of water availability, water use, and water stress at the global scale has been the subject of ongoing research, the water requirements of aquatic ecosystems have not been considered explicitly or estimated globally (Smakhtin, Revenga, and Döll 2004). It could be possible to establish an environmental allocation beyond which substantial degradation of ecosystem services and human well-being results (King, Tharme, and Sabet 2000). Defining this allocation entails also defining what constitutes a degraded ecosystem.

Poff and others (1997) emphasize that analysis of environmental flows should consider both the quantity and the timing of flows to maintain "naturally variable flow regimes" with the aim of retaining the benefits provided by seasonally low and high flows. Several methods have been used to establish environmental flow allocations and to reduce or remediate problems caused by previous water regulation. King, Brown, and Sabet (2003) emphasize that monitoring and management adjustments are a necessary component of such methods. There are many methods for estimating the amount of water that is critical for preserving aquatic ecosystems and resources (Annear and others 2002).

> Most of the tools for dealing with tradeoffs involving ecosystem services work best in environments where ecosystem behavior is well understood, but mechanisms are needed for dealing with uncertainty

In addition to determining the suitable quantity and timing of an environmental flow, it may be necessary to consider how to deliver flows. The engineering structures along rivers can constrain flow releases and may need adjustment. The rate and volume of releases and the temperature and oxygen content of the water are all important components of a flow release. Tools have been developed to assist in making decisions for allocating water for both economic and environmental purposes. The Downstream Response to Imposed Flow Transformation framework (box 6.14) differs from others such as the Instream Flow Incremental Methodology and Catchment Abstraction Management Strategies in its explicit consideration of the socioeconomic implications of different release scenarios.

Conceptualizing uncertainty

Most of the tools that have been developed for dealing with tradeoffs involving ecosystem services work best in environments where ecosystem behavior and response to change are well understood and the problems and benefits are already known. But ecosystem

---

box 6.14 | **Guiding environmental flows: the Downstream Response to Imposed Flow Transformation framework**

The Downstream Response to Imposed Flow Transformation (DRIFT) framework is an interactive and holistic approach for providing advice on environmental flows in rivers. It incorporates knowledge from experienced scientists from a range of biophysical disciplines as well as socioeconomic information to establish flow-related scenarios that describe a modified flow regime, the resulting condition of the river or species, the effect on water resource availability for off-stream users, and the social and economic costs and benefits. DRIFT highlights the importance of maintaining groundwater ecosystems along with surface water ecosystems in securing streamflows for ecosystem purposes. The process is developed through interactive and multidisciplinary stakeholder workshops to develop agreed biophysical and socioeconomic scenarios.

The development of scenarios requires an assessment of biophysical, social, and economic data and draws on results from other predictive models that assess the responses of specific biota to flow conditions (such as the Physical Habitat Simulation model). To be effective DRIFT should be run in parallel with a macroeconomic assessment of the wider implications of each scenario and in conjunction with a public participation process that enables people other than direct users to contribute to finding the best solution for the river.

Source: Acreman and King 2003; MEA 2005b.

Agriculture, water, and
ecosystems: avoiding the
costs of going too far

6

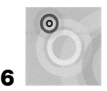

complexity and variability are common, so uncertainty is high, resulting in outcomes that are unpredictable and difficult to control. Mechanisms are needed for dealing with uncertainty that enable proactive rather than reactive responses to change.

Two interrelated approaches, adaptive management and scenario planning (see chapter 3 on scenarios), have been suggested for dealing with unpredictability (figure 6.5). Adaptive management and scenario planning both examine alternative models of how the world might work and seek to develop policies that are robust to this uncertainty. What distinguishes them is that the models used in adaptive management build in management experiments. The approaches are complementary to the integrated approaches described above and can be used together.

Adaptive management. Adaptive management emphasizes learning and flexibility in management institutions to cope with situations that involve unknown and uncertain ecological management tradeoffs (Walters 1986; Holling 1973; figure 6.6). Treating management policies as hypotheses rather than solutions, adaptive management has been a highly visible

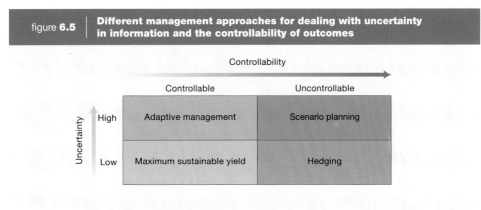

figure **6.5** | **Different management approaches for dealing with uncertainty in information and the controllability of outcomes**

Source: Adapted from Peterson, Cumming, and Carpenter 2003.

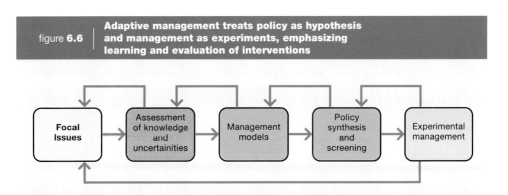

figure **6.6** | **Adaptive management treats policy as hypothesis and management as experiments, emphasizing learning and evaluation of interventions**

policy instrument in the management of major river systems, including the Columbia (Lee 1993), Colorado (Walters and others 2000), San Pedro and the Apalachicola-Chattahoochee-Flint River (Richter and others 2003), and rivers in Kruger National Park (Rogers and Biggs 1999) and the Everglades (Walters, Gunderson, and Holling 1992). The key is identifying management-relevant uncertainties that underlie policies and then evaluating the management alternatives through scientific assessment, modeling, and if necessary, experimental management.

Successful adaptive management requires time, resources for learning, and social support (Richter and others 2003; Walters 1986). Consequently, it often focuses on building ecological resilience, establishing knowledge for ecological management by working to integrate knowledge from many different scientific and local sources, and developing connections between the system being managed and its larger context (Berkes, Colding, and Folke 2003).

In an example of adaptive management Carpenter (2002) describes how a partnership of university researchers and state ecological managers collaborated to design and operate a management experiment to improve water quality in Lake Mendota, Wisconsin, by altering the fish community dynamics in the lake to increase predation of algae. The experiment was made possible by a history of collaboration between lake managers and academics and supported by the availability of decades of lake monitoring.

> Scenario planning offers a structured way of coping with complex systems and outcomes through learning and preparing for change

Scenario planning. Many problems related to management of water for agriculture and other ecosystem services are too complex and involve too many interest groups to be solved through narrowly focused experiments or computer model projections. Scenario planning offers a structured way of coping with complex systems and outcomes through learning and preparing for change (Peterson, Cumming, and Carpenter 2003; MEA 2005c). Decisions about how, when, and where to act are typically based on expectations for the future. When the world is highly unpredictable and when we are working from a limited range of experiences, our expectations may be proved wrong. Scenario planning provides a means to examine these expectations through a set of contrasting plausible futures described though a set of narratives. It has been applied in recent assessments such as the Intergovernmental Panel on Climate Change, the Millennium Ecosystem Assessment, and the International Assessment on Agricultural Science and Technology for Development.

Ideally, scenarios should build understanding of the potential costs and benefits of alternative futures. Scenario planning integrates diverse qualitative and quantitative information into a set of plausible narratives to explore policy-relevant futures. A scenario planning process functions similarly to an adaptive management process, but uses scenarios rather than computer models or management experiments to develop and test policy alternatives. One of the biggest shortcomings of scenario planning is the inability of participants to perceive their own assumptions (Keepin and Wynne 1984) and the potential consequences of being wrong. This problem cannot be completely avoided, but more robust scenarios can be created if a wide diversity of stakeholders and perspectives are included and if the exercise is repeated several times.

Agriculture, water, and
ecosystems: avoiding the
costs of going too far

6

Conclusions

Human society depends on an array of services provided by ecosystems, including agro-ecosystems. However, agriculture has resulted in the serious degradation of the components and processes of many other ecosystems, including processes that are essential for food production. These include:

- River depletion and consequent degradation of downstream aquatic ecosystems, including effects on groundwater and fisheries.
- Drainage of wetlands and runoff or discharge of wastewater to surface water– and groundwater-dependent ecosystems.
- Groundwater depletion by overexploitation for irrigation, causing damage to groundwater-dependent ecosystems.
- Land degradation and alterations of local to regional climate from land-use changes.
- Pollution from overuse of nutrients and agrochemicals, with consequences for terrestrial and aquatic ecosystems and for human health because of water pollution.
- A worsening of water pollution problems by river depletion, decreasing possible river dilution, as illustrated in the tributaries to the Aral Sea and in the severe health problems caused to downstream populations.

There are four ways to respond to these adverse impacts:

- By rehabilitating lost or degraded ecosystems and ecological processes.
- By improving agricultural practices using existing and improved technology.
- By ensuring more careful forward planning that includes conscious striking of trade-offs between water for food production and for other ecosystem services and dealing with uncertainty.
- By addressing the underlying social issues and divisions that affect how decisions are made in many communities, especially within poor rural communities that often disproportionately suffer the effects of environmental degradation.

It is also essential that unknown, poorly understood, or uncertain phenomena be brought into these tradeoffs. The social context for addressing these issues can be important, especially when such issues as culture, gender, health, and education come to the fore.

Where ecosystem degradation has not progressed too far, it may be possible to rehabilitate ecosystems, for instance, to reduce severe eutrophication of lakes and coastal waters or important wetlands and to secure, by reallocation, enough residual stream flow to restore environmental flows that support downstream ecosystems and ecosystem services. More essential are actions that focus on preventing further degradation and loss of important ecosystems.

Because food production will have to increase to alleviate undernutrition and to feed a projected 50% increase in the world population (before it stabilizes by the middle of the present century), many challenges remain for land and water managers. The type of responses available will differ depending on whether the effects of particular instances of ecosystem degradation are avoidable or unavoidable. Avoidable effects can be minimized largely through concerted responses, while unavoidable effects have to be considered when striking tradeoffs.

> A more cautious approach toward water management and food production will be essential to ensure social and ecological sustainability

A catchment-based and integrated approach to land use, water, and ecosystems will be essential for a knowledge-based balancing of water among different ecological processes and the provision of ecosystem services. It will be necessary to develop the scientific and administrative capability and capacity to analyze the conditions necessary for securing social and ecological resilience to change in ecosystems, including in those that are particularly vulnerable to large or episodic events, such as drought, storms, and floods, and those that are subject to multiple and cumulative impacts. Climate change raises questions about how the future use of water and land for agriculture will constrain the ability of ecosystems to respond. That is, will water and land uses adversely affect ecosystem resilience and responses to climate change?

We are dependent on the ecological components and processes and ecosystem services that provide or support much of our food. Thus a more cautious approach toward water management and food production will be essential to ensure social and ecological sustainability. While food production will continue to be at the forefront of our endeavors to support human well-being, sustainability can be achieved only through a more conscious striking of tradeoffs between different interests. Underlying all must be a clear understanding of the vital role that ecosystems and ecosystem services play in supporting human well-being and the recognition that much past ecological change has undermined the provision of many vital ecosystem services, often with complex social and economic inequities.

Reviewers

Chapter review editor: Rebecca D'Cruz.
Chapter reviewers: Maria Angelica Algeria, Andrew I. Ayeni, Donald Baird, Thorsten Blenckner, Stuart Bunn, Zhu Defeng, Rafiqul M. Islam, Ramaswamy R. Iyer, Mostafa Jafari, Joan Jaganyi, Hillary Masundhire, Randy Milton, A.D. Mohile, Jorge Mora Portuguez, V.J. Paranjpye, Bernt Rydgren, Marcel Silvius, Elizabeth Soderstrom, Douglas Taylor, and Yunpeng Xue.

References

Acreman, M.C., and J.M. King. 2003. "Defining Water Requirements." In M. Dyson, G. Bergkamp, and J. Scanlon, eds., *Flow: The Essentials of Environmental Flows*. Gland, Switzerland, and Cambridge, UK: World Conservation Union.

Adams, W.M., R. Aveling, D. Brockington, B. Dickson, J. Elliott, J. Hutton, D. Roe, B. Vira, and W. Wolmer. 2004. "Biodiversity Conservation and the Eradication of Poverty." *Science* 306 (5699): 1146–49.

Agardy, T., and J. Alder. 2005. "Coastal Systems." In *Millennium Ecosystem Assessment*. Vol. 1, *Ecosystems and Human Well-being: Current State and Trends. Findings of the Conditions and Trends Working Group*. Washington, D.C.: Island Press.

Alam, M., and W. Kabir. 2004. "Irrigated Agriculture in Bangladesh and Possible Impact Due to Inter-Basin Water Transfer as Planned by India." Paper presented at the Annual Meeting of the American Society of Agricultural and Biological Engineers, 1–4 August, Ottawa, Canada.

Alexander, R.B., R.A. Smith, and G.E. Schwarz. 2000. "Effect of Stream Channel Size on the Delivery of Nitrogen to the Gulf of Mexico." *Nature* 403 (6771): 758–61.

Anderies, J.M. 2005. "Minimal Models and Agroecological Policy at the Regional Scale: An Application to Salinity Problems in Southeastern Australia." *Regional Environmental Change* 5 (1): 1–17.

Anderies, J.M., G. Cumming, M. Janssen, L. Lebel, J. Norberg, G. Peterson, and B. Walker. 2001. "A Resilience Centered Approach for Engaging Stakeholders about Regional Sustainability: An Example from the Goulburn Broken Catchment in Southeastern Australia." Technical Report. Commonwealth Scientific and Industrial Research Organisation Sustainable Ecosystems, Canberra, Australia.

Annear, T., I. Chisholm, H. Beecher, A. Locke, P. Aarrestad, C. Coomer, C. Estes, and others. 2002. *Instream Flows for Riverine Resource Stewardship*. Bozeman, Mont.: Instream Flow Council.

Agriculture, water, and
ecosystems: avoiding the
costs of going too far

6

Arrow, K., B. Bolin, R. Costanza, P. Dasgupt, C. Folke, C.S. Holling, B-O. Jansson, S. Levin, K-G. Maler, C. Perrings, and D. Pimentel. 1995. "Economic Growth, Carrying Capacity, and the Environment." *Science* 268 (28 April): 520–21.

Balmford, A., A. Bruner, P. Cooper, R. Costanza, S. Farber, R.E. Green, M. Jenkins, and others. 2002. "Economic Reasons for Conserving Wild Nature." *Science* 297 (9 August): 950–53.

Baron, J.S., M.D. Hartman, T.G.F. Kittel, L.E. Band, D.S. Ojima, and R.B. Lammers. 1998. "Effects of Land Cover, Water Redistribution, and Temperature on Ecosystem Processes in the South Platte Basin." *Ecological Applications* 8 (4): 1037–51.

Baron, J.S., N. LeRoy Poff, P.L. Angermeier, C.N. Dahm, P.H. Gleick, N.G. Hairston, Jr., R.B. Jackson, C.A. Johnston, B.D. Richter, and A.D. Steinman. 2002. "Meeting Ecological and Societal Needs for Freshwater." *Ecological Applications* 12 (5): 1247–60.

Bennett, E.M., S.R. Carpenter, and N.F. Caraco. 2001. "Human Impact on Erodable Phosphorus and Eutrophication: A Global Perspective." *BioScience* 51 (3): 227–34.

Bennett, E.M., G.S. Cumming, and G.D. Peterson. 2005. "A Systems Model Approach to Determining Resilience Surrogates for Case Studies." *Ecosystems* 8 (8): 945–57.

Berg, H., M. Kilbus, and N. Kautsky. 1992. "DDT and Other Insecticides in the Lake Kariba Ecosystem." *Ambio* 21 (7): 444–50.

Berkes, F., and C. Folke. 1998. *Linking Social and Ecological Systems: Management Practices and Social Mechanisms for Building Resilience.* Cambridge, UK: Cambridge University Press.

Berkes, F., J. Colding, and C. Folke, eds. 2003. *Navigating Social-ecological Systems: Building Resilience for Complexity and Change.* Cambridge, UK: Cambridge University Press.

Berndes, G. 2002. "Bioenergy and Water—The Implications of Large-scale Bioenergy Production for Water Use and Supply." *Global Environmental Change* 12 (4): 7–25.

Bosch, J.M., and J.D. Hewlett. 1982. "A Review of Catchment Experiments to Determine the Effect of Vegetation Changes on Water Yield and Evapotranspiration." *Journal of Hydrology* 55 (1–4): 3–23.

Bravo de Guenni, L. 2005. "Regulation of Natural Hazards: Floods and Fires." In *Millennium Ecosystem Assessment.* Vol. 1, *Ecosystems and Human Well-being: Current State and Trends. Findings of the Conditions and Trends Working Group.* Washington, D.C.: Island Press.

Briggs, S.V., and N. Taws. 2003. "Impacts of Salinity on Biodiversity—Clear Understanding or Muddy Confusion?" *Australian Journal of Botany* 51 (6): 609–17.

Bruijnzeel, L.A. 1990. *Hydrology of Moist Tropical Forests and Effects of Conversion: A State of Knowledge Review.* Paris and Amsterdam: United Nations Education, Scientific and Cultural Organization, International Hydrological Program, Humid Tropics Program, and Free University.

Bullock, A., and M. Acreman. 2003. "The Role of Wetlands in the Hydrological Cycle." *Hydrology and Earth System Sciences* 7 (3): 358–89.

Calder, I. 2005. *Blue Revolution: Integrated Land and Water Resource Management.* 2nd ed. London: Earthscan.

Carbonell, M., N. Nathai-Gyan, and C.M. Finlayson, eds. 2001. *Science and Local Communities: Strengthening Partnerships for Effective Wetland Management.* Memphis, Tenn.: Ducks Unlimited.

Carpenter, S.R. 2002. "Ecological Futures: Building an Ecology of the Long Now." *Ecology* 83 (8): 2069–83.

Carpenter, S.R., and M.G. Turner. 2000. "Hares and Tortoises: Interactions of Fast and Slow Variables in Ecosystems." *Ecosystems* 3 (6): 495–97.

Carpenter S.R., F. Westley, M.G. Turner. 2005. "Surrogates for Resilience of Social-Ecological Systems." *Ecosystems* 8 (8): 941–44.

Carpenter, S.R., B.H. Walker, J.M. Anderies, and N. Abel. 2001. "From Metaphor to Measurement: Resilience of What to What?" *Ecosystems* 4 (8): 765–81.

Carson, R. 1962. *Silent Spring.* Boston, Mass.: Houghton Mifflin.

Chase, T.N., R.A. Pielke, T.G.F. Kittel, J.S. Baron, and T.J. Stohlgren. 1999. "Potential Impacts on Colorado Rocky Mountain Weather Due to Land Use Changes on the Adjacent Great Plains." *Journal of Geophysical Research—Atmospheres* 104 (D14): 16673–90.

Coe, M.T., and J.A. Foley. 2001. "Human and Natural Impacts on the Water Resources of the Lake Chad Basin." *Journal of Geophysical Research—Atmospheres* 106 (D4): 3349–56.

Cohen, M. 2002. "Managing Across Boundaries: The Case of the Colorado River Delta." In P. Gleick, W.C.G. Burns, E.L. Chalecki, M. Cohen, K.K. Cushing, A.S. Mann, R. Reyes, G.H. Wolff, and A.K. Wong, eds., *The World's Water: 2002–03: The Biennial Report on Freshwater Resources.* Washington, D.C.: Island Press.

Cumming, G.S., and B.J. Spiesman. 2006. "Regional Problems need Integrated Solutions: Pest Management and Conservation Biology in Agroecosystems." *Biological Conservation* 131: 533–43.

Cumming, G.S., G. Barnes, S. Perz, M. Schmink, K.E. Sieving, J. Southworth, M. Binford, M.D. Holt, C. Stickler, and T.V. Holt. 2005. "An Exploratory Framework for the Empirical Measurement of Resilience." *Ecosystems* 8 (8): 975–87.

Daily, G.C., S. Alexander, P.R. Ehrlich, L. Goulder, J. Lubchenco, P.A. Matson, H.A. Mooney, S. Postel, S.H. Schneider, D. Tilman, and G.M. Woodwell. 1997. *Ecosystem Services: Benefits Supplied to Human Societies by Natural Ecosystems.* Washington, D.C.: Island Press.

Davidson, N.C., and D.A. Stroud. Forthcoming. "African-Eurasian Flyways: Current Knowledge, Population Status, and Future Challenges." In G. Boere, C. Galbraith, and D. Stroud, eds., *Waterbirds around the World.* Proceedings of the Global Flyways Conference 2004, Waterbirds around the World, Edinburgh, 3–8 April. London: CBI.

Davies, B.R., and J.A. Day. 1998. *Vanishing Waters.* Cape Town: UCT Press.

Davis, J.A., M. McGuire, S.A. Halse, D. Hamilton, P. Horwitz, A.J. McComb, R. Froend, M. Lyons, and L. Sim. 2003. "What Happens When You Add Salt: Predicting Impacts of Secondary Salinisation on Shallow Aquatic Ecosystems By Using an Alternative-States Model." *Australian Journal of Botany* 51 (6): 715–24.

Döll, P., and S. Siebert. 2002. "Global Modeling of Irrigation Water Requirements." *Water Resources Research* 38 (4): 1037.

Dybas, C.L. 2005. "Dead Zones Spreading in World Oceans." *BioScience* 55 (7): 552–57.

Dyson, M., G. Bergkamp, and J. Scanlon, eds. 2003. *The Essentials of Environmental Flows.* Gland, Switzerland, and Cambridge, UK: World Conservation Union.

Elder, S., and D. Schmidt. 2004. "Global Employment Trends for Woman, 2004." Employment Strategy Papers. International Labour Organisation, Geneva.

Elmqvist, T., C. Folke, M. Nystrom, G. Peterson, J. Bengtsson, B. Walker, and J. Norberg. 2003. "Response Diversity, Ecosystem Change, and Resilience." *Frontiers in Ecology and the Environment* 1 (9): 488–94.

Falconer, I.R. 2001. "Toxic Cyanobacterial Bloom Problems in Australian Waters: Risks and Impacts on Human Health." *Phycologia* 40 (3): 228–33.

Falkenmark, M. 1979. "Main Problems of Water Use and Transfer of Technology." *GeoJournal* 3 (5): 435–43.

———. 1999. Forward to the Future: A Conceptual Framework for Water Dependence. *Ambio* 28 (4): 356–61.

———. 2003. "Freshwater as Shared between Society and Ecosystems: From Divided Approaches to Integrated Challenges." *Philosophical Transactions of the Royal Society B* 358 (1440): 2037–49.

Falkenmark, M., and M. Lannerstad. 2005. "Consumptive Water Use to Feed Humanity—Curing a Blind Spot." *Hydrology and Earth System Sciences* 9 (1/2): 15–28.

Falkenmark, M., and J. Rockström. 1993. "Curbing Rural Exodus from Tropical Drylands." *Ambio* 22 (7): 427–37.

Farrington, P., and R.B. Salama. 1996. "Controlling Dryland Salinity by Planting Trees in the Best Hydrogeological Setting." *Land Degradation & Development* 7 (3): 183–204.

FAO and UNESCO (Food and Agriculture Organization and United National Educational, Scientific, and Cultural Organization). 2003. Digital Soil Map of the World and Derived Soil Properties. Rev.1. FAO, Rome. [www.fao.org/AG/agl/agll/dsmw.htm].

Fernandez, R.J., E.R.M. Archer, A.J. Ash, H. Dowlatabadi, P.H.Y. Hiernaux, J.F. Reynolds, C.H. Vogel, B.H. Walker, and T. Wiegand. 2002. "Degradation and Recovery in Socio-ecological Systems." In F. Reynolds and D.M. Stafford Smith, eds., *Global Desertification: Do Humans Cause Deserts?* Berlin: Dahlem University Press.

Finlayson, C.M., and R. D'Cruz. 2005. "Inland Water Systems." In R. Hassan, R. Scholes, and N. Ash, eds., *Ecosystems and Human Well-being: Current State and Trends: Findings of the Condition and Trends Working Group.* Washington, D.C.: Island Press.

Finlayson, C.M., H. Gitay, M.G. Bellio, R.A. van Dam, and I. Taylor. Forthcoming. "Climate Variability and Change and Other Pressures on Wetlands and Waterbirds—Impacts and Adaptation." In G. Boere, C. Galbraith, and D. Stround, eds., *Waterbirds around the World.* London: CBI Press.

Foley, J., R. DeFries, G.P. Asner, C. Barford, G. Bonan, S.R. Carpenter, F.S. Chapin, and others. 2005. "Global Consequences of Land Use." *Science* 309 (22 July): 570–74.

Folke, C., T. Hahn, P. Olsson, and J. Norberg. 2005. "Adaptive Governance of Social-Ecological Systems." *Annual Review of Environment and Resources* 30: 441–73.

Folke, C., Å. Jansson, J. Larsson, and R. Costanza. 1997. "Ecosystem Appropriation by Cities." *Ambio* 26 (3): 167–72.

Folke, C., S. Carpenter, B. Walker, M. Scheffer, T. Elmqvist, L. Gunderson, and C.S. Holling. 2004. "Regime Shifts, Resilience, and Biodiversity in Ecosystem Management." *Annual Review of Ecology, Evolution, and Systematics* 35: 557–81.

Folke C., S. Carpenter, T. Elmqvist, L. Gunderson, C.S. Holling., B. Walker, J. Bengtsson, F. Berkes, J. Colding, K. Danell, M. Falkenmark, L. Gordon, and others. 2002 *Resilience and Sustainable Development: Building Adaptive Capacity in a World of Transformations.* Report for the Swedish Environmental Advisory Council, Ministry of the Environment, Stockholm.

Agriculture, water, and
ecosystems: avoiding the
costs of going too far

6

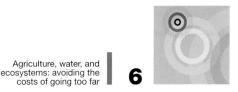

Fu, C. 2003. "Potential Impacts of Human-induced Land Cover Change on East Asia Monsoon." *Global and Planetary Change* 37 (3–4): 219–29.

Galloway, J.N., F.J. Dentener, D.G. Capone, E.W. Boyer, R.W. Howarth, S.P. Seitzinger, G. Asner, and others. 2004. "Global and Regional Nitrogen Cycles: Past, Present and Future." *Biogeochemistry* 70 (2): 153–226.

Gammelsrod, T. 1992. "Variation in Shrimp Abundance on the Sofala Bank, Mozambique, and its Relation to the Zambezi River Runoff." *Estuarine, Coastal and Shelf Science* 35 (1): 91–103.

Gitay, H., A. Suarez, R.T. Watson, and D.J. Dokken, eds. 2002. "Climate Change and Biodiversity." IPCC Technical Paper V. Intergovernmental Panel on Climate Change, Washington, D.C.

Glover, D., and T. Jessup, eds. 1999. *Indonesia's Fires and Haze: The Cost of Catastrophe.* Singapore and Ottawa: Institute of South East Asian Studies and International Development Research Centre.

Gordon, L., M. Dunlop, and B. Foran. 2003. "Land Cover Change and Water Vapour Flows: Learning from Australia." *Philosophical Transactions of the Royal Society B* 358 (1440): 1973–84.

Gordon, L.J., W. Steffen, B.F. Jönsson, C. Folke, M. Falkenmark, and Å. Johannesen. 2005. Human Modification of Global Water Vapor Flows from the Land Surface. *Proceedings of the National Academy of Sciences* 102 (21): 7612–17.

Green, P., C. J. Vörösmarty, M. Meybeck, J. Galloway, and B.J. Peterson. 2004. "Pre-industrial and Contemporary Fluxes of Nitrogen through Rivers: A Global Assessment Based on Typology." *Biogeochemistry* 68 (1): 71–105.

Gunderson, L.H. 2001. "Managing Surprising Ecosystems in Southern Florida." *Ecological Economics* 37 (3): 371–78.

Gunderson, L.H., and C.S. Holling. 2002. *Panarchy: Understanding Transformations in Human and Natural Systems.* Washington, D.C.: Island Press.

Gupta, S.K., and R.D. Deshpande. 2004. "Water for India in 2050: First-order Assessment of Available Options." *Current Science* 86 (9): 1216–24.

Hall, S.J. 2002. "The Continental Shelf Benthic Ecosystem: Current Status, Agents for Change and Future Prospects." *Environmental Conservation* 29 (3): 350–74.

He, C., S.-K. Cheng, and Y. Luo. 2005. "Desiccation of the Yellow River and the South Water Northward Transfer Project." *Water International* 30 (2): 261–68.

Hertzman, T., and T. Larsson. 1999. *Lake Hornborga: The Return of a Bird Lake.* Publication 50. Wageningen, Netherlands: Wetlands International.

Hoffman, W.A., and R.B. Jackson. 2000. "Vegetation—Climate Feedbacks in the Conversion of Tropical Savanna to Grassland." *American Meteorological Society* 13 (9): 1593–1602.

Holling, C.S. 1973. "Resilience and Stability of Ecological Systems." *Annual Review of Ecology and Systematics* 4: 1–23
———. 1986. "The Resilience of Terrestrial Ecosystems: Local Surprise and Global Change." In W.C. Clark and R.E. Munn, eds., *Sustainable Development of the Biosphere.* Cambridge, UK: Cambridge University Press.

Holling, C.S., and G.K. Meffe. 1996. "On Command-and-Control and the Pathology of Natural Resource Management." *Conservation Biology* 10 (2): 328–37.

Holling, C.S., D.W. Schindler, B.W. Walker, and J. Roughgarden. 1995. "Biodiversity in the Functioning of Ecosystems: An Ecological Synthesis." In C. Perrings, K.-G. Mähler, C. Folke, C.S. Holling, and B.-O. Jansson, eds., *Biodiversity Loss: Economic and Ecological Issues.* Cambridge, UK: Cambridge University Press.

Hollis, G.E. 1994. "Halting and Reversing Wetland Loss and Degradation: A Geographical Perspective on Hydrology and Land Use." Thomas Telford Services and Institution of Engineers, London.

International Council for Science. 2002. *Biodiversity, Science and Sustainable Development.* Series on Science for Sustainable Development 10. Paris.

Italy, Ministry for the Environment and Territory, and Free Iraq Foundation. 2004. The New Eden Project: Final Report. Paper presented at the United Nations Commission for Sustainable Development CSD-12 meeting April 14–30, New York. [www.edenagain.org/publications/pdfs/newedenfinalreportcsd12rev0.pdf].

IUCN (World Conservation Union). 2003. The Pangani River Basin. A Situation Analysis. Gland, Switzerland.

Jackson, R.B., E.G. Jobbágy, R. Avissar, S. Baidya Roy, D. Barrett, C.W. Cook, K.A. Farley, D.C. le Maitre, B.A. McCarl, and B.C. Murray. 2005. "Trading Water for Carbon with Biological Carbon Sequestration." *Science* 310 (23 December): 1944–47.

Jansson, Å., C. Folke, J. Rockström, and L. Gordon. 1999. "Linking Freshwater Flows and Ecosystem Services Appropriated by People: The Case of the Baltic Sea Drainage Basin." *Ecosystems* 2 (4): 351–66.

Jansson, A.M., M. Hammer, C. Folke, and R. Costanza, eds. 1994. *Investing in Natural Capital: The Ecological Economics Approach to Sustainability.* Washington, D.C.: Island Press.

Jewitt, G. 2002. "The 8%–4% Debate: Commercial Afforestation and Water Use in South Africa." *Southern African Forestry Journal* 194 (2): 1–6.

Junk, W. 2002. "Long-term Environmental Trends and the Future of Tropical Wetlands." *Environmental Conservation* 29 (4): 414–435.

Kabat, P., M. Claussen, P.A. Dirmeyer, J.H.C. Gash, L. Bravo de Guenni, M. Meybeck, R.A. Pielke, Sr., C.J. Vörösmarty, R.W.A. Hutjes, and S. Lütkemeier, 2004, *Vegetation. Water. Humans and the Climate: A New Perspective on an Interactive System.* Berlin: Springer-Verlag.

Keepin, B., and B. Wynne. 1984. "Technical Analysis of IIASA Energy Scenarios." *Nature* 312 (5996): 691–95.

King, J.M., C. Brown, and H. Sabet. 2003. "A Scenario-based Holistic Approach to Environmental Flow Assessments for Rivers." *River Research and Applications* 19 (5/6): 619–39.

King, J.M., R.E. Tharme, and H. Sabet. 2000. "Environmental Flow Assessments for Rivers: Manual for the Building Block Methodology." Water Research Commission, Pretoria.

Kremen, C. 2005. "Managing for Ecosystem Services: What Do We Need to Know About Their Ecology?" *Ecology Letters* 8 (5): 468–479.

Kremen, C., N.M. Williams, and R.W. Thorp. 2002. "Crop Pollination From Native Bees at Risk from Agricultural Intensification." *Proceedings of the National Academy of Sciences* 99 (26): 16812–16.

Kura, Y., C. Revenga, E. Hoshino, and G. Mock. 2004. *Fishing for Answers.* Washington D.C.: World Resources Institute.

Lansing, J.S. 1991. *Priests and Programmers: Technologies of Power in the Engineered Landscape of Bali.* Princeton, N.J.: Princeton University Press.

Le Maitre, D.C., B.W. van Wilgen, R.A. Chapman, and D.H. McKelly. 1996. "Invasive Plants and Water Resources in the Western Cape Province, South Africa: Modelling the Consequences of a Lack of Management." *Journal of Applied Ecology* 33 (1): 161–172.

Lee, K. 1993. *Compass and Gyroscope: Integrating Science and Politics for the Environment.* Washington, D.C.: Island Press.

Lemly, A.D., R.T. Kingsford, and J.R. Thompson. 2000. "Irrigated Agriculture and Wildlife Conservation: Conflict on a Global Scale." *Environmental Management* 25 (5): 485–512.

Lemoalle, J. 2003. "Lake Chad: A Changing Environment." In J.C.J. Nihoul, P.O. Zavialov, and P.P. Micklin, eds, *Dying and Dead Seas.* NATO Advanced Research Workshop, Advanced Study Institute Series, Dordrecht, Netherlands: Kluwer Publishers.Levin, S. 1999. *Fragile Dominion: Complexity and the Commons.* Reading, Mass.: Perseus Books.

Levin, S.A. 1999. *Fragile Dominion: Complexity and the Commons.* Reading, Mass.: Perseus Books.

L'vovich, M.I. 1979. *World Water Resources and their Future.* Chelsea, UK: LithoCrafters Inc.

Lukatelich, R. J., and A.J. McComb. 1986. "Nutrient Levels and the Development of Diatom and Blue-Green Algal Blooms in a Shallow Australian Estuary." *Journal of Plankton Research* 8 (4): 597–618.

Magadza, C.H.D. 1995. "Special Problems in Lakes/Reservoir Management in Tropical Southern Africa." Presented at the 6th International Conference on the Conservation and Management of Lakes, 23–27 October, University of Tsukuba, Japan.

Marland, G., R.A. Pielke, Sr., M. Apps, R. Avissar, R.A. Betts, K.J. Davis, P.C. Frumhoff, S.T. Jackson, and others. 2003. "The Climatic Impacts of of Land Surface Change and Carbon Management, and the Implications for Climate-Change Mitigation Policy." *Climate Policy* 3 (2): 149–57.

McCulloch, J.S.G., and M. Robinson. 1993. "History of Forest Hydrology." *Journal of Hydrology* 150 (2–4): 189–216.

McNeely, J.A., and S.J. Scherr. 2003. *Ecoagriculture: Strategies to Feed the World and Save Wild Biodiversity.* Washington, D.C.: Island Press.

MEA (Millennium Ecosystem Assessment). 2003. *Ecosystems and Human Well-being: A Framework for Assessment.* Washington D.C.: Island Press.

———. 2005a. *Ecosystems and Human Well-being: Health Synthesis.* Washington, D.C.: World Resources Institute.

———. 2005b. *Ecosystems and Human Well-being: Wetlands and Water Synthesis.* Washington, D.C.: World Resources Institute.

———. 2005c. *Millennium Ecosystem Assessment Synthesis Report.* Washington D.C.: Island Press.

Meybeck, M., and A. Ragu. 1997. "Presenting the GEMS-GLORI, A Compendium of World River Discharge to the Oceans." In B. Webb, ed., *Freshwater Contamination. Proceedings of a Symposium Held During the Fifth IAHS Scientific Assembly at Rabat, Morocco, April–May 1997.* Publication 243. Wallingford, UK: International Association of Hydrological Sciences.

Milliman, J.D. 1991. "Flux and Fate of Fluvial Sediment and Water in Coastal Seas." In R.F.C. Mantoura, J.-M. Martin, and R. Wollast, eds., *Ocean Margin Processes in Global Change.* Chichester, UK: John Wiley & Sons.

Mirza, M.M.Q. 1998. "Diversion of the Ganges Water at Farakka and its Effects on Salinity in Bangladesh." *Environmental Management* 22 (5): 711–22.

Molden, D., and C. de Fraiture. 2004. "Investing in Water for Food, Ecosystems and Livelihoods." Comprehensive Assessment of Water Management in Agriculture Blue Paper. International Water Management Institute, Colombo.

Agriculture, water, and
ecosystems: avoiding the
costs of going too far

6

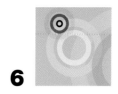

Nemani, R.R., S.W. Running, R.A. Pielke, and T.N. Chase. 1996. "Global Vegetation Cover Changes from Coarse Resolution Satellite Data." *Journal of Geophysical Research* 101 (D3): 7157–62.

North American Waterfowl Management Plan. 2004. *Strengthening the Biological Foundation.* Ottawa, Washington, D.C., and Mexico City: Environment Canada; US Department of the Interior, Fish and Wildlife Services; and Secretaria de Medio Ambente Recursos Naturales.

OECD (Organisation for Economic Co-operation and Development) 1996. *Guidelines for Aid Agencies for Improved Conservation and Sustainable Use of Tropical and Subtropical Wetlands.* Paris.

Olsson, P., C. Folke, and T. Hahn. 2004. "Social-ecological Transformation for Ecosystem Management: The Development of Adaptive Co-management of a Wetland Landscape in Southern Sweden." *Ecology and Society* 9 (4): 2.

Oyama, M.D., and C.A. Nobre. 2003. "A New Climate-Vegetation Equilibrium State for Tropical South America." *Geophysical Research Letters* 30 (23) 2199–203.

Page, S.E., F. Siegert, J.O. Rieley, H.D. Boehm, A. Jaya, and S. Limin. 2002. "The Amount of Carbon Released from Peat and Forest Fires in Indonesia during 1997." *Nature* 420 (6911): 61–65.

Pala, C. 2006. "Once a Terminal Case, the Aral Sea Shows New Signs of Life." *Science* 312 (5771): 183.

Partow, H. 2001. *The Mesopotamian Marshlands: Demise of an Ecosystem.* Nairobi: United Nations Environment Programme.

Peterson, G.D., G.S. Cumming, and S.R. Carpenter. 2003. "Scenario Planning: A Tool for Conservation in an Uncertain World." *Conservation Biology* 17 (2): 358–66.

Pielke, R.A., T.J. Lee, J.H. Copeland, J.L. Eastman, C.L. Ziegler, and C.A. Finley. 1997. "Use of USGS–Provided Data to Improve Weather and Climate Simulations." *Ecological Applications* 7 (1): 3–21.

Pielke, R.A., R.L. Walko, L. Steyaert, P.L. Vidale, G.E. Liston, W.A. Lyons, and T.N. Chase. 1999. "The Influence of Anthropogenic Landscape Changes on Weather in South Florida." *Monthly Weather Review* 127 (7): 1663–73.

Pielke, R.A., Sr., R. Avissar, M. Raupach, A.J. Dolman, X. Zeng, and A.S. Denning. 1998. "Interactions between the Atmosphere and Terrestrial Ecosystems: Influence on Weather and Climate." *Global Change Biology* 4 (5): 461–75.

Poff, N.L., J.D. Allan, M.B. Bain, J.R. Karr, K.L. Prestegaard, B.D. Richter, R.E. Sparks, and J.C. Stromberg. 1997. "The Natural Flow Regime: A Paradigm for River Conservation and Restoration." *Bioscience* 47 (11): 769–84.

Postel, S. 1996. *Last Oasis: Facing Water Scarcity.* New York: W.W. Norton & Company.

———. 1999. *Pillar of Sand: Can the Irrigation Miracle Last?* New York: W.W. Norton & Company.

Postel, S., and S.R. Carpenter. 1997. "Freshwater Ecosystem Services." In G. Daily, ed., *Nature's Services.* Washington, D.C.: Island Press.

Rahman, M.M, M.Q. Hassan, M. Islam, and S.Z.K.M. Shamsad. 2000. "Environmental Impact Assessment on Water Quality Deterioration Caused by the Decreased Ganges Outflow and Saline Water Intrusion in South-western Bangladesh." *Environmental Geology* 40 (1–2): 31–40.

Revenga, C., J. Brunner, N. Henniger, K. Kassem, and R. Payner. 2000. *Pilot Analysis of Global Ecosystems, Freshwater Systems.* Washington, D.C.: World Resources Institute.

Richardson, C.J., P. Reiss, N.A. Hussain, A.J. Alwash, and D.J. Pool. 2005. "The Restoration Potential of the Mesopotamian Marshes of Iraq." *Science* 307 (5713): 1307–11.

Richter, B.D., R. Mathews, D.L. Harrison, and R. Wigington. 2003. "Ecological Sustainable Water Management: Managing River Flows for Ecological Integrity." *Ecological Applications* 13 (1): 206–24.

Rogers, K., and H. Biggs. 1999. "Integrating Indicators, Endpoints and Value Systems in Strategic Management of the Rivers of the Kruger National Park." *Freshwater Biology* 41 (2): 439–52.

Salati, E., and C.A. Nobre. 1991. "Possible Climatic Impacts of Tropical Deforestation." *Climate Change* 19 (1–2): 177–96.

Savenije, H.H.G. 1995. "New Definitions for Moisture Recycling and the Relation with Land-use Changes in the Sahel." *Journal of Hydrology* 167 (1): 57–78.

———. 1996. "Does Moisture Feedback Affect Rainfall Significantly?" *Physical Chemistry of the Earth* 20 (5–6): 507–51.

Scheffer, M., S. Carpenter, J. A. Foley, C. Folke, and B. Walker. 2001. "Catastrophic Shifts in Ecosystems." *Nature* 413 (11 October): 591–96.

Shiklomanov, I.A., and J. Rodda. 2003. *World Water Resources at the Beginning of the 21st Century.* Paris: United Nations Educational, Scientific and Cultural Organization.

Silvius, M.J., M. Oneka, and A. Verhagen. 2000. "Wetlands: Lifeline for People at the Edge." *Physical Chemistry of the Earth B* 25 (7–8): 645–52.

Silvius, M.J., B. Setiadi, W.H. Diemont, F. Sjarkowi, H.G.P. Jansen, H. Siepel, J.O. Rieley, A. Verhagen, A. Beintema, L. Burnhill, and S.H. Limin. 2003. "Financial Mechanisms for Poverty-Environment Issues. The Bio-rights System." Alterra and Wetlands International, Wageningen, Netherlands.

SIWI (Stockholm International Water Institute), IFPRI (International Food Policy Research Institute), IUCN (World Conservation Union), and IWMI (International Water Management Institute). 2005. *Let It Reign: The New Water Paradigm for Global Food Security.* Final report to CSD-13. Stockholm: Stockholm International Water Institute.

Smakhtin, V., C. Revenga, and P. Döll. 2004. "Taking into Account Environmental Water Requirements in Global-scale Water Resources Assessments." Comprehensive Assessment of Water Management in Agriculture. International Water Management Institute, Colombo.

Snaddon, C.D., B.R. Davies, and M.J. Wishart. 1999. "A Global Overview of Inter-basin Water Transfer Schemes, with an Appraisal of their Ecological, Socio-Economic and Socio-Political Implications, and Recommendations for their Management." Water Research Commission Technology Transfer Report TT 120/00. Water Research Commission, Pretoria.

Steffen, W., A. Sanderson, P.D. Tyson, J. Jäger, P.A. Matson, B. Moore, F. Oldfield, K. Richardson, H.J. Schellnhuber, B.L. Turner, and R.J. Wasson. 2004. *Global Change and the Earth System: A Planet Under Pressure.* Berlin: Springer-Verlag.

Strehlow, K., J. Davis, L. Sim, J. Chambers, S. Halse, D. Hamilton, P. Horwitz, A. McComb, and R. Froend. 2005. "Temporal Changes between Ecological Regimes in a Range of Primary and Secondary Salinised Wetlands." *Hydrobiologia* 552 (1): 17–31.

Taylor, G.J., D.J. Baird, and A.M.V.M. Soares. 2002. "Ecotoxicology of Contaminants in Tropical Wetlands: The Need for Greater Ecological Relevance in Risk Assessment." *SETAC Globe* 3 (1): 27–28.

Tharme, R.E. 2003. "A Global Perspective on Environmental Flow Assessment: Emerging Trends in the Development and Application of Environmental Flow Methodologies for Rivers." *River Research and Applications* 19 (5–6): 397–441.

Tilman, D., J. Knops, D. Wedin, P. Reich, M. Ritchie, and E. Siemann. 1997. "The Influence of Functional Diversity and Composition on Ecosystem Processes." *Science* 277 (5330): 1300–02.

Trenberth, K.E. 1999. "Conceptual Framework for Changes of Extremes of the Hydrological Cycle with Climate Change." *Climatic Change* 42 (1): 327–39.

UNEP (United Nations Environment Programme). 2002. *Africa Environment Outlook: Past, Present and Future Perspectives.* Hertfordshire, UK: Earthprint.

UNESCO (United Nations Educational, Scientific and Cultural Organization). 2000. *Water Related Vision for the Aral Sea Basin for the Year 2025.* Paris.

Van Dam, R., H. Gitay, M. Finlayson, N.J. Davidson, and B. Orlando. 2002. "Climate Change and Wetlands: Impacts, Adaptation and Mitigation." Background document DOC.SC26/COP8–4 for the 26th Meeting of the Standing Committee of the Convention on Wetlands (Ramsar Convention), 3–7 December, Gland, Switzerland.

Van den Brink, P.J., S.N. Sureshkumar, M.A. Daam, I. Domingues, G.K. Milwain, W.H.J. Beltman, M. Warnajith, P. Perera, and K. Satapornvanit. 2003. Environmental and Human Risks of Pesticide Use in Thailand and Sri Lanka: Results of a Preliminary Risk Assessment. Alterra-rapport 789. MAMAS Report Series No. 3/2003. Green World Research. Wageningen, Netherlands: Alterra.

Verhoeven, J.T.A., B. Arheimer, C. Yin, and M.M. Hefting. 2006. "Regional and Global Concerns over Wetlands and Water Quality." *Trends in Ecology and Evolution.* 21 (2): 96–103.

Vörösmarty, C.J., and D. Sahagian 2000. "Anthrogenic Disturbance of the Terrestrial Water Cycle." *BioScience* 50: 753–65.

Vörösmarty, C.J., C. Lévêque, and C. Revenga. 2005. "Fresh Water." In R. Hassan, R. Scholes, and N. Ash, eds., *Ecosystems and Human Well-being: Current State and Trends: Findings of the Condition and Trends Working Group.* Washington, D.C.: Island Press.

Vörösmarty, C.J., M. Meybeck, B. Fekete, K. Sharma, P. Green, and J. Syvitski. 2003. "Anthropogenic Sediment Retention: Major Global Impact from Registered River Impoundments." *Global and Planetary Change* 39 (1–2): 169–90.

Walling, D.E., and D. Fang. 2003. "Recent trends in the suspended sediment loads of the world's rivers." *Global and Planetary Change* 39 (1–2): 111–26.

Walters, C.J. 1986. *Adaptive Management of Renewable Resources.* New York: MacMillan Publishing Co.

Walters, C.J., L.H. Gunderson, and C.S. Holling. 1992. "Experimental Policies for Water Management in the Everglades." *Ecological Applications* 2 (2): 189–202.

Walters, C., J. Korman, L.E. Stevens, and B. Gold. 2000. "Ecosystem Modeling for Evaluation of Adaptive Management Policies in the Grand Canyon." *Conservation Ecology* 4 (2): 1.

WCD (World Commission on Dams). 2000. *Dams and Development: A New Framework for Decision-Making.* London: Earthscan.

Wester, P., C.A. Scott, and M. Burton. 2005. "River Basin Closure and Institutional Change in Mexico's Lerma-Chapala Basin." In M. Svendsen, ed., *Irrigation and River Basin Management: Options for Governance and Institutions.* Wallingford, UK: CABI Publishing.

Williams, W.D. 2002. "Environmental Threats to Salt Lakes and the Likely Status of Inland Saline Wetlands by 2025." *Environment Conservation* 29 (2): 154–67.

Agriculture, water, and
ecosystems: avoiding the
costs of going too far

6

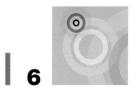

Wollheim, W.M., B.J. Peterson, L.A. Deegan, J.E. Hobbie, B. Hooker, W.B. Bowden, K.J. Edwardson, D.B. Arscott, A.E. Hershey, and J. Finlay. 2001. "Influence of Stream Size on Ammonium and Suspended Particulate Nitrogen Processing." *Limnology and Oceanography* 46 (1): 1–13.

Wooster, M.J., and N. Strub. 2002. "Study of the 1997 Borneo Fires: Quantitative Analysis Using Global Area Coverage (GAC) Satellite Data." *Global Biogeochemical Cycles* 16 (1): 1009.

WMO (World Meteorological Organization). 1997. *Comprehensive Assessment of the Freshwater Resources of the World.* Stockholm: World Meteorological Organization and Stockholm Environment Institute.

Wösten, J.H.M., J. van den Berg, P. van Eijk, G.J.M. Gevers, W.B.J.T. Giesen, A. Hooijer, A. Idris, P.H. Leenman, D.S. Rais, C. Siderius, M.J. Silvius, N. Suryadiputra, and I.T. Wibisono. 2006. "Interrelationships between Hydrology and Ecology in Fire Degraded Tropical Peat Swamp Forests." *International Journal of Water Resources Development* 22 (1): 157–74.

WRI (World Resources Institute), UNDP (United Nations Development Programme), UNEP (United Nations Environment Programme), and World Bank. 2005. *World Resources 2005: The Wealth of the Poor—Managing Ecosystems to Fight Poverty.* Washington, D.C.: World Resources Institute.

WWF. 2006. *Payments for Environmental Services: An Equitable Approach for Reducing Poverty and Conserving Nature.* Gland, Switzerland.

Zavaleta, E. 2000. "The Economic Value of Controlling an Invasive Shrub." *Ambio* 29 (8): 462–67.

Zheng, X., and E.A.B. Eltathir. 1998. "The Role of Vegetation in the Dynamics of West African Monsoons." *Journal of Climate* 11 (8): 2078–96.

Zwarts, L., P. Van Beukering, B. Kone, E. Wymenga, and D. Taylor. 2006. "The Economic and Ecological Effects of Water Management Choices in the Upper Niger River: Development of Decision Support Methods." *International Journal of Water Resources Development* 22 (1): 135–56.

Water use and productivity in a river basin

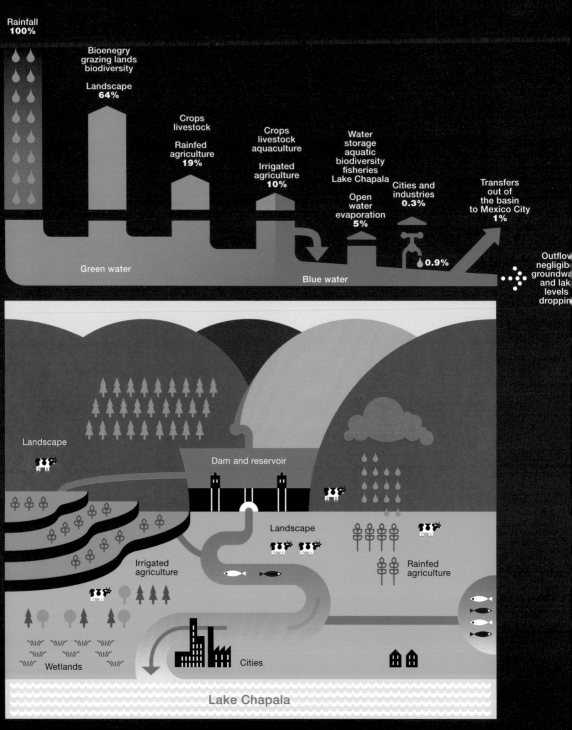

Lerma-Chapala Basin, Mexico
(average annual basis)

Rainfall
100%

Bioenegry
grazing lands
biodiversity

Landscape
64%

Crops
livestock

Rainfed
agriculture
19%

Crops
livestock
aquaculture

Irrigated
agriculture
10%

Water
storage
aquatic
biodiversity
fisheries
Lake Chapala

Open
water
evaporation
5%

Cities and
industries
0.3%

Transfers
out of
the basin
to Mexico City
1%

Green water

Blue water

0.9%

Outflow
negligib
groundwa
and lak
levels
droppin

Landscape

Dam and reservoir

Landscape

Irrigated
agriculture

Rainfed
agriculture

Wetlands

Cities

Lake Chapala

Source: Wester and others forthcoming.

Grow more food with less water

Artist: Monique Chatigny, Quebec, Canada

7 | Pathways for increasing agricultural water productivity

Coordinating lead authors: David Molden and Theib Y. Oweis

Lead authors: Pasquale Steduto, Jacob. W. Kijne, Munir A. Hanjra, Prem S. Bindraban

Contributing authors: Bas Antonius Maria Bouman, Simon Cook, Olaf Erenstein, Hamid Farahani, Ahmed Hachum, Jippe Hoogeveen, Henry Mahoo, Vinay Nangia, Don Peden, Alok Sikka, Paula Silva, Hugh Turral, Ashutosh Upadhyaya, and Sander Zwart

Overview

Water productivity is defined as the ratio of the net benefits from crop, forestry, fishery, livestock, and mixed agricultural systems to the amount of water required to produce those benefits. In its broadest sense it reflects the objectives of producing more food, income, livelihoods, and ecological benefits at less social and environmental cost per unit of water used, where *water use* means either water delivered to a use or depleted by a use. Put simply, it means growing more food or gaining more benefits with less water. *Physical water productivity* is defined as the ratio of the mass of agricultural output to the amount of water used, and *economic productivity* is defined as the value derived per unit of water used. Water productivity is also sometimes measured specifically for crops *(crop water productivity)* and livestock *(livestock water productivity)*.

To feed a growing and wealthier population with more diversified diets will require more water for agriculture on an average annual basis [well established]. Evapotranspiration from agricultural land is estimated at 7,130 cubic kilometers and without increases in water productivity could increase by 60%–90% by 2050 (see chapter 3 on scenarios). Agricultural water withdrawals from natural systems are estimated at 2,664 cubic kilometers, or about 70% of water withdrawn for human purposes. Additional water for agriculture will strain terrestrial and aquatic ecosystems and intensify competition for water resources. Improving physical water productivity in agriculture reduces the need for additional water and land in irrigated and rainfed systems and is thus a critical response to increasing water scarcity, including the need to leave enough water to sustain ecosystems and to meet the growing demands of cities and industries.

There is considerable scope for improving physical water productivity, but not everywhere [established but incomplete]. In areas of the world that already exhibit high physical water productivity, the scope for improvements is limited. But scope for improvement remains in high potential areas in many rainfed, irrigated, livestock, and fisheries systems in many regions of the world. Many farmers in developing countries could raise water productivity by adopting proven agronomic and water management practices because raising land productivity generally leads to increases in water productivity. Many promising pathways for raising water productivity are available over the continuum from fully rainfed to fully irrigated farming systems. These include supplemental irrigation (some irrigation to supplement rainfall); soil fertility maintenance; deficit irrigation; small-scale affordable management practices for water storage, delivery, and application; modern irrigation technologies (such as pressured systems and drip irrigation); and soil-water conservation through zero or minimum tillage. Breeding and biotechnology can help indirectly by reducing biomass losses through increased resistance to pests and diseases, vigorous early growth for fast ground cover, and reduced susceptibility to drought. But water productivity gains are context dependent and can be properly assessed only by taking an integrated basin perspective.

> **Many farmers in developing countries could raise water productivity by adopting proven agronomic and water management practices because raising land productivity generally leads to increases in water productivity**

Increasing water productivity, especially the value produced per unit of water, can be an important pathway for poverty reduction [established but incomplete]. Increasing the value derived per unit of water, especially the opportunities for employment, income generation, nutrition, and opportunities for women, is important for poverty reduction. But carefully crafted programs are required to ensure that these gains reach the poor, especially rural women, and are not captured only by wealthier or more powerful users.

There is significant scope to improve physical and economic water productivities in livestock and aquaculture [established but incomplete]. Rising demand for livestock and fish products leads to rising demand for water. Water productivity gains can be made by carefully considering feed sources and feeding strategies, improving the quality of produce, and integrating fisheries and livestock into farm production systems. Because capture fisheries are increasingly threatened by reductions in streamflows *[established but incomplete]*, basin water productivity analysis should consider the social and ecological values generated by fisheries before reducing river flows that support them.

Increasing the value generated by water use and decreasing associated costs require understanding and interventions that look beyond the direct production benefits and investment costs of agricultural water management to the livelihood and ecological benefits and costs. Integrated and multiple-use systems—in which water serves crops, fish, livestock, and domestic purposes—can increase the value derived per unit of water used. Gains in crop production have often come, for instance, at the expense of fisheries. Values generated by fisheries, including ecosystem sustenance values, are routinely underestimated. Understanding values helps us to understand where there are win-win situations and what tradeoffs will have to be made. But these values are poorly understood and rarely enter into decisionmaking.

The adoption of techniques to improve water productivity requires an enabling policy and institutional environment that aligns the incentives of producers, resource managers, and society and provides a mechanism for dealing with tradeoffs. Despite adequate technologies and management practices, achieving net gains in water productivity is difficult for numerous reasons. The price of most agricultural produce is low, and the risks for farmers are high. Productivity gains tend to suppress market prices by increasing supply. Gains achieved by one group often come at the expense of another (crop farmers taking water out of fisheries). Incentive systems do not support the adoption and uptake of existing technologies (who pays for the water-saving practices by farmers that ultimately benefit city users?). The incentives of producers (more water for more income) are often much different than the incentives of broader society (more water for cities and the environment). Gains are often captured by more powerful users, and the poor are left behind (those who can afford drip irrigation tend to gain more). Strategies must recognize these tradeoffs and provide incentives and compensation for greater equity among winners and losers. Many incentives will come from outside the water sector and address issues of vulnerability and risk, markets, and the profitability of the agriculture enterprise. Research should explore ways to limit the magnitude of the tradeoffs, while inclusive processes for involving interest groups should balance the ways in which these tradeoffs are dealt with.

> Integrated and multiple-use systems—in which water serves crops, fish, livestock, and domestic purposes—can increase the value derived per unit of water used

There are four high priority areas for water productivity gains:

- Areas where poverty is high and water productivity is low, where improvements could particularly benefit the poor, as in much of Sub-Saharan Africa and parts of South Asia and Latin America.
- Areas of physical water scarcity where there is intense competition for water, such as the Aral Sea Basin and the Yellow River, especially where gains in economic water productivity are possible.
- Areas with little water resources development where high returns from a little water can make a big difference.
- Areas of water-driven ecosystem degradation, such as falling groundwater tables, river desiccation, and intense competition for water.

What is water productivity and why is it important?

In the broadest sense water productivity relates to the net socioeconomic and environmental benefits achieved through the use of water in agriculture, including fisheries, livestock, crops, agroforestry, and mixed systems. The concept reflects the desire to do better using less of scarce water resources.

There are important reasons to improve agricultural water productivity:

- To meet the rising demand for food from a growing, wealthier, and increasingly urbanized population, in light of water scarcity.
- To respond to pressures to reallocate water from agriculture to cities and to ensure that water is available for environmental uses.
- To contribute to poverty reduction and economic growth. For the rural poor more productive use of water can mean better nutrition for families, more income, productive employment, and greater equity. Targeting high water productivity can reduce investment costs by reducing the amount of water that has to be withdrawn.

Globally, the additional amount of water needed to support agriculture directly will depend on the gains in water productivity. With no gains in water productivity current average annual agricultural evapotranspiration of 7,130 cubic kilometers could nearly double in the next 50 years. But with appropriate practices in livestock, aquaculture, rainfed, and irrigated systems the increase could be held down to 20%–30%. Increases in withdrawals for irrigation, now at 2,664 cubic kilometers, could range from zero to 55% depending on investments in increasing water productivity and on how much rainfed and irrigated agriculture expand.

Within the broad definition of water productivity there are interrelated and cascading sets of definitions useful for different purposes. Physical water productivity relates the mass of agricultural output to water use—"more crop per drop." Economic water productivity relates the economic benefits obtained per unit of water used and has also been applied to relate water use in agriculture to nutrition, jobs, welfare, and the environment. Water productivity depends on a number of nonwater factors, such as fertilizer use and labor, as well as on water. Increasing water productivity is particularly appropriate where water is scarce compared with other resources involved in production.

This chapter presents a framework for water productivity analysis and highlights how the framework can be used in different situations. Physical water productivity is presented in detail because it underpins many of the broader concepts and has the largest impact on the amount of water required to produce food. The chapter then examines promising pathways to achieving higher water productivity, implications for poverty reduction, and the constraints to achieving high water productivity. The chapter concludes with investment priorities for increasing water productivity.

To understand water productivity, it is essential to follow the flow of water through a basin and to understand how water supports life and livelihoods

A framework for water productivity

Water productivity analysis can be applied to crops, livestock, tree plantations, fisheries, and mixed systems at selected scales—crop or animal, field or farm, irrigation system, and basin or landscape, with interacting ecosystems (table 7.1). The objectives of water productivity analysis range from assessing agricultural production (kilograms of grain per unit of water depleted by a crop on a field) to assessing incremental welfare per unit of water used in the agricultural sector. Because expressions for water productivity differ in each context, it is important to be clear about the agriculture output and input terms used.

To understand water productivity, it is essential to follow the flow of water through a basin and to understand how water supports life and livelihoods (see chapter frontispiece). The natural source of basin water is rain. Interbasin transfers, conveying water from one river basin to another, are an increasingly common source of water. As water moves downstream, a drop may be transpired by a plant, be evaporated from the land, or continue to flow downstream to be used and reused by cities, agriculture, and fisheries.

The denominator of the water productivity equation is expressed as water either supplied or depleted. Water is depleted when it is consumed by evapotranspiration, is incorporated into a product, flows to a location where it cannot be readily reused (to saline groundwater, for example), or becomes heavily polluted (Seckler 1996; Molden and others 2003).

table **7.1**	Water productivity interests at different scales				
	Crop, plant, or animal	Field or pond	Farm or agricultural enterprise	Irrigation system	Basin and landscape
Processes	Energy conversion, nutrient uptake and use, photosynthesis, and the like	Soil, water, nutrient management	Balancing risks and rewards, managing farm inputs including water	Distribution of water to users, operation and maintenance, fees, drainage	Allocation across uses, regulation of pollution
Interests	Agricultural producers, breeders, plant and animal physiologists	Agricultural producers; soil, crop, fish, livestock scientists	Agricultural producers, agriculturalists, agriculture economists	Irrigation engineers, social scientists, water managers	Economists, hydrologists, social scientists, engineers, water managers
Production terms (numerator)	Kilograms of produce	Kilograms of produce	Kilograms, $	Kilograms, $, value, ecosystem services	$, value, eco-system services
Water terms (denominator)	Transpiration	Transpiration, evaporation, water application	Evapotranspiration, irrigation supply	Irrigation deliveries, depletion, available water	Deliveries, flows, depletion

Note: The $ sign represents marketable financial values, while the word *value* includes other intrinsic values such as the value of livelihood support, ecological benefits, and cultural significance.

This notion of water productivity evolved from two disciplines. Crop physiologists defined *water use efficiency* as carbon assimilated and crop yield per unit of transpiration (Viets 1962), and then later as the amount of produce per unit of evapotranspiration. Irrigation specialists have used the term *water use efficiency* to describe how effectively water is delivered to crops and to indicate the amount of water wasted. But this concept provides only a partial and sometimes misleading view because it does not indicate the benefits produced, and water lost by irrigation is often gained by other uses (Seckler, Molden, and Sakthivadivel 2003).

The current focus of water productivity has evolved to include the benefits and costs of water used for agriculture in terrestrial and aquatic ecosystems (table 7.2). Water productivity analysis can be seen as part of an ecosystem approach to managing water. Rain, natural flows, withdrawals, and evaporation support terrestrial and aquatic ecosystems, which produce numerous services for people. The primary service of agroecosystems is food and fiber production, but other important services are produced as well (see chapter 6 on ecosystems).

Crop water productivity basics

An assessment of the potential for reducing water needs and increasing production and values requires an understanding of basic biological and hydrological crop-water relations. Answering the question of how much more water will be needed for agriculture requires understanding the connections among water, food, and diets. The amount of water that we consume when eating food depends on diet and on the water productivity of the agriculture production system (box 7.1) The amount of water required for field crops and the relation to yield dominates the equation on the need for additional water for food.

table **7.2**

A framework for linking water productivity with ecosystem approaches				
Ecosystems	**Agricultural activities**	**Water source and depletion**	**Services (provisioning, regulating, cultural, and supporting services)**	**Ways to increase water productivity**
Terrestrial: forests, grasslands	Livestock grazing, forest products	Rain, evaporation, transpiration	Biodiversity, climate and water flow regulation, cultural values	• Increase services • Decrease water depletion • Decrease negative impacts on other ecosystems
Agroecosystems	Crops, agroforestry, livestock, aquaculture	Rain plus water diversion, evaporation, transpiration	Provision of food and fiber plus other services	
Aquatic: wetlands, rivers, lakes	Capture fisheries, aquatic plants	Runoff, return flows, evaporation, transpiration	Biodiversity, water regulation, recreational, and cultural values	

box **7.1** | **How much water do we eat?**

It is possible to calculate how much water in terms of evapotranspiration is required to sustain different diets based on knowledge of the relations between evaporation, transpiration, and yield. Depending on climate and management, it takes 400–2,000 liters of evapotranspiration to produce a kilogram of wheat. After taking into consideration the amount of evapotranspiration for grazing or feed and how much of this food livestock consume, it is possible to calculate the water required to produce eggs or meat. The amount is highly variable, depending on the type of animal, feed, and management practices, but it is on the order of 1,000–20,000 liters per kilogram of meat (see chapter 13 on livestock).

Based on these estimates, researchers have reported values of daily water requirements to support diets of 2,000–5,000 liters of water a day (Renault and Wallender 2000), with a rule of thumb of about 3,000 liters per person per day, or 1 calorie per liter of water evapotranspired. High-calorie, protein-rich diets require more water than do vegetarian diets. Where water productivity is quite low, as in much of Sub-Saharan Africa, the amount of water required to sustain a balanced daily diet can be quite high despite low calorie intake and undernutrition.

Estimated daily water consumption from primary dietary components for Ethiopia, Thailand, and Italy

Product	**Description**	**Ethiopia**	**Thailand**	**Italy**
	Calories per person per day	1,253	1,180	1,166
	Water use (liters per kilogram)	1,576	3,523	949
	Daily per capita use (liters)	573	1,141	428
Cereals[a]	Share of diet (% of total calorie intake)	68	50	32

(continues on facing page)

| box **7.1** | **How much water do we eat?** (continued) |

Product	Description	Ethiopia	Thailand	Italy
Starchy roots[b]	Calories per person per day	229	47	72
	Water use (liters per kilogram)	375	279	152
	Daily per capita use (liters)	57	12	1
	Share of diet (% of total calorie intake)	12	2	2
Vegetable oil	Calories per person per day	31	151	652
	Water use (liters per kilogram)	17,842	3,764	1,719
	Daily per capita use (liters)	27	305	683
	Share of diet (% of total calorie intake)	2	6	17
Vegetables	Calories per person per day	10	36	93
	Water use (liters per kilogram)	418	264	108
	Daily per capita use (liters)	13	30	44
	Share of diet (% of total calorie intake)	1	1	3
Fruits[c]	Calories per person per day	13	108	172
	Water use (liters per kilogram)	507	851	440
	Daily per capita use (liters)	10	144	239
	Share of diet (% of total calorie intake)	2	5	5
Animal products[d]	Calories per person per day	102	295	950
	Water use from grazing land (liters per kilogram)	23,289	2,486	1,474
	Daily per capita use (liters)	2,238	605	1,611
	Share of diet (% of total calorie intake)	6	12	26
Other[e]	Calories per person per day	200	566	498
	Daily per capita water use (liters)	225	718	230
	Share of diet (% of total calorie intake)	11	24	14
Total	Total calories supplied per person per day	1,838	2,383	3,603
	Total daily water consumption (liters)	3,143	2,955	3,236

Note: Values are based on national averages and include losses from retail to consumer so do not reflect what is actually ingested. Values for share of diet may not sum to 100% because of rounding.

a. Predominant cereal crop is tef in Ethiopia, rice in Thailand, and wheat in Italy.

b. Predominant starchy root is cassava in Thailand, various in Ethiopia, and potatoes in Italy.

c. Predominant fruit is bananas in Ethiopia and Thailand and citrus in Italy.

d. Predominant animal products are beef and milk in Ethiopia, pork and fish in Thailand, and milk and pork in Italy.

e. Other includes sugar, oil crops, alcohol, spices, and pulses.

Source: Analysis by Food and Agriculture Organization for the Comprehensive Assessment of Water Management in Agriculture.

Thus this section starts with a fundamental but somewhat technical presentation of the relations among transpiration, evaporation, delivery, drainage, biomass, and yield shown in figure 7.1.

As figure 7.1 shows, the supply of water is from rain and irrigation. Water is depleted by productive transpiration and evaporation—together known as evapotranspiration. Water in excess of evapotranspiration runs off the field (runoff), drains into soil water

figure **7.1** | **Crop and water balance**

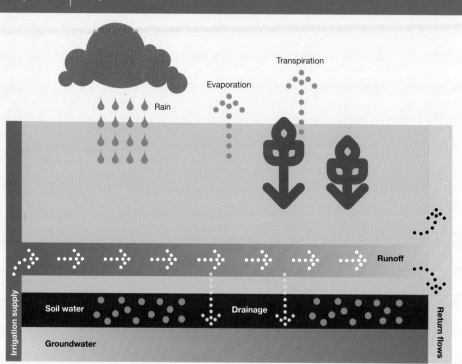

(green water source), or percolates to groundwater. These return flows are not necessarily wastage, as other users downstream may depend on that water.

Transpiration, biomass, and yield

For a given crop variety, fertility level, and climate there is a well established linear relation between plant biomass (leaves, stems, roots, grain) and transpiration (Tanner and Sinclair 1983; Steduto and Albrizio 2005), a process by which plants convert liquid water to water vapor. More biomass production requires more transpiration because when stomata open, carbon dioxide flows into the leaves for photosynthesis and water flows out. Water outflow is essential for cooling and for creating liquid movement in the plant for transporting nutrients. Stomata close during drought, limiting transpiration, photosynthesis, and production. Different kinds of plants are more water efficient in terms of the ratio between biomass and transpiration. The most common crops, C_3 crops such as wheat and barley, are least efficient. C_4 crops such as maize and sugarcane are more efficient, while the most efficient are CAM (crassulacean acid metabolism) crops such as cactus and pineapple.

To boost economic yield, plant breeders have developed varieties with a higher harvest index, or the proportion of economic produce (such as food grains) to total biomass. In doing so, they have also achieved more economic produce per unit of transpiration.

This breeding strategy has probably raised the potential for water productivity gains more than any other agronomic practice over the last 40 years (Keller and Seckler 2004). The harvest index for wheat and maize rose from about 0.35 before the 1960s to 0.5 in the 1980s (Sayre, Rajaram, and Fischer 1997) when green revolution breeders focused their attention on these crops. But the rate of increase has slowed over the last 20 years as physiological limits are being reached. In situations of low yield, however, values for harvest index are less than the maximum achievable because of suboptimal management practices.

This relation between transpiration and crop production has far-reaching consequences for water. Increases in food production are achieved with a near proportionate increase in transpired water. That is why increases in food production have taken water from ecosystems, reducing the amount of water transpired by forests and grass and reducing water flows to the sea, and why future production will continue to do the same. Feeding more people will require more water to be transpired.

> Increases in food production are achieved with a near proportionate increase in transpired water

Evaporation and transpiration

Agriculture depletes the water resource base mainly through evapotranspiration, the combination of productive transpiration and collateral evaporation from land and water surfaces (photo 7.1). It is a commonly used concept partly because it is difficult to separately measure evaporation and transpiration. Evapotranspiration is critically important because it is essential for crop production and because raising agricultural evapotranspiration means that less water is available for ecological and other human uses. Ultimately, the extent of agriculture is limited by the available water resources that can be depleted by evapotranspiration.

Climate plays a central role in water productivity per unit of evapotranspiration. Higher productivity is achievable at lower vapor pressure deficits (the difference between the actual and maximum amount of water vapor in the air) (Tanner and Sinclair 1983) [well established], which are common at higher latitudes (Zwart and Bastiaanssen 2004). It has been speculated that the higher carbon dioxide levels associated with climate change will raise water productivity per unit of evapotranspiration because more carbon can enter the plant for more photosynthesis (Droogers and Aerts 2005; IPCC 2001), but more recent evidence that productivity gains will be substantially offset by increased temperature (Long and others 2006) casts doubts on claims that increased carbon dioxide from climate change will enhance yield and water productivity.

While there is a fixed relation between biomass and transpiration, there is substantial variability in yield (here, the marketable produce of a crop) relative to transpiration because of differences in evaporation, harvest index, climate conditions, cultivars, water stress, pest and diseases, nutritional and soil status, and other management and agronomic practices (figure 7.2). Thus there seems to be considerable scope for raising the amount of yield relative to evapotranspiration before reaching the upper limit (the straight line in figure 7.2 that coincides with the reputed linear relationship between transpiration and yield). That much of the variability is due to management practices (French and Schultz 1984) is important because it offers hope of possible improvements in the ratio between marketable produce and evapotranspiration.

Photo 7.1 Crop evapotranspiration: water is transpired through leaves and evaporated from soil surfaces

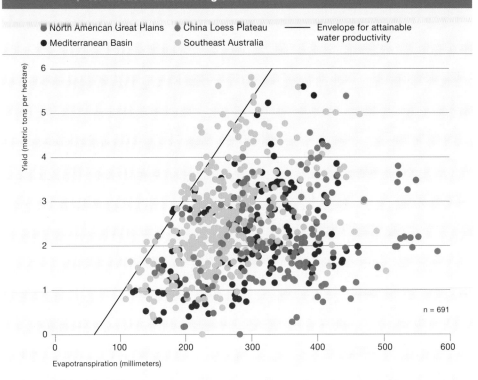

figure **7.2** | **There are large variations between yield and evapotranspiration for wheat in different regions of the world**

North American Great Plains ● China Loess Plateau —— Envelope for attainable water productivity
● Mediterranean Basin ● Southeast Australia

Yield (metric tons per hectare)

Evapotranspiration (millimeters)

n = 691

Source: Adapted from Sadras and Angus 2006.

In situations where yield is less than 40%–50% of potential, nonwater factors such as soil fertility limit yield and crop water productivity per unit of evapotranspiration (Tanner and Sinclair 1983). Land degradation and nutrient depletion significantly constrain opportunities to increase water productivity (see chapter 15 on land). In these situations there is a synergistic effect when water practices that increase access to water at the right time or reduce land degradation processes are combined with other agronomic practices such as maintaining soil health and fertility, controlling weeds and disease, and timing planting. Such synergistic interactions between production factors raise water productivity, especially when yield values are low, because most production resources are used more efficiently as yield levels rise (de Wit 1992). When yields are above 40%–50% of their potential, however, yield gains come at a near proportionate increase in the amount of evapotranspiration (figure 7.3).

Deliveries and drainage

Much attention has been given to reducing water deliveries to agriculture (blue water focus), while less has been given to the depletion of water, especially through evapotrans-

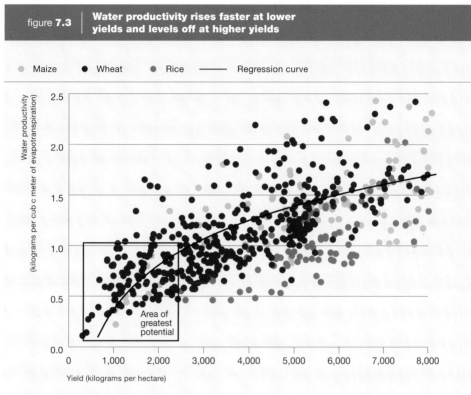

| figure **7.3** | **Water productivity rises faster at lower yields and levels off at higher yields** |

Maize   ● Wheat   ● Rice   —— Regression curve

Water productivity (kilograms per cub c meter of evapotranspiration)

Area of greatest potential

Yield (kilograms per hectare)

Source: Adapted from Zwart and Bastiaanssen 2004.

piration. Both are important, but both have different implications. A crucial point is that strategies to increase water productivity per unit of water delivered must also consider what happens to drainage flows.

Several farm water management practices such as shorter furrows, alternating wet and dry irrigation, and sprinkler irrigation are intended to convert more of the water input into transpiration to increase yield and consequently to reduce drainage flows. Similarly, concrete lining or pipes in irrigation systems are employed to reduce seepage from canals and so to reduce drainage flows.

To know whether more precise farm and irrigation management practices "save" water that can be used for something else, it is important to know what happens to drainage flows. Drainage flows are undesirable in situations where flows are directed to a saline aquifer, contribute to waterlogging, or are directed away from an important ecosystem. But drainage flows can also be desirable, when they are a source of water for downstream farmers, reach shallow groundwater for home gardens (Bakker and others 1999) and domestic wells (Meijer and others 2006), or support other important ecosystem services. Misguided investments to "save" water in such cases can be detrimental to livelihoods and well-being. What is needed is more analysis in a basin context.

Water productivity as value per unit of water

Increasing net benefits or value per unit of water has key implications for farmer decisions, economic growth, poverty reduction, equity, and the environment. There is much more scope for increasing value per unit of water use in agriculture (economic water productivity) than in physical water productivity, which is becoming increasingly constrained. Strategies for increasing the value of water used in agriculture include:

- Increasing yield per unit of supply or depletion.
- Changing from low- to high-value crops—from wheat to strawberries, for example (photo 7.2)
- Reallocating water from low to higher valued uses (for example, from agriculture to cities).
- Lowering the costs of inputs (labor, water technologies).
- Increasing health benefits and the value of ecological services of agriculture.
- Decreasing social, health, and environmental costs (for example, minimizing degradation of other ecosystems).
- Obtaining multiple benefits per unit of water (for example, using water for drinking and agriculture).
- Achieving more livelihood support per unit of water (more jobs, nutrition, and income for the same amount of water).

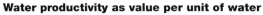

Photo by Mats Lannerstad

Photo 7.2 Growing higher valued crops, such as irrigated bananas and cabbage, improves economic water productivity

Pathways to improving water productivity

Pathways to improving water productivity include improving the productivity of green and blue water; improving the water productivity of livestock and fisheries; applying an integrated approach to increase the value per unit of water; and adopting an integrated basin perspective to understand water productivity tradeoffs.

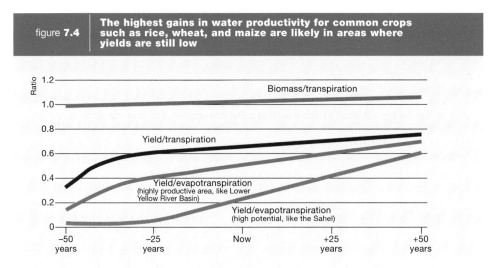

figure 7.4 The highest gains in water productivity for common crops such as rice, wheat, and maize are likely in areas where yields are still low

Source: Schematic developed for the Comprehensive Assessment of Water Management in Agriculture.

Improving water productivity with respect to evapotranspiration

Physical water productivity can be increased for the most common grain crops like rice, wheat, and maize in three fundamental ways (figure 7.4). There is controversy over the potential for future increases in the harvest index (ratio of grain weight to biomass) or the ratio of biomass to transpiration for common crops like wheat and rice, ranging from deep skepticism (Tanner and Sinclair 1983) to slight optimism (Bindraban 1997; Bennett 2003). Much of the potential for increasing the harvest index for common grains such as wheat, maize, and rice was met during the green revolution. But surprises do happen, which could lead to unexpected changes in these relations (box 7.2).[1] There are greater opportunities to improve the harvest index in other crops like sorghum and millet, important crops for many poor people. Breeding, targeting early growth vigor to reduce evaporation, and increasing resistance to drought, disease, or salinity could all improve water productivity per unit of evapotranspiration.

The two lower lines of figure 7.4 indicate that improvements in physical water productivity are possible through improved management that increases the ratio of yield to evapotranspiration. But in many of the most productive areas of the world, such as the lower Yellow River Basin, large improvements have already been made and the remaining scope is small. The implication is that for these areas achieving higher yields will require more evapotranspiration.

The areas with the highest potential gains are those with very low yields, such as Sub-Saharan Africa and South Asia. These are also areas of extreme poverty, with the largest

---

box **7.2**	**Can biotechnology improve water productivity?**

Crop breeding has been responsible for tremendous gains in water productivity through interventions that have increased the harvest index. Common grains such as wheat, maize, and rice, which achieved such gains during the 1960s to 1980s, are less likely to make further gains in this area. But there are several indirect means to improve physical water productivity in which biotechnology can play a role:

- Targeting rapid early growth to shade the soil and reduce evaporation.
- Breeding drought-resistant varieties. The gains are clear when crop failure is avoided, but where yield is increased, so is evapotranspiration, and therefore the gain in water productivity is ambiguous.
- Breeding for resistance to disease, pests, and salinity.
- Boosting the harvest index for crops such as millet and sorghum that have not received as much attention as the green revolution grains.

More value per unit of evapotranspiration can be achieved by:

- Improving the nutritional quality of crops.
- Reducing agrochemical inputs by planting disease- and pest-resistant crops.

For this Comprehensive Assessment and a time scale of 15–20 years we therefore conclude that only moderate impacts on crop water productivity should be expected from improvements in plant genetics. But such improvements can reduce the risk of crop failure. This can be achieved slowly through conventional breeding or more quickly using appropriate biotechnological tools. Genetic modification, still highly contentious, is but one possible means championed by some people for its potential benefits. Because the gap between actual practice and biophysical potential is so large, greater gains are possible through better management *[competing explanations]*.

concentration of poor people and high dependence of the poor on agriculture. This is a heartening conclusion because a focus on these areas can both reduce the amount of additional water needed for agriculture globally and help to reduce poverty. Current levels of water productivity show large variation by commodity, implying scope for improvement (table 7.3).

Improving soil fertility. For arid and semiarid regions, in particular for the Sahel, model analysis and field experiments have shown that nutrient limitations set a stronger ceiling on yield than water availability (Breman, Groot, and van Keulen 2001). In much of Africa fertilizer use is low—only 9 kilograms of nutrients per hectare in Sub-Saharan Africa compared with 73 kilograms in Latin America, 100 kilograms in South Asia, and 135 kilograms in East and Southeast Asia (Kelly 2006, p. 1)—and a constraint to water productivity (Twomlow and others 1999). Bindraban and others (1999, 2000) found that the biophysical opportunity to increase yields in semiarid West Africa is high. Extremely low yields in West African rainfed agriculture (map 7.1; top) because of limited availability

table **7.3**	**Value produced from a unit of water for selected commodities**			
	Water productivity			
Product	**Kilograms per cubic meter**	**Dollars per cubic meter**	**Protein grams per cubic meter**	**Calories per cubic meter**
Cereal				
Wheat ($0.2 per kilogram)	0.2–1.2	0.04–0.30	50–150	660–4,000
Rice ($0.31 per kilogram)	0.15–1.6	0.05–0.18	12–50	500–2,000
Maize ($0.11 per kilogram)	0.30–2.00	0.03–0.22	30–200	1,000–7,000
Legumes				
Lentils ($0.3 per kilogram)	0.3–1.0	0.09–0.30	90–150	1,060–3,500
Fava beans ($0.3 per kilogram)	0.3–0.8	0.09–0.24	100–150	1,260–3,360
Groundnut ($0.8 per kilogram)	0.1–0.4	0.08–0.32	30–120	800–3,200
Vegetables				
Potatoes ($0.1 per kilogram)	3–7	0.3–0.7	50–120	3,000–7,000
Tomatoes ($0.15 per kilogram)	5–20	0.75–3.0	50–200	1,000–4,000
Onions ($0.1 per kilogram)	3–10	0.3–1.0	20–67	1,200–4,000
Fruits				
Apples ($0.8 per kilogram)	1.0–5.0	0.8–4.0	Negligible	520–2,600
Olives ($1.0 per kilogram)	1.0–3.0	1.0–3.0	10–30	1,150–3,450
Dates ($2.0 per kilogram)	0.4–0.8	0.8–1.6	8–16	1,120–2,240
Others				
Beef ($3.0 per kilogram)	0.03–0.1	0.09–0.3	10–30	60–210
Fish (aquaculture[a])	0.05–1.0	0.07–1.35	17–340	85–1,750

a. Includes extensive systems without additional nutritional inputs to superintensive systems.

Source: Muir 1993; Verdegem, Bosma, and Verreth 2006; Renault and Wallender 2000; Oweis and Hachum 2003, Zwart and Bastiaanssen 2004.

of nutrients could be much higher with soil fertility improvements combined with better management of rainfall (bottom). With improvements in soil fertility and management of rainwater to reduce evaporation and divert more flows to transpiration, yields can double or even quadruple.

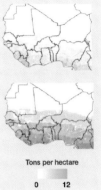

Using international trade to increase global water productivity. Global gains in water productivity can be achieved by growing crops in places where climate and management practices enable high water productivity and trading them to places with lower water productivity. In 1995 global trade from high water productivity areas to low water productivity areas resulted in an estimated 6% less evapotranspiration and 11% less depletion of irrigation water to grow the same amount of crops (de Fraiture and others 2004) than would have been required without trade. But trade takes place for other economic and political reasons, and water productivity gains are merely a by-product. A more detailed analysis of trade that considers payment for imports, rural employment, and environmental impacts must be considered (see chapter 3 on scenarios).

Tons per hectare

0   12

Map 7.1 Simulated yields before and after soil fertility and rainfall management improvements in West Africa

Source: Bindraban and others 2000.

Reducing evaporation. Reducing evaporation while increasing productive transpiration can enhance water productivity. Evaporation varies with agricultural practices (Burt and others 2005) and ranges from 4% to 15%–25% in sprinkler irrigation systems (Burt, Howes, and Mutziger 2001) up to 40% and more in rainfed systems (Rockström, Barron, and Fox 2003). The amount of evaporation depends on climate, soils, and the extent of the crop canopy, which shades the soil (photo 7.3). Evaporation can be a very high share of evapotranspiration in rainfed systems with low plant densities. Surprisingly, drip and sprinkler irrigation systems do not necessarily result in less evaporation than good surface irrigation systems (Burt, Howes, and Mutziger 2001). Practices such as mulching,

Photo by David Molden

Photo 7.3 Water left standing after irrigation evaporates quickly. Reducing evaporation saves water.

plowing, or breeding for fast leaf expansion in order to shade the ground as rapidly as possible reduce evaporation and increase productive transpiration.

In some agricultural landscapes there is significant scope for reducing evaporation from water bodies, high water tables, and water-logged areas, taking care that these do not support important wetland functions. Drainage or reduced water applications are key practices. In many areas high water tables are a result of agricultural practices, and drainage could have positive benefits such as reduction of mosquito breeding sites. Using groundwater instead of reservoirs for storage reduces evaporation. In the Mexican Lerma-Chapala Basin an annual average of 1.8 cubic kilometers evaporates from water bodies under current conditions, about 54% of the amount used by irrigated agriculture and 38% of annual runoff from the basin (IMTA 2002).

In arid environments up to 90% of rainfall evaporates back into the atmosphere, leaving just 10% for productive transpiration. Micro- and macro-catchment water-harvesting techniques can capture more of this water for crops and livestock before it evaporates, increasing beneficial rainwater available for transpiration to 20%–50% (Oweis, Hachum, and Kijne 1999).

The water-saving benefits of reducing deliveries are often overestimated because return flows and reuse are not properly brought into the analysis

Improving the water productivity of water deliveries

Reducing or limiting water withdrawals from rivers and groundwater through water-saving practices and demand management remains an important strategy to control water resources, limit damage to aquatic ecosystems, and in some cases release water from agriculture to other uses. Excess water deliveries generate excess drainage that is hard to control, require energy for pumping, reduce the quality of water, and can provide breeding grounds for disease vectors. Moreover, reduced deliveries can mean that more surface water remains in rivers to support ecosystem functions and biodiversity. Using more precise water delivery practices gives water managers more flexibility to deliver water where it is needed, when it is needed. But the water-saving benefits of reducing deliveries are often overestimated because return flows and reuse are not properly brought into the analysis (box 7.3).

Because timing, amount, and reliability of blue water application influence yield and the quality of produce, blue water productivity can be improved through better management. Applying irrigation water at a time when a crop is susceptible to water stress raises yield per unit of water delivered and per unit of evapotranspiration; missing the application has the reverse effect. The quality of some fruits and vegetables is better under conditions of water stress at key times, and farmers fetch a higher market price for them.

Enhanced reliability of deliveries and greater flexibility in the timing and amount of water provided are important factors in farmers' investment decisions. When the supply of water is unpredictable, farmers will not invest in inputs and will tend to cultivate crops that are resilient to water stress and variable irrigation timing and thus that tend to have low yield and low monetary value (Hussain and others 2004).

Supplemental irrigation—the addition of small amounts of water at the right time to supplement rain—is an excellent way to increase the productivity of water supplies and evapotranspiration. Water productivity can also be increased with deficit irrigation—supplying less water than the maximum level of crop evapotranspiration

---

| box **7.3** | **Are the water savings real?** |

Saving water, especially releasing water from irrigated agriculture, can make it available to other, higher value uses in cities, industries, ecosystems, or more agriculture. Investments in improving irrigation efficiency by lining canals, installing drip and sprinkler irrigation, harvesting water, and applying on-farm water management practices are important when they prevent salinization and water-logging or improve overall water management.

But many people question whether these practices promote real water savings, in which water can be transferred to other users without affecting production levels, or whether they simply "rob Peter to pay Paul" (Seckler 1996; Perry 1999; Seckler, Molden, and Sakthivadivel 2003; Molle, Mamanpoush, and Miranzadeh 2005).

Practices that reduce deliveries typically also reduce drainage outflows. Farmers downstream may be using these drainage flows or the flows may be supporting important ecosystems. What often happens is that the perceived gain is offset by a loss (Gichuki 2004) that is difficult to recognize. In other cases, where the deliveries to farms are not reduced, farmers will have a high incentive to use "saved" water on their own farm, resulting in more evapotranspiration and thus more food but less water available to other users in the basin.

Whether reducing water deliveries results in real water savings depends on what happens to drainage flows. Reducing deliveries and drainage works well in situations where drainage flows damage, pollute, or flow to a saline sink (Molden, Sakthivadivel, and Keller 2001). In other cases a basin perspective is needed to determine whether savings are real.

(Zhang 2003). In western Syria wheat yields increased from 2 to 5 metric tons per hectare with the timely application of 100–200 millimeters of water and water productivity improved from 0.6 kilograms per cubic meter to 1.85 (Oweis and Hachum 2003). Yields of sorghum in Burkina Faso and maize in Kenya were increased from 0.5 metric tons per hectare to 1.5–2.0 metric tons with supplemental irrigation plus soil fertility management (Rockström, Barron, and Fox 2003). These practices work particularly well when water supplies are constrained by the limited supply or high costs of water.

There is substantial scope to reduce water deliveries to irrigation through a range of technical and management practices: drip and sprinkle irrigation, more precise application practices (level basins, surge irrigation), canal lining or delivery through pipes, reduced allocations of water to farmers, or pricing to influence demand. Many of these practices increase yields (table 7.4). Several practices are applicable to rice irrigation, such as alternate wet and dry irrigation (Bouman and others 2003; see chapter 14 on rice). But, again, whether these practices are warranted requires examination from a larger, basin context.

A common misperception is that irrigation is wasteful because of highly inefficient practices (typical irrigation system efficiencies are reported at 40%–50%). But because so much drainage flow is reused downstream, especially in closed basins (see chapter 16 on river basins), there is actually much less scope in saving water in irrigation than is commonly believed [*established, but incomplete*]. In fact, in irrigated regions in dry areas it is common to document ratios of evapotranspiration to irrigation plus rain much greater than 60%, often depleting more water than is renewable and leading to aquifer mining. Such areas include the Gediz Basin in Turkey (Droogers and Kite 1999), Egypt's Nile (Keller and Keller 1995)

table **7.4**	**Water productivity gains for various crops from shifting from conventional surface irrigation to drip irrigation in India** (percent)		
Crop	Increase in yield	Decline in water application	Gains in water productivity
Bananas	52	45	173
Cabbage	2	60	150
Cabbage (evapotranspiration)	54	40	157
Cotton	27	53	169
Cotton	25	60	212
Cotton (evapotranspiration)	35	15	55
Cotton	10	15	27
Grapes	23	48	134
Okra (evapotranspiration)	72	40	142
Potatoes	46	~0	46
Sugarcane	6	60	163
Sugarcane	20	30	70
Sugarcane	29	47	143
Sugarcane	33	65	280
Sugarcane	23	44	121
Sweet potatoes	39	60	243
Tomatoes	5	27	44
Tomatoes	50	39	145

Note: Water productivity is measured as crop yield per unit of irrigation water supplied or as the ratio of yield to evapotranspiration where evapotranspiration is indicated in parentheses.

Source: Adapted from Postel and others 2001; Tiwari, Singh, and Mal 2003 for cabbage row 2; Rajak and others 2006 for cotton row 3; Shah and others 2003 for cotton row 4; Tiwari and others 1998 for okra; and Narayanmoorthy 2004 for sugarcane row 5.

and Fayoum (Bos 2004), the Christian subdivision in Pakistan (Molden, Sakthivadivel, and Habib 2000), the Bhakra irrigation system in India (Molden, Sakthivadivel, and Habib 2000), the Liu Yuan Ku irrigation system in China (Hafeez and Khan 2006), the Tunuyuan irrigated area in Argentina (Bos 2004), the Nilo Coelho in Brazil (Bos 2004), and the Rio Grande Basin in Mexico and the United States (Booker, Michelsen, and Ward 2005).

Irrigation systems are under increased pressure to produce more with reduced supplies of water. Frequently, allocations to irrigation are diminishing because of increased demands by cities and the environment, and increases in blue water productivity are often a response to this reduced allocation so that farmers can continue to produce. Reducing water delivered to irrigation requires two actions: a change in agricultural practice combined with a change in water allocation. If farmers increase blue water productivity, they are more likely to use the saved water on their own land than to give it to cities. But if farmers have to adjust to reduced allocations, they may try to achieve at least the same value of production with the reduced supplies.

A complete assessment of irrigation performance requires a view beyond crops that includes other functions of irrigation and their value. Renault, Hemakumara, and Molden (2001) showed that the perennial vegetation at Kirindi Oya system in Sri Lanka evapotranspires about the same amount of water as rice and generates valuable ecosystem services, giving a different picture (65% of inflows beneficially depleted) than if paddy rice were considered alone (22% of inflows depleted by rice). Home gardens at Kirindi Oya, a key source of livelihood for women, depend almost entirely on the seepage flows from the irrigation channels. In these cases the problem is not wastage but high withdrawals and evapotranspiration rates that reduce drainage and tend to dry up rivers and wetlands, leaving little to downstream use. It is important to view each case from a basin perspective, considering the quality and equity dimensions of water and how drainage flows are used downstream.

In addition to producing more food, there are ample opportunities in irrigation to generate more value and incur fewer social and environmental costs (see chapter 6 on ecosystems) in new and established irrigation. Achieving this will require more integrated approaches promoting multiple uses and multiple ecosystem services (Scherr and McNeely forthcoming; Matsuno and others 2006; Groenfeldt 2006).

Increasing the water productivity of livestock

Globally, livestock production accounts for some 20% of agricultural evapotranspiration, and this proportion could grow with the increasing consumption of animal products (see chapter 3 on scenarios). Reducing the amount of water required for livestock production could thus contribute considerably to reducing future agricultural water needs.

The physical water productivity of animal products is derived mainly from the water required for the food that animals consume; the drinking water requirements of livestock are negligible by comparison. Estimates of the amount of evapotranspiration required to produce 1 kilogram of animal products vary widely, depending on management practices, the kind of feed, how crop residues are used, the processing system, and how well the animals convert feed and plants into the animal product. Gains in livestock water productivity can be made by adjusting each of these factors (see chapter 13 on livestock).

The information on diets in the table in box 7.1 is instructive. While only 6% of the average Ethiopian diet consists of animal products, three-quarters of the daily water requirement for food is from animal requirements. One-quarter of the Italian diet consists of meat products, with half the water consumed coming from meat products. While there is considerable uncertainty about these estimates, there is a pattern. Where livestock productivity is low, as in Ethiopia, animal products require a lot of water. Where meat is a high proportion of the diet, dietary water requirements are high, but this can be offset by intensive livestock management practices, as in Italy.

But a focus solely on water requirements for livestock can be misleading. Livestock add value in many ways to production systems and play an important role in livelihood strategies, contributing to overall productivity and welfare gains. A reason that livestock water use is so high in Ethiopia is that livestock are used for transport, plowing, and fertilizer generation (manure). Keeping livestock reduces vulnerability to food shortages and agroclimatic risk (Fafchamps, Udry, and Czukas 1998). Livestock production is a key strategy for livelihood diversification in the smallholder irrigated systems in India and Pakistan, where livestock generate productive employment for the landless, especially women, and income, especially for the poor, important for improving equity (Adams and Alderman 1992).

> The physical water productivity of animal products is derived mainly from the water required for the food that animals consume; the drinking water requirements of livestock are negligible by comparison

There is considerable scope for increases in livestock productivity, in both physical and economic water productivity. Water productivity–enhancing strategies include improving feed sourcing of animals; enhancing animal production (milk, meat, eggs) services, and cultural values from livestock; and conserving water resources to lessen the amount of water required for grazing and reduce negative environmental impacts.

Increasing water productivity in fisheries and aquaculture

Fish can often be integrated into water management systems with the addition of little or no water

As with livestock, there is considerable scope for better integrating fisheries and aquaculture with water management systems to improve water productivity and reduce poverty (see chapter 12 on fisheries).

The two major components of water use in aquaculture are the water required for feed and the blue water required for aquaculture. Water productivity is the mass or value of the aquaculture produce divided by the amount of water required for feed plus the amount of evaporation from the pond. On-farm water use in aquaculture can be as low as 500–700 liters in superintensive recirculation systems and as high as 45,000 liters of water (evaporation plus seepage plus feed) per kilogram of produce in extensive ponds (Verdegem, Bosma, and Verreth 2006).

Fish can often be integrated into water management systems with the addition of little or no water (Prein 2002). Renwick (2001) found that the fisheries in irrigation reservoirs at Kirindi Oya, Sri Lanka, contributed income equal to 18% of the rice production in the system. Haylor (1994, 1997) assessed the potential for aquaculture in small and large irrigated farming systems in the Punjab, Pakistan, and noted that aquaculture was almost entirely pond culture of carp fed with tubewell water and that there was economic justification for expanding such aquaculture using local shallow tubewells. The revenue potential for cage aquaculture in irrigation canals was also attractive, but operational conflicts in the use of water for agriculture would need to be resolved. Murray and others (2002) pointed out that traditional power structures may undermine attempts to integrate aquaculture in irrigation systems and that changes in laws and regulations would be required from community to national levels. In coastal areas aquaculture may severely degrade land and water quality and biodiversity, requiring special attention (Gowing, Tuong, and Hoanh 2006).

Fisheries in lakes, rivers, and wetlands present a special case for water productivity assessment because fish are only one of the many ecosystem services provided by aquatic ecosystems (see chapter 12 on fisheries). The values and livelihood benefits of fisheries are high and often ignored or underestimated, but considering only the values of fish produce would grossly underestimate the value of water in these aquatic ecosystems. The water productivity of fisheries systems needs to be considered in terms of the ecosystem services and livelihoods supported per unit of water. Thus maintenance of wetlands and biodiversity should be considered potential benefits of leaving water in these aquatic ecosystems.

Applying integrated approaches to increasing the value per unit of water

Designing and managing agricultural water for multiple uses—drinking water, industries, livestock, fisheries—can raise the social and economic productivity of water in water management systems (Meinzen-Dick 1997; Bhatnagar and others 2004; Nguyen-Khoa, Smith, and Lorenzen 2005; van Koppen, Moriarty, and Boelee 2006; photo 7.4). Irrigation provides water for fruit and shade trees, habitat to sustain biodiversity, and is a source of recharge for groundwater, a common source of rural drinking water supporting the livelihoods of smallholders. Multifunctional farm ponds that store water for crop irrigation and for domestic purposes may be suitable for raising fish to improve household nutrition and provide a ready source of income. Integrated agriculture-aquaculture provides a means of recycling water and nutrients and obtaining more value and income from farm enterprises (Gupta and others 1999). On-farm pounds may serve as nutrient traps for surface runoff (from crops and livestock) that may be recycled by fish, with the residue used as fertilizer for crops grown on pond dikes, helping to upgrade smallholder agriculture.

Agricultural water management practices can provide multiple ecosystem services beyond food production (see chapter 6 on ecosystems). The value of paddy cultivation is underestimated unless its multifunctional roles are taken into consideration (see chapter 14 on rice). Practices that reduce environmental costs and enhance ecosystem services increase the value derived from agricultural water management (Matsuno and others 2006; Scherr and McNeely forthcoming).

> Designing and managing agricultural water for multiple uses—drinking water, industries, livestock, fisheries—can raise the social and economic productivity of water in water management systems

Adopting an integrated basin perspective for understanding water productivity tradeoffs

A change in basin water use will result in winners and losers. Putting water into the service of agriculture by expanding rainfed systems or adding irrigation takes water away from other uses—forests, grasslands, rivers (photo 7.5). Expanding agriculture upstream through better rainfall capture and artificial storage can reduce downstream flows supporting other

Photo by Mats Lannerstad

Photo 7.4 Using irrigation water for multiple purpose means more value per unit of water

agriculturalists, fishers, and household users. Producing more food means putting more water into production and taking it out of other uses. Water productivity analysis at a basin scale can illuminate these tradeoffs to help decisionmakers develop strategies in which benefits exceed costs (box 7.4).

Instead, most basin-level water use strategies today are guided by individual political, economic, and social factors, with water productivity issues barely considered (see chapter 16 on river basins). Typically, with urbanization, water is reallocated from agriculture to cities (Molle and Berkoff 2006) and from natural uses like rivers and wetlands to agriculture. Rarely are the intrinsic values generated by ecosystems and agriculture considered in these reallocations, and often the transfers are made without negotiation or adequate compensation. Thus changes in farmers' practices are typically a response to reallocation of supplies rather than the driver behind reallocation.

In sum, basin water productivity can be improved by improving water productivity for crops, irrigation, livestock, and fish per unit of water use; reducing nonproductive evaporation or flows to sinks; tapping into more available water while also addressing tradeoffs with others uses; and generating higher economic benefits through comanagement or reallocation of water to activities with a higher monetary value or increased social and ecological values; or in any of these activities reducing social and environmental costs associated with changes in water use patterns (see table 7.2).

At larger scales water productivity issues become increasingly complex, particularly for multisector systems where competition among water users, recycling of water, resource degradation, and opportunity costs and equity issues of water come into play. Assessing the impact of a change in basin water use requires analysis of the changes in benefits and costs and their distribution among stakeholders. The first part of the analysis requires a hydrological examination to understand the changes in quality, quantity, and timing of water for different uses. This is not always obvious because of complex hydrologic interconnections. People who tap into a stream in the hills may have no idea of the consequences for downstream agriculture or wetlands.

The second part requires a comprehensive valuation exercise to assess marginal water productivity and the nonmarketable values associated with water use—livelihood support

> Most basin-level water use strategies today are guided by individual political, economic, and social factors, with water productivity issues barely considered

Photo 7.5 Water use within a landscape

Photo by Karen Conniff

box **7.4** | **Means of increasing productivity of water in a basin context**

There are four primary ways to increase the productivity of water in a basin context.

- Increasing the productivity per unit of evapotranspiration:
    - Improving soil and water management and agronomic practices that promote soil fertility, reduce salinity, or improve the environment for fish and livestock.
    - Changing plant varieties to those that can provide increased yields or values for each unit of water consumed or that consume less water.
    - Using deficit, supplemental, or precision irrigation to achieve higher yields per unit of evapotranspiration, especially when combined with other management practices.
    - Improving irrigation water management by providing better timing of supplies to reduce stress at critical crop growth stages or by increasing the reliability of water supply so farmers invest more in other agricultural inputs, leading to higher output per unit of water.
    - Managing water and improving feed sourcing in fish and livestock production.
    - Lessening nonproductive evaporation by mulching, enhancing soil infiltration and storage properties, enhancing canopy cover, subsurface drip irrigation, matching planting dates with periods of less evaporative demand, and reducing evaporation from fallow land and high water tables by decreasing areas of exposed water surface and decreasing vegetation (weed control).
- Minimizing nonproductive depletion of blue water flows (taking care that these are not serving other important purposes like wetlands or other farmers):
    - Reducing water flows to sinks by interventions that reduce irrecoverable deep percolation and surface runoff, such as canal lining, drip irrigation, and alternating wet and dry irrigation of rice.
    - Minimizing salinization and pollution of return flows by minimizing flows through saline or polluted soils, drains, and groundwater, and managing the mixing of saline or polluted water with freshwater (see chapter 11 on marginal-quality water).
    - Shunting polluted water to sinks to avoid the need to dilute with freshwater; saline or polluted water should be shunted directly to sinks.
- Providing additional supplies for human uses by tapping uncommitted outflows, taking care to address possible tradeoff with downstream human and ecological uses:
    - Adding water storage facilities (reservoirs, groundwater aquifers, small tanks, ponds on farmers' fields, and soil moisture storage) so that more water is available when it can be more productively used.
    - Improving management of existing irrigation facilities to reduce drainage flows that contribute to uncommitted outflow. Possible interventions are reducing delivery requirements by improving application efficiency, water pricing, and allocation and distribution practices. Policy, design, management, and institutional interventions may allow for an expansion of irrigated area, increased cropping intensity, or increased yields within service areas.
    - Reusing return flows by controlling, diverting, and storing drainage flows and using them again.
- Reallocating and comanaging water among uses:
    - Reallocating water from lower value to higher value uses within and between sectors, for example by allocating water from agriculture to cities or industries, but taking care of compensation and consequences to other users and uses.
    - Identifying and managing committed outflows for environment and downstream water allocation.
    - Comanaging among multiple uses, recognizing multiple uses, and reaping multiple benefits while mitigating adverse impacts.
    - Incorporating aquaculture, fisheries, and livestock considerations into basin management.

and values derived from ecosystem services (Ward and Michelsen 2002). The concept of marginal water productivity is simple. For example, if a small amount of water is moved from agriculture to higher value industry, it can generate a large net gain because water in support of, say, computer chips generates much more value than water provided to wheat. But industries typically have a very low consumptive water requirement, and after enough water is given for the industrial process, the value of additional water flowing to industry falls to zero—or becomes negative if industry pollutes return flows. Similarly, taking a little water from rivers for agriculture may result in very small changes in ecosystem services delivered by the river but provide a large gain in agricultural value. But when rivers are reduced to minimum levels, the next drop taken out of the river may be at considerable ecosystem cost. Such analysis is not common in part because the integrated hydrological and valuation tools are complex and imprecise (box 7.5), but also because there are too few institutional arrangements where such information enters the decisionmaking process.

<blockquote>Most water productivity interventions can be tailored to benefit the poor</blockquote>

Nevertheless, it is possible to make much more informed decisions than are being made today. Stakeholders representing each use should be involved in decisions on reallocating water, and the types of information discussed should be available to them. Valuation of nonmarketable functions and services calls for stakeholder processes to decide how to balance the needs of the various groups. Disagreements about actual allocation will always remain because people's values, goals, priorities, and aspirations differ (Warner, Bindraban, and van Keulen 2006). Thus informed multistakeholder decisionmaking processes are needed to address conflicts and find constructive solutions (Emerton and Bos 2004).

Water productivity pathways for reducing poverty

Water productivity improvement can provide two pathways to poverty alleviation. First, targeted water interventions can enable poor and marginalized people to gain access to water and use it more effectively. Second, across-the-board increases in water productivity may benefit poor people through multiplier effects on food security, employment, and income.

Targeting techniques range from a combination of agronomic and water management practices to raise grain yields in high-potential areas, to strategies to increase the value per unit of scarce water, to strategies to reduce vulnerability to drought, polluted water, or loss of water allocations. Most water productivity interventions can be tailored to benefit the poor (see chapter 4 on poverty and photo 7.6). For example, efforts to reduce the cost of drip irrigation have made it affordable for smallholders (Postel and others 2001). Poverty alleviation efforts may drive water productivity gains in areas where access to water is difficult—in economically water-scarce areas. Interventions targeted to the rural poor can help them get the most out of limited water supplies. Examples include treadle pumps providing low-cost access, drip lines reducing the amount of water needed, and water bags for storage. With access to a little water and some precision technologies smallscale farmers can produce high-value crops such as vegetables and fruits. Microcredit and private commercial investments can help people use water. Access to markets is essential.

More effort is needed to tailor practices to the requirements of women, who play a large role in agriculture. Adapting water systems for home gardens and domestic needs improves

box **7.5** | **Tools for water productivity analysis**

Increasing demand for basin analysis and the complexity of interlinked hydrologic, socioeconomic, and ecological systems require new tools for analysis to better inform stakeholder decisions (van Dam and others 2006). These range from economic valuation, modeling, remote sensing, and geographic information system analysis to more participatory approaches. To influence investment and management information these tools needs to be closely integrated into political decisionmaking processes.

For example, remote sensing analysis has proven useful in identifying the range of possible values for crop water productivity and, combined with ground analysis, can help to pinpoint constraints to improvements. At the Yaqui irrigation district in Mexico remote sensing images have captured wide variations in water productivity (see photo).

The image shows water productivity per unit of evapotranspiration. Wheat yields and actual evapotranspiration were assessed with the surface energy balance algorithm for land methodology using high-resolution Landstat and low-resolution U.S. National Oceanic and Atmospheric Administration Advanced Very High Resolution Radiometer satellite images. The map depicts strong variation in water productivity across fields, with water productivity varying from 1.1 kilograms per cubic meter of evapotranspiration (yellow) to 1.6 kilograms per cubic meter (dark red). This variation is attributed to the management decisions of individual farmers, such as choice of seeds, fertilization, and amount and timing of irrigation.

Remote sensing image displaying variations in crop water productivity in wheat, Yaqui Valley, Sonora State, Mexico

<1.10   1.35   1.60>

Kilograms per cubic meter of evapotranspiration

Source: Zwart and others 2006.

nutrition and contributes to better health, improving the productivity of water and greatly helping rural women (Moriarty, Butterworth, and van Koppen 2004). But these interventions can only be pro-poor and sustainable when they really target the poor, are crafted to meet local needs, and are an integral part of a long-term development program and not merely a short-term relief effort (Polak and Yoder 2006; Moyo and others 2006).

There is ample evidence to conclude that women are as efficient producers as men, provided that they have similar access to inputs and markets and that they control the fruits of their labor (van Koppen 2000). It should be possible to reap higher productivity gains by addressing the concerns of women as well as men. Clearly, this is the case in farming systems dominated by women, but also, more subtly, in mixed and male-dominated systems where a focus on women could raise the value per unit of water.

Improvements in water productivity that indirectly increase food security and generate employment opportunities and income through multiplier effects can also reduce poverty. The full range of economic benefits from agricultural production are much greater than the simple measure of the value of local production (Hussain and Hanjra 2004).

Photo 7.6 Irrigation technology made affordable—a low-cost sprinkler

Photo by Sharni Jayawardena

Estimates of economywide farm and nonfarm multipliers vary widely. Estimates for India suggest a multiplier as low as 1.2 for local irrigation schemes to as high as 3 for the country as a whole. Multipliers tend to be higher in Asia than in Africa and higher in developed countries (estimated as high as 6 for Australia and Canada; Hill and Tollefson 1996).

Moreover, pro-poor gains in water productivity also come from outside water management—through better credit and insurance, support for better farm practices, improved links to markets and support services, and basic education and healthcare—thus calling for approaches that look beyond water management alone.

> Water productivity itself is unlikely to feature prominently among the many considerations facing agricultural producers

Establishing enabling conditions

While many strategies exist for improving water productivity, adoption rates remain low. There are many reasons why. Reliable, low-cost supplies of sufficient water enable high levels of productivity and reduce risk, so why should producers reduce water inputs? And while incentives for agriculture to deplete less water are high for society and river basin managers trying to allocate limited supplies, they are low for individual agricultural producers (Luquet and others 2005). These complex factors can be organized according to three types of uncertainty.

One type of uncertainty concerns the practical benefits of increasing water productivity relative to other factors that influence decisions. Water productivity itself is unlikely to feature prominently among the many considerations facing agricultural producers. Farmers rarely manage to increase water productivity; rather they manage to make their entire enterprise profitable. Factors that influence the uptake of water productivity–enhancing practices include:

- Cost and affordability—the ability to pay for a management practice or technology is an important determinant of whether farmers will adopt it.
- Price and profitability—will there be a payback on the investment?
- Risk—returns from a particular strategy may vary greatly from year to year, based on market, climate, and availability of water.
- Markets—can a farmer sell the produce and make a profit (photo 7.7)?
- Availability of a reliable supply of water—knowing when water is available may be more important for management decisions than the total quantity.
- Education—knowing about a product and its use may encourage uptake.
- Incentives and institutional structures—support for water productivity–enhancing measures can influence farmers' decisions.

A second type of uncertainty concerns the scale of potential benefits. Until decisionmakers are clear about the degree, timing, and cost of the potential improvement, prospects for a concerted effort seem limited. Who stands to gain from improvements? Who are the winners and losers in proposed redistributions? What are the risks of change, for example, through loss of "nonproductive" environmental flows? Surprisingly few detailed measurements exist of current water productivity on which to gauge the scope for improvement. Nor is it clear how *potential* water productivity—which expresses the upper limit of gain—varies spatially. This uncertainty can be removed by continuing measurement and analysis.

Photo by Sanjini de Silva

Photo 7.7 Market access is an enabling condition for improved water productivity

The scale of decision can be critical. Increases in water productivity at the farm level can actually increase basin water depletion, especially where water is scarce compared with land. Farmers may see water productivity–enhancing technologies like drip irrigation as an opportunity to expand areas using the same amount of water, ultimately increasing the amount of water depleted by agriculture and reducing the amount of water available for other users.

A third type of uncertainty concerns how people value water productivity improvement collectively. Water scarcity is a key driver behind water productivity gains, with agriculture under pressures from increased use by cities and a demand for more allocations for the environment. Because this driver does not directly influence the decisions of individuals who have water access, economic instruments have been considered to reflect physical scarcity values. Some people argue that because the price of agricultural water is so low, farmers do not feel the scarcity and that therefore raising the price would lower the demand for water by farmers, releasing some water for cities. Others argue that there is little evidence that pricing is an effective means of controlling demand within irrigation because the price increase would have to be so substantial, because of a lack of water rights and monitoring systems, and because there is typically strong political opposition within agrarian societies (Hellegers and Perry 2006; Molle and Berkhoff 2006; Berbel and Gómez-Limón 2000). Administrative allocation has been shown to be an effective option. Farmers adopt water productivity practices in response to less supply.

There are a variety of actors with different incentives, all with an interest in water productivity gains and reallocation. Society has an incentive to allocate water to various uses. Cities in search of more water may set their sights on cheap agricultural water. Farmers have an incentive to retain their supply for more production relative to costs. Raising prices for water can be seen as a further penalty for producers who are already struggling to make a living. Understanding incentives, the tradeoffs of different management options, and the proper alignment of incentives across various actors is a key to adoption. One strategy for bringing farmers into alignment with urban and broader social concerns is to compensate them for releasing water out of agriculture and to invest in water saving and profitability-enhancing farming technologies.

Thus adoption of water-productivity enhancements requires understanding potential tradeoffs, identifying winners and losers, and aligning the incentives of all actors. Many incentives will come from outside the water sector and address issues of the vulnerability and risk and markets and profitability of the agriculture enterprise and the equity and welfare of stakeholders.

> Adoption of water-productivity enhancements requires understanding potential tradeoffs, identifying winners and losers, and aligning the incentives of all actors

Investment priorities

Water productivity hotspots that need special attention are:
- Areas where poverty is high and water productivity is low, where attention could particularly benefit the poor, as in much of Sub-Saharan Africa and parts of South Asia and Latin America.

- Areas of physical water scarcity where there is intense competition for water, such as the Aral Sea Basin and the Yellow River Basin, especially where gains in economic water productivity are possible.
- Areas with little water resources development, where high returns from a little water can make a big difference.
- Areas of water-driven ecosystem degradation, such as falling groundwater tables, river desiccation, and intense competition for water.

Some actions can be taken up immediately, while others will require more time and persistence:

- Diagnosing reasons for high or low water productivity, and setting standards through benchmarking (fast).
- Concentrating on major factors limiting production (fertilizers, pests and diseases, water) and perpetuating poverty (fast).
- Building infrastructure and institutional capacity for better governance (slow).
- Strengthening producers' skills in managing systems (slow).
- Improving water resources management skills at different levels to deal with the diversity of competing water uses (slow).

Reviewers

Chapter review editor: David Seckler.
Chapter reviewers: George Ayad, Andrew I. Ayeni, Wim Bastiaanssen, Paul Belder, Thorsten Blenckner, Eline Boelee, Walter Bowen, Stuart Bunn, David Dent, Peter Droogers, Peter Edwards, Molly Hellmuth, Rafiqul M. Islam, Gunnar Jacks, Joan Jaganyi, Dinesh Kumar, Mats Lannerstad, A.D. Mohile, François Molle, Minh-Long Nguyen, V.J. Paranjpye, Sawaeng Ruaysoongnern, Lisa Schipper, Marcel Silvius, Sylvia Tognneti, Steven Twomlow, and Jos van Dam.

Note

1. For example, putting the characteristics of more water-efficient C_4 or CAM crops into less efficient C_3 crops would be a breakthrough.

References

Adams, R.H., and H. Alderman. 1992. "Sources of Income Inequality in Rural Pakistan: A Decomposition Analysis." *Oxford Bulletin of Economics and Statistics* 54 (4): 591–608.

Bakker, M., R. Barker, R. Meinzen-Dick, and F. Konradsen, eds. 1999. *Multiple Uses of Water in Irrigated Areas: A Case Study from Sri Lanka.* SWIM Paper 8. Colombo: International Water Management Institute.

Bennett, J. 2003. "Opportunities for Increasing Water Productivity of CGIAR Crops through Plant Breeding and Molecular Biology." In J.W. Kijne, R. Barker, and D. Molden, eds., *Water Productivity in Agriculture: Limits and Opportunities for Improvement.* Wallingford, UK, and Colombo: CABI Publishing and International Water Management Institute.

Berbel, J., and J.A. Gómez-Limón. 2000. "The Impact of Water-Pricing Policy in Spain: An Analysis of Three Irrigated Areas." *Agricultural Water Management* 43 (2): 219–38.

Bhatnagar, P.R., A.K. Sikka, L.K. Prassad, B.R. Sharma, and S.R. Singh. 2004. "Water Quality Dynamics in Secondary Reservoir for Intensive Fish Production." Abstract 176. Paper presented at International Association of Theoretical and Applied Limnology (SIL) Congress 2004, 8–14 August, Lahti, Finland.

Bindraban, P.S. 1997. "Bridging the Gap between Plant Physiology and Breeding: Identifying Traits to Increase Wheat Yield Potential Using Systems Approaches." Ph.D. thesis. Wageningen Agricultural University, The Netherlands.

Bindraban, P.S., A. Verhagen, P.W.J. Uithol, and P. Henstra. 1999. "A Land Quality Indicator for Sustainable Land Management: The Yield Gap." Report 106. Research Institute for Agrobiology and Soil Fertility, Wageningen, Netherlands.

Bindraban, P.S., J.J. Stoorvogel, D.M. Jansen, J. Vlaming, and J.J.R. Groot. 2000. "Land Quality Indicators for Sustainable Land Management: Proposed Method for Yield Gap and Soil Nutrient Balance." *Agriculture, Ecosystems and Environment* 81 (2): 103–12.

Booker, J.F., A.M. Michelsen, and F.A. Ward. 2005. "Economic Impact of Alternative Policy Responses to Prolonged and Severe Drought in the Rio Grande Basin." *Water Resources Research* 41 (2), W02026, doi: 10.1029/2004WR003486

Bos, M.G. 2004. "Using the Depleted Fraction to Manage the Groundwater Table in Irrigated Areas." *Irrigation and Drainage Systems* 18 (3): 201–09.

Bouman, B.A.M., H. Hengsdijk, B. Hardy, P.S. Bindraban, T.P. Tuong, and J.K. Ladha, eds. 2003. *Water-wise Rice Production.* Los Baños, Philippines: International Rice Research Institute.

Breman, H., J.J.R. Groot, and H. van Keulen. 2001. "Resource Limitations in Sahelian Agriculture." *Global Environmental Change* 11 (1): 59–68.

Burt, C.M., D.J. Howes, and A. Mutziger. 2001. "Evaporation Estimates for Irrigated Agriculture in California." Presented at the 2001 Irrigation Association Conference, 4–6 November, San Antonio, Tex.

Burt, C.M., A.J. Mutziger, R.G. Allen, and T.A. Howell. 2005. "Evaporation Research: Review and Interpretation." *Journal of Irrigation and Drainage Engineering* 131 (1): 37–58.

De Fraiture, C., X. Cai, U. Amarasinghe, M. Rosegrant, and D. Molden. 2004. "Does International Cereal Trade Save Water? The Impact of Virtual Water Trade on Global Water Use." Comprehensive Assessment of Water Management in Agriculture, Colombo.

De Wit, C.T. 1992. "Resource Use Efficiency in Agriculture." *Agricultural Systems* 40 (1–3): 125–51.

Droogers, P., and J. Aerts. 2005. "Adaptation Strategies to Climate Change and Climate Variability: A Comparative Study between Seven Contrasting River Basins." *Physics and Chemistry of the Earth, Parts A/B/C* 30 (6–7): 339–46.

Droogers, P., and G. Kite. 1999. "Water Productivity form Integrated Basin Modeling." *Irrigation and Drainage Systems* 13 (3): 275–90.

Emerton, L., and E. Bos. 2004. *Value: Counting Ecosystems as Water Infrastructure.* Gland, Switzerland and Cambridge, UK: World Conservation Union.

Fafchamps, M., C. Udry, and K. Czukas. 1998. "Drought and Saving in West Africa: Are Livestock a Buffer Stock?" *Journal of Development Economics* 55 (2): 273–305.

French, R.J., and J.E. Schultz. 1984. "Water Use Efficiency of Wheat in a Mediterranean-type Environment. I: The Relation between Yield, Water Use and Climate." *Australian Journal of Agricultural Research* 35 (6): 743–64.

Gichuki, F. 2004. "Managing the Externalities of Declining Dry Season River Flow: A Case Study from the Ewaso Ngiro North River Basin, Kenya." *Water Resources Research* 40 (8), W08S03, doi: 10.1029/2004WR003106.

Gowing, J.W., T.P. Tuong, and C.T. Hoanh. 2006. "Land and Water Management in Coastal Zones: Dealing with Agriculture-Aquaculture-Fishery Conflicts." In C. T. Hoanh, T.P. Tuong, J.W. Gowing, and B. Hardy, eds., *Environment and Livelihoods in Tropical Coastal Zones: Managing Agriculture-Fishery-Aquaculture Conflicts.* Wallingford, UK, and Colombo: CABI Publishing and International Water Management Institute.

Groenfeldt, D. 2006. "Multifunctionality of Agricultural Water: Looking beyond Food Production and Ecosystem Services." *Irrigation and Drainage* 55 (1):73–83.

Gupta M.V., J.D. Sollows, M.A. Maxid, M. Rahman, and M.G. Hussain. 1999. *Integration of Aquaculture with Rice Farming in Bangladesh: Feasibility and Economic Viability—Its Adoption and Impact.* Technical Report 55. Penan, Malaysia: WorldFish Center.

Hafeez, M., and S. Khan. 2006. "Tracking Fallow Irrigation Water Losses Using Remote-Sensing Techniques: A Case Study from the Liuyuankou Irrigation System, China." In I.R. Willett and Z. Gao, eds., *Agricultural Water Management in China: Proceedings of a Workshop Held in Beijin China, 14 September 2005.* Canberra: Australian Centre for International Agricultural Research.

Haylor, G.S. 1994. "Fish Production from Engineered Water Systems in Developing Countries." In J.F. Muir and R.J. Roberts, eds., *Recent Advances in Aquaculture V.* London: Blackwell Science.

Haylor, G. S. 1997. "Aquaculture Systems Research: Participatory Research Projects Involving Fish Production in Agro-eco-systems in Asia." *Aquaculture News* 23: 18–20.

Hellegers, P.J.G.J., and C.J. Perry. 2006. "Can Irrigation Water Use Be Guided by Market Forces? Theory and Practice." *Water Resources Development* 22 (1): 79–86.

Hill, H., and L. Tollefson. 1996. "Institutional Questions and Social Challenges." In L.S. Pereira, R.A. Feddes, J.R. Gilley, and B. Lesaffre, eds., *Sustainability of Irrigated Agriculture.* NATO ASI Series. Dordrecht, Netherlands: Kluwer Academic Publishers.

Hussain, I., M. Mudasser, M.A. Hanjra, U. Amrasinghe, and D. Molden. 2004. "Improving Wheat Productivity in Pakistan: Econometric Analysis Using Panel Data from Chaj in the Upper Indus Basin." *Water International* 29(2): 189–200.

Hussain, I., and M.A. Hanjra. 2004. "Irrigation and Poverty Alleviation: Review of the Empirical Evidence." *Irrigation and Drainage* 53(1) 115.

IMTA (Mexican Institute of Water Technology). 2002. "Estudio Tecnico para la Reglamentacion de la Cuenca Lerma-Chapala." IMTA, National Water Commission (CAN) and Secretariat of the Environment and Natural Resources (SEMARNAT), Mexico City.

IPCC (Intergovernmental Panel on Climate Change). 2001. *Climate Change 2001: Impacts, Adaptation and Vulnerability.* Third Assessment Report. Geneva.

Keller, A., and J. Keller. 1995. "Effective Efficiency: A Water Use Efficiency Concept for Allocating Freshwater Resources." Brief for the Center for Economic Policy Studies. Winrock International, Arlington, Va.

Keller, A., and D. Seckler. 2004. *Limits to Increasing the Productivity of Water in Crop Production.* Arlington, Va.: Winrock Water.

Kelly, V.A. 2006. "Factors Affecting Demand for Fertilizer in Sub-Saharan Africa." Agriculture and Rural Development Discussion Paper 23. World Bank, Washington, D.C.

Long, S.P., E.A. Ainsworth, A.D.B. Leakey, J. Nosberger, and D.R. Ort. 2006. "Food for Thought: Lower-than-expected Crop Yield Stimulation with Rising CO_2 Concentrations." *Science* 312 (5782): 1918–21.

Luquet, D., A. Vidal, M. Smith, and J. Dauzatd. 2005. "'More Crop per Drop': How to Make it Acceptable for Farmers?" *Agricultural Water Management* 76 (2): 108–19.

Matsuno, Y., K. Nakamura, T. Masumoto, H. Matsui, T. Kato, and Y. Sato. 2006. "Prospects for Multifunctionality of Paddy Rice Cultivation in Japan and Other Countries in Monsoon Asia." *Paddy and Water Environment* 4 (4): 189–97.

Meijer, K., E. Boelee, D. Augustijn, and I. van der Molen. 2006. "Impacts of Concrete Lining of Irrigation Canals on Availability of Water for Domestic Use in Southern Sri Lanka." *Agricultural Water Management.* 83 (3): 243–51.

Meinzen-Dick, R. 1997. "Valuing the Multiple Uses of Water." In M. Kay, T. Franks, and L. Smith, eds., *Water: Economics, Management and Demand.* London: E&FN Spon.

Molden, D. J., R. Sakthivadivel, and Z. Habib. 2000. *Basin Level Use and Productivity of Water: Examples from South Asia.* Research Report 49. Colombo: International Water Management Institute.

Molden, D.J., R. Sakthivadivel, and J. Keller. 2001. *Hydronomic Zones for Developing Basin Water Conservation Strategies.* Research Report 56. Colombo: International Water Management Institute.

Molden, D., H. Murray-Rust, R. Sakthivadivel, and I. Makin. 2003. "A Water-Productivity Framework for Understanding and Action." In J.W. Kijne, R. Barker, and D. Molden, eds., *Water Productivity in Agriculture: Limits and Opportunities for Improvement.* Wallingford, UK, and Colombo: CABI Publishing and International Water Management Institute.

Molle, F., and J. Berkoff. 2006. "Cities versus Agriculture: Revisiting Intersectoral Water Transfers, Potential Gains and Conflicts." Comprehensive Assessment of Water Management in Agriculture, Colombo.

Molle, F., A. Mamanpoush, and M. Miranzadeh. 2005. *Robbing Yadullah's Water to Irrigate Saeid's Garden: Hydrology and Water Rights in a Village of Central Iran.* Research Report 80. Colombo: International Water Management Institute.

Moriarty, P., J.A. Butterworth, and B. van Koppen, eds. 2004. *Beyond Domestic: Case Studies on Poverty and Productive Uses of Water at the Household Level.* IRC Technical Paper Series 41. Delft, Netherlands: IRC International Water and Sanitation Centre.

Muir, J.F. 1993. "Water Management for Aquaculture and Fisheries; Irrigation, Irritation or Integration?" In *Priorities for Water Resources Allocation and Management.* Proceeding of the Natural Resources and Engineering Advisers Conference, Overseas Development Authority, July 1992, Southampton, UK. Chatham, UK: Natural Resources Institute.

Moyo, R., D. Love, M. Mul, W. Mupangwa, and S. Twomlow 2006. "Impact and Sustainability of Low-Head Drip Irrigation Kits in the Semi-Arid Gwanda and Beitbridge Districts, Mzingwane Catchment, Limpopo Basin, Zimbabwe." *Physics and Chemistry of the Earth, Parts A/B/C,* 31(15–16): 885–92.

Murray, F., D.C. Little, G. Haylor, M. Felsing, J. Gowing, and S.S. Kodithuwakku. 2002. "A Framework for Research into the Potential for Integration of Fish Production in Irrigation Systems." In P. Edwards, D.C. Little, and H. Demaine, eds., *Rural Aquaculture.* Wallingford, UK: CABI Publishing.

Narayanamoorthy, A. 2004. "Impact Assessment of Drip Irrigation in India: The Case of Sugarcane." *Development Policy Review* 22 (4): 443–62.

Nguyen-Khoa, S., L. Smith, and K. Lorenzen. 2005. "Impacts of Irrigation on Inland Fisheries: Appraisals in Laos and Sri Lanka." Comprehensive Assessment of Water Management in Agriculture, Colombo.

Oweis, T., and A. Hachum. 2003. "Improving Water Productivity in the Dry Areas of West Asia and North Africa." In J.W. Kijne, R. Barker, and D. Molden, eds., *Water Productivity in Agriculture: Limits and Opportunities for Improvement.* Wallingford, UK, and Colombo: CABI Publishing and International Water Management Institute.

Oweis, T., A. Hachum, and J. Kijne. 1999. *Water Harvesting and Supplemental Irrigation for Improved Water Use Efficiency in Dry Areas.* SWIM paper 7. Colombo: International Water Management Institute.

Perry, C.J. 1999. "The IWMI Water Resources Paradigm—Definitions and Implications." *Agricultural Water Management* 40 (1): 45-50.

Polak, P., and R. Yoder. 2006. "Creating Wealth from Groundwater for Dollar-a-Day Farmers: Where the Silent Revolution and the Four Revolutions to End Rural Poverty Meet." *Hydrogeology Journal* 14(3): 424–32.

Postel, S., P. Polak, F. Gonazales, and J. Keller. 2001. "Drip Irrigation for Small Farmers: A New Initiative to Alleviate Hunger and Poverty." *Water International* 26 (1): 3–13.

Prein, M. 2002. "Integration of Aquaculture into Crop-Animal Systems in Asia." *Agriculture Systems* 71 (1) 127–46.

Rajak, D., M.V. Manjunatha, G.R. Rajkumar, M. Hebbara, and P.S. Minhas. 2006. "Comparative Effects of Drip and Furrow Irrigation on the Yield and Water Productivity of Cotton (*Gossypium hirsutum* L.) in a Saline and Waterlogged Vertisol." *Agricultural Water Management* 83 (1–2): 30–36.

Renault, D., and W.W. Wallender. 2000. "Nutritional Water Productivity and Diets." *Agricultural Water Management* 45 (3): 275–96.

Renault, D., M. Hemakumara, and D. Molden. 2001. "Importance of Water Consumption by Perennial Vegetation in Irrigated Areas of the Humid Tropics: Evidence from Sri Lanka." *Agricultural Water Management* 46 (3): 215–30.

Renwick, M.E. 2001. "Valuing Water in a Multiple-Use System—Irrigated Agriculture and Reservoir Fisheries." *Irrigation and Drainage Systems* 15 (2): 149–71.

Rockström, J., J. Barron, and P. Fox. 2003. "Water Productivity in Rain-fed Agriculture: Challenges and Opportunities for Smallholder Farmers in Drought-prone Tropical Agroecosystems." In J.W. Kijne, R. Barker, and D. Molden, eds., *Water Productivity in Agriculture: Limits and Opportunities for Improvement.* Wallingford, UK, and Colombo: CABI Publishing and International Water Management Institute.

Sadras, V.O., and J.F. Angus. 2006. "Benchmarking Water Use Efficiency of Rainfed Wheat in Dry Environments." *Australian Journal of Agricultural Research* 57 (8): 847–56.

Sayre, K.D., S. Rajaram, and R.A. Fischer. 1997. "Yield Potential Progress in Short Bread Wheats in Northwest Mexico." *Crop Science* 37 (1): 36–42.

Scherr, S.J., and J.A. McNeely, eds. Forthcoming. *Farming with Nature: The Science and Practice of Ecoagriculture.* Washington, D.C.: Island Press.

Seckler, D. 1996. *The New Era of Water Resources Management: From 'Dry' to 'Wet' Water Savings.* Research Report 1. Colombo: International Irrigation Management Institute.

Seckler, D., D. Molden, and R. Sakthivadivel. 2003. "The Concept of Efficiency in Water Resources Management and Policy." In J.W. Kijne, R. Barker, and D. Molden, eds., *Water Productivity in Agriculture: Limits and Opportunities for Improvement.* Wallingford, UK, and Colombo: CABI Publishing and International Water Management Institute.

Shah, T., S. Verma, V. Bhamoriya, S. Ghosh, and R. Sakthivadivel. 2003. *Social Impact of Technical Innovations: Study of Organic Cotton and Low-cost Drip Irrigation in the Agrarian Economy of West Nimar Region.* International Water Management Institute, Colombo. [www.fibl.net/english/cooperation/projects/documents/social-impact-report.pdf].

Steduto, P., and R. Albrizio. 2005. "Resource-use Efficiency of Field-grown Sunflower, Sorghum, Wheat and Chickpea. II. Water Use Efficiency and Comparison with Radiation Use Efficiency." *Agricultural and Forest Meteorology* 130 (2005): 269–81.

Tanner, C.B., and T.R. Sinclair. 1983. "Efficient Water Use in Crop Production: Research or Re-search?" In H.M. Taylor, W.A. Jordan, and T.R. Sinclair, eds., *Limitations to Efficient Water Use in Crop Production.* Madison, Wisc.: American Society of Agronomy.

Tiwari, K.N., A. Singh, and P.K. Mal. 2003. "Effect of Drip Irrigation on Yield of Cabbage (*Brassica oleracea* L.var. *capitata*) under Mulch and Non-mulch Conditions." *Agricultural Water Management* 58 (1): 19–28.

Tiwari, K.N., P.K. Mal, R.M. Singh, and A. Chattopadhyay. 1998. "Response of Okra (*Abelmoschus esculentus* (L.) Moench.) to Drip Irrigation under Mulch and Non-mulch Condition." *Agricultural Water Management* 38 (2): 91–102.

Twomlow, S., C. Riches, D. O'Neill, P. Brookes, and J. Ellis-Jones. 1999. "Sustainable Dryland Smallholder Farming in Sub-Saharan Africa." *Annals of Arid Zone* 38 (2): 93–135.

Van Dam, J.C., R. Singh, J.J.E. Bessembinder, P.A. Leffelaar, W.G.M. Bastiaanssen, R.K. Jhorar, J.G. Kroes, and P. Droogers. 2006. "Assessing Options to Increase Water Productivity in Irrigated River Basins Using Remote Sensing and Modelling Tools." *Water Resources Development* 22 (1): 115–33.

Van Koppen, B. 2000. *From Bucket to Basin: Managing River Basins to Alleviate Water Deprivation.* The Contribution of the International Water Management Institute to the World Water Vision for Food and Rural Development. Colombo: International Water Management Institute.

Van Koppen, B., P. Moriarty, and E. Boelee. 2006. *Multiple-use Water Services to Advance the Millennium Development Goals.* Research Report 98. Colombo: International Water Management Institute.

Verdegem, M.C.J., R.H. Bosma, and J.A.J. Verreth. 2006. "Reducing Water Use for Animal Production through Aquaculture." *Water Resources Development* 22 (1): 101–13.

Viets, F.G., Jr. 1962. "Fertilizers and the Efficient Use of Water." *Advances in Agronomy* 14: 223–64.

Ward, F.A., and A. Michelsen. 2002. "The Economic Value of Water in Agriculture: Concepts and Policy Applications." *Water Policy* 4 (5): 423–46.

Warner, J.F., P.S. Bindraban, and H. van Keulen. 2006. "Water for Food and Ecosystems: How to Cut Which Pie?" *Water Resources Development* 22 (1): 3–13.

Wester, Philippus, Sergio Vargas-Velázquez, Eric Mollard, and Paula Silva-Ochoa. Forthcoming. "Negotiating Surface Water Allocations to Achieve a Soft Landing in the Closed Lerma-Chapala Basin, Mexico." *International Journal of Water Resources Development.*

Zhang, H. 2003. "Improving Water Productivity through Deficit Irrigation: Examples from Syria, the North China Plain and Oregon, USA." In J.W. Kijne, R. Barker, and D. Molden, eds., *Water Productivity in Agriculture: Limits and Opportunities for Improvement.* Wallingford, UK, and Colombo: CABI Publishing and International Water Management Institute.

Zwart, S.J., W.G.M. Bastiaanssen, J. Garatuza-Payan, C.J. Watts. 2006. "SEBAL for Detecting Spatial Variation of Water Productivity for Wheat in the Yaqui Valley, Mexico." Paper presented at the International Conference on Earth Observation for vegetation monitoring and water management, 10–11 November 2005, Naples, Italy.

Zwart, S.J., and W.G.M. Bastiaanssen. 2004. "Review of Measured Crop Water Productivity Values for Irrigated Wheat, Rice, Cotton and Maize." *Agricultural Water Management* 69 (2): 115–33.

Part 4 | Thematic issues

These chapters assess trends, conditions, and response options for managing critical resources for agriculture.

Unlocking the potential of rainfed agriculture

Artist: Surendra Pradhan, Nepal

8 | Managing water in rainfed agriculture

Coordinating lead author: Johan Rockström

Lead authors: Nuhu Hatibu, Theib Y. Oweis, and Suhas Wani

Contributing authors: Jennie Barron, Adriana Bruggeman, Jalali Farahani, Louise Karlberg, and Zhu Qiang

Overview

Facing the food and poverty crises in developing countries will require a new emphasis on small-scale water management in rainfed agriculture involving the redirection of water policy and large new investments. Rainfed systems dominate world food production, but water investments in rainfed agriculture have been neglected over the past 50 years. Upgrading rainfed agriculture promises large social, economic, and environmental paybacks, particularly in poverty reduction and economic development. Rainfed farming covers most of the world's cropland (80%) and produces most of the world's cereal grains (more than 60%), generating livelihoods in rural areas and producing food for cities. Estimates suggest that about 25% of the increased water requirement needed to attain the 2015 hunger reduction target of the Millennium Development Goal can be contributed from irrigation. The remaining 75% will have to come from water investments in rainfed agriculture.

There is a close correlation between hunger, poverty, and water: most hungry and poor people live in regions where water challenges pose a particular constraint to food production. The world's hotspots for hunger and poverty are concentrated in the arid, semiarid, and dry subhumid regions of the world. There, water is a key challenge for food production due to the extreme variability of rainfall, long dry seasons, and recurrent droughts, floods, and dry spells. These regions cover some 40% of the world's land area and host roughly 40% of the world's population. The water challenge in these rainfed areas is to enhance yields by improving water availability and the water uptake capacity of crops.

Investments in rainfed agriculture have large payoffs in yield improvements and poverty alleviation through income generation and environmental sustainability. This is an important conclusion of the Comprehensive Assessment of Water Management in Agriculture, given that rainfed agriculture, particularly in the world's most water-challenged regions, is a risky business, with current yields generally less than half of those in irrigated systems and in temperate regions where water risks are much lower.

The key challenge is to reduce water-related risks posed by high rainfall variability rather than coping with an absolute lack of water. There is generally enough rainfall to double and often even quadruple yields in rainfed farming systems, even in water-constrained regions. But it is available at the wrong time, causing dry spells, and much of it is lost. Apart from water, upgrading rainfed agriculture requires investments in soil, crop, and farm management. However, to achieve these, rainfall-related risks need to be reduced, which means that investments in water management are the entry point to unlock the potential in rainfed agriculture.

> **Small investments for supplemental irrigation in combination with improved soil, nutrient, and crop management can more than double water productivity and yields in small-scale rainfed agriculture**

A new era of water investments and policy is required for upgrading rainfed agriculture. The focus of the past 50 years on managing rainfall in farmers' fields, through soil and water conservation, cannot alone reduce the risk of frequent dry spells. Needed are investments in water resources management in smallholder rainfed farming systems that add new freshwater through local management of rainfall and runoff. Upgrading rainfed agriculture thus involves investments in the continuum between rainfed and irrigated agriculture.

The Comprehensive Assessment shows that the potential for improving water productivity is particularly high in smallholder rainfed agriculture, with water savings of 15%–20% already possible over the coming decade. Such large water savings are possible because water productivity is very low in rainfed agriculture in poverty-stricken rural areas. Small investments (providing 1,000 cubic meters of extra water per hectare per season) for supplemental irrigation in combination with improved soil, nutrient, and crop management can more than double water productivity and yields in small-scale rainfed agriculture.

Investments in rainfed agriculture can improve environmental sustainability. Expansion of land under agriculture, particularly rainfed crops and grazing, is a key driver of the severe degradation of ecosystem services over the past 50 years. Poor management of rainwater in rainfed systems generates excessive runoff, causing soil erosion and poor yields due to a shortage of soil moisture. Investments to maximize rainfall infiltration and the water-holding capacity of soils minimize land degradation while increasing the water available in the soil for crop growth. This will result in improvements in the quality of natural ecosystems and of water in aquatic ecosystems.

There is an urgent need for widening the policy scope to include explicit strategies for water management in rainfed agriculture, including grazing and forest systems. Policy on water resources management for agriculture remains focused on irrigation, while the framework for integrated water resources management at watershed and basin scales concentrates primarily on allocation and management of blue water in rivers, groundwater, and lakes. What is needed is effective integration that focuses on investment options for water management across the continuum from rainfed to irrigated agriculture. Now is the time to abandon the sectoral divide between irrigated and rainfed agriculture and to place water resources management and planning more centrally in the policy domain of agriculture at large. The current focus on water resources planning at the river basin scale does not put enough emphasis on water management in rainfed agriculture, which overwhelmingly occurs below the river basin scale, on farms of less than 5 hectares (ha), at the scale of small catchments. Therefore, an equally strong focus is needed on managing water at the watershed level and at the basin scale. This shift in focus opens up space for much needed investments in water resources management in rainfed agriculture.

Even where the potential gains from water investments in rainfed agriculture are greatest, improving water management alone is not enough to achieve significant and sustainable increases in yield. At the farming systems level full response to water investments is achievable only if other production factors, such as soil fertility, crop varieties, and tillage practices, are improved simultaneously. Important yield improvements can be achieved through synergies, particularly when water management is linked to organic fertilization from agroforestry and livestock systems, for example. Attention to land tenure, water ownership, and market access is also needed to ensure the full benefits from water management interventions.

The knowledge already exists to at least double yields in rainfed agriculture, even where water poses a particular challenge: the key is adaptation and adoption strategies. Needed for success are human capacity building and stronger institutions. Due to the general perception that water takes care of itself in rainfed systems, the emphasis has been on on-farm management of soil, plants, trees, and animals. Thus, farmers in many regions of the world still practice rainfed farming with no explicit water management strategies. Investments are needed in institutional and human capacities to plan and manage water for rainfed agriculture at the catchment scale, where local runoff water resources can be diverted, stored, and managed. The Comprehensive Assessment has found that while many countries have written off rainfed agriculture in arid, semiarid, and dry subhumid areas as marginal with limited potential, and invested little in institutional and human capacities to support water investments by farmers, other countries have invested in tapping the potential that lies in the availability of an adequate but erratic water resource provided by the rain.

> Rainfed agriculture will continue to produce the bulk of the world's food. And because water productivity is very low in rainfed agriculture, there are significant opportunities for producing more food with less freshwater

Major water investments required in rainfed agriculture

When it comes to ensuring food security for all, two major water realities face humankind. Rainfed agriculture will continue to produce the bulk of the world's food. And water productivity is very low in rainfed agriculture, thus providing significant opportunities for producing more food with less freshwater. Rainfed agriculture is practiced in 80% of the world's physical agricultural area and generates 62% of the world's staple food (FAOSTAT 2005).

Addressing malnourishment and poverty requires a new green revolution (Conway 1997) in small-scale rainfed agriculture in arid, semiarid, and dry subhumid regions of the world (Falkenmark and Rockström 2004). A key to success is to invest in the often untapped potential of upgrading rainfed agriculture through integrated water investments. The Comprehensive Assessment indicates that water investments in rainfed agriculture are required to attain the Millennium Development Goals, as most hungry people live in regions subject to frequent water stress and extreme water shocks, such as droughts, floods, and dry spells (short periods of water stress during critical growth stages).

Water management to upgrade rainfed agriculture encompasses a wide spectrum, from water conservation practices for improving rainwater management on the farmer's field to managing runoff water (surface and subsurface) for supplying supplemental irrigation water to rainfed food production. There is no clear demarcation between rainfed and irrigated systems (see conceptual framework annex). This chapter addresses water management in all agricultural systems where direct rainwater is the main water source for crop production. It describes the major trends, drivers, and current conditions for key water management challenges facing rainfed agriculture from the perspectives of water productivity, wealth creation and poverty eradication, and environmental sustainability. While applying a global outlook, the chapter focuses on temperate and tropical arid, semiarid, and dry subhumid regions in developing countries, regions where rainfed farming systems and agriculture-based livelihoods are common, where water stress–related constraints in agriculture are concentrated, and where rural poverty and malnourishment are greatest. Since the most unreliable and often scarce resource in agricultural production in these areas is soil moisture for plant growth ("green water"), the challenge is to enhance the availability and productivity of water used for biomass production.

> Most food for poor communities in developing countries is produced in rainfed agriculture

The chapter first details the gaps in the management of water under rainfed systems. It then evaluates opportunities for investment in managing water in rainfed systems together with evidence on the potential returns on these investments with respect to livelihoods and environmental sustainability. The final section assesses the policy shifts needed to support the necessary investments.

Most food is produced in rainfed agriculture

The importance of rainfed agriculture varies regionally, but most food for poor communities in developing countries is produced in rainfed agriculture. Some 93% of farmed land is rainfed in Sub-Saharan Africa, 87% in Latin America, 67% in the Near East and North Africa, 65% in East Asia, and 58% in South Asia (FAO 2002). Most countries depend primarily on rainfed agriculture for their grain food.

Yield increase is the key to future food production from rainfed agriculture. In the past 40 years agricultural land use has expanded 20%–25%, contributing approximately 30% of the overall growth in grain production during the period (FAO 2002; Ramankutty, Foley, and Olejniczak 2002). The remaining yield gains originated from intensification through yield increases per unit of land area. However, regional variation is large, as are the differences between irrigated and rainfed agriculture. In developing countries rainfed grain yields are on average 1.5 metric tons per hectare, compared with 3.1 metric tons per hectare for irrigated yields (Rosegrant and others 2002), and increases in production from rainfed agriculture have originated mainly from land expansion.

Trends differ by region. Sub-Saharan Africa, with 97% rainfed production of staple cereals such as maize, millet, and sorghum, has doubled cultivated cereal area since 1960, while yield per unit of land has barely changed (figures 8.1 and 8.2; FAOSTAT 2005).

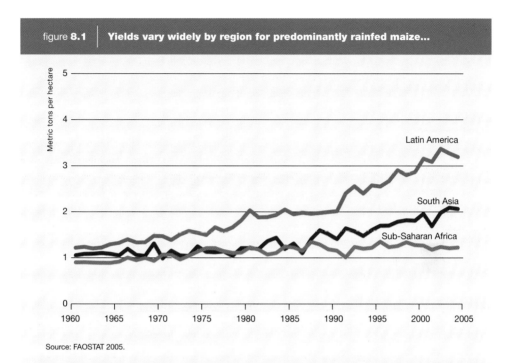

figure **8.1** | **Yields vary widely by region for predominantly rainfed maize...**

Source: FAOSTAT 2005.

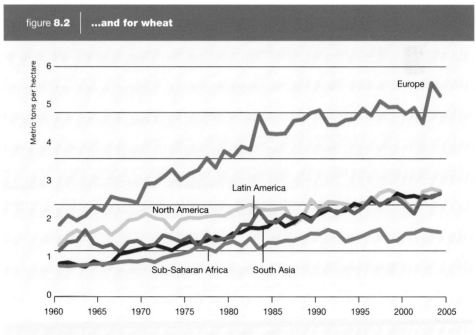

figure **8.2** | **...and for wheat**

Source: FAOSTAT 2005.

South Asia has experienced a major shift from more drought-tolerant low-yielding crops such as sorghum and millet, to wheat and maize, for which area planted and yield per unit of land have doubled since 1961 (FAOSTAT 2005). In Latin America and the Caribbean area expansion of 25% in the last 40 years has been less than the gain in yield per unit of land (FAOSTAT 2005). In many predominantly rainfed regions of the world grain yields have doubled or tripled during the same period (see figures 8.1 and 8.2).

Rainfed maize yields differ substantially across regions from just over 1 metric ton per hectare in Sub-Saharan Africa to 3 metric tons per hectare in Latin America and the Caribbean (see figure 8.1). By comparison, in the United States and Europe, yields are 7–10 metric tons per hectare. Similar variation is found for wheat (see figure 8.2). In view of these regional differences in yield development there appears to be significant potential for boosting yields in rainfed agriculture, particularly in South Asia and Sub-Saharan Africa.

> A majority of poor people in the world are dependent on rainfed agriculture for food, incomes, and thus livelihood security

Rainfed agriculture—large untapped potential. In several regions of the world rainfed agriculture has some of the highest yields. These are predominantly temperate regions, with relatively reliable rainfall and inherently productive soils. But even in tropical regions, particularly in subhumid and humid zones, agricultural yields in commercial rainfed agriculture exceed 5–6 metric tons per hectare (Rockström and Falkenmark 2000; Wani and others 2003a, b). At the same time the dry subhumid and semiarid regions have experienced the lowest yields and weakest yield improvements per unit of land. Yields for rainfed agriculture are in the range of 0.5–2 metric tons per hectare, with an average of 1 metric ton per hectare in Sub-Saharan Africa, and 1–1.5 metric tons per hectare in South Asia and Central and West Asia and North Africa (Rockström and Falkenmark 2000; Wani and others 2003a, b).

Analyses by the Comprehensive Assessment of major rainfed crops in semiarid regions in Africa and Asia and rainfed wheat in North Africa and West Asia reveal large yield gaps, with farmers' yields being 2–4 times lower than achievable yields for major rainfed crops (figure 8.3). Historic trends show a growing yield gap between farmers' practices and farming systems that benefit from management advances (Wani and others 2003a).

Upgrading rainfed agriculture—a key to poverty reduction?

Rainfed agriculture generates most of the food in the world *[well established]* and plays a key role in poverty reduction *[established but incomplete]*. A majority of poor people in the world are dependent on rainfed agriculture for food, incomes, and thus livelihood security *[established but incomplete]*. The importance of rainfed sources of food weighs disproportionately on women, who make up some 70% of the world's poor (WHO 2000). Agriculture plays a key role in economic development (World Bank 2005) and poverty reduction (Irz and Roe 2000), with every 1% increase in agricultural yields translating into a 0.6–1.2 percentage point decrease in the absolute poor by some estimates (Thirtle and others 2002). In Sub-Saharan Africa agriculture accounts for 35% of GDP and employs 70% of the population (World Bank 2000), and more than 95% of the agricultural area is rainfed (box 8.1; FAOSTAT 2005).

There is a correlation between poverty, hunger, and water stress (Falkenmark 1986). The UN Millennium Project (2005) has identified "hotspot" countries suffering from the

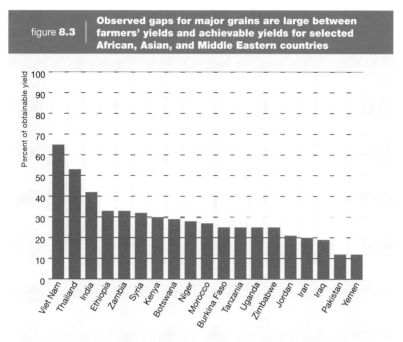

figure **8.3** | **Observed gaps for major grains are large between farmers' yields and achievable yields for selected African, Asian, and Middle Eastern countries**

Source: Analysis done for the Comprehensive Assessment of Water Management in Agriculture.

highest prevalence of malnutrition. These countries coincide closely with those that contain the major semiarid and dry subhumid hydroclimates in the world (savannahs and steppe ecosystems), where rainfed agriculture is the dominant source of food and where water constitutes a key limiting factor to crop growth (map 8.1; SEI 2005). Nearly all of the world's 850 million undernourished people live in poor developing countries, which are located predominantly in tropical regions (FAO 2004b).

box **8.1** | **Agricultural growth is an underlying factor for economic growth**

Agriculture, the sector in which a large majority of poor people in Africa make their living, is the engine of overall economic growth and, therefore, of broad-based poverty reduction (Johnston and Mellor 1961; World Bank 1982; Timmer 1988; Abdulai and Hazell 1995; IFAD 2001; DFID 2002; Koning 2002). Recent international reports have reaffirmed this conclusion, which is based on analysis of the historical development paths of countries worldwide (IAC 2004; Commission for Africa 2005; UN Millennium Project 2005). Higher farm yields enhanced producer incomes, in cash and in kind, and created demand for agricultural labor. Thus, agricultural growth typically preceded economic growth in the high-income industrial countries and the more recent growth in the Asian Tigers such as Indonesia, Malaysia, Thailand, Viet Nam, and parts of China.

Source: van Koppen, Namara, and Stafilios-Rothschild 2005.

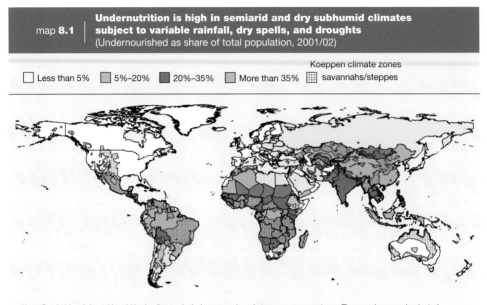

map 8.1

Undernutrition is high in semiarid and dry subhumid climates subject to variable rainfall, dry spells, and droughts
(Undernourished as share of total population, 2001/02)

Koeppen climate zones

☐ Less than 5%   ☐ 5%–20%   ■ 20%–35%   ☐ More than 35%   ▦ savannahs/steppes

Note: Semiarid and dry subhumid hydroclimates include savannah and steppe agroecosystems. These regions are dominated by sedentary farming subject to the world's highest rainfall variability and occurrence of dry spells and droughts.
Source: UNStat 2005.

Lack of focus on water management has led to missed opportunities

Increasingly, evidence shows that the amount of water is not the key limiting factor for improved yields, even in so-called drylands (Klaij and Vachaud 1992; Agarwal 2000; Wani and others 2003b; Hatibu and others 2003) *[established but incomplete]*. Savannah regions have rainfall levels that sometimes exceed rainfall in the temperate zone—500–1,000 millimeters (mm) per growing season compared with 500–700 mm per growing season for temperate regions. Instead, the major water-related challenge for rainfed agriculture in semiarid and dry subhumid regions is the extreme variability in rainfall, characterized by few rainfall events, high-intensity storms, and high frequency of dry spells and droughts. It is therefore critical to understand how hydroclimatic conditions and water management affect yields in rainfed agriculture.

Water availability has shaped rainfed agriculture. Farming systems have adapted to hydroclimatic gradients, from pastoral systems in arid environments to multiple-cropping systems in humid agroecosystems (table 8.1). Though based on the same fundamental principles across the world, farming systems also exhibit variations based in history and culture that result in differences in crops, tillage systems, and soil and water management systems.

Even if rainfed agriculture can be categorized generically, it is critical to distinguish among hydroclimatic zones, which vary widely from a few hundred millimeters of rainfall per year to more than 1,000 mm, with aridity index values ranging from below 0.2 to

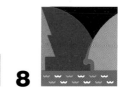

| table 8.1 | Classification of hydroclimatic zones by aridity index, typical agricultural land use, and ecosystem gradients |

	Arid		Semiarid	
	Temperate	**Tropical**	**Temperate**	**Tropical**
Area (%)	0.5	4.0	2.6	13.0
Population (%)	2.5	9.5	5.6	11.7
Major production constraints	■ Precipitation amount ■ Precipitation distribution ■ Soil chemistry	■ Precipitation amount ■ Precipitation distribution ■ Potential greater than actual evapotranspiration ■ Soil chemistry	■ Precipitation amount ■ Precipitation distribution ■ Temperature	■ Precipitation amount ■ Precipitation distribution ■ Precipitation intensity ■ Potential greater than actual evapotranspiration ■ Soil physiology and chemistry
Hotspots	■ West Asia ■ North Africa	■ Sub-Saharan Africa ■ Northeast Brazil ■ Mexico	■ Central and West Asia ■ North Africa ■ Southern Europe ■ Mongolia ■ Northern China	■ Sub-Saharan Africa ■ South Asia ■ Northeast Brazil ■ Southern China
Ecosystem gradient	■ Desert ■ Desert shrubland	■ Desert	■ Steppe ■ Grassland	■ Grassland ■ Savannah ■ Parkland savannah
Typical rainfed farming systems	■ Pastoral ■ Rainfed winter crop	n.a.	■ Pastoral ■ Rainfed winter crop ■ Rainfed mixed	■ Pastoral ■ Rainfed cereal, mixed, rice-wheat
	Subhumid		Humid	
	Temperate	**Tropical**	**Temperate**	**Tropical**
Area (%)	7.3	9.0	19.3	41.9
Population (%)	5.7	7.1	9.2	26.8
Major production constraints	■ Precipitation distribution ■ Temperature	■ Precipitation distribution ■ Precipitation intensity ■ Soil physiology and chemistry	■ Temperature	■ Precipitation intensity
Hotspots	■ Central Asia	■ Sub-Saharan Africa ■ South Asia ■ Southeast Asia ■ Latin America		■ Southeast Asia
Ecosystem gradient	■ Steppe ■ Shrubland ■ Forest	■ Parkland savannah ■ Woodland savannah	■ Forest	■ Forest ■ Rain forest
Typical rainfed farming systems	■ Rainfed winter crop ■ Rainfed mixed	■ Rainfed cereal ■ Rainfed mixed ■ Rice-wheat	n.a.	■ Rainfed rice-wheat

n.a. is not available

Note: Climate is defined according to the aridity index: precipitation/potential evapotranspiration less than 0.2 arid (including hyperarid); 0.2 to less than 0.5 semiarid; 0.5 to less than 1 subhumid; more than 1 humid (Deichmann and Eklundh 1991). Temperature classification follows FAO/IIASA (2000) climatic zones, with temperate meaning at least one month with monthly mean temperatures, corrected to sea level, below 5° Celsius (C) and four or more months above 10°C, and tropical and subtropical as all months with monthly mean temperatures, corrected to sea level, above 18°C, and one or more months with monthly mean temperatures, corrected to sea level, below 18°C but above 5°C.

Source: Compiled for the Comprehensive Assessment of Water Management in Agriculture using population data from LandScan (2004) and aggregated farming systems classification as defined by Dixon, Gulliver, and Gibbon (2001).

more than unity. Key constraints to rainwater productivity (total amount of rainfall per grain yield) will differ greatly across this wide range of rainfall zones. In the arid regions it is the absolute amount of water that constitutes the major limiting factor in agriculture. In the semiarid and dry subhumid tropical regions seasonal rainfall is generally adequate to significantly improve yields, and managing extreme rainfall variability over time and space is the largest water challenge. Only in the dry semiarid and arid zones, even when considering the standard deviation around the mean, is absolute water stress common (figure 8.4). In the wetter part of the semiarid zone and into the dry subhumid zone, rainfall generally exceeds crop water needs.

> "Agricultural" droughts are due primarily to management-related problems with the on-farm water balance and are an indicator of large opportunities to improve yields through better water management

Thus, the large observed differences between farmers' yields and attainable yields cannot be explained by differences in rainfall. Rather, they are a result of differences in water, soil, and crop management. In a global analysis of more than 100 agricultural development projects, Pretty and Hine (2001) found that in projects that focused on improving rainfed agriculture, yields doubled on average and often increased several hundred percent. This illustrates the large potential for investments in upgrading rainfed agriculture.

Meteorological and agricultural droughts: water stress in agriculture is often human induced. Though the absolute amount of water scarcity is rarely the major problem for rainfed agriculture, water scarcity is a key reason behind low agricultural productivity. To identify management options for upgrading rainfed agriculture, it is essential to assess different types of water stress in food production. Especially important is distinguishing between climate- and human-induced water stress and between droughts and dry spells (table 8.2). In semiarid and dry subhumid agroecosystems rainfall variability generates dry spells (short periods of water stress during critical growth stages) almost every rainy season (Barron and others 2003). Meteorological droughts (periods of inadequate rainfall to grow a crop), by contrast, occur on average only once every decade in moist semiarid regions and up to twice every decade in dry semiarid regions. Investments in water management can bridge dry spells, which generally last two to four weeks (Barron and others 2003). Meteorological droughts cannot be bridged through agricultural water management and instead require social coping strategies, such as cereal banks, relief food, local food storage, and livestock sales.

Even in regions with low variability in rainfall, not all of the rain reaches farmers' fields as soil moisture. In general, only 70%–80% of the rainfall is available to plants as soil moisture, and on poorly managed land the share of plant-available water can be as low as 40%–50% (Falkenmark and Rockström 2004). This leads to agricultural dry spells and droughts, which are due primarily to management-related problems with the on-farm water balance and are thus an indicator of large opportunities to improve yields through better water management.

Agarwal (2000) argues that India would not have to suffer from droughts if local water balances were better managed. Even during drought years better rainfall management has benefited Indian farmers; villages benefiting from watershed management projects increased food production and market value by 63% compared with those without such projects (Wani and others 2006b). In Malawi over the past three decades only a few of the years that

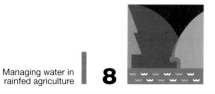

figure **8.4**

Range of rainfall variability across hydroclimatic zones from arid to humid agroecosystems

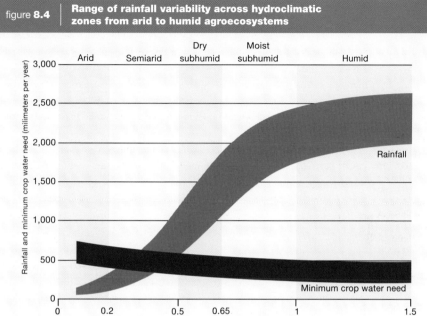

Note: The ecosystem gradient is shown as the aridity index (ratio of annual precipitation to annual potential evapotranspiration). The range in total rainfall is expressed as plus or minus one standard deviation.

Source: Minimum crop water need is estimated from Doorenbos and Pruitt (1992) and adjusted for aridity index.

table **8.2** | **Types of water stress and underlying causes in semiarid and dry subhumid tropical environments**

	Dry spell	Drought
Meteorological		
Frequency	Two out of three years	One out of ten years
Impact	Yield reduction	Complete crop failure
Cause	Rainfall deficit of two- to five-week periods during crop growth	Seasonal rainfall below minimum seasonal plant water requirement
Agricultural		
Frequency	More than two out of three years	One out of ten years
Impact	Yield reduction or complete crop failure	Complete crop failure
Cause	Low plant water availability and poor plant water uptake capacity	Poor rainfall partitioning, leading to seasonal soil moisture deficit for producing harvest (where poor partitioning refers to a high proportion of runoff and nonproductive evaporation relative to soil water infiltration at the surface)

Source: Falkenmark and Rockström 2004.

were politically proclaimed to be drought years actually suffered meteorological droughts (Mwale 2003). Glantz (1994) has pointed out that agricultural droughts, caused primarily by a poorly performing water balance, are more common than meteorological droughts.

Why is drought so commonly blamed when there are famines and food shortages? The answer is that even if there is no shortage of rain, crops may suffer from drought in the root zone. Often, land degradation and poor management of soil fertility and crops are the major causes of "droughts." These are referred to as agricultural droughts when available water as rainfall is not fully used for plant growth.

Evidence from water balance analyses on farmers' fields around the world shows that only a small fraction of rainfall (generally less than 30%) is used as productive green water flow (plant transpiration) supporting plant growth (Rockström 2003). In Sub-Saharan Africa this varies from 15% to 30% of rainfall, even in regions generally perceived as water scarce (figure 8.5). On severely degraded land or land where yields are lower than 1 metric ton per hectare, as little as 5% of rainfall may be used productively to produce food. In arid areas typically as little as 10% of rainfall is consumed as productive green water flow, with most of the remainder going to nonproductive evaporation flow (Oweis and Hachum 2001). For temperate arid regions, such as North Africa and West Asia, a larger portion of the rainfall is generally consumed in the farmers' fields as productive transpiration (45%–55%) as a result of higher yield levels (3–4 metric tons per hectare compared with 1–2 metric tons per hectare). Still, 25%–35% of the rainfall flows as nonproductive evaporation, with only some 15%–20% generating blue water flow (runoff).

> Evidence from water balance analyses on farmers' fields around the world shows that generally less than 30% of rainfall is used as plant transpiration supporting plant growth

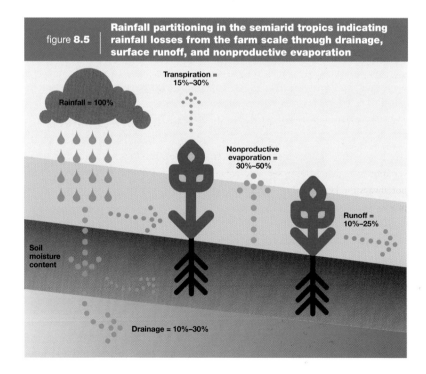

figure 8.5 | Rainfall partitioning in the semiarid tropics indicating rainfall losses from the farm scale through drainage, surface runoff, and nonproductive evaporation

Transpiration = 15%–30%

Rainfall = 100%

Nonproductive evaporation = 30%–50%

Runoff = 10%–25%

Soil moisture content

Drainage = 10%–30%

Many factors limit yields in rainfed agriculture. Often, soil fertility is the limiting factor (Stoorvogel and Smaling 1990). Soil degradation, through nutrient depletion and loss of organic matter, causes serious yield decline closely related to water determinants. It affects water availability for crops through poor rainfall infiltration and plant water uptake due to weak roots. Nutrient mining is a serious problem in smallholder rainfed agriculture, particularly in Sub-Saharan Africa. An estimated 85% of African farmland experienced a loss of more than 30 kilograms per hectare of nutrients annually in 2002–04 (Henao and Baanante 2006).

Investments in soil fertility directly improve water management. In India watershed management trials in more than 300 villages found that subsistence farming practices had depleted soils not only of macronutrients but also of such micronutrients as zinc and boron and secondary nutrients such as sulphur beyond critical limits. When both micronutrients and adequate nitrogen and phosphorus were applied, crop yields increased substantially for a number of rainfed crops (maize, sorghum, mung bean, pigeonpea, chickpea, castor, and groundnut) (Rego and others 2005). Rainwater productivity for maize, groundnut, greengram, castor, and sorghum increased 70%–100% as a result of the micronutrient amendment, and net economic returns were 1.5–1.75 times higher (Rego and others 2005). Similarly, rainwater productivity increased significantly when integrated land and water management options were adopted along with the use of improved cultivars in semi-arid regions of India (Wani and others 2003b).

What *can* be produced on farms *will* not always be produced, however, especially by resource-poor small-scale farmers. The farmers' reality is influenced by other constraints such as labor shortages, insecure land ownership, capital constraints, and limitations in human capacities. All these factors affect how farming is done, in terms of the timing of operations, the effectiveness of farm operations, investments in fertilizers and pesticides, use of improved crop varieties, and water management. What is produced in the field is thus strongly affected by social, economic, and institutional conditions.

Risks are high and will increase with climate change. Rainfall is concentrated in short rainy seasons (3–5 months), with a few intensive rainfall events that are unreliable in temporal distribution and with high deviations from the mean (coefficients of variation as high as 40% in semiarid regions; Wani and others 2004). Even if water is not always the key limiting yield factor, rainfall is the only truly random agricultural production factor.

The temporal and spatial variability of climate, especially rainfall, is a major constraint to yield improvements, competitiveness, and commercialization of rainfed crops, tree crops, and livestock systems in most of the tropics. The high risk for water-related yield loss makes farmers risk averse, influencing their other investment decisions, including labor, improved seed, and fertilizers *[established but incomplete]*. Smallholder farmers are usually aware of the effects of the shortage and variability of soil moisture on the variety, quantity, and quality of production, leading to a narrow range of options for commercialization. Combined with the fluctuations in yields, this makes it hard for resource-poor men and women in semiarid areas to respond effectively to opportunities made possible by

> The temporal and spatial variability of climate, especially rainfall, is a major constraint to yield improvements, competitiveness, and commercialization of rainfed crops, and evidence is emerging that climate change is increasing rainfall variability

emerging markets, trade, and globalization. Management options should therefore start by focusing on reducing rainfall-induced risks.

Evidence is emerging that climate change is increasing rainfall variability and the frequency of extreme events such as drought, floods, and hurricanes (IPCC 2001). In a recent study of rainfed cereal potential under different climate change scenarios and varying rainfall, losses of rainfed production potential in the most vulnerable developing countries was predicted under most scenarios. Losses were estimated at 10%–20% of production area, with some 1–3 billion people possibly affected in 2080 (Fischer, Shah, and van Velthuizen 2002). In particular, Sub-Saharan Africa is estimated to lose 12% of its cultivation potential, mostly in the Sudan-Sahelian zone, which is already subject to high climate variability and adverse crop conditions. Because of the risk associated with climate variability, smallholder farmers generally (and rationally) prefer to reduce the risk of crop failure due to dry spells and drought before investing in soil fertility, improved crop varieties, and other yield-enhancing inputs (Hilhost and Muchena 2000).

> Even with improvements in water productivity, investments in upgrading rainfed agriculture will require assessing tradeoffs with downstream users and ecosystems

Large new investments needed in water management in rainfed agriculture

The largest amount of new consumptive water use in crop production needed to attain the Millennium Development Goal for reducing hunger (more than 900 cubic kilometers a year; see chapter 3 on scenarios) will have to take place on current farmland through investments in upgrading rainfed agriculture or on land converted from natural ecosystems and grazing lands to agriculture. Land conversion would correspond to an expansion of rainfed agriculture of at least 70 million hectares, and possibly much more (see chapter 3).

Closing basins (when more water is being used than is environmentally desirable or renewably available) leave fewer degrees of freedom for blue water development and may redirect attention to green water flows upstream, before rainfall turns into blue runoff flow. Even with expansion of agricultural land, development of irrigated agriculture, and significant improvements in green water productivity, rainfed agriculture will have to shoulder the largest burden of providing food in developing countries, and large water investments are required for success. This calls for increased efforts to upgrade rainfed systems.

At the same time, even with improvements in water productivity, investments in upgrading rainfed agriculture, including technologies such as small-scale supplemental irrigation and conservation agriculture (as described later), will result in the capture of local blue water resources and an increased consumption of green water. Thus, tradeoffs with downstream users and ecosystems will have to be assessed.

The challenges of broadening the reach of investments and policies

Past investments in agricultural research in savannah agroecosystems have been disappointing (Seckler and Amarasinghe 2004). One reason is the lack of focus on water resources management in rainfed agriculture. Instead, the focus over the past 50 years at the farm level has been mainly on crop research, soil conservation, and to a lesser extent in-situ water conservation (maximizing rainfall infiltration) through various strategies of terracing, bunding, and ridging.

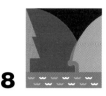

Failure of innovation to achieve widespread adoption. Upgrading rainfed agriculture requires that technologies be adapted to local biophysical and sociocultural conditions and that institutional and behavioral transformations accompany the technological changes (Harris, Cooper, and Pala 1991; van Duivenbooden and others 2000). As researchers have noted, it is difficult to assess the impact of natural resources management interventions using the econometric methods applied for assessing the impact of commodity-based interventions (Shiferaw, Freeman, and Swinton 2004).

Social and ecological crises often spur the adoption of new ways of thinking and of system transformation *[established]*. The adoption of conservation agriculture in several parts of the world was driven by crises—in the United States as a response to the Dust Bowl in the 1930s, in parts of Latin America as a response to an agrarian yield crisis, and in Zambia as a response to droughts. Recent widespread adoption of soil and water management practices in Burkina Faso and Niger forms part of a response to crisis-related land degradation and possible climate change *[established but incomplete]*.

There are many challenges to investments in rainfed agriculture. Large numbers of households are small, with marginal farmers. Most rainfed areas have poor infrastructure facilities because large investments have historically tended to go to high-potential irrigated areas. Local institutions engaged in agricultural development and extension have limited capacity to promote rainwater management. This knowledge-intensive extension effort suffers from limited information of the options available, social and economic constraints to adoption, lack of enabling environments and backup services, poor market linkages, and weak infrastructure.

Focus on blue water has led to weak policies for water investments in rainfed agriculture. One result of the historic focus on blue water in agricultural policy is a legacy of weak water governance and policies for rainfed agricultural development. Water resources management is normally governed under ministries for water affairs and focuses on developing and allocating water for large-scale irrigation, drinking water, and hydropower. This has resulted in a downstream focus, with upper catchment areas, where rainfed agriculture is generally practiced, being seen primarily as runoff or blue water–generating zones. Ministries of agriculture have focused on the "dry" parts of agricultural development and tended to give priority to erosion control over water management in general (box 8.2). Thus, although proven knowledge for better management of rainwater exists, investments for turning this knowledge into innovations in governance, policy, institutions, practices, and technologies to support smallholder farmers have been very limited.

Recently, management of green water resources and other investments to upgrade rainfed agriculture have begun to receive increased priority from state and central governments (see box 8.2). Important efforts have been made under watershed development programs in India, for example. Originally, these programs were implemented by different ministries (Agriculture, Rural Development, Forestry) making integrated water management difficult. Recently, steps were taken to unify the program (Wani and others 2006b). In 2005 the National Commission on Farmers adopted an integrated watershed management approach, with a focus on harvesting rainwater and improving soil health for sustainable development of drought-prone rainfed areas (India 2005).

> Water management for rainfed agriculture requires a landscape perspective and involves cross-scale interactions from farm households to watersheds

In Kenya, Tanzania, and Uganda national food security is achieved largely by smallholder farmers in rainfed agricultural-livestock systems. Population growth rates are high, and land for agricultural expansion is no longer abundant. Traditionally, national water management has been the responsibility of different ministries—agriculture, water, environment, tourism, and energy—with adverse impacts on local strategies to improve water management for cultivation and food production. A review by the Comprehensive Assessment of water and food policy-related documents in Kenya, Tanzania, and Uganda found that there was no clear policy on rainwater harvesting for agricultural production to improve food security among the rural poor.

Tanzania implemented a major soil and water conservation program in the semiarid central part of the country in 1973–95. An evaluation in 1995 noted several weaknesses of the program, including these (Hatibu and others 1999):

- The program was oriented toward the land rather than the people in the project area.
- The work on croplands focused on water runoff disposal and addressed rainwater productivity only in marginal ways.
- Key extension messages were quite conventional (improved seed, row planting), and soil-water conservation did not figure prominently among the messages.
- There should have been more emphasis on rainwater management than on erosion control considering that shortage of soil moisture was the bigger problem for crop yields in the dry land of central Tanzania.
- On-farm soil and water conservation measures promoted by the project have done very little to increase land productivity.
- The strategy needs to shift from a narrow focus on erosion control to a broader, holistic land husbandry approach.

The 2002 National Water Policy in Tanzania sets a goal of making more water available to rural communities through rainwater harvesting technologies (Tanzania Ministry of Agriculture and Food Security 2002). The Agricultural Sector Development Strategy recognizes integrated soil-water management as the solution to the drought problems of semiarid areas (Tanzania Ministry of Agriculture and Food Security 2001). This comprehensive program includes integrated soil and water conservation, rainwater harvesting and storage, irrigation, and drainage. As a result, rainwater harvesting forms an important part of the national irrigation master plan adopted in 2003 (Tanzania Ministry of Agriculture and Food Security 2003).

There is thus growing evidence of the importance of water investments in rainfed agriculture and of the gradual redirection of water governance and management toward upgrading rainfed agriculture as a key strategy for reducing poverty and increasing agricultural production. It is further becoming increasingly clear that water management for rainfed agriculture requires a landscape perspective and involves cross-scale interactions from farm households to watersheds.

Investing in rainfed agriculture to improve livelihoods and environmental sustainability

Although proven knowledge for better management of rainwater exists, investments in turning this knowledge into innovations in governance, policy, institutions, practices, and technologies to support smallholder farmers have been limited. Opportunities within rainfed systems include increasing the productivity of green water depleted in rainfed systems and increasing yields in rainfed systems by capturing more soil moisture for plant water uptake. Taking advantage of both opportunities requires large investments in rainfed agriculture. While the focus here is on management options at the farm level to upgrade rainfed agriculture, the required policy, governance, and market strategies have to operate at a higher scale, from the watershed to national and regional levels.

Investing in water management in rainfed agriculture

There are several rainwater management strategies to improve crop yields and green water productivity (table 8.3; Critchley and Siegert 1991). One set of strategies aims at maximizing plant water availability in the root zone (maximizing the green water resource) through practices that reduce surface runoff (blue water flow) and that redirect upstream runoff to the farm (local storage of blue water for supplemental irrigation). A second set aims at maximizing plant water uptake capacity, which involves crop and soil management practices that increase root water uptake (and thus minimize drainage to the water table). There is a wide spectrum of integrated land and water management options to achieve these aims. Some focus on increasing water productivity, such as mulch practices, drip irrigation techniques, and crop management to enhance canopy cover, while most aim at improving crop production by capturing more water (water productivity increases

table **8.3**	**Rainwater management strategies and corresponding management options to improve yields and water productivity**		
Aim	**Rainwater management strategy**	**Purpose**	**Management options**
Increase plant water availability	External water harvesting systems	Mitigate dry spells, protect springs, recharge groundwater, enable off-season irrigation, permit multiple uses of water	Surface microdams, subsurface tanks, farm ponds, percolation dams and tanks, diversion and recharging structures
	In-situ water-harvesting systems, soil and water conservation	Concentrate rainfall through runoff to cropped area or other use	Bunds, ridges, broad-beds and furrows, microbasins, runoff strips
		Maximize rainfall infiltration	Terracing, contour cultivation, conservation agriculture, dead furrows, staggered trenches
	Evaporation management	Reduce nonproductive evaporation	Dry planting, mulching, conservation agriculture, intercropping, windbreaks, agroforestry, early plant vigor, vegetative bunds
Increase plant water uptake capacity	Integrated soil, crop and water management	Increase proportion of water balance flowing as productive transpiration	Conservation agriculture, dry planting (early), improved crop varieties, optimum crop geometry, soil fertility management, optimum crop rotation, intercropping, pest control, organic matter management

Source: Authors' compilation.

simultaneously because the on-farm water balance is used more effectively) as crop production increases.

The focus of the water management strategies discussed here is on water harvesting, because most of the new, innovative investment options are in this area. There is a particular emphasis therefore on external water-harvesting systems. Moreover, the description of in-situ water-harvesting techniques is limited to what has been assessed as a particularly promising avenue, namely conservation agriculture systems. A comprehensive assessment of in-situ soil and water-conservation methods is given in Liniger and Critchley (forthcoming).

' Capturing local runoff upstream in water-harvesting systems addresses problems of frequent drought and prevailing poverty in upper watersheds

Reinventing small-scale water harvesting. Rainwater harvesting (concentrating runoff from watersheds for beneficial use) was practiced in the Negev Desert as early as the 10th century (Evanari, Shanan, and Tadmor 1971). Encompassing any practice that collects runoff for productive purposes (Siegert 1994), rainwater harvesting includes three components: a watershed area to produce runoff, a storage facility (soil profile, surface reservoirs, or groundwater aquifers), and a target area for beneficial use of the water (agriculture, domestic, or industry). The classification varies depending on the spatial scale of runoff collection, from in-situ practices managing rain on farmland (often defined as water conservation) to external systems collecting runoff from watersheds outside the cultivated area (Oweis, Prinz, and Hachum 2001). Rainwater harvesting practices are further defined by storage strategies, from direct runoff concentration in the soil (photo 8.1) to collection and storage of water in structures (surface, subsurface tanks, and small dams; Fox and Rockström 2000).

In India water development policies aimed at large-scale water infrastructure and motorized pumping of surface and groundwater for agriculture resulted in the abandoning of a widespread historic water-harvesting legacy (Agarwal and Narain 1997) *[established*

Photo 8.1 Small-scale rainwater harvesting can bridge intraseasonal dry spells and stabilize food supplies in periods of poor rainfall

Photo by Lisa Schipper

but incomplete]. The situation is now changing. Watershed programs are being recognized as a potential engine for agricultural growth and development in fragile and marginal rainfed areas. Several factors explain the shift. Blue water investments are located mainly downstream in watersheds and basins, because they depend on the concentration of large volumes of stable runoff (in lakes and rivers). Large-scale irrigation therefore benefits predominantly downstream communities, while water harvesting offers an appropriate water management complement for agriculture for wide spatial coverage across watersheds and basins. Capturing local runoff upstream in water-harvesting systems addresses problems of frequent drought and prevailing poverty in upper watersheds.

Increasing and stabilizing yields through drought proofing and dry spell mitigation.
Supplemental irrigation systems are external rainwater-harvesting systems that collect runoff from watershed areas external to the cultivated land and add it to the rainfed cropland. These systems, developed in different parts of the world, collect runoff at different watershed scales and use various methods to store it. Supplemental irrigation is a key strategy, still underused, for unlocking rainfed yield potential and water productivity (box 8.3).

Since rainfall is the principal source of water for rainfed crops, supplemental irrigation is applied only when rainfall fails to provide essential moisture for improved and stable production (photo 8.2). The amount and timing of supplemental irrigation, particularly in water-scarce areas, are not scheduled to provide moisture-stress-free conditions throughout the growing season but to ensure a minimum amount of water during critical stages of crop growth to permit optimal (in water use or in economic terms) rather than maximum yield (as limited by external conditions that cannot be influenced by management). Supplemental irrigation systems can provide multiple irrigation opportunities during the course of a rainy season (microdams can be filled and emptied several times) and can be used for full-scale off-season irrigation of small gardens for market crops such as vegetables (box 8.4).

The critical importance of supplemental irrigation lies in its capacity to bridge dry spells and thereby reduce risks in rainfed agriculture. In many farming systems supplemental irrigation provides the only strategy for dry spell mitigation in rainfed agriculture. In-situ management of rainwater, for example, through water conservation methods to increase rainfall infiltration, cannot provide plants with adequate water through dry spells long enough to cause water stress. Evidence indicates that supplemental irrigation of 50–200 mm (500–2,000 cubic meters per hectare) a season is sufficient to bridge critical yield-reducing dry spells and stabilize yield levels (Oweis 1997). Such small amounts can be collected using water in local springs, shallow groundwater, or conventional water resource schemes during the rainy season. By reducing risk, supplemental irrigation may provide the necessary incentive for investments in other production factors such as crop varieties, fertilizer, labor, and tillage techniques and for diversification (staple food crops and cash crops).

Several studies have shown that supplemental irrigation systems are affordable and appropriate for single household or small community investments. A cost-benefit study on supplemental irrigation of maize-tomato cropping systems in Burkina Faso and Kenya found net profits of $73 and $390 per hectare annually, compared with net income losses

> Supplemental
> irrigation is a
> key strategy,
> still underused,
> for unlocking
> rainfed yield
> potential
> and water
> productivity

Photo 8.2 Supplemental
irrigation supports normal
yields among crops ruined by
insufficient rainfall

Photo by Jennie Barron

| box **8.3** | **Supplemental irrigation increases yields and water productivity in rainfed systems** |

When rainfall is scarce, supplemental irrigation can increase yields significantly compared with completely rainfed systems (figure 1), and in arid regions this increase can be substantial. In water-scarce regions deficit irrigation (only partly meeting plant water demand when adding water) may also be practiced. Experiments in arid regions show that water productivity is higher using deficit supplemental irrigation than with full supplemental irrigation (figure 2). However, yield improvements are greater with full supplemental irrigation. Thus, there is a tradeoff between maximizing yield and maximizing water productivity.

Figure 1 Yield increase with supplemental irrigation at different rainfall amounts

Figure 2 Relationship between yield increase with supplemental irrigation and water productivity

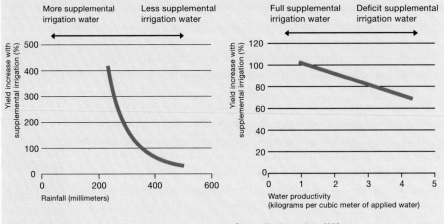

Source: Oweis 1997.

Source: Ilbeyi and others 2006.

The implications of dry spell occurrence in smallholder farming systems were investigated using a crop-soil water simulation model (APSIM) in semiarid Kenya and Tanzania. In more than half of crop seasons the conventional maize system resulted in poor yields (less than 200 kilograms per hectare). Improved water management alone, using supplemental irrigation for dry spell mitigation, was not enough to improve farmers' yields. When supplemental irrigation was combined with fertilizer (60 kilograms of nitrogen per hectare), however, yields doubled (from 0.4 to 0.9 metric tons per hectare per season), and water productivity was also significantly improved. The number of seasons with crop failure decreased by 25%, with potentially strong impacts on household food security among the smallholder farming systems prevalent in tropical savannah agroecosystems (Barron forthcoming).

of $165 and $221 in traditional systems (Fox, Rockström, and Barron 2005). Moreover, the study found a strong mutual dependence between investments in supplemental irrigation and fertilizers. Studies of supplemental irrigation of maize and cabbage using farm ponds in Kenya (Ngigi and others 2005a, b) and a rice-mustard cropping system in India (Panigrahi, Panda, and Agrawal 2005) also concluded that supplemental irrigation was an economically viable option for improving livelihoods of smallholder farmers. In general,

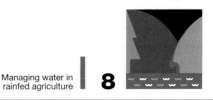

In Rajasthan, India, an arid region receiving 200–300 mm of rainfall, farmers commonly harvest runoff from large field areas upstream. The runoff is concentrated into smaller areas at lower elevations for use in growing crops. In most of South India tanks are traditionally used to harvest and store runoff water. The stored water is used communally for supplemental irrigation during dry spells or for growing a post–rainy season crop.

A promising technology that has been widely adapted in India is the percolation tank, a small reservoir that captures runoff and holds the water for percolation into shallow water tables. The water is subsequently pumped onto the fields when needed. Groundwater storage avoids the high evaporation losses of surface storage and provides a low-cost water distribution system to farms. However, since groundwater is a limited and shared resource, there is a risk for unequal distribution among farmers unless water withdrawal is regulated.

Source: Sreedevi and others 2006; Wani and others 2006b.

investments in rainfed agriculture exhibit higher marginal returns from additional investments in technology and infrastructure compared with investments in irrigated agriculture (Fan, Hazell, and Haque 2000).

Although supplemental irrigation has great potential, realizing maximum benefits depends on its proper application as one element in a package that includes other farm inputs and management practices. Consequently, farmers need to be involved in the development and testing of the technology within the local community and possibly also at the water basin level. Water-harvesting systems have been widely adopted by commercial farmers. Examples include farm ponds in the upper Murray Darling Basin in Australia and on vineyards (for supplemental irrigation of grape production) and livestock farms (for drinking) in the relatively water-scarce Western Cape region in South Africa (van Dijk and others 2006). In India smallholder farmers in several semiarid regions have adopted water harvesting on a large scale.

Using the local field-water balance more effectively. Most water management investments in rainfed agriculture over the past 50 years have focused on improving management of the rain that falls on farmers' fields. Soil and water conservation or in-situ water-harvesting systems (see table 8.3) form the logical entry point for improved water management in rainfed agriculture.

Since in-situ rainwater management strategies are often relatively cheap and can be applied on any piece of land, they should be optimized before water from external sources is considered. Investing first in management of the local field-water balance increases the likelihood of success with supplemental irrigation systems based on rainwater harvesting, river-flow diversion, and groundwater sources *[established but incomplete]*. Studies of the drivers of collective action in successful watersheds found tangible economic benefits to farmers through in-situ rainwater conservation (Wani and others 2003b; Sreedevi, Shiferaw, and Wani 2004).

Conservation agriculture is one of the most important strategies for enhancing soil productivity and moisture conservation *[well established]*. Noninversion systems, which replace conventional plowing with ripping, subsoiling, and no-till systems using direct planting techniques, combined with mulch management, build organic matter and improve soil structure. Conservation agriculture is practiced in approximately 40% of rainfed agriculture in the United States and has generated an agricultural revolution in several countries in Latin America (Derpsch 1998, 2005; Landers and others 2001). There has been wide adoption of conservation agriculture systems among small-scale rainfed and irrigated farmers cultivating rice and wheat on the Indo-Gangetic plains in Asia (Hobbs and Gupta 2002).

Conservation agriculture is of key importance for upgrading rainfed agriculture among the world's resource-poor farmers. It reduces traction requirements (by tractors or draft animals), which saves money and is strategic from a gender perspective, as it generally gives women, particularly in female-headed households, a chance to carry out timely and effective tillage. Conservation agriculture can be practiced on all agricultural land, since it does not suffer from limitations related to the need for watershed areas and storage capacity for water harvesting. A particularly important soil and water management strategy in hot tropical regions subject to water constraints, conservation agriculture avoids the rapid oxidation of organic matter and increased soil erosion that occur with soil inversion (using plows) in hot tropical environments *[established but incomplete]*. Some drawbacks of the method are the high initial costs of specialized planting equipment and the need for new management skills. Another challenge is to find strategies to control weeds, particularly for poor farm households for which herbicides are not an option. However, while the use of pesticides might be necessary during the first years, the level normally falls below that of the original farming system after several years.

Converting from plowing to conservation agriculture using subsoiling and ripping has resulted in major improvements in yield and water productivity in parts of semiarid to dry subhumid East Africa, with a doubling of yields in good years due to increased capture of rainwater (box 8.5). Further increases in grain yield have been achieved by applying manure. These interventions can be implemented on all agricultural land. Evidence from East Africa and Southern Africa shows that conservation agriculture can reduce labor needs and improve yields in smallholder rainfed agriculture (box 8.5) *[established but incomplete]*. Yield improvements range from 20% to 120%, with rainwater productivity improving 10%–40%.

In-situ water-harvesting options also include techniques to concentrate runoff to plants, such as terracing, bunds, ridges, and microbasins. The productivity of rain in arid environments can be substantially increased with water-harvesting techniques that concentrate runoff to plants and trees (photo 8.3). Small basins *(negarim)* have supported almond trees for more than 17 years in the Muwaqqar area of Jordan, where the mean annual rainfall is 125 mm, even during several years of drought (Oweis and Taimeh 1996). In the Mehasseh area of the Syrian steppe, with an average annual rainfall of 120 mm, the survival rate of rainfed shrubs rose from less than 10% to more than 90% when the shrubs were grown in microcatchments. In northwest Egypt, with an average annual rainfall of

> Soil and water conservation or in-situ water-harvesting systems form the logical entry point for improved water management in rainfed agriculture

Photo 8.3 Supplemental irrigation: furrow irrigation and gravitational water supply

Photo by Jennie Barron

box **8.5**

Water and soil productivity improvement through conservation agriculture in East Africa

Trials with farmers on innovative conservation agriculture in semiarid to dry subhumid areas in Ethiopia, Kenya, Tanzania, and Zambia during 1999–2003 indicate large potential to substantially improve yields and rainwater productivity of staple food crops (Rockström and others forthcoming). Limited fertilizer (manure and chemical fertilizer) was applied along permanently ripped planting lines. Yields increased significantly in all countries (see figure). The conservation agriculture systems maximized rainfall infiltration into the soil and cut the need for draft animal traction by at least half.

Maize yield improvements from conservation agriculture in on-farm trials

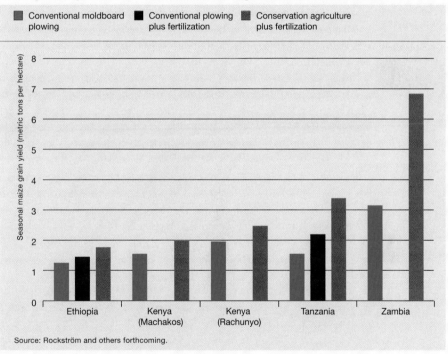

Source: Rockström and others forthcoming.

130 mm, small water-harvesting basins with 200 square meter watersheds support olive trees, and rainwater harvested from greenhouse roofs can provide about half the water required by vegetables grown inside the greenhouse (Somme and others 2004).

Shifting nonproductive evaporation to productive transpiration. In semiarid areas up to half the rainwater falling on agricultural land is lost as nonproductive evaporation. This is a key window for improving green water productivity through shifting nonproductive evaporation to productive transpiration, with no downstream blue water tradeoff, through management of soil physical conditions, soil fertility, crop varieties, and agronomy. This vapor shift (or transfer) of the evaporative loss into useful transpiration by plants is a particular opportunity in arid, semiarid, and dry subhumid regions.

Field measurements of rainfed grain yields and green water flows (evapotranspiration) indicate that when yields double from 1 to 2 metric tons per hectare in semiarid tropical agroecosystems, green water productivity may improve from approximately 3,500 cubic meters per metric ton to less than 2,000 cubic meters per metric ton (figure 8.6; Rockström 2003; Oweis, Pala, and Ryan 1998), a result of the dynamic nature of water productivity improvements when moving from very low yields to higher yields. At low yields evaporative losses of water from the soil are high because the sparse canopy coverage of the soil. When yield levels increase, soil shading improves (thanks to larger canopies), and when yields reach 4–5 metric tons per hectare and greater, the canopy density is so high that the opportunity to reduce evaporation in favor of increased transpiration declines, lowering the relative improvement of water productivity. This indicates that large opportunities for improving water productivity are found in low-yielding farming systems, particularly in rainfed agriculture (water productivity is already higher in irrigated agriculture because of better yields).

In arid areas evidence shows that adoption of in-situ (microcatchment) water harvesting for rainfall infiltration can raise productive transpiration from 10%–30% to 60%, a

> In semiarid areas up to half the rainwater falling on agricultural land is lost as nonproductive evaporation

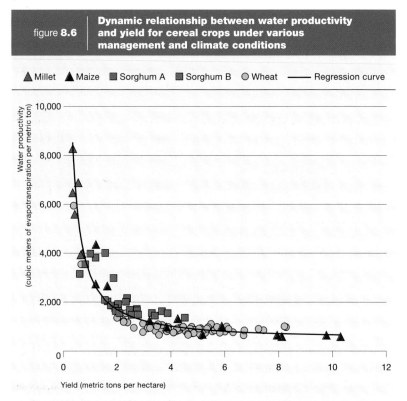

figure **8.6**   **Dynamic relationship between water productivity and yield for cereal crops under various management and climate conditions**

△ Millet   ▲ Maize   ▣ Sorghum A   ■ Sorghum B   ○ Wheat   —— Regression curve

Source: Millet, Rockström, Jansson, and Barron 1998; maize, Stewart 1988; sorghum A, Dancette 1983; sorghum B, Pandey, Maranville, and Admou 2000; durum wheat, Zhang and Oweis 1999; regression line after Rockström 2003.

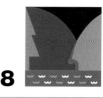

substantial change. Moreover, with supplemental irrigation for dry spell mitigation nonproductive evaporation can be reduced to 50% of total green water flow.

Crop breeding is important for improving the response to water availability. Using both Mendelian breeding techniques and modern genetic engineering, new crop varieties can be developed that can increase water productivity while maintaining or even increasing yield.

In sum, there seems to be ample room for improvements in water productivity through management. Reducing nonproductive water losses can make more water available in the root zone without sacrificing blue water formation. Moreover, increasing yield results in a simultaneous increase in water productivity, although in this case more blue water is diverted to evapotranspiration.

Evidence shows
not only large
opportunities to
upgrade rainfed
agriculture, but
also substantial
payoffs for
society

Applying a holistic approach to agroecosystems

Investments in rainfed and irrigated agriculture are important for meeting not only the Millennium Development Goal on reducing hunger but also the goals on reducing poverty and ensuring environmental sustainability. Increased yields in agriculture have raised consumptive water use dramatically (from approximately 1,000 cubic kilometers a year in 1960 to 4,500 cubic kilometers a year today) and have resulted in large expansions of agricultural area in developing countries (from some 26–32 million square kilometers to 56 million square kilometers over the past 45 years; FAOSTAT 2005). As the Millennium Ecosystem Assessment notes, changes in land use due to expansion of agriculture were the main reason behind the degradation of 65% of ecosystem services over the past 50 years (MEA 2005). Thus, investments in upgrading rainfed agriculture need to take a holistic approach to agroecosystems.

Investments in rainfed agriculture promise substantial payoffs. Evidence shows not only large opportunities to upgrade rainfed agriculture, but also substantial payoffs for society. An exhaustive review of 311 case studies on watershed programs in India focusing on rainwater management found that the mean cost-benefit ratio of watershed programs was relatively high, at 1:2.14 (Joshi and others 2005). The watershed programs generated large employment opportunities, augmented irrigated area and cropping intensity, and conserved soil and water resources.

Returns to labor and profitability at the farm household scale are key drivers behind decisions to invest in rainfed agriculture, especially in water management. An evaluation of farming practices in water harvesting in Tanzania found that upgrading rainwater management is a critical factor in increasing returns to labor and thus for poverty reduction (Hatibu and others 2006). Similarly, case studies in Asia have amply demonstrated that investments in managing rainwater and enhancing its use efficiency increased profitability for the farmers (Wani and others 2006b). In the Adarsha watershed, Kothapally, India, returns to family labor and land (net income) from rainfed cereals and pulses almost doubled in large part because of a watershed development approach based on integrated genetic and natural resources management (Wani and others 2006b). Per capita income was 1,900 rupees ($43) in villages without investments in upgrading rainfed farming and 3,400 rupees ($77) in the Adarsha watershed. These examples show clearly that continued failure to bridge the gap between potential yields, returns to labor, and profitability and those achieved on farmers' fields in rainfed farming is a major factor explaining the perpetuation of poverty.

Water management is a key investment for diversification of agricultural income. Off-farm employment in rural areas usually expands in parallel with agricultural growth *[established but incomplete]*. Each 1% growth in agricultural yields brings about an estimated 0.5%–0.7% reduction in number of poor people (World Bank 2005). Thus rural employment, both on and off the farm, is strongly conditioned by the rate of agricultural growth.

Investments in water management in rainfed systems can have important additional benefits that arise from the multiple roles of water for livelihoods and health

A recent study in the developed Rajasamadhiyala watershed in Gujarat, India, revealed that public investments in rainwater harvesting enabled farmers to invest in wells, pump sets, sprinkler sets, and drip irrigation systems in addition to fertilizers and improved pest and disease management (Wani and others 2006a; Sreedevi and others 2006). Development in integrated watersheds triggered a shift toward commercial cereal crop production, such as maize, whereas in the surrounding villages without watershed development farmers continued to grow low-value cereals like sorghum. In addition, farmers in the developed watershed village in Andhra Pradesh put more area under vegetables and horticultural crops than did farmers in the surrounding villages, contributing to income stability and resilience (figure 8.7; Wani and others 2006b). A prerequisite for such diversification is access to markets. In India the output from rainfed agriculture, including that from high yielding varieties, has increased rapidly in many areas and at the same pace as in irrigated areas (Kerr 1996).

In many parts of Tanzania rainwater harvesting has enabled farmers in semiarid areas to upgrade rainfed farming by growing a marketable crop, thus helping to reduce poverty. Farmers upgraded from sorghum and millet to rice or maize with follow-up legume crops that exploit residual moisture in the field. Currently, production of rice in semiarid areas using rainwater harvesting accounts for more than 35% of the rice produced in the country (Gowing and others 1999; Meertens, Ndgege, and Lupeja 1999).

Farm-scale water management improvements yield multiple benefits. Investments in water management in rainfed systems can have important additional benefits that arise from the multiple roles of water for livelihoods and health. In supporting all forms of biomass growth for cultivated crops—pasture for livestock, noncultivated food plants, and fuel and construction wood—rainwater influences the resilience of rural communities practicing rainfed agriculture. Rural livelihoods also depend on nonagricultural incomes (remittances, seasonal off-farm work, rural complementary sources of income) that reduce vulnerability to variations in rainfall.

A study in East Africa shows that strategies for reducing poverty to meet the Millennium Development Goals require investments that promote productivity growth in three areas (ASARECA and IFPRI 2005). Major staples were found to be the key for overall economic growth and poverty reduction. Rainfed systems dominate the production of staples, underscoring the importance of investing in the upgrading of rainfed systems. The livestock sector, which consists predominantly of rainfed systems, is a key livelihood source for people in South Asia. And many nonfarm rural enterprises are linked to value-adding processing of crop and livestock products.

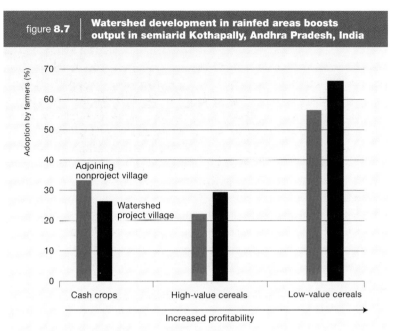

| figure **8.7** | **Watershed development in rainfed areas boosts output in semiarid Kothapally, Andhra Pradesh, India** |

Source: Wani and others 2006b.

There are also other options for generating more benefits from systems such as forests and rangelands, which deplete rainwater naturally. They include investments to add further value to rain, such as the development of microenterprises associated with natural resources such as vermicomposting, plant nurseries, biodiesel plantations, oil extraction, and processing of farm produce. These help to ensure diversified livelihood options for women and youth and increase resilience during drought years (Wani and others 2003a; Joshi and others 2005; Wani and others 2006b).

Intensified rainfed agriculture requires balancing water for food and for ecosystems. Every increase in water used in agriculture will affect water availability for other uses, both for direct human use (water supply) and for ecosystem use (terrestrial and aquatic ecosystems). In overcommitted watersheds upgrading rainfed agriculture through investments in water-harvesting systems may result in severe water tradeoffs with downstream users and ecosystems (Calder 1999), although other evidence points to limited or no downstream impacts on stream flow even from broad implementation of small-scale water storage systems (Evanari, Shanan, and Tadmor 1971; Schreider and others 2002; Sreedevi and others 2006) *[competing explanations]*. Investing in water management in rainfed agriculture can have positive environmental impacts on other ecosystems as a result of reduced land degradation and improvements in water quality downstream.

Basinwide gains are possible from investments in upstream water harvesting in rainfed agricultural systems. Improvements in water productivity, which are expected to be particularly large in rainfed agricultural areas where yields often are low (see figure 8.6), partially offset the reduction of water availability downstream that would have resulted without any improvements in water productivity. Thus, although blue water availability downstream will likely decrease, the total amount of green water consumed per unit of crop yield is lower from a basin perspective. Moreover, capturing water close to the source (where the raindrop hits the ground), as is common in water-harvesting systems, reduces evaporative losses of blue water during its journey from field to watershed to river basin. Energy savings is another important advantage in investing in storage of water as close as possible to the source. Storage investments as far upstream as possible in a watershed permit using gravitational energy, whereas storage downstream may require new energy to lift water back to the farm land. However, more research is needed to assess the downstream water effects of upgrading rainfed agriculture.

The evidence on rainfed agriculture conveys two key messages: rainfed agriculture will play a major role in global food security and sustainable economic growth, and there are large opportunities for gains from new investments in water management

The dramatic increase in land degradation over the past half century as a result of deforestation and poor land use, often in upstream locations in river basins, has upset hydrological performance (chapter 15 on land; Vörösmarty, Lévêque, and Revenga 2005). The reduced water-holding capacity of upper watersheds and disrupted partitioning of rainfall between green and blue water flows (lower green flows and higher blue storm flows) have affected both upstream rural communities (more recurrent water stress) and downstream communities (faster runoff because of lower base flow and higher surface flow; siltation of dams; Bewket and Sterk 2005). Investments in upgrading rainfed agriculture in upper watersheds, by slowing the release of water and thus taming the erosive flows of blue water, can reduce land degradation. Furthermore, good management of water in rainfed agriculture will increase slow subsurface water flows in the landscape. This improves the release of freshwater downstream over time and reduces land degradation from water-induced soil erosion.

Investments in improved water and land management upstream yield economic payoffs for communities downstream *[established but incomplete]*. Most documented experiences have so far considered afforestation in the upstream watershed (Perrot-Maître and Davis 2001; Landell-Mills and Porras 2002), but examples are emerging in different parts of the world of downstream communities compensating upstream communities for the economic gains of environmental services received downstream as a result of water management investments upstream (FAO 2004a).

New investment opportunities and policy options

The evidence on rainfed agriculture presented in this chapter conveys two key messages: rainfed agriculture will play a major role in global food security and sustainable economic growth, and there are large opportunities for gains from new investments in water management. Furthermore, the knowledge exists to substantially increase long-term yields in rainfed agriculture in regions subject to recurrent water-related productivity challenges. But there is a gap in the uptake and use of this knowledge among all stakeholders, from policymakers to small-scale farmers. A number of constraints interfere, including technical, socioeconomic, and policy factors, but inadequate investment in knowledge sharing and scaling-up of best practices is the major impediment.

A new approach to agricultural water policy is needed that views rainfall as the freshwater resource and that considers both green and blue water for livelihood options at the appropriate scale for local communities. Unlocking the potential in rainfed agriculture requires large new investments in human capacity, supporting research, and institutional development as well as specific technologies. A new set of extension services are needed, with staff trained to support farmers in water management investments at the smaller rainfed farming scale (water management skills are now embedded in water resource development for large-scale irrigation). The knowledge-intensive nature of this undertaking means that successful dissemination will require large investments.

A policy focus on rainwater management, not just runoff management

Rainfed agriculture has suffered from insufficient policy and institutional support for improving water management for production. Investments have focused on remediating the negative effects of water upstream (erosion control and water conservation) to reduce the downstream impact. In recent decades, however, the focus has shifted from water management for conservation to water management for production upstream, changing the perception from water as a foe, to be disposed of through erosion control measures, to water as a friend, to be supplied for productive purposes at the local scale.

A green and blue water paradigm for strategic investments. Today, the focus of water policy is primarily at the river basin or large watershed scale, while agricultural policy often targets the individual farm, but not in terms of water investments. A new water policy paradigm needs to focus more explicitly at the smaller watershed scale, which often corresponds to the community, small township, or village (tens to thousands of hectares). This scale corresponds to the relevant water resource management scale of rainfed farmers, where a new green revolution will have to occur over the next decades in order to achieve the Millennium Development Goal of reducing poverty and hunger by half and ensuring environmental sustainability.

Introducing a water policy focus on green water resources widens the scope to include water planning in upper watersheds and land use impacts on blue water availability downstream. Conventionally, in policy, management, and legal terms, only liquid, blue water in rivers, groundwater, lakes, wetlands, and estuaries is included in water resources management. Water investments in rainfed agriculture involve management of water that is not considered to be water. The green water resource needs to be placed centrally in water resource investments. This requires a shift in water policy focus from permanent blue water flow in rivers, lakes, and groundwater to rainfall and intermittent and local surface runoff flow in rills and gullies, local shallow water tables, and temporary impoundments of surface water. Rainfall needs to be viewed as an economic water resource, rather than only the blue water component.

Such a shift in policy perspective took place recently in India, in recognition of the importance of rainfed agriculture for development and its contribution to the overall economic growth of the country. The government established an independent National

> Water investments in rainfed agriculture involve management of water that is not considered to be water: rainfall also needs to be viewed as an economic water resource

Authority for Development of Rainfed Agriculture in 2005. This shift has also reached the state level. The government of Tamil Nadu, for example, established a Mission on Rainfed Agriculture in 2005.

A new meso-scale for water management. Water resources management focuses mainly on the larger watershed or river basin scale, while agricultural interventions for rainfed agriculture remain focused at the farm or field level. To capitalize on the untapped potential of rainfed agriculture for small-scale farmers, water management investments are required at the small watershed scale—the tributary scale in river basins—where runoff often flows only during short periods after rainfall events.

' A new water policy framework for integrated water resources management is required for planning and allocating rainwater at the watershed scale

A new water policy framework for integrated water resources management is required for planning and allocating rainwater at the watershed scale. Moving toward the gray area between rainfed and irrigated agriculture at the watershed scale requires new skills and data on water availability and use at the meso-scale. Essential data on important processes, especially runoff, are needed to properly design and implement landscape or community-level approaches to water harvesting and delivery systems for integrated water management. New approaches to legal ownership of rainwater at the watershed levels will also have to be developed. Water policies and regulations are designed for allocating irrigation water from large rivers, groundwater, and dams and not for collecting rainfall at the meso-watershed scale in small microdams, farm ponds, and percolation tanks. To succeed a new water paradigm in agriculture is required, which promotes water investments at the appropriate scale for particularly small-scale farmers in tropical and subtropical developing countries.

New efforts to promote innovation and adaptive adoption

Upgrading rainfed agriculture requires integrated approaches to social and ecological management. A challenge facing low-productive rainfed agriculture is the need for innovations in management of water that require novel technologies and practices such as water harvesting and conservation agriculture. Both innovation and adaptation are needed for successful adoption and out-scaling. One promising approach is adaptive comanagement between local communities and knowledge agents, in which knowledge sharing and transformation occur as an iterative process. Important tools for adaptive comanagement include participatory approaches, farmer field schools, and action research methods.

An integrated approach to rainwater management must address links between investments and risk reduction, between rainwater management and multiple livelihood strategies, and between land, water, and crops. Strategies for upgrading, including technologies and management, are generally known. However, the missing links for scaling-up and scaling-out are social and economic processes and institutions that can link to suitable policies.

India has experienced important success from integrated watershed management, with local ownership combined with tangible economic benefits among rural households (Wani and others 2003c). However, India's experience also highlights the limitation of a compartmental approach. The benefits of increased productivity were not realized to the desired extent, equity issues were not addressed, and community participation was not achieved, resulting in neglect of the various water-harvesting structures in the watersheds.

An integrated approach to land, water, and crop management is required on farm at the same time that watershed and basin development strategies are employed to increase yields in rainfed agriculture. Successes are not directly transferable to other socioecological contexts but require adaptation and comanagement. Investments in upgrading rainfed agriculture need to consider the wide range of benefits from rainwater that contribute to the overall resilience of rural communities—support for all forms of biomass growth, including cultivated crops, pasture for livestock, noncultivated food plants, and fuel and construction wood.

Strategies to enable investments in rainwater management

Governance of agricultural development should give more attention to resource management and intersectoral approaches, including at the local level, to counteract the focus on inputs that has dominated in the past. This is challenging, as it requires the integration of socioecological understanding in institutional capacity so that the rain, land, and crop complexities, potentials, and risks involved in rainfed agriculture are integrated in economic planning. Broader knowledge is needed for investments at national, regional, and district levels.

Institutional reform is required at the national level to bridge the divide in governance of water resources, agriculture, and the environment. Relevant departments and ministries need to be more closely connected in legal, policy, and management areas.

Investments are required in local institutions for resource management. Opportunities to make investments in rainfed agriculture bankable need to be promoted. Land tenure reforms and development of local markets and transport infrastructure are crucial. Farmer organizations, small-scale credit schemes, private banking partnerships, and other institutional arrangements need to go hand in hand with policy advances.

Microcredit schemes for water management investments are especially important. Farm households generally cannot afford the large (relative to financial capacity) initial investments required even for small-scale water-harvesting systems for crop production, despite high benefit to cost ratios and the positive impact on long-term risk reduction.

Enabling environments are important. Well targeted economic support is essential in agriculture development. Improved water management needs to be supported by investments in infrastructure, markets, access roads, and secure land tenure.

Providing complementary public sector investments. To support farmers' efforts of gradual intensification, participatory approaches should be combined with public investments in governance, management, and infrastructure.

In rainfed areas strategic public investments in rainwater management are urgently needed to encourage the private sector (individual as well as corporate) to take investment risks. India has demonstrated that once public investments in rainwater harvesting have ensured soil moisture and increased groundwater availability, individuals and industries will increase their investments in rainfed agriculture (Wani and others 2006a). As private investments tend to follow the path of minimum risk, once the highest risk for growing economic biomass—rainfall variability—was reduced, private investments flowed.

Investments in infrastructure supporting agricultural development are important. Evidence shows that investments in roads and education targeted to rainfed areas had a larger

> In rainfed areas strategic public investments in rainwater management are urgently needed to encourage the private sector to take investment risks

effect on poverty than those directed to irrigated areas (Fan, Hazell, and Haque 2000; Fan, Zhang, and Zhang 2002). Work by Hatibu and Rockström (2005) has shown that investments in rainwater management generate significant impacts on poverty if accompanied by linkages to profitable markets. In the Machakos District in Kenya the social and economic success over the past 50 years among rainfed farming communities originated in investments in soil and water conservation, particularly terracing (Tiffen, Mortimore, and Gichuki 1994), combined with investments in infrastructure that enabled farmers to diversify and penetrate local markets (Zaal and Oostenrup 2002). Linking crop and livestock producers in semiarid areas with markets and marketing systems enables them to obtain high returns on their investments in rainwater management, increasing the benefits from existing systems while promoting wider adoption. This agrees with findings in India that complementary investments in road infrastructure in rainfed areas resulted in much higher impacts on poverty (Wani and others 2006b).

> Linking crop and livestock producers in semiarid areas with markets and marketing systems enables them to obtain high returns on their investments in rainwater management

Increasing the profitability of private sector investments. Profitability is a key factor determining all investment. Rainfed agriculture has suffered from particularly low profitability as a result of the strong focus on staple grains and the trend of declining world market prices for grain. By contrast, irrigated agriculture has diversified into specialized commercial crops such as cut flowers and other horticultural crops. Rainfed agriculture similarly needs to shift toward greater diversification to boost investment. This could be achieved through investments in water resources management *[established but incomplete]*. Investment in small water-harvesting structures for storage of local runoff for supplemental irrigation, for example, could support diversification by enabling off-season full irrigation of high-value vegetables and fruits.

Investmenting in capacity building. Agricultural extension services and other service institutions need to adjust their skills mix to meet the needs of rainfed agriculture. Today, capacity is focused on the local field scale (agriculture, livestock, and soil and water conservation at the local farm scale) or the larger watershed or river basin scale for irrigation development, management, and planning. The capacity to upgrade rainfed agriculture through water investments, which requires skill at the meso-watershed scale, is very limited.

Adaptation to climate change to increase resilience

There is growing confidence in the scientific predictions of the impacts of anthropogenic climate change. Water resources are severely affected, and evidence indicates, despite large standard deviations, that rainfall in tropical regions will become even more unreliable. Larger and more intensive storms will become more common, and several regions, including Southern Africa, will suffer from reduced rainfall. Furthermore, advances in climate science over the past five years also point with growing certainty to the unavoidability of climate change impacts in the coming decades, not just in a distant future.

Increasingly, this has resulted in a growing concern for the need to adapt to climate change. Investments in water management in rainfed agriculture should form a cornerstone of any country's strategy for adapting to climate change, particularly in developing countries in tropical regions where rainfed agriculture plays such an important economic role. Poor countries are more vulnerable to climate change, and poor communities are hit hardest by social and environmental shocks. Investments that reduce water-related risks build more resilient communities better able to face increased occurrence of floods, droughts, and dry spells under a changing climate. The National Adaptation Programmes of Action under the UN Framework Convention on Climate Change need to address both small- and large-scale investments in water management to meet a future with a higher frequency of water-related climate shocks. For agricultural water management this includes a strategic balance between investments to reduce vulnerability to droughts and floods at the local scale through small water storage systems as well as large-scale infrastructure investments. Building water resilience to climate change adds a new and urgent dimension to the need for large new investments in water management to upgrade rainfed agriculture.

> Investments in water management in rainfed agriculture should form a cornerstone of any country's strategy for adapting to climate change

Comprehensive evidence for action to improve livelihoods

Diverse forces and comprehensive evidence point to the urgency of concerted and strategic investments in upgrading rainfed agriculture in developing countries where water is a constraint to food production. They also highlight the large opportunities. Achieving the Millennium Development Goals of reducing poverty and hunger by half and ensuring environmental sustainability is not possible without major contributions from rainfed agriculture. Low yields today are an opportunity for the future, given the wide evidence of large volumes of unused water, even in water-scarce regions, and the wide knowledge base of appropriate, effective, and affordable water management practices ready to be adopted by farmers at a large scale. Nothing less than a new green revolution is required in Sub-Saharan Africa, and significant agricultural productivity improvements are needed in large parts of South, Southeast, and East Asia as well as in parts of Latin America.

Water alone will not do the job. But this chapter shows that in rainfed farming, where water is a highly variable production factor, risk reduction through water management is a key to unlocking the potential of managing crops, soil fertility, and pests and allowing for diversification. A crucial finding is the possibility of improving livelihoods as well as water productivity through water management in rainfed agriculture. More food can be produced with relatively less water, particularly in the low-yielding farming systems of the world.

It is time for governments and development organizations to abandon the notion that rainfed farming in semiarid and dry subhumid regions is a marginal activity practiced on drylands and instead invest in tapping the potential for doubling and often tripling or quadrupling productivity in these systems. This will contribute to fighting poverty, reducing environmental degradation, and building resilience to climate change; allow for a more balanced rural-urban development; and ultimately contribute to sustainability.

Reviewers

Chapter review editor: Jean Boroto.
Chapter reviewers: Mintesinot Behailu, Meena Bilgi, Eline Boelee, James Chimphamba, Guy Evers, John Gowing, Dorothy Hamada, Ingrid Hartman, Peter Hobbs, Dyno Keatinge, Henry Mahoo, Douglas J. Merrey, Tony Peacock, Bharat R. Sharma, Jonathan Woolley, and Yali E. Woyessa.

References

Abdulai, A., and P. Hazell. 1995. "The Role of Agriculture in Sustainable Development in Africa." *Journal of Sustainable Agriculture* 7 (2/3): 101–19.

Agarwal, A. 2000. *Drought: Try Capturing the Rain*. Briefing Paper. New Delhi: Centre for Science and Environment.

Agarwal, A., and S. Narain. 1997. *Dying Wisdom: Rise, Fall and Potential of India's Traditional Water Harvesting System*. Faridabad, India: Thomson Press Ltd.

ASARECA (Association for Strengthening Agricultural Research in Eastern and Central Africa) and IFPRI (International Food Policy Research Institute). 2005. "Strategic Priorities for Agricultural Research-for-Development in Eastern and Central Africa." Entebbe, Uganda, and Washington, D.C.

Barron, J. Forthcoming. "Water Productivity and Rainwater Management in Smallholder Farming Systems: Simulations for Cereals in Semiarid Sub-Sahara Africa with APSIM." Contribution to the Comprehensive Assessment project "Water Use in Agriculture on Water Scarcity and Food Security in Tropical Rainfed Water Scarcity Systems: A Multi-level Assessment of Existing Conditions, Response Options and Future Potentials." International Crops Research Institute for the Semi-Arid Tropics, Andhra Pradesh, India.

Barron, J., J. Rockström, F. Gichuki, and N. Hatibu. 2003. "Dry Spell Analysis and Maize Yields for Two Semiarid Locations in East Africa." *Agricultural and Forest Meteorology* 117 (1–2): 23–37.

Bewket, W., and G. Sterk. 2005. "Dynamics in Land Cover and its Effect on Stream Flow in the Chemoga Watershed, Blue Nile Basin, Ethiopia." *Hydrological Processes* 19 (2): 445–58.

Calder, I.R. 1999. *The Blue Revolution: Land Use and Integrated Water Resources Management*. London: Earthscan.

Commission for Africa. 2005. *Our Common Interest: Report of the Commission for Africa*. Accessed May 2005. [www.commissionforafrica.org/english/report/introduction.html].

Conway, G. 1997. *The Doubly Green Revolution: Food for All in the Twenty-first Century*. London: Penguin Books.

Critchley, W., and K. Siegert. 1991. *Water Harvesting: A Manual for the Design and Construction of Water Harvesting Schemes for Plant Production*. Rome: Food and Agriculture Organization.

Dancette, C. 1983. "Estimation des besoins en eau des principales cultures pluviales en zone soudano-sahélienne." *L'Agronomie Tropicale* 38 (4): 281–94.

Deichmann, U., and L. Eklundh. 1991. "Global Digital Data Sets for Land Degradation Studies: A GIS Approach." GRID Case Study Series 4. United Nations Environment Programme, Global Environmental Monitoring System and Global Resource Information Database, Nairobi. Accessed February 2006. [http://geodata.grid.unep.ch/].

Derpsch, R. 1998. "Historical Review of No-tillage Cultivation of Crops." In J. Benites, E. Chuma, R. Fowler, J. Kienzle, K. Molapong, J. Manu, I. Nyagumbo, K. Steiner, and R. van Veenhuizen, eds., *Conservation Tillage for Sustainable Agriculture*. Proceedings from an International Workshop, Harare, 22–27 June. Part II (Annexes). Eschborn, Germany: Deutsche Gesellschaft fur Technische Zusammenarbeit.

———. 2005. "The Extent of Conservation Agriculture Adoption Worldwide: Implications and Impact." Keynote Paper at the 3rd World Congress on Conservation Agriculture, Regional Land Management Unit, World Agroforestry Centre, 3–7 October, Nairobi.

DFID (Department for International Development). 2002. "Better Livelihoods for Poor People: The Role of Agriculture." Issues Paper. Consultation Document Draft A4. Rural Livelihoods Department, London.

Dixon, J., A. Gulliver, and D. Gibbon. 2001. *Farming Systems and Poverty: Improving Farmers' Livelihoods in a Changing World*. Rome and Washington, D.C.: Food and Agriculture Organization and World Bank.

Doorenbos, J., and W.O. Pruitt. 1992. *Crop Water Requirements*. FAO Irrigation and Drainage Paper. Rome: Food and Agriculture Organization.

Evenari, M., L. Shanan, and N.H. Tadmor. 1971. *The Negev: The Challenge of a Desert*. Cambridge, Mass.: Harvard University Press.

Falkenmark, M. 1986. "Fresh Water—Time for a Modified Approach." *Ambio* 15 (4): 192–200.

Falkenmark, M., and J. Rockström. 2004. *Balancing Water for Humans and Nature: The New Approach in Ecohydrology*. London: Earthscan.

Fan, S., P. Hazell, and T. Haque. 2000. "Targeting Public Investments by Agro-ecological Zone to Achieve Growth and Poverty Alleviation Goals in Rural India." *Food Policy* 25 (4): 411–28.

Fan, S., L. Zhang, and X. Zhang. 2002. *Growth, Inequality, and Poverty in Rural China*. Research Report 125. Washington, D.C.: International Food Policy Research Institute.

FAO (Food and Agriculture Organization). 2002. *World Agriculture: Towards 2015/2030: Summary Report*. Rome.

———. 2004a. *Payment Schemes for Environmental Services in Watersheds*. Regional Forum, 9–12 June 2003 in Arequipa, Peru. Land and Water Discussion Paper 3. Rome.

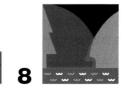

———. 2004b. *The State of Food Insecurity in the World 2004.* Rome.

FAO (Food and Agriculture Organization)/IIASA (International Institute for Applied Systems Analysis). 2000. *Global Agro-Ecological Zones (Global-AEZ).* CD-ROM. Rome and Laxenburg, Austria. Accessed February 2006. [www.iiasa. ac.at/Research/LUC/GAEZ].

FAOSTAT. 2005. Database. Food and Agriculture Organization, Rome. Accessed November 2005. [http://faostat.fao. org/].

Fischer, G., M. Shah, and H. van Velthuizen. 2002. *Climate Change and Agricultural Vulnerability.* Special report for the UN World Summit on Sustainable Development, 26 August–4 September, Johannesburg. Laxenburg, Austria: International Institute for Applied Systems Analysis. [www.iiasa.ac.at/Research/LUC/JB-Report.pdf].

Fox, P., and J. Rockström. 2000. "Water Harvesting for Supplemental Irrigation of Cereal Crops to Overcome Intra-seasonal Dry-spells in the Sahel." *Physics and Chemistry of the Earth, Part B Hydrology, Oceans and Atmosphere* 25 (3): 289–96.

Fox, P., J. Rockström, and J. Barron. 2005. "Risk Analysis and Economic Viability of Water Harvesting for Supplemental Irrigation in Semiarid Burkina Faso and Kenya." *Agricultural Systems* 83 (3): 231–50.

Glantz, M.H. 1994. *Drought Follows the Plough: Cultivating Marginal Areas.* Cambridge, UK: Cambridge University Press.

Gowing, J.W., H. Mahoo, O.B. Mzirai, and N. Hatibu. 1999. "Review of Rainwater Harvesting Techniques and Evidence for Their Use in Semiarid Tanzania." *Tanzania Journal of Agriculture Science* 2 (2): 171–80.

Harris, H.C., P.J.M. Cooper, and M. Pala. 1991. *Soil and Crop Management for Improved Water Use Efficiency in Rainfed Areas.* Proceedings of an International Workshop sponsored by the Ministry of Agriculture, Forestry, and Rural Affairs, International Center for Agricultural Research in the Dry Areas, and International Maize and Wheat Improvement Center, 15–19 May, 1989. Ankara: International Center for Agricultural Research in the Dry Areas.

Hatibu, N., and J. Rockström. 2005. "Green-Blue Water System Innovations for Upgrading of Smallholder Farming Systems—A Policy Framework for Development." *Water Science and Technology* 51 (8): 121–32.

Hatibu, N., E.A. Lazaro, H.F. Mahoo, F.B. Rwehumbiza, and A.M. Bakari. 1999. "Soil and Water Conservation in Semiarid Areas of Tanzania: National Policies and Local Practices." *Tanzania Journal of Agricultural Sciences* 2 (2): 151–70.

Hatibu, N., M.D.B. Young, J.W. Gowing, H.F. Mahoo, and O.B. Mzirai. 2003. "Developing Improved Dryland Cropping Systems for Maize in Semiarid Tanzania. Part 1: Experimental Evidence of the Benefits of Rainwater Harvesting." *Journal of Experimental Agriculture* 39 (3): 279–92.

Hatibu, N., K. Mutabazi, E.M. Senkondo, and A.S.K. Msangi. 2006. "Economics of Rainwater Harvesting for Crop Enterprises in Semiarid Areas of East Africa." *Agricultural Water Management* 80 (1–3): 74–86.

Henao, J., and C. Baanante. 2006. *Agricultural Production and Soil Nutrient Mining in Africa: Implications for Resource Conservation and Policy Development.* IFDC Technical Bulletin. Muscle Shoals, Ala: International Fertilizer Development Center.

Hilhost, T., and F. Muchena. 2000. *Nutrients on the Move: Soil Fertility Dynamics in African Farming Systems.* London: International Institute for Environment and Development.

Hobbs, P.R., and R.K. Gupta. 2002. "Rice-wheat Cropping Systems in the Indo-Gangetic Plains: Issues of Water Productivity in Relation to New Resource Conserving Technologies." In J.W. Kijne, ed., *Water Productivity in Agriculture: Limits and Opportunities for Improvement.* Wallingford, UK: CABI Publishing.

IAC (InterAcademy Council). 2004. *Realizing the Promise and Potential of African Agriculture: Science and Technology Strategies for Improving Agricultural Productivity and Food Security in Africa.* Amsterdam: InterAcademy Secretariat.

IFAD (International Fund for Agricultural Development). 2001. *Rural Poverty Report 2001: The Challenge of Ending Rural Poverty.* Oxford, UK: Oxford University Press.

Ilbeyi, A., H. Ustun, T. Oweis, M. Pala, and B. Benli. 2006. "Wheat Water Productivity and Yield in a Cool Highland Environment: Effect of Early Sowing with Supplemental Irrigation." *Agricultural Water Management* 82 (3): 399–410.

India, Government of. 2005. *Serving Farmers and Saving Farming—2006: Year of Agricultural Renewal.* Third Report. New Delhi: Ministry of Agriculture, National Commission on Farmers.

IPCC (Intergovernmental Panel on Climate Change). 2001. *Climate Change 2001.* Third Assessment Report. Cambridge, UK: Cambridge University Press.

Irz, X., and T. Roe. 2000. "Can the World Feed Itself? Some Insights from Growth Theory." *Agrekon* 39 (3): 513–28.

Johnston, D.G., and J.W. Mellor. 1961. "The Role of Agriculture in Economic Development." *American Economic Review* 51 (4): 566–93.

Joshi, P.K., A.K. Jha, S.P. Wani, L. Joshi, and R.L. Shiyani. 2005. *Meta-analysis to Assess Impact of Watershed Program and People's Participation.* Comprehensive Assessment of Water Management in Agriculture Research Report 8. Colombo: International Water Management Institute.

Kerr, J. 1996. "Sustainable Development of Rainfed Agriculture in India." EPTD Discussion Paper 20. International Food Policy Research Institute, Environment and Production Technology Division, Washington, D.C. [www.ifpri.org/divs/eptd/dp/papers/eptdp20.pdf].

Klaij, M.C., and G. Vachaud. 1992. "Seasonal Water Balance of a Sandy Soil in Niger Cropped with Pearl Millet, Based on Profile Moisture Measurements." *Agricultural Water Management* 21 (4): 313–30.

Koning, N. 2002. "Should Africa Protect Its Farmers to Revitalise its Economy?" Working Paper North-South Centre. Wageningen University and Research Centre, Wageningen, Netherlands.

Landell-Mills, N., and T.I. Porras. 2002. *Silver Bullet or Fools' Gold? A Global Review of Markets for Forest Environmental Services and Their Impact on the Poor*. Instruments for Sustainable Private Sector Forestry Series. London: International Institute for Environment and Development. [www.iied.org/pubs/pdf/full/9066IIED.pdf].

Landers, J.N., H. Mattana Saturnio, P.L. de Freitas, and R. Trecenti. 2001. "Experiences with Farmer Clubs in Dissemination of Zero Tillage in Tropical Brazil." In L. García-Torres, J. Benites, and A. Martínez-Vilela, eds., *Conservation Agriculture, A Worldwide Challenge*. Rome: Food and Agriculture Organization.

LandScan. 2004. Global Population Database. Oak Ridge National Laboratory, Oak Ridge, Tenn. Accessed November 2005.

Liniger, H.P., and W. Critchley. Forthcoming. *Where the Land Is Greener: Case Studies and Analysis of Soil and Water Conservation Initiatives Worldwide*. Berne, Switzerland: World Overview of Conservation Approaches and Technologies.

MEA (Millennium Ecosystem Assessment). 2005. *Ecosystems and Human Wellbeing: Synthesis*. Washington, D.C.: Island Press.

Meertens, H., L. Ndege, and P. Lupeja. 1999. "The Cultivation of Rainfed Lowland Rice in Sukumaland, Tanzania." *Agriculture, Ecosystems, and Environment* 76 (1): 31–45.

Mwale, F. 2003. "Drought Impact on Maize Production in Malawi." UNESCO–IHE Report. United Nations Educational, Scientific and Cultural Organization Institute for Water Education, Delft, Netherlands.

Ngigi, S.N., H.H.G. Savenije, J. Rockström, and C.K. Gachene. 2005a. "Hydro-economic Evaluation of Rainwater Harvesting and Management Technologies: Farmers' Investment Options and Risks in Semiarid Laikipia District of Kenya." *Physics and Chemistry of the Earth* 30 (11–16): 772–82.

Ngigi, S.N., H.H.G. Savenije, J.N. Thome, J. Rockström, and F.W.T. Penning de Vries. 2005b. "Agro-hydrological Evaluation of On-farm Rainwater Storage Systems for Supplemental Irrigation in Laikipia District, Kenya." *Agricultural Water Management* 73 (1): 21–41.

Oweis, T. 1997. *Supplemental Irrigation: A Highly Efficient Water-use Practice*. Aleppo, Syria: International Center for Agricultural Research in the Dry Areas.

Oweis, T., and A. Hachum. 2001. "Reducing Peak Supplemental Irrigation Demand by Extending Sowing Dates." *Agricultural Water Management* 50 (2):109–23.

Oweis, T., and A. Taimeh. 1996. "Evaluation of a Small Basin Water-Harvesting System in the Arid Region of Jordan." *Water Resources Management* 10 (1): 21–34.

Oweis, T., M. Pala, and J. Ryan. 1998. "Stabilizing Rainfed Wheat Yields with Supplemental Irrigation and Nitrogen in a Mediterranean Climate." *Agronomy Journal* 90 (5): 672–81.

Oweis, T., D. Prinz, and A. Hachum. 2001. *Water Harvesting: Indigenous Knowledge for the Future of the Drier Environments*. Aleppo, Syria: International Center for Agricultural Research in the Dry Areas.

Pandey, R.K., J.W. Maranville, and A. Admou. 2000. "Deficit Irrigation and Nitrogen Effects on Maize in a Sahelian Environment: I. Grain Yield and Yield Components." *Agricultural Water Management* 46 (1): 1–13.

Panigrahi, B., S.N. Panda, and A. Agrawal. 2005. "Water Balance Simulation and Economic Analysis for Optimal Size of On-farm Reservoir." *Water Resources Management* 19 (3): 233–50.

Perrot-Maître, D., and P. Davis. 2001. *Case Studies: Developing Markets for Water Services from Forests*. Washington D.C.: Forest Trends.

Pretty, J., and R. Hine. 2001. *Reducing Food Poverty with Sustainable Agriculture: A Summary of New Evidence*. Final Report of the "Safe World" Research Project. University of Essex, UK.

Ramankutty, N., J.A. Foley, and N.J. Olejniczak. 2002. "People and Land: Changes in Global Population and Croplands during the 20th Century." *Ambio* 31(3): 251–57.

Rego, T.J., S.P. Wani, K.L. Sahrawat, and G. Pardhasardhy. 2005. *Macro-benefits from Boron, Zinc, and Sulphur Application in Indian SAT: A Step for Grey to Green Revolution in Agriculture*. Global Theme on Agroecosystems Report 16. Andhra Pradesh, India: International Crops Research Institute for the Semi-Arid Tropics.

Rockström, J. 2003. "Water for Food and Nature in Drought-prone Tropics: Vapour Shift in Rain-fed Agriculture." *Royal Society Transactions B Biological Sciences* 358 (1440): 1997–2009.

Rockström, J., and M. Falkenmark. 2000. "Semiarid Crop Production from a Hydrological Perspective: Gap between Potential and Actual Yields." *Critical Reviews in Plant Science* 19 (4): 319–46.

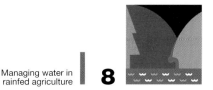

Rockström, J., P-E. Jansson, and J. Barron. 1998. "Seasonal Rainfall Partitioning under Runon and Runoff Conditions on Sandy Soil in Niger. On-farm Measurements and Water Balance Modelling." *Journal of Hydrology* 210 (1–4): 68–92.

Rockström, J., P. Kaumbutho, J. Mwalley, A.W. Nzabi, M. Temesgen, L. Mawenya, J. Barron, and S. Damgaard-Larsen. Forthcoming. "Conservation Farming Strategies in East and Southern Africa: A Regional Synthesis of Crop and Water Productivity from On-farm Action Research." Submitted to *Soil and Tillage Research*.

Rosegrant, M., C. Ximing, S. Cline, and N. Nakagawa. 2002. "The Role of Rainfed Agriculture in the Future of Global Food Production." EPTD Discussion Paper 90. International Food Policy Research Institute, Environment and Production Technology Division, Washington, D.C. [www.ifpri.org/divs/eptd/dp/papers/eptdp90.pdf].

Schreider, S.Y., A.J. Jakeman, R.A. Letcher, R.J. Nathan, B.P. Neal, and S.G. Beavis. 2002. "Detecting Changes in Streamflow Response to Changes in Non-climatic Catchment Conditions: Farm Dam Development in the Murray-Darling Basin, Australia." *Journal of Hydrology* 262 (1–4): 84–98.

Seckler, D., and U. Amarasinghe. 2004. "Major Problems in the Global Water-Food Nexus." In C. Scanes and J. Miranowski, eds., *Perspectives in World Food and Agriculture 2004*. Ames, Iowa: Iowa State Press.

SEI (Stockholm Environment Institute). 2005. "Sustainable Pathways to Attain the Millennium Development Goals—Assessing the Role of Water, Energy and Sanitation." Document prepared for the UN World Summit, 14 September, New York. Stockholm.

Shiferaw, B., H.A. Freeman, and S. Swinton. 2004. *Natural Resource Management in Agriculture: Methods for Assessing Economic and Environmental Impacts*. Wallingford, UK: CABI Publishing.

Siegert, K. 1994. "Introduction to Water Harvesting: Some Basic Principles for Planning, Design and Monitoring." In *Water Harvesting for Improved Agricultural Production*. Proceedings of the FAO Expert Consultation, 21–25 November 1993, Cairo. Water Report 3. Rome: Food and Agriculture Organization.

Somme, G., T. Oweis, Q. Abdulal, A. Bruggeman, and A. Ali. 2004. *Micro-catchment Water Harvesting for Improved Vegetative Cover in the Syrian Badia*. On-farm Water Husbandry Research Reports Series 3. Aleppo, Syria: International Center for Agricultural Research in the Dry Areas.

Sreedevi, T.K., B. Shiferaw, and S.P. Wani. 2004. *Adarsha Watershed in Kothapally: Understanding the Drivers of Higher Impact*. Global Theme on Agroecosystems Report 10. Andhra Pradesh, India: International Crops Research Institute for the Semi-Arid Tropics.

Sreedevi, T.K., S.P. Wani, R. Sudi, M.S. Patel, T. Jayesh, S.N. Singh, and T. Shah. 2006. *On-site and Off-site Impact of Watershed Development: A Case Study of Rajasamadhiyala, Gujarat, India*. Global Theme on Agroecosystems Report 20. Andhra Pradesh, India: International Crops Research Institute for the Semi-Arid Tropics.

Stewart, J.I. 1988. *Response Farming in Rainfed Agriculture*. Davis, Calif.: The WHARF Foundation Press.

Stoorvogel, J.J., and E.M.A. Smaling. 1990. *Assessment of Soil Nutrient Depletion in Sub-Saharan Africa: 1983–2000*. Vol. 1, Main Report. Report 28. Wageningen, Netherlands: Winand Staring Centre.

Tanzania, Ministry of Agriculture and Food Security. 2001. "Agricultural Sector Development Strategy." Dar es Salaam.

——— . 2002. "Water Policy." Dar es Salaam.

——— . 2003. "Study on Irrigation Master Plan." Dar es Salaam.

Thirtle, C., L. Beyers, L. Lin, V. Mckenzie-Hill, X. Irz, S. Wiggins, and J. Piesse. 2002. *The Impacts of Changes in Agricultural Productivity on the Incidence of Poverty in Developing Countries*. DFID Report 7946. London: Department for International Development.

Tiffen, M., M. Mortimore, and F. Gichuki. 1994. *More People, Less Erosion—Environmental Recovery in Kenya*. Nairobi: ACTSPRESS, African Centre for Technology Studies.

Timmer, C.P. 1988. "The Agricultural Transformation." In H. Chenery, and T.N. Srinivasan, eds., *Handbook of Development Economics*. Vol. 1. Amsterdam: Elsevier.

UN Millennium Project. 2005. *Investing in Development: A Practical Plan to Achieve the Millennium Development Goals*. New York. Accessed May 2005. [www.unmilenniumproject.org].

UNStat. 2005. United Nations Statistics Division, Statistical databases. Accessed December 2005. http://unstats.un.org/unsd/default.htm.

Van Dijk, A., R. Evans, P. Hairsine, S. Khan, R. Nathan, Z. Paydar, N. Viney, and L. Zhang. 2006. *Risks to the Shared Water Resources of the Murray-Darling Basin*. Part II. Prepared for the Murray-Darling Basin Commission. MDBC Publication 22/06. Clayton South, Victoria, Australia: Commonwealth Scientific and Industrial Research Organization.

Van Duivenbooden, N., M. Pala, C. Studer, C.L. Bielders, and D.J. Beukes. 2000. "Cropping Systems and Crop Complementarity in Dryland Agriculture to Increase Soil Water Use Efficiency: A Review." *Netherlands Journal of Agricultural Science* 48 (3/4): 213–36.

Van Koppen, B., R. Namara, and C. Stafilios-Rothschild. 2005. "Reducing Poverty through Investments in Agricultural Water Management: Poverty and Gender Issues and Synthesis of Sub-Saharan Africa Case Study Reports." Working Paper 101. International Water Management Institute, Colombo.

Vörösmarty, C.J., C. Lévêque, and C. Revenga. 2005. "Fresh Water." In R. Hassan, R. Scholes, and N. Ash, eds., *Millenium Ecosystem Assessment*. Ecosystems and Human Well-being Vol. 1. Current Status and Trends. Washington, D.C.: Island Press.

Wani, S.P., S.S. Balloli, A.V.R. Kesava Rao, and T.K. Sreedevi. 2004. "Combating Drought through Integrated Watershed Management for Sustainable Dryland Agriculture." Presented at Regional Workshop on Agricultural Drought Monitoring and Assessment Using Space Technology, 4 May, National Remote Sensing Agency, Hyderabad, India.

Wani, S.P., M. Reddy, T.K. Sreedevi, and D. Raju, eds. 2006a. "Corporate Science and Technology Institutions—Partnerships for Inclusive and Sustainable Development and Economic Growth." Proceedings of the CII-ICRISAT Workshop, 27 February, International Crops Research Institute for the Semi-Arid Tropics, Andhra Pradesh, India.

Wani, S.P., P. Pathak, L.S. Jangawad, H. Eswaran, and P. Singh. 2003a. "Improved Management of Vertisols in the Semiarid Tropics for Increased Productivity and Soil Carbon Sequestration." *Soil Use and Management* 19 (3): 217–22.

Wani, S.P., P. Pathak, T.K. Sreedevi, H.P. Singh, and P. Singh. 2003b. "Efficient Management of Rainwater for Increased Crop Productivity and Groundwater Recharge in Asia." In J.W. Kijne, R. Barker, and D. Molden, eds., *Water Productivity in Agriculture: Limits and Opportunities for Improvement*. Wallingford, UK, and Colombo: CABI Publishing and International Water Management Institute.

Wani, S.P., H.P. Singh, T.K. Sreedevi, P. Pathak, T.J. Rego, B. Shiferaw, and S.R. Iyer. 2003c. "Farmer-participatory Integrated Watershed Management: Adarsha Watershed, Kothapally India. An Innovative and Scalable Approach." In R.R. Harwood and A.H. Kassam, eds., *Research towards Integrated Natural Resources Management: Examples of Research Problems, Approaches and Partnerships in Action in the CGIAR*. Washington, D.C.: Consultative Group on International Agricultural Research, Interim Science Council.

Wani, S.P., Y.S. Ramakrishna, T.K. Sreedevi, T.D. Long, T. Wangkahart, B. Shiferaw, P. Pathak, and A.V.R. Kesava Rao. 2006b. "Issues, Concepts, Approaches and Practices in Integrated Watershed Management: Experience and Lessons from Asia." In B. Shiferaw and K.P.C. Rao, eds., *Integrated Management of Watersheds for Agricultural Diversification and Sustainable Livelihoods in Eastern and Central Africa: Lessons and Experiences from Semi-Arid South Asia*. Proceedings of the International Workshop held at International Crops Research Institute for the Semi-Arid Tropics, Nairobi, 6–7 December 2004. Andhra Pradesh, India: International Crops Research Institute for the Semi-Arid Tropics.

WHO (World Health Organization). 2000. "Gender, Health and Poverty." Factsheet 251. June. [www.who.int/mediacenter/factsheets/fs251/en/].

World Bank. 1982. *World Development Report 1982*. New York: Oxford University Press.

———. 2000. "Spurring Agricultural and Rural Development." In *Can Africa Claim the 21st Century?* Washington, D.C.

———. 2005. *Agricultural Growth for the Poor: An Agenda for Development*. Washington, D.C.: World Bank.

Zaal, F., and R.H. Oostenrup. 2002. "Explaining a Miracle: Intensification and the Transition towards Sustainable Small-scale Agriculture in Dryland Machakos and Kitui Districts, Kenya." *World Development* 30 (7): 1221–87.

Zhang, H., and T. Oweis. 1999. "Water-yield Relations and Optimal Irrigation Scheduling of Wheat in the Mediterranean Region." *Agricultural Water Management* 38 (3): 195–211.

Multiple uses of water

Artists: Jhun Jhun Jha and Hira Karn, Nepal

9 | Reinventing irrigation

Coordinating lead author: Jean-Marc Faurès

Lead authors: Mark Svendsen and Hugh Turral

Contributing authors: Jeremy Berkoff, Madhusudan Bhattarai, Ana Maria Caliz, Salah Darghouth, Mohammed Rachid Doukkali, Mona El-Kady, Thierry Facon, M. Gopalakrishnan, David Groenfeldt, Chu Thai Hoanh, Intizar Hussain, Jean-Yves Jamin, Flemming Konradsen, Alejandro León, Ruth Meinzen-Dick, Kathleen Miller, Monirul Mirza, Claudia Ringler, Lisa Schipper, Aidan Senzanje, Girma Tadesse, Rebecca Tharme, Paul van Hofwegen, Robina Wahaj, Consuelo Varela-Ortega, Robert Yoder, and Gao Zhanyi

Overview

The conditions that led to large public investment in irrigation in the second half of the 20th century have changed radically, and today's circumstances demand substantial shifts in irrigation strategies. Irrigation has ensured an adequate global food supply and raised millions out of poverty, especially in Asia, thanks to massive investments. But a stable world food supply, declining population growth rates, continuing declines in the real price of food, and the rising importance of investment in other sectors diminish the need to maintain similar levels of irrigation investment today. The era of rapid expansion of public irrigation infrastructure is over.

For many developing countries investment in irrigation will continue to represent a substantial share of investment in agriculture, but the pattern of investment will change substantially from previous decades. New investment will focus much more on enhancing the productivity of existing systems through upgrading infrastructure and reforming management processes. Irrigation will need to adapt to serve an increasingly productive agriculture, and investments will be needed to adapt yesterday's systems to tomorrow's needs. Substantial productivity gains are possible across the spectrum of irrigated agriculture through modernization and better responses to market demand. These gains will be driven by the market and financial incentives that will lead to higher farm incomes.

Large surface irrigation systems will need to incorporate improvements in water control and delivery, automation and measurement, and training of staff to better respond to farmers'

needs. Conjunctive use of canal water and groundwater will remain an attractive option to enhance flexibility and reliability in water service provision. Under pressure from other sectors, the irrigation sector will find it increasingly hard to secure public finance for irrigation and drainage infrastructure. This situation will increase the financial burden on local government and users and is likely to have severe consequences for the irrigation sector. Cost-recovery mechanisms that guarantee the sustainability of systems will become imperative. At the same time, private investment in irrigation will likely grow in response to new opportunities for agricultural production.

> Irrigation and drainage will be more site-specific and much more closely linked with policies and plans in agriculture and other sectors

Irrigation and drainage will still expand on new land, but at a much slower pace. They will be more site-specific and much more closely linked with policies and plans in agriculture and other sectors. Irrigation will remain critical in supplying cheap, high-quality food, and its share of world food production will rise to more than 45% by 2030, from 40% today. Farmers around the world will increasingly integrate into a global market, which will dictate their choices and behavior. New market opportunities will emerge where suitable national policies, infrastructure, and institutions are in place. Countries will need to tailor irrigation investment more closely to the stage of national development, degree of integration into the world economy, availability of land and water resources, share of agriculture in the national economy, and comparative advantage in local, regional, and world markets.

In regions that rely heavily on agriculture irrigation is likely to remain important in rural poverty reduction strategies. But irrigation's contribution to poverty reduction remains contentious, with some experts arguing that there are more effective ways to address rural poverty. In these regions increasing productivity in agriculture is often the only way out of poverty, and new irrigation development can be a springboard for economic development. The type and scale of intervention will vary considerably from one region to another. In Sub-Saharan Africa the best option to enhance food security and reduce people's vulnerability to external shocks and climate variability is investment in both rainfed and irrigated agriculture, combined with programs to improve soil fertility; increase access to inputs, information, and markets; and strengthen local institutions. Public investment in bulk infrastructure will be required to support private initiatives, especially those in small-scale irrigation.

The changing demand for agricultural products and the increasing understanding of the impacts of climate change on agriculture and the water cycle will also influence future investment in irrigation and water control. Rapidly rising incomes and urbanization in many developing countries are shifting demand from staples to fruits or vegetables, which typically require irrigation technologies that improve reliability, raise yields, and improve product quality. But as the century unfolds, weather events will become more variable—extreme events will increase, rainfall distribution will change, and glaciers and mountain snowpacks will shrink. Investment will be required to respond to these changes; especially where average precipitation declines and shrinking glacial and snowpack storage reduces summer streamflows. Adaptation strategies will generally require more storage capacity and new operating rules for reservoirs, posing onerous tradeoffs between allocations for environmental and agricultural water.

As competition for water from other sectors intensifies, irrigation will increasingly be under pressure to release water for higher value uses. Increased water scarcity will be an incentive for irrigation to perform better. The number of regions where water availability limits food production is on the rise, and intersectoral competition for water will increase almost universally with urbanization and economic development. Environmental water allocations will steadily increase and present a much greater challenge to irrigation than will cities and industries, because the volumes at stake are likely to be larger. Transfers of water from irrigation to higher value uses will occur and require oversight to ensure that they are transparent and equitable. Water measurement, assessment, and accounting will likely grow in importance, and water rights will need to be formalized, especially to protect the interests of marginal and traditional water users. The use of water pricing as an economic tool for demand management remains low and is not a workable option in the prevailing economic conditions for most irrigation schemes.

> The overall performance of irrigation has been acceptable but at considerable cost

Irrigation and drainage performance will increasingly be assessed against the full range of their benefits and costs, not only against commodity production. The overall performance of irrigation has been acceptable, as judged by the current stability in world food supply and continually declining real prices for food. But this global gain has come at considerable financial cost, and in many cases irrigation systems have failed to meet their performance targets. Some have failed completely. The success of irrigation has also often come at the environment's expense, degrading ecosystems and reducing water supplies to wetlands. It has also had mixed impacts on human health. Better nutrition and improved water availability for domestic needs have improved hygiene and reduced infections and diseases. But irrigation is also associated with higher prevalence of malaria, schistosomiasis, and other waterborne diseases.

Decentralized and more transparent governance will be important in irrigation and drainage water management, and the role of governments will change. The recent trend to devolve the responsibility for irrigation management and the associated costs to local institutions, with more direct involvement of farmers, is likely to intensify. The many possible outcomes will range from full farmer ownership and operation, to contracted professional management, to joint management by government and farmers. As governments withdraw from direct managerial functions they will need to develop compensating regulatory capacities to oversee service provision and to protect public interests. While control of system infrastructure will likely be devolved, bulk water supply infrastructure, because of its multiple functions and strategic value, will usually remain the responsibility of the state.

Irrigation: a key element in the 20th century's agricultural revolution

The last 50 years have seen massive investments in large-scale public surface irrigation infrastructure as part of a global effort to rapidly increase staple food production, ensure food self-sufficiency, and avoid devastating famine. Private and community-based investment in developing countries, particularly groundwater pumping, has grown rapidly since the 1980s, propelled by cheap drilling technology, rural electrification, and inexpensive small pumps.

Trends in irrigation development

Investment in irrigation accelerated rapidly in the 1960s and the 1970s, with area expansion in developing countries at 2.2% a year reaching 155 million hectares (ha) in 1982 (figure 9.1). Global irrigated area rose from 168 million ha in 1970 to 215 million ha over the same time frame (Carruthers, Rosegrant, and Seckler 1997). Rapid growth in irrigated area, together with other components of the green revolution package, such as improved crop varieties and substantial growth in fertilizer use, particularly in Asia, led to a steady increase in staple food production and a reduction of real world food prices. More recently, agricultural subsidizes in developed countries have helped keep food prices low (Rosegrant and others 2001).

The annual growth rate of irrigation development, particularly in large-scale public schemes, has decreased since the late 1970s due to several factors. The areas best suited to irrigation have already been developed, leading to increased construction costs for future

| figure **9.1** | **Irrigation expanding, food prices falling** |

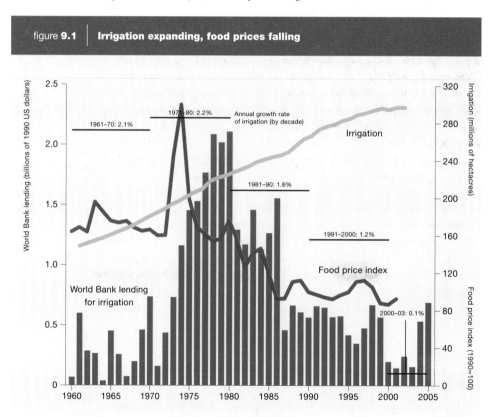

Source: Based on World Bank and Food and Agriculture Organization data.

dams and related infrastructure, and prices of staple cereals have declined. Both of these factors have made irrigated agriculture progressively less economically attractive than in the past. The underperformance of large-scale irrigation (Chambers 1988) has also reduced donor interest (Merrey 1997). Concerns over negative social and environmental impacts, particularly the dislocation of residents in affected communities and the calls for increased in-stream flows for environmental purposes have received heavy publicity and discouraged lenders from investing in irrigation. More competition for water from other sectors has also reduced the scope for further development of irrigation. Declining cereal prices have slowed growth in input use and investment in crop research and irrigation infrastructure, with consequent effects on yield growth (Rosegrant and Svendsen 1993; Carruthers, Rosegrant, and Seckler 1997; Sanmuganathan 2000).

Irrigation is particularly crucial in sustaining agriculture across the "dry belt" that extends from the Middle East through Northern China to Central America and parts of the United States (map 9.1). Asia alone has over 60% of the world's irrigated land, both in semiarid and humid tropical conditions. By contrast, irrigation has remained limited in most of Sub-Saharan Africa, with a few large commercial schemes developed during the colonial period and a relatively modest small-scale irrigation subsector. The 1990s saw a substantial rise in private irrigated peri-urban agriculture in Sub-Saharan Africa in response to higher demand from growing cities for fresh fruits and vegetables (FAO 2005).

The advent of affordable drilling and pumping technologies in India and Pakistan in the mid-1980s led to rapid development of shallow tubewells and conjunctive use of

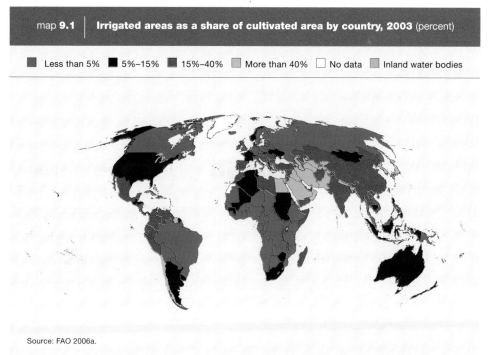

map **9.1** | **Irrigated areas as a share of cultivated area by country, 2003** (percent)

■ Less than 5% ■ 5%–15% ■ 15%–40% ▨ More than 40% ☐ No data ▨ Inland water bodies

Source: FAO 2006a.

table **9.1**	**Irrigated land, total and as share of arable land, 1980, 1990, and 2002**					
	Total irrigated area (thousands of hectares)			**As share of arable land** (percent)		
Region	**1980**	**1990**	**2002**	**1980**	**1990**	**2002**
World	210,222	244,988	276,719	15.7	17.6	19.7
Developed countries	58,926	66,286	68,060	9.1	10.2	11.1
Industrialized countries	37,355	39,935	43,669	9.9	10.5	11.9
Transition economies	21,571	26,351	24,391	7.9	9.8	10.0
Developing countries	151,296	178,702	208,659	21.9	24.1	26.3
Latin America and the Caribbean	13,811	16,794	18,622	10.8	12.5	12.6
Near East and North Africa	17,982	24,864	28,642	21.8	28.8	32.3
Sub-Saharan Africa	3,980	4,885	5,225	3.2	3.7	3.6
East & Southeast Asia	59,722	65,624	74,748	37.0	33.9	35.1
South Asia	55,798	66,529	81,408	28.6	33.9	41.7
Oceania, developing	3	6	14	0.7	1.2	2.4

Source: FAO 2004a.

surface water and groundwater (Shah 1993; Palmer Jones and Mandal 1987). Direct control of farmers' water sources—either through groundwater pumping, drainage reuse, or direct pumping from canals and rivers—brought the flexibility and reliability in water delivery that most large-scale surface distribution systems did not offer. It also brought new challenges in managing irrigation schemes under conjunctive use, falling groundwater tables, and indirect subsidies though cheap or free electricity from public distribution systems (see chapter 10 on groundwater).

Official statistics indicate a total of 277 million ha of land under irrigation in 2002 worldwide (table 9.1; FAO 2006a), but the extent of land under irrigation is likely to be higher when unreported private investment in irrigation is taken into account. Irrigation covers 20% of all cultivated land and about 40% of agricultural production. In 1995, 38% of cereals grown in developing countries were on irrigated land, accounting for just under 60% of cereal production (Ringler and others 2003). Rainfed cereal yields averaged 1.5 metric tons per hectare in the developing world in 1995, but irrigated yields were 3.3 metric tons per hectare (Rosegrant, Cai, and Cline 2002). The difference in productivity between irrigated and rainfed agriculture varies widely, depending on the climate, combination of crops, and technologies. Typically, land productivity is two to four times higher in irrigated agriculture.

Moreover, cropping intensity is typically higher under irrigation, with up to three rice crops per year in parts of Southeast Asia and two crops per year in most of the Asian subcontinent. Figure 9.2 shows the distribution of crops under irrigation worldwide.

A diversity of systems

The term *irrigation system* covers a diversity of situations associated with a variety of crops, leading to multiple development and management strategies. There are fundamental

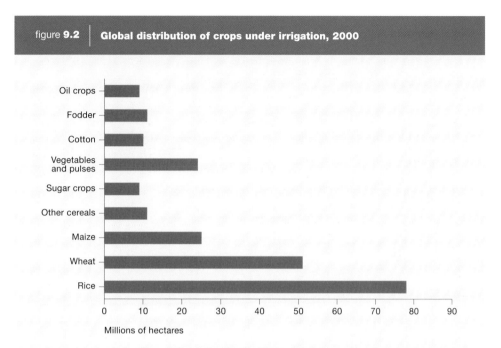

figure **9.2** | **Global distribution of crops under irrigation, 2000**

Millions of hectares

Source: Food and Agriculture Organization estimates based on data and information for 230 million hectares in 100 countries.

differences between public and privately managed schemes, between cash crop and food grain production, and between the humid tropics and arid areas. Irrigation plays different roles in different climatic contexts, supplying full, partial, or supplementary irrigation. To organize the discussion here, a simplified typology with five categories of irrigation systems is used, based principally on mode of governance (table 9.2 and appendix).

The analysis of irrigation systems and its implication in political terms must also take into account the economic environment. This typology is thus further refined by defining three stages of economic development of a particular region or country:

- Stage 1: Countries or regions within countries where agriculture accounts for a substantial share of the economy and employs a large proportion of the population (including most of Sub-Saharan Africa; Diao and others 2005).

table **9.2** | **Typology of irrigation systems**

Type	Description
1	Large-scale public irrigation systems in dry areas, growing mostly staple crops.
2	Large-scale public paddy irrigation systems in humid areas.
3	Small- to medium-scale community-managed (and -built) systems.
4	Commercial privately managed systems, producing for local and export markets.
5	Farm-scale individually managed systems, producing for local markets, often around cities.

- Stage 2: Countries in transition to more market-based and industrial economies where the relative importance of agriculture is falling in economic terms but where a large part of the population still derives its livelihood from it (including most of Southeast Asia and the Middle East);

- Stage 3: Countries where agriculture contributes only a small share of the economy and further large-scale investment is unlikely (Republic of Korea, Malaysia, and Taiwan). The farming sector in these countries may follow divergent paths: from a competitive international market orientation (such as Australia or Brazil) to redefining the role of farmers as "guardians of the landscape," as in Europe, Japan, the Republic of Korea, and Taiwan (Hung and Shih 1994). In large countries all these outcomes can occur, and national policies must account for regional specificities.

Trajectories of change within and between categories of irrigation farmers are shaped not only by agricultural policies but also by the capacity to ensure allocations of water in all three stages, by wider financial restrictions, and by local capacity to overcome pollution and environmental damage in countries moving through stages 2 and 3.

> Private and informal irrigation is important in terms of both food production and food security

Past investment in irrigation

Irrigation has received most of the public agricultural investment in the developing world—and most of the public operating subsidies (Jones 1995). In the early 1980s irrigation investment peaked at 60% of total agricultural expenditures in the Philippines and more than 50% in Sri Lanka (Kikuchi and others 2002). In Viet Nam slightly more than half of public agricultural expenditures were still devoted to irrigation during the 1990s (Barker and others 2004). In most cases direct cost recovery has not fully covered either investment costs or operations and maintenance costs, making these investments subsidies to the agriculture sector. The investments have, however, helped balance the typically adverse agricultural terms of trade (agricultural price controls, taxes, and the like) also operating within the sector and eventually indirectly supported all food consumers.

Private investment (private entrepreneurs, commercial irrigation, farmers' investment in public irrigation) is significant (and in some places even larger than public investment) and generally growing. In parts of Latin America, where the private irrigation sector is most dynamic, 56% of irrigation is private (FAO 2000). Recognition and knowledge of farmer-managed and private irrigation, its importance, and its success are growing, and these forms of investment are likely to grow faster than public investment (Shah 2003). But government departments, having served primarily large public irrigation schemes, have rarely had the opportunity to learn from them and to provide them with the required support. Yet private and informal irrigation is important in terms of both food production and food security.

Economic benefits and costs of irrigation

Through increased productivity irrigation produces secondary benefits for the economy at all levels, including increased productivity of rural labor, promotion of local agro-enterprises, and stimulation of the agriculture sector as a whole. The overall multiplier effect on the economy has been estimated at 2.5–4 (Bhattharai, Barker, and Narayanamoorthy forthcoming; Lipton, Litchfield, and Faurès 2003; Huang and others 2006).

Under these conditions the multiplier effects are so broad that irrigation's impacts need to be viewed from the context of rural development rather than simply agricultural development. Road systems, education, health, and the entire way of life in rural areas are transformed by irrigation. Public investment in irrigation has been crucial in agricultural growth in many Asian countries: in Viet Nam it accounted for 28% of growth in overall agricultural output during the 1990s. Investments in agricultural research closely follows, accounting for 27% of total growth (Barker and others 2004).

Irrigation has historically had a large positive impact on poverty reduction (see chapter 4 on poverty) (Hussain 2005; Lipton and others 2003). At the same time, growing prosperity has highlighted the plight of those who have not benefited from irrigation. The largest positive impacts of irrigation on poverty and livelihoods, in both urban and rural areas, have been relatively cheap food for everyone and employment opportunities for the landless poor. Many recent studies agree that an increase in farm income from enhanced farm productivity creates an increase in demand for local nontradable goods and services, which offer labor opportunities to the poorest segments of the rural population (see chapter 4). The growth induced by increases in agricultural productivity that raise farm income does not worsen income distribution and therefore decreases the level of absolute poverty (Mellor 2002). Recent studies in India have found that irrigation and farmer's education level are the two main factors in improving agricultural productivity and alleviating rural poverty (Bhattarai and Narayanamoorthy 2003).

In addition to these large and far-reaching benefits there are many direct and indirect costs associated with irrigation. The budgetary costs are the easiest to document: irrigation-related development was the biggest budgetary item for some Asian countries in the 1980s. The environmental and social costs of irrigation are partly intrinsic to the nature of irrigation (for example, transformation of natural habitats) and partly due to choices about the type of agricultural practices that irrigation supports. Negative impacts can outweigh the positive ones, for example, when pollution, displacement of populations, increased inequity, reduced biodiversity, and waterborne diseases are not compensated for by substantial increases in productivity and well-being (Dougherty and Hall 1995; MEA 2005b). Important challenges for irrigation are to acknowledge, account for, and mitigate the unavoidable alterations of ecological systems while ensuring that negative impacts are minimized.

> The largest positive impacts of irrigation on poverty and livelihoods have been relatively cheap food for everyone and employment opportunities for the landless poor

Beyond production: the multiple functions of irrigation

Economic assessments of irrigation projects are typically based on the internal rate of return, which compares the costs and benefits of irrigation development. But this approach does not capture the intangible benefits associated with irrigation (Tiffen 1987). In addition, multiple uses of irrigation water are also rarely taken into account (see chapter 4 on poverty). Irrigation development is usually associated with intensive agriculture and the forces of modernization, but it has a long history and in some places is closely linked to local culture and tradition, acting as a stable agroecosystem. As economies develop, the relationships among food production, food consumption, and food security become more complex.

Irrigation affects the material and the cultural life of society and the environment in four main ways: economic, social, environmental, and cultural (table 9.3). The impact in

table 9.3	Impact of irrigation by type of system				
Impact	Large-scale public, dry zone	Large-scale public, paddy-based	Small- or medium-size community-managed	Private, commercial	Smallholder, individual
Economic					
Production	Low positive	Low positive	Low positive	High positive	High positive
Food security	High positive	High positive	High positive	Low positive	High positive
Rural employment	High positive	High positive	High positive	Low positive	High positive
Social					
Settlement strategies	Mixed	Mixed	High positive	None	None
Social capital	None	Low positive	High positive	None	None
Health	Mixed	Mixed	Mixed	Low negative	Mixed
Environmental					
Biological diversity	Mixed	Mixed	Mixed	Mixed	None
Soil and water conservation	Mixed	Mixed	Mixed	Mixed	None
Water quality	High negative	Mixed	Mixed	High negative	Low negative
Cultural					
Religious ceremonies	Low negative	None	Low positive	None	None
Landscape, aesthetics	Mixed	High positive	High positive	Low negative	None
Cultural heritage	Mixed	Mixed	High positive	None	None

Note: Mixed indicates a large variability of local situations.

each area varies with the type of irrigation system, and the magnitude (positive or negative) is subjective, but there is value in highlighting the complex and diverse roles of irrigation and in remembering that in many places, particularly Asia, the Near East, and South America, irrigation is embedded in the culture and history.

The next era of irrigation investments

The rapid expansion of irrigation in the 20th century is unlikely to be repeated because the economic justification for irrigation has changed with falling food prices and the overall adequacy of current food production levels. This section analyses the main factors that will influence future investments in irrigation and drainage.

The context has changed

While most major changes affecting public irrigation are progressive, the end of the cold war and acceleration of globalization have certainly intensified some of these trends (table 9.4). Population pressures are now easing. The world food system can now satisfy the needs of a slower growing population, and fears of food shortages and famines are receding in most places outside of Sub-Saharan Africa, though local shortages may intensify, leading to increased food trade (FAO 2003). Technology, including biotechnology, will

table **9.4**	**Evolution of public irrigation since the 1960s**	
Context	1960s to 1980s	1990s to present
Goals: drivers	Food security	Livelihood, income
Resources: land, water, and labor	Abundant	Increased scarcity
Hydraulic development stages	Construction, utilization	Utilization, allocation
Dominant expertise	Hydraulic engineering, agronomy	Multidisciplinary, sociology, economics
Irrigation governance	Public	Mixed
Irrigation technology	Surface	Conjunctive use, pressurized
System management	Supply-driven	Farmer-oriented
Crops	Fixed, cereals and cotton	Diversified
Cropping intensity[a]	1–1.5	1.5–2.5
Value of water	Low	Increasing
Concern for environment	Low	Increasing

a. Average number of crops per year on area equipped for irrigation.
Source: Adapted from Barker and Molle 2004.

further enhance the productive capacity of agriculture and most crop yields will continue to increase. However, compared with the last two decades, the food supply may become tighter as a result of declining public expenditure on irrigation and agricultural research, leading to stagnation and increases in world food prices and to further degradation of the agricultural resource base.

Other changes will characterize the coming era as well. While food grain prices should continue to fall, perhaps eventually stabilizing at historically low levels, rising incomes will lead to shifts in food preferences, away from grains and toward fruits, vegetables, meat, and dairy products, all of which are higher value commodities and require more water and energy inputs. The population will continue to urbanize, and agriculture's share of GDP will fall in most countries. Finally, global climate change will disrupt existing cycles and patterns in various ways, including increased variability in precipitation (IPCC 2001) and reduced snowpack storage in mountains (Barnett, Adams, and Lettenmaier 2005).

Projections of developing country irrigation expansion by the Food and Agriculture Organization (FAO), International Food Policy Research Institute, and the International Water Management Institute predict much lower rates of expansion of irrigated land over the next 20–30 years (FAO 2003; Rosegrant, Cai, and Cline 2002; IWMI 2000). The FAO (2003) predicts an average increase of 0.6% a year between 1997/99 and 2030 in developing countries, compared with 1.6% a year from 1960 to 1990. Such projections are systematically lower than those given by most national irrigation departments, which generally rely more on past trends than on a careful analysis of demand for agricultural outputs. Nevertheless, irrigation's contribution to total agricultural production is expected to exceed 45% by 2030 as yields continue to increase and cropping patterns shift to higher value crops (FAO 2003). This means 12%–17% more water withdrawn for irrigation.

The situation will vary substantially from one region to another, and places where water is already stretched to the limit will see reductions in allocations for agriculture, a trend that will intensify as competition for water increases (Molle and Berkoff 2006).

Rationale for future investments in irrigation

This section considers investment in a broad sense, covering capital, institutional, and operational investments (box 9.1). There are five principal reasons to invest in irrigation over the next three to five decades.

> Irrigation's contribution to total agricultural production is expected to exceed 45% by 2030 as yields continue to increase and cropping patterns shift to higher value crops

First is to preserve and modernize the present stock of irrigation infrastructure. Continuing investment will be required to preserve the safety and improve the functionality of existing irrigation. Different elements have different lifetimes. Large dams may last hundreds of years with proper maintenance and attention to safety (unless rapid siltation reduces their lifespan), while pumps and other equipment may last only a decade.

Second, irrigation can be a path out of poverty for the rural poor. Where pockets of rural poverty exist within an irrigated agricultural context, intensification and shifts to higher value crops will create new employment opportunities, as will value-added post-harvest processing and water-dependent off-farm rural employment in handicrafts, livestock raising, and similar activities (Bakker and others 1999). Where rural poverty is widespread, other employment options are absent, and climate variability affects production (figure 9.3), as in parts of Sub-Saharan Africa, soil moisture control, along with complementary investments in rural infrastructure (such as roads and stronger local institutions), provides new farming opportunities. However, the extent to which irrigation contributes to poverty alleviation remains a contentious issue, with alternative vigorous arguments about ways to address rural poverty (Lipton, Litchfield, and Faurès 2003; Bhattarai and Narayanamoorthy 2003; Berkoff 2003).

Third is to adapt to changing food preferences and changing social priorities. Most of the increased production of staple crops in the coming decades will come from intensification in existing irrigated areas, with higher yields per unit of water and land and higher cropping intensities. This implies investment in modernizing equipment and in

---

box 9.1 | What do we mean by investment?

Investment in irrigation usually means public expenditure on new irrigation systems (capital investment). A broader definition is used here to include public investment in irrigation and drainage development, modernization, institutional reform, improved governance, capacity building, management improvement, creation of farmer organizations, and regulatory oversight, as well as farmers' investment in joint facilities, wells, and on-farm water storage and irrigation equipment.

Financing for major capital works has historically come from international development banks with varying levels of contribution from national budgets, as low-income countries typically lack sufficient resources to invest in large capital projects (Winpenny 2003) such as large dams. There has been significant experimentation with financing packages to attract private investment to developing countries through design, build, and operate contracts and franchises. But the niche for these instruments is limited, and expected financing levels have not been, and are unlikely to be, achieved.

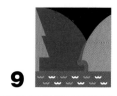

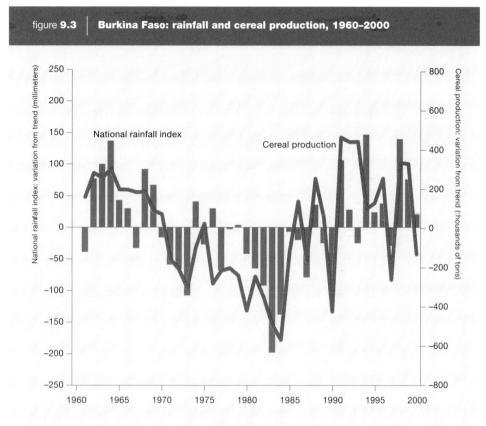

figure **9.3** | **Burkina Faso: rainfall and cereal production, 1960–2000**

Note: The national rainfall index is a measure of annual precipitation in the agricultural areas of a country (Gommes 1993). Both the national rainfall index and cereal production are presented here as the deviation from the long-term trend to better illustrate the impact of the interannual variation of precipitation on production.

Source: Food and Agriculture Organization statistics.

improved water control. Irrigated basic food grain production will remain a priority in some countries. Rising incomes and growing urbanization in many developing countries are shifting demand from staple crops to fruits, vegetables, and "luxury" goods such as wine, as in China, for example (figure 9.4). These shifts are typically associated with investment in supply reliability and precision water application, but—more important for farmers—they also raise yields and improve product quality. Other shifts, such as increased meat and milk demand, also require increased grain production. Increased global trade also opens developed country markets to these commodities. Notably, these production shifts also require major investment in the entire post-harvest marketing chain.

Fourth, rapidly expanding urban populations and industrialization increase demand for both surface water and groundwater (Molle and Berkoff 2006). Changing social values that emphasize natural ecosystem protection will increase water allocations to the environment. In many cases these competing uses will take water directly away from agriculture, requiring compensating investment in new supplies or increased water productivity (see chapter 7 on water productivity). Reusing urban and industrial wastewater in agriculture will require new investment in water treatment and conveyance.

Fifth, investment will probably be needed to respond to climate change. Predictions by global climate models are gradually converging, and several characteristics now seem clear (IPCC 2001). Weather patterns will become more variable and will include more extreme events. The assured supply of water will decline and the need for additional storage, above or below ground, will increase to compensate. Rainfall distribution and volumes will change, and investment in groundwater and surface storage will be required in response. Finally, in several important locations high mountain snowfields serve as frozen reservoirs, releasing water gradually over the summer. The most notable example is the Himalayan Mountains, which source seven major rivers of East and South Asia. Climate change is shrinking these snowfields, reducing their storage capacity, and causing more precipitation to fall as rain, increasing spring flows and flooding while reducing summer flows (Barnett, Adams, and Lettenmaier 2005). With more than one-sixth of the Earth's population relying on glaciers and seasonal snow packs for their water supply, the consequences of these hydrological changes are likely to be severe.

figure **9.4** | **Evolution of harvested area for major crop groups in China, 1980–2004**

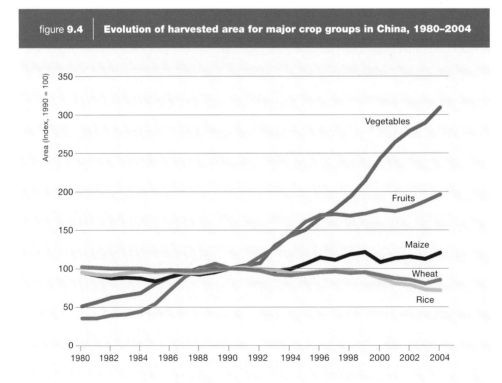

Source: FAO 2006a.

The most vulnerable people are the poor, landless, and marginal farmers in rural areas dependent on isolated rainfed agricultural systems in humid, semiarid, and arid regions. Small changes in rainfall will result in big changes in river flows and soil moisture. The African continent has the largest number of countries that are already vulnerable to climate variability and extremes because of a lack of surface water and groundwater resources in the semiarid and arid regions. Further compensatory irrigation development will be necessary in these regions, to supplement both existing irrigation systems and rainfed systems. Necessary changes to fixed capital associated with irrigation may represent one of the largest costs associated with climate change adaptation and will present considerable challenges to the poorest farmers (Quiggin and Horowitz 1999).

Types of investment

The environment in which irrigation investment decisions will be made is far more complex today than in the past: more stakeholders, more competing demands for water, and no single overwhelming driver for investment. Irrigation investment will thus be more carefully tailored to particular circumstances, reflecting stage of national development, market opportunities, degree of integration into the world economy, land and water availability, share of agriculture in the national economy, and comparative advantage in regional and world markets.

Farmers around the world will continue to integrate into a global market that will increasingly dictate their choices and behavior. While irrigated grain production will remain important, a variety of niche markets will emerge, creating opportunities for innovative entrepreneurial farmers where suitable national policies are in place. By contrast, smallholder farmers in Sub-Saharan Africa have few opportunities to take advantage of global markets. Water control investment could be an important part of rural development strategies in many Sub-Saharan countries, but it should be made in connection with policies that allow farmers to better serve local or regional markets (FAO 2006b).

Countries with a legacy of aging irrigation infrastructure will need to invest more in technical and managerial upgrading and less in new development, progressively improving the performance of irrigation in response to growing demand for more reliable water service. Investment in drainage will continue at relatively modest levels, although regional waterlogging and salinization problems resulting from past development will continue to require remediation. Thus there will be considerable tension arising from these financial needs compared with government's willingness and ability to finance them.

New development will still take place where enough land and water resources are available and where national priorities support it. It will be more site-specific and more closely linked with policies and plans in other sectors. Table 9.5 shows projections of expansion of irrigated land and investments in new development and rehabilitation between 1998 and 2030 based on unit costs provided by various lending agencies. Irrigation investment costs vary widely in developing countries, from less than $1,000 per hectare to as much as $20,000, averaging $3,500 in 2000 (Inocencio and others forthcoming; FAO data). Irrigation investment costs are generally much higher in Sub-Saharan Africa than in Asia, reflecting the challenging environment of the region, unfavorable geomorphological

> While irrigated grain production will remain important, a variety of niche markets will emerge, creating opportunities for innovative entrepreneurial farmers where suitable national policies are in place

table **9.5**	Projections of capital investment needs in irrigation development and rehabilitation in 93 developing countries, 1998–2030							
	Irrigated area (thousands of hectares)			Unit cost (US dollars per hectare)		Total cost (millions of US dollars)		
Region	1998	2030	Change (percent)	New	Rehabili-tated	New	Rehabili-tated	Total
East & South East Asia	71,500	85,300	19	2,900	700	40,000	46,400	86,500
Latin America & Caribbean	18,400	22,000	20	3,700	1,300	13,400	23,900	37,300
Near East & North Africa	26,400	33,100	25	6,000	2,000	40,100	52,800	92,900
South Asia	80,500	95,000	18	2,600	900	37,600	68,500	106,100
Sub-Saharan Africa	5,300	6,800	30	5,600	2,000	8,900	10,500	19,400
Total	202,000	242,200	20	3,500	1,000	140,100	202,000	342,100

Source: Based on FAO 2003 and Inocencio and others forthcoming.

conditions, higher infrastructure development costs, and differences in the scale of irrigation development projects. These factors seriously constrain attempts to develop irrigation in the region.

Priorities for investment by type of system

In large-scale public surface irrigation systems in dry areas most investment in existing systems should improve water control capability and supply predictability and increase transparency and accountability to the user. Areas with incomplete drainage and high water tables will probably see investment in completing these networks and associated salt disposal works to mitigate secondary soil salinization. Investment will typically involve a mix of technological and managerial upgrading.

In large-scale public surface irrigation systems in humid areas investment should enhance flexibility in the service of water in existing systems and the potential for operation to enhance the multifunctionality of the system. The level of flexibility needed in irrigation is subject to debate (Ankum 1996; FAO 1999a; Horst 1998; Perry and Narayanamurthy 1998). It will likely be determined case by case based on farmers' needs and cropping opportunities, local agricultural policies, and the availability of financial resources for investment. Flexible service will be increasingly important as off-season cropping expands, as in Viet Nam's Red River Delta (Malano, George, and Davidson 2004). It may be achieved through private investment in low-lift pumps or on-farm storage reservoirs, for example, or through public investment in intermediate in-system storage reservoirs. Investment in flexibility will also support new cultural practices for rice which may, for example, involve alternate wet and dry irrigation as opposed to continuous ponding (see chapter 14 on rice). Some countries in humid regions that did not participate in the construction boom of the 1960s and 1970s may continue to construct storage to enhance basin-level water control, including for irrigation, far into the 21st century.

Further dramatic private investment in groundwater irrigation and on-farm storage can be anticipated in large-scale surface irrigation systems (photo 9.1) in both dry and humid areas, as well as in very small (farm) systems. A major challenge in national investment strategies will be arriving at a balance of polices that allow equitable development (for instance, policies favoring cheap imported pumps and motors) but constrain overuse (for instance, by limiting or withholding energy subsidies for abstraction) (see chapter 10 on groundwater). Investment will be required to more effectively monitor and regulate such private development.

In areas of small- to medium-scale community-managed irrigation, mostly traditional subsistence schemes, complementary investments in roads, communications, and other supporting infrastructure that enhances information flows and market access usually offer high payoffs. Additional investment in new small-scale development is warranted in some circumstances, and incorporating small-scale irrigation development into comprehensive rural development programs may offer better chances of success and sustainability (Ward, Peacock, and Gamberelli 2006). These systems are also fertile ground for low-pressure irrigation technologies. Low-cost technologies, including small pumps, marketed through the private sector have rapidly expanded in several countries over the last decade (Shah and others 2000; Heierli and Polak 2000; Barker and Molle 2004).

For private commercial irrigation responding to local and export markets, water will become more of a commercial commodity than a common good. Improving connectivity, in combination with well specified water rights, will allow regular water transactions among users and more extensive reuse of drainage and treated wastewater. Growers will likely continue to make major investments in on-farm water application technology to improve productivity and product quality. Governments and individuals would need to invest in measurement and control technology.

> For private commercial irrigation responding to local and export markets, water will become more of a commercial commodity than a common good

Photo by G. Bizzarri/FAO

Photo 9.1 Farmer pumping groundwater for irrigation

table 9.6	Focus for investment by type of irrigation system		

System type and category	Agriculture economy, large rural population	Transition	Industrial, market-based economy
Large-scale public irrigation systems in dry and humid areas			
Policy focus	Integrated rural development	Linking water and agriculture policies	Implementing integrated water resources management approach
Capital investment, water	Small and large dams, gravity irrigation development, drainage development, on-farm groundwater development		Upgrading irrigation and drainage infrastructure
Capital investment, other	Rural infrastructure, roads, markets, social and health infrastructure, electrification		Upgrading rural infrastructure
Regulation	Land tenure and water rights, stakeholder involvement in scheme management	Water rights, local institutions regulations, participatory irrigation management	Irrigation management transfer
Management	Increased reliability in system operation	Restructuring, improved accountability and transparency, improved system control and operations, enhanced flexibility of water service, enhancing system multifunctionality	
Capacity building	Training irrigation staff and farmers, water user association formation and strengthening		Strengthening of professional organizations, market information systems
Finance	Term finance, rural credit and micro-credit, grants	Term finance, agricultural savings and loans	Commercial financing
Technology	Land leveling, shallow wells, small-scale pumping technology, conjunctive use of surface water and groundwater		Automation, pressurized irrigation systems, water quality monitoring
Small- to medium-scale community-managed systems			
Policy focus	Integrated rural development	Linking water and agriculture policies	
Capital investment, water	Runoff river, weirs, diversion, local storage and small dams	Local storage and small dams, improved water distribution infastructure	
Capital investment, other	Rural infrastructure, roads, market access and information, social and health infrastructure, electrification		
Regulation	Water rights, including traditional water rights	Recognition and formalization of water rights and bulk water allocation	
Management	Conflict management, on-farm water management		
Capacity building	Training of extension staff, water user association formation and empowerment	Water user association monitoring and support, staff training	
Finance	Grants, targeted subsidies	Rural finance	
Technology	Small-scale microirrigation systems, tanks	Mechanized agriculture, deep tubewell drilling, pressurized irrigation systems	

table **9.6**	**Focus for investment by type of irrigation system** (continued)		
System type and category	**Agriculture economy, large rural population**	**Transition**	**Industrial, market-based economy**
Commercial privately managed systems			
Policy focus	Market chain; negotiating favorable trade policies		
Capital investment, water	Diversion dams, deep tubewells	Runoff recycleing, automation of water supply	Automation
Capital investment, other	Markets, communication and storage infrastructure, including for export		
Regulation	Bulk water allocation, water rights, tariffs		
Management	Irrigation scheduling, soil moisture monitoring		
Capacity building	Water quality monitoring		
Finance	Commercial finance		
Technology	Overhead irrigation, sprinkler and micro-irrigation technologies	Precision farming, pivots, lateral moves, microirrigation, fertigation	
Farm-scale individually managed systems for local markets			
Policy focus	Food safety, food security and nutrition policies		
Capital investment, water	Shallow well drilling, canals		
Capital investment, other	Market and infrastructure development	Rural electrification, energy pricing	Market and infrastructure development, wastewater treatment
Regulation	Tenure security, water rights, food safety control		Tenure security, food safety control, environmental control
Management	Wastewater reuse		
Capacity building	Training on on-farm water management and food and water quality control		
Finance	Micro-finance		
Technology	Low-cost, robust irrigation technology	Mechanized groundwater use	Water measurement and control, automation, low pressure irrigation

Note: *Term finance* refers to equity or medium- and long-term loan finance.

For individual smallholder irrigation responding to local markets, private investment in water application technology should be able to support improved output and product quality. Complementary public investment in governance and improved markets and infrastructure should strengthen this sector. Public intervention will also be needed in regulatory fields, including tenure security and specification and registration of equitable water rights, and in health-related monitoring and education. The link among smallholders, the private sector, and governments for the provision of services (technical advisory, finance, and marketing) needs to be better developed. Innovative approaches, such as the farmer field school, will be needed to compensate for the reduction of public extension services.

In nearly all situations significant investment will be required in training, particularly to manage the transition from construction to management orientation in irrigation systems. There will be a strong demand for well trained professionals at all levels of water management, with increasingly multidisciplinary perspectives and the acquisition of a learning culture (see chapter 5 on policies and institutions). Table 9.6 summarizes possible focuses for investment by type of irrigation system.

Investment in irrigation has not always been driven by the need to increase food supply or to stabilize production; other hidden political agendas have also considerably influenced investment decisions

Adapting yesterday's systems to tomorrow's needs

The recent rapid development of irrigation has been the subject of many controversies, and experts disagree strongly on its overall performance. Rehabilitation, modernization, and a range of institutional reforms including irrigation management transfer and participatory irrigation management have been advocated over the last 20 years as ways to improve the delivery of water services, reduce recurrent costs, and boost productivity in large irrigation schemes. The results have been mixed, and it is important to understand the reasons behind the failures and successes to distinguish which options can be pursued, what can be further improved upon, and what innovations can replace them (see chapter 5 on policies and institutions).

Overall performance of public irrigation schemes

On average, the economic performance of public irrigation projects has been relatively good. About 67% of World Bank–financed irrigation projects from 1961 to 1987 were rated satisfactory by the Bank's Operations Evaluation Department, with an average internal rate of return of 15% (Jones 1995). Large investment projects tended to show higher returns than small ones, mainly because of economies of scale, but small-scale irrigation projects within them had lower costs and offered higher returns (Lipton, Litchfield, and Faurès 2003; Inocencio and others forthcoming).

This positive view is often contested, and there are numerous cases of poor performance, mostly relating to failure to meet design performance targets (ODI various years). In addition, there are several cases of significant failure of large-scale irrigation schemes for reasons varying from overcommitment of water resources to poor design and construction, to lack of market, labor, managerial skills, or financial resources for operations and maintenance. In Sub-Saharan Africa, for instance, about 18% of land under irrigation is not used (FAO 2005), and many Asian countries have large amounts of unused irrigable land.

Indeed, investment in irrigation has not always been driven by the need to increase food supply or to stabilize production. Other hidden political agendas have also considerably influenced investment decisions, with obvious implications for the systems' overall economic performance. Public funding aimed at benefiting a particular area for electoral purposes has influenced investment priorities, with politicians promising new irrigation schemes to villages even when such schemes are not feasible in technical or economic terms (Mollinga 1998; Reisner 1986). In other places large public irrigation schemes are being constructed to lay claim to transboundary water even when rivers are already overcommitted. Moreover, perverse incentives for lending institutions increase

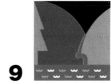

project budgets beyond requirements. Corruption and rent-seeking have also led to higher project costs and lower economic returns on irrigation investments in many cases (Wade 1982; Repetto 1986; Rinaudo 2002). Land tenure, where it favors absentee land-lords, can also seriously constrain the development of productive irrigated agriculture (Hussain 2005).

Planning and design flaws are among the main causes of irrigation schemes' poor performance and often lead to nonfunctioning systems, unreliable water supplies, and excessive management complexity (Plusquellec 2002; Albinson and Perry 2002; Bos, Burton, and Molden 2005; IFAD and IWMI forthcoming). Possible future developments of irrigation technology are summarized in box 9.2.

---

box 9.2 | **Technologies and irrigation in the future**

Technological improvements will happen at all levels and affect all types of irrigation systems. Better technologies do not necessarily mean new, expensive, or sophisticated options, but ones that are appropriate to the agricultural needs and demands, the managerial capacity of system managers and farmers, and the financial and economic capacity needed to ensure proper operation and maintenance. We can expect better design and better matching of technologies, management, and institutional arrangements.

Technological innovation will occur in broadly two categories:

- At the irrigation system level: water level, flow control, and storage management within surface irrigation systems at all scales.
- On farm: storage, reuse, water lifting (manual and mechanical), and the adoption of precision application technologies such as overhead sprinkler and localized irrigation. As farms consolidate, particularly in larger more formal systems, increasing mechanization will require greater attention to land forming and farm layout. In Africa the emerging pattern of development and adoption of low-cost, microirrigation technologies will likely continue and strengthen (see chapter 4 on poverty).

Many of the technologies already exist, particularly the hardware. Considerable change can be expected on the soft technology side as electronics, communication systems, computers, and instrumentation become cheaper, more reliable, more accessible, and more available throughout the developing world. Automation for monitoring and control (including supervisory control and data acquisition in formal canal systems) and measurement (of groundwater levels, canal discharges, and even on-farm and water-course deliveries) will become more widespread. Over time this technology will be adopted in smaller informal systems and in groundwater irrigation, as well as more quickly by more commercially oriented growers at all scales.

Satisfying real-time demand more quickly and improving flexibility in formal canal systems will be achieved largely by further expansion of conjunctive use of groundwater and assisted by better canal management, mostly likely through intermediate service options such as "arranged demand." Software for managing lower system level demands will become more commonplace.

Some irrigation systems may continue with simple infrastructure and management systems, provided that they are well understood and appropriate to cropping patterns and user needs. Islands of minimal technology development in irrigation are also likely, especially where water remains abundant. There will be increasing interest in affordable technologies of all types (Keller and Keller 2003), well adapted to private investments.

Engineering designs sometimes do not match the management capacities of agency staff, water user associations, or farmers (Murray-Rust and Snellen 1993). Even simply structured large-scale irrigation systems with proportional division of flows through branching networks of canals (typically in Asia) require well trained professional managers and operators to achieve acceptable levels of performance in water delivery service (Horst 1998).

Institutional reforms and prospects for future water management

Many attempts to privatize water services have failed, and the extent to which such a model should be widely promoted remains highly controversial

The last 15–20 years have seen the development of institutional reforms for public irrigation management in more than 50 countries (FAO 1997; FAO 1999b; Johnson, Svendsen, and Gonzalez 2004), with a focus on withdrawing government from management and devolving responsibilities from centralized bureaucratic management to lower levels, including water user associations. Positive outcomes have been reported in Armenia, Australia, China, Colombia, Malaysia, Mexico, Peru, and Turkey, where reforms have improved maintenance standards of irrigation infrastructure. In most cases the transfer of costs from government to farmers improved maintenance, equity, yields, and income, thus at least partially fulfilling the purpose of the reforms. But the nature and degree of success is contested (Rap, Wester, and Pérez-Prado 2004; Vermillion 1997; Shah 2003), and there are many cases of wholesale nonperformance in irrigation management transfer.

In the context of irrigation management transfer, public-private partnership and the scope for professional "third-parties" between farmers and government are receiving increasing attention (Tardieu and others 2005). In Chile, China, Iran, and Viet Nam experiments are being conducted where farmers contract private or semiprivate companies to provide irrigation services. In China legally established water user associations establish operating franchises with public water bureaus.

But many attempts to privatize water services have failed (Qian 1994), and the extent to which such a model should be widely promoted remains highly controversial. To be viable, private water services must be based on reliable and measurable provision of service and include a reliable source of funding. Also needed are adequate regulations and dispute settlement mechanisms and training for water user associations and local service providers. Of particular concern are the difficulties in assessing operation and maintenance costs and ensuring that private managers do not delay rehabilitation and maintenance to show reduced management costs. The transfer of responsibilities for collecting water taxes from government to local institutions also presents challenges in financial accountability.

Sectoral reforms in irrigation management cannot succeed in a vacuum and depend heavily on broader reforms in governance and transparency at the national level and on agricultural policies (see chapter 5 on policies and institutions). The necessary legal reforms have often not happened or have been enacted only on paper and thus fail to give a solid and practical underpinning to irrigation management reforms. The main conditions for success and reasons for failure of institutional reforms are presented in table 9.7.

Another reason for failure often lies in the emphasis on water by irrigation departments. Poor performance of irrigated agriculture may be the result of non-water-related constraints, in which case irrigation management reforms will attract little attention from

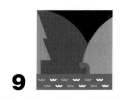

table **9.7**	Main conditions for success and reasons for failure of institutional reforms	
Conditions for success		**Reasons for failure**
▪ Strong political backing. ▪ A clear role for the different stakeholders. ▪ Support for the empowerment of institutions at all levels (including water user associations and local governments). ▪ The autonomy of the water user associations. ▪ The legal framework needed to accommodate the proposed changes in authority. ▪ Capacity building of the people governing the transferred system. ▪ Functioning infrastructure. ▪ Success in recovering operation and maintenance costs.		▪ Lack of political support. ▪ Resistance of public agencies and water users. ▪ Insufficient resources. ▪ Poor water quality. ▪ Lack of proper involvement of water users. ▪ Transfer of dilapidated or badly designed infrastructure that is dysfunctional and needs major improvement.

Source: FAO forthcoming

farmers. The broad sociotechnical environment of irrigation is summarized in figure 9.5 to illustrate the importance of matching technology and institutional development in a specific context. Reality is inevitably far more complex, and the intention of the figure is to show key issues that need to be addressed to achieve good irrigation system performance rather than to offer a prescription with neat cause and effect links. Underlying this set of links are the incentives, vested interests, and communication pathways that are more intangible and hard to include in a simple diagram.

The historical bias toward infrastructure investment to the neglect of training, capacity building (for farmers and for irrigation service providers), and institutional strengthening interventions is one cause of poor irrigation performance. But training, personnel policies, and salaries are still major problems in many countries (see chapter 5 on policies and institutions). A more balanced approach should characterize future interventions as the synergies are recognized and the cost effectiveness of an approach balancing soft and hard investment is demonstrated.

Most reforms have been based on the assumption that greater user participation will result in improved responsiveness and performance and that users will be increasingly interested in the management of their irrigation service as the state retreats from providing and financing its provision. However, much has to be learned about how to do this effectively in practice without resorting to simplistic and prescriptive "magic bullets" that have been prevalent over the last 15–20 years.

Cost recovery, water charging, and sustainability

Cost recovery and associated water charges have been the subject of intense debate and controversy (Molle and Berkoff forthcoming). As financial resources become scarcer, the issue is becoming critical and will have a major impact on the sector in the near future. Evidence confirms that most governments in developing countries already face a serious funding crisis with broad consequences for rural services, including irrigation. Funding for housing, infrastructure, education, and social services in urban centers competes with

figure **9.5** **Factors affecting the performance of irrigation schemes**

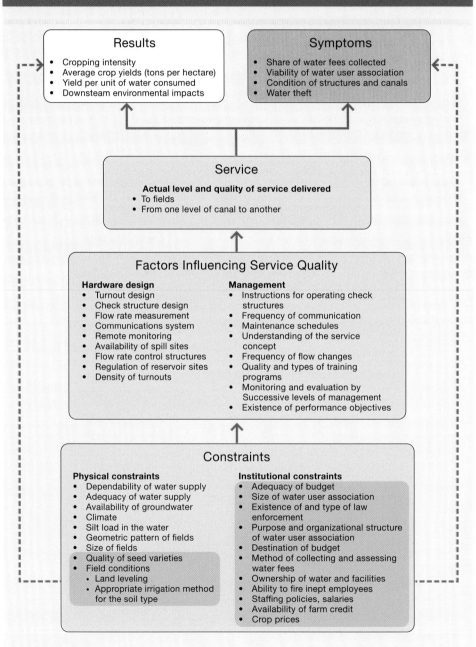

Results
- Cropping intensity
- Average crop yields (tons per hectare)
- Yield per unit of water consumed
- Downsteam environmental impacts

Symptoms
- Share of water fees collected
- Viability of water user association
- Condition of structures and canals
- Water theft

Service
Actual level and quality of service delivered
- To fields
- From one level of canal to another

Factors Influencing Service Quality

Hardware design
- Turnout design
- Check structure design
- Flow rate measurement
- Communications system
- Remote monitoring
- Availability of spill sites
- Flow rate control structures
- Regulation of reservoir sites
- Density of turnouts

Management
- Instructions for operating check structures
- Frequency of communication
- Maintenance schedules
- Understanding of the service concept
- Frequency of flow changes
- Quality and types of training programs
- Monitoring and evaluation by Successive levels of management
- Existence of performance objectives

Constraints

Physical constraints
- Dependability of water supply
- Adequacy of water supply
- Availability of groundwater
- Climate
- Silt load in the water
- Geometric pattern of fields
- Size of fields
- Quality of seed varieties
- Field conditions
  - Land leveling
  - Appropriate irrigation method for the soil type

Institutional constraints
- Adequacy of budget
- Size of water user association
- Existence of and type of law enforcement
- Purpose and organizational structure of water user association
- Destination of budget
- Method of collecting and assessing water fees
- Ownership of water and facilities
- Ability to fire inept employees
- Staffing policies, salaries
- Availability of farm credit
- Crop prices

Source: FAO 1999a.

requirements in rural areas. Given these conditions, a drastic reduction of government funding can be expected for irrigation programs in many countries. The irrigation land-scape will undoubtedly change in response to this pressure, but in ways that are hard to predict, ranging from gradual disuse and disbandment to dynamic self-financing.

The current school of thought in the water sector is well illustrated by the Global Water Partnership (GWP 2000): full cost recovery should be the goal for all water uses. However, assessment of the full cost of water is often out of reach (figure 9.6), and the Global Water Partnership also argues that while all efforts need to be made to estimate costs in order to ensure rational allocation and management decisions, these costs should not necessarily be charged to the user (GWP 2000). In irrigation the relevant question therefore is how users (through water charges) and taxpayers (through subsidies) should share the costs associated with irrigation (ICID 2004).

In addition to a thorough understanding of the costs associated with irrigation, information on economywide benefits of irrigation is critical to efficiently allocate irrigation cost across sectors. Indeed, in many cases society as a whole gets a much larger share of irrigation benefits through induced and indirect benefits than a typical irrigated farmer gets through increased crop productivity (Mellor 2002). This is evidenced by the high multiplier of investment in irrigation—between 2.5 and 4 in India (Bhattarai, Barker, and Narayanamoorthy forthcoming)—a factor to consider in setting cost-recovery policies for irrigation.

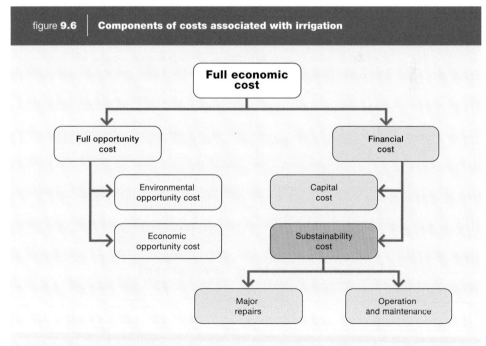

figure **9.6** | **Components of costs associated with irrigation**

Source: Adapted from ICID 2004; Rogers, Bhatia, and Huber 1998; FAO 2004b.

Contention usually focuses on whether and what to charge: service, operation, and maintenance only, or those plus the full cost of capital investment, either in the past or as future replacement annuity. The answer varies widely according to the role irrigation plays in the country's economy: while some advanced economies may seek full cost recovery from irrigation, others may consider subsidies in irrigation as part of wider rural development strategies. In both cases the concept of sustainable cost recovery (see figure 9.6), which is gaining increasing attention, remains valid and deserves decisionmakers' attention: ensuring the sustainability of existing irrigation infrastructure requires that operation, maintenance, administrative, and renewal costs be adequately covered.

> Users often enjoy the benefits of water use while passing on the environmental and social costs to others, leading to problems of equity, groundwater mining, pollution of drainage water, poor health of farm workers, and contamination of consumer products

Programs aimed at increasing cost recovery will not be accepted by farmers if they result in an overall reduction in benefits. Any substantial increase in cost recovery should be discussed and agreed on with representatives of farmers as part of an overall package of management reform, linking increased charges with guarantees of improved water service (Murray-Rust, and Snellen 1993). Under such conditions a progressive rise in water charges, corresponding to increased accountability and transparency on the part of service providers and progressive transfer of authority to users, matched by increased profitability of irrigated agriculture, is a sensible option for reducing public funding in irrigation. The fact that farmers bear the full financial cost of irrigation under private irrigation shows that irrigation systems are economically viable in some settings. Irrigation service provision in large public systems will increasingly need to incorporate accountability systems based on explicit or implicit contracts and financial arrangements (Huppert and others 2001).

Modes of charging for water service vary widely and must be adapted to the level of development of the irrigation scheme. While volumetric water charging may epitomize the service-payment concept and allow for possible demand management (Malano and Hofwegen 1999), the transaction costs associated with volumetric measurement are rarely justified. Semivolumetric measurement methods, or area-based water charges, which are often added to other land taxes, may be appropriate as long as transparency and equity are guaranteed.

In addition to the controversy over cost-recovery levels, considerable confusion prevails in the public debates on the distinction between water charges (aimed at covering all or part of the costs associated with irrigation) and water pricing (FAO 2004b). The issue of pricing as a demand management tool for irrigation is discussed later, but evidence suggests that in most cases the incremental leap that would be required to reach levels of water charges that would affect demand would be politically unmanageable in the prevailing economic conditions of most irrigation schemes (Molle and Berkoff forthcoming).

The changing role of government

With the general decline in construction of new systems and the increasing shift of management responsibilities to users, the role of public irrigation agencies is rapidly changing. Past activities involving planning and designing systems, contracting for and supervising civil works, and delivering water to farms will be less important than in the past. New responsibilities will include resource allocation, bulk water delivery, basin-level management, sector regulation, and the achievement of global social and environmental goals such as the Millennium Development Goals (see chapter 5 on policies and institutions).

Regulation and oversight

Because water is generally regarded as a public good, the state has a duty to sustain its availability and quality. Users often enjoy the benefits of water use while passing on environmental and social costs to others, leading to problems of equity, groundwater mining, pollution of drainage water, poor health of farm workers, and contamination of consumer products. The state should play an important role in regulating these externalities. Moreover, water will increasingly become a commodity, quantified and governed by agreements among users and between public authorities and users. Governments will play important roles in sanctioning and regulating these agreements.

Most governments will need to modify their water-related agencies to carry out these new responsibilities. There will be a tendency to separate regulatory agencies from water management and supply agencies to avoid conflicts of interest. Private or client-controlled organizations are likely to be responsible for water supply to users in an increasing number of cases. Adjudication mechanisms will be needed to resolve disputes among parties over water allocation, quality, and use. These mechanisms may be a part of the national legal system or a separate set of institutions that rely more on mediation and consensus. In all cases, institutional development should be shaped by context and the existing laws, regulations, and approaches to water rights and priorities.

Assessing and collecting fees and taxes have been a key role for many public agencies in the past. With the devolution of irrigation system management, financing structures will need to change as well to allow sufficient funds to sustain operations to those who actually run them: therefore, there will be increasingly complicated cost-recovery mechanisms in large irrigation systems involving local service charges as well as bulk water supply costs.

Governments will continue to play the role of water wholesaler by operating or contracting to private service providers large and strategic facilities such as dams (in particular multipurpose dams) and major irrigation infrastructure such as main canals and pumping stations.

The problems of the private irrigation sector are more directly related to questions of equity and environmental sustainability, including mining of groundwater, land subsidence, pollution, and health for farm workers, consumers, and other water users downstream. These issues require public intervention, and regulatory frameworks are needed for equitable and secured use of land and water resources. Public interventions are also likely to be sought to stimulate the private sector through marketing policies and targeted investment in bulk infrastructure and to enable private sector provision of farm-level water technology.

Resources allocation and management

Changing demand patterns for water will require reallocating water among competing uses as well as investing in appropriate infrastructure. This may be done either administratively or through market mechanisms established and regulated by the government. In both

> Changing demand patterns for water will require not only investing in appropriate infrastructure but also reallocating water among competing uses, either administratively or through market mechanisms established and regulated by the government

cases, great strides are required in quantifying water supplies, water deliveries, and uses. Without quantification, neither more careful allocation nor reallocation is possible.

Integrated management of water resources at the basin level will be an important task involving government, users, and other stakeholders. Although dedicated river basin management agencies are often proposed as a key solution, well orchestrated institutional development between existing agencies can be as effective (Turral 1998). Basin management entities will often be cross-sectoral and multidisciplinary, with a governing body that includes representatives from agriculture, municipal authorities, industry, and the environment, along with significant civil society representation (consumers and producers).

Governments will need to improve conflict management skills and mechanisms to deal with increasing competition for water. Transboundary water management will become more important with growing water scarcity, and governments will need dialogue and negotiation on transboundary water allocation.

‘

Where agriculture contributes significantly to GDP and employs many people, irrigation can ensure pro-poor growth and fuel nonagricultural growth

Sustaining growth and reducing poverty in rural areas

While macroeconomic conditions are changing, there are still many settings in which irrigation is an important element of poverty reduction strategies: areas of slow rates of rural outmigration; high prevalence of unemployed and underemployed labor; and high dependence on agriculture for livelihoods (photo 9.2). Poverty reduction and rural employment strategies may justify investments in agriculture-dependent areas that cannot be justified in direct economic terms.

Where agriculture contributes significantly to GDP and employs many people, irrigation can ensure pro-poor growth and fuel nonagricultural growth. Farmers with higher incomes tend to spend a high proportion locally, a stimulus to local employment. But where irrigation is controlled by large-scale absentee farmers who have consumption patterns intensive in capital and imports, the local impact on rural poverty reduction is much lower. In very low-income societies without a well developed rural economy, as in much of Sub-Saharan Africa, the multiplier from agricultural growth to the nonfarm sector is much weaker (Mellor 2002).

Investments in irrigation and related interventions for agricultural development are, under certain conditions, preferred means of creating jobs and reducing rural poverty (Dhawan 1988; Mellor 1999, 2002; Hussain 2005). Equity and security of rights to land and irrigation resources matter for larger poverty impacts. Where the distribution of land and water is equitable, irrigation has larger poverty-reducing impacts (Brabben and others 2004; Hussain 2005).

Designs and investment in irrigation improvement that allow for multiple uses of water are also good for poverty reduction. Often the use of water for domestic water supply, irrigation, and other farm and nonfarm enterprises may have higher benefits than separate investments. Many recent studies have highlighted the significant benefits and contributions to livelihoods from these multiple uses, especially for poor households (Van Koppen, Moriarty, and Boelee 2006).

Photo 9.2 Water tank for irrigation on a small Andean farm

Photo by G. Bizzarri/FAO

Water-application technologies and improved production practices offer promise. Some technologies are scale-neutral and may even self-select the poor (treadle pumps, labor-intensive agricultural activities). Some can be redesigned to better serve the poor (microirrigation technologies). Others, such as resource-conservation technologies, can be made available to the poor through efficient institutional arrangements or efficient rental markets for the machinery. The benefits of these technologies to the poor can be enhanced through initial targeted subsidy schemes, targeted training opportunities, private participation in the input-supply chain, quick payback technologies, and strengthened public research systems.

One aspect of poverty alleviation and equity that has been hotly debated, but with little progress, is women's access to and use of water and the benefits this brings (Boelens and Zwarteveen 2002). There are well documented cases of women being disenfranchised by poorly targeted irrigation development, mainly in Africa (Van Koppen 2000) but also in Asia (Udas and Zwarteveen 2005). Better targeting of female farmers is likely to increase agricultural productivity and growth (see chapter 5 on policies and institutions). There has also been a progressive feminization of agriculture due to urban and seasonal migration (Buechler 2004): women represent 54% of the agricultural and related labor force in Sub-Saharan Africa and 65% in Southern Asia, and their role in agriculture is likely to grow (photo 9.3). But the design, operation, and management of systems have rarely accommodated such changes (Vera 2005). Some simple gender-related questions for irrigation management suggest where to direct practical efforts for better services to female farmers (box 9.3) (Bruins and Heijmans 1993; Meinzen-Dick and Zwarteveen 1998; Van Koppen 2002).

In many countries women may be responsible for domestic and livestock water use and for irrigation of garden plots that make a vital contribution to the variety and nutritional quality of diets (FAO 1999a). If these needs are not explicitly understood, there may be too much bias toward field crop irrigation at the expense of household needs, especially when the volumes required are small but have relatively high value (Meinzen-Dick and van der Hoek 2001).

> One aspect of poverty alleviation and equity that has been hotly debated, but with little progress, is women's access to and use of water and the benefits this brings

Photo 9.3 A group of female farmers planting rice seedlings by hand

Photo by J. Boethling/FAO

| box **9.3** | **Gender and irrigation—issues that matter** |

Some specific questions to better target irrigation service to women are:
- Do women have recognized access to land and water?
- Are women represented in formal water user associations?
- How are women's needs expressed and communicated?
- Is it safe for women to irrigate at night?
- Do irrigation schedules accommodate women's needs for flexibility?
- How can structures be improved so that women can easily operate them?
- Are irrigated plots close to households?
- Do women have the same access to credit and inputs as men?
- Are separate financial mechanisms required?
- Are household nutritional needs being met by the chosen cropping pattern?
- Is the importance of backyard gardening recognized and adequately promoted?

Managing the impacts of irrigation on health and the environment

Irrigation's health and environmental impacts are closely linked. For health, the negative impacts of irrigation development can be mitigated through better design and operation of new and existing systems, especially through multiple uses of irrigation water. For the environment, the impacts of irrigation can be positive but they more usually are negative (Goldsmith and Hildyard 1992; Dougherty and Hall 1995; Petermann 1996). Better identification and understanding of the externalities related to irrigation during design or redesign and management of irrigation systems can enhance the positive impacts and mitigate the negative ones (Bolton 1992).

> Potentially the greatest negative health impact of intensified agriculture at a global scale is from pesticide use. Integrated pest and plant fertility management can reduce the negative impacts of agrochemicals in irrigated systems

Health impacts of irrigation

A potentially negative impact of irrigation on human health is the increased incidence of vectorborne diseases, such as malaria and schistosomiasis, with the expansion of suitable habitat for the disease-transmitting organisms. While irrigation systems may significantly increase the number of malaria mosquito vectors in an area, that does not necessarily result in a greater incidence of malaria, especially when the introduction of an irrigation system leads to higher income, better access to health care, improved housing, and greater use of mosquito nets. Vulnerable community members not benefiting from the irrigation development may, however, face an increased malaria burden, and in certain cases the introduction of irrigation has been found to prolong the malaria transmission season.

Upgrading irrigation can improve health. Water management strategies, such as alternate wet and dry irrigation, and water-saving irrigation technologies reduce sites for the breeding of intermediary host snails of schistosomiasis and insect vectors of diseases. Clever modernization of irrigation infrastructure to minimize standing water can do the same. Institutional reforms, such as creating water user associations or improving extension services, can facilitate multiple uses and bridge the divide between agricultural and health departments (Bakker and others 1999).

In Africa irrigation development is associated with the spread of schistosomiasis and the intensification of human infections (McCartney and others 2005). Medical and engineering options exist to deal with the problem. Irrigation water management and weed control (including maintenance of drains and canals and night storage dams) can reduce the burden of schistosomiasis, in both large- and small-scale irrigation systems.

Irrigation water is an important potential source of domestic water supplies, but satisfying both needs often poses management problems. Access to irrigation water close to homesteads can have significant health benefits, especially in the reduction of hygiene-related diarrheal or skin and eye diseases (van der Hoek, Feenstra, and Konradsen 2002). Water-saving strategies and the increasing use of low-quality water for irrigation in situations where people are fully dependent on canal water for most domestic purposes can have negative health impacts. High water tables may severely limit the options for safe sanitation, and therefore drainage in waterlogged areas will have positive results.

Potentially the greatest negative health impact of intensified agriculture at a global scale is from pesticide use. Banning the use of the most toxic pesticides would be the first priority in preventing poisoning episodes (Eddleston and others 2002). Inappropriate pest management policies in developing countries increasingly hamper their exports of goods to Organisation for Economic Co-operation and Development markets because of high pesticide residues. Integrated pest and plant fertility management can considerably reduce the negative impacts of agrochemicals in irrigated systems.

Environmental impacts of irrigation

Policies and practices associated with irrigated agriculture continue to be a major driver of change in both terrestrial and aquatic ecosystems, exerting a wide range of largely detrimental impacts globally. The impacts, ranging from local and subtle to long distance and severe, have adverse effects on human well-being through reductions in ecosystem services and resilience (MEA 2005a,b).

Many of irrigation's negative environmental effects arise from withdrawal, storage, and diversion from natural aquatic ecosystems and the resultant changes to the natural pattern and timing of hydrological flows (Rosenberg, McCully, and Pringle 2000; also see chapter 6 on ecosystems). Rivers have in many instances become disconnected from their floodplains and from downstream estuaries and wetlands—with, in some instances, total and irreversible wetland loss (MEA 2005b). The routes and systems of infrastructure for water transfer and storage have also led to the introduction and proliferation of invasive species, such as aquatic weeds, in both water management systems and natural wetlands.

Wetland water quality has deteriorated in all regions, particularly in areas under high-intensity irrigation (MEA 2005b). Nutrient loading—primarily from fertilizers (nitrogen and phosphorus) applied to irrigated (and rainfed) areas—is one of the most important drivers of ecosystem change, resulting in eutrophication, hypoxia, and algal blooms. Total pesticide use is still increasing, and though many of the more persistent chemicals used in irrigated agriculture are being phased out and replaced by ones with less environmental impact, this is not necessarily so in developing countries.

The extent to which irrigation induces waterlogging and salinization is imperfectly known but estimated at 10% of the total irrigated area worldwide. In large river basins in arid regions the picture is much more severe, with salinity buildups in drainage water and the consequent salinization of the land and rivers (Smedema and Shiati 2002). Salinization causes the loss of natural vegetation, reduces crop yields, and leaves drinking water unfit for human and animal consumption. Drainage is systematically neglected until salinity problems are manifest, because of the additional capital cost it incurs. If drainage is constructed early, the likelihood of accumulating salts is much lower and the loads disposed in natural streams and rivers are smaller. Adapting farming systems through the use of salt-tolerant varieties may provide short-term respite for producers but is likely to increase the negative environmental impacts in the long run.

Irrigation can also create or enhance wetland ecosystems, generating habitats to support biodiversity conservation and ecosystem services. This is particularly so where irrigation-based agroecosystems have developed over centuries and function as wetlands

> Irrigation can also create or enhance wetland ecosystems, generating habitats to support biodiversity conservation and ecosystem services

(Wiseman, Taylor, and Zingstra 2003; Fernando, Göltenboth, and Margraf 2005; photo 9.4). There is a school of thought that argues for the positive biodiversity impacts of water management and irrigation systems in their own right, as for waterbirds in rice systems in Asia (Galbraith, Amerasinghe, and Huber-Lee 2005). In several instances, however, the biodiversity of irrigated systems is of less ecological and socioeconomic value than that of the natural system it replaced (see chapter 6 on ecosystems).

> The scope for water conservation strategies that free water from agriculture to satisfy the requirements of other sectors is limited

Another positive impact of irrigation is the higher agricultural productivity through which irrigation has contained some of the expansion of rainfed agricultural areas into forested or marginal lands (Carruthers 1996).

Developing countries with significant irrigation have paid relatively little attention to safeguarding flows for the environment, but this is changing rapidly, with more countries embedding environmental flow principles in policy and legislation (for example, the South African National Water Act and the Mekong Agreement) and undertaking local assessments of environmental water needs in basins (Tharme 2003). The scope and expertise now exist to reallocate water in major rivers to restore downstream ecosystems, including highly productive riverine floodplains. Water management techniques can create substantial flexibility in how infrastructure is operated, opening possibilities to restore lost ecological functions and processes. In particular, changing the operating rules for dams can improve environmental performance while allowing continuing provision of water, power, and flood control.

A growing range of ecoagriculture strategies can be applied in irrigation systems to prevent or mitigate habitat fragmentation—for example, through corridors of natural or seminatural vegetation to enhance connectivity for biodiversity conservation (Molden and others 2004). Systems need to accommodate the multiple uses of water, including environmental uses, by understanding their role and importance.

Photo 9.4 Rice terraces in Indonesia

Photo by R. Faidutti/FAO

Adapting to sectoral competition

In the growing political and economic tussles over access to water, agriculture is perceived as the low-value residual user. Experience shows that water conservation in agriculture does not drive transfers of water from agriculture to other sectors. Transfers occur in a variety of ways—including land and water purchase, appropriation by default as cities expand into peri-urban irrigated areas, competitive development, and water conservation investment in return for "saved" water. This mostly ad hoc set of mechanisms will lead to a framework of rules and practices that will gradually regularize the process. Under conditions of increasing competition the stakes are high for all current and prospective water users, and governments bear responsibility to ensure a level playing field for these processes to play out.

The scope for water conservation strategies that free water from agriculture to satisfy the requirements of other sectors is rather limited. Focusing on water conservation alone is certainly not sufficient to sustain agricultural production while releasing the water for environmental, urban, and other uses. Rather, a strategy that provides farmers with the means to increase their productivity within the broader context of agricultural modernization is more likely to succeed (Kijne, Molden, and Barker 2003).

In countries where water rights exist and are separate from land rights, markets can theoretically lead to efficient reallocation of water among sectors. In practice, water trading has so far reallocated only small volumes of the resource

Water saving and water-use efficiency in irrigation

The concept of water-use efficiency (the ratio between effective water consumption by crops and water abstracted from its source for irrigation) is subject to controversy and misinterpretation. Developed initially for use in the design of physical structures of water storage and conveyance in irrigation systems (Israelsen 1932), the concept was later interpreted as a measure of irrigation inefficiency and waste: because only 30%–50% of the water withdrawn from its source is actually transpired by crops in a typical irrigation system, many conclude that substantial gains in water volumes can be obtained by increasing water-use efficiency in irrigation.

However, most investments aiming primarily at increasing water-use efficiency (in particular through canal lining) result in little real water savings, especially when there is little degradation in water quality. Large surface irrigation systems circulate massive volumes of water through canals and drains. Because a substantial portion of these flows is recaptured downstream, water-saving technologies on farms upstream may make only minor contributions to savings considered on a larger scale, such as at the irrigation system or river basin level (Seckler, Molden, and Sakthivadivel 2003). This is most evident where irrigation efficiencies are low in a fully allocated basin, such as the Yellow River in China, and there is little outflow to the sea (see chapter 16 on river basins).

For the Nile River in Egypt conveyance and field application efficiencies are low, but about 75%–87% of the water withdrawn from the Nile is ultimately evaporated by irrigation (figure 9.7; Abu Zeid and Seckler 1992; Molden, el Kady, and Zhu 1998). In some situations reducing percolation from irrigated fields can lower groundwater tables and reduce the water available to crops from below, while increasing the cost of

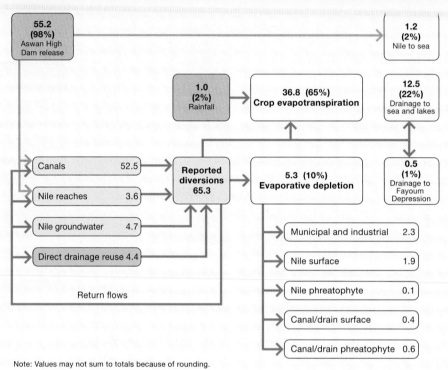

figure 9.7 | **Nile water balance in Egypt, 1993–94 (cubic kilometers per year)**

55.2 (98%) Aswan High Dam release

1.2 (2%) Nile to sea

1.0 (2%) Rainfall

36.8 (65%) Crop evapotranspiration

12.5 (22%) Drainage to sea and lakes

Canals 52.5

Nile reaches 3.6

Reported diversions 65.3

5.3 (10%) Evaporative depletion

0.5 (1%) Drainage to Fayoum Depression

Nile groundwater 4.7

Direct drainage reuse 4.4

Return flows

Municipal and industrial 2.3

Nile surface 1.9

Nile phreatophyte 0.1

Canal/drain surface 0.4

Canal/drain phreatophyte 0.6

Note: Values may not sum to totals because of rounding.

Source: Adapted from Molden, el Kady, and Zhu 1998.

pumping for reuse downstream. So when planning programs to conserve water in irrigated agriculture, it is vital to have a full understanding of the regional hydrology to avoid expensive solutions that simply move water from one location to another within the irrigation system.

Nevertheless, the concept of water-use efficiency is site-, scale- and purpose-specific (Lankford 2006). Efficiencies matter locally, in terms of irrigation design, for satisfactory operation and monitoring of existing systems (Bos, Burton, and Molden 2005), equitable access to water within the irrigation schemes, energy saving, and control of waterlogging and salinization (see chapter 7 on water productivity).

Tools for demand management in irrigation

Many economists argue that the low prices paid for irrigation water are a disincentive to efficient use and that improved water pricing policies could save water and increase productivity. But there are almost no examples of pricing as a primary mechanism for efficiency gains in irrigation (see chapter 5 on policies and institutions).

There are two reasons for this. First, water pricing must be based on measured deliveries. In the vast majority of irrigation schemes, delivered volumes of water are not measured, making volumetric water pricing impossible, and measuring them would involve huge investments. It is now more widely recognized that the applicability of volumetric water pricing to individual farms is limited to a small subset of technologically and managerially advanced irrigation schemes. Second, the water charges currently levied in most irrigation schemes have rarely reached even a fraction of that needed to constrain demand (Perry, Rock, and Seckler 1997). In these systems the political consequences of increasing water charges to the point that the demand elasticity becomes significant can be expected to be severe and constraining.

In countries where water rights exist and are separate from land rights, markets can theoretically lead to efficient reallocation of water among sectors. In practice, water trading has so far reallocated only small volumes of the resource (less than 1% a year of permanent entitlements in Australia and the western United States) (Turral and others 2005). It is unlikely that water markets will affect irrigation water use and reallocation in most countries of Asia or Sub-Saharan Africa in the coming 20–30 years because of the time lag in the development of suitable water rights and allocation frameworks and the marginal nature of markets once established. A major challenge in formalizing water rights is to include traditional (often small) systems and to avoid disenfranchising established small-scale water users (Bruns and Meinzen-Dick 2000; Bruns, Ringler, and Meinzen-Dick 2005). Water markets will also need to adopt more comprehensive water valuation approaches that encompass the broad range of benefits and costs of water management in agriculture—and that include payment for environmental services.

> In the future the magnitude of environmental reallocations and their impact on agriculture will be greater than incremental demands rising from cities and industry

In the interim, consultative and participatory arrangements for water allocation will be required. Consultation is a key process in water allocation—along with data collection, analysis, and promulgation, and negotiation—to find optimal sharing of benefits. The challenge over the next 20 years is to develop cost-effective arrangements for doing this and erect a functional framework of facilitating laws, treaties, and regulations. Since the water allocation process is inherently political, effective representation is crucial. A major challenge for the coming decades is to develop strong and effective representative voices on behalf of those stakeholders now underrepresented, including small-scale farmers, women, and the environment (Ostrom, Schroeder, and Wynne 1993; Blomquist 1992).

Governments will have to be proactive in managing the growing competition for water, by establishing effective water rights systems, setting out targeted policies on conservation, and implementing appropriate land-use restrictions to facilitate equitable transfers from irrigation to other sectors. In the case of environmental demands, some public recognition of its value is necessary prior to any reallocation. The degree of recognition and the magnitude of the unmet environmental need for additional water varies considerably from country to country. In the future the magnitude of environmental reallocations and their impact on agriculture will be greater than incremental demands rising from cities and industry, as is already the case in many higher income countries such as Australia and the United States, since environmental uses are essentially consumptive.

Appendix: Typology of irrigation systems

The following typology of irrigation systems is based primarily on mode of governance.

■ *Large-scale public irrigation systems in dry areas, growing staple crops.* They include most of the large public schemes of Northern China, the dry part of the Indo-Gangetic Plain, Central Asia, Sudan, the Middle East, the Nepalese Terai, and Mexico. These schemes are mostly run by public management agencies and for the last 10–15 years have been the focus of irrigation management transfer programs. In these schemes water delivery services are typically rather inflexible and inequities between the head and tail ends of the schemes are marked. In response to poor service, farmers typically seek to improve the reliability of supply by stealing water, pumping from drains, or using shallow groundwater in conjunction with canal water. These schemes were built with the purpose of providing large numbers of people with either full or partial irrigation to stabilize and augment staple food production and were usually not expected to pay their own operating expenses. Today, they face the challenge of economic and financial viability, and of the technical and managerial upgrading that would allow them to respond to the new needs of their farmers.

■ *Large-scale public paddy irrigation systems in humid areas.* These irrigation systems were progressively developed to produce paddy rice and have in most cases gone through a process of accretionary development, leading progressively to increased water control and increased cropping intensity. Typical of this type of systems are the large terrace systems of Southeast Asia or the tank and delta systems of East and South India and Sri Lanka. While they face similar challenges for viability and upgrading as do the dry area systems, they also have unique features and properties related to their high rainfall environment and paddy cultivation.

■ *Small- to medium-scale community-managed (and -built) systems.* Such systems are found across the world in Afghanistan, Indonesia, Nepal, the Philippines, the Andes Mountains, the Atlas Mountains, Sub-Saharan Africa, and highland areas in general. While this category covers a wide range of situations, it is characterized by the small size of the systems, private or community investment, and management. Public sector involvement focuses on rehabilitation, consolidation, or improvement. These systems form the basis of the economies of their communities and typically show a large variety of cropping patterns.

■ *Commercial privately managed systems, producing for local and export markets.* These systems do not represent a large share of irrigated areas worldwide but can be important locally. They can be found in Latin America (Argentina, Brazil, Chile, northern Mexico), Morocco, Turkey, and industrialized countries. They are governed by cultivators, employ paid staff, often use advanced technologies, and are responsive to local and international market opportunities. Sugar production is a special case of commercial irrigation, where management of irrigation and cultivation is often combined in a single entity.

■ *Farm-scale individually managed systems, producing for local markets, often around cities.* These systems develop around cities to take advantage of local markets for high-value

crops like fruits and vegetables. They are highly dynamic and volatile, face land tenure problems as cities grow, and are often characterized by large short-term returns on investment. They rely on groundwater or wastewater and often face environmental and health related problems, for both consumers and field workers.

Reviewers

Chapter review editor: Linden Vincent.
Chapter reviewers: Charles Abernethy, Ger Bergkamp, Belgin Cakmak, Evan Christen, Bert Clemmens, Biksham Gujja, Hammond Murray-Rust, Ursula Oswald Spring, Shaheen Khan Qabooliya, Jorge Ramirez Vallerjo, Ranjith Ratnayake, Juan Sagardoy, R. Sakthivadivel, Jose Trava, Pranita Udas, and Xiaoliu Yang.

References

Abu Zeid, M., and D. Seckler, eds. 1992. "Roundtable on Egyptian Water Policy." Conference Proceedings. Ministry of Public Works and Water Resources, Water Research Centre, Cairo, and Winrock International, Arlington, Va.

Aerts, J., and P. Droogers, eds. 2004. *Climate Change in Contrasting River Basins: Adaptation Strategies for Water, Food and Environment.* Oxfordshire, UK and Cambridge, Mass.: CABI Publishing.

Albinson, B., and C.J. Perry. 2002. "Fundamentals of Smallholder Irrigation: The Structured System Concept." Research Report 58. International Water Management Institute, Columbo.

Ankum, P. 1996. "Selection of Operation Methods in Canal Irrigation Delivery Systems." In *Irrigation Scheduling: From Theory to Practice.* Water Reports 8. Proceedings of the International Commission on Irrigation and Drainage and Food and Agriculture Organization Workshop on Irrigation Scheduling, 12–13 September, Rome.

Bakker, M., R. Barker, R.S. Meinzen-Dick, and F. Konransen, eds. 1999. *Multiple Uses of Water in Irrigated Areas: A Case Study from Sri Lanka.* SWIM Report 8. Colombo: International Water Management Institute.

Barker, R., and F. Molle. 2004. *Evolution of Irrigation in South and Southeast Asia.* Comprehensive Assessment Research Report 5. Colombo: International Water Management Institute.

Barker, R., C. Ringler, N.M. Tien, and M.W. Rosegrant. 2004. *Macro Policies and Investment Priorities for Irrigated Agriculture in Viet Nam.* Comprehensive Assessment Research Report 6. Colombo: International Water Management Institute.

Barnett, T.P., J.C. Adams, and D.P. Lettenmaier. 2005. "Potential Impacts of a Warming Climate on Water Availability in Snow-Dominated Regions." *Nature* 438 (7066): 303–09.

Berkoff, J. 2003. "Prospects for Irrigated Agriculture: Has the International Consensus Got It Right?" Alternative Water Forum, May 1–2, Bradford, UK.

Bhattarai, M., and A. Narayanamoorthy. 2003. "Impact of Irrigation on Rural Poverty in India: An Aggregate Panel-Data Analysis." *Water Policy* 5 (5–6): 443–58.

Bhattarai M., R. Barker, and A. Narayanamoorthy. Forthcoming. "Who Benefits from Irrigation Development in India? Implication of Irrigation Multipliers for Irrigation Financing." *Irrigation and Drainage.*

Blomquist, W. 1992. *Dividing the Waters: Governing Groundwater in Southern California.* San Francisco, Calif.: ICS Press.

Boelee, E., and H. Laamrani. 2004. "Environmental Control of Schistosomiasis through Community Participation in a Moroccan Oasis." *Tropical Medicine and International Health* 9 (9): 997–1004.

Boelens, R., and M. Zwarteveen. 2002. "Gender Dimensions of Water Control in Andean Irrigation." In R. Boelens and P. Hoogendam, eds., *Water Rights and Empowerment.* Assen, Netherlands: Van Gorcum.

Bolton, P. 1992. "Environmental and Health Aspects of Irrigation." OD/P 116. Hydraulics Research, Wallingford, UK.

Bos, M.G, M.A. Burton, and D.J. Molden. 2005. *Irrigation and Drainage Performance Assessment: Practical Guidelines.* Wallingford, UK: CABI Publishing.

Brabben, T., C. Angood, J. Skutch, and L. Smith. 2004. *Irrigation can Sustain Rural Livelihoods: Evidence from Bangladesh and Nepal.* Wallingford, UK: HR Wallingford.

Brohan, P., J. Kennedy, I. Harris, S.F.B. Tett, and P.D. Jones. Forthcoming. "Uncertainty Estimates in Regional and Global Observed Temperature Changes: A New Dataset from 1850." *Journal of Geophysical Research.*

Bruins, B., and A. Heijmans. 1993. "Gender Biases in Irrigation Projects: Gender Considerations in the Rehabilitation of Bauraha Irrigation System in the District of Dang." SNV Nepal, Kathmandu.

Bruns, B.R., and R. Meinzen-Dick, eds. 2000. *Negotiating Water Rights.* London: Intermediate Technology Press.

Bruns, B.R., C. Ringler, and R.S. Meinzen-Dick, eds. 2005. *Water Rights Reform: Lessons for Institutional Design.* Washington, D.C.: International Food Policy Research Institute.

Buechler, S. 2004. "Women at the Helm of Irrigated Agriculture in Mexico: The Other Side of Male Migration." In V. Bennett, S. Dávila-Poblete, and M. Nieves Rico, eds., *Swimming Against the Current: Gender and Water in Latin America.* Pittsburgh, Pa.: Pittsburgh University Press.

Carruthers, I. 1996. "Economics of Irrigation." In L. Pereira, R. Feddes, J. Gilley, and B. Lesaffre, eds., *Sustainability of Irrigated Agriculture.* Dordrecht, Netherlands: Kluwer Academic.

Carruthers, I., M.W. Rosegrant, and D. Seckler. 1997. "Irrigation and Food Security in the 21st Century." *Irrigation and Drainage Systems* 11: 83–101.

Chambers, R. 1988. *Managing Canal Irrigation: Practical Analysis from South Asia.* New York: Cambridge University Press.

de Fraiture, C. 2005. *Assessment of Potential of Food Supply and Demand Using the Watersim Model.* Columbo: International Water Management Institute.

Dhawan, B.D. 1988. *Irrigation in India's Agricultural Development: Productivity, Stability, Equity.* New Delhi: Sage Publications.

Diao, X., and A. Nin Pratt with M. Gautam, J. Keough, J. Chamberlin, L. You, D. Puetz, D. Resnick, and B. Yu. 2005 "Growth Options and Poverty Reduction in Ethiopia: A Spatial, Economywide Model Analysis for 2004–15." DSGD Discussion Paper 20. International Food Policy Research Institute, Washington, D.C.

Dougherty, T.C., and A.W. Hall. 1995. "Environmental Impact Assessment of Irrigation and Drainage Projects." Irrigation and Drainage Paper 53. Food and Agriculture Organization, Rome.

Eddleston, M., L. Karalliedde, N. Buckley, R. Fernando, G. Hutchinson, G. Isbister, F. Konradsen, D. Murray, J.C. Piola, N. Senanayake, R. Sheriff, S. Singh, S.B. Siwach, and L. Smit. 2002. "Pesticide Poisoning in the Developing World: A Minimum Pesticides List." *Lancet* 12 (360): 1163–67.

FAO (Food and Agriculture Organization). 1997. "Modernization of Irrigation Schemes: Past Experiences and Future Options." FAO Technical Paper 12. Rome.

———. 1999a. "Modern Water Control and Management Practices in Irrigation: Impact on Performance." FAO Water Report 19. International Program for Technology and Research in Irrigation and Drainage, Rome.

———. 1999b. "Transfer of Irrigation Management Services. Guidelines." FAO Irrigation and Drainage Paper 58. Rome.

———. 2000. *Irrigation in Latin America and the Caribbean in Figures.* Rome.

———. 2003. *World Agriculture towards 2015/2030: An FAO Perspective.* Rome and London: Food and Agriculture Organization and Earthscan Publishers.

———. 2004a. *Compendium of Food and Agriculture Indicators.* Rome.

———. 2004b. *Water Charging in Irrigated Agriculture: An Analysis of International Experience.* FAO Water Report 28. Rome.

———. 2005. *Irrigation in Africa in Figures. Aquastat Survey—2005.* FAO Water Report 29. Rome.

———. 2006a. FAOSTAT database. [http://faostat.fao.org/].

———. 2006b. "Demand for Products of Irrigated Agriculture in Sub-Saharan Africa." FAO Water Report 31. Rome.

———. Forthcoming. "Irrigation Management Transfer: Worldwide Efforts and Results." Rome.

Fernando, C.H., F. Göltenboth, and J. Margraf, eds. 2005. *Aquatic Ecology of Rice Fields: A Global Perspective.* Ontario, Canada: Volumes Publishing.

Galbraith, H., P. Amerasinghe, and A. Huber-Lee. 2005. *The Effects of Agricultural Irrigation on Wetland Ecosystems in Developing Countries: A Literature Review.* CA Discussion Paper 1. Comprehensive Assessment Secretariat, Colombo.

Gerrards, J. 1994. "Irrigation Service Fees (ISF) in Indonesia: Towards Irrigation Co-Management with Water Users Associations through Contributions, Voice, Accountability, Discipline, and Plain Hard Work." Proceedings of the International Conference on Irrigation Management Transfer, 20–24 September, Wuhan, China. International Irrigation Management Institute, Colombo.

Goldsmith, E., and N. Hildyard. 1992. *The Social and Environmental Effects of Large Dams. Volume III: A Review of the Literature.* Bodmin, UK: Wadebridge Ecological Centre.

Gommes, René. 1993. "Current Climate and Population Constraint on Agriculture." In H. Kaiser and T.E. Drennen, eds., *Agricultural Dimension of Global Climatic Change.* Delray Beach, Fla.: St. Lucie Press.

Grey, D., and C. Sadoff. 2005. "Water Resources, Growth and Development." A Working Paper for discussion at the UN Commission on Sustainable Development, Panel of Finance Ministers. World Bank, Washington, D.C.

GWP (Global Water Partnership). 2000. "Integrated Water Resources Management." TAC Background Paper 4. Technical Advisory Committee, Stockholm.

Heierli, U., and P. Polak. 2000. "Poverty Alleviation as Business: The Market Creation Approach to Development." Swiss Agency for Development and Cooperation, Bern.

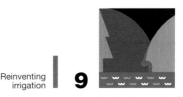

Horst, L. 1998. *The Dilemmas of Water Division, Considerations and Criteria for Irrigation System Design.* Colombo: International Water Management Institute.

Huang, Qiuqiong, S. Rozelle, B. Lohmar, Jikun Huang, and Jinxia Wang. 2006. "Irrigation, Agricultural Performance and Poverty Reduction in China." *Food Policy* 31 (1): 30–52.

Hung, Tun Yueh, and C. Shih. 1994. "Development and Outlook for Irrigation Water Management in Taiwan." Proceedings of the International Conference on Irrigation Management Transfer, 20–24 September, Wuhan, China. International Irrigation Management Institute, Colombo.

Huppert, Walter, Mark Svendsen, and Douglas L. Vermillion with Birgitta Wolff, Martin Burton, Paul van Hofwegen, Ruth Meinzen-Dick, Waltina Scheumann, and Klaus Urban. 2001. *Governing Maintenance Provision in Irrigation: A Guide to Institutionally Viable Maintenance Strategies.* Eschborn, Germany: GTZ.

Hussain, I. 2005. *Pro-poor Intervention Strategies in Irrigated Agriculture in Asia. Poverty in Irrigated Agriculture: Issues, Lessons, Options and Guidelines.* Asian Development Bank and International Water Management Institute, Colombo.

ICID (International Commission on Irrigation and Drainage). 2004. "Irrigation and Drainage Services: Some Principles and Issues towards Sustainability." ICID Position Paper. New Delhi.

IFAD (International Fund for Agricultural Development). 2001. *Rural Poverty Report 2001: The Challenge of Ending Rural Poverty.* New York: Oxford University Press.

IFAD (International Fund for Agricultural Development) and IWMI (International Water Management Institute). Forthcoming. "Study on Agricultural Water Development and Poverty Reduction in Eastern and Southern Africa." Rome and Colombo.

Inocencio, A., D. Merrey, M. Tonasaki, A. Maruyama, I. de Jong, and M. Kikuchi. Forthcoming. "Costs and Performance of Irrigation Projects: A Comparison of Sub-Saharan Africa and Other Developing Countries." IWMI Research Report. International Water Management Institute, Colombo.

IPCC (Intergovernmental Panel on Climate Change). 2001. *Climate Change 2001: The Scientific Basis.* Contribution of Working Group I to the Third Assessment Report of the Intergovernmental Panel on Climate Change. New York: Cambridge University Press.
[HYPERLINK "http://www.grida.no/climate/ipcc_tar/wg1/index.htm" www.grida.no/climate/ipcc_tar/wg1/index.htm].

IPTRID (International Program for Technology and Research in Irrigation and Drainage). 1999. *Poverty Reduction and Irrigated Agriculture.* Issues Paper 1. Rome.

Israelsen, O.W. 1932. *Irrigation Principles and Practices,* 1st ed. New York: John Wiley and Sons.

IWMI (International Water Management Institute). 2000. *World Water Supply and Demand.* Colombo.

Johnson, S., III, M. Svendsen, and F. Gonzalez. 2004. *Institutional Reform Options in the Irrigation Sector.* Agriculture and Rural Development Discussion Paper 5. World Bank, Washington, D.C.

Jones, W.I. 1995. *The World Bank and Irrigation.* Operations Evaluation Study. World Bank, Washington, D.C.

Keller, J., and A.A. Keller. 2003. "Affordable Drip Irrigation Systems for Small Farms in Developing Countries." Proceedings of the Irrigation Association Annual Meeting, 18–20 November, San Diego, Calif.

Kendy, Eloise, D.J. Molden, T.S. Steenhuis, and C.M. Liu. 2003. *Policies Drain the North China Plain: Agricultural Policy and Groundwater Depletion in Luancheng County, 1949–2000.* Research Report 71. International Water Management Institute, Colombo.

Kijne, J.W., D. Molden, and R. Barker, eds. 2003. *Water Productivity in Agriculture: Limits and Opportunities for Improvement.* Comprehensive Assessment of Water Management in Agriculture Series, No. 1. Wallingford, UK: CABI Publishing.

Kikuchi, M., R. Barker, P. Weligamage, and M. Samad. 2002. *Irrigation Sector in Sri Lanka: Recent Investment Trends and the Development Path Ahead.* Research Report 62. International Water Management Institute, Colombo.

Lankford, B. 2006. "Localising Irrigation Efficiency." *Irrigation and Drainage* 55: 1–18.

Lipton, M., J. Litchfield, and Jean-Marc Faurès. 2003. "The Effects of Irrigation on Poverty: A Framework for Analysis." *Water Policy* 5 (5): 413–27.

Lipton, M., Julie Litchfield, Rachel Blackman, Darshini De Zoysa, Lubina Qureshy, and Hugh Waddington. 2003. *Preliminary Review of the Impact of Irrigation on Poverty.* AGL/MISC/34/2003. Rome: Food and Agriculture Organization.

Loeve, R., L. Hong, B. Dong, G. Mao, C.D. Chen, D. Dawe, and R. Barker. 2004. "Long Term Trends in Intersectoral Water Allocation and Crop Water Productivity in Zhanghe and Kaifeng, China." *Paddy and Water Environment* 2 (4): 237–45.

Malano, H., and P.V. Hofwegen. 1999. *Management of Irrigation and Drainage Systems: A Service Approach.* IHE Monograph 3. Rotterdam: A.A. Balkema.

Malano, H.M., B.A. George and B. Davidson, eds. 2004. "A Framework for Improving the Management of Irrigations Schemes in Vietnam." Australian Centre for International Agricultural Research, Canberra.

McCartney, M., Boelee, E., Cofie, O., F. Amerasinghe, and C. Mutero. 2005. "Agricultural Water Development in Sub-Saharan Africa: Planning and Management to Improve the Benefits and Reduce the Environmental and Health Costs." Final Report (Health). Investments in Agricultural Water Management in Sub-Saharan Africa: Diagnosis of Trends and Opportunities Project. International Water Management Institute, Colombo.

MEA (Millennium Ecosystem Assessment). 2005a. *Ecosystems and Human Well-being: Biodiversity Synthesis.* Washington D.C. : World Resources Institute,

———. 2005b. *Ecosystem and Human Well-being: Wetlands and Water Synthesis.* Washington D.C.: World Resources Institute.

Meinzen-Dick, Ruth, and Wim van der Hoek. 2001. "Multiple Uses of Water in Irrigated Areas." *Irrigation and Drainage Systems* 15 (2): 93–98.

Meinzen-Dick, R., and Margreet Zwarteveen. 1998. "Gendered Participation in Water Management: Issues and Illustrations from Water Users' Associations in South Asia." *Agriculture and Human Values* 15 (4): 337–45.

Mellor, John W. 1999. "Faster More Equitable Growth—The Relation Between Growth in Agriculture and Poverty Reduction." Paper prepared for United States Agency for International Development, Bureau for Global Programs, Center for Economic Growth and Agricultural Development, Division of Agriculture and Food Security. Abt Associates Inc., Cambridge, Mass.

———. 2002. "Irrigation, Agriculture and Poverty Reduction: General Relationships and Specific Needs." In I. Hussain and E. Biltonen, eds., *Managing Water for the Poor: Proceedings of the Regional Workshop on Pro-Poor Intervention Strategies in Irrigated Agriculture in Asia, Bangladesh, China, India, Indonesia, Pakistan and Vietnam.* Colombo: International Water Management Institute.

Merrey, D.J. 1997. *Expanding the Frontiers of Irrigation Management Research: Results of Research and Development at the International Irrigation Management Institute 1984–1995.* Colombo: International Water Management Institute.

Molden, D.J., M. el Kady, and Z. Zhu. 1998. "Use and Productivity of Egypt's Nile Water." In J.I. Burns and S.S. Anderson, eds., *Contemporary Challenges for Irrigation and Drainage: Proceedings from the USCID 14th Technical Conference on Irrigation, Drainage and Flood Control, Phoenix, Arizona, June 3-6, 1998.* Denver, Colo.: U.S. Committee on Irrigation and Drainage.

Molden, D., R. Tharme, I. Abdullaev, and R. Puskur. 2004. "Water, Food, Livelihoods and Environment: Maintaining Biodiversity in Irrigated Landscapes." Proceedings of the International Ecoagriculture Conference, 27 September–1 October, Nairobi.

Molle, F., and J. Berkoff. 2006. "Cities versus Agriculture: Revisiting Intersectoral Water Transfers, Potential Gains, and Conflicts." Comprehensive Assessment of Water Management in Agriculture Research Report 10. International Water Management Institute, Colombo.

Molle, F., and J. Berkoff., eds. Forthcoming. *Irrigation Water Pricing Policy in Context: Exploring the Gap between Theory and Practice.* Colombo: CABI Publishing and International Water Management Institute.

Mollinga, P. 1998. "On the Waterfront; Water Distribution, Technology and Agrarian Change in a South Indian Canal Irrigation System." PhD diss., Wageningen Agricultural University, Netherlands.

Murray-Rust, D.H., and W.B. Snellen. 1993. *Irrigation System Performance Assessment and Diagnosis.* Colombo: International Irrigation Management Institute.

ODI (Oversees Development Institute). Various years. Irrigation Management Network Papers. Overseas Development Institute, London.

Ostrom, E., L. Schroeder, and S.G. Wynne. 1993. *Institutional Incentives and Sustainable Development: Infrastructure Policies in Perspective.* Boulder, Colo.: Westview Press.

Palmer Jones, R.W., and M.A.S. Mandal. 1987. *Irrigation Groups in Bangladesh.* Irrigation Management Network Paper 87/2c. Overseas Development Institute, London.

Peel, M. C, Thomas A. McMahon, and Brian L. Finlayson. 2004. "Continental Differences in the Variability of Annual Runoff – Update and Reassessment." *Journal of Hydrology* 295 (1–4): 185–97.

Peel, M.C., Thomas A. McMahon, and Geoffrey G.S. Pegram. 2004. "Global Analysis of Runs of Annual Precipitation and Runoff Equal to or Below the Median: Run Magnitude and Severity." *International Journal of Climatology* 25 (5): 549–68.

Peel, M.C., T.A. McMahon, B.L. Finlayson, and F.G.R. Watson. 2001. "Identification and Explanation of Continental Differences in the Variability of Annual Runoff." *Journal of Hydrology* 250 (1–4): 224–40.

Perry, C.J., and S.G. Narayanamurthy. 1998. *Farmer Response to Rationed and Uncertain Irrigation Supplies.* IWMI Research Report 24. International Water Management Institute, Colombo.

Perry, C.J., Michael Rock, and D. Seckler. 1997. *Water as an Economic Good: A Solution or a Problem?* IWMI Research Report 14. International Water Management Institute, Colombo.

Petermann, T. 1996. *Environmental Appraisals for Agricultural and Irrigated Land Development.* Zschortau, Germany: German Foundation for International Development and Food and Agriculture Development Centre.

Plusquellec, Hervé. 2002. *How Design, Management and Policy Affect the Performances of Irrigation Projects.* Food and Agriculture Organization, Regional Office for Asia and the Pacific, Bangkok.

Qian, Zhengying. 1994. *Water Resources Development in China.* Beijing: China Water and Power Press.

Quiggin, John, and John K. Horowitz. 1999. "The Impact of Global Warming on Agriculture: A Ricardian Analysis: Comment." *American Economic Review* 89 (4): 1044–45.

Rap, E., P. Wester, and L.N. Pérez-Prado. 2004. "The Politics of Creating Commitment: Irrigation Reforms and the Reconstitution of the Hydraulic Bureaucracy in Mexico." In P. Mollinga and A. Bolding, eds., *The Politics of Irrigation Reform: Contested Policy Formulation and Implementation in Asia, Africa, and Latin America.* Hans, UK: Ashgate.

Reisner, M. 1986. *Cadillac Desert: The American West and its Disappearing Water.* London: Secker and Warburg.

Repetto, R. 1986. *Skimming the Water: Rent-seeking and the Performance of Public Irrigation Systems.* Research Report 4. World Resources Institute, Washington, D.C.

Revenga, C., and Y. Kura. 2003. *Status and Trends of Biodiversity of Inland Water Ecosystems.* Technical Series 11. Secretariat of the Convention on Biological Diversity, Montreal, Canada.

Rinaudo, J.D. 2002. "Corruption and Allocation of Water: The Case of Public Irrigation in Pakistan." *Water Policy* 4 (2002): 405–22.

Ringler, C., M. Rosegrant, X. Cai, and S. Cline. 2003. "Auswirkungen der zunehmenden Wasserverknappung auf die globale und regionale Nahrungsmittelproduktion." *Zeitschrift für angewandte Umweltforschung (ZAU)* 15/16 (3–5): 604–19.

Rogers, P., R. Bhatia, and A. Huber. 1998. *Water as a Social and Economic Good: How to Put the Principle into Practice.* Technical Advisory Committee Working Papers 2. Stockholm: Global Water Partnership.

Rosegrant, Mark W., and Mark Svendsen. 1993. "Asian Food Production in the 1990s: Irrigation Investment and Management Policy." *Food Policy* 18 (2): 13–32.

Rosegrant, M.W., X. Cai, and S. Cline. 2002. *World Water and Food to 2025: Dealing with Scarcity.* Washington, D.C.: International Food Policy Research Institute and International Water Management Institute.

Rosegrant, M.W., M.S. Paisner, S. Meijer, and J. Witcover. 2001. *Global Food Projections to 2020: Emerging Trends and Alternative Futures.* Washington, D.C.: International Food Policy Research Institute.

Rosenberg, D.M., P. McCully, and C.M. Pringle. 2000. "Global-scale Environmental Effects of Hydrological Alterations: Introduction." *BioScience* 50 (9): 746–51.

Sanmuganathan, K. 2000. *Assessment of Irrigation Options.* WCD Thematic Review Options Assessment IV.2. World Commission on Dams, Cape Town. [www.dams.org/docs/kbase/thematic/drafts/tr42_finaldraft.pdf].

Seckler, D., D. Molden, and R. Sakthivadivel. 2003. "The Concept of Efficiency in Water-resources Management and Policy." In J.W. Kijne, R. Barker, and D. Molden, eds., *Water Productivity in Agriculture: Limits and Opportunities for Improvement.* Wallingford, UK: CABI Publishing.

Shah, T. 1993. *Groundwater Markets and Irrigation Development: Political Economy and Practical Policy.* Mumbai: Oxford University Press.

———. 2003. "Governing the Groundwater Economy: Comparative Analysis of National Institutions and Policies in South Asia, China and Mexico." *Water Perspectives* 1 (1): 2–27.

Shah, T., M. Alam, D. Kumar, R.K. Nagar, and M. Singh. 2000. *Pedaling out of Poverty: Social Impacts of a Manual Irrigation Technology in South Asia.* IWMI Research Report 45. International Water Management Institute, Colombo.

Shah, T., B. Van Koppen, D. Merrey, M. de Lange, and M. Samad. 2002. *Institutional Alternatives in African Smallholder Irrigation: Lessons from International Experience with Irrigation Management Transfer.* IWMI Research Report 60. Colombo: International Water Management Institute.

Smedema, L.K., and K. Shiati. 2002. "Irrigation and Salinity: A Perspective Review of the Salinity Hazards of Irrigation Development in the Arid Zone." *Irrigation and Drainage Systems* 16 (2): 161–74.

Tardieu, H., B. Prefol, A. Vidal, and S. Darghouth. 2005. "Public Private Partnerships in Irrigation and Drainage: Need for a Professional Third Party between Farmers and Governments." Draft paper prepared for the World Bank, 8th International Seminar on Participatory Irrigation Management, 9–13 May, Tarbes, France.

Tharme, R.E. 2003. "A Global Perspective on Environmental Flow Assessment: Emerging Trends in the Development and Application of Environmental Flow Methodologies for Rivers." *River Research and Applications* 19 (5–6): 397–441.

Thenkabail, P.S., C.M. Biradar, H. Turral, and M. Schull. Forthcoming. *A Global Irrigated Area Map (GIAM) at the End of the Last Millennium using Multi-sensor, Time-series Satellite Sensor Data.* Research Report. International Water Management Institute, Colombo.

Tiffen, M. 1987. "Dethroning the Internal Rate of Return: The Evidence from Irrigation Projects." Development Policy Review 5 (4): 361–77.

Turral, H.N. 1998. *Hydro Logic? Reform in Water Resources Management in Developed Countries with Major Agricultural Water Use: Lessons for Developing Nations.* ODI Research Study. Overseas Development Institute, London.

Turral, H.N., T. Etchells, H.M.M. Malano, H.A. Wijedasa, P. Taylor, T.A.M. McMahon, and N. Austin. 2005. "Water Trading at the Margin: The Evolution of Water Markets in the Murray-Darling Basin." *Water Resources Research* 41 (7): W07011.1–W07011.8, doi:10.1029/2004WR003463.

Udas, P.B., and M. Zwarteveen. 2005. "Prescribing Gender Equity? The Case of Tukucha Nala Irrigation System, Central Nepal." In D. Roth, R. Boelens, and M. Zwarteveen, eds., *Liquid Relations: Contested Water Rights and Legal Complexity.* Piscataway, N.J.: Rutgers University Press.

UK Met Office. 2006. Global Temperatures. [www.met-office.gov.uk/research/hadleycentre/obsdata/globaltemperature.html].

Van der Hoek, W., S.G. Feenstra, and F. Konradsen. 2002. "Availability of Irrigation Water for Domestic Use in Pakistan: Its Impact on Prevalence of Diarrhoea and Nutritional Status of Children." *Journal of Health, Population and Nutrition* 20 (1): 77–84.

Van der Hoek, W., R. Sakthivadivel, M. Renshaw, J.B. Silver, M.H. Birley, and F. Konradsen. 2001. *Alternate Wet/Dry Irrigation in Rice Cultivation: A Practical Way to Save Water and Control Malaria and Japanese Encephalitis?* IWMI Research Report 47. International Water Management Institute, Colombo.

Van Koppen, B. 2000. "Discussion Note: Policy Issues and Options for Gender-balanced Irrigation Development." Proceedings of the 6th International Microirrigation Congress, October 22–27, Cape Town.

Van Koppen, B. 2002. *A Gender Performance Indicator for Irrigation: Concepts, Tools and Applications.* IWMI Research Report 59. International Water Management Institute, Colombo.

Van Koppen, B., P. Moriarty, and E. Boelee. 2006. *Multiple-use Water Services to Advance the Millennium Development Goals.* Research Report 98. International Water Management Institute, Colombo.

Vera, J. 2005. "Irrigation Management, the Participatory Approach and Equity in an Andea Community." In V. Bennett, S. Davila-Poblete, and M. Nieves Rico, eds., *Opposing Currents: The Politics of Water and Gender in Latin America.* Pittsburgh, Pa.: University of Pittsburgh Press.

Vermillion, D.L. 1997. *Impacts of Irrigation Management Transfer: A Review of the Evidence.* IWMI Research Report 11. International Water Management Institute, Colombo.

Wade, R. 1982. "The System of Administrative and Political Corruption: Canal Irrigation in South India." *Journal of Development Studies* 18 (3): 287–328.

Ward, C., A. Peacock, and G. Gamberelli. 2006. "Investment in Agricultural Water for Poverty Reduction and Economic Growth in Sub-Saharan Africa." Synthesis Report. African Development Bank, World Bank, International Fund for Agricultural Development, and Food and Agriculture Organization Consultative Group.

WCD (World Commission on Dams). 2000. *Dams and Development: A New Framework for Decision Making.* London: Earthscan Publications Ltd.

Winpenny, J. 2003. *Financing Water for All.* Report of the World Panel on Financing Water Infrastructure, chaired by Michel Camdessus. Kyoto: World Water Council, 3rd World Water Forum, and Global Water Partnership.

Wiseman, R., D. Taylor, and H. Zingstra, eds. 2003. *Wetlands and Agriculture. Proceedings of the Workshop on Agriculture, Wetlands, and Water Resources. 17th Global Biodiversity Forum, Valencia, Spain, November 2002.* New Delhi: National Institute of Ecology and International Scientific Publications.

Groundwater boom and bust?

Artist: Supriyo Das, India

10 | Groundwater: a global assessment of scale and significance

Coordinating lead author: Tushaar Shah

Lead authors: Jacob Burke and Karen Villholth

Contributing authors: Maria Angelica, Emilio Custodio, Fadia Daibes, Jaime Hoogesteger, Mark Giordano, Jan Girman, Jack van der Gun, Eloise Kendy, Jacob Kijne, Ramon Llamas, Mutsa Masiyandama, Jean Margat, Luis Marin, John Peck, Scott Rozelle, Bharat Sharma, Linden Vincent, and Jinxia Wang.

Overview

Intensive groundwater use in agriculture has become a dominant, yet underperceived aspect of contemporary water use. While the use of groundwater has its roots in many ancient civilizations, it has grown exponentially in scale and intensity over recent decades. Global abstraction of groundwater grew from a base level of 100–150 cubic kilometers in 1950 to 950–1,000 cubic kilometers in 2000. The bulk of this growth is concentrated in agriculture, particularly in Asia *[established but incomplete]*.

Groundwater has contributed significantly to growth in global irrigated areas since the 1970s. The irrigated areas supplied wholly or partly by groundwater are officially reported at 69 million hectares (ha), but independent studies suggest a higher figure, closer to 100 million ha, up from approximately 30 million ha during the 1950s *[established but incomplete]*.

While millions of farmers and pastoralists in Africa and Asia have significantly improved their livelihoods and household food security, aquifer depletion and groundwater pollution are also a direct result of this intensive use of groundwater, implying that existing trends cannot be sustained unless accompanied by far more intensive regimes of resource management than are currently deployed. The groundwater boom has been driven by supply-push factors, such as government subsidies and easy availability of inexpensive pumps and drilling technologies. Demand-pull factors have also contributed, arising from groundwater's capacity to provide flexible, on-demand irrigation to support vibrant, wealth-creating agriculture in all climate zones and from the growing need to provide food for urban populations. By far the most powerful pull has been in South Asia and North China, where the land-augmenting impact of groundwater has proved irresistible.

Globally, agricultural groundwater use of around 900 cubic kilometers a year supports annual output valued at $210–$230 billion, yielding a gross productivity of about $0.23–$0.26 per cubic meter of water abstracted [speculative]. However, much of this use is concentrated in Bangladesh, China, India, Iran, Pakistan, and the United States, which account for well over 80% of global groundwater use. The dynamic impacts of intensive groundwater use are best understood by recognizing four types of groundwater-in-agriculture systems:

' The groundwater boom has been driven by supply-push factors, such as government subsidies and easy availability of inexpensive pumps and drilling technologies. Demand-pull factors have also contributed

■ *Arid agricultural systems,* such as in the Middle East and North Africa, where groundwater is increasingly needed and demanded in higher value nonfarm uses.

■ *Industrial agricultural systems,* such as Australia, Europe, and the western United States, where groundwater supports wealth-creating agriculture and attracts more scientific and material resources to manage its negative externalities.

■ *Smallholder farming systems,* such as South Asia and the North China plains, where groundwater irrigation creates relatively little wealth but is the mainstay of 1–1.2 billion poor female and male farmers.

■ *Groundwater-supported extensive pastoralism,* such as much of Sub-Saharan Africa and Latin America, where groundwater abstractions are less than in other systems but are crucial for water supply schemes and for an extensive pastoral economy that supports a large share of its female and male herders.

In smallholder agrarian systems and groundwater-supported extensive pastoralism the socioeconomic impacts of groundwater irrigation are unassailable.

Overwhelming evidence from Asia suggests that groundwater irrigation promotes greater interpersonal, intergender, interclass, and spatial equity than do large irrigation projects. Evidence from Africa, Asia, and Latin America also suggests that groundwater is important in settings where poor farmers find opportunities to improve their livelihoods through small-scale farming based on shallow groundwater circulation. Once these inherently vulnerable shallow groundwater circulations are threatened, so too are the millions of rural livelihoods tied to them.

This intensive—but essentially unplanned—groundwater use faces several challenges. Pumping costs are rising, and irrigation-supporting subsidies are compromising the viability of rural energy providers. India is a prime example. Moreover, the impacts of groundwater depletion on water quality, stream flows, wetlands, and downgradient users in certain pockets are rapidly nullifying the widely dispersed beneficial impacts on livelihoods and food security at the society level. In arid regions, where fossil groundwater is a primary source of water for all uses, intensive groundwater irrigation may threaten future water security. In addition, with anticipated shifts in precipitation patterns induced by climate change, groundwater's value as a strategic reserve is set to increase worldwide. The challenges bring the central issue of the sustainability of groundwater use systems into sharp focus.

The long-term sustainability of groundwater systems is not easily determined. And a debate has emerged among hydrogeologists over the widely used notion of sustainable yield of aquifers. To manage groundwater resources properly and to identify effective resource management strategies urgently needed among the poorest agrarian societies, an improved

Groundwater: a global
assessment of scale
and significance 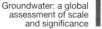 **10**

understanding of aquifer behavior has to be combined with an appreciation of the socio-economic drivers of intensive groundwater use.

In the face of such growing concerns, groundwater use in agriculture is showing no sign of ebbing. It will continue to grow in many parts of the developing world. Participatory approaches to sustainable groundwater management will need to combine supply-side measures—such as artificial recharge, aquifer recovery, interbasin transfer of water, and the like—with demand-side measures—such as groundwater pricing, legal and regulatory control, water rights and withdrawal permits, and promotion of water-saving crops and technologies. But not all these measures are immediately suited to developing countries if approached from a formal water management perspective. Supply-side measures have proved easier to implement than demand-side measures, even in technologically advanced countries. In the absence of supply augmentation the only way to adequately ease the strain on aquifer systems may be to reduce irrigated areas, improve farming practices, and shift to water saving crops—but this may be difficult to implement in socioeconomic and political terms in developing countries.

The long-term strategy to ease pressure on groundwater resources may be to increase opportunities for off-farm livelihoods and ease population pressure on agriculture. In the medium term key priorities in Latin America and Sub-Saharan Africa are to develop groundwater for improving the livelihoods of poor male and female farmers but in a regulated and planned manner. In Asia's groundwater hotspots key priorities are to develop effective indirect and direct means to regulate aggregate groundwater withdrawals; step up investments in groundwater management, including widescale managed aquifer recharge and scientific conjunctive management; and conduct judicious and well planned interbasin transfers of water. In all parts of the developing world a key common priority is to improve the data base, upgrade the understanding of groundwater supply and demand conditions, and create effective programs for public education in the sustainable use of groundwater resources.

> The opportunities and challenges presented by the growth in intensive groundwater use in agriculture are often underrepresented in global discussions of the challenges of water scarcity

Global trends in groundwater irrigation

Rapid growth in groundwater irrigation has dominated expansion in global agricultural water use during recent decades. Global abstraction of groundwater grew from 100–150 cubic kilometers in 1950 to 950–1,000 cubic kilometers in 2000, largely concentrated in agriculture, particularly in Asia. The opportunities and challenges presented by the growth in intensive groundwater use in agriculture are often underrepresented in global discussions on the challenges of water scarcity. The goal of this chapter is to assess this revolutionary phenomenon in terms of its socioeconomic, hydrogeological, and environmental fallouts. The chapter also explores where the global groundwater irrigation economy is headed in the coming years and the options available for socioecological sustainability.

Historical context

With the introduction of the tubewell and mechanical pump technology in the early decades of the 20th century and their growing popularity after 1950, groundwater use soared to previously unthinkable levels after 1950 in many parts of the world. In Spain groundwater use increased from 2 cubic kilometers per year to 6 over 1960–2000 (Martinez-Cortina and Hernandez-Mora 2003). In the Indian subcontinent groundwater use soared from around 10–20 cubic kilometers per year before 1950 to 240–260 by 2000 (Shah and others 2003). In the United States groundwater's share in irrigation water increased from 23% in 1950 to 42% in 2000 (Winter and others 1998). Chinese history records occasional cases of farmers lifting water from shallow wells by barrels to irrigate vegetables. But North China had very little irrigation until 1950, and its tubewell irrigation revolution took off only after 1970. In sum, then, the silent revolution in groundwater irrigation is essentially a story of the past 50 years (Llamas and Custodio 2003).

Groundwater has increasingly come to dominate agriculture in many parts of the irrigating world

Despite this exponential growth in groundwater use in agriculture, the world is still using only a fraction of earth's known groundwater reserves. At less than 1,000 cubic kilometers per year global groundwater use is a quarter of total global water withdrawals but just 1.5% of the world's annually renewable freshwater supplies, 8.2% of annually renewable groundwater, and 0.0001% of global groundwater reserves (estimated to be 7–23 million cubic kilometers) (Howard 2004). Yet its contribution to human welfare is huge. Groundwater has historically supplied domestic water requirements in numerous human settlements, urban and rural, around the world. According to one estimate, more than half the world's population relies on groundwater for its drinking water supply (Coughanowr 1994).

Irrigated agriculture, however, remains the major user of groundwater, which is often of high quality, suitable for direct human consumption. Understandably, the competition for such high-quality water is now intense, especially for shallow groundwater circulation that can be readily accessed by individual farmers and rural communities for livelihoods and food security. The explosion in groundwater irrigation in some key regions of the world presents a complex resource management challenge. Though global in purview, this chapter emphasizes developing countries where groundwater use in agriculture is high and increasing and where the associated challenges of sustainable resource management are critical for rural livelihoods.

Temporal patterns

Data on groundwater use are scarce. Data on the impact of agricultural groundwater use on food security, rural livelihoods, and ecological systems are even more so. But there is little doubt that groundwater has increasingly come to dominate agriculture in many parts of the irrigating world. Moreover, groundwater irrigation around the world over the past century has emerged and proceeded in waves. The first wave was in Italy, Mexico, Spain, and the United States, where large-scale groundwater use began in the early parts of the 1900s and seems to have peaked—or at least to have stopped growing. The second wave began in South Asia, parts of the North China plains, and parts of the Middle East and North Africa during the 1970s and is still continuing (figure 10.1).

In other regions of the world, however, groundwater use in agriculture has been slight but shows signs of rapid growth in the near future. In northeast Sri Lanka groundwater irrigation took off only during the early 1990s (Kikuchi and others 2003) and is still growing. Groundwater use in agriculture in much of Sub-Saharan Africa is still very slight and concentrated on commercial farms. But groundwater is increasingly important in supporting extensive pastoralism. A third wave of growth in groundwater use is thus likely

Groundwater: a global
assessment of scale
and significance

10

| figure **10.1** | **Development in groundwater withdrawal in selected countries** |

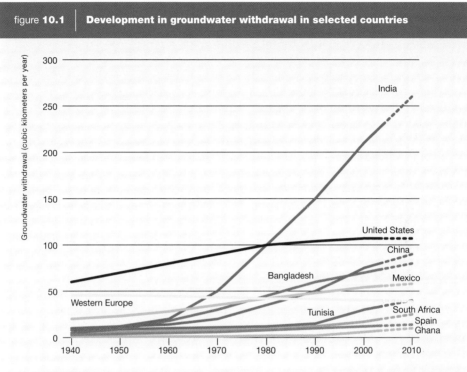

Source: Shah 2005.

| table **10.1** | **Groundwater irrigation in a global context** |

| | | Groundwater-irrigated area | |
Continent	Area under groundwater irrigation (thousands of hectares)	Share of total irrigated area (percent)	Share of cultivated area (percent)
Africa	2,472	19.8	1.0
Latin America & Caribbean	3,383	18.6	2.1
Asia	51,863	28.9	9.0

Source: FAO 2005a.

in many regions of Africa and in some South and Southeast Asian countries such as Sri Lanka and Viet Nam (Molle, Shah, and Barker 2003), although a good deal of pumping of water there takes place from surface water.

Scale of groundwater use in agriculture

A complete global picture of groundwater use in agriculture is not available. The Food and Agriculture Organization's AQUASTAT database provides national data on irrigated areas supplied by groundwater and surface water as reported by national agencies from developing countries and countries in transition (table 10.1). But since many of these countries do not regularly report data on groundwater-irrigated areas, this coverage is not comprehensive and does not necessarily present an up-to-date picture.

Taking just the developing countries and countries in transition from central planning, some 58 million ha—just 4% of total farm land—are under groundwater irrigation. But 25% of global irrigation depends upon groundwater, and 75% of groundwater-irrigated areas of the world are in Asia.

Information from other sources, however, suggests that total area under groundwater irrigation in 2005 may be 25%–40% higher than reported by the Food and Agriculture Organization.[1] For many countries accurate official estimates are simply not available.[2] For many other countries available estimates are out of date by a decade or longer. For India, the largest groundwater irrigator in the world, official estimates of area under groundwater irrigation are based on a 1993–94 census of groundwater structures. But recent large-scale nationwide surveys suggest that groundwater irrigation in India has experienced explosive growth during the past decade (see, for example, India NSSO 1999, 2003; Shah, Singh, and Mukherji 2006).[3] The 2001 Census of Minor Irrigation by the government of India suggests that gross area irrigated by groundwater wells in India is 53 million ha (India Ministry of Water Resources 2005). Similar trends are noted by researchers in the North China

figure **10.2** | **Top 20 groundwater irrigating countries**

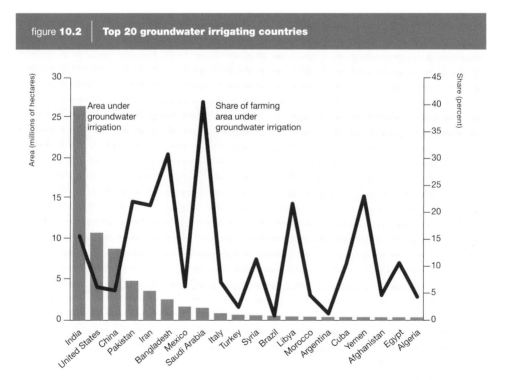

Source: FAO 2005a.

Groundwater: a global
assessment of scale
and significance **10**

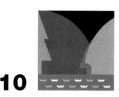

plains (Wang and others 2006a). If these estimates are accurate, groundwater-irrigated areas in Asia may well be in excess of 70 million ha, and global groundwater irrigation may well approach 100 million ha *[established but incomplete]*.

Global pockets of intensive groundwater use in agriculture

Since groundwater use in agriculture is concentrated in a few countries—and often in pockets within them—disaggregated analysis is necessary. Based on AQUASTAT data, of the 20 countries with the largest areas registered under groundwater irrigation and accounting for 99% of recorded groundwater irrigated areas, six of them—Bangladesh, China, India, Iran, Pakistan, and the United States—account for 83% of the world's groundwater-irrigated areas (figure 10.2, table 10.2). Because this chapter's assessment is about groundwater use in agriculture, these global pockets of intensive groundwater irrigation are of special interest.

table **10.2**	Top 20 groundwater-irrigating countries					
Country	Cultivated land per agricultural worker (hectares)	Area under groundwater irrigation (thousands of hectares)	Share of global ground-water-irrigated area (percent)	Groundwater-irrigated area		Ground-water-irrigated area (percent of total area)
				Share of irrigated area (percent)	Share of total culti-vated area (percent)	
India	0.6	26,538	38.6	53.0	15.6	8.1
United States	63.8	10,835	15.8	45.5	6.1	1.1
China	0.3	8,863	12.3	16.0	5.5	0.9
Pakistan	0.8	4,871	7.1	30.8	22.0	6.1
Iran	2.6	3,639	5.3	50.1	21.3	2.2
Bangladesh	0.2	2,592	3.8	69.1	30.8	18.0
Mexico	3.2	1,689	2.5	27.0	6.2	0.9
Saudi Arabia	6.0	1,538	2.2	95.6	40.5	0.7
Italy	11.2	865	1.3	27.2	7.0	2.9
Turkey	1.9	672	1.0	16.0	2.4	0.9
Syria	3.3	610	0.9	60.2	11.3	3.3
Brazil	5.9	545	0.8	19.0	0.8	0.1
Libya	22.9	464	0.7	98.7	21.6	0.3
Morocco	2.4	430	0.6	29.0	4.6	1.0
Argentina	24.1	403	0.6	27.7	1.2	0.1
Cuba	5.2	393	0.6	45.1	10.4	3.5
Yemen	0.6	383	0.6	79.6	23.0	0.7
Afghanistan	1.2	367	0.5	11.5	4.6	0.6
Egypt	0.4	361	0.5	10.6	10.6	0.4
Algeria	3.0	352	0.5	61.8	4.3	0.1

Two other categories of area are also of interest. First are regions where the dominant source of water for all uses is fossil groundwater, such as the Middle East and North Africa. Some countries in these regions—with significant areas under groundwater irrigation—are in the list of top 20. Another region of interest is Sub-Saharan Africa, where groundwater use is small relative to the resource potential. Careful and planned development of the resource can make groundwater an important part of a poverty-reduction toolkit for this region. There is already movement in this direction. The general impression among researchers is that groundwater use is insignificant in Sub-Saharan Africa, and its role in supporting livelihoods equally so. Recent explorations, however, suggest that quantities of groundwater annually withdrawn may be smaller than in South Asia or the United States, but groundwater already plays a significant role in supporting livelihoods in Sub-Saharan Africa by sustaining extensive pastoralism (Giordano 2006), irrigated agriculture, and water supply.

> Careful and planned development of groundwater can make it an important part of a poverty reduction toolkit for Sub-Saharan Africa

Driving forces

Ready access to groundwater drilling technology and borehole mechanization led to the widespread uptake of groundwater in the second half of the 20th century. This trend was anticipated as early as the mid-1950s (UN 1960). What has not been so easily explicable is the intense regional differentiation, that is, rapid growth in Asia and the notable absence of growth in much of Africa and Latin America. This section attempts to review the principal drivers behind such regional disparities.

Water scarcity

The global groundwater boom in recent decades has occurred in regions with limited rainfall and hence recharge. The countries where pressures to intensify agricultural production have been acute have witnessed intensive groundwater use in agriculture.

A new global map developed by researchers at the Technical University of Dresden shows the average annual groundwater recharge in different parts of the world (map 10.1). None of the 20 countries listed in table 10.2 falls in areas with high average annual recharge of 300–1,000 millimeters (mm). Groundwater use in agriculture is absent or minimal in regions with high recharge, and it is intensive where the recharge is too small to sustain intensive groundwater use. Notable exceptions are Bangladesh, eastern India, and Nepal's Terai region—humid areas with abundant surface water resources where large pockets of intensive groundwater irrigation have emerged and played a significant role in improving food and livelihood security for the rural poor.

On-demand groundwater services

Another argument explaining the groundwater revolution emphasizes groundwater's many favorable characteristics. First, it is ubiquitous, available in lesser or greater degree, almost everywhere. Second, unlike large surface irrigation structures that may necessitate government initiative or cooperative effort on a large scale, groundwater irrigation can be developed quickly by individual farmers or small groups. Third, while operating costs of groundwater may be higher, the capital costs of groundwater structures are much lower per

Groundwater: a global
assessment of scale
and significance **10**

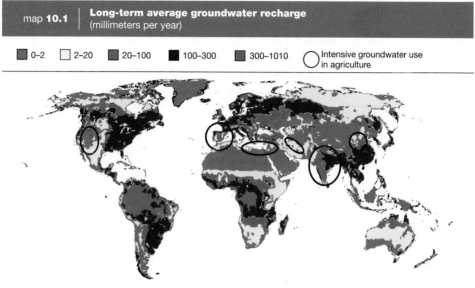

| map **10.1** | **Long-term average groundwater recharge** (millimeters per year) |

☐ 0–2   ☐ 2–20   ☐ 20–100   ☐ 100–300   ☐ 300–1010   ⃝ Intensive groundwater use in agriculture

Source: Döll and Flörke 2005.

hectare of irrigation than those of surface structures. Fourth, groundwater irrigation also demonstrates greater drought-resilience; groundwater aquifers keep yielding during a dry year even when all surface water bodies dry up. Fifth, and most important, groundwater provides irrigation on demand, offering a high-class captive irrigation source that provides farmers freedom to apply water when their crops need it the most. Sixth, due to its reliability in time and space, transmission and storage losses (for example, leakage and evaporation) from groundwater irrigation are lower than with surface irrigation. As a result, farmers tend to economize on its use, optimize other inputs (such as seeds, fertilizers, and pesticides), and diversify crops to more higher valued crops, thereby yielding significantly higher water productivity (in terms of kilograms per cubic meter of water and of dollars per cubic meter of water) than with surface water sources (Shah 1993; Burke and Moench 2000; Deb Roy and Shah 2003; Hernandez-Mora, Martinez-Cortina, and Fornes 2003).

These unique advantages of groundwater are important in explaining why millions of farmers throughout the world have taken to groundwater irrigation. However, these are not enough to stimulate intensive groundwater use in the vast high-recharge regions that are well endowed with groundwater (see map 10.1). This suggests that other drivers of the groundwater revolution are at play.

Access to cheap drilling, pumps, and electricity

The extensive use of groundwater in agriculture has been limited by the labor intensity and high cost of lifting groundwater with human labor and animal traction. Advances in and easy access to pumping and drilling technologies and spread of rural electrification have meant that groundwater development has offered opportunities to tap this beneficial resource for improving agriculture and livelihoods. In many Asian countries, especially China and India, growth in groundwater structures gave rise to a large and competitive industry to manufacture pumps, engines, motors, and drilling rigs, resulting in progressive decline in real prices of this equipment. Governments in many countries, such as India, Jordan, Mexico, Syria, and for some years Pakistan, stimulated groundwater irrigation by subsidizing energy for pumping (photo 10.1). Others, such as Bangladesh and later Sri Lanka, supported groundwater irrigation first by subsidizing equipment costs and more recently by opening their markets to cheap Chinese pumps. One reason that smallholder irrigation experienced explosive growth in South Asia but has grown very slowly in Sub-Saharan Africa is the absence of rural electrification combined with the prohibitive costs of importing pump and irrigation equipment in Africa.

> The unique advantages of groundwater are important in explaining why millions of farmers throughout the world have taken to groundwater irrigation

Pressures of feeding an urbanizing population

As towns and cities grow, their demand for food grows too. Urban consumers need quantity and demand quality. Irrigation has been the principal strategy to maintain national food security in Malaysia and Morocco. Increasing year-round global consumption of fruit and vegetables has prompted the mobilization of groundwater near urban centers such as Lusaka and several cities of China to furnish both urban markets and also feed into export markets.

As the global demand for animal protein increases, groundwater is increasingly called on to provide more water for livestock on rangeland without surface water or for irrigating fodder under zero-grazing systems. Many arid and semiarid rangelands depend entirely on access to groundwater to sustain stocking ratios. But groundwater structures both encourage stocking ratios higher than the range (fodder) capacity and concentrate livestock around boreholes. The self-limiting balance of rangelands can be severely disrupted by the

Photo 10.1 Supplemental irrigation in Syria

Photo by David Molden

introduction of mechanized boreholes. Gomes (2005) cites examples from Somalia and northern Kenya where boreholes have encouraged overstocking and resulted in disputes between borehole owners and local communities. The oversized groundwater economy of northern Gujarat and many other arid and semiarid regions in India centers around zero-grazed dairy production (Singh and others 2004). Groundwater is intensively used here to produce fodder and other cash crops, with manure being returned to the land to improve soil quality. This white revolution has been pulled by the establishment of large and highly successful dairy cooperatives that offer reliable and stable markets for milk produced by smallholders in the region. However, the apparent success is limited by aquifer reserves, which in some parts of the state are showing signs of overdevelopment.

Agricultural demand in arid and semiarid regions

Many arid and semiarid regions of the world offer excellent farming conditions suitable for intensive cultivation: good alluvial soils, flat lands, and climate with sunshine suitable for supporting two or more crops per year. The North China plains, the Indus Basin, California, and central Mexico are examples. The only input that these areas have lacked for supporting vibrant agriculture was water. Agriculture in many of these regions performed below its potential under rainfed conditions. For millennia farmers in the North China plains harvested three crops every two years using rain and soil moisture (Dong 1991), and the vast and fertile Indus Basin supported extensive pastoralism but was sparsely populated and hardly cultivated. Many of these regions are also located above abundant aquifers, but lifting water manually or with animal labor has restricted the use of these aquifers. The rise of groundwater irrigation with tubewells and mechanical pumps transformed many of these into highly productive agricultural areas. The key driver of the groundwater revolution here was the demand pull for water control through irrigation—the only missing input that kept agriculture in these areas from performing at full potential.

> Many arid and semiarid regions of the world offer excellent farming conditions suitable for intensive cultivation. The only missing input was water

Pressures of rural populations struggling to survive

A widely prevalent view is that intensive groundwater irrigation emerges only in arid and semiarid areas otherwise suitable for intensive agriculture. However, Bangladesh, Nepal's Terai region, and eastern India—all of them humid and endowed with ample surface water resources—challenge this view. And these observations cannot be brushed aside as outliers because they account for a large share of the global groundwater economy, no matter which criterion is used: groundwater-irrigated area, groundwater abstraction, or number of people affected.

The groundwater revolution in these pockets is also driven by demand pull but of a different kind. The massive demand pull for groundwater irrigation in these areas has been powered by tremendous increases in population pressure on agriculture since 1960. Intensive agriculture based on groundwater irrigation has emerged in all densely populated pockets, such as Punjab in India and Pakistan, eastern India, Bangladesh, and Tamil Nadu and Andhra Pradesh in India. By contrast, sparsely populated regions—such as the central Indian highlands and Sindh and Baluchistan in Pakistan—make far less intensive use of groundwater irrigation. Bangladesh, eastern India, and Nepal's Terai region are the only areas where high average annual recharge of 300–1,000 mm is matched by intensive use. But there are also vast regions, especially in peninsular India, with intensive groundwater irrigation but very small average annual recharge. South Asia is thus a region where groundwater development has had little to do with the availability of recharge; the revolution has been driven primarily by the capacity of borewell irrigation to make multiple cropping of land possible and thereby serve as a land-augmenting technology (Mukherji and Shah 2005).

Socioeconomic impacts

> In South Asia groundwater development has had little to do with the availability of recharge; the revolution has been driven primarily by the capacity of borewell irrigation to make multiple cropping of land possible and thereby serve as a land-augmenting technology

Global use of about 900 cubic kilometers of groundwater a year in agriculture indicates annual final output of about $210–$230 billion, with gross productivity of $0.23–$0.26 per cubic meter abstracted. In the global economy groundwater-supported output would be a tiny part, and if groundwater irrigation around the world suddenly halted, the global economy would hardly notice. But the socioeconomic impacts of intensive groundwater use in agriculture are important to understand because of the critical links to the livelihoods and food security of some 1.2–1.5 billion rural households in some of the poorest regions of Africa and Asia (photo 10.2). To understand these impacts, it is important to explore the dynamic of groundwater use in agriculture in different regions of the world.

Global typology of groundwater irrigation and impacts

The drivers for intensive groundwater use in agriculture—as well as its broader socioeconomic impacts—differ throughout the world. A meaningful approach to understanding the global economics of groundwater irrigation needs to distinguish between four types of agricultural groundwater use situations: arid agricultural systems, industrial agricultural systems, smallholder farming systems, and groundwater-supported extensive pastoralism (table 10.3). These situations differ from each other in overall climatic, hydrological, and

Photo by David Molden

Photo 10.2 Use of groundwater in Asia is critical to livelihoods, especially for the poor

Groundwater: a global
assessment of scale
and significance | **10**

demographic parameters; land-use patterns; organization of agriculture; and relative importance of irrigated and rainfed farming. They also differ in the drivers of expansion in groundwater irrigation and the nature and level of societies' involvement in groundwater-based irrigated agriculture.

Arid agricultural systems have low population pressure on land and a tiny fraction of their geographic area under cultivation. Farming depends on irrigation, mostly from fossil—or limitedly renewable—groundwater, which is the only source of irrigation. But growing competition for fossil groundwater from higher value uses, especially urban water supply, will crowd out its agricultural use. The virtual water thinking pioneered by Allan and others (Allan 2003; Delgado and others 2003; Warner 2003) best applies to arid agricultural systems.

In industrial agricultural systems—as in Australia, Italy, Spain, and the United States—groundwater sustains some highly productive industrial agriculture. Irrigated agriculture is a small proportion of total agriculture, and groundwater is, in turn, a relatively small proportion of irrigated agriculture. Few people depend on groundwater-based agriculture, but more people depend on agribusiness. Industrial agricultural systems have pockets of severe groundwater depletion and pollution due to groundwater irrigation. But agribusiness is a high-value use and creates massive wealth. California's $90 billion agricultural economy depends heavily on groundwater use, as does Spain's export economy of grapes, citrus, olives, fruit, and vegetables. Industrial agricultural systems bring vast financial and scientific resources to ameliorate problems of groundwater abuse, offering a scientific and institutional knowledge base for sustainable groundwater management.

In South Asia and the North China plains intensive groundwater irrigation reflects the population pressure on agriculture (Bruinsma 2003). Smallholder farming systems cultivate a larger proportion of their geographic area, irrigate more of their cultivated area,

table **10.3**	**Four types of groundwater economies**			
	Arid agricultural systems	**Industrial agricultural systems**	**Smallholder farming systems**	**Groundwater-supported extensive pastoralism**
Countries	Algeria, Egypt, Iran, Iraq, Libya, Morocco, Tunisia, Turkey	Australia, Brazil, Cuba, Italy, Mexico, South Africa, Spain, United States	Afghanistan, Bangladesh, North China, India, Nepal, Pakistan	Botswana, Burkina Faso, Chad, Ethiopia, Ghana, Kenya, Malawi, Mali, Namibia, Niger, Nigeria, Senegal, South Africa, Sudan, Tanzania, Zambia
Groundwater-irrigated areas	Less than 6 million hectares	6–70 million hectares	71–500 million hectares	More than 500 million hectares of grazing area supported by boreholes for stock watering
Climate	Arid	Semiarid	Semiarid to humid, monsoon climate	Arid to semiarid areas
Aggregate national water resources	Very small	Good to very good	Good to moderate	Mixed rainfed livestock and cropping systems

(continues on next page)

table **10.3** | **Four types of groundwater economies** (continued)

	Arid agricultural systems	Industrial agricultural systems	Smallholder farming systems	Groundwater-supported extensive pastoralism
Population pressure on agriculture	Low to medium	Low to very low	High to very high	Population density is low but pressure on grazing areas is high
Share of total land area under cultivation	1%–5%	10%–50%	40%–60%	5%–8%
Share of culti-vated areas under irrigation	30%–90%	2%–15%	40%–70%	Less than 5%
Share of irri-gated area under groundwater irrigation	40%–90%	5%–20%	10%–60%	Less than 1%
Share of total geographic area under groundwater	0.12%–4.0%	0.001%–1.5%	1.6%–25.0%	Less than 0.001%, but groundwater-supported grazing areas are about 17% of total area
Organization of agriculture	Small to medium-size farms under market-based agriculture	Medium-size to large-scale farms under industrial, export-oriented farming	Very small landhold-ings, subsistence-oriented, mixed peasant farming systems	Small-scale pastoralists, often seasonally con-nected with small-scale agriculturalists
Driver of groundwater irrigation	Lack of alterna-tive irrigation or livelihood	Highly profitable market-based farming	Need to absorb surplus labor in farming through land-augmenting technologies	Stock watering
Significance of groundwater ir-rigation to national economy	Low (less than 2%–3% of GDP)	Low (less than 0.5% of GDP)	Moderate (5%–20% of GDP)	Moderate (5%–20% of GDP)
Significance of groundwater irrigation economy to welfare of national population	Low to moderate	Low to very low	Very high (40%–50% of rural population and 40%–80% of food production involve groundwater irrigation)	Low in terms of numbers of pastoralists involved, sometimes moderate in terms of national food supply
Significance of groundwater irrigation for poverty reduction	Moderate	Very low	Very high	Groundwater central to pastoral livelihood sys-tems, but limited scope for using more groundwater for poverty reduction
Gross value of output supported by groundwater irrigation	$6–$8 billion	$100–$120 billion	$100–$110 billion	$2–$3 billion

Source: Data on cultivated areas under irrigation are from FAO 2005b; data on irrigated areas under groundwater irrigation are from FAO 2005a. Other data are preliminary estimates by the authors.

and use groundwater over more areas for intensive agriculture than do arid agricultural systems and industrial agricultural systems. While in arid agricultural systems and industrial agricultural systems groundwater is used on 0.1%–4% of geographic area, in pockets of smallholder farming systems—such as the Indo-Gangetic Basin—up to a quarter of the total geographic area can be under groundwater irrigation.

In terms of groundwater quantity and number of people involved, the smallholder farming systems in Bangladesh, China, India, Iran, Nepal, and Pakistan have experienced the largest growth by far in groundwater use over the past 35–40 years. Of the global annual groundwater diversion of 950–1,000 cubic kilometers half or more is likely accounted for by these countries. By stabilizing rainfed peasant farming and facilitating multiple cropping, groundwater use in smallholder farming systems affects a larger proportion of population, of cultivated area, and of gross domestic product than in arid agricultural systems and industrial agricultural systems. The challenge of sustainably managing groundwater resources is most serious here, but it is also the most complex.

Groundwater-supported extensive pastoralism is concentrated predominantly in Africa. In Sub-Saharan Africa groundwater resources are modest, but a very small proportion of what is available is currently developed and plays a critical role in supporting extensive livestock (Sonou 1994; Giordano 2006). Groundwater abstraction per hectare is small and is mainly used for stock-watering. The absolute number of poor people who depend on groundwater-supported extensive pastoralism may be smaller than the number who depend on groundwater-irrigated agriculture in Asia. But pastoralists account for a substantial proportion of Africa's population. In Sub-Saharan Africa, where the challenge of improving rural livelihoods persists, groundwater-supported extensive pastoralism is critical in creating a global picture of groundwater's contribution to human welfare (box 10.1).

> In terms of groundwater quantity and number of people involved, the smallholder farming systems in Bangladesh, China, India, Iran, Nepal, and Pakistan have experienced the largest growth by far in groundwater use over the past 35–40 years

Groundwater-intensive, market-driven irrigated agriculture

The specific value of groundwater to agriculture is apparent only where irrigation schemes depend entirely on groundwater sources. Burke and Moench (2000) have summarized accounts of the boost that groundwater gives to agricultural production and the attendant environmental stability that groundwater confers. Specific studies are also captured in the Food and Agriculture Organization's 2004 inventory of valuation studies (FAO 2004). Key characteristics are:

- *Available on site*. Groundwater that is available on site needs little conveyance infrastructure thus leading to decentralized management.
- *Storage and reliability*. Groundwater storage provides an important interannual buffer at a fraction of the cost of conventional surface water storage.
- *Flexibility*. Pumped groundwater is a perfect delivery system for farmers. The on-demand, just-in-time characteristics of the system overcome the uncertainty and risk often associated with surface water deliveries. Few surface irrigation schemes can be as perfect and low risk, even if they have good downstream control.
- *Conjunctive use*. In surface water irrigation schemes conjunctive use of surface water and groundwater can make categorical attribution difficult, although farmers in

surface water commands who also have access to groundwater are clearly able to boost overall productivity (see below on conjunctive management of groundwater and surface water).

Groundwater irrigation and rural poverty

In smallholder farming systems the advantages of groundwater irrigation translate into reduced poverty, better food security, and improved livelihoods. In India more than 70% of irrigated agricultural production is attributed to groundwater irrigation (Deb Roy and Shah 2003; India NSSO 2005). Many have dubbed the green revolution in India a "tube-well revolution" (Repetto 1985). And Bangladesh's *boro* rice revolution, which transformed the country from a rice importer to an exporter, is also attributed to its shallow tubewell revolution (Palmer-Jones 1999). For a long time North China farmers raised only three rainfed crops of maize and wheat in a two-year cycle. But the expansion of groundwater irrigation made two crops every year of maize and wheat the standard practice in most of the North China plains (photo 10.3; Wang and others 2006a).

In these regions productivity-enhancing impacts of groundwater irrigation worked through several pathways:

Photo 10.3 Groundwater provides flexible and reliable supply in China

- *Increased cropping intensity.* Groundwater irrigation made double—or even triple—cropping of farm land possible, making it a land-augmenting intervention in these land-poor regions.
- *Stabilized rainfed* kharif (*monsoon season*) *crop.* Because of the high variability in amount and timing of rainfall from the southwest monsoon, the *kharif* crop always suffered from high production risks. Groundwater irrigation reduced these risks.

---

box **10.1** | **Groundwater and poverty alleviation in Africa**

Use of agricultural groundwater is lower in Sub-Saharan Africa than in Asia, but it is critical for livestock production in large parts of the Sahel and East Africa (Burke 1996), and it supports small-scale but highly valuable irrigation and stabilizes the drinking water supply (BGS 2004; Calow and others 1997; Carter and Howsam 1994). While the volumes used may be small, a majority of poor rural households, which make up most agricultural producers in Sub-Saharan Africa, depend on groundwater in some way—for direct crop production, livestock watering, or domestic supplies.

In many parts of Sub-Saharan Africa groundwater is not yet used; in others it has been sustainably used over long periods of time; and in still others depletion is already a problem. For groundwater to contribute more to poverty alleviation, it is important to consider the links between technical feasibility and economic and political realities. Where it makes economic sense, farmers are quick to take to groundwater use. For instance, despite the supposed high costs of irrigation development in Africa, farmers in southeastern Ghana have transitioned from hand-dug wells to diesel pumps to electrification over a relatively short period. Similarly, diesel pump technology introduced in Nigeria after the oil boom spread quickly elsewhere in the region. The point of future development policy as related to groundwater in Sub-Saharan Africa should thus be to understand both where additional development is possible and where and why it is not (Giordano 2006).

Photo by Tushaar Shah

Groundwater: a global
assessment of scale
and significance **10**

- *Reliability.* Supplemental groundwater irrigation's reliability promoted agricultural diversification. High-value crops like fruits and vegetables require more frequent, on-demand irrigation than well owners are able to provide.
- *Geographically widespread benefits of supplemental irrigation.* In Sub-Saharan Africa groundwater has played—and will continue to play—a much less direct role in agriculture, affecting perhaps less than 1% of cultivated area (Giordano 2006). But almost 20% of the irrigated area in Africa is served by groundwater (30% in North Africa and 10% in Sub-Saharan Africa). This is 0.35% of the continent's cultivated area (FAO 2005a).[4] Groundwater sustains Africa's pastoral economy and small pockets of value-added peri-urban agriculture.

Gender and equity issues in groundwater use in agriculture and pastoralism

Especially in Asia the evidence is overwhelming that the groundwater boom has demonstrated greater interpersonal, interclass, and interregional equity in access to irrigation—and thereby to benefits of intensive agriculture—than large canal irrigation projects that have created pockets of prosperity in command areas (Shah 1993; Deb Roy and Shah 2003; Bhattarai and Narayanamoorthy 2004; Moench 2003).

Some researchers have found that women have little to say or do in managing canal irrigation (van Koppen 1998; van Koppen, Parthasarathy, and Safiliou 2002; Shah and others 2000). However, numerous studies in Africa, Asia, and Latin America show that when women explore ways to improve their livelihood through smallholder agriculture or livestock, groundwater and small pumps are commonly involved. Conversely, poor women and men are hardest hit by groundwater depletion or quality deterioration.

Prospects for sustainable groundwater management

Given the trends in groundwater use and the current set of drivers, overall groundwater use in agriculture is not expected to decline in the foreseeable future. But there are signs that the patterns and styles of use are changing. These changes present both threats and opportunities.

Making the transition from development to management

In many parts of the world where the sustainability of groundwater irrigation is in serious question governments and management agencies have operated in resource development mode far too long. Before tubewell technology became popular, government policies aimed to encourage groundwater use in agriculture through subsidies for capital and operating costs and at times through government installation and operation of tubewells, as in South Asia (Shah 2000), China (Wang, Zhang, and Cai 2004), and Central Asia. Many governments—such as in Sri Lanka and in several African countries—are still in that mode.

However, where intensive groundwater irrigation is already well established, concern is growing among governments, nongovernmental organizations, media, and the general

> Given the trends in groundwater use and the current set of drivers, overall groundwater use in agriculture is not expected to decline in the foreseeable future—but there are signs that the patterns and styles of use are changing

public about the consequences of groundwater depletion and degradation. Country responses are similar: a groundwater organization is set up merely to monitor and study groundwater changes. Once threats are visible, there is a clamor to pass laws to regulate groundwater development by establishing a system of permits to install tubewells and withdraw groundwater. Unfortunately, such measures in isolation are not adequate to curb further groundwater development.

Where intensive groundwater irrigation is already well established, concern is growing about the consequences of groundwater depletion and degradation

Managing groundwater supply

A natural response to groundwater scarcity is to search for new water sources. However, since development of groundwater is usually secondary to development of surface water, new options for expansion of water supply sources become increasingly limited and costly.

Managed aquifer recharge and rainwater harvesting. Rainwater harvesting and artificial (or enhanced) recharge are popular attempts to capture and store underground rainwater and discharge, termed "excess runoff" or "rejected recharge" (photo 10.4) Rainwater harvesting increases groundwater recharge at the expense of immediate runoff. It may increase stream flow later in the season, when the artificially recharged groundwater discharges to streams. Thus, artificial recharge can be used to mitigate floods and to enhance late-season stream flows.

In India rainwater harvesting is a bylaw in urban construction regulations in such cities as Chennai, Delhi, and Rajkot, and artificial recharge is promoted and financially supported by the government. At the local level rainwater harvesting has gained the character of a mass movement, especially in such regions as western India, where groundwater exhaustion is a real impediment for agricultural activities (Shah 2000; Shah and Desai 2002; Sakthivadivel and Nagar 2003; Agarwal and Narain 1999). This has not been without controversy. The ability of rainwater harvesting to generate new water services in upstream areas will always need to be set against the reduction of downstream flows (Rao and others 2003).

Photo 10.4 Recharging aquifers through rainwater harvesting in Dudhara, India

Photo by Tushaar Shah

Groundwater: a global
assessment of scale
and significance | **10**

Augmenting groundwater with wastewater. In many parts of the developing world cities depend increasingly on groundwater, often to the detriment of farmers in suburban and rural areas. In turn, steadily increasing amounts of wastewater generated by cities, often discharged into streams, have given rise to a new water resource that farmers have opted to use as an alternative (Scott, Faruqui, and Raschid-Sally 2004; Bhamoriya 2002; Buechler, Devi, and Raschid-Sally 2002). This resource is dependable in quantity but poor in quality because untreated wastewater from cities in the developing world can contain harmful pathogenic micro-organisms, excessive nutrients, and toxic chemicals. In most places wastewater use is not subject to any control or surveillance (see chapter 11 on marginal-quality water), posing health risks to farmers using the water and people eating crops grown with wastewater—and causing environmental impacts such as groundwater contamination and disruption of ecosystems in downstream areas. An alternative is to deliberately infiltrate wastewater into groundwater, thereby augmenting the groundwater resource and obtaining partial treatment through filtering processes within soil and aquifer materials (Foster and others 2003).

> As opportunities for developing newer sources of irrigation are rapidly exhausted, sustainable aquifer management depends greatly on better planning and management of conjunctive use of surface water and groundwater

Conjunctive management of surface water and groundwater. Conjunctive water use refers to the coordinated use of surface water and groundwater to meet demand. Conjunctive management refers to deliberate and planned efforts to comanage surface water and groundwater resources to optimize benefits from new water development projects in terms of productivity, equity, and environmental sustainability. As opportunities for developing newer sources of irrigation are rapidly exhausted, sustainable aquifer management depends greatly on better planning and management of conjunctive use of surface water and groundwater.

A key strategy in conjunctive management of surface water and groundwater is the planned drawing down of the water table in the pre-monsoon dry months to enhance recharge from monsoon rainwater as well as from irrigation return flows. The conjunctive water management scheme in China's People's Victory Canal used water from wells and canals for irrigation, recharged groundwater with canal water, and used groundwater for nonagricultural purposes. It successfully reduced waterlogging and salinization, alleviated conflicts over low stream flows, reduced sedimentation problems in canals and drainage ditches, assured timely delivery of irrigation water, and increased agricultural production (Cai 1988). This win-win arrangement has, however, broken down in recent years (Pearce 2005).

In the developing world conjunctive use is ubiquitous by default. For example, Dhawan (1988) showed that the mushrooming number of wells in India changed the profile of water use in Mula command in Maharashtra and argued that the indirect benefits of canal irrigation through groundwater recharge are even greater than the direct benefits of flow irrigation. Similarly, Scott and Restrepo (2001, p. 176) concluded that in the Lerma-Chapala Basin in central Mexico, "the sustainability of groundwater trends is inextricably linked to the management of surface water, and is highly sensitive to the area and type of crops irrigated, as well as surface water management practices." The pumping of water from drainage canals for rice planting is routinely observed in South Asian commands, and the use of shallow groundwater pumping from waterlogged soil along leaky conveyance canals is also commonplace. Recent reviews of progress in the Indus Basin note the impact of conjunctive use on farmer incomes but point out that there has been no attempt at conjunctive management (Van Halsema 2002; Wahaj 2001; Strosser 1997).

Scavenging of surplus groundwater on the margins of surface-supplied schemes points to conjunctive use, but not management (FAO 2001). The Loukos pressurized scheme in Morocco effectively provides groundwater at its margin to private irrigators beyond the scheme perimeter, a supply that is sustained through free draining soils. Realizing the multiple uses of irrigation water, this scavenging of leakage water through wells may also provide farming households with better drinking water than other local sources, as in Pakistan and Sri Lanka (Boelee and van der Hoek 2002; Ensink and others 2002; Meijer and others 2006; Shortt and others 2003).

Conjunctive management is rare in developing countries. But in high-income countries conjunctive management is highly developed—enough to even out spatial and temporal variations in regional water availability (Blomquist, Heikkila, and Schlager 2001). In the Phoenix, Arizona, irrigation commands surface water has been banked for future use by agriculture (Lluria and Fisk 1995). Surface irrigation practices have a direct impact on groundwater recharge. Key to effective conjunctive management of surface water and groundwater resources is improved main system management, which sometimes requires changes in infrastructure but is more a question of capacity building, efficient organization, and better information and communication.

In regions with primary salinity—such as the Indus Basin in Pakistan and northwest India, the Nile Basin, the Yellow River Basin in North China—the objective of conjunctive management is to maintain both water and salt balances. System managers require more control and precision in canal water deliveries to different parts of the command to maintain an optimal ratio of fresh and saline water for irrigation (Murray-Rust and Vander Velde 1992). Depending on the aquifer characteristics and water quality parameters, it may make sense to divide the command areas into surface water irrigation zones and groundwater irrigation zones. Recharge structures within a surface system are often useful for rehabilitation and modernization. Another benefit of integrated groundwater and surface water use in irrigation commands has been reduced waterlogging problems in areas where groundwater is pumped to control groundwater level rise and to augment irrigation potential, as in Pakistan (Van Steenbergen and Oliemans 2002).

The benefits of conjunctive management have been realized for municipal water supply to protect stressed aquifers (Todd and Priestadt 1997). But aquifer storage and recovery as tools for managing supply have so far been restricted to municipal uses, where water quality standards have to be maintained and the injection and cycling of treated water does not suffer any loss of quality (Pyne 1995). Given the high costs of injection and recovery, this application is unlikely to benefit low-value agriculture that is indifferent to quality.

The prospects for conjunctive management in agriculture alone look bleak. Where conjunctive use is applied with good results, the legacy of the surface water design and overall management of surface water commands rarely permits precision application of surface water, let alone planned recharge of aquifers whose storage has been opened up.

> Key to effective conjunctive management of surface water and groundwater resources is improved main system management, which sometimes requires changes in infrastructure but is more a question of capacity building, efficient organization, and better information and communication

Groundwater: a global
assessment of scale
and significance **10**

Only the proximity of higher value uses is likely to prompt more active management of groundwater recharge and discharge.

Interbasin water transfers. In countries with vastly contrasting climate conditions another management strategy for dealing with water deficiency is large interbasin water transfer schemes that attempt to level out and democratize overall access to water resources by transferring water from water-rich regions to water-deficient ones. One example is the San Joaquin Valley of California (box 10.2).

China is similarly planning transbasin diversions from the Yangtze in the water-surplus south to the water-short Yellow River Basin in the north (Liu and Zheng 2002; Keller, Sakthivadivel, and Seckler 2000; Liu and You 1994). India has talked about a garland canal to link Himalayan rivers with Cauveri and other South Indian rivers, but these have remained at the idea level. Generally, supply augmenting interventions (such as rainwater harvesting and enhanced recharge) are more acceptable because they do not emphasize reduction in present water use. However, when supply augmentation measures take the dimension of mega-water transfer schemes, the propositions become highly political and contentious as have India's plans to link Himalayan and peninsular rivers.

> When supply augmentation measures take the dimension of mega-water transfer schemes, the propositions become highly political and contentious

Managing demand for groundwater

Many Middle East and North Africa countries, which developed intensive groundwater-irrigated agriculture based on nonrenewable groundwater, have begun to save their aquifers for the more pressing drinking water needs of present and future generations. Saudi Arabia expanded wheat irrigation during the 1970s, eventually becoming an exporter. In 1992 Saudi Arabia spent $2 billion to subsidize local production of 4 million metric tons of wheat, which it could have bought at a fifth of the cost in the global wheat market (Postel 1992).

---

box 10.2 | **Interbasin water transfer in the San Joaquin Valley of California**

In the San Joaquin Valley of California groundwater irrigation was managed to create a tax base that would support water imports. Thanks to rapid agricultural growth, by the early 1950s well irrigators were pumping more than 1.2 billion cubic meters of water. Percolation of irrigation water became the main source of recharge, exceeding natural recharge by 40 times. The drawdown to 30–60 meters changed the direction of water flow in the confined zone, and pumping lifts increased to 250 meters in many areas. Land subsidence soon emerged as a widespread problem. These costs justified the import of water through the California Aqueduct. After 1967 surface water irrigation increased substantially, and hydraulic head increased by 30–100 meters. Throughout the area the recovery in potentiometric surface from 1967 to 1984 was nearly half the drawdown that occurred from pre-development years to 1967. Increased recharge with surface irrigation and reduced groundwater draft raised water tables to less than 1.5 meters in some parts, causing drainage problems. A regional tile drain installed in 1988 over a 150 square kilometer area lowered the water table but also diverted water that could have been used to increase recharge.

Source: Llamas, Back, and Margat 1992.

More recently, Saudi Arabia has successfully reduced wheat irrigation through administrative controls (Abderrahman 2001). Oman has similarly used stringent administrative regulation to control groundwater withdrawals for irrigation. And Iran has banned new irrigation tube-wells in a third of its plains for nearly a decade (Hekmat 2002). Mexico and Spain's experience with a communitarian model of groundwater management is described in box 10.3. Some efforts to manage demand for groundwater in Asia are discussed in box 10.4.

Elsewhere—as in Jordan, Syria, and Yemen—efforts to regulate groundwater irrigation have been made but have had limited success. However, the urgency of the need to do so is widely accepted. Algeria, Morocco, and Tunisia depend on renewable groundwater, but their well numbers have increased at South Asian rates, leading to serious problems of contamination and saline water intrusion (Bahri 2002).

Moving toward precision irrigation and water-saving technologies

Water-saving technologies—drip and sprinkler systems, pipes rather than open furrows to transport water from well-heads, mulch, and the like—are often recommended to ease pressure on groundwater. However, many researchers question these technologies. First, water leakage is not always a loss but may be a source for other users downstream. Second, only cutting down on excessive evaporation (such as evaporation from bare soil, open canals, and water-logged areas) holds any promise of alleviating groundwater declines. If farmers use the freed water to expand irrigation, the net effect may actually be more evapotranspiration (and groundwater decline) rather than relief. Kendy (2003) holds that only cutting down on

| box **10.3** | **Groundwater management in Mexico and Spain** |

Mexico and Spain have recently experimented with a communitarian model of groundwater management. The underlying premise is that organized and empowered groundwater users will mobilize their collective strength to monitor groundwater behavior and take the steps necessary to protect the resource and ensure its long-term sustainability. Mexico's 1993 Water Law declared water to be federal property, and a more recent Supreme Court verdict applied that provision to groundwater. The Mexican National Water Commission has been registering all irrigation wells and issuing concessions (permits) to farmers to withdraw specified quotas of groundwater. The commission has also organized groundwater users in aquiferwide Technical Committees for Groundwater Management (Marin 2005, personal communication).

Spain has tried a similar strategy. Spanish authorities have formed groundwater user associations to manage resources at the local level. A new mandate from the EU Framework Directive to protect groundwater has given these associations more significance.

However, in Mexico, Spain, and elsewhere the impact of these strategies on groundwater conservation and protection seems uncertain. If anything, the impact is perverse in some regions. In Mexico, for instance, a recent use-it-or-lose-it move by the National Water Commission to withdraw unused portions of groundwater quotas encouraged farmers to pump more groundwater than they would have otherwise, lest they lose their quota (Marin 2005, personal communication). In Spain studies show that most groundwater user associations are defunct and the water law is widely bypassed (Lopez and Llamas 1999).

Groundwater: a global
assessment of scale
and significance **10**

---

box 10.4 | **Groundwater management in Asia**

If countries in the industrial agricultural systems category (see table 10.3) find sustainable ground-water management difficult, countries in the smallholder farming system category—including those in South Asia—have not even begun to seriously address the problem. China has done more, but it will take time before its initiatives bear fruit (Shah, Giordano, and Wang 2004). Mexico's model is being held out as a panacea to smallholder farming system countries, but there is no evidence that this model has helped Mexico move toward sustainability (see box 10.3). Mexico's efforts need to produce better results before they can be held out as a model for other groundwater-using countries to follow.

Cross-country analysis suggests that governing the groundwater economy in a sustainable manner concerns not only the hydrogeology of aquifers but also the larger political and social institutions of a country. How countries respond to the challenge of sustainable management of groundwater depends on factors related to the context of each country. These factors can have a decisive impact on whether an approach that has worked in one country will work in another with a different context.

Consider attempts to ban tubewells. Mexico has been trying to ban new tubewells in its central plains for 50 years and has yet to succeed. China has a large number of tubewells scattered over a vast countryside. Chances are that over the coming decade, the government will be able not only to bring them within the ambit of its permit system but also to influence their operation. Accomplishing the same thing in India or Pakistan will remain unrealistic for a long time because of the countries' political structures and systems. The Indian states of Maharashtra and Uttar Pradesh already have elaborate legislation to control groundwater overdraft, but implementation has been patchy (Phansalkar and Kher 2003; Narayana and Scott 2004).

---

irrigated farming in stressed areas, as witnessed in parts of the United States, will be effective. Precision strategies save water when they reduce evaporation, when they prevent water from becoming salinized or polluted, or when the percolation does not readily recharge aquifers.

Microirrigation technologies are likely to increase in popularity all the same. Many countries, such as India, however, are less concerned about saving water than saving energy. Energy subsidies make up a large proportion of government budgets. Microirrigation definitely improves energy efficiency in groundwater irrigation if not water efficiency. Moreover, worldwide, farmers take to microirrigation technologies not so much to save water but to improve crop yields and quality. This is beginning to become evident among farmers in Asia as well. Microirrigation systems used to be capital intensive because they included sophisticated control mechanisms appropriate for large farms. Nongovernmental organizations and irrigation equipment companies are now discovering that Asian farms can do without these expensive mechanisms, and as a result the costs of microirrigation systems are dropping to a fraction of what they were a decade ago. Many nongovernmental organizations are promoting low-cost microirrigation systems to poor women farmers in Africa and Asia. Again, the key idea is not so much to save groundwater but to improve livelihoods.

Water-saving crops and technologies. Though controversial, a big breakthrough in water saving is promised by the system of rice intensification, a package of agronomic practices that suggest that the rice plant can withstand flooding but does not need it to thrive.

Whether the system of rice intensification results in significant real water savings is debatable (see chapter 14 on rice). But many governments—including those in China and the south Indian states of Andhra Pradesh, Karnataka, and Tamil Nadu—are promoting the system as an answer to growing water stress in rice systems (Jothimani and Thiyagarajan 2005; Satyanarayana 2005). A real issue that the system tackles is the energy costs of groundwater irrigation. In rice growing regions such as Bangladesh, West Bengal, and Assam—where an agrarian revolution of sorts was ushered in by groundwater irrigation of boro rice with diesel pumps—an increase in diesel prices and a drop in rice prices have led to a precipitous decline in the area growing boro rice. The system of rice intensification offers an opportunity for its revival by curtailing irrigation costs. Zero tillage, alternate wet and dry irrigation of paddy, and other such agronomic practices also hold promise for water saving in field crops.

> Precision strategies save water when they reduce evaporation, when they prevent water from becoming salinized or polluted, or when the percolation does not readily recharge aquifers.

Other examples of cropping pattern changes that save groundwater are replacement of irrigated rice with rainfed maize and of irrigated maize with Bt cotton on a large scale in many parts of the North China plains. In Liaoning Province, for example, rising costs of electricity and chemical fertilizers and falling international rice prices have resulted in large-scale substitution of groundwater-irrigated rice with rainfed maize, leading to substantial recovery in groundwater levels (Shah, Giordano, and Wang 2004).

Crop diversification and more cash per drop. In the groundwater-irrigated North China plains there has been a large-scale shift from maize to cotton, especially Bt cotton, which grows extremely well under drip irrigation and polythene mulch. Just as pronounced is the unprecedented shift to production of high-value fruits and vegetables for sale in both domestic and export markets. This production is also especially well supported by groundwater. In many groundwater-irrigated areas of India the shift is evident in the rapid expansion of dairy production systems under groundwater use. In groundwater-stressed Andhra Pradesh the value of dairy production has surpassed the combined value of all crops in recent years (Tukker 2005, personal communication). Likewise, in groundwater-stressed North Gujarat dairying has expanded rapidly under groundwater-irrigated fodder crops, becoming the mainstay of rural livelihood systems (Kumar and Singh 2004). In Tamil Nadu's groundwater-stressed areas rice paddy is giving way to exotic crops such as vanilla. Whether these shifts toward value-added farming will ease the pressure on groundwater is uncertain, but they will help improve livelihoods and raise income per cubic meter of groundwater use.

Occupational diversification. Groundwater stress in smallholder farming systems essentially reflects population pressure on agriculture. In some arid or semiarid parts of India where intensive groundwater has sustained high population pressures, declining groundwater availability and reliability have forced farmers out of farming. The transition may also be planned, in the sense that farmers intentionally keep overdrafting the aquifers to build sufficient wealth from their fields to support their children's education and permanent transition and settlement in the cities (Moench and Dixit 2004). In the medium to long run transferring the population to the nonfarm sector will ease pressure on land and groundwater.

Groundwater: a global
assessment of scale
and significance **10**

*   *   *

In conclusion, in regions of the world where groundwater use in agriculture is expected
to grow, people will have to be a part of the solution. No resource management strategy
will work unless it is embraced by millions of users. As Noam Chomsky, one of the great
living philosophers, said:

> At this stage of history either one of two things is possible. Either the general popu-
> lation will take control of its own destiny and will concern itself with community
> interests, guided by values of solidarity and sympathy, and concern for others; or
> alternatively there will be no destiny for anyone to control (*Manufacturing Consent:
> Noam Chomsky and the Media* 2:40:53).

Reviewers

Chapter review editor: Fatma Attia.
Chapter reviewers: Zafar Altaf, John Chilton, Ramaswamy R. Iyer, Gunnar Jacks, Todd Jarvis, Simi Kamal, Flemming
Konradsen, Aditi Mukherji, James Nachbur, Lisa Schipper, and Dennis Wichelns.

Notes

1. There are other data sets compiled by private researchers often under the aegis of international organizations. Margat (2005,
personal communication) has compiled estimates of groundwater irrigated areas. They use mostly data from the Food and
Agriculture Organization's (FAO) AQUASTAT database, with refinements or updates for specific countries. Zekster and Everett's
(2004) report for the United Nations Educational, Scientific and Cultural Organization's (UNESCO) International Hydrological
Programme is another, but it relies solely on national government sources, which are also the sources for FAO's AQUASTAT.

2. AQUASTAT lacks data on groundwater-irrigated areas. Since leaving out China from this analysis would distort
the picture greatly, we have used the estimate of 8.46 million ha provided in China National Bureau of Statistics (2002).
However, Wang and others (2006b) cite a Chinese government source that suggests that groundwater-irrigated area in China
was about 15 million ha in 2000. They go on to estimate, based on their own large-scale survey, that this figure may be as
high as 23 million ha.

3. The International Water Management Institute's (IWMI) global irrigated area map (Thenkabail and others 2006),
which is based on remote sensing data, estimated gross global irrigated area to be 480 million ha in 1999, far above FAO's
more recent estimates of 257–280 million ha. According to the IWMI map, groundwater gets involved—either as the sole
source of irrigation or in conjunctive use mode—in 132 million ha of global gross irrigated area, which is over 50% higher
than FAO estimates of groundwater irrigated area.

4. These figures do not include the fadama and bas fonds areas, since these styles of irrigation are not classified as
equipped irrigated areas but as areas under water management.

References

Abderrahman, W.A. 2001. "Water Demand Management in Saudi Arabia." In N.I. Faruqui, A.K. Biswas, and M.J. Bino,
    eds., *Water Management in Islam*. Tokyo: United Nations University.
Agarwal, A., and S. Narain. 1999. *Making Water Management Everybody's Business: Water Harvesting and Rural Development
    in India*. Gatekeeper Series 87. International Institute for Environment and Development, London.
Allan, J.A. 2003. "Virtual Water—The Water, Food, and Trade Nexus: Useful Concept or Misleading Metaphor?" *Water
    International* 28 (1): 106–12.
Bahri, A. 2002. "Integrated Management of Limited Water Resources in Tunisia—Research Topic Priorities." In R.
    Rodríguez, ed., *Identifying Priorities and Tools for Cooperation. INCO-MED Workshops*. Brussels: European Commission
    and Spanish National Research Council.
BGS (British Geological Survey). 2004. *Community Management of Groundwater Resources: An Appropriate Response to
    Groundwater Overdraft in India?* London: British Geological Survey.

Bhamoriya, V. 2002. "Wastewater and Welfare: Pump Irrigation Economy of Peri-urban Vadodara." Discussion Paper. Annual Partners' Meet 2002. IWMI-Tata Water Policy Research Program, Mumbai and Colombo.

Bhattarai, M., and A. Narayanamoorthy. 2004. "Dynamics of Irrigation Impacts on Rural Poverty in India." Paper presented at the Third IWMI-Tata Annual Water Policy Workshop, 17–19 February, 2004, Anand, India.

Blomquist, W., T. Heikkila, and E. Schlager. 2001. "Institutions and Conjunctive Water Management Among Three Western States." *Natural Resources Journal* 41 (3): 653–83.

Boelee, E., and W. van der Hoek. 2002. "Impact of Irrigation on Drinking Water Availability in Sri Lanka / Impact de l'irrigation sur la disponibilité de l'eau potable au Sri Lanka." ICID-CIID 18th Congress on Irrigation and Drainage, 21–28 July, Montreal, Canada. Q. 51, R. 5.04. International Commission on Irrigation and Drainage.

Bruinsma, J., ed. 2003. *World Agriculture: Towards 2015/2030, An FAO Perspective.* London and Rome: Earthscan and Food and Agriculture Organization.

Buechler, S., G. Devi and L. Raschid-Sally. 2002. "Livelihoods and Wastewater Irrigated Agriculture along the Musi River in Hyderabad City, Andhra Pradesh, India." *Urban Agriculture Magazine* 8 (Wastewater Reuse in Urban Agriculture): 14–17.

Burke, J.J. 1996. "Hydrogeological Provinces in Central Sudan: Morphostructural and Hydrogeomorphological Controls." In A.G. Brown, ed., *Geomorphology and Groundwater.* Chichester, UK: Wiley.

Burke, J.J., and M. Moench. 2000. *Groundwater and Society: Resources, Tensions and Opportunities.* New York: United Nations.

Cai, L. 1988. "Efficient Conjunctive Use of Surface and Groundwater in the People's Victory Canal." In G.T. O'Mara, ed., *Efficiency in Irrigation.* Washington, D.C.: World Bank.

Calow, R.C., N.S. Robins, A.M. Macdonald, D.M.J. Macdonald, B.R. Gibbs, W.R.G. Orpen, P. Mtembezeka, A.J. Andrews and S.O. Appiah. 1997. "Groundwater Management in Drought-prone Areas of Africa." *Water Resources Development* 13 (2): 241–61.

Carter, R.C., and P. Howsam. 1994. "Sustainable Use of Groundwater for Small Scale Irrigation: With Special Reference to Sub-Saharan Africa." *Land Use Policy* 11 (4): 275–85.

China, National Bureau of Statistics. 2002. *China Statistical Year Book 2002.* Beijing: China Statistical Publishing House

Coughanowr, C. 1994. *Ground Water.* Water-related Issues of the Humid Tropics and Other Warm Humid Regions. IHP Humid Tropics Programme Series 8. United Nations Educational, Scientific and Cultural Organization, Paris.

Deb Roy, A., and T. Shah. 2003. "Socio-Ecology of Groundwater Irrigation in India." In R. Llamas and E. Custodio, eds., *Intensive Use of Groundwater: Challenges and Opportunities.* Lisse, Netherlands: Swets and Zeitlinger.

Delgado, C., M. Rosegrant, H. Steinfed, S. Ehui, and C. Courbois. 2003. *Livestock to 2020: The Next Food Revolution.* Food, Agriculture and Environment Discussion Paper 28. International Food Policy Research Institute, Washington, D.C.

Dhawan, B.D. 1988. *Irrigation in India's Agricultural Development: Productivity-Stability-Equity.* New Delhi: India: Commonwealth Publishers.

Döll, P., and M. Flörke. 2005. "Global-Scale Estimation of Diffuse Groundwater Recharge." Hydrology Paper 3. Frankfurt University, Insitute of Physical Geography, Germany.

Dong, K.C. 1991. "The Historical and Social Background." In G. Xu and L.J. Peel, eds., *The Agriculture of China.* New York: Oxford University Press.

Ensink, J.H.J., M.R. Aslam, F. Konradsen, P.K. Jensen, and W. van der Hoek. 2002. "Linkages between Irrigation and Drinking Water in Pakistan." Working Paper 46. International Water Management Institute, Colombo.

FAO (Food and Agriculture Organization). 2001. "La valorisation de l'eau d'irrigation dans un grand périmètre irrigué. Le cas du Loukkos au Maroc." Food and Agriculture Organization Ministry of Agriculture, Forestry, and Water Management, Rome.

———. 2004. *Economic Valuation of Water Resources in Agriculture: From the Sectoral to a Functional Perspective of Natural Resource Management.* FAO Water Report 27. Rome.

———. 2005a. AQUASTAT database. [www.fao.org/ag/agl/aglw/aquastat/main/index.stm].

———. 2005b. Global Map of Irrigated Areas Version 3.0 [www.fao.org/ag/agl/aglw/aquastat/irrigationmap/index.stm].

Foster, S., M. Nanni, K. Kemper, H. Garduño, and A. Tuinhof. 2003. "Utilization of Non-Renewable Groundwater—A Socially-sustainable Approach to Resource Management." GW-Mate Briefing Note 11. World Bank, Washington, D.C.

Giordano, M. 2006. "Agricultural Groundwater Use and Rural Livelihoods in Sub-Saharan Africa: A First-cut Assessment." *Hydrogeology Journal* 14 (3): 310–18.

Gomes, N. 2005. "Access to Water, Pastoral Resource Management and Pastoralists Livelihoods: Lessons from Water Development in Selected Areas of Eastern Africa (Kenya, Ethiopia, Somalia)." Food and Agriculture Organization Livelihoods Support Programme, Rome.

Groundwater: a global
assessment of scale
and significance | **10**

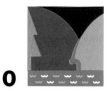

Hekmat, A. 2002. "Overexploitation of Groundwater in Iran: Need for an Integrated Water Policy." Paper for the IWMI–ICAR–Colombo Plan Policy Dialogue "Forward-Thinking Policies for Groundwater Management: Energy, Water Resources, and Economic Approaches." India International Center, 2–6 September, New Delhi.

Hernandez-Mora, N., L. Martinez-Cortina, and J. Fornes. 2003. "Intensive Groundwater Use in Spain." In M.R. Llamas and E. Custodio, eds, *Intensive Use of Groundwater: Challenges and Opportunities.* Leiden, Netherlands: Balkema.

Howard, K. 2004. "Strategic Options and Priorities in Groundwater Resources: Workshop Context." Presented at the STAP-GEF Technical Review Workshop on Strategic Options and Priorities in Groundwater Resources, United Nations Educational, Scientific and Cultural Organization, 5–7 April, Paris.

India, Ministry of Water Resources, Minor Irrigation Division. 2005. *Report on 3rd Census of Minor Irrigation Schemes (2000-01).* New Delhi.

India, NSSO (National Sample Survey Organisation). 1999. *Cultivation Practices in India.* Report 451 (54/31/3), 54th round, January-June 1998. New Delhi.

———. 2003. *Report on Village Facilities.* Report 487 (58/3.1/1) 58th round, July-December, 2002. New Delhi.

———. 2005. *Situation Assessment Survey of Farmers: Some Aspects of Farming,* Report 496(59/33/3) 59th National Sample Survey Round, January–December 2003. New Delhi.

Jothimani, S., and T.M. Thiyagarajan. 2005. "Optimization of Water for Crop Quality and Grain Yield of Rice under System of Rice Intensification." Paper presented at the Fourth IWMI-Tata Annual Water Policy Workshop, 24–26 February, Anand, India.

Keller, A., R. Sakthivadivel, and D. Seckler. 2000. *Water Scarcity and the Role of Storage in Development.* IWMI Research Report 39. Colombo: International Water Management Institute.

Kendy, E. 2003. "The False Promise of Sustainable Pumping Rates." *Ground Water* 41 (1): 2–4.

Kikuchi, M., P. Weligamage, R. Barker, M. Samad, H. Kono, and H.M. Somaratne. 2003. *Agro-Well and Pump Diffusion in the Dry Zone of Sri Lanka—Past Trends, Present Status and Future Prospects.* IWMI Research Report 66. Colombo: International Water Management Institute.

Kumar, M.D., and O.P. Singh. 2004. "Virtual Water in Global Food and Water Policy Making: Is There a Need for Rethinking?" *Water Resources Management* 19 (6): 759–89.

Liu, C., and H. Zheng. 2002. "South-to-North Water Transfer Schemes for China." *Water Resources Development* 18 (3): 453–71.

Liu, C.M., and M.Z. You. 1994. "The South-to-North Water Transfer Project and Sustainable Agricultural Development on the North China Plain." In C.M. Liu and K.C. Tan, eds., *Chinese Environment and Development 5, No. 2.* New York: M.E. Sharp, Inc.

Llamas, R., and E. Custodio, eds. 2003. *Intensive Use of Groundwater—Challenges and Opportunities.* Leiden, Netherlands: Balkema.

Llamas, R., W. Back, and J. Margat. 1992. "Groundwater Use: Equilibrium Between Social Benefits and Potential Environmental Costs." *Hydrogeology Journal* 1 (2): 1431–2174.

Lluria, M.R., and M. Fisk. 1995. "A Large Aquifer Storage Facility for the Phoenix Area." In I. Johnson and D. Pyne, eds., *Artificial Recharge of Ground Water II.* New York: American Society of Civil Engineers.

Lopez, G., and M.R. Llamas. 1999. "New and Old Paradigms in Spain's Water Policy." In U. Farinelli, V. Kouzminov, M. Martellini, and R. Santesso, eds., *Water Security in the Third Millennium: Mediterranean Countries Towards a Regional Vision.* United Nations Educational, Scientific and Cultural Organization, Science for Peace Series, Como, Italy.

"Manufacturing Consent: Noam Chomsky and the Media." 2006. Directed by Mark Archbar and Peter Wintonick, 1992. Necessary Illusions. *Wikipedia.*

Margat, J. 2005. Personal communication on groundwater resources. Hydrogeologist, Geological and Mining Research, Orleans, France.

Marin, L. 2005. Personal communication on groundwater use and management. Universidad Nacional Autónoma de México, Mexico City, 23 June.

Martinez-Cortina, L., and N. Hernandez-Mora. 2003. "The Role of Groundwater in Spain's Water Policy." *International Water Resources Association* 28 (3): 313–20.

Meijer, K., E. Boelee, D. Augustijn, and I. van der Molen. 2006. "Impacts of Concrete Lining of Irrigation Canals on Availability of Water for Domestic Use in Southern Sri Lanka." *Agricultural Water Management* 83 (3): 243–51.

Moench, M. 2003. "Groundwater and Poverty: Exploring the Connections." In M.R. Llamas and E. Custodio, eds., *Intensive Use of Groundwater: Challenges and Opportunities.* Leiden, Netherlands: Balkema Publishers.

Moench, M., and A. Dixit. 2004. *Adaptive Capacity and Livelihood Resilience: Adaptive Strategies for Responding to Floods and Droughts in South Asia.* Nepal and Boulder, Colo.: Institute for Social and Environmental Transition.

Molle, F., T. Shah, and R. Barker. 2003. "The Groundswell of Pumps: Multi-level Impacts of a Silent Revolution." In *ICID Asian Regional Workshop, Sustainable Development of Water Resources and Management and Operation of Participatory Irrigation Organizations, November 10–12, 2003, the Grand Hotel, Taipei.* Vol.1. Taipei: International Commission on Irrigation and Drainage.

Mukherji, A., and T. Shah. 2003. "Socio-Ecology of Groundwater Irrigation in South Asia: An Overview of Issues and Evidence." In A. Sahuquillo, J. Capilla, L.M. Cortina, X.S. Vila, eds., Groundwater: Intensive Use. International Association of Hydrogeologists. *Selected Papers on Hydrogeology* 7. Leiden, Netherlands: Taylor & Francis.

Murray-Rust, H., and E. Vander Velde. 1992. "Conjunctive Use of Canal and Groundwater in Punjab, Pakistan: Management and Policy Options." In *Advancements in IIMI's Research 1992.* A selection of papers presented at the Internal Program Review. Colombo: International Irrigation Management Institute.

Narayana, P., and C. Scott. 2004. "Effectiveness of Legislative Controls on Groundwater Extraction." Paper presented at the Third IWMI-Tata Annual Water Policy Workshop, 17–19 February, Anand, India.

Palmer-Jones, R. 1999. " Slowdown in Agricultural Growth in Bangladesh: Neither a Good Description nor a Description Good to Give." In Ben Rogaly, Barbara Harris-White, and Sugata Bose, eds., 1999. *Sonar Bangla? Agricultrural Growth and Agrarian Change in West Bengal and Bangladesh.* New Delhi: SAGE Publications

Pearce, G. 2005. *Investing in Building Capacity in Agricultural Water Management in Shaping the Future of Water for Agriculture: A Sourcebook for Investment in Agricultural Water Management.* Washington, D.C.: World Bank, Agriculture and Rural Development Department.

Phansalkar, S., and V. Kher. 2003. "A Decade of Maharashtra Groundwater Legislation: Analysis of Implementation Process in Vidarbha." In S. Phansalkar, ed., *Issues in Water Use in Agriculture in Vidarbha.* Nagpur, India: Amol Management Consultants.

Postel, S. 1992. *Last Oasis: Facing Water Scarcity.* New York: W.W. Norton.

Pyne, R.G.D. 1995. *Groundwater Recharge and Wells. A Guide to Aquifer Storage and Recovery.* Boca Raton, Fla.: Lewis Publishers.

Rao, M.S.R.M, C.H. Batchelor, A.J. James, R. Nagaraja, J. Seeley, and J.A. Butterworth. 2003. Andhra Pradesh Rural Livelihoods Programme Water Audit Report. Andhra Pradesh Rural Livelihoods Programme, Rajendranagar, Hyderabad, India.

Repetto, R., ed. 1985. *The Global Possible: Resources, Development, and the New Century.* New Haven, Conn.: Yale University Press.

Sakthivadivel, R., and R.K. Nagar. 2003. *Private Initiative for Groundwater Recharge—Case of Dudhada Village in Saurashtra.* Water Policy Research Highlight 15. Discussion Paper. Annual Partners' Meet 2002. IWMI-Tata Water Policy Research Program, Mumbai and Colombo.

Satyanarayana, A. 2005. System of Rice Intensification—An Innovative Method to Produce More with Less Water and Inputs. Paper presented at the Fourth IWMI-Tata Annual Water Policy Workshop, 24–26 February, Anand, India.

Scott, C.A., and C.G. Restrepo. 2001. "Conjunctive Management of Surfacewater and Groundwater in the Middle Rio Lerma Basin, Mexico." In A.K. Biswas and C. Tortajada, eds., *Integrated River Basin Management.* Oxford, UK: Oxford University Press.

Scott, C.A., N.I. Faruqui, and L. Raschid-Sally. 2004. *Wastewater Use in Irrigated Agriculture: Confronting the Livelihood and Environmental Realities.* Wallingford, UK: CABI Publishing, International Water Management Institute, and International Development Research Centre.

Shah, T. 1993. *Water Markets and Irrigation Development: Political Economy and Practical Policy.* Bombay, India: Oxford University Press.

———. 2000. "Mobilizing Social Energy against Environmental Challenge: Understanding the Groundwater Recharge Movement in Western India." *Natural Resources Forum* 24 (3): 197–209.

———. 2005. "Groundwater and Human Development: Challenges and Opportunities in Livelihoods and Environment." *Water, Science & Technology* 51 (8): 27–37.

Shah, T., and R. Desai. 2002. "Creative Destruction: Is That How Gujarat is Adapting to Groundwater Depletion? A Synthesis of ITP Studies." Discussion Paper. Annual Partners' Meet 2002. IWMI-Tata Water Policy Research Program, Mumbai and Colombo.

Shah, T., M. Giordano, and J. Wang. 2004. "Irrigation Institutions in a Dynamic Economy: What Is China Doing Differently from India?" *Economic and Political Weekly* 39 (31): 3452–61.

Shah, T., O.P. Singh, and A. Mukherji. 2006. "Groundwater Irrigation and South Asian Agriculture: Empirical Analyses from a Large-scale Survey of India, Pakistan, Nepal Terai and Bangladesh." *Hydrogeology Journal* 14 (3): 286–309.

Shah, T., A. DebRoy, A.S. Qureshi, and J. Wang. 2003. "Sustaining Asia's Groundwater Boom: An Overview of Issues and Evidence." *Natural Resources Forum* 27 (2): 130–40.

Groundwater: a global
assessment of scale
and significance **10**
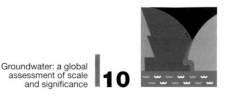

Shah, T., M. Alam, M.D. Kumar, R.K. Nagar, and M. Singh. 2000. *Pedaling Out of Poverty: Social Impact of a Manual Irrigation Technology in South Asia.* IWMI Research Report 45. Colombo: International Water Management Institute.

Shortt, R., E. Boelee, Y. Matsuno, C. Faubert, C. Madramootoo, and W. van der Hoek. 2003. "Evaluation of Thermotolerant Coliforms and Salinity in the Four Available Water Sources of an Irrigated Region of Southern Sri Lanka." *Irrigation and Drainage* 52 (2): 133–46.

Singh, O.P., A. Sharma, R. Singh, and T. Shah. 2004. "Virtual Water Trade in Dairy Economy: Irrigation Water Productivity in Gujarat." *Economic and Political Weekly* 39 (31): 3492–97.

Sonou, M. 1994. "An Overview of Lowlift Irrigation in West Africa: Trends and Prospects." Food and Agriculture Organization, Rome.

Strosser, P. 1997. "Analysing Alternative Policy Instruments for the Irrigation Sector. An Assessment of the Potential for Water Market Development in the Chistian Sub-division." Wageningen Agricultural University, Department of Water Resources, Netherlands

Thenkabail, P.S., C.M. Biradar, H. Turral, P. Noojipady, Y.J. Li, J. Vithanage, V. Dheeravath, M. Velpuri, M. Schull, X.L. Cai, and R. Dutta, R. 2006. *An Irrigated Area Map of the World (1999) Derived from Remote Sensing.* Research Report 105. Colombo: International Water Management Institute.

Todd, D.K., and I. Priestadt. 1997. "Role of Conjunctive Use in Groundwater Management." In D.R. Kendall, ed., *Conjunctive Use of Water Resources: Aquifer Storage and Recovery.* AWRA Symposium Proceedings. American Water Resources Association Technical Publication Series 97 (2): 139–45.

Tukker, S.P. 2005. Personal communication. Secretary (Water Resources), Government of Andhra Pradesh, Hyderabad, Presentation made in a meeting in Hotel Ashoka, Delhi on 13th January, 2005.

UN (United Nations). 1960. *Large-Scale Groundwater Development.* Water Resources Development Centre. New York.

van Halsema, G.E. 2002. "Trial and Re-trial: The Evolution of Irrigation Modernisation in NWFP, Pakistan." PhD diss. Wageningen University, Department of Water Resources, Netherlands. [http://library.wur.nl/wda/dissertations/dis3246.pdf].

van Koppen, B. 1998. *More Jobs per Drop: Targeting Irrigation to Poor Women and Men.* Wageningen, Netherlands, and Amsterdam, Netherlands: Wageningen Agricultural University and Royal Tropical Institute.

van Koppen, B., R. Parthasarathy, and C. Safiliou. 2002. *Poverty Dimensions of Irrigation Management Transfer in Large-scale Canal Irrigation in Andhra Pradesh and Gujarat, India.* IWMI Research Report 61. Colombo: International Water Management Institute.

van Steenbergen, F., and W. Oliemans. 2002. "A Review of Policies in Groundwater Management in Pakistan 1950–2000." *Water Policy* 4 (4): 323–44.

Wahaj, R. 2001. "Farmers Actions and Improvements in Irrigation Performance Below the Mogha: How Farmers Manage Water Scarcity and Abundance in a Large Scale Irrigation System in South-eastern Punjab, Pakistan." PhD diss. Wageningen University, Department of Water Resources, Netherlands.

Wang, J., L. Zhang, and S. Cai. 2004 "Assessing the Use of Pre-paid Electricity Cards for the Irrigation Tube Wells in Liaoning Province, China." Anand, India, and Beijing: IWMI-Tata Water Policy Program and Chinese Centre for Agricultural Policy.

Wang, J., L. Zhang, C. Rozelle, A. Blanke, and Q. Huang. 2006a. "Groundwater in China: Development and Response." In Mark Giordano and Villholth, K.G., eds., *The Agricultural Groundwater Revolution: Opportunities and Threats to Development.* Wallingford, UK: CABI Publishing.

Wang, J., J. Huang, Q. Huang, and S. Rosalle. 2006b. "Privatization of Tubewells in North China: Determinants and Impacts on Irrigated Area, Productivity and the Water Table." *Hydrogeology Journal* 14 (3): 275–85.

Warner, J. 2003. "Virtual Water—Virtual Benefits? Scarcity, Distribution, Security and Conflict Reconsidered." In A.Y. Hoekstra, ed., *Virtual Water Trade: Proceedings of the International Expert Meeting on Virtual Water Trade.* Value of Water Research Reports Series 12. Delft, Netherlands: Institute for Water Education.

Winter, T.C., J.W. Harvey, O.L. Franke, and W.M. Alley. 1998. *Ground Water and Surface Water: A Single Resource.* U.S. Geological Survey Circular 1139. U.S. Department of the Interior, U.S. Geological Survey, Denver, Colo.

Zekster, I.S., and L. Everett. 2004. *Groundwater Resources of the World and Their Uses.* IHP-VI Series on Groundwater 6. Paris: United Nations Educational, Scientific, and Cultural Organization.

Feed the cities

Artist: Titilope Shittu, Nigeria

11 | Agricultural use of marginal-quality water— opportunities and challenges

Coordinating lead author: Manzoor Qadir

Lead authors: Dennis Wichelns, Liqa Raschid-Sally, Paramjit Singh Minhas, Pay Drechsel, Akiça Bahri, and Peter McCornick

Contributing authors: Robert Abaidoo, Fatma Attia, Samia El-Guindy, Jeroen H.J. Ensink, Blanca Jimenez, Jacob W. Kijne, Sasha Koo-Oshima, J.D. Oster, Lekan Oyebande, Juan Antonio Sagardoy, and Wim van der Hoek

Overview

Millions of small-scale farmers around the world irrigate with marginal-quality water, often because they have no alternative. There are two major types of marginal-quality water: wastewater from urban and peri-urban areas, and saline and sodic agricultural drainage water and groundwater. Around cities in developing countries, farmers use wastewater from residential, commercial, and industrial sources, sometimes diluted but often without treatment. Sometimes farmers in deltaic areas and tailend sections of large-scale irrigation schemes irrigate with a blend of canal water, saline drainage water, and wastewater. Still others irrigate with saline or sodic groundwater, either exclusively or in conjunction with higher quality surface water. Many of those farmers cannot control the volume or quality of water they receive.

Wastewater often contains a variety of pollutants: salts, metals, metalloids, pathogens, residual drugs, organic compounds, endocrine disruptor compounds, and active residues of personal care products. Any of these components can harm human health and the environment. Farmers can suffer harmful health effects from contact with wastewater, while consumers are at risk from eating vegetables and cereals irrigated with wastewater. Application of wastewater has to be carefully managed for effective use.

In contrast to wastewater, saline and sodic water contains salts that can impair plant growth but rarely contains metals or pathogens. However, it can lead to soil salinization and waterlogging, which impair productivity on millions of hectares of agricultural land. Irrigating successfully with saline or sodic water requires careful management to prevent near-term reductions in crop yield and long-term reductions in productivity.

Many of the small-scale farmers in developing countries using untreated or diluted waste-water for irrigation likely feel fortunate to have any water supply, given their inability to purchase higher quality surface water or to pump groundwater. Farmers unquestionably prefer to irrigate with nonsaline water, but in many areas only saline or sodic water is available. The irrigation supply for farmers in tailend portions of irrigation schemes often includes saline drainage water from headend farmers. In some areas of industrialized countries farmers reuse saline drainage water because environmental policies prevent them from discharging the water into rivers or lakes.

> The challenge for public officials is to set policies that enable farmers to maximize the values generated with limited water resources while protecting public health and the environment

Both the demand for and supply of wastewater for irrigation are increasing in many areas [well established but incomplete]. Demand is driven by the attractive returns farmers can earn from producing fruits and vegetables in urban and peri-urban settings. Demand also rises with increasing competition for limited water resources in deltaic areas and large-scale irrigation schemes. The supply of wastewater expands with population growth in large cities, towns, and villages throughout the developing world. In many communities the volume of wastewater has increased faster than the ability to build and operate treatment facilities, and as a result more wastewater is released into open ditches or discharged into agricultural drains.

Public officials in many areas likely have mixed views about the increasing demand for and supply of wastewater and its increasing use for irrigation, and the long-term health effects may eventually affect public budgets [speculative]. Where public budgets are inadequate for treating wastewater, farmers provide a service by using untreated wastewater for irrigation. The revenue this generates enables farmers to support their families, perhaps enhancing local and regional economic activity. In addition, city residents have access to a local supply of fruits and vegetables that might not be available if farmers were unable to irrigate with wastewater. The downside of the increasing supply is the rising aggregate risk to farmers, consumers, and the environment. The long-term health effects of the increasing use of untreated wastewater might eventually weigh on public budgets, either directly through public expenditures to protect health and welfare or indirectly through the declining productivity of lands regularly irrigated with low-quality wastewater.

The use of wastewater and saline or sodic water in agriculture increases the total volume of irrigation water in many areas, but the off-farm and long-term negative implications can be substantial [established but incomplete]. Wastewater use can have health impacts for farmers and consumers, while sustained use of saline and sodic water can impair soil quality and productivity, reducing crop yields. The challenge for public officials is to set policies that enable farmers to maximize the values generated with limited water resources while protecting public health and the environment.

Irrigation with wastewater is risky, although the link between specific pathogens and risk is not always clear. The health risks of wastewater use must be evaluated in conjunction with the potential benefits *[competing explanations]*. Both private and public benefits and risks are associated with wastewater use. Optimal treatment strategies will vary by country and situation. Economics, science, and politics will influence wastewater treatment programs and use. Policies that attempt to prevent any irrigation with wastewater, if enforceable, might eliminate desirable economic benefits from the associated crop production.

Agricultural use of
marginal-quality water—
opportunities and challenges **11**

Public agencies should consider wastewater and saline or sodic water when evaluating na-tional water management strategies to optimize the use of limited water resources [established but incomplete]. There are three opportunities for implementing policies to improve the management of marginal-quality water in agriculture and minimize risks from its use: before marginal-quality water is generated, while the water is being used, and after crops have been irrigated and products are prepared for sale and consumption. Treatment and disposal costs can be reduced in many areas by minimizing the volume of marginal-quality water. Efforts to improve the use of wastewater and the handling of agricultural products after harvest can reduce public health impacts. Women have special roles in agriculture and in food preparation, particularly in areas where wastewater is used for irrigation, so special efforts should be made to include women in education programs that promote hygiene and address risk minimization methods.

Two features complicate policies pertaining to wastewater use in agriculture: most waste-water is generated outside the agricultural sector, and many individuals and organizations have policy interests pertaining to wastewater use [established but incomplete]. Strong institutional coordination is vital, accompanied by flexible control and regulation mechanisms. Public concern regarding wastewater reuse varies with the types of water involved, treatment lev-els, and information available. Effluent standards, taxes, and tradable permits can motivate improvements in water management by households and industries discharging wastewater from point sources. Pertinent policies include effective water allocation and pricing, water rights, restrictions on groundwater pumping, full-cost energy pricing, and incentives for farm-level investments in water-saving irrigation methods.

Public agencies in several countries already implement policies on marginal-quality water [well established]. Egypt plans to increase its official reuse of marginal-quality water from 10% in 2000 to about 17% by 2017 (Egypt MWRI 2004). In Tunisia in 2003 about 43% of wastewater was used after treatment. Wastewater use will increase in India, as the proportion of freshwater in agricultural deliveries declines from 85% today to 77% by 2025, reflecting rising demand for freshwater in cities (India CWC 2002). Worldwide, marginal-quality water will become an increasingly important component of agricultural water supplies, particularly in water-scarce countries (Abdel-Dayem 1999). Water supply and water quality degradation are global concerns that will intensify with increasing water demand, the unexpected impacts of extreme events, and climate change in resource-poor countries (Watson, Moss, and Zinyowera 1998).

> Worldwide, marginal-quality water will become an increasingly important component of agricultural water supplies, particularly in water-scarce countries

Situation and outlook

This section examines the main types of marginal-quality water: wastewater from urban and peri-urban areas and saline or sodic agricultural drainage water and groundwater (box 11.1).

Wastewater—minimizing risks while achieving livelihood goals

Water use by households, cities, and industries generates wastewater containing undesir-able constituents. Industrial wastewater often contains metals, metalloids, and volatile or semivolatile compounds, while domestic wastewater often contains pathogens. Wastewater

box **11.1** | **Marginal-quality water resources**

Marginal-quality water includes urban wastewater, agricultural drainage water, and saline or sodic surface water and groundwater.

- *Urban wastewater* usually refers to domestic effluent, wastewater from commercial establishments and institutions, industrial effluent, and stormwater. Many farmers use treated or untreated wastewater for irrigation. In some areas wastewater is discharged into agricultural drains, and farmers use the commingled water for irrigation.
- *Agricultural drainage water* includes surface runoff and deep percolation that move through surface ditches or are collected in artificial drainage systems. Drainage water often contains salts, agricultural chemicals and nutrients, and soil amendments such as gypsum.
- *Saline or sodic surface water and groundwater* contain salts that originate from reactions that occur as water moves through the soil profile and reactions that occur within the layers where groundwater is located. Saline and sodic water also can contain metals, metalloids, and pathogens that enter groundwater from land-based activities.

from households, cities, and industries must be treated before disposal or reuse to prevent negative health and environmental impacts, particularly where farmers use wastewater for irrigation.

The volume of wastewater increases with urbanization, improved living conditions, and economic development. Large volumes of wastewater are returned to the hydrologic system in urban areas, where only 15%–25% of water diverted or withdrawn is consumed. In most cities in developing countries there is little or no wastewater treatment (WHO and UNICEF 2000). In Asia 35% of wastewater is treated; in Latin America, 14% is treated.

Photo by Liqa Raschid-Sally

Photo 11.1 Vietnamese women harvest edible aquatic plants from polluted water sources

Agricultural use of
marginal-quality water—
opportunities and challenges **11**

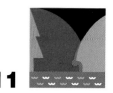

box **11.2** | **Urban and peri-urban agriculture and wastewater use**

Worldwide more than 800 million farmers are engaged in urban and peri-urban agriculture (UNDP 1996). Many of the 200 million farmers who specialize in market gardening depend on irrigation. In developing countries these farmers rely on raw or diluted wastewater when higher quality sources are unavailable (see figure).

Irrigated agriculture is important in hot climates of the developing world where refrigerated transport and storage are limited. Farmers enhance household income by producing perishable crops such as leafy vegetables for sale in local markets, providing a supply of vitamin-rich vegetables. In many cities 60%–90% of vegetables are produced within the city or at the city's edge. Although salads diversify urban diets, many residents are at risk when consuming vegetables irrigated with wastewater. This is a major concern for city authorities. Interim health risk reduction strategies are needed where wastewater treatment facilities are not yet available.

Sources of irrigation water in urban and peri-urban areas

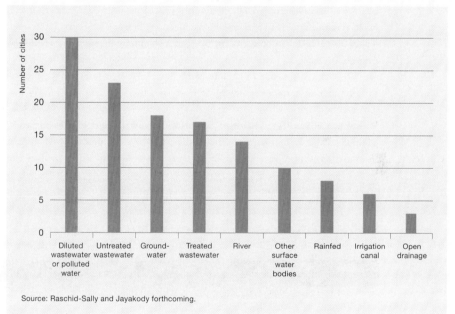

Source: Raschid-Sally and Jayakody forthcoming.

Urban drainage systems in developing countries mix domestic and industrial waste-water and stormwater, often discharging the wastewater into natural waterways, polluting water used by farmers and other downstream users (Scott, Faruqui, and Raschid-Sally 2004). Such water pollution and the use of this wastewater for irrigation in urban and peri-urban areas are rising in many countries (photo 11.1 and box 11.2).

Government priorities influence wastewater treatment and management. In many cities in Asia and Africa population growth has outpaced improvements in sanitation and wastewater infrastructure, making management of urban wastewater ineffective. In India only 24% of wastewater from households and industry is treated, and in Pakistan, only 2% (IWMI 2003; Minhas and Samra 2003). In Accra, Ghana, only 10% of wastewater is collected in piped sewage systems and receives primary or secondary treatment (Drechsel, Blumenthal, and Keraita 2002; Scott, Faruqui, and Raschid-Sally 2004). Even these small volumes of wastewater are not always adequately treated because of lack of capacity or treatment plants that are out of commission. Most developing countries cannot afford to build and operate treatment plants or sewer systems with sufficient capacity, so most wastewater is discharged into waterways without treatment.

Reliable estimates of projected wastewater use are needed for planning and management. Except for a few assessments conducted in India, Pakistan, and Viet Nam, limited information on the extent of wastewater use in agriculture makes estimating future use difficult. Data collection and comparison are challenging, in part because of the lack of a universally accepted typology (Van der Hoek 2004). In some cases information on agricultural use of wastewater exists, but government policies make access difficult or the information is available only in local or national literature. Jimenez and Asano (2004) suggest that at least 2 million hectares (ha) are irrigated with untreated, partly treated, diluted, or treated wastewater. The estimated area would be larger if the land irrigated from rivers and canals that receive wastewater were considered. Box 11.3 gives examples of the importance of wastewater use in some countries.

Wastewater is used for agriculture, aquaculture, and nonagricultural purposes. In addition to the use of wastewater by small-scale farmers to produce fresh vegetables and other crops in urban and peri-urban areas, wastewater is used to produce grains,

| box **11.3** | **The importance of wastewater use in selected countries** |

Wastewater has been recycled in agriculture for centuries as a means of disposal in cities such as Berlin, London, Milan, and Paris (AATSE 2004). In China, India, and Viet Nam wastewater has been used to provide nutrients and improve soil quality. In recent years wastewater has gained importance in water-scarce regions. In Pakistan 26% of national vegetable production is irrigated with wastewater. Any changes to this practice would reduce the supply of vegetables to cities (Ensink and others 2004). In Hanoi 80% of vegetable production is from urban and peri-urban areas irrigated with wastewater and water from the Red River Delta, which receives drainage effluent from the city (Lai 2000). Around Kumasi, Ghana, informal irrigation involving diluted wastewater from rivers and streams occurs on an estimated 11,500 ha, an area larger than the reported extent of formal irrigation in the country (Keraita and Drechsel 2004). In Mexico about 260,000 ha are irrigated with wastewater, mostly untreated (Mexico CNA 2004).

In the United States municipal water reuse accounted for 1.5% of water withdrawals in 2000. California residents reuse 656 million cubic meters of municipal wastewater annually. In Tunisia reclaimed water accounted for 4.3% of available water resources in 1996 and could reach 11% by 2030. In Israel wastewater accounted for 15% of water resources in 2000 and could reach 20% by 2010.

Agricultural use of
marginal-quality water—
opportunities and challenges
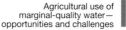 **11**

fodder, and industrial crops. In developed countries treated wastewater is used in parks, on sporting grounds, and on road plantings. Wastewater is used in aquaculture in Africa, Central Asia, and South and Southeast Asia (Bangladesh, Cambodia, China, India, Indonesia, and Viet Nam). Treated wastewater is also used for environmental purposes (wetlands, wildlife refuges, riparian habitats, urban lakes and ponds), industrial functions (cooling, boiling, processing), nonpotable applications (fire fighting, air conditioning, dust control, toilet flushing), and groundwater recharge (Asano 1998; Lazarova and Bahri 2005).

Emphasizing livelihoods sometimes leads to neglect of wastewater regulations in agriculture. Many farmers in developing countries irrigate with diluted, untreated, or partly treated wastewater. Some farmers know the health risks, but not all do. Wastewater is the only reliable or affordable source of irrigation water for many farmers. Farmers who cannot purchase supplemental fertilizer appreciate the nutrient content of wastewater. Public officials recognize the employment opportunities and livelihood benefits made possible by wastewater irrigation (Jimenez and Garduño 2001; IWMI 2003; Keraita and Drechsel 2004). Where farmers already face substantial risks to their welfare and livelihoods, some farmers and public officials likely discount the incremental risk of exposure to wastewater.

> Farmers who cannot purchase supplemental fertilizer appreciate the nutrient content of wastewater

In many areas there is a laissez-faire attitude toward wastewater use, as authorities face more important challenges of urbanization and poverty alleviation. With little allocation of funds for wastewater collection and treatment, countries cannot enforce bans on agricultural use of wastewater. Some public officials regard agricultural use as a viable disposal option for wastewater. Some agencies sell wastewater to farmers. However, officials occasionally expel farmers from their fields or uproot vegetables irrigated with wastewater. Officials are challenged to find ways to minimize potential health and environmental risks while allowing communities to achieve livelihood goals. There are also potential impacts on international trade. Some countries might reject shipments of agricultural commodities produced with polluted water.

Saline and sodic water—rising use with increasing competition for freshwater

Surface runoff and subsurface drainage water can be reused for irrigation, provided sufficient care is taken to minimize harm to crops and maintain salt balance. Artificial drainage systems have been installed in many arid areas to prevent crop damage from saline high water tables. In some areas increases in cropping intensities, excessive use of agricultural chemicals, inappropriate irrigation methods, and irrigation of saline soils have caused increases in the salinity of drainage water (Skaggs and Van Schilfgaarde 1999). To maintain salt balance in the root zone, drainage water salinity must be higher than irrigation water salinity. Where drainage water flows through saline geologic deposits or displaces saline groundwater, the salt load in drainage water exceeds that projected to occur from irrigation alone. In some cases drainage water may dissolve and displace potentially toxic elements.

With increasing competition for freshwater many communities in water-scarce countries use saline and sodic groundwater for household needs and irrigation. Groundwater resources are overexploited in many areas, due partly to increasing competition for surface water supplies and partly to policies that encourage excessive use, such as free or cheap electricity for pumping groundwater. In some areas groundwater quality has deteriorated with increasing rates of withdrawal. In India an estimated 32 billion of the 135 billion cubic meters of groundwater withdrawn annually are saline (Minhas and Samra 2003). Saline groundwater results from reactions that occur as water moves through the soil profile and from reactions that occur within groundwater layers. Irrigating with saline groundwater can degrade land quality, causing long-term impacts on crop growth and yields. Substantial investments in land reclamation are needed to restore productivity in some areas.

> The reuse of agricultural drainage water has increased with the expansion of irrigated agriculture

In Bangladesh and West Bengal in India groundwater contains elevated levels of arsenic, a potentially toxic metalloid (Adeel 2001). Persistent use of arsenic-contaminated water for drinking causes health problems whose full effects become apparent only at later stages of development. In India about 66 million people drink groundwater containing excessive fluoride, which causes mottling of teeth and, in severe cases, crippling skeletal deformities and other health problems.

No regional or global estimates are available of the volumes of saline drainage water and groundwater or the areas irrigated with them. The reuse of agricultural drainage water has increased with the expansion of irrigated agriculture, particularly since 1950. Global irrigated area has grown from 140 million ha in 1960 to about 270 million ha today. About 20% of the global irrigated area is affected by varying levels of salinity and sodicity (Ghassemi, Jakeman, and Nix 1995). Globally, irrigation efficiency is on the order of 50%, suggesting the use of substantial volumes of drainage water in agriculture. Saline groundwater is also used increasingly for irrigation in water-scarce areas. Analysts generally agree that agricultural use of these waters will gain importance in the overall water balance. With pressures to produce more, the overexploitation of good-quality water in many developing countries and the alarming rate of decline in groundwater levels are putting aquifers at risk of contamination from adjoining poor-quality aquifers. In addition, recent trends in climate change and salt-water intrusion suggest the influence of even greater volumes of these waters in agricultural production in coastal areas in coming years.

Use of saline and sodic drainage water and groundwater varies greatly among countries. Egypt uses an estimated 5 billion cubic meters of drainage water for irrigation in the Nile Delta, mixing drainage water with freshwater. In addition, farmers at the tailends of irrigation schemes reuse an estimated 2.8 billion cubic meters of drainage water unofficially. The drainage system also collects treated and untreated wastewater (APP 2002). In India, as noted, an estimated 32 billion cubic meters of saline and sodic groundwater are withdrawn annually.

In agriculture saline or sodic water is used to produce many conventional grain, forage, and feed crops and salt-tolerant plants and trees, particularly in Bangladesh, China, Egypt, India, Iran, Pakistan, Syria, and the United States. Recently, as areas have been

Agricultural use of
marginal-quality water—
opportunities and challenges **11**

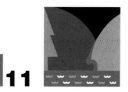

box **11.4** | **Drainage water use in aquaculture and horticulture**

Agricultural drainage water has been used for fish production for more than 20 years in the southern part of Lake Edko, Egypt. Fish ponds cover more than 3,200 ha of land that is too saline to support crop production. Typical pond size is 4 ha, and the average annual production of tilapia, silver carp, and eels is 0.8 tons per hectare, generating annual revenue of about $400 per hectare.

Farmers in the coastal area near Lake Edko use drainage water to irrigate vegetables and fruits, including onions, tomatoes, peppers, cucumbers, watermelons, apples, guava, pomegranates, and grapes. Land is enhanced by adding sand from nearby dunes to the topsoil. The annual rainfall of about 200 millimeters occurs in winter. Wastewater irrigation with drip systems supports crop production in other seasons. The average investment cost is about $2,700 per hectare (IPTRID 2005).

abandoned for agriculture because of waterlogging and salinity, inland saline aquaculture has been adopted on a small scale in several developing countries, as in the Nile Delta of Egypt (Stenhouse and Kijne 2006; box 11.4).

Impacts of using marginal-quality water

Risk management is essential for preventing adverse impacts when irrigating with wastewater or saline and sodic water. Untreated wastewater disposal pollutes freshwater and causes harmful health and environmental impacts, while inappropriate use of saline and sodic water causes soil salinization and water quality degradation that can limit crop choices and reduce yields.

Wastewater—human health, environmental, and economic impacts

Disposal of untreated wastewater pollutes freshwater, affecting other potential beneficial uses, and causes human health and environmental impacts. The failure to properly treat and manage wastewater generates adverse health effects (table 11.1). In low-income countries women and children are most vulnerable to waterborne diseases. In India the Ganges River receives about 120,000 cubic meters of sewage effluent per day, affecting downstream domestic and agricultural use and threatening human health. In addition, groundwater is contaminated by land disposal of wastewater (Foster, Gale, and Hespanhol 1994).

Risk management is needed to prevent adverse environmental, health, and gender-related impacts. Irrigation with wastewater without applying risk management measures may cause contamination of groundwater beneath irrigated fields or during groundwater recharge, particularly when wastewater contains untreated industrial effluent (Ensink and others 2002); accumulation of pathogens with high associated risk where groundwater is used for drinking (Attia and Fadlelmawla 2005); and gradual accumulation of salts, metals, and metalloids in the soil solution and on cation exchange sites to levels that might become toxic to plants.

table **11.1**	Annual global mortality and disability-adjusted life years lost due to some diseases of relevance to wastewater use in agriculture		
Disease	Number of deaths	DALYs[a]	Comments
Diarrhea	1,798,000	61,966,000	Almost all (99.8%) deaths occur in developing countries, most (90%) of them among children
Typhoid fever	600,000	—	Estimated 16 million cases a year
Ascariasis	3,000	1,817,000	Estimated 1.45 billion infections; 350 million suffer adverse health effects
Hookworm disease	3,000	59,000	Estimated 1.3 billion infections; 150 million suffer adverse health effects
Lymphatic filariasis	0	5,777,000	Mosquito vectors of filariasis breed in contaminated water; does not cause death but leads to severe disability
Hepatitis A	—	—	Estimated 1.4 million cases a year; serological evidence of prior infection ranges from 15% to nearly 100%

— not available

Note: The table considers diseases potentially attributable to pollution caused by wastewater use in agriculture.

a. DALYs, or disability-adjusted life years lost due to disease, reflect the time lost due to disability or death from a disease, compared with a long life free of disability in the absence of the disease. DALYs describe the health of a population or burden of disease due to a specific disease or risk factor.

Source: Adapted from WHO 2006.

Human health risks from wastewater include exposure to pathogens, helminth infections, and heavy metals. Leafy vegetables, eaten raw, can transmit contamination from farm fields to consumers. Hookworm infections are transmitted by direct exposure to contaminated water and soils. A survey along the Musi River in India revealed the transfer of metal ions from wastewater to cow's milk through fodder (para grass) irrigated with wastewater. About 4% of grass samples showed excessive amounts of cadmium, and all samples showed excessive lead. Milk samples were contaminated with metal ions ranging from 1.2 to 40 times permissible levels (Minhas and Samra 2004). Leafy vegetables accumulate greater amounts of certain metals like cadmium than do nonleafy species. Generally, metal concentrations in plant tissue increase with metal concentrations in irrigation water, and concentrations in roots usually are higher than concentrations in leaves.

Farmers and their families using untreated wastewater are exposed to health risks from parasitic worms, viruses, and bacteria. Many farmers cannot afford treatment for some of the health problems caused by exposure. Generally, farmers irrigating with wastewater have higher rates of helminth infections than farmers using freshwater, but there are exceptions (Trang and others 2006). In addition, skin and nail problems occur more frequently among farmers using wastewater (Van der Hoek and others 2002). The relationship among possible health risks, pathogen concentrations, and water quality guidelines is described in box 11.5.

The gender implications of wastewater use arise from women's roles in agriculture. Women provide much of the labor required to produce vegetables, particularly in developing countries. They also perform much of the weeding and transplanting, tasks that can expose them to long periods of contact with wastewater. Women also are more

Agricultural use of
marginal-quality water—
opportunities and challenges **11**

susceptible than other household members to health impacts when domestic water supplies are polluted by wastewater. Women generally prepare meals, creating the opportunity for transferring pathogens to other family members unless good hygiene is maintained. The incremental risk of pathogen transfer is larger in households that normally practice good hygiene. In many areas of low-income countries wastewater is just one of several sources of pathogens. Nonetheless, improvements in the hygiene of food preparation can reduce the risk of health impacts due to consuming crops irrigated with wastewater. Women also have the opportunity to promote risk reduction interventions in vegetable production and marketing, given their key roles in those activities.

The size of area irrigated with wastewater and the volume of water used are not sufficient statistics for judging the potential implications of wastewater use in agriculture. Fear of economic repercussions in the trade of agricultural products may make

---

box 11.5 | **Health risk and water quality guidelines**

The general perception among policymakers and the public is that using untreated wastewater in agriculture is unsanitary and unhealthy and that the practice should not be promoted. Shuval and others (1986) and Blumenthal and others (2001) showed that wastewater use can increase the risk of intestinal nematode infections, particularly *Ancylostoma* (hookworm) and *Ascaris,* in farmers in India and Mexico. Others have shown that in Egypt, Germany, and Israel consumption of vegetables irrigated with wastewater can increase the risk of *Ascaris* and *Trichyris* infections in the general public (Khalil 1931; Krey 1949; Shuval, Yekutiel, and Fattal 1984). Outbreaks of typhoid fever and an increased risk of enteric disease also have been associated with the consumption of vegetables irrigated with wastewater.

Many studies showing negative health impacts lack statistical rigor, however (Blumenthal and Peasey 2002), and have not measured the concentrations of pathogens in the water used. In addition, most studies that have investigated the risk from consumption of vegetables irrigated with wastewater have linked a high prevalence of infection in a population with the widespread use of wastewater in agriculture. The studies are epidemiologically flawed, as they do not assess the risk of exposure at the individual level. Too few studies have combined an epidemiological component with a water quality assessment and a quantitative microbial risk assessment. Some of the studies meeting that criterion have been conducted under different environmental, cultural and climatic conditions, making comparison and extrapolation of findings difficult.

An expert committee of the World Health Organization first examined the health concerns of wastewater use in aquaculture and agriculture in 1971. Microbial water quality guidelines for irrigation water were established (WHO 1973) but were relaxed in 1989 to 1,000 fecal coliforms per 100 milliliters, based on the findings of epidemiological studies of wastewater irrigation. In addition, a quality guideline for intestinal nematodes was recommended as less than 1 intestinal nematode egg per liter (WHO 1989). The revised guidelines were criticized as being both too lenient and too strict. Recent studies conducted in India, Pakistan, and Viet Nam have challenged the validity of the global (helminth) water quality guideline.

The latest guidelines (2006) for the safe use of wastewater in agriculture have been revised considerably. The fecal coliform guideline has been replaced by a focus on attributable risks and disability-adjusted life years. In addition, governments in developing countries have been given greater flexibility in applying the guidelines (WHO 2006).

governments reluctant to acknowledge the use of wastewater for irrigation and so prevent them from implementing mitigation measures. Jordan's export market was seriously affected in 1991 when countries in the region restricted imports of fruits and vegetables irrigated with inadequately treated wastewater (McCornick, Hijazi, and Sheikh 2004) Jordan implemented an aggressive campaign to rehabilitate and improve wastewater treatment plants and introduced enforceable standards to protect the health of fieldworkers and consumers. The government continues to focus on this sensitive situation, given the importance of international trade. This example reveals that the impacts of wastewater use can be indirect and wide-ranging.

Most farmers, consumers, and government agents in developing countries are not fully aware of the impacts of using wastewater for irrigation. Many farmers in low-income countries irrigating with wastewater do not understand the risks or the potential environmental consequences. Many farmers are illiterate, lack adequate information, and have been exposed to poor sanitary conditions for most of their lives. Poverty also motivates many farmers to use any available water for irrigation, regardless of its quality. Many consumers are not aware that farm products have been irrigated with wastewater, while the authorities often have insufficient knowledge of the technical and management options available for reducing environmental and health risks.

> Many farmers in low-income countries irrigating with wastewater do not understand the risks or the potential environmental consequences

Saline and sodic water—impacts on soil, crop choices, and yields

Water allocation policies in many countries have not been sufficiently rigorous to prevent the overirrigation that causes salinization and waterlogging. Many large-scale irrigation systems have been constructed without adequate drainage systems.

The risks of using saline and sodic water inappropriately include soil salinization and water quality degradation. Inappropriate irrigation with saline or sodic water causes salt accumulation in soils, resulting in secondary salinity or sodicity. Salinity affects crop growth through increased osmotic pressure and lower availability of water in the soil to plants and through the specific effects of some elements on plants. Sodicity, as measured by the sodium adsorption ratio or exchangeable sodium percentage, is primarily a soil problem. Sodic soils exhibit structural problems created by certain physical processes (slaking, swelling, and dispersion of clay) and surface crusting that affect erosion, seedling emergence, root penetration, tillage operations, water and air movement, and plant-available water-holding capacity. In addition, imbalances in plant-available nutrients in salt-affected soils impair plant growth.

Elevated levels of salts in irrigation water and soils may restrict planting to crops that can withstand ambient salinity levels. Farmers using saline water must manage irrigation carefully to minimize potential losses due to crop sensitivity to salinity, chloride toxicity, plant-available nutrient deficiency, and structural deterioration of soils (Ayers and Westcot 1985).

Disposal of saline or sodic water into freshwater bodies impairs environmental quality. The disposal of saline drainage water into canals and rivers disperses salts and

Agricultural use of
marginal-quality water—
opportunities and challenges **11**

potentially toxic substances over a much wider area. About 1 billion cubic meters of saline drainage water are discharged annually into the Euphrates River in Syria, causing a doubling of salinity (from about 0.5 to 1.0 deciSiemen per meter) when the river enters Iraq. In Jordan water quality in the Amman-Zarqa Basin and the Jordan Valley has been affected for several decades, with consequences for irrigated agriculture (McCornick, Grattan, and Abu-Eisheh 2003). Anticipated increases in the region's population and growth in economic activity will exacerbate the situation. National agencies have gathered extensive datasets, including water quality data, for many years at strategic locations (Grabow and McCornick forthcoming). Analysis of those data will enhance understanding of salinity dynamics and guide the development of policies to minimize the negative impacts of salinity and other wastewater constituents on irrigated agriculture.

Response options and management strategies for marginal-quality water

Many options are available to manage the risks in using marginal-quality water.

Wastewater—reducing risk

In resource-poor situations it might be wiser to manage or minimize risk, rather than trying to eliminate risk. Wastewater needs treatment prior to its use or discharge to the environment (Pescod 1992, Ongley 1996). Public agencies usually determine water quality objectives by considering health risks and requiring wastewater treatment to achieve those goals. The goal of treatment is to remove or reduce unwanted toxic substances, pathogens, and nutrients. Most public agencies evaluate potential risks to individuals and communities when establishing water quality goals. Risk assessments are revised over time with improvements in science and changes in public preferences (see box 11.5).

In many developing countries the costs of operation and maintenance and the lack of required skills are the primary limitations on wastewater treatment capacity. In these situations treatment can be phased in by first introducing primary treatment facilities, particularly where wastewater is used directly for irrigation. Secondary treatment can be implemented in some areas using low-cost options, such as waste-stabilization ponds, constructed wetlands, and up-flow anaerobic sludge blanket reactors (Mara 2003).

Because constraints are greater for large, centralized wastewater collection and treatment systems, decentralized systems that are more flexible and compatible with local demands for effluent use have emerged in many areas. Some communities prefer to operate and maintain local systems to ensure long-term operation and financial sustainability (Raschid-Sally and Parkinson 2004). However, small-scale treatment plants are ineffective when their capacity is exceeded.

Water quality can be improved by storing reclaimed water in reservoirs that provide peak-equalization capacity, which increases the reliability of supply and improves the rate of reuse. Long retention times in the King Talal Reservoir in the Amman-Zarqa Basin of

> In most developing countries wastewater treatment is a long-term strategy; interim solutions may be needed to protect farmers and public health

Jordan reduce fecal coliform levels in water downstream of the dam, although it was not initially intended for that purpose (Grabow and McCornick forthcoming).

In most developing countries wastewater treatment is a long-term strategy. Interim solutions may be needed to protect farmers and public health (IWMI 2006). Though unpopular, protective measures such as wearing boots and gloves can reduce farmers' exposure. Farmers also can wash their arms and legs after immersion in wastewater to prevent the spread of infection. Improvements in irrigation methods and in personal and domestic hygiene can be encouraged through public awareness campaigns. Drip irrigation can protect farmers and consumers by minimizing crop and human exposure, but pretreatment of wastewater is needed to avoid clogging of emitters. A combination of farm-level and post-harvest measures can be used to protect consumers, such as producing industrial or nonedible crops or products that require cooking before consumption. Farmers also can stop applying wastewater long before harvest, to reduce potential harm to consumers. Vegetables can be washed before sale or consumption, and storage methods can be improved. Public agencies can implement child immunization campaigns against diseases that can be transmitted through wastewater use and target selected populations for periodic antihelminthic campaigns (USEPA and USAID 2004; WHO 2006).

> The farm-level nutrient value of wastewater will vary with constituent loads, soil conditions, crop choices, and the cost and availability of inorganic fertilizers

The nutrients in municipal wastewater can contribute to crop growth, but periodic monitoring is needed to avoid imbalanced nutrient supply. Excessive nutrients can cause undesirable vegetative growth and delayed or uneven maturity (Jensen and others forthcoming), reduce crop quality, and pollute groundwater and surface water. Periodic monitoring is required to estimate the nutrient loads in wastewater and adjust fertilizer applications. The amount of nutrients in 1,000 cubic meters of wastewater irrigation per hectare can vary considerably: 16–62 kilograms (kg) total nitrogen, 4–24 kg phosphorus, 2–69 kg potassium, 18–208 kg calcium, 9–110 kg magnesium, and 27–182 kg sodium. Nitrogen and sodium levels often exceed plant requirements. The farm-level nutrient value of wastewater will vary with constituent loads, soil conditions, crop choices, and the cost and availability of inorganic fertilizers. Studies of the farm-level and aggregate implications of nutrient uptake from untreated wastewater are rare. One study in Viet Nam reports a 40% increase in rice grain protein content in a wastewater irrigation system (Jensen and others forthcoming).

Farmers in Mexico's Mezquital (Tula) Valley appreciate wastewater because it allows agricultural development in an area with annual precipitation of just 550 millimeters and soils that are low in organic matter. Irrigation and supplemental nutrients are required to ensure productivity. Wastewater irrigation in the valley provides 2,400 kg of organic matter, 195 kg of nitrogen, and 81 kg of phosphorus per hectare per year, contributing to significant increases in crop yields (Jimenez 2005). Farmers in the valley oppose wastewater treatment because they do not want nutrients removed from the water they use for irrigation. The farmers may be wrong, however, as even secondary treatment, while removing organic matter, leaves enough nutrients (nitrogen and potassium) to satisfy crop requirements. Box 11.6 provides insight into the costs and benefits of using wastewater in agriculture.

Agricultural use of
marginal-quality water—
opportunities and challenges | **11**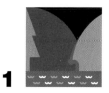

| box **11.6** | **The costs and benefits of using wastewater in agriculture** |

Market prices and standard analytical methods can be used to assess the financial implications for farmers, any negative environmental and health impacts, and any benefits society might derive from wastewater use (Hussain and others 2001; Ul-Hassan 2002; Ul-Hassan and Ali 2002; Scott, Zarazua, and Levine 2000). Ul-Hassan and Ali (2002) estimated the direct benefits to farmers from nutrient reuse and fertilizer savings in Haroonabad, Pakistan. They compared vegetable production with freshwater and untreated wastewater and found that the gross margins with wastewater were significantly higher ($150 per hectare), because farmers spent less on chemical fertilizer and achieved higher yields. No other costs or benefits were measured, but a potential tradeoff calculation showed that each cubic meter of wastewater used for irrigation released three to four times the volume of freshwater for use elsewhere, generating a net monetary gain for society.

Scott, Zarazua, and Levine (2000) estimated nutrient enrichment gains from wastewater application in Guanajuato, Mexico. The estimated cost of replacing the nitrogen and phosphorus received from the wastewater after construction of a treatment plant was $900 per hectare. This was an overestimate as the nutrients in the wastewater exceeded plant requirements; a more realistic value is $135 per hectare. With the plant in operation the total cost to farmers was estimated at $18,900 a year in forgone nutrients (Drechsel, Giordano, and Gyiele 2004).

Estimates of nonmarket costs and benefits, such as health and environmental effects, can inform policies on regulatory targets and intervention programs (WHO 2005). In developed countries most nonmarket evaluations pertain to environmental rather than health issues. The most common is contingent valuation, which uses measures of willingness to pay or willingness to accept to quantify nonpriced goods and services, including nonbeneficial ones, in cases where health and environmental impacts interact in order to evaluate policy choices more comprehensively. Topics to explore include:

- Valuation of the benefits of environmental and health risk reduction, with an emphasis on health disparities within a population and in the context of many risk sources, including irrigation with wastewater.
- Assessment of the full costs and benefits (including productivity impacts) of
    - Environmental technology choices that affect human health at the individual or household level.
    - Policy choices for wastewater management with environmental and health impacts at the aggregate or city level.
- Assessment of how cultural and social factors and individual socioeconomic status affect the discounting of future health and environmental costs and benefits.

Hussain and others (2001, 2002) present a framework and review the literature on the economic impacts of wastewater use.

With safeguards to protect groundwater quality, treated wastewater can be used for groundwater recharge. Aquifer recharge with wastewater can occur through deep percolation in irrigated fields (as in Mexico's Mezquital Valley) or through intentional recharge programs. Recharge with wastewater should be conducted under controlled conditions and with continuous monitoring and, if wastewater is injected into an aquifer, treatment. The estimated unintentional recharge due to deep percolation beneath irrigated fields is as large as 1 meter in Jordan, Mexico, Peru, and Thailand, a depth that exceeds average annual rainfall in some areas (Foster and others 2004). Studies in Tula Valley, Mexico, suggest that almost half of the untreated wastewater infiltrates through soil, which acts as a filter and removes pollutants. However, salinity and nitrate levels in groundwater are increasing. Continuous monitoring of the aquifer is needed to identify emerging health problems (Jimenez and Chávez 2004).

Aquifers have been recharged intentionally with treated wastewater for many years in the United States, with no recorded unacceptable impacts. Israel has been recharging an aquifer south of Tel Aviv with reclaimed wastewater for 20 years. About 120 million cubic meters of reclaimed water have been infiltrated into the aquifer each year, using intermittently operated spreading basins (Idelovitch 2001). Water withdrawn from the aquifer is used for unrestricted irrigation of crops.

Groundwater recharge through soil percolation removes microorganisms provided that an appropriate flooding-drying cycle and an adequate microbiological population are maintained. California has proposed criteria for groundwater recharge with reclaimed water combining aspects such as source control, wastewater treatment processes, water quality, recharge methods, recharge area, depth to groundwater, underground retention time of the recharged water, reclaimed water contribution to the aquifer, and extraction well proximity (Asano and Cotruvo 2004).

Untreated wastewater should not be used on crops that are likely to transmit contaminants or pathogens to consumers. In many developing countries restrictions on crops (particularly those consumed raw) that are most likely to transmit contaminants and pathogens to consumers are helpful in reducing human health hazards. In the Aleppo region of Syria less than 7% of the area under wastewater irrigation is cultivated with vegetables because government restrictions are enforced by officials who uproot any vegetables found to be growing there. Usually, restrictions are difficult to enforce because demand for vegetables is high in cities and because only vegetables achieve the level of profits farmers need to maintain their livelihoods. A recent global survey found that vegetables (32% frequency of responses) and cereals (27%) are the most common crops produced by farmers using wastewater for irrigation (Raschid and Jayakody forthcoming).

Pragmatic approaches are needed to protect water quality and achieve sustainable use of wastewater. Many developing countries have adopted legislation and policies to protect water quality and regulate wastewater use. However, the inclusion of unrealistic criteria makes implementation difficult. A more pragmatic approach would combine provisional guidelines with continuing improvements to enhance wastewater quality or the ability to use wastewater in an environmentally safe manner. Meaningful criteria need to be established in accordance with local, technical, economic, social, and cultural contexts (IWMI 2006). Several countries are integrating management of wastewater reuse to reduce costs and increase agricultural productivity (box 11.7).

Strategies for managing mixed marginal-quality water (wastewater mixed with saline or sodic water) should apply a multiple-barrier approach that incorporates more than one intervention at various points in the water cycle and in crop handling (box 11.8). The multiple-barrier approach has recently been adopted in new Israeli standards and guidelines and

Agricultural use of
marginal-quality water—
opportunities and challenges | **11**

| box **11.7** | **Integrated wastewater treatment and use for irrigation in Morocco and Tunisia** |

Integrating management of wastewater reuse to minimize treatment costs and increase agricultural productivity is gaining interest in many countries. In Drarga, Morocco, untreated wastewater was being discharged into the environment, contaminating drinking water supplies. To deal with this problem a public participation program created an institutional partnership involving local water management stakeholders, urban water users, and farmers water user groups (USEPA and USAID 2004). Wastewater treatment now includes screening, anaerobic basins, sand filters, and denitrification. To ensure the sustainability of the treatment and reuse program, a fee was imposed for domestic water supply and other cost-recovery mechanisms have been implemented.

Tunisia launched a national water reuse programme in the early 1980s to increase the country's usable water resources. Most municipal wastewater is from domestic sources and receives secondary biological treatment. Several treatment plants are located along the coast to protect coastal resorts and prevent marine pollution. In 2003, 187 million cubic meters of the 240 million cubic meters of wastewater collected in Tunisia received treatment. About 43% of the treated wastewater was used for agricultural and landscape irrigation. Reusing wastewater for irrigation is viewed as a way to increase water resources, provide supplemental nutrients, and protect coastal areas, water resources, and sensitive receiving bodies. Reclaimed water is used on 8,000 ha to irrigate cereals, vineyards, citrus and other fruit trees, and fodder crops. Regulations allow the use of secondary-treated effluent on all crops except vegetables, whether eaten raw or cooked. Regional agricultural departments supervise the water reuse decree and collect charges (about $0.01 per cubic meter). Golf courses also irrigate with treated effluent, while industrial use and groundwater recharge opportunities are being investigated.

| box **11.8** | **Integrated approaches to managing mixed wastewater** |

The concentration of salts in sewage, soils, and aquifers in some areas of Israel has increased in recent decades. There are no inexpensive ways to remove salts from sewage. The government and farmers are coping with the problem by reducing the salt content of water supplies and treated effluent; reducing salt addition during industrial and residential water use; reducing evaporation losses during wastewater storage; using drip irrigation; adequately draining irrigated fields; discharging saline, first-flood waters of the rainy season; applying calcium soil amendments; and planting salt-tolerant crops (Weber and Juanicó 2004).

in guidelines developed by the World Health Organization. Wastewater treatment levels are categorized on a scale of 1 to 5, with level 5 the lowest quality and usable only on crops that require no barriers. Barriers can be either physical (buffer zones, plastic mulches, or subsurface drip) or process oriented (selecting the right crops; processing, cooking, or peeling prior to consumption). No-barrier crops include cotton, forages, and those harvested at least 60 days after the last irrigation with wastewater (USEPA and USAID 2004).

Saline and sodic water—improving management

Leaching and drainage are required to maintain salt balance in the soil profile and to sustain crop yields in arid areas. Irrigation is essential in arid areas, but it generates saline drainage water that must be disposed of or reused. The salinity of drainage water is a function of the salinity of the applied water, soil salinity, and the salinity of shallow groundwater (Ayers and Westcot 1985; Pescod 1992). In water-abundant areas farmers prefer to discharge saline **drainage** water. In arid, water-scarce areas drainage water is a resource that can extend farm-level and regional water supplies. Careful management is required to maximize the value of saline drainage water while minimizing negative impacts on downstream areas (Minhas and Samra 2003).

There are different types of drainage systems: natural drainage, subsurface drainage systems (tiles or perforated pipes), tubewell-based drainage, and biodrainage. The choice of drainage system influences the quality of drainage effluent (Tanji and Kielen 2002). Subsurface drainage systems that enhance water flow through the soil quickly remove soluble salts and toxic trace elements from the root zone. The potential for reusing drainage water is reduced by the high salt content of the effluent. Drainage water can be reused if it is blended with freshwater or used to irrigate salt-tolerant crops.

Most subsurface drainage systems are installed 1–3 meters below the surface. Most tubewell-based drainage systems operate at 6–10 meters, but some reach depths of 100 meters, such as the deep tubewell drains in India and Pakistan. The quality of subsurface drainage water is influenced by the type and concentration of salts in irrigation water, the agricultural chemicals used, and the quality of shallow groundwater. With tubewell drains the quality of drainage water is affected by salt-water intrusion, the type and concentration of salts in groundwater, and to a lesser extent the quality of irrigation water (Tanji and Kielen 2002).

Biodrainage involves deep-rooted crops and trees that modify water flux through evapotranspiration. Biodrainage is less costly than conventional drainage and can provide fuel wood, timber, fruit, windbreaks, shade and shelter, and organic matter (Heuperman, Kapoor, and Dencke 2002). Biodrainage also can remove ponds that form along canal embankments. The sustainability of biodrainage is not guaranteed in all settings. The gradual accumulation of salinity might eventually harm deep-rooted crops and trees, reducing their effectiveness. In addition, the decline or harvesting of biodrainage plants will enable salts that have accumulated below the root zone to move upward through capillary action. A combination of biodrainage and a conventional drainage system might delay or minimize the impacts of salt accumulation.

Water conservation and drainage water reuse, treatment, and disposal can improve management of agricultural drainage water. Water conservation can reduce the volume of drainage water and constituent loads and make water available for other beneficial uses. Strategies include source reduction, minimization of deep percolation, and groundwater management. Land retirement should be considered where competition for water is intense and where disposal of drainage water is constrained (as in a closed basin) or threatens ecologically sensitive areas.

Drainage water can be reused in conventional agriculture or in saline agriculture and in wildlife habitats and wetlands (Rhoades and Kandiah 1992). Reuse can be combined with conservation measures, particularly when drainage water management cannot be

Agricultural use of
marginal-quality water—
opportunities and challenges **11**

achieved by source reduction alone. Attention must be given to measures that minimize long- and short-term effects of elevated salinity on soil productivity and water quality. Integrated planning and management approaches at district or basin scales can maximize social and economic benefits while safeguarding ecological values (Abdel-Dayem and others 2004).

The cost of drainage water treatment usually exceeds the incremental value of water use in agriculture. However, treatment might be sensible when environmental regulations prevent drainage water disposal or when water scarcity justifies the high cost of treatment. Desalination of drainage water is suitable for high-value purposes only, such as drinking water (box 11.9). Constructed wetlands are a relatively low-cost option for protecting aquatic ecosystems and fisheries, either downstream from irrigated areas or in closed basins.

The volume of drainage water requiring disposal can be reduced by treatment and cyclic reuse. Disposal options include direct discharge into rivers, streams, lakes, deserts, and oceans and discharge into evaporation basins.

Saline and sodic waters can be used directly or blended with freshwater, but careful management is required to sustain productivity. Many farmers irrigate with a mixture of saline or sodic water and higher quality water in large areas of Egypt, India, Pakistan, the United States, and Central Asia (Ayers and Westcot 1985; Tanji and Kielin 2002). As long as the salinity of applied water does not exceed threshold levels and good drainage exists, use of saline water will not severely reduce yields. In areas such as India heavy rainfall during a portion of the year prevents the long-term accumulation of salts in the soil.

Where drainage water salinity exceeds crop threshold levels the water can be blended with freshwater. Blending, which can be done before or during irrigation, enables farmers to extend the volume of water available (Rhoades 1999; Oster and Grattan 2002).

In Egypt almost all agricultural land is served by surface or subsurface drainage systems that control soil salinity and reduce crop losses from direct use of saline water. A monitoring program was started in the 1970s to identify spatial and temporal changes in drainage water volume and quality. In 1995 a program was initiated in the Nile Delta to

| box **11.9** | **Desalination of seawater and highly brackish groundwater** |

Seawater desalination has been practiced for more than 50 years, mainly in oil-rich Middle Eastern countries. Elsewhere, a few countries with dense populations, substantial industry and tourism, and inadequate drinking water resources also produce freshwater from seawater and brackish groundwater. Desalination plants worldwide produce about 30 million cubic meters of freshwater daily, about two-thirds from seawater and the rest from brackish groundwater.

Distillation, the oldest process for desalting seawater, separates the water from salt and other impurities through evaporation and condensation. Reverse osmosis, which involves tightly bound semipermeable membranes that separate freshwater from seawater, has been used since the 1970s and is more energy efficient than distillation. Interest in desalination has increased in recent years as the cost of producing freshwater has declined from about $5.50 per cubic meter in the late 1970s to $0.50–$0.60. Desalination is not yet affordable for agricultural purposes in most countries.

assess the impacts of drainage water use on soil and water quality and crop yields. According to government policy the salinity of blended water should not be higher than 1.56 deciSiemen per meter. Crop yields using blended water are similar to those obtained using freshwater (table 11.2). Where drainage water is the only irrigation source, however, crop yields are 20%–60% lower (El-Guindy 2003).

The cyclic approach involves crop rotations that include both moderately salt-sensitive and salt-tolerant crops. Typically, nonsaline water is used before planting and during initial growth stages of the salt-tolerant crop while saline water is used after seedling establishment (Rhoades 1999). A crop rotation plan is needed to optimize the use of saline and nonsaline water, given the salt sensitivities of crops at different growth stages. Examples of yields obtained when irrigating with saline water in cyclic and blended fashion are shown in table 11.3 (Minhas, Sharma, and Chauhan 2003). There were nonsignificant losses in wheat yield when two initial canal water irrigations were followed by two saline water irrigations. For a given amount of salt input, yields were higher with cyclic use than when blending saline water and canal water. In addition, cyclic use likely is less costly than blending, which might require infrastructure for combining water from two sources.

table **11.2**	**Average irrigation water salinity, soil salinity, and yields of selected crops in the Nile Delta, 1997**		
	Eastern delta	**Middle delta**	**Western delta**
Irrigation water salinity (deciSiemens per meter)			
Freshwater	0.75	0.71	0.65
Blended water	1.70	1.75	0.97
Drainage water	2.87	2.07	2.89
Soil salinity (deciSiemens per meter)			
Freshwater	2.03	2.63	2.15
Blended water	2.70	4.06	2.27
Drainage water	4.16	3.96	3.68
Cotton yield (metric tons per hectare)			
Freshwater	1.73	1.82	2.40
Blended water	1.51	1.68	2.30
Drainage water	1.06	1.56	2.09
Wheat yield (metric tons per hectare)			
Freshwater	9.36	5.76	5.52
Blended water	8.40	4.32	5.28
Drainage water	5.52	4.56	4.80
Maize yield (metric tons per hectare)			
Freshwater	5.52	5.04	3.60
Blended water	3.84	6.24	3.36
Drainage water	3.60	6.96	2.40

Source: Adapted from DRI, Louis Berger International, Inc., and Pacer Consultants 1997.

Agricultural use of
marginal-quality water—
opportunities and challenges **11**

| table **11.3** | **Crop yields under varying modes of irrigation with canal water and saline water, 1990s** (metric tons per hectare) |

| | Deep water table (more than 6.0 meters) | | | | | | Shallow water table (1.5–2.0 meters) |
| | Cotton-wheat rotation | | Pearl millet-mustard rotation | | Mustard-sunflower rotation | | |
Treatment	Cotton	Wheat	Pearl millet	Mustard	Mustard	Sunflower	Wheat[a]
Canal water only	1.63	4.88	3.15	2.07	2.42	1.34	6.0
Cyclic mode							
Pre-planting irrigation with canal water and rest with saline water	0.98	4.05	2.99	1.88	2.25	0.71	5.3
Pre-planting irrigation with saline water and rest with canal water	ni	ni	ni	ni	2.39	0.99	ni
One irrigation each with saline and canal water and rest with saline water	0.72	4.08	2.80	1.67	ni	ni	ni
Alternate irrigations with canal and saline water, starting with canal water	1.23	4.72	2.96	1.96	2.54	0.99	5.8
Alternating two irrigations with canal water and saline water, starting with canal water	1.28	4.62	ni	ni	ni	ni	5.1
Alternating two irrigations with canal water and one with saline water, starting with canal water	ni	ni	ni	ni	2.47	0.98	ni
Alternate irrigations with saline water and canal water, starting with canal water	0.76	4.02	ni	ni	2.31	0.81	ni
Alternating two irrigations with saline water and one with canal water, starting with canal water	ni	ni	2.91	1.41	ni	ni	ni
Blended mode							
Irrigation with a blend of canal water and saline water in a 1:1 ratio	1.04	4.37	2.80	1.81	ni	ni	ni
Irrigation with a blend of canal water and saline water in a 1:2 ratio	ni	ni	ni	ni	2.60	0.72	ni
Irrigation with a blend of canal water and saline water in a 2:1 ratio	ni	ni	ni	ni	2.50	0.89	ni
All irrigations with saline water	0.46	3.59	2.91	1.18	2.52	0.29	4.5
Least square difference ($p = 0.05$)	0.32	0.35	ns	0.36	ns	0.15	ni

ni is not included in the respective treatment; ns is not significant.

Note: Salinity of canal water is 0.4–0.7 deciSiemens (dS) per meter. Saline water is 9 dS per meter for cotton and wheat, 12 dS per meter for pearl millet and mustard, 8 dS per meter for mustard and sunflower, and 12–17 dS per meter for wheat.

a. Under shallow water table conditions, cyclic use is for post-plant irrigations since wheat received pre-plant irrigation with canal water.

Source: Minhas, Sharma, and Chauhan 2003.

The cyclic option involves applying relatively better quality water to a crop with low salt tolerance, then using drainage water from that field to irrigate crops with greater salt tolerance. This strategy minimizes the volume of drainage water requiring disposal by reusing drainage water on fields located downslope of those where drainage water is first collected (Rhoades 1999). The number of cycles depends on the concentrations of salt and other elements in drainage water, the volume of water available, economic values, and acceptable yields (figure 11.1). Implementing cyclic reuse on a regional scale, rather than on individual farms, enhances long-term feasibility. Drainage water reuse can be concentrated on a small portion of a regional irrigation scheme, minimizing the areal extent of land degradation from salt accumulation. In every reuse sequence the volume of drainage water decreases and the salt concentration increases. The final sequence produces brine that can be discharged to a solar evaporator or an alternative repository.

Cropping choices are key decisions when irrigating with saline or sodic water. Crops vary considerably in their ability to tolerate saline conditions (table 11.4). Factors such as the type and concentration of salts, expected rainfall and its distribution, groundwater levels and quality, and irrigation management practices must be considered when irrigating with saline or sodic water. Irrigation with saline water can improve the quality of some crops, as the sugar content in sugarbeets, tomatoes, and melons is increased (Moreno and others 2001).

figure **11.1**	**Sequential reuse of drainage water on drainage-affected lands as proposed in the San Joaquin Valley Drainage Implementation Program, California**

1 Drainage water   3 Salt-tolerant crops   5 Halophytes
2 Salt-sensitive crops   4 Salt-tolerant trees   6 Solar evaporator

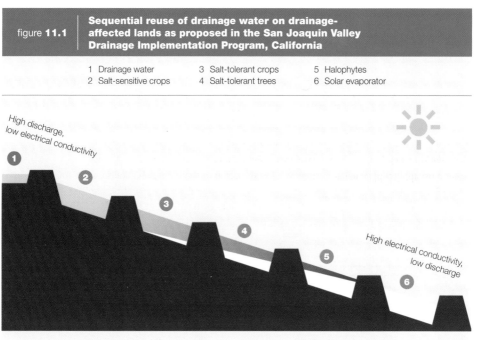

High discharge, low electrical conductivity

High electrical conductivity, low discharge

Source: Adapted from Tanji and Kielen 2002.

Agricultural use of
marginal-quality water—
opportunities and challenges | 11

table **11.4**	**Yield potential of selected crops as a function of average root zone salinity**			
		Average root zone salinity at specified yield potentials (deciSiemens per meter)		
Common name	**Botanical name**	**50%**	**80%**	**100%**
Triticale (grain)	*X Triticosecale*	26	14	6
Wheat (forage)	*Triticum aestivum* L.	24	12	4
Kallar grass	*Leptochloa fusca* (L.) Kunth	22	14	9
Durum wheat	*Triticum durum* Desf.	19	11	6
Tall wheat grass	*Agropyron elongatum* (Host) Beauv.	19	12	8
Barley (grain)	*Hordeum vulgare* L.	18	12	8
Cotton	*Gossypium hirsutum* L.	17	12	8
Rye (grain)	*Secale cereale* L.	16	13	11
Sugar beet	*Beta vulgaris* L.	16	10	7
Bermuda grass	*Cynodon dactylon* L.	15	10	7
Sudan grass	*Sorghum sudanese* (Piper) Stapf	14	8	3
Sesbania	*Sesbania bispinosa* (Jacq.) W. Wight	13	9	6
Wheat (grain)	*Triticum aestivum* L.	13	9	6
Barley (forage)	*Hordeum vulgare* L.	13	9	6
Sorghum	*Sorghum bicolor* (L.) Moench	10	8	7
Alfalfa	*Medicago sativa* L.	9	5	2
Corn (forage)	*Zea mays* L.	9	5	2
Rice (paddy)	*Oryza sativa* L.	7	5	3
Corn (grain)	*Zea mays* L.	6	3	2

Note: The data on yield potential serve only as a guideline to relative tolerances among crops. Absolute salt tolerances vary and depend on climate, soil conditions, and cultural practices.
Source: Adapted from Maas and Grattan 1999.

Chemical or biological amendments are needed over time to prevent soil structural degradation when irrigating exclusively with sodic water. Farmers irrigating with sodic water must apply supplemental calcium to offset the effects of sodium on soils and crops. Many farmers use gypsum ($CaSO_4 \cdot 2H_2O$), which usually is available and affordable, and the amount needed can be estimated using simple analytical tests.

On calcareous soils that contain appreciable amounts of precipitated or native calcite ($CaCO_3$), the dissolution of calcite in the root zone is enhanced by adding acid formers and by the actions of plant roots that increase the levels of carbon dioxide, thereby providing soluble calcium to offset sodium effects (Qadir and others 2005). Sodic soils can also be improved by leaving plant residues and adding organic matter from other sources (box 11.10).

Saline drainage water can support wildlife habitat and wetlands. Drainage water can be reused to support water birds, fish, mammals, and aquatic vegetation. Typical native marsh plants grown with drainage water include smartweed (*Polygonum lapothefolium*), swamp

box **11.10** | **Sesbania improves soil conditions in India**

Sesbania, a legume, has shown promise for biomass production and biological amelioration of soils degraded by irrigation with sodic water, in part because nitrogen is a limiting nutrient in many saline areas. If grown for 45 days and used as a green manure, sesbania improves soil fertility and enriches soils by creating up to 120 kg of nitrogen per hectare. Sesbania decomposes rapidly, producing organic acids and increased levels of carbon dioxide, which enhance dissolution of calcite in sodic soils. The fibrous stems help open voids and channels, and young branches of the tree provide fodder. Sesbania is gaining popularity among farmers who use saline and sodic groundwater from tubewells in India.

timothy (*Heleochloa schenoides*), tule or hardstem bulrush (*Scirpus fluviatilis*), cattails (*Typha spp*), alkali bulrush (*Scirpus robustus*), brass buttons (*Cotula corinopifola*), salt grass (*Distichilis spicata*), and tules (*Scirpus acutus*). Water is applied in autumn and held until spring. When the soil begins to warm, the ponds are drained to mudflat conditions to stimulate seed germination.

It is not always economically feasible to use highly saline water for agriculture, especially on degraded lands. The planting of permanent vegetation might be the best use of land in those situations, including such tree species as *Tamarix articulata, Prosopis juliflora, Acacia nilotica, Acacia tortilis, Feronia limonia, Acacia farnesiana* and *Melia azadirach*. Halophytic plant species have also been identified for use in biosaline agriculture (Minhas and Samra 2003).

Policies and institutions relating to marginal-quality water

Policies to improve the management of marginal-quality water in agriculture can be implemented before marginal-quality water is generated, while it is being used, and after crops have been irrigated and products are prepared for sale and consumption. Reducing the volume of marginal-quality water can reduce treatment and disposal costs, but where wastewater is not treated, reducing the volume could increase its concentration, with negative impacts.

Two features complicate policymaking pertaining to wastewater use in agriculture: most wastewater is generated outside the agricultural sector, and many individuals and organizations have an interest in policies pertaining to wastewater use. In addition, public concern varies with the type of water involved, treatment levels, and the amount of information available (Toze 2006). Where possible, it is helpful to distinguish between industrial and domestic wastewater. Removing pathogens from domestic wastewater can be less costly than removing chemicals from industrial wastewater.

Particularly in industrialized countries, households, communities, and industries generate excessive volumes of wastewater because there is little incentive to minimize volume or to reuse wastewater. Improving the institutions and policies that influence the use of freshwater can reduce the cost of treating and managing wastewater. Often the

Agricultural use of
marginal-quality water—
opportunities and challenges **11**

institutional framework is adequate, but public agencies have overlapping jurisdictions that prevent optimal implementation of desirable policies. Effluent standards, taxes, and tradable permits can be used to motivate improvements in water management by households and firms discharging wastewater from point sources.

The discharge of saline drainage water into surface water and groundwater is a nonpoint source pollution problem. The policy challenge is to motivate many diffuse farmers to reduce surface runoff and deep percolation by improving water management. Helpful policies include taxes and standards involving inputs such as irrigation water, fertilizer, and other chemicals. Financial incentives including low-interest loans and cost-sharing can also encourage desirable production methods.

The volume of saline and sodic drainage water can be reduced through policies affecting water withdrawals and deliveries. Pertinent policies include effective water allocation and pricing, assignment of water rights, restrictions on groundwater pumping, full-cost energy pricing, and incentives for farm-level investments in water-saving irrigation methods.

Establish property rights to wastewater

In regions where farmers and others compete for a limited supply of wastewater, assigning property rights can motivate efficient use. Property rights can be coupled with responsibility for using wastewater appropriately and managing discharges from irrigated farmland. Special attention is needed in areas where wastewater is treated by a municipality or water company. If a water treatment agency assumes property rights after treating the wastewater, the agency might view treated wastewater as a new resource, for allocation to new users, without consideration of the farmers who previously used the wastewater for irrigation.

Consider wastewater a resource requiring good management

Within the framework of integrated water resources management wastewater can be viewed as both an effluent and a resource. Where wastewater is used for irrigation, society gains value from the crops produced and the improvements in livelihoods in urban and peri-urban farming using wastewater. Irrigation also provides a method of using wastewater that might otherwise require further treatment or disposal.

The challenge for public agencies is to determine the best mix of policies to reduce wastewater generation and ensure safe and efficient use of wastewater (Huibers and Van Lier 2005; Martijn and Redwood 2005; Raschid-Sally, Carr, and Buechler 2005). There are costs to reducing wastewater volume. The optimal treatment strategy will vary with wastewater source and constituents, and with the crops being irrigated (Emongor and Ramolemana 2004; Fine, Halperin, and Hadas 2006; Tidåker and others 2006).

Implement economic incentives

Incentives for reusing treated wastewater are helpful in areas where water users can choose among water sources of different quality. Lower water prices and subsidies for purchasing new equipment can speed the pace at which farmers and firms begin using marginal-quality water. Incentives can be combined with monitoring to ensure compliance with incentive programs and safe use of wastewater.

Farmers facing low prices or abundant supplies of irrigation water will not strive to reduce the volumes of saline or sodic drainage water leaving their farms. Water prices and allocations that reflect water scarcity and externalities will encourage farmers to consider the off-farm impacts of their irrigation and drainage activities.

In some areas subsidies for farm-level investments in irrigation equipment will be more effective than higher water prices in reducing effluent. For example, farmers can be encouraged to use drip systems instead of sprinklers when irrigating with water that is saline or contains other undesirable constituents (Oron and others 1999a, 1999b, 2002; Capra and Scicolone 2004).

The challenge for public agencies is to determine the best mix of policies to reduce wastewater generation and ensure safe and efficient use of wastewater

Improve financial management

Public agencies in many developing countries have limited ability to invest in wastewater treatment plants and programs to optimize wastewater reuse. Policies and institutions can be helpful in raising the funds needed for those activities. Volumetric charges for wastewater will encourage reuse and discourage discharge into natural waterways or facilities operated by a wastewater agency. There is conceptual justification for programs that generate revenue by charging water users a fee per unit of effluent they generate (the polluter pays principle), particularly when the revenue is used to construct facilities for collecting, treating, and reusing wastewater.

Protect and compensate the poor

Policies to protect the poor will be needed in conjunction with successful reductions in wastewater volume and improvements in wastewater management. Public officials must consider potential impacts on the poor when designing policies and programs. The greatest challenge might be ensuring that low-income residents of peri-urban and rural areas who rely on wastewater for crop production are not deprived of their livelihoods. Many poor farmers have been using wastewater for years without formal water rights. Improving water management practices in upper portions of a watershed or urban area, to reduce wastewater volume, will also reduce a portion of the irrigation supply for those farmers. Improvements in water treatment can also reduce water supply if the treated water is transferred from its original point of use. Policies can be implemented to compensate poor farmers by providing them with alternative sources of irrigation water or giving them payments or training that would enable them to pursue alternative livelihood activities. Policies that enable the poor to reduce wastewater use gradually, while seeking other livelihood activities, might be wiser than policies that cause sharp disruptions in wastewater supply.

Consult widely with individuals and organizations

Public agencies must consult broadly with individuals, firms, and organizations that might be affected by policies on wastewater generation and use. Stakeholder involvement can improve the dissemination of information and enhance the success of wastewater reuse projects (Janosova and others 2006). Much of the wastewater used in crop production in peri-urban areas in developing countries is applied untreated by small-scale farmers. Their

Agricultural use of
marginal-quality water—
opportunities and challenges **11**

knowledge and experience might be helpful in designing effective policies. Improvements in communication among government agencies and environmental organizations with expertise in wastewater issues also can enhance public policies for wastewater management.

Conduct public awareness programs

Many farmers and consumers in developing countries are not aware of the potential health impacts of wastewater. Many also lack information on appropriate food hygiene practices. Public programs that inform farmers and consumers about potential health impacts and mitigation measures can reduce health problems and social costs. Information on postharvest handling practices will also enhance consumer safety. Context-sensitive guidelines need to describe the types and amounts of wastewater that can be used effectively for irrigation (IWMI 2006), while in many areas inspection and certification programs are needed to ensure consumer safety regarding vegetables and other produce sold in urban markets.

> Policies to protect the poor will be needed in conjunction with successful reductions in wastewater volume and improvements in wastewater management

Special attention should be paid to gender when designing these education programs on farmer and consumer safety. Educational efforts pertaining to wastewater will be most successful if they are designed to match the roles and availabilities of men and women in farming communities. In many farm households women are directly involved in agriculture besides being responsible for food preparation. Women also might have limited time for attending special classes or training sessions.

Support research, development, and outreach

Many farmers might use the nutrient content of wastewater more effectively if they had better information about constituent loads in their water supply and nutrient levels in soils. Public funding of research, development, and outreach on farm-level reuse strategies is justified by the public benefits gained from using wastewater more effectively in agriculture.

Better data on the nature and extent of wastewater use for irrigation can enhance the efforts of public agencies and researchers. Information describing the volume and quality of wastewater used and the geographic distribution of wastewater use within peri-urban areas can be helpful when designing policies to improve water management and protect public health. Incentives might be offered to small-scale farmers to report wastewater reuse, yields, and observable impacts on humans, plants, and soils. Public agencies also might work with farmers to establish wastewater monitoring programs.

Strengthen political will

Inadequate efforts to improve wastewater management, treatment, and reuse cannot be attributed only to a lack of technical information or inadequate knowledge of policy impacts. In many areas inadequate public involvement reflects a lack of political will, inadequate investment, or insufficient institutional capacity or coordination.

There is no simple formula for strengthening political will. Public officials must appreciate the scarcity value of water and the impacts of poor water quality and inefficient use on public health, economic growth, the environment, and rural and urban households. Leaders must appreciate the potential for improving livelihoods and enhancing public welfare by improving land and water management practices. International agencies, donors, and nongovernmental organizations can provide political leaders with information, encourage innovative policy choices, and motivate greater public involvement in water management efforts.

Minimize risk and uncertainty

Some of the implications of irrigating with wastewater are uncertain. Farmers, consumers, and researchers will gain knowledge of the potential impacts of wastewater and on health and the environment as experience increases. Given the inherent uncertainty and potential social costs, public agencies should adopt the precautionary principle when designing policies for wastewater use. Policies should minimize the potentially harmful long-term impacts, even at the cost of lower near-term financial gains to farmers and consumers. Public awareness campaigns might be helpful in gaining support for policies that reflect the precautionary principle. Special efforts will be needed in areas where many residents are not literate and where farmers depend on wastewater to support their livelihoods.

> Much of the wastewater used in crop production in peri-urban areas in developing countries is applied untreated by small-scale farmers. Their knowledge and experience might be helpful in designing effective policies

Improve the management of saline and sodic water

Policies such as requiring farmers to reuse or dispose of saline drainage water within their farming operation can motivate farmers to improve their management of saline and sodic water. Water quality agencies might limit the discharge of drainage water to surface streams or enforce ambient water quality standards pertaining to drainage water. In many areas enforcement of water quality standards will encourage farmers and water user associations to improve water management practices.

The discharge of saline drainage water by farmers at the headends of many irrigation schemes degrades the quality of water available to farmers at the tailends. Salt accumulation in the soils of tailend farmers causes yield to decline and reduces crop choices. Scheme-level planning is thus required. Aggregate productivity in many irrigation schemes can be increased by improving water management on headend farms. Policies that improve the distribution of higher quality water among headend and tailend farmers can reduce drainage water volume and enhance crop production in tailend portions of irrigation schemes.

Research and development of new methods for using saline and sodic water will also be helpful. More research is needed on the optimal management of salt-tolerant crops, particularly when high- and low-salt content irrigation water is combined. Blending irrigation water is appropriate in some applications, while cyclic reuse is appropriate in others. Improvements in extension services are also needed to inform farmers about new methods of using saline and sodic water.

Strengthen regional policies and institutions

Regional institutions such as federations of water user associations will be helpful in motivating farmers to minimize harmful impacts on downstream users (Beltrán 1999). Regional associations can be formed to encourage farmers to reduce surface runoff and subsurface drainage. In some areas existing water user associations can expand their activities

Agricultural use of
marginal-quality water—
opportunities and challenges

11

to include drainage water management. Regional associations can manage the generation, collection, and reuse of drainage water.

River basin authorities can implement data collection programs and coordinate analysis to enhance policy efforts. In areas lacking institutional support for a river basin authority, it might be necessary to improve coordination among ministries and agencies responsible for managing land and water resources.

Invest in infrastructure and institutional capacity

Optimal management of wastewater and saline and sodic water requires supporting infrastructure. Public investments are needed in many areas to enhance the ability of water users to improve management practices. Improvements in physical infrastructure are needed in some areas to increase the efficiency of water delivery systems and the management and disposal of wastewater. In other areas institutional capacity must be increased to enable efficient use of existing infrastructure and natural resources.

Reviewers

Chapter review editor: David Seckler and Sawfat Abdel-Dayem.
Chapter reviewers: Paul Appasamy, Netij Ben Mechlia, Shashikant Chopde, Peter Cookey, Caroline Gerwe, Frans Huibers, Elisabeth Kvarnstrom, Ghulam Murtaza, Julian Martinez Beltran, Lisa Schipper, Michel Soulie, John Stenhouse, Farhana Sultana, and Girma Tadesse.

References

AATSE (Australian Academy of Technological Sciences and Engineering). 2004. *Water Recycling in Australia.* Victoria, Australia.

Abdel-Dayem, S. 1999. "A Framework for Sustainable Use of Low Quality Water in Irrigation." Proceedings of the 17th International Congress on Irrigation and Drainage, 11–19 September, Granada, Spain.

Abdel-Dayem, S., J. Hoevenaars, P.P. Mollinga, W. Scheumann, R. Slootweg, and F. van Steenbergen. 2004. *Reclaiming Drainage: Toward an Integrated Approach.* Agricultural and Rural Development Report 1. Washington D.C.: World Bank.

Adeel, Z. 2001. *Arsenic Crisis Today—A Strategy for Tomorrow.* UNU Policy Paper. United Nations University, Tokyo.

APP (Advisory Panel Project on Water Management). 2002. "Egyptian-Dutch Advisory Panel Project: Revision of the Reuse Mixing Policy." Consultancy Report Submitted to the 36th Panel Meeting. Kaliubia, Egypt.

Asano, T., ed. 1998. *Wastewater Reclamation and Reuse.* Water Quality Management Library Series. Vol. 10. Lancaster, Pa.: Technomic Publishing Co., Inc.

Asano, T., and J.A. Cotruvo. 2004. "Groundwater Recharge with Reclaimed Municipal Wastewater: Health and Regulatory Considerations." *Water Research* 38 (8): 1941–51.

Attia, F., and A. Fadlelmawla. 2005. *Development of Groundwater Protection Criteria.* International Hydrological Programme-Regional Network on Groundwater Protection in the Arab Region. United Nations Educational, Scientific, and Cultural Organization, Cairo.

Ayers, R.S., and D.W. Westcot, eds. 1985. *Water Quality for Agriculture.* FAO Irrigation and Drainage Paper 29 (Rev. 1). Rome: Food and Agriculture Organization of the United Nations.

Beltrán, J.M. 1999. "Irrigation with Saline Water: Benefits and Environmental Impact." *Agricultural Water Management* 40 (2–3):183–94.

Blumenthal, U., and A. Peasey. 2002. "Critical Review of Epidemiological Evidence of the Health Effects of Wastewater and Excreta Use in Agriculture." World Health Organization, Geneva.

Blumenthal, U.J., E. Cifuentes, S. Bennett, M. Quigley, and G. Ruiz-Palacios. 2001. "The Risk of Enteric Infections Associated with Wastewater Reuse: The Effect of Season and Degree of Storage of Wastewater." *Transactions of the Royal Society of Tropical Medicine and Hygiene* 95 (2): 131–37.

Capra, A., and B. Scicolone. 2004. "Emitter and Filter Tests for Wastewater Reuse by Drip Irrigation." *Agricultural Water Management* 68 (2): 135–49.

Drechsel, P., U.J. Blumenthal, and B. Keraita. 2002. "Balancing Health and Livelihoods: Adjusting Wastewater Irrigation Guidelines for Resource-poor Countries." *Urban Agricultural Magazine* 8: 7–9.

Drechsel, P., M. Giordano, and L.A. Gyiele. 2004. *Valuing Nutrients in Soil and Water: Concepts and Techniques with Examples from IWMI Studies in the Developing World.* Research Report 82. International Water Management Institute, Colombo.

DRI (Drainage Research Institute), Louis Berger International, Inc., and Pacer Consultants. 1997. *Drainage Water Irrigation Project (Final Report).* Cairo.

Egypt, MWRI (Ministry of Water Resources and Irrigation). 2004. *The National Water Resources Plan.* Cairo.

El-Guindy, S. 2003. "Requested Protections and Safe Guards against Misuse of the Agricultural Drainage Water for Irrigation Purposes in Egypt." In R. Ragab, ed., *Sustainable Strategies for Irrigation in Salt-prone Mediterranean Region: A System Approach: Proceedings of an International Workshop. Cairo, Egypt, 8–10 December 2003.* Wallingford, UK: Centre for Ecology and Hydrology.

Emongor, V.E., and G.M. Ramolemana. 2004. "Treated Sewage Effluent (Water) Potential to Be Used for Horticultural Production in Botswana." *Physics and Chemistry of the Earth A/B/C* 29 (15–18): 1101–08.

Ensink, J.H.J., T. Mehmood, W. Van der Hoek, L. Raschid-Sally, and F.P. Amerasinghe. 2004. "A Nation-wide Assessment of Wastewater Use in Pakistan: An Obscure Activity or a Vitally Important One?" *Water Policy* 6: 197–206.

Ensink, J.H.J., W. Van der Hoek, Y. Matsuno, S. Munir, and M.R. Aslam. 2002. *Use of Untreated Wastewater in Peri-urban Agriculture in Pakistan: Risks and Opportunities.* Research Report 64. International Water Management Institute, Colombo.

Fine, P., R. Halperin, and E. Hadas. 2006. "Economic Considerations for Wastewater Upgrading Alternatives: An Israeli Test Case." *Journal of Environmental Management* 78 (2): 163–69.

Foster, S.S.D., H. Gale, and I. Hespanhol. 1994. *Impacts of Wastewater Use and Disposal on Groundwater.* Technical Report WD/94/55. Nottingham, UK: British Geological Survey.

Foster, S.S.D., H. Garduño, A. Tuinhof, K. Kemper, and M. Nanni. 2004. "Urban Wastewater as Groundwater Recharge: Evaluating and Managing the Risks and Benefits." Briefing Note 12. World Bank, Washington, D.C.

Ghassemi, F., A.J. Jakeman, and H.A. Nix. 1995. *Salinisation of Land and Water Resources: Human Causes, Extent, Management and Case Studies.* Wallingford, UK: CABI Publishing.

Grabow, G., and P.G. McCornick. Forthcoming. "Planning for Water Allocation and Water Quality Using a Spreadsheet-Based Model." *Journal of Water Resources Planning and Management.*

Heuperman, A.F., A.S. Kapoor, and H.W. Denecke. 2002. *Biodrainage—Principles, Experiences and Applications.* Knowledge Synthesis Report 6. Rome: International Programme for Technology and Research in Irrigation and Drainage.

Huibers, F.P., and J.B. Van Lier. 2005. "Use of Wastewater in Agriculture: The Water Chain Approach." *Irrigation and Drainage* 54 (Suppl. 1): S-3–S-9.

Hussain, I., L. Raschid, M.A. Hanjra, F. Marikar, and W. van der Hoek. 2001. "A Framework for Analyzing Socioeconomic, Health and Environmental Impacts of Wastewater Re-use in Agriculture in Developing Countries." Working Paper 26. International Water Management Institute, Colombo.

———. 2002. "Wastewater Use in Agriculture: Review of Impacts and Methodological Issues in Valuing Impacts." Working Paper 37. International Water Management Institute, Colombo.

Idelovitch, E. 2001. "Wastewater Reclamation for Irrigation: The Dan Region Project in Israel." World Bank, Washington, D.C.

India CWC (Central Water Commission). 2002. *Water and Related Statistics.* New Delhi: Ministry of Water Resources, Central Water Commission, Water Planning and Projects Wing.

IPTRID (International Programme for Technology and Research in Irrigation and Drainage). 2005. *Towards Integrated Planning of Irrigation and Drainage in Egypt.* Rapid assessment study in support of the Integrated Irrigation Improvement Project. Rome.

IWMI (International Water Management Institute). 2003. *Confronting the Realities of Wastewater Use in Agriculture.* Water Policy Briefing 9. Colombo.

———. 2006. *Recycling Realities: Managing Health Risks to Make Wastewater an Asset.* Water Policy Briefing 17. Colombo.

Janosova, B., J. Miklankova, P. Hlavinek, and T. Wintgens. 2006. "Drivers for Wastewater Reuse: Regional Analysis in the Czech Republic." *Desalination* 187 (1–3): 103–14.

Jensen, J.R., N.C. Vinh, N.D. Minh, and R.W. Simmons. Forthcoming. "Wastewater Use in Irrigated Rice Production—A Case Study from the Red River Delta, Vietnam." Proceedings of the workshop on "Wastewater Reuse in Agriculture in Vietnam: Water Management, Environment and Human Health Aspects." Working Paper. International Water Management Institute, Columbo.

Agricultural use of
marginal-quality water—
opportunities and challenges 11

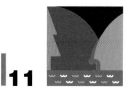

Jimenez, B. 2005. "Treatment Technology and Standards for Agricultural Wastewater Reuse: A Case Study in Mexico." *Irrigation and Drainage* 54 (Suppl. 1): S22–S33.

Jimenez, B., and T. Asano. 2004. "Acknowledge All Approaches: The Global Outlook on Reuse." *Water21* December 2004: 32–37.

Jimenez, B., and A. Chávez. 2004. "Quality Assessment of an Aquifer Recharged with Wastewater for its Potential Use as Drinking Source: El-Mezquital Valley Case." *Water Science and Technology* 50 (2): 269–76.

Jimenez, B., and H. Garduño. 2001. "Social, Political and Scientific Dilemmas for Massive Wastewater Reuse in the World." In C.K. Davis and R.E. McGinn, eds., *Navigating Rough Waters: Ethical Issues in the Water Industry.* Denver, Colo.: American Water Works Association.

Keraita, B.N., and P. Drechsel. 2004. "Agricultural Use of Untreated Urban Wastewater in Ghana." In C.A. Scott, N.I. Faruqui, and L. Raschid-Sally, eds., *Wastewater Use in Irrigated Agriculture.* Wallingford, UK: CABI Publishing.

Khalil, M. 1931. "The Pail Closet as an Efficient Means of Controlling Human Helminth Infection as Observed in Tura Prison, Egypt, with a Discussion on the Source of Ascaris Infection." *Annals of Tropical Medicine and Parasitology* 25: 35–62.

Krey, W. 1949. "The Darmstadt Ascariasis Epidemic and Its Control." *Zeitschrift fur Hygiene und Infektions Krankheiten* 129: 507-18

Lai, T.V. 2000. "Perspectives of Peri-urban Vegetable Production in Hanoi." Background paper prepared for the Action Planning Workshop of the CGIAR Strategic Initiative for Urban and Peri-Urban Agriculture (SIUPA), Hanoi, 6–9 June. Convened by International Potato Center (CIP), Lima.

Lazarova, V., and A. Bahri, eds. 2005. *Water Reuse for Irrigation: Agriculture, Landscapes, and Turf Grass.* Boca Raton, Fla.: CRC Press.

Maas, E.V., and S.R. Grattan. 1999. "Crop Yields as Affected by Salinity." In R.W. Skaggs and J. van Schilfgaarde, eds., *Agricultural Drainage.* Madison, Wisc.: American Society of Agronomy–Crop Science Society of America–Soil Science Society of America.

Mara, D. 2003. *Domestic Wastewater Treatment in Developing Countries.* London, UK: Earthscan.

Martijn, E., and M. Redwood. 2005. "Wastewater Irrigation in Developing Countries—Limitations for Farmers to Adopt Appropriate Practices." *Irrigation and Drainage* 54 (Suppl. 1): S-63–S-70.

McCornick, P. G., S. R. Grattan, and I. Abu-Eisheh. 2003. "Water Quality Challenges to Irrigated Agriculture Productivity in the Jordan Valley." In A.J. Clemmens and S.S. Anderson, eds., *Water for a Sustainable World—Limited Supplies and Expanding Demand: Proceeding of the Second International Conference on Irrigation and Drainage.* Phoenix, Ariz.: U.S. Commission on Irrigation and Drainage.

McCornick, P. G., A. Hijazi, and B. Sheikh. 2004. "From Wastewater Reuse to Water Reclamation: Progression of Water Reuse Standards in Jordan." In C. Scott, N.I. Faruqui, and L. Raschid, eds., *Wastewater Use in Irrigated Agriculture: Confronting the Livelihood and Environmental Realities.* Wallingford, UK: CABI Publishing.

Mexico CNA (Comisiòn Nacional del Agua). 2004. *Water Statistics.* Mexico City: National Water Commission. (In Spanish).

Minhas, P.S., and J.S. Samra. 2003. *Quality Assessment of Water Resources in the Indo-Gangetic Basin Part in India.* Karnal, India: Central Soil Salinity Research Institute.

———. 2004. *Wastewater Use in Peri-urban Agriculture: Impacts and Opportunities.* Karnal, India: Central Soil Salinity Research Institute.

Minhas, P.S., D.R. Sharma, and C.P.S. Chauhan. 2003. "Management of Saline and Alkali Waters for Irrigation." In *Advances in Sodic Land Reclamation.* International Conference on Management of Sodic Lands for Sustainable Agriculture, 9–14 February, Lucknow, India.

Moreno, F., F. Cabrera, E. Fernandez-Boy, I.F. Giron, J.E. Fernandez, and B. Bellido. 2001. "Irrigation with Saline Water in the Reclaimed Marsh Soils of South-west Spain: Impact on Soil Properties and Cotton and Sugar Beet Crops." *Agricultural Water Management* 48 (2): 133–50.

Ongley, E.D., ed. 1996. *Control of Water Pollution from Agriculture.* FAO Irrigation and Drainage Paper 55. Rome: Food and Agriculture Organization of the United Nations.

Oron, G., C. Campos, L. Gillerman, and M. Salgot. 1999a. "Wastewater Treatment, Renovation and Reuse for Agricultural Irrigation in Small Communities." *Agricultural Water Management* 38 (3): 223–34.

Oron, G., Y. DeMalach, L. Gillerman, I. David, and V.P. Rao. 1999b. "Improved Saline-water Use Under Subsurface Drip Irrigation." *Agricultural Water Management* 39 (1): 19–33.

Oron, G., Y. DeMalach, L. Gillerman, I. David, and S. Lurie. 2002. "Effect of Water Salinity and Irrigation Technology on Yield and Quality of Pears." *Biosystems Engineering* 81 (2): 237–47.

Oster, J.D., and S.R. Grattan. 2002. "Drainage Water Reuse." *Irrigation and Drainage Systems* 16 (4): 297–310.

Pescod, M.B., ed. 1992. *Wastewater Treatment and Use in Agriculture.* FAO Irrigation and Drainage Paper 47. Rome: Food and Agriculture Organization of the United Nations.

Qadir, M., A.D. Noble, J.D. Oster, S. Schubert, and A. Ghafoor. 2005. "Driving Forces for Sodium Removal during Phytoremediation of Calcareous Sodic and Saline-sodic Soils: A Review." *Soil Use and Management* 21 (2): 173–80.

Raschid-Sally, L., and D. Jayakody. Forthcoming. "Understanding the Drivers of Wastewater Agriculture in Developing Countries—Results from a Global Assessment." Comprehensive Assessment Research Report Series. International Water Management Institute, Colombo.

Raschid-Sally, L., and J. Parkinson. 2004. "Wastewater Reuse for Agriculture and Aquaculture—Current and Future Perspectives for Low-income Countries." *Waterlines Journal* 23 (1): 2–4.

Raschid-Sally, L., R. Carr, and S. Buechler. 2005. "Managing Wastewater Agriculture to Improve Livelihoods and Environmental Quality in Poor Countries." *Irrigation and Drainage* 54 (Suppl. 1): 11–22.

Rhoades, J.D. 1999. "Use of Saline Drainage Water for Irrigation." In R.W. Skaggs and J. van Schilfgaarde, eds., *Agricultural Drainage.* Madison, Wisc.: American Society of Agronomy, Crop Science Society of America, and Soil Science Society of America.

Rhoades, J.D., and A. Kandiah, eds. 1992. *The Use of Saline Waters for Crop Production.* FAO Irrigation and Drainage Paper 48. Rome: Food and Agriculture Organization of the United Nations.

Scott, C.A., N. I. Faruqui, and L. Raschid-Sally. 2004. "Wastewater Use in Irrigated Agriculture: Management Challenges in Developing Countries." In C.A. Scott, N.I. Faruqui, and L. Raschid-Sally, eds., *Wastewater Use in Irrigated Agriculture: Confronting the Livelihood and Environmental Realities.* Wallingford, UK; Colombo; and Ottawa, Canada: CABI Publishing, International Water Management Institute, and International Development Research Centre.

Scott, C.A., J.A. Zarazua, and G. Levine. 2000. *Urban Wastewater Reuse for Crop Production in the Water-short Guanajuato River Basin, Mexico.* IWMI Research Report 41. Colombo: International Water Management Institute.

Shuval, H.I., P. Yekutiel, and B. Fattal. 1984. "Epidemiological Evidence for Helminth and Cholera Transmission by Vegetables Irrigated with Wastewater: Jerusalem—A Case Study." *Water Science and Technology,* 17: 433–42.

Shuval, H.I., A. Adin, B. Fattal, E. Rawitz, and P. Yekutiel. 1986. *Wastewater Irrigation in Developing Countries: Health Effects and Technical Solutions.* Technical Paper 51. World Bank, Washington, D.C.

Skaggs, R.W., and J. Van Schilfgaarde, eds. 1999. *Agricultural Drainage.* Madison, Wisc.: American Society of Agronomy, Crop Science Society of America, and Soil Science Society of America.

Stenhouse, J., and J. Kijne. 2006. *Prospects for Productive Use of Saline Water in West Asia and North Africa.* Research Report 11 of the Comprehensive Assessment of Water Management in Agriculture. Colombo: International Water Management Institute.

Tanji, K., and N.C. Kielen, eds. 2002. *Agricultural Drainage Water Management in Arid and Semiarid Areas.* FAO Irrigation and Drainage Paper 61. Rome: Food and Agriculture Organization of the United Nations.

Tidåker, P., F. Kärrman, A. Baky, and H. Jönsson. 2006. "Wastewater Management Integrated with Farming—An Environmental Systems Analysis of a Swedish Country Town." *Resources, Conservation and Recycling* 47 (4): 295–315.

Toze, S. 2006. "Reuse of Effluent Water—Benefits and Risks." *Agricultural Water Management* 80 (1–3): 147–59.

Trang, D.T., W. van der Hoek, P.D. Cam, K.T. Vinh, N.V. Hoa, and A. Dalsgaard. 2006. "Low Risk for Helminth Infection in Wastewater-fed Rice Cultivation in Vietnam." *Journal of Water and Health* 4 (3): 321–331.

Ul-Hassan, M. 2002. "Maximising Private and Social Gains of Wastewater Agriculture in Haroonabad." *Urban Agriculture Magazine* 7 (August): 29–31.

Ul-Hassan, M., and N. Ali. 2002. "Potential for Blue-gray Water Trade-offs for Irrigation in Small Towns of Pakistan: A Case Study of Farmers' Costs and Benefits in Haroonabad." *The Pakistan Development Review* 41 (2): 161–77.

UNDP (United Nations Development Program). 1996. *Urban Agriculture: Food, Jobs and Sustainable Cities.* Publication Series for Habitat II, Volume One. New York.

USEPA (U.S. Environmental Protection Agency) and USAID (U.S. Agency for International Development). 2004. *Guidelines for Water Reuse.* Washington D.C.

Van der Hoek, W. 2004. "A Framework for a Global Assessment of the Extent of Wastewater Irrigation: The Need for a Common Wastewater Typology." In C.A. Scott, N.I. Faruqui, L. Raschid-Sally, eds., *Wastewater Use in Irrigated Agriculture: Confronting the Livelihood and Environmental Realities.* Wallingford, UK; Colombo; and Ottawa, Canada: CABI Publishing, International Water Management Institute, and International Development Research Centre.

Van der Hoek, W., M. Ul Hassan, J.H.J. Ensink, S. Feenstra, L. Rashid-Sally, S. Munir, M.R. Aslam, N. Ali, R. Hussain, and Y. Matsuno. 2002. *Urban Wastewater: A Valuable Resource for Agriculture.* Research Report 63. Colombo: International Water Management Institute.

Agricultural use of
marginal-quality water—
opportunities and challenges **11**

Watson, R.T., R.H. Moss, and M.C. Zinyowera, eds. 1998. *The Regional Impacts of Climate Change: An Assessment of Vulnerability.* Intergovernmental Panel on Climate Change. Cambridge, UK: Cambridge University Press.

Weber, B., and M. Juanicó. 2004. "Salt Reduction in Municipal Sewage Allocated for Reuse: The Outcome of a New Policy in Israel." *Water Science and Technology* 50 (2): 17–22.

WHO (World Health Organization). 1973. *Reuse of Effluents: Methods of Wastewater Treatment and Health Safeguards.* Technical Report Series 517. Geneva.

———. 1989. *Health Guidelines for the Use of Wastewater in Agriculture and Aquaculture.* Technical Report Series 778. Geneva.

———. 2005. *Using Economic Valuation Methods for Environment and Health Assessment.* The Health and Environment Linkages Initiative. World Health Organization and United Nations Environment Programme, Geneva and Nairobi. [www.who.int/heli/economics/valmethods/en/].

———. 2006. *Guidelines for the Safe Use of Wastewater, Excreta and Grey Water.* Volume 2. *Wastewater Use in Agriculture.* Geneva.

WHO (World Health Organization) and UNICEF (United Nations Children's Fund). 2000. *Global Water Supply and Sanitation Assessment 2000 Report.* Geneva and New York.

Freshwater fisheries

Artist: Supriyo Das, India

12 | Inland fisheries and aquaculture

Coordinating lead author: Patrick Dugan

Lead authors: Veliyil Vasu Sugunan, Robin L. Welcomme, Christophe Béné, Randall E. Brummett, and Malcolm C.M. Beveridge

Contributing authors: Kofi Abban, Upali Amarasinghe, Angela Arthington, Marco Blixt, Sloans Chimatiro, Pradeep Katiha, Jackie King, Jeppe Kolding, Sophie Nguyen Khoa, and Jane Turpie

Overview

Fish and other living aquatic resources of inland water ecosystems provide important services that are seriously undervalued [well established]. Inland fisheries and aquaculture contribute about 25% to the world's production of fish. In addition, many important estuarine and coastal fisheries are strongly linked to the ecological processes that occur in freshwater systems *[well established]*. The value of freshwater production to human nutrition and incomes is much greater than gross national production figures suggest. The bulk of production is generated by small-scale activities, with exceedingly high levels of participation not only in catching and farming, but also in processing and marketing. Inland fisheries are often critical to local food security *[well established]*.

  Most inland fisheries in the developing world are heavily exploited. While the fisheries are not necessarily overexploited in terms of gross production, individual species are often seriously overexploited. However, inland fisheries suffer greatly from environmental pressures, in particular deteriorating water quality and habitat *[well established]*. Many coastal and inshore marine systems are also affected by lower water quality and reduced availability of freshwater.

  Competition for water and aquatic habitat is the most critical challenge facing inland fisheries in many countries [well established]. The need for water to support fish and fisheries can conflict with the needs of other sectors, in particular agriculture, in both water quality and flow requirements for sustaining aquatic habitat. Decisions on water management frequently do not take into account the impact on fish and fisheries and on the rural livelihoods of the populations that depend on them. In part this is because inland fisheries are greatly undervalued in water management at local, national, and basin levels. Equally, there is a lack of knowledge of how to optimize ecosystem services, for example, through environmental flow and water productivity approaches that are needed to guide the allocation of sufficient water to sustain fish and fisheries.

Improving the consideration of fisheries in water management decisions requires better valuation methods and improved governance [established but incomplete]. Valuations need to pay more attention to nonformal values, especially those concerning livelihoods, food security, and biodiversity. Governance systems need to incorporate such values into cross-sectoral water management that recognizes the importance of ecosystem services. Decentralization may be a possible avenue toward these governance improvements but should be planned and implemented with care if equity in access to the resource, and its full development value, is to be fostered.

There are two broad challenges for fisheries production. The first is to sustain current levels of fisheries production and other ecosystem services through the provision of target-directed environmental flows that sustain or restore the aquatic environment, including its diversity *[established but incomplete]*, and improved management of capture fisheries. The second is to increase current levels of fisheries production through the wider adoption of methods for enhancing and intensifying production, such as stocking and aquaculture, that require adequate quantities of clean water, suitable habitat, and appropriate management arrangements *[established but incomplete]*. These challenges will be more successfully addressed by building partnerships between fisheries and other interest groups concerned with water management, especially those engaged in water management for agriculture, which are also searching for more efficient ways to increase the overall benefits of water productivity to food security and poverty reduction.

> There is a tradeoff between the use of water for agriculture and the provision of water in the quality and quantity required for fish production and the other goods and services generated by inland aquatic ecosystems

What inland fisheries and aquaculture contribute to economic and social development

Freshwater supplies are not only vital to river fisheries; they also sustain the fisheries of associated wetlands and influence estuarine and inshore marine fisheries.[1] Although fisheries are usually nonconsumptive users of water, they require particular quantities and seasonal timing of flows in rivers and their dependent wetlands, lakes, and estuaries. There is, therefore, a tradeoff between the use of water for agriculture and the provision of water in the quality and quantity required for fish production and the other goods and services generated by inland aquatic ecosystems (see chapter 6 on ecosystems).

Fisheries and aquaculture from lakes, reservoirs, rivers, ponds, and wetlands contributed about 25% (34 million metric tons) of reported world fisheries production in 2003 (FAO 2004). However, catches in rivers and associated wetlands are easy to underestimate because the contributions of numerous fisheries on smaller tributaries and water bodies are generally overlooked (Coates 2002) *[established but incomplete]*. Reported harvests from river fisheries alone have been shown to account for only some 30%–50% of actual catch (Kolding and van Zwieten forthcoming), and the contribution from inland fisheries is therefore believed to be significantly higher. In addition, the benefits of inland fisheries tend to accrue to local communities, in particular the rural poor, and their socioeconomic value is disproportionately high compared with other fisheries sectors such as high seas fisheries *[established but incomplete]*.

Despite the high productivity, water resources development planners give little recognition to freshwater-dependent fishery production or its ecological basis. Several factors contribute to this. One is the dearth of reliable data and scientific literature compared with that on industrial marine fisheries. The majority of freshwater fisheries are small-scale, spatially diffuse activities, and a significant part of the production is not commercialized or is marketed only through informal channels and is therefore not properly reflected in national economic statistics. As a consequence, these fisheries are often perceived as a low-value activity (Allan and others 2005). Aquaculture is better defined, although the reporting of fisheries that interface between enhanced natural fisheries and extensive aquaculture is less clear and makes the relative contribution of each sector difficult to assess. In addition, hydrological approaches to water management have tended to focus on in-stream quantitative flows, often ignoring the more important impacts on the quality and extent of adjacent wetlands.

> Despite the high productivity, water resources development planners give little recognition to freshwater-dependent fishery production or its ecological basis

The poor appreciation of the importance of the fishery sector has several consequences. It has exacerbated the lack of data, which has in turn hampered research and management (Misund, Kolding, and Fréon 2002) and may have biased policies and the allocation of national development resources away from fisheries. The contribution of fish to national GDP is underestimated in many countries, despite the importance to income and livelihoods. In turn, the legislative and policy frameworks for the management of inland fisheries and aquaculture development have either been absent or tended to focus on overexploitation as the primary issue when the priority need has been to improve environmental management. This impedes the role that these sectors can play at the scales of both national and local economies and in food security.

Contribution to the global economy

Fish is a highly traded commodity: roughly 33% of global fish output by value was traded across international borders in 2001 (Dey and others 2005), and it is now the fastest growing agricultural trade commodity on international markets *[well established]*. Since production remains more limited than for staple agricultural crops, and consumer demand for a healthier diet—often defined to include more fish—is increasing, the relative importance of fish is likely to continue to rise. In value terms the growth of trade in world fish products is greater than the increase in the net exports of other staple agricultural commodities such as coffee, bananas, rice, and tea (FAO 2002). In 2002 the value of world exports of fish and fish products increased to $58.2 billion—a 5% increase over 2000 (FAO 2004). At an estimated 8 million metric tons, the contribution of inland capture fisheries to total world fish production is small in comparison with marine capture fisheries and marine and inland aquaculture (figure 12.1). Nevertheless, inland fisheries have sustained annual growth of about 2% worldwide (FAO 2002), and the potential for further increases in production is high in some systems (Kolding and van Zwieten forthcoming) *[established but incomplete]*.

This overall growth, however, masks the more complex reality at the regional level (figure 12.2). The main increases have been in Africa and Asia. In Africa gains reflect

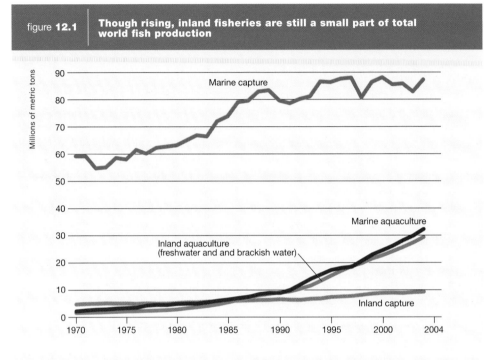

figure 12.1 | **Though rising, inland fisheries are still a small part of total world fish production**

Marine capture

Marine aquaculture

Inland aquaculture
(freshwater and and brackish water)

Inland capture

Millions of metric tons

90
80
70
60
50
40
30
20
10
0

1970   1975   1980   1985   1990   1995   2000   2004

Source: FAO 2004.

increased yield from lakes, especially of Nile perch (*Lates niloticus*) from Lake Victoria. Production in Asia has increased for a number of reasons, notably because of the proliferation of culture-based fisheries in Bangladesh and China, but also because of improved catch statistics from the Mekong River Basin countries, among others. In contrast, declines in catches are observed in Canada and the United States, as well as in Europe, although there the economic values of recreational fisheries dominate.

With a farmgate value of $28 billion in 2003, some three times that of inland capture fisheries, the contribution of freshwater aquaculture has increased rapidly in recent decades (FAO 2004). It is now the major contributor to inland fisheries production, having overtaken inland capture fisheries in 1986. The geographic significance of aquaculture is still uneven, with the major developments concentrated in Asia and production relatively low in Africa and some parts of Latin America.

Contribution to the national economy

Inland fisheries, and related export and regional trade, can play a significant role in the economy of regions and countries. The sector contributes 7% to GDP in Cambodia (photo 12.1) and 4% in Bangladesh. In Africa inland fisheries provide employment and income for several million people. A recent estimate of employment and income for seven major river basins finds that in West and Central Africa alone fisheries provide a livelihood to

Photo by C. Bene

Photo 12.1 In Cambodia inland fisheries play a major role in the livelihoods of millions of people

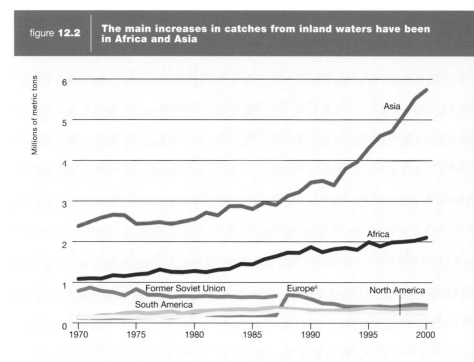

figure **12.2** | **The main increases in catches from inland waters have been in Africa and Asia**

a. Includes data for the countries of the former Soviet Union from 1988 onward, including countries in Central Asia.
Source: FAO 2002.

more than 227,000 full-time fishers and yield an annual catch of about 570,000 tons with a first-sale value of $295 million (table 12.1; Neiland and Béné forthcoming). The study also estimates that the total potential annual fisheries production for the region (about 1.34 million tons with an annual value of $750 million) is more than twice the estimated actual production.[2] Freshwater and brackish water aquaculture also play a major macroeconomic role in some Asian countries, notably as a source of foreign exchange and employment.

Contribution to the local economy

Where small-scale inland fisheries or aquaculture has been supported and well managed, fish-related activities play a critical role in generating wealth and sustaining economic growth (Béné 2006) [*well established*]. For example, research in the Zambezi floodplain reveals that inland fisheries generate more cash for households than cattle rearing in most cases and more than crop production in some cases (table 12.2). In Sri Lanka recent economic valuations have put the value of fisheries at about 18% of total economic returns to water in irrigated paddy production (Renwick 2001). This capacity of small-scale fisheries to generate cash, however, is still poorly recognized by both academics and decisionmakers. In addition, because fishers and, to a lesser extent, fish-farmers, can access cash year-round by selling fish, fisheries provide a "bank in the water" for remote rural populations that

table **12.1**	Contribution of fisheries of the major river basins and lakes in West and Central Africa to employment and income				
		Actual production		Potential production	
River basins and lakes	**Employment** (fishers)	**Volume** (metric tons per year)	**Value** (millions of US dollars per year)	**Volume** (metric tons per year)	**Value** (millions of US dollars per year)
River basins					
Senegal-Gambia	25,500	30,500	16.78	112,000	61.60
Volta (rivers)	7,000	13,700	7.12	16,000	8.32
Niger-Benue	64,700	236,500	94.60	205,610	82.24
Logone-Chari	6,800	32,200	17.71	130,250	71.64
Congo-Zaire	62,000	119,500	47.80	520,000	208.00
Atlantic coastal	6,000	30,700	46.66	118,000	179.30
Lakes					
Volta	20,000	40,000	28.40	62,000	44.02
Chad	15,000	60,000	33.00	165,000	90.75
Kainji	20,000	6,000	3.30	6,000	3.30
Total	227,000	569,100	295.17	1,334,860	749.17

Note: Table excludes the numerous men and women who engage in part-time (seasonal or occasional) fishing.

Source: Neiland and Béné forthcoming.

lack access to formal financial systems. This contrasts with agriculture, where farmers have to invest and then wait for harvest before earning cash returns.

In some river basins recreational fisheries also contribute significantly to the local economy. In Europe, for instance, the inland recreational fishing industry has been valued as high as $25 billion a year (Cowx 2002). Increasing numbers of developing countries, such as Argentina, Brazil, Chile, India, and several states of the Zambezi River Basin, are also using part of their fishery resource for recreational fisheries to boost their local tourist economy.

Contribution to gender empowerment

The water sector is often presented as a key entry point for poverty alleviation and gender empowerment (see chapter 4 on poverty). While professional fish capture (harvesting) is dominated by men, post-harvest activities (fish processing, fish retailing, and trading) are often done by women, in particular in Africa but also in many other parts of the world (photo 12.2) [*well established*]. Uneducated and poor women are often involved in post-harvest activities, which do not require large capital investments or high technical skills. A large proportion of small-scale (household) fishers are women and children. Some may be so successful in running their fish trade that they become owners of boats or outboard engines or are able to provide loans to fishers to purchase fishing equipment.

For millions of other women, however, fish processing and trade are more about economic survival. They often operate in an informal environment, making their contributions

table **12.2**	Contribution of fisheries and other activities to households' cash income in different parts of the Zambezi River Basin (US dollars per household per year)							
	Barotse floodplain		Caprivi-Chobe wetlands		Lower Shire wetlands		Zambezi Delta	
Activity	Value	Share (%)	Value	Share (%)	Value	Share (%)	Value	Share (%)
Cattle	120	28	422	37	31	7	0	..
Crops	91	22	219	19	298	66	121	48
Fish	180	43	324	28	56	12	100	39
Wild animals	6	1	49	4	1	..	0.4	..
Wild plants	24	6	121	11	48	11	29	11
Wild foods	0	..	11	1	7	2	4	2
Clay[a]	2	..	0	..	8	2	0.1	..

.. Less than one.
a. For pots and other utensils.
Source: Turpie and others 1999.

less visible than those of the rest of the sector. For these women, the income generated by post-harvest activities is often their only source of cash income, in particular in societies where men control a large part of the household's main cash-generating activities *[established but incomplete]*. Studies have shown that a disproportionately high number of vulnerable women, such as female heads of households, are involved in post-harvest fishery activities, which then play a crucial safety-net function.

These fish-related activities represent a vital element of the day to day struggle for economic and social empowerment. That struggle is often exacerbated by the fact that women are rarely recognized as legitimate stakeholders in the sector and the management

Photo 12.2 Fish trade can contribute to the economic empowerment of women

process, and their specific needs and aspirations are not systematically integrated into the design of fisheries and aquaculture policies and management.

Aquaculture

'
Aquaculture contributes directly to increasing the productivity of water

Aquaculture is the farming of fish and other aquatic organisms and contributes directly to increasing the productivity of water. Aquaculture consists of a flexible and adaptable set of technologies, species, and systems ranging from simple ponds receiving no inputs and infrequent stocking to massive, high-technology cage or raceway systems that can produce up to 100 kilograms (kg) per cubic meter of fish. Many of these systems are relevant to the needs and contexts of developing countries and water-stressed countries (table 12.3).

Most aquaculture is conducted in earthen ponds, but at a wide range of intensities. At the low end are small ponds of less than 500 square meters, which contribute to the stability and durability of small-scale farming systems in Africa, Asia, and Latin America. When regularly stocked and fertilized, these units produce 1,000–2,000 kg per hectare per year of fish for household consumption and sale or barter. Even on this scale aquaculture has been shown to substantially improve the economic and biophysical functioning of farms (Dey and others 2006).

At the higher end of the pond aquaculture spectrum are intensive systems that use mechanical aeration and pelleted feeds to overcome natural constraints to productivity. When the necessary inputs (feeds, fingerlings, fuel, electricity, spare parts) and infrastructure (roads, markets) are available, these systems regularly produce more than 10,000 kg per hectare per year and proportionally large returns to investment (figure 12.3). However, overloading ecosystems in this way decreases the sustainability of other ecosystem services. Catastrophic disease problems have been known to devastate the industry, as occurred in Asian penaeid shrimp farming in the 1990s. Destruction of mangroves for

| table **12.3** | Productivity from aquaculture systems in developing countries |

Production system	Production volume (kilograms per hectare)
Tilapia, unfertilized ponds (Diana 1997)	320
Red Swamp Crayfish, extensive rice paddies (Arringnon and others 1994)	750
Malaysian prawn, fed ponds (Lake Harvest Aquaculture, Ltd. 2003)	2,500
Tilapia, fertilized ponds (Diana 1997)	3,200
Tilapia, fed ponds (Diana 1997)	5,900
Tilapia, intensive ponds (Diana 1997)	10,000
Indian carp polyculture (Murthy 2002)	13,600
Clarias, flow-through ponds (Hatch and Hanson 1992)	40,000
Tilapia, fed cages (Arringnon and others 1994)	500,000
Common carp, intensive cages (Akiyama 1991)	1,100,000
Clarias, flow-through tanks (Hatch and Hanson 1992)	8,500,000

figure **12.3**	**Production from different capture and culture systems varies greatly**

1	Recirculation systems	8	Heavily stocked, fertilized ponds
2	Raceways	9	Extensive stocked unfertilized ponds
3	Cages	10	Drain-in ponds
4	Completely fed and aerated ponds	11	Extensively stocked natural systems
5	Fertilized and fed ponds	12	Tropical lakes and rivers
6	Brush parks and pens	13	Temperate lakes and rivers
7	Fertilized ponds	14	Cold temperate lakes and rivers

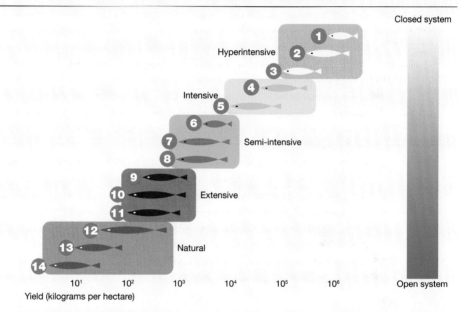

Source: Adapted from Welcomme and Bartley 1998.

pond construction, although now curtailed in most places, has also had serious negative social and economic effects on rural communities (Primavera 1997). Between these two extremes lies a wide variety of productive and sustainable fish culture systems. Ponds can produce 3,000–5,000 kg per hectare per year on agricultural by-products such as brewery waste, oilseed cakes, brans, and manures and can add value to processing while transforming low-value products into high-value animal protein. Fish are cold blooded and neutrally buoyant, so they do not waste energy on keeping warm or resisting gravity, making them more energy efficient to grow than other animals.

Integrated agriculture-aquaculture—taking advantage of economic synergies

Aquaculture probably began in Asia as a modification of an existing farming system to include fish (Beveridge and Little 2002). Many farmers who do not consider themselves aquaculturists stock fish into reservoirs or livestock watering ponds for mosquito and weed control, but benefit additionally through recreational fishing and improved household food security. Rice farmers in Asia have traditionally managed the aquatic fauna of paddy fields as a valuable supplement to rice production. Examples of integrated agriculture-aquaculture systems are now found throughout the world. The basic principles are to use the nutrients found in agricultural by-products for fish production and to optimize the agricultural use of water. Fish production has been successfully integrated into row crops (especially rice), hydroponic horticultural systems, silkworm production, and animal husbandry (pigs, poultry, rabbits, small ruminants, cattle).

> As with other agricultural diversification strategies, integrated agriculture and aquaculture systems also reduce risks to vulnerable, often rain-fed, small-scale farming systems

Driving integrated agriculture-aquaculture systems are the economic synergies to be had by amortizing capital and labor investments over a wider range of production units. Although these systems are knowledge intensive, overall costs for inputs, weed control, and waste disposal are reduced while profits are enhanced *[well established]*. As with other agricultural diversification strategies (intercropping, crop rotations), integrated agriculture and aquaculture systems also reduce risks to vulnerable, often rain-fed, small-scale farming systems by adding a production module that:

- Does not require daily feeding (fish may not grow, but will not normally regress with irregular feeding).
- Requires minimal labor (less than 10% of that needed for crops and 30% of that needed for other types of animal husbandry).
- Holds water for emergency use by the household or other production units.
- Produces a high-value crop that can be eaten by the family or sold.

A widespread type of integrated agriculture and aquaculture is the integration of fish into rice paddies. As most rice is grown in standing water, a certain number of fish are always present in the system, although this has been reduced in some areas by the need to use pesticides and herbicides with high-yielding systems. Typically, "natural" rice paddies produce 120–300 kg per hectare per year of diverse mixed fish and other animals that contribute directly to household diets and in some cases to profit margins. More intensively managed fish stocking and harvesting have been shown to increase rice yields (through weed control and soil aeration) by some 10% while producing up to 1,500 kg per hectare of fish and reducing both the need for pesticides and the cost (dela Cruz 1994; Halwart and Gupta 2004).

China (3.3 million hectares) and India (2.5 million hectares) have the largest areas under rice-fish cultivation, followed by Indonesia, Malaysia, Thailand, and Viet Nam. The community-based management of fisheries, aquaculture, and rice farming practiced in Bangladesh (photo 12.3) and Sri Lanka is a good example of how to achieve maximum synergy through appropriate technical and management interventions (Dey and Prein 2003). Fish production on these floodplains has increased from the traditional 50–70 kg per hectare to 650–1700 kg per hectare, while maintaining rice production at 6–7 metric tons per hectare.

Aquatic invertebrates, including mosquito larvae, form a major part of the food chain in rice paddy ecosystems, and fish predation on these has been shown to reduce the incidence of malaria and possibly other diseases (Nalim 1994).

Photo by R. Welcomme

Photo 12.3 Rice-fish integrated culture in Bangladesh

Cage aquaculture—flexible, but experiencing setbacks

Tilapia, carp, catfish, and a number of other species are produced in cages (Beveridge 2004). Provided that water currents are sufficient to disperse metabolic wastes from the cages, production can be adapted to the overall carrying capacity of the river, lake, or reservoir in which they are situated to prevent excessive environmental change. Sustainable production per cycle in such systems is typically in the range of 10–50 kg per cubic meter, depending on the natural productivity of the water, the ability of the ecosystem to absorb wastes, and other uses for the water, such as for drinking. The fish in these systems must be fed more or less complete diets, meaning that substantial inputs of nutrients to natural waters are sometimes unavoidable, which can increase the risk of surface water pollution and eutrophication. On the other hand, in irrigated systems the introduction of caged fish and their feeds, by increasing nutrient concentrations, can reduce fertilizer costs and increase yields of the irrigated crops (Beveridge and Muir 1999).

Cage culture technology can increase the overall production of valuable table fish and mitigate the effects of environmental changes. It also has social advantages in that landless people can find habitation and employment in cage aquaculture (Costa Pierce 2002). Small-scale cage aquaculture has been shown to be a flexible technology adaptable to the needs of poor people, as in Bangladesh. By placing only the cages and their contents under the ownership of the landless, cage aquaculture is not reliant on ownership or leasing of land or a water body and promotes the use of otherwise "fallow" water bodies (Hambrey, Beveridge, and McAndrew 2001). Operations carried out over shorter periods, such as fish overwintering, nursing, and fattening in small cages, fit well with the income-generating strategies of the poor by providing them with a potential source of income in periods of hardship and shortage (McAndrew, Little, and Beveridge 2000).

There are also a number of associated industries such as cage construction, feed supply, and transport of products that can serve as a nucleus for the development of whole regions, as happened with the Chilean salmon industry. When integrated in ponds, cage culture allows the simultaneous farming of fish species at different trophic levels (caged fish are fed high-protein diets, while open-pond filter feeding species depend on caged-fish wastes), enabling incremental production of biomass per unit of water while recycling nutrients (Yang and Lin 2000).

Cage culture has suffered setbacks, however, as conflicts with other users and environmental externalities (pollution) have arisen, prompting planners to adopt a more integrated approach (Beveridge and Muir 1999). It has proved difficult to estimate environmental capacity or to implement environmental management plans, resulting in overexploitation of lake environments, with occasional fish kills and economic hardship for those involved (Beveridge 2004; Abery and others 2005). A further problem has been the guarantee of access rights for landless poor people who can benefit from cage technology once it has proved economically viable. There are also fears that placing cages in canals might reduce water currents, thereby increasing deposition of solids and increasing canal maintenance costs. As a result, cage farming in irrigation canals is prohibited in some countries.

> Cage culture technology can increase the production of valuable table fish, mitigate the effects of environmental changes, and provide habitation and employment for landless people

Water use in aquaculture—wide variability in requirements

Surprisingly, fish production uses no more water—and in many cases much less—than the production of other animal foods (Phillips, Beveridge, and Clarke 1991; Brummett 1997, 2006; Verdegem, Bosma, and Verreth 2006) and, for the case of rainfed systems, the periodicity of water supply is also much less critical for fish than for crops such as maize. However, care must be taken in comparing water consumption by various types of aquaculture and livestock and crops (table 12.4). Data come from different sources and cover a considerable period of time, and assumptions are often unstated.

Although aquaculture has tended to become more efficient in use of water, it is nonetheless highly variable, with water use for intensive aquaculture generally being higher where there are no incentives to reduce use. Water use includes both consumptive use (losses in pond systems associated with seepage and evaporation) and nonconsumptive

table 12.4	Water requirements for various types of aquaculture	
Food crop/production system	Water requirement (metric tons per cubic meter)	Relative importance of nonconsumptive water losses in aquaculture
Potatoes	500	
Wheat	900	
Sorghum	1,110	
Corn (maize)	1,400	
Rice	1,912	
Soybeans	2,000	
Broiler chickens	3,500	
Beef	100,000	
Clarias; intensive, static ponds	50–200	Low to medium
Tilapia; extensive, static ponds	3,000–5,000	Medium to high
Tilapia; sewage, minimal exchange ponds	1,500–2,000	Medium to high
Tilapia; intensive, aerated ponds	21,000	Low to medium
Carp/tilapia polyculture; conventional ponds	12,000	Medium to high
Carp/tilapia polyculture; semi-intensive ponds	5,000	Low to medium
Carp/tilapia polyculture; intensive ponds	2,250	Low to medium
Carp; intensive raceways	740,000	Low
Channel catfish; intensive ponds	3,000–6,000	Low to medium
Trout; raceways	63,000–252,000	Low
Salmonids; ponds/tanks	252,000	Low to medium
Salmonids; cages	2,260,000	None
Penaeid shrimp; semi-intensive ponds	11,000–21,430	Low to medium
Penaeid shrimp; intensive ponds	29,000–43,000	Low
Penaeid shrimp; intensive raceways	55,125	Low

Source: Philipps, Beveridge, and Clarke 1991; Piemental and others 1997; Brummett 2006.

use (water that passes through the aquaculture system and is returned to the river or lake from which it was taken with little need for treatment). Unlike the case in agriculture, nonconsumptive losses can be high in aquaculture. Data in table 12.4 also do not include indirect water use associated with aquaculture feeds (see Brummett 2006 and Verdegem, Bosma, and Verreth 2006 for discussions). (For more detailed consideration of water use in agriculture, readers should consult the appropriate chapters in this volume.) Note too that there are various ways to express water consumption: water use per unit of biomass production or per unit of protein or in energy production terms (see Brummett 2006 for discussion).

Keeping water flowing

Freshwater fish resources are probably among the most resilient harvestable natural resources, provided their habitat, including the quantity, timing, and variability of river flow, is maintained (Welcomme and Petr 2004) *[well established]*. Their management and conservation can be approached only at the ecosystem level (figure 12.4), as changes in flow and water quality in rivers and river-dependent water bodies can have major impacts on fisheries production there and downstream. These changes may arise naturally, due to climatic variability, as in Sahelian rivers (Dansoko, Breman, and Daget 1976; Lae and others 2004). More commonly, they result from human modifications to the flow regime and the functioning of the ecosystem, in particular from reduced extent and duration of flooding that undermine biological production and reduce the potential for fisheries *[well established]*.

> Many species of fish and other aquatic organisms are sensitive to variations in the timing, quantity, quality, and temperature of water

Rivers and associated wetlands—maintaining environmental flows

Reduced flows in main river channels lead to significant changes, in particular reductions in area of associated wetlands (floodplains and floodplain swamps and lakes). This results in net production losses through direct habitat loss. The direct conversion of wetlands to agricultural use has similar consequences.

Many species of fish and other aquatic organisms are sensitive to variations in the timing, quantity, quality, and temperature of water, which are important, for example, as essential triggers to migration and breeding *[well established]*. Different fish species generally use different parts of the aquatic system, including the main channels of rivers, seasonally attached wetlands, lakes and reservoirs, and estuaries and near-shore marine areas. Some species use all or many of these areas and need to migrate between them. All these areas have to be treated as a continuum. Different species have different flow needs, and most species react negatively to changes in the hydrograph (Bunn and Arthington 2002).

Changes to river morphology due to altered flows may interfere with the connectivity and channel diversity that are essential for the survival of many species (Dollar 2004). Other changes include silting or removal of critical substrates that act as spawning sites for many species and a source of invertebrate food for others (Arthington and others 2004). Where water quality is poor, reduced flows increase the risk of deoxygenation and other effects of contamination. Hydrological conditions that fall outside the range of natural variation in rivers may cause the fauna to become simplified, with the replacement of

figure **12.4** **Schematic view of a river basin showing ecological zones and their role in fisheries and some activities that interact with water use**

1 Many species of fish are specialized for life in the upper basins of rivers. Other species from downriver migrate to upriver sites to spawn.

2 Dams heavily affect downstream fish fauna but also create opportunities for new fisheries. Where native species are not well adapted to lake conditions, new species may need to be introduced.

3 Mid-basin braided reaches often have specialized faunas adapted to the rapidly changing and unpredictable hydrological conditions found there.

4 Agricultural dams provide an opportunity for fisheries as a parallel crop, usually by stocking.

5 Lakes have specialized fauna adapted to still water conditions and support valuable fisheries.

6 Floodplains are essential habitats for many species of fish that migrate onto them during floods to reproduce and feed. Floodplain water bodies and rice fields also support distinctive fauna.

7 Estuarine areas and coastal lagoons are among the most productive fisheries. They depend on a specific balance of fresh and marine waters.

8 Aquaculture ponds can occur throughout the river basin associated with aquaculture or on their own.

9 Inland coastal and near-shore marine areas are influenced by inflows of freshwater, silt, and nutrients and by the access to upstream areas for migratory species.

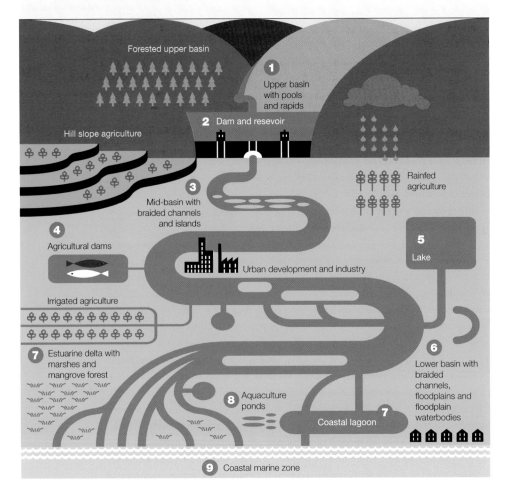

larger species by less valuable small generalists or introduced species, and may lead to the elimination of migratory and other sensitive species and a general loss of biodiversity (Welcomme 1999). Maintaining environmental flows must therefore include sustaining ecosystem service provision as well as sustaining broader ecosystem connectivity and functioning for conserving biodiversity.

Lakes and reservoirs—a dependence on river flows

All reservoirs and most lakes depend on flow from rivers for their productivity or their very existence. Year to year fluctuations in the productivity of Lake Kariba (Zambia and Zimbabwe) and Lake Turkana (Kenya) illustrate the dependence of even large water bodies on river inflows, which provide both variation in area and inflow of nutrients (Karenge and Kolding 1995; Kolding 1992). Other lakes, such as Lake Chilwa (Malawi) and Lake Chad (Cameroon, Chad, Niger, and Nigeria), depend on inflow for their existence—a reduction or failure in flooding from inflowing rivers results in diminished area and failure of their fisheries, although these are restored when more normal flow conditions reappear (van Zwieten and Njaya 2003). In the Aral Sea water abstractions in support of irrigated agriculture for non-food crops led to the loss of about 50,000 metric tons of food fish per year (Petr 2004).

> **All reservoirs and most lakes depend on flow from rivers for their productivity or their very existence. Coastal fisheries are also vulnerable to changes in freshwater inputs**

The productivity of reservoirs and dams can be influenced by filling, drawdown, and abstraction regimes. Abrupt changes in water level can be detrimental to certain species. For example, tilapia species, which are commonly present in reservoirs and lakes, nest on the shallow bottom, and rapid changes in level may submerge or expose the nests, resulting in breeding failure (Amarasinghe and Upasena 1985; De Silva 1985; De Silva and Sirisena 1988) *[established but incomplete]*.

Marine and brackish water areas—vulnerability to changes in freshwater inputs

Coastal fisheries are also vulnerable to changes in freshwater inputs. For example, the pelagic fisheries of the eastern Mediterranean experienced a marked downturn following the regulation of the Nile River's flow by the Aswan High Dam (Nixon 2004). There is also evidence that coral reefs and their fish populations can be affected when freshwater discharge patterns are modified *[established but incomplete]*, particularly where land use results in excessive sedimentation. In fresh-salt water transitional zones in estuaries, changes to flow can affect the intrusion of salt water into the freshwater system and associated soils (photo 12.4). This affects not only the distribution, reproduction, larval development, and growth of many freshwater, brackish water, and marine fish, crustacea, and molluscs but also the suitability of land for agriculture. Mangrove forests are particularly at risk in areas where coastal transition zones suffer changes in salinity by reductions in freshwater inputs or are degraded by declining sediment deposition.

Aquaculture—reliance on consistent inputs of clean water

Many forms of aquaculture are viable only if flow conditions are suitable. Successful rearing of fish generally depends on reliable supplies of clean water, although many rainfed stillwater ponds and more advanced recirculation systems may be extremely economical

Photo 12.4 Shrimp aquaculture can greatly affect soil quality by increasing salinity

Photo by C. Béné

of water use. Intensive running water culture systems need constant inputs of high-quality water to ensure sufficient oxygen for the fish and removal of wastes; sufficient flow is needed in rivers into which farm effluents are discharged to dilute wastes and nutrients without damaging ecosystems (Brown and King 1996). In many parts of the world certain flow criteria must be met before farm licenses are granted, and alterations to flow can place farms in jeopardy.

Water management—an ecosystem approach is crucial

The ecosystem approach to managing watersheds, with the rivers, wetlands, lakes, estuarine areas, and land viewed as part of a continuum, is fundamental to managing water for inland fisheries. This approach should consider not only water quantity and quality but also the connectivity of the system because many species of fish must be able to move between spawning, nursery, and feeding areas within a basin. This management approach needs to consider land-use practices, such as agriculture and forestry, as well as the needs of industry, urban areas, and waterborne transport that affect basin processes and the quality, quantity, and timing of flows. The approach is further complicated by the fact that many river basins are transboundary and may be located within several countries, necessitating international mechanisms to regulate and manage river flows.

Evaluating the amount of water needed in the system

The negative impact of alterations in flows means that efforts have to be made to maintain the flow in rivers and other flow-sensitive systems if fisheries are to be sustained. This flow is termed an environmental flow and, for fishery purposes, is defined as that portion of the original flow of a river that is needed to maintain specific valued features of its ecosystem or the quantity of water that must be maintained in a river system at all times to protect the species of interest for fisheries or for conservation of the environments on which they

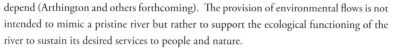
depend (Arthington and others forthcoming). The provision of environmental flows is not intended to mimic a pristine river but rather to support the ecological functioning of the river to sustain its desired services to people and nature.

A range of methods has been developed to determine the environmental flow requirements for rivers, wetlands, and estuaries (Tharme 2003; Arthington and others forthcoming), but most are used only in small rivers in temperate zones. Methods are beginning to be developed and used for large systems as well, but they are still incomplete (Tharme 2003).

Environmental flows are an important tool for assessing ecological requirements for water. The desired environmental flow for a river depends on the management objective. The environmental flow for sustaining biota is not the same as that for optimal ecosystem service provision, for example. If developed and applied properly, measures of environmental flow have considerable potential to improve the technical basis of tradeoff decisions for water allocation.

The type of environmental flow regulation needed to maintain fisheries depends on the primary cause of flow modification and the desired nature of the fishery. Restrictive management is required where water is abstracted directly from a donor waterbody. Licenses to abstract water should be granted only when sufficient water will remain in the system to guarantee flows that allow the fish and fisheries to function at desired levels, including during periods of low flow. Active management is required where releases from dams are involved. Artificial flow regimes are needed to create peak flows timed to act as triggers for breeding and to provide water of sufficient depth and duration to flood riparian wetlands long enough for young fish to grow. The flows should also allow fish to migrate, access riparian floodplains, and otherwise complete their normal life cycles. Active management can also be applied to poldered systems, where the floodplain is enclosed to control flow for rice and other crops. Correct management of the sluices controlling flow can favor fish as well as rice (Halls 2005) *[established but incomplete]*.

> Damming has proved particularly detrimental to downstream fisheries by suppressing flood peaks and preventing the periodic inundations of floodplains downstream, altering their timing and preventing instream migration

Impact of water management schemes

Damming for power generation, flood control, and urban supply and leveeing and poldering to control flooding for urban development and agriculture all affect flow regimes and habitat availability, which in turn can affect the contributions of fish and fisheries to water productivity *[well established]*. Damming has proved particularly detrimental to downstream fisheries (World Commission on Dams 2000) by suppressing flood peaks and preventing the periodic inundations of floodplains downstream, altering their timing and preventing instream migration (Bunn and Arthington 2002), with negative consequences for fishing communities. The growing trend in Bangladesh of enclosing lowland floodplains with polders, for example, is denying many species of migratory fish access to large areas of floodplain. Cross-basin transfers may be particularly damaging as they rob one river, whose fauna is degraded as a consequence, to discharge the water into another system, where the new hydrograph may exceed the capacity of the fauna to deal with it *[speculative]*, and transfer alien species or genotypes from one system to the other.

The volume of water removed for irrigated agriculture can also harm downstream fisheries. Irrigation accounts for some 70% of all water removed from rivers (gross abstraction).[3] Although some of this water may be returned to the donor river, the discharged water may be of lower quality and the timing may be inappropriate. The net impact of these high levels of removal on fisheries has rarely been investigated, although it is assumed from knowledge of the dynamics of fish populations in rivers that such effects are generally deleterious *[established but incomplete]*. However, in some irrigated landscapes such as rice farming systems, aggregated impacts of irrigation on fisheries production and on the livelihoods of fishing communities are not always negative at the catchment level, as demonstrated in Lao PDR and Sri Lanka (Nguyen-Khoa, Smith, and Lorenzen 2005b). Further investigation of such impacts is urgently needed.

Realizing the opportunities

The chapter has highlighted the value of inland fisheries and aquaculture and the opportunities for improving water productivity. The chapter also identified several constraints that need to be overcome. To ensure optimal benefits, appropriate mechanisms for evaluation, decisionmaking, and governance regarding fisheries and aquaculture need to be fully incorporated into water allocation processes.

Improving evaluation of fisheries

There is an urgent need for more holistic evaluation techniques that take into account the different contributions of fisheries to water productivity. Environmental economics theory has made tremendous progress in incorporating the nonmarket goods and services provided by ecosystems into economic frameworks and decisionmaking—for example, the development and implementation of valuation techniques and concepts such as total economic value, existence or option values, and contingency valuation (see, for example, Barbier 1989 and Willis and Corkindale 1995). Still needed, however, are approaches to resource valuation that quantify less tangible social functions and services, such as food security, provision of financial safety nets, and the spreading of risk, a need that is particularly acute for fisheries. Where better valuation has occurred, the profile of fisheries has been raised and national policies on water allocation to support fisheries have been adjusted accordingly.

These new evaluation techniques need to draw on innovative approaches that attempt to include community perceptions of these different social services and functions through an integrated participatory assessment (Nguyen-Khoa, Smith, and Lorenzen 2005a). The challenge is to internalize these overlooked benefits, collectively for all services provided by water including fisheries, into a new interpretation of water productivity.

Accommodating new investment approaches

The private sector is increasingly involved in the economic development of fisheries and aquaculture, in particular at the micro level. This is illustrated by the exponential increase in private sector–led aquaculture farming in Asia and Latin America. Private investment in fisheries and aquaculture is driven by several factors. The increasing demand of urban markets for fish is turning the focus of inland fisheries away from rural subsistence, and this is

> Environmental economics theory has made tremendous progress in incorporating the nonmarket goods and services provided by ecosystems into economic frameworks and decisionmaking; still needed are approaches to resource valuation that quantify less tangible social functions and services

driving changes in fisheries practice and in the social and economic orientation of many fisheries. This tends to favor the intensification of production systems, leading eventually to monoculture. Securing a return on investment is accompanied by increasing control over resources (including fish habitat) by individuals or limited groups.

Privatization of the common-pool resource is a form of enclosure of the commons. This can have tremendous negative impacts on vulnerable socioeconomic groups (usually the poorest, with a large number of women), which rely more heavily on these resources to sustain their livelihoods through subsistence harvesting, generally under informal communal access rights. In Asia this enclosure has already occurred following the aquaculture boom and the development of enhanced fisheries in oxbows and ponds (Ahmed and others 1998). It is now taking place in Africa through the privatization of the large lakes in East and Southern Africa (for example, Lake Kariba and Lake Malawi) by commercial cage culture ventures and by brush park fisheries in West Africa.

Export-oriented policies have also been a major catalyst for private investors to develop commercial, high-value, large-scale fish production systems. These new export-oriented commercial strategies raise concerns about local food security and livelihood equity, including for a large number of women (Abila 2003).

The processing sector is also being transformed by greater vertical integration and sophistication and intensification of the processing technologies in response to more stringent international food quality standards (such as Hazard Analysis Critical Control Point certification, or HACCP). This trend is accompanied by growing consumer demand for environmental and, increasingly, social, standards for production. Certification or labeling requirements may deny or reduce access to international or even national markets to small-scale producers. These producers may, however, continue to supply local consumers, thereby slowing the current trend in declining domestic fish availability observed in certain developing countries.

An increasing number of governments and development organizations are promoting institutional frameworks that draw on private sector dynamism, while at the same time allowing a certain degree of pro-poor growth and limiting the risks of exclusion. Public-private partnership has been identified as one potential option in this search for pro-poor growth.

> An increasing number of governments and development organizations are promoting institutional frameworks that draw on private sector dynamism, while allowing a certain degree of pro-poor growth and limiting the risks of exclusion

Improving governance

A broader policy and improved governance environment is needed to stimulate pro-poor growth, including through adequate support to investment and public-private partnerships that optimize the benefits of fisheries. These should ensure high levels of participation in decisionmaking by all stakeholder groups, including fishery interests at all levels (photo 12.5). Such an improved governance environment should create and enforce mechanisms to ensure the accountability of the different public and private actors whose actions affect the allocation of water and water productivity, including that reflected through fisheries.

Effective governance of aquatic resources is rare, especially in developing countries. Most governments and institutions have failed to design governance mechanisms and policy processes that account for the aspirations and needs of the rural populations that depend on inland aquatic resources for their livelihoods. In an effort to address this weakness, an increasing number of governance reforms have been launched since the early 1990s.

<blockquote>
Most governments and institutions have failed to design governance mechanisms and policy processes that account for the aspirations and needs of the rural populations that depend on inland aquatic resources for their livelihoods
</blockquote>

Photo 12.5 Improving water governance is critical to the participation of all stakeholders in the decisionmaking process

Photo by R. Welcomme

Decentralization and participatory democratization, in particular, are seen as necessary to improve governance mechanisms. Reforms are often associated with improvements in public accountability, environmental sustainability, and empowerment of poor and vulnerable groups. Decentralization is perceived as a possible means of improving rural livelihoods and reducing poverty (World Bank 2000; IFAD 2001).

The most common argument is that decentralization is by definition a mechanism for inclusion and empowerment because it involves bringing government closer to the governed, making government more knowledgeable about, and hence more responsive to, the needs of the poorest and most marginalized people, including women, who are rarely recognized as legitimate stakeholders. This mechanism of inclusion is expected to lead to greater empowerment and stronger pro-poor policies and outcomes. In fisheries community-based management and comanagement arrangements are now frequently promoted successfully as part of this governance reform (Pomeroy 2001; Berkes and others 2001).

Recent reviews suggest, however, that decentralization reforms raise a number of challenges for natural resources management, particularly water use (Dupar and Badenoch 2002; Ribot 2002). The decentralized level provides little opportunity to address issues of transboundary resources, including water and shared and migratory fish stocks. It is more difficult to create the managerial conditions and knowledge necessary to integrate the water flow requirements of fisheries into watershed or basinwide integrated water resource management. The level of coordination and information necessary for a sustainable and equitable allocation of water among the different users across a basin is rarely achieved.

Many proposed reforms contravene legislation in many countries, particularly on access to fisheries and land and water tenure. Decentralization reforms need to embrace legislative reform to support the rights and responsibilities of local communities to stewardship of resources and to provide capacity building for both resource users and decentralized officers. Improved information flows, lower transaction costs, and clearly defined goals and responsibilities of government units at all levels will be necessary to deal in an integrated way with complex and potentially conflicting resource management issues emerging at basin, national, and international levels (Brugere 2006).

Decentralization should not be seen as a universal panacea to improve equity and empowerment. As empirical evidence demonstrates, when human capacity and social capital at the community level are low, decentralization may exacerbate unequal power distribution and reinforce the marginalization of some groups because elite groups capture decisionmaking mechanisms (Abraham and Platteau 2000; Béné and Neiland 2006). As a result, policy decisions at the local level still frequently favor powerful groups such as large landowners (through irrigation schemes and water user associations, for example) or even large herd owners, to the detriment of the vast majority of society, especially fisher groups (Ratner 2003).

Developing an intersectoral policy framework adapted to inland fisheries

The consensus among practitioners and scholars is clearly that new evaluation techniques, investment approaches, and governance reforms can support and improve the contribution of fisheries and aquaculture to water productivity. Implementation of these approaches still represents an enormous challenge for a large number of institutions in developing countries, however. Adaptive policy support mechanisms are required to ensure that reforms realize the potential local economic development and improved food security benefits. Many countries lack a wider integrated natural resource management framework into which inland fisheries can fit. Effective policies for the conservation and sustainable use of freshwater biodiversity are also generally absent despite the increased recognition of its role.

Many countries have yet to develop national policy and legal frameworks tailored to inland fisheries. More commonly, inland fisheries continue to be placed under policy frameworks that evolved to address coastal and marine fisheries. There is an urgent need for all countries to develop and implement frameworks specific to inland fisheries. These should have explicit links to integrated approaches to sustaining aquatic environments.

An essential attribute of an effective inland fishery policy framework is an ecosystem approach to fisheries, which includes fisheries considerations and related environmental concerns in integrated planning, particularly for water use. This is still a major challenge in the low-capacity and data-deficient environment in developing countries. However, an ecosystem approach offers a much better adapted framework for fishery management than the sector-based approach still prevalent in most developing countries. One mechanism to promote such integrated, multisectoral approaches is participatory scenario-based negotiations, which can better integrate the needs of stakeholder groups within fisheries with those of other interests and take account of gender perspectives. These processes should facilitate the establishment of intersectoral consensus mechanisms through collective negotiation of land and water issues and consideration of their relationship to aquaculture and fisheries.

> An essential attribute of an effective inland fishery policy framework is an ecosystem approach to fisheries, which includes fisheries considerations and related environmental concerns in integrated planning, particularly for water use

Reviewers

Chapter review editor: David Coates.
Chapter reviewers: Edward Barbier, Devin Bartley, Cecile Brugere, Jane Dowling, Mark Giordano, Nancy Gitonga, Brij Gopal, John Gowing, Brian Harvey, Chu Thai Hoanh, Daniel Jamu, Kai Lorenzen, Niklas S. Mattson, Ruth Meinzen-Dick, Patricia Ocampo-Thomason, Tomi Petr, Sawaeng Ruaysoongnern, Sena de Silva, Simon Funge Smith, John Valbo-Jørgensen, and Paul van Zwieten.

Notes

1. The word *fishery* includes finfish, crustaceans, molluscs, and other miscellaneous animals but excludes the harvest of plants.

2. Potential production is calculated using standard coefficients relating the surface of water bodies (river or floodplain) to potential production rates (metric tons per hectare per year) as typically observed for these water bodies and classically used in the literature (see, for example, Welcomme 2001).

3. See www.fao.org/ag/agl/aglw/aquastat/water_use/index6.stm.

References

Abery, N.W., F. Sukadi, A.A. Budhiman, E.S. Karamihardja, S. Koeshendrajana, and S.S. De Silva. 2005. "Fisheries and Cage Culture of Three Reservoirs in West Java: A Case Study of Ambitious Development and Resulting Interactions." *Fisheries Management and Ecology* 12 (5): 315–30.

Abila, R.O. 2003. "Fish Trade and Food Security: Are They Reconcilable in Lake Victoria?" In *Report of the Expert Consultation on International Fish Trade and Food Security. Casablanca, Morocco, 27–30 January.* FAO Fisheries Report 708. Rome: Food and Agriculture Organization.

Abraham, A., and J.-P. Platteau. 2000. "The Central Dilemma of Decentralized Rural Development." Conference on New Institutional Theory, Institutional Reform, and Poverty Reduction, London School of Economics, 7–8 September, London.

Ahmed, I., S.R. Bland, C.R. Price, and R. Kershaw. 1998. "Open Water Stocking in Bangladesh: Experiences from the Third Fisheries Project." In Tomi Petr, ed., *Inland Fishery Enhancements.* FAO Fisheries Technical Paper 374. Rome: Food and Agriculture Organization and UK Department for International Development.

Akiyama, D.M. 1991. "The Use of Soybean Meal Based Feeds for High Density Cage Culture of Common Carp in Indonesia and the People's Republic of China." ASA Technical Bulletin AQ 28-1991. American Soybean Association, Singapore.

Allan, JD., R. Abell, Z. Hogan, C. Revenga, B.W. Taylor, R.L. Welcomme, and K. Winemiller. 2005. "Overfishing of Inland Waters." *Bioscience* 55 (12): 1041–51

Amarasinghe, U.S., and T. Upasena. 1985. "Morphometry of a Man-made Lake in Sri Lanka: A Factor Influencing Recruitment to Cichlid Fishery." *Journal of the National Aquatic Resources Agency* 32: 121–29.

Arrignon, J.C.V., J.V. Huner, P.J. Laurent, J.M. Griessinger, D. Lacroix, P. Gondouin, and M. Autrand. 1994. *Warm-water Crustaceans.* Wageningen, Netherlands: Technical Centre for Agriculture and Rural Cooperation.

Arthington, A.H., R. Tharme, S.O. Brizga, B.J. Pusey, and M.J. Kennard. 2004. "Environmental Flow Assessment with Emphasis on Holistic Methodologies." In R. Welcomme and T. Petr, eds., *Proceedings of the Second International Symposium on the Management of Large Rivers for Fisheries Volume II.* Food and Agriculture Organization, Regional Office for Asia and the Pacific, Bangkok.

Arthington, A.H., E. Baran, C.A. Brown, P. Dugan, A.S. Halls, J.M. King, C.V. Minte-Vera, R.E. Tharme, and R.L. Welcomme. Forthcoming. "Water Requirements of Floodplain Rivers and Fisheries: Existing Decision-Support Tools and Pathways for Development." Comprehensive Assessment of Water Management in Agriculture Research Report 17. International Water Management Institute, Colombo.

Barbier, E. 1989. "The Economic Value of Ecosystems: Tropical Wetlands." Briefing papers on key issues in environmental economics. LEEC Gatekeeper 89–92. International Institute for Environment and Development, London.

Béné, C. 2006. "Small-scale Fisheries: Assessing Their Contribution to Rural Livelihoods in Developing Countries." FAO Fisheries Circular 1008. Food and Agriculture Organization, Rome.

Béné, C., and A.E. Neiland. 2006. *From Participation to Governance: A Critical Review of the Concepts of Governance, Co-management, and Participation and Their Implementation in Small-scale Inland Fisheries in Developing Countries.* Penang,

Malaysia, and Colombo: WorldFish Center and Consultative Group on International Agricultural Research Challenge Program on Water and Food.

Berkes, F., R. Mahon, P. McConney, R. Pollnac, and R. Pomeroy. 2001. *Managing Small-scale Fisheries: Alternative Directions and Methods*. Ottawa: International Development Research Center.

Beveridge, M.C.M. 2004. *Cage Aquacul ture*, 3rd ed. Oxford: Blackwell Publishing.

Beveridge, M.C.M., and D.C. Little. 2002. "Aquaculture in Traditional Societies." In B.A. Costa-Pierce, ed., *Ecological Aquaculture*. Oxford: Blackwell Publishing.

Beveridge, M.C.M., and J. F. Muir. 1999. "Environmental Impacts and Sustainability of Cage Culture in Southeast Asian Lakes and Reservoirs." In W.L.T. van Densen and M.J. Morris, eds., *Fish and Fisheries of Lakes and Reservoirs in Southeast Asia and Africa*. Otley, UK: Westbury Publishing.

Brown, C.A., and J.M. King. 1996. "The Effects of Trout-farm Effluent on Benthic Invertebrate Community Structure in South-western Cape Rivers." *South African Journal of Aquatic Science* 21 (91/2): 3–21.

Brugere, C. 2006. "Can Integrated Coastal Management Solve Agriculture-Fisheries-Aquaculture Conflicts at the Land-Water Interface? A Perspective from New Institutional Economics." In C.T. Huong, T.P. Tuong, J.W. Gowing, and B. Hardy, eds., *Environment and Livelihoods in Coastal Tropical Zones: Managing Agriculture-Fishery-Aquaculture Conflicts*. Wallingford, UK: CABI Publishing.

Brummett, R. E. 1997. "Farming Fish to Save Water." *Bioscience* 47 (7): 402.

———. 2006. "Comparative Analysis of the Environmental Costs of Fish Farming and Crop Production in Arid Areas: A Materials Flow Analysis." Paper presented to the International Workshop on the Environmental Costs of Aquaculture, April 25–28, Vancouver, Canada.

Bunn, S.E., and A.H. Arthington. 2002. "Basic Principles and Ecological Consequences of Altered Flow Regimes for Aquatic Biodiversity." *Environmental Management* 30 (4): 492–507.

Coates, D. 2002. *Inland Capture Fishery Statistics of Southeast Asia: Current Status and Information Needs*. RAP Publication 2002/11. Food and Agriculture Organization, Regional Office for Asia and the Pacific, Asia-Pacific Fishery Commission, Bangkok.

Costa Pierce, B.A. 2002. "Sustainability of Cage Aquaculture Ecosystems for Large-scale Resettlement from Hydropower Dams: An Indonesian Case Study." In B.A. Costa-Pierce, ed., *Ecological Aquaculture: The Evolution of the Blue Revolution*. Oxford: Blackwell Publishing.

Cowx, I.G. 2002. "Recreational Fishing." In P.J.B. Hart and J.D. Reynolds, eds., *Handbook of Fish Biology and Fisheries*. Oxford: Blackwell Publishing.

Dansoko, D.D., H. Breman, and J. Daget. 1976. "Influence de la secheresse sur les populations d'*hydrocynus* dans le delta centrale du Niger." *Cahier ORSTOM (Hydrobiol)* 10 (2): 71–76.

dela Cruz, C.R., ed. 1994. *Role of Fish in Enhancing Ricefield Ecology and in Integrated Pest Management*. International Center for Living Aquatic Resources Management Conference Proceedings 43. WorldFish Center, Penang, Malaysia.

De Silva, S.S. 1985. "Observations on the Abundance of the Exotic Cichlid *Sarotherodon mossambicus* (Peters) in Relation to Fluctuations in the Water-level in a Man-made Lake in Sri Lanka." *Aquaculture and Fisheries Management* 16: 265–72.

De Silva, S.S., and H.K.G. Sirisena. 1988. "Observations on the Nesting Habits of *Oreochromis mossambicus* (Peters) (Pisces: Cichlidae) in Sri Lankan Reservoirs." *Journal of Fish Biology* 33 (5): 689–96.

Dey, M.M., and M. Prein. 2003. "Participatory Research at Landscape Level: Flood-prone Ecosystems in Bangladesh and Vietnam." In B. Pound, S.S. Snapp, C. McDougall, and A. Braun, eds., *Managing Natural Resources for Sustainable Livelihoods: Uniting Science and Participation*. London and Ottawa: Earthscan and International Development Research Centre.

Dey, M.M., P. Kambewa, M. Prein, D. Jamu, and F.J. Paraguas. 2006. "Impact of the Development and Dissemination of Integrated Aquaculture-Agriculture (IAA) Technologies in Malawi." In D. Zilberman and H. Waibel, eds., *The Impact of NRM Research in the CGIAR*. Wallingford, UK: CABI Publishing.

Dey M.M., M.A. Rab, A. Kumar, A. Nisapa, and M. Ahmed. 2005. "Food Safety Standard and Regulatory Measures: Implications for Selected Fish Exporting Asian Countries." *Aquaculture Economics and Management* 9 (1–2): 217–36.

Diana, J. 1997. "Feeding Strategies." In H.S. Egna and C.E. Boyd, eds., *Dynamics of Pond Aquaculture*. Boca Raton, La.: CRC Press.

Dollar, E.S.J. 2004. "Fluvial Geomorphology." *Progress in Physical Geography* 28 (3): 405–50.

Dupar, Mari, and Nathan Badenoch. 2002. *Environment, Livelihoods, and Local Institutions—Decentralization in Mainland Southeast Asia*. Washington, D.C.: World Resources Institute.

FAO (Food and Agriculture Organization). 2002. *The State of World Fisheries and Aquaculture*. Fisheries Department. Rome.

———. 2004. *The State of World Fisheries and Aquaculture.* Fisheries Department. Rome.

Halls, A.S. 2005. "The Use of Sluice Gates for Stock Enhancement and Diversification of Livelihoods." Project R8210. Fisheries Management Science Programme. Marine Resources Assessment Group, London.

Halwart, M., and M.V. Gupta, eds. 2004. *Culture of Fish in Rice Fields.* Penang, Malaysia: Food and Agriculture Organization and the WorldFish Center.

Hambrey, J., M. Beveridge, and K. McAndrew. 2001. "Aquaculture and Poverty Alleviation 1. Cage Culture in Freshwater in Bangladesh." *World Aquaculture* 32 (1): 50–55, 67.

Hatch, L.U., and T.R. Hanson. 1992. "Economic Viability of Farm Diversification through Tropical Freshwater Aquaculture in Less Developed Countries." International Center for Aquaculture, Auburn University, Ala.

IFAD (International Fund for Agricultural Development). 2001. *Rural Poverty Report 2001: The Challenge of Ending Rural Poverty.* Oxford, UK: Oxford University Press.

Karenge, L.P., and J. Kolding. 1995. "On the Relationship between Hydrology and Fisheries in Man-made Lake Kariba, Central Africa." *Fisheries Research* 22 (3): 205–26.

Kolding, J. 1992. "A Summary of Lake Turkana: An Ever-changing Mixed Environment." *Mitteilungen-Internationale Vereinigung für Theoretische und Angewandte Limnologie* 23: 25–35.

Kolding, J., and P.A.M van Zwieten. Forthcoming. "Improving Productivity in Tropical Lakes and Reservoirs." Consultative Group on International Agricultural Research Challenge Program on Water and Food, Bergen, Norway.

Lae, R., S. Williams, A. Malam Massou, P. Morand, and O. Mikolasek. 2004. "Review of the Present State of the Environment, Fish Stocks and Fisheries of the River Niger (West Africa)." In R. Welcomme and T. Petr, eds., *Proceedings of the Second International Symposium on the Management of Large Rivers for Fisheries* Vol. I. RAP Publication 2004/16. Bangkok: Food and Agriculture Organization, Regional Office for Asia and the Pacific.

Lake Harvest Aquaculture, Ltd. 2003. "Key Production Parameters." Zimbabwe.

McAndrew, K.I., D. Little, and M.C.M. Beveridge. 2000. "Entry Points and Low Risk Strategies Appropriate for the Resources Poor to Participate in Cage Aquaculture: Experiences from CARE-CAGES Project, Bangladesh." In I.C. Liao and C. Kwei Lin, eds., *Cage Aquaculture in Asia: Proceedings of the First International Symposium on Cage Aquaculture in Asia.* Manila and Bangkok: Asian Fisheries Society and World Aquaculture Society, Asia Branch.

Misund, O.A., J. Kolding, and P. Fréon. 2002. "Fish Capture Devices in Industrial and Artisanal Fisheries and their Influence on Management." In P.J.B. Hart and J.D. Reynolds, eds., *Handbook of Fish Biology and Fisheries.* Vol. II. London: Blackwell Publishing.

Murthy, H.S. 2002. "Culture and Feeding of Indian Major Carps." American Soybean Association, New Delhi.

Nalim, S. 1994. "The Impact of Fish in Enhancing Ricefield Ecosystems." In C.R. dela Cruz, ed., *Role of Fish in Enhancing Ricefield Ecology and in Integrated Pest Management.* International Center for Living Aquatic Resources Management Conference Proceedings 43. WorldFish Center, Penang, Malaysia.

Neiland, A., and C. Béné, eds. Forthcoming. "Tropical River Fisheries Valuation: A Global Synthesis and Critical Review." WorldFish Center and International Water Management Institute, Penang, Malaysia and Colombo.

Nguyen Khoa, S., L. Smith, and K. Lorenzen. 2005a. "Adaptive, Participatory and Integrated Assessment (APIA) of the Impacts of Irrigation on Fisheries: Evaluation of the Approach in Sri Lanka." Working Paper 89. International Water Management Institute, Colombo.

———. 2005b. "Impacts of Irrigation on Inland Fisheries: Appraisals in Laos and Sri Lanka." Comprehensive Assessment of Water Management in Agriculture Research Report 7. Comprehensive Assessment Secretariat, Colombo.

Nixon, S.W. 2004. "The Artificial Nile." *American Scientist* 92 (2): 158–65.

Petr, T. 2004. "Irrigation Systems and their Fisheries in the Aral Sea Basin, Central Asia." In R.L. Welcomme and T. Petr, eds., *Proceedings of the Second International Symposium on the Management of Large Rivers for Fisheries.* Vol. I. RAP Publication 2004/16. Bangkok: Food and Agriculture Organization, Regional Office for Asia and the Pacific.

Phillips, M.J., M.C.M. Beveridge, and R.M. Clarke. 1991. "Impact of Aquaculture on Water Resources." In D.R. Brune and J.R. Tomasso, eds., *Aquaculture and Water Quality.* Advances in World Aquaculture Series. Vol. 3. Baton Rouge, La.: World Aquaculture Society.

Piemental, D., J. Houser, E. Preiss, O. White, H. Fang, L. Mesnick, T. Barsky, S. Tariche, J. Schreck, and S. Alpert. 1997. "Water Resources: Agriculture, the Environment and Society." *Bioscience* 47 (2): 97–106.

Pomeroy, R. 2001. "Devolution and Fisheries Co-management." In R. Meinzen-Dick, A. Knox, and M. Di Gregorio, eds., *Collective Action, Property Rights and Devolution of Natural Resource Management: Exchange of Knowledge and Implications for Policy.* Feldafing, Germany: Deutsche Stiftung für Internationale Entwicklung/Zentralstelle für Ernährung und Landwirtschaft (DSE/ZEL).

Primavera, J.H. 1997. "Socio-economic Impacts of Shrimp Culture." *Aquaculture Research* 28 (10): 815–27.

Ratner, B. 2003. "The Politics of Regional Governance in the Mekong River Basin." *Global Change* 15 (1): 59–76.

Renwick, M.E. 2001. *Valuing Water in Irrigated Agriculture and Reservoir Fisheries: A Multiple-use Irrigation System in Sri Lanka.* Research Report 51. Colombo: International Water Management Institute.

Ribot, Jesse. 2002. *Democratic Decentralization of Natural Resources: Institutionalizing Popular Participation.* Washington, D.C.: World Resources Institute.

Tharme, R.E. 2003. "A Global Perspective on Environmental Flow Assessment: Emerging Trends in the Development and Application of Environmental Flow Methodologies for Rivers." *River Research and Applications* 19 (5-6): 397–441.

Turpie, J., B. Smith, L. Emerton, and B. Barnes. 1999. *Economic Value of the Zambezi Basin Wetlands.* Cape Town: World Conservation Union.

van Zwieten, P.A.M, and F. Njaya. 2003. "Environmental Variability, Effort Development and the Regenerative Capacity of the Fish Stock in Lake Chilwa, Malawi." In E. Jul-Larsen, J. Kolding, J.R. Nielsen, R. Overa, and P.A.M. van Zwieten, eds., *Management, Co-management or No Management? Major Dilemmas in Southern African Freshwater Fisheries.* Part 2: Case Studies. FAO Fisheries Technical Paper 426/2. Rome: Food and Agriculture Organization.

Verdegem, M.C.J., R.H. Bosma, and J.A.V. Verreth. 2006. "Reducing Water Use for Animal Production through Aquaculture." *Water Resources Development* 22 (1): 101–13.

Welcomme, R.L. 1999. "A Review of a Model for Qualitative Evaluation of Exploitation Levels in Multi-species Fisheries." *Journal of Fisheries Ecology and Management* 6 (1): 1–20.

Welcomme, R.L., and D.M. Bartley. 1998. "An Evaluation of Present Techniques for the Enhancement of Fisheries." *Journal of Fisheries Ecology and Management* 5: 351–82.

Welcomme, R.L., and T. Petr, eds. 2004. *Proceedings of the Second International Symposium on the Management of Large Rivers for Fisheries Volume I.* RAP Publication 2004/16/17. Bangkok: Food and Agriculture Organization, Regional Office for Asia and the Pacific.

Willis, K.G., and J.T. Corkindale, eds. 1995. *Environmental Valuation, New Perspectives.* Wallingford, UK: CABI Publishing.

World Bank. 2000. *World Development Report 2000/2001: Attacking Poverty.* New York: Oxford University Press.

World Commission on Dams. 2000. *Dams and Development: A New Framework for Decision-making.* Report of the Word Commission on Dams. London: Earthscan.

Yang, Y., and C.K. Lin. 2000. "Integrated Cage Culture in Ponds: Concepts, Practices and Perspectives." In I. C. Liao and C. Kwei Lin, eds., *Cage Aquaculture in Asia. Proceedings of the First International Symposium on Cage Aquaculture in Asia.* Manila and Bangkok: Asian Fisheries Society and World Aquaculture Society, Asia Branch.

**Livestock help the world's
poor escape poverty**

Artist: Shittu Titilope, Nigeria

13 | Water and livestock for human development

Coordinating lead author: Don Peden

Lead authors: Girma Tadesse and A.K. Misra

Contributing authors: Faisal Awad Ahmed, Abiye Astatke, Wagnew Ayalneh, Mario Herrero, Gabriel Kiwuwa, Tesfaye Kumsa, Bancy Mati, Denis Mpairwe, Tom Wassenaar, and Asfaw Yimegnuhal

Overview

Livestock production, one of the most important agricultural subsectors worldwide, is practiced in rangeland areas and in mixed crop-livestock systems that cover about 60% of the land area of developing countries [well established]. In developing countries cattle, sheep, and goats total about 1.2 billion tropical livestock units (converted at the rate of 250 kilograms of live animal weight per tropical livestock unit). Animal densities are strongly correlated with human densities and are highest in areas of intensified agriculture, especially in and around irrigation systems. Animals are heavily dependent on water for feed production, using an estimated 500 billion cubic meters or more a year for maintenance. Total water needed may be more than double this amount, with drinking water less than 2% of that required for feed production. Inappropriate grazing and watering practices contribute to widespread degradation of water and land resources, particularly around watering sites. Investments in water and livestock have often failed to achieve maximum and sustainable returns because of a lack of integration of the two.

Despite many efforts to develop water and livestock in developing countries over the past 50 years, sustainability and gender-equitable returns on investments have been disappointing [established but incomplete]. Global experience indicates that integrating water and livestock development creates opportunities to sustainably increase benefits in ways that independent development efforts cannot achieve. Without integration, opportunities to achieve maximum and sustainable returns on investments in both sectors will be lost.

Livestock are an important part of global agriculture, providing meat, milk, eggs, blood, hides, cash income, farm power, and manure for fuel and soil nutrient replenishment [well established]. Livestock also have important cultural values and are a means for poor people to accumulate wealth. Large numbers of poor farmers and herders depend on livestock for their livelihoods. Livestock depend on water, but when poorly managed, they contribute to the degradation and contamination of water resources.

Livestock keeping represents a diverse set of geographically varying livelihoods that benefit both poor and wealthy people in rangelands and in rainfed and irrigated crop-livestock farming systems [well established]. Agricultural intensification often correlates with higher livestock densities. Understanding spatial changes in the distribution and structure of livestock production systems in relation to agricultural water can help to identify areas where considerations of livestock-water interactions can enhance the sustainability and returns on livestock investments. South Asia and Sub-Saharan Africa are priority regions for integrating livestock and water development for poverty reductions, but benefits can be expected elsewhere as well.

' Rapidly growing demand for meat and milk in urban areas of developing countries will place substantial new demands on agricultural water resources, especially for feed production

Rapidly growing demand for meat and milk in urban areas of developing countries will place substantial new demands on agricultural water resources, especially for feed production [well established]. Meeting this demand will require much more water but will also provide opportunities for rural farmers to generate needed income. This trend may also increase competition for agricultural water, marginalizing some farmers and herders, provoking conflict, and driving them deeper into poverty. Households will need adequate agricultural water to maintain animals that remain important providers of quality nutrition and on-farm power and a preferred means of wealth savings.

A livestock water productivity framework, with a gender dimension, enables a better understanding of livestock-water interactions [established but incomplete]. The framework identifies four basic livestock development strategies that can lead to more productive and sustainable use of water resources: improving the sourcing of animal feeds; enhancing animal productivity (products, services, and cultural values) through better veterinary care, genetics, marketing of animal products, and value-added enterprise; improving watering and grazing practices to avoid degradation of land and water resources; and providing quality drinking water. These strategies are often needed simultaneously.

Little is known about water depleted to produce feed, the efficiency with which feed is converted into animal products and services, and the impact animals have on water resources [established but incomplete]. A seventyfold difference in feed-water productivity (ratio of the benefits of livestock goods and services produced to the water depleted in producing them) is reported in the scientific literature. There are also large variations in animal productivity and animal impacts on water resources. Thus, generalized estimates of livestock water productivity require scrutiny, and global assessments of livestock water productivity are needed. While there is still much to learn about site- and production system-specific policy, technologies, and practices that can lead to increased and sustainable livestock water productivity, integration of existing knowledge of animal production with range and water resources management options affords good opportunities to increase sustainability and the productivity of water used for livestock production.

Drinking water is essential for animal survival, but the amount needed is small compared with other uses of agricultural water [well established]. Investing in drinking water makes strategic sense given the high value of animals and animal products and the small amount of water used. One liter of drinking water provided in areas of surplus feed effectively makes available an additional 100 liters of otherwise unusable agricultural water evapotranspired from rangeland vegetation and greatly increases livestock water productivity. Strategic placement and provision of adequate quality drinking water enables animals, particularly cattle, to source feed in otherwise inaccessible grazing areas and enhances the production of meat and milk. Selecting animals adapted to dryland conditions may reduce the need for drinking water. Careful management of areas adjacent to drinking water is necessary to avoid water and land degradation.

The widespread perception that livestock production is a wasteful use of the world's water resources does not apply to conditions in many developing country contexts [established but incomplete]. Livestock can be efficient and effective users of water when they depend largely on crop residues and by-products and on well managed rangelands unsuitable for crop production. Application of livestock water productivity concepts may lead to some of the greatest enhancements in productivity of future agricultural water use in developing countries. Achieving this requires improved integrated governance of livestock and water resources.

The overarching message of this chapter is that livestock-water interactions are important and under-researched and that huge opportunities exist to improve the productivity of water associated with livestock production. In contrast to the large body of knowledge related to crop-water interactions, research on livestock-water interactions remains in its infancy. Of necessity, this chapter takes a "broad brush" approach and a global overview of some general principles that are likely to be most applicable in the poorest regions of the world, especially in Sub-Saharan Africa. Readers are advised to examine their specific cases and situations in detail, to be vigilant for new and unexpected ways that animals and water use affect each other, and to consult with qualified and diverse disciplinary experts before intervening in national and local contexts.

> One of the quickest ways to aggravate poverty is to deprive smallholder livestock keepers and herders in developing countries of their animals

Water, livestock, and human development

Livestock keeping is one of the most important, complex, and diverse subsectors of world agriculture and a primary means of escaping poverty in rural areas. The very poor often do not keep animals, but many would likely do so given the opportunity (van Hoeve and van Koppen 2005). One of the quickest ways to aggravate poverty is to deprive smallholder livestock keepers and herders in developing countries of their animals. Little systematic integration of water and livestock development has taken place, a failure that has undermined investments in both subsectors (Peden and others 2006). Future development of agricultural water will benefit from effective integration and consideration of animal use of and impact on water resources *[established but incomplete]*.

Much popular and environmental literature considers livestock production to be among the greatest threats to sustainable water use over the coming decades. The large volumes of water thought necessary to produce human food from livestock is the major concern. For example, the *Times of India* (2004) reports that one liter of milk requires 3,000 liters of water, and it attributes rapid declines in groundwater to wasteful dairy production. Goodland and Pimental (2000) and Nierenberg (2005) state that producing 1 kilogram (kg) of grainfed beef requires about 100,000 liters of water, while producing 1 kg of potatoes takes only 500 liters. However, SIWI and others (2005) estimate that grainfed beef uses only 15,000 liters of water. Thus, while there is little agreement on the precise amount of water needed for grainfed beef production, the literature does agree that it takes much more water to produce 1 kg of grainfed beef than 1 kg of crops (Chapagain and Hoekstra 2003; Hoekstra and Hung 2003). Much of the literature is flawed, however, in comparing water used for production (kilogram fresh weight) of human foods without correcting for their water content and in using data of questionable relevance to developing countries.

> The contributions of livestock to rural livelihoods have been underestimated because of a past focus on productivity, limited consideration of nonmonetized products and services, and neglect of small stock

The water productivities of dry weight protein from crops and animal products differ less than those of fresh weight production. For example, Renault and Wallender (2000) estimate protein water productivity at 41 grams per cubic meter for eggs, 40 for milk, 33 for poultry meat, 21 for pork, and 10 for beef compared with 150 grams per cubic meter for potatoes, 77 for maize, 76 for bean, 74 for wheat, 49 for rice, and 14 for groundnuts. And the 10 grams per cubic meter refers to California grainfed beef. In poverty-prone regions of the world farmers' and herders' cattle graze or feed mostly on crop residues, processes that require much less water than does grain for production.

Furthermore, the amino acid mix of crop proteins is less suitable for human nutrition unless people consume appropriate mixtures of grains and pulses or obtain quality protein from other sources. And some crop foods such as potatoes, although their protein water productivity is high, have a very low protein content. Adults would have to consume 2,700 kilocalories a day of potato energy to obtain minimal daily protein requirements of 75 grams (Beaton 1991). Meat consumed beyond the 75 grams of protein needed daily tends to be used by the human body as an energy source. Thus, the water used to meet the first 75 grams of dietary protein is more effectively used than the water used to produce additional protein if the body converts it to energy. Modest amounts of meat in the diets of African children appear to improve mental, physical, and behavioral development (Sigman and others 2005; Neumann and others 2003), demonstrating that meat should not be evaluated only in terms of weight produced. However, the literature on livestock-water interactions does not address this important topic *[established but incomplete]*.

The contributions of livestock to rural livelihoods have been underestimated because of a past focus on productivity, limited consideration of nonmonetized products and services, and neglect of small stock, such as goats and poultry. But poor and subsistence households obtain multiple benefits from the use of livestock (Shackleton and others 1999; Landefeld and Bettinger 2005).

Beyond meat production and consumption, water used to support animals provides great value. Livestock contribute to the livelihoods of at least 70% of the world's rural poor and strengthen their capacity to cope with income shocks (Ashley, Holden, and Bazeley 1999). They provide milk, blood, manure, hides, and farm power essential to cultivation and marketing of crops. Livestock assets are often an important source of wealth security.

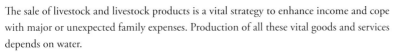

The sale of livestock and livestock products is a vital strategy to enhance income and cope with major or unexpected family expenses. Production of all these vital goods and services depends on water.

This chapter describes the global distribution of livestock production systems and the implications for the use of agricultural water, outlines major trends affecting animal production, and links this distribution and production to the use of agricultural water. It introduces a livestock water productivity framework to help understand how livestock keeping in diverse production systems affects the depletion and degradation of water resources and uses this understanding to suggest strategies and options for more efficient, productive, and sustainable use of water. It concludes with brief case studies of the practical application of these strategies.

> The sale of livestock and livestock products is a vital strategy to enhance income and cope with major or unexpected family expenses

This chapter emphasizes animal keeping in developing countries, especially in South Asia and Sub-Saharan Africa, where poverty and livestock keeping converge, and it emphasizes ruminants, particularly cattle, since these are the animals most commonly associated with high rates of water use and degradation. The chapter draws on relevant developed country research when appropriate. Many breeds and species of animals constitute what is collectively known as livestock, but space does not allow discussion of all of them. Poultry and swine are particularly important but are not addressed here in any detail. This study is among the first to examine livestock-water interactions in diverse poverty-stressed developing countries, and much more research is needed to tailor specific policy and research options applicable to national and local areas.

Where are livestock kept by the poor?

Livestock keeping varies greatly by the livelihoods, environments, and cultures in which it takes place. The nature of livestock-water interactions also differs, including livestock use of water resources and impact on them and options for better management of both resources and their interactions. A global assessment requires an understanding of all these variations.

Livestock production systems

This chapter uses Thornton and others' (2002) description of nine livestock production systems and global distributions of tropical livestock units (defined in box 13.1) and poor livestock keepers (table 13.1). Production systems are defined according to water availability, agricultural intensification, and presence of livestock. In addition, "landless" livestock production is rapidly increasing in developing countries. Landless systems include industrial-scale and smallholder production in which animals are confined to pens. The producers, living in livestock-supporting landscapes, neither graze their animals nor produce the feed for them but rather purchase the feed and usually sell animal products for profit. *Poor livestock keepers* are defined as people who live in rural areas, keep livestock, and live below the national poverty lines established by the World Bank for each country. Descriptions of production systems, livestock, and the distribution of poor livestock keepers in the chapter provide a valid broad global overview, but substantive variation will occur at local levels.

box **13.1** | **Tropical livestock units**

Livestock consist of many species and breeds of big and small animals that are raised worldwide in diverse production systems. To enable comparisons and to synthesize results, livestock are converted into tropical livestock units. One tropical livestock unit is equivalent to a 250 kg live-weight animal. The tropical livestock unit is a useful estimator of animal biomass, but it is imprecise because of significant variation of animal weights within species, across herds, and across production systems. For that reason, some sources cited in the chapter use different tropical livestock unit equivalents. The table shows indicative tropical livestock unit equivalents for domestic animals considered in this chapter. Also shown are basal metabolic rates based on Kleiber's "three-quarters law" that underpins discussion on water requirements for livestock feed production (see discussion later in chapter).

Indicative tropical livestock unit equivalents and basal metabolic rates

Species	Tropical livestock units per head	Basal metabolic unit (kilocalories per tropical livestock unit)	Species	Tropical livestock units per head	Basal metabolic unit (kilocalories per tropical livestock unit)
Camel	1.4	4,046	Pig	0.20	6,581
Cattle	1.0	4,401	Sheep or goats	0.10	7,826
Donkey	0.5	5,234	Poultry (chicken)	0.01	13,917

Source: FAO 2004; Kleiber 1975; Jahnke 1982.

Animal census data are notably incomplete for many countries, and methods for conducting them vary. Caution is needed in applying this information to smaller areas.

Developing countries cover about 80 million square kilometers of the world's land area. Of this about 48 million square kilometers are used for livestock keeping (23 square kilometers is rangeland, 20 square kilometers is mixed rainfed crop-livestock production, and 5 square kilometers is mixed irrigated crop-livestock). About half of the rangelands and a third of the mixed rainfed production systems are in Sub-Saharan Africa. Diseases limit animal keeping in very hot and humid areas such as the Amazon and Congo Basins. Extreme aridity, such as in the Sahara Desert, also constrains animal production. Otherwise, livestock are widespread across the developing world.

Landless animal production is most evident in the Indo-Gangetic region of South Asia, China, and Indonesia. It will likely expand in and around urban areas of Sub-Saharan Africa in coming years (Peden and others 2006).

Livestock keepers and their animals

Human and animal demographics vary greatly across production systems and regions of the world. Livestock production systems support about 4 billion people (see table 13.1). Of these, about 1.3 billion (32%) people are poor and about 509 million people (13%) are poor livestock keepers (map 13.1). Sub-Saharan Africa and South Asia are home to 63% (800 million) of the poor and about 68% (344 million) of the poor livestock keepers. About half

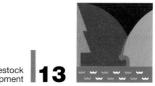

table **13.1**	Area, people, poverty, and livestock within animal production systems of developing country regions							
	Sub-Saharan Africa	Central and South America	West Asia and North Africa	East Asia	South-east Asia	South Asia	Newly independent states of Central Asia	Total
Animal production system area (millions of square kilometers)								
Rangeland	8.97	5.47	1.81	4.33	0.21	0.35	2.05	23.19
Mixed irrigated	0.12	0.40	0.83	1.37	0.48	1.52	0.41	5.13
Mixed rainfed	6.53	5.23	1.56	2.47	1.41	1.72	1.01	19.93
Other lands with some livestock	8.45	9.24	8.09	2.80	2.65	0.80	0.57	32.60
Total	24.2	20.3	12.3	11.0	4.8	4.4	4.0	80.8
People and poverty in production systems								
Number of people (millions)	506	329	310	1,187	401	1,256	64	4,053
Number of people below national poverty lines (millions)	268	132	85	111	127	533	17	1,273
Number of poor livestock keepers[a] (millions)	152	45	34	24	52	192	10	509
Share of total who are poor (percent)	53	40	27	9	32	42	27	44
Share of total who are poor livestock keepers (percent)	30	14	11	2	13	15	16	13
Cattle, sheep, and goats (tropical livestock units[b])								
Number (millions)	246	391	57	111	85	276	24	1,190
Density (number per square kilometer)	10.2	19.3	4.6	10.1	17.7	62.7	6.0	14.7
Estimated water needs for maintenance of livestock[c] (billions of cubic meters a year)								
Drinking	2.2	3.7	0.5	1.0	0.8	2.5	0.2	0.9
Feed production	111	176	26	50	38	124	11	536

a. Refer to map 13.1 for geographic distribution.

b. One tropical livestock unit = 250 kg of live animal weight.

c. Maintenance refers to minimum amount of water needed to keep animals alive without weight loss but excludes extra feed needed for growth, lactation, and work; see text for explanation.

Source: Adapted from Thornton and others 2002.

of the 500 million people who reside in livestock-producing areas of Sub-Saharan Africa live below the poverty line and about 30% of them are poor livestock keepers. About 40% (533 million) of South Asians are poor and 15% (192 million) are poor livestock keepers. In summary, South Asia has the highest level of absolute poverty and Sub-Saharan Africa has the highest prevalence of poverty. The poor in these two regions, for whom livestock are often very important as both critical livelihood opportunities and constraints, are the focus of this chapter although important livestock-water-poverty interactions are widespread globally.

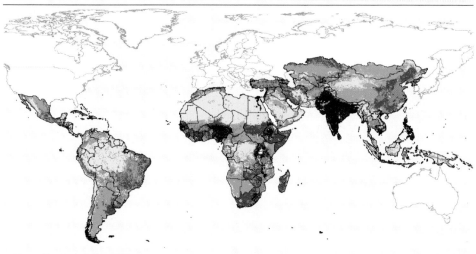

| map **13.1** | **Developing country distribution of livestock keepers who are poor** (per square kilometer) |

☐ 0 ▨ 1–2 ▨ 2–5 ▨ 5–20 ■ More than 20

Source: Thornton and others 2002.

Understanding how livestock, water resources, and poverty are intertwined holds promise of ensuring that livestock and water development can be encouraged in a coherent and balanced way to sustainably improve human well-being.

In many countries livestock holdings are more equitably distributed than land holdings. Livestock have greater economic and social importance in poor households than in less poor ones (Heffernan and Misturelli 2001). For example, in India smallholders with less than 2 hectares (ha) of land make up 62.5% the rural households, possess only 32.8% of the cultivated land, but account for 74% of poultry, 70% of pigs, 67% of bovines, and 65% of small ruminants (Taneja and Brithal 2004). In Ethiopia smallholder farmers account for 98% of milk production (Redda 2002). In North, Central, and South America, most beef is produced on medium-size and large ranches but a significant share is produced on small farms (Jarvis 1986).

Although about 165 million poor livestock keepers live in East and Southeast Asia, the newly independent states of Central Asia, West Asia and North Africa, and Central and South America, they constitute a smaller share of the population in livestock-producing areas compared with South Asia and Sub-Saharan Africa, and average poverty levels are less severe (see table 13.1).

Cattle, sheep, and goats in the production systems of developing countries total about 1.2 billion tropical livestock units (see table 13.1). The convergence of high livestock density (more than 40 tropical livestock units per square kilometer) and poverty occurs mostly in South Asia and Sub-Saharan Africa in a band stretching from Senegal across the Sahel to Ethiopia and southward through East Africa and into Southern Africa (map 13.2).

| map **13.2** | **Developing country distribution of livestock** (tropical livestock units per square kilometer) |

□ 0–5 ⬜ 6–10 ◼ 11–20 ⬜ 21–40 ⬛ More than 40

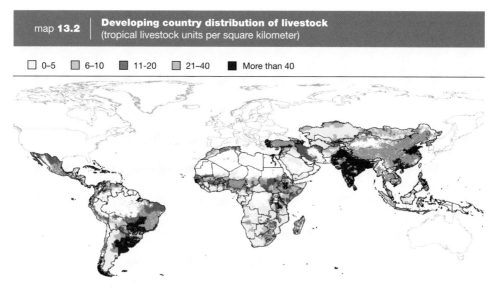

Source: Thornton and others 2002.

High animal densities also exist in the Cone of South America, Turkey and the eastern Mediterranean, and East Asia, but poverty in these areas is less severe.

The global livestock population requires considerable amounts of water, but estimates of these amounts are crude. When considering livestock and water, most people think of drinking water. Drinking water requirements total about 900 million cubic meters per year within developing country production systems (see table 13.1), assuming a need for about 25 liters a day per tropical livestock unit, though the amount is highly variable. However, by far more water is required to produce feed for animals. Evapotranspiration associated with the production of maintenance feed totals about 450 cubic meters per tropical livestock unit a year, an amount that can underestimate the actual value by as much as 50% depending on animals' growth, reproduction, work, environment, and lactating states. The total water required for cattle, sheep, and goat feed in developing countries will exceed 530 billion cubic meters a year, with additional water required for other livestock species.

Livestock and intensified agriculture

Animal densities are often correlated with human densities, the intensification of agriculture, proximity to markets, and the use of water for crop production (table 13.2; Peden and others 2006). For example, in Africa the highest animal densities are associated with intensive crop production, especially large-scale irrigation systems. This may suggest that livestock keepers are already responding to the driving forces of urbanization, or it may simply be that people and animals are more prevalent where food crop production is highest and where people are wealthy enough to own animals. However, evidence suggests that successful intensification of agriculture, including irrigated crop production, generates new farm income and helps reduce poverty. This enables farmers to invest in livestock as a

table **13.2**

	African livestock densities in irrigated, rainfed, and rangeland production systems in relation to market access and human density (tropical livestock units per square kilometer)			
	Production system			
Criterion	Mixed irrigated	Mixed rainfed	Livestock dominant	Weighted mean[a]
Market access				
Poor	14.0[b]	14.1	9.7	10.9
Good	38.7	23.0	16.7	21.8
Human population density				
High	45.1	31.2	38.8	33.0
Low	26.1[b]	13.6	10.9	12.1
Weighted mean	32.4	19.7	11.3	

a. Weighted according to total area covered by the associated criterion.

b. Irrigated area was so small that comparison with data in the rest of the table may not be reliable.

Source: Peden and others 2006.

preferred means of wealth savings and an opportunity to further increase income through sales of animal products (chapter 4 on poverty; Peden and others 2006).

In South Asia water and land availability determine the types and numbers of live-stock (Chawla, Kurup, and Sharma 2004). In India livestock densities are higher in irrigated areas than in rainfed areas (Sastry 2000; Misra and Mahipal 2000), but the average number of animals per household may be fewer (Chawla, Kurup, and Sharma 2004) and animal feed may be more limiting. Intensification of crop production through the development of agricultural water will attract livestock production and heighten competition for water resources.

Demand for livestock products

World consumption of animal products is growing. Projected demand for animal production and rates of change in demand vary by region (table 13.3). Consumption and production are rising at about 2.5%–4% a year in developing countries, but at less than 0.5% a year in developed ones. Rising demand and consumption are closely linked to the increased purchasing power of rapidly urbanizing populations. In developed countries per capita demand for animal products has leveled off and may decline in the future, reflecting consumers' concern about prices, the ethics of keeping animals, and perceptions about the harmful impact of excessive use of animal products on human health and the environment. Despite faster growth in consumption of meat and milk in South Asia and Sub-Saharan Africa, where poverty and food security remain critical, by 2020 per capita consumption will still be far below levels in developed countries.

Demand for animal products originates in the same markets that drive demand for high-value horticultural crops and other products of intensified agriculture and likely competes for the same agricultural water needed to produce them. Three challenges for the future are allocating water required to satisfy urban demands for both meat and crop

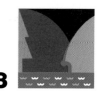

table **13.3**	Projected trends in meat and milk consumption and production, 1997–2020					
	Projected annual growth rate 1997–2020 (percent)		Projected amount in 2020 (million metric tons)		Projected per capita amount in 2020 (kilograms a year)	
Region	Meat	Milk	Meat	Milk	Meat	Milk
Consumption						
China	3.1	3.8	107	24	73	16
India	3.5	3.5	10	133	8	105
Other East Asia	3.2	2.5	5	2	54	29
Other South Asia	3.5	3.1	7	42	13	82
Southeast Asia	3.4	3.0	19	12	30	19
Latin America	2.5	1.9	46	85	70	130
West Asia and North Africa	2.7	2.3	13	42	26	82
Sub-Saharan Africa	3.2	3.3	11	35	12	37
Developing countries	3.0	2.9	217	375	36	62
Developed countries	0.8	0.6	117	286	86	210
World	2.1	1.7	334	660	45	89
Production						
China	2.9	3.2	86	19	60	13
Other East Asia	2.4	3.9	7	3	55	29
India	2.8	1.6	8	172	6	135
Other South Asia	2.6	3.1	4	46	9	92
Southeast Asia	3.1	2.9	16	3	25	5
Latin America	2.2	2.0	39	80	59	121
West Asia and North Africa	2.5	2.6	11	46	18	72
Sub-Saharan Africa	3.4	4.0	11	31	10	30
Developing countries	2.7	3.2	183	401	29	63
Developed countries	0.7	0.4	121	371	87	267
World	1.8	1.6	303	772	39	100

Source: Delgado 2003.

production in intensified agricultural systems; making livestock production a more water efficient and sustainable livelihood option, particularly for the poor; and ensuring that policy focused on meeting demands from urban markets does not divert attention from rural livestock keepers, for whom livestock have many uses beyond the sale of meat and milk.

Livestock water productivity—an integrated approach to managing animal-water interactions

Livestock water productivity is defined as the ratio of net beneficial livestock-related products and services to the water depleted in producing them. It acknowledges the importance of competing uses of water but focuses on livestock-water interaction. Livestock water productivity is a systems concept, with each production system having a unique dynamic structure and mix of processes. Production systems are complex, and an integrating framework can help to identify sets of options to enable more effective and sustainable use of water for livestock. Key livestock water productivity principles are illustrated in figure 13.1.

Regardless of the size of the land area covered, water enters an agricultural system in the form of rain or surface inflow. Water is depleted or lost through transpiration, evaporation, and downstream discharge and cannot be readily used again. Degradation and contamination also deplete water in the sense that the water may be too costly to purify for reuse. Agricultural output depends primarily on transpiration. Animal production depends on the use of feed produced by transpiration (unless it has been imported, in which case the feed incorporates "virtual" water, reflecting transpiration occurring in another country). Introducing animal management practices that promote useful transpiration or infiltration of available water will likely increase livestock water productivity. Livestock water productivity differs from water or rain use efficiency because it looks at water depleted rather than at applied or inflowing water.

> Three basic strategies help to increase livestock water productivity directly: improving feed sourcing, enhancing animal productivity, and conserving water

Three basic strategies help to increase livestock water productivity directly: improving feed sourcing, enhancing animal productivity, and conserving water (see figure 13.1). Providing sufficient drinking water of adequate quality also improves livestock water productivity. However, it does not factor directly into the livestock water productivity equation because water that has been drunk remains inside the animal and thus within the production system, although subsequent evaporative depletion may follow.

Focusing on a single strategy may not be effective. A balanced, site-specific approach that considers all four strategies will help to increase the benefits derived from the use of agricultural water for the production of animal products and services. Children, women, and men often receive different benefits from animal keeping and have different roles in managing livestock-water interactions, considerations that need to be taken into account in attempts to improve livestock water productivity. Livestock water productivity does not seek to maximize the number of livestock or the production of animal products and services. Rather, it opens opportunities to produce the same benefits with fewer animals and less demand for agricultural water.

Improving feed sourcing

Animal production depends on access to sufficient supplies of quality feed—grains, crop residues and by-products, pasture, tree fodder, and forage crops. Production of feeds is one of the world's largest uses of agricultural water. The entry point for improving global livestock water productivity must be strategic sourcing of animal feed, an issue that has largely been ignored during the past 50 years of research on livestock and water management. Judicious selection of feed sources is potentially one of the most effective ways of improving global agricultural water productivity.

Science-based knowledge of water use for feed remains contradictory and highly variable. The discussion here focuses on three important issues: the water productivity of feeds and forages, conversion of feed to animal products and services, and the distribution of feed resources.

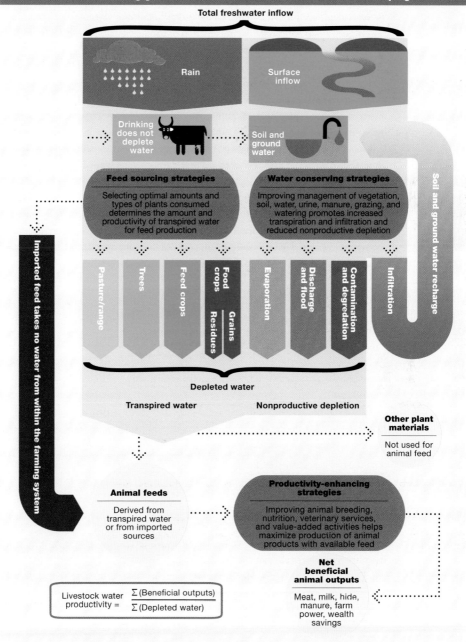

Source: Authors' schematization derived from research for the Comprehensive Assessment of Water Management in Agriculture and the Challenge Program on Water and Food of the Consultative Group on International Agricultural Research.

Water productivity of feeds and forages. Available literature indicates that evapotranspired water used to produce 1 kg of dry animal feed is highly variable, ranging from about 0.5 kg per cubic meter of water to about 8 kg (table 13.4). Many factors affect the amount of water depleted through evapotranspiration, including the vegetative leaf area index, animal preferences for specific fodder plants, root depth, rainfall, plant genetics, and soil structure, moisture, and chemistry.

Sala and others (1988) analyzed 9,500 sites throughout the central United States and found that the water productivity of diverse temperate grasslands receiving 200–1,200 millimeters (mm) of annual rainfall was similar, at about 0.5 kg of aerial biomass per cubic meter of evapotranspiration, with productivity slightly higher in wetter sites than in drier ones. The higher levels of water productivity for forage sorghum in Sudan, for various crops and pasture in Ethiopia, and for *Pennisetum* reflect experimental studies in which cumulative evapotranspiration was measured only during plant growth. The remaining cases represent year-round calculations of evapotranspiration in cooler climates where growing seasons were less than one year in length. Clearly, no accurate estimates of evapotranspiration used for feed are possible without standardizing the methodology, but for illustrative purposes we have used the figure of 4 kg per cubic meter. This figure, based on experimental evidence, may overestimate water productivity in the real world. There is great need for a systematic global evaluation of the water productivity of forage plants.

table **13.4**	**Dry matter water productivity of selected forage and rangeland vegetation**	
Forage and feed plants	**Above ground dry matter water productivity (kilograms per cubic meter)**	**Source**
Irrigated forage sorghum, Sudan	6–8[a]	Saeed and El-Nadi 1997
Various crops and pastures, Ethiopia	4[a]	Astatke and Saleem 1998
Pennisetum purpureum (1,200 mm evapotranspiration)	4.33	Ferraris and Sinclair 1980
Pennisetum purpureum (900 mm evapotranspiration)	4.27	Ferraris and Sinclair 1980
Pennisetum purpureum (600 mm evapotranspiration)	4.15	Ferraris and Sinclair 1980
Irrigated alfalfa, Sudan	1.3–1.7	Saeed and El-Nadi 1997
Irrigated alfalfa, Wyoming, United States	1.22–1.47[b]	Claypool and others 1997
Alfalfa, California, United States	1.11	Renault and Wallender 2000
Irrigated pasture, California, United States	0.72	Renault and Wallender 2000
Rangeland, California, United States	0.72	Renault and Wallender 2000
Grasslands, United States (1,200 mm rain)	0.57	Sala and others 1988
Grasslands, United States (900 mm rain)	0.56	Sala and others 1988
Grasslands, United States (600 mm rain)	0.54	Sala and others 1988
Grasslands, United States (300 mm rain)	0.49	Sala and others 1988

a. Relatively high values may reflect experimental design, ambient temperature, annual versus growing season water budget, leaf area index, solar energy, and other variables.
b. Estimates transpiration rather than evapotranspiration.

Keller and Seckler (2005) suggest that transpiration efficiency (dry matter production per unit of transpired water) is relatively constant for particular plant species and that variability in crop water efficiency depends on site- and season-specific differences in the evaporation component of evapotranspiration. Some opportunity exists to select water-efficient forage species and varieties (Claypool and others 1997). C_4 plants may have higher water productivity than C_3 species.[1] However, reducing the evaporation component of evapotranspiration will be one of the most important and practical pathways for increasing feed water productivity and thus livestock water productivity.

Crop residues and by-products present a unique opportunity for feed sourcing. Because efforts to improve crop water productivity have focused on grains and fruits that people consume, any residues and by-products that can be used by animals represent a potential feed source that requires no additional evapotranspiration. To the extent that animal production can take advantage of this feed source, huge gains in livestock water productivity are possible. Figure 13.2 demonstrates how the livestock water productivity for a group of Ethiopian farmers is positively correlated with the share of crop residues in their animals' diets. Use of crop residues can boost farm income without the use of additional water [*established but incomplete*].

Theoretically, if livestock production were based solely on the use of crop residues and by-products, water for feed production would be nil. However, this extreme may not be economically and environmentally desirable if sufficient residues and manure are not left

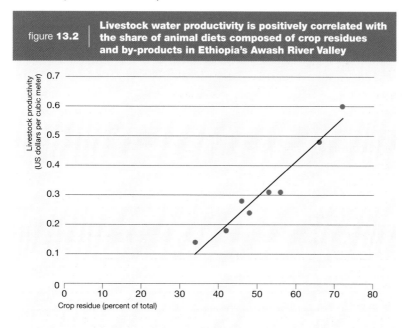

figure **13.2** | **Livestock water productivity is positively correlated with the share of animal diets composed of crop residues and by-products in Ethiopia's Awash River Valley**

Note: This example takes into account livestock's multiple values in terms of providing milk, meat, and farm power. Evapotranspiration enabling grain production also results in valuable stover for use as animal feed without using more water.

Source: Authors' analysis based on data from Ayalneh 2004.

in or returned to the soil to maintain soil productivity. Furthermore, crop residues tend to be relatively indigestible and to have lower nutritional quality. These limitations will have to be overcome. Options include making urea-treated silage from residues and providing high quality supplemental foods containing limited grains or leguminous forage crops Studies are needed of the tradeoffs associated with different options for using residues and by-products.

Improving livestock water productivity requires assessing the feed requirements of livestock and selecting feeds with high water productivity relative to other uses for agricultural water

Conversion of feed to animal products and services. Improving livestock water productivity requires assessing the feed requirements of livestock and selecting feeds with high water productivity relative to other uses for agricultural water. This in turn requires estimates of the feed energy and nutrient needs for maintenance, growth, reproduction, lactation, work, thermoregulation, and symbiotic micro-organisms and parasites of the digestive tract. The digestibility of feed varies between 20% and 70%, and the indigestible component is returned to the ecosystem in the form of manure. Should the transpired water used to produce undigestible feed that ends up as manure be attributed to livestock production when this manure contributes to the fertility replenishment of soil, household fuel, and construction material for homes? In this study we include the value of manure among the benefits attributed to animal production. We could also have reduced the estimated water depleted for animal production. Either way, recognizing the value of manure will lead to increased estimates of livestock water productivity where there is demand for manure. In cases where excess deposition of manure damages the environment, the environmental cost should be included in estimating the net benefits associated with livestock production.

The basal metabolic rate is the intracellular energy consumption of a fasting animal (not in a state of reproduction or lactation) at rest in a thermoneutral environment. In 1932 Kleiber (1932) demonstrated that the basal metabolic rate of mammals ranging in size from mice to elephants is proportional to their live weight$^{0.75}$. Kleiber's "three-quarters law" is the conceptual basis for estimating maintenance feed energy requirements of livestock. The basal metabolic rate is a common denominator for comparing the energy requirements of individual animals of all livestock species, breeds, and age classes. The basal metabolic rate for one animal weighing 250 kg (1 tropical livestock unit) is 4,401 kilocalories (Kcal) a day. The basal metabolic rate per tropical livestock unit can be much greater for small animals than for big animals. The basal metabolic rate of chickens, for example, is about three times that of cattle or camels. The three-quarters law has been confirmed by numerous scientists, but small deviations from this predictor can still be expected [well established].

Taking into account other energy and nutrient needs of livestock is a complex task. Maintenance energy consumption is greater than the basal metabolic rate and includes energy needs for thermoregulation, gut function, loss of energy in urine, and modest work for feeding and drinking. Maintenance energy varies by livestock species and breeds and the environments in which they are kept (tables 13.2 and 13.5).

A synthesis by the International Livestock Research Institute (ILRI) (Fernandez-Rivera 2006) suggests an estimate of animal maintenance energy of 11,000 Kcal per tropical livestock unit per day for grazing cattle in Africa, but diverse environments, species,

table **13.5**	Estimated maintenance energy consumption of selected animals	
Animal and location	**Maintenance energy[a]**	**Source**
Broiler chickens, United States, at 13°C	157	Sakomura and others 2005
Broiler chickens, United States, at 32°C	127	Sakomura and others 2005
Holstein cattle, Japan	116	Odai 2003
Broiler chickens, United States, at 23°C	112	Sakomura and others 2005
Swine, average	106	NRC 1998
Holstein crossbreed, Thailand	98	Odai 2003
Cows, crossbred, Ethiopia	93	Zerbini and others 1992
Beef cattle	77	NRC 1996
Zebu oxen, Nigeria	76	Dijkman 1993
Mice to elephant, basal metabolic rate	70	Kleiber 1975
Draft oxen, West Africa	56	Fall and others 1997
Zebu oxen, Niger	48	Becker and others 1993

a. Kilocalories divided by live weight$^{0.75}$.

and breeds lead to wide variations. Animals also require additional energy for growth, reproduction, labor, and milk production.

Astatke, Reed, and Butterworth (1986) suggest that digestible energy in African hay is about 1,900–2,000 kcal per kilogram of dry weight and that 1 cubic meter of evapotranspiration will produce about 4 kg of dry weight hay (see table 13.4). Taking the ILRI estimate of 11,000 Kcal per tropical livestock unit per day for maintenance energy, this implies that grazing cattle in Africa would require about 5 kg per tropical livestock unit per day of feed for maintenance. The amount of evapotranspiration required to produce this feed would be about 1.25 cubic meters per tropical livestock unit per day or 450 cubic meters per tropical livestock unit per year. This compares with 25–50 liters a day or 9–18 cubic meters per tropical livestock unit per year for drinking water.

We recognize that actual energy use and water for feed will be about double this when factoring in growth, work, lactation, reproduction, herd structure, and thermoregulation. Considering the range of forage water productivity values cited in table 13.4, the uncertainties in estimating feed intake, and the varying digestibility of animal feeds, any estimates of worldwide use of agricultural water for livestock production are highly uncertain. Nevertheless, we can conclude that water transpired for feed production will be about 50 times or more the amount of drinking water intake. Increasing livestock water productivity will depend strongly on increasing the amount of feed animals use for production relative to the amounts used for maintenance.

Distribution of feed resources. Almost 50 million ha of agricultural land in developing countries is used to produce livestock (see table 13.1), but animal production is not optimally distributed within production systems to take advantage of many feed resources. Some areas are overgrazed, and some have surplus feeds that remain unused. Rangelands and drier rainfed cropping areas often lack drinking water for animals. Without drinking water, livestock, especially cattle, cannot access available forages and crop residues. Feeds that have been produced but cannot be consumed constitute a major loss of potential benefits and productivity of agricultural water. Global, regional, and national map inventories are needed that quantify the gaps between feed production and animal demands for feed. This knowledge can be used to identify options to enhance livestock water productivity by balancing animal stocking rates with sustainable feed supplies. Interventions may include bailing and transporting surplus feed to livestock or providing drinking water (discussed later in this chapter) so that animals can remain near feed sources.

> Global, regional, and national map inventories are needed that quantify the gaps between feed production and animal demands for feed to identify options to enhance livestock water productivity

Global use of water for feed production. Global evapotranspiration to produce feed to maintain cattle, sheep, and goats may be about 536 billion cubic meters a year in developing countries. Taking into account water for other livestock species and requirements beyond maintenance, we conclude that water used for global feed production ranges from 1 to 2 trillion cubic meters per year plus that used in developed countries. These estimates remain quite imprecise and are lower than some other estimates [competing explanations].

Enhancing animal productivity

Water transpired to produce maintenance feed is a fixed input required for animal keeping whether or not animals are gaining weight, producing milk, or working. Additional water is needed for production. A key livestock water productivity strategy requires increasing the productivity of each animal. This is the domain of the traditional animal science disciplines of nutrition, genetics, veterinary health, marketing, and animal husbandry. Typical interventions include:

- Providing continuous access to quality drinking water (Muli 2000; Staal and others 2001).
- Selecting and breeding cattle for improved feed conversion efficiency and thus increased livestock water productivity (Basarab 2003).
- Providing veterinary health services as part of investments in irrigation development in dryland areas to reduce the risk of waterborne animal and zoonotic diseases (Peden and others 2006) and to meet animal health safety standards for marketing animals and animal products (Perry and others 2002).
- Adding value to animal products, such as farmers' production of butter (box 13.2).

Conserving water resources

As early as 1958 Love (cited in Sheehy and others 1996, section 2.1.1.2) noted that, "There is a large body of information leading to the conclusion that heavy grazing has had bad hydrologic consequences. It is doubtful that more investigations are needed to emphasize this conclusion." A half century later this still holds true. Sheehy and others (1996), in a comprehensive overview of the impact of grazing livestock on water and associated land resources, conclude that livestock must be managed in ways that maintain vegetative ground cover because vegetation loss results in increased soil erosion,

box **13.2**

Integrated water-livestock resources management increases the income and assets of a poor rural household

Many Ethiopian farmers subsist on less than $300 a year. With support from Sasakawa-Global 2000, a few farmers have adopted household water harvesting systems involving catchment areas of about 2,500 square meters that channel water into underground storage tanks with capacities of about 65 cubic meters each. For one female farmer (photo) this investment eliminated the daily 7 km trek for water. With two underground tanks, she meets her year-round domestic needs, provides drinking water for an improved hybrid milk cow, and provides supplemental irrigation for cash-generating onion, garlic, and citrus crops. Milk production increased from less than 2 liters a day to more than 40 liters a day from her crossbred cow. Time freed up from fetching water enabled her to produce butter and cheese, further increasing the cash generated from each liter of milk. Her children appear healthier and spend more time in school. The integration of dairying into this water harvesting-based livelihood strategy increased the financial, human, social, and physical assets of this poor rural household to a level exceeding that possible through crop production alone.

Household water harvesting integrated with livestock production helped secure family assets and reduce poverty and vulnerability

In the villages the increased cash flow enabled more farmers to diversify their incomes and to open a small shop serving the village area. With year-round income men spend more time at home on productive tasks and less time drinking.

Source: ILRI 2005.

downslope sedimentation, reduced infiltration, and less pasture production. While they find that low to moderate grazing pressure has little negative impact on hydrology, they also find that there is an optimal or threshold site-specific level of grazing intensity above which water and land degradation become problematic and animal production declines. Within this limit livestock water productivity can be maximized by balancing enhanced leaf to land area ratios that shift water depletion from evaporation to transpiration (Keller and Seckler 2005), with profitable levels of animal production and offtake.

The species composition and stocking levels of grazing animals affect the species composition of the vegetation (Sheehy and others 1996). High grazing pressure causes loss of palatable species suitable for animal production, but very low grazing pressure may encourage encroachment of woody vegetation. Either way, vegetation shifts can reduce the amount of useful vegetation and increase transpiration channeled through plant species that have little value for animals or other users.

Livestock grazing interacts with animal drinking. Cattle, especially, concentrate and often overgraze near water resources, leaving more distant areas undergrazed. Apart from removing vegetation as feed, animals aggravate runoff sedimentation by trampling and trekking on paths. Riparian areas, including streams, natural and artificially created ponds and lakes, wetlands, and irrigation infrastructure are all subject to degradation by inappropriately managed livestock (photos 13.1 and 13.2). Animals potentially affect water resources by causing chemical, physical, and bacteriological changes in water; modifying habitat and associated vegetation; and changing water flow patterns (Sheehy and others 1996).

Although overgrazing is a major threat to water resources, converting grazing land into cropland only within mixed crop-livestock systems presents a greater risk (Hurni 1990). Cultivation exposes soil to erosive rain and lack of vegetation. Under intensified Ethiopian farming systems poor farmers depend on animal power for cultivation (photos 13.3 and 13.4). Without oxen crop production would decline. Oxen are highly dependent on crop residues for feed, which is otherwise in short supply. Under customary land tenure farmers' lands revert to common grazing after crops have been harvested. Farmers' invest heavily in removing all residues from crop lands because if they do not do so neighbors' animals will consume the residues anyway. The production system, and not just the livestock, makes these crop lands highly vulnerable to runoff and erosion, lowering livestock water productivity and putting downstream water resources at risk.

Water used for meat processing and rendering (slaughtering animals and fowl, curing, canning meat products, transforming inedible and discarded remains into useful by-products such as lards and oils) is variable, but likely less than 2% of that needed for feed production (World Bank 1998). However, effluents originating from meat processing are often point sources of pollution, potentially degrading water resources and putting human health at risk.

Livestock grazing interacts with animal drinking

Photo 13.1 · Photo by Don Peden · Photo 13.2 · Photo by Don Peden

Uncontrolled use of water for livestock drinking contaminates water supplies, degrades riparian vegetation, and puts people's health at risk. Providing watering places that are physically separated from the water supply can restore habitat and improve domestic water quality (see photo 13.7 later in chapter).

Photo 13.3 · Photo by Don Peden · Photo 13.4 · Photo by Don Peden

Horses, cattle, and buffalo are important sources of farm power for poor farmers. Much of the water used to maintain farm animals is an input to crop production.

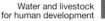
Providing sufficient drinking water

Water constitutes about 60%–70% of an animal's live weight (Faries, Sweeten, and Reagor 1997; Pallas 1986). This level must be maintained through water intake from drinking water and the water content of ingested feed. Animals also take advantage of metabolic water that results from intracellular respiration (which consumes oxygen and releases carbon dioxide and water). Animals lose water through evaporation, urine, feces, and lactation. Drinking is not a water-depleting process because the water remains in the production system. However, drunk water may be subsequently depleted through evaporation from pulmonary tissues and sweating. Water lost in urine passes to the soil (at least in pastures) and that lost in milk passes to young animals (unless processed for human consumption) and remains in the system. Subsequent depletion through evapotranspiration and milk export is possible, however.

> Livestock drink about 20–50 liters per tropical livestock unit per day

Livestock drink about 20–50 liters per tropical livestock unit per day (table 13.6). Drinking water volumes vary greatly by species and breed, ambient temperature, water quality, levels and water content of feed, and animal activity, pregnancy, and lactation (Pallas 1986; Seleshi, Tegegne, and Tsadik 2003; King 1983). Water drunk per kilogram of food intake ranges from 3.6 liters at ambient temperatures below 15° Celsius (C) to 8.5 liters at temperatures above 27°C (Pallas 1986; Sreeramulu 2004). In tropical areas air temperature may be greater than 32°C, and drinking increases greatly (NRC 1978; Shirley 1985). Thus, in the range of 5°–32°C water intake per degree Celsius per kilogram of dry matter will be about 0.118 liters, and intake above 32°C will be about 1.3 liters. For *Bos taurus* cattle water intake for heifers will be about 5% and for dry cows 10% of animal live weight in rainy and dry seasons, and for *Bos indicus* about half that. Water deprivation

table **13.6**	Estimated water requirement and voluntary intake of livestock under Sahelian conditions and chickens in India (liters per tropical livestock unit per day)						
Animal	**Tropical livestock unit per head**	**Wet season and air temperature of 27°C**		**Dry season and air temperature of 15°–21°C**		**Dry season and air temperature of 27°C**	
		Needed	**Voluntary intake**[a]	**Needed**	**Voluntary intake**[a]	**Needed**	**Voluntary intake**[a]
Sahelian livestock							
Camels	1.6	31	9	23	22	31	31
Cattle	0.7	36	14	29	27	39	39
Sheep	0.1	50	20	40	40	50	50
Goats	0.1	50	20	40	40	50	50
Donkeys	0.4	40	13	30	28	40	40
Indian chickens							
Laying hens[b]	0.01						32
Nonlaying hens[b]	0.01						18

a. Voluntary water intake is the daily amount of water drunk by an animal assuming that liquid water is continuously available to the animal and that feed plants have 70%–75% moisture during the wet season and 10–20% moisture during the dry season.
b. Water in feed is not known.
Source: For livestock, Pallas 1986; for chickens, Sreeramulu 2004.

reduces feed intake and lowers production. For lactating cows water deprivation can great-ly lower milk production (Staal and others 2001; Muli 2000).

Lactating cows require additional drinking water. For example, Indian lactating cows drink on average 70 liters of water daily; dry cows drink 45 liters and calves 22 liters (Sreeramulu 2004). In Canada lactating Holstein cows drink on average 85 liters of water daily and dry cows drink 40 liters (Irwin 1992). Drinking water is an important tool for enhancing animal production, but the volume drunk is a small fraction of the total water used for feed production.

Animals adapted to dryland conditions tend to drink less and to have high urinary osmolar concentrations[2] when dehydrated in contrast with those adapted to more temper-ate conditions (table 13.7). Most domesticated animals can survive about 60 days without feed but less than a week without drinking water. The best adapted species can rely on water in succulent plants and use little or no additional drinking water even in arid en-vironments. Domestication and breeding for productivity may have made livestock more dependent on drinking water and less able to withstand dry conditions.

Feces are a potentially larger source of water loss than urine. Half the body's total water pool can pass through the salivary glands and rumen each day. Therefore the ability to extract and reabsorb fecal water in the colon is important (Seleshi, Tegegne, and Tsadik 2003). *Bos taurus* cattle can reduce fecal moisture content to 60%, sheep to 50%, and camels to 45% (Macfarlane 1964, cited in King 1983). The feces of zebu cattle contain less water than those of European cattle (Quartermain, Phillips, and Lampkin 1957, cited in King 1983), partly explaining the lower water requirement of the zebu (Phillips 1960, cited in King 1983). One-third to one-half of the total daily water loss in cattle is in the feces (Schmidt-Nielsen 1965, cited in King 1983). Animals with high water reabsorption capacity will be better adapted to water-stressed environments and be able to graze farther from drinking water sources.

Cattle prefer to graze close to drinking water. Strategic placement of watering points encourages more complete and uniform grazing of entire pastures. In Missouri cattle pro-duction on 65 ha pastures was experimentally sustained and maximized by ensuring that distance to drinking water was less than 244 meters (Gerrish, Peterson, and Morrow 1995).

> Drinking water is an important tool for enhancing animal production, but the volume drunk is a small fraction of the total water used for feed production

table 13.7	Maximal urinary osmolar concentrations of selected East African mammals after severe dehydration	
Animal	**Maximal urinary osmolar concentration**
Dikdik	4,100
Camel	3,200
Oryx	3,000
Fat-tailed sheep	2,950
Goat	2,800
Impala	2,600
Donkey	1,500
Zebu cow	1,400

Source: Maloiy 1972, as cited in King 1983.

A study in Wyoming found that 77% of cattle grazing took place within 366 meters of the watering source, whereas 65% of available pasture was more than 730 meters from water (Gerrish and Davis 1999). In Sudan, to enable more effective use of vast quantities of underutilized grazing land, the government places priority on the strategic establishment of water harvesting to supply drinking water in pastoral areas.

Livestock water productivity and estimates of the virtual water content of meat and milk

The concept of virtual water attempts to integrate the water productivity of forage and feed with the conversion efficiency of these feeds into meat or milk. The complexity and diversity of livestock production systems create great uncertainty regarding the actual amounts of water used by livestock.

Chapagain and Hoekstra's (2003) estimates of the virtual water content of a number of animal products (table 13.8) generally support the view that animal production requires more water than crop production, but their estimates suggest that water usage is lower than that estimated by others (for example, Goodland and Pimental 2000) *[established but incomplete]*. In our view there are no reliable estimates of livestock water productivity for most situations in which livestock are kept. Existing estimates of water use by livestock have many limitations. Among the most salient are the following:

- Livestock production systems are highly diverse biophysically and socioeconomically and subject to many unresearched factors, making existing estimates of livestock water productivity unreliable generalizations. The knowledge gap is especially large for developing countries, where it impedes the introduction of targeted interventions that could bring about significant gains in agricultural water productivity.
- The water productivity of forage reported in the literature varies at least seventyfold, implying that estimates of livestock water productivity could vary accordingly.

> The complexity and diversity of livestock production systems create great uncertainty regarding the actual amounts of water used by livestock

table **13.8**	Virtual water content of sample meat and milk products expressed as livestock water productivity

Animal product	Virtual water content expressed as livestock water productivity (kilograms per cubic meters of freshwater)
Horse meat	0.082
Beef	0.082
Sheep and goat meat	0.118
Pork	0.291
Poultry meat	0.22–0.51
Cow's milk	0.788

Note: These estimates represent fresh weights only and do not examine nutritionally important components of meat and milk. Livestock water productivity is a function of forage water productivity, feed conversion efficiency, values of multiple animal products and services, values of competing uses of water, and the impact of livestock watering and grazing on water resources. Feed conversion efficiency is a function of animal genetics, animal health, availability of drinking water, temperature, work loads, and feed quality.

Source: Chapagain and Hoekstra 2003.

> **Much new research is required to provide reliable estimates of livestock water productivity**

- In rangelands, especially dry ones, forage water productivity is low, but there are few alternate uses of agricultural water, and livestock keeping may be one of the best uses of agricultural water. Furthermore, only a small part of the evapotranspiration typically attributed to pasture production is actually used by grazing animals. Typically, about half of plant biomass production takes place below ground. In well managed pastures only about half of the above biomass is consumed by grazing animals. Of the amount consumed only about half is digested, with the remainder being returned to the soil. Thus, only about one-eighth of depleted evapotranspiration contributes to animal production. The rest contributes to maintaining the pasture ecosystem and providing ecosystem services *[established but incomplete]*.

- In irrigated and mixed crop-livestock systems crop residues and by-products have very high water productivity because little or no water is used to produce them and manure provides additional value.

- Developing countries often have large herds with low productivity so that most water depleted by animals is associated with maintenance rather than with the production of goods and services.

- The literature describing water use by livestock usually focuses on meat or milk and ignores the multiple uses of animals, thereby underestimating livestock water productivity, especially in developing countries. For example, without animal power, crop production would decline in some countries.

- The literature describing water use by livestock usually ignores the impact of livestock grazing and watering on water contamination, degradation, and depletion, implying that livestock water productivity may be overestimated. However, the conversion of livestock to annual crop production for the purpose of increasing water productivity may result in lower water productivity because of enhanced depletion through runoff from cropland.

- Our understanding of livestock water productivity is in its infancy, and a transdisciplinary global effort is required to fully and meaningfully asses it worldwide.

We believe that much new research is required to provide reliable estimates of livestock water productivity *[established but incomplete]*.

Livestock water productivity and gender

Livestock help satisfy poor farmers' demands for financial and natural capital and depend on human and physical capital for their management. Efforts to improve livestock water productivity through feed sourcing, production enhancing, and water conserving and provisioning activities will affect children, women, and men and various ethnic groups uniquely, and the various products and services provided by animals will benefit people differently *[established but incomplete]* (photos 13.5–13.6).

Van Hoeve and Van Koppen (2005) have examined the gender dimensions of the livestock water productivity framework and have concluded that efforts to improve animal production must take into account gender differences within livestock producing communities. A key lesson is the potential of smallholder dairying to enable rural and peri-urban

Photo 13.5   Photo by Don Peden   Photo 13.6   Photo by Don Peden

Children play a major role in caring for grazing livestock in developing countries, which may reduce school attendance

farming women to increase their disposable income through the production and sale of dairy products (see Upadhyay 2004 for India; Muriuki 2002 and Staal and others 2001 for Kenya; Kurwijila 2002 for Tanzania; and box 13.2 for Ethiopia). Such opportunities to improve the livelihoods of women and help bring them out of poverty depend on effective investments in water resources, an issue discussed later in the chapter.

The distribution of labor in livestock raising in India shows the variation in gender roles that is common around the world. Indian women and children dominate many areas of animal production. Women contribute 71% of the labor in the livestock sector (Anthra 1999; Chawla, Kurup, and Sharma 2004; Devendra and others 2000; Ragnekar 1998, as cited in Parthasarathy, Birthal, and Ndjeunga 2005; Upadhyay 2004) and spend 20%–25% of their time attending to livestock. Women influence household decision-making, although following up on decisions is generally left to men. Key tasks shouldered by women include feeding and watering animals kept at home, managing domestic water for all uses including animals, care of sick animals, cleaning sheds and pens, collecting manure and eggs, and selling produce locally. One reason women dominate in animal keeping is that, because they are generally less educated than men, they are assigned to the low-paying, labor-intensive activities. Men tend to handle grazing, watering grazed animals, taking sick animals to veterinary clinics, and selling animal products to agents and in larger, more distant markets. Men also have easier access to critical inputs such as extension, veterinary care, credit, and training.

Applying livestock water productivity principles

Livestock-water interactions have been largely neglected in both water and livestock research and planning (Peden and others 2006). Unlike the case in irrigation and crop sciences, there are few examples of research and assessments that attempt to understand the total water needs of livestock and how animal production affects water resources. The consequence has been lost opportunities to maximize investment returns in past investments in water and livestock development. This chapter has briefly considered the distribution of livestock keeping in developing countries in relation to the need for water, anticipated demand for animal products, and four strategies that can collectively improve livestock water productivity (improving feed sourcing, enhancing animal productivity, conserving water, and providing drinking water). Following are three brief examples drawn from pastoral, rainfed mixed crop-livestock systems, and irrigated mixed systems to illustrate the potential application of these four strategies.

Pastoral market chains

Kordofan and Darfur, Sudan, are homes to pastoralists who depend on grazing livestock, but the markets for their animals are in Khartoum, hundreds of kilometers to the east. Migration corridors supplied with water and feed enable animals to trek to markets and arrive in relatively good condition. Watering points require effective management, such as the provision of drinking troughs, physically separated from wells and other water sources (photo 13.7) to mitigate the degradation of water sources, and vegetation buffers to protect riparian areas. Once in Khartoum buyers fatten animals with crop residues and feed supplements procured from the irrigation systems of the Nile.

This case exemplifies the interconnection of pastoral and irrigated production systems and the need for areawide approaches to their management. Improving feed sourcing, enhancing production, conserving water, and providing drinking water are all important intervention strategies *[established but incomplete]*.

Rainfed mixed crop-livestock systems

The Ethiopian highlands are home to millions of poor grain farmers who keep cattle, sheep, goats, equines, and poultry. Feed sourcing is a priority activity, and much value is placed on harvesting crop residues that are widely used by oxen and equines (photo 13.8). Farmers are also taking other steps to improve livestock water productivity such as using veterinary care and improved hybrid dairy cattle and providing water at home (see box 13.2).

Irrigated mixed crop-livestock systems

Gezira, Sudan, Africa's largest contiguous irrigation scheme, was constructed about 1920. For more than 60 years there were no policies or plans to accommodate animal keeping. Now, livestock keeping provides 36% of farm income (Elzaki 2005). In a study on the feasibility of integrating livestock production with irrigated agriculture in Gezira, Elzaki (2005) argues that adding fodder in the crop rotation could increase farm income, provide animal feed, and boost milk production. She stresses the need for improved feed sourcing strategies within irrigation systems and improved veterinary care. She concludes that the main constraint facing improved investment returns in the irrigation system is the unclear and contradictory policy of the Gezira irrigation scheme management and the conflict between animal keepers and crop farmers. Strategic use of crop residues for feed and enhanced productivity of animals are key entry points for increased livestock water productivity, but contamination of water with pathogens now threatens both people and their animals *[well established]*.

Integration of livestock and water management and improved governance

This chapter briefly described the developing country distribution of cattle, sheep, and goats, their implied needs for water resources, and probable trends in demand for animal

Photo 13.7 Providing drinking water in troughs helps prevent contamination of well and surface water

Photo 13.8 Crop residues help maximize evapotranspiration use by grain crops

Photo by Don Peden

products. The principles outlined in the chapter presented the basics for a livestock water productivity framework that can help to systematize thinking about the nature of livestock-water interactions. The framework consists of four basin entry points or strategies for improving livestock water productivity. The case examples drawn from East Africa highlight the major differences among production systems and the need for integrated site-specific interventions to ensure that livestock production contributes to sustainable and productive use of water resources and to improved livelihoods of the poor. The existing quantitative data on livestock water productivity are not adequate to characterize livestock use of water on a global scale.

During the past 50 years investments in agricultural water and livestock development often failed to achieve potential and sustainable returns. Evidence suggests that the livestock water productivity approach can help to identify opportunities for integrating livestock and water development for the benefit of both. Realizing these opportunities requires intersectoral and interdisciplinary planning, development, and management of water and livestock resources. Integration demands location-specific adjustments in institutional arrangements and integrated cost-benefit, enterprise budget, and land-use analyses. In communities integration of pasture management and water user associations will be needed. Integrated governance at and across various scales has great potential for increasing the productivity and sustainability of water use and livestock production worldwide *[established but incomplete]*.

Reviewers

Chapter review editor: Richard Harwood.
Chapter reviewers: Michael Blummel, Eline Boelee, Lisa Deutsch, Ade Freeman, Anita Idel, Ralph von Kaufmann, Violet Matiru, Ian Maudlin, Odo Primavesi, and Shirley Tarawali.

Notes

1. Most broadleaf and temperate zone plants are C_3. C_4 plants such as sugar cane and maize exhibit more efficient photosynthesis than C_3 plants, making them better adapted to very sunny conditions and to higher levels of crop water productivity.

2. In biochemistry this refers to the concentration of osmotically active particles in solution, which may be quantitatively expressed in osmoles of solute per liter of solution. Used here as an indicator of animals' capacity to concentrate urine and reduce water loss through urination.

References

Anthra. 1999. "Role of Women in Animal Husbandry in Orissa." ISPO Gender Study Series. Hyderabad, India.
Ashley, S., S. Holden, and P. Bazeley. 1999. *Livestock in Poverty-focused Development*. Livestock in Development. Crewkerne: United Kingdom.
Astatke, A., and M. Saleem. 1998. "Effect of Different Cropping Options on Plant-available Water of Surface-drained Vertisols in the Ethiopian Highlands." *Agricultural Water Management* 36 (2): 111–20.
Astatke, A., J. Reed, and M. Butterworth. 1986. "Effect of Diet Restriction on Work Performance and Weight Loss of Local Zebu and Friesian x Boran Crossbred Oxen." *ILCA Bulletin* 23 (January): 11–14.
Ayalneh, W. 2004. "Socio Economic and Environmental Impact Assessment of Community Based Small-scale Irrigation in the Upper Awash Basin: A Case Study of Four Community Based Irrigation Schemes." MSc Thesis. Addis Ababa University, School of Graduate Studies, Environmental Science. [www.iwmi.cgiar.org/Assessment/files/pdf/PhDThesis/Wagnew-thesis.pdf].

Basarab, J. 2003. "Feed Efficiency in Cattle." Press release. Alberta Beef Industry Development Fund, Calgary, Canada. [https://mail.une.edu.au/lists/archives/beef-crc-technet/2003-November/000016.html].

Beaton, G. 1991. "Human Nutrient Requirement Estimates: Derivation, Interpretation and Application in Evolutionary Perspective." *Food, Nutrition and Agriculture* 1(2/3): 3–15.

Becker, K., M. Rometsch, A. Susenbeth, U. Roser, and P. Lawrence. 1993. "Characterisation of the Physiological Performance and Determination of the Efficiency of Draught Oxen." In *Adapted Farming in West Africa*. Special Research Program 308. Report of Results, Interim Report 1991–1993. University of Hohenheim, Germany.

Chapagain, A., and A. Hoekstra. 2003. "Virtual Water Trade: A Quantification of Virtual Water Flows between Nations in Relation to International Trade of Livestock and Livestock Products." In A.Y. Hoekstra, ed., *Virtual Water Trade. Proceedings of the International Expert Meeting on Virtual Water Trade*. Value of Water Research Report Series 12. Delft, Netherlands: United Nations Educational, Scientific and Cultural Organization, Institute for Water Education.

Chawla, N., M. Kurup, and V. Sharma. 2004. *State of the Indian Farmer—A Millennium Study: Animal Husbandry*. Vol. 12. New Delhi: Ministry of Agriculture.

Claypool, D., R. Delaney, R. Ditterline, and R. Lockerman. 1997. *Genetic Improvement of Alfalfa to Conserve Water*. Proceedings of the 36th North American Alfalfa Improvement Conference, 2–6 August, Bozeman, Mont.

Delgado, C. 2003. "Rising Consumption of Meat and Milk in Developing Countries Has Created a New Food Revolution." *Journal of Nutrition* 133 (11): 3907S–3910S.

Devendra, C., D. Thomas, M. Jabbar, and E. Zerbini. 2000. *Improvement of Livestock Production in Crop-animal Systems in Agro-ecological Zones of South Asia*. Nairobi: International Livestock Research Institute.

Dijkman, J. 1993. "The Measurement of Draught Ruminant Energy Expenditure in the Field." PhD thesis. University of Edinburgh, Centre for Tropical Veterinary Medicine.

Elzaki, R. 2005. "The Feasibility of Integration of Livestock Production in Irrigated Agriculture in Sudan: Case Study: The Gezira Scheme." PhD Thesis. University of Giessen, Department of Project and Regional Planning.

Fall, A., R. Pearson, P. Laurence, and S. Fernández-Rivera. 1997. *Feeding and Working Strategies for Oxen Used for Draught Purposes in Semiarid West Africa*. Nairobi: International Livestock Research Institute.

FAO (Food and Agriculture Organization). 2004. "Tropical Livestock Units (TLU)." Virtual Livestock Centre, Livestock and Environment Toolbox. Rome. [http://lead.virtualcentre.org/en/dec/toolbox/Mixed1/TLU.htm].

Faries, F., J. Sweeten, and J. Reagor. 1997. *Water Quality: Its Relationship to Livestock*. College Station, Tex.: Texas A&M University System, Texas Agricultural Extension Service.

Fernandez-Rivera, S. 2006. Personal communication summarizing the experience of the International Livestock Research Institute, Addis Ababa, Ethiopia, covering diverse animal feeding trials and production studies conducted in Sub-Saharan Africa.

Ferraris, R., and B. Sinclair. 1980. "Factors Affecting the Growth of Pennisetum purpureum in the Wet Tropics. II. Uninterrupted Growth." *Australian Journal of Agricultural Research* 31 (5): 915–25.

Gerrish, J., and M. Davis. 1999. "Water Availability and Distribution." In J. Gerrish and C. Roberts, eds., *Missouri Grazing Manual*. Columbia, Miss.: University of Missouri Extension.

Gerrish, J., P. Peterson, and R. Morrow. 1995. "Distance Cattle Travel to Water Affects Pasture Utilization Rate." Proceedings of the American Forage and Grassland Council Conference, 12–14 March, Lexington, Ky, 4: 61–65.

Goodland, R., and D. Pimental. 2000. "Environmental Sustainability and Integrity in Natural Resources Systems." In D. Pimental, L. Westra and R. Noss, eds., *Ecological Integrity*. Washington, D.C.: Island Press.

Heffernan, C., and F. Misturelli. 2001. "Perceptions of Poverty among Poor Livestock Keepers in Kenya: A Discourse Analysis Approach." *Journal of International Development* 13 (7): 863–75.

Hoekstra, A., and P. Hung. 2003. *Virtual Water Trade: A Quantification of Virtual Water Flows between Nations in Relation to International Crop Trade*. Value of Water Research Report Series 11. Delft, Netherlands: United Nations Educational, Scientific and Cultural Organization, Institute for Water Education.

Hurni, H. 1990. "Degradation and Conservation of Soil Resources in the Ethiopian Highlands." In B. Messerli and H. Hurni, eds., *African Mountains and Highlands: Problems and Perspectives*. Marceline, Miss.: African Mountains Association.

Irwin, R. 1992. "Water Requirements of Livestock." Rev. ed. Factsheet. Ontario Ministry of Agriculture, Food and Rural Affairs, Ontario.

Jahnke, H. 1982. *Livestock Production Systems and Livestock Development in Tropical Africa*. Kiel, Germany: Kieler Wissenschaftsverlag Vauk.

Jarvis, L. 1986. *Livestock Development in Latin America*. Washington, D.C.: World Bank.

Keller, A., and D. Seckler. 2005. "Limits to the Productivity of Water in Crop Production." In *California Water Plan Update 2005*. Vol. 4. Sacramento, Calif.: California Department of Water Resources.

King, J. 1983. *Livestock Water Needs in Pastoral Africa in Relation to Climate and Forage.* ILCA Research Report 7. Addis Ababa: International Livestock Centre for Africa.

Kleiber, M. 1932. "Body Size and Metabolism." *Hilgardia* 6: 315–53.

———. 1975. *The Fire of Life: An Introduction to Animal Energetics.* New York: Robert E. Krieger Publishing Co.

Kurwijila L. 2002. "An Overview of Dairy Development in Tanzania." In D. Rangnekar D and W. Thorpe, eds., *Smallholder Dairy Production and Marketing Opportunities and Constraints.* Nairobi: International Livestock Research Institute.

Landefeld, M., and J. Bettinger. 2005. "Water Effects on Livestock Performance." Fact Sheet ANR-13-02. Ohio State University, Agriculture and Natural Resources. Columbus, Ohio.

Love, L.D. 1958. "Rangeland Watershed Management." *Proceedings of the Society of American Foresters*: 198–200.

Macfarlane, W. 1964. "Terrestrial Animals in Dry Heat: Ungulates." In D.B. Dill, ed., *Handbook of Physiology-environment.* Washington, D.C.: American Physiological Society.

Maloiy, G.M.O. 1972. "Renal Salt and Water Excretion in the Camel (Camelus dromedarius)." *Symposium of the Zoological Society,* London 21: 243–59.

Misra, A.K. and Mahipal. 2000. "Strategies of Livestock Management for Improving Productivity Under Rainfed Farming Situations." In K.H. Vedini, ed., *Management Issues in Rainfed Agriculture in India.* Hyderabad, India: MANAGE.

Muli, A. 2000. "Factors Affecting Amount of Water Offered to Dairy Cattle in Kiambu District and Their Effects on Productivity." B.Sc. thesis, Range Management, University of Nairobi.

Muriuki, H. 2002. "Smallholder Dairy Production and Marketing in Kenya." In D. Rangnekar and W. Thorpe, eds., *Smallholder Dairy Production and Marketing Opportunities and Constraints.* Nairobi: International Livestock Research Institute.

Neumann, C., N. Bwibo, S. Murphy, M. Sigman, S. Whaley, L. Allen, D. Guthrie, R. Weiss, and M. Demment. 2003. "Animal Source Foods Improve Dietary Quality, Micronutrient Status, Growth and Cognitive Function in Kenyan School Children: Background, Study Design and Baseline Findings." *Journal of Nutrition* 133 (11): 3941S–3949S.

Nierenberg, D. 2005. *Happier Meals: Rethinking the Global Meat Industry.* Worldwatch Paper 171. Washington, D.C.: Worldwatch Institute.

NRC (National Research Council). 1978. *Nutrient Requirements of Dairy Cattle.* 5th ed. Washington, D.C.: National Academy of Science.

———. 1996. *Nutrient Requirements of Beef Cattle.* 7th ed. Washington, D.C.: National Academy of Science.

———. 1998. *Nutrient Requirements of Swine.* 10th ed. Washington, D.C.: National Academy of Science.

Odai, M. 2003. "Energy Requirement for the Maintenance of Dairy Cows in Northeast Thailand." *Jircas Newsletter* 34: 5.

Pallas, P. 1986. *Water for Animals.* Rome: Food and Agriculture Organization.

Parthasarathy, R.P., P. Birthal, and J. Ndjeunga. 2005. *Crop-Livestock Economies in the Semi-Arid Tropics: Facts, Trends, and Outlook.* Hyderabad, India: International Crops Research Institute for the Semi-Arid Tropics.

Peden, D., A. Freeman, A. Astatke, and A. Notenbaert. 2006. "Investment Options for Integrated Water-Livestock-Crop Production in Sub-Saharan Africa." Working Paper 1. Nairobi: International Livestock Research Institute.

Perry, B., T. Randolph, J. McDermott, K. Sones, and P. Thornton. 2002. *Investing in Animal Health to Alleviate Poverty.* International Livestock Research Institute, Nairobi.

Phillips, G. 1960. "The Relationship between Water and Food Intakes of European and Zebu Type Steers." *Journal of Agricultural Science* 54: 231–34.

Quartermain, A., G. Phillips, and G. Lampkin. 1957. "A Difference in the Physiology of the Large Intestine between European and Indigenous Cattle in the Tropics." *Nature* 180 (4585): 552–53.

Ragnekar, S. 1998. "The Role of Women in Smallholder Rainfed Mixed Farming in India." In *Women in Agriculture and Animal Production: Proceedings of a Workshop, Tune, Landboskole, Denmark, 30 March–3 April.*

Redda, T. 2002. "Small-scale Milk Marketing and Processing in Ethiopia." In D. Rangnekar and W. Thorpe, eds., *Smallholder Dairy Production and Marketing Opportunities and Constraints.* Proceedings of a South-South Workshop, 13–16 March 2001. Anand, India and Nairobi: National Dairy Development Board and International Livestock Research Institute.

Renault, D., and W. Wallender. 2000. "Nutritional Water Productivity and Diets." *Agricultural Water Management* 45 (3): 275–96.

Saeed, I., and A. El-Nadi. 1997. "Irrigation Effects on the Growth, Yield and Water Use Efficiency of Alfalfa." *Irrigation Science* 17 (2): 63–68.

———. 1998. "Forage Sorghum Yield and Water Use Efficiency under Variable Irrigation." *Irrigation Science* 18 (2): 67–71.

Sakomura, N., F. Longo, E. Oviedo-Rondon, C. Boa-Viagem, and A. Ferraudo. 2005. "Modeling Energy Utilization and Growth Parameter Description for Broiler Chickens." *Poultry Science* 84 (9): 1363–69.

Sala, O., W. Parton, A. Joyce, and W. Lauenroth. 1988. "Primary Production of the Central Grasslands of the United States." *Ecology* 69 (1): 40–45.

Sastry, N. 2000. "Regional Considerations for Appropriate Livestock Development Strategies in India." *Journal of Indian Veterinary Association* 5 (3): 16–29.

Schmidt-Nielsen, K. 1965. Desert Animals: Physiological Problems of Heat and Water. Oxford, UK: Clarendon Press.

Seleshi, Z., A. Tegegne, and T. Tsadik. 2003. "Water Resources for Livestock in Ethiopia: Implications for Research and Development." In P. McCornick, A. Kamara, and G. Tadesse, eds., *Integrated Water and Land Management Research and Capacity Building Priorities for Ethiopia*. Proceedings of a Ministry of Water Resources, Ethiopian Agricultural Research Organization, International Water Management Institute, and International Livestock Research Institute International Workshop, 2–4 December 2002. Addis Ababa: International Livestock Research Institute.

Shackleton, C., S. Shackleton, T. Netshiluvhi, F. Mathabela, and C. Phiri. 1999. "The Direct Use Value of Goods and Services Attributed to Cattle and Goats in the Sand River Catchment, Bushbuckridge." Report ENV-P-C 99003. Council for Scientific and Industrial Research, Pretoria.

Sheehy, D., W. Hamilton, U. Kreuter, J. Simpson, J. Stuth, and J. Conner. 1996. *Environmental Impact Assessment of Livestock Production in Grassland and Mixed Rainfed Systems in Temperate Zones and Grassland and Mixed-Rainfed Systems in Humid and Subhumid Tropic and Subtropic Zones*. Vol. II. Rome: Food and Agriculture Organization.

Shirley, R. 1985. "Water Requirements for Grazing Ruminants and Water as a Source of Minerals." In L.R. McDowell, ed., *Nutrition of Grazing Ruminants in Warm Climates*. Orlando, Fla.: Academic Press.

Sigman, M., S. Whaley, M. Kamore, N. Bwibo, and C. Neumann. 2005. *Supplementation Increases Physical Activity and Selected Behaviors in Rural Kenyan Schoolchildren*. CRSP Research Brief 05-04-CNP. University of California, Global Livestock Collaborative Research Support Program, Davis, Calif.

SIWI (Stockholm International Water Institute), IFPRI (International Food Policy Research Institute), IUCN (World Conservation Union), and IWMI (International Water Management Institute). 2005. *Let it Reign: The New Water Paradigm for Global Food Security*. Final report to CSD-13. Stockholm: Stockholm International Water Institute.

Sreeramulu, P. 2004. "Fodder, Water and Livestock Issues in Andhra Pradesh, India." Paper presented at a workshop on Fodder, Water and Livestock for Better Livelihoods, 27 August, cosponsored by the Department of Animal Husbandry, Andhra Pradesh, and Water Conservation Mission, Andhra Pradesh. State Management Institute for Livestock Development, Directorate of Animal Husbandry, Hyderabad, India.

Staal, S., M. Owango, G. Muriuki, B. Lukuyu, F. Musembi, O. Bwana, K. Muriuki, G. Gichungu, A. Omore, B. Kenyanjui, D. Njubi, I. Baltenweck, and W. Thorpe. 2001. "Dairy Systems Characterization of the Greater Nairobi Milk-shed." SDP Research Report. Ministry of Agriculture and Rural Development, Kenya Agricultural Research Institute, and International Livestock Research Institute, Nairobi.

Taneja, V.K., and P. S. Birthal. 2004. "Role of Buffalo in Food Security in Asia." *Asian Buffalo* 1 (1): 1–13.

Thornton, P., R. Kruska, N. Henninger, P. Kristjanson, R. Reid, F. Atieno, A. Odero, and T. Ndegwa. 2002. *Mapping Poverty and Livestock in the Developing World*. Nairobi: International Livestock Research Institute.

Times of India. 2004. "Holy Cow! Milk's a Groundwater Guzzler." Times of India Online. 3 June.

Upadhyay, B. 2004. "Gender Roles and Multiple Uses of Water in North Gujarat." Working Paper 70. International Water Management Institute, Colombo.

Van Hoeve, E., and B. van Koppen. 2005. "Beyond Fetching Water for Livestock: A Gendered Sustainable Livelihood Framework to Assess Livestock-Water Productivity." ILRI Working Paper 1. International Livestock Research Institute, Nairobi.

World Bank. 1998. *Meat Processing and Rendering. Pollution Prevention and Abatement Handbook*. Washington, D.C.

Zerbini, E., T. Gemeda, D. O'Neill, P. Howell, and R. Schroter. 1992. "Relationship Between Cardio-respiratory Parameters and Draught Work Output in F1 Crossbred Dairy Cows Under Field Conditions." *Animal Production* 55: 1–10.

The culture of rice

Artist: Supriyo Das, India

14 | Rice: feeding the billions

Coordinating lead author: Bas Bouman

Lead authors: Randolph Barker, Elizabeth Humphreys, and To Phuc Tuong

Contributing authors: Gary Atlin, John Bennett, David Dawe, Klaus Dittert, Achim Dobermann, Thierry Facon, Nao Fujimoto, Raj Gupta, Stephan Haefele, Yasukazu Hosen, Abdel Ismail, David Johnson, Sarah Johnson, Shabaz Khan, Lin Shan, Ilyas Masih, Yutaka Matsuno, Sushil Pandey, Shaobing Peng, Thruppayathangudi Mutukumarisami Thiyagarajan, and Reiner Wassman.

Overview

Because rice is critical for food security in so many of the poorest countries, investments in the rice sector should be designed to alleviate poverty and meet the food demands of still growing—and increasingly urbanized—populations. In all rice environments vital ecosystem services—such as biodiversity, groundwater recharge, and flow regulation—in addition to food production should be explicitly recognized and protected. Rice may be relatively benign to the environment compared with other crops: more methane emission but less nitrous oxide, little to no nitrate leaching, and little herbicide use. The food security of many poor consumers depends on the productive capacity of irrigated areas. Increasing water scarcity is expected to further shift rice production to more water-abundant delta areas and to lead to crop diversification and more aerobic soil conditions in rice fields in water-short areas. Investments in these areas should support the adoption of water-saving technologies and the improvement of irrigation supply systems, while sustaining the resource base of the rice fields. There is no single solution for all circumstances, and investments need to be selective and specifically targeted to the different rice environments.

Between a quarter and a third of the world's tapped freshwater resources have already been developed to irrigate rice, the staple food for 3 billion people. More than 90% of the world's rice is produced and consumed in Asia, where rice is a political commodity and where millennia-old practices of growing rice have resulted in specific rice cultures. These cultures need a collective, community-based approach to decisionmaking about the investments in rice fields and about their operation and maintenance. Rice is grown on some 250 million farms, mostly family owned, averaging from less than 0.5 hectares (ha) to 4 ha. Rice grows in a wide range of environments and is productive in many situations where other crops would fail. Worldwide, there are about 79 million ha of irrigated lowlands with average yields of 5 metric tons per hectare, 54 million ha of rainfed lowlands with average yields of 2.3 metric tons per hectare, 14 million ha of rainfed uplands with average yields of 1 metric ton per hectare, and 11 million ha of flood-prone areas with average yields of 1.5 metric tons per hectare. The highly productive irrigated lowlands provide 75% of the world's rice supply. Rice environments also provide unique but as yet poorly understood ecosystem services, such as regulation of water and preservation of aquatic and terrestrial biodiversity.

> The key to achieving food security and alleviating poverty is increasing rice productivity while lowering production costs

Because of the unprecedented growth in production during the past five decades the supply of rice has kept pace with population growth, and the price of rice has fallen and is currently at a historic low. In recent years, however, the growth in productivity has slowed in many countries in Asia. World annual rice production is currently some 550–600 million metric tons (rough, unhusked, and unmilled), and the world market price of top quality (nonaromatic) indica rice has fluctuated at about $250 a metric ton for the past five to six years. The high yields and low prices have helped to alleviate poverty among poor rice consumers.

To meet the food demands of growing populations, rice production needs to continue to increase in coming decades. Although consumer food preferences tend to change as incomes rise, poverty remains in rural irrigated and rainfed rice-growing areas and is increasing in urban areas. To meet the dual challenge of producing enough food and alleviating poverty, more rice needs to be produced at a low unit cost so that producers can be ensured of reasonable profits, poor consumers can have the benefit of low prices, and the environment and ecosystem services can be safeguarded. All this needs to be achieved as urbanization, wages, and the feminization of the rural workforce are increasing and the supply of labor is decreasing. At the same time the productive capacity of rice environments is being threatened by increasing water scarcity in irrigated systems and by droughts, salinity, uncontrolled flooding, and climate change. Approximately 25 million ha of rainfed rice are frequently affected by drought, and 9–12 million ha by salinity, and 15–20 million ha of irrigated rice are projected to suffer some degree of water scarcity over the next 25 years.

The key to achieving food security and alleviating poverty is increasing rice productivity while lowering production costs. Because many stresses on rice production are related to water, increasing water productivity is especially important. The various ecosystem services of rice environments must also be recognized and protected to sustain their capacity to produce food. In irrigated lowlands with ample water supply the development of hybrid rice has the potential to increase the yield of rice plants by 5%–15%. Integrated management approaches could narrow gaps between potential yields and current farmers' yields. A suite of water-saving technologies can help farmers reduce combined losses from percolation, drainage, and evaporation by 15%–20% without reducing yields. The efficiency of irrigation systems can be increased by the conjunctive use of surface water and groundwater and the reuse of percolation and drainage water. We still need to improve our understanding of the effects of increasingly aerobic (nonflooded) field conditions—induced by water scarcity—on the environment, ecosystem services, and the sustainability of rice growing.

In environments prone to drought, salinity, and floods the combination of improved varieties and specific management packages has the potential to increase on-farm yields by 50%–100% in the coming 10 years, provided that investment in research and extension is intensified. Development and delivery of better technologies need to be science based, participatory, gender inclusive, and aware of indigenous farmers' knowledge.

Trends and conditions

Rice, a staple food for almost half the world's population (Maclean and others 2002), grows in a wide range of environments (photo 14.1). More than 90% of global rice production is harvested from irrigated or rainfed lowland rice fields. There is growing awareness that lowland rice environments provide a rich variety of ecosystem services. Rice production also has environmental impacts, largely by releasing or sequestering gases and compounds to the atmosphere and troposphere and by changing the chemical composition of the water flowing through the rice fields. Rice production also has health impacts, mainly mediated through the use of agrochemicals.

Rice is a staple food for almost half the world's population

The economy of rice

Rice production and consumption. Ninety percent of the world's rice is produced and consumed in Asia (table 14.1), where it accounts for 20%–70% of total caloric intake. Brazil and the United States are also major rice producers; each produces some 10 million metric tons a year. Rice is grown on an estimated 250 million farms, most of them family owned, with country average farm sizes varying from less than 0.5 ha to 4 ha (Hossain and Fischer 1995). In many countries in Asia rice accounts for more than half of the harvested area of all crops.

Photo 14.1

Photo by International Rice Research Institute

Historically, an important political objective in most rice-growing countries has been to achieve self-sufficiency in rice production and maintain price stability through domestic procurement and adjustment of stocks. In recent years this has been less necessary because the world rice market has become deeper and more stable (Dawe 2002). International trade in rice is about 7% of production compared with 11% for maize and 18% for wheat (FAOSTAT). With increasing demand for rice (see chapter 2 on trends) and subregional shifts in production, however, we expect that international trade in rice will increase in coming years. Since the 1960s rice imports in West and Central Africa have increased eightfold, to 4 million metric tons a year currently, at an annual cost of more than $1 billion, and now represent more than 25% of the value of total food imports. The relatively cheap imports of rice from Asia pose extra challenges to poor rice farmers in remote areas of Africa.

In the 1960s the combination of new high-yielding rice varieties and increased use of water, fertilizer, and biocides (to protect the crop from pests, disease, and weeds) led to the rapid increase in productivity known as the green revolution. Because of this increased productivity and an increase in cropped area, total rice production over the past 40 years has more than kept pace with the tremendous growth in population in Asia (figure 14.1).

table **14.1**	Rice production and consumption statistics worldwide, 2002				
Country	Rough rice[a] production (millions of metric tons)	Rice area[b] (thousands of hectares)	Rough rice yield[c] (metric tons per hectare)	Annual milled rice consumption (kilograms per capita)	Share of calories from rice in diet (percent)
China	176.34	28,509	6.19	83	28
India	116.50	40,280	2.89	83	34
Indonesia	51.49	11,521	4.47	149	50
Bangladesh	37.59	10,771	3.49	164	74
Viet Nam	34.45	7,504	4.59	169	65
Thailand	26.06	9,988	2.61	103	41
Myanmar	21.81	6,381	3.42	205	68
Philippines	13.27	4,046	3.28	105	43
Japan	11.11	1,688	6.58	58	22
Brazil	10.46	3,146	3.32	35	12
United States	9.57	1,298	7.37	9	3
Pakistan	6.72	2,225	3.02	18	8
Korea, Rep.	6.69	1,053	6.35	83	29
Egypt	6.11	613	9.97	38	12
Nepal	4.13	1,545	2.67	102	38
Cambodia	3.82	1,995	1.92	149	69
Nigeria	3.19	3,160	1.01	24	9
Iran, Islamic Rep.	2.89	611	4.73	37	12
Sri Lanka	2.86	820	3.49	91	37
Madagascar	2.60	1,216	2.14	95	49
Lao PDR	2.42	783	3.09	168	64
Colombia	2.35	469	5.01	30	12
Malaysia	2.20	677	3.25	73	25
Korea, Dem. Rep.	2.19	583	3.75	70	32
Peru	2.12	317	6.69	49	19
Italy	1.38	219	6.31	6	2
Ecuador	1.29	327	3.93	47	16
Australia	1.19	150	7.95	10	3
Côte d'Ivoire	1.08	470	2.30	63	22
World	577.97	147,633	3.91	57	20

Note: Data are for countries producing more than 1 million metric tons of rice annually.

a. Unhulled and unmilled rice.

b. Harvested area, includes multiple cropping.

c. Total production divided by total area averaged across all seasons and areas.

Source: FAOSTAT online updated 14 July 2005 (http://faostat.fao.org/faostat/collections).

| figure **14.1** | **Rice production has kept pace with population growth in Asia over the past 40 years, while world prices have been falling in the past 25 years** |

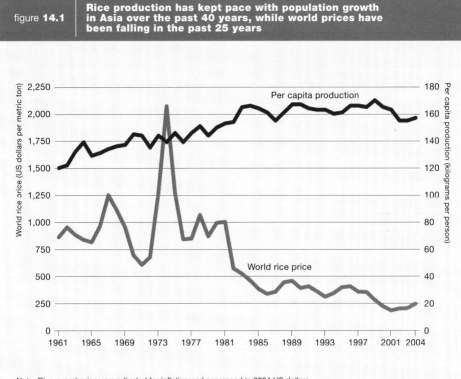

Note: Rice export prices are adjusted for inflation and expressed in 2004 US dollars.

Source: FAOSTAT online statistical service (http://faostat.fao.org/faostat/collections); World Rice Statistics (www.irri.org/science/ricestat/index.asp); IMF International Financial Statistics online service (www.imf.org)

In recent years, however, the growth in productivity has slowed in many countries in Asia. Declining per capita demand as Asians diversify their diets has also contributed to a stabilization of per capita production.

The falling price of rice. Increasing rice production has led to declining rice prices. World rice prices (adjusted for inflation) fluctuated at around $1,000 a metric ton between 1961 and 1981, declined sharply between 1981 and 1984, and then declined gradually, reaching a record low of less than $250 a metric ton in 2002 (see figure 14.1). Prices rose again slightly in 2004 to about 25% of their level in the early 1980s, with another increase in 2005 as import demand increased.

Shifting comparative advantages. Within Asia the comparative regional advantage in rice production is shifting (Barker and Dawe 2002; Dawe 2005). Before World War II the delta regions (in Bangladesh, Cambodia, eastern India, Myanmar, Thailand, and Viet Nam) held the comparative advantage in rice production and were the main sources of rice exports. The early beneficiaries of the green revolution technology of the 1960s and

1970s were areas where it was possible to irrigate two crops of rice with the construction of reservoir storage. Also benefiting was the northwest Indo-Gangetic Plain, where private investment in groundwater pumping and public investment in irrigation systems and other government policies (subsidies for inputs and minimum price support schemes for grain) favored rice production.

> Rice grows in a wide range of environments and is productive in many situations where other crops would fail

For political reasons and because of the inability to manage floods, the deltas initially were unable to take advantage of the new rice technologies. Over the past 15–20 years, however, with the availability of low-cost pump technology and new cropping systems based on short-duration rice varieties that can avoid the floods, the delta areas have regained their comparative advantage and shown the most rapid growth in rice production and exports. With the improved water control provided by pumps, the delta regions have been able to shift out of low-yielding deep water and floating rice by planting one crop before and one after the floods. In short, rice production is gaining in regions with plentiful water supply and cheap labor relative to areas of water scarcity, and this trend is expected to continue. In the northwest Indo-Gangetic Plain there are now grave concerns about the sustainability of irrigated rice production because of rapidly falling groundwater tables and the government's need to reduce the large fiscal costs associated with policies that promote rice production.

Changes in demography and the rice economy. As economies develop, the rural sector undergoes major changes. The younger members of rural communities, particularly the men, leave in search of jobs in urban areas or overseas and send remittances back to their rural homes. These rural economies are becoming older and more feminized (box 14.1), and this trend is likely to continue. In some countries, especially in Africa, HIV/AIDS is also exacting a toll on the rural labor force. As a consequence, labor availability is declining and wages are increasing in many rice-growing areas (Barker and Dawe 2002). Farm employment is less attractive, and labor is harder to find at peak periods for key operations such as transplanting, weeding, and harvesting. With rising wages and labor shortages, mechanization is becoming more common for both land preparation and harvesting, especially in irrigated areas. Also, farmers are shifting from hand weeding to the use of herbicides, and from transplanting to direct seeding. By the late 1990s an estimated one-fifth of the rice area in Asia was direct seeded (Pandey and Velasco 2002), and this proportion is expected to rise.

The rice environments

Rice grows in a wide range of environments and is productive in many situations where other crops would fail. Most classifications of rice environments are based on hydrological characteristics (Huke and Huke 1997; Maclean and others 2002). Irrigated lowland rice is grown in bunded fields with ensured irrigation for one or more crops a year. Farmers generally try to maintain 5–10 centimeters (cm) of water ("floodwater") on the field. Rainfed lowland rice is grown in bunded fields that are flooded with rainwater for at least part of the cropping season to water depths that exceed 100 cm for no more than 10 days. In both irrigated and rainfed lowlands fields are predominantly puddled (harrowing or rotavating under shallow submerged conditions) and plants are transplanted. Deepwater rice and floating rice are found in flood-prone environments, where the fields suffer periodically from excess

box **14.1** | **Gender issues**

As in agriculture in general, gender issues in rice production are complex and site specific. Women participate in various degrees in the cultivation of rice and often have specific tasks such as transplanting, weeding, or harvesting. In Central and West Africa women constitute the majority of upland rice farmers.

Increasing water scarcity and technological response options affect women in different ways, depending on whether they are paid or unpaid laborers. For example, a shift from transplanting to direct seeding may specifically affect the livelihoods of women since transplanting is their traditional task in most African and Asian societies. If they are unpaid laborers, the shift will remove the drudgery and back-breaking burden of transplanting. But if they are paid laborers, it will deprive them of a source of income. The same reasoning holds for weeding. Water scarcity and response options such as alternate wetting and drying and aerobic rice may promote weed growth and increase the need for manual weeding. In Africa women's preference for using water to control weeds arises from their being unpaid laborers.

Thus it is important to include a gender perspective in the development of alternative response options or technologies of rice production. The same holds true for the development and deployment of new rice varieties. Women should be specifically included in activities such as participatory varietal selection, as they often have different perceptions of relevant crop traits, for example, grain quality and feed quality of the straw (in many cases, it is women who tend the livestock).

water and uncontrolled, deep flooding. Upland rice is grown under dryland conditions (no ponded water) without irrigation and without puddling, usually in nonbunded fields.

Irrigated environments. Worldwide, about 79 million ha of irrigated lowland rice provide 75% of the world's rice production (Maclean and others 2002). Some 56% of the world's irrigated area of all crops is in Asia, where rice accounts for 40%–46% of the irrigated area of all crops (Dawe 2005). Rice occupies 64%–83% of the irrigated area in Southeast Asia, 46%–52% in East Asia, and 30%–35% in South Asia. At the field level rice receives up to 2–3 times more water per hectare than other irrigated crops (Tuong, Bouman, and Mortimer 2005), but an unknown portion of the water losses is reused by other fields downstream (Loeve and others 2004a). Assuming a reuse rate of 25%, we estimate that irrigated rice receives 34%–43% of the world's irrigation water and some 24%–30% of the world's developed freshwater resources.

Irrigated rice is grown mostly with supplementary irrigation in the wet season and is reliant entirely on irrigation in the dry season. The proportion of the Asian rice area that is irrigated (excluding China, where essentially all rice is irrigated) increased substantially from the late 1970s (35%) to the mid-1990s (44%) because of an increase in the irrigated area coupled with a large decline in upland and deepwater rice cultivation (Dawe 2005). In many irrigated areas rice is grown as a monoculture with two crops a year. However, significant areas of rice are also grown in rotation with a range of other crops, including about 15–20 million ha of rice-wheat systems. At the turn of the millennium, country average irrigated rice yields in Asia ranged from 3 metric tons to 9 metric tons per hectare, with an overall average of about 5 metric tons per hectare.

Rainfed environments. Worldwide, about 54 million ha rainfed lowlands supply about 19% of the world's rice production, and 14 million ha rainfed uplands contribute about 4% of the world's total rice production (Maclean and others 2002). Rainfed rice environments experience multiple abiotic stresses and high levels of uncertainty in timing, duration, and intensity of rainfall. Some 27 million ha of rainfed rice are frequently affected by drought, the largest, most frequently, and severely affected areas being eastern India (about 20 million ha) and northeastern Thailand and Lao PDR (7 million ha) (Huke and Huke 1997). Drought is also widespread in Central and West Africa. Further constraints arise from the widespread prevalence of problem soils with poor physical and chemical properties. Country average rice yields are only some 2.3 metric tons per hectare in the lowlands and 1 metric ton per hectare in the uplands.

> **Rainfed rice environments experience multiple abiotic stresses and high levels of uncertainty in timing, duration, and intensity of rainfall**

In *rainfed lowlands* small to moderate topographic differences can have important consequences for water availability, soil fertility, and flooding risk. The unpredictability of rainfall often results in field conditions that are too dry or too wet. Besides imposing water-related stresses on crop growth, these conditions prevent timely and effective management operations such as land preparation, transplanting, weed control, and fertilizer application. If such operations are delayed or skipped, yield losses can be large, even though the plants have not suffered physiological water stress.

Rainfed uplands are highly heterogeneous, with climates ranging from humid to subhumid, soils from relatively fertile to highly infertile, and topography from flat to steeply sloping. With low population density and limited market access, shifting cultivation with long (more than 15 years) fallow periods was historically the dominant land-use system. Increasing population and improved market access have put pressure on these systems, but shifting cultivation with 3–5 year fallow periods still accounts for 14% of the Asian upland rice area, mainly in northeastern India, Lao PDR, and Viet Nam. However, some 70% of Asia's upland rice areas have made the transition to permanent systems where rice is grown every year and is closely integrated with other crops and livestock. In Central and West Africa, the rice belt of Africa, upland areas represent about 40% of the area under rice cultivation and employ about 70% of the region's rice farmers. As market access remains limited, most of the world's upland rice farmers tend to be self-sufficient by producing a range of agricultural outputs.

Research efforts to increase yields and yield stability in rainfed environments, limited in the past, have been intensified in the past 10–15 years, especially in the lowlands. Together with socioeconomic developments this has considerably improved rainfed systems through better access to information and markets for inputs and outputs, more opportunities for off-farm income, improved varieties, and (partial) mechanization.

Flood-prone environments. Flood-prone environments include deepwater areas submerged under more than 100 cm of water from 10 days to a few months, areas that are affected by flash floods of longer than 10 days, extensive low-lying coastal areas where plants are subject to daily tidal submergence, and areas with problem soils (acid-sulphate and sodicity) where the problem is often excess water but not necessarily prolonged submergence (Maclean and others 2002). Altogether, there are some 11 million ha of flood-prone rice areas with average yields of about 1.5 metric tons per hectare.

Salinity-prone environments. Salinity is widespread in coastal areas, and salinity, alkalinity, or sodicity is widespread in inland areas of arid regions (Garrity and others 1986). These problems occur in irrigated as well as rainfed environments. In coastal areas rice can suffer from salinity because of seawater ingress during high tides. In inland areas salinity arises from salt deposits present in the soil or bedrock or from the use of salty irrigation water. In the mid-1980s an estimated 1.3 million ha of rice-growing areas were affected by salinity or alkalinity. Today, we estimate that some 9–12 million ha are affected, with 5–8 million ha in India; 1 million ha each in Bangladesh, Thailand, and Viet Nam; and about 1 million ha in Indonesia and Myanmar combined.

Water use and water productivity

More than 90% of the world's rice production is harvested from irrigated or rainfed lowland (or paddy) rice fields (photo 14.2). Traditionally, lowland rice is raised in a seedbed and then transplanted into a main field that is kept under continuous (irrigated) or intermittent (rainfed) ponded water conditions to help control weeds and pests. Land preparation consists of soaking, plowing, and puddling. Puddling is also done for weed control, to reduce soil permeability and percolation losses, and to ease field leveling and transplanting. The water balance of lowland rice, because of its flooded nature, is different from that of other cereals such as wheat (box 14.2).

Water use. Total seasonal water input to rice fields (rainfall plus irrigation, but excluding capillary rise, which is rarely quantified) is up to 2–3 times more than that for other cereals (Tuong, Bouman, and Mortimer 2005). It varies from as little as 400 mm per field in heavy clay soils with shallow groundwater tables that supply water for crop transpiration by capillary rise, to more than 2,000 mm in coarse-textured (sandy or loamy) soils with deep groundwater tables (Bouman and Tuong 2001). About 1,300 millimeters (mm) seems to be a typical average value for irrigated rice in Asia. Nonproductive outflows of water by runoff, seepage, and percolation are about 25%–50% of all water input in heavy soils with shallow water tables of 20–50 cm depth and 50%–85% in coarse-textured soils with deep water tables of 1.5 meter depth or more. Though runoff, seepage, and percolation are losses at the field level, they are often captured and reused downstream and do not necessarily lead to true water depletion at the irrigation area or basin scales. However, the proportion and magnitude of reuse of these flows are not generally known.

Water productivity. Modern rice varieties, when grown under flooded conditions, are similar in transpiration efficiency to other C_3 cereals (box 14.3) such as wheat, at about 2 kilograms (kg) grain per cubic meter of water transpired (Bouman and Tuong 2001). What few data are available indicate that water productivity of rice as measured by evapotranspiration is also similar to that of wheat, ranging from 0.6 kg to 1.6 kg grain per cubic meter of evapotranspired water, with a mean of 1.1 kg grain per cubic meter (Zwart and Bastiaanssen 2004). The higher evaporation rates from the water layer in rice than from the underlying soil in wheat are apparently compensated for by the higher yields of rice. Maize, as a C_4 crop, has a higher evapotranspiration efficiency (ranging from 1.1 kg to 2.7 kg grain per cubic

More than 90% of the world's rice production is harvested from irrigated or rainfed lowland (or paddy) rice fields

Photo 14.2

Photo by B.A.M. Bouman

box **14.2** | **Water flows from a rice field**

For lowland rice, water is needed to prepare the land and to match the outflows seepage, percolation, and evapotranspiration during crop growth (see figure). The amount of water used for wet land preparation can be as low as 100–150 mm (depth of water per surface area) when the time lag between soaking and transplanting is only a few days or when the crop is directly wet seeded. But it can be as high as 940 mm in large-scale irrigation systems with poor water control, where the time lag between soaking and transplanting is as long as two months (Tabbal and others 2002).

After the crop is established, the soil is usually kept ponded until shortly before harvest. *Seepage* is the lateral subsurface flow of water, and *percolation* is the flow of water down below the root zone. Typical combined values for seepage and percolation vary from 1–5 mm a day in heavy clay soils to 25–30 mm a day in sandy and sandy loam soils (Bouman and Tuong 2001). *Evaporation* is water lost into the air as vapor from the ponded water layer or from the surface of the soil, and *transpiration* is water released into the air as vapor through the plants. Typical combined evapotranspiration rates of rice fields are 4–5 mm a day in the wet season and 6–7 mm a day in the dry season, but can be as high as 10–11 mm a day in subtropical regions before the onset of the monsoon. *Over-bund flow* or *surface runoff* is the spillover when water depths rise above the bunds of the fields. Seepage, percolation, evaporation, and over-bund flow are all nonproductive flows of water and are considered losses at the field level.

Water inflows and outflows in a lowland rice field

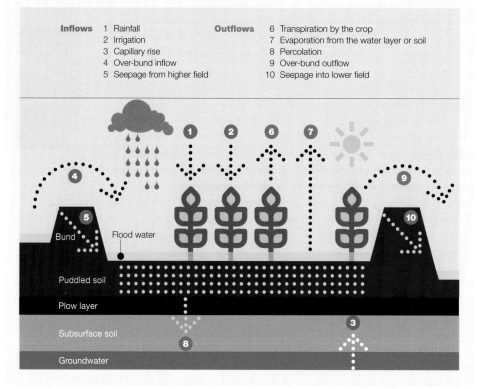

Inflows		Outflows	
1	Rainfall	6	Transpiration by the crop
2	Irrigation	7	Evaporation from the water layer or soil
3	Capillary rise	8	Percolation
4	Over-bund inflow	9	Over-bund outflow
5	Seepage from higher field	10	Seepage into lower field

Bund

Flood water

Puddled soil

Plow layer

Subsurface soil

Groundwater

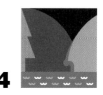

---

box **14.3** | **The rice plant**

All plants fall into two main categories according to how they assimilate carbon dioxide into their system. Rice, together with cereals such as wheat and barley, belongs to the group of C_3 grasses, whereas cereals such as maize and sorghum belong to the group of C_4 grasses. The C_4 species have a more efficient photosynthetic pathway than the C_3 species and produce more biomass per unit of intercepted radiation and per unit of transpiration. The wetland ancestry of rice is reflected in a number of morphological and physiological characteristics that are unique among crop species and set it apart from other cereals (Lafitte and Bennet 2002).

Rice is extremely sensitive to water shortage. When soil water content drops below saturation, growth and yield formation are affected, mainly through reduced leaf surface area, photosynthesis rate, and sink size. The most sensitive stage to drought is around flowering (see photo), when drought induces spikelet sterility.

While rice is adapted to water logging, complete submergence can be lethal. Most rice varieties can survive complete submergence of only 3–4 days, though some rainfed lowland rice can survive up to 10 days. Germination especially is sensitive to submergence. During later vegetative develop-

ment rice can adapt to complete submergence, though it hastens the plant's energy depletion and increases mortality. Tall plants tend to lodge (fall down) when the water level recedes, resulting in yield losses and poor grain quality.

Rice is a salt-sensitive crop and yield reductions start at electric conductivity values of 3 decisiemens (dS) per meter, rising to 50% at 6 dS per meter and 90% at 10 dS per meter (Shannon 1997). For comparison, yield reductions start at about 2 dS per meter for maize, 6 dS per meter for wheat, and 8 dS per meter for barley. Rice is relatively tolerant of salinity during germination, active tillering, and toward maturity but is sensitive during early seedling and reproductive stages.

Rice is especially sensitive to drought at flowering

---

meter of water, with a mean of 1.8). The water productivity of rice for total water input (irrigation plus rainfall) ranges from 0.2 kg to 1.2 kg grain per cubic meter of water, with an average of 0.4, about half that of wheat (Tuong, Bouman, and Mortimer 2005).

Unique ecosystem services

Though only a few studies have been conducted so far, awareness is growing that lowland rice environments provide an unusually rich variety of ecosystem services. Studies on the value of rice ecosystems beyond crop production have recently received a boost by the threat to rice price supports and trade restrictions in many countries presented by multilateral trade negotiations under the World Trade Organization (PAWEES 2005).

Provisioning services. The most important provisioning function of the rice environment is the production of rice. Irrigated rice culture has been sustained for thousands of years in various parts of Asia. Recent findings of 30 long-term continuous cropping experiments at 24 sites in Asia confirm that, with an assured water supply, lowland rice fields are extremely sustainable and able to produce continuously high yields (Dawe and others 2000). Flooding has beneficial effects on soil acidity; phosphorus, iron, and zinc availability; and biological nitrogen fixation (Kirk 2004). Other provisioning services are the raising of fish and ducks in rice fields, ponds, or canals. Frogs and snails are collected for consumption in some countries.

Regulating services. Bunded rice fields may increase the water storage capacity of catchments and river basins, lower the peak flow of rivers, and increase groundwater flow. For example, in 1999 and 2000, 20% of the floodwater in the lower Mekong River Basin was estimated to be temporarily stored in upstream rice fields (Masumoto, Shimizu, and Hai 2004). The many irrigation canals and reservoirs associated with the lowland rice landscape have a similar buffering function.

> Many traditional festivals and religious practices are associated with rice cultivation

Other regulatory services of bunded rice fields and terraces include trapping of sediments and nutrients and the prevention or mitigation of land subsidence, soil erosion, and landslides. Percolation from rice fields, canals, and storage reservoirs recharges groundwater systems. Such recharge may also provide a means of sharing water equitably among farmers, who can pump from shallow aquifers at relatively low cost rather than suffer from inequitably shared or poorly managed surface irrigation systems. The moderation of air temperature by rice fields has been recognized as a regulating service in peri-urban areas where paddy and urban land are intermingled. This function is attributed to relatively high evapotranspiration rates that lower the ambient temperature of the surrounding area in the summer and result in lateral heat emission from the water body in winter. Rice can be used as a desalinization crop because of its ability to grow well under flooded conditions where continuously percolating water leaches salts from the topsoil.

Photo by International Rice Research Institute

Photo 14.3

Supporting services. Flooded rice fields and irrigation channels form a comprehensive water network, which together with their contiguous dry land provides a complex mosaic of landscapes. The Ramsar Convention on wetlands classified irrigated rice land as a human-made wetland (Ramsar Convention Secretariat 2004). Surveys show that such landscapes sustain a rich biodiversity, including unique and threatened species (Fernando, Goltenboth, and Margraf 2005), and enhance biodiversity in urban and peri-urban areas. In parts of the United States, such as California, rice fields are ponded in winter and used to provide habitat for ducks and other water birds.

Cultural services. The cultural services of rice environments are especially valued in Asian countries, where rice has been the main staple food and the single most important source of employment and income for rural people for centuries if not millennia. Many old kingdoms as well as small communities have been founded on the construction of irrigation facilities to stabilize rice production. The collective approach needed to invest in rice systems (construction of terraces, tank systems for irrigation) and operation and maintenance (terraces, but also cropping calendar) requires strong community approaches. Rice affects daily life in many ways, and the social concept of rice culture gives meaning to rice beyond

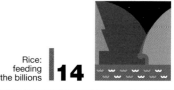

its role as an item of production and consumption (Hamilton 2003). Many traditional festivals and religious practices are associated with rice cultivation (photo 14.3), and rice fields are valued for their scenic beauty. Rice is also an integral part of the history and culture of Africa, where it has been grown for more than 3,000 years.

Environmental impacts

Rice production affects the environment mainly by releasing or sequestering gases or compounds that are active in the atmosphere or troposphere and by changing the chemical composition of the water flowing through rice fields. Rice is in turn affected by environmental changes, such as global climate change (box 14.4).

Ammonia volatilization. Ammonia volatilization is the major pathway of nitrogen loss from applied nitrogen fertilizer in rice systems. Across irrigated environments in Asia, nitrogen fertilizer input averages 118±40 kg per hectare, with the highest levels in southern China, at up to 300 kg per hectare (Witt and others 1999). In tropical transplanted rice nitrogen losses from ammonia volatilization can be 50% or higher, while in direct-seeded rice in temperate regions losses are generally negligible because most of the fertilizer is incorporated into the soil before flooding. Ammonia-nitrogen volatilizations from lowland rice fields are estimated at 3.6 teragrams (Tg) a year (compared with 9 Tg a year emitted from all agricultural fields worldwide), which is some 5%–8% of the estimated 45–75 Tg of globally emitted ammonia-nitrogen each year (Kirk 2004). The magnitude of ammonia volatilization depends largely on climatic conditions, field water management, and method

---

box **14.4** | **Projected effects of climate change on rice**

Climate change is expected to raise carbon dioxide levels and temperatures and increase the frequency of extreme climatic events, such as storms, droughts, and heavy rainfall in monsoon climates that will increase the incidence of flooding. Rising sea levels are expected to increase flood risk and salinity intrusion in rice growing environments in delta areas (Wassman and others 2004).

Simulations for the major rice-growing regions of Asia find that yield decreases 7% for every 1° Celsius (C) rise in temperature above current mean temperature at existing atmospheric carbon dioxide concentration. Elevated carbon dioxide levels increase yield and water productivity by increasing dry matter production, number of panicles, and grain filling percentage (Ziska and others 1997). However, elevated carbon dioxide also increases spikelet susceptibility to high temperature–induced sterility. Overall, the beneficial effect of elevated carbon dioxide on the yield and water productivity of rice disappears under high temperatures. Recently, yield reduction in rice has been correlated with increased nighttime temperatures: grain yield declined 10% for each 1°C increase in growing-season minimum temperature in the dry season in irrigated tropical rice (Peng and others 2004).

Intraspecific variations in yield response to changes in carbon dioxide levels in rice could be exploited to maximize the beneficial effect of increased carbon dioxide levels. Similarly, genotypic variation in the sensitivity to warm nighttime temperature and high daytime temperatures opens up the possibility of developing rice varieties that are less sensitive to higher temperatures. Selection of rice varieties that flower early in the morning can be an effective way to avoid high daytime temperatures and reduced spikelet sterility.

of nitrogen fertilizer application. Volatilized ammonium can be deposited on the earth by rain. This can be a beneficial source of (free) nitrogen fertilizer in agricultural lands, but it can also lead to soil acidification and unintended nitrogen inputs into natural ecosystems.

Greenhouse gases. Of the three main greenhouse gases, rice production reduces carbon dioxide levels through carbon sequestration and has relatively low nitrous oxide emissions but relatively high methane emissions.

Rice contributes 3%–10% to global methane emissions

Carbon sequestration. Rice soils that are flooded for long periods of the year tend to sequester carbon, even with the complete removal of above-ground plant biomass (Bronson and others 1997). Significant carbon accumulation results from biological activity in the soil-floodwater system. Average soil organic carbon content in irrigated double and triple rice systems in Asia is about 14–15 grams of carbon per kilogram in the upper 20–25 cm of soil (Dobermann and others 2003). Assuming an average bulk density of about 1.25 metric tons per cubic meter of soil and a physical land area of about 24 million ha, these monoculture systems alone store about 45 metric tons of carbon per hectare or a total of 1.1 petagrams of carbon (109 metric tons) in the topsoil. Additional carbon is stored in other irrigated rice systems (such as single rice and rice-maize), although typically in smaller amounts than in monoculture systems. However, reliable information on soil carbon stocks is not available for rice systems in most countries, and it is not known how soil organic carbon levels will change in response to changing climate or management practices.

Nitrous oxide. Few accurate assessments have been made of nitrous oxide emissions from rice fields, so the contribution to global emissions has not been assessed. In irrigated rice systems with good water control, nitrous oxide emissions are very small except when nitrogen fertilizer rates are excessively high (Bronson and others 1997; Wassmann and others 2000). In irrigated rice fields the bulk of nitrous oxide emissions occur during fallow periods and immediately after flooding of the soil at the end of the fallow period. In rainfed systems, however, nitrate accumulation in aerobic phases might contribute to considerable emission of nitrous oxide.

Methane. In the early 1980s it was estimated that lowland rice fields emitted 50–100 Tg of methane per year, or about 10%–20% of the then-estimated global methane emissions (Kirk 2004). Recent measurements show that many rice fields emit substantially less methane, especially in northern India and China, both because methane emissions have decreased with changes in rice production systems and because techniques for upscaling greenhouse gas emissions have improved with the use of simulation models and geographic information systems (GIS) (Matthews and others 2000).

The uncertainty in methane emissions from rice fields is among the highest of all sources in the global methane budget. Current estimates of annual methane emissions from rice fields are in the range of 20–60 Tg, or 3%–10% of global emissions of about 600 Tg (Kirk 2004). Estimates of annual methane emissions from the principal rice producers China and India are in the range of 10–30 Tg. The magnitude and pattern of methane emissions from rice fields are determined mainly by the water regime and organic inputs and to a lesser extent by soil type, weather, tillage practices, residue management, fertilizer use, and rice cultivar (Bronson and others 1997; Wassmann and others 2000). Use of

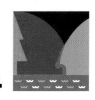

organic manure generally enhances methane emissions. Flooding of the soil is a prerequisite for sustained emissions of methane. Mid-season drainage, a common irrigation practice in the major rice-growing regions of China and Japan, greatly reduces methane emissions. Similarly, rice environments with an uneven supply of water, such as rainfed environments, have a lower emission potential than environments where rice is continuously flooded.

Surface water pollution. The changes in water quality associated with rice production may be positive or negative, depending on the quality of the incoming water and on management practices relating to fertilizer and biocide use, among others. The quality of the water leaving rice fields may be improved by the capacity of the wetland ecosystem to remove nitrogen and phosphorus. On the other side of the ledger, nitrogen transfers from flooded rice fields by direct flows of dissolved nitrogen in floodwater through runoff or drainage warrant more attention. The pollution of groundwater is covered below in the discussion of human health.

> Contamination of groundwater with arsenic has recently emerged as a major health issue in Asia

Salinization. Percolating water from lowland rice fields usually raises the water table. Where the groundwater is saline, this can salinize the rootzone of nonrice crops in the area and cause waterlogging and salinity in lower areas in the landscape, such as in parts of Australia and the northwest Indo-Gangetic Plain. Where irrigation water is relatively fresh, flooded rice can be used in combination with adequate drainage to leach salts that had previously accumulated under nonrice crops out of the rootzone, as in parts of northern China, and to reclaim sodic soils when used in combination with gypsum, as in parts of the northwest Indo-Gangetic Plain.

Rice and health—pollution and nutrition

Many of the rural poor in Asia obtain water for drinking and household use from shallow aquifers under agricultural land. Among the agrochemicals that pose the greatest threats to domestic use of groundwater are nitrate and biocide residues. In addition, contamination of groundwater with arsenic has recently emerged as a major health issue in Asia. Other health aspects concern malnutrition and vector-borne diseases related to rice production.

Nitrates. Nitrate leaching from flooded rice fields is normally negligible because of rapid denitrification under anaerobic conditions. In the Philippines, for example, nitrate pollution of groundwater under rice-based cropping systems exceeded the 10 milligrams (mg) per liter limit for safe drinking water only when highly fertilized vegetables were included in the cropping system (Bouman, Castañeda, and Bhuiyan 2002). In the Indian Punjab, however, an increase in nitrate of almost 2 mg per liter was recorded between 1982 and 1988, with a simultaneous increase in nitrogen fertilizer use from 56 kg to 188 kg per hectare, most of it on combined rice-wheat cultivation (Bijay-Singh, Sadana, and Arora 1991). The relative contribution to this increase from rice, however, is not clear.

Biocides. Mean biocide use in irrigated rice systems varies from some 0.4 kg active ingredients per hectare in Tamil Nadu, India, to 3.8 kg per hectare in Zhejiang Province, China (Bouman, Castañeda, and Bhuiyan 2002). In the warm and humid conditions of the tropics volatilization is the major process of biocide loss, especially when biocides are applied on the water surface or on wet soil. Relatively high temperatures favor rapid transformation of the remaining biocides by photochemical and microbial degradation, but little is known about the toxicity of the residual components. In case studies in the Philippines mean biocide concentrations in groundwater under irrigated rice-based cropping systems were one to two orders of magnitude below the single (0.1 micrograms per liter) and multiple (0.5 micrograms per liter) biocide limits for safe drinking water, although temporary peak concentrations of 1.14–4.17 micrograms per liter were measured (Bouman, Castañeda, and Bhuiyan 2002).

'
Human micronutrient deficiencies are relatively severe in areas where rice is the major staple

Biocides and their residues may be directly transferred to open water bodies through drainage water that flows overland from rice fields. The potential for water pollution from biocides is greatly affected by field water management. Different water regimes result in different pest and weed populations and densities, which farmers may combat with different amounts and types of biocides. In traditional rice systems relatively few herbicides are used because puddling, transplanting, and ponding water are effective weed control measures.

Arsenic. Arsenic in groundwater has been reported in many countries in Asia. Severe problems of aresenicosis occur in rural areas in Bangladesh and in West Bengal in India. In the past two decades the number of shallow tubewells for irrigation in these areas has increased dramatically, and the dry season rice production (Boro rice) depends heavily on groundwater. It is unclear whether groundwater extraction for irrigation influences arsenic behavior in the shallow aquifers, but irrigation from arsenic-contaminated aquifers may pose several risks. Arsenic accumulates in the topsoil as a result of irrigation water input. Because rice fields receive higher inputs of irrigation water than other crops, they accumulate more arsenic than other fields. Moreover, arsenic is potentially more bioavailable under flooded than nonflooded conditions.

It is not yet possible to predict arsenic uptake by plants from the soil, and significant correlations are not often found between total arsenic in the soil and in plants (Abedin, Cotter-Howells, and Meharg 2002). Arsenic that is taken up by rice is found mostly in roots and shoot tissue, and very little in the grains. In Bangladesh no milled rice samples have been found to contain more arsenic than the government threshold of 1 part per million for safe consumption, although straw samples have, raising concerns about arsenic toxicity in animal feed.

Arsenic in the soil may also affect crop production, but this aspect has not received much attention yet, and understanding of the long-term aspects of arsenic in agriculture is too limited to assess the risks. Water-saving irrigation techniques for rice (such as alternate wetting and drying irrigation and aerobic rice) reduce the irrigation inputs and arsenic contamination risk of the topsoil. As the soil becomes more aerobic, the solubility and uptake of arsenic is also reduced.

Nutrition. Human micronutrient deficiencies are relatively severe in areas where rice is the major staple. Increasing the density of provitamin A carotenoid, iron, and zinc in rice can help alleviate these deficiencies, especially among the urban and rural poor people who have little access to alternatives such as enriched foods and diversified diets. Promising examples are the development of golden rice to combat vitamin A deficiency (Potrykus 2003) and of iron-rich rice to combat iron deficiency (Haas and others 2005), although it is still debated whether such increases in the endosperm are sufficient to significantly affect human nutrition. To drive the adoption of micronutrient-rich varieties, the improved traits will need to be combined with other traits that are attractive to farmers, such as tolerance to drought, salinity, or submergence.

Vector-borne diseases. Irrigated rice fields can serve as breeding sites for mosquitoes and snail intermediate hosts capable of transmitting human parasites (see also chapter 9 on irrigation). In particular, before transplanting and after harvest, puddles in rice fields are attractive breeding grounds for the mosquito *Anopheles gambiae,* Africa's most efficient malaria vector. Factors that determine whether the introduction of irrigated rice increases or reduces the incidence of malaria are known, and technical options exist to mitigate this impact, including alternate wetting and drying irrigation. Moreover, countries such as Sri Lanka have made great strides in controlling epidemics through broad-based public health campaigns. Japanese B-encephalitis is highly correlated with rice irrigation in Asia, especially where pigs are also reared, as in China and Viet Nam. Again, alternate wetting and drying can help reduce the breeding of vectors (Keiser and others 2005).

> Future demand for rice will depend on population growth and on the age structure, income, and urbanization of the population

The challenges

The main challenge facing most rice-producing and -consuming countries is to provide sufficient affordable food for growing and urbanizing populations and to alleviate rural and urban poverty. This has to be done under increasing pressure on land, water, and labor resources that threaten the sustainability of the rice production base. At the same time, the importance of the nonfood services provided by rice environments is increasingly recognized. And the negative externalities of rice production on the environment need to be minimized where water scarcity forces production to rely on more aerobic systems rather than permanent flooding.

Feeding the billions

Future demand for rice will depend on population growth and on the age structure, income, and urbanization of the population. Annual population growth in rice-producing Asia was about 1.2% from 2000 to 2005 but is forecast to decline to 0.1% by 2050 (FAO-STAT). As incomes rise, particularly in urban areas, per capita rice consumption declines. At the national level per capita consumption is declining not only in East Asia (China, Japan, and the Republic of Korea) but also in Malaysia and Thailand. For the next two decades, however, an increasing demand for rice in response to increasing populations is still expected to outstrip this decline in per capita consumption. Assuming a mild decline in world rice prices, rice demand in Asia is expected to grow by about 1% a year until 2025 (Sombilla, Rosegrant, and Meijer 2002). In West and Central Africa demand for rice is currently growing at 6% a year, faster than anywhere else in the world. This growth is largely the result of urbanization and changing consumer preferences favoring rice.

Alleviating poverty

Despite declining poverty rates in the past few decades in much of Asia, the absolute number of poor people has declined very little, especially in South Asia and Sub-Saharan Africa. Poverty still exists in rural areas in both the irrigated and the rainfed rice environments. Asia is rapidly urbanizing, and more people will shift from being net rice producers to net rice consumers. Also, the total number of urban poor people is expected to increase. A major challenge will be not only to produce more rice, but to keep its price low to improve the well-being of poor people (box 14.5). Because a low rice price depresses the profitability of rice farming, particularly for small-scale producers, the simultaneous challenge is to decrease the cost of rice production (per kilogram) to boost the profitability of rice farming. Support schemes for small farmers can also help in coping with low prices.

Sustaining the resource base and protecting the environment

Irrigated environments. Worldwide, water for agriculture is increasingly scarce. Although there is no systematic definition, inventory, or quantification of water scarcity in rice-growing areas, there is evidence that water scarcity is encroaching on irrigated lowlands. It is estimated that by 2025, 15–20 million ha of irrigated rice will suffer some degree of water scarcity

---

box 14.5 | **Rice's contribution to poverty alleviation**

Access to irrigation, fertilizer, and the high-yielding varieties of the green revolution increased productivity and profits and contributed to food security and poverty reduction among farmers with irrigated land. The growth in rice production outstripped the growth in population, thus lowering prices (see figure 14.1), which reduced the daily expenses for food of poor consumers such as the rural landless, urban laborers, fishers, and farmers of crops other than rice. The contribution of lower prices is not trivial, because many of these people spend 20%–40% of their income on rice alone. Furthermore, low rice prices make labor costs in the industrial and service sectors more competitive, fueling job growth and catalyzing economic development (Dawe 2000).

But low rice prices can hurt some farmers, especially those who have not adopted modern varieties and thus have not benefited from productivity increases. Indeed, despite the successes of the green revolution poverty or hunger still occurs among considerable numbers of rice farmers within irrigated areas (Magor 1996), because even in highly productive systems it is difficult to escape poverty with only a small plot of land. Poverty is still widespread among farmers in rainfed areas, especially in the remote uplands of Laos, Nepal, Viet Nam, and northeastern India and in Sub-Saharan Africa. For many poor farming households, however, increasing rice productivity is often the first step out of poverty as it provides food security and frees up land and labor resources (Hossain and Fischer 1995). With increased rice yields part of the farm land can be taken out of rice production and converted into more profitable cash crops. Freed-up labor can be invested in off-farm employment. Increased income can be used to invest in the education of children, which is a potential pathway out of farming and poverty.

(Tuong and Bouman 2003). Even in areas generally considered water abundant, several case studies indicate that there are local hotspots of water scarcity. This water scarcity is expected to further shift rice production to more water-abundant delta areas, to lead to crop diversification, and to result in more aerobic soil conditions in rice fields in water-short areas.

There are indications that soil-borne pests and diseases (such as nematodes, root aphids, and fungi) and nutrient disorders occur more in nonflooded than in flooded rice systems (George and others 2002). Rice that is not permanently flooded tends to have more weed growth and a broader weed spectrum than rice that is (Mortimer and Hill 1999), likely leading to more frequent use of herbicides. With less water the numbers and types of pests and predators may change as well as predator-pest relationships. Possible shifts in the use of pesticides by farmers in response to these changes, and what this means for the environment, are as yet unknown.

> **Better understanding of the ecosystem services of the rice environment is needed**

Less ammonia volatilization and methane emissions are expected under nonflooded conditions, but also higher nitrous oxide emissions and more leaching of nitrate. The net greenhouse gas impact is as yet unknown. While direct evidence from converted paddy fields is still missing, it is likely that growing rice under increasingly aerobic conditions will reduce soil carbon contents and release carbon dioxide into the atmosphere. This change in soil organic matter will be accompanied by changes in the microbial community, shifting from predominately anaerobic to aerobic organisms. It is not clear how these changes will affect soil fertility, if at all. The transformation of rice fields to upland crops will likewise have consequences for sustainability and the environment.

Rainfed environments. A major challenge is to minimize the negative environmental consequences of intensification in rainfed environments. Intensification through increased fertilizer use, cropping intensity, and changes in methods of crop establishment will affect soil and environmental processes. Increased productivity, based initially on better varieties and subsequently on unbalanced use of inorganic fertilizer and reduced organic fertilizer, changes nutrient balances and increases the mining of soil nutrients. Reports of rapidly emerging severe nutrient deficiencies after intensification testify to the relative fragility of rainfed systems because of frequently low natural soil fertility and low buffering capacity.

Photo 14.4

Photo by B.A.M. Bouman

Valuing the ecosystem services of rice environments

There is growing recognition of the need for a better understanding of the ecosystem services of the rice environment (photo 14.4). Although some methodologies have been developed to measure and estimate different services of agricultural systems, quantifying and valuing the positive and negative externalities are still major challenges. Many countries lack relevant data at the appropriate geographic level.

Response options

Most of the increase in rice production to meet food security and alleviate poverty has to come from higher yields on existing cropland (irrigated and rainfed) to avoid environmental degradation, destruction of natural ecosystems, and loss of biodiversity (Tilman and others 2002). Most of the rice surplus will continue to come from irrigated environments. In some major rice-producing countries, such as Bangladesh, the Philippines, and Thailand, there is still a large gap between actual and potential yields, and efforts need to be directed at crop management technologies to narrow the yield gap. In other countries, such as China, Japan, and the Republic of Korea, the yield gap is closing, and further yield increases can come only from increased genetic yield potential.

Increased yields and total production mean that, with current management practices, more water will be needed to meet increased transpiration requirements. With increasing water shortage, this means that the water productivity of rice needs to increase.

> The scope to increase the water productivity of rice through increased transpiration efficiency of the plant is small compared with decreased water losses from the field

Varietal improvement

Yield potential. The key attributes of the high-yielding varieties of the green revolution were semidwarf stature (which increased harvest index and lodging resistance) and photoperiod insensitivity. There are no indications that these factors can be further exploited to significantly increase the yield potential of inbred varieties under fully irrigated conditions (Peng and others 1999). For example, since the introduction of IR8 in the 1960s the yield potential of semidwarf tropical indica inbred varieties has stagnated at about 10 metric tons per hectare. Substantial yield improvement has recently come only from the development of hybrid rice, which has increased yield potential by 5%–15% over inbred varieties in the same environment. China's "super" rice–breeding program has developed several hybrid varieties with a yield of 12 metric tons per hectare in on-farm demonstration fields, which is 8%–15% higher than the hybrid check varieties. Transforming the C_3 rice plant into a C_4 plant through genetic engineering could be a long-term approach for increasing rice yield potential, but the feasibility and potential benefits of this approach are still being debated (Sheehy, Mitchell, and Hardy 2000).

Traditional breeding programs for irrigated environments have selected varieties under conditions of continuously ponded water. With increasing water scarcity in irrigated systems, breeding programs should include selection under conditions of water-saving technologies such as alternate wetting and drying or aerobic cultivation. Some success has been recorded with the development of high-yielding aerobic rice varieties in northern China, as discussed later (see section on "Tolerance to abiotic stresses").

Water productivity. The modern improved japonica varieties have a 25%–30% higher transpiration efficiency than the older indica varieties, suggesting considerable variation for this trait in rice germplasm (Peng and others 1998). The potential for exploiting this trait has not been investigated, however. Proposals to increase the waxiness of rice leaves to reduce nonstomatal transpiration have demonstrated no notable progress. Transforming the C_3 rice plant into a C_4 plant could potentially increase transpiration efficiency, but again, not much progress has been made.

Overall, the scope to increase the water productivity of rice through improved transpiration efficiency of the plant seems to be small compared with the scope to increase water productivity through reduced total water inputs (irrigation, rainfall). The shorter growth duration of modern high-yielding rice varieties has reduced outflows of evaporation, seepage, and percolation from individual rice fields. The combined effect of increased yield and reduced growth duration is that these varieties have a water productivity related to total inputs that is three times higher than that of traditional varieties grown under similar water management (Tuong and Bouman 2003). A range of breeding strategies can be explored to further increase water productivity through increased evapotranspiration efficiency, such as early vigor to reduce soil evaporation and weed suppression to reduce weed transpiration (Bennett 2003).

Tolerance to abiotic stresses. Other routes to increased yields and total production are through greater tolerance to abiotic stresses, including drought, submergence, and salinity.

Drought. Most progress so far has come from the development of short-duration varieties that escape drought at the end of the rainy season (Bennett 2003). But during the last decade substantial genetic variability for grain yield under drought stress has been documented in both cultivated Asian rice, *Oryza sativa*, and its hardy African relative, *Oryza glaberrima*. New breeding approaches are resulting in the development of both upland and lowland rice varieties with improved tolerance to severe water stress during the sensitive stages of flowering and grain-filling, while retaining the ability to produce high yields when water supplies are not limiting. Two examples for upland environments are aerobic rice and Nerica (New Rice for Africa). Aerobic rice is higher yielding than traditional upland varieties and combines input responsiveness with improved lodging resistance and harvest index (Atlin and others 2006). These new varieties are designed for nonflooded, aerobic soil conditions in either rainfed or water-short irrigated environments. (Examples of adoption in Brazil and China are discussed later in the section on "Managing rice fields better.") Nerica is the result of crossing *Oryza glaberrima* with *Oryza sativa* species at the African Rice Centre (WARDA) beginning in the mid-1990s to combine the toughness of *glaberrima* with the productivity of *sativa* (Jones and others 1997). The aim was to combine resistance to local stresses with higher yield, shorter growth duration, and higher protein content than traditional rice varieties. The first Nerica series (1–18) were upland varieties; 8 varieties have been officially released. There are now 60 lowland Nerica varieties, 2 of which have been officially released in Burkina Faso and Mali.

Submergence. Though breeding for submergence tolerance and enhanced yield in flash-flood areas has been going on for more than three decades, only a few tolerant lines with improved agronomic characteristics have been developed so far. Recently, a few tolerant landraces were discovered that can withstand complete submergence for 10–14 days. New submergence-tolerant breeding lines with improved agronomic characteristics are now being developed by transferring this tolerance into semidwarf breeding lines using marker-assisted selection (box 14.6). Some breeding progress has been made for deepwater areas, and a few new lines with reasonable yield and grain quality have been released. Recently, three main quantitative trait loci (QTL; a region of DNA associated with a particular trait) were identified for elongation ability (Sripongpangkul and others 2000). Fine-mapping and tagging of these QTLs will facilitate their efficient incorporation into modern popular varieties through marker-assisted selection.

Other routes to increased yields and total production are through greater tolerance to abiotic stresses, including drought, submergence, and salinity

The complete sequencing of the rice genome is expected to accelerate the discovery and exploitation of useful genes in breeding programs. Molecular tools were used in the development of Nerica to overcome hybrid sterility, accelerating the breeding program from 5–7 years to about two years. For drought tolerance molecular tools are starting to identify genes controlling the responses of plants to water stress, but so far no quantitative trait loci (QTL) have been identified for tolerance to either reproductive- or vegetative-stage drought stress with effects large enough to be useful in breeding (Bennett 2003).

Molecular tools are contributing successfully to breeding for tolerance to salinity and submergence. An example is the recent advance in tolerance to flash flooding. Using a population developed from a cross between an indica submergence-tolerant line (IR40931) and a susceptible japonica line (PI543851) a major QTL was mapped to chromosome 9, designated as Sub1 (Mackill and Xu 1996). This QTL accounted for a large proportion of the phenotypic variation in submergence tolerance. The Sub1 QTL was fine mapped, and markers were developed and successfully used to transfer it into Swarna, a popular rainfed lowland variety sensitive to submergence, which became substantially tolerant to flooding under field conditions without changing its agronomic or quality traits. Efforts are ongoing to transfer the Sub1 QTL into other "Mega" varieties in rainfed lowlands such as BR11, IR64, Mahsuri, Samba Mahsuri, and CR1009.

Salinity. Despite a general sensitivity to salinity rice has considerable variation in tolerance. Combining new screening techniques with conventional, mutation, and anther culture techniques, salinity tolerance was successfully introduced into high-yielding plant types (Gregorio and others 2002). Some newly released varieties have demonstrated more than 50% yield advantage over current salt-sensitive varieties. Breeding cultivars with much higher tolerance is possible if component traits are combined in a suitable genetic background. The opportunity to improve salinity tolerance through the incorporation of useful genes or pyramiding of superior alleles appears very promising. A major QTL, designated Saltol, was recently mapped. It accounted for more than 70% of the variation in salt uptake in this population. Marker-assisted backcrossing is currently used to incorporate this QTL into popular high-yielding varieties.

To enhance adoption of improved varieties, farmers' preferences need to be taken into account. This was done for the delivery of aerobic rice in Asia and Nerica in Africa through participatory varietal selection and community-based seed production systems.

Managing rice fields better

Irrigated environments. Increasingly, technologies that aim to close the gap between actual yields and potential yield need to apply holistic approaches that integrate crop, soil, and water management. An example is the system of rice intensification (Stoop, Uphoff, and Kassam 2002). As with all such approaches, care must be taken in promoting a single solution across environments, and site-specific adaptation must be allowed for. For example, the system of rice intensification in the original form developed in Madagascar has strict rules about the use of young seedlings, wide plant spacing, transplanting of single seedlings, transplanting in squares, alternate wetting and drying, manual or mechanic weeding, and large amounts of organic fertilizer. Though the validity of the principles behind the system are still questioned (Sheehy and others 2004; McDonald, Hobbs, and Riha 2006), many farmers pioneer the system in new areas by modifying it to suit their local needs and environments, often to the extent that the original approach is no longer recognizable.

Though water flows have hardly been studied in these integrated technologies, it is likely that yield increases are accompanied by relative increases in transpiration and by relative decreases in evaporation, seepage, and percolation. In terms of water savings any agronomic practice that increases the harvest index (ratio of crop yield to aboveground weight of the plant) will result in more grains per unit of water transpired and thus in increased water productivity.

> **Technologies that aim to close the gap between actual and potential yield need to apply holistic approaches that integrate crop, soil, and water management**

Water-saving technologies. Various water-saving technologies exist or are being developed to help farmers cope with water scarcity in irrigated environments (Tuong, Bouman, and Mortimer 2005; Humphreys and others 2005). These technologies increase the productivity of water inputs (rainfall, irrigation) mainly by reducing unproductive seepage and percolation losses and to a lesser extent by reducing evaporation. Mechanical soil compaction can reduce percolation flows in certain soil types but may be too expensive for large-scale implementation and may adversely affect the growth of any upland crop following rice. General measures such as land leveling, farm channels, and good puddling and bund maintenance improve water control and reduce seepage and percolation outflows. Minimizing the turnaround time between wet land preparation and transplanting reduces the time when no crop is present and outflows of water from the field do not contribute to production.

Especially in large-scale irrigation systems with plot to plot irrigation the water losses during the turnaround time can be high when farmers maintain seedbeds in their main fields and keep the whole area flooded for the full duration of the seedbeds (Tabbal and others 2002). The losses can be minimized by installing field channels, adopting common seedbeds, or direct seeding. With field channels water can be delivered separately to individual seedbeds, and the main field does not need to be flooded. Common seedbeds, either communal or privately managed, can be located strategically close to irrigation canals and irrigated as one block. With direct seeding the crop starts growing and using water from the moment of establishment onwards. Direct dry seeding can also increase the effective use of rainfall and reduce irrigation needs (Cabangon, Tuong, and Abdullah 2002).

Water management techniques such as saturated soil culture and moderate alternate wetting and drying (without imposing drought stress) reduce field water application 15%–20% without significantly affecting yield and increase the productivity of total water input (Belder and others 2004; Tabbal and others 2002). For example, in experiments on alternate wetting and drying in China in a clay loam soil with shallow groundwater depths of 0 0.3 meters, alternate wetting and drying saved 10% 15% water with no effect on yield (table 14.2). More water can be saved and water productivity further increased by prolonging the periods of dry soil and imposing slight drought stress on the plants, but this usually comes at the expense of some loss of yield (Bouman and Tuong 2001). In experiments on alternate wetting and drying in the Philippines in a silty clay loam with

table **14.2**		Yield and water use of alternate wetting and drying and aerobic rice systems, China, India, and the Philippines			
Country and source	Year	Treatment[a]	Yield (metric tons per hectare)	Total water input[b] (millimeters)	Water productivity (grams of grain per kilogram of water)
Philippines (Tabbal and others 2002)	1988	Flooded	5.0	2,197	0.23
		AWD	4.0	880	0.46
	1989	Flooded	5.8	1,679	0.35
		AWD	4.3	700	0.61
	1990	Flooded	5.3	2,028	0.26
		AWD	4.2	912	0.46
	1991	Flooded	4.9	3,504	0.14
		AWD	3.3	1,126	0.29
China (Belder and others 2004)	1999	Flooded	8.4	965	0.90
		AWD	8.0	878	0.95
	2000	Flooded	8.1	878	0.92
		AWD	8.4	802	1.07
India (Mishra and others 1990)	1983	Flooded	6.3	1,991	0.32
		AWD 1d	5.8	1,891	0.31
		AWD 3d	5.5	1,748	0.31
		AWD 5d	5.1	1,747	0.29
		AWD 7d	4.8	1,747	0.27
	1984	Flooded	6.3	1,890	0.33
		AWD 1d	5.9	1,569	0.38
		AWD 3d	5.6	1,426	0.39
		AWD 5d	5.1	1,352	0.38
		AWD 7d	5.0	1,352	0.38
Philippines (Bouman and others 2005)	2001	Flooded	5.1	1,718	0.29
		Aerobic	4.4	787	0.55
	2002	Flooded	7.3	1,268	0.58
		Aerobic	5.7	843	0.67
	2003	Flooded	6.8	1,484	0.46
		Aerobic	4.0	980	0.41
China (Yang and others 2005)	2001	Flooded	5.4	1,351	0.40
		Aerobic wet	4.7	644	0.73
		Aerobic dry	3.4	524	0.66
	2002	Flooded	5.3	1,255	0.42
		Aerobic wet	5.3	917	0.58
		Aerobic dry	4.6	695	0.66

a. AWD is alternate wetting and drying. In India the irrigation interval is given in days (d).
b. Rainfall plus irrigation, from crop establishment till harvest, excluding any contribution from groundwater.

groundwater depths of 0.7–2.0 meters water inputs in flooded rice were relatively high, and the alternate wetting and drying treatment saved more than 50% water with some 20% yield loss. In an experiment on clay loam in India, with a groundwater table fluctuating between 0.1 and 1.2 meters, increasing the number of days without ponded water progressively reduced both water inputs and yields.

Alternate wetting and drying reduce evaporation by 0%–30%, whereas the other water savings arise from reduced seepage and percolation loss (Belder and others 2005). The technique is a mature technology that has been widely adopted in China and can now be considered the common practice of lowland rice production in that country (Li and Barker 2004). It is also being recommended in northwestern India and parts of the Philippines.

In the system of *aerobic* rice specially adapted input-responsive rice varieties are grown under dryland conditions just like other cereals such as wheat, with or without supplemental irrigation (photo 14.5). In experiments in clay soil with groundwater at depths of 0.6–1.4 meters in the Philippines and in sandy soil with groundwater at 20 meters depth in northern China water inputs in aerobic rice systems were 30%–50% less than in flooded systems and yields were 20%–30% lower with a maximum of about 5.5 metric tons per hectare (see table 14.2). Reductions in evaporation losses were 50%–75%. Aerobic rice systems are currently being pioneered by farmers on an estimated 80,000 ha in north China (Wang and others 2002).

> In the system of aerobic rice specially adapted input-responsive rice varieties are grown under dryland conditions just like other cereals

However, the development of aerobic rice systems for irrigated environments is in its infancy, and more research is needed to develop high-yielding varieties and sustainable management systems. In aerobic rice systems resource-conserving technologies, as practiced in upland nonrice crops, become available to rice farmers as well, such as mulching and zero or minimum tillage. Various methods of mulching are being experimented with in nonflooded rice systems in China and have been shown to reduce evaporation (Dittert and others 2002). Growing rice under aerobic conditions on raised beds shows promise but is also still in its infancy (Humphreys and others 2005).

Photo 14.5

Sustainability and environmental protection. While more work has been done on the development of technologies to increase crop productivity under water scarcity, little attention has been paid to their long-term sustainability and environmental impacts. Studies are needed on the relationships between the use of organic and inorganic fertilizers and crop residue management on the one hand, and yield sustainability, greenhouse gas emissions, and pathways of nutrient losses on the other. The effectiveness and environmental impacts of fertilizer management technologies such as site-specific nutrient management, slow-release fertilizers, and deep placement need to be evaluated under various scenarios of water availability.

Water-saving technologies can have different effects on the emission of greenhouse gases, depending on environmental site conditions and management practices (box 14.7). With less water, weed management practices need to be developed that reduce the reliance on herbicides by anticipating weed species "shifts" and developing preventive strategies that integrate management interventions such as manual weeding, increased seed density (in direct-seeded systems), and mechanical weeding.

Little is known about changing pest and disease dynamics when field conditions change from water abundant to water short, although initial reports suggest an increase

The following figure shows the variability in greenhouse gas emissions from conventional flooded rice fields (control) and from two water-saving systems, unsaturated soil covered by plastic film (film) and unsaturated soil covered by straw mulch (straw) at three sites in China. Methane emission is highest from flooded rice at all three sites. Nitrous oxide emission is lowest from flooded rice at Nanjing and Guangzhou, but similar among all three systems at Beijing. When both methane and nitrous oxide emission are converted into equivalent carbon dioxide emission and summed, flooded rice has the lowest global warming potential at Nanjing and the highest global warming potential at Guangzhou, whereas all three systems had similar global warming potential at Beijing. The overall impact of the adoption of water-saving management practices in rice production on global warming is unknown and needs more study.

Variability in greenhouse gas emissions from conventional and water-saving systems 2002

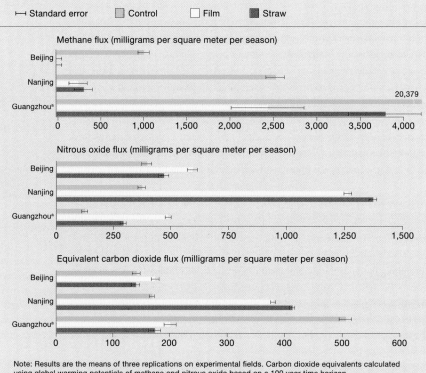

Note: Results are the means of three replications on experimental fields. Carbon dioxide equivalents calculated using global warming potentials of methane and nitrous oxide based on a 100 year time horizon.

a. Only the late rice crop was evaluated.

Source: Dittert and others 2002.

in soil-borne pests such as nematodes. It is to be expected that under fully aerobic soil conditions rice cannot be grown continuously on the same piece of land each year (as can be successfully done with flooded rice) without yield decline (Peng and others 2006; Piñheiro and others 2006). Suitable crop rotation will be needed as well as varieties that are tolerant of soil-borne pests and diseases. The experiences of upland rice and other dryland crops with pest and disease management have to be exploited in the development of sustainable management systems for water-short irrigated environments. Under completely aerobic conditions salts may accumulate in the root zone as in any other dryland crop, and flooded rice could be included as a rotation crop to periodically flush down salts.

> The high variability of rainfed environments exposes farmers to great risk of yield loss

Stress-prone environments. The high variability of rainfed environments exposes farmers to great risk of yield loss. The development of stress-tolerant and input-responsive varieties will reduce this risk and increase the incentive to use external inputs and intensify the cropping system. Adjusted cropping systems and management technologies will be needed to make the most efficient use of the possibilities offered by the new varieties. The combination of the improved rice varieties that are in the pipeline and specific management technologies has the potential to increase yields by 0.5–1.0 metric tons per hectare in environments prone to drought, flood, and salinity within the next 10 years.

Rainfed lowlands. Two promising technologies are direct seeding and improved nutrient management. Direct seeding potentially offers better use of early-season rainfall, better drought tolerance, lower risk from late season droughts, better use of indigenous soil nitrogen supply, and an increased possibility for a second crop. Site- and season-specific nutrient management can reduce nutrient losses and pollution of the environment. Both technologies have already enabled substantial productivity increases in some more favorable rainfed areas. In Lombok, Indonesia, the introduction of short-duration and input-responsive varieties with direct seeding and the use of inorganic fertilizer increased and stabilized yields (Fagi and Kartaatmadja 2002). In Lao PDR production in rainfed lowlands contributed considerably to achieving self-sufficiency in rice within a decade after the introduction of improved varieties and crop management (Pandey 2001).

Uplands. Strategies should aim at sustainable intensification to break the spiral of resource degradation caused by shorter fallow periods in shifting cultivation systems. For rice a promising option is the establishment of lowland fields in valley bottoms in mountainous areas, also referred to as "montane paddy rice" (Castella and Erout 2002). These lowland fields could benefit from irrigation water supplied by mountain streams that converge in the valley bottoms. Rainfed lowland rice fields are also found in shallow inland valleys in Sub-Saharan Africa, which have been identified as offering the greatest potential for expansion and intensification.

The aerobic rice production system offers scope where seasonal rainfall is some 600 mm or more or where farmers have access to supplementary irrigation. In the hilly regions of Yunnan Province in southern China farmers grow rainfed aerobic rice under intensified management, realizing yields of 3–4 metric tons per hectare (Atlin and others 2006). The combination of aerobic rice and terraces offers even greater scope for intensification. Aerobic rice also holds promise for permanent arable production systems in rotation with other crops. In Brazil a breeding program to improve upland rice has resulted in aerobic varieties with a yield potential of up to 6 metric tons per hectare (Piñheiro and others 2006). Farmers grow these varieties in rotation with crops such as soybean and fodder on large commercial farms with supplemental sprinkler irrigation on an estimated 250,000 ha of flatlands in the Cerrado region, realizing yields of 3–4 metric tons per hectare.

Submergence-prone environments. The new submergence-tolerant varieties need to be combined with adapted crop and nutrient management to improve seedling and plant survival as well as the ability to recover after submergence. Seedlings of submergence-tolerant varieties that are enriched in nutrients, particularly zinc and phosphorus, and possibly silicon, have a greater chance of survival. Application of nutrients after the recession of floodwater also speeds recovery, improves tillering, and boosts yield.

Salt- or sodic-affected areas. New salt-tolerant varieties need to be integrated with specific nursery, crop, and nutrient management strategies to mitigate the effects of salt stress and to improve soil quality. Soil amendments, particularly gypsum, can help in reclaiming sodic-affected soils, but they require large investments. The combined use of farmyard manure or pressmud from industrial waste with improved varieties can cut the need for gypsum by more than half. Relatively fresh irrigation water can leach salts accumulated in the root zone during previous nonrice crops.

> Aerobic rice holds promise for permanent arable production systems in rotation with other crops

Lowering the cost of production. There are many options to lower the costs of production, but few are directly related to water management. Where irrigation water is supplied by pumping, water-saving technologies reduce water inputs, pumping costs, and energy consumption. Whether this actually increases profitability depends on the yield obtained and the relative price of rice and water. Reducing irrigation frequency reduces the labor used for irrigation, but when fields are not continuously flooded, weed infestation may increase, requiring more labor or herbicides. The system of rice intensification has relatively high labor requirements and, partly as a result, there are reports of the system's abandonment in its country of origin, Madagascar (Moser and Barrett 2003). Dry seeding and aerobic rice technologies offer possibilities for mechanization of farm operations such as sowing, weed control, and combine harvesting, although adoption of these technologies seems to be driven more by labor shortage than by water shortage. Increased labor productivity also lowers the cost of production.

Options at the landscape level

Irrigation system efficiency and water reuse. Large volumes of water outflows through surface drainage, seepage, and percolation characterize irrigated rice fields. Although the outflows are losses from individual fields, there is great scope for reuse of these flows within a landscape that consists of many interconnected fields (figure 14.2). Surface drainage and seepage water usually flows into downstream fields and is lost only at the bottom of a toposequence when it flows into drains or ditches. Even then farmers can use small pumps to lift water from drains to irrigate fields that are inadequately serviced by irrigation canals. In many irrigation systems in low-lying deltas or flood plains with impeded drainage, the continuous percolation of water has created shallow groundwater tables close to the surface (Belder and others 2004;

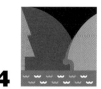

Cabangon and others 2004). Again, farmers can either directly pump water from the shallow groundwater or pump groundwater when it becomes surface water as it flows into creeks or drains. Recent studies of rice-based irrigation systems in China indicate that irrigation efficiency improves with increasing spatial scale because of the reuse of water (Loeve and others 2004a; box 14.8). Much of this reuse is informal, as farmers take the initiative to pump up water, block drains, or construct small on-farm reservoirs for secondary storage.

Although water can be efficiently reused this way, it does come at a cost and may not alleviate inequities among farmers in irrigation systems. The current debate on the improvement of irrigation systems focuses on the benefits and costs of system modernization relative to those of mostly informal reuse of water. System modernization aims to improve the irrigation system delivery infrastructure and operation scheme to supply each farmer with the right amount of water at the right time.

Stress-prone environments. There are many interventions at the landscape level that are effective in alleviating abiotic stresses. On-farm water harvesting can reduce drought risk and increase productivity in drought-prone rainfed environments by making small amounts of extra water available to bridge critical periods of dry spells. Developing reservoirs and canal networks to store rainwater or freshwater from rivers before it becomes

figure **14.2**	**There is great scope for reuse of water flows in a rice landscape of interconnected fields**

Water flows	1 Water flows into the fields by irrigation
	2 Water flows across fields by surface drainage
	3 Water flows across fields by lateral seepage
	4 Water recharges the groundwater through percolation
	5 Water may be reused by pumping from ditches and from the groundwater that collects drainage, seepage, and percolation flows.

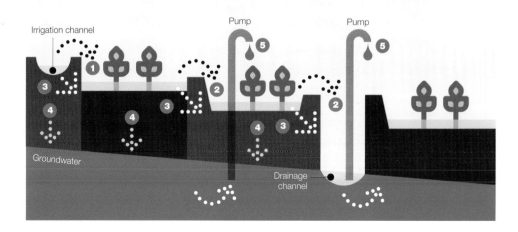

box **14.8** | **Producing more rice using less water**

The Zanghe Irrigation System (ZIS) in the middle reaches of the Yangtze Basin has a command area of about 160,000 ha and services mainly rice in the summer season. Since the early 1970s the amount of water released to agriculture has been steadily reduced in favor of increased releases to cities, industry, and hydropower. By the mid-1990s the amount of water received by agriculture had declined to less than 30% of the amount received in the early 1970s. In the same period, however, rice production increased, peaking at about 650,000 metric tons in the late 1980s, or nearly twice the amount produced in the late 1960s (see figure). Although rice production has leveled off to a stable 500,000 metric tons in the last decade, more rice has been produced with less water over the past 30 years, thanks to a variety of integrated measures:

- Replacing double rice cropping by more water-efficient single rice cropping.
- Promoting alternate wetting-drying water-saving technology.
- Introducing volumetric water pricing and such institutional reforms as water user associations, which promote efficient use of water by farmers.
- Upgrading the irrigation system (for example, canal lining).
- Developing secondary storage through the creation of thousands of small- to large-size ponds and reservoirs.

The ZIS case study suggests that win-win situations are possible where rice production can be maintained, or even increased, while freeing up water for other purposes. A thorough understanding of the boundary conditions under which the ZIS success was accomplished may identify entry points for successful replication in other systems.

Water supply and rice production in the Zanghe Irrigation System in the Yangtze Basin

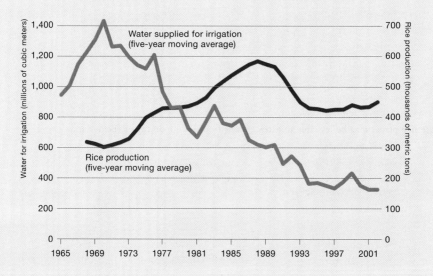

Source: Adapted from Loeve and others 2004b.

saline can extend the growing season in saline coastal areas and substantially improve productivity. Managing water by constructing large-scale coastal embankments and sluices has been reasonably successful in preventing seawater intrusion in many deltaic coastal areas, substantially reducing soil salinity in the wet season. The technology also opens up the possibility of growing high-yielding, modern rice varieties, as in the coastal areas of the Mekong Delta in Viet Nam (Tuong and others 2003).

However, water needs to be managed judiciously to avert undesirable long-term environmental consequences and local conflicts with other water users, especially landless poor people who depend on brackish water fisheries for their livelihood. The use of pumps for shallow groundwater (as in Bangladesh) or surface water (as in the Mekong Delta) allows cultivation of short-duration varieties in nonflooded periods in many deltas. Farmers in the flood-prone areas of the Mekong Delta also build community dikes, protecting areas of ten to a few hundred hectares and allowing them to harvest the crop before floods arrive. These dikes delay the onset of floods rather than prevent the peak of the flood from entering the protected area, thus avoiding the potentially adverse environmental consequences of absolute flood protection.

> Water needs to be managed judiciously to avert undesirable long-term environmental consequences and local conflicts with other water users

Relationship between water use at field- and irrigation-system levels. The relationships between water use at the field- and irrigation-system level are complex and involve hydrologic, infrastructural, and economic aspects. At the field level farmers can increase water productivity and reduce water use by adopting water-saving technologies. For farmers who pay for the water they use, any savings in water translates directly into a reduction in costs, thus increasing the profitability of rice farming.

At the irrigation-system level the adoption of field-level water-saving technologies by farmers will reduce the amount of evaporative losses from rice fields, but by relatively small amounts (see section on "Water-saving technologies"). The biggest water savings at the field level come from reducing seepage, percolation, and surface drainage flows. But while this retains more water at the surface (in the irrigation canals), which is available for downstream farmers, it reduces the amount of water re-entering the hydrological cycle and thus reduces options for informal reuse downstream. Reducing percolation from rice fields can lower groundwater tables. While deeper groundwater tables can adversely affect yields, because rice plants may be less able to extract water from the groundwater (Belder and others 2004), and increase the cost of pumping for reuse downstream, deeper groundwater tables also reduce nonproductive evaporation flows from fallow land.

Any adoption of water-saving technologies requires considerable water control by the farmer. This is not much of a problem for farmers using their own pumps, but can be a problem for farmers in large-scale, unreliable surface irrigation systems that lack flexibility in water delivery and for farmers using electric pumps for groundwater in areas where electricity supply is unreliable. For farmers to profit from water-saving technologies, irrigation systems need to be modernized, which has an economic cost. Integrated approaches that take into account the options for reuse of water and for conjunctive use of surface water and groundwater seem to be the best way forward to improve total water use efficiency at the system scale (see box 14.8).

Reviewers

Chapter review editor: David Seckler.

Chapter reviewers: Gelia Castillo, M.A. Ghani, Nobumasa Hatcho, Chu Thai Hoanh, Paul Kiepe, Barbara van Koppen, Yuanhua Li, Noel Magor, Paul van Mele, K. Palanisamy, S.A. Prathapar, Daniel Renault, Lisa Schipper, Anil Singh, Douglas Taylor, Paul Vlek, and Ian Willett.

Note

Valuable input was also obtained from participants at two conferences at which the first draft of the chapter was presented, the International Conference on Management of Paddy and Water Environment for Sustainable Rice Production, organized by the Paddy and Water Environment Engineering Society, 7–8 September 2005, Kyoto University, Kyoto, Japan, and the Regional Workshop on the Future of Large Rice-Based Irrigation Systems in Southeast Asia, organized by the Food and Agriculture Organization, 26–28 October 2005, Ho Chi Minh City, Viet Nam.

References

Abedin, M.J., J. Cotter-Howells, and A.A. Meharg. 2002. "Arsenic Uptake and Accumulation in Rice (*Oryza sativa* L.) Irrigated with Contaminated Water." *Plant and Soil* 240 (2): 311–19.

Atlin, G.N., H.R. Lafitte, D. Tao, M. Laza, M. Amante, and B. Courtois. 2006. "Developing Rice Cultivars for High-Fertility Upland Systems in the Asian Tropics." *Field Crops Research* 97 (1): 43–52.

Barker, R., and D. Dawe. 2002. "The Transformation of the Asian Rice Economy and Directions for Future Research: The Need to Increase Productivity." In M. Sombilla, M. Hossain, and B. Hardy, eds., *Developments in the Asian Rice Economy*. Los Baños, Philippines: International Rice Research Institute.

Belder, P., J.H.J. Spiertz, B.A.M. Bouman, G. Lu, and T.P. Tuong. 2005. "Nitrogen Economy and Water Productivity of Lowland Rice under Water-Saving Irrigation." *Field Crops Research* 93 (2–3): 169–85.

Belder, P., B.A.M. Bouman, R. Cabangon, G. Lu, E.J.P. Quilang, Y. Li, J.H.J. Spiertz, and T.P. Tuong. 2004. "Effect of Water-Saving Irrigation on Rice Yield and Water Use in Typical Lowland Conditions in Asia." *Agricultural Water Management* 65 (3): 193–210.

Bennett, J. 2003. "Status of Breeding for Tolerance of Water Deficit and Prospects for Using Molecular Techniques." In J.W. Kijne, R. Baker, and D. Molden, eds., *Water Productivity in Agriculture: Limits and Opportunities for Improvement*. Wallingford, UK: CABI Publishing.

Bijay-Singh, U.S. Sadana, and B.R. Arora. 1991. "Nitrate Pollution of Ground Water with Increasing Use of Nitrogen Fertilizers and Animal Wastes in the Punjab, India." *Indian Journal of Environmental Health* 33: 57–67.

Bouman, B.A.M., and T.P. Tuong. 2001. "Field Water Management to Save Water and Increase Its Productivity in Irrigated Rice." *Agricultural Water Management* 49 (1): 11–30.

Bouman, B.A.M., A. Castañeda, and S.I. Bhuiyan. 2002. "Nitrate and Pesticide Contamination of Groundwater under Rice-Based Cropping Systems: Evidence from the Philippines." *Agriculture, Ecosystems and Environment* 92 (2–3): 185–99.

Bouman, B.A.M., S. Peng, A.R. Castaneda, and R.M. Visperas. 2005. "Yield and Water Use of Irrigated Tropical Aerobic Rice Systems." *Agricultural Water Management* 74 (2): 87–105.

Bronson, K.F., H.U. Neue, U. Singh, and E.B.J. Abao. 1997. "Automated Chamber Measurement of Methane and Nitrous Oxide Flux in Flooded Rice Soil: I. Residue, Nitrogen, and Water Management." *Soil Science Society of America Journal* 61 (3): 981–87.

Cabangon, R.J., T.P. Tuong, and N.B. Abdullah. 2002. "Comparing Water Input and Water Productivity of Transplanted and Direct-Seeded Rice Production Systems." *Agricultural Water Management* 57 (1): 11–31.

Cabangon, R.J., T.P. Tuong, E.G. Castillo, L.X. Bao, G. Lu, G.H. Wang, Y. Cui, B.A.M. Bouman, Y. Li, C. Chen, and J. Wang. 2004. "Effect of Irrigation Method and N-Fertilizer Management on Rice Yield, Water Productivity, and Nutrient-Use Efficiencies in Typical Lowland Rice Conditions in China." *Paddy and Water Environment* 2 (4): 195–206.

Castella, J.C., and A. Erout. 2002. "Montane Paddy Rice: The Cornerstone of Agricultural Production Systems in Bac Kan Province, Vietnam." In J.C. Castella and D.D. Quang, eds., *Doi Moi in the Mountains: Land Use Changes and Farmers' Livelihood Strategies in Bac Kan Province Vietnam*. Ha Noi, Vietnam: The Agricultural Publishing House.

Dawe, D. 2000. "The Contribution of Rice Research to Poverty Alleviation." In J.E. Sheehy, P.L. Mitchell, and B. Hardy, eds., *Redesigning Rice Photosynthesis to Increase Yield*. Los Baños, Philippines, and Amsterdam: International Rice Research Institute and Elsevier Science B.V.

———. 2002. "The Changing Structure of the World Rice Market, 1950–2000." *Food Policy* 27 (4): 355–70.

———. 2005. "Increasing Water Productivity in Rice-Based Systems in Asia—Past Trends, Current Problems, and Future Prospects." *Plant Production Science* 8 (3): 221–30.

Dawe, D., A. Dobermann, P. Moya, S. Abdulrachman, B. Singh, P. Lal, S.Y. Li, B. Lin, G. Panaullah, O. Sariam, Y. Singh, A. Swarup, P.S. Tan, and Q.X. Zhen. 2000. "How Widespread Are Yield Declines in Long-Term Rice Experiments in Asia?" *Field Crops Research* 66 (2): 175–93.

Dittert, K., S. Lin, C. Kreye, X.H. Zheng, Y.C. Xu, X.J. Lu, Q.R. Shen, X.L. Fan, and B. Sattelmacher. 2002. "Saving Water with Ground Cover Rice Production Systems (GCRPS) at the Price of Increased Greenhouse Gas Emissions?" In B.A.M. Bouman, H. Hengsdijk, B. Hardy, P.S. Bindraban, T.P. Tuong, J.K. Ladha, eds., *Water-Wise Rice Production*. Los Baños, Philippines: International Rice Research Institute.

Dobermann, A., C. Witt, S. Abdulrachman, H.C. Gines, R. Nagarajan, T.T. Son, P.S. Tan, G.H. Wang, N.V. Chien, V.T.K. Thoa, C.V. Phung, P. Stalin, P. Muthukrishnan, V. Ravi, M. Babu, G.C. Simbahan, and M.A.A. Adviento. 2003. "Soil Fertility and Indigenous Nutrient Supply in Irrigated Rice Domains of Asia." *Agronomy Journal* 95 (4): 913–23.

Fagi, A.M., and S. Kartaatmadja. 2002. "Gogorancah Rice in Indonesia: A Traditional Method in the Modern Era." In S. Pandey, M. Mortimer, L. Wade, T.P. Tuong, K. Lopez, and B. Hardy, eds., *Direct Seeding: Research Strategies and Opportunities*. Los Baños, Philippines: International Rice Research Institute.

FAOSTAT. Food and Agriculture Organization statistical databases. [http://faostat.fao.org/].

Fernando, C.H., F. Goltenboth, and J. Margraf, eds., 2005. *Aquatic Ecology of Rice Fields*. Kitchener, Canada: Volumes Publishing.

Garrity, D.P., L.R. Oldeman, R.A. Morris, and D. Lenka. 1986. "Rainfed Lowland Rice Ecosystems: Characterization and Distribution." In *Progress in Rainfed Lowland Rice*. Los Baños, Philippines: International Rice Research Institute.

George, T., R. Magbanua, D.P. Garrity, B.S. Tubaña, and J. Quiton. 2002. "Rapid Yield Loss of Rice Cropped Successively in Aerobic Soil." *Agronomy Journal* 94 (5): 981–89.

Gregorio, G.B., D. Senadhira, R.D. Mendoza, N.L. Manigbas, J.P. Roxas, and C.Q. Guerta. 2002. "Progress in Breeding for Salinity Tolerance and Associated Abiotic Stresses in Rice." *Field Crops Research* 76 (2–3): 91–101.

Haas, J.D., J.L. Beard, L.E. Murray-Kolb, A.M. del Mundo, A. Felix, and G.B. Gregorio. 2005. "Iron-Biofortified Rice Improves the Iron Stores of Nonanemic Filipino Women." *Journal of Nutrition* 135 (12): 2823–30.

Hamilton, R.W., ed. 2003. *The Art of Rice: Spirit and Sustenance in Asia*. Los Angeles: UCLA Fowler Museum of Cultural History.

Hossain, M., and K.S. Fischer. 1995. "Rice Research for Food Security and Sustainable Agricultural Development in Asia: Achievements and Future Challenges." *GeoJournal* 35 (3): 286–98.

Huke, R.E., and E.H. Huke. 1997. *Rice Area by Type of Culture: South, Southeast, and East Asia; A Revised and Updated Database*. Los Baños, Philippines: International Rice Research Institute.

Humphreys, E., C. Meisner, R. Gupta, J. Timsina, H.G. Beecher, T.Y. Lu, Y. Singh, M.A. Gill, I. Masih, Z.J. Guo, and J.A. Thompson. 2005. "Water Saving in Rice-Wheat Systems." *Plant Production Science* 8 (3): 242–58.

International Financial Statistics. International Monetary Fund online service. [www.imf.org/].

Jones, M.P., M. Dingkuhn, G.K. Aluko, and M. Semon. 1997. "Interspecific Oryza Sativa L. X. O. Glaberrima Steud. progenies in Upland Rice Improvement." *Euphytica* 94 (2): 237–46.

Keiser, J., M.F. Maltese, T.E. Erlanger, R. Bos, M. Tanner, B.H. Singer, and J. Utzinger. 2005. "Effect of Irrigated Rice Agriculture on Japanese Encephalitis, Including Challenges and Opportunities for Integrated Vector Management." *Acta Tropica* 95 (1): 40–57.

Kirk, G. 2004. *The Biochemistry of Submerged Soils*. Chichester, UK: John Wiley and Sons.

Lafitte, H.R., and J. Bennet. 2002. "Requirements for Aerobic Rice: Physiological and Molecular Considerations." In B.A.M. Bouman, H. Hengsdijk, B. Hardy, P.S. Bindraban, T.P. Tuong, and J.K. Ladha, eds., *Water-Wise Rice Production*. Los Baños, Philippines: International Rice Research Institute.

Li, Y.H., and R. Barker. 2004. "Increasing Water Productivity for Paddy Irrigation in China." *Paddy and Water Environment* 2 (4): 187–93.

Loeve, R., B. Dong, D. Molden, Y.H. Li, C.D. Chen, and J.Z. Wang. 2004a. "Issues of Scale in Water Productivity in the Zhanghe Irrigation System: Implications for Irrigation in the Basin Context." *Paddy and Water Environment* 2 (4): 227–36.

Loeve, R., L. Hong, B. Dong, G. Mao, C. Chen, D. Dawe, and R. Barker. 2004b. "Long-Term Trends in Intersectoral Water Allocation and Crop Water Productivity in Zanghe and Kaifeng, China." *Paddy and Water Environment* 2 (4): 237–45.

Mackill, D., and K. Xu. 1996. "Genetics of Seedling-Stage Submergence Tolerance in Rice." In G. Khush, ed., *Rice Genetics III*. Manila: International Rice Research Institute.

Maclean, J.L., D. Dawe, B. Hardy, and G.P. Hettel, eds. 2002. *Rice Almanac.* 3rd ed. Wallingford, UK: CABI Publishing.

Magor, N.P. 1996. "Empowering Marginal Farm Families in Bangladesh." Ph.D. dissertation. University of Adelaide, Adelaide, Australia.

Masumoto, T., K. Shimizu, and P.T. Hai. 2004. "Roles of Floods for Agricultural Production in and around Tonle Sap Lake." In V. Seng, E. Craswell, S. Fukai, and K. Fischer, eds., *ACIAR Proceedings 116: Water in Agriculture.* Canberra, Australia: Australian Centre for International Agricultural Research.

Matsuno, Y., and W. van der Hoek. 2000. "Impact of Irrigation on an Aquatic Ecosystem." *International Journal of Ecology and Environmental Science* 26 (4): 223–33.

Matthews, R.B., R. Wassmann, J. Knox, and L.V. Buendia. 2000. "Using a Crop/Soil Simulation Model and GIS Techniques to Assess Methane Emissions from Rice Fields in Asia. IV. Upscaling to National Levels." *Nutrient Cycling Agroecosystems* 58 (1–3): 201–17.

McDonald, A.J., P.R. Hobbs, and S.J. Riha. 2006. "Does the System of Rice Intensification Outperform Conventional Best Management? A Synopsis of the Empirical Record." *Field Crops Research* 96 (1): 31–36.

Mishra, H.S., T.R. Rathore, and R.C. Pant. 1990. "Effect of Intermittent Irrigation on Groundwater Table Contribution, Irrigation Requirements, and Yield of Rice in Mollisols of the Tarai region." *Agricultural Water Management* 18 (3): 231–41.

Mortimer, A.M., and J.E. Hill. 1999. "Weed Species Shifts in Response to Broad Spectrum Herbicides in Sub-Tropical and Tropical Crops." In British Crop Protection Council, *The 1999 Brighton Conference—Weeds: Proceedings of an International Conference Held at the Brighton Metropole Hotel, Brighton, U.K., 15–18 November 1999.* Vol. 2. Alton, UK.

Moser, C.M., and C.B. Barrett. 2003. "The Disappointing Adoption Dynamics of a Yield-Increasing, Low External-Input Technology: The Case of SRI in Madagascar." *Agricultural Systems* 76 (3): 1085–100.

Pandey, S. 2001. "Economics of Lowland Rice Production in Laos: Opportunities and Challenges." In S. Fukai and J. Basnayake, eds., *ACIAR Proceedings 101: Increased Lowland Rice Production in the Mekong Region.* Canberra, Australia: Australian Centre for International Agricultural Research.

Pandey, S., and L. Velasco. 2002. "Economics of Direct Seeding in Asia: Patterns of Adoption and Research Priorities." In S. Pandey, M. Mortimer, L. Wade, T.P. Tuong, K. Lopez, and B. Hardy, eds., *Direct Seeding: Research Strategies and Opportunities.* Los Baños, Philippines: International Rice Research Institute.

PAWEES (International Society of Paddy and Water Environment Engineering). 2005. "Management of Paddy and Water Environment for Sustainable Rice Production." Proceedings of the International Conference, September 7–8, Kyoto, Japan.

Peng, S., K.G. Cassman, S.S. Virmani, J. Sheehy, and G.S. Khush. 1999. "Yield Potential Trends of Tropical Rice since the Release of IR8 and the Challenge of Increasing Rice Yield Potential." *Crop Science* 39 (6): 1552–59.

Peng, S., B.A.M. Bouman, R.M. Visperas, A. Castañeda, L. Nie, and H.-K. Park. 2006. "Comparison between Aerobic and Flooded Rice in the Tropics: Agronomic Performance in an Eight-Season Experiment." *Field Crops Research* 96 (2–3): 252–59.

Peng, S., R.C. Laza, G.S. Khush, A.L. Sanico, R.M. Visperas, and F.V. Garcia. 1998. "Transpiration Efficiencies of Indica and Improved Tropical Japonica Rice Grown under Irrigated Conditions." *Euphytica* 103 (1): 103–08.

Peng, S., J. Huang, J.E. Sheehy, R.C. Laza, R.M. Visperas, X. Zhong, G.S. Centeno, G.S. Khush, and K.G. Cassman. 2004. "Rice Yields Decline with Higher Night Temperature from Global Warming." *Proceedings of the National Academy of Sciences of the United States of America* 101 (27): 9971–75.

Piñheiro, B. da S., E. da M. de Castro, and C.M. Guimarães. 2006. "Sustainability and Profitability of Aerobic Rice Production in Brazil." *Field Crops Research* 97 (1): 34–42.

Potrykus, I. 2003. "Golden Rice: Concept, Development, and Its Availability to Developing Countries." In T.W. Mew, D.S. Brar, S. Peng, D. Dawe, and B. Hardy, eds., *Rice Science: Innovations and Impacts for Livelihood.* Los Baños, Philippines: International Rice Research Institute.

Ramsar Convention Secretariat. 2004. *Ramsar Handbooks for the Wise Use of Wetlands: Handbook 7; Designating Ramsar Sites.* 2nd ed. Gland, Switzerland. [http://indaba.iucn.org/ramsarfilms/lib_handbooks_e07.pdf]

Shannon, M.C. 1997. "Adaptation of Plants to Salinity." *Advances in Agronomy* 60: 75–120.

Sheehy, J.E., P.L. Mitchell, and B. Hardy, eds. 2000. *Redesigning Rice Photosynthesis to Increase Yield.* Amsterdam: Elsevier Science.

Sheehy, J.E., S. Peng, A. Dobermann, P.L. Mitchell, A. Ferrer, J. Yang, Y. Zou, X. Zhong, and J. Huang. 2004. "Fantastic Yields in the System of Rice Intensification: Fact or Fallacy?" *Field Crops Research* 88 (1): 1–8.

Sombilla, M., M.W. Rosegrant, and S. Meijer. 2002. "A Long-Term Outlook for Rice Supply and Demand Balances." In M. Sombilla, M. Hossain, and B. Hardy, eds., *Developments in the Asian Rice Economy.* Los Baños: International Rice Research Institute.

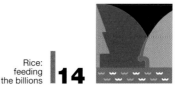

Sripongpangkul, K., G.B.T. Posa, D.W. Senadhira, D. Brar, N. Huang, G.S. Khush, and Z.K. Li. 2000. "Genes/QTLs Affecting Flood Tolerance in Rice." *TAG Theoretical and Applied Genetics* 101 (7): 1074–81.

Stoop, W., N. Uphoff, and A. Kassam. 2002. "A Review of Agricultural Research Issues Raised by the System of Rice Intensification (SRI) from Madagascar: Opportunities for Improving Farming Systems for Resource-Poor Farmers." *Agricultural Systems* 71 (3): 249–74.

Tabbal, D.F., B.A.M. Bouman, S.I. Bhuiyan, E.B. Sibayan, and M.A. Sattar. 2002. "On-Farm Strategies for Reducing Water Input in Irrigated Rice: Case Studies in the Philippines." *Agricultural Water Management* 56 (2): 93–112.

Tilman, D., K.G. Cassman, P.A. Matson, R. Naylor, and S. Polasky. 2002. "Agricultural Sustainability and Intensive Production Practices." *Nature* 418 (6898): 671–77.

Tuong, T.P., and B.A.M. Bouman. 2003. "Rice Production in Water Scarce Environments." In J.W. Kijne, R. Barker, and D. Molden, eds., *Water Productivity in Agriculture: Limits and Opportunities for Improvement.* Wallingford, UK: CABI Publishing.

Tuong, T.P., B.A.M. Bouman, and M. Mortimer. 2005. "More Rice, Less Water—Integrated Approaches for Increasing Water Productivity in Irrigated Rice-Based Systems in Asia." *Plant Production Science* 8 (3): 231–41.

Tuong, T.P., S.P. Kam, C.T. Hoanh, L.C. Dung, N.T. Khiem, J. Barr, and D.C. Ben. 2003. "Impact of Seawater Intrusion Control on the Environment, Land Use, and Household Incomes in a Coastal Area." *Paddy Water Environment* 1 (2): 65–73.

Wang, H., B.A.M. Bouman, D. Zhao, C. Wang, and P.F. Moya. 2002. "Aerobic Rice in Northern China: Opportunities and Challenges." In B.A.M. Bouman, H. Hengsdijk, B. Hardy, P.S. Bindraban, T.P. Tuong, and J.K. Ladha, eds., *Water-Wise Rice Production.* Los Baños, Philippines: International Rice Research Institute.

Wassmann, R., N.X. Hien, C.T. Hoanh, and T.P. Tuong. 2004. "Sea Level Rise Affecting Vietnamese Mekong Delta: Water Elevation in Flood Season and Implications for Rice Production." *Climatic Change* 66 (1): 89–107.

Wassmann, R., H.U. Neue, R.S. Lantin, K. Makarim, N. Chareonsilp, L.V. Buendia, and H. Renneberg. 2000. "Characterization of Methane Emissions from Rice Fields in Asia. II. Differences among Irrigated, Rainfed, and Deepwater Rice." *Nutrient Cycling in Agroecosystems* 58 (1–3): 13–22.

Witt, C., A. Dobermann, S. Abdulrachman, H.C. Gines, G.H. Wang, R. Nagarajan, S. Satawatananont, T.T. Son, P.S. Tan, L.V. Tiem, G.C. Simbahan, and D.C. Olk. 1999. "Internal Nutrient Efficiencies of Irrigated Lowland Rice in Tropical and Subtropical Asia." *Field Crops Research* 63 (2): 113–38.

Yang, X., B.A.M. Bouman, H. Wang, Z. Wang, J. Zhao, and B. Chen. 2005. "Performance of Temperate Aerobic Rice under Different Water Regimes in North China." *Agricultural Water Management* 74 (2): 107–22.

Ziska, L.H., O. Namuco, T. Moya, and J. Quilang. 1997. "Growth and Yield Response of Field-Grown Tropical Rice to Increasing Carbon Dioxide and Air Temperature." *Agronomy Journal* 89: 45–53.

Zwart, S.J., and W.G.M. Bastiaanssen. 2004. "Review of Measured Crop Water Productivity Values for Irrigated Wheat, Rice, Cotton, and Maize." *Agricultural Water Management* 69 (2): 115–33.

Conserving land

Artist: Luis Armando Piña Anaya, Mexico

15 | Conserving land— protecting water

Coordinating lead author: Deborah Bossio

Lead authors: William Critchley, Kim Geheb, Godert van Lynden, and Bancy Mati

Contributing authors: Pranita Bhushan, Jon Hellin, Gunnar Jacks, Annette Kolff, Freddy Nachtergaele, Constance Neely, Don Peden, Jorge Rubiano, Gemma Shepherd, Christian Valentin, and Markus Walsh

Overview

The key to effective management of water resources is understanding that the water cycle and land management are intimately linked. Every land-use decision is a water-use decision. Improving water management in agriculture and the livelihoods of the rural poor requires mitigating or preventing land degradation. Erosion, pollution, nutrient depletion, reduced plant cover, loss of soil organic matter, and other forms of degradation resulting from faulty agricultural land-use decisions threaten ecosystems, change regional and global hydrological cycles, and have enormous negative implications for water productivity, quantity, quality, and storage *[well established]*. Up to half the world's agricultural land and half its river systems are now degraded to some degree *[established but incomplete]*. The chief cause of land degradation is the unsuitable use of agricultural land. Because 80% of the world's poor rely directly on agriculture, degradation is particularly deleterious to small-scale farmers in developing countries. For farming communities key issues are declining returns to labor; the impacts of land degradation on human health, including rising malnutrition rates; and the increasing pollution of drinking water.

Land degradation is driven by the complex sociopolitical and economic context in which land use occurs. Policy and livelihood decisions that fail to account for the long-term relationships between processes and consequences drive degradation. Sociopolitical and economic systems often result in insecure land tenure, political environments can discourage innovation and adaptation, and inequitable gender relationships often distance resource users from management decisions. In some cases development projects insist on land husbandry techniques that are ill-suited to the environment and poorly matched to local capacity. In other cases suppression of innovation may be more subtle—innovation is an expression of freedom that may sit uneasily with dominant political thought.

Smallholder agricultural systems are an important intervention point for measures aimed at preventing or mitigating land degradation in the developing world. Smallholder agriculture is the mainstay of most developing country rural economies and is likely to remain so into the foreseeable future. In many vulnerable areas smallholder farmers possess the greatest unexploited potential to directly influence land- and water-use management. Smallholders make up the majority of the world's rural poor and often occupy marginal and vulnerable land. It makes sense, therefore, to concentrate development and conservation investments in land and water sectors and human capacity at this level. Supporting small-scale agriculture probably offers the best chance for achieving many of the Millennium Development Goals in developing countries.

> In many vulnerable areas smallholder farmers possess the greatest unexploited potential to directly influence land- and water-use management

Integrated solutions that support participation in sustainable land management are needed to achieve balance in food production, poverty alleviation, and resource conservation. Policy and administrative actions are needed to create sociopolitical environments conducive to good governance and to activities that combat and mitigate land degradation. They are also needed to support such initiatives through appropriate technologies, integrating soil and water management, marketing infrastructure, and institutional environments. Traditional land-use systems are not static. Provided that the opportunity and enabling environment exist, land users can alter their land husbandry techniques to ameliorate or even reverse land degradation. Many useful lessons can be drawn from success stories involving both traditional methods of cultivation and local innovation and providing a basket of options for land users. Sustainable increases in land and water productivity are possible through resource-conserving agricultural approaches that can increase the resilience of systems otherwise susceptible to extreme climate events and climate variability. This is important, because it can reduce the vulnerability and uncertainty to which the rural poor are frequently exposed.

Enhancing the multifunctionality of agricultural land is a point of convergence for poverty reduction, resource conservation, and international concerns for global food security, biodiversity conservation, and carbon sequestration. Too much land-use policy and research fails to appreciate the interlinked nature of landscapes. Addressing land degradation from the individual farm up to the landscape level requires a series of integrated measures that focus on resource-conserving farming strategies and on sustainable soil and water productivity. Ecoagricultural approaches can create synergies among agricultural production, water, and wild biodiversity, benefiting ecosystems as a whole. Integrated land and water management drawing on such strategies has carbon sequestration and clean water benefits *[well established]*, although the quantitative and site-specific evidence is still incomplete.

Research is needed to underpin and stimulate the development of land-use systems that can absorb and sustain high population densities. The global population is unlikely to stabilize soon, with the highest population growth occurring in developing countries. Although opinions differ, population growth is not necessarily synonymous with land and water degradation. In many places, population growth has led to land-improving investments and conservation management. National efforts to address this issue must couple population

policies with research on land-use systems that can accommodate high population densities by increasing labor productivity and wealth generation per parcel of land. Rigorous measurement of land and water interactions, especially at watershed scales, is required to understand the drivers of land degradation, to identify appropriate ways to manage them, and to assess the impact of previous interventions.

Key elements of land degradation

The Global Assessment of Human-Induced Soil Degradation (GLASOD), conducted during the 1980s, was the first attempt to estimate the extent of soil degradation globally (Oldeman, Hakkeling, and Sombroek 1991) and remains today the only uniform global source of degradation data. GLASOD paints a stark picture (box 15.1). According to GLASOD estimates, degradation of cropland appears to be most extensive in Africa, affecting 65% of cropland areas, compared with 51% in Latin America and 38% in Asia. Degradation of pasture is also most extensive in Africa, affecting 31% of pasturelands, compared with 20% in Asia and 14% in Latin America. Forestland degradation is most extensive in Asia, affecting 27% of forestlands, compared with 19% in Africa and 14% in Latin America. Based on GLASOD, Wood, Sebastian, and Scherr (2000) estimate that 40% of agricultural land in the world is moderately degraded and a further 9% strongly degraded, reducing global crop yield by 13%. In 1992 the UN Convention to Combat Desertification, supported by GLASOD's findings and concentrating particularly on

---

| box **15.1** | **The Global Assessment of Human-Induced Soil Degradation— the first global assessment** |

The Global Assessment of Human-Induced Soil Degradation (GLASOD) project set out to map global soil degradation in the 1980s (Oldeman, Hakkeling, and Sombroek 1991). The assessment was based on expert opinion—experts' assessments of the status of soil degradation in the countries or regions with which they were familiar. The final statistics, based on continental trends worldwide, revealed that erosion by water is the most prominent degradation feature worldwide (see table). Other causes, accounting for smaller areas of degradation, are various forms of chemical deterioration, such as soil fertility decline and soil pollution, and physical deterioration, such as compaction and waterlogging. The GLASOD study was the first comprehensive soil degradation overview at the global scale. It raised awareness of various further needs, still relevant today:

- An assessment of measures to control degradation.
- A more objective, quantitative approach (especially for more detailed scales).
- Data validation and updating.

GLASOD had several limitations. It was too large for national-level breakdowns. It was based on qualitative and subjective expert judgment, with perhaps too much emphasis on visible and spectacular land degradation problems, such as erosion. And it was too problem focused.

Since GLASOD there have been some regional studies, such as the Assessment of the Status of Human-Induced Soil Degradation in South and South East Asia (van Lynden and Oldeman 1997) and the World Atlas of Desertification (Middleton and Thomas 1997). The Land Degradation Assessment in Drylands project is expected to provide more land degradation data in the future.

(continues on next page)

Human induced soil degradation for the world
(millions of hectares)

Type	Light	Moderate	Strong	Extreme	Total
Water	343.2	526.7	217.2	6.6	1,093.7 (55.6)
Loss of top soil	301.2	454.5	161.2	3.8	920.3
Terrain deformation (such as gully formation)	42.0	72.2	56.0	2.8	173.3
Wind	268.6	253.6	24.3	1.9	548.3 (27.9)
Loss of top soil	230.5	213.5	9.4	0.9	454.2
Terrain deformation (such as dune formation)	38.1	30.0	14.4	—	82.5
Overblowing	—	10.1	0.5	1.0	11.6
Chemical	93.0	103.3	41.9	0.8	239.1 (12.2)
Loss of nutrients	52.4	63.1	19.8	—	135.3
Salinization	34.8	20.4	20.3	0.8	76.3
Pollution	4.1	17.1	0.5	—	21.8
Acidification	1.7	2.7	1.3	—	5.7
Physical	44.2	26.8	12.3	—	83.3 (4.2)
Compaction	34.8	22.1	11.3	—	68.2
Waterlogging	6.0	3.7	0.8	—	10.5
Subsidence organic soils	3.4	1.0	0.2	—	4.6
Total	749.0 (38)	910.4 (46)	295.7 (15)	9.3 (1)	1,964.4 (100)

— zero or negligible

Note: Numbers in parentheses are percentages of totals. A *light* degree of soil degradation, implying somewhat reduced productivity but manageable in local farming systems, is identified for 38% of all degraded soils worldwide. A somewhat larger percentage (46%) has a *moderate* degree of soil degradation, with greatly reduced productivity. Major improvements, often beyond the means of local farmers in developing countries, are required to restore productivity. More than 340 million hectares (ha) of this moderately degraded terrain are found in Asia and more than 190 million ha in Africa. Some 15% of degraded soils are *strongly* degraded. No longer reclaimable at the farm level and virtually lost, they will require major engineering work or international assistance to restore them. Some 124 million ha are in Africa and 108 million ha in Asia. *Extremely* degraded soils are considered irreclaimable. They make up about 0.5% of total degraded soils worldwide, of which more than 5 million ha are in Africa.

Source: Oldeman, Hakkeling, and Sombroek 1991.

desertification, was signed at the United Nations Conference on the Environment and Development. While land degradation is not confined to desertification (box 15.2), this convention placed land degradation processes firmly on the global agenda for addressing negative environmental trends. Estimates of land-use degradation *rates* are even more uncertain than estimates of the extent of degradation, varying from 5 to 10 million hectares a year (Scherr and Yadav 1996).

The root cause of land degradation is poor land use. Land degradation represents a diminished ability of ecosystems or landscapes to support the functions or services required for sustaining livelihoods. When agriculture is introduced in place of natural vegetation and

| box **15.2** | **What is desertification?** |

Desertification does not simply mean "expanding deserts" but covers a more complex concept. The United Nations Convention to Combat Desertification defines it as the degradation of land in arid, semiarid, and subhumid dry areas caused by climate change and human activities. It is accompanied by a reduction in the natural potential of the land and a depletion of surface water and groundwater resources. The phenomenon is global in scope, threatening about two-thirds of the countries of the world and one-third of the earth's surface on which a fifth of the world population lives. The vulnerability of land to desertification is due mainly to climate, land relief, the state of the soil and the natural vegetation, and the ways these two resources are used by farmers and pastoralists. Because many of the poorest land users live in drier areas, programs to combat desertification simultaneously address poverty.

is then intensified to maximize yields, farmers simplify agroecosystem structures by limiting the variety of vegetation. Such vegetation changes immediately affect water use and cycling in landscapes and result in biodiversity loss and the development of a less complex network of ecosystem interrelations than occurs naturally (see chapter 6 on ecosystems). Over time, continuing agricultural production, particularly on marginal or fragile lands, results in degradation of the natural resource base, with increasing impacts on water resources.

This section considers primarily the relationships between major forms of soil degradation and water:

- *Loss of organic matter and physical degradation of soil.* Soil organic matter is integral to managing water cycles in ecosystems. Depleted levels of organic matter have significant negative impacts on infiltration and porosity, local and regional water cycles, water productivity, plant productivity, the resilience of agroecosystems, and global carbon cycles.
- *Nutrient depletion and chemical degradation of soil.* Pervasive nutrient depletion in agricultural soils is a primary cause of decreasing yields, low on-site water productivity, and off-site water pollution. Salinity, sodicity, and waterlogging threaten large areas of the world's most productive land and pollute groundwater.
- *Soil erosion and sedimentation.* Accelerated on-farm soil erosion leads to substantial yield losses and contributes to downstream sedimentation and the degradation of water bodies, a major cause of investment failure in water and irrigation infrastructure.
- *Water pollution.* Globally, agriculture is the main contributor to non-point-source water pollution, while urbanization contributes increasingly large volumes of wastewater. Water quality problems can often be as severe as those of water availability, but have yet to receive as much attention in developing countries.

Loss of organic matter and physical degradation of soil

Soil organic matter is integral to managing water cycles in ecosystems. Among the best documented examples are organic matter losses that occur when land is cleared of forest and farmed intensively—especially when accompanied by burning—and productivity declines rapidly. Less visible is the loss of organic matter through interrill erosion, a process

that selectively removes organic matter and inorganic nutrient-rich particles, leaving impoverished topsoil behind. The impact of organic matter loss is not confined to production loss, but also disturbs water cycles.

The decrease of soil organic matter, along with the associated decline of faunal activities (aggravated by the use of pesticides and tillage practices), favors the collapse of soil aggregates and thus the crusting, and sealing, of the soil surface (Valentin and Bresson 1997). The result is reduced porosity, less infiltration, and more runoff. Compaction of the soil surface, by heavy machinery or overgrazing, for example, can cause overland flow, even on usually permeable soils (Hiernaux and others 1999). Such changes increase the risk of flooding and water erosion. On sloping terrain, intense rainfall and associated runoff increase interrill erosion (photo 15.1). Higher runoff concentrates in channels, causing rills and then gullies.

Degradation thus changes the proportion of water flowing along pathways within catchments, with a tendency to promote rapid surface overland flow (runoff) and decrease subsurface flow. In pristine or well managed environments higher infiltration rates are the norm. As these environments are degraded, a negative, self-accelerating feedback loop is created (figure 15.1).

By controlling infiltration rates and water-holding capacity, soil organic matter plays a vital function in buffering yields through climate extremes and uncertainty. Significantly, it is one of the most important biophysical elements that can be managed to improve resilience. Soil organic matter, furthermore, holds about 40% of the overall terrestrial carbon pool—twice the amount contained in the atmosphere (Robbins 2004). Poor agricultural practices are thus a significant source of carbon emissions and contribute to climate change.

Nutrient depletion and chemical degradation of soil

One-way nutrient flows occur from forest to farm, from rural to urban areas, from terrestrial ecosystems to the ocean and increasingly even across continents (Craswell and others

Photo 15.1 Cultivated hillside in Mexico with rill erosion

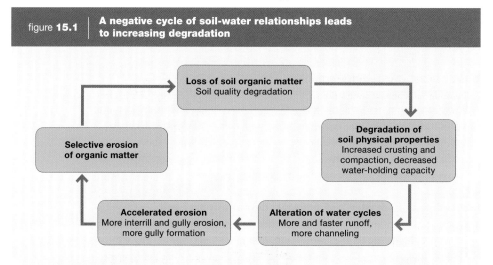

figure **15.1** | **A negative cycle of soil-water relationships leads to increasing degradation**

Loss of soil organic matter
Soil quality degradation

Degradation of soil physical properties
Increased crusting and compaction, decreased water-holding capacity

Selective erosion of organic matter

Accelerated erosion
More interrill and gully erosion, more gully formation

Alteration of water cycles
More and faster runoff, more channeling

Photo by William Critchley

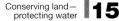

2004). This results in nutrient depletion at the sources and pollution at the sinks. Closing some of these loops will be vital, especially as urbanization continues and these imbalances in nutrient movement accelerate (Vlek 2005).

Globally, only half of the nutrients that crops take from the soil are replaced. This depletion of soil nutrients often leads to fertility levels that limit production and severely reduce water productivity. Shorter fallow periods do not compensate for losses in soil organic matter and nutrients, leading to the mining of soil nutrients. For instance, in southern Mali an estimated 40% of farmers' incomes come from soil mining, while only 11% of gross income is reinvested into agricultural production (Steiner 1996). In many African, Asian, and Latin American countries, the nutrient depletion of agricultural soils is so high that current agricultural land use is not sustainable (Craswell and others 2004). Nutrient balance analysis demonstrates nutrient depletion in many Asian countries on the order of 50 kilograms (kg) of macronutrients per hectare per year (Sheldrick, Syers, and Lingard 2002).

Trends are even worse in Africa, where nutrient depletion in some East and Southern African countries is estimated to average 47 kg of nitrogen, 6 kg of phosphorous, and 37 kg of potassium per hectare a year (figure 15.2; Smaling 1993; Stoorvogel, Smaling, and Jansen 1993). Country averages hide important site-specific variation. Where farmers are poor and cannot afford inputs to replenish fertility, nutrient loss through soil mining (and selective erosion) is much higher. Nutrient depletion is now considered the chief biophysical factor limiting small-scale farm production in Africa (Drechsel, Giordano, and Gyiele 2004).

Other important forms of chemical degradation are the depletion of trace metals such as zinc, causing productivity declines and affecting human nutrition (Cakmak and others 1999; Ezzati and others 2002), acidification, and salinization. Secondary salinization is a serious threat to sustainable irrigated agricultural production. Although data are poor, estimates indicate that 20% of irrigated land worldwide suffers from secondary salinization and waterlogging (Wood, Sebastian, and Scherr 2000) induced by the build-up of salts introduced through irrigation water (see chapter 9 on irrigation).

> **Globally, only half of the nutrients that crops take from the soil are replaced. This depletion of soil nutrients often leads to fertility levels that limit production and severely reduce water productivity**

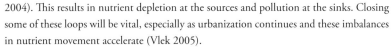

Soil erosion and sedimentation

Soil erosion rates almost always rise substantially with agricultural activity. This is especially the case with annual systems, where the soil surface is seasonally exposed to rainfall and wind. With a fivefold increase in the global area under crop production and livestock grazing over the past 200 years, this has become a serious problem, both onsite and downstream.

Onsite, soil erosion reduces crop yields by removing nutrients and organic matter. Yield impacts can be severe and vary with soil type. They are particularly evident in the early stages of erosion. In Ethiopia soil erosion reduces yields by an average of 1%–2% annually, although over 20 years of observation base yields have not fallen below 300–500 kg per hectare (Hurni 1993). Stocking (2003), however, demonstrated much more dramatic declines on a wide range of soils (figure 15.3). Erosion also interferes with soil-water relationships: the depth of soil is reduced, diminishing water storage capacity and damaging

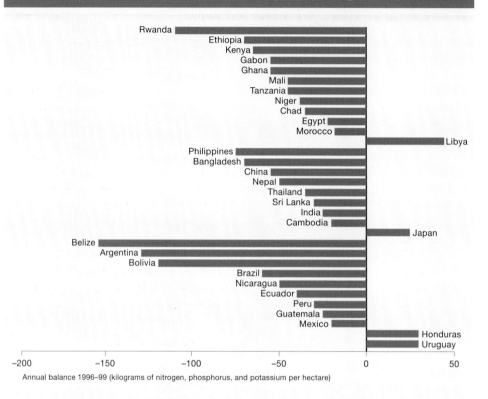

| figure **15.2** | **Nutrient balance estimates for selected countries in Africa, Asia, and Latin America show nutrient depletion in many countries** |

Annual balance 1996–99 (kilograms of nitrogen, phosphorus, and potassium per hectare)

Source: Craswell and others 2004: Sheldrick, Syers, and Lingard 2002.

soil structure, thus reducing soil porosity. Surface sealing and crusting reduce infiltration and increase surface runoff, which is a problem in itself and results in a net loss of water for crops.

Downstream, the main impact of soil erosion is sedimentation, a major form of human-induced water pollution. The increased sediment load in rivers can create important practical and economic problems, such as the sedimentation of reservoir navigation channels and the impairment of turbines, irrigation schemes, and water treatment facilities. Sedimentation causes storage loss within the world's major reservoirs at a rate of 1% of gross capacity a year. The effects on small dams and reservoirs can be even more acute. In Tigray, Ethiopia, most of the reservoirs built to improve the livelihoods of poor people lost more than half their water storage capacity within five years of entering service due to sedimentation arising from erosion in upper catchments, although the dams had a designed life of 20 years (Lulseged 2005). In response, the government has all but stopped its dam building activities in Tigray (Vlek 2005). An estimated 25% or more of the world's

| figure **15.3** | **Erosion results in large yield declines for a selection of tropical soils** |

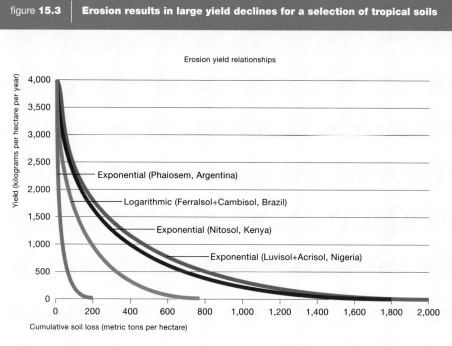

Erosion yield relationships

Source: Stocking 2003.

freshwater storage capacity will be lost in the next 25–50 years unless measures are taken to control sedimentation in reservoirs (Palmieri, Shah, and Dinar 2001).

Controlling sedimentation in large reservoirs requires soil conservation at the catchment scale. Because sediment sources vary considerably, a variety of strategies may be required. In the Himalayan region, as in other tectonically active zones, mass wasting processes—landslides (most of them natural, others triggered by poor road construction practices), riverbank erosion, and gullies—contribute far more sediment than do the hill farmers who have historically received the blame (Ives and Messerli 1989). Under certain circumstances gully erosion is the main source of sediment at the catchment scale and is usually triggered or accelerated by a combination of poor land use and extreme rainfall (Lulseged 2005). Poorly maintained or degraded pastures can also contribute substantially to sedimentation in some areas. Although erosion rates may be lower than from cropland, pasture areas are often much larger (see chapter 13 on livestock).

Water pollution

Every day more than 2 million metric tons of waste are dumped into rivers and lakes (WWAP 2003). There are now about 12,000 cubic kilometers of polluted water on the planet, a volume greater than the contents of the world's 10 biggest river basins and equivalent to six years' worth of global irrigation needs. In India less than 35% of wastewater receives primary treatment, and there is little if any treatment in smaller cities and rural areas. Scenarios are similar—if not worse—in other developing countries.

Recent assessments (WWAP 2003; MEA 2005; UNEP 1999, 2004) detail alarming trends in pollution of the world's freshwater and emphasize the destructive effects of eutrophication caused by increased anthropogenic nitrogen and phosphorus loading and increasing pollution by pesticides, heavy metals, and bacteria, among other pollutants. Many of this second group of agents are persistent and can have human health impacts even in very low concentrations and over long periods of time.

Agricultural activities can exacerbate these problems by increasing the proportion of water that flows rapidly over land. Surface runoff picks up microbes, nutrients, organic matter, pesticides, and heavy metals, which tend to concentrate in surface layers. Phosphorus, for example, can be approximately 10 times higher in surface runoff than in groundwater (Gelbrecht and others 2005). Agricultural chemicals—pesticides, herbicides, and fertilizers—are also readily transported by runoff and drainage water or may infiltrate groundwater. The destruction of riparian forests, wetlands, and estuaries allows unbuffered flows of nutrients between terrestrial and water ecosystems. Excess nutrients leak into groundwater, rivers, and lakes and are transported to the coast.

> Agricultural activities can exacerbate pollution problems by increasing the proportion of water that flows rapidly over land

Drivers of land degradation

Linked sociopolitical, economic, demographic, and biophysical drivers of land degradation have resulted in the accelerated degradation of resources and diminished ecosystem resilience. Three key drivers are considered here:

- *Sociopolitical and economic drivers.* People make decisions about water and land use based on sociopolitical and economic contexts, as well as the physical characteristics of land. Land tenure, markets and commodity prices, and gender relations all affect decisionmaking. In addition, political environments may be so repressive as to undermine the readiness of land users to develop and implement innovative land and water management practices.

- *Demographic trends.* Under certain circumstances high and growing population densities can have serious impacts on water and land. This is particularly evident where populations spill over into previously uncultivated marginal dry lands (as has been happening rapidly in parts of East Africa) and where poor farmers are pushed further uphill onto ever steeper slopes (as is the case in parts of Asia and Central America). In both cases this land is especially vulnerable to degradation.

- *Biophysical forces.* Major biophysical events, such as hurricanes, cyclones, and tectonic activity, probably have a greater role to play in land degradation than previously believed. Usually, such events have a considerable impact on poor people, who live in more vulnerable areas and who are less able to recover from these events.

Sociopolitical and economic drivers

The sociopolitical and economic factors that influence human decisionmaking about land use are deeply intertwined. Together, they determine which people and how many of them

inhabit and use what land and how access to resources is defined, negotiated, and managed. The ways national and regional policies are articulated at local levels are often unanticipated and may have profound impacts on land use and concomitant degradation (see Blakie 1985 for pioneering work on this topic). In many cases policies addressing land use push vulnerable sections of the population on to the poorest land, which is particularly vulnerable to degradation.

Misguided policy may have unintended effects. In Lao PDR the average population density is less than 15 inhabitants per square kilometer. In one representative village in the north, however, natural growth coupled with resettlement and conservation policies has led to a population density exceeding 350 inhabitants per square kilometer of arable land (figure 15.4). Land degradation in these resettlement areas has been severe (Lestrelin, Giordano, and Keohavong 2005). Policy influences on land use and degradation tend to be more nuanced, but examples as extreme as this are not altogether uncommon (Homewood and Brockington 1999; Wily 1999).

In Mexico, as in many other areas of the developing world, there is a clear tendency for poorer rural communities to be located on sloping lands (figure 15.5; see also photo 15.1). Policies favor the nonpoor, 80% of whom inhabit more desirable flat lands, while 66% of the rural poor live on lands with a greater than 5% slope (Bellon and others 2005).

figure **15.4** | **Resettlement programs and policies that restrict access to land have had enormous impacts on population density in a village in Northern Lao PDR**

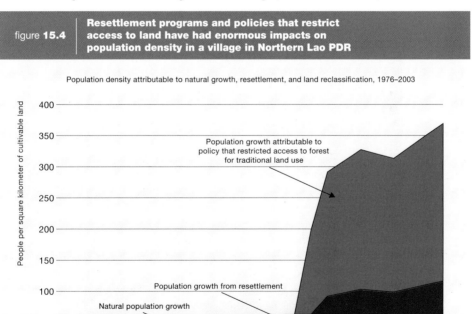

Population density attributable to natural growth, resettlement, and land reclassification, 1976–2003

Source: Lestrelin, Giordano, and Keohavong 2005.

Policymakers need to anticipate such consequences if they are to prevent a further spiral of land degradation and poverty.

The type of tenure system often influences how land is managed and used (Mc-Cay and Acheson 1987; Berkes 1989). Well functioning common property regimes are governed by widely agreed land management practices and rules, with no free-riding by resource users. Competition among community users is low, and cooperation is high (McCay and Acheson 1987). But where no governance mechanisms are in place or where they have broken down, open-access conditions may arise, leading to "tragedy of the commons" scenarios (Hardin 1968). The result is almost always overexploitation and degradation. Among natural resources examples are global fisheries and denuded parts of the Amazon forest. Competition between users, especially for access to resources, may be expressed through violence (box 15.3). Where small-scale mixed farming is the dominant form of land use, investments in sustainable land management are most likely where there is security of tenure, which means security of access, although not necessarily private ownership.

| figure **15.5** | **In rural Mexico most of the poor live on sloping land and most of the nonpoor live on flat land** |

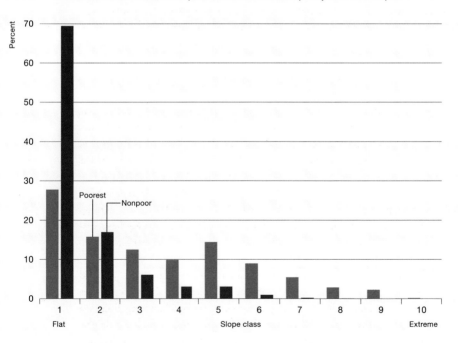

Share of rural communities in Mexico predicted to be below the food poverty line or to be nonpoor

Source: Bellon and others 2005.

The pastoralists of northern Kenya, which include the Borana, Rendille, Samburu, and Turkana, graze their cattle in an area that is underadministered and whose borders with neighboring Somalia, Sudan, and Uganda are porous. Improvements in veterinary medicine and disease control have ensured that for many pastoral communities, herds experience less disease, increased lifespan, and improved survival under difficult conditions. Herd sizes have increased, so that traditional boundaries separating ethnic groups are under severe pressure as herders seek new grazing areas.

Unrest in Somalia, southern Sudan, and northeastern Uganda, much of which has continued for decades, has meant that the struggle to obtain additional grazing is now assisted by modern weaponry. During periods of drought or Kenya's dry season, armed conflict ("AK47 herding") between the region's ethnic groups and nomads from neighboring countries is common (Gray and others 2003). Such raiding is intended not only to secure grazing but also, as has traditionally been the case, to rustle cattle. For the victorious raiders, these raids can improve livelihoods considerably by ensuring additional cattle and opening up new grazing. For the attacked, however, the raids can have very serious consequences for their livelihoods. Because raiding is so common in this part of the world, it plays a pivotal role in the success or failure of livelihood strategies here (Hendrickson, Armond, and Mearns 1998).

Relations between men and women are a key component of the sociopolitical conditions that underpin land and water use. Women produce nearly all the food in developing countries. Women constitute up to 90% of the rice-producing labor force in Southeast Asia and produce up to 80% of basic household food stuffs in Sub-Saharan Africa, where they make a similar contribution to the agricultural labor force (Lado 1992). Despite women's major contribution to cultivation, harvesting, and processing, men—particularly in Africa—retain most ownership, control, and decisionmaking power over agricultural resources—and even over women's labor (Ellis 2000).

Many parts of the developing world are in a state of transition between an economy dominated by subsistence objectives to a cash and surplus production economy. As cash income assumes a more prominent role in households, many rurally based men migrate to find wage labor, leaving women a greater share of household agricultural responsibilities (von Bulow and Sørensen 1993; Francis 1995). Yet traditional patterns of land ownership and access remain, leaving women with principal responsibility for farming but few decisionmaking powers. As the cash economy grows, more of women's labor is taken up growing cash crops controlled by men, potentially taking female labor away from food production and giving men even greater control over the product of women's labor (von Bulow and Sørensen 1993; Mearns 1995).

The result is that women, who have the most intimate relationship with the land and who are best positioned to manage it on a daily basis, are often excluded from decisions that affect its use. Paradoxically, women may be even better at land husbandry than men (see box 15.7 later in the chapter). Where higher yields are seen to be generated mainly by men, yield differences are the result mainly of gender inequalities in access to agricultural inputs. In Sub-Saharan Africa women have less access to education (including agricultural training) and to cash for inputs such as fertilizers than do men. Therefore, unequal assets could have a greater impact on food and nutrition security in this region than in others. In Burkina Faso men have greater access to fertilizer and to household and nonhousehold labor for their farm plots. Reallocating these resources to women could increase household agricultural output by 10%–20% (Alderman and others 2003). In Kenya, if female farmers had the same levels of education, experience, and farm inputs as their male counterparts, their maize, bean, and cowpea yields could increase by 22% (Alderman and others 2003).

Because women have less control over land and what is cultivated on it, this may also have profound implications for household nutrition. The role of women in rearing livestock and marketing livestock products is equally important for household food security (see chapter 13 on livestock). As the primary caregivers in the developing world, women, through their access to food, may also determine children's nutritional well-being.

> Because women have less control over land than men, this may have profound implications for household nutrition

Demographic drivers

Land degradation is rarely a problem under conditions of low population pressure and high per capita resource abundance. But land degradation accelerates as population increases, a process often attributed to the breaching of the land's "carrying capacity" by excess populations of people and their livestock. The relationship between population pressure and land (and other resource) degradation is controversial, however, and spans Malthusian thinkers who insist on a positive correlation (Ehrlich 1968), to others who emphasize that rising populations can trigger innovation in land management (a perspective initially advanced by Boserup 1965; see also Tiffen, Mortimore, and Gichuki 1994; Scherr 1999). If conditions are conducive, high population densities can stimulate conservation and good land husbandry.

In the absence of conducive conditions, however, high population densities can represent a serious problem (box 15.4). Despite the trend toward urbanization, populations are still increasing in most rural areas of developing countries, and the consequences are

| box **15.4** | **Contrasting examples of population growth and land degradation from Africa** |

Using current relations between soil erosion and population growth, Planchon and Valentin (forthcoming) calculated that West Africa's degraded area would increase by 202,000 square kilometers over the next 30 years, a 13% increase in the area occupied by degraded soils. The area affected by water erosion would increase 26%, mainly in the moist savannah zone (1,000–1,500 millimeters of annual rainfall). Although far less densely populated than the wettest region, many areas in the moist savannah may have a population density exceeding 70 inhabitants per square kilometer, which is a critical threshold in a region vulnerable to severe water erosion. In the wettest zone (more than 1,500 millimeters of annual rainfall), pristine areas are expected to erode abruptly as a result of land clearing using heavy machinery (Valentin 1996).

In contrast, Reij, Scoones, and Toulmin (1996) have demonstrated that in response to increased population pressure, farmers in parts of Burkina Faso have invested substantially in improving their natural resource base. The result, associated with an upturn in rainfall, has been a remarkable recovery in vegetation and conservation status over the last decade or so.

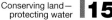

typically a reduction in plot size and spillovers onto marginal lands, such as steep hillsides or areas with poor or erratic rainfall. Larger rural populations make more demands on resources, and this is exacerbated by the parallel growth in urban inhabitants. Together, these ingredients can result in serious land degradation.

Too few farmers can also result in problems. When young farmers move to urban areas, the agricultural labor pool shrinks, making maintenance of structures such as terraces and irrigation channels uneconomical. Ancient terracing systems may collapse (Critchley, Reij, and Willcocks 1994). Analysis of the relationship between degradation and population in the Machakos District of Kenya suggests that a minimum population density is required for development to take off; if the number is too low, investments do not pay off and resource degradation continues (Templeton and Scherr 1999).

The complex relations among growing population density, the context within which it occurs, and land degradation are not well understood. For now, most interventions designed to mitigate land degradation are based on the premise that high and growing population density constitutes a key driver of land degradation.

> Few land-use systems will be able to adjust to the impacts of climate change, and new systems will have to evolve to cope with disturbed rainfall patterns

Biophysical drivers

Natural fluctuations in weather patterns (such as the El Niño/La Niña phenomena) resulting in extreme events occur regardless of land use and have a profound impact on land. Landslides brought on by Hurricane Mitch in Honduras, for example, caused sedimentation 600 times greater than the normal annual average for the region and enormous loss of life (Perotto-Bladiviezo and others 2004).

Human-induced climate change is likely to increase the incidence of extreme events by changing rainfall and temperature patterns and upsetting existing equilibriums. For example, while average rainfall in some areas may not increase (and may even decrease), its distribution may be affected, with intensive and concentrated periods of rainfall followed by extended drier seasons. Few land-use systems will be able to adjust to the impacts of climate change, and new systems will have to evolve to cope with these disturbed rainfall

box **15.5**	**Climate change has increased the vulnerability of agriculture on Mt. Kilimanjaro, Tanzania**

One of Africa's most established and oldest irrigation systems lies on Mt. Kilimanjaro. Massively increased agricultural intensification has meant that this system cannot meet irrigation demand. Up to 85% of water, however, is being lost. Canals are poorly constructed and leaky, while plots are inadequately prepared to receive the irrigation water. In the past, such inefficiency was masked by an abundance of water and relatively low agricultural intensity. Although current rainfall on the mountain's slopes remains good (1,200–2,000 millimeters a year), competition among farmers has reduced the relative amount of water per farmer. The importance of melt-water from the mountain's famous ice cap has increased proportionally. The ice cap, however, is close to disappearing as average temperatures have risen, threatening centuries-old land-use systems and markedly increasing human vulnerability in the area.

Source: IUCN 2003.

patterns. Developed countries account for most greenhouse gas and other global warming emissions. Although developing countries contribute very little to global greenhouse gas emissions, it is these very vulnerable countries that will feel the brunt of the impact from climate change (box 15.5). Where land degradation is already a problem, this vulnerability is substantially increased.

Poverty and livelihoods

By causing land productivity to decline, land degradation has implications for food security. While the relationship between land degradation and food insecurity is difficult to demonstrate, there is no question that the poor are clustered on the most degraded and fragile land. Such land is also often very vulnerable to climate factors such as drought or flooding. The kinds of risks that these farmers face in tilling such land cannot typically be mitigated by investments, because farmers are too poor to make the necessary investments. Risk aversion is costly, and to reduce the time over which these costs are incurred, small-scale farmers may choose to intensify their land-use practices at the expense of land sustainability, contributing further to land degradation.

> By causing land productivity to decline, land degradation has implications for food security

As smallholders struggle against these odds, land productivity declines, having implications for health through malnutrition and exposure to agricultural chemicals in an effort to reduce risk, and increasing the amount of labor required per unit of agricultural output.

The main elements and drivers of land degradation and their impacts pervade the societies that rely on land, rendering them more vulnerable and potentially destroying them. This section considers two key areas of concern with respect to the human impact of land degradation: health and labor.

Impacts of land degradation on human health

An estimated 1.7 billion rural people live on marginal land (Scherr 1999) in areas with noticeable land and water degradation. Areas with the greatest potential for land and water degradation—areas with highly weathered soils, steep slopes, inadequate or excess rainfall, and high temperatures—appear to correspond closely with areas of the highest rural poverty and malnutrition (table 15.1). There are strong indications that the consequences

table **15.1**	**Relationship between rural poor and marginal land in developing country regions**		
	Rural poor on favored lands (millions)	**Rural poor on marginal lands**	
Region		**Number** (millions)	**Share of total** (percent)
Sub-Saharan Africa	65	175	73
Asia	219	374	63
Central and South Africa	24	47	66
West Asia and North Africa	11	35	76
Total	319	613	66

Source: Scherr 1999.

of land degradation for food security at the household level already significantly affect many people (Bridges and others 2001). Land degradation implies a reduction in land productivity and the need for purchased inputs to maintain productivity.

The negative impact of soil degradation on productivity has a more profound effect on food security and hunger in areas cultivated primarily by smallholders than in areas where farmers have larger landholdings. In Honduras, for example, much steep land is cultivated mainly by smallholder farmers. Policies that resulted in inequitable land distribution and an increase in the absolute number of farmers have resulted in 10% of producers holding 90% of land designated as agricultural. Land shortages and external pressures for land make subsistence agriculture all the more difficult. By 1989 the area in southern Honduras cultivated with maize had declined to 49% of its 1952 level, while per capita production fell to 28% of its previous level. The area cultivated with beans fell to 15% of its 1952 level and to 5% of its per capita production (Stonich 1993, p. 73). Conroy, Murray, and Rosset (1996, p. 30) report that throughout Central America in the 1980s, per capita maize production fell 14% and bean production fell 25%.

In Sub-Saharan Africa the burden of disease is especially severe. Malaria and HIV/AIDS are more prevalent in Africa than on other continents. Inadequate nutrition and inadequate healthcare render these diseases all the more crippling. There is also a negative feedback for land degradation in that the debilitating effect of illness on people of all ages has a direct impact on their capacity to look after the land.

These patterns are characteristic of much of the developing world. An additional concern for the health of smallholder farmers is the impact of agrochemicals, particularly pesticides, which can be severe. In the 1940s farmers in the lowland areas of Mexico's Yaqui Valley adopted irrigation agriculture that relied heavily on chemical fertilizers and pesticides (Guillette and others 1998). In studies in 1990 high levels of multiple pesticides were found in the umbilical cord blood of newborns and in breast milk, with alarming implications for the physical and mental development of the area's children.

> Areas with the greatest potential for land and water degradation appear to correspond closely with areas of the highest rural poverty and malnutrition

Impacts of land degradation on labor

As land degradation worsens, the time needed to produce the same or better harvests increases, along with the need to increase inputs. Land degradation, therefore, has serious cost implications in terms of time, labor, and agricultural inputs. In a resettled village of northern Lao PDR yields have plummeted while associated annual work time has soared (Pelletreau 2004). Under a slash and burn agricultural system with decreased fallow (from approximately nine to three years), lengthened cropping period (figure 15.6; Lestrelin, Giordano, and Keohavong 2005), and no use of fertilizers and herbicides, the yield decline is associated with fertility exhaustion and soil erosion. As land degrades, new opportunities open up for hardier types of vegetation—such as weeds. In the Laotian case labor increases were due primarily to weed invasion, with the number of hand weeding operations increasing from one to four (de Rouw, Baranger, and Soulilad 2002). Yields have declined 75% over the last 30 years.

As described above, land degradation has profound affects on hydrology (both through the soil and at catchment scales) and on water quality. As permanent water courses

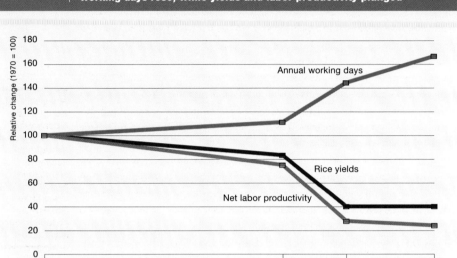

figure 15.6 As land degradation worsened in a northern village in Lao PDR, annual working days rose, while yields and labor productivity plunged

Source: Adapted from Pelletreau 2004.

become seasonal, wells dry up or water quality declines, and access to adequate water resources for household and livestock needs declines. The time and effort expended in obtaining water supplies therefore increasese. In this way, too, land degradation contributes to increased labor costs.

As is the case with negative health impacts, labor increases have severe implications for livelihood success. The success of rural livelihoods has always been dependent on diversity as well as agricultural productivity. Farming communities might also fish, collect forest products, herd, engage in petty commerce, and so on. As land degrades, however, the need for diverse income sources is accentuated, forcing many rural people to search for alternative income streams from urban areas, plantations, and other sources. And as the most productive resources become increasingly scarce, competition for them can reach the point where violence erupts among different users. Whatever the cause, the impacts of land degradation on those who rely most heavily on ecological services and natural capital are severe, widespread, and reach upwards and outwards to national and regional scales (MEA 2005).

Response options

Many land degradation problems arise because of the simplification of agroecosystem structures. To increase yields, farmers must be able to control weeds, wild herbivores, and pathogens and make nutrients accessible to their crops. All types of agricultural systems have negative environmental impacts of varying degrees over time, with some systems yielding no detectable land degradation for long periods and others developing symptoms very quickly. As a general rule, the greater the effort to control ecological processes, the more rapidly is degradation likely to occur. Typically, if manipulation is extensive, degradation can be compensated for through the addition of substantial agricultural inputs far beyond the reach of most smallholder agriculturalists. The sensible solution, therefore, is to advocate agricultural systems with complex structures and a minimal ecological footprint. This section considers various options for doing this:

- *Focusing on smallholder agriculture.* With smallholder agriculture likely to persist for some time to come in developing countries, development and conservation investments should treat the smallholder as the most promising unit around which land and water management can occur.
- *Applying integrated solutions for sustainable land management.* Multiple and synergistic measures should be attempted to treat land degradation at the landscape level. These need to focus on resource-conserving strategies and technologies supported by enabling policy and institutional environments to achieve sustainable increases in land and water productivity and reduce vulnerability to climate change.
- *Enhancing the multifunctionality of agricultural landscapes.* When agricultural land use is understood as an integral part of broader landscapes, synergies can be enhanced with other ecosystem functions. Ecoagricultural approaches offer significant benefits. Landscape success stories (so-called bright spots) provide multiple functions through increased carbon sequestration and reduced water pollution.
- *Creating opportunities from high population densities.* Global population increases are unlikely to be curtailed any time soon. Research needs to focus on identifying land-use systems that can tolerate such densities, while policy needs to promote their implementation.

> The smallholder unit is the single most promising sector for influencing land- and water-use managemont to have a discernable, positive impact on rural livelihoods

Focusing on smallholder agriculture

Smallholders carry out 60% of global agriculture, providing 80% of food in developing countries (Cosgove and Rijsberman 2000). Most developing economies are not growing fast, so it is unlikely that alternative or supporting income-earning opportunities will keep pace with population growth. The largest proportion of the developing world's undernourished people are concentrated among smallholder agricultural groups (figure 15.7). Thus, it makes sense to concentrate land and water sector development investments at this level. The importance of such a focus is reflected in several recent strategy papers (see, for example, the 2004 Copenhagen Consensus and Beijing Consensus). While forests, rangelands, and other common property areas are important, the smallholder unit is the single most promising sector for influencing land- and water-use management to have a discernable, positive impact on rural livelihoods. It is the most productive sector of the rural economy in most countries and the most sensitive to land degradation. Land and its use represent vital buffers for poor people in the developing world, shielding them against the vagaries of the delicate economies in which they live. It is important then to consolidate the security that land use represents and to improve its sustainability.

box **15.7** | **Smallholder farmers constitute the largest share of the developing world's undernourished, 2004**

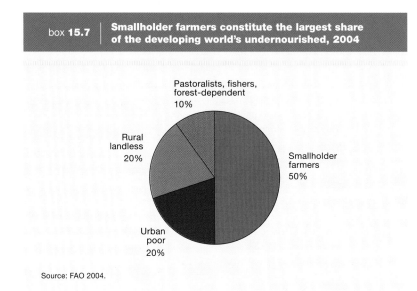

Source: FAO 2004.

Applying integrated solutions for sustainable land management

Over the last two decades new thinking has emerged on resource-conserving agriculture (box 15.6; Shaxson 1988; Hudson 1992; Hurni and others 1996; Pretty 1995). It calls for the introduction of participatory methods in decisionmaking and implementation that emphasize training and capacity building and ensure high levels of voluntary engagement by those who should have a stake in what is done. This approach recognizes that indigenous skills and the innovative capacity of smallholders represent a vital localized resource for managing and conserving land (Richards 1985; Warren, Slikkerveer, and Brokensha 1995) and that participatory methods allow these skills and technologies to be tapped.

This new approach aims to provide a basket of options to small-scale farmers, rather than a single technical panacea to the problems of land degradation. It recognizes that production rather than conservation itself is the priority of resource-poor farmers. Thus, in-field practices such as mulching (photo 15.2), composting, cover cropping, mixed cropping, and agroforestry receive emphasis. These can simultaneously improve the soil, reduce its vulnerability to erosion, and improve production, thus achieving the objectives of both productivity and conservation. Furthermore, cross-slope vegetative barriers, which can do double duty as livestock fodder, are increasingly promoted in place of inert structures of earth or stone.

Such structures still have a role to play, however, as part of a package of measures to augment soil depth, reduce off-site sedimentation, and enhance the biological, chemical, and physical health of the soil. There is also a widely acknowledged need to move away from the narrow spatial and temporal confines of blueprint projects to longer term and more responsive programs or processes. The basket of options approach will require changes in attitude by extensionists and decisionmakers, because less standard approaches

Photo 15.2 Mulching can improve productivity and conservation

Photo by William Critchley

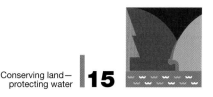

| box **15.6** | **Resource-conserving agriculture covers a broad range of systems** |

The term *resource-conserving agriculture* covers farming systems that aim to conserve natural resources and minimize negative environmental impacts. There are several close similarities in approach. These include plant diversification, plant and animal integration, and an emphasis on soil quality, especially soil organic matter, and on biological solutions to fertility and pest control where possible. A selection of strategies ranging from overall holistic systems to more specific situation-oriented forms, typically used in conjunction, are as follows:

- Organic farming, where artificial additions to the farming system (inorganic fertilizers and agrochemicals) are avoided, and the role of nature is emphasized.
- Conservation agriculture, which combines noninversion tillage (minimum or zero tillage in place of plowing) with mulching or cover cropping and crop rotation to improve soil quality and reduce erosion and costs.
- Ecoagriculture, which emphasizes managing agricultural landscapes to enhance production while conserving or restoring ecosystem services and biodiversity.
- Agroforestry, which incorporates trees into agricultural systems and stresses the multifunctional value of trees within those systems (see photo).
- Integrated pest management, which uses ecosystem resilience and diversity for pest, disease, and weed control and seeks to use pesticides only when other options are ineffective.
- Integrated nutrient management, which seeks both to balance the need to fix nitrogen within farm systems with the need to import inorganic and organic sources of nutrients and to reduce nutrient losses through erosion control.

Agroforestry system in Kenya
Photo by William Critchley

- Integrated livestock systems, especially those that incorporate stallfed dairy cattle, small stock, and poultry, which raise overall productivity, diversify production, use crop by-products, and produce manure.
- Aquaculture, which brings fish, shrimp, and other aquatic resources into farm systems—irrigated rice fields and fishponds—and increases protein production.
- Water harvesting in dryland areas, which maximizes the use of scarce rainfall by capturing runoff (and sediments) for productive purposes.

call for more flexibility and acceptance of indigenous knowledge. In addition, empowering farmers may mean disempowering others.

Better monitoring and evaluation of land degradation underpinning a broader knowledge base are crucial to support these efforts (a forerunner is the World Overview of Conservation Approaches and Technologies, WOCAT; see www.wocat.net).

New policy emphases on institutions and gender. Much policy that relates to land use and degradation suffers from a lack of integration. For example, policies to tackle one aspect of land use, such as conservation, may fail to anticipate spinoff consequences, such as resettlement, that suddenly increase local population density and result in land degradation. Policy needs to anticipate indirect consequences. Of particular concern, here, are impacts on institutions and gender.

Institutions are regular patterns of behavior between individuals and groups in a society that serve a collective purpose (Leach, Mearns, and Scoones 1997; see chapter 5 on policies and institutions). Identifying and fostering responsive, local-level institutions as the basis for decisionmaking and governing land and its use are a powerful response option that managers, administrators, and policymakers can exploit (Ayre and Callway 2005). Achieving an understanding of local-level institutions and how they can be harnessed to tackle land degradation is central to developing effective responses at the community level. Recognizing the role of women in local institutions may be particularly crucial for achieving successful resource management (box 15.7). As already noted, nearly all the food in developing countries is produced by women, and evidence presented here and previously suggests that women can manage resources equitably (Alderman and others 2003).

Bright spots—local contexts, institutions, and policy environments. Agricultural production must increase to feed growing populations. With increasing restrictions on land and water availability, this goal will have to be achieved through intensification—by increasing the productivity of land and water. This may require focusing on the most resilient lands and accepting that certain areas are too fragile for sustainable farming or herding. To make such initiatives sustainable in the long term, resource degradation needs to be mitigated or prevented, while the ecosystem services of the land need to be increased (McNeely and Scherr 2003).

There is ample evidence that it is possible to intensify agriculture in ways that are sustainable and that balance the various goods and services we expect from agricultural landscapes. Success stories have received considerable attention in recent years.[1] One study compiled evidence from bright spots (Noble and others 2006) in 438 recent cases from 57 countries across 11 million farms covering 32 million hectares (table 15.2). Productivity increases were demonstrated across a wide range of farming systems. One of the most

box **15.7**	**Women's leadership of community forestry leads to improved watershed management**

Nepalese forest policy encourages women to take a leading role in forest management, and there are several examples of forests being effectively managed by women. The first women's forest user committee was formed in 1990. By 2002, 442 of 10,901 forest user committees in 53 districts were women's groups. The women's groups range from 11 members to 843 members.

Women appear to take a broader view of managing forest resources than do men. The women's committees apply the concept of ecological sustainability to the management of community forests, taking into account the multiple needs that communities have for forest resources. For example, women instituted the protection of Ahal, ponds in which domestic buffalo swim downstream of the forest. They established nurseries to promote agroforestry in forests and villages to increase wood availability. In contrast, male-dominated committees tended to protect forests simply by restricting access, without taking into account the needs of the community for fuel wood and fodder. This often led to continued exploitation and degradation of forest margins.

Source: Pranita Bhushan, Nepal Water Conservation Foundation, Nepal, personal communication.

table 15.2	Summary of global adoption and impact of sustainable agricultural technologies and practices on 438 projects in 57 countries		
Food and Agriculture Organization farm system category[a]	Number of farmers	Number of hectares under sustainable agriculture	Average increase in crop yields[b] (percent)
Smallholder irrigated	172,389	357,296	169.8 (±197.2)
Wetland rice	7,226,414	4,986,284	21.9 (±32.3)
Smallholder rainfed humid	1,708,278	1,122,840	129.3 (±167.3)
Smallholder rainfed highland	387,265	702,313	112.3 (±122.3)
Smallholder rainfed dry/cold	579,413	719,820	98.6 (±95.3)
Dualistic mixed[c]	466,292	23,515,847	55.3 (±32.4)
Coastal artisanal	220,000	160,000	62.0 (±28.3)
Urban-based and kitchen garden	206,492	35,952	158.8 (±98.6)
Total	10,966,543	31,600,351	
Weighted mean[d]			156.4

a. Based on the farming systems classification of Dixon, Gulliver, and Gibbon (2001) .

b. Increase from levels before initiation of the project.

c. Mixed large commercial and smallholder farming systems, mainly from southern Latin America.

d. Based on the area occupied by each farming system.

Source: Noble and others 2006.

important features of these documented success cases is that they have developed within local contexts and associated market, institutional, and policy environments.

The cases represent a wide variety of farming systems and innovations. They all incorporate resource-conserving technologies (see box 15.6) assisted in various ways, such as extension advice directed at individuals or extension contact with community-based watershed management institutions. Support has come from both nongovernmental organizations and government services. These cases and those from other sources provide compelling evidence that improvement is possible, even though global degradation trends remain a major concern.

These cases also show that it is possible to preserve and restore resources while simultaneously boosting productivity. This means that it is not necessary to trade off resource conservation to achieve increased production. Significantly, the area of greatest impact was found in smallholder agricultural systems (see table 15.2), and the greatest relative yield increases were achieved where original yield levels were very low, less than 1.5 metric tons per hectare (figure 15.8). Thus, the win-win potential is greatest in the "one ton" agricultural systems that dominate rainfed farming in Sub-Saharan Africa. In these very low-yielding and degraded systems adopting resource-conserving agricultural methods of the sort described in box 15.6 often means an increase in inputs of organic and inorganic fertilizers, water, and sometimes labor. Thus, the lag time in productivity stabilization or gains that is often experienced when transitioning from high input-intensive systems to organic or lower input systems is not necessarily a factor. The largest areas of land adopting resource-conserving agriculture, however, were primarily in Latin American mixed large-scale commercial and smallholder farming systems that had adopted conservation

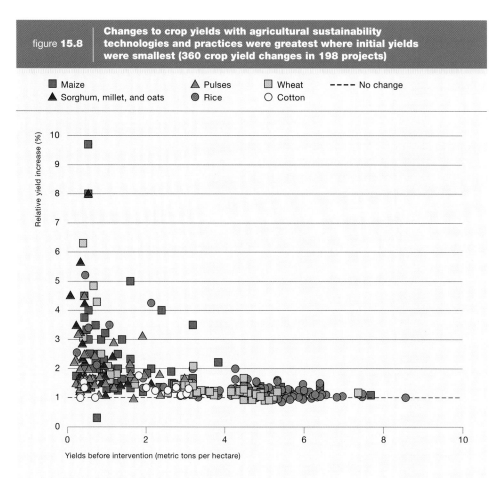

figure 15.8 | **Changes to crop yields with agricultural sustainability technologies and practices were greatest where initial yields were smallest (360 crop yield changes in 198 projects)**

■ Maize   ▲ Pulses   ▢ Wheat   ‑ ‑ ‑ ‑ No change
▲ Sorghum, millet, and oats   ● Rice   ○ Cotton

Relative yield increase (%)

Yields before intervention (metric tons per hectare)

Source: Pretty and others 2006.

tillage. Priming factors in these successful cases included investment, secure land tenure, appropriate integrated land and water technologies, aspirations for change among local populations, and effective leadership.

An important feature of many of the bright spots examples is that they are embedded in traditional agricultural systems. These traditions have evolved—often through local innovation—within very specific localized environmental conditions and therefore yield important clues to the characteristics of appropriate land use for these environments. Thus, bright spots often result from improving on local traditions and knowledge through innovation and adaptation (Critchley, Reij, and Willcocks 1994).

Increasing soil and water productivity. Many soil conservation initiatives have focused narrowly on capturing eroded soil without integrating productivity improvements (box 15.8) or addressing the causes of degradation. Accelerated runoff and erosion are essentially

---

box **15.8** | **The relationship between soil loss and onsite productivity**

It is often assumed that soil erosion is linearly related to reduced soil fertility and hence to a reduction in productivity. Thus soil productivity declines are often equated with the quantity of soil particles lost through erosion. As a result, many soil conservation programs simply seek to control soil and water loss, expecting a predictable return.

There is not, however, a clear and linear relationship between soil loss and soil productivity. In Ethiopia, for example, cross-slope soil conservation technologies substantially reduced soil loss compared with control plots over a three- to five-year period. There was, however, no increase in productivity in the short term (Herweg and Ludi 1999). Similar results were obtained with contour hedgerows in Peru (Shaxson and Barber 2003). Nevertheless, Stocking (2003) graphically demonstrate how the negative impact of erosion on yield differs considerably from soil to soil, though the rate of decline is most rapid initially (see figure 15.3). The key is to prevent early degradation, when erosion (especially interrill erosion, which selectively removes nutrient-rich particles) is most damaging to production. The downstream impacts of erosion are much more closely related to the quantity of soil eroded, however, than are the onsite impacts that are discussed here.

---

consequences of declining soil quality. Improving soil quality by increasing organic matter has the additional benefit of providing significant resilience in systems otherwise vulnerable to extreme climate events and climate variability.

Investing in improved soil management and quality can considerably improve water productivity in both rainfed and irrigated agricultural systems. Soil management practices to improve infiltration and soil water storage (such as zero till) can boost water use efficiency by an estimated 25%–40%, while nutrient management can boost water use efficiency by 15%–25% (Hatfield, Sauer, and Prueger 2001). Water productivity improvement can range from 70% to 100% in rainfed systems and from 15% to 30% in irrigated systems using resource-conserving agricultural techniques that enhance soil fertility and reduce water evaporation through conservation tillage (table 15.3; Pretty and others 2006).

Rehabilitating degraded soils can improve water productivity even more. Some sandy soils in northeastern Thailand display severe nutrient and carbon depletion after 40 or more years of agricultural production. Crops often fail because nutrients and water are unavailable. Annual precipitation of about 1,100 millimeters is sufficient for rainfed farming, but this amount of freshwater is often consumed with zero productivity, when crops fail. Fertilizers or supplemental irrigation does not stabilize yields because of the soil's very low capacity to retain water and nutrients. The application of clay materials can significantly improve the soil's nutrient- and water-holding capacities (Noble and Suzuki 2005), dramatically increase the system's water productivity, and restore yields.

Water productivity can be improved by implementing better adapted cropping systems, particularly in semiarid environments (Hatfield, Sauer, and Prueger 2001). Examples such as the documented bright spots (Noble and others 2006) suggest that improved land management is one of the most promising ways of increasing water productivity in low-yielding rainfed systems (Falkenmark and Rockström 2004).

table **15.3**	**Changes in water productivity from the adoption of sustainable agricultural practices in 144 projects, by crop type** (kilogram of produce per cubic meter of water used by evapotranspiration)			
Crop	Before intervention	After intervention	Gain	Increase (percent)
Irrigated agriculture				
Rice (18 projects)	1.03 (±0.52)	1.19 (±0.49)	0.16 (±0.16)	15.5
Cotton (8 projects)	0.17 (±0.10)	0.22 (±0.13)	0.05 (±0.05)	29.4
Rainfed agriculture				
Cereals (80 projects)	0.47 (±0.51)	0.80 (±0.81)	0.33 (±0.45)	70.2
Legumes (19 projects)	0.43 (±0.29)	0.87 (±0.68)	0.44 (±0.47)	102.3
Roots and tubers (14 projects)	2.79 (±2.72)	5.79 (±4.04)	3.00 (±2.43)	107.5

Note: Numbers in parentheses are standard errors.

Source: Pretty and others 2006.

Enhancing the multifunctionality of agricultural landscapes

Enhancing the multifunctionality of agricultural landscapes means increasing the types of ecosystem services derived or supported by the landscape, while maintaining agricultural production as a primary function. The dominant trend in food production systems has been to radically simplify landscapes, greatly increasing the single service of food production (often a single commodity) while reducing other provisioning and supporting services (see chapter 6 on ecosystems). When this simplification is accompanied by detrimental land-use practices, the result is degradation. In initially high productive-potential areas, degradation may be slow, but on low quality soils or otherwise fragile lands even modest levels of simplification and use can be degrading. Awareness of the full range of services of improved land-use systems is growing (MEA 2005), and efforts to quantify and value these services are important for reversing these trends.

Multifunctionality can be enhanced at both farm and landscape scales. On-farm diversification, as in many resource-conserving farming systems (see box 15.6), is one way to diversify livelihoods, reduce vulnerability, and achieve other ecosystem benefits, such as carbon sequestration (Pretty and others 2006). Integrated pest management systems use specialized on-farm niches to increase overall landscape functionality. They use the borders of fields for plants that attract pollinators and other beneficial insects, for example, thus providing more sustainable pest control, with the added benefit that these often perennial vegetation strips provide habitat for small animals (Earles and Williams 2005).

Landscape approaches that go beyond farm scale are also necessary because land degradation has causes and impacts beyond the location where it is observed. Land degradation often arises because of the failure to integrate the agroecological system into the broader landscape in which it is located. Vital ecosystem functions, particularly related to water cycling, cannot be maintained without a larger scale approach within an ecosystem context. Landscape approaches take into account the ecology and function of the landscape's components and make strategic use of their potential, integrating agriculture into an ecosystematic whole (Ryszkowski and Jankowiak 2002).

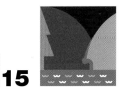
At the landscape level there are several ways to increase multifunctionality with over-all benefit. One way is to actively manage nonfarmed land in and around farmed land. This includes waste land and riparian zones. In a system widespread in the Eastern Himalayas

box **15.9**	**Meeting diverse needs through alder-cardamom agroforestry in riparian zones**

In the Eastern Himalayas (Sikkim and Assam in India and in Nepal) steep slopes, low soil fertility, tectonic activity, and intense precipitation cause erosion and slumping. Together with increasing population pressures, this makes land management difficult. One response was the strategic planting of an alder-cardamom agroforestry system in riparian zones (see figure), which satisfied a diversity of farmers' needs while protecting the land from severe biophysical pressures (Zomer and Menke 1993).

Riparian buffers trap sediment and reduce bank erosion, providing significant water quality benefits. This type of conservation-production system increases the provision of ecosystem goods and services at the landscape scale, which cannot always be achieved when management targets only lands under annual cropping systems.

Alder-cardamom agroforestry system

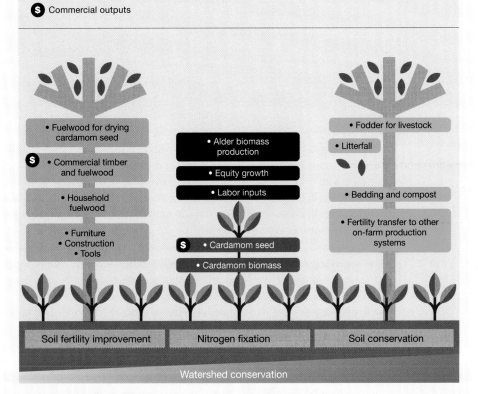

Source: Adapted from Zomer and Menke 1993.

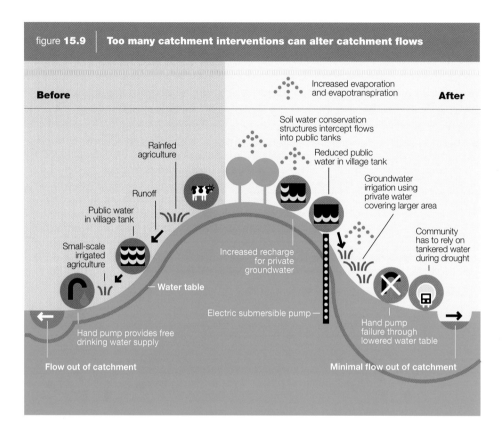

figure **15.9** | **Too many catchment interventions can alter catchment flows**

Increased evaporation and evapotranspiration

Before

After

Rainfed agriculture

Soil water conservation structures intercept flows into public tanks

Reduced public water in village tank

Runoff

Groundwater irrigation using private water covering larger area

Public water in village tank

Small-scale irrigated agriculture

Increased recharge for private groundwater

Community has to rely on tankered water during drought

— Water table

Electric submersible pump —

Hand pump provides free drinking water supply

Hand pump failure through lowered water table

Flow out of catchment

Minimal flow out of catchment

riparian zones become productive parts of the landscape, protecting steep hillsides and river banks from accelerated erosion (box 15.9). Another way is to make greater use of perennials in the farm landscape, creating land-use mosaics, interspersing perennials and small patches of annuals or high-disturbance systems. A mosaic of perennials usually provides more stable plant cover, protecting the soil and increasing infiltration, thus mitigating or reversing some of the negative effects described above. There are often many opportunities to substitute perennials for current annuals (especially to produce livestock feed and oils), and they can also provide new income-earning potential. These approaches may be the only option for sustainable production on degradation-prone lands.

It should be noted, however, that using more perennials will also typically boost local water consumption through increased evapotranspiration, reducing water that might otherwise be available for alternative uses. In semiarid areas, for example, the understanding is growing of the potential for "excessive" implementation of catchment interventions involving irrigation, forestry, and soil water conservation measures to alter catchment flows and the availability of "private" and "public" water, thus becoming a governance and water rights issue (figure 15.9; Calder 2005). The magnitude of such water-use reallocation effects will vary across ecosystems and climate zones (see chapter 16 on river basins) and will also depend on such factors as how much locally used

water was previously lost through unproductive evaporation, changes in groundwater recharge, and any impact on local precipitation patterns. This is an area that requires research attention.

Creating opportunities from high population densities

Despite continuing rural-urban migration, it is unlikely that rural populations in developing countries have peaked. National policies cannot afford to focus on controlling population growth alone but must also emphasize research on land-use systems that can accommodate high population densities.

Small-scale farmers in developing countries facing the constraint of high population pressure and known to be innovators should be acknowledged as allies in developing land husbandry systems appropriate under these conditions (Tiffen, Mortimore, and Gichuki 1994). Appropriate interventions need to be stimulated by creating enabling sociopolitical environments. Where political contexts favor secure access to land, and adequate marketing opportunities for produce exist, land users are more willing to develop and implement land husbandry innovations. A review of 70 empirical studies on farming on tropical hillsides found that in many places population growth, especially at higher population densities, led to extensive land-improving investments and conservation management (Templeton and Scherr 1999).

> Where political contexts favor secure access to land, and adequate marketing opportunities for produce exist, land users are more willing to develop and implement land husbandry innovations

Conclusion

This chapter has detailed the global extent of land degradation, particularly as viewed from the perspective of livelihoods in developing countries. It makes clear that considerably more research is needed—particularly at water catchment scales—to better understand the multiple drivers underpinning land degradation and the ways in which land users respond to these drivers. It has focused on the sociopolitical and economic contexts within which land degradation occurs to reveal the drivers that cause it and the solution: sociopolitical and economic environments that foster innovative responses to mitigate and prevent land degradation and that are often resource conserving. In addition, the local-level context in which land use occurs reveals important dynamics between different actors at this scale. This includes power relationships between men and women and the importance of tenure—the guarantee of access to resource bases—as a pivotal component in the way land is used and managed (photo 15.3).

Photo 15.3 Gender relations affect land use

Photo by William Critchley

The solutions proposed here call for a policy focus at the small scale capable of providing latitude and encouragement for the development and evolution of local strategies and institutions able to prevent and mitigate land degradation. In addition, the chapter calls for policy and local-level interventions that can stimulate resource-conserving agriculture that improves land and water productivity, relies less on artificial inputs and more on ecosystem services, and works with ecosystem sustainability and contributes to it in the long term. In addition, the chapter calls for an understanding of land use at the landscape level, managing these as a suite of potential activities with ecosystems in common.

Reviewers

Chapter review editor: Robert Wasson.

Chapter reviewers: Miguel Ayarza, Olivier Briet, Ian Calder, Mark Giordano, Michael Hauser, Hans Hurni, Patricia Kabatabazi, Joke Muylwijk, Sawaeng Ruyasoongerng, Lech Ryszkowski, Sara Scherr, Vladmir Starodubtsev, Girma Tadesse, Samyuktha Varma, and Paul Vlek.

Note

1. Groups with projects cataloguing and detailing success stories include the Centre for Development and Environment, Berne; Centre for Environment and Society, University of Essex; Ecoagriculture Partners; Food and Agriculture Organization Land and Water Development Division; Food and Agriculture Organization/Land and Water Development Division Gateway Project; Centre for International Cooperation, Vrije Universiteit Amsterdam; Institute for Regional Community Development; Sustainability Institute, Stockholm Environment Institute; and the World Overview of Conservation Approaches and Technologies, Berne. See Bridges and others (2001); McNeely and Scherr (2003); and WOCAT (2006).

References

Alderman, H., J. Hoddinott, L. Haddad, and C. Udry. 2003. "Gender Differentials in Farm Productivity: Implications for Household Efficiency and Agricultural Policy." In A. Quisumbing, ed., *Household Decisions, Gender, and Development: A Synthesis of Recent Research.* Baltimore, Md.: Johns Hopkins University Press.

Alegre, J.C., and M.R. Rao. 1996. "Soil and Water Conservation by Contour Hedging in the Humid Tropics of Peru." *Agriculture, Ecosystem, and Environment* 57 (1): 17–25.

Ayre, G., and R. Callway, eds. 2005. *Governance for Sustainable Development: A Foundation for the Future.* London: Earthscan.

Bellon, M.R., D. Hodson, D. Bergvinson, D. Beck, E. Matinez-Romero, and Y. Montoya. 2005. "Targeting Agricultural Research to Benefit Poor Farmers: Relating Poverty Mapping to Maize Environments in Mexico." *Food Policy* 30 (5–6): 476–92.

Berkes, F., ed. 1989. *Common Property Resources: Ecology and Community-Based Sustainable Development.* London: Belhaven Press.

Blakie, P.M. 1985. *The Political Economy of Soil Erosion in Developing Countries.* London: Longman.

Boserup, E. 1965. *The Condition of Agricultural Growth: The Economics of Agrarian Change under Population Pressure.* London: Earthscan.

Bridges, E.M., I.D. Hannam, L.R. Oldeman, F.W.T. Penning de Vries, S.J. Scherr, and S. Sombatpanit, eds. 2001. *Response to Land Degradation.* Enfield, N.H.: Science Publishers.

Cakmak, I., M. Kalayci, H. Ekiz, H.J. Braun, Y. Kilinc, and A. Yilmaz. 1999. "Zinc Deficiency as a Practical Problem in Plant and Human Nutrition in Turkey." *Field Crops Research* 60 (1–2): 175–88.

Calder, I.R. 2005. *Blue Revolution.* London: Earthscan.

Conroy, M.E., D.L. Murray, and P.M. Rosset. 1996. *A Cautionary Tale: Failed U.S. Development Policy in Central America.* Food First Development Studies. Boulder and London: Lynne Rienner.

Cosgrove, W.J., and F.R. Rijsberman. 2000. *World Water Vision—Making Water Everybody's Business.* London: Earthscan.

Craswell, E.T., U. Grote, J. Henao, and P.L.G. Vlek. 2004. "Nutrient Flows in Agricultural Production and International Trade: Ecological and Policy Issues." ZEF Discussion Paper on Development Policy 78. Center for Development Research, Bonn, Germany.

Critchley, W.R.S., C. Reij, and T.J. Willcocks. 1994. "Indigenous Soil and Water Conservation: A Review of the State of Knowledge and Prospects for Building on Traditions." *Land Degradation and Rehabilitation* 5 (4): 293–314.

De Rouw, A., P. Baranger, and B. Soulilad. 2002. "Upland Rice and Job's Tear Cultivation in Slash and Burn Systems under Very Short Fallow Periods in Luangprabang Province." *The Lao Journal of Agriculture and Forestry* 5: 2–10.

Derpsch, R., and J.R. Benites. 2003. "Situation of Conservation Agriculture in the World." Presented at the Second Global Congress of Conservation Agriculture, August 11–15, Foz do Iguassu, Brazil.

Dixon, J., A. Gulliver, and D. Gibbon. 2001. "Farming Systems and Poverty: Improving Farmers' Livelihoods in a Changing World." Food and Agriculture Organization and World Bank, Rome and Washington, D.C.

Drechsel, P., M. Giordano, and L. Gyiele. 2004. *Valuing Nutrients in Soil and Water: Concepts and Techniques with Examples from IWMI Studies in the Developing World.* IWMI Research Report 82. Colombo: International Water Management Institute.

Earles, R., and P. Williams. 2005. "Sustainable Agriculture: An Introduction." Attra Publication IPO43/121. National Center for Appropriate Technology, Butte, Mont.

Ehrlich, P. 1968. *The Population Bomb.* New York: Ballantine.

Ellis, F. 2000. *Rural Livelihoods and Diversity in Developing Countries.* Oxford, UK: Oxford University Press.

Ezzati, M., A.D. Lopez, A. Rodgers, S. Vander Hoorn, and C.J.L. Murray. 2002. "Selected Major Risk Factors and Global and Regional Burden of Disease." *Lancet* 360 (9343): 1347–60.

FAO (Food and Agriculture Organization). 2004. "The State of Food Insecurity in the World 2004." Rome.

Falkenmark, M., and J. Rockström. 2004. *Balancing Water for Humans and Nature.* London: Earthscan.

Francis, E. 1995. "Migration and Changing Divisions of Labour: Gender Relations and Economic Change in Kogutu, Western Kenya." *Africa* 65 (2): 197–216.

Gelbrecht J., H. Lengsfeld, R. Pöthig, and D. Opitz D. 2005. Temporal and Spatial Variation of Phosphorus Input, Retention, and Loss in a Small Catchment of NE Germany. *Journal of Hydrology* 304 (1/2): 151–65.

Gray, S., M. Sundal, B. Wiebusch, M.A. Little, P.W. Leslie, and I.L. Pike. 2003. "Cattle Raiding, Cultural Survival, and Adaptability of East African Pastoralists." *Current Anthropology* 44 (suppl.): S3–S30.

Guillette, E., M. Meza, M. Aquilar, A. Soto, and I. Enedina. 1998. "An Anthropological Approach to the Evaluation of Preschool Children Exposed to Pesticides in Mexico." *Environmental Health Perspectives* 106 (6): 347–53.

Hardin, G. 1968. "The Tragedy of the Commons." *Science* 162: 1243–48.

Hatfield, J.L., T.J. Sauer, and J.H. Prueger. 2001. "Managing Soils to Achieve Greater Water Use Efficiency: A Review." *Agronomy Journal* 93 (2): 271–80.

Hendrickson, D., J. Armond, and R. Mearns. 1998. "The Changing Nature of Conflict and Famine Vulnerability: The Case of Livestock Raiding in Turkana District, Kenya." *Disasters* 22 (3): 185–99.

Herweg, K., and E. Ludi. 1999. "The Performance of Selected Soil and Water Conservation Measures—Case Studies from Ethiopia and Eritrea." *Catena* 36 (1–2): 99–114.

Hiernaux, P., C.L. Bielders, C. Valentin, A. Bationo, and S.P. Fernández-Rivera. 1999. "Effects of Livestock Grazing on Physical and Chemical Properties of Sandy Soils in Sahelian Rangelands." *Journal of Arid Environment* 41 (3): 231–45.

Homewood, K., and D. Brockington. 1999. "Biodiversity, Conservation, and Development in Mkomazi Game Reserve, Tanzania. " *Global Ecology and Biogeography* 8 (3–4): 301–13.

Hudson, N.W. 1992. *Land Husbandry.* London: Batsford.

Hurni, H. 1993. "Land Degradation, Famine, and Land Resource Scenarios in Ethiopia." Paper presented to the National Conference on a Disaster Prevention and Preparedness Strategy for Ethiopia, December 5–8, Addis Ababa.

Hurni, H. (with the assistance of an international group of contributors). 1996. *Precious Earth: From Soil and Water Conservation to Sustainable Land Management.* Berne: International Soil Conservation Organization and Centre for Development and Environment.

IUCN (World Conservation Union). 2003. *Pangani Basin: A Situation Analysis.* Nairobi.

Ives, J.D., and B. Messerli. 1989. *The Himalaya Dilemma: Reconciling Development and Conservation.* London: John Wiley and Sons.

Kennedy, E., and L. Haddad. 1994. "Are Preschoolers from Female-Headed Households Less Malnourished? A Comparative Analysis of Results from Ghana and Kenya." *Journal of Development Studies* 30 (3): 680–95.

Kennedy, E., and P. Peters. 1992. "Household Food Security and Child Nutrition: The Interaction of Income and Gender of Household Head." *World Development* 20 (8): 1077–85.

Lado, C. 1992. "Female Labour Participation in Agricultural Production and the Implications for Nutrition and Health in Rural Africa." *Social Science and Medicine* 34 (7): 789–807.

Leach, M., R. Mearns, and I. Scoones. 1997. "Challenges to Community-Based Sustainable Development: Dynamics, Entitlements, Institutions." *IDS Bulletin* 28 (4): 4–14.

Lestrelin, G., M. Giordano, and B. Keohavong. 2005. *When "Conservation" Leads to Land Degradation: Lessons from Ban Lak Sip, Laos.* IWMI Research Report 91. Colombo: International Water Management Institute.

Lotter, D.W., R. Seidel, and W. Liebhardt. 2002. "The Performance of Organic and Conventional Cropping Systems in an Extreme Climate Year." *American Journal of Alternative Agriculture* 18 (3): 146–54.

Lulseged, T. 2005. "Catchment Erosion—Reservoir Siltation: Processes in the Highlands of Ethiopia." Ph.D. Dissertation. University of Bonn, Bonn, Germany.

McCay, B.J., and J.M. Acheson, eds. 1987. *The Question of the Commons: The Culture and Ecology of Communal Resources.* Tucson, Ariz.: University of Arizona Press.

McNeely, J.A., and S.J. Scherr. 2003. *Eco-agriculture: Strategies to Feed the World and Save Wild Biodiversity.* Washington, D.C.: Island Press.

MEA (Millennium Ecosystem Assessment). 2005. *Living Beyond Our Means: Natural Assets and Human Well-Being.* Washington, D.C.: Island Press.

Mearns, R. 1995. "Institutions and Natural Resource Management: Access to and Control over Woodfuel in East Africa." In T. Binns, ed., *People and Environment in Africa.* Chichester, UK: John Wiley and Sons.

Middleton, N., and D. Thomas, eds. 1997. *World Atlas of Desertification.* Nairobi: United Nations Environment Programme.

Noble, A.D., and S. Suzuki. 2005. "Improving the Productivity of Degraded Cropping Systems in Northeast Thailand: Improving Farmer Practices with Innovative Approaches." Proceedings of the Joint Meeting on Environmental Engineering in Agriculture, September 12–15, Kanazawa, Japan.

Noble, A.D., D.A. Bossio, F.W.T. Penning de Vries, J. Pretty, T.M. Thiyagarajan. 2006. "Intensifying Agricultural Sustainability: An Analysis of Impacts and Drivers in the Development of 'Bright Spots'." Comprehensive Assessment of Water Management in Agriculture Research Report 13. International Water Management Institute, Colombo.

Oldeman, L.R., R.T.A. Hakkeling, and W.G. Sombroek. 1991. *World Map of the Status of Human-Induced Soil Degradation.* An Explanatory Note. Global Assessment of Soil Degradation, October 1991. Second revised ed. Wageningen, Netherlands: International Soil Reference and Information Centre and United Nations Environment Programme.

Onyango, A., K. Tucker, and T. Eisemon. 1994. "Household Headship and Child Nutrition: A Case Study in Western Kenya." *Social Science and Medicine* 39 (12): 1633–39.

Palmieri, A., F. Shah, and A. Dinar. 2001. "Economics of Reservoir Sedimentation and Sustainable Management of Dams." *Journal of Environmental Management* 61 (2): 149–63.

Pelletreau, A. 2004. "Pricing Soil Degradation in Uplands: The Case of the Houay Pano Catchment, Lao PDR." Internship Report. Institut de Recherche pour le Développement, International Water Management Institute, National Agriculture and Forestry Research Institute, Vientiane.

Perotto-Baldiviezo, H.L., T.L. Thurow, C.T. Smith, R.F. Fisher, and X.B. Wu. 2004. "GIS-Based Spatial Analysis Modelling for Landslide Hazard Assessment in Steeplands, Southern Honduras." *Agriculture, Ecosystems, and the Environment* 103 (1): 165–76.

Planchon, O., and C. Valentin. Forthcoming. "Soil Erosion in West Africa: Present and Future." In D. Favis-Mortlock and J. Boardman, eds., *Soil Erosion and Climatic Change.* Oxford, UK: Imperial College Press.

Pretty, J. 1995. *Regenerating Agriculture: Policies and Practices for Sustainability and Self-Reliance.* London: Earthscan.

Pretty, J., A. Noble, D. Bossio, J. Dixon, R. Hine, F.T.W. Penning de Vries, and J. Morison. 2006. "Resource-Conserving Agriculture Increases Yields in Developing Countries." *Environmental Science and Technology* 40 (4): 1114–19.

Reij, C., and A. Waters-Bayer, eds. 2001. *Farmer Innovation in Africa: A Source of Inspiration for Agricultural Development.* London: Earthscan.

Reij, C., I. Scoones, and C. Toulmin, eds. 1996. *Sustaining the Soil: Indigenous Soil and Water Conservation in Africa.* London: Earthscan.

Richards, P. 1985. *Indigenous Agricultural Revolution.* London: Unwin Hyman.

Robbins, M. 2004. *Carbon Trading, Agriculture, and Poverty.* Special Publication 2. World Association of Soil and Water Conservation, Bangkok.

Ryszkowski, L., and J. Jankowiak. 2002. "Development of Agriculture and Its Impacts on Landscape Functions." In L. Ryszkowski, ed., *Landscape Ecology in Agroecosystems Management.* Boca Raton, Fla.: CRC Press.

Scherr, S.J. 1999. "Poverty-Environment Interactions in Agriculture: Key Factors and Policy Implications." Paper 3. United Nations Development Program and the European Community, Policy and Environment Initiative, New York.

Scherr, S.J., and S. Yadav. 1996. "Land Degradation in the Developing World: Implications for Food, Agriculture, and the Environment to 2020." Food, Agriculture and the Environment Discussion Paper 14. International Food Policy Research Institute, Washington, D.C.

Shaxson, T.F. 1988. "Conserving Soil by Stealth." In W.C. Moldenhauer and N.W. Hudson, eds., *Conservation Farming on Steep Lands.* Ankeny, Iowa: World Association of Soil and Water Conservation.

Shaxson, T.F., and R. Barber. 2003. "Optimizing Soil Moisture for Plant Production." Soils Bulletin 79. Food and Agriculture Organization, Rome.

Sheldrick, W.F., J.K. Syers, and J. Lingard. 2002. "A Conceptual Model for Conducting Nutrient Audits and the National, Regional, and Global Scales." *Nutrient Cycling in Agroecosystems* 62 (1): 61–72.

Smaling, E.M.A. 1993. "An Agro-ecological Framework for Integrated Nutrient Management." Ph.D. thesis. Wageningen Agricultural University, Wageningen, Netherlands.

Steiner, K.G. 1996. *Causes of Soil Degradation and Development Approaches to Sustainable Soil Management.* Eschborn, Germany: Deutsche Gesellschaft fur Technische Zusammenarbeit.

Stocking, M.A. 2003. "Tropical Soils and Food Security: The Next 50 Years." *Science* 302 (5649): 1356–59.

Stonich, S. 1993. *I Am Destroying the Land: The Political Ecology of Poverty and Environmental Destruction in Honduras.* Boulder, Colo.: Westview Press.

Stoorvogel, J.J., E.M.A. Smaling, and B.H. Jansen. 1993. "Calculating Soil Nutrient Balances in Africa at Different Scales: I; Supranational Scales." *Fertiliser Research* 35: 227–35.

Templeton, S.R., and S.J. Scherr. 1999. "Effects of Demographic and Related Microeconomic Change on Land Quality in Hills and Mountains of Developing Countries." *World Development* 27 (6): 903–18.

Tiffen, M., M. Mortimore, and F. Gichuki. 1994. *More People, Less Erosion: Environmental Recovery in Kenya.* London: Wiley.

UNEP (United Nations Environment Programme). 1999. *Global Environmental Outlook 2000.* Nairobi.

———. 2004. *Freshwater in Europe.* Nairobi.

Utting, P. 1991. "The Social Origins and Impact of Deforestation in Central America." United Nations Research Institute for Social Development, Geneva, Switzerland.

Valentin, C. 1996. "Soil Erosion under Global Change." In B.H. Walker and W.L. Steffen, eds., *Global Change and Terrestrial Ecosystems.* Cambridge, UK: Cambridge University Press.

Valentin, C. and L.-M. Bresson. 1997. "Soil Crusting." In R. Lal, W.E.H. Blum, C. Valentin, and B.A. Stewart, eds., "Methodology for Assessment of Soil Degradation." Boca Raton, CRC

van Lynden, G.W.J., and L.R. Oldeman. 1997. "Assessment of the Status of Human-Induced Soil Degradation in South and South East Asia." International Soil Reference and Information Centre, Wageningen, Netherlands. [http://lime.isric.nl/Docs/ASSODEndReport.pdf].

Vlek, P. 2005. "Nothing Begets Nothing: The Creeping Disaster of Land Degradation." Policy Brief 1. United Nations University, Institute for Environment and Human Security, Bonn, Germany.

von Bulow, D., and A. Sørenson. 1993. "Gender and Contract Farming: Tea Outgrower Schemes in Kenya." *Review of African Political Economy* 56 (4): 38–52.

Warren, D.M., L.J. Slikkerveer, and D. Brokensha, eds. 1995. *The Cultural Dimension of Development: Indigenous Knowledge Systems.* London: Intermediate Technology Publications Ltd.

Wily, L. 1999. "Moving Forward in African Community Forestry: Trading Power, Not Use Rights." *Society & Natural Resources* 12 (1): 49–61.

WOCAT (World Overview of Conservation Approaches and Technologies). 2006. *Where the Land is Greener: Case Studies and Analysis of Soil and Water Conservation Initiatives Worldwide.* Berne: Technical Centre for Agricultural and Rural Cooperation, United Nations Environment Programme, Food and Agriculture Organization, Centre for the Comparative Study of Culture, Development and the Environment.

Wood, S., K. Sebastian, and S.J. Scherr. 2000. "Soil Resource Condition." In S. Wood, K. Sebastian, and S.J. Scherr, eds., *Pilot Analysis of Global Ecosystems: Agroecosystems.* Washington, D.C.: IFPRI and World Resources Institute.

WWAP (World Water Assessment Program). 2003. *Water for People, Water for Life.* Barcelona, Spain: UNESCO Publishing and Berghahn Books.

Zomer, R., and J. Menke. 1993. "Site Index and Biomass Productivity Estimates for Himalayan Alder-Large Cardamom Plantations: A Model Agroforestry System of the Middle Hills of Eastern Nepal." *Mountain Research and Development* 13 (3): 235–55.

Water for food, water for life

Artist: Andrea Nittu, Albania

16 | River basin development and management

Coordinating lead author: François Molle

Lead authors: Philippus Wester and Phil Hirsch

Contributing authors: Jens R. Jensen, Hammond Murray-Rust, Vijay Paranjpye, Sharon Pollard, and Pieter van der Zaag

Overview

In many river basins use of water for human purposes through investments in water infrastructure for urban, industrial, and agricultural growth is approaching or exceeding the amount of renewable water available. Such overcommitment of water resources is caused by a disregard for environmental water requirements, incomplete hydrological knowledge, fuzzy water rights, and politically motivated projects with weak economic rationale *[well established]*. The results are overbuilt river basins and basin closure, the situation where more water is used than is environmentally desirable or, in some cases, than is renewably available. The challenge for water management in agriculture is to do more with less water in river basins that are already stressed and to provide much stricter scrutiny by decisionmakers and civil society of new infrastructure development in relatively open river basins to avoid overcommitment of water resources.

River basins are experiencing multiple constraints. Expanding water supply is constrained by the cost and potential impact of new projects and by the reduction of available renewable freshwater due to contamination, overdraft of aquifers, and climate change, which increases variability and imposes more conservative management of dams. On the demand side, nonagricultural requirements increase, irrigation often expands, and more water needs to be reserved or reallocated to environmental flow regimes *[well established]*.

A first response for escaping this impasse is too often to seek supply-side approaches for capturing more water. In both open and closing basins informed decisions need to be made about whether more infrastructure is needed, where, and of which type. In closing basins further increases in water withdrawals for human purposes will lead to irreversible losses of biodiversity and ecosystems services *[established but incomplete]*. In closed basins interbasin transfers or new dams are often inappropriate responses, exacerbating problems or shifting costs to the donor area. River basin management therefore needs political reforms and a commitment to more open, accountable, and inclusive governance; increased public scrutiny of traditional evaluation tools such as cost-benefit analyses and environmental impact assessments; and enabling policy and political environments that allow negotiated agreements.

With basin closure the interconnectedness of the water cycle, aquatic ecosystems, and water users increases greatly. Local interventions such as tapping more groundwater, lining canals, or using microirrigation often have third-party impacts and unexpected consequences elsewhere in the basin. In closing basins users and managers tend to adapt to scarcity, conserve water, and resort to multiple sources, while local "losses" are reused elsewhere in the basin. Thus the scope for using water more efficiently at the basin level is frequently much smaller than assumed *[established but incomplete]*. Based on a solid hydrological analysis, planners need to gauge whether there is scope for saving water or simply for redistributing it and to make sure that possible third-party impacts are avoided or compensated for.

Water policies and interventions need to take into account the social and political aspects of basin interconnectedness and the imbalances they create. The population groups that manage water, make or influence decisions, receive benefits, or bear costs and risk have different levels of access to resources, knowledge, political representation, or courts.

> **Basins should have a three-tiered allocation framework for surface water: a tier for basic human needs and the environment, a tier for productive water for the poor, and a tier for other productive uses**

Sustainable river basin management needs water allocation mechanisms based on a comprehensive understanding of hydrological interactions and on recognition of customary rights. To prevent negative impacts on weak constituencies, a good starting point for redesigning water allocation mechanisms is to define environmental water requirements and water entitlements for the poor. Both open and closed river basins should have a three-tiered allocation framework for surface water: a tier for basic human needs and the environment, a tier for productive water for the poor, and a tier for other productive uses. Stakeholders must participate in defining entitlements, which should remain flexible and adaptive, with possible evolution toward a more formal water rights system.

Progress in establishing integrated water resources management strategies has been undermined by such factors as the lack of fit between hydrologic and politico-administrative jurisdictions, conflicts between line agencies and policy fields, as well as erratic financing and lack of hydrological data or technical capacity [well established]. Basins facing complex problems of conflicting societal values and pressure on resources will probably not be well managed by a single body. In such cases institutional arrangements for river basin management should focus on consultation and coordination instead of pursuing an ideal organizational model for river basin management through a centralized river basin organization. Although institutional arrangements should be based on existing organizations, customary practices, and administrative structures, this will often require reshaping the role of traditional hydraulic bureaucracies and seeking political support for more polycentric and collaborative modes of governance.

Many international rivers are the subject of shared agreements, but results have fallen short of expectations because of historical factors, lack of shared hydrological data, and the absence of nonstate actors in negotiations [established but incomplete]. Permanent platforms, data sharing, or the introduction of other issues of common interest in the negotiations may assist in building trust and achieving equitable agreements.

Not all problems can or should be solved at the river basin level. Water quality or flood problems may be more local in scope. Watershed initiatives also signal that local governance is more effective, but how to integrate scattered initiatives within the larger basin remains a crucial question. While river basins are relevant units for planning water resource development, many problems affecting them—and their solution—may well lie beyond the basins themselves. Agricultural policies, free trade agreements, demographic changes, and shifts in ideologies or societal values can all have a bearing on water use and call for dynamic and adaptive river basin management.

An introduction to river basins

Except for a few islands or desert areas all land on the Earth's surface is part of one river basin or another

During much of the 20th century the water needs of growing populations were met through the construction of infrastructure to increase water withdrawals from rivers and aquifers. Water was perceived to be abundant, and impacts on the environment were incremental and little noticed at first. Today, water resources in many river basins are fully or almost fully committed to a variety of human uses, water quality is degraded, river-dependent ecosystems are threatened, and expanding demand for water is leading to intense competition and even at times to strife. In agriculture the challenge for water management is to do more with less water in river basins that are already stressed, while in relatively open river basins judicious assessments of new water infrastructure is needed. Compounding this challenge is the widespread poverty in river basins in developing countries and the pressure this places on the reallocation of water to the poor for productive uses. This chapter reviews the drivers and impacts of river basin development and outlines the challenges facing agricultural water management in closing river basins.

Except for a few islands or desert areas all land on the Earth's surface is part of one river basin or another. River basins are the geographic area contained within the watershed limits of a system of streams and rivers converging toward the same terminus, generally the sea or sometimes an inland water body. Tributary subbasins or basins more limited in size (typically from tens of square kilometers to 1,000 square kilometers) are often called *watersheds* (in American English), while *catchment* is frequently used in British English as a synonym for river basins, *watershed* being more narrowly defined as the line separating two river basins. This chapter is mainly concerned with river basins.

While efforts to control rivers go back many thousands of years, the concept of river basins as units for planning, developing, and managing water emerged in the late 19th and early 20th centuries (Teclaff 1996; Molle 2006). River basin development was boosted by technological changes in dam construction at the beginning of the 20th century. During the second half of the century multipurpose development of river basins focused primarily on the construction of large dams (whose numbers increased from 5,000 in 1950 to 45,000 in 2000, an average of two new large dams each day; WCD 2000) for hydropower generation, flood control, and water storage for irrigation. During the same period irrigated areas doubled from 140 million hectares (ha) to 280 million ha (see chapter 9 on irrigation).

Enthusiastic—and optimistic—large-scale development of river basins yielded unexpected results, however. River systems turned out to be interconnected transfer and transport systems (Newson 1997) carrying not only water, but also sediment, nutrients, contaminants, and biota across space and time. Control of water, estimation of extreme events, and management of annual variability posed many problems unanticipated by engineers. The intricacies of surface water and groundwater interactions led to unexpected impacts and conflicts, while drastic alterations of the natural water regime provoked severe ecological degradation.

> The intricacies of surface water and groundwater interactions led to unexpected impacts and conflicts, while drastic alterations of the natural water regime provoked severe ecological degradation

Human interventions in the water cycle have placed many river basins under growing stress. When water resources are increasingly committed, the interconnectedness of the water cycle, aquatic ecosystems, and water users rises greatly. Interventions such as groundwater development, canal lining, drip irrigation, and reforestation generally have unexpected third-party effects elsewhere in the basin. Because users adjust to water scarcity and reuse water in the basin, closing basins tend to have much less "slack" than is often assumed, and the potential for net water savings at the basin level is often overstated. In addition, the social and environmental costs of supply-side approaches to capturing more water, such as interbasin transfers and construction of more dams, are seldom fully identified and in many cases—especially in closing basins—will only exacerbate problems. This double squeeze demands care and judgment in designing solutions and requires decisionmakers to deal with sociohydrological complexity and avoid overcommitment of water resources.

In moving toward sustainable river basin management there is a growing interest in institutional processes that can bring together fragmented water uses and water users into an integrated planning, allocation, and management framework. This has led to the rise of integrated river basin management for reconciling hydrologic and ecosystem complexity, uncoordinated development interventions, and sociopolitical and administrative fragmentation. Despite the orderliness and rationality conveyed by the approach, it is apparent that the diversity of values and interests (water, power asymmetries, and wealth stratification) combined with natural risk and variability defines a framework in which sociopolitical processes engage in a struggle for resources and a constant reordering of the water regime. Thus, the politics of governance are embedded in sociopolitical realities and lie at the heart of river basin development and management.

With mounting pressure on water, allocation takes center stage. The call for clear, secure, and transferable water rights has been made many times, but creating property rights to water that are just, equitable, and feasible (both technically and politically) and account for legal pluralism is never straightforward. That demands sophisticated knowledge of hydrological interactions among surface water, groundwater, and wastewater, with corresponding data management, and respect for prior customary rights to water. As the environment and the poor tend to be short-changed in existing water allocations, the definition of environmental flows and water entitlements for the poor is a good starting point for redesigning water allocation mechanisms.

The next section describes common and emerging problems affecting river basins, how societies have responded, and how users are increasingly interconnected through the hydrological cycle. It also addresses trends in management and governance in more detail.

The following section looks at how effective river basin management can address issues of further water resources development, allocation, conflict resolution, poverty alleviation, and environmental sustainability. It also stresses the limits of basin approaches and draws attention to the links between river basins and their wider economic and sociopolitical environments.

Mounting pressure on water

The growing abstraction of water by individual users and state-initiated projects has approached or even exceeded the threshold of renewable water resources in a number of river basins. Water shortages and conflicts have increased accordingly. This trend has been paralleled by a degradation of the quality of both surface water and groundwater through the combined effluents of cities, industries, and agricultural activities.

> The growing abstraction of water has approached or even exceeded the threshold of renewable water resources in a number of river basins

Basin closure and other water challenges

The roots of the resulting crisis lie beyond mere notions of dwindling per capita endowments, and its consequences have been coped with in various ways.

Committed and degraded water resources. As societies develop, water resources within a given basin become increasingly diverted, controlled, and used. Water flowing out of subbasins is often committed to other downstream uses, and outflow to the sea has several often overlooked functions: flushing out sediments (Yellow River in China), diluting polluted water (Chao Phraya River in Thailand), controlling salinity intrusion (many deltas), and sustaining estuarine and coastal ecosystems. When river discharges fall short of meeting such commitments during part of or all of the year, basins (or subbasins) are said to be closing or closed (figure 16.1).[1] In many cases (as in Europe and the Eastern United States) basin closure has been accompanied by severe pollution, as increasing effluent and declining flows have outstripped the dilution capacity of many rivers and led to wider ecosystem degradation.

Many closing basins are typically under stress for one to six months a year. The Yellow River (China) dried up for the first time in 1972, but in 1997 the dry-up lasted 226 days and reached 700 kilometers (km) upstream (Ren and Walker 1998). The Colorado (United States), the Indus (India and Pakistan), the Murray-Darling (Australia) and most rivers in the Middle-East and Central Asia are also severely overcommitted. Even basins in monsoon regions, such as the Chao Phraya River (Thailand) and the Cauvery River (India) experience months of closure, when salinity creeps inland or outflows are zeroed as a result of upstream diversions. River basins that terminate in lakes are not closed if they can replenish and sustain these wetlands, but many basins are situated in arid regions with large diversions and are also closed (for example, the Jordan River and Dead Sea, the Amu Darya and Syr Darya Rivers and Aral Sea, and the Tarim River and Lop Nor Lake).

Closure and scarcity can also occur in subbasins or small catchments, while the wider basin remains open. The Greater Ruaha Basin in Tanzania is a classic example of a subbasin under stress that contributes to a river (the Rufiji) that is fed by many other tributaries

figure **16.1** | **Closing and closed basins—rivers under stress**

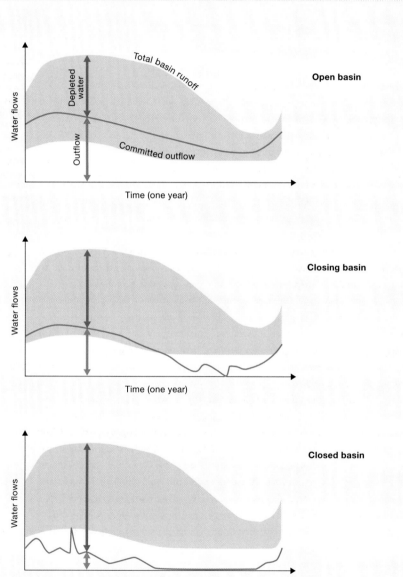

with still abundant flow. The Yamuna River at Delhi is dry part of the year, but the basin reopens further downstream. Likewise, the need to ensure water quality standards in the whole basin has led managers in the United Kingdom and France, for example, to define minimum flows at several nodal points of the river network to avoid local or tributary closure.

The definition of closure depends on the definition of the flow that is committed to flushing, diluting, and sustaining ecosystems. This definition is controversial but challenges the idea that any water in excess of human requirements is "lost," often expressed in declarations by engineers (or politicians) that not a single drop of water should be lost to the sea. The opposite position argues that all the river flow is necessary to sustain ecosystems, as they are intricately attuned to the natural flow regime. In many cases the flood regime is indeed part of ecosystem functioning and crucial for inland fisheries and can be considered as part of the fraction of water "used" (for example, the Rufiji floodplain, the inland Niger Delta, the lower Mekong, the Senegal Valley). Thus defining acceptable, if not optimal, environmental flows is a critical issue. One useful definition is "water that is purposefully left in or released into an aquatic ecosystem to maintain it in a condition that will support its direct and indirect use values" (Brown and King 2002, p. 1; see below and chapter 6 on ecosystems).

> The definition of closure depends on the definition of the flow that is committed to flushing, diluting, and sustaining ecosystems—a definition that challenges the idea that any water in excess of human requirements is "lost"

While problems and conflicts tend to increase with basin closure, challenges also arise in open basins. Flood damage, aquifer depletion, and pollution (for example, effluents from mines in southern Africa or diffuse agricultural pollution in Europe) occur widely and in all types of basins. These problems can be local or confined to one part of the basin without relevance for the entire river basin (Moench and others 2003). Situations of poverty due to lack of infrastructure (economic water scarcity) or exclusion (social or political water scarcity) are also common: villagers along the São Francisco River (Brazil), around Lake Victoria (Uganda), or in many parts of Africa suffer from deprivation although they live alongside plentiful waters.

Basin closure can be sketched schematically, as in figure 16.2,[2] which shows how over the years the development of facilities to abstract surface water and groundwater allows human water use to approach the total annual renewable water resources in the basin.[3] The fraction of water that can be stored or pumped under existing economic and technological constraints is generally under the total annual renewable resource when, for example, a large part of floods cannot be controlled and flows to the sea. But it may be higher in some cases when dams can capture all or most of the runoff and aquifers are overexploited. The Lerma-Chapala Basin (Mexico) is a telling example of a closed basin, with water depletion exceeding annual renewable water by 9% on average, even without including environmental flows, because of overabstraction of groundwater and excessive surface water withdrawals (Wester, Scott, and Burton 2005).

The apparent linearity and inexorability of basin closure give this process a "natural" gloss. Just as Malthusian thinking associates high population density with the specter of famines, many analysts associate declining per capita water endowments with environmental degradation, food insecurity, and wars (Starr 1991; Klare 2001). Such an approach overlooks both the political dimension of poverty and deprivation and the scope

figure **16.2** | **Development of water resources can lead to basin closure**

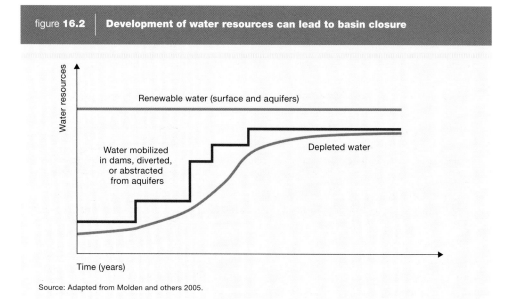

Source: Adapted from Molden and others 2005.

for change. Just as local adaptability and global innovations have helped food production catch up with needs through intensification, so societies may respond to water challenges in many ways.

Drivers of basin closure. Basin closure is by definition a human-induced process: a host of driving forces work to produce developed and often overbuilt basins. Overdevelopment of river basins is a common phenomenon that goes beyond the mere continuation of supply-oriented strategies accompanied by disregard for demand-management strategies and the environment. It includes the development of infrastructure with a potential demand for water that outstrips basin resources and ecosystem resilience. Unpacking the logic that drives the overbuilding of basins is essential because of its major impact on water management and allocation.

Development of river basins in the second half of the 20th century unfolded under the banner of integrated, or unified, river basin development, out of enthusiasm for large-scale undertakings as epitomized by the creation of the Tennessee Valley Authority (TVA) after the Great Depression. The vision of integrated development was confined mainly to constructing infrastructure that would serve multiple purposes, in general hydropower generation, flood control, navigation, irrigation, and urban water supply. Newly independent nations, with priorities of food security, rural poverty alleviation, regional unification, and nation building through iconic large-scale projects, embraced this vision. The modernist belief in the potential of technology transfer to trigger development in the developing world, the concept of development projects as strategic assets in the cold war (Ekbladh 2002; Barker and Molle 2004), strong financial interests from the development industry (Saha and Barrows 1981), and the specter of hunger in a world undergoing spectacular population growth contributed to fueling large investments in dams, flood protection, and irrigation infrastructure (see chapters 2 on trends and 9 on irrigation for more detail).

While these influences explain the initial emphasis on infrastructure development, they do not necessarily explain why it continued to the point of provoking basin closure. The first investments in a river basin are generally made in areas with a favorable combination of soils and water resources. Typically large alluvial plains and deltas are developed first, accentuating their natural advantage for crop production. But state investment at a national level is a highly politicized process. Regions with little irrigation infrastructure generally lag behind, exhibit higher rates of poverty, fuel migration to cities, and build up their claim to a share of investment, arguing that they have been discriminated against and that the river that traverses their land is also "theirs." This leads to further development plans in subregions with sometimes only marginal land and to tapping resources that are partly appropriated by downstream users. Equity, in terms of spreading benefits, is promoted at the cost of basic economic principles.

Several factors make this possible: the fuzziness of water rights, the supply-driven logic of development banks, the malleability of cost-benefit analyses, and the overriding political nature of decisions taken before feasibility studies start (McCully 1996; WCD 2000; box 16.1). The complexity of river basins as ecosystems has also made it difficult to identify externalities, so projects are allowed to go ahead because externalities are not fully factored into decisionmaking (WCD 2000). In some cases competition between regions, states, or countries within the same basin generates a race for water appropriation that results in uncoordinated investments and overdeveloped water-use infrastructures, as can be seen in the Cauvery and Krishna River Basins in India (Weber 2005).

Basin closure is accelerated and compounded by unchecked disposal of waste and contaminants into river systems that outstrips the dilution capacity of streams and renders water unfit for further use. Ignoring social, health, and environmental externalities enhances private gains and the competitiveness of firms, but it decreases water availability. Who can pollute and to what extent are questions of political economy and are therefore human-defined rather than the result of inexorable mounting pressure on resources.

> The complexity of river basins as ecosystems has made it difficult to identify externalities, so infrastructure projects are allowed to go ahead because externalities are not fully factored into decisionmaking

Coping with the water squeeze. As basin water resources are committed, challenges posed by water quality and scarcity arise. Societies respond to basin closure in many ways, at both the individual and community level and the state level. While the emphasis is often on the coping strategies of the state or technocratic elites (Turton and Ohlsson 1999), the multileveled responses of society are often overlooked. In particular, local adjustments by individual users or groups of individuals and by local managers and officials are insufficiently recognized. These uncoordinated adjustments frequently contradict measures taken at the macro level or even make them irrelevant.

A first category of responses consists of augmenting the supply from existing sources (foremost, increasing the quantity of controlled water), as well as tapping additional sources. Typically, this is done by constructing new dams or sinking more tubewells and by diverting water from neighboring basins, desalinizing seawater, artificially recharging groundwater, and seeding clouds. At the local level farmers may tap shallow or deep aqui-

| box **16.1** | **Overbuilding river basins: you've got your irrigation scheme, now what about my scheme?** |

Irrigation in the Chao Phraya River Basin in Thailand started with small valley floors in the upper watersheds but developed on a large scale only in the first half of the 20th century, with the progressive reclamation of the delta. In the 1950s the Chao Phraya Dam was constructed in Chai Nat Province to divert water through major distributors east and west of the river. In the 1960s and early 1970s two major dams were constructed on two of the four major tributaries (Ping and Nan Rivers), gradually allowing the development of dry season irrigation on half of the delta on average. The provinces located between these dams and the delta naturally claimed parts of the benefits of the water flowing at their feet and feasibility studies for the Phitsanulok project, conceived to irrigate 217,000 ha on the lower Nan River, started in the late 1970s.

The project was initiated in 1982 and funded by the World Bank. Because water was already committed to downstream uses in the dry season, most of the scheme was supposed to grow only one crop (securing existing rainfed crops) and cropping intensity was targeted at 121%. Since only a quarter of the project would be economically justified based on existing efficiencies, ad hoc hypotheses on expected "improvement of practices and facilities" were made. In the 1980s similar development took place on the lower Ping River, downstream of the second dam.

Currently, not only do these schemes in the middle basin claim an equitable share of dry season stocks but they sometimes receive more than the delta (proportionally to area). The combined abstraction of water by these projects and by pumping schemes established independently by the Department of Energy Development and Promotion amounted to 38% of dam releases during the dry season of 1998. In an internal report consultants to the World Bank admitted that the basin was "overbuilt." Other developments also took place in the upper part of the basin, although on a reduced scale. Finally, recurring water shortages and farmer unrest are used as a basis for justifying more supply augmentation projects, including diversions from the Salween and Mekong Basins.

Source: Molle and others 2001.

fers or invest in local storage facilities (such as farm ponds, which store excess irrigation flows or rainfall). They also develop conjunctive uses of water, using water from drains, rivers, and ponds and pumping water from irrigation canals when the water level is too low to allow for gravity inflow to their plot. At the macro level importing food is an indirect way to increase water supply into the country, a transaction often referred to as use of virtual water because the water comes embedded in the imported food (Allan 2003).

A second category of responses relates to conservation, or improving the efficiency of use of already controlled water resources without increasing supply. Line agencies or resource managers may implement structural measures, such as lining canals, controlling leakage in pipe systems, and treating wastewater for reuse. They may also resort to such nonstructural measures as improving dam or canal management (so that nonbeneficial releases are reduced) and establishing rotations or other arrangements for higher supply reliability. The state may also elicit water savings through policies (volumetric water pricing, quotas) or through innovations derived from research (plot-level water management, improved varieties and cultivation techniques).

Farmers and groups of farmers may actually conserve water at the local level as well. They may shift calendars or raise bunds around rice fields (to make better use of direct rainfall or canal water when available), adopt better cultivation techniques (such as mulching, deficit irrigation, the alternate wet-dry water regime in rice farming, shortening of furrows, and improved leveling), choose crop varieties with a shorter cycle, or invest in water-saving technologies, such as microirrigation. Improved management also requires managerial and institutional change, and often better infrastructure. Better collective management of scarcity also results from closer monitoring of flows, involvement of users, participatory planning, stricter rotations and scheduling, and definition of entitlements.

A third strategy consists of reallocating water from one user to another, either within the same sector (for example, within or between irrigation schemes) or across sectors. This reallocation may be justified by a concern for raising water productivity, but the objective may also be to enhance food security, redress inequities, or restore natural river flows. Reallocation can occur within the farm (when a farmer chooses to direct limited water resources to the crops that give a higher return per unit of water), between farmers (typical short-term transactions), or at the irrigation system level. Bribery, water theft, and tampering with hydraulic infrastructure are also ways to reallocate water and augment individual supply. At the basin level managers may reallocate water according to a given priority system. Within the agriculture sector water can be shifted from one area to another according to comparative advantages in water productivity (typically, areas with orchards or aquaculture).

> Water allocation issues brought by basin closure make politics, governance, and the distribution of power central issues

The rationale for intersectoral transfers is generally economic: cities are accorded priority to water for domestic uses and industries, where the economic return to 1 cubic meter of water is much higher than elsewhere and political power is concentrated. Agricultural uses can cope with a higher variability in supply and tend to receive the remaining water in the basin (this residual part also regularly happens to be the largest). Unfortunately, agriculture also often responds by further displacing nature. Reallocation is sometimes decided bureaucratically, but the definition of a new pattern of access to resources often stirs opposition and conflicts. This is why water allocation issues brought by basin closure make politics, governance, and the distribution of power central issues (see discussion of allocation issues later in this chapter).

Conservation and allocation responses are often pooled together as *demand management,* which can be typified as "doing better with what we have," as opposed to supply augmentation strategies (Winpenny 1994).

These three categories of responses to water scarcity can be further identified by level of actors—local and global or state level (figure 16.3)—as a way to stress that actors are not passive and respond individually and collectively to growing water scarcity, just as agrarian systems respond to changes in the relative scarcity of other production factors. This has been shown by case studies such as Zilberman and others (1992) for California, Loeve and others (2003) for China, and Molle (2004) for Thailand. State-driven responses are only a part of the transformation, although officials tend to see rural areas as static and malleable through public interventions (infrastructures or otherwise; Long and van der Ploeg 1989; Scott 1998). They overlook the constant endogenous adjustment of rural households and communities, as well as of line managers, to changing conditions. Because of such manifold adjustments and the gradual tapping of the water that remains available, water-short basins tend to have much less "slack" than is often supposed, and the potential for demand management is thus often overstated (Seckler 1996).

Typically, the first responses to water problems are capital-intensive solutions and augmentation of supply. When options for augmentation get scarcer or more costly, the emphasis is likely to shift to improved management and conservation. Once gains in efficiency have been realized, reallocation to higher value or other uses may appear necessary. These three responses do not always occur in this sequence, and when the fraction of water that is effectively consumed approaches the available supply, the three strategies are resorted to in tandem because none can solve the problem alone (Molle 2003).

figure 16.3 | **Three types of responses to water scarcity and the level of actors involved**

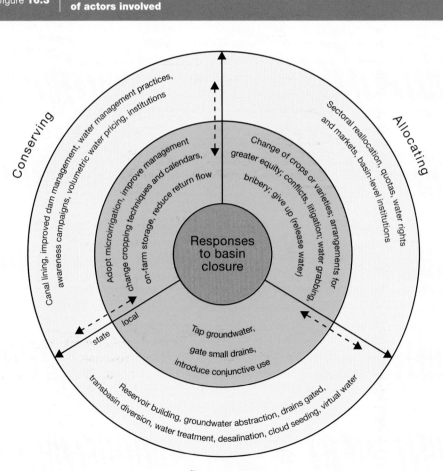

Source: Molle 2003.

Which responses are selected depends on the interests of the various stakeholders, the distribution of power and agency in the basin, and other factors, including the nature of state-citizenry relations (governance), and whether the agrarian transition has been smooth (defining the relative weight of rural interests). Responses are also often encouraged or forced by shock events (extreme floods, droughts, pollution), mediated by competing discourses, and shaped by dominant ideologies. Mass media and infrastructure-oriented government departments often call for supply-based solutions, while environmentalists and fiscal conservatives call for demand management. Science is often mobilized to legitimize particular agendas, but the quality of the science and the scientific basis of assumptions brought to bear are highly variable. The project nature of water resource development tends to involve consultancy rather than peer-reviewed scientific expertise, with attendant biases and conflicts of interest.

> Basin closure brings about increasing interdependence of users and ecosystems that are dependant on the hydrological cycle

Interconnectedness and complexity in river basins

Basin closure brings about increasing interdependence of users and ecosystems that are dependant on the hydrological cycle. The literature identifies four interlinked manifestations of this interconnectedness: spatial and hydrological interplay, sociopolitical dimensions, ecological interactions, and wider complexity derived from interactions with the outside world.

Hydrological interconnectedness within river basins. The typology of responses presented above misses a very crucial point in the functioning of river basins: the temporal and spatial interconnectedness across scales in both hydrologic and governance terms. While each of the strategies described as local can be associated with a clear objective, things get blurred when looking at the broader picture. For example, increasing supply locally through farm ponds, groundwater use, water harvesting, or small tanks may be tantamount to capturing water that would have been used downstream. Overall, there is little or no increase of controlled water but a mere spatial redistribution of the resource. Likewise, while transbasin diversions and even cloud-seeding can be considered supply augmentation from a narrow local point of view, they can be viewed as spatial redistribution (or reallocation) from a wider scale. Interventions by the state and adjustments by local actors are also interrelated. For example, subsidies for the adoption of microirrigation will foster local conservation by farmers, while farmers' development of groundwater use will elicit interventions or policies at the national level. (This is symbolized in figure 16.3 by the arrows that link the two layers.)

These examples show that the measures taken at the two levels schematized in figure 16.3—local and state—are not purely additive. Nor should they be treated as noise. Rather, the relationship between micro- and macro-processes lies at the heart of river basin management. Because the closure of river basins results in a growing interdependence of the users within the basin, many interactions must be clearly identified and analyzed, to avoid misconceived policies and faulty decisions. Thus it is important to analyze how rainfall is partitioned between green water (evaporated or stored in the soil) and blue water (flowing), how the paths of the different surface and underground flows are interrelated, and how any local intervention that modifies the quantity, quality, or timing of one of these flows affects the whole system. There are numerous examples of such interactions that need to be properly comprehended:

- *Win-win or win-lose?* Efficiency in water use is most commonly understood at the user or canal level. Return flows are generally called "losses," although they are often reused downstream. Thus reducing losses may merely reduce the water available to downstream users. Canal lining projects frequently reduce groundwater recharge, affecting those who use these sources. The lining of the Upper Ganga (India) and All-American Canals (United States), which were designed to achieve water savings and redistribute them to urban use, are good examples of "paper savings" (box 16.2), which amount to a mere reallocation of resources across space and categories of users. An individual user (or a system) who becomes more efficient may compound the overconsumption of water resources and deprive downstream users.

- *Microirrigation can make things worse.* Microirrigation technologies are invariably held as the conservation measure par excellence. However, such technologies often result in better control of irrigation doses and an increase in the amount of water depleted by crop transpiration (Burt, Howes, and Mutziger 2001). In countries where land is not the limiting factor, farmers will generally use the water saved through reduced application to increase their irrigated area (see Feuillette 2001 for Tunisia; García-Mollá 2000 for Spain; Moench and others 2003 for India). In both cases, local water depletion is increased, return flows available to downstream users are reduced, and expected water savings at the basin level do not occur. However, when water returning to the system is degraded in quality, is costly to abstract, or flows to a sink, conservation may be real.

- *Groundwater is not an additional renewable source of water.* Hydrological interconnectedness is often hard to comprehend: contamination is invisible, solid transport is cumulative, and groundwater flows are hidden. A widespread misconception is that aquifers are additional water waiting to be tapped. Although hydrogeological situations are varied and complex, water that infiltrates into the ground generally returns to the surface (through springs or as baseflow to rivers) or to the sea (Sophocleous 2002). Aquifers are large assets as underground reservoirs, providing a buffer during droughts, but the amount of water withdrawn from them generally corresponds to an equivalent reduction in the amount stocked or restituted to the river system. A typical case (for example, in India, Iran, or the United States) is that of rivers that normally receive a net positive inflow from adjacent aquifers and that—because of a dramatic drop in the water level of aquifers—end up recharging them instead. Notions of safe yields are fuzzy and often used to justify mismanagement (see chapter 10 on groundwater).

- *Forests and the "sponge myth."* The runoff collected by rivers is by and large the leftover from rain after evapotranspiration of cultivated crops, natural vegetation, and water bodies. Surface water resources are therefore linked to land use and management, and closing basins become more susceptible and vulnerable to changes in land cover. Common wisdom often links perceived declining river flows, as well as floods, to

> Well intentioned water conservation measures are frequently tantamount to reallocation or reappropriation of water—recognized or not, the transfers often amount to robbing Peter to pay Paul

---

box **16.2** | **Win-win or win-lose? The Imperial Valley deal**

The Los Angeles–San Diego urban area is a well known water-thirsty region that relies on interbasin transfers, particularly diversion from the Colorado River. Celebrated as a win-win agreement between the Southern California Metropolitan Water Authority (MWA) and the Imperial Irrigation District (IID), this 1998 agreement is a good example of a conservation intervention that amounts to reallocation.

Under the agreement MWA would fund the lining of the All-American Canal, which diverts water from the Colorado River to the district, in exchange for a usufructory right to an estimated 100 million cubic meters a year conserved through this intervention (CGER 1992). In fact, the so-called savings are detrimental to the recharge and quality of the aquifer that is tapped by Mexican farmers on the other side of the border in the Mexicali Valley (Cortez-Lara and García-Acevedo 2000). Of the total 100 million cubic meters a year to be saved, 30 million cubic meters a year are currently captured by the La Mesa drain (which has been excavated to control the level of the aquifer), while 70 million cubic meters a year recharge the aquifer. The aquifer and the La Mesa drain are tapped by individual and federal wells that irrigate a total of 19,800 ha. However, because the reduction of freshwater percolation will increase the salinity of groundwater, it is likely that negative impacts will eventually affect an area of 33,400 ha (Cortez-Lara 2004). The decrease in groundwater resources also renders the future supply of the growing urban areas more critical (Castro-Ruíz 2004).

Officially, the arrangement is said to be in accordance with the Colorado River Compact, which deals only with surface water allocation between the two countries, and therefore to conform to existing legal agreements. Focusing on the US side of the deal allows decisionmakers to picture the arrangement as a win-win situation, while ignoring surface water–groundwater interactions and overlooking the "lose" side of the agreement.

---

deforestation in upper catchments. Forests are believed to control flooding and to act as sponges, absorbing excess water and releasing it in the dry season. Despite contrary evidence in many regions, particularly in wet areas, and the critical negative impacts of species like pines, eucalyptus, and exotic tree plantations on water resources, the sponge myth drives large investments based on uncritical examination of local conditions (CLUFR 2005; Forsyth 1996). Trees do not produce water but consume it and therefore often diminish streamflows. Effects of land use on low flows, erosion, and floods are very complex and site specific (FAO and CIFOR 2005), so much caution is needed before blaming particular hydrological events or particular land use practices.

What these examples show is that well intentioned water conservation measures are frequently tantamount to reallocation or reappropriation of water. Recognized or not, desirable or not, compensated or not, the transfers often amount to robbing Peter to pay Paul (Molle and others 2004). Local efficiency concerns eventually translate into macro-level allocation and equity concerns. As basins close, the complexity of water paths increases and management becomes more arduous. Figure 16.4 illustrates the changes in water flows observed in the lower Jordan River Valley between 1950 and 2000 (Courcier, Venot, and Molle 2005).

Socioeconomic and political interdependency within river basins. As hydrologic interactions increasingly manifest themselves through competitive uses between upstream and downstream users, agriculturalists and urbanites, subsistence-oriented farmers and fishers

figure **16.4** | **Lower Jordan River Basin water balance**

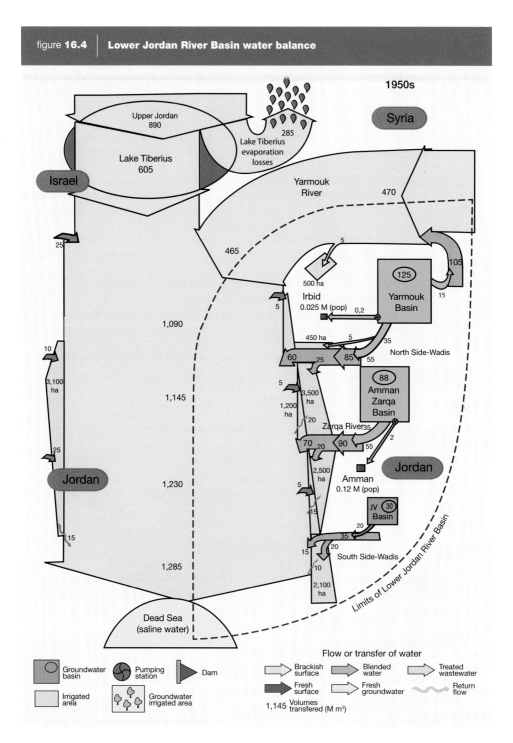

figure **16.4** | **Lower Jordan River Basin water balance** (continued)

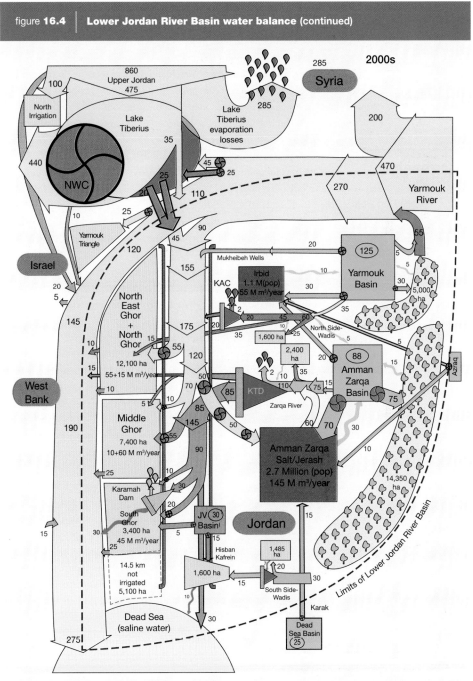

Source: Courcier, Venot, and Molle 2006.

and commercial enterprises, and off-stream and on-stream uses, so river basins become internally interdependent socially, economically, and politically.

Social and economic externalities of stressed river basins are accentuated by the fact that the categories of people who find themselves in competition often have varied priorities, objectives, and political power. Externalities occur when more powerful actors secure water at the expense of economically and politically marginal groups. For example, pine plantations in the upper Sand catchment in South Africa affect domestic water availability for high-density rural settlements, or Thai golf courses and orchards used and owned by well-off urbanites deplete water available to nearby rice farmers (Both ENDS and Gomukh 2005; Flatters and Horbulyk 1995). Industrialists generally have greater political clout and severely affect other uses, notably through pollution of waterways. Fishers are often displaced by water projects and are seldom compensated for the loss of their livelihoods (WCD 2000, chap. 3). Cities and industries generally get preferential allocation and adversely affect agriculture (though the reverse also occurs), and all three groups adversely affect the environment. Externalities are particularly salient in times of scarcity.

' How relations between basin users are managed is shaped by the sociopolitical and development context of the basin

Intergenerational externalities occur when the costs of current consumption are borne by future generations. Examples are the cumulative impact of progressive basin closure on riverine fisheries (such as in the Columbia River Basin), the contamination or exhaustion of aquifers, and the loss of wildlife diversity. Similarly, the past diversion of certain rivers to adjacent basins result in forgone benefits that are invariably glossed over but are already apparent in places like the Piracicaba Basin (diverted to São Paulo, Brazil; Braga 2000) or the Snowy River (diverted to the Murray-Darling) or that may surface in the mid-term in such places as the Mae Klong Basin (diversion to Bangkok) or the Karum Basin in Iran (diversion to Isfahan Province and beyond) or the long run in the Melamchi Basin (diversion to Katmandu; Bhattarai, Pant, and Molden 2002).

Water scarcity and resource capture (forcing other users to resort to more costly sources), emission of pollutants, or the displacement of flood damage to other areas by diking all generate externalities that travel across space and time and sociopolitical categories of stakeholders. They amount to a constant redistribution of costs and benefits along lines of power that eventually tend to determine who are the winners and losers among diverse stakeholders. Third-party impacts must be regulated, and the state usually has a critical role.

River basin problems also involve the interaction of—or even competition between—administrative bodies that often overlap at various levels (states or regions, districts, and subdistricts) and between sectors (various government ministries and agencies that deal with water issues, typically the ministries of water resources, agriculture, and environment) (Barrows 1998; Moss 2004). How relations between basin users are managed is shaped by the sociopolitical and development context of the basin. In a country such as Thailand the combination of political space for an active civil society and the long-standing experience of development-induced displacement from dams has meant that no single government-appointed river basin authority can achieve the legitimacy to represent all basin users. At the same time the bureaucratic and Bangkok-centric history of water management makes it difficult for the state to accept more open governance of water as an acceptable framework (Both ENDS and Gomukh 2005; Sneddon 2002). In Viet Nam, by contrast, the embryonic river basin organizations, to whose design not even provincial water authorities have made a significant contribution, are largely international agency–driven bodies established through a centralized state.

River basins as interconnected ecosystems. The third-party effects described earlier often focus on human use. Viewing a river basin as a continuum of nested ecosystems assists in understanding how changes in one part of a basin affect both water availability and environmental health in other parts of the basin. For example, the functions of seasonal and permanent wetlands are controlled by changes in flow regime as a result of impoundments and diversions elsewhere in the system. An ecosystem approach, defined by the Convention on Biological Diversity (CBD 2000) as a strategy for the integrated management of land, water, and living resources that promotes conservation and sustainable use in an equitable way, provides an analytical framework for examining tradeoffs between interventions in the hydrological cycle and ecological integrity and between nutritional values derived from alternative uses of water. Exclusive concern for increasing cereal production through water impoundment and extraction comes at the cost of neglecting impacts on fisheries, for example. In the Mekong River Basin fish typically provide 40%–80% of dietary animal protein, and this dependence is especially high among the rural poor (see chapter 6 on ecosystems).

> Viewing a river basin as a continuum of nested ecosystems assists in understanding how changes in one part of a basin affect both water availability and environmental health in other parts of the basin

Major ecological changes have been brought about by water resource development (see chapters 2 on trends and 6 on ecosystems). Dams, especially, have radically altered the flow of most large rivers. In some places these developments have undermined or destroyed elaborate human uses of ecosystems, at the cost of overall economic losses, declining food security, environmental degradation, and loss of ecosystem services (see the case of the Hadejia' Jama'a River in Nigeria, Barbier and Thompson 1998; or of the Kafue flats in Zambia, WWF 2003). It is also the case, however, that many flood-prone areas lie close to densely populated areas, so that flood control has allowed urbanization, and more intensive agriculture, and interseasonal regulation has allowed higher cropping intensities. The economic, environmental, and social record of these (often multipurpose) dams has been mixed and will not be addressed here in detail (see McCully 1996; WCD 2000; and chapters 2 and 6).

The systemic and complex nature of river basin ecosystems has often compounded the direct impact of dams, irrigation, and pumping schemes and led to a series of destructive effects that were not identified at the outset or have frequently been overlooked. These include the loss of springs (overdraft of aquifers in the Azraq Oasis in Jordan) or of wetland productivity, as the connectivity between river and floodplain is diminished through altered flood regimes (the impact of the Aswan Dam on the Nile Delta or of irrigated cotton development in New South Wales on the Macquarie Marshes). Many of the benefits associated with floods—fertility enhancement, replenishment of aquifers, support of wetlands, ecosystem sustainability, flood recession agriculture, and fecundity of fisheries—have been severely curtailed (WCD 2000).

Because most environmental assessments of large projects miss many of these ecosystemic impacts and fail to fully factor externalities into decisionmaking, projects whose overall costs may exceed their benefits are allowed to go ahead (WCD 2000). Each project tends to be accounted for without reference to its impacts on other projects—not to mention other river basin values—thereby ignoring the finite supply of water and often leading to multiple accounting of benefits at the basin level.

The value attributed to a pristine environment by urbanites and environmental nongovernmental organizations, when translated into political clout, has moderated overly developmentalist approaches. Environmentalists have increasingly influenced the definition of landscapes and water regimes. In Europe environmental concerns have been the major force behind the recent European Water Framework Directive (Kaika 2003). In a bid to combat the neglect of ecological impacts derived from land and water development, environmentalists have centered their efforts on several issues:

■ *Economic valuation.* Many environmentalists have developed methodologies for valuing ecosystem services both to make the hidden costs of interventions explicit and to influence cost-benefit analysis and feasibility studies in favor of environmental preservation (see chapter 6 on ecosystems). They also argue that higher water prices could encourage conservation (thus increasing river flows) and have developed the concept of payments for environmental services.

■ *Opposition to dams.* Many dam projects have been shelved because of heightened opposition from civil society, but many others in countries like China (Three Gorges Dam), Turkey, and Viet Nam or on upper reaches of international rivers, such as the Lancang-Mekong in China, are under construction.

■ *Dam removal.* Shifts in societal values and their internalization into politics and public choice have resulted in the removal of some smaller dams (for example, in the United States and on the Loire River in France) to restore fisheries and riverine ecosystems.

■ *Negotiated flow regimes.* Following a similar dynamic, negotiated flow regimes from some dams have partly restored wetlands and other ecological values, for example in the Senegal River Valley (Fraval and others 2002) and in Canada (Ryder 2005). Elsewhere, affected people have pressed for alteration of dam operating regimes from peak to baseload production on a seasonal basis (for example, along the Se San River in Cambodia; Hirsch and Wyatt 2004).

■ *Environmental flows.* The notion of environmental flow, defined as the flow regime required to ensure the maintenance of particular environmental functions in a river ecosystem, is an attempt to find a compromise between productive uses and some protection threshold. The scientific determination of these environmental flows is problematic (see chapter 6), and the values considered in practice are more often the outcome of negotiated tradeoffs than of scientific studies.

■ *National parks and reservation areas.* Such designations as in the Okavango Delta, at the end of one of Africa's undeveloped rivers, have allowed some areas to be preserved, although sometimes at the cost of the livelihoods of local residents (Swatuk 2005a).

> The notion of environmental flow—the flow regime needed to maintain environmental functions in a river ecosystem—is an attempt to find a compromise between productive uses and some protection threshold

The river basin and beyond. Although determining the physical boundaries of river basins appears straightforward, the complexity of both nature and societies places limitations on river basins as territories of governance. Surface waters are interconnected with aquifer systems that may span several basins. Deltas are geographic entities that often fuse several rivers and make watershed boundaries irrelevant. Surface waters are frequently diverted to cities or to irrigated areas that belong to other basins. But even these cases can generally be accommodated as extensions of the original concept of river basin without diminishing its usefulness and relevance.

More crucially perhaps, many other factors and processes originating in wider spheres have critical impacts on water use and management within the basin. Climate change, for example, may increase hydrologic variability and the frequency of extreme events. These seemingly extraneous factors are sometimes so crucial that the causes of some basin problems—and their solutions—may lie well outside the basin or even the water sector (Allan 2004).

> The causes of some basin problems—and their solutions—may lie well outside the basin or even the water sector

First, river basins are part of a national and transnational economy. Sectoral and market linkages have spatial implications for basin agricultural production and water use, while relative or shifting factor prices, taxation or subsidies, migration, the World Trade Organization or other free trade agreements, and the evolution of world markets sometimes have sweeping consequences. Economic incentives established by state policies may encourage or discourage certain water uses. For example, EU subsidies through the Common Agricultural Policy have prompted the development of cereal cultivation in Spain, contributing to the depletion of aquifers (Garrido 2002). The North American Free Trade Agreement led to intensive development of water-intensive export cash crops in northern Mexico, at the cost of severe aquifer depletion (Barker and others 2000).

Second, politics also have a direct bearing on water resource development in river basins. Territories conquered by Israel during wars with its neighbors allowed it to divert the full flow of the upper Jordan river to its own benefit. In other countries water infrastructure has sometimes been used as a geopolitical tool to control certain regions or as a buffer against guerillas. Impacts of political events are sometime unexpected and indirect. The influx of several hundred thousand Yemeni and Palestino-Jordanian citizens working in the Gulf to their home countries after the first Gulf War led to a dramatic increase in the number of wells and in groundwater abstraction, with a severe impact on aquifers (Mohieldeen 1999). Conversely, the Mekong River Basin is "underdeveloped" largely because the wars in the region have prevented realization of the TVA-like development plans drawn up after the second world war (Bakker 1999).

Third, shifts in ideologies, worldviews, or values also often have unexpected impacts. Food security or nationalism-driven self-sufficiency policies were achieved at the cost of sustainability, as in China where promotion of winter wheat resulted in the overdraft of aquifers. The growth of environmentalism in western countries has translated into the sanctuarization of pristine natural areas for tourism, to the detriment of local users, such as in the Okavango Delta (Swatuk 2005a). The emergence of environmentalism in developing countries has fueled successful opposition to dams, as occurred recently in China on the upper Salween River.

Some arid countries have established piped water systems that span large areas and tend to do away with the physical notion of a river basin (for example, Cyprus, Israel, Jordan, and Tunisia). Basins have been challenged as obsolete at a time when technology allows interbasin transfers that demand wider planning perspectives (Teclaff 1996). Several large-scale capital-intensive diversion projects have been initiated or are under discussion (the South-North project in China, Berkoff 2003; the interlinking of rivers in India; the diversion of the São Francisco in Brazil; the Red Sea–Dead Sea project in the Middle East), perhaps signaling growing recourse to such options.

> **Basin management is currently more about mediating conflicts and allocating water than about development**

Trends in the governance and management of river basins

The growing pressure on water resources and the increasing hydrological, social, and ecological interdependencies in closing river basins has led to widespread recognition of the need for holistic approaches to water management. There is a renewed emphasis on river basins as the most appropriate spatial unit for water management. The decision to manage water on the basis of river basins is a political choice, and river basins thus become a scale of governance in which tensions arise between effectiveness, participation, and legitimacy (Barham 2001; Schlager and Blomquist 2000; Wester and Warner 2002). Progress in establishing adaptive, multilevel, collaborative governance arrangements for river basin management has been weak, with undue emphasis on form (setting up river basin organizations) over process.

From river basin development to river basin management. The idea of using river basins as the unit for water development and management has evolved over the past 150 years. The first conceptualizations, born with the progress in natural sciences and tinged with utopianism and scientism, emerged in the late 19th century and gathered force in colonial undertakings (particularly in the Nile and Indus basins) and in the Western United States (Teclaff 1996; Molle 2006). The idea of constructing numerous dams on a river for multiple purposes (navigation, power, irrigation, flood control) took hold and led to the formulation of water development plans for the entire river basin.

These conceptions coalesced in the creation of the TVA in 1933, where the establishment of a river basin authority was seen as necessary for the unified planning and full development of water resources on a river basin scale in order to achieve regional development (Lilienthal 1944; White 1957). The strong appeal of the TVA model to engineers, planners, and diplomats (Ekbladh 2002), and the political constellation after World War II led to the global spread of river basin authorities, primarily to developing countries. While the TVA and its clones achieved little in terms of unified, bottom-up development (Newson 1997; Scudder 1989), they served as an enabling concept for building dams on a massive scale and sometimes for entrenching authority in the hands of large hydraulic bureaucracies. To date, most river basin organizations are manager/operators (Millington 2000).

River basin development started to lose momentum in industrialized countries in the early 1970s, with the growing recognition of associated social and environmental costs, but also with the decreasing availability of suitable dam sites. Priority shifted toward management of water quality and environmental sustainability. In the early 1990s these concerns were reflected in the Dublin Principles (ACC/ISGWR 1992) and the formulation of integrated water resources management approaches, and later formalized by the European Union in its Water Framework Directive (EU 2000) (box 16.3). Once again the river basin was sanctioned as the appropriate unit for managing water.

As river basin management becomes more holistic, it has to come to grips with a much more complex set of issues, such as population growth, urbanization, and the diversity of competing values, livelihoods, and economic interests, all depending on the same hydrological cycle. This means that river basin management is currently more about mediating conflicts and allocating water in contexts of skewed distribution of wealth and power, critical environmental changes, and increasing variability in water supplies due to climate change. This reorientation from development to management, however, is driven mostly by western countries that have already largely developed their river basins and is sometimes resented by countries that believe that their infrastructure is still insufficient (Thatte 2005).

| box **16.3** | **The challenges of integrated approaches to water management** |

Pervasive conflicts, environmental degradation, administrative bickering, and contradictory water policies have prompted the need for more integrated approaches to water management. The principles of integrated water resources management were internationally endorsed during the 1992 United Nations Conference on Environment and Development in Rio de Janeiro (Earth Summit), as formulated under point 18.8 of Agenda 21:

> Integrated water resources management is based on the perception of water as an integral part of the ecosystem, a natural resource, and a social and economic good, whose quantity and quality determine the nature of its utilization. To this end, water resources have to be protected, taking into account the functioning of aquatic ecosystems and the perennial nature of the resource, in order to satisfy and reconcile needs for water in human activities. In developing and using water resources, priority has to be given to the satisfaction of basic needs and the safeguarding of ecosystems. (UN 1992, p. 197)

As summarized by Millington (2000), integrated water resources management is about allocating water between competing uses, safeguarding aquatic ecosystems, and supplying clean drinking water to all people. It aims to reconcile economic efficiency, equity, and environmental preservation goals (including ecosystem services). This assumes that these values can be harmonized. Yet they are often mutually exclusive: the partial attainment of one has negative effects for the attainment of the others. Integrated water resources management offers a principled and normative vision of what water management should be (van der Zaag 2005), but few guidelines on how to get there (Biswas 2004) and even fewer successful examples in the real world (Biswas, Varis, and Tortajada 2005). That its objectives rarely add up in practice is frequently obfuscated, and mechanisms to balance economic, social, and environmental values are weak or not present.

The integrated water resources management literature tends to promote a technocratic vision of reforms. Experts are to supply the right institutions, establishing proper policies and legislation, creating adequate administrative and coordinating mechanisms, ensuring law enforcement and participatory decisionmaking, and so on. But reforms are essentially political processes (Mollinga and Bolding 2004; Swatuk 2005b), both in the sense of bureaucratic changes permeated by politics and in the wider sense of a continuous reshaping of the access to resources and the power structure.

While it has long been argued that management of land and water resources requires a basin perspective, examples of integrated river basin management are rare (Barrows 1998; WCD 2000). Several reasons are said to account for their rarity. First, political and administrative jurisdictions do not correspond to basin boundaries, making accommodation between different states or provinces difficult. River basin management is a classic example of the problem of fitting biophysical systems to political-administrative territories (Moss 2004). Second, river basin institutions set up to overcome this dilemma frequently create new boundary problems with existing line agencies and other policy fields that have a major impact on water use, such as urban development, land-use planning, transportation, energy, and forestry (Mitchell 1990; Millington 2000). Third, many local problems do not have to be addressed at the basin level (Moench and others 2003), and the articulation between different scales is often problematic, in both hydrologic and governance terms. Fourth, river basin management needs to be financed, whether out of user or polluter fees or through government subsidies, and this revenue is often precarious or uncertain (Abernethy 2005). Last, basin management may be undermined by several other factors, such as political infighting, lack of awareness or interest in problems, and insufficient hydrological data.

Although there may not be a central basin manager, this does not mean that river basins are not managed (Schlager and Blomquist 2000). This can be brought out by identify the roles of the various actors engaged in water management in a river basin, asking who does what, where, to what end, and how well. In any river basin essential functions are partly or wholly carried out, with their sum constituting basin governance (table 16.1).

table **16.1**	**Essential functions for river basin management**
Function	**Definition**
Plan	Formulation of medium- to long-term plans for managing and developing water resources in the basin.
Construct facilities	Activities executed for the design and construction of hydraulic infrastructure.
Maintain facilities	Activities executed to maintain the serviceability of the hydraulic infrastructure in the basin.
Allocate water	Mechanisms and criteria by which water is apportioned among different use sectors, including the environment.
Distribute water	Activities executed to ensure that allocated water reaches its point of use.
Monitor and enforce water quality	Activities executed to monitor water pollution and salinity levels and ensure that they remain at or below accepted standards.
Preparedness against water disasters	Flood and drought warning, prevention of floods, and development of emergency works, drought preparedness, and coping mechanisms.
Resolve conflicts	Provision of space or mechanisms for negotiation and litigation.
Protect ecosystems	Priorities and actions to protect ecosystems, including awareness campaigns.
Coordinate	Harmonization of policies and actions undertaken in the basin by state and nonstate actors relevant to land and water management.

Note: The functions listed here subsume supporting functions such as data collection and resource mobilization, which are not ends in themselves, but rather facilitate the higher level functions listed.

Source: Adapted from Svendsen, Wester, and Molle 2005.

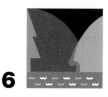

How well functions are carried out, from whose perspective, and for whose benefit are empirical questions. Since many organizations and stakeholders are involved with water management in a river basin, a number that generally grows with basin closure, more than one organization may be involved in performing individual functions. This points to the importance of finding ways to get the multitude of water management stakeholders to work together in a river basin.

Trends in institutional arrangements for river basin governance. Much attention has been given to the ideal organizational model for river basin management, while much less emphasis has been placed on the process of developing, managing, and maintaining collaborative relationships for river basin governance. More fundamentally, the essential function in river basin management—allocating water between competing uses and users, including the environment—has not received sufficient attention, although it is at the heart of integrated water resources management.

> The essential function in river basin management—allocating water between competing uses and users, including the environment—has not received sufficient attention

There are two main trends in basin governance. One trend concerns watersheds, or subbasins, of a limited size (typically from tens of square kilometers to 1,000 square kilometers), where local stakeholders and agencies attempt to solve their land- and water-related problems (box 16.4). A second trend concerns the management of wider river basins. This trend has three salient aspects (Svendsen and Wester 2005). First is the consensus that integrated water resources management should be carried out at the river basin level. This, together with the desire to realize the promise of integration, has placed river basin management on the agenda of governments and international funding agencies and has led to many new river basin initiatives (see box 16.4).

Second, the number of public and private sector actors involved in, or concerned with basin planning and management is increasing, from environmental agencies and civil society or interest groups to regulatory bodies and service providers for agricultural, municipal, and industrial water users. With rising standards of living, urbanization, and continuing environmental deterioration more diverse stakeholders and worldviews need to be integrated.

Third, organizations associated with basin planning and management have become more specialized and differentiated into regulators, resource managers, and service providers (Millington 2000). Regulation and standard-setting are carried out in the public interest and are necessarily functions of government, but other tasks may be fulfilled by commercial or hybrid public-private organizations.

In many people's minds river basin management requires a unitary basin management organization. River basin organizations have emerged as a consensual pillar of the integrated water resources management toolbox. However, they cover a wide gamut of organizations with quite varied roles and structures. At first sight this seems a source of confusion, but it also suggests that both the nature of the problems faced (for example, development or management) and the particular history and context of each basin reflect on each river basin organization. The following typology can be inferred from a broad-brush review of river basin organizations, keeping in mind that there are no clear-cut definitions and that there is a large variation in roles and power even within the same category (the generic terms may not correspond to particular bodies):

In developing countries watershed management has gained increasing importance since the 1970s as a response for arresting land degradation, securing downstream water-related services, and improving agriculture and natural resources management (Tiffen and others 1996; Joy and Paranjape 2004). In Australia and the United States growth of watershed management initiatives was linked to efforts to adopt more holistic and regionalized ecosystem approaches to resource assessment and management and to restore environmental quality in line with new values and uses, such as recreation and aesthetics (Omernik and Bailey 1997; Lane, McDonald, and Morrison 2004; Kenney 1997).

Watershed management is based on recognition of the watershed area as the spatial integrator and appropriate unit for managing land and water resources based on hydrological principles of upstream-downstream linkages. Thus, watershed management projects generally aim at establishing an enabling environment for such integrated management to accomplish resource conservation and biomass production objectives (Jensen 1996). A coordinated, multiobjective dynamic involving many sectors and stakeholders is implied, with an emphasis on community-level activities in governance and improved production and conservation technology.

The concept of watershed management has evolved over the past 40 years in response to implementation experiences and changing policies and development paradigms on land husbandry, good governance, and poverty alleviation. Generalizing, the projects of the 1970s and 1980s may be characterized as top-down watershed protection projects aimed at arresting land degradation and securing downstream water supply, using a soil and water conservation engineering approach driven by physical targets. The impact of most of these projects was small and limited to the project period. A lack of people's participation and a technical focus on conservation were broadly identified as major causes of failure (Doolette and Magrath 1990; Chenoweth, Ewing, and Bird 2002; Kerr, Pangare, and Pangare 2002).

A new generation of projects, generally referred to as participatory watershed management projects, emerged in the 1990s with a more complex mix of strategic concerns: poverty alleviation, local participation and ownership, collective action and institution building, production system and land husbandry, cost sharing, programmatic approaches with policy linkages, and sustainability (Farrington, Turton, and James 1999). These projects are generally considered likely to be more successful and are being further developed within the context of political and administrative decentralization, privatization, and the wider perspective of sustainable rural livelihoods to enhance equity, institutional sustainability, and replicability.

This evolution parallels that on river basins—the second trend in basin governance—and reflects an adaptation of the watershed management concept from a narrow focus on hydrological linkages to a wider recognition of the human element and interconnectedness of ecosystems. A major lesson, relevant to all scales (field, farm, village, watershed, and basin), is that conservation or environmental objectives can be achieved only in combination with an upstream-oriented development objective: conservation through use (Badenoch 2002). Watershed initiatives also signal a type of fragmentation of river basin management, and the links between these scattered initiatives and the larger basin remain a crucial question.

■ *Basin authorities* are autonomous executive organizations with extensive mandates for their river basin, undertaking most water-related development and management functions. They are regulator, resource manager, and service provider all in one. The TVA is the epitome of this type of organization and has been exported as a model to many countries, with large variations and mixed success. The Damodar Valley Corporation in India, the Mahaweli Authority in Sri Lanka, the Companhia de Desenvolvimento dos Vales de São Franciscoe do Parnaiba in Brazil, and the Confederaciones Hidrograficas in Spain are other examples. Authorities generally show poor responsiveness to local demands and are often undermined by bureaucratic conflict because they infringe on the competence of other government agencies and line ministries.

Some of these authorities received a basinwide, multifunctional mandate covering various domains but were not endowed with the legal, political, or administrative power to achieve them. They generally ended up focusing on construction works and dam management (mostly for hydropower or flood control). Examples include the Damodar Valley Corporation in India (Saha 1979), the River Basin Development Authorities in Nigeria (Adams 1985), and the China River Commissions (Millington 2000). Some authorities were designed to ensure regional infrastructure development (the early River Basin Commissions in Mexico), others endured as powerful manager/operators (Brantas basin in Indonesia, Tarim in China), while others shrank and were confined to one issue or degenerated into powerless parallel structures with narrow scope and erratic funding (A. Dourojeanni, personal communication).

- *Basin commissions or committees* focus on policy setting, basinwide planning, water allocation, and information management, with varying degrees of stakeholder participation. They are usually endowed with authority to manage water resources (allocating permits, defining taxation, negotiating water allocations, defining effluent standards) and sometimes to plan future developments, but are not involved in operation or construction. Examples include the Delaware Commission in the United States, the Murray-Darling Commission in Australia, the British water authorities, and the French agences de l'eau.

- *Coordinating councils* are deliberative decisionmaking bodies incorporating public and private stakeholders and integrating policymaking across different policy areas. They are not organizations in the strict sense, but rather bring together stakeholders from various agencies and water-use sectors. Their role is coordination, conflict resolution, and review of water resources allocation or management. Examples include the river basin councils in Mexico (Wester, Scott, and Burton 2005), the proposed catchment management agencies in South Africa (Waalewijn, Wester, and von Straaten 2005), the Zimbabwean catchment councils (Jaspers 2001), the river basin committees and users commissions in Brazil (Lemos and Oliveira 2004), and several river commissions in the United States.

- *International river commissions* may be set apart because coordination is achieved between countries rather than among stakeholders and because political dimensions are pervasive. They were frequently established as part of a treaty signed between riparian countries or to manage dams on shared rivers (for example, Senegal, Volta, or Zambezi Rivers) (Barrows 1998; see below). They mediate water conflicts through consultation and cooperation but may also manage common databases, and their work may lead to concrete agreements.

From a governance perspective institutional arrangements for river basin management may be distributed along two axes, one that distinguishes between state-driven and stake-

> Institutional arrangements for river basin management may be distributed along two axes, one that distinguishes between state-driven and stakeholder-driven functioning, and one that contrasts centralized and decentralized modes

holder-driven functioning, and one that contrasts centralized and decentralized modes (figure 16.5). This yields four models for basin governance: unicentric (state-driven, centralized), deconcentrated (state-driven, decentralized), coordination (stakeholder-driven, centralized) and polycentric (stakeholder-driven, decentralized). Under the unicentric model a basin authority or line ministry manages the river basin. In the polycentric model the actions of existing organizations, layers of government, and stakeholder initiatives are coordinated to cover an entire river basin or subbasin.

Integrated management at the basin level tends toward the unicentric model, as it implies a degree of centralization of data, water allocation decisions, and decisionmaking power in order to internalize third-party effects and to address interactions between users across the basin. This reinforces state control and may militate against the integration of the values and interests of all stakeholders. Decentralization, involvement, and participation of users and stakeholders, local community management of upper watersheds, and the principle of subsidiarity point toward polycentric governance. This poses a challenge for the definition and emergence of institutional arrangements that can ensure that water use is consistent with available resources and ecosystem integrity, upstream-downstream interactions are balanced, and asymmetries of power between stakeholders are recognized.

The polycentric model leads to a more responsive governance process and improves intersectoral linkages, as coordination is among stakeholders, agencies, and other jurisdictions responsible for a range of policy sectors. However, decisionmaking can be cumbersome, coordination costs may be high, and political changes in participating jurisdictions can upset agreements. Polycentric and multilevel governance seek to reconcile stakeholder

figure **16.5** | **Typology of river basin governance**

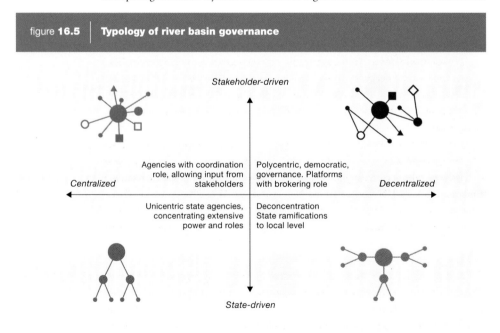

Stakeholder-driven

Centralized · Decentralized

| Agencies with coordination role, allowing input from stakeholders | Polycentric, democratic, governance. Platforms with brokering role |
| Unicentric state agencies, concentrating extensive power and roles | Deconcentration State ramifications to local level |

State-driven

values and objectives by ensuring that information becomes available to all stakeholders and that conflicting actions are flagged in advance and duly debated (Svendsen, Wester, and Molle 2005; Schlager and Blomquist 2000). This requires a culture of democratic debate and not too severe imbalances of power, and it becomes more difficult to achieve as the size of the basin increases.

River basin management without a unicentric manager is the prevailing mode of basin governance in the Netherlands and in the Western United States (Schlager and Blomquist 2000). In the United States formal bodies for managing river basins are rare, with policymaking authority distributed among a variety of federal and state agencies and departments. Coordination is achieved through multiple committees and working groups linking stakeholders into discussion and decisionmaking forums. Legislation and negotiated legally binding agreements are important instruments for establishing policy and practices, and the court system is routinely invoked to resolve disagreements and disputes. Thus, a more dispersed set of organizations can also manage a basin effectively if they are knit together with suitable processes, rules, and other institutions.

> Some 158
> international
> river basins
> lack any type
> of cooperative
> management
> framework

Challenges and trends in managing transboundary river basins. For international rivers as for river basins contained in one country, there is a growing need for collaboration and cooperation. More than 45% of Earth's land area lies within the world's 263 river basins that cross national boundaries. These international river basins are home to about 40% of the world's people and account for 60% of the flow in the world's rivers (Wolf 2002). During the twentieth century 145 treaties were signed concerning nonnavigational uses of international rivers (Wolf 1998), with most of the treaties between two countries, even in river basins shared by three or more countries. Very few of the treaties deal with water allocation, only one in five has enforcement mechanisms, and only one in two has any monitoring provisions (Wolf 1998). Classical examples of functioning institutional arrangements for transboundary river basins include the Danube, Elbe, and Rhine (pollution and navigation); the Colorado, Ganges, Indus, and Nile, (arrangements for water allocation); and the Mekong, Niger, Senegal, and Lake Chad Basin (agreements for joint management).

Despite these achievements 158 international river basins lack any type of cooperative management framework (Wolf 2002). In the absence of treaties states are still bound by the general rules of customary international law governing the use of shared freshwater resources. The 1997 UN Convention on Nonnavigational Uses of International Watercourses establishes two main principles: "equitable and reasonable use" and the obligation not to cause "significant harm" to neighbors. However, as of March 2003 only 12 countries were party to the Convention, far short of the 35 needed for it to enter into force (Giordano and Wolf 2003).

Reaching agreement on sharing the waters of an international basin proves difficult. Most treaties ignore issues of water allocation, and the treaties that do often allocate water in fixed amounts (Giordano and Wolf 2003). Riparian relations are embedded within more immediate, and often more influential, dimensions of historical political relations between neighboring countries. Sentiments of territorial sovereignty often override notions of territorial integrity in a shared basin, eliciting unilateral actions in the name of national development and poverty alleviation. When negotiations stall, it may help to introduce issues unrelated to water, such as trade, or issues related to another river basin, which helped Mozambique, South Africa, and Swaziland to successfully conclude a water-sharing agreement over the Incomati and Maputo Basins in 2002 (van der Zaag and Carmo Vaz 2003).

A recurring complaint in transboundary management is that the mandate of the basin organization is too limited to allow for effective joint management. It may be questioned, however, whether the scaling up of executive powers beyond the riparian states will increase effectiveness if the basin organization is seen primarily as a TVA-style facilitator for infrastructure construction rather than as a regulatory body for ensuring fair and sustainable allocation of water among different users (not just different riparian states). Because of their shaky record on transparency, accountability, and representation of multiple stakeholder interests, a further concentration of power in multilateral organizations may not be the way to go. More emphasis should be placed on negotiating water allocation treaties that ensure "equitable and reasonable use."

A striking omission in many transboundary basin agreements is in mechanisms of monitoring and enforcement. Monitoring through remote sensing may be a strong confidence builder. Data sharing, whether from remotely sensed sources or from hydrometric networks and national sources, is a basic condition of cooperation and transboundary water management. Without knowing and understanding the complexity of both the hydrology and the benefits derived from water, it is difficult to reach agreement over the equitable use of the water resources of an international river.

The emphasis on stakeholder participation exposes the lack of public involvement in interstate water agreements, which have often been concluded between a narrow group of actors and interests after behind the scenes negotiations. International river basin agencies such as the Mekong River Commission still have only minimal ties to civil society or involvement in the key dimensions of competition and conflict over water. The new river basin councils, platforms, and forums in which water user representatives discuss plans and allocation issues within a country provide the necessary deepening of superficial interstate agreements—and an important counterbalance. The Zambezi Basin is an example of a genuine, albeit costly, attempt to develop a basin strategy that actively involves stakeholder groups in all eight riparian countries.

Easing the pressure: response options for governing river basins

River basin management in the future will seek varying expressions within a spectrum bounded by two water paradigms: the water development approach and the ecosystem approach. The development approach focuses on harnessing nature and controlling water for human benefit through infrastructure development, while the ecosystem approach promotes restoring and maintaining the integrity of the water cycle and aquatic ecosystems. It is well established that political choices need to be made to initiate a transition toward more balanced practices, with more attention for ecosystems and for the tradeoffs in the

> River basin management in the future will seek varying expressions within a spectrum bounded by two water paradigms: the water development approach and the ecosystem approach

development and management of water resources. In closing river basins continuing the emphasis on supply-side approaches will only intensify the pressure on water. Doing better with what we have has profound implications for the choice of responses to basin closure end for the traditional engineering approach; for the allocation of scarce water resources, with a view to sustaining ecosystems and ensuring equity; for the emergence of patterns of governance that will ensure these goals; and for the need to manage water resources in a context of growing complexity and multiple worldviews. This section points to some ways forward and offers recommendations on these four issues.

Developing and conserving water resources

Developing more infrastructure to withdraw more water, as discussed earlier, is often an attractive option for decisionmakers and politicians, even if this is an expensive way to respond to water stress. In several countries, including many in Sub-Saharan Africa, increasing storage to improve water regulation over time and to expand productive uses is often seen as necessary. In closing river basins the cost of mobilizing additional water resources rises steeply because only marginal or distant resources remain available. With existing resource commitments already high, such mobilization also tends to have increasing environmental impacts.

> Subsidized projects increasingly create economic distortions and incentives for uses of water that do not reflect the real cost of providing water, let alone other social or environmental costs

Interbasin transfers are another way to reopen closed basins by bringing in large amounts of water. This can improve the balance between supply and demand in the receiving basin, but it usually implies large losses in terms of direct impact and long-term forgone opportunities for the donor basin, may foster lavish use of water in low-return activities, and may have substantial ecological impacts in the receiving and donor basins (Davies, Thoms, and Meador 1992). Such transfers pose specific problems that tend to be proportional to their scale but they are almost invariably designed in secrecy and imposed by strong political will rather than discussed publicly and openly.

To varying degrees, all impoundment or diversion projects, whether in open basins (avoid past mistakes) or in closed basins (deal with increased interconnectedness), face the same challenges. They must be based on a thorough understanding of their hydrological and ecological impacts and ramifications for water management and water entitlements, and choices must be informed by a review of alternatives (see the rights and risks approach developed by the World Commission on Dams, WCD 2000). Increased scrutiny and openness must be brought to bear on projects stemming primarily from hydraulic bureaucracies seeking to perpetuate themselves or states looking for national icons, politicians for votes, or private operators for financial benefits.

The costs of water resource development or interbasin transfers should be fully accounted for, and full compensations of losers should be ensured. Subsidized projects may have been justified in the past, but they increasingly create economic distortions and incentives for uses of water that do not reflect the real cost of providing water, let alone other social or environmental costs. The political logic of such projects should be countered through greater economic rigor and more stringent environmental impact assessments. These tools have so far achieved only moderate success, even in developed countries, and are of limited use if not accompanied by openness and public scrutiny.

However, the recent freezing of the Ebro River diversion in Spain shows that economic rationality and environmentalism, if backed by political clout, may counterbalance the arguments put forward to justify such projects (Embid 2003). Decisionmakers are urged to comprehend the mechanisms that generate overbuilt basins and the negative consequences of such processes.

The main alternative responses to water overexploitation in closed basins revolve around water demand management. While the scope for real water savings diminishes as basins close, this should not deter efforts to identify situations where real gains are possible and others where reallocations associated with conservation are desirable. City distribution networks often have losses as high as 40%. And even though these losses may return to the aquifer and be reused, this costly treated water should be conserved as much as possible. Outdoor domestic use and industrial use are also amenable to substantial water savings (Gleick 2000). Slack irrigation management may increase nonproductive losses (such as evaporation during lengthy land preparation periods in rice cultivation; see chapter 14 on rice), and the quality of drainage water may become degraded or even flow to sinks (for example, saline aquifer) and become unrecoverable. Some return flows through aquifers may also have long time lags and not be readily available. Reuse also often involves pumping, which increases overall costs. Each situation must therefore be analyzed individually, through a thorough quantitative description of water fluxes and paths.

> Water balances often consider only surface water. Water accounting, water quality assessment, ecosystem approaches, and similar exercises are needed for a more complete picture

Understanding hydrological and ecological interconnections requires more effort than is usually thought. Water balances often consider only surface water. Water accounting, water quality assessment, ecosystem approaches, and similar exercises are needed for a more complete picture. Because basin management increasingly resembles a zero-sum game as the basin closes, it is important to identify implicit spatial reappropriation caused by interventions, notably conservation efforts, especially the final impact on the environment. The use of wastewater in agriculture is also a way to increase beneficial use in the basin and is a promising path (see chapter 11 on marginal-quality water). In sum, demand management and conservation options are important responses in closing basins, but their pervasive third-party impacts at the basin level must be fully examined.

Water allocation: sharing costs and benefits

Water allocation, which is a scarcity-sharing mechanism, is the core issue in closing basins. Sharing the "water pie," however, is often wrongly equated with more concrete issues such as the division or distribution of (nearly) static assets like land. Water allocation is characterized by contingent levels of variability and uncertainty, both temporal and spatial. In the mid- to long term hydrologic regimes may vary because of changes in rainfall, temperature, land use, and runoff patterns; in the short term they reflect the variability of seasonal rainfall patterns. Climate variability tends to increase with aridity and with climate change. Allocation is also spatially distributed and has to be defined at several nested levels that are made interdependent by the nature of the hydrological cycle. Allocation arrangements must therefore be defined at several levels in the basin, principally between sectors and bulk users (but also within irrigation schemes), and must take temporal variability into account.

Three modes of allocation are commonly recognized (Dinar, Rosegrant, and Meinzen-Dick 1997). First, the state allocates water administratively according to rules that may, or may not, be very transparent or explicit. Allocation is sometimes volumetric, in general at the bulk level, and various (often fuzzy) mechanisms are used to reduce entitlements in times of shortage. Second, allocation can be ensured by a group of users among themselves. This case is more common in smaller systems (for example, a tank in India, a qanat in the Middle East), but users may also manage large schemes. Third, water may be allocated through markets of tradable rights, as in Australia or Chile. Underlying all three modes of water allocation are water rights, either de facto or usufruct rights, or more legally defined ownership rights.

> Water allocation mechanisms should not emerge from ideological inclination but from a sound understanding of each context and situation

These three modalities are not necessarily exclusive. Markets, for example, need strong state involvement for law enforcement or control of environmental externalities, while users may still have to share water allocated in bulk. Each has prerequisites, advantages, and drawbacks related to their impact on equity, economic efficiency, and environmental sustainability (Meinzen-Dick and Rosegrant 1977). It is often believed that markets, because they are assumed to be impersonal and neutral, provide an efficient way to allocate water to high-value uses while circumventing resource capture by powerful parties. However, skewed political or social power, lack of accountability and transparency, and a weak state with weak law enforcement capacity preclude fair markets just as much as they warp the outcomes of administrative or collective allocation. Societies with a capacity to keep such negative factors under reasonable control can more successfully allocate or manage water, whether through markets (Australia), public bodies (France), or people's associations (Taiwan). In sum, allocation mechanisms should not be based on ideological inclination but on a sound understanding of each context and situation.

Considering the confusion and conflicts commonly generated by water-sharing mechanisms, it is tempting to propose state definition of ownership rights to water as a way out. It is hoped that defining state-sanctioned water rights for all users, or all groups of users, will transform chaotic and confrontational situations into a clear-cut list of numbers defining—and matching—supply and demand. Many consultant reports, national water policies, or even water laws emphasize the need to formalize water rights but tend to overlook the prerequisites for such arrangements to be effective:

- Sound knowledge of the resource (in particular surface-groundwater interactions, return flows, water quantity and quality interactions) and of existing users.
- Means to control effective diversions and abstraction and to prevent increased water use.
- Technical capacity to share water volumetrically, and mechanisms to adjust these shares in deficit years.

Instead of trying to establish formal water rights at once, it may be preferable first to define seasonal entitlements based on existing usufruct rights, both within irrigation systems and between bulk users of the same basin. These entitlements can be flexible and negotiated with users' participation and may constitute a desirable first step toward defining more formal water rights that may be amenable to some form of trade or financial compensation in times of scarcity.

Currently, the main trend in the allocation of water is the transfer of water out of nature to agriculture and out of agriculture to urban uses (Meinzen-Dick and Rosegrant

1997; Molle and Berkoff 2005). The first transfer needs to be stalled or reverted, while the second is going to continue and its consequences must be addressed. The environment tends to be the ultimate loser. The definition of environmental flows is a starting point for negotiations and, when enforced, incorporates the environment into allocation. Average allocations often pose few problems in a normal year. But the rather incompressible needs of industries and cities are salient in times of droughts, when agriculture and nature are squeezed and appear to be the residual users in the system. Planning for such contingencies, rather than hiding the fact that some parties will be affected more than others, should include defining temporary compensation mechanisms.

> **River basin governance is about the emergence of the appropriate blend of government, civil society, and markets in decisionmaking and regulation**

A desirable water allocation mechanism for surface water has three tiers: a reserve for basic human needs and the environment (as in South Africa), a reserve for productive water for the poor, and a reserve for productive use, including water for urban areas and agriculture. After the first two tiers have been satisfied, proportional (or otherwise) allocation on an annual basis would determine the water available for other productive use. In any case, designing and enforcing allocation rules or priorities that are socially—and not just bureaucratically sanctioned—require that stakeholders be represented in forums with decisionmaking powers. More generally, the values of water for local stakeholders may vary and may not always be amenable to economic evaluation; they should be at the center of decisionmaking.

The basin governance challenge

River basin governance is about the emergence of the appropriate blend of government, civil society, and markets in decisionmaking and regulation. In addition to greater control, rigor, and openness for water resource planning and allocation, as just described, integrated river basin management demands adequate governance. This brings out two main challenges: ensuring that all stakeholders, including the environment, have a voice, and coordinating uses and policies within the basin.

Although frequently advocated as a key to achieving effective water management (Rogers and Hall 2003), stakeholder participation in river basin management is not straightforward, and including the poor and achieving substantive stakeholder representation have proven elusive in practice (Wester, Merrey, and de Lange 2003). Emphasizing participation in river basin management may draw attention away from the very real social and economic differences between people and the need for redistributing resources, entitlements, and opportunities. This is unlikely to happen without challenges, and decisionmakers committed to social equity need to devise mechanisms that strengthen the representation of marginal groups in river basin management and empower them.

Stakeholder platforms, whether river basin councils, catchment management agencies, or watershed councils, democratize river basin management by giving voice to multiple actors. However, much depends on the institutional arrangements from which these river basin management institutions emerge, as many roles, rights, and technologies and physical infrastructure for controlling water are already in place. Stakeholders have different levels and kinds of education, differ in access to resources and politics, hold different beliefs about how nature and society function, and often speak different languages

(Edmunds and Wollenberg 2001). If these differences are not taken into account when creating new rules, roles, and rights, the institutional outcome can easily privilege those who are literate and have access to the legal system and eventually institutionalize inequality and power differentials instead of giving voice to marginal groups (Wester and Warner 2002).

While the complexity of integrated management of sizable river basins invites centralization and technocracy, participation suggests subsidiarity (delegation of decisions and management to the lowest appropriate level) and small-scale operations, inviting people to think creatively about the issues with which their lives are intimately linked (Green and Warner 1999). However, subsidiarity may work against integrated management if local users take decisions that disregard spatial, ecological, and social interconnections across scales. Watershed management may be achieved by groups of people who are spatially connected, but links and coordination with other scales must be ensured. In large basins management would thus entail a layered system of representation and management, with local actions subjected to normative regulations and supervision (or direct support) of both technical and political bodies.

> Basins facing complex problems of conflicting societal values and pressure on resources will probably not be well managed by a single body

This review of basin governance patterns identified the various types of organizations and arrangements for basin management. A strong civil engineering body capable of planning, designing, and constructing infrastructure to tap available water is useful and effective when resources are plentiful and management is not a strong requirement. In later phases of basin closure, however, experience shows that large civil engineering organizations (and agricultural or other line agencies) are not well suited to dealing with the challenges of basin governance. They have limited experience in political negotiation or interacting with key stakeholders and lack the breadth of experience in dealing with complex, broad-based issues and multiple values. Further, they often tend to adopt stances based on vested interest in continuing infrastructure development, a position antagonistic to that of stakeholders with ecosystem concerns. Countries that have strong civil engineering organizations reluctant to cede any power will face intense negotiations and struggles before an acceptable form of river basin coordination emerges that is capable of undertaking the key tasks required. But wherever the scope for construction is reduced and societal values have changed, the trend is likely to follow that of countries such as Australia and the United States, where engineering bodies have contracted and evolved into environmental agencies.

Decisionmakers should not infer from the integrated water resources management message that river basin management needs a strong centralized organization. Basins facing complex problems of conflicting societal values and pressure on resources will probably not be well managed by a single body. Nested or polycentric patterns of basin governance, in which user and community organizations, layers of government, and stakeholder initiatives are coordinated at the basin level, perform better and can be especially effective in settings where participation and democratic practices are well established (see chapter 5 on policies and institutions). Moving toward sustainable river basin management requires much more emphasis on developing, managing, and maintaining collaborative relationships for river basin governance, building on existing organizations, customary practices, and administrative structures.

Concluding remarks

The focus on river basins and on river basin organizations must not distract decisionmakers from the evidence that many external events or changes in wider economic and political spheres can also have large impacts on basin water use. Changes in import and export tariffs, for example, may alter crop choices and the amount of water used. Importing food grown from water-demanding crops may amount to importing virtual water, but other factors such as food security and geopolitics also have a bearing on such choices. The impact of climate change on resource variability may exacerbate conflicts. Societal preferences change with time, leading to shifts in the balance of political power. Ecosystem dynamics are hard to comprehend, are often nonlinear, and require adaptive management. In other words, both basin-based arrangements and wider policies must remain flexible and capable of incorporating change.

Reflecting on the challenges facing basin governance, it is clear that where poverty is widespread, river basin management needs a strong developmental dimension. At a minimum, strategies for river basin management should detail mechanisms for addressing imbalances in access to water and establishing recognized and secure water entitlements for the poor. While much can be learned from institutional arrangements for river basin management in affluent countries, these arrangements do not operate in the same way in the conditions of low-income countries: dominance of smallholder agriculture, weak institutions, insufficient financial and human resources, marked social inequity, and extreme poverty. Water management can only partly address these issues, which must explicitly form the points of departure in the reform of institutional arrangements for river basin management in developing countries.

Reviewers

Chapter review editor: Paul Appasamy and Jean Boroto.
Chapter reviewers: Charles Abernethy, Luna Baharathi, Mohammed Bazza, Seleshi Bekele, Ger Bergkamp, Deborah Bossio, Cate Brown, David Coates, Declan Conway, Mark Giordano, Line J. Gordon, Molly Hellmuth, Chu Thai Hoanh, Ramaswamy R. Iyer, Eiman Karar, Bruce Lankford, Monirul Mirza, Marcus Moench, David Molden, James Nachbaur, Andreas Neef, Malcolm Newson, Lekan Oyebande, Krishna C. Prasad, Wim van der Hoek, Sergio Vargas, Jeroen Warner, Saskia Werners, Dennis Wichelns, Yunpeng Xue, and Margareet Zwarteveen.

Notes

1. This definition differs from the hydrologic definition of a closed basin, where rivers do not discharge into the ocean but to internal seas, lakes or other sinks.

2. Conceptualizations of basin trajectories have been developed by Keller, Keller, and Davids (1998), Keller (2000), Turton and Ohlsson (1999), Ohlsson and Turton (1999), and further by Molden and others (2005) and Molle (2003).

3. Total annual renewable water resources in the basin are defined as total runoff in the basin plus the safe yield of the aquifer, where the safe yield is the level of abstraction whose consequences, in average reduction in groundwater stocks and base flow, are considered acceptable.

References

Abernethy, C. 2005. "Financing River Basin Organizations." In M. Svendsen, ed., *Irrigation and River Basin Management: Options for Governance and Institutions.* Wallingford, UK: CABI Publishing.

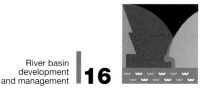

ACC/ISGWR (United Nations Administrative Coordination Council Inter-Secretariat Group on Water Resources). 1992. "The Dublin Statement and Report of the Conference." Prepared for the International Conference on Water and the Environment: Development Issues for the 21st Century, 26–31 January, Dublin.

Adams, W.M. 1985. "River Basin Planning in Nigeria." *Applied Geography* 5 (4): 297–308.

Allan, J.A. 2003. "Virtual Water—The Water, Food, and Trade Nexus: Useful Concept or Misleading Metaphor?" *Water International* 28 (1): 4–11.

———. 2004. "Beyond the Watershed: Avoiding the Dangers of Hydro-centricity and Informing Water Policy." Paper presented at the Israel-Palestine Center for Research and Information Conference on Middle East Water, October 10–14, Antalya, Turkey. [www.ipcri.org/watconf/papers/allan.pdf].

Badenoch, N. 2002. *Transboundary Environmental Governance: Principles and Practice in Mainland Southeast Asia.* Washington, D.C.: World Resources Institute.

Bakker, K. 1999. "The Politics of Hydropower: Developing the Mekong." *Political Geography* 18 (2). 209–32.

Barbier, E.B., and J.R. Thompson. 1998. "The Value of Water: Floodplain versus Large-Scale Irrigation Benefits in Northern Nigeria." *Ambio* 27 (6): 434–40.

Barham, E. 2001. "Ecological Boundaries as Community Boundaries: The Politics of Watersheds." *Society & Natural Resources* 14 (3): 181–91.

Barker, R., and F. Molle. 2004. *Evolution of Irrigation in South and Southeast Asia.* Comprehensive Assessment of Water Management in Agriculture Research Report 5. Colombo: International Water Management Institute. [www.iwmi. cgiar.org/assessment/files/pdf/publications/ResearchReports/CARR5.pdf]

Barker, R., C. Scott, C. de Fraiture, and U. Amarasinghe. 2000. "Global Water Shortages and the Challenge Facing Mexico." *Water Resources Development* 16 (4): 525–42.

Barrows, C.J. 1998. "River Basin Development Planning and Management: A Critical Review. *World Development* 26 (1): 171–86.

Berkoff, J. 2003. "China: The South-North Water Transfer Project—Is It Justified?" *Water Policy* 5 (1): 1–28.

Bhattarai, M., D. Pant, and D. Molden. 2002. "Socio-Economics and Hydrological Impacts of Intersectoral and Interbasin Water Transfer Decisions: Melamchi Water Transfer Project in Nepal." Asian Institute of Technology. Paper presented at "Asian Irrigation in Transition—Responding to the Challenges Ahead," 22–23 April, Bangkok.

Biswas, A.K. 2004. "Integrated Water Resources Management: A Reassessment." *Water International* 29 (2): 248–56.

Biswas, A.K., O. Varis, and C. Tortajada. 2005. *Integrated Water Resources Management in South and Southeast Asia.* New Delhi: Oxford University Press.

Both ENDS and Gomukh. 2005. *River Basin Management: A Negotiated Approach.* Amsterdam: Both ENDS. [www. bothends.org/strategic/RBM-Boek.pdf].

Braga, B.P.F. 2000. "The Management of Urban Water Conflicts in the Metropolitan Region of São Paulo." *Water International* 25 (2): 208–213.

Brown, C.A., and J.M. King. 2002. "Environmental Flows: Requirements and Assessment." In R. Hirji, P. Johnson, P. Maro, and T. Matiza Chiuta, eds., *Defining and Mainstreaming Environmental Sustainability in Water Resources Management in Southern Africa.* Maseru, Lesotho; Harare, Zimbabwe; Washington, D.C.: Southern African Development Community, World Conservation Union, Southern Africa Research and Documentation Centre, and World Bank.

Burt, C.M., D.J. Howes, and A. Mutziger, A. 2001. "Evaporation Estimates for Irrigated Agriculture in California." ITRC Paper P 01-002. Irrigation Training and Research Center, San Luis Obispo, Calif.

Castro-Ruíz, J.L. 2004. "El revestimiento del Canal Todo Americano y la oferta de agua urbana en el valle de Mexicali: escenarios futuros." In V. Sánchez Munguía, coord., *El revestimiento del Canal Todo Americano: la competicion o cooperacion por el agua en la frontera Mexico-Estados Unidos.* Mexico City: Playa y Valdez.

CBD (Convention on Biological Diversity). 2000. Conference of the Parties to the Convention on Biological Diversity, May 2000 [www.biodiv.org/programmes/cross-cutting/ecosystem/default.asp].

CGER (Commission on Geosciences, Environment, and Resources). 1992. "California's Imperial Valley: A 'Win-Win' Transfer?" In *Water Transfers in the West: Efficiency, Equity, and the Environment.* Washington, D.C.: National Academy Press.

Chenoweth, J., S. Ewing, and J. Bird. 2002. "Procedures for Ensuring Community Involvement in Multi-Jurisdictional River Basins: A Comparison of the Murray-Darling and Mekong River Basins." *Environmental Management* 29 (4): 497–509.

CLUFR (Center for Land Use and Forestry Research, University of Newcastle). 2005. *From the Mountain to the Tap: How Land Use and Water Management can Work for the Rural Poor.* London: UK Department for International Development.

Cortez-Lara, A.A. 2004. "El revestimiento del Canal Todo Americano y el Valle de Mexicali: ¿equilibrio estatico de mercado ó equilibrio de Nash?" In V. Sánchez Munguía, coord., *El revestimiento del Canal Todo Americano: la competicion o cooperacion por el agua en la frontera mexico-Estados Unidos.* Mexico City: Playa y Valdez.

Cortez-Lara, A.A., and M.R. García-Acevedo. 2000. "The Lining of the All-American Canal: The Forgotten Voices." *Natural Resources Journal* 40 (2): 261–79.

Courcier, R.; J-P Venot, and F. Molle. 2006. *Historical Transformations of the Lower Jordan River Basin: Changes in Water Use and Projections (1950–2025).* Comprehensive Assessment of Water Management in Agriculture Research Report 9. Colombo: International Water Management Institute. [www.iwmi.cgiar.org/assessment/hles/pdf/publications/ResearchReports/CARR9.pdf]

Davies, B., M. Thoms, and M. Meador. 1992. "An Assessment of the Ecological Impacts of Inter-Basin Water Transfers, and Their Threats to River Basin Integrity and Conservation." *Aquatic Conservation: Marine and Freshwater Ecosystems* 2 (4): 325–49.

Dinar, A., M.W. Rosegrant, and R. Meinzen-Dick. 1997. "Water Allocation Mechanisms: Principles and Examples." Policy Research Working Paper 1779. World Bank, Washington, D.C.

Doolette, J.B., and W.B. Magrath, eds. 1990. *Watershed Development in Asia: Strategies and Technologies.* World Bank Technical Paper 127. Washington, D.C.: World Bank.

Edmunds, D., and E. Wollenberg. 2001. "A Strategic Approach to Multistakeholder Negotiations." *Development and Change* 32 (2): 231–53.

Ekbladh, D. 2002. "'Mr. TVA': Grass-Root Development, David Lilienthal, and the Rise and Fall of the Tennessee Valley Authority as a Symbol for U.S. Overseas Development, 1933–1973." *Diplomatic History* 26 (3): 335–74.

Embid, A. 2003. "The Transfer from the Ebro Basin to the Mediterranean Basins as a Decision of the 2001 National Hydrological Plan: The Main Problems Posed." *Water Resources Development* 19 (3): 399–411.

EU (European Union). 2000. "Directive 2000/60/ec of the European Parliament and of the Council of 23 October 2000 Establishing a Framework for Community Action in the Field of Water Policy." *Official Journal of the European Communities* 43 (L327): 1–72. [europa.eu.int/eur-lex/pri/en/oj/dat/2000/l_327/l_32720001222en00010072.pdf].

FAO (Food and Agriculture Organization) and CIFOR (Center for International Forestry Research). 2005. *Forests and Floods: Drowning in Fiction or Thriving on Facts.* RAP Publication 2005/03. Bogor Barat, Indonesian, and Bangkok, Thailand.

Farrington, J., C. Turton, and A.J. James, eds. 1999. *Participatory Watershed Development: Challenges for the Twenty-First Century.* New Delhi : Oxford University Press.

Feuillette, S. 2001. "Vers une gestion de la demande sur une nappe en accès libre : exploration des interactions ressources usages par les systèmes multi-agents ; application à la nappe de Kairouan, Tunisie Centrale." Ph.D. thesis. Université Montpellier II, Montpellier, France.

Flatters, F., and T. Horbulyk. 1995. "Economic Perspectives on Water Conflicts in Thailand." *TDRI Quarterly* 10 (3): 3–10.

Forsyth, T. 1996. "Science, Myth, and Knowledge: Testing Himalayan Environmental Degradation Northern Thailand." *Geoforum* 27 (3): 375–92.

Fraval, P., J.-C. Bader, L.K. Mané, H. David-Benz, J.P. Lamagat, and O.D. Diagne. 2002. "The Quest for Integrated and Sustainable Water Management in the Senegal River Valley." Paper presented at the 5th Inter-Regional Conference on Environment and Water ENVIROWATER 2002, November 5–8, Ouagadougou, Burkina Faso.

García-Mollá, M. 2000. "Análisis de la influencia de los costes en el consumo de agua en la agricultura valenciana: Caracterización de las entidades asociativas para riego." Ph.D. thesis. Universidad Politecnica de Valencia, Department of Economics and Social Sciences, Valencia, Spain.

Garrido, A. 2002. "Transition to Full-Cost Pricing of Irrigation Water for Agriculture in OECD Countries." COM/ENV/EPOC/AGR/CA(2001)62/FINAL. Organisation for Economic Co-operation and Development, Paris.

Giordano, M.A., and A.T. Wolf. 2003. "Sharing Waters: Post-Rio International Water Management." *Natural Resources Forum* 27 (2): 163–71.

Gleick, P.H. 2000. "The Changing Water Paradigm: A Look at Twenty-First Century Water Resources Development." *Water International* 25 (1): 127–38

Green, C., and J.F. Warner. 1999. "Flood Management: Towards a New Paradigm." Paper presented at the 9th Stockholm Water Symposium, 9–12 August, Stockholm.

Hirsch, P., and A. Wyatt. 2004. "Negotiating Local Livelihoods: Scales of Conflict in the Se San River Basin." *Asia Pacific Viewpoint* 45 (1): 51–68.

Jaspers, F.G.W. 2001. "The New Water Legislation of Zimbabwe and South Africa— Comparison and Legal and Institutional Reform." *International Environmental Agreements: Politics, Law, and Economics* 1 (3): 305–25

Jensen, J.R. 1996. "Introduction to Danida Workshop on Watershed Development." In J.R. Jensen, S.L. Seth, T. Sawhney, and P. Kumar, eds., *Proceedings of Danida's International Workshop on Watershed Development.* WDCU Publication 1. New Delhi: Danida Watershed Development Coordination Unit.

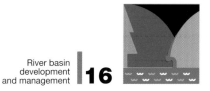

Joy, K.J., and S. Paranjape. 2004. "Watershed Development Review: Issues and Prospects." CISED Technical Report. Center for Interdisciplinary Studies in Environment and Development, Bangalore, India.

Kaika, M. 2003. "The Water Framework Directive: A New Directive for a Changing Social, Political, and Economic European Framework." *European Planning Studies* 11 (3): 299–316.

Keller, J. 2000. "Reengineering Irrigation to Meet Growing Freshwater Demands." Proceedings of the 4th Decennial Symposium of the American Society of Agricultural Engineers. American Society of Agricultural Engineers, St. Joseph, Mich.

Keller, J., A. Keller, and G. Davids. 1998. "River Basin Development Phases and Implications of Closure." *Journal of Applied Irrigation Science* 33 (2): 145–64.

Kenney, D.S. 1997. "Resource Management at the Watershed Level: An Assessment of the Changing Federal Role in the Emerging Era of Community-Based Watershed Management." University of Colorado School of Law, Natural Resources Law Center, Boulder, Colo.

Kerr, J., G. Pangare, and V.L. Pangare. 2002. "Watershed Development Projects in India: An Evaluation." Research Report 127. International Food Policy Research Institute, Washington, D.C.

Klare, M.T. 2001. "The New Geography of Conflict." *Foreign Affairs* 80 (4): 49–61.

Lane, M.B., G.T. McDonald, and T. Morrison. 2004. "Decentralisation and Environmental Management in Australia: A Comment on the Prescriptions of the Wentworth Group." *Australian Geographical Studies* 42 (1): 103–15.

Lemos, M.C., and J.L.F. Oliveira. 2004. "Can Water Reform Survive Politics? Institutional Change and River Basin Management in Ceará, Northeast Brazil." *World Development* 32 (12): 2121–37.

Lilienthal, D.E. 1944. *TVA: Democracy on the March.* New York and London: Harper and Brothers Publishers.

Loeve, R., L. Hong, B. Dong, G. Mao, C.D. Chen, D. Dawe, and R. Barker. 2003. "Long-Term Trends in Agricultural Water Productivity and Intersectoral Water Allocations in Zhanghe, Hubei, China, and in Kaifeng, Henan, China." Prepared for the Asian Regional Workshop "Sustainable Development of Water Resources and Management and Operation of Participatory Irrigation Organizations," 10–12 November, Taipei, Taiwan.

Long, N., and J.D. van der Ploeg. 1989. "Demythologizing Planned Intervention: An Actor Perspective." *Sociologia Ruralis* 29 (3/4): 226–49.

McCully, P. 1996. *Silenced Rivers: The Ecology and Politics of Large Dams.* London: Zed Books.

Meinzen-Dick, R.S., and M.W. Rosegrant. 1997. "Alternative Allocation Mechanisms for Intersectoral Water Management." In J. Richter, P. Wolff, H. Franzen, and F. Heim, eds., *Strategies for Intersectoral Water Management in Developing Countries—Challenges and Consequences for Agriculture.* Feldafing, Germany: Deutsche Stiftung für internationale Entwicklung, Zentralstelle für Ernährung und Landwirtschaft.

Millington, P. 2000. *River Basin Management: Its Role in Major Water Infrastructure Projects.* Thematic Review V.3. Cape Town: World Commission on Dams.

Mitchell, Bruce. 1990. "Integrated Water Management." In: Bruce Mitchell, ed., *Integrated Water Management: International Experiences and Perspectives.* London and New York: Belhaven Press.

Moench, M., A. Dixit, M. Janakarajan, S. Rathore, and S. Mudrakartha. 2003. *The Fluid Mosaic: Water Governance in the Context of Variability, Uncertainty, and Change.* Katmandu: Water Conservation Foundation.

Mohieldeen, Y. 1999. "Responses to Water Scarcity: Social Adaptive Capacity and the Role of Environmental Information; A Case Study from Ta'iz, Yemen." Occasional Paper 23. University of London, School of Oriental and African Studies, Water Issues Study Group, London.

Molden, D., R. Sakthivadivel, M. Samad, and M. Burton. 2005. "Phases of River Basin Development: The Need for Adaptive Institutions." In M. Svendsen, ed., *Irrigation and River Basin Management: Options for Governance and Institutions.* Wallingford, UK: CABI Publishing.

Molle, F. 2003. *Development Trajectories of River Basins: A Conceptual Framework.* Research Report 72. Colombo: International Water Management Institute. [www.iwmi.cgiar.org/pubs/pub072/Report72.pdf].

———. 2004. "Technical and Institutional Responses to Basin Closure in the Chao Phraya River Basin, Thailand." *Water International* 29 (1): 70–80.

———. 2006. *Planning and Managing Water Resources at the River Basin Level: Emergence and Evolution of a Concept.* Comprehensive Assessment of Water Management in Agriculture. Research Report 16. Colombo: International Water Management Institute.

Molle, F., and J. Berkoff. 2005. *Cities versus Agriculture: Revisiting Intersectoral Water Transfers, Potential Gains, and Conflicts.* Comprehensive Assessment Research Report 10. Colombo: International Water Management Institute.

Molle, F., C. Chompadist, T. Srijantr, and J. Keawkulaya. 2001. "Dry-Season Water Allocation and Management in the Chao Phraya Basin." Research Report 8. Institut de Recherche pour le Développement, Paris, and Kasetsart University, DORAS Centre, Bankok.

Molle, F., A. Mamanpoush, and M. Miranzadeh. 2004. *Robbing Yadullah's Water to Irrigate Saeid's Garden: Hydrology and Water Rights in a Village of Central Iran.* Research Report 80. Colombo: International Water Management Institute.

Mollinga, P.P., and A. Bolding. 2004. *The Politics of Irrigation Reform: Contested Policy Formulation and Implementation in Asia, Africa, and Latin America.* Aldershot, UK: Ashgate.

Moss, T. 2004. "The Governance of Land Use in River Basins: Prospects for Overcoming Problems of Institutional Interplay with the EU Water Framework Directive." *Land Use Policy* 21 (1): 85–94.

Narcy, J.B., and L. Mermet. 2003. "Nouvelles justifications pour une gestion spatiale de l'eau." *Natures, Sciences, Sociétés* 11 (2): 135–45.

Newson, M. 1997. *Land, Water, and Development: Sustainable Management of River Basin Systems.* 2nd ed. London: Routledge.

Ohlsson, L., and A.R. Turton. 1999. "The Turning of a Screw: Social Resource Scarcity as a Bottle-Neck in Adaptation to Water Scarcity." Occasional Paper 19. University of London, School of Oriental and African Studies, Water Issues Study Group, London.

Omernik, J.M., and R.G. Bailey. 1997. "Distinguishing between Watersheds and Ecoregions." *Journal of the American Water Resources Association* 33 (5): 935–49.

Ren, M., and H.J. Walker. 1998. "Environmental Consequences of Human Activity on the Yellow River and Its Delta, China." *Physical Geography* 19 (5): 421–32.

Rogers, P., and A.W. Hall. 2003. "Effective Water Governance." TEC Background Papers 7. Global Water Partnership, Stockholm.

Ryder, G. 2005. "Negotiating Riparian Recovery: Applying BC Hydro Water Use Planning Experience in the Transboundary Se San River Basin." Paper presented at the International Symposium on the Role of Water Sciences in Transboundary River Basin Management, Ubon Ratchathani, 10–12 March, Thailand.

Saha, S.K. 1979. "River Basin Planning in the Damodar Valley of India." *Geographical Review* 69 (3): 273–87.

Saha, S.K., and C.J. Barrows. 1981. "Introduction." In S.K. Saha and C.J. Barrow, eds., *River Basin Planning: Theory and Practice.* New York: John Wiley & Sons.

Schlager, E., and W. Blomquist. 2000. "Local Communities, Policy Prescriptions, and Watershed Management in Arizona, California, and Colorado." Paper presented at the Eighth Conference of the International Association for the Study of Common Property, 31 May–4 June, Bloomington, Indiana.

Scott, J.C. 1998. *Seeing Like a State: How Certain Schemes to Improve the Human Condition Have Failed.* Yale Agrarian Studies Series. New Haven, Conn.: Yale University Press.

Scudder, T. 1989. "The African Experience with River Basin Development." *Natural Resources Forum* 13 (2): 139–48.

Seckler, D. 1996. "The New Era of Water Resources Management: From 'Dry' to 'Wet' Water Savings." IIMI Research Report 1. International Irrigation Management Institute, Colombo, Sri Lanka.

Sneddon, C. 2002. "Water Conflicts and River Basins: The Contradictions of Comanagement and Scale in Northeast Thailand." *Society and Natural Resources* 15 (8): 725–41.

Sophocleous, M. 2002. "Interactions between Groundwater and Surface Water: The State of the Science." *Hydrogeology Journal* 10 (2): 52–67.

Starr, J.R. 1991. "Water Wars." *Foreign Policy* 82: 17–36.

Svendsen, M., and P. Wester. 2005. "Managing River Basins: Lessons from Experience." In M. Svendsen, ed., *Irrigation and River Basin Management: Options for Governance and Institutions.* Wallingford, UK: CABI Publishing.

Svendsen, M., P. Wester, and F. Molle. 2005. "Managing River Basins: An Institutional Perspective." In M. Svendsen, ed., *Irrigation and River Basin Management: Options for Governance and Institutions.* Wallingford, UK: CABI Publishing.

Swatuk, L.A. 2005a. "Whose Values Matter Most? Water and Resource Governance in the Okavango River Basin." Paper presented at the conference "Value of Water—Different Approaches in Transboundary Water Management," March 10–11, Koblenz, Germany.

———. 2005b. "Political Challenges to Implementing IWRM in Southern Africa." *Physics and Chemistry of the Earth* 30 (11–16): 872–80.

Teclaff, L.A. 1996. "Evolution of the River Basin Concept in National and International Water Law." *Natural Resources Journal* 36 (2): 359–91.

Thatte, C.D. 2005. "Sabarmati River Basin: Problems and Prospects for Integrated Water Resource Management." In A.K. Biswas, O. Varis, and C. Tortajada, eds., *Integrated Water Resources Management in South and Southeast Asia.* Delhi: Oxford University Press.

Tiffen, M., R. Purcell, F. Gichuki, C. Gachene, and J. Gatheru. 1996. "National Soil and Water Conservation Programme." SIDA Evaluation 96/25. Swedish International Development Cooperation Agency, Department for Natural Resources and the Environment, Stockholm.

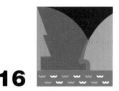

Turton, A.R., and L. Ohlsson. 1999. "Water Scarcity and Social Stability: Towards a Deeper Understanding of the Key Concepts Needed to Manage Water Scarcity in Developing Countries." Occasional Paper 17. University of London, School of Oriental and African Studies, Water Issues Study Group, London.

UN (United Nations). 1992. *Agenda 21.* United Nations Conference on Environment and Development, Rio de Janeiro, Brazil, 3–14 June 1992. [www.un.org/esa/sustdev/ documents/agenda21/english/Agenda21.pdf].

Van der Zaag, P. 2005. "Integrated Water Resources Management: Relevant Concept or Irrelevant Buzzword? A Capacity Building and Research Agenda for Southern Africa." *Physics and Chemistry of the Earth* 30 (11–16): 867–71.

Van der Zaag, P., and Á. Carmo Vaz. 2003. "Sharing the Incomati Waters: Cooperation and Competition in the Balance." *Water Policy* 5 (4): 349–68.

Vandergeest, P., and N.L. Peluso. 1995. "Territorialization and State Power in Thailand." *Theory and Society* 24 (3): 385–426.

Waalewijn, P., P. Wester, and K. van Straaten. 2005. "Transforming River Basin Management in South Africa: Lessons from the Lower Komati River." *Water International* 30 (2): 184–96.

WCD (World Commission on Dams). 2000. *Dams and Development: A New Framework for Decision-Making.* London: Earthscan.

Weber, E. 2005. "The Cauvery: A River of Power and Dispute." Paper presented at the 4th IWHA Conference on Water and Civilization, 1–4 December, Paris.

Wester, P., and J. Warner. 2002. "River Basin Management Reconsidered." In A. Turton and R. Henwood, eds., *Hydropolitics in the Developing World: A Southern African Perspective.* Pretoria: African Water Issues Research Unit.

Wester, P., D.J. Merrey, and M. de Lange. 2003. "Boundaries of Consent: Stakeholder Representation in River Basin Management in Mexico and South Africa." *World Development* 31 (5): 797–812.

Wester, P., C.A. Scott, and M. Burton. 2005. "River Basin Closure and Institutional Change in Mexico's Lerma-Chapala Basin." In M. Svendsen, ed., *Irrigation and River Basin Management: Options for Governance and Institutions.* Wallingford, UK: CABI Publishing.

White, G.F. 1957. "A Perspective of River Basin Development." *Law and Contemporary Problems* 22 (2): 156–87.

Winpenny, J. 1994. *Managing Water as an Economic Resource.* London: Routledge.

Wolf, A. 1998. "Conflict and Cooperation along International Waterways." *Water Policy* 1 (2): 251–65.

———. 2002. "Atlas of International Freshwater Agreements." United Nations Environment Programme, Nairobi. [www.transboundarywaters.orst.edu/publications/atlas/].

WWF (World Wildlife Fund). 2003. "Kafue Flats." Washington, D.C. [www.panda.org/about_wwf/what_we_do/freshwater/oursolutions/rivers/irbm/index.cfm]

Zilberman, D., A. Dinar, K. MacDougall, M. Khanna, C. Brown, and F. Castillo. 1992. "Individual and Institutional Responses to the Drought: The Case of California Agriculture." ERS Staff Paper. US Department of Agriculture, Washington, D.C.

About the coordinating lead authors, lead authors, and review editors

Safwat Abdel-Dayem

Emeritus Professor at the National Water Research Center of Egypt. Formerly World Bank Senior Drainage Advisor (1998–2005); Chairman of the Egyptian Drainage Authority (1997–98) and Director of the Drainage Research Institute, Egypt (1992–97); Honorary Vice President of the International Commission on Irrigation and Drainage; and member of the Governing Board of the Arab Water Council. Water resources management specialist, with a major interest in land drainage.

Paul Appasamy

Professor and Head of the Centre of Excellence in Environmental Economics, Madras School of Economics, India. Has been engaged in research in water and urban environmental studies in India since obtaining his PhD in urban and regional planning at the University of Michigan, United States, in 1983. His recent research has focused on the environmental aspects of water management, urban and rural water supply, and basin management.

Fatma Attia

Professor Emeritus, National Water Research Center of Egypt, and Director of the Water Boards Project. Was Deputy Chair of the National Water Research Center of Egypt; First Under-Secretary, Head of the Groundwater Sector, Ministry of Water Resources and Irrigation; and Director of the Research Institute for Groundwater of the National Water Research Center of the Egyptian Ministry of Public Works and Water Resources, among other positions. Her research focuses on the institutional development of systems and organizational structures to suit cultural and working conditions in Egypt and the management of water resources, with special emphasis on groundwater and wadi systems. Has a PhD in groundwater hydrology.

Akissa Bahri

Joined the International Water Management Institute in 2005 as Director for Africa. Has been working for the National Research Institute for Agricultural Engineering, Water, and Forestry of Tunisia, where she was in charge of research management in agricultural water use. An agronomy engineer with PhD degrees from universities in France and Sweden, she has been involved in policy and legislative issues regarding water reuse and land application of sewage sludge and is a member of different international scientific committees. Has also worked on agricultural uses of marginal-quality water and sewage sludge and their impacts on the environment.

Randolph Barker

Professor Emeritus, Cornell University. Served as head of the Economics Department, International Rice Research Institute, during 1966–78. Was a principal researcher at the International Water Management Institute during 1995–2004.

Christophe Béné

Senior Advisor on Small-Scale Fisheries and Development for the WorldFish Center. Has 15 years of experience in research and management of aquatic resources in developing countries. His work focuses on socioeconomic and policy issues related to the contribution of small-scale fisheries and aquaculture to the livelihoods of rural populations, with an emphasis on poverty reduction, governance, and rural development. Has recently been involved in several Food and Agriculture Organization of the United Nations expert consultations on poverty issues in small-scale fisheries.

Malcolm C.M. Beveridge

Discipline Director for Aquaculture and Genetic Improvement at the WorldFish Center. An aquatic ecologist by training, has worked extensively in the tropics, particularly on the environmental impacts of aquaculture. He left the University of Stirling, Scotland, in 2001 to become Director of the Fisheries Research Services Freshwater Fisheries Laboratory in Pitlochry, Scotland. Joined WorldFish in 2006 and is based in Cairo. Is also a visiting Research Fellow at Imperial College, London.

Prem S. Bindraban

Educated in theoretical production ecology, has worked on the interface between plant physiology and breeding using comprehensive systems approaches such as modeling. Has calculated world food production potentials and the associated requirement of land, water, and nutrients, including environmental implications. Is involved in projects on water for food and ecosystems. As an Associate Study Director made a substantial contribution to the strategic plan on the role of science and technology in harnessing agricultural productivity in Sub-Saharan Africa at the request of UN Secretary-General Kofi Annan.

About the coordinating lead
authors, lead authors, and
review editors

Jean Boroto

Consultant to government departments, development agencies, and research institutions. Previously served as the Water Expert for the Global Water Partnership, Southern Africa, and as Director of Project Planning at the Department of Water Affairs and Forestry in South Africa. A Democratic Republic of the Congo–born water engineer, has worked for 17 years in the management of water resources.

Deborah Bossio

Senior Researcher at the International Water Management Institute. A soil scientist with a broad background in soil fertility, sustainable agriculture, soil ecology, nutrient cycling, and soil carbon dynamics, with a particular interest in the environmental impacts of different land-use systems and the ecosystems services they provide. Has more than 10 years of professional experience working in East Africa, South America, and the United States, where she has done research on sustainable farming systems, indigenous soil fertility maintenance, trace gas fluxes, and carbon and nutrient cycling at various scales.

Bas Bouman

Senior Scientist at the International Rice Research Institute (IRRI), Los Banos, the Philippines, and Theme Leader, Crop Water Productivity (2004–006) of the Consultative Group on International Agricultural Research Challenge Program on Water and Food. His main field of work is water management in rice production systems, with an emphasis on the development of water-saving technologies to mitigate water scarcity. Before moving to IRRI, worked 2 years in Costa Rica on quantitative land-use analysis and 10 years at Plant Research International (and its predecessors) as an agroecologist developing remote sensing-based technologies for crop growth

Randall E. Brummett

Senior Scientist with the WorldFish Center in Africa. Has been working on sustainable aquatic resource management in developing countries for more than 30 years. His project portfolio includes commercial aquaculture, capture fisheries management, sport and aquarium fisheries, integrated farming systems, and conservation biology. His development and promotion of action and participatory research protocols has contributed to a new impact-oriented focus for the national research systems in many of the countries in which he has worked.

Jacob Burke

Senior Water Policy Officer at the Land and Water Division of the Food and Agriculture Organization of the United Nations (FAO). Before joining FAO Headquarters in Rome in 2000, was a technical adviser in groundwater at the United Nations Secretariat in New York. Has more than 25 years of groundwater management experience in the Africa, Asia, and the Middle East.

Gina E. Castillo

Policy Advisor at Oxfam Novib. With a PhD in anthropology, works on the right to a sustainable livelihood. Has done research on a variety of livelihood issues, including water. In her spare time, she practices urban agriculture on her balcony.

David Coates

Program Officer at the Secretariat of the Convention on Biological Diversity in Montreal, Canada. Is responsible for inland waters, the ecosystem approach, and mainstreaming of relevant issues into other program areas, particularly agriculture, and is the focal point for the Ramsar Convention. Previously worked on diverse environment and water management issues in Africa and South and Southeast Asia. His main interest is the contribution of aquatic biodiversity to sustainable development.

William Critchley

Head of the Natural Resource Management Section of the Centre for International Co-operation at Vrije University in Amsterdam. Began his working life in 1973 as a volunteer agriculturalist in Kenya, where he worked for 13 years under a series of projects and programs. With a PhD in soil and water conservation he travels globally supporting and evaluating projects, teaching and supervising students, and writing.

Rebecca D'Cruz

Executive Director of Aonyx Environmental, a natural resources management consultancy based in Kuching, Sarawak, Malaysia. Has extensive experience in wetlands conservation and wise use, ranging from policy development and strategic planning to site assessment, monitoring and management planning, training, and communications. Other posts include Co-Chair of the Wetlands Synthesis, and co-lead author of the chapter on inland waters for the Millennium Ecosystem Assessment.

Charlotte de Fraiture

Senior Researcher and Head of the Global Change and Environment group at the International Water Management Institute (IWMI), based in Colombo. Working for IWMI since 1996, has been involved in research projects related to watershed development, irrigation performance and irrigation management transfer. Over the past four years has been working primarily on modeling scenarios of global water and food supply and demand.

Pay Drechsel

Principal Scientist at the International Water Management Institute (IWMI), leading the research theme Agriculture, Water and Cities. Is based in IWMI's Africa Office in Ghana and has nearly 20 years of working experience as an environmental scientist, especially in urban and rural Sub-Saharan Africa. Is on the steering committee of Urban Harvest (Consultative Group on International Agricultural Research) and is a board member of the Resource Centres on Urban Agriculture and Food Security Foundation. Is involved in

About the coordinating lead
authors, lead authors, and
review editors

adapting and implementing the new World Health Organization guidelines for the safe use of wastewater, excreta, and graywater in agriculture.

Patrick Dugan

Deputy Director General of the WorldFish Center. Has more than 25 years of experience in research and management of aquatic ecosystems, working primarily in Africa, Asia, and Latin America.

Malin Falkenmark

Senior Scientific Adviser at the Stockholm International Water Institute. Her interests are interdisciplinary, with a focus on regional differences; linkages among land, water, and ecosystems; and the crucial role of the global water cycle as the bloodstream of the biosphere, deeply involved in human life support and in generating environmental side effects of human activities. Has been awarded the International Hydrology Prize, the Volvo Environment Prize, and the International Water Resources Association's 2005 Crystal Drop Award.

Jean-Marc Faurès

Senior Water Resources Management Officer at the Land and Water Division of the Food and Agriculture Organization of the United Nations. An agricultural engineer specializing in water resources management, he has spent most of his career working on issues related to improved productivity of water in agriculture, with an emphasis on the Mediterranean region. In close collaboration with national governments, works on the analysis and policy implications of agricultural water use and water demand management. Also participates in global perspective studies on the impact of irrigated agriculture on water scarcity and intersectoral competition for water.

C. Max Finlayson

A wetland ecologist with the International Water Management Institute, with research and management experience covering environmental protection, multiple land and water uses, and the provision of multiple ecosystem services in support of human well-being. Has participated in international assessments, including the Millennium Ecosystem Assessment, that have promoted the concept of ecosystem services and the interconnectedness of human well-being and ecological change. Has participated on the Scientific and Technical Panel of the Ramsar Convention on Wetlands and provided scientific support and advice to nongovernmental groups and community-based organizations.

Karen Franken

Water Resources Management Officer at the Land and Water Division of the Food and Agriculture Organization of the United Nations (FAO) and Coordinator of the AQUASTAT Programme, FAO's global information system on water and agriculture. Worked for 20 years as an irrigation engineer and water resources development and management officer in different countries and regions, more than 15 of them in Africa.

Kim Geheb

With a PhD from the University of Sussex, Brighton, United Kingdom, is currently Research Coordinator for the Mekong River Commission, based in Vientiane, Lao PDR. A natural resource management specialist, with most of his experience gained in East Africa and Southeast Asia. His main experience and interest have been the development of research-based management systems for fisheries, wildlife, water, and river basins.

Habiba Gitay

Researcher and a Senior Lecturer for 10 years at the Australian National University, where she remains a Visiting Fellow. Since 2002 has been an independent consultant providing technical advice and leading capacity development initiatives on adaptation and natural resource management. An ecologist who has worked in many ecosystems in many parts of the world, with an emphasis on the effect of disturbances such as fire, grazing, and climate change. Has been a coordinating lead author in various science policy assessments, including the Intergovernmental Panel on Climate Change and the Millennium Ecosystem Assessment.

Line J. Gordon

Assistant Professor at Stockholm Resilience Center, Stockholm University. Her research addresses interactions among freshwater, food, and ecosystem services, focusing primarily on how agricultural changes in water flows alter the resilience of agricultural landscapes and trigger regime shifts in ecosystems at various scales. Does fieldwork in the drylands of Sub-Saharan Africa and models global hydrological change. Is an associate member of the Resilience Alliance, a member of the Swedish National Committee for the International Geosphere-Biosphere Program, World Climate Research Program, and a subject editor of the journal *Ecology and Society.*

John Gowing

Reader in Agricultural Water Management at the School of Agriculture, Food, and Rural Development in Newcastle University, United Kingdom. His professional experience spans 30 years of work on land and water resources development in Africa, Asia, and the Middle East. Originally from an engineering background with an interest in design and management of irrigation and drainage systems. More recent work has pushed out the discipline boundaries to embrace all aspects of water management in agriculture.

Munir A. Hanjra

An international development economist with more than 15 years of experience in research and development in socioeconomic issues, land and water resources management, rural-agricultural development policy analysis, agricultural productivity growth, rural poverty alleviation, pro-poor intervention strategies, impact assessment of rural-agricultural development interventions, poverty mapping, environmental sustainability and equity analysis, and the economics of information technology, agribiotechnology, nanotechnology, and global climate change. Has lived and worked in Australia, Canada, Pakistan, and Sri Lanka

About the coordinating lead
authors, lead authors, and
review editors

and has project-related experience in Africa and Asia. He is currently affiliated with the International Centre of Water for Food Security, Charles Sturt University, Australia.

Richard Harwood

Professor and C.S. Mott Chair of Sustainable Agriculture Emeritus at Michigan State University, United States. A production systems agronomist and ecologist with 15 years of systems research and project management in tropical Asia and more than 20 years in the Midwestern United States. Recently completed nine years of service on the Technical Advisory Committee and Science Council of the Consultative Group on International Agricultural Research, where his specialty was integrated natural resources management in production systems. He serves on the Science Advisory Panel to the International Live-stock Research Institute and on the Board of Winrock International.

Nuhu Hatibu

Founding Regional Coordinator of the Soil and Water Management Research Network (SWMnet) for East and Central Africa. A professor at Sokoine University of Agriculture in Tanzania, where he founded and led the Soil and Water Management Research Group, which is credited with research and promotion of rainwater harvesting, making it a central water management strategy in Tanzania. Also at Sokoine University provided research leadership as Dean of one of the largest Faculties of Agriculture in East and Southern Africa. Has experience in project development and management, knowledge management, and strategy formulation. Since 1987 has planned and coordinated implementation of several action-oriented research-for-development projects. Has published a book, 12 book chapters, and more than 20 papers in international refereed journals.

Phil Hirsch

Associate Professor of Geography at the School of Geosciences, University of Sydney and Director of the Australian Mekong Resource Centre. Has more than 25 years of experience working on rural development and environment issues in Southeast Asia and has published widely. Has been engaged in a number of collaborative research projects on water governance in Cambodia, Thailand, and the wider Mekong Region.

Elizabeth Humphreys

Recently commenced as Theme Leader for Improving Crop Water Productivity in the Challenge Program on Water and Food, based at the International Rice Research Institute in the Philippines. Was a research scientist for 21 years with the Commonwealth Scientific and Industrial Research Organisation, Australia, undertaking field-based research to increase the land and water productivity of irrigated crops, especially rice-based systems in Australia and South Asia.

Maliha H. Hussein

Works as an independent development consultant leading diverse teams covering a wide range of development projects and sectors. An economist with a broad range of sectoral experience including agriculture, irrigation, forestry, water, microfinance, rural development, health, and education. Was a career diplomat with the Pakistan Foreign Service and worked with the Aga Khan Rural Support Programme in the high mountain areas of Pakistan. Has an MSc in agricultural economics from Michigan State University, United States, and a certificate in international law, economics, and politics from Oxford University, United Kingdom.

Eiman Karar

Director of Water Resources Management at the Water Research Commission of South Africa. Obtained her post-graduate qualifications in Sudan and has good experience in the region. Has more than 15 years of experience in water management in South Africa as well. As a registered professional natural scientist, has worked with the South African Water Affairs Department for five years as the National Director for Water Management Institutional Governance.

Eric Kemp-Benedict

Senior Scientist at the Stockholm Environment Institute. Has been involved with sustainability scenarios at the global level since 1997, when he began working with the Global Scenario Group. Has a PhD in physics and a degree in education. His current work focuses on scenario analysis as a tool for sustainability planning at scales ranging from local to global.

Jacob W. Kijne

Former Director of Research of the International Water Management institute (IWMI) and now a part-time consultant on water management issues. Based on his fieldwork for IWMI in Pakistan, has written on the link between irrigation system management and the prevalence of salinity. Was an editor of *Water Productivity in Agriculture: Limits and Opportunities for Improvement,* published jointly in 2006 by the Comprehensive Assessment of Water Management in Agriculture and CABI Publishing.

Jan Lundqvist

Professor in the Department of Water and Environmental Studies, Linköping University, Sweden, and has a part-time assignment at the Stockholm International Water Institute, where he chairs the Scientific Program Committee. Trained as a social scientist, he has been involved in interdisciplinary research and training activities for some 25 years. Has extensive experience in research and policy-related work in Africa, Asia, and the Middle East. His main current interest is in the dynamic interplay between consumption trends and implication for production orientation and what happens in this chain.

Bancy Mati

Regional Facilitator for the Improved Management of Agricultural Water in Eastern and Southern Africa program of the Soil Water Management Network (SWMNet), and Professor of Soil and Water Engineering at Jomo Kenyatta University of Agriculture and Technology, Kenya. Is a member of the Steering Committees of the Global Water Partnership and Nile–IWRM Net and serves on the Advisory Board of the International Rainwater

About the coordinating lead
authors, lead authors, and
review editors

Harvesting Alliance. Has been a part-time researcher with the International Water Management Institute. Is also a corporate member of the Institution of Engineers of Kenya and a former member of the Council of IEK.

Peter McCornick

Asia Director and Principal Researcher with the International Water Management Institute based in Sri Lanka. Is a water resources engineer with more than 27 years of experience in research, implementation, teaching, and capacity building in the water and agricultural sectors throughout Africa, Asia, the Middle East, and North America.

Ruth Meinzen-Dick

Senior Research Fellow at the International Food Policy Research Institute and Coordinator of the Consultative Group on International Agricultural Research Systemwide Program on Collective Action and Property Rights. Is a development sociologist who has done extensive interdisciplinary research and has published widely on water policy, land and water rights, local organizations, gender analysis, and the impact of agricultural research on poverty in Africa and Asia.

Douglas J. Merrey

Director for Research at the Southern African Food, Agriculture, and Natural Resources Policy Analysis Network. A social anthropologist by training, during 20 years at the International Water Management institute (IWMI) held increasingly senior positions including Deputy Director General (Programs). As Director for Africa established IWMI's well regarded African program. His research area is institutional arrangements and policies for water resources management, especially for irrigation. Has experience in numerous African and Asian countries.

Paramjit Singh Minhas

Assistant Director General, Irrigation Water Management, Indian Council of Agricultural Research, New Delhi. Has 28 years of research experience with a specialization in soil physics, irrigation water quality management, and reclamation of salt-affected lands. His scientific contributions have led to a better understanding of soil-water-plant interactions in saline environments and development of management strategies for the judicious use of marginal-quality water.

A.K. Misra

Senior Scientist, Livestock Production and Management, at the Central Research Institute for Dryland Agriculture, Hyderabad, India. His main areas of research are livestock development, farming system research, and natural resources management. Has a PhD in animal nutrition from the Indian Veterinary Research Institute, Izatnagar. Has been a consultant on livestock development and forage production to many national and international organizations such as the UK Department for International Development, World Bank, and the state government of Andhra Pradesh, India.

David Molden

Deputy Director General, Research, at the International Water Management Institute and Coordinator of the Comprehensive Assessment for Water Management in Agriculture. His passion for water issues was sparked while helping villagers organize to develop a drinking water well in Lesotho. With a PhD from Colorado State University, United States, and specialties in groundwater hydrology and irrigation, has since developed broader interests in integrating social and technical aspects of water management. Has lived and worked closely with local communities and governments in Botswana, Egypt, India, Lesotho, and Nepal.

François Molle

Senior Researcher at the Institut de Recherche pour le Développement, France, he holds a joint appointment with the International Water Management Institute. Has experience in Africa, Asia, and South America on irrigation and river basin management and now focuses his research on water policy and governance issues.

Peter P. Mollinga

Senior Researcher at the Centre for Development Studies (ZEF) in Bonn, Germany, and Convenor of the South Asia Consortium for Interdisciplinary Water Resources Studies, based in Hyderabad, India. Was Associate Professor at the Irrigation and Water Engineering group at Wageningen Agricultural University, the Netherlands. Has worked on irrigation management and reform and the politics of water. Is involved in land- and water-management research in Afghanistan, India, and Uzbekistan and previously in China. His academic interest lies in the integration of natural and social science perspectives through the interdisciplinary study of water resources.

Joke Muylwijk

Executive Director of the Gender and Water Alliance. An agrarian sociologist with a gender specialization. Has experience in broad areas of agriculture and environment. Lived and worked in East African and Asian countries for many years; was a lecturer in Wageningen Agricultural University, the Netherlands; and was an advisor on the social aspects of development cooperation for the Netherlands in India.

Regassa E. Namara

Research Scientist at the International Water Management Institute. Has a PhD from the University of Goettingen, Germany. His expertise includes agricultural economics, economics of agricultural water management, socioeconomics of rural development, and research and development impact evaluations.

Theib Y. Oweis

Director of Research Program, Water and Drought Management, at the International Center for Agricultural Research in the Dry Areas, Aleppo, Syria. As an irrigation engineer, has been involved with agriculture and irrigation since 1972, with experience managing water under scarcity especially in the dry areas of the world and with a special focus on Central and West

About the coordinating lead
authors, lead authors, and
review editors

Asia and North Africa. Has extensive experience in water harvesting, supplemental irrigation, agricultural water productivity, integrated water resources management, and education.

Don Peden

Researcher with the International Livestock Research Institute (ILRI) in Addis Ababa, Ethiopia. Currently leads ILRI's research on sustaining water productivity of livestock systems with a focus on Sub-Saharan Africa. Has a PhD in range management and systems ecology from Colorado State University, United States. Has conducted research on livestock, wildlife, agricultural water management, and agroforestry in Africa and Canada with the government of the Republic of Kenya, Canada's International Development Research Centre (IDRC), and ILRI. Has worked closely with the Comprehensive Assessment of Water Management in Agriculture and the Challenge Program on Water and Food.

Manzoor Qadir

Has a joint appointment with the International Water Management Institute and the International Center for Agricultural Research in the Dry Areas to work on multidisciplinary projects addressing assessment and management of marginal-quality water resources. Was Associate Professor at the University of Agriculture, Faisalabad, Pakistan, and Visiting Professor at the Justus Liebig University, Giessen, Germany. Is a fellow of the Alexander von Humboldt Foundation and serves on the editorial boards of *Agricultural Water Management* and the *Journal of Plant Nutrition and Soil Science.*

Liqa Raschid-Sally

An environmental engineer with the International Water Management Institute. Has worked extensively on wastewater management and reuse in developing countries. "It's funny how you don't think of the value of wastewater, till you see people actually using it and fighting over it," she says.

Helle Munk Ravnborg

Senior Researcher at the Danish Institute for International Studies. Was a Research Fellow at the International Center for Tropical Agriculture, Colombia. Has a PhD in environmental planning and social studies. Her current research focuses on access to water and water-related conflict and cooperation from a poverty perspective.

Johan Rockström

Associate Professor in Natural Resources Management and Executive Director of the Stockholm Environment Institute (SEI). Director of the Stockholm Resilience Centre, a joint research initiative by SEI, the Swedish Royal Academy of Sciences, and Stockholm University. Has more than 15 years of experience in integrated agricultural water management in developing countries, with more than 50 scientific publications in areas related to water, agriculture, and sustainability. Has extensive experience with on-farm participatory research on upgrading rainfed agriculture in developing countries and has pioneered the concepts of green and blue water management for sustainable livelihoods.

Claudia Sadoff

Lead Economist with the World Bank, currently on external service as an Economic Advisor on joint appointment to the International Water Management Institute and the World Conservation Union (IUCN). Areas of expertise are development and natural resource economics, with an emphasis on international waters and the dynamics of water, wealth, and poverty.

Lisa Schipper

Her research focuses on adaptation to climate change. Has worked in El Salvador and Ethiopia, examining the underlying causes of vulnerability to floods and droughts. Has a PhD in development studies from the University of East Anglia/Tyndall Centre for Climate Change Research, United Kingdom. Completed a post-doctoral fellowship at the International Water Management Institute in 2007, which focused on the Comprehensive Assessment of Water Management in Agriculture.

David Seckler

Emeritus Professor of Resource Economics at Colorado State University, United States, and Director of Winrock Water, a research and informational website in water resources. Former Director General of the International Water Management Institute. Has worked for the Ford Foundation in India and the US Agency for International Development in Indonesia. Has published 3 books and more than 50 papers and has 3 patents in irrigation technology and waste recycling.

Mahendra Shah

Senior Scientist and Coordinator of United Nations Relations at the International Institute for Applied Systems Analysis. Engaged in work on sustainable agricultural development and integrated social, environmental, climate change, and economic policy analysis; international negotiations; and Millennium Development Goals. Served as Executive Secretary to the Third Consultative Group on International Agricultural Research System Review, Senior Advisor to the Secretary General of the United Nations Conference on Environment and Development, Director of the UN Office of the Coordinator for Afghanistan, and Director of the UN Office for Emergency Operations in Africa. Has a PhD from the University of Cambridge, United Kingdom, and started his career at the University of Nairobi and the Kenya Ministry of Economic Planning.

Tushaar Shah

Principal Researcher at the International Water Management Institute. Former Director of the Institute of Rural Management at Anand, India. Trained as an economist and public policy specialist, over the past 20 years his main research interests have been in water institutions and policies in South Asia, particularly Bangladesh, India, Nepal, Pakistan, and Sri Lanka. Has conducted extensive studies on groundwater governance in this region and in the North China Plains. Has also explored groundwater management models in China, Mexico, and Spain to distill practical lessons for improving groundwater management in

About the coordinating lead
authors, lead authors, and
review editors

South Asia. Received the Outstanding Scientist award from the Consultative Group of
International Agricultural Research in 2002.

Laurence Smith

Senior Lecturer in the Centre for Environmental Policy at Imperial College London. As an
economist he specializes in natural resource management, rural development, agricultural
sector policy, and water resources. Has extensive experience in research and advisory work
in about a dozen developing countries, with particular expertise in South Asia.

Miguel Solanes

Has worked as a water lawyer with the United Nations Global Water Partnership and on
various advisory missions. Has published on water law and governance, interactions between law and economics, regulation of water utilities, structural elements in water services
sustainability, international investment law, and water and water-related services. Has law
degrees from universities in Argentina and the United States.

Pasquale Steduto

Chief of the Water Development and Management Unit in the Land and Water Division
of the Food and Agriculture Organization of the United Nations. Has been working for
more than 20 years on crop-water relations and ecophysiology, with an emphasis on agricultural water-use efficiency and water productivity. Has written many scientific publications and book chapters. Has a PhD in soil-plant-water relations from the University of
California, Davis, United States.

Veliyil Vasu Sugunan

Assistant Director General of the Indian Council of Agricultural Research, New Delhi. With
34 years of research and research management experience in inland aquatic ecosystems, is
noted for his contributions to reservoir ecosystems and fisheries. Served as the Theme Leader
of the Consultative Group on Agricultural Research Challenge Program on Water and Food,
Andre Mayer Fellow of the Food and Agriculture Organization of the United Nations, and the
Director of the Central Inland Fisheries Research Institute, Calcutta, India. He has written 6
books and 124 papers and has received many prestigious national and international awards.

Mark Svendsen

An independent consultant with more than 30 years of experience in irrigation and water
resource management. Has worked in 26 countries in Africa, Asia, and North and South
America and holds degrees in physics, water resource systems engineering, and soil and
water engineering.

Girma Tadesse

Research Officer in Environment and the International Livestock Research Institute in Addis Ababa, Ethiopia. Has a PhD in soil and water management and ample on the ground
experience with water, food, and livestock issues.

To Phuc Tuong

Division Head, Crop and Environmental Sciences Division, International Rice Research Institute. Is a soil and water engineer with a wide and varied research experiences in water management for agriculture, problem soil amelioration, and environmental management. Was a member of the Steering Committee of the Comprehensive Assessment of Water Management in Agriculture until December 2002 and Leader of Theme 1: Improving Crop Water Productivity of the Challenge Program on Water for Food during 2001–03. He is a member of the editorial boards of *Irrigation Science Journal* and *Paddy and Water Environment Journal*.

Hugh Turral

Theme Leader for Basin Water Management at the International Water Management Institute. As a water resources and irrigation engineer has worked on development projects for agriculture (9 years) and in research (16 years), with long-term experience in Australia, Asia, and Europe. Research interests cover technical, environmental, institutional, and economic aspects of water, agriculture, and development, including surface water and groundwater, modeling, and applications of remote sensing.

Domitille Vallée

During 2002–06 coordinated the Dialogue on Water, Food, and the Environment at the International Water Management Institute and was deeply involved in facilitating the assessment process of the Comprehensive Assessment of Water Management in Agriculture. Holds degrees in environmental technology, agronomy, and water and forestry management. Has focused on environmental impact assessment, monitoring and evaluation of pressures on the environment, and solutions for mitigating them in Africa, Europe (particularly the Mediterranean region), the Middle East, and South America.

Godert van Lynden

Senior Researcher in sustainable land management at World Soil Information in Wageningen, the Netherlands, where he focuses on Africa, Asia, and Europe. A physical geographer with expertise in soil degradation and soil conservation, he has worked as General Manager, Summit Nepal Trekking (tourism); as Assistant Professional Officer for the Food and Agriculture Organization of the United Nations (FAO), Soil and Water Conservation in Togo; Assistant Professional Officer at FAO; and Information Officer at Asia Soil Conservation Network in Indonesia.

Karen Villholth

A groundwater specialist with a background in physical, chemical, and numerical sciences and with broad knowledge and experience in groundwater research and management from professional work in Africa, America, Asia, and Europe. Her interests and recent assignments span from research on tsunami impacts on groundwater to large-scale interdisciplinary capacity-building programs on groundwater management in Asia.

About the coordinating lead
authors, lead authors, and
review editors

Linden Vincent

Professor of Irrigation and Water Engineering at Wageningen University, the Netherlands. Previous appointments include Research Fellow with the Irrigation Management Network at the Overseas Development Institute in London. Has a strong interest in interdisciplinary research in irrigation and water management and is currently involved in research programs studying the relationships between irrigation technology and institutions in water management, the evolution of irrigation design concepts and choices in different ecological and agrarian contexts, and water scarcity.

Suhas Wani

Regional Theme Coordinator for the GT-Agroecosystems theme in Asia in the International Crops Research Institute for the Semi-Arid Tropics, Patancheru, India, with expertise in the area of integrated watershed management, carbon sequestration, and soil biology in the semiarid tropics. Has 30 years of experience and has published more than 200 articles in national and international journals.

Robert Wasson

Deputy Vice Chancellor for Research at Charles Darwin University, Northern Territory, Austrailia. As a geomorphologist he has specialized in analysis of the impact of land use on soils and river catchment processes in Australia, India, Indonesia, New Zealand, Pakistan, and Timor-Leste. Has also contributed to the development of transdisciplinary research methods.

Robin L. Welcomme

Senior Research Advisor in Imperial College, London, where he works on inland fisheries management, river fisheries, and inland water biodiversity. With a PhD from Makerere College, University of East Africa, he began his scientific career in 1963 working on Lake Victoria and later in Benin. In 1971 he joined the Food and Agriculture Organization of the United Nations as a Fishery Resources Officer and later became Chief of Inland Fishery Resources and Aquaculture Service.

Phillipus Wester

Assistant Professor of Water Reforms at the Irrigation and Water Engineering Group, Wageningen University, the Netherlands. Trained as an interdisciplinary water management researcher, he has studied water governance processes in Bangladesh, Mexico, the Netherlands, Pakistan, and Senegal. His current research focuses on river basin governance and environmental and institutional change processes.

Dennis Wichlens

Professor of Economics at Hanover College, in Indiana, United States, and Joint Editor-in-Chief of the international journal *Agricultural Water Management.* Has studied the economics of agriculture, irrigation, and drainage for many years. Also works on poverty, food security, and international development.

Institutional affiliations of authors and reviewers and cross-cutting theme reviewers

Institutional affiliations

Authors and reviewers participating in the Comprehensive Assessment of Water Management in Agriculture are affiliated with numerous organizations worldwide. These organizations have contributed to the assessment through their support of their staff. This involvement does not necessarily mean an endorsement of the results of the assessment.

Africa Rice Centre (WARDA); Ankara University Faculty of Agriculture; Aonyx Environmental; ARD Inc; Argentina University; Arid Land Agricultural Research Center; Asian Institute of Technology, Bankok; Australia Centre for International Agricultural Research; Brazilian Agricultural Research Corporation (EMBRAPA); British Geological Survey; Central American Freshwater Action Network; Central Soil Salinity Research Institute; Central University of Technology, Free State; Centre de Cooperation Internationale en Recherche Agronomique pour le Developpement; Centre for Development and Environment (Switzerland); Centre for Development Research, University of Bonn (ZEF); Centre for Development Studies (India); Centre for Environment, Agriculture and Development (South Africa); Centre for Policy Research, (India); Centre for Tropical Veterinary Medicine, University of Edinburgh; Centre for Water and Climate, Alterra; Centro Internacional de la Papa, Lima; Charles Darwin University; China National Rice Research Institute; Chinese Academy of Sciences; Chinese National Committee on Irrigation and Drainage; Columbia University; Commonwealth Scientific and Industrial Research Organization; Compagnie d'Aménagement des Coteaux de Gascogne; Consultative Group on International Agricultural Research (CGIAR) Challenge Program on Water and Food; Cornell University; Cranfield University; Danish Institute for International Studies; Deakin University; Ecoagriculture Partners; Environment and Natural Resource Management; Environment Canada.

Environment Liaison Centre International; Federal Ministry of Environment, Nigeria; Fisheries Department, Kenya; Food Agriculture and Natural Resource Policy Analysis Network; Food and Agriculture Organization of the United Nations (FAO); Foundation for Australian Agricultural Women; FutureWater; Gender and Water Alliance; German Technical Cooperation Agency (GTZ); Global Water Partnership (GWP); Global Water Policy Project; Gomukh Trust; Griffith University; Hanover College; Imperial College, London; Inland Water Resources and Aquaculture Service; Institut de Recherche pour le Développement (IRD); Institut National Agronomique de Tunisie; Institute of Environment Policy and Rural Development; Institute Hassan II; Institute for Social and Environmental Transition; Institute for Water and Watersheds; Institutional and Social Innovations in the Management of Mediterranean Irrigation (MEDA-ISIIMM); Instituto Mexicano de Tecnología del Agua; Instituto Nacional Reforma y Desarrollo Agrario; Integrated Coastal Zone Management; International Association for Ecology; International Atomic Energy Agency (IAEA); International Center for Agricultural Research in the Dry Areas (ICRISAT); International Center for Biosaline Agriculture; International Center for Soil Fertility and Agricultural Development; International Center for Tropical Agriculture (CIAT); International Commission on Irrigation and Drainage (ICID); International Development Enterprises (IDE); International Development Research Centre (IDRC); International Food Policy Research Institute (IFPRI); International Fund for Agricultural Development (IFAD); International Institute for Applied Systems Analysis (IIASA); International Livestock Research Institute (ILRI); International Maize and Wheat Improvement Center (CIMMYT); International Plant Genetic Resources Institute (IPGRI); International Rice Research Institute (IRRI); International Secretariat of the Dialogue on Water and Climate (DWC); International Water Management Institute (IWMI); Iowa State University; ISRIC World Soil Information;

Jawaharlal Nehru University; Jomo Kenyatta University of Agriculture and Technology; Kent University; Khon Kaen University; King's College, London; Kinki University; Lanka Jalani, Sri Lanka National Water Partnership; Latin American Council of Peace Research; Linköping University; Livestock Production and Management at the Central Research Institute for Dryland Agriculture, Iran; Madras School of Economics; Mediterranean Agronomic Institute of Bari; Mekelle University; Mekong River Commission (MRC); Melkassa Agricultural Research Center; Michigan State University; Ministry of Public Works, Chile; Ministry of the Environment and Spatial Planning, Slovenia; National Agricultural University of Ukraine; National Association of Professional Environmentalists, Uganda; National Center for Atmospheric Research, Colorado; National University of Mexico; National Water Research Center, South Africa; Natural Heritage Institute, California; Oxfam Novib; Polytechnic University of Madrid; Raasta Development Consultants; Research Centre for Agricultural and Forest Environment, Polish Academy of Sciences; Royal Institute of Technology, Stockholm; School of Development Studies, University of East Anglia.

Secretariat of the Convention on Biological Diversity; Smallholder Flood Plains Development Programme, Malawi; Soil and Water Management Research Network (SWMNet); Sokoine University of Agriculture; Southern Waters; Stockholm Environment Institute (SEI); Stockholm International Water Institute (SIWI); Stockholm University; Sultan Qaboos University; SwedPower AB; Thailand Water Resources Association; Tropical Soil Biology and Fertility Institute; United Nations Educational, Scientific

Institutional affiliations of
authors and reviewers and
cross-cutting theme reviewers

and Cultural Organization, Institute for Water Education (UNESCO-IHE); United Nations System Network on Rural Development and Food Security; United States Agency for International Development (USAID); Universidad de Chile; Universidad de Los Andes, Bogota; University of Agriculture, Faisalabad, Pakistan; University of Botswana; University of Bradford; University of California, Santa Barbara; University of Copenhagen; University for Development Studies (Ghana); University of Hohenheim; University of Lagos; University of Malawi; University of Natural Resources and Applied Life Sciences, Vienna; University of Newcastle; University of Sussex; University of Sydney; University of Tamil Nadu; University of Toronto; University of Wyoming; University of Zimbabwe; Uppsala University; Vrije Universiteit, Amsterdam; Wageningen University; Water Research Commission, South Africa; Wetlands and Coastal Habitats Program, Nova Scotia; Wetlands International; Winrock International India; World Conservation Union (IUCN); World Water Council; WorldFish Center; World Wildlife Fund International (WWF); Wychwood Economic Consulting Limited; Yellow River Conservancy Commission (YRCC).

Cross-cutting theme reviewers

Review teams were formed to assist the chapter writing teams with cross-cutting issues of gender, health, and climate change. In addition, a team of Latin American specialists reviewed chapter key messages from a regional perspective. Also, Margaret Catley-Carlson, Alexander Müller, and Frank Rijsberman provided additional review comments and input on the summary.

Health
Priyanie Amerasinghe, Eline Boelee, Olivier Briet, Jeroen Ensink, Flemming Konradsen, and Wim van der Hoek

Gender
Maria Angelica Algeria, Meena Bilgi, Jane Dowling, Violet Matiru, Joke Muylwijk, Shaheen Khan Qabooliyo, Farhana Sultana, Pranita Udas, Juana Vera, Samyuktha Varma, and Barabara van Koppen

Climate
Declan Conway, Molly Helmuth, C.T. Hoanh, Kathleen Miller, Monirul Mirza, Lisa Schipper, and Saskia Werners

Latin American specialists
(organized by Freshwater Action Network Central America and coordinated by Jorge Mora Portuguez)

René Barreno, Jeannette de Noack, Norma Ferris, Marta Franco, Lourdes García, Josè Guevara, Raul López, Freddy Miranda, Jorge Mora Portuguez, Renè Orellana, Mariana Sell, Alejandra Salazar, and Mario Sotomayor